GREGORY G. DESS
University of Texas at Dallas
GERRY McNAMARA
Michigan State University
ALAN B. EISNER
Pace University
SEUNG-HYUN (SEAN) LEE
University of Texas at Dallas
With contributions by **Steve Sauerwald**
University of Illinois at Chicago

tenth edition

STRATEGIC MANAGEMENT

text & cases

Mc Graw Hill

Nico Muller Art/Shutterstock

RATEGIC MANAGEMENT: TEXT AND CASES, TENTH EDITION

Published by McGraw-Hill Education, 2 Penn Plaza, New York, NY 10121. Copyright © 2021 by McGraw-Hill Education. All rights reserved. Printed in the United States of America. Previous editions © 2016, 2014, and 2012. No part of this publication may be reproduced or distributed in any form or by any means, or stored in a database or retrieval system, without the prior written consent of McGraw-Hill Education, including, but not limited to, in any network or other electronic storage or transmission, or broadcast for distance learning.

Some ancillaries, including electronic and print components, may not be available to customers outside the United States.

This book is printed on acid-free paper.

1 2 3 4 5 6 7 8 9 0 LWI 21 20

ISBN 978-1-260-07508-3 (bound edition)
MHID 1-260-07508-7 (bound edition)

ISBN 978-1-260-70658-1 (loose-leaf edition)
MHID 1-260-70658-3 (loose-leaf edition)

Portfolio Director: *Michael Ablassmeir*
Lead Product Developer: *Kelly Delso*
Product Developer: *Anne Ehrenworth*
Executive Marketing Manager: *Debbie Clare*
Content Project Managers: *Harvey Yep* (Core), *Bruce Gin* (Assessment)
Buyer: *Susan K. Culbertson*
Design: *Matt Diamond*
Content Licensing Specialist: *Traci Vaske* (Image and Text)
Cover Image: *Nico Muller Art/Shutterstock*
Compositor: *Aptara®, Inc.*

All credits appearing on page or at the end of the book are considered to be an extension of the copyright page.

Library of Congress Control Number: 2019920213

The Internet addresses listed in the text were accurate at the time of publication. The inclusion of a website does not indicate an endorsement by the authors or McGraw-Hill Education, and McGraw-Hill Education does not guarantee the accuracy of the information presented at these sites.

mheducation.com/highered

dedication

To my family, Margie, Taylor, Alex - our new son-in-law, and my parents, the late Bill and Mary Dess

To my first two academic mentors–Charles Burden and Les Rue (of Georgia State University)

–Greg

To my wonderful wife, Gaelen, and my children, Megan and AJ

–Gerry

To my family, Helaine, Rachel, and Jacob

–Alan

To my family, Hannah, Paul, and Stephen; and my parents, Kenny and Inkyung

–Sean

about the authors

Gregory G. Dess

©He Gao

Gregory G. Dess

is the Andrew R. Cecil Endowed Chair in Management at the University of Texas at Dallas. His primary research interests are in strategic management, organization environment relationships, and knowledge management. He has published numerous articles on these subjects in both academic and practitioner-oriented journals. He also serves on the editorial boards of a wide range of practitioner-oriented and academic journals. In August 2000, he was inducted into the *Academy of Management Journal's* Hall of Fame as one of its charter members. Professor Dess has conducted executive programs in the United States, Europe, Africa, Hong Kong, and Australia. During 1994 he was a Fulbright Scholar in Oporto, Portugal. In 2009, he received an honorary doctorate from the University of Bern (Switzerland). He received his PhD in Business Administration from the University of Washington (Seattle) and a BIE degree from Georgia Tech.

Gerry McNamara

is the Eli Broad Professor of Management at Michigan State University. His research draws on cognitive and behavioral theories to explain strategic phenomena, including strategic decision making, mergers and acquisitions, and environmental assessments. His research has been published in the *Academy of Management Journal,* the *Strategic Management Journal, Organization Science, Organizational Behavior and Human Decision Processes,* the *Journal of Applied Psychology,* the *Journal of Management,* and the *Journal of International Business Studies.* Gerry's research has also been abstracted in the *Wall Street Journal, Harvard Business Review, New York Times, Bloomberg Businessweek,* the *Economist*, and *Financial Week*. He serves as an Associate Editor for the *Strategic Management Journal* and previously served as an Associate Editor for the *Academy of Management Journal.* He received his PhD from the University of Minnesota.

Alan B. Eisner

Seung-Hyun Lee

Alan B. Eisner

is Professor of Management and Associate Dean for Graduate Programs at the Lubin School of Business, Pace University. He received his PhD in management from the Stern School of Business, New York University. His primary research interests are in strategic management, technology management, organizational learning, and managerial decision making. He has published research articles and cases in journals such as *Advances in Strategic Management, International Journal of Electronic Commerce, International Journal of Technology Management, American Business Review, Journal of Behavioral and Applied Management, and Journal of the International Academy for Case Studies.* He is the former Associate Editor of the Case Association's peer-reviewed journal, The CASE Journal.

Seung-Hyun Lee

is a Professor of strategic management and international business and the Area Coordinator of the Organization, Strategy, and International Management area at the Jindal School of Business, University of Texas at Dallas. His primary research interests lie on the intersection between strategic management and international business spanning from foreign direct investment to issues of microfinance and corruption. He has published in numerous journals including *Academy of Management Review, Journal of Business Ethics, Journal of International Business Studies, Journal of Business Venturing, and Strategic Management Journal.* He received his MBA and PhD from the Ohio State University.

preface

Welcome to the Tenth Edition of *Strategic Management: Text and Cases!* We always appreciate the constructive and helpful feedback that we have received on our work. And, later in the Preface, we are happy to acknowledge the reviewers for all of the 10 editions of *Strategic Management* by name. The following are some examples of the encouraging feedback we have received:

Dess and colleagues have crafted a globally compelling, innovatively current, and poignantly challenging strategic tool for those of us passionate about teaching strategy. Educators will be inspired and impressed by the portfolio of relevant concepts linked to practical applications through Learning From Mistakes (my favorite), Strategy Spotlights, Insights from Executives, Reflecting on Career Implications, and Cases. Nicely done!

Marta Szabo White, Georgia State University

We like to change up our cases each term so this gives us a good variety to pick from and rotate through. I feel like each case offers a different learning experience so it is good to incorporate variety.

Nicole Lowes, Liberty University

The Dess book comprehensively covers the fundamentals of strategy and supports concepts with research and managerial insights.

Joshua J. Daspit, Mississippi State University

Very engaging. Students will want to read it and find it hard to put down.

Amy Gresock, University of Michigan, Flint

Strategic Management by Dess, McNamara, Eisner, and Lee is the most engaging and relevant strategy text on the market. The information is convincingly presented and with enough timely examples that students will be engaged. The text also provides thorough, accurate coverage of strategy concepts. These factors combined are a recipe for student learning.

Drake Mullens, Tarleton State University

I use *Strategic Management* in a capstone course required of all business majors, and students appreciate the book because it synergizes all their business education into a meaningful and understandable whole. My students enjoy the book's readability and tight organization, as well as the contemporary examples, case studies, discussion questions, and exercises.

William Sannwald, San Diego State University

The content is current and my students would find the real-world examples to be extremely interesting. My colleagues would want to know about it and I would make extensive use of the following features: Learning from Mistakes, Strategy Spotlights, Issues for Debate, and I especially like the Reflecting on Career Implications feature. Bottom line: the authors do a great job of explaining complex material and at the same time their use of up-to-date examples promotes learning.

Jeffrey Richard Nystrom, University of Colorado at Denver

The examples in each chapter are extremely useful to the students and the choice of cases are excellent for case study analysis.

Michael L. Sloan, San Diego State University

We always endeavor to improve our work and we are most appreciative of the extensive and thoughtful feedback that many strategy professionals have graciously given us. The author team has worked hard to incorporate many of their ideas into the Tenth Edition.

We believe we have made valuable improvements throughout our many revised editions of *Strategic Management.* At the same time, we strive to be consistent and "true" to our original overriding objective: a book that satisfies three Rs–rigor, relevance, and readable. And we are pleased that we have received feedback (such as the comments on the previous page) that is consistent with what we are trying to accomplish.

What are some of the features in *Strategic Management* that reinforce the three Rs? First, we build in rigor by drawing on the latest research by management scholars and insights from management consultants to offer a current and comprehensive view of strategic issues. We reinforce this rigor with our Issues for Debate and Reflecting on Career Implications that require students to develop insights on how to address complex issues and understand how strategy concepts can enhance their career success. Second, to enhance relevance, we provide numerous examples from management practice in the text and Strategy Spotlights (sidebars). We also increase relevance by relating course topic and examples to current business and societal themes, including environmental sustainability, ethics, globalization, entrepreneurship, and data analytics. Third, we stress readability through an engaging writing style with minimal jargon to ensure an effective learning experience. This is most clearly evident in the conversational presentations of chapter opening Learning from Mistakes and chapter ending Issues for Debate.

Unlike other strategy texts, we provide three separate chapters that address timely topics about which business students should have a solid understanding. These are the role of intellectual assets in value creation (Chapter 4), entrepreneurial strategy and competitive dynamics (Chapter 8), and fostering entrepreneurship in established organizations (Chapter 12). We also provide an excellent and thorough chapter on how to analyze strategic management cases.

In developing *Strategic Management: Text and Cases*, we certainly didn't forget the instructors. As we all know, you have a most challenging (but rewarding) job. We did our best to help you. We provide a variety of supplementary materials that should help you in class preparation and delivery. For example, our chapter notes do not simply summarize the material in the text. Rather (and consistent with the concept of strategy), we ask ourselves: "How can we add value?" Thus, for each chapter, we provide numerous questions to pose to help guide class discussion, at least 12 boxed examples to supplement chapter material, and three detailed "teaching tips" to further engage students. For example, we provide several useful insights on strategic leadership from one of Greg's colleagues, Charles Hazzard (formerly Executive Vice President, Occidental Chemical). Also, we completed the chapter notes ourselves. That is, unlike many of our rivals, we didn't simply farm the work out to others. Instead, we felt that such efforts help to enhance quality and consistency–as well as demonstrate our personal commitment to provide a top-quality total package to strategy instructors. With the Tenth Edition, we also benefited from valued input by our strategy colleagues to further improve our work.

Let's now address some of the key substantive changes in the Tenth Edition. Then we will cover some of the major features that we have had in previous editions.

WHAT'S NEW? HIGHLIGHTS OF THE TENTH EDITION

We have endeavored to add new material to the chapters that reflects the feedback we have received from our reviewers as well as the challenges today's managers face. Thus, we all invested an extensive amount of time carefully reviewing a wide variety of books, academic and practitioner journals, and the business press.

We also worked hard to develop more concise and tightly written chapters. Based on feedback from some of the reviewers, we have tightened our writing style, tried to eliminate redundant examples, and focused more directly on what we feel is the most important content in each chapter for our audience. The overall result is that we were able to update our material, add valuable new content, and–at the same time–shorten the length of the chapters.

PREFACE

Here are some of the major changes and improvements in the Tenth Edition:

- **Digital Economy.** We discuss and illustrate how the rise in digital technologies is changing the competitive environment and how firms are enhancing their strategic position by leveraging elements of the digital economy. A few examples include:
  - How Alibaba has created a sprawling e-commerce giant in Chapter 1
  - How Zara is restructuring its operations to serve online customers in Chapter 3
  - How Unilever uses artificial intelligence to hire the best talent in Chapter 4
  - How firms use data analytics to enhance organizational control in Chapter 9
- **Sustainability.** With sustainability being an increasing concern of our students, customers, and investors, sustainability has become a key driver of organizational success. We illustrate how firms have incorporated sustainability as a core element of their strategy. A few examples include:
  - How firms proactively incorporate environmental concerns in their business practices by eliminating plastic waste in Chapter 2
  - How firms are focusing on sustainability across a range of elements of the value chain and how these efforts support the attainment of long-term financial performance in Chapter 3
  - How sustainable business strategies can attract and retain talent in Chapter 4
  - How entrepreneurial firms are working to produce more environmentally sustainable batteries in Chapter 12
- **The importance of human and social capital for career and firm success.** We enhance our discussion of how building and leveraging human and social capital is a core strategic activity. A few examples include:
  - How to network more effectively in Chapter 4
  - How firms can build and leverage independent work teams in Chapter 9
  - How firms can inspire passion in their employees in Chapter 9
  - How superbosses can help employees working for them accomplish more than they ever thought possible in Chapter 11
- **Executive Insights: The Strategic Management Process.** Here, we introduce an in-depth interview with Mr. Usman Ghani, an internationally recognized consultant who is Chairman of ConfluCore LLP. Usman provides several practical insights into the strategic management process based on his extensive consulting experience and academic background at the Massachusetts Institute of Technology, where he earned three graduate degrees.
- **Over half of the 12 opening Learning from Mistakes vignettes that lead off each chapter are totally new.** Unique to this text, they are all examples of what can go wrong, and they serve as an excellent vehicle for clarifying and reinforcing strategy concepts. After all, what can be learned if one simply admires perfection?
- **Over half of our Strategy Spotlights (sidebar examples) are brand new, and many of the others have been thoroughly updated.** Although we have reduced the number of Spotlights from the previous edition to conserve space, we still have a total of 60–among the most in the strategy market. We focus on bringing the most important strategy concepts to life in a concise and highly readable manner. And we work hard to eliminate unnecessary detail that detracts from the main point we are trying to make. Also, consistent with our previous edition, many of the Spotlights focus on two "hot" issues that are critical in leading today's organizations–ethics and environmental sustainability–as well as the digital economy in this edition.

Key content changes for the chapters include:

- **Chapter 1 addresses why executives must communicate their long-term thinking to help ensure the support of investors and other stakeholders.** Such an initiative has many benefits. Among these are to provide investors with two critical elements: a long-term value creation *story* (the past) and a long term-value creation *plan* (the future). Further, when a company espouses an authentic, sustainable purpose, it is more likely to attract, motivate, and retain talent–a core objective in the knowledge economy. We also address how research by Andrew Winston, founder of Winston Eco-Strategies, has demonstrated the dramatic increase in the percentage of S&P companies that have produced detailed and rigorous reports on how they manage environmental and social issues as well as how they have incorporated them into their financial reports.
- **Chapter 2 discusses the importance of the digital economy as a fundamental shift in the business environment.** The term *digital economy* refers to economic transactions and business operations that are based on digital computing technologies. We highlight how the rise of the digital economy has disrupted existing industries by, for instance, reducing the asset intensity of business operations. Embracing the opportunities created by the digital economy has allowed entrepreneurs to create new business models such as ride sharing services and social networks.
- **Chapter 3 discusses how firms are leveraging artificial intelligence to increase the sustainability of their competitive advantages.** Firms are beginning to use artificial intelligence (AI) to better assess the preferences of their customers, how customers use their products, and how to best structure the firm's operations to build and maintain competitive advantages. Using AI, these firms are able to build sustainable advantages because their resource sets are built on path dependent and socially complex processes, making imitation difficult.
- **Chapter 4 discusses some of the challenges that women face when it comes to networking, an activity that is vital for career advancement.** Given that there are relatively fewer women in positions of leadership, it often becomes more difficult for them to find sponsors in order to make introductions and referrals. Professor Herminia Ibarra, of the London Business School, has proposed some suggestions on how women can more successfully engage in networking activities. These include making connections across diverse circles, investing time in extracurricular activities, and joining a professional women's network. We also provide examples of how companies have overcome the geographic preferences of talented professionals by building dispersed facilities and creating and maintaining formal relationships with research institutions.
- **Chapter 5 introduces the concept of unscaling and how firms are using it to create a combination strategy.** While firms have traditionally built large-scaled operations to run as efficiently as possible in order to dominate markets, firms that pursue unscaling turn things on their head. Unscaled firms look to build small scale operations that meet the needs of particular customers as efficiently as possible, at times even more efficiently than scaled competitors. Unscaling involves both the leveraging of technology, such as artificial intelligence, and the reliance on suppliers or customers to provide critical inputs to the process. We illustrate the concept by showing how Waze, P&G, and Indochino all use unscaling to efficiently offer differentiated products and services.
- **Chapter 6 discusses how CEO underpayment can be a trigger for acquisitions.** Research shows that when CEOs are underpaid relative to their peer CEOs, they undertake acquisitions to grow the size of the firm and increase their compensation. Further, it appears to work for the acquiring CEOs. They do benefit by seeing their pay rise. Thus, this research provides evidence that CEOs sometimes undertake acquisitions to benefit themselves, not the stockholders of the firm.

- **Chapter 7 illustrates the potential of reverse innovation for the health care sector in high-income countries such as the United States.** Reverse innovation refers to innovations that flow from low-income to high-income countries rather than the other way around. We illustrate how Indian hospital groups reconfigured their healthcare delivery to achieve high quality care at prices that are much lower than in the United States. These heathcare innovations subsequently found great success in parts of the United States that resemble the problems found in low-income countries.
- **Chapter 8 challenges the conventional view that entrepreneurial firms are typically started by tech savvy college students or young adults.** Research shows that the average age at which entrepreneurs start businesses is in their early forties. Further, the fastest growing firms were started by entrepreneurs who were even older, with founders of fast growing firms almost three times more likely to be over fifty than under thirty.
- **Chapter 9 outlines disadvantages associated with outsider dominated boards of directors**. The dominant view of boards of directors is that having boards that are primarily populated with outsiders, those not employed by or tied to the firm, is beneficial since the board will then be able to better monitor the firm's CEO. However, we outline a number of disadvantages that arise with outsider dominated boards. First, the board receives less information about the firm's operations since all information is filtered through the CEO. Second, the board has greater difficulty identifying who should be the next CEO of the firm since they don't regularly interact with any executives other than the current CEO. Third, non-CEO executives miss out on opportunities to develop their strategic decision making skills by being part of the board.
- **Chapter 10 discusses the power of small, independent teams in keeping the firm innovative and agile.** We draw on consultants' insights on how to structure and manage teams to make them more effective. Recommendations include keeping the size of the team small, staffing the team with top performers, empowering the team to spend their budget, holding the team accountable for their goals, and having an engaged manager.
- **Chapter 11 delves into the attributes of superbosses.** Superbosses not only build strong firms but also help those around them accomplish more than they ever thought possible. How do they do it? First, they strive to hire the best employees and surround themselves with unusually gifted people. They have no desire to be the smartest person in the room. Instead, Lorne Michaels, the producer of Saturday Night Live, reflected the mindset of a superboss when he said, "If you look around the room and think, 'God, these people are amazing,' then you're probably in the right room." Once they have these highly skilled individuals on their team, superbosses also figure out how to develop employees. We discuss several actions managers can take to identify the best candidates for their firm and ways they can act to best develop their employees.
- **Chapter 12 discusses the mindset needed to leverage the value of technologies in different markets.** Firms often struggle in their efforts to leverage their existing technologies in new markets. We discuss a four-step process firms can employ to increase their effectiveness in leveraging their technologies in new markets. The steps redefine the technology or competency in general terms, identify new applications of the technology, select the most promising applications, and choose the best entry mode. We discuss these steps in more detail and provide an example of each in the chapter.
- **Chapter 13 updates our Appendix: Sources of Company and Industry Information.** As always, the authors owe a huge debt of gratitude to Ms. Ruthie Brock, of the University

of Texas at Arlington. She has provided us with comprehensive and updated information for the Tenth Edition that is organized on a wide range of issues. These include competitive intelligence, annual report collections, company rankings, business websites, as well as strategic and competitive analysis. She has always been very gracious when we impose on her every two years!

- **We have worked hard to further enhance our excellent case package with a major focus on fresh and current cases on familiar firms.**
  - More than half of our cases are author-written (much more than the competition).
  - While many of the titles look familiar, we have created fresh stories and added interesting data about the companies to minimize instructor preparation time and "maximize freshness" of the content.
  - We have added several exciting new cases to the lineup including a return of Southwest Airlines with a fresh story, The Movie Exhibition industry, Lime (bicycle ride-sharing), Venmo (mobile payments), FlipKart (Amazon competitor in India) and Alibaba (e-commerce).
  - These new cases along with 32 fresh stories about familiar firms and classics such as Robin Hood give instructors many great options.

WHAT REMAINS THE SAME: KEY FEATURES OF EARLIER EDITIONS

Let's now briefly address some of the exciting features that remain from the earlier editions.

- **Traditional organizing framework with three other chapters on timely topics.** Crisply written chapters cover all of the strategy bases and address contemporary topics. First, the chapters are divided logically into the traditional sequence: strategy analysis, strategy formulation, and strategy implementation. Second, we include three chapters on such timely topics as intellectual capital/knowledge management, entrepreneurial strategy and competitive dynamics, and fostering corporate entrepreneurship and new ventures.
- **Learning from Mistakes chapter-opening cases.** To enhance student interest, we begin each chapter with a case that depicts an organization that has suffered a dramatic performance drop, or outright failure, by failing to adhere to sound strategic management concepts and principles. We believe that this feature serves to underpin the value of the concepts in the course and that it is a preferred teaching approach to merely providing examples of outstanding companies that always seem to get it right. After all, isn't it better (and more challenging) to diagnose problems than admire perfection? As Dartmouth's Sydney Finkelstein, author of *Why Smart Executives Fail*, notes: "We live in a world where success is revered, and failure is quickly pushed to the side. However, some of the greatest opportunities to learn—for both individuals and organizations—come from studying what goes wrong."* We'll see how, for example, Mattress Firm grew to more than 3,200 stores and $3 billion in annual revenue—but then crashed into bankruptcy. Clearly, the advent of nimble internet rivals, such as Casper Sleep, Inc., led to their downfall. However, their demise was hastened by their aggressive expansion and the accumulation of excessive debt to fund it. We'll also explore the bankruptcy of storied law firm Dewey & LeBoeuf LLP. Their failure can be attributed to three major issues: a reliance on borrowed money,

*Personal Communication, June 20, 2005.

PREFACE

making large promises about compensation to incoming partners (which didn't sit well with their existing partners!), and a lack of transparency about the firm's financials.

- **Issue for Debate at the end of each chapter.** We find that students become very engaged (and often animated!) in discussing an issue that has viable alternate points of view. It is an exciting way to drive home key strategy concepts. For example, in Chapter 4, we ask whether or not providing financial incentives to employees to lose weight actually works. And, in Chapter 10 we address a trend that is taking place in many large corporations: the flattening of hierarchical organizational structures. In fact, one survey found that 93 percent of polled firms indicate that they intend to flatten their organization in the near future. On the one hand, such restructuring has its advantages–it can offer cost savings, flexibility, and quicker response times. However, some of these benefits may be offset by some negative consequences that can occur. These include the overstretching of management attention, additional friction among managers at various levels since there are fewer middle managers to resolve conflicts, and demotivating effects caused by reduced opportunities for managers to advance through the management ranks. Clearly, one size does not fit all. Firms must consider the relative benefits and costs of flattening their structures as well as take into account such factors as a firm's size, technology, and culture as well as the industry in which it competes.
- **Insights from Research.** We include six of these features in the Tenth Edition–and half of them are entirely new. Here, we summarize key research findings on a variety of issues and, more importantly, address their relevance for making organizations (and managers!) more effective. For example, in Chapter 2 we discuss findings from a meta-analysis (research combining many individual studies) to debunk several myths about older workers–a topic of increasing importance, given the changing demographics in many developed countries. In Chapter 4, we address a study that explored the viability of re-hiring employees who had previously left the organizations. Such employees, called "boomerangs" may leave an organization for several reasons and such reasons may strongly influence their willingness to return to the organization. And in Chapter 6, we explore a study that investigates how closely CEOs attend to media assessments of actions that they take. Using a large database of 745 large acquisitions undertaken by S&P 500 firms, researchers find that CEOs do pay attention to media evaluations of acquisitions. However, the extent to which they are future- or past-focused influences whether and how they learn from the media.
- **Reflecting on Career Implications . . .** We provide insights that are closely aligned with and directed to three distinct issues faced by our readers: prepare them for a job interview (e.g., industry analysis), help them with current employers or their career in general, or help them find potential employers and decide where to work. We believe this will be very valuable to students' professional development.
- **Consistent chapter format and features to reinforce learning.** We have included several features in each chapter to add value and create an enhanced learning experience. First, each chapter begins with an overview and a list of key learning objectives. Second, as previously noted, the opening case describes a situation in which a company's performance eroded because of a lack of proper application of strategy concepts. Third, at the end of each chapter there are four different types of questions/exercises that should help students assess their understanding and application of material:

1. Summary review questions.
2. Experiential exercises.
3. Application questions and exercises.
4. Ethics questions.

Given the centrality of online systems to business today, each chapter contains at least one exercise that allows students to explore the use of the Internet in implementing a firm's strategy.

- **Key Terms.** Approximately a dozen key terms for each chapter are identified in the margins of the pages. This addition was made in response to reviewer feedback and improves students' understanding of core strategy concepts.
- **Clear articulation and illustration of key concepts.** Key strategy concepts are introduced in a clear and concise manner and are followed by timely and interesting examples from business practice. Such concepts include value-chain analysis, the resource-based view of the firm, Porter's five forces model, competitive advantage boundaryless organizational designs, digital strategies, corporate governance, ethics, data analytics, and entrepreneurship.
- **Extensive use of sidebars.** We include 60 sidebars (or about five per chapter) called Strategy Spotlights. The Strategy Spotlights not only illustrate key points but also increase the readability and excitement of new strategy concepts.
- **Integrative themes.** The text provides a solid grounding in ethics, globalization, environmental sustainability, and technology. These topics are central themes throughout the book and form the basis for many of the Strategy Spotlights.
- **Implications of concepts for small businesses.** Many of the key concepts are applied to start-up firms and smaller businesses, which is particularly important since many students have professional plans to work in such firms.
- **Not just a product, but an entire package.** *Strategic Management* features the best chapter teaching notes available today. Rather than merely summarizing the key points in each chapter, we focus on value-added material to enhance the teaching (and learning) experience. Each chapter includes dozens of questions to spur discussion, teaching tips, in-class group exercises, and about a dozen detailed examples from business practice to provide further illustrations of key concepts.

TEACHING RESOURCES

Instructor's Manual (IM)

Prepared by the textbook authors, along with valued input from our strategy colleagues, the accompanying IM contains summary/objectives, lecture/discussion outlines, discussion questions, extra examples not included in the text, teaching tips, reflecting on career implications, experiential exercises, and more.

Test Bank

Revised by Christine Pence of the University of California-Riverside, the test bank contains more than 1,000 true/false, multiple-choice, and essay questions. It is tagged with learning objectives as well as Bloom's Taxonomy and AACSB criteria.

- **Assurance of Learning Ready**. Assurance of Learning is an important element of many accreditation standards. The Tenth Edition is designed specifically to support your Assurance of Learning initiatives. Each chapter in the book begins with a list of numbered learning objectives that appear throughout the chapter. Every test bank question is also linked to one of these objectives, in addition to level of difficulty, topic area, Bloom's Taxonomy level, and AACSB skill area. *Test Builder*, an easy-to-use, cloud-based test bank software, can search the test bank by these and other categories, providing an engine for targeted Assurance of Learning analysis and assessment.

PREFACE

- **AACSB Statement.** McGraw-Hill is a proud corporate member of AACSB International. Understanding the importance and value of AACSB accreditation, the Tenth Edition has sought to recognize the curricula guidelines detailed in the AACSB standards for business accreditation by connecting selected questions in Dess 10e and the test bank to the general knowledge and skill guidelines found in the AACSB standards. The statements contained in this new edition are provided only as a guide for the users of this text. The AACSB leaves content coverage and assessment within the purview of individual schools, the mission of the school, and the faculty. While this new edition and the teaching package make no claim of any specific AACSB qualification or evaluation, we have labeled selected questions within the title according to the six general knowledge and skills areas.
- **Test Builder.** A comprehensive bank of test questions is provided within a computerized test bank powered by *Test Builder,* a cloud-based tool that enables instructors to format tests that can be printed or administered within a LMS. Available in Connect, *Test Builder* offers a modern, streamlined interface for easy content configuration that matches course needs, without requiring a download. *Test Builder* allows you to:
    - access all test bank content from a particular title.
    - easily pinpoint the most relevant content through robust filtering options.
    - manipulate the order of questions or scramble questions and/or answers.
    - pin questions to a specific location within a test.
    - determine your preferred treatment of algorithmic questions.
    - choose the layout and spacing.
    - add instructions and configure default settings.

Test Builder provides a secure interface for better protection of content and allows for just-in-time updates to flow directly into assessments.

PowerPoint Presentation

Prepared by Pauline Assenza of Western Connecticut State University, it consists of more than 400 slides incorporating an outline for the chapters tied to learning objectives. Also included are instructor notes, multiple-choice questions that can be used as Classroom Performance System (CPS) questions, and additional examples outside the text to promote class discussion.

The Business Strategy Game and GLO-BUS Online Simulations

Both allow teams of students to manage companies in a head-to-head contest for global market leadership. These simulations give students the immediate opportunity to experiment with various strategy options and to gain proficiency in applying the concepts and tools they have been reading about in the chapters. To find out more or to register, please visit **www.bsg-online.com or www.glo-bus.com.**

COURSE DESIGN AND DELIVERY RESOURCES

Craft your teaching resources to match the way you teach! With McGraw-Hill *Create, www.mcgrawhillcreate.com*, you can easily rearrange chapters, combine material from other content sources, and quickly upload content you have written, like your course syllabus or teaching notes. Find the content you need in Create by searching through thousands of leading McGraw-Hill textbooks. Arrange your book to fit your teaching style. *Create* even allows you to personalize your book's appearance by selecting the cover and adding your name, school, and course information. Order a *Create* book and you'll receive a complimentary print review copy in three to five business days or a complimentary electronic review copy (eComp) via email in about one hour. Go to *www.mcgrawhillcreate.com* today and register. Experience how McGraw-Hill *Create* empowers you to teach *your* students your way.

At McGraw-Hill, we understand that getting the most from new technology can be challenging. That's why our services don't stop after you purchase our products. You can email our product specialists 24 hours a day to get product training online. Or you can search our knowledge bank of Frequently Asked Questions on our support website. For customer support, call 800-338-3987 or visit *www.mheducation.com/contact.html.* One of our technical support analysts will be able to assist you in a timely fashion.

ACKNOWLEDGMENTS

Strategic Management represents far more than just the joint efforts of the four co-authors. Rather, it is the product of the collaborative input of many people. Some of these individuals are academic colleagues, others are the outstanding team of professionals at McGraw-Hill, and still others are those who are closest to us—our families. It is time to express our sincere gratitude.

First, we'd like to acknowledge the dedicated instructors who have graciously provided their insights since the inception of the text. Their input has been very helpful in both pointing out errors in the manuscript and suggesting areas that needed further development as additional topics. We sincerely believe that the incorporation of their ideas has been critical to improving the final product. These professionals and their affiliations are:

The Reviewer Hall of Fame

Moses Acquaah,
University of North Carolina-Greensboro

Todd Alessandri,
Northeastern University

Larry Alexander,
Virginia Polytechnic Institute

Thomas H. Allison,
Washington State University

Brent B. Allred,
College of William & Mary

Allen C. Amason,
Georgia Southern University

Kathy Anders,
Arizona State University

Jonathan Anderson,
University of West Georgia

Peter H. Antoniou,
California State University-San Marcos

Dave Arnott,
Dallas Baptist University

Marne L. Arthaud-Day,
Kansas State University

Dr. Bindu Arya,
University of Missouri-St. Louis

Jay A. Azriel,
York College of Pennsylvania

Jeffrey J. Bailey,
University of Idaho

David L. Baker, PhD,
John Carroll University

PREFACE

Dennis R. Balch,
University of North Alabama

Bruce Barringer,
University of Central Florida

Barbara R. Bartkus,
Old Dominion University

Barry Bayon,
Bryant University

Brent D. Beal,
Louisiana State University

Dr. Patricia Beckenholdt,
Business and Professional Programs, University of Maryland, University College

Joyce Beggs,
University of North Carolina-Charlotte

Michael Behnam,
Suffolk University

Kristen Bell DeTienne,
Brigham Young University

Eldon Bernstein,
Lynn University

Lyda Bigelow,
University of Utah

David Blair,
University of Nebraska at Omaha

Daniela Blettner,
Tilburg University

Dusty Bodie,
Boise State University

William Bogner,
Georgia State University

David S. Boss, PhD,
Ohio University

Scott Browne,
Chapman University

Jon Bryan,
Bridgewater State College

Charles M. Byles,
Virginia Commonwealth University

Mikelle A. Calhoun,
Valparaiso University

Thomas J. Callahan,
University of Michigan-Dearborn

Samuel D. Cappel,
Southeastern Louisiana State University

Gary Carini,
Baylor University

Shawn M. Carraher,
University of Texas-Dallas

Tim Carroll,
University of South Carolina

Don Caruth,
Amberton University

Maureen Casile,
Bowling Green State University

Gary J. Castrogiovanni,
Florida Atlantic University

Radha Chaganti,
Rider University

Erick PC Chang,
Arkansas State University

Tuhin Chaturvedi,
Joseph M. Katz Graduate School of Business, University of Pittsburgh

Jianhong Chen,
University of New Hampshire

Tianxu Chen,
Oakland University

Andy Y. Chiou,
SUNY Farmingdale State College

Theresa Cho,
Rutgers University

Timothy S. Clark,
Northern Arizona University

Bruce Clemens,
Western New England College

Betty S. Coffey,
Appalachian State University

Wade Coggins,
Webster University-Fort Smith Metro Campus

Susan Cohen,
University of Pittsburgh

George S. Cole,
Shippensburg University

Jennifer Collins,
Florida A&M University

Joseph Coombs,
Virginia Commonwealth University

Christine Cope Pence,
University of California-Riverside

James J. Cordeiro,
SUNY Brockport

Stephen E. Courter,
University of Texas at Austin

Jeffrey Covin,
Indiana University

Keith Credo,
Auburn University

Joshua J. Daspit, PhD,
Mississippi State University

Deepak Datta,
University of Texas at Arlington

James Davis,
Utah State University

Justin L. Davis,
University of West Florida

David Dawley,
West Virginia University

Daniel DeGravel,
California State University Northridge, David Nazarian College of Business and Economics

Helen Deresky,
State University of New York-Plattsburgh

Rocki-Lee DeWitt,
University of Vermont

Jay Dial,
Ohio State University

Michael E. Dobbs,
Arkansas State University

Jonathan Doh,
Villanova University

Dr. John Donnellan,
NJCU School of Business

Tom Douglas,
Clemson University

Jon Down,
Oregon State University

Meredith Downes,
Illinois State University

Mohinder Dugal,
Western Connecticut State University

Alan E. Ellstrand,
University of Arkansas

Dean S. Elmuti,
Eastern Illinois University

Clare Engle,
Concordia University

Mehmet Erdem Genc,
Baruch College, CUNY

Tracy Ethridge,
Tri-County Technical College

William A. Evans,
Troy State University-Dothan

Frances H. Fabian,
University of Memphis

Angelo Fanelli,
Warrington College of Business

Michael Fathi,
Georgia Southwestern University

Carolyn J. Fausnaugh,
Florida Institute of Technology

Tamela D. Ferguson,
University of Louisiana at Lafayette

David Flanagan,
Western Michigan University

Kelly Flis,
The Art Institutes

Karen Ford-Eickhoff,
University of North Carolina Charlotte

Dave Foster,
Montana State University

Isaac Fox,
University of Minnesota

Charla S. Fraley,
Columbus State Community College-Columbus, Ohio

Deborah Francis,
Brevard College

Steven A. Frankforter,
Winthrop University

Harold Fraser,
California State University-Fullerton

Vance Fried,
Oklahoma State University

Karen Froelich,
North Dakota State University

Naomi A. Gardberg,
Baruch College, CUNY

Joe Gerard,
Western New England University

J. Michael Geringer,
Ohio University

Diana L. Gilbertson,
California State University-Fresno

Matt Gilley,
St. Mary's University

Debbie Gilliard,
Metropolitan State College-Denver

Yezdi H. Godiwalla,
University of Wisconsin-Whitewater

Sanjay Goel,
University of Minnesota-Duluth

Sandy Gough,
Boise State University

Amy Gresock, PhD
The University of Michigan, Flint

Vishal K. Gupta,
The University of Mississippi

Dr. Susan Hansen,
University of Wisconsin-Platteville

Allen Harmon,
University of Minnesota-Duluth

Niran Harrison,
University of Oregon

Paula Harveston,
Berry College

Ahmad Hassan,
Morehead State University

Donald Hatfield,
Virginia Polytechnic Institute

Kim Hester,
Arkansas State University

Scott Hicks,
Liberty University

John Hironaka,
California State University-Sacramento

Anne Kelly Hoel,
University of Wisconsin-Stout

Alan Hoffman,
Bentley College

Gordon Holbein,
University of Kentucky

Stephen V. Horner,
Pittsburg State University

Jill Hough,
University of Tulsa

John Humphreys,
Eastern New Mexico University

James G. Ibe,
Morris College

Jay J. Janney,
University of Dayton

Lawrence Jauch,
University of Louisiana-Monroe

Dana M. Johnson,
Michigan Technical University

Homer Johnson,
Loyola University, Chicago

Hyungu Kang,
Central Michigan University

Patricia Kanishiro,
Loyola University, Maryland

Marilyn R. Kaplan,
Naveen Jindal School of Management, University of Texas-Dallas

James Katzenstein,
California State University-Dominguez Hills

Joseph Kavanaugh,
Sam Houston State University

Franz Kellermanns,
University of Tennessee

Craig Kelley,
California State University-Sacramento

Donna Kelley,
Babson College

Dave Ketchen,
Auburn University

John A. Kilpatrick,
Idaho State University

Dr. Jaemin Kim,
Stockton University

Brent H. Kinghorn,
Emporia State University

Helaine J. Korn,
Baruch College, CUNY

Stan Kowalczyk,
San Francisco State University

Daniel Kraska,
North Central State College

Donald E. Kreps,
Kutztown University

Jim Kroeger,
Cleveland State University

Subdoh P. Kulkarni,
Howard University

Ron Lambert,
Faulkner University

Theresa Lant,
New York University

Jai Joon Lee,
California State University Sacramento

Ted Legatski,
Texas Christian University

David J. Lemak,
Washington State University-Tri-Cities

Cynthia Lengnick-Hall,
University of Texas at San Antonio

Donald L. Lester,
Arkansas State University

Wanda Lester,
North Carolina A&T State University

Krista B. Lewellyn,
University of Wyoming

Benyamin Lichtenstein,
University of Massachusetts at Boston

Jun Lin,
SUNY at New Paltz

Zhiang (John) Lin,
University of Texas at Dallas

Dan Lockhart,
University of Kentucky

John Logan,
University of South Carolina

Franz T. Lohrke,
Samford University

Eduardo Lopez,
Belmont University

Kevin B. Lowe,
Graduate School of Management, University of Auckland

Nicole Lowes,
Liberty University

Leyland M. Lucas,
Morgan State University

Doug Lyon,
Fort Lewis College

Rickey Madden, PhD,
Presbyterian College

James Maddox,
Friends University

Ravi Madhavan,
University of Pittsburgh

Paul Mallette,
Colorado State University

Santo D. Marabella,
Moravian College

Catherine Maritan,
Syracuse University

Daniel Marrone,
Farmingdale State College, SUNY

Sarah Marsh,
Northern Illinois University

Jim Martin,
Washburn University

John R. Massaua,
University of Southern Maine

Hao Ma,
Bryant College

Eric Shaunn Mattingly,
Boise State University

Larry McDaniel,
Alabama A&M University

Jean McGuire,
Louisiana State University

Abagail McWilliams,
University of Illinois-Chicago

Ofer Meilich,
California State University-San Marcos

John E. Merchant,
California State University-Sacramento

John M. Mezias,
University of Miami

Michael Michalisin,
Southern Illinois University at Carbondale

Elouise Mintz,
St. Louis University

Doug Moesel,
University of Missouri-Columbia

Fatma Mohamed,
Morehead State University

Mike Montalbano,
Bentley University

Debra Moody,
University of North Carolina-Charlotte

Gregory A. Moore,
Middle Tennessee State University

James R. Morgan,
Dominican University and UC Berkeley Extension

Ken Morlino,
Wilmington University

Sara A. Morris,
Old Dominion University

Todd W. Moss, PhD,
Syracuse University

Carolyn Mu,
Baylor University

Stephen Mueller,
Northern Kentucky University

John Mullane,
Middle Tennessee State University

Chandran Mylvaganam,
Northwood University

Sucheta Nadkarni,
Cambridge University

Anil Nair,
Old Dominion University

V.K. Narayanan,
Drexel University

Maria L. Nathan,
Lynchburg College

Louise Nemanich,
Arizona State University

Kent Neupert,
Boise State University

Charles Newman,
University of Maryland, University College

Stephanie Newport,
Austin Peay State University

Gerry Nkombo Muuka,
Murray State University

Bill Norton,
University of Louisville

Dr. Jill E. Novak
Texas A&M University

Roman Nowacki,
Northern Illinois University

Yusuf A. Nur,
SUNY Brockport

Jeffrey Richard Nystrom,
University of Colorado-Denver

William Ross O'Brien,
Dallas Baptist University

d.t. ogilvie,
Rutgers University

Floyd Ormsbee,
Clarkson University

Dr. Mine Ozer,
SUNY-Oneonta

Dr. Eren Ozgen,
Troy University-Dothan Campus

Karen L. Page,
University of Wyoming

Jacquelyn W. Palmer,
University of Cincinnati

Julie Palmer,
University of Missouri-Columbia

Daewoo Park,
Xavier University

Gerald Parker,
Saint Louis University

Ralph Parrish,
University of Central Oklahoma

Vijay Patel,
University of North Carolina-Charlotte

Amy Patrick,
Wilmington University

John Pepper,
The University of Kansas

Douglas K. Peterson,
Indiana State University

Edward Petkus,
Mary Baldwin College

Michael C. Pickett,
National University

Peter Ping Li,
California State University-Stanislaus

Michael W. Pitts,
Virginia Commonwealth University

Laura Poppo,
Virginia Tech

PREFACE

Steve Porth,
Saint Joseph's University

Jodi A. Potter,
Robert Morris University

Tobias Pret,
Pace University

Scott A. Quatro,
Grand Canyon University

Ranfeng Qiu,
California State University-San Bernadino

Nandini Rajagopalan,
University of Southern California

Annette L. Ranft,
North Carolina State University

Abdul Rasheed,
University of Texas at Arlington

Devaki Rau,
Northern Illinois University

George Redmond,
Franklin University

Kira Reed,
Syracuse University

Clint Relyea,
Arkansas State University

Barbara Ribbens,
Western Illinois University

Maurice Rice,
University of Washington

Violina P. Rindova,
University of Texas-Austin

Ron Rivas,
Canisius College

David Robinson,
Indiana State University-Terre Haute

Kenneth Robinson,
Kennesaw State University

Simon Rodan,
San Jose State University

Patrick R. Rogers,
North Carolina A&T State University

John K. Ross III,
Texas State University-San Marcos

Robert Rottman,
Kentucky State University

Matthew R. Rutherford,
Gonzaga University

Carol M. Sanchez,
Grand Valley State University

Doug Sanford,
Towson University

William W. Sannwald,
San Diego State University

Yolanda Sarason,
Colorado State University

Marguerite Schneider,
New Jersey Institute of Technology

Roger R. Schnorbus,
University of Richmond

Terry Sebora,
University of Nebraska-Lincoln

John Seeger,
Bentley College

Jamal Shamsie,
Michigan State University

Mark Shanley,
University of Illinois at Chicago

Ali Shahzad,
James Madison University

Lois Shelton,
California State University-Northridge

Herbert Sherman,
Long Island University

Weilei Shi,
Baruch College, CUNY

Chris Shook,
Auburn University

Jeremy Short,
University of Oklahoma

Mark Simon,
Oakland University-Michigan

Rob Singh,
Morgan State University

Bruce Skaggs,
University of Massachusetts

Lise Anne D. Slattern,
University of Louisiana at Lafayette

Michael Sloan,
San Diego State University

Wayne Smeltz,
Rider University

Anne Smith,
University of Tennessee

Andrew Spicer,
University of South Carolina

James D. Spina,
University of Maryland

John Stanbury,
George Mason University & Inter-University Institute of Macau, SAR China

Timothy Stearns,
California State University-Fresno

Elton Stephen,
Austin State University

Charles E. Stevens,
University of Wyoming

Alice Stewart,
Ohio State University

Christopher Stewart,
Metropolitan State University of Denver

Mohan Subramaniam,
Carroll School of Management Boston College

Ram Subramanian,
Grand Valley State University

Roy Suddaby,
University of Iowa

Michael Sullivan,
UC Berkeley Extension

Marta Szabo White,
Georgia State University

Stephen Takach,
University of Texas at San Antonio

Justin Tan,
York University, Canada

Qingjiu Tao, PhD,
James Madison University

Renata A. Tarasievich,
University of Illinois at Chicago

Linda Teagarden,
Virginia Tech

Bing-Sheng Teng,
George Washington University

Alan Theriault,
University of California-Riverside

Tracy Thompson,
University of Washington-Tacoma

Karen Torres,
Angelo State University

Mary Trottier,
Associate Professor of Management, Nichols College

Robert Trumble,
Virginia Commonwealth University

Francis D. (Doug) Tuggle,
Chapman University

K.J. Tullis,
University of Central Oklahoma

Craig A. Turner, PhD,
East Tennessee State University

Beverly Tyler,
North Carolina State University

Rajaram Veliyath,
Kennesaw State University

S. Stephen Vitucci,
Tarleton State University-Central Texas

Jay A. Vora,
St. Cloud State University

Valerie Wallingford, Ph.D.,
Bemidji State University

Jorge Walter,
Portland State University

Bruce Walters,
Louisiana Tech University

Edward Ward,
St. Cloud State University

N. Wasilewski,
Pepperdine University

Andrew Watson,
Northeastern University

Larry Watts,
Stephen F. Austin University

Marlene E. Weaver,
American Public University System

Paula S. Weber,
St. Cloud State University

Kenneth E. A. Wendeln,
Indiana University

Robert R. Wharton,
Western Kentucky University

Laura Whitcomb,
California State University-Los Angeles

Marta Szabo White,
Georgia State University

Scott Williams,
Wright State University

Ross A. Wirth,
Franklin University

Gary Wishniewsky,
California State University East Bay

Diana Wong,
Bowling Green State University

Beth Woodard,
Belmont University

John E. Wroblewski,
State University of New York-Fredonia

Anne York,
University of Nebraska-Omaha

Michael Zhang,
Sacred Heart University

Monica Zimmerman,
Temple University

Second, we would like to thank the people who have made our two important features possible. The information found in our six Insights from Research was provided courtesy of www.businessminded.com, an organization founded by K. Matthew Gilley, PhD (St. Mary's University) that transforms empirical management research into actionable insights for business leaders. We appreciate Matt's graciousness and kindness in helping us out. And, of course, our Executive Insights: The Strategic Management Process would not have been possible without the gracious participation of Usman Ghani, a premier international consultant, and Chairman of ConfluCore, LLP.

PREFACE

Third, the authors would like to thank several faculty colleagues who were particularly helpful in the review, critique, and development of the book and supplementary materials. Greg's and Sean's colleagues at the University of Texas at Dallas also have been helpful and supportive. These individuals include Mike Peng, Joe Picken, Kumar Nair, John Lin, Larry Chasteen, Tev Dalgic, and Livia Markoczy. Administrative assistant, Shalonda Hill, has been extremely helpful. Four doctoral students, Brian Pinkham, Steve Sauerwald, Kyun Kim, and Canan Mutlu, have provided many useful inputs and ideas. They also appreciate the support of his dean and associate dean, Hasan Pirkul and Varghese Jacob, respectively. Greg wishes to thank a special colleague, Abdul Rasheed at the University of Texas at Arlington, who certainly has been a valued source of friendship and ideas for us for many years. He provided valuable contributions to many of the editions. Gerry thanks all of his colleagues at Michigan State University for their help and support over the years. He also thanks his mentor, Phil Bromiley, as well as the students and former students he has had the pleasure of working with. Alan thanks his colleagues at Pace University and the Case Association for their support in developing these fine case selections. Special thanks go to Jamal Shamsie at Michigan State University for his support in developing the case selections for this edition.

Fourth, we would like to thank the team at McGraw-Hill for their outstanding support throughout the entire process. As we work on the book through the various editions, we always appreciate their hard work and recognize how so many people add value to our final package. This began with John Biernat, formerly publisher, who signed us to our original contract. He was always available to us and provided a great deal of support and valued input throughout several editions. Presently, in editorial, Terri Schiesl, managing director, editorial director Mike Ablassmeir, and senior product developer Anne Ehrenworth kept things on track, responded quickly to our seemingly endless needs and requests, and offered insights and encouragement. We appreciate their expertise–as well as their patience! Once the manuscript was completed and revised, content project manager Harvey Yep expertly guided it through the content and assessment production process. Matt Diamond provided excellent design and artwork guidance. We also appreciate executive marketing manager Debbie Clare and marketing coordinator Julia Blankenship for their energetic, competent, and thorough marketing efforts. Last, but certainly not least, we thank MHE's outstanding book reps–who serve on the front lines–as well as many in-house sales professionals. Clearly, they deserve a lot of credit (even though not mentioned by name) for our success.

Fifth, we acknowledge the valuable contributions of many of our strategy colleagues for their excellent contributions to our supplementary and digital materials. Such content really adds a lot of value to our entire package! We are grateful to Pauline Assenza at Western Connecticut State University for her superb work on case teaching notes as well as chapter and case PowerPoints. Patrick McGuigan, Pace University, deserves our thanks for his hard work in developing excellent digital materials for Connect. We thank Christine Pence, University of California-Riverside, for her important contributions in revising our test bank and chapter quizzes, and Todd Moss, Oregon State University, for his hard work in putting together an excellent set of videos online, along with the video grid that links videos to chapter material. Finally, we thank Steve Sauerwald, University of Illinois- Chicago, for his excellent contributions to the content in some of the chapters.

Finally, we would like to thank our families. For Greg this includes his parents, the late William and Mary Dess, who have always been there for him. His wife, Margie, and daughter, Taylor, have been a constant source of love and companionship. Our family is also thrilled to welcome a new member–Alex, who married Taylor in December 2018. Gerry thanks his wife, Gaelen, for her love,

support, and friendship; and his children, Megan and AJ, for their love and the joy they bring to his life. He also thanks his current and former PhD students who regularly inspire and challenge him. Alan thanks his family—his wife, Helaine, and his children, Rachel and Jacob—for their love and support. He also thanks his parents, Gail Eisner and the late Marvin Eisner, for their support and encouragement. Sean thanks his wife, Hannah, and his two boys, Paul and Stephen, for their unceasing love and care. He also thanks his parents, Kenny and Inkyung Lee, for being there whenever needed.

FOR INSTRUCTORS

You're in the driver's seat.

Want to build your own course? No problem. Prefer to use our turnkey, prebuilt course? Easy. Want to make changes throughout the semester? Sure. And you'll save time with Connect's auto-grading too.

65%
Less Time Grading

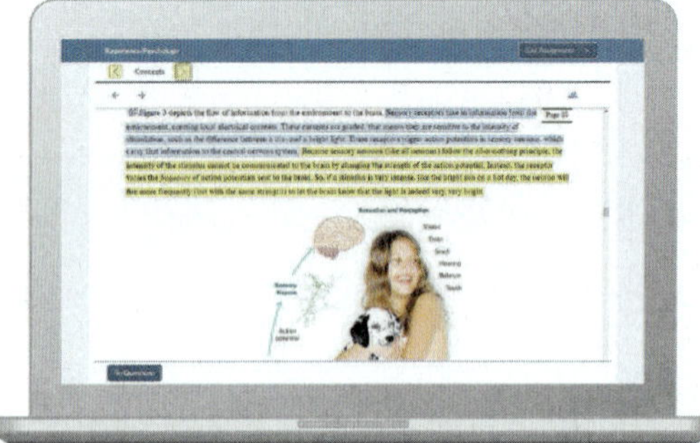

Laptop: McGraw-Hill; Woman/dog: George Doyle/Getty Images

They'll thank you for it.

Adaptive study resources like SmartBook® 2.0 help your students be better prepared in less time. You can transform your class time from dull definitions to dynamic debates. Find out more about the powerful personalized learning experience available in SmartBook 2.0 at **www.mheducation.com/highered/connect/smartbook**

Make it simple, make it affordable.

Connect makes it easy with seamless integration using any of the major Learning Management Systems—Blackboard®, Canvas, and D2L, among others—to let you organize your course in one convenient location. Give your students access to digital materials at a discount with our inclusive access program. Ask your McGraw-Hill representative for more information.

Padlock: Jobalou/Getty Images

Solutions for your challenges.

A product isn't a solution. Real solutions are affordable, reliable, and come with training and ongoing support when you need it and how you want it. Our Customer Experience Group can also help you troubleshoot tech problems—although Connect's 99% uptime means you might not need to call them. See for yourself at **status.mheducation.com**

Checkmark: Jobalou/Getty Images

FOR STUDENTS

Effective, efficient studying.

Connect helps you be more productive with your study time and get better grades using tools like SmartBook 2.0, which highlights key concepts and creates a personalized study plan. Connect sets you up for success, so you walk into class with confidence and walk out with better grades.

Study anytime, anywhere.

Download the free ReadAnywhere app and access your online eBook or SmartBook 2.0 assignments when it's convenient, even if you're offline. And since the app automatically syncs with your eBook and SmartBook 2.0 assignments in Connect, all of your work is available every time you open it. Find out more at **www.mheducation.com/readanywhere**

"I really liked this app—it made it easy to study when you don't have your text-book in front of you."

- Jordan Cunningham, Eastern Washington University

Calendar: owattaphotos/Getty Images

No surprises.

The Connect Calendar and Reports tools keep you on track with the work you need to get done and your assignment scores. Life gets busy; Connect tools help you keep learning through it all.

Learning for everyone.

McGraw-Hill works directly with Accessibility Services Departments and faculty to meet the learning needs of all students. Please contact your Accessibility Services office and ask them to email accessibility@mheducation.com, or visit **www.mheducation.com/about/accessibility** for more information.

Top: Jenner Images/Getty Images, Left: Hero Images/Getty Images, Right: Hero Images/Getty Images

a guided tour

CHAPTER 1

Strategic Management

Creating Competitive Advantages

Learning Objectives

LO1-1 Define strategic management and its four key attributes.

LO1-2 Understand the strategic management process and its three interrelated and principal activities.

LO1-3 Identify the vital role of corporate governance and stakeholder management, as well as how "symbiosis" can be achieved among an organization's stakeholders.

LO1-4 Understand the importance of social responsibility, including environmental sustainability, and how it can enhance a corporation's innovation strategy.

LO1-5 Recognize the need for greater empowerment throughout the organization.

LO1-6 Explain how an awareness of a hierarchy of strategic goals can help an organization achieve coherence in its strategic direction.

We encourage you to reflect on how the concepts presented in this chapter can enhance your career success (see "Reflecting on Career Implications..." at the end of the chapter).

LEARNING OBJECTIVES

Learning Objectives numbered LO 1-1, LO 1-2, LO 1-3, etc., with corresponding icons in the margins to indicate where learning objectives are covered in the text.

LEARNING FROM MISTAKES

What makes the study of strategic management so interesting? Things can change so rapidly! Some start-ups can disrupt industries and become globally recognized names almost overnight and the rankings of the world's most valuable firms can dramatically change in a brief period of time. On the other hand, many impressive, high-flying firms can struggle to reclaim past glory—or fail altogether. As colorfully (and ironically!) noted by Arthur Martinez, Sears's former Chairman: "Today's peacock is tomorrow's feather duster."[1]

Consider the following:[2]

- The 33-year average tenure of companies on the S&P 500 in 1962 narrowed to 24 years by 2016 and is forecast to shrink to merely 12 years by 2027.
- At the beginning of 2000, the four firms in the world with the highest market values were General Electric, Exxon Mobil, Pfizer, and Citigroup. By late 2019, four tech firms headed the list: Apple, Alphabet (parent of Google), Amazon, and Microsoft.
- Record private equity activity, a strong M&A market, and the growth of start-ups with billion dollar market caps (called "unicorns") are often viewed as leading factors to increase disruptions in a wide variety of industries.
- A quarter century ago, few would have predicted that a South Korean firm would be a global car giant, an Indian firm would be one of the world's largest technology firms, and a huge Chinese Internet firm would list on an American stock exchange.
- In 1995, only about 3 percent of the companies on the Fortune 500 list were from emerging markets. This number has increased to 26 percent in 2013, and is predicted to grow to 45 percent by 2025.
- With the emergence of the digital economy, new entrants are shaking up long-standing industries. After all, Alibaba has become the world's most valuable retailer—but holds no inventory; Airbnb is the world's largest provider of accommodations—but owns no real estate; and Uber is the world's largest car service—but owns no cars.

Retail has become one of the prime examples of an industry that has been impacted by the digital disruption and the emergence of online competitors. Many brick-Bath & Beyond, Urban Outfitters, Sears, Radio Shack, and J.C. Penney have either filed for bankruptcy, or have become mere shadows of their former selves.

Let's take a closer look at another retailer, Mattress Firm, which filed for bankruptcy on October 5, 2018.[3]

Houston-based Mattress Firm was founded in 1986 and eventually grew to more than 3,200 stores and $3 billion in annual revenues. However, its pursuit of growth and dominance—largely via acquisition–in the industry led to its eventual demise.

A turning point came in 2015 when it purchased one of its chief rivals, Sleepy's, for $780 million. Steve Stagner, Mattress Firm's CEO at the time asserted, "This transformational acquisition unites the nation's two largest mattress specialty retailers providing customers with convenience, value, and choice."

However, things certainly didn't turn out as he had hoped. Acquiring Sleepy's 1,000 stores left Mattress Firm severely over-retailed. As store traffic slowed, costly leases turned into an albatross around the firm's neck. In bankruptcy court filings, the rapid expansion led to the "cannibalization" of stores that were clustered too closely and put them in direct competition with each other. This was poignantly stated by Hendre Ackermann, the firm's CFO: "There are many examples of a Mattress Firm store being located literally across the street from another Mattress Firm store."

Mattress Firm's fortunes were also eroded by a set of more nimble competitors: online upstarts, including Casper, Lessa, Tuft & Needle, and Sapira. For example, Casper Sleep, Inc., founded in 2014, raised $240 million to sell mattresses directly to consumers. It provided easy online ordering, hassle-free delivery, and returns of reasonably affordable mattresses. Within a year, Casper booked sales of $100 million.

The online rivals also had another major advantage over Mattress Firm: Shoppers had grown weary of the traditional mattress-buying experience. This involved going into a store, testing out a slew of mattresses for a few minutes, and rushing into a decision on an expensive item

LEARNING FROM MISTAKES

Learning from Mistakes vignettes are examples of where things went wrong. Failures are not only interesting but also sometimes easier to learn from. And students realize strategy is not just about "right or wrong" answers, but requires critical thinking.

1.1 STRATEGY SPOTLIGHT

AMBIDEXTROUS BEHAVIORS: COMBINING ALIGNMENT AND ADAPTABILITY

A study involving 41 business units in 10 multinational companies identified four ambidextrous behaviors in individuals. Such behaviors are the essence of ambidexterity, and they illustrate how a dual capacity for alignment and adaptability can be woven into the fabric of an organization at the individual level.

They take time and are alert to opportunities beyond the confines of their own jobs. A large computer company's sales manager became aware of a need for a new software module that nobody currently offered. Instead of selling the customer something else, he worked up a business case for the new module. With management's approval, he began working full time on its development.

They are cooperative and seek out opportunities to combine their efforts with others. A marketing manager for Italy was responsible for supporting a newly acquired subsidiary. When frustrated about the limited amount of contact she had with her peers in other countries, she began discussions with them. This led to the creation of a European marketing forum

They are multitaskers who are comfortable wearing more than one hat. Although an operations manager for a major coffee and tea distributor was charged with running his plant as efficiently as possible, he took it upon himself to identify value-added services for his clients. By developing a dual role, he was able to manage operations and develop a promising electronic module that automatically reported impending problems inside a coffee vending machine. With corporate funding, he found a subcontractor to develop the software, and he then piloted the module in his own operations. It was so successful that it was eventually adopted by operations managers in several other countries.

A recent *Harvard Business Review* article provides some useful insights on how one can become a more ambidextrous leader. Consider the following questions:

- **Do you meet your numbers?**
- **Do you help others?**
- **What do you do for your peers?** Are you just their in-house competitor?
- **When you manage up, do you bring problems—or**

1.2 STRATEGY SPOTLIGHT

ENVIRONMENTAL SUSTAINABILITY IN THE FASHION INDUSTRY

The $3 trillion fashion industry employs over 60 million people along its global value chain. Although it makes 100 billion accessories and garments each year, three-fifths of them are thrown away within a year, according to McKinsey & Company. Further, a vast amount of cotton, water, and power is used to make their products, but less than 1 percent is recycled into new clothes, according to an environmental research group in England. Amazingly, the United Nations Economic Commission for Europe estimates that about 40 percent of clothes in the wardrobes of developed countries are never worn! To provide some perspective, Rob Opsomer, a sustainability researcher asserts that "the equivalent of a dump truck filled with textiles gets landfilled or incinerated every single second."

Inditex SA, the company that owns Zara and several other brands, made 1.6 billion garments in 2016—a scale that has helped its stock price quintuple over a recent 10-year period. However, recently industry growth has slowed, in part because millennials have become sensitive to fast fashion's impact on the environment. (In fact, according to Boston Consulting Group, one-third of this demographic consistently identifies sustainability as a

This situation creates an opportunity for companies to use sustainability to differentiate their brands. With growing concerns over the waste, retailers have begun placing recycling bins prominently in many stores, using greener materials, etc., to help win over customers. Let's look at some of Inditex's initiatives:

- Began disassembling old clothing to spin into yarns for fashions it markets as "garments with a past."
- Grouped many of its sustainability efforts—clothes made from organic cotton and repurposed fabrics into a sub-brand called Join Life.
- To boost the share of greener textiles in its mix, the firm has funded research programs at MIT and universities in Spain. One initiative is to try using 3D printing to make textiles using by-products from timber operations.

Inditex says that for now they're absorbing the extra costs of using recycled or reconstituted garments. The Join Life line is priced competitively with other items in the Zara stores—T-shirts cost less than $10 and jeans are priced under $40. The firm is striving to keep a lid on prices of its greener materials and it expects the cost to fall as production increases. Anna Gedda, an

STRATEGY SPOTLIGHT

These boxes weave themes of ethics, globalization, and technology into every chapter of the text, providing students with a thorough grounding necessary for understanding strategic management. Select boxes incorporate the digital economy, environmental sustainability, and ethical themes.

INSIGHTS

Chapter 1's "Insights from Executive" contains an interview with a worldwide organization about current issues salient to strategic management. "Insights from Research" throughout the text summarize key research findings relevant to maintaining the effectiveness of an organization and its management.

THE STRATEGIC MANAGEMENT PROCESS

Usman Ghani, Chairman, ConfluCore

Biosketch

Usman Ghani has held leadership roles in strategic planning, marketing, operations, organization development, IT, and executive education, as well as led cross-functional, multicultural core business process teams to effective implementations. He is a former Fortune 100 executive distinguished by his record of developing powerful board policies and business strategies for a variety of industry leaders, including McKinsey & Company, Royal Dutch/Shell Group, Exxon Mobil Corporation, and HP/Electronic Data Systems.

Characterized as a high-energy visionary, Usman is passionat...

Question 2. Looking at it from the other side, what are some of the key pitfalls you've seen firms fall prey to that have resulted in strategic failures?

Beware! While not broadly published, strategic failures outnumber strategic successes in all sizes and types of organizations. It is only when the acclaimed ones (like Borders, GE, Kodak, and Sears) result in large-scale failures that we become aware and then only for a while. Often, it is the dysfunctional strategic management of these organizations that fail them.

Successes and failures occur every day, but only for the attentive. These accumulate and, upon crossing some threshold, successes are cele-...

3.1 INSIGHTS from Research

THE BENEFITS OF BALANCE

Overview

Business leaders face strong pressures to produce financial results, but they also know that ignoring other areas of the firm can cause trouble down the line. This study speaks on that topic and shows that having balance in performance pays off for the firm financially.

What the Research Shows

Researchers from the Drucker Institute have compiled a dataset on 693 large, publicly-traded companies from 2012 to 2017. They collected information on 37 indicators of performance in five specific areas: customer satisfaction, employee engagement, innovation, social responsibility, and financial performance. Companies were scored on a range of 0 to 100 in each of these five areas. The scores were standardized so that the mean score on each scale was 50. The researchers were specifically focused on...

So, why is consistency beneficial? The researchers suggest that when a firm has uneven performance across these measures, there may be particular areas of weakness that could become major problems for the firm in coming years. The researchers use the metaphor of an elite athlete. If the athlete neglects endurance and focuses exclusively on strength and speed, she will not be able to sustain performance over time.

Key Takeaways

- Five key areas of performance for firms to focus on are customer satisfaction, employee engagement and development, innovation, social responsibility, and financial strength.
- Firms tend to perform better over time if they perform consistently across these five areas.
- Weakness on any of the five areas indicates an issue...

EXHIBIT 3.2 The Value Chain: Some Factors to Consider in Assessing a Firm's Primary Activities

Inbound Logistics
• Location of distribution facilities to minimize shipping times. • Warehouse layout and designs to increase efficiency of operations for incoming materials.
Operations
• Efficient plant operations to minimize costs. • Efficient plant layout and workflow design. • Incorporation of appropriate process technology.
Outbound Logistics
• Effective shipping processes to provide quick delivery and minimize damages. • Shipping of goods in large lot sizes to minimize transportation costs.
Marketing and Sales
• Innovative approaches to promotion and advertising. • Proper identification of customer segments and needs.
Service
• Quick response to customer needs and emergencies. • Quality of service personnel and ongoing training.

Source: Adapted from Porter, M. E. 1985. *Competitive Advantage: Creating and Sustaining Superior Performance.* New York: Free Press.

EXHIBITS

Both new and improved exhibits in every chapter provide visual presentations of the most complex concepts covered to support student comprehension.

REFLECTING ON CAREER IMPLICATIONS

This section before the summary of every chapter consists of examples on how understanding of key concepts helps business students early in their careers.

Reflecting on Career Implications . . .

This chapter addresses the importance of the internal environment for strategic managers. As a strategic manager, you should fully understand how you can leverage your competencies to both bring value to your firm and enhance your career opportunities.

- **The Value Chain:** It is important that you develop an understanding of your firm's value chain. What activities are most critical for attaining competitive advantage? Think of ways in which you can add value in your firm's value chain. How might your firm's support activities (e.g., information technology, human resource practices) help you accomplish your assigned tasks more effectively? How will you bring your value-added contribution to the attention of your superiors?
- **The Value Chain:** Consider the most important linkages ... ization with ... en your firm and its suppliers, customers, and alliance partners. Understanding and strengthening these linkages can contribute greatly to your career advancement within your current organization.
- **Resource-Based View of the Firm:** Are your skills and talents rare, valuable, and difficult to imitate, and do they have few substitutes? If so, you are in the better position to add value for your firm—and earn rewards and incentives. How can your skills and talents be enhanced to help satisfy these criteria to a greater extent? Get more training? Change positions within the firm? Consider career options at other organizations?
- **Balanced Scorecard:** Can you design a balanced scorecard for your life? What perspectives would you include in it? In what ways would such a balanced scorecard help you attain success in life?

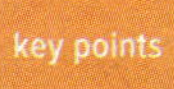

LO3-1 The primary and support activities of a firm's value chain.

- Primary activities include all parts of the organization that are involved in the direct physical creation, distribution, sale, or servicing of the firms products and services, including inbound logistics, operations, outbound logistics, marketing and sales, and service.
- Support activities either add value themselves or in combination with both primary and other support activities, including procurement, technology development, human resource management, and general administration.

LO3-2 How value-chain analysis can help managers create value by investigating relationships among

- Interrelationships improve overall firm value when they involve the effective coordination of actions and exchange of resources, such as information, technology, and people.

LO3-3 The resource-based view of the firm and the different types of tangible and intangible resources, as well as organizational capabilities.

- The resource-based view of the firm considers the firm as a bundle of resources: tangible resources, intangible resources, and organizational capabilities.
- Competitive advantages that are sustainable over time generally arise from the creation of bundles of resources and capabilities.

LO3-4 The four criteria that a firm's resources must

CASES

Updated case lineup provides six new cases. The majority of the remaining cases have been revised to "maximize freshness" and minimize instructor preparation time. New cases for this edition include well-known companies such as LimeBike, Alibaba, and Venmo.

CASES

CASE 4

ZYNGA: IS THE GAME OVER?*

CASE 9

KICKSTARTER AND CROWDFUNDING 2

CASE 15

WEIGHT WATCHERS IS NOW WW*

brief contents

contents

PART 1 STRATEGIC ANALYSIS

CHAPTER 1

CHAPTER 2

CHAPTER 3

CHAPTER 4

CONTENTS

CONTENTS

CONTENTS

cases

CASES

The Strategic Management Process

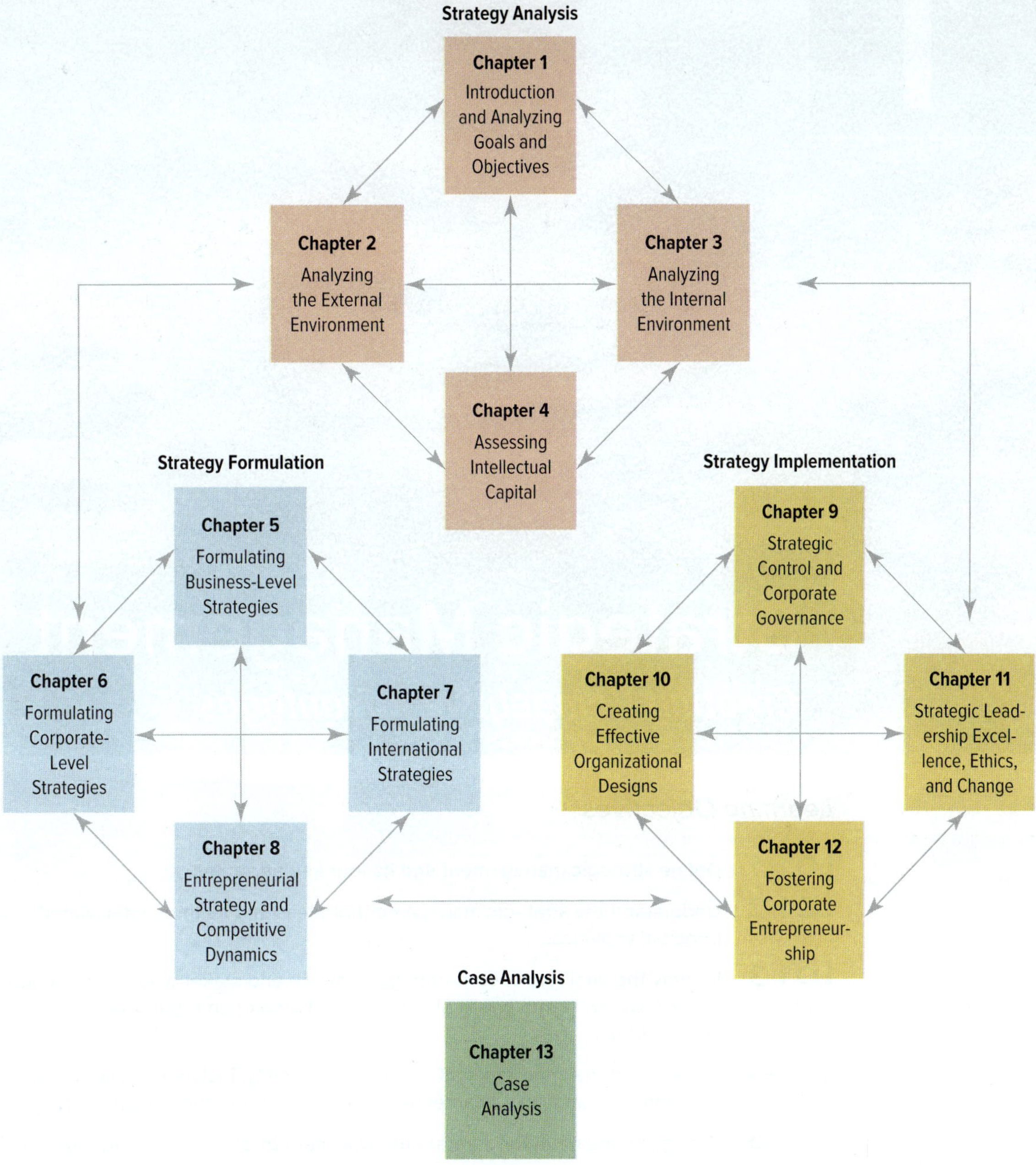

©Nico Muller Art/Shutterstock

Strategic Management

Creating Competitive Advantages

Learning Objectives

LO1-1 Define strategic management and its four key attributes.

LO1-2 Understand the strategic management process and its three interrelated and principal activities.

LO1-3 Identify the vital role of corporate governance and stakeholder management, as well as how "symbiosis" can be achieved among an organization's stakeholders.

LO1-4 Understand the importance of social responsibility, including environmental sustainability, and how it can enhance a corporation's innovation strategy.

LO1-5 Recognize the need for greater empowerment throughout the organization.

LO1-6 Explain how an awareness of a hierarchy of strategic goals can help an organization achieve coherence in its strategic direction.

We encourage you to reflect on how the concepts presented in this chapter can enhance your career success (see "Reflecting on Career Implications..." at the end of the chapter).

LEARNING FROM MISTAKES

What makes the study of strategic management so interesting? Things can change so rapidly! Some start-ups can disrupt industries and become globally recognized names almost overnight and the rankings of the world's most valuable firms can dramatically change in a brief period of time. On the other hand, many impressive, high-flying firms can struggle to reclaim past glory—or fail altogether. As colorfully (and ironically!) noted by Arthur Martinez, Sears's former Chairman: "Today's peacock is tomorrow's feather duster."[1]

Consider the following:[2]

- The 33-year average tenure of companies on the S&P 500 in 1962 narrowed to 24 years by 2016 and is forecast to shrink to merely 12 years by 2027.
- At the beginning of 2000, the four firms in the world with the highest market values were General Electric, Exxon Mobil, Pfizer, and Citigroup. By late 2019, four tech firms headed the list: Apple, Alphabet (parent of Google), Amazon, and Microsoft.
- Record private equity activity, a strong M&A market, and the growth of start-ups with billion dollar market caps (called "unicorns") are often viewed as leading factors to increase disruptions in a wide variety of industries.
- A quarter century ago, few would have predicted that a South Korean firm would be a global car giant, an Indian firm would be one of the world's largest technology firms, and a huge Chinese Internet firm would list on an American stock exchange.
- In 1995, only about 3 percent of the companies on the Fortune 500 list were from emerging markets. This number has increased to 26 percent in 2013, and is predicted to grow to 45 percent by 2025.
- With the emergence of the digital economy, new entrants are shaking up long-standing industries. After all, Alibaba has become the world's most valuable retailer—but holds no inventory; Airbnb is the world's largest provider of accommodations—but owns no real estate; and Uber is the world's largest car service—but owns no cars.

Retail has become one of the prime examples of an industry that has been impacted by the digital disruption and the emergence of online competitors. Many brick-and-mortar (i.e., high asset intensive) firms such as Bed, Bath & Beyond, Urban Outfitters, Sears, Radio Shack, and J.C. Penney have either filed for bankruptcy, or have become mere shadows of their former selves.

Let's take a closer look at another retailer, Mattress Firm, which filed for bankruptcy on October 5, 2018.[3]

Houston-based Mattress Firm was founded in 1986 and eventually grew to more than 3,200 stores and $3 billion in annual revenues. However, its pursuit of growth and dominance—largely via acquisition–in the industry led to its eventual demise.

A turning point came in 2015 when it purchased one of its chief rivals, Sleepy's, for $780 million. Steve Stagner, Mattress Firm's CEO at the time asserted, "This transformational acquisition unites the nation's two largest mattress specialty retailers providing customers with convenience, value, and choice."

However, things certainly didn't turn out as he had hoped. Acquiring Sleepy's 1,000 stores left Mattress Firm severely over-retailed. As store traffic slowed, costly leases turned into an albatross around the firm's neck. In bankruptcy court filings, the rapid expansion led to the "cannibalization" of stores that were clustered too closely and put them in direct competition with each other. This was poignantly stated by Hendre Ackermann, the firm's CFO: "There are many examples of a Mattress Firm store being located literally across the street from another Mattress Firm store."

Mattress Firm's fortunes were also eroded by a set of more nimble competitors: online upstarts, including Casper, Lessa, Tuft & Needle, and Sapira. For example, Casper Sleep, Inc., founded in 2014, raised $240 million to sell mattresses directly to consumers. It provided easy online ordering, hassle-free delivery, and returns of reasonably affordable mattresses. Within a year, Casper booked sales of $100 million.

The online rivals also had another major advantage over Mattress Firm: Shoppers had grown weary of the traditional mattress-buying experience. This involved going into a store, testing out a slew of mattresses for a few minutes, and rushing into a decision on an expensive item designed to last for years. And, customers were often annoyed by complicated and expensive delivery options. As noted by Casper's co-founder and CEO, Philip Krim, "Traditional mattress retailers have been alienating customers for decades and are now buckling under pressure. Casper has turned a tired industry on its head with innovative products and a superior shopping experience." Recently, Casper expanded its direct-to-consumer online business into a wide variety of products including bed frames, sheets, pillows, and dog mattresses.

Discussion Questions

1. What actions should Mattress Firm have taken when it became apparent that there were some nimble, online rivals entering the industry?
2. Casper Sleep Inc. has certainly become a strong competitor in this industry. In your view, what could they do to further strengthen their position?

romantic view of leadership situations in which the leader is the key force determining the organization's success—or lack thereof.

Today's leaders face a large number of complex challenges in the global marketplace. In considering how much credit (or blame) they deserve, two perspectives of leadership come immediately to mind: the "romantic" and "external control" perspectives.[4] First, let's look at the **romantic view of leadership.** Here, the implicit assumption is that the leader is the key force in determining an organization's success—or lack thereof.[5] This view dominates the popular press in business magazines such as *Fortune, Bloomberg Businessweek,* and *Forbes,* wherein the CEO is either lauded for his or her firm's success or chided for the organization's demise.[6] Consider, for example, the credit that has been bestowed on leaders such as Bill Gates, Andrew Grove, and Jeff Bezos for the tremendous accomplishments when they led their firms—Microsoft, Intel, and Amazon, respectively.

Similarly, Apple's emergence as one of the world's most valuable firms has been attributed almost entirely to the late Steve Jobs, its former CEO, who died on October 5, 2011.[7] Apple's string of hit products, such as iMac computers, iPods, iPhones, and iPads, is a testament to his genius for developing innovative, user-friendly, and aesthetically pleasing products. In addition to being a perfectionist in product design, Jobs was a master showman with a cult following. During his time as CEO between 1997 and 2011, Apple's market value soared by over $300 billion!

On the other hand, when things don't go well, much of the failure of an organization can also, rightfully, be attributed to the leader.[8] Clearly, the aggressive acquisition of its rival, Sleepy's, by Mattress Firm's CEO, Steve Stagner, led to a steep decline in the firm's performance because of the resulting oversaturation of its retail outlets and the associated costly leases. In contrast, Apple fully capitalized on emerging technology trends with a variety of products, including sophisticated smartphones.

The effect—for good or for bad—that top executives can have on a firm's market value can be reflected in what happens when one of them leaves their firm.[9] For example, look what occurred when Kasper Rorsted stepped down as CEO of the German packaged-goods firm Henkel in January, 2016 to become CEO of Adidas: Henkel immediately lost $2 billion in market capitalization, and Adidas gained $1 billion. On the other hand, when Viacom announced that executive chairman Sumner Redstone was stepping down, the firm gained $1.1 billion of market valuation in 30 minutes!

external control view of leadership situations in which external forces—where the leader has limited influence—determine the organization's success.

However, such an emphasis on the leader reflects only part of the picture. Consider another perspective, called the **external control view of leadership.** Here, rather than making the implicit assumption that the leader is the most important factor in determining organizational outcomes, the focus is on external factors that may positively (or negatively) affect a firm's success. We don't have to look far to support this perspective. Developments in the general environment, such as economic downturns, new technologies, governmental legislation, or an outbreak of major internal conflict or war, can greatly restrict the choices that are available to a firm's executives. For example, several book retailers, such as Borders and Waldenbooks, found the consumer shift away from brick-and-mortar bookstores to online book buying (e.g., Amazon) and digital books an overwhelming environmental force against which they had few defenses.

Looking back at the opening Mattress Firm case, Mr. Stagner faced some challenges from the external environment over which the firm had relatively little control. As noted, the online upstarts, such as Casper Sleep, Inc., had multiple competitive advantages such as lower capital investments and labor costs, as well as a superior customer shopping experience. At the same time, of course, Mattress Firm was encumbered with the high costs associated with physical locations.[10]

Before moving on, it is important to point out that successful executives are often able to navigate around the difficult circumstances that they face. At times it can be refreshing to see the optimistic position they take when they encounter seemingly insurmountable odds. Of course, that's not to say that one should be naive or Pollyannaish. Consider, for example, how one CEO, discussed next, is handling trying times.[11]

Name a general economic woe, and chances are that Charles Needham, CEO of Metorex, is dealing with it.

- Market turmoil has knocked 80 percent off the shares of South Africa's Metorex, the mining company that he heads.
- The plunge in global commodities is slamming prices for the copper, cobalt, and other minerals Metorex unearths across Africa. The credit crisis makes it harder to raise money.
- Fighting has again broken out in the Democratic Republic of Congo, where Metorex has a mine and several projects in development.

Such problems might send many executives to the window ledge. Yet Needham appears unruffled as he sits down at a conference table in the company's modest offices in a Johannesburg suburb. The combat in northeast Congo, he notes, is far from Metorex's mine. Commodity prices are still high, in historical terms. And Needham is confident he can raise enough capital, drawing on relationships with South African banks. "These are the kinds of things you deal with, doing business in Africa," he says.

WHAT IS STRATEGIC MANAGEMENT?

LO 1-1

Define strategic management and its four key attributes.

Given the many challenges and opportunities in the global marketplace, today's managers must do more than set long-term strategies and hope for the best.[12] They must go beyond what some have called "incremental management," whereby they view their job as making a series of small, minor changes to improve the efficiency of their firm's operations.[13] Rather than seeing their role as merely custodians of the status quo, today's leaders must be proactive, anticipate change, and continually refine and, when necessary, make dramatic changes to their strategies. The strategic management of the organization must become both a process and a way of thinking throughout the organization.

Defining Strategic Management

strategic management the analyses, decisions, and actions an organization undertakes in order to create and sustain competitive advantages.

Strategic management consists of the analyses, decisions, and actions an organization undertakes in order to create and sustain competitive advantages. This definition captures two main elements that go to the heart of the field of strategic management.

First, the strategic management of an organization entails three ongoing processes: *analyses, decisions,* and *actions.* Strategic management is concerned with the *analysis* of strategic goals (vision, mission, and strategic objectives) along with the analysis of the internal and external environments of the organization. Next, leaders must make strategic decisions. These *decisions,* broadly speaking, address two basic questions: What industries should we compete in? How should we compete in those industries? These questions also often involve an organization's domestic and international operations. And last are the *actions* that must be taken. Decisions are of little use, of course, unless they are acted on. Firms must take the necessary actions to implement their **strategies.** This requires leaders to allocate the necessary resources and to design the organization to bring the intended strategies to reality.

strategy
the ideas, decisions, and actions that enable a firm to succeed.

Second, the essence of strategic management is the study of why some firms outperform others.[14] Thus, managers need to determine how a firm is to compete so that it can obtain advantages that are sustainable over a lengthy period of time. That means focusing on two fundamental questions:

competitive advantage
a firm's resources and capabilities that enable it to overcome the competitive forces in its industry(ies).

- ***How should we compete in order to create* competitive advantages *in the marketplace?*** Managers need to determine if the firm should position itself as the low-cost producer or develop products and services that are unique and will enable the firm to charge premium prices. Or should they do some combination of both?
- ***How can we create competitive advantages in the marketplace that are unique, valuable, and difficult for rivals to copy or substitute?*** That is, managers need to make such advantages sustainable, instead of temporary.

Sustainable competitive advantage cannot be achieved through operational effectiveness alone.[15] The popular management innovations of the last two decades–total quality, just-in-time, benchmarking, business process reengineering, outsourcing–are all about operational effectiveness. **Operational effectiveness** means performing similar activities better than rivals. Each of these innovations is important, but none lead to sustainable competitive advantage because everyone is doing them.

operational effectiveness
performing similar activities better than rivals.

Strategy is all about being different. Sustainable competitive advantage is possible only by performing different activities from rivals or performing similar activities in different ways. Companies such as Walmart, Southwest Airlines, and IKEA have developed unique, internally consistent, and difficult-to-imitate activity systems that have provided them with sustained competitive advantages. A company with a good strategy must make clear choices about what it wants to accomplish. Trying to do everything that your rivals do eventually leads to mutually destructive price competition, not long-term advantage.

The Four Key Attributes of Strategic Management

Before discussing the strategic management process, let's briefly talk about four attributes of strategic management.[16] It should become clear how this course differs from other courses that you have had in functional areas, such as accounting, marketing, operations, and finance. Exhibit 1.1 provides a definition and the four attributes of strategic management.

EXHIBIT 1.1
Strategic Management Concepts

Definition: Strategic management consists of the analyses, decisions, and actions an organization undertakes in order to create and sustain competitive advantages.

Key Attributes of Strategic Management

- Directs the organization toward overall goals and objectives.
- Includes multiple stakeholders in decision making.
- Needs to incorporate short-term and long-term perspectives.
- Recognizes trade-offs between efficiency and effectiveness.

First, strategic management is *directed toward overall organizational goals and objectives.* That is, effort must be directed at what is best for the total organization, not just a single functional area. Some authors have referred to this perspective as "organizational versus individual rationality."[17] That is, what might look "rational" or ideal for one functional area, such as operations, may not be in the best interest of the overall firm. For example, operations may decide to schedule long production runs of similar products to lower unit costs. However, the standardized output may be counter to what the marketing department needs to appeal to a demanding target market. Similarly, research and development may "overengineer" the product to develop a far superior offering, but the design may make the product so expensive that market demand is minimal.

As noted by David Novak, former CEO of Yum Brands:[18]

> I tell people that once you get a job you should act like you run the place. Not in terms of ego, but in terms of how you think about the business. Don't just think about your piece of the business. Think about your piece of the business and the total business. This way, you'll always have a broader perspective.

Second, strategic management *includes multiple stakeholders in decision making.*[19] **Stakeholders** are those individuals, groups, and organizations that have a "stake" in the success of the organization, including owners (shareholders in a publicly held corporation), employees, customers, suppliers, the community at large, and so on. (We'll discuss this in more detail later in this chapter.) Managers will not be successful if they focus on a single stakeholder. For example, if the overwhelming emphasis is on generating profits for the owners, employees may become alienated, customer service may suffer, and the suppliers may resent demands for pricing concessions.

stakeholders
individuals, groups, and organizations that have a stake in the success of the organization. These include owners (shareholders in a publicly held corporation), employees, customers, suppliers, and the community at large.

Third, strategic management *requires incorporating both short-term and long-term perspectives.*[20] Peter Senge, a leading strategic management author, has referred to this need as a "creative tension."[21] That is, managers must maintain both a vision for the future of the organization and a focus on its present operating needs. However, financial markets can exert significant pressures on executives to meet short-term performance targets. Studies have shown that corporate leaders often take a short-term approach to the detriment of creating long-term shareholder value.

Andrew Winston addresses this issue in his recent book, *The Big Pivot:*[22]

> Consider the following scenario: You are close to the end of the quarter and you are faced with a project that you are certain will make money. That is, it has a guaranteed positive net present value (NPV). But it will reduce your earnings for this quarter. Do you invest?
>
> A research study posed this question to 400 CFOs and a majority said they would not do it. Further, 80 percent of the executives would decrease R&D spending, advertising, and general maintenance. So, what occurs when you cut back on these investments to prop up short-term earnings *every* quarter? Logically, you don't invest in projects with favorable paybacks and you underspend on initiatives that build longer-term value. Thus, your earnings targets in the future quarters actually get more difficult to hit.

Fourth, strategic management *involves the recognition of trade-offs between effectiveness and efficiency.* Some authors have referred to this as the difference between "doing the right thing" **(effectiveness)** and "doing things right" **(efficiency).**[23] While managers must allocate and use resources wisely, they must still direct their efforts toward the attainment of overall organizational objectives. As noted by Meg Whitman, Hewlett-Packard's former CEO, "Less than perfect strategy execution against the right strategy will probably work. A 100 percent execution against the wrong strategy won't."[24]

effectiveness
tailoring actions to the needs of an organization rather than wasting effort, or "doing the right thing."

efficiency
performing actions at a low cost relative to a benchmark, or "doing things right."

Successful managers must make many trade-offs. It is central to the practice of strategic management. At times, managers must focus on the short term and efficiency; at other times, the emphasis is on the long term and expanding a firm's product-market scope in order to anticipate opportunities in the competitive environment.

To summarize, leaders typically face many difficult and challenging decisions. In a recent article in the *Harvard Business Review*, Wendy Smith and her colleagues provide some valuable insights in addressing such situations.[25] The author team studied corporations over many years and found that senior executives are often faced with similar sets of opposing goals, which can polarize their organizations. Such tensions or paradoxes fall into three categories, which may be related to three questions that many leaders view as "either/or" choices.

- *Do we manage for today or for tomorrow?* A firm's long-term survival requires taking risks and learning from failure in the pursuit of new products and services. However, companies also need consistency in their products and services. This depicts the tension between existing products and new ones, stability and change. This is the *innovation paradox*. For example, in the late 1990s, IBM's senior leaders saw the Internet wave and felt the need to harness the new technology. However, the firm also needed to sustain its traditional strength in client-server markets. Each strategy required different structures, cultures, rewards, and metrics–which could not easily be executed in tandem.
- *Do we stick to boundaries or cross them?* Global supply chains can be very effective, but they may also lack flexibility. New ideas can emerge from innovation activities that are dispersed throughout the world. However, not having all the talent and brains in one location can be costly. This is the tension between global connectedness and local needs, the *globalization paradox*. In 2009, NASA's director of human health and performance started an initiative geared toward generating new knowledge through collaborative cross-firm and cross-disciplinary work. Not too surprisingly, he faced strong pushback from scientists interested in protecting their turf and their identities as independent experts. Although both collaboration and independent work were required to generate new innovations, they posed organizational and cultural challenges.
- *Whom do we focus on, shareholders or stakeholders?* Clearly, companies exist to create value. But managers are often faced with the choice between maximizing shareholder gains while trying to create benefits for a wide range of stakeholders–employees, customers, society, etc. However, being socially responsible may bring down a firm's share price, and prioritizing employees may conflict with short-term shareholders' or customers' needs. This is the *obligation paradox*. Paul Polman, Unilever's CEO, launched the Unilever Sustainable Living Plan in 2010. The goal was to double the size of the business over 10 years, improve the health and well-being of more than a billion people, and cut the firm's environmental impact in half. He argued that such investments would lead to greater profits over the long term; whereas a singular focus on short-term profits would have adverse effects on society and the environment. His arguments were persuasive to many; however, there have been many challenges in implementing the plan. Not surprisingly, it has caused uncertainty among senior executives that has led to anxiety and fights over resource allocation.

ambidexterity
the challenge managers face of both aligning resources to take advantage of existing product markets and proactively exploring new opportunities.

Some authors have developed the concept of **"ambidexterity"** (similar to the aforementioned "innovation paradox"), which refers to a manager's challenge to both align resources to take advantage of existing product markets and proactively explore new opportunities.[26] Strategy Spotlight 1.1 discusses ambidextrous behaviors that are essential for success in today's challenging marketplace.

1.1 STRATEGY SPOTLIGHT

AMBIDEXTROUS BEHAVIORS: COMBINING ALIGNMENT AND ADAPTABILITY

A study involving 41 business units in 10 multinational companies identified four ambidextrous behaviors in individuals. Such behaviors are the essence of ambidexterity, and they illustrate how a dual capacity for alignment and adaptability can be woven into the fabric of an organization at the individual level.

They take time and are alert to opportunities beyond the confines of their own jobs. A large computer company's sales manager became aware of a need for a new software module that nobody currently offered. Instead of selling the customer something else, he worked up a business case for the new module. With management's approval, he began working full time on its development.

They are cooperative and seek out opportunities to combine their efforts with others. A marketing manager for Italy was responsible for supporting a newly acquired subsidiary. When frustrated about the limited amount of contact she had with her peers in other countries, she began discussions with them. This led to the creation of a European marketing forum that meets quarterly to discuss issues, share best practices, and collaborate on marketing plans.

They are brokers, always looking to build internal networks. When visiting the head office in St. Louis, a Canadian plant manager heard about plans for a $10 million investment for a new tape manufacturing plant. After inquiring further about the plans and returning to Canada, he contacted a regional manager in Manitoba, who he knew was looking for ways to build his business. With some generous support from the Manitoba government, the regional manager bid for, and ultimately won, the $10 million investment.

They are multitaskers who are comfortable wearing more than one hat. Although an operations manager for a major coffee and tea distributor was charged with running his plant as efficiently as possible, he took it upon himself to identify value-added services for his clients. By developing a dual role, he was able to manage operations and develop a promising electronic module that automatically reported impending problems inside a coffee vending machine. With corporate funding, he found a subcontractor to develop the software, and he then piloted the module in his own operations. It was so successful that it was eventually adopted by operations managers in several other countries.

A recent *Harvard Business Review* article provides some useful insights on how one can become a more ambidextrous leader. Consider the following questions:

- **Do you meet your numbers?**
- **Do you help others?**
- **What do you do for your peers?** Are you just their in-house competitor?
- **When you manage up, do you bring problems—or problems with possible solutions?**
- **Are you transparent?** Managers who get a reputation for spinning events gradually lose the trust of peers and superiors.
- **Are you developing a group of senior managers who know you and are willing to back your original ideas with resources?**

Sources: Birkinshaw, J. and C. Gibson. 2004. Building ambidexterity into an organization. *MIT Sloan Management Review,* 45(4): 47–55; and Bower, J. L. 2007. Solve the succession crisis by growing inside-out leaders. *Harvard Business Review,* 85(11): 90–99.

THE STRATEGIC MANAGEMENT PROCESS

LO 1-2

Understand the strategic management process and its three interrelated and principal activities.

We've identified three ongoing processes–analyses, decisions, and actions–that are central to strategic management. In practice, these three processes–often referred to as strategy analysis, strategy formulation, and strategy implementation–are highly interdependent and do not take place one after the other in a sequential fashion in most companies.

Intended versus Realized Strategies

Henry Mintzberg, a management scholar at McGill University, argues that viewing the strategic management process as one in which analysis is followed by optimal decisions and their subsequent meticulous implementation neither describes the strategic management process accurately nor prescribes ideal practice.[27] He sees the business environment as far from predictable, thus limiting our ability for analysis. Further, decisions are seldom based on optimal rationality alone, given the political processes that occur in all organizations.[28]

EXHIBIT 1.2 Realized Strategy and Intended Strategy: Usually Not the Same

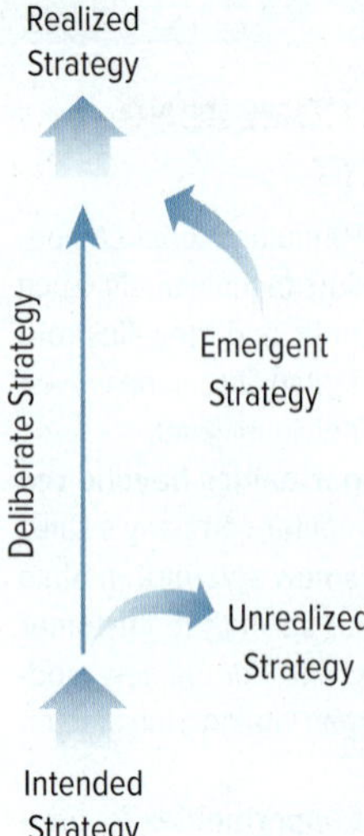

Source: Adapted from Mintzberg, H., and Waters, J. A. 1985. Of strategies: Deliberate and emergent. *Strategic Management Journal,* 6: 257–272.

intended strategy strategy in which organizational decisions are determined only by analysis.

Taking into consideration the limitations discussed previously, Mintzberg proposed an alternative model. As depicted in Exhibit 1.2, decisions following from analysis, in this model, constitute the **intended strategy** of the firm. For a variety of reasons, the intended strategy rarely survives in its original form. Unforeseen environmental developments, unanticipated resource constraints, or changes in managerial preferences may result in at least some parts of the intended strategy remaining *unrealized.*

Consider how a factor clearly outside of management's control–weather–can impact a firm and lead to changes in its strategy:[29]

> Superdry PLC, a British clothing brand, suffered a 21 percent drop in its share price on October 15, 2018. Why? The firm said that unseasonably hot weather in the UK, continental Europe, and on the East Coast of the U.S. over the summer and autumn had significantly affected demand for its cold-weather clothing–which generates 45 percent of its annual sales. As noted by its former Chief Executive Euan Sutherland, "Superdry is a strong brand with significant growth opportunities...but we are not immune to the challenges presented by this extraordinary period of unseasonably hot weather."
>
> In response to the weather change, the firm said that it is seeking to address its reliance on autumn and winter clothing by expanding into dresses, skirts, and women's tops. In addition, it plans to move into new market segments such as sports products, giving the company's global consumers broader choices.

realized strategy strategy in which organizational decisions are determined by both analysis and unforeseen environmental developments, unanticipated resource constraints, and/or changes in managerial preferences.

Thus, the final **realized strategy** of any firm is a combination of deliberate and emergent strategies.

Next, we will address each of the three key strategic management processes–strategy analysis, strategy formulation, and strategy implementation–and provide a brief overview of the chapters.

Exhibit 1.3 depicts the strategic management process and indicates how it ties into the chapters in the book. Consistent with our previous discussion, we use two-way arrows to convey the interactive nature of the processes.

Before moving on, we point out that analyzing the environment and formulating strategies are, of course, important activities in the strategic management process. However, nothing happens until resources are allocated and effective strategies are successfully

EXHIBIT 1.3 The Strategic Management Process

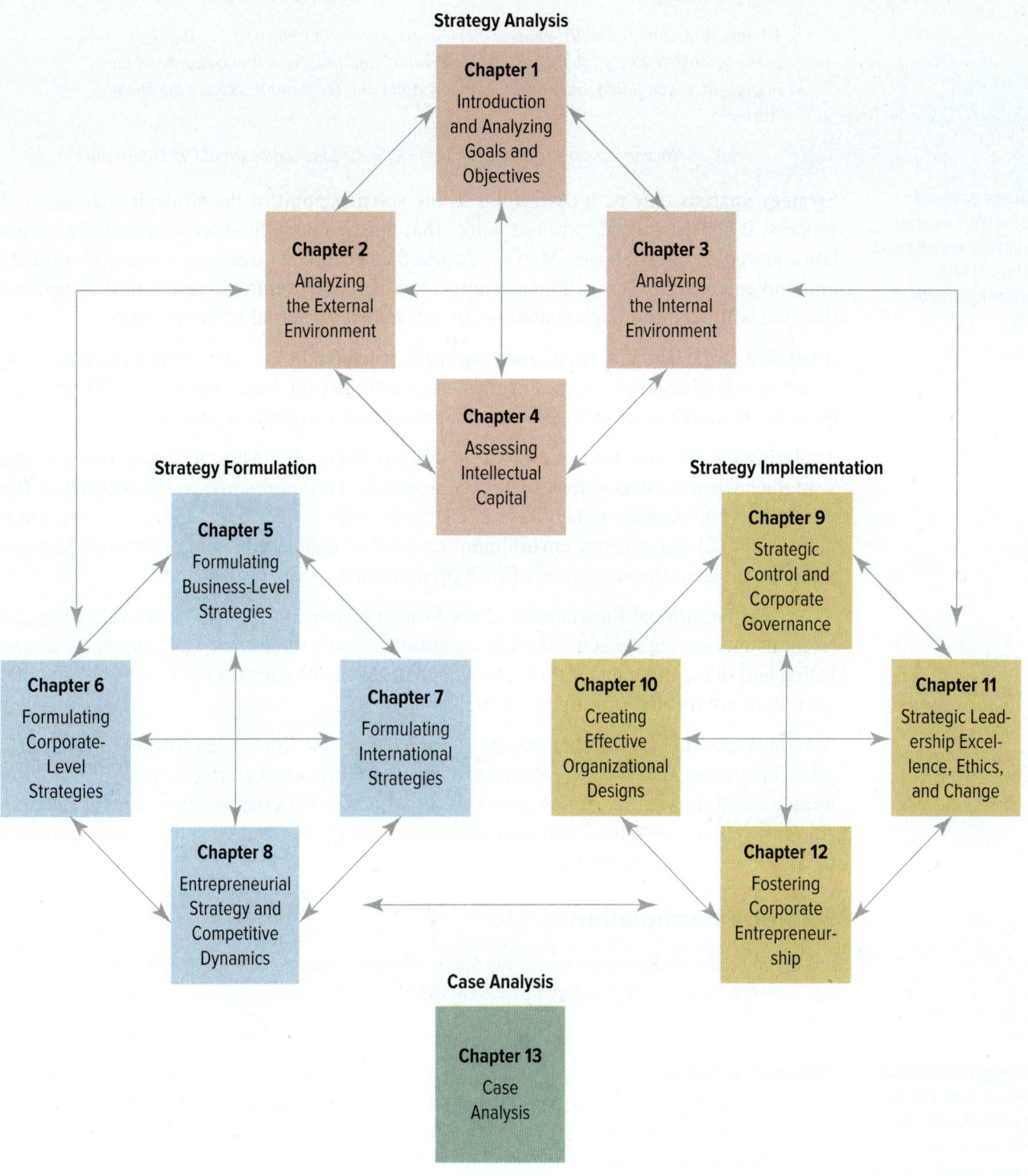

implemented. Rick Spielman, General Manager of the Minnesota Vikings (of the National Football League), provides valuable insight on this issue.[30] He recalls the many quarterbacks that he has interviewed over the past 25 years and notes that many of them can effectively draw up plays on the whiteboard and "you sit there and it's like listening to an offensive coordinator." However, that is not enough. He points out, "Now can he translate that and make those same decisions and those same type of reads in the two and a half seconds he has to get rid of the ball?"

Strategy Analysis

We measure, study, quantify, analyze every single piece of our business. . . . But then you've got to be able to take all that data and information and transform it into change in the organization and improvements in the organization and the formalization of the business strategy.

–Richard Anderson, former CEO of Delta Air Lines and current CEO of Amtrack[31]

strategy analysis study of firms' external and internal environments, and their fit with organizational vision and goals.

Strategy analysis may be looked upon as the starting point of the strategic management process. It consists of the "advance work" that must be done in order to effectively formulate and implement strategies. Many strategies fail because managers may want to formulate and implement strategies without a careful analysis of the overarching goals of the organization and without a thorough analysis of its external and internal environments.

Analyzing Organizational Goals and Objectives (Chapter 1) A firm's vision, mission, and strategic objectives form a hierarchy of goals that range from broad statements of intent and bases for competitive advantage to specific, measurable strategic objectives.

Analyzing the External Environment of the Firm (Chapter 2) Managers must monitor and scan the environment as well as analyze competitors. Two frameworks are provided: (1) The general environment consists of several elements, such as demographic and economic segments, and (2) the industry environment consists of competitors and other organizations that may threaten the success of a firm's products and services.

Assessing the Internal Environment of the Firm (Chapter 3) Analyzing the strengths and relationships among the activities that constitute a firm's value chain (e.g., operations, marketing and sales, and human resource management) can be a means of uncovering potential sources of competitive advantage for the firm.[32]

Assessing a Firm's Intellectual Assets (Chapter 4) The knowledge worker and a firm's other intellectual assets (e.g., patents) are important drivers of competitive advantages and wealth creation. We also assess how well the organization creates networks and relationships as well as how technology can enhance collaboration among employees and provide a means of accumulating and storing knowledge.[33]

Strategy Formulation

"You can have the best operations. You can be the most adept at whatever it is that you're doing. But, if you have a bad strategy, it's all for naught."

–Fred Smith, CEO of FedEx[34]

strategy formulation decisions made by firms regarding investments, commitments, and other aspects of operations that create and sustain competitive advantage.

Strategy formulation is developed at several levels. First, business-level strategy addresses the issue of how to compete in a given business to attain competitive advantage. Second, corporate-level strategy focuses on two issues: (a) what businesses to compete in and (b) how businesses can be managed to achieve synergy; that is, they create more value by working together than by operating as standalone businesses. Third, a firm must develop international strategies as it ventures beyond its national boundaries. Fourth, managers must formulate effective entrepreneurial initiatives.

Formulating Business-Level Strategy (Chapter 5) The question of how firms compete and outperform their rivals and how they achieve and sustain competitive advantages goes to the heart of strategic management. Successful firms strive to develop bases for competitive advantage, which can be achieved through cost leadership and/or differentiation as well as by focusing on a narrow or industrywide market segment.[35]

Formulating Corporate-Level Strategy (Chapter 6) Corporate-level strategy addresses a firm's portfolio (or group) of businesses. It asks: (1) What business (or businesses) should we compete in? and (2) How can we manage this portfolio of businesses to create synergies among the businesses?

Formulating International Strategy (Chapter 7) When firms enter foreign markets, they face both opportunities and pitfalls.[36] Managers must decide not only on the most appropriate entry strategy but also how they will go about attaining competitive advantages in international markets.[37]

Entrepreneurial Strategy and Competitive Dynamics (Chapter 8) Entrepreneurial activity aimed at new value creation is a major engine for economic growth. For entrepreneurial initiatives to succeed, viable opportunities must be recognized and effective strategies must be formulated.

Strategy Implementation

"Without strategy, execution is aimless. Without execution, strategy is useless."

–Morris Chang, Founding Chairman of Taiwan Semiconductor Manufacturing Company [38]

Clearly, sound strategies are of no value if they are not properly implemented.[39] **Strategy implementation** involves ensuring proper strategic controls and organizational designs, which includes establishing effective means to coordinate and integrate activities within the firm as well as with its suppliers, customers, and alliance partners.[40] Leadership plays a central role to ensure that the organization is committed to excellence and ethical behavior. It also promotes learning and continuous improvement and acts entrepreneurially in creating new opportunities.

strategy implementation
actions made by firms that carry out the formulated strategy, including strategic controls, organizational design, and leadership.

Strategic Control and Corporate Governance (Chapter 9) Firms must exercise two types of strategic control. First, informational control requires that organizations continually monitor and scan the environment and respond to threats and opportunities. Second, behavioral control involves the proper balance of rewards and incentives as well as cultures and boundaries (or constraints). Further, successful firms (those that are incorporated) practice effective corporate governance.

Creating Effective Organizational Designs (Chapter 10) Firms must have organizational structures and designs that are consistent with their strategy. In today's rapidly changing competitive environments, firms must ensure that their organizational boundaries–those internal to the firm and external–are more flexible and permeable.[41] Often, organizations develop strategic alliances to capitalize on the capabilities of other organizations.

Creating a Learning Organization and an Ethical Organization (Chapter 11) Effective leaders set a direction, design the organization, and develop an organization that is committed to excellence and ethical behavior. In addition, given rapid and unpredictable change, leaders must create a "learning organization" so that the entire organization can benefit from individual and collective talents.

Fostering Corporate Entrepreneurship (Chapter 12) Firms must continually improve and grow as well as find new ways to renew their organizations. Corporate entrepreneurship and innovation provide firms with new opportunities, and strategies should be formulated that enhance a firm's innovative capacity.

Chapter 13, "Analyzing Strategic Management Cases," provides guidelines and suggestions on how to evaluate cases in this course. Thus, the concepts and techniques discussed in the first 12 chapters can be applied to real-world organizations.

In the "*INSIGHTS* from Executives" sidebar we include an interview that the authors conducted with Usman Ghani, Chairman of ConfluCore, a large and successful consulting firm that has offices and affiliates on six continents.

1.1 ***INSIGHTS*** **from Executives**

THE STRATEGIC MANAGEMENT PROCESS

Usman Ghani, Chairman, ConfluCore

Biosketch

Usman Ghani has held leadership roles in strategic planning, marketing, operations, organization development, IT, and executive education, as well as led cross-functional, multicultural core business process teams to effective implementations. He is a former Fortune 100 executive distinguished by his record of developing powerful board policies and business strategies for a variety of industry leaders, including McKinsey & Company, Royal Dutch/Shell Group, Exxon Mobil Corporation, and HP/Electronic Data Systems.

Characterized as a high-energy visionary, Usman is passionate about helping complex organizations see the big picture so that they are capable of transformation. He consistently applies fresh thinking, refined dynamic strategy models, organizational approaches, and futuristic technologies to reveal the best solutions to compound challenges. His advisory firm, ConfluCore, integrates multiple concepts to generate *confluence* at the core of organizations to generate superior synergies. ConfluCore is headquartered in Las Colinas, Texas. It has offices and affiliates on all six continents and has been serving boards and senior executives worldwide for two decades.

Usman A. Ghani

With three Master's degrees from MIT and multiple certifications, courses, and diplomas, Usman has strived to undertake the tutelage of some of the world's premier thought leaders in each field he has taken on. These include Robert Blake, Peter Drucker, Jay Forrester, David McClelland, Edgar Schein, and Peter Senge. Believing in lifelong learning, he continues his own development personally and professionally.

Question 1. In your experience working with organizations, what have you found to be key attributes of successful strategies?

Successful strategies have not a few but *several* attributes and all of them must operate *in concert.* The three aspects I emphasize are, that: (a) *considered* strategic processes are applied, (b) strategies display systematic *adaptability,* and (c) customer offerings are effectively *differentiated* by the organizations. To ensure this, strategic management should itself also be *regularly assessed.*

Question 2. Looking at it from the other side, what are some of the key pitfalls you've seen firms fall prey to that have resulted in strategic failures?

Beware! While not broadly published, strategic failures outnumber strategic successes in all sizes and types of organizations. It is only when the acclaimed ones (like Borders, GE, Kodak, and Sears) result in large-scale failures that we become aware and then only for a while. Often, it is the dysfunctional strategic management of these organizations that fail them.

Successes and failures occur every day, but only for the attentive. These accumulate and, upon crossing some threshold, successes are celebrated while failures are shunned. So, the top pitfall is that strategic management often lacks a critiquing process to leverage *both* successes and "failures" as active learning. Both can contribute effectively if acknowledged by management. Bill Gates said there is nothing more dangerous than not knowing why and how you have succeeded. I would add to that statement that failures are learning steps and opportunities to leapfrog ahead; without knowing the why and how of your failures, over time organizations are bound to repeat their past failures or accumulate the negative consequences from their smaller failures, eventually becoming big failures. However, very few organizations realize this and management may hide failures to avoid negative consequences and also to exaggerate successes to beget recognition.

The most dangerous pitfalls in strategic management are often attitudinal and behavioral. These include disallowing changes to static/fixed strategies, becoming comfortable with average benchmarks, overconfident executives, complacent management, groupthink cultures, playing favorites, etc. All these can be checked if management so desires to avert attitudinal and behavioral pitfalls.

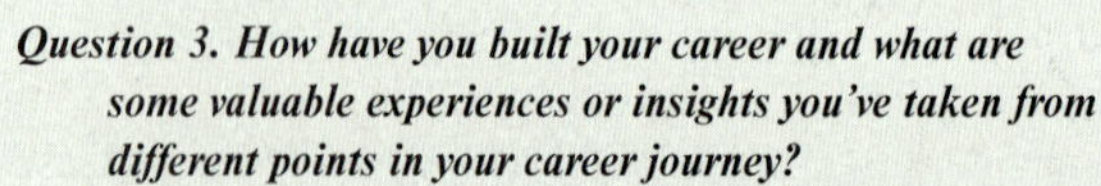

Question 3. How have you built your career and what are some valuable experiences or insights you've taken from different points in your career journey?

My career is atypical. Being fortunate to get guidance of great minds early on, I avoided singular specialization and aspired to understand a wide range of subjects and strove to integrate across these. By choice,

continued

I pursued multiple cross-disciplinary academic programs at the best institutions and took on challenging integrative management projects with the finest and largest global corporations. Never tilting with one discipline alone, I kept experimenting with inclusive ideas that have ensued for me into one powerful concept: confluence–*the dynamic integration of core actions and decisions of an organization.*

Most companies and departments like to try integrative notions (like cross-functional communication), but these do not herald fullest potential synergy. Applying innovative methods, my company, ConfluCore (stands for *confluence at the core*) has effected real integration providing boards and management deeper insights into the workings of their organizations, meeting their crucial challenges, and developing self-convincing practicable, productive solutions. I say that when a sprinter wins a race, we do not kiss his feet; nor wish to pat his heart; nor praise his determined mind, nor admire any other one function of his. The whole human accomplished the win and gets the award (typically a medal around the neck). Similarly, an organization is a whole: we should never run it believing that we have one or two excellent departments. This is dangerous as we have seen in many corporate failures of the 21st century. We must have all functions and departments confluent at the organizational core. As we have seen, reasonably well-run departments that are mutually and dynamically integrated *for confluence* outdo those organizations that have one or a few excellent functions but lack dynamic integration.

Question 4. Based on your experience, what are some of the most critical attributes of effective strategic leaders?

Effective strategic leaders underscore strategic management as having three overlapping functions and are not biased toward any one function. They advance strategic analysis, formulation, and implementation in proper proportions. They become orchestra conductors, using Peter Drucker's metaphor. I am known for saying that a CEO is a Chief Everything Officer and so, responsible for *creating confluence* among all aspects of the organization, never tilting to one at the expense of the others. I have seen that executives who tilt eventually end up performing poorly and not really leaving a legacy.

The roles of effective strategic leaders includes developing visions, designing organizations, building integrative cultures, and inspiring all organizational stakeholders to attain greater heights. These roles carry huge influence and convey power. So, when done ethically, they advance the organization's power to innovate and redefine their excellence in serving customers. As these roles are more interactive and social, they are neither executed either alone nor with a small group in isolation. Effectiveness demands deep interaction skills, principally listening, empathizing, reflecting, motivating, resolving conflicts, and teambuilding. Effective strategic leaders use appropriate metaphors at appropriate times to resonate with the stakeholders. Additionally, an effective leader is open to critique to develop deeper self-awareness, which is rather uncommon. I have seen that the few leaders who yearn for deeper self-awareness and candid interactions, far outperform others who don't or those who are afraid to be perceived as vulnerable.

Question 5. How do you see the growing focus on advanced technologies, such as data analytics and artificial intelligence, influencing firms and industries over the next decade?

Advanced technologies and technical innovation are helpful when they are strategically deployed by an organization. Two effective approaches for this include: (a) changing the method and quality of an organization's *offerings,* and (b) developing better *support systems* to advance actions and decisions of the board and management to the next level. These two should also be included in an organization's technology strategy.

Offering-focused technologies enhance the value of the company's products and services and provide renewed competitive positioning while also advancing the state of its industry. Support-systems technologies also provide significant competitive advantage (if these are not adopted hurriedly or taken as "we too") by supplying real information faster and more meaningfully to the right people. Organizations should define the role (and processes) of their support systems *to establish and rekindle these* over time with the right advanced technologies.

The strategic management of support systems is increasingly important and must incorporate "soft" factors that are "invisible" or the intangible aspects of organizations. Such factors are not typically captured in classic accounting practices. For example, elements of corporate culture, level of organizational morale, stock of talent capability, and the like are the social aspects that should be included in strategic management. Additionally, boards and leadership should apply smart simulations to anticipate the consequences of their decisions, develop alternative strategies, indulge in scenario planning, and, in the process, also actively seek to acquire new learning themselves.

continued

Question 6. How important have you found integrity and organizational ethics to be for leaders and organizations? Can you provide any examples of times where integrity played a pivotal role in organizations you've worked with?

Organizations are social entities. Hence, ethics and values are paramount to establishing trust that rallies sound action by its people. When ethics are evident in actions of leaders, people walk the talk and live the values. But when ethics and values are "written on paper only", then terrible things happen. A recent example of the latter is Wells Fargo where the espoused theory was customer service and trust, while the strategy-in-action was compelling customers to open multiple accounts so the bank could project the market perception of growth, while in reality the number of customers remained the same. The fall from grace that the bank faced is still ongoing.

Ethical strategic leaders know that convergence of espoused values with values that are practiced fosters tremendous trust and mobilizes an unstoppable cultural momentum that spawns innovation, loyalty, and progress, and loyalty. But when these are dissimilar, not only do the most ambitious of strategies fail, they also take a long time to recover, if ever. For example, Enron never recovered and disappeared leaving behind its ghastly mark on corporate America.

Let's now address two concepts–corporate governance and stakeholder management–that are critical to the strategic management process.

LO 1-3

Identify the vital role of corporate governance and stakeholder management, as well as how "symbiosis" can be achieved among an organization's stakeholders.

THE ROLE OF CORPORATE GOVERNANCE AND STAKEHOLDER MANAGEMENT

corporate governance the relationship among various participants in determining the direction and performance of corporations. The primary participants are (1) the shareholders, (2) the management (led by the chief executive officer), and (3) the board of directors.

Most business enterprises that employ more than a few dozen people are organized as corporations. As you recall from your finance classes, the overall purpose of a corporation is to maximize the long-term return to the owners (shareholders). Thus, we may ask: Who is really responsible for fulfilling this purpose? Robert Monks and Neil Minow provide a useful definition of **corporate governance** as "the relationship among various participants in determining the direction and performance of corporations. The primary participants are (1) the shareholders, (2) the management (led by the chief executive officer), and (3) the board of directors."[42] This relationship is illustrated in Exhibit 1.4.

EXHIBIT 1.4 The Key Elements of Corporate Governance

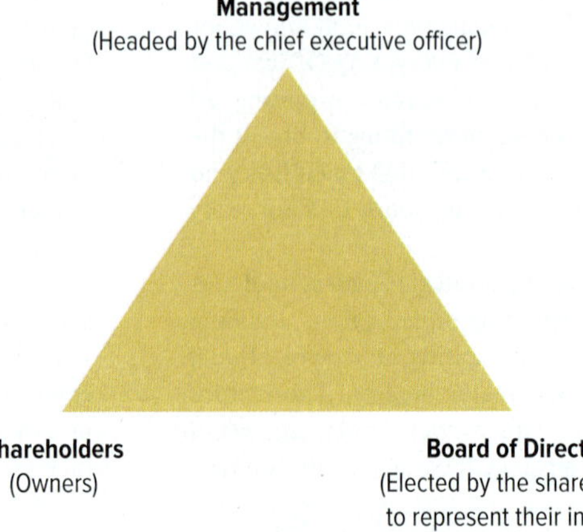

The board of directors (BOD) are the elected representatives of the shareholders charged with ensuring that the interests and motives of management are aligned with those of the owners (i.e., shareholders). In many cases, the BOD is diligent in fulfilling its purpose. For example, Intel Corporation, the giant $59 billion maker of microprocessor chips, practices sound governance. Its BOD follows guidelines to ensure that its members are independent (i.e., are not members of the executive management team and do not have close personal ties to top executives) so that they can provide proper oversight; it has explicit guidelines on the selection of director candidates (to avoid "cronyism"). It provides detailed procedures for formal evaluations of directors and the firm's top officers.[43] Such guidelines serve to ensure that management is acting in the best interests of shareholders.[44]

Recently, there has been much criticism as well as cynicism by both citizens and the business press about the poor job that management and the BODs of large corporations are doing. We only have to look at the scandals at firms such as Arthur Andersen, Best Buy, Olympus, Enron, Volkswagen, and Wells Fargo.[45] Such malfeasance has led to an erosion of the public's trust in corporations. For example, according to the 2014 CNBC/Burson-Marsteller Corporation Perception Indicator, a global survey of 25,000 individuals, only 52 percent of the public in developed markets has a favorable view of corporations.[46] Forty-five percent felt corporations have "too much influence over the government." More than half of the U.S. public said "strong and influential" corporations are "bad" even if they are promoting innovation and growth, and only 9 percent of the public in the United States says corporate CEOs are "among the most respected" in society.

Perhaps, part of the responsibility—or blame—lies with boards of directors who are often not delivering on their core mission: providing strong oversight and strategic support for management's efforts to create long-term value.[47] In a recent study by McKinsey & Co., only 34 percent of 772 directors agreed that the boards on which they served fully comprehended their firm's strategies. And only 22 percent claimed their boards were completely aware of how their firms created value. Finally, a mere 16 percent claimed their boards had a strong understanding of the dynamics of their firms' industries.

One area in which public anger is most pronounced is the excessive compensation of the top executives of well-known firms. It is now clear that much of the bonus pay awarded to executives on Wall Street in the past was richly undeserved.[48] Case in point, 2011 was a poor year for financial stocks: 35 of the 50 largest financial company stocks fell that year. The sector lost 17 percent—compared to flat performance for the Standard & Poor's 500. However, even as the sector struggled, the average pay of finance company CEOs rose 20.4 percent. For example, JPMorgan CEO Jamie Dimon was the highest-paid banker—with $23.1 million in compensation, an 11 percent increase from the previous year. The firm's shareholders didn't do as well—the stock fell 20 percent.[49]

Of course, executive pay is not restricted to financial institutions. A study released in 2016 entitled "The 100 Most Overpaid CEOs" addressed what it viewed as the "fundamental disconnect between CEO pay and performance."[50] It found that CEO pay grew 997 percent over the most recent 36-year period—a rate that outpaced the growth in the cost of living, the productivity of the economy, and the stock market. The lead author, Rosanna Weaver, argues that the latter point disproves "the claim that the growth in CEO pay reflects the 'performance' of the company, the value of its stock, or the ability of the CEO to do anything but disproportionately raise the amount of his pay."

Clearly, there is a strong need for improved corporate governance, and we will address this topic in Chapter 9.[51] We focus on three important mechanisms to ensure effective corporate governance: an effective and engaged board of directors, shareholder activism, and proper managerial rewards and incentives.[52] In addition to these internal controls, a key role is played by various external control mechanisms.[53] These include the auditors, banks, analysts, an active financial press, and the threat of hostile takeovers.

Alternative Perspectives of Stakeholder Management

Generating long-term returns for the shareholders is the primary goal of a publicly held corporation.[54] As noted by former Chrysler vice chairman Robert Lutz, "We are here to serve the shareholder and create shareholder value. I insist that the only person who owns the company is the person who paid good money for it."[55]

Despite the primacy of generating shareholder value, managers who focus solely on the interests of the owners of the business will often make poor decisions that lead to negative, unanticipated outcomes.[56] For example, decisions such as mass layoffs to increase profits, ignoring issues related to conservation of the natural environment to save money, and exerting excessive pressure on suppliers to lower prices can harm the firm in the long run. Such actions would likely lead to negative outcomes such as alienated employees, increased governmental oversight and fines, and disloyal suppliers.

Clearly, in addition to *shareholders,* there are other *stakeholders* (e.g., suppliers, customers) who must be taken into account in the strategic management process.[57] A stakeholder can be defined as an individual or group, inside or outside the company, that has a stake in and can influence an organization's performance. Each stakeholder group makes various claims on the company.[58] Exhibit 1.5 provides a list of major stakeholder groups and the nature of their claims on the company.

stakeholder management
a firm's strategy for recognizing and responding to the interests of all its salient stakeholders.

Zero Sum or Symbiosis? There are two opposing ways of looking at the role of **stakeholder management**.[59] The first one can be termed "zero sum." Here, the various stakeholders compete for the organization's resources: the gain of one individual or group is the loss of another individual or group. For example, employees want higher wages (which drive down profits), suppliers want higher prices for their inputs and slower, more flexible delivery times (which drive up costs), customers want fast deliveries and higher quality (which drive up costs), the community at large wants charitable contributions (which take money from company goals), and so on. This zero-sum thinking is rooted, in part, in the traditional conflict between workers and management, leading to the formation of unions and sometimes ending in adversarial union-management negotiations and long, bitter strikes.

Consider, for example, the many stakeholder challenges facing Walmart, the world's largest retailer.

> Walmart strives to ramp up growth while many stakeholders are watching nervously: employees and trade unions; shareholders, investors, and creditors; suppliers and joint venture partners; the governments of the United States and other nations where the retailer operates; and customers. In addition many non-governmental organizations (NGOs), particularly in countries where the retailer buys its products, are closely monitoring Walmart. Walmart's stakeholders have different interests, and not all of them share the firm's goals.

EXHIBIT 1.5
An Organization's Key Stakeholders and the Nature of Their Claims

Stakeholder Group	Nature of Claim
Stockholders	Dividends, capital appreciation
Employees	Wages, benefits, safe working environment, job security
Suppliers	Payment on time, assurance of continued relationship
Creditors	Payment of interest, repayment of principal
Customers	Value, warranties
Government	Taxes, compliance with regulations
Communities	Good citizenship behavior such as charities, employment, not polluting the environment

There will always be conflicting demands on organizations. However, organizations can achieve mutual benefit through stakeholder symbiosis, which recognizes that stakeholders are dependent upon each other for their success and well-being.[60] Consider Procter & Gamble's "laundry detergent compaction," a technique for compressing even more cleaning power into ever smaller concentrations.

P&G perfected a technique that could compact two or three times as much cleaning powder into a liquid concentration. This remarkable breakthrough has led to not only a change in consumer shopping habits but also a revolution in industry supply chain economics. Here's how several key stakeholders are affected:

> *Consumers* love concentrated liquids because they are easier to carry, pour, and store. *Retailers,* meanwhile, prefer them because they take up less floor and shelf space, which leads to higher sales-per-square-foot–a big deal for Walmart, Target, and other big retailers. *Shipping and wholesalers,* meanwhile, prefer reduced-sized products because smaller bottles translate into reduced fuel consumption and improved warehouse space utilization. And, finally, *environmentalists* favor such products because they use less packaging and produce less waste than conventional products.[61]

Social Responsibility and Environmental Sustainability: Moving beyond the Immediate Stakeholders

LO 1-4

Understand the importance of social responsibility, including environmental sustainability, and how it can enhance a corporation's innovation strategy.

Organizations cannot ignore the interests and demands of stakeholders such as citizens and society in general that are beyond its immediate constituencies–customers, owners, suppliers, and employees. The realization that firms have multiple stakeholders and that evaluating their performance must go beyond analyzing their financial results has led to a new way of thinking about businesses and their relationship to society.

First, *social responsibility* recognizes that businesses must respond to society's expectations regarding their obligations to society. Second, the *triple bottom line approach* evaluates a firm's performance. This perspective takes into account financial, social, and environmental performance. Third, *making the case for sustainability initiatives* addresses some of the challenges managers face in obtaining approvals for such projects–and how to overcome them.

social responsibility the expectation that businesses or individuals will strive to improve the overall welfare of society.

Social Responsibility **Social responsibility** is the expectation that businesses or individuals will strive to improve the overall welfare of society.[62] From the perspective of a business, this means that managers must take active steps to make society better by virtue of the business being in existence.[63] What constitutes socially responsible behavior changes over time. In the 1970s, affirmative action was a high priority; during the 1990s and up to the present time, the public has been concerned about environmental quality. Many firms have responded to this by engaging in recycling and reducing waste. And in the wake of terrorist attacks on New York City and the Pentagon, as well as the continuing threat from terrorists worldwide, a new kind of priority has arisen: the need to be vigilant concerning public safety.

In order to maximize the positive impact of corporate social responsibility (CSR) initiatives, firms need to create coherent strategies.[64] Research has shown that companies' CSR activities are generally divided across three theaters of practice and assigning the activities accordingly is an important initial step.

- *Theater one: Focusing on philanthropy*. Here, programs are not designed to increase profits or revenues. Examples include financial contributions to civic and charity organizations as well as the participation and engagement of employees in community programs.
- *Theater two: Improving operational effectiveness*. Initiatives in this theater function within existing business models to provide social or environmental benefits and support a company's value creating activities in order to enhance efficiency and effectiveness. They typically can increase revenue or decrease costs–or both. Examples

include sustainability initiatives that can reduce the use of resources, waste, or emissions–to cut costs. Or, firms can invest in employee health care and working conditions to enhance retention and productivity–as well as a firm's reputation.

- *Theater three: Transforming the business model.* Improved business performance is a requirement of programs in this theater and is predicated on social and environmental challenges and results. An example would be Hindustan Unilever's Project Shakti in India. Rather than use the typical wholesaler-retailer distribution model to reach remote villages, the firm recruited village women who were provided with training and microfinance loans in order to sell soaps, detergents, and other products door-to-door. More than 65,000 women were recruited and not only were they able to typically double their household's income but it also contributed to public health via access to hygiene products. The project attained more than $100 million in revenues and has led the firm to roll out similar programs in other countries.

A key stakeholder group that appears to be particularly susceptible to corporate social responsibility (CSR) initiatives is customers.[65] Surveys indicate a strong positive relationship between CSR behaviors and consumers' reactions to a firm's products and services.[66] For example:

- Corporate Citizenship's poll conducted by Cone Communications found that "84 percent of Americans say they would be likely to switch brands to one associated with a good cause, if price and quality are similar."[67]
- Hill & Knowlton/Harris's Interactive poll reveals that "79 percent of Americans take corporate citizenship into account when deciding whether to buy a particular company's product and 37 percent consider corporate citizenship an important factor when making purchasing decisions."[68]

Such findings are consistent with a large body of research that confirms the positive influence of CSR on consumers' company evaluations and product purchase intentions across a broad range of product categories.

triple bottom line assessment of a firm's financial, social, and environmental performance.

The Triple Bottom Line: Incorporating Financial as Well as Environmental and Social Costs Many companies are now measuring what has been called a **"triple bottom line."** This involves assessing financial, social, and environmental performance. Shell, NEC, Procter & Gamble, and others have recognized that failing to account for the environmental and social costs of doing business poses risks to the company and its community.[69]

Social and environmental issues can ultimately become financial issues. According to Lars Sorensen, CEO of Novo Nordisk, a $17 billion global pharmaceutical firm based in Denmark:[70]

> If we keep polluting, stricter regulations will be imposed, and energy consumption will become more costly. The same thing applies to the social side. If we don't treat employees well, if we don't behave as good corporate citizens in our local communities, and if we don't provide inexpensive products for poorer countries, governments will impose regulations on us that will end up being very costly.

The environmental revolution has been almost four decades in the making.[71] In the 1960s and 1970s, companies were in a state of denial regarding their firms' impact on the natural environment. However, a series of visible ecological problems created a groundswell for strict governmental regulation. In the United States, Lake Erie was "dead," and in Japan, people died of mercury poisoning. More recently, Japan's horrific tsunami that took place on March 11, 2011, Hurricane Sandy's devastation on the East Coast of the United States in late October 2012, and Hurricane Michael's heavy destruction of Florida's Gulf Coast in October 2018 have raised alarms.

As noted by Andrew Winston, founder of Winston Eco-Strategies, the norms and expectations about how firms manage environmental and social issues are rapidly changing.[72] For example, in 2011, only 20 percent of the S&P companies produced sustainability reports. However, by 2016, 82 percent did, providing public, detailed looks at their environmental and social initiatives and performance. A growing number have integrated these sustainability reports into their annual financial reports.

Winston's company maintains a public database on the sustainability goals set by multinational firms. Such commitments include objectives such as "reduce greenhouse gas emissions by 50 percent by 2025," and "ensure women make up 40 percent of management roles." Greater than 90 percent of the 200 largest companies in the world now have public targets on social or environmental performance–and it is nearly 100 percent if we exclude Chinese state-owned enterprises, which typically only follow government mandates. More than 130 of the world's largest companies are now committed to 100 percent renewable energy. Ten years ago, the number of large firms with renewable energy goals, or any sustainability objectives, was negligible.

For many successful firms, environmental values are now becoming a central part of their cultures and management processes.[73] And, as noted earlier, environmental impacts are being audited and accounted for as the third bottom line. According to a recent corporate report, "If we aren't good corporate citizens as reflected in a Triple Bottom Line that takes into account social and environmental responsibilities along with financial ones–eventually our stock price, our profits, and our entire business could suffer."[74] Also, a CEO survey on sustainability by Accenture debunks the notion that sustainability and profitability are mutually exclusive corporate goals. The study found that sustainability is being increasingly recognized as a source of cost efficiencies and revenue growth. In many companies, sustainability activities have led to increases in revenue and profits.

Strategy Spotlight 1.2 discusses some of the challenges and initiatives directed toward environmental sustainability in the fashion industry.

Many firms have profited by investing in socially responsible behavior, including those activities that enhance environmental sustainability. However, how do such "socially responsible" companies fare in terms of shareholder returns compared to benchmarks such as the Standard & Poor's 500 Index? Let's look at some of the evidence.

> SRI (socially responsible investing) is a broad-based approach to investing that now encompasses an estimated $3.7 trillion, or $1 out of every $9 under professional management in the United States.[75] SRI recognizes that corporate responsibility and societal concerns are considerations in investment decisions. With SRI, investors have the opportunity to put their money to work to build a more sustainable world while earning competitive returns both today and over time.
>
> And, as the saying goes, nice guys don't have to finish last. The ING SRI Index Fund, which tracks the stocks of 50 companies, enjoyed a 47.4 percent return in a recent year. That easily beat the 2.65 percent gain of the Standard & Poor's 500 stock index. A review of the 145 socially responsible equity mutual and exchange-traded funds tracked by Morningstar also shows that 65 percent of them outperformed the S&P 500.[76]

Making the Business Case for Sustainability Initiatives We mentioned many financial and nonfinancial benefits associated with sustainability initiatives in the previous section. However, in practice, such initiatives often have difficulty making it through the conventional approval process within corporations. This is primarily because, before companies make investments in projects, managers want to know their return on investment.[77]

The ROIs on sustainability projects are often very difficult to quantify for a number of reasons. Among these are:

1. ***The data necessary to calculate ROI accurately are often not available when it comes to sustainability projects.*** However, sustainability programs may often find their success beyond company boundaries, so internal systems and process metrics can't capture all the relevant numbers.

1.2 STRATEGY SPOTLIGHT

ENVIRONMENTAL SUSTAINABILITY IN THE FASHION INDUSTRY

The $3 trillion fashion industry employs over 60 million people along its global value chain. Although it makes 100 billion accessories and garments each year, three-fifths of them are thrown away within a year, according to McKinsey & Company. Further, a vast amount of cotton, water, and power is used to make their products, but less than 1 percent is recycled into new clothes, according to an environmental research group in England. Amazingly, the United Nations Economic Commission for Europe estimates that about 40 percent of clothes in the wardrobes of developed countries are never worn! To provide some perspective, Rob Opsomer, a sustainability researcher asserts that "the equivalent of a dump truck filled with textiles gets landfilled or incinerated every single second."

Inditex SA, the company that owns Zara and several other brands, made 1.6 billion garments in 2016—a scale that has helped its stock price quintuple over a recent 10-year period. However, recently industry growth has slowed, in part because millennials have become sensitive to fast fashion's impact on the environment. (In fact, according to Boston Consulting Group, one-third of this demographic consistently identifies sustainability as a factor that influences their purchasing habits.) Plus, they exhibit a preference for spending on experiences rather than goods.

Despite their strong past performance, Inditex has missed analysts' revenue expectations in recent quarters and its shares have lost about one third of their value since the summer of 2017. As noted by Edwin Keh, CEO of the Hong Kong Research Institute of Textiles and Apparel, "Their business model is fundamentally unsustainable. We all have enough stuff."

This situation creates an opportunity for companies to use sustainability to differentiate their brands. With growing concerns over the waste, retailers have begun placing recycling bins prominently in many stores, using greener materials, etc., to help win over customers. Let's look at some of Inditex's initiatives:

- Began disassembling old clothing to spin into yarns for fashions it markets as "garments with a past."
- Grouped many of its sustainability efforts—clothes made from organic cotton and repurposed fabrics into a sub-brand called Join Life.
- To boost the share of greener textiles in its mix, the firm has funded research programs at MIT and universities in Spain. One initiative is to try using 3D printing to make textiles using by-products from timber operations.

Inditex says that for now they're absorbing the extra costs of using recycled or reconstituted garments. The Join Life line is priced competitively with other items in the Zara stores—T-shirts cost less than $10 and jeans are priced under $40. The firm is striving to keep a lid on prices of its greener materials and it expects the cost to fall as production increases. Anna Gedda, an executive at rival H&M, whose firm has undertaken similar initiatives, asserts, "We take it as a long-term investment instead of charging it to our customers. We believe sustainable fashion should be affordable for all."

Sources: Hirtenstein, A., and D. Wei. 2018. The greening of throwaway stuff. *Bloomberg BusinessWeek*, May 7: 18-19; Kell, G. 2018. Can fashion be sustainable? *forbes.com*, June 4: np; and Mellery-Pratt, R. 2017. 5 sustainability threats to fashion. *businessfashion.com*, May 26: np.

2. ***Many of the benefits from such projects are intangible.*** Traditional financial models are built around relatively easy-to-measure, monetized results. Yet many of the benefits of sustainability projects involve fuzzy intangibles, such as the goodwill that can enhance a firm's brand equity.
3. ***The payback period is on a different time frame.*** Even when their future benefits can be forecast, sustainability projects often require longer-term payback windows.

Clearly, the case for sustainability projects needs to be made on the basis of a more holistic and comprehensive understanding of all the tangible and intangible benefits rather than whether or not they meet existing hurdle rates for traditional investment projects. For example, 3M uses a lower hurdle rate for pollution prevention projects. When it comes to environmental projects, IKEA allows a 10- to 15-year payback period, considerably longer than it allows for other types of investment. And Diversey, a cleaning products company, has employed a portfolio approach. It has established two hurdles for projects in its carbon reduction plan: a three-year payback and a cost per megaton of carbon avoided. Out of 120 possible projects ranging from lighting retrofits to solar photovoltaic systems, only 30 cleared both hurdles. Although about 60 of the other ideas could reach *one,* an expanded 90-project portfolio, all added together, met the double hurdle. Subsequently, Diversey was able to increase its carbon reduction goal from 8 to 25 percent and generated a higher net present value.

Such approaches are the result of the recognition that the intangible benefits of sustainability projects–such as reducing risks, staying ahead of regulations, pleasing communities, and enhancing employee morale–are substantial even when they are difficult to quantify. Just as companies spend large fortunes on launching advertising campaigns or initiating R&D projects without a clear quantification of financial returns, sustainability investments are necessary even when it is difficult to calculate the ROI of such investments. The alternative of not making these investments is often no longer feasible.

THE STRATEGIC MANAGEMENT PERSPECTIVE: AN IMPERATIVE THROUGHOUT THE ORGANIZATION

LO 1-5

Recognize the need for greater empowerment throughout the organization.

Strategic management requires managers to take an integrative view of the organization and assess how all of the functional areas and activities fit together to help an organization achieve its goals and objectives. This cannot be accomplished if only the top managers in the organization take an integrative, strategic perspective of issues facing the firm and everyone else "fends for themselves" in their independent, isolated functional areas. Instead, people throughout the organization must strive toward overall goals.

To develop and mobilize people and other assets, leaders are needed throughout the organization.[78] No longer can organizations be effective if the top "does the thinking" and the rest of the organization "does the work." Everyone must be involved in the strategic management process. There is a critical need for three types of leaders:

- ***Local line leaders*** who have significant profit-and-loss responsibility.
- ***Executive leaders*** who champion and guide ideas, create a learning infrastructure, and establish a domain for taking action.
- ***Internal networkers*** who, although they have little positional power and formal authority, generate their power through the conviction and clarity of their ideas.[79]

Top-level executives are key in setting the tone for the empowerment of employees. Consider Richard Branson, founder of the Virgin Group, whose core businesses include retail operations, hotels, communications, and an airline. He is well known for creating a culture and an informal structure where anybody in the organization can be involved in generating and acting upon new business ideas. In an interview, he stated: "If someone has an idea, they can pick up the phone and talk to me. I can vote, 'Done, let's do it.' Or, better still, they can just go ahead and do it. They know that they are not going to get a mouthful from me if they make a mistake."[80]

To inculcate a strategic management perspective, managers must create management processes to foster change. This involves planning, leading, and holding people accountable. At Netflix, leading people is not based on one's position in the hierarchy, nor an individual trait that is taught to people identified as "high potentials."[81] The expectation is that anyone can take initiative, make decisions, and influence others consistent with the firm's strategy. Everyone gets–and receives–feedback from team members, supervisors, managers, and customers. As part of the overall system that emphasizes transparency, there is the shared belief at Netflix that good results depend on people providing their insights and perspectives. Getting alignment, direction, and obtaining results the right way is essential. Those who fail to achieve this are asked to leave the firm.

We'd like to close with our favorite example of how inexperience can be a virtue. It further reinforces the benefits of having broad involvement throughout the organization in the strategic management process (see Strategy Spotlight 1.3).

1.3 STRATEGY SPOTLIGHT

STRATEGY AND THE VALUE OF INEXPERIENCE

Peter Guber, chairman of Mandalay Entertainment, discovered that great ideas can come from the least expected sources. During the filming of the movie *Gorillas in the Mist*, his production company faced many problems. Rwanda—the site of the filming—was on the verge of revolution, the film needed to use 200 animals, and the screenplay required the gorillas to follow a script, that is, do what the script called for and "act." If that failed, the fallback position was to use dwarfs in gorilla suits on a soundstage—a strategy that usually failed.

Guber explains how the "day was saved" by someone with very limited experience:

> We called an emergency meeting to solve these problems. In the middle of it, a young intern asked, "What if you let the gorillas write the story?" Everyone laughed and wondered what she was doing in the meeting with experienced filmmakers. Hours later, someone casually asked her what she had meant. She said, "What if you send a really good cinematographer into the jungle with a ton of film to shoot the gorillas, then you could write a story around what the gorillas did on film." It was a brilliant idea. And we did exactly what she suggested: We sent Alan Root, an Academy Award–nominated cinematographer into the jungle for three weeks. He came back with phenomenal footage that practically wrote the story for us.

The upshot? The film cost $20 million to shoot—half the original budget. And it was nominated for five Academy Awards—including Sigourney Weaver for best actress—and it won two Golden Globe Awards.

Source: Guber, P. 1998. My greatest lesson. *Fast Company,* 14: 88–90; and *imdb.com.*

LO 1-6

Explain how an awareness of a hierarchy of strategic goals can help an organization achieve coherence in its strategic direction.

ENSURING COHERENCE IN STRATEGIC DIRECTION

Employees and managers must strive toward common goals and objectives.[82] By specifying desired results, it becomes much easier to move forward. Otherwise, the organization's stakeholders would not know what the firm is striving to accomplish. And, employees and managers would have no idea of what to work toward. Alan Mulally, former CEO at Ford Motor Company, stressed the importance of perspective in creating a sense of mission: "What are we? What is our real purpose? And then, how do you include everybody so you know where you are on that plan, so you can work on areas that need special attention."[83]

Why Share a Firm's Strategic Direction?

Despite pressure for short-term results, executives should communicate their long-term thinking to help ensure the support of investors and other stakeholders. Many have suggested the benefits that firms can obtain when they communicate their perspectives and priorities. Among these are:[84]

- Investor presentations of long-term plans provide an opportunity for discussions to take place regarding the continuing corporate performance on two critical elements: a long-term value creation story (drawing on the past) and a long-term value creation plan (looking to the future). This involves a good deal of research about the market, product development, fiscal and attitudinal changes, and regulatory changes. In addition, it also helps to signal credibility as to the corporation's preparedness to deal with anticipated environmental changes. When Aled Smith, an award-winning fund manager with M&G Investments, was asked how he decides if a corporation's management was trustworthy, he responded, "What matters to me is that companies can explain their strategy...And unfortunately, probably 80 percent of the corporate presentations fall into the same trap, confusing strategy with objectives or aims with ambitions. Their explanations are like...'We're going to build this great platform, and then we're going to monetize it and make lots of money.' The steps in between are not well laid out."

- Investors are increasingly seeing ESG (environmental, social, governance) issues as financially material and expect sound management of such factors in order to deliver better performance over the long term. Thus, communicating such matters enables investors to view them "through the eyes of management" and reduces uncertainty about a firm's initiatives and insight regarding their resource allocations. It also demonstrates that the company can anticipate as well as capitalize on megatrends. A long-term plan enables the CEO to outline, for example, how the firm is responding to significant trends such as technological disruption, an aging society, and the transition to a low-carbon economy.
- A corporation can obtain many collateral benefits when it communicates a long-term purpose. Among these are the ability to inspire—and retain—managers and employees. When a company espouses an authentic, sustainable purpose, it is more likely to attract, motivate, and retain talent—a core objective in the knowledge economy. However, in a recent MIT Sloan School survey of more than 4,000 managers, only 28 percent could correctly list three of their firms' top strategic priorities. Similarly, in another study, only 14 percent of the organizations that were polled reported that their employees had a good understanding of their company's strategy and direction. The Metrus Group identified several factors that can enhance the attainment of alignment in the purpose and objectives throughout an organization—an agreed upon strategy; strategic measures or a balanced scorecard; and, linking to business functions with targets, individual accountabilities, and rewards.

Organizations express priorities best through stated goals and objectives that form a **hierarchy of goals,** which includes the firm's vision, mission, and strategic objectives.[85] What visions may lack in specificity, they make up for in their ability to evoke powerful and compelling mental images. On the other hand, strategic objectives tend to be more specific and provide a more direct means of determining if the organization is moving toward broader, overall goals.[86] Visions, as one would expect, also have longer time horizons than either mission statements or strategic objectives. Exhibit 1.6 depicts the hierarchy of goals and its relationship to two attributes: general versus specific and time horizon.

hierarchy of goals
organizational goals ranging from, at the top, those that are less specific yet able to evoke powerful and compelling mental images to, at the bottom, those that are more specific and measurable.

Organizational Vision

A **vision** is a goal that is "massively inspiring, overarching, and long term."[87] It represents a destination that is driven by and evokes passion. For example, Wendy Kopp, founder of Teach for America, notes that her vision for the organization, which strives to improve the quality of inner-city schools, draws many applicants: "We're looking for people who are magnetized to this notion, this vision, that one day all children in our nation should have the opportunity to attain an excellent education."[88]

vision
organizational goal(s) that evoke(s) powerful and compelling mental images.

Leaders must develop and implement a vision. A vision may or may not succeed; it depends on whether or not everything else happens according to an organization's strategy.

EXHIBIT 1.6 A Hierarchy of Goals

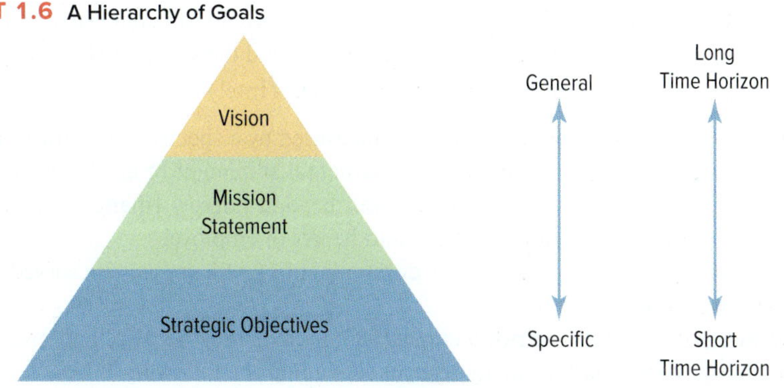

1.4 STRATEGY SPOTLIGHT — DIGITAL ECONOMY

ALIBABA'S VISION CREATED THE WORLD'S MOST VALUABLE ONLINE ECOSYSTEM

Alibaba has become one of the leading online retailers in the world with a market capitalization of more than $400 billion, exceeding the value of more traditional retailers such as Walmart. Jack Ma started Alibaba in 1999 as a business-to-business (B2B) portal connecting Chinese manufacturing companies with the world. Ma quickly replicated the initial success of the B2B portal to other e-commerce areas, such as consumer-to-consumer (C2C) markets with the Taobao marketplace launched in 2003. However, while Alibaba's initial business model was very successful, it was not until 2007 that Alibaba became the world-beater it is today. This was when Jack Ma and his management team agreed on a new vision for the Chinese e-commerce giant: "foster the development of an open, coordinated, prosperous e-commerce ecosystem." This vision transformed Alibaba's business model from simply connecting sellers and buyers into an ecosystem providing all resources that Chinese online businesses would need to succeed. Over time, Alibaba moved more and more retail functions to its sprawling online platform. Alibaba's ecosystem today includes a startling array of businesses, including commerce, payment, advertising, lending, and shipping. In other words, Alibaba does what Amazon, eBay, PayPal, Google, LendingClub, and FedEx do in the United States, but in a coordinated and data-driven network controlled by Alibaba. Bringing these varied businesses into the Alibaba ecosystem is not only customer-centric, but also efficient. Alibaba uses machine-learning technology to leverage the data created in its ecosystem. For instance, Alibaba's lending business—called Ant Financial—automates lending decisions to small businesses, allowing Alibaba to make lending decisions in a matter of minutes without the input or supervision of a banker. This data-driven lending business assesses the strengths of the borrower's business, the competitive pressure from rival vendors, and the overall likelihood of repayment, all with the data available in the Alibaba ecosystem. Alibaba's leadership team understands the value of its ecosystem and invests heavily in protecting it. For instance, a recent loyalty program, called 88VIP, either costs 88 RMB ($13) or 888 RMB ($130). Members who contribute more to the value of the ecosystem by writing reviews or shopping at different Alibaba businesses are charged the lower price. Alibaba not only realizes direct benefits from this membership model by collecting membership fees, but also reaps indirect benefits by creating an engaged and credible customer base, which further raises the value of the Alibaba ecosystem in a virtuous cycle.

Sources: Ming, Z. 2018. Alibaba and the future of business. *Harvard Business Review*, 96(5): 88-96; Saiidi, U. 2017. Alibaba is much more than just China's e-commerce platform. cnbc.com, September 22: np; and Laubscher, H. 2018. Is Alibaba's 88VIP loyalty program the final straw for competitors? forbes.com, August 14: np.

As the late Mark Hurd, Hewlett-Packard's former CEO, humorously pointed: "Without execution, vision is just another word for hallucination."[89]

In a survey of executives from 20 different countries, respondents were asked what they believed were a leader's key traits.[90] Ninety-eight percent responded that "a strong sense of vision" was the most important. Similarly, when asked about the critical knowledge skills, the leaders cited "strategy formulation to achieve a vision" as the most important skill. In other words, managers need to have not only a vision but also a plan to implement it. Regretfully, 90 percent reported a lack of confidence in their own skills and ability to conceive a vision.[91]

One of the most famous examples of a vision is Microsoft's (at its founding): "A computer on every desk in every home." Other examples are:

- "Transforming technology to save lives." (Medtronic)
- "To move with velocity to drive profitable growth and become an even better McDonald's serving more customers delicious food each day around the world." (McDonald's)
- "If it is smart and connected, it is best with Intel." (Intel)

Although such visions cannot be accurately measured by a specific indicator of how well they are being achieved, they do provide a fundamental statement of an organization's values, aspirations, and goals. Such visions go well beyond narrow financial objectives, of course, and strive to capture both the minds and hearts of employees.

Strategy Spotlight 1.4 discusses how the development of Alibaba's vision served to create a more expansive view of their future.

Clearly, vision statements are not a cure-all. Sometimes they backfire and erode a company's credibility. Visions fail for many reasons, including the following:[92]

The Walk Doesn't Match the Talk An idealistic vision can arouse employee enthusiasm. However, that same enthusiasm can be quickly dashed if employees find that senior management's behavior is not consistent with the vision. Often, vision is a sloganeering campaign of new buzzwords and empty platitudes like "devotion to the customer," "teamwork," or "total quality" that aren't consistently backed by management's action.

Irrelevance Visions created in a vacuum–unrelated to environmental threats or opportunities or an organization's resources and capabilities–often ignore the needs of those who are expected to buy into them. Employees reject visions that are not anchored in reality.

Not the Holy Grail Managers often search continually for the one elusive solution that will solve their firm's problems–that is, the next "holy grail" of management. They may have tried other management fads only to find that they fell short of their expectations. However, they remain convinced that one exists. A vision simply cannot be viewed as a magic cure for an organization's illness.

Too Much Focus Leads to Missed Opportunities The downside of too much focus is that in directing people and resources toward a grandiose vision, losses can be significant. It is analogous to focusing your eyes on a small point on a wall. Clearly, you would not have very much peripheral vision. Similarly, organizations must strive to be aware of unfolding events in both their external and internal environment when formulating and implementing strategies.

An Ideal Future Irreconciled with the Present Although visions are not designed to mirror reality, they must be anchored somehow in it. People have difficulty identifying with a vision that paints a rosy picture of the future but does not account for the often hostile environment in which the firm competes or that ignores some of the firm's weaknesses.

Mission Statements

A company's **mission statement** differs from its vision in that it encompasses both the purpose of the company and the basis of competition and competitive advantage.

mission statement a set of organizational goals that identifies the purpose of the organization, its basis of competition, and competitive advantage.

Exhibit 1.7 contains the vision statement and mission statement of The Walt Disney Company, a $60 billion giant entertainment and media enterprise. Note that while the vision statement is broad-based, the mission statement is more specific and focused on the means by which the firm will compete.

Effective mission statements incorporate the concept of stakeholder management, suggesting that organizations must respond to multiple constituencies. Customers, employees, suppliers, and owners are the primary stakeholders, but others may also play an important role. Mission statements also have the greatest impact when they reflect an organization's enduring, overarching strategic priorities, and competitive positioning. Mission statements also can vary in length and specificity. The following two mission statements illustrate these issues.

- "To produce superior financial returns for our shareholders by providing high value-added logistics, transportation, and related business services through focused operating companies." (Federal Express)

EXHIBIT 1.7 Comparing The Walt Disney's Vision and Mission

Vision
To be one of the world's leading producers and providers of entertainment and information.
Mission
To be one of the world's leading producers and providers of entertainment and information. Using our portfolio of brands to differentiate our content, services, and consumer products, we seek to develop the most creative, innovative, and profitable entertainment experiences and related products in the world.

Source: Walt Disney company records.

- "To be the very best in the business. Our game plan is status go . . . we are constantly looking ahead, building on our strengths, and reaching for new goals. In our quest of these goals, we look at the three stars of the Brinker logo and are reminded of the basic values that are the strength of this company . . . People, Quality, and Profitability. Everything we do at Brinker must support these core values. We also look at the eight golden flames depicted in our logo, and are reminded of the fire that ignites our mission and makes up the heart and soul of this incredible company. These flames are: Customers, Food, Team, Concepts, Culture, Partners, Community, and Shareholders. As keeper of these flames, we will continue to build on our strengths and work together to be the best in the business." (Brinker International, whose restaurant chains include Chili's and On the Border)[93]

Few mission statements identify profit or any other financial indicator as the sole purpose of the firm. Indeed, many do not even mention profit or shareholder return.[94] Employees of organizations or departments are usually the mission's most important audience. For them, the mission should help to build a common understanding of purpose and commitment to nurture.

A good mission statement, by addressing each principal theme, must communicate why an organization is special and different. Two studies that linked corporate values and mission statements with financial performance found that the most successful firms mentioned values other than profits. The less successful firms focused almost entirely on profitability.[95] In essence, profit is the metaphorical equivalent of oxygen, food, and water that the body requires. They are not the point of life, but without them, there is no life.

Vision statements tend to be quite enduring and seldom change. However, a firm's mission can and should change when competitive conditions dramatically change or the firm is faced with new threats or opportunities.

Strategic Objectives

strategic objectives
a set of organizational goals that are used to put into practice the mission statement and that are specific and cover a well-defined time frame.

Strategic objectives are used to operationalize the mission statement.[96] That is, they help to provide guidance on how the organization can fulfill or move toward the "higher goals" in the goal hierarchy–the mission and vision. Thus, they are more specific and cover a more well-defined time frame. Setting objectives demands a yardstick to measure the fulfillment of the objectives.[97]

Exhibit 1.8 lists several firms' strategic objectives–both financial and nonfinancial. While most of them are directed toward generating greater profits and returns for the owners of the business, others are directed at customers or society at large.

EXHIBIT 1.8
Strategic Objectives

Strategic Objectives (Financial)
• Increase sales growth 6 percent to 8 percent and accelerate core net earnings growth from 13 percent to 15 percent per share in each of the next 5 years. (Procter & Gamble)
• Generate Internet-related revenue of $1.5 billion. (AutoNation)
• Cut corporate overhead costs by $30 million per year. (Fortune Brands)
Strategic Objectives (Nonfinancial)
• Reduce volatile emissions 15 percent over a 5-year period, indexed to net sales. (3M)
• Our goal is to help save 100,000 more lives each year. (Varian Medical Systems)
• We want to be the top-ranked supplier to our customers. (PPG)

Sources: Company documents and annual reports.

For objectives to be meaningful, they need to satisfy several criteria. An objective must be:

- ***Measurable.*** There must be at least one indicator (or yardstick) that measures progress against fulfilling the objective.
- ***Specific.*** This provides a clear message as to what needs to be accomplished.
- ***Appropriate.*** It must be consistent with the organization's vision and mission.
- ***Realistic.*** It must be an achievable target given the organization's capabilities and opportunities in the environment. In essence, it must be challenging but doable.
- ***Timely.*** There must be a time frame for achieving the objective. As the economist John Maynard Keynes once said, "In the long run, we are all dead!"

When objectives satisfy the given criteria, there are many benefits. First, they help to channel all employees' efforts toward common goals. This helps the organization concentrate and conserve valuable resources and work collectively in a timely manner.

Second, challenging objectives can help to motivate and inspire employees to higher levels of commitment and effort. Much research has supported the notion that people work harder when they are striving toward specific goals instead of being asked simply to "do their best."

Third, as we noted earlier in the chapter, there is always the potential for different parts of an organization to pursue their own goals rather than overall company goals. Although

ISSUE FOR DEBATE

Seventh Generation's Decision Dilemma

A strike idled 67,300 workers of the United Food and Commercial Workers (UFCW) who worked at Albertsons, Ralphs, and Vons–all large grocery store chains. These stores sold natural home products made by Seventh Generation, a socially conscious company. Interestingly, the inspiration for its name came from the Great Law of the Haudenosaunee. (This Law of Peace of the Iroquois Confederacy in North America has its roots in the 14th century.) The law states that "in our every deliberation we must consider the impact of our decisions on the next seven generations." Accordingly, the company's mission is "To inspire a revolution that nurtures the health of the next seven generations," and its values are to "care wholeheartedly, collaborate deliberately, nurture nature, innovate disruptively, and be a trusted brand."

Clearly, Seventh Generation faced a dilemma: On the one hand, it believed that the strikers had a just cause. However, if it honored the strikers by not crossing the picket lines, the firm would lose the shelf space for its products in the stores it had worked so hard to secure. Honoring the strikers would also erode its trust with the large grocery stores. On the other hand, if Seventh Generation ignored the strikers and proceeded to send its products to the stores, it would be compromising its values and thereby losing trust and credibility with several stakeholders–its customers, distributors, and employees.

Discussion Questions

1. How important should the Seventh Generation values be considered when deciding what to do?
2. How can Seventh Generation solve this dilemma?

Sources: Russo, M. V. 2010. *Companies on a mission: Entrepreneurial strategies for growing sustainably, responsibly, and profitably.* Stanford: Stanford University Press, 94–96; Seventh Generation. 2012. Seventh generation's mission–Corporate social responsibility. www.seventhgeneration.com, np; Foster, A. C. 2004. Major work stoppage in 2003. U.S. Bureau of Labor and Statistics: Compensation and Working Conditions. www.bls.gov, November 23: np; Fast Company. 2008. 45 social entrepreneurs who are changing the world. Profits with purpose: Seventh Generation. www.fastcompany, np; and Ratical. n.d. The six nations: Oldest living participatory democracy on earth. www.ratical.org, np.

well intentioned, these may work at cross-purposes to the organization as a whole. Meaningful objectives thus help to resolve conflicts when they arise.

Finally, proper objectives provide a yardstick for rewards and incentives. They will ensure a greater sense of equity or fairness when rewards are allocated.

A caveat: When formulating strategic objectives, managers need to remember that too many objectives can result in a lack of focus and diminished results:

> A few years ago CEO Tony Petrucciani and his team at Single Source Systems, a software firm in Fishers, Indiana, set 15 annual objectives, such as automating some of its software functions. However, the firm, which got distracted by having so many items on its objective list, missed its $8.1 million revenue benchmark by 11 percent. "Nobody focused on any one thing," he says. Going forward, Petrucciani decided to set just a few key priorities. This helped the company to meet its goal of $10 million in sales. Sometimes, less is more![100]

Reflecting on Career Implications . . .

This chapter discusses both the long-term focus of strategy and the need for coherence in strategic direction. The following issues extend these themes by asking students to consider their own strategic goals and how they fit with the goals of the firms in which they work or would seek employment.

- **Attributes of Strategic Management:** The attributes of strategic management described in this chapter are applicable to your personal careers as well. What are your overall goals and objectives? Who are the stakeholders you have to consider in making your career decisions (family, community, etc.)? What trade-offs do you see between your long-term and short-term goals?
- **Intended versus Emergent Strategies:** While you may have planned your career trajectory carefully, don't be too tied to it. Strive to take advantage of new opportunities as they arise. Many promising career opportunities may "emerge" that were not part of your intended career strategy or your specific job assignment. Take initiative by pursuing opportunities to get additional training (e.g., learn a software or a statistical package), volunteering for a short-term overseas assignment, etc. You may be in a better position to take advantage of such emergent opportunities if you take the effort to prepare for them. For example, learning a foreign language may position you better for an overseas opportunity.
- **Ambidexterity:** In Strategy Spotlight 1.1, we discussed the four most important traits of ambidextrous individuals. These include looking for opportunities beyond the description of one's job, seeking out opportunities to collaborate with others, building internal networks, and multitasking. Evaluate yourself along each of these criteria. If you score low, think of ways in which you can improve your ambidexterity.
- **Strategic Coherence:** What is the mission of your organization? What are the strategic objectives of the department or unit you are working for? In what ways does your own role contribute to the mission and objectives? What can you do differently in order to help the organization attain its mission and strategic objectives?
- **Strategic Coherence:** Setting strategic objectives is important in your personal career as well. Identify and write down three or four important strategic objectives you want to accomplish in the next few years (finish your degree, find a better-paying job, etc.). Are you allocating your resources (time, money, etc.) to enable you to achieve these objectives? Are your objectives measurable, timely, realistic, specific, and appropriate?

key points

LO1-1 The definition of strategic management and its four key attributes.

- Strategic management is defined as "consisting of the analyses, decisions, and actions an organization undertakes to create and sustain a competitive advantage."
- The issue of how and why some firms outperform others in the marketplace is central to the study of strategic management.
- Strategic management has four attributes: It is directed at overall organizational goals, involves multiple stakeholders, includes both short-term and long-term perspectives, and incorporates trade-offs between efficiency and effectiveness.

LO1-2 The strategic management process and its three interrelated and principal activities.

- The three principal activities in the strategic management process are: strategy analysis, strategy formulation, and strategy implementation.
- All of these activities are highly interrelated and interdependent on the others.

LO1-3 The vital role of corporate governance and stakeholder management, as well as how "symbiosis" can be achieved among an organization's stakeholders.

- Corporate governance can be broadly defined as the relationship among various participants in determining the direction and performance of corporations.
- Internal governance mechanisms include shareholders (owners), management (led by the chief executive officer), and the board of directors.
- External control is exercised by auditors, banks, analysts, an active business press, as well as the threat of takeovers.
- We identify five key stakeholder groups in an organization: owners, customers, suppliers, employees, and society at large.
- Although inherent conflicts may arise among the demands of various stakeholders, managers must endeavor to achieve "symbiosis," that is, interdependence and mutual benefit among the multiple stakeholder groups.

LO1-4 The importance of social responsibility, including environmental sustainability, and how it can enhance a firm's innovation strategy.

- Social responsibility recognizes that businesses must respond to society's expectations regarding their obligations to society.
- Many firms have become more innovative by investing in initiatives that incorporate socially responsible behavior, including activities that enhance environmental sustainability.
- The triple bottom line approach evaluates a firm by taking into account its financial, social, and environmental performance.

LO1-5 The need for greater empowerment throughout the organization.

- Effective strategic management cannot be achieved if only the organization's top managers take an integrative, strategic perspective of issues facing the firm and everyone else "fends for themselves" in their independent, isolated functional areas.
- To develop and mobilize people and other assets, leaders are needed throughout the organization.
- Organizations cannot be effective if the top "does the thinking" and the rest of the organization "does the work."

LO1-6 How an awareness of a hierarchy of strategic goals can help an organization achieve coherence in its strategic direction.

- Organizations need to have consistency among their hierarchy of goals: their vision, mission, and strategic objectives.
- Visions should evoke powerful and compelling mental images.
- A company's mission statement differs from its vision in that it encompasses both the purpose of the company and the basis of competition and competitive advantage.
- Strategic objectives are used to operationalize the mission statement. They serve to provide guidance on how the organization can fulfill or move toward the "higher goals" in the goal hierarchy—the mission and the vision. Thus, they are more specific and cover a well-defined time frame.

SUMMARY REVIEW QUESTIONS

1. How is "strategic management" defined in the text, and what are its four key attributes?
2. Briefly discuss the three key activities in the strategic management process. Why is it important for managers to recognize the interdependent nature of these activities?
3. Explain the concept of "stakeholder management." Why shouldn't managers be solely interested in stockholder management, that is, maximizing the returns for owners of the firm—its shareholders?
4. What is "corporate governance"? What are its three key elements, and how can it be improved?
5. How can "symbiosis" (interdependence, mutual benefit) be achieved among a firm's stakeholders?
6. Why do firms need to have a greater strategic management perspective and empowerment in the strategic management process throughout the organization?
7. What is meant by a "hierarchy of goals"? What are the main components of it, and why must consistency be achieved among them?

key terms

romantic view of leadership 4
external control view of leadership 4
strategic management 5
strategy 6
competitive advantage 6
operational effectiveness 6
stakeholders 7
effectiveness 7
efficiency 7
ambidexterity 8
intended strategy 10
realized strategy 10
strategy analysis 12
strategy formulation 12
strategy implementation 13
corporate governance 16
stakeholder management 18
social responsibility 19
triple bottom line 20
hierarchy of goals 25
vision 25
mission statement 27
strategic objectives 28

EXPERIENTIAL EXERCISES AND APPLICATION QUESTIONS

1. Strategy Spotlight 1.1 discusses four activities that underlie ambidextrous behaviors–a dual capacity for alignment and adaptability. Interview two managers in a public, private, or volunteer organization and ask them the following questions: (1) How often do you engage in each of these activities? (2) In your view, which are most important and why? and (3) How would the most effective managers you know "score" on each of these activities? Do you think that the differences in the responses you obtain are due to differences with regard to the managers' personalities, the particular position they have within the organization, or the type of industry in which they work?
2. Using the Internet or library sources, select four organizations–two in the private sector and two in the public sector. Find their mission statements. Complete the following exhibit by identifying the stakeholders that are mentioned. Evaluate the differences between firms in the private sector and those in the public sector.

Organization Name

Mission Statement

Stakeholders (√ = mentioned)

A. Customers

B. Suppliers

C. Managers/employees

D. Community-at-large

E. Owners

F. Others?

G. Others?

3. Go to the Internet and look up one of these company sites: *www.walmart.com*, *www.ge.com*, or *www.fordmotor.com*. What are some of the key events that would represent the "romantic" perspective of leadership? What are some of the key events that depict the "external control" perspective of leadership?
4. Select a company that competes in an industry in which you are interested. What are some of the recent demands that stakeholders have placed on this company? Can you find examples of how the company is trying to develop "symbiosis" (interdependence and mutual benefit) among its stakeholders? (Use the Internet and library resources.)
5. Provide examples of companies that are actively trying to increase the amount of empowerment in the strategic management process throughout the organization. Do these companies seem to be having positive outcomes? Why? Why not?
6. Look up the vision statements and/or mission statements for a few companies. Do you feel that they are constructive and useful as a means of motivating employees and providing a strong strategic direction? Why? Why not? (*Note:* Annual reports, along with the Internet, may be good sources of information.)

ETHICS QUESTIONS

1. A company focuses solely on short-term profits to provide the greatest return to the owners of the business (i.e., the shareholders in a publicly held firm). What ethical issues could this raise?
2. A firm has spent some time–with input from managers at all levels–on developing a vision statement and a mission statement. Over time, however, the behavior of some executives is contrary to these statements. Could this raise some ethical issues?

REFERENCES

1. Gunther, M. 2010. Fallen angels. *Fortune,* November 1: 75-78.
2. These examples draw on: Anthony, S. D., Viguerie, S. P., Schwartz, E. I., and V. Van Landeghem. 2018. 2018 Corporate longevity forecast: Creative destruction is accelerating. *innosight.com,* np; Colvin, G. 2015. The 21st century corporation. *Fortune*. November 1: 103-122; Anonymous. 2016. The rise of superstars. *The Economist,* September 17: 3-16; and Harjani, A. 2013. Emerging markets to shake up Fortune 500 list. *cnbc.com,* October 3: np.
3. This example draws on the following sources: Biswas, S., and B. Yerak. 2018. Mattress firm to cut stores in Chapter 11. *The Wall Street Journal,* October 6-7: B3; Meyersohn, N. 2018. How Casper drove Mattress Firm into bankruptcy. *cnn.com*. October 6: np; Griswold, A. 2018. Mattress Firm never understood how much Americans hate mattress shopping. *qz.com*. October 6: np; and Blunt, K. 2018. Mattress Firm CEO to step down. *houstonchronicle.com*. January 26, np. We note that Mattress' parent, Steinhoff International Holdings, had taken the firm private two years ago, and had been involved recently in an accounting scandal. Its creditors had agreed to suspend all payments on its debt for three years and Steinhoff is expected to soon commence a debt restructuring for its European business.
4. For a discussion of the "romantic" versus "external control" perspective, refer to Meindl, J. R. 1987. The romance of leadership and the evaluation of organizational performance. *Academy of Management Journal,* 30: 92-109; and Pfeffer, J., and G.R. Salancik. 1978. *The external control of organizations: A resource dependence perspective.* New York: Harper & Row.
5. A recent perspective on the "romantic view" of leadership is provided by Mintzberg, H. 2004. Leadership and management development: An afterword. *Academy of Management Executive,* 18(3): 140-142.
6. For a discussion of the best and worst managers for 2008, read Anonymous. 2009. The best managers. *BusinessWeek,* January 19: 40-41; and The worst managers, on page 42 in the same issue.
7. Burrows, p. 2009. Apple without its core? *BusinessWeek,* January 26/ February 2: 31.
8. For a study on the effects of CEOs on firm performance, refer to Kor, Y. Y., and V. F. Misangyi. 2008. *Strategic Management Journal,* 29(11):1357-1368.
9. Colvin, G. 2016. Developing an internal market for talent. *Fortune.* March 1: 22.
10. Kapner, S., and Lublin, *op. cit.*
11. Ewing, J. 2008. South Africa emerges from the shadows. *BusinessWeek,* December 15: 52-56.
12. For an interesting perspective on the need for strategists to maintain a global mind-set, refer to Begley, T. M., and D. Boyd. 2003. The need for a global mind-set. *MIT Sloan Management Review,* 44(2): 25-32.
13. Porter, M. E. 1996. What is strategy? *Harvard Business Review,* 74(6): 61-78.
14. See, for example, Barney, J. B., and A. M. Arikan. 2001. The resource-based view: Origins and implications. In Hitt, M. A., Freeman, R. E., and J. S. Harrison (Eds.), *Handbook of strategic management:* 124-189. Malden, MA: Blackwell.
15. Porter, M. E. 1996. What is strategy? *Harvard Business Review,* 74(6): 61-78; and Hammonds, K. H. 2001. Michael Porter's big ideas. *Fast Company,* March: 55-56.
16. This section draws upon Dess, G. G., and A. Miller. 1993. *Strategic management.* New York: McGraw-Hill.
17. See, for example, Hrebiniak, L. G., and W. F. Joyce. 1986. The strategic importance of managing myopia. *Sloan Management Review,* 28(1): 5-14.
18. Bryant, A. 2011. *The corner office.* New York: Times Books.
19. For an insightful discussion on how to manage diverse stakeholder groups, refer to Rondinelli, D. A., and T. London. 2003. How corporations and environmental groups cooperate: Assessing cross-sector alliances and collaborations. *Academy of Management Executive,* 17(1): 61-76.
20. Some dangers of a short-term perspective are addressed in Van Buren, M. E., and T. Safferstone. 2009. The quick wins paradox. *Harvard Business Review,* 67(1): 54-61.
21. Senge, p. 1996. Leading learning organizations: The bold, the powerful, and the invisible. In Hesselbein, F., Goldsmith, M., and R. Beckhard (Eds.), *The leader of the future:* 41-58. San Francisco: Jossey-Bass.
22. Winston, A. S. 2014. *The big pivot.* Boston: Harvard Business Review.
23. Loeb, M. 1994. Where leaders come from. *Fortune,* September 19: 241 (quoting Warren Bennis).
24. Ignatius, A. 2016. The HBR Interview: Hewlett Packard Enterprise CEO Meg Whitman. *Harvard Business Review,* 94(5): 100.
25. This section draws on: Smith, W., Lewis, M., and M. Tushman. 2016. "Both/and" leadership. *Harvard Business Review,* 94(5): 63-70.
26. New perspectives on "management models" are addressed in Birkinshaw, J., and J. Goddard. 2009. What is your management model? *MIT Sloan Management Review,* 50(2): 81-90.
27. Mintzberg, H. 1985. Of strategies: Deliberate and emergent. *Strategic Management Journal,* 6: 257-272.
28. Some interesting insights on decision-making processes are found in Nutt, P. C. 2008. Investigating the success of decision making processes. *Journal of Management Studies,* 45(2): 425-455.
29. Zhang, D., and Clark, A. 2018. Clothing brand feels heat. *The Wall Street Journal,* October 16: B3.
30. Machota, J. 2016. Job description varies for NFL QBs," *The Dallas Morning News,* March 20: 4C.
31. Bryant, A. 2009. *The corner office, The New York Times,* April 25: np.
32. A study investigating the sustainability of competitive advantage is Newbert, S. L. 2008. Value, rareness, competitive advantages, and performance: A conceptual-level empirical investigation of the resource-based view of the firm. *Strategic Management Journal,* 29(7): 745-768.
33. Good insights on mentoring are addressed in DeLong, T. J., Gabarro, J. J., and R. J. Lees. 2008. Why mentoring matters in a hypercompetitive world. *Harvard Business Review,* 66(1): 115-121.
34. Karlgaard, R. 2014. *The soft edge.* San Francisco: Jossey-Bass.
35. A unique perspective on differentiation strategies is Austin, R. D. 2008. High margins and the quest for aesthetic coherence. *Harvard Business Review,* 86(1): 18-19.
36. Some insights on partnering in the global area are discussed in MacCormack, A. & Forbath, T. 2008. *Harvard Business Review,* 66(1): 24, 26.

37. For insights on how firms can be successful in entering new markets in emerging economies, refer to Eyring, M. J., Johnson, M. W., & Nair, H. 2011. New business models in emerging markets. *Harvard Business Review,* 89(1/2): 88-95.
38. Martinez, M. 2014. 14 inspirational quotes on strategy implementation. khorus.com.
39. An interesting discussion of the challenges of strategy implementation is Neilson, G. L., Martin, K. L., and E. Powers. 2008. The secrets of strategy execution. *Harvard Business Review,* 86(6): 61-70.
40. Interesting perspectives on strategy execution involving the link between strategy and operations are addressed in Kaplan, R. S. and D. Norton. 2008. Mastering the management system. *Harvard Business Review,* 66(1): 62-77.
41. An innovative perspective on organizational design is found in Garvin, D. A., and L. C. Levesque. 2008. The multiunit enterprise. *Harvard Business Review,* 86(6): 106-117.
42. Monks, R., and N. Minow. 2001. *Corporate governance* (2nd ed.). Malden, MA: Blackwell.
43. Intel Corp. 2007. Intel corporation board of directors guidelines on significant corporate governance issues. *www.intel.com*
44. Jones, T. J., Felps, W., and G. A. Bigley. 2007. Ethical theory and stakeholder-related decisions: The role of stakeholder culture. *Academy of Management Review,* 32(1): 137-155.
45. For example, see: The best (& worst) managers of the year, 2003. *BusinessWeek,* January 13: 58-92; and Lavelle, M. 2003. Rogues of the year. *Time,* January 6: 33-45.
46. Baer, D. A. 2014. The West's bruised confidence in capitalism. *The Wall Street Journal,* September 22: A17; and Miller, D. 2014. Greatness is gone. *Dallas Morning News,* October 26: 1D.
47. Barton, D., and M. Wiseman. 2015. Where boards fall short. *Harvard Business Review,* 93(1/2): 100.
48. Hessel, E., and S. Woolley. 2008. Your money or your life. *Forbes,* October 27: 52.
49. Task, A. 2012. Finance CEO pay rose 20% in 2011, even as stocks stumbled. *www.finance.yahoo.com,* June 5: np.
50. Rosenberg, Y. 2016. This CEO got $142 million more than he deserved. *finance.yahoo.com,* February 17: np.
51. Some interesting insights on the role of activist investors can be found in Greenwood, R., and M. Schol. 2008. When (not) to listen to activist investors. *Harvard Business Review,* 66(1): 23-24.
52. For an interesting perspective on the changing role of boards of directors, refer to Lawler, E., and D. Finegold. 2005. Rethinking governance. *MIT Sloan Management Review,* 46(2): 67-70.
53. Benz, M., and B.S. Frey. 2007. Corporate governance: What can we learn from public governance? *Academy of Management Review,* 32(1): 92-104.
54. The salience of shareholder value is addressed in Carrott, G. T., and S. E. Jackson. 2009. Shareholder value must top the CEO's agenda. *Harvard Business Review,* 67(1): 22-24.
55. Stakeholder symbiosis. 1998. *Fortune,* March 30: S2.
56. An excellent review of stakeholder management theory can be found in Laplume, A. O., Sonpar, K., and R. A. Litz. 2008. Stakeholder theory: Reviewing a theory that moves us. *Journal of Management,* 34(6): 1152-1189.
57. For a definitive discussion of the stakeholder concept, refer to Freeman, R. E., and J. McVae. 2001. A stakeholder approach to strategic management. In Hitt, M. A., Freeman, R. E., &and J. S. Harrison (Eds.), *Handbook of strategic management:* 189-207. Malden, MA: Blackwell.
58. Harrison, J. S., Bosse, D. A., and R. A. Phillips. 2010. Managing for stakeholders, stakeholder utility functions, and competitive advantage. *Strategic Management Journal,* 31(1): 58-74.
59. For an insightful discussion on the role of business in society, refer to Handy, op. cit.
60. Stakeholder symbiosis. op. cit., p. S3. The Walmart example draws on: Camillus, J. 2008. Strategy as a wicked problem. *Harvard Business Review,* 86(5): 100-101.
61. Sidhu, I. 2010. *Doing both.* Upper Saddle River, NJ: FT Press, 7-8.
62. Thomas, J. G. 2000. Macroenvironmetal forces. In Helms, M. M. (Ed.), *Encyclopedia of management* (4th ed.): 516-520. Farmington Hills, MI: Gale Group.
63. For a strong advocacy position on the need for corporate values and social responsibility, read Hollender, J. 2004. What matters most: Corporate values and social responsibility. *California Management Review,* 46(4): 111-119.
64. Rangan, K., Chase, L., and S. Karim. 2015. The truth about CSR. *Harvard Business Review,* 93(1/2): 41-49.
65. Bhattacharya, C. B., and S. Sen. 2004, Doing better at doing good: When, why, and how consumers respond to corporate social initiatives. *California Management Review,* 47(1): 9-24.
66. For some findings on the relationship between corporate social responsibility and firm performance, see Margolis, J. D., and H. A. Elfenbein. 2008. *Harvard Business Review,* 86(1): 19-20.
67. Cone Corporate Citizenship Study, 2002, *www.coneinc.com.*
68. Refer to *www.bsr.org.*
69. For an insightful discussion of the risks and opportunities associated with global warming, refer to Lash, J., and F. Wellington. 2007. Competitive advantage on a warming planet. *Harvard Business Review,* 85(3): 94-102.
70. Ignatius, A. 2015. Leadership with a conscience. *Harvard Business Review,* 93(11): 50-63.
71. This section draws on Hart, S. L. 1997. Beyond greening: Strategies for a sustainable world. *Harvard Business Review,* 75(1): 66-76; and Berry, M. A., and D. A. Rondinelli. 1998. Proactive corporate environmental management: A new industrial revolution. *Academy of Management Executive,* 12(2): 38-50.
72. Winston, A. 2018. Stop focusing on what other businesses do. *MIT Sloan Management Review.* 59(3): 34-35
73. Winston, A. 2018. Stop focusing on what other businesses do. *MIT Sloan Management Review.* 59(3): 34-35.
74. Vogel, D. J. 2005. Is there a market for virtue? The business case for corporate social responsibility. *California Management Review,* 47(4): 19-36.
75. Chamberlain, M. 2013. Socially responsible investing: What you need to know. *Forbes.com,* April 24: np.
76. Kaahwarski, T. 2010. It pays to be good. *Bloomberg Businessweek,* February 1 to February 8: 69.
77. This discussion draws on Kuehn, K., and L. McIntire. 2014. Sustainability a CFO can love. *Harvard Business Review,* 92(4): 66-74; and Esty, D. C., and A. S. Winston. 2009. *Green to gold.* Hoboken, NJ: Wiley.
78. For an interesting perspective on the role of middle managers in the strategic management process, refer to Huy, Q. H. 2001. In praise of middle managers. *Harvard Business Review,* 79(8): 72-81.

79. Senge, 1996, op. cit., pp. 41–58.
80. Kets de Vries, M. F. R. 1998. Charisma in action: The transformational abilities of Virgin's Richard Branson and ABB's Percy Barnevik. *Organizational Dynamics,* 26(3): 7–21.
81. Worley, C. G., Williams, T., and E. E. Lawler. III. 2016. Creating management processes built for change. *MIT Sloan Management Review,* 58(1): 77–82.
82. An interesting discussion on how to translate top management's goals into concrete actions is found in Bungay, S. 2011. How to make the most of your company's strategy. *Harvard Business Review,* 89(1/2): 132–140.
83. Bryant, A. 2011. *The corner office.* New York: St. Martin's/Griffin, 171.
84. This section draws on several sources. These include: Youmans, T., and B. Tomlinson. 2018. Share your long-term thinking. *MIT Sloan Management Review*, 59(3): 36–38; Kummerli, B. C., Anthony, S. D., and M. Messerer. 2018. Unite your senior team. *Harvard Business Review*, 96(6): 60–69; Goedhart, M., and T. Koller. 2013. How to attract long-term investors: An interview with M&G's Aled Smith. mckinsey.com, June: np; Matta, V. 2016. Do your employees know your mission statement? This is why it's important. careershift.com, August 29: np; and Davies, P. 2017. What are the main advantages of medium and long term planning in a commercial firm? Who should be most involved in the making of these plans? quora.com, October 19: np.
85. An insightful discussion about the role of vision, mission, and strategic objectives can be found in Collis, D. J., and M. G. Rukstad. 2008. Can you say what your strategy is? *Harvard Business Review,* 66(4): 82–90.
86. Our discussion draws on a variety of sources. These include Lipton, M. 1996. Demystifying the development of an organizational vision. *Sloan Management Review,* 37(4): 83–92; Bart, C. K. 2000. Lasting inspiration. *CA Magazine,* May: 49–50; and Quigley, J. V. 1994. Vision: How leaders develop it, share it, and sustain it. *Business Horizons,* September–October: 37–40.
87. Lipton, op. cit.
88. Bryant, A. 2011. *The corner office.* New York: St. Martin's/Griffin, 34.
89. Hardy, Q. 2007. The uncarly. *Forbes,* March 12: 82–90.
90. Some interesting perspectives on gender differences in organizational vision are discussed in Ibarra, H., and O. Obodaru. 2009. Women and the vision thing. *Harvard Business Review,* 67(1): 62–70.
91. Quigley, op. cit.
92. Lipton, op. cit. Additional pitfalls are addressed in this article.
93. Pederson, J. P. 2001. International Directory of Company Histories, 38: 101.
94. Lipton, op. cit.
95. Sexton, D. A., and P. M. Van Aukun. 1985. A longitudinal study of small business strategic planning. *Journal of Small Business Management,* January: 8–15, cited in Lipton, op. cit.
96. For an insightful perspective on the use of strategic objectives, refer to Chatterjee, S. 2005. Core objectives: Clarity in designing strategy. *California Management Review,* 47(2): 33–49.
97. Ibid.
98. Harnish, V. 2011. Five ways to get your strategy right. *Fortune,* April 11: 42.

CHAPTER

2

©Nico Muller Art/Shutterstock

Analyzing the External Environment of the Firm

Learning Objectives

LO2-1 Understand the importance of developing forecasts of the business environment.

LO2-2 Explain why environmental scanning, environmental monitoring, and collecting competitive intelligence are critical inputs to forecasting.

LO2-3 Explain why scenario planning is a useful technique for firms competing in industries characterized by unpredictability and change.

LO2-4 Recognize the impact of the general environment on a firm's strategies and performance.

LO2-5 Explain how forces in the competitive environment can affect profitability, and how a firm can improve its competitive position by increasing its power vis-à-vis these forces.

LO2-6 Explain how the Internet and digitally based capabilities are affecting the five competitive forces and industry profitability.

LO2-7 Understand the concept of strategic groups and their strategy and performance implications.

We encourage you to reflect on how the concepts presented in this chapter can enhance your career success (see "Reflecting on Career Implications..." at the end of the chapter).

LEARNING FROM MISTAKES

When the European aircraft maker Airbus announced the development of the world's largest passenger airplane A380 in 2000, it was the answer to Boeing's decade-long dominance of the jumbo jet market. Singapore Airlines took delivery of the first A380 in 2007 after two years of production delays due to technical challenges. Passengers loved the superjumbo for its spacious cabins and quiet interior, but airlines did not share the same enthusiasm. After Airbus invested more than $17 billion into the project, the company announced in 2019 that it would discontinue the A380 production by 2021. At that time, Airbus estimates to have sold fewer than half the A380s it expected to deliver. What went wrong?

Airplane projects have extremely long life cycles, with some airliners flying for more than 30 years. When the A380 development started, Airbus bet that the market demands in the airline industry persisted. At that time, airlines used a hub-and-spoke approach, requiring large jetliners to fly between hub airports such as New York and London. However, this model is increasingly supplemented by direct long-haul routes that can be served more economically by smaller (and more fuel-efficient) airplanes.

In addition, the size and luxury of the A380 have contributed to its demise, even on routes connecting hubs. The A380 was often described as a "hotel in the sky," which was able to transport at least 500 passengers and allowed airlines to offer onboard perks such as bars and beauty salons. Yet, such amenities added weight and proved incompatible with the changing business model of airlines. It also proved difficult to fill the seats on such a large aircraft due to lower than expected passenger demand. As a result, airlines offered discounted fares to boost demand and ensure high capacity utilization.

Around the same time that Airbus developed the A380 superjumbo, Boeing set out to develop the midsized 787 Dreamliner with a different vision of clients' future needs. Instead of focusing on size and perks as Airbus did, Boeing focused on fuel efficiency and comfort. Airlines flocked to the Dreamliner because it works better in an economy with higher fuel prices and allows for easier booking to ensure jetliners fly full. Airlines are also able to use the Dreamliner to bypass hub airports and connect distant cities directly, offering airlines more flexibility.

Discussion Questions

1. Given that it is difficult to predict future market needs and trends in industries with long product life cycles (such as jetliners), how should managers deal with this uncertainty?
2. How should Airbus compete against Boeing going forward?

Sources: Wall, R., and D. Michaels. 2019. Airbus jet leaves legacy of flubs. *Wall Street Journal*, February 20: B2; Bedingfield, W. 2019. Why did the Airbus A380 fail? *wired.com*, February 16; and Halsey, A. 2018. Is the Airbus 380 the future of air travel or a relic of the past? *washingtonpost.com*, August 19.

> *"We built a better mousetrap but there were no mice" (commenting on his firm's development of blue windshield glass for the automobile industry).*[1]
>
> *Gary W. Weber, PPG Industries*

Successful managers must recognize opportunities and threats in their firm's external environment. They must be aware of what's going on outside their company. If they focus exclusively on the efficiency of internal operations, the firm may degenerate into the world's most efficient producer of buggy whips, typewriters, or carbon paper. But if they miscalculate the market, opportunities will be lost—hardly an enviable position for their firm. As we saw from the Airbus A380 example, miscalculating the market demands can lead to negative consequences.

In *Competing for the Future,* Gary Hamel and C. K. Prahalad suggest that "every manager carries around in his or her head a set of biases, assumptions, and presuppositions about the structure of the relevant 'industry,' about how one makes money in the industry, about who the competition is and isn't, about who the customers are and aren't, and so on."[2] Environmental analysis requires you to continually question such assumptions. Peter Drucker, considered the father of modern management, labeled these interrelated sets of assumptions the "theory of the business."[3] Mattress Firm was blindsided by startups such as Casper, which recognized how miserable mattress shopping could be and promised a better experience—as we discussed in the opening case in Chapter 1.

A firm's strategy may be good at one point in time, but it may go astray when management's frame of reference gets out of touch with the realities of the actual business situation. This results when management's assumptions, premises, or beliefs are incorrect or when internal inconsistencies among them render the overall "theory of the business" invalid. As Warren Buffett, investor extraordinaire, colorfully notes, "Beware of past performance 'proofs.' If history books were the key to riches, the Forbes 400 would consist of librarians."

In the business world, many once-successful firms have fallen. Today we may wonder who will be the next Blockbuster, Toys "R" Us, Circuit City, or Sears.

LO 2-1

Understand the importance of developing forecasts of the business environment.

ENHANCING AWARENESS OF THE EXTERNAL ENVIRONMENT

perceptual acuity
the ability to sense what is coming before the fog clears.

So how do managers become environmentally aware?[4] Ram Charan, an adviser to many Fortune 500 CEOs, provides some useful insights with his concept of **perceptual acuity**.[5] He defines it as "the ability to sense what is coming before the fog clears." He draws on Ted Turner as an example: Turner saw the potential of 24-hour news before anyone else did. All the ingredients were there, but no others connected them until he created CNN. Like Turner, the best CEOs are compulsively tuned to the external environment and seem to have a sixth sense that picks up anomalies and detects early warning signals that may represent key threats or opportunities.

How can perceptual acuity be improved? Although many CEOs may complain that the top job is a lonely one, they can't do it effectively by sitting alone in their office. Instead, high-performing CEOs are constantly meeting with people and searching out information. Charan provides three examples:

- One CEO gets together with his critical people for half a day every eight weeks to discuss what's new and what's going on in the world. The setting is informal, and outsiders often attend. The participants look beyond the lens of their industry because some trends that affect one industry may impact others later on.
- Another CEO meets four times a year with about four other CEOs of large, but noncompeting, diverse global companies. Examining the world from multiple perspectives, they share their thinking about how different trends may develop. The CEO then goes back to his own weekly management meeting and throws out "a bunch of hand grenades to shake up people's thinking."
- Two companies ask outsiders to critique strategy during their board's strategy sessions. Such input typically leads to spirited discussions that provide valued input on the hinge assumptions and options that are under consideration. Once, the focus was on pinpointing the risk inherent in a certain strategy. Now, discussions have led to finding that the company was missing a valuable opportunity.

We will now address three important processes—scanning, monitoring, and gathering competitive intelligence—used to develop forecasts.[6] Exhibit 2.1 illustrates relationships among these important activities. We also discuss the importance of scenario planning in anticipating major future changes in the external environment and the role of SWOT analysis.[7]

EXHIBIT 2.1 Inputs to Forecasting

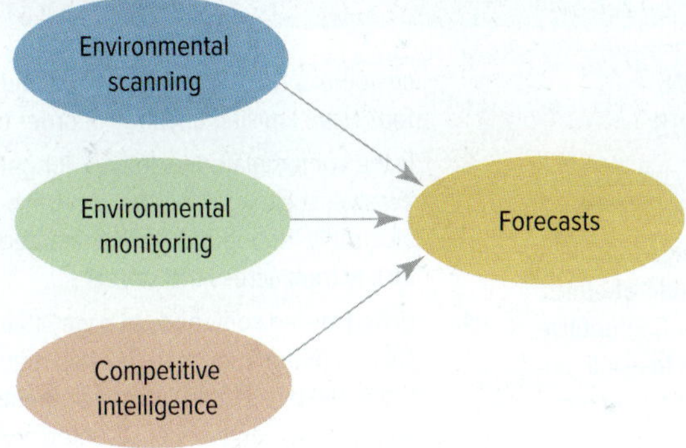

The Role of Scanning, Monitoring, Competitive Intelligence, and Forecasting

Environmental Scanning **Environmental scanning** involves surveillance of a firm's external environment to predict environmental changes and detect changes already underway.[8,9] This alerts the organization to critical trends and events before changes develop a discernible pattern and before competitors recognize them.[10] Otherwise, the firm may be forced into a reactive mode.[11]

Experts agree that spotting key trends requires a combination of knowing your business and your customer as well as keeping an eye on what's happening around you. Such a big-picture/small-picture view enables you to better identify the emerging trends that will affect your business.

Leading firms in an industry can also be a key indicator of emerging trends.[12] For example, with its wide range of household goods, Procter & Gamble is a barometer for consumer spending. Any sign that it can sell more of its premium products without cutting prices sharply indicates that shoppers may finally be becoming less price-sensitive with everyday purchases. In particular, investors will examine the performance of beauty products like Olay moisturizers and CoverGirl cosmetics for evidence that spending on small, discretionary pick-me-ups is improving.

LO 2-2

Explain why environmental scanning, environmental monitoring, and collecting competitive intelligence are critical inputs to forecasting.

environmental scanning
surveillance of a firm's external environment to predict environmental changes and detect changes already under way.

Environmental Monitoring **Environmental monitoring** tracks the evolution of environmental trends, sequences of events, or streams of activities. They may be trends that the firm came across by accident or ones that were brought to its attention from outside the organization.[13] Monitoring enables firms to evaluate how dramatically environmental trends are changing the competitive landscape.

environmental monitoring
a firm's analysis of the external environment that tracks the evolution of environmental trends, sequences of events, or streams of activities.

One of the authors of this text has conducted on-site interviews with executives from several industries to identify indicators that firms monitor as inputs to their strategy process. Examples of such indicators included:

- ***A Motel 6 executive.*** The number of rooms in the budget segment of the industry in the United States and the difference between the average daily room rate and the consumer price index (CPI).
- ***A Pier 1 Imports executive.*** Net disposable income (NDI), consumer confidence index, and housing starts.
- ***A Johnson & Johnson medical products executive.*** Percentage of gross domestic product (GDP) spent on health care, number of active hospital beds, and the size and power of purchasing agents (indicates the concentration of buyers).

Such indices are critical for managers in determining a firm's strategic direction and resource allocation.

2.1 STRATEGY SPOTLIGHT — ETHICS

ETHICAL GUIDELINES ON COMPETITIVE INTELLIGENCE: UNITED TECHNOLOGIES

United Technologies (UT) is a global conglomerate composed of world-leading businesses with rich histories of technological pioneering, such as Otis Elevator, Carrier Air Conditioning, and Sikorsky (helicopters). UT believes strongly in a robust code of ethics. One such document is the Code of Ethics Guide on Competitive Intelligence. This encourages managers and workers to ask themselves these five questions whenever they have ethical concerns.

1. Have I done anything that coerced somebody to share this information? Have I, for example, threatened a supplier by indicating that future business opportunities will be influenced by the receipt of information with respect to a competitor?
2. Am I in a place where I should not be? If, for example, I am a field representative with privileges to move around in a customer's facility, have I gone outside the areas permitted? Have I misled anybody in order to gain access?
3. Is the contemplated technique for gathering information evasive, such as sifting through trash or setting up an electronic "snooping" device directed at a competitor's facility from across the street?
4. Have I misled somebody in a way that the person believed sharing information with me was required or would be protected by a confidentiality agreement? Have I, for example, called and misrepresented myself as a government official who was seeking some information for some official purpose?
5. Have I done something to evade or circumvent a system intended to secure or protect information?

Sources: Nelson, B. 2003. The thinker. *Forbes,* March 3: 62–64; and The Fuld war room–Survival kit 010. Code of ethics (printed 2/26/01).

competitive intelligence
a firm's activities of collecting and interpreting data on competitors, defining and understanding the industry, and identifying competitors' strengths and weaknesses.

Competitive Intelligence **Competitive intelligence** (CI) helps firms define and understand their industry and identify rivals' strengths and weaknesses.[14] This includes the intelligence gathering associated with collecting data on competitors and interpreting such data. Done properly, competitive intelligence helps a company avoid surprises by anticipating competitors' moves and decreasing response time.[15]

Examples of competitive analysis are evident in daily newspapers and periodicals such as *The Wall Street Journal, Bloomberg Businessweek,* and *Fortune.* For example, banks continually track home loan, auto loan, and certificate of deposit (CD) interest rates charged by rivals. Major airlines change hundreds of fares daily in response to competitors' tactics. Car manufacturers are keenly aware of announced cuts or increases in rivals' production volume, sales, and sales incentives (e.g., rebates and low interest rates on financing). This information is used in their marketing, pricing, and production strategies.

Keeping track of competitors has become easier today with the amount of information that is available on the Internet. The following are examples of some websites that companies routinely use for competitive intelligence gathering.[16]

- ***Slideshare.*** A website for publicly sharing PowerPoint presentations. Marketing teams have embraced the platform and often post detail-rich presentations about their firms and products.
- ***Quora.*** A question-and-answer site popular among industry insiders who embrace the free flow of information about technical questions.
- ***iSpionage.*** A site that reveals the ad words that companies are buying, which can often shed light on new campaigns being launched.
- ***YouTube.*** Great for finding interviews with executives at trade shows.

At times, a firm's aggressive efforts to gather competitive intelligence may lead to unethical or illegal behaviors.[17] Strategy Spotlight 2.1 provides an example of a company, United Technologies, that has set clear guidelines to help prevent unethical behavior.

A word of caution: Executives must be careful to avoid spending so much time and effort tracking the actions of traditional competitors that they ignore new competitors. Further, broad environmental changes and events may have a dramatic impact on a firm's viability. Peter Drucker, wrote:

> Increasingly, a winning strategy will require information about events and conditions outside the institution: noncustomers, technologies other than those currently used by the company and its present competitors, markets not currently served, and so on.[18]

Consider the failure of specialized medical lab Sleep HealthCenters.[19] Until recently, patients suffering from sleep disorders, such as apnea, were forced to undergo expensive overnight visits to sleep clinics, including Sleep HealthCenters, to diagnose their ailments. The firm was launched in 1997 and quickly expanded to over two dozen locations. Revenue soared from nearly $10 million in 1997 to $30 million in 2010.

However, the rapid improvements in the price and performance of wearable monitoring devices changed the business, gradually at first and then suddenly. For one thing, the more comfortable home setting produced more effective measurements. And the quick declines in the cost of wearable monitoring meant patients could get the same results at one-third the price of an overnight stay at a clinic. By 2011, Sleep HealthCenters' revenue began to decline, and the firm closed 20 percent of its locations. In 2012, its death knells sounded: Insurance companies decided to cover the less expensive option. Sleep HealthCenters abruptly closed its doors.

Environmental Forecasting Environmental scanning, monitoring, and competitive intelligence are important inputs for analyzing the external environment. **Environmental forecasting** involves the development of plausible projections about the direction, scope, speed, and intensity of environmental change.[20] Its purpose is to predict change.[21] It asks: How long will it take a new technology to reach the marketplace? Will the present social concern about an issue result in new legislation? Are current lifestyle trends likely to continue?

environmental forecasting
the development of plausible projections about the direction, scope, speed, and intensity of environmental change.

Some forecasting issues are much more specific to a particular firm and the industry in which it competes. Consider how important it is for Motel 6 to predict future indicators, such as the number of rooms, in the budget segment of the industry. If its predictions are too optimistic, it will build too many units, creating a surplus of room capacity that would drive down room rates.

A danger of forecasting is that managers may view uncertainty as black and white and ignore important gray areas.[22] The problem is that underestimating uncertainty can lead to strategies that neither defend against threats nor take advantage of opportunities.

LO 2-3

Explain why scenario planning is a useful technique for firms competing in industries characterized by unpredictability and change.

In 1977 one of the colossal underestimations in business history occurred when Kenneth H. Olsen, president of Digital Equipment Corp., announced, "There is no reason for individuals to have a computer in their home." The explosion in the personal computer market was not easy to detect in 1977, but it was clearly within the range of possibilities at the time. And, historically, there have been underestimates of the growth potential of new telecommunication services. The electric telegraph was derided by Ralph Waldo Emerson, and the telephone had its skeptics. More recently, an "infamous" McKinsey study in the early 1980s predicted fewer than 1 million cellular users in the United States by 2000. Actually, there were nearly 100 million.[23]

Obviously, poor predictions about technology change never go out of vogue. Consider some other "gems"—predicted by very knowledgeable people: [24]

- (1981) "Cellular phones will absolutely not replace local wire systems." Inventor Marty Cooper
- (1995) "I predict the Internet will soon go spectacularly supernova and in 1996 catastrophically collapse." Robert Metcalfe, founder of 3Com
- (1997) "Apple is already dead." Former Microsoft CTO Nathan Myhrvold
- (2005) "There's just not that many videos I want to watch." Steve Chen, CTO and co-founder of YouTube, expressing concerns about the firm's long-term viability

- (2006) "Everyone's always asking me when Apple will come out with a cell phone. My answer is 'Probably never.'" David Pogue, *The New York Times*
- (2007) "There's no chance that the iPhone is going to get significant market share." Steve Ballmer, Microsoft

Jason Zweig, an editor at *The Wall Street Journal,* provides an important cautionary note (and rather colorful example!) regarding the need to question the reliability of forecasts: "Humans don't want accuracy; they want assurance . . . people can't stand ignoring all predictions; admitting that the future is unknowable is just too frightening."[25]

> The Nobel laureate and the late Stanford University economist Kenneth Arrow did a tour of duty as a weather forecaster for the U.S. Air Force during World War II. Ordered to evaluate mathematical models for predicting the weather one month ahead, he found that they were worthless. Informed of that, his superiors sent back another order: "The Commanding General is well aware that the forecasts are no good. However, he needs them for planning purposes."

scenario analysis an in-depth approach to environmental forecasting that involves experts' detailed assessments of societal trends, economics, politics, technology, or other dimensions of the external environment.

Scenario Analysis **Scenario analysis** is a more in-depth approach to forecasting. It draws on a range of disciplines and interests, among them economics, psychology, sociology, and demographics. It usually begins with a discussion of participants' thoughts on ways in which societal trends, economics, politics, and technology may affect an issue.[26] Scenario analysis involves the projection of future possible events. It does not rely on extrapolation of historical trends. Rather, it seeks to explore possible developments that may only be connected to the past. That is, several scenarios are considered in a scenario analysis in order to envision possible future outcomes.

Consider PPG Industries.[27] The Pittsburgh-based producer of paints, coatings, specialty materials, chemicals, glass, and fiberglass has paid dividends each year since 1899. One of the key tools it uses today in its strategic planning is scenario analysis.

> PPG has developed four alternative futures based on differing assumptions about two key variables: the cost of energy (because its manufacturing operations are energy-intensive) and the extent of opportunity for growth in emerging markets. In the most favorable scenario, cost of energy will stay both moderate and stable and opportunities for growth and differentiation will be fast and strong. In this scenario, PPG determined that its success will depend on having the resources to pursue new opportunities. On the other hand, in the worst case scenario, the cost of energy will be high and opportunities for growth will be weak and slow. Such a scenario would call for a complete change in strategic direction.
>
> Between these two extremes lies the possibility of two mixed scenarios. First, opportunity for growth in emerging markets may be high, but the cost of energy may be volatile. In this scenario, the company's success will depend on coming up with more efficient processes. Second, cost of energy may remain moderate and stable, but opportunities for growth in emerging markets may remain weak and slow. In this situation, the most viable strategy may be one of capturing market share with new products.

SWOT Analysis

To understand the business environment of a particular firm, you need to analyze both the general environment and the firm's industry and competitive environment. Generally, firms compete with other firms in the same industry. An industry is composed of a set of firms that produce similar products or services, sell to similar customers, and use similar methods of production. Gathering industry information and understanding competitive dynamics among the different companies in your industry is key to successful strategic management.

SWOT analysis a framework for analyzing a company's internal and external environments and that stands for strengths, weaknesses, opportunities, and threats.

One of the most basic techniques for analyzing firm and industry conditions is **SWOT analysis.** SWOT stands for strengths, weaknesses, opportunities, and threats. It provides "raw material"—a basic listing of conditions both inside and surrounding your company.

The Strengths and Weaknesses refer to the internal conditions of the firm—where your firm excels (strengths) and where it may be lacking relative to competitors (weaknesses). Opportunities and Threats are environmental conditions external to the firm. These could be factors in either the general or the competitive environment. In the general environment, one might experience developments that are beneficial for most companies, such as improving economic conditions that lower borrowing costs, or trends that benefit some companies and harm others. An example is the heightened concern with fitness, which is a threat to some companies (e.g., tobacco) and an opportunity to others (e.g., health clubs). Opportunities and threats are also present in the competitive environment among firms competing for the same customers.

The general idea of SWOT analysis is that a firm's strategy must:

- Build on its strengths.
- Remedy the weaknesses or work around them.
- Take advantage of the opportunities presented by the environment.
- Protect the firm from the threats.

Despite its apparent simplicity, the SWOT approach has been very popular. First, it forces managers to consider both internal and external factors simultaneously. Second, its emphasis on identifying opportunities and threats makes firms act proactively rather than reactively. Third, it raises awareness about the role of strategy in creating a match between the environmental conditions and the firm's internal strengths and weaknesses. Finally, its conceptual simplicity is achieved without sacrificing analytical rigor.

While analysis is necessary, it is also equally important to recognize the role played by intuition and judgment. Steve Jobs, the legendary former chairman of Apple, took a very different approach in determining what customers *really* wanted:[28]

> Steve Jobs was convinced market research and focus groups limited one's ability to innovate. When asked how much research was done to guide Apple when he introduced the iPad, Jobs famously quipped: "None. It isn't the consumers' job to know what they want. It's hard for (consumers) to tell you what they want when they've never seen anything remotely like it."
>
> Jobs relied on his own intuition—his radarlike feel for emerging technologies and how they could be brought together to create, in his words "insanely great products, that ultimately made the difference." For Jobs, who died in 2011 at the age of 56, intuition was no mere gut call. It was, as he put it in his often-quoted commencement speech at Stanford, about "connecting the dots, glimpsing the relationships among wildly disparate life experiences and changes in technologies."

THE GENERAL ENVIRONMENT

LO 2-4

Recognize the impact of the general environment on a firm's strategies and performance.

The **general environment** is composed of factors that can have dramatic effects on firm strategy.[29] We divide the general environment into six segments: demographic, sociocultural, political/legal, technological, economic, and global. Exhibit 2.2 provides examples of key trends and events in each of the six segments of the general environment.

general environment factors external to an industry, and usually beyond a firm's control, that affect a firm's strategy.

Before addressing each of the six segments in turn, consider Dominic Barton's insights in response to a question posed to him by an editor of *Fortune* magazine: *What are your client's worries right now?* (Barton is global managing director emeritus of McKinsey, the giant consulting firm.)[30] He highlights four challenges for CEOs. First, geopolitical tensions around the globe have replaced the political stability of the past decades. Second, technology moves several times faster than management, which not only creates new opportunities but also threats for many companies. Third, cybersecurity and the related efforts to protect computer systems and networks is a big priority for CEOs. Finally, economic powers around the world are shifting, with more than 2 billion new middle-class customers emerging in the next 15 years, many of them in Asia and Africa.

EXHIBIT 2.2

General Environment: Key Trends and Events

Demographic
• Aging population • Rising affluence • Changes in ethnic composition • Geographic distribution of population • Greater disparities in income levels
Sociocultural
• More women in the workforce • Increase in temporary workers • Greater concern for fitness • Greater concern for environment • Postponement of family formation
Political/Legal
• Tort reform • Americans with Disabilities Act (ADA) of 1990 • Deregulation of utility and other industries • Increases in federally mandated minimum wages • Taxation at local, state, federal levels • Legislation on corporate governance reforms in bookkeeping, stock options, etc. (Sarbanes-Oxley Act of 2002) • Affordable Care Act (Obamacare)
Technological
• Genetic engineering • Three-dimensional (3D) printing • Research in synthetic and exotic materials • Pollution/global warming • Miniaturization of computing technologies • Wireless communications • Nanotechnology • Big Data Analytics
Economic
• Interest rates • Unemployment rates • Consumer price index • Trends in GDP • Changes in stock market valuations • National debt
Global
• Changes in global trade • Currency exchange rates • Emergence of the Indian and Chinese economies • Trade agreements among regional blocs (e.g., NAFTA, EU, ASEAN) • Creation of WTO (leading to decreasing tariffs/free trade in services) • Increased risks associated with terrorism

The Demographic Segment

Demographics are the most easily understood and quantifiable elements of the general environment. They are at the root of many changes in society. Demographics include elements such as the aging population,[31] rising or declining affluence, changes in ethnic composition, geographic distribution of the population, and disparities in income level.[32]

The impact of a demographic trend, like all segments of the general environment, varies across industries. Rising levels of affluence in many developed countries bode well for brokerage services as well as for upscale pets and supplies. However, this trend may adversely affect fast-food restaurants because people can afford to dine at higher-priced restaurants. Fast-food restaurants depend on minimum-wage employees to operate efficiently, but the competition for labor intensifies as more attractive employment opportunities become prevalent, thus threatening the employment base for restaurants. Let's look at the details of one of these trends.

The aging population in the United States and other developed countries has important implications. Although the percentage of those 65 and over in the U.S. workforce bottomed in the 1990s, it has been rising ever since.[33] According to the Bureau of Labor Statistics, adults 55 years and older will make up 25 percent of the U.S. workforce by 2024, compared to just 12 percent of workers in 1990.[34] And, according to a 2014 study by Merrill Lynch and the Age Wave Consulting firm, 72 percent of preretirees aged 50 and over wanted to work during their retirement. "Older workers are to the first half of the 21st century what women were to the last half of the 20th century," says Eugene Steuerle, an economist at the Urban Institute.

There are a number of misconceptions about the quality and value of older workers. The Insights from Research box on page 46, however, debunks many of these myths.

demographic segment of the general environment genetic and observable characteristics of a population, including the levels and growth of age, density, sex, race, ethnicity, education, geographic region, and income.

The Sociocultural Segment

Sociocultural forces influence the values, beliefs, and lifestyles of a society. Examples include a higher percentage of women in the workforce, dual-income families, increases in the number of temporary workers, greater concern for healthy diets and physical fitness, greater interest in the environment, and postponement of having children. Such forces enhance sales of products and services in many industries but depress sales in others. The increased number of women in the workforce has increased the need for business clothing merchandise but decreased the demand for baking product staples (since people would have less time to cook from scratch). The health and fitness trend has helped industries that manufacture exercise equipment and healthful foods but harmed industries that produce unhealthful foods.

Increased educational attainment by women in the workplace has led to more women in upper-management positions.[35] Given such educational attainment, it is hardly surprising that companies owned by women have been one of the driving forces of the U.S. economy; as of 2018, these companies (more than 12 million in number) account for around 40 percent of all U.S. businesses and have generated $1.8 trillion in annual revenue.[36] In addition, women have a tremendous impact on consumer spending decisions. Not surprisingly, many companies have focused their advertising and promotion efforts on female consumers.

Strategy Spotlight 2.2 provides examples of how advocacy groups and public opinion can put pressure on companies to address environmental sustainability concerns such as waste reduction in a proactive manner.

sociocultural segment of the general environment the values, beliefs, and lifestyles of a society.

The Political/Legal Segment

Political processes and legislation influence environmental regulations with which industries must comply.[37,38] Some important elements of the political/legal arena include tort reform, the Americans with Disabilities Act (ADA) of 1990, the repeal of the Glass-Steagall

political/legal segment of the general environment how a society creates and exercises power, including rules, laws, and taxation policies.

2.1 *INSIGHTS* from Research

NEW TRICKS: RESEARCH DEBUNKS MYTHS ABOUT OLDER WORKERS

Overview

People often think that older workers are less motivated and less healthy, resist change and are less trusting, and have more trouble balancing work and family. It turns out these assumptions just aren't true. By challenging these stereotypes in your organization, you can keep your employees working.

What the Research Shows

In a 2012 paper published by *Personnel Psychology,* researchers from the University of Hong Kong and the University of Georgia examined 418 studies of workers' ages and stereotypes. A meta-analysis–a study of studies–was conducted to find out if any of the six following stereotypes about older workers–as compared with younger workers–was actually true:

- They are less motivated.
- They are less willing to participate in training and career development.
- They are more resistant to change.
- They are less trusting.
- They are less healthy.
- They are more vulnerable to work-family imbalance.

After an exhaustive search of studies dealing with these issues, the investigators' meta-analytic techniques turned up some interesting results. Older workers' motivation and job involvement are actually slightly higher than those of younger workers. Older workers are slightly more willing to implement organizational changes, are not less trusting, and are not less healthy than younger workers. Moreover, they're not more likely to have issues with work-family imbalance. Of the six investigated, the only stereotype supported was that older workers are less willing to participate in training and career development.

Children born today in advanced economies have a more than 50 percent chance of living past their 100th birthday. Companies must proactively address the opportunities and challenges that come with greater longevity. Most companies today use a three-stage career model of education, work, and retirement. However, longer lives will result in multistage career models that encompass new periods of explorations in younger years, additional career transitions, and the need to maintain intangible assets such as health and professional skills. Companies are well advised to adapt their human resource practices to address these changes in the demographic segment of the general environment.

Key Takeaways

- The percentage of American workers 55 years old and older is expected to increase from 19.5 percent in 2010 to 25.2 percent in 2020.
- Many stereotypes exist about older workers. A review of 418 studies reveals these stereotypes are largely unfounded.
- Older workers subjected to negative stereotypes are more likely to retire and more likely to report lower quality of life and poorer health.
- When business leaders accept stereotypes about older workers, they lose out on these workers' wisdom and experience. And by 2020 employers may have a smaller pool of younger workers than they do today.
- Solutions include creating opportunities for younger and older workers to work together and having frank, open discussions about stereotypes.

Questions

1. Given that employees and firms need to update existing skills and develop new knowledge, how can managers encourage older employees to close the training and development gap with younger employees?
2. How should companies adapt their human resource practices to ensure that they attract and retain the best employees when people are living and working longer?

Research Reviewed

Gratton, L., and A. Scott. 2017. The corporate implications of longer lives. *MIT Sloan Management Review,* 58(3): 63-70; Ng, T. W. H., and D. C. Feldman. 2012. Evaluating six common stereotypes about older workers with meta-analytical data. *Personnel Psychology,* 65: 821–858. We thank Matthew Gilley, PhD, of *businessminded.com* for contributing this research brief.

Act in 1999 (banks may now offer brokerage services), deregulation of utilities and other industries, and increases in the federally mandated minimum wage.[39]

Government legislation can also have a significant impact on the governance of corporations. The U.S. Congress passed the Sarbanes-Oxley Act in 2002, which greatly increases

2.2 STRATEGY SPOTLIGHT — ENVIRONMENTAL SUSTAINABILITY

ENVIRONMENTAL AWARENESS DRIVES SUSTAINABLE BUSINESS PRACTICES

Customers and regulators around the world are increasingly challenging companies to find new ways to deal with plastic waste. For instance, the European Union recently banned a range of single-use plastics such as plastic cutlery, plates, and straws by 2021. China halted the import of plastic waste from foreign countries, potentially leaving 111 million tons of plastic waste to go nowhere by 2030. On a local level, some cities such as Chicago now impose fees on customers using plastic bags. In addition to regulatory forces, non-governmental organizations such as Greenpeace call for abandoning single-use plastics that pollute the world's oceans to the tune of eight million metric tons annually. Given these recent developments, it is safe to say that many societies around the world increasingly demand more sustainable business practices.

Many companies proactively respond to these societal concerns by adopting environmentally sustainable business models. Kroger, the large U.S. grocery chain, announced plans to eliminate plastic shopping bags by 2025. Other retailers even go a step further in their efforts to reduce plastic waste. Walmart, for instance, plans to eliminate all non-recyclable packaging materials from its stores. This would make Walmart a "zero waste" store in their U.S. operations by 2025. Walmart already made significant strides toward this goal by diverting 81 percent of its U.S. waste from landfill and incineration in 2018.

In addition to banning plastic waste, some companies experiment with innovative ways to reduce plastic use altogether. For example, Starbucks invested millions to invent and design a strawless lid to replace plastic straws by 2020. The coffee chain anticipates that this change will eliminate one billion straws annually. Similarly, Burger King rolled out biodegradable drinking straws; and Hyatt instructed its employees to only offer plastic straws to customers who explicitly ask for straws.

While many companies proactively address changing attitudes toward plastic waste, other companies are lagging behind. Some companies fear that more environmentally sustainable offerings such as banning plastic bags and redesigning coffee lids can alienate customers. However, waiting until strict environmental expectations become the norm may be a risky proposition as customer expectations about environmental issues can change fast. Companies that proactively adapt to environmental trends can experiment with different approaches to meet customer demands. For instance, Kroger is trying to ease its customers into a world without plastic bags. The supermarket chain offers paper bags instead of plastic and sells reusable shopping bags with the goal of getting its customers familiarized with reusable bags.

Sources: Haddon, H. 2018. Kroger bags plastic packaging. *Wall Street Journal*, August 24: B6; Jargon, J., and K. Chin. 2018. Plastic straws bend to criticism. *Wall Street Journal*, July 10: B1-B2; Anonymous. 2018. Walmart global responsibility report. *Walmart*, 2018: np.

the accountability of auditors, executives, and corporate lawyers. This act responded to the widespread perception that existing governance mechanisms failed to protect the interests of shareholders, employees, and creditors. Clearly, Sarbanes-Oxley has also created a tremendous demand for professional accounting services.

Legislation can also affect firms in the high-tech sector of the economy by expanding the number of temporary visas available for highly skilled foreign professionals.[40] For example, a bill passed by the U.S. Congress in October 2000 allowed 195,000 H-1B visas for each of the following three years–up from a cap of 115,000. However, beginning in 2006 and continuing through 2019, the annual cap on H-1B visas has shrunk to only 65,000–with an additional 20,000 visas available for foreigners with a master's or higher degree from a U.S. institution. Many of the visas are for professionals from India with computer and software expertise. In 2014, companies applied for 172,500 H-1B visas. This means that at least 87,500 engineers, developers, and others couldn't take jobs in the United States.[41] As one would expect, this is a political "hot potato" for industry executives as well as U.S. labor and workers' rights groups. The key arguments against H-1B visas are that H-1B workers drive down wages and take jobs from Americans.

The Technological Segment

technological segment of the general environment innovation and state of knowledge in industrial arts, engineering, applied sciences, and pure science; and their interaction with society.

Developments in technology lead to new products and services and improve how they are produced and delivered to the end user.[42] Innovations can create entirely new industries and alter the boundaries of existing industries.[43] Technological developments and trends include genetic engineering, Internet technology, research in artificial and exotic materials, and, on the downside, pollution and global warming.[44] Petroleum and primary metals industries spend significantly to reduce their pollution. Engineering and consulting firms that work with polluting industries derive financial benefits from solving such problems.

Nanotechnology is becoming a very promising area of research with many potentially useful applications.[45] Nanotechnology takes place at industry's tiniest stage: one-billionth of a meter. Remarkably, this is the size of 10 hydrogen atoms in a row. Matter at such a tiny scale behaves very differently. Familiar materials–from gold to carbon soot–display startling and useful new properties. Some transmit light or electricity. Others become harder than diamonds or turn into potent chemical catalysts. What's more, researchers have found that a tiny dose of nanoparticles can transform the chemistry and nature of far bigger things.

Another emerging technology is physiolytics, which is the practice of linking wearable computing devices with data analysis and quantified feedback to improve performance.[46] An example is sensors in shoes (such as Nike+, used by runners to track distance, speed, and other metrics). Another emerging application of wearable devices is medical monitoring, a domain in which Apple established an early lead. Apple Watch Series 4 is able to measure heart rate in ways that is normally restricted to bulky electrocardiogram (ECG) devices. Apple promotes the Apple Watch 4 as a device that can take an electrocardiogram to diagnose heart failure. A promising sign that Apple's efforts in this domain will pay off comes from the U.S. Food and Drug Administration (FDA), which cleared the Apple Watch 4 as a medical device.[47]

economic segment of the general environment characteristics of the economy, including national income and monetary conditions.

The Economic Segment

The economy affects all industries, from suppliers of raw materials to manufacturers of finished goods and services, as well as all organizations in the service, wholesale, retail, government, and nonprofit sectors.[48] Key economic indicators include interest rates, unemployment rates, the consumer price index, the gross domestic product, and net disposable income.[49] Interest rate increases have a negative impact on the residential home construction industry but a negligible (or neutral) effect on industries that produce consumer necessities such as prescription drugs or common grocery items.

Other economic indicators are associated with equity markets. Perhaps the most watched is the Dow Jones Industrial Average (DJIA), which is composed of 30 large industrial firms. When stock market indexes increase, consumers' discretionary income rises and there is often an increased demand for luxury items such as jewelry and automobiles. But when stock valuations decrease, demand for these items shrinks.

global segment of the general environment influences from foreign countries, including foreign market opportunities, foreign-based competition, and expanded capital markets.

The Global Segment

More firms are expanding their operations and market reach beyond the borders of their "home" country. Globalization provides both opportunities to access larger potential markets and a broad base of production factors such as raw materials, labor, skilled managers, and technical professionals. However, such endeavors also carry many political, social, and economic risks.[50]

Examples of key elements include currency exchange rates, increasing global trade, the economic emergence of China, trade agreements among regional blocs (e.g., North American Free Trade Agreement, European Union), and the General Agreement on Tariffs and Trade (GATT) (lowering of tariffs).[51] Increases in trade across national boundaries also provide benefits to air cargo and shipping industries but have a minimal impact on service industries such as bookkeeping and routine medical services.

A key factor in the global economy is the rapid rise of the middle class in emerging countries. The number of consumers in Asia's middle class is rapidly approaching the number in Europe and North America combined. An important implication of this trend is the dramatic change in hiring practices of U.S. multinationals. For example, many U.S.-based multinational firms have recently added jobs faster than other U.S. employers.

Relationships among Elements of the General Environment

In our discussion of the general environment, we see many relationships among the various elements.[52] For example, a demographic trend in the United States, the aging of the population, has important implications for the economic segment (in terms of tax policies to provide benefits to increasing numbers of older citizens). Another example is the emergence of information technology as a means to increase the rate of productivity gains in the United States and other developed countries. Such use of IT results in lower inflation (an important element of the economic segment) and helps offset costs associated with higher labor rates.

The effects of a trend or event in the general environment vary across industries. Governmental legislation (political/legal) to permit the importation of prescription drugs from foreign countries is a very positive development for drugstores but a very negative event for U.S. drug manufacturers. Exhibit 2.3 provides other examples of how the impact of trends or events in the general environment can vary across industries.

EXHIBIT 2.3

The Impact of General Environmental Trends on Various Industries

Segment/Trends and Events	Industry	Positive	Neutral	Negative
Demographic				
Aging population	Health care	✓		
	Baby products			✓
Rising affluence	Brokerage services	✓		
	Fast foods			✓
	Upscale pets and supplies	✓		
Sociocultural				
More women in the workforce	Clothing	✓		
	Baking products (staples)			✓
Greater concern for health and fitness	Home exercise equipment	✓		
	Meat products			✓
Political/legal				
Tort reform	Legal services			✓
	Auto manufacturing	✓		
Americans with Disabilities Act (ADA)	Retail			✓
	Manufacturers of elevators, escalators, and ramps	✓		
Technological				
Genetic engineering	Pharmaceutical	✓		
	Publishing		✓	
Pollution/global warming	Engineering services	✓		
	Petroleum			✓
Economic				
Interest rate decreases	Residential construction	✓		
	Most common grocery products		✓	
Global				
Increasing global trade	Shipping	✓		
	Personal service		✓	
Emergence of China as an economic power	Soft drinks	✓		
	Defense			✓

DIGITAL ECONOMY: A FUNDAMENTAL SHIFT IN THE BUSINESS ENVIRONMENT

Digital Economy
The term Digital Economy refers to economic transactions and business operations that are based on digital computing technologies.

Before moving on, let us consider the influence of the growth of the **Digital Economy.** The term Digital Economy refers to economic transactions and business operations that are based on digital computing technologies. It reflects the economic activity and means of organizing that results from billions of everyday online connections among people, businesses, devices, and processes. The rise of the digital economy has disrupted existing industries, altering how firms structure themselves and how they interact with business partners and customers. As Professor Walter Brenner of the University of St. Gallen in Switzerland states, "*The aggressive use of data is transforming business models, facilitating new products and services, creating new processes, generating greater utility, and ushering in a new culture of management.*"[53] It has also grown dramatically and by 2016, represented about one-sixth of the US economy.[54]

The effects of the digital economy include the following:

- **Globalization of business.** By facilitating transactions with suppliers and customers through online and mobile systems, firms large and small are now able to interact with business partners on a global scale.
- **Disintermediation of markets.** Through online transactions, firms are able to more directly interact with suppliers and customers. As a result, firms are less reliant on distributors and retailers to reach end consumers as well as on intermediaries when interacting with suppliers. These changes have increased the efficiency of the vertical chain that spans from raw material and component suppliers to end customers by cutting out multiple middlemen from the process.
- **Reducing the asset intensity of business operations.** By facilitating the ease of transactions and allowing distant firms to coordinate operations, firms can more easily ally with outside firms to provide critical business operations. This has reduced the need of firms to invest in expensive operations, such as R&D facilities, technology infrastructure, manufacturing plants, and physical stores.
- **Increasing collaboration.** Online systems allow greater connectedness and collaboration both within and across firm boundaries. This has facilitated greater collaboration not only between suppliers and customers but also with complementary product and service firms to meet evolving customer needs.
- **Increasing customer expectations.** With the availability of information on products and services, the perceived increase in the rate of new technology introduction, and the availability of a larger number of global suppliers, customers are more knowledgeable and more fickle than in the past.[55] For example, by interacting directly with suppliers, customers perceive the opportunity to push for customized services and products.
- **Infusion of Internet technology into products.** The ease of connection to the Internet has facilitated the rise of the "Internet of Things," which allows devices to interact with each other and users to access products from anywhere in the world. This has led to products, such as trucks, that send performance information to manufacturers who then communicate with users about service needs. It also includes smart home systems, such as lighting systems, that allow users to access the system and adjust settings from anywhere in the world.

The digital economy has also led to the creation of completely new markets. As technology advances have allowed people to connect with each other in new ways, it has fostered the creation of the social network industry, platform-oriented retailers such as Etsy and Priceline, sharing economy businesses such as ride sharing services, and the cloud computing industry.

2.3 STRATEGY SPOTLIGHT — DIGITAL ECONOMY

HOW BIG DATA CAN MONITOR FEDERAL, STATE, AND LOCAL GOVERNMENT EXPENDITURES

Open The Books is a new initiative that uses big data to make the work of city, state, and the federal government more transparent. It was founded in Illinois by Adam Andrzejewski, a big-data expert. He and his team have amassed the computing power to capture a great share of the federal checkbook's vendor spending in the United States, as well as more than 48 states and many local governments.

Open The Books can also trace public salaries, pensions, and donations to political campaigns. Perhaps not too surprisingly, donors and subsidy recipients frequently turn out to be one of the same! Open The Books has created an app that can be quite revealing—the beauty school that receives more than 100 times in grants and student loans what it charges in tuition, and the $1.67 million in federally guaranteed loans received by the brother of a former Illinois director of agriculture.

Let's take a closer look to see what Andrzejewski has uncovered in his study of expenditures by the state of Illinois. He found that it has been two years since Illinois state government had a full-year budget and more than 70,000 vendors are owed $8.2 billion. However, despite a deadlock by the legislature and apparent fiscal insolvency, more than $50 billion has been paid to providers and other entities during the 2016 fiscal year. Who are some of these recipients?

- Comptroller Leslie Munger paid a lobbyist $50,000 out of her budget. The lobbyist—Shea, Paige and Rogal—has garnered more than $370,000 in payments since 2009. A key executive is the chairman emeritus of the Republican Party.
- Since 2005, J. Walter Thompson (JWT), one of the world's largest advertising agencies, has received $178.1 million.
- The Illinois Department of Transportation (IDOT) employs 1,133 civil engineers and 1,155 engineering technicians. Given this bank of talent, one might question why civil engineering firms such as ESI Consultants were paid $3.7 million, as well as other firms at large hourly rates.
- One could claim that IDOT engages in political patronage. On August 31, 2016, Munger paid $4.1 million in "performance bonuses" to 1,230 IDOT employees—members of the Teamsters. However, it may hardly be called a "performance bonus" because one of every two employees qualified for the pay enhancement.

As noted by Andrzejewski, "The Illinois credit ranking is the lowest of all 50 states. But the public patronage machine rolls on."

Sources: Shales, A. 2015. Pulling down state credit ratings. *Forbes*, November 2: 52; and Andrzejewski, A. 2016. The $50 billion Illinois favor factory hums along. *www.forbes.com*, August 31: np.

With the increasing centrality of online interactions and the infusion of products with Internet connectivity, firms have been able to collect increasingly large sets of information on their customers, including customer characteristics, purchasing patterns, and their use of the firm's products and services. Internally, firms are able to collect large amounts of data on employee activity and productivity, create social networks within the firm, and analyze physical asset utilization.

This has facilitated the rise of **data analytics** (or alternatively "Big Data"), the analysis of large data sets to uncover hidden patterns, market trends, and customer preferences. These efforts enable firms to better customize their product and service offerings to customers and to better differentiate the firm from its rivals while simultaneously using the firm's resources more efficiently. For example, Pepsi used data analytics to develop an algorithm that lowers the rate of stock outs and has shared the algorithm with its partners and retailers. Similarly, Kaiser Permanente collects petabytes of data on the health treatments of its 8 million healthcare members. This has allowed Kaiser to develop insights on the cost, efficiency, and safety of the treatments provided by doctors and procedures in hospitals.

data analytics
the process of examining large data sets to uncover hidden patterns, market trends, and customer preferences.

With elements of the digital economy affecting a wide range of industries, we examine digital economy as an integrating theme that affects all aspects of strategy. We discuss how firms are employing digital economy elements in different ways throughout the text. Examples of this include the discussion of how Alibaba has created an e-commerce giant in Chapter 1, how Zara is restructuring its operations to serve online customers in Chapter 3, how Unilever uses artificial intelligence to hire the best talent in Chapter 4, and how firms use data analytics to enhance organizational control in Chapter 9.

Spotlight 2.3 is an example of how data analytics can play a key role in monitoring spending in the public sector of the economy.

LO 2-5

Explain how forces in the competitive environment can affect profitability, and how a firm can improve its competitive position by increasing its power vis-à-vis these forces.

THE COMPETITIVE ENVIRONMENT

I remember listening to the senior executives in the room conclude, 'Walmart can't touch us.'

–Lynn Walsh, Former Vice President, Sears[56]

Managers must consider the competitive environment (also sometimes referred to as the task or industry environment). The nature of competition in an **industry,** as well as the profitability of a firm, is often directly influenced by developments in the competitive environment.

industry
a group of firms that produce similar goods or services.

The **competitive environment** consists of many factors that are particularly relevant to a firm's strategy. These include competitors (existing or potential), customers, and suppliers. Potential competitors may include a supplier considering forward integration, such as an automobile manufacturer acquiring a rental car company, or a firm in an entirely new industry introducing a similar product that uses a more efficient technology.

competitive environment
factors that pertain to an industry and affect a firm's strategies.

Next, we will discuss key concepts and analytical techniques that managers should use to assess their competitive environments. First, we examine Michael Porter's five forces model that illustrates how these forces can be used to explain an industry's profitability.[57] Second, we discuss how the five forces are being affected by the capabilities provided by Internet technologies. Third, we address some of the limitations, or "caveats," that managers should be familiar with when conducting industry analysis. Finally, we address the concept of strategic groups, because even within an industry it is often useful to group firms on the basis of similarities of their strategies. As we will see, competition tends to be more intense among firms *within* a strategic group than between strategic groups.

Porter's Five Forces Model of Industry Competition

Porter's five forces model of industry competition
a tool for examining the industry-level competitive environment, especially the ability of firms in that industry to set prices and minimize costs.

The **"five forces" model** developed by Michael E. Porter has been the most commonly used analytical tool for examining the competitive environment. It describes the competitive environment in terms of five basic competitive forces:[58]

1. The threat of new entrants.
2. The bargaining power of buyers.
3. The bargaining power of suppliers.
4. The threat of substitute products and services.
5. The intensity of rivalry among competitors in an industry.

Each of these forces affects a firm's ability to compete in a given market. Together, they determine the profit potential for a particular industry. The model is shown in Exhibit 2.4. A manager should be familiar with the five forces model for several reasons. It helps you decide whether your firm should remain in or exit an industry. It provides the rationale for increasing or decreasing resource commitments. The model helps you assess how to improve your firm's competitive position with regard to each of the five forces.[59] For example, you can use insights provided by the five forces model to understand how higher entry barriers discourage new rivals from competing with you.[60] Or you can see how to develop strong relationships with your distribution channels. You may decide to find suppliers who satisfy the price/performance criteria needed to make your product or service a top performer.

Consider, for example, some of the competitive forces affecting the hotel industry.[61] Airbnb, a room-sharing site, offers more rooms than even Marriott. Online travel agencies take a hefty cut of hotel bookings; and price-comparison sites make it difficult to raise room rates. Growing supply may make it harder still. In 2018, supply additions outpaced the demand growth for hotel rooms, further putting pressure on hotels and their profit margins.

EXHIBIT 2.4 Porter's Five Forces Model of Industry Competition

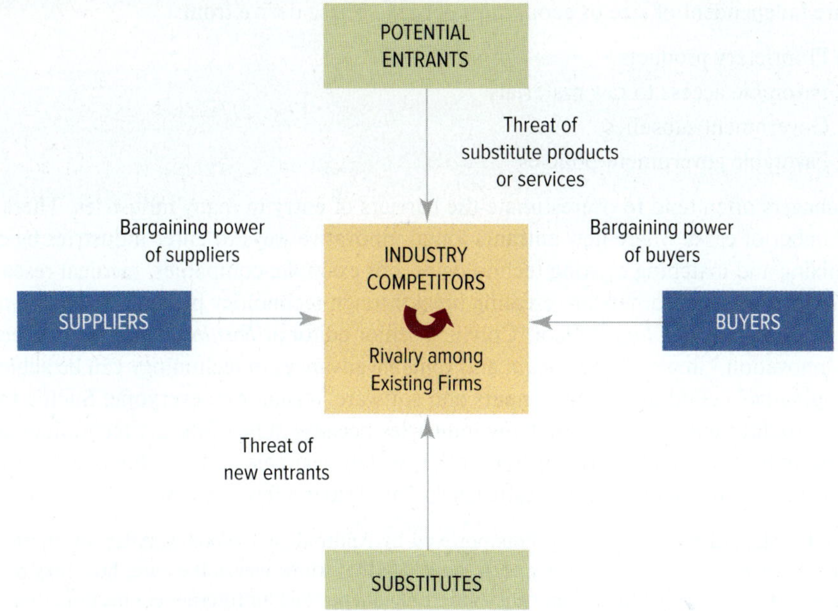

Source: Porter, M. E. 2008. The five competitive forces that shape strategy. Special Issue on HBS Centennial. *Harvard Business Review,* 86(1): 78-93.

The Threat of New Entrants The **threat of new entrants** refers to the possibility that the profits of established firms in the industry may be eroded by new competitors.[62] The extent of the threat depends on existing barriers to entry and the combined reactions from existing competitors.[63] If entry barriers are high and/or the newcomer can anticipate a sharp retaliation from established competitors, the threat of entry is low. These circumstances discourage new competitors. There are six major sources of entry barriers.

threat of new entrants the possibility that the profits of established firms in the industry may be eroded by new competitors.

Economies of Scale **Economies of scale** refers to spreading the costs of production over the number of units produced. The cost of a product per unit declines as the absolute volume per period increases. This deters entry by forcing the entrant to come in at a large scale and risk strong reaction from existing firms or come in at a small scale and accept a cost disadvantage. Both are undesirable options.

economies of scale decreases in cost per unit as absolute output per period increases.

Product Differentiation When existing competitors have strong brand identification and customer loyalty, **product differentiation** creates a barrier to entry by forcing entrants to spend heavily to overcome existing customer loyalties.

product differentiation the degree to which a product has strong brand loyalty or customer loyalty.

Capital Requirements The need to invest large financial resources to compete creates a barrier to entry, especially if the capital is required for risky or unrecoverable up-front advertising or research and development (R&D).

Switching Costs A barrier to entry is created by the existence of one-time costs that the buyer faces when switching from one supplier's product or service to another.

switching costs one-time costs that a buyer/supplier faces when switching from one supplier/buyer to another.

Access to Distribution Channels The new entrant's need to secure distribution for its product can create a barrier to entry.

Cost Disadvantages Independent of Scale Some existing competitors may have advantages that are independent of size or economies of scale. These derive from:

- Proprietary products
- Favorable access to raw materials
- Government subsidies
- Favorable government policies

Managers often tend to overestimate the barriers of entry in many industries. There are any number of cases where new entrants found innovative ways to enter industries by cleverly mixing and matching existing technologies. For example, companies, medical researchers, governments, and others are creating breakthrough technology products *without having to create any new technology.*[64] Geoff Colvin, a senior editor at *Fortune,* calls this "the era of Lego Innovation," in which significant and valuable advances in technology can be achieved by imaginatively combining components and software available to everyone. Such a trend serves to reduce entry barriers in many industries because state-of-the-art technology does not have to be developed internally–rather, it is widely available and, Colvin asserts, "we all have access to a really big box of plastic bricks." Consider a few examples:

> MIT's Media Lab has created robots powered by Android smartphones. After all, those devices can see, hear, recognize speech, and talk; they know where they are, how they're oriented, and how fast they're moving. And, through apps and an Internet connection, they can do a nearly infinite number of other tasks, such as recognize faces and translate languages. Similarly, teams at the University of South Carolina combined off-the-shelf eye-tracking technology with simple software they wrote to detect whether a driver was getting drowsy; any modern car has enough computing power to handle this job easily.

bargaining power of buyers
the threat that buyers may force down prices, bargain for higher quality or more services, and play competitors against each other.

The Bargaining Power of Buyers Buyers threaten an industry by forcing down prices, bargaining for higher quality or more services, and playing competitors against each other. These actions erode industry profitability.[65] The power of each large buyer group depends on attributes of the market situation and the importance of purchases from that group compared with the industry's overall business. A buyer group is powerful when:

- ***It is concentrated or purchases large volumes relative to seller sales.*** If a large percentage of a supplier's sales are purchased by a single buyer, the importance of the buyer's business to the supplier increases. Large-volume buyers also are powerful in industries with high fixed costs (e.g., steel manufacturing).
- ***The products it purchases from the industry are standard or undifferentiated.*** Confident they can always find alternative suppliers, buyers play one company against the other, as in commodity grain products.
- ***The buyer faces few switching costs.*** Switching costs lock the buyer to particular sellers. Conversely, the buyer's power is enhanced if the seller faces high switching costs.
- ***It earns low profits.*** Low profits create incentives to lower purchasing costs. On the other hand, highly profitable buyers are generally less price-sensitive.
- ***The buyers pose a credible threat of backward integration.*** If buyers either are partially integrated or pose a credible threat of backward integration, they are typically able to secure bargaining concessions.
- ***The industry's product is unimportant to the quality of the buyer's products or services.*** When the quality of the buyer's products is not affected by the industry's product, the buyer is more price-sensitive.

At times, a firm or set of firms in an industry may increase its buyer power by using the services of a third party. FreeMarkets Online is one such third party.[66] Pittsburgh-based FreeMarkets has developed software enabling large industrial buyers to organize online auctions for qualified suppliers of semistandard parts such as fabricated components, packaging materials, metal stampings, and services. By aggregating buyers, FreeMarkets increases the buyers' bargaining power. The results are impressive. In its first 48 auctions, most participating companies saved over 15 percent; some saved as much as 50 percent.

The Bargaining Power of Suppliers Suppliers can exert bargaining power by threatening to raise prices or reduce the quality of purchased goods and services. Powerful suppliers can squeeze the profitability of firms so far that they can't recover the costs of raw material inputs.[67] The factors that make suppliers powerful tend to mirror those that make buyers powerful. A supplier group will be powerful when:

bargaining power of suppliers the threat that suppliers may raise prices or reduce the quality of purchased goods and services.

- ***The supplier group is dominated by a few companies and is more concentrated (few firms dominate the industry) than the industry it sells to.*** Suppliers selling to fragmented industries influence prices, quality, and terms.
- ***The supplier group is not obliged to contend with substitute products for sale to the industry.*** The power of even large, powerful suppliers can be checked if they compete with substitutes.
- ***The industry is not an important customer of the supplier group.*** When suppliers sell to several industries and a particular industry does not represent a significant fraction of its sales, suppliers are more prone to exert power.
- ***The supplier's product is an important input to the buyer's business.*** When such inputs are important to the success of the buyer's manufacturing process or product quality, the bargaining power of suppliers is high.
- ***The supplier group's products are differentiated, or it has built up switching costs for the buyer.*** Differentiation or switching costs facing the buyers cut off their options to play one supplier against another.
- ***The supplier group poses a credible threat of forward integration.*** This provides a check against the industry's ability to improve the terms by which it purchases.

The formation of Delta Pride Catfish is an example of the power a group of suppliers can attain if they exercise the threat of forward integration.[68] Catfish farmers in Mississippi historically supplied their harvest to processing plants run by large agribusiness firms such as ConAgra and Farm Fresh. When the farmers increased their production of catfish in response to growing demand, they found, much to their chagrin, that processors were holding back on their plans to increase their processing capabilities in hopes of higher retail prices for catfish.

What action did the farmers take? About 120 of them banded together and formed a cooperative, raised $4.5 million, and constructed their own processing plant, which they supplied themselves. ConAgra's market share quickly dropped from 35 percent to 11 percent, and Farm Fresh's market share fell by over 20 percent. Within 10 years, Delta Pride controlled over 40 percent of the U.S. catfish market. Recently, Delta Pride changed its ownership structure and became a closely-held corporation. In 2014, it had revenues of $80 million, employed 600 people, and processed 80 million pounds of catfish.

The Threat of Substitute Products and Services All firms within an industry compete with industries producing **substitute products and services.**[69] Substitutes limit the potential returns of an industry by placing a ceiling on the prices that firms in that industry can profitably charge. The more attractive the price/performance ratio of substitute products, the tighter the lid on an industry's profits.

threat of substitute products and services the threat of limiting the potential returns of an industry by placing a ceiling on the prices that firms in that industry can profitably charge without losing too many customers to substitute products.

Identifying substitute products involves searching for other products or services that can perform the same function as the industry's offerings. This may lead a manager into businesses seemingly far removed from the industry. For example, the airline industry might not consider video cameras much of a threat. But as digital technology has improved and wireless and other forms of telecommunication have become more efficient, teleconferencing has become a viable substitute for business travel. That is, the rate of improvement in the price-performance relationship of the substitute product (or service) is high.

substitute products and services products and services outside the industry that serve the same customer needs as the industry's products and services.

intensity of rivalry among competitors in an industry
the threat that customers will switch their business to competitors within the industry.

The Intensity of Rivalry among Competitors in an Industry Firms use tactics like price competition, advertising battles, product introductions, and increased customer service or warranties. Rivalry occurs when competitors sense the pressure or act on an opportunity to improve their position.[70]

Some forms of competition, such as price competition, are typically highly destabilizing and are likely to erode the average level of profitability in an industry.[71] Rivals easily match price cuts, an action that lowers profits for all firms. On the other hand, advertising battles expand overall demand or enhance the level of product differentiation for the benefit of all firms in the industry. Rivalry, of course, differs across industries. In some instances it is characterized as warlike, bitter, or cutthroat, whereas in other industries it is referred to as polite and gentlemanly. Intense rivalry is the result of several interacting factors, including the following:

- ***Numerous or equally balanced competitors.*** When there are many firms in an industry, the likelihood of mavericks is great. Some firms believe they can make moves without being noticed. Even when there are relatively few firms, and they are nearly equal in size and resources, instability results from fighting among companies having the resources for sustained and vigorous retaliation.
- ***Slow industry growth.*** Slow industry growth turns competition into a fight for market share, since firms seek to expand their sales.
- ***High fixed or storage costs.*** High fixed costs create strong pressures for all firms to increase capacity. Excess capacity often leads to escalating price cutting.
- ***Lack of differentiation or switching costs.*** Where the product or service is perceived as a commodity or near commodity, the buyer's choice is typically based on price and service, resulting in pressures for intense price and service competition. Lack of switching costs, described earlier, has the same effect.
- ***Capacity augmented in large increments.*** Where economies of scale require that capacity must be added in large increments, capacity additions can be very disruptive to the industry supply/demand balance.
- ***High exit barriers.*** Exit barriers are economic, strategic, and emotional factors that keep firms competing even though they may be earning low or negative returns on their investments. Some exit barriers are specialized assets, fixed costs of exit, strategic interrelationships (e.g., relationships between the business units and others within a company in terms of image, marketing, shared facilities, and so on), emotional barriers, and government and social pressures (e.g., governmental discouragement of exit out of concern for job loss).

Rivalry between firms is often based on price. Companies facing intense competition may find themselves unable to raise prices to account for inflation or finance technology upgrades.

Strategy Spotlight 2.4 illustrates how U.S. grocery chains struggle to raise prices in the face of intense competition.

Exhibit 2.5 summarizes our discussion of industry five-forces analysis. It points out how various factors, such as economies of scale and capital requirements, affect each "force."

LO 2-6

Explain how the Internet and digitally based capabilities are affecting the five competitive forces and industry profitability.

How the Internet and Digital Technologies Are Affecting the Five Competitive Forces

The Internet is having a significant impact on nearly every industry. Internet-based and digital technologies have fundamentally changed the ways businesses interact with each other and with consumers. In most cases, these changes have affected industry forces in ways that have created many new strategic challenges. In this section, we will evaluate Michael Porter's five forces model in terms of the actual use of the Internet and the new technological capabilities that it makes possible.

2.4 STRATEGY SPOTLIGHT

INTENSE RIVALRY PREVENTS U.S. GROCERS FROM RAISING PRICES

Few industries in the U.S. are more competitive than the grocery industry. One reason for the cut-throat competition is the market entrance of European discounters such as Aldi and Lidl. These discounters keep costs low by focusing on a narrow product offering and private-label products, allowing them to undercut the prices of U.S. grocers such as Kroger or Albertsons. Another reason for the intense rivalry is the fragmented nature of the grocery industry. While in the UK the top four grocers account for more than 60 percent of grocery sales, in the United States this figure is only 42 percent.

While this competition is great for customers, grocers are struggling to grow and keep the doors open. Some regional supermarket chains such as Southeastern Grocers (the owner of Bi-Lo) have filed for bankruptcy. Even larger chains struggle with intense price competition. For one, consumers have become accustomed to low prices and are less loyal to brand names. At the same time, the return of inflation and the need to invest in new technologies to fend off Amazon's forays into the grocery industry require grocers to find new ways to raise their margins.

As a response, large supermarket chains such as Kroger try to shift competition to non-price aspects such as dining options and in-store pickup of online orders. In addition, supermarkets take a page out of the Aldi playbook and increase the share of private-label products in their product offering. The hope is that a combination of increased differentiation and lower costs will allow grocery chains to reduce the intense rivalry and raise profitability.

Sources: Giammona, C., and A. Back. 2018. Raising prices can be costly move for grocers. *Wall Street Journal,* April 26: 3D; and Wilmot, S., and A. Back. 2018. Grocers feel the squeeze. *Wall Street Journal,* June 13: B1–B2.

EXHIBIT 2.5 Competitive Analysis Checklist

Threat of New Entrants Is High When:	High	Low
Economies of scale are		X
Product differentiation is		X
Capital requirements are		X
Switching costs are		X
Incumbent's control of distribution channels is		X
Incumbent's proprietary knowledge is		X
Incumbent's access to raw materials is		X
Incumbent's access to government subsidies is		X

Power of Buyers Is High When:	High	Low
Concentration of buyers relative to suppliers is	X	
Switching costs are		X
Product differentiation of suppliers is		X
Threat of backward integration by buyers is	X	
Extent of buyer's profits is		X
Importance of the supplier's input to quality of buyer's final product is		X

Power of Suppliers Is High When:	High	Low
Concentration relative to buyer industry is	X	
Availability of substitute products is		X
Importance of customer to the supplier is		X
Differentiation of the supplier's products and services is	X	
Switching costs of the buyer are	X	
Threat of forward integration by the supplier is	X	

Threat of Substitute Products Is High When:	High	Low
Differentiation of the substitute product is	X	
Rate of improvement in price–performance relationship of substitute product is	X	

Intensity of Competitive Rivalry Is High When:	High	Low
Number of competitors is	X	
Industry growth rate is		X
Fixed costs are	X	
Storage costs are	X	
Product differentiation is		X
Switching costs are		X
Exit barriers are	X	
Strategic stakes are	X	

The Threat of New Entrants In most industries, the threat of new entrants has increased because digital and Internet-based technologies lower barriers to entry. For example, businesses that reach customers primarily through the Internet may enjoy savings on other traditional expenses such as office rent, sales-force salaries, printing, and postage. This may encourage more entrants who, because of the lower start-up expenses, see an opportunity to capture market share by offering a product or performing a service more efficiently than existing competitors. Thus, a new cyber entrant can use the savings provided by the Internet to charge lower prices and compete on price despite the incumbent's scale advantages.

Alternatively, because digital technologies often make it possible for young firms to provide services that are equivalent or superior to an incumbent, a new entrant may be able to serve a market more effectively, with more personalized services and greater attention to product details. A new firm may be able to build a reputation in its niche and charge premium prices. By so doing, it can capture part of an incumbent's business and erode profitability.

Another potential benefit of web-based business is access to distribution channels. Manufacturers or distributors that can reach potential outlets for their products more efficiently by means of the Internet may enter markets that were previously closed to them. Access is not guaranteed, however, because strong barriers to entry exist in certain industries.[72]

The Bargaining Power of Buyers The Internet and wireless technologies may increase buyer power by providing consumers with more information to make buying decisions and by lowering switching costs. But these technologies may also suppress the power of traditional buyer channels that have concentrated buying power in the hands of a few, giving buyers new ways to access sellers. To sort out these differences, let's first distinguish between two types of buyers: end users and buyer channel intermediaries.

End users are the final customers in a distribution channel. Internet sales activity that is labeled "B2C"–that is, business-to-consumer–is concerned with end users. The Internet is likely to increase the power of these buyers for several reasons. First, the Internet provides large amounts of consumer information. This gives end users the information they need to shop for quality merchandise and bargain for price concessions. Second, an end user's switching costs are potentially much lower because of the Internet. Switching may involve only a few clicks of the mouse to find and view a competing product or service online.

In contrast, the bargaining power of distribution channel buyers may decrease because of the Internet. *Buyer channel intermediaries* are the wholesalers, distributors, and retailers who serve as intermediaries between manufacturers and end users. In some industries, they are dominated by powerful players that control who gains access to the latest goods or the best merchandise. The Internet and wireless communications, however, make it much easier and less expensive for businesses to reach customers directly. Thus, the Internet may increase the power of incumbent firms relative to that of traditional buyer channels. Strategy Spotlight 2.5 illustrates some of the changes brought on by the Internet that have affected the legal services industry.

The Bargaining Power of Suppliers Use of the Internet and digital technologies to speed up and streamline the process of acquiring supplies is already benefiting many sectors of the economy. But the net effect of the Internet on supplier power will depend on the nature of competition in a given industry. As with buyer power, the extent to which the Internet is a benefit or a detriment also hinges on the supplier's position along the supply chain.

The role of suppliers involves providing products or services to other businesses. The term "B2B"–that is, business-to-business–often refers to businesses that supply or sell to other businesses. The effect of the Internet on the bargaining power of suppliers is a

2.5 STRATEGY SPOTLIGHT

BUYER POWER IN LEGAL SERVICES: THE ROLE OF THE INTERNET

The $276 billion U.S. legal services industry, which includes about 180,000 firms, historically was a classic example of an industry that leaves buyers at a bargaining disadvantage. One of the key reasons for the strong bargaining position of law firms is high information asymmetry between lawyers and consumers, meaning that highly trained and experienced legal professionals know more about legal matters than the average consumer of legal services.

The Internet provides an excellent example of how unequal bargaining power can be reduced by decreasing information asymmetry. A new class of Internet legal services providers tries to accomplish just that and is challenging traditional law services along the way. For instance, *LawPivot.com*, a recent start-up backed by Google Ventures and cofounded by a former top Apple Inc. lawyer, allows consumers to interact with lawyers on a social networking site. This service allows customers to get a better picture of a lawyer's legal skills before opening their wallets. As a result, information asymmetry between lawyers and consumers is reduced and customers find themselves in a better bargaining position. Another example is *LegalZoom.com*, a service that helps consumers to create legal documents. Customers familiar with *LegalZoom.com* may use their knowledge of the time and effort required to create legal documents to challenge a lawyer's fees for custom-crafted legal documents.

Sources: Anonymous. 2016. The size of the U.S. legal market: Shrinking piece of a bigger pie: An LEI Graphic. *www.legalexecutiveinstitute.com,* January 11: np; Jacobs, D. L. 2011. Google takes aim at lawyers. *Forbes,* August 8: np; Anonymous. 2011. Alternative law firms: Bargain briefs. *The Economist,* August 13: 64; and Anonymous. 2014. Legal services industry profile. *First Research,* August 25: np.

double-edged sword. On the one hand, suppliers may find it difficult to hold on to customers because buyers can do comparative shopping and price negotiations so much faster on the Internet.

On the other hand, several factors may also contribute to stronger supplier power. First, the growth of new web-based business may create more downstream outlets for suppliers to sell to. Second, suppliers may be able to create web-based purchasing arrangements that make purchasing easier and discourage their customers from switching. Online procurement systems directly link suppliers and customers, reducing transaction costs and paperwork.[73] Third, the use of proprietary software that links buyers to a supplier's website may create a rapid, low-cost ordering capability that discourages the buyer from seeking other sources of supply. *Amazon.com*, for example, created and patented One-Click purchasing technology that speeds up the ordering process for customers who enroll in the service.[74]

Finally, suppliers will have greater power to the extent that they can reach end users directly without intermediaries. Previously, suppliers often had to work through intermediaries who brought their products or services to market for a fee. But a process known as *disintermediation* is removing the organizations or business process layers responsible for intermediary steps in the value chain of many industries.[75] Just as the Internet is eliminating some business functions, it is creating an opening for new functions. These new activities are entering the value chain by a process known as *reintermediation*—the introduction of new types of intermediaries. Many of these new functions are affecting traditional supply chains. For example, delivery services are enjoying a boom because of the Internet. Many more consumers are choosing to have products delivered to their door rather than going out to pick them up.

The Threat of Substitutes Along with traditional marketplaces, the Internet has created a new marketplace and a new channel. In general, therefore, the threat of substitutes is heightened because the Internet introduces new ways to accomplish the same tasks.

Consumers will generally choose to use a product or service until a substitute that meets the same need becomes available at a lower cost. The economies created by Internet technologies have led to the development of numerous substitutes for traditional ways of doing business.

Another example of substitution is in the realm of electronic storage. With expanded desktop computing, the need to store information electronically has increased dramatically. Until recently, the trend has been to create increasingly larger desktop storage capabilities and techniques for compressing information that create storage efficiencies. But a viable substitute has emerged: storing information digitally on the Internet. Companies such as Dropbox and Amazon Web Services are providing web-based storage that firms can access simply by leasing space online. Since these storage places are virtual, they can be accessed anywhere the web can be accessed. Travelers can access important documents and files without transporting them physically from place to place.

The Intensity of Competitive Rivalry Because the Internet creates more tools and means for competing, rivalry among competitors is likely to be more intense. Only those competitors that can use digital technologies and the web to give themselves a distinct image, create unique product offerings, or provide "faster, smarter, cheaper" services are likely to capture greater profitability with the new technology.

Rivalry is more intense when switching costs are low and product or service differentiation is minimized. Because the Internet makes it possible to shop around, it has "commoditized" products that might previously have been regarded as rare or unique. Since the Internet reduces the importance of location, products that previously had to be sought out in geographically distant outlets are now readily available online. This makes competitors in cyberspace seem more equally balanced, thus intensifying rivalry.

The problem is made worse for marketers by the presence of shopping robots ("bots") and infomediaries that search the web for the best possible prices. Consumer websites like mySimon seek out all the web locations that sell similar products and provide price comparisons.[76] Obviously, this focuses the consumer exclusively on price. Some shopping infomediaries, such as CNET, not only search for the lowest prices on many different products but also rank the customer service quality of different sites that sell similarly priced items.[77] Such infomediary services are good for consumers because they give them the chance to compare services as well as price. For businesses, however, they increase rivalry by consolidating the marketing message that consumers use to make a purchase decision into a few key pieces of information over which the selling company has little control.

Using Industry Analysis: A Few Caveats

For industry analysis to be valuable, a company must collect and evaluate a wide variety of information. As the trend toward globalization accelerates, information on foreign markets as well as on a wider variety of competitors, suppliers, customers, substitutes, and potential new entrants becomes more critical. Industry analysis helps a firm not only to evaluate the profit potential of an industry but also to consider various ways to strengthen its position vis-à-vis the five forces. However, we'd like to address a few caveats.

First, *managers must not always avoid low-profit industries (or low-profit segments in profitable industries).*[78] Such industries can still yield high returns for some players who pursue sound strategies. As an example, consider WellPoint Health Network (now Anthem, Inc.), a huge health care insurer:[79]

> In 1986, WellPoint Health Network (then known as Blue Cross of California) suffered a loss of $160 million. That year, Leonard Schaeffer became CEO and challenged the conventional wisdom that individuals and small firms were money losers. (This was certainly "heresy" at the time–the firm was losing $5 million a year insuring 65,000 individuals!) However, by the early 1990s, the health insurer was leading the industry in profitability. The firm has continued to grow and outperform its rivals even during economic downturns. By 2017, its revenues and net income were over $90 billion and $3.8 billion, respectively.

Second, five-forces analysis implicitly *assumes a* **zero-sum game**, *determining how a firm can enhance its position relative to the forces.* Yet such an approach can often be shortsighted; that is, it can overlook the many potential benefits of developing constructive win-win relationships with suppliers and customers. Establishing long-term mutually beneficial relationships with suppliers improves a firm's ability to implement just-in-time (JIT) inventory systems, which let it manage inventories better and respond quickly to market demands. A recent study found that if a company exploits its powerful position against a supplier, that action may come back to haunt the company.[80] Consider, for example, General Motors' heavy-handed dealings with its suppliers:[81]

zero-sum game
a situation in which multiple players interact, and winners win only by taking from other players.

> In 2014, GM was already locked in a public relations nightmare as a deadly ignition defect triggered the recall of over 2.5 million vehicles.[82] At the same time, it was faced with another perception problem: poor supplier relations. GM is now considered the worst big automaker to deal with, according to a new survey of top suppliers in the car industry in the United States.
>
> The annual survey, conducted by the automotive consultant group Planning Perspectives Inc., asks the industry's biggest suppliers to rate the relationships with the six automakers that account for more than 85 percent of all cars and light trucks in the U.S. Those so-called "Tier 1" suppliers say GM is their least favorite big customer–less popular than even Chrysler, the unit of Fiat Chrysler Automobiles that had "earned" the dubious distinction since 2008.
>
> The suppliers gave GM low marks on all kinds of measures, including its overall trustworthiness, its communication skills, and its protection of intellectual property. The suppliers also said that GM was the automaker least likely to allow them to raise prices to recoup unexpected materials cost increases. In return, parts executives have said they tend to bring hot new technology to other carmakers first–certainly something that makes it more difficult for GM to compete in this hotly contested industry.

Third, the five-forces analysis also has been criticized for *being essentially a static analysis.* External forces as well as strategies of individual firms are continually changing the structure of all industries. The search for a dynamic theory of strategy has led to greater use of game theory in industrial organization economics research and strategy research.

Based on game-theoretic considerations, Brandenburger and Nalebuff recently introduced the concept of the value net,[83] which in many ways is an extension of the five-forces analysis. It is illustrated in Exhibit 2.6. The value net represents all the players in the game and analyzes how their interactions affect a firm's ability to generate and appropriate value. The vertical dimension of the net includes suppliers and customers. The firm has direct transactions with them. On the horizontal dimension are substitutes and complements, players with whom a firm interacts but may not necessarily transact. The concept of complementors is perhaps the single most important contribution of value net analysis and is explained in more detail below.

Complements typically are products or services that have a potential impact on the value of a firm's own products or services. Those who produce complements are usually referred to as complementors.[84] Powerful hardware is of no value to a user unless there is software that runs on it. Similarly, new and better software is possible only if the hardware on which it can be run is available. This is equally true in the video game industry, where the sales of game consoles and video games complement each other. Nintendo's success in the early 1990s was a result of its ability to manage its relationship with its complementors. Nintendo built a security chip into the hardware and then licensed the right to develop games to outside firms. These firms paid a royalty to Nintendo for each copy of the game sold. The royalty revenue enabled Nintendo to sell game consoles at close to their cost, thereby increasing their market share, which, in turn, caused more games to be sold and more royalties to be generated.[85]

complements
products or services that have an impact on the value of a firm's products or services.

We would like to close this section with some recent insights from Michael Porter, the originator of the five-forces analysis.[86] He addresses two critical issues in conducting a good industry analysis, which will yield an improved understanding of the root causes of

EXHIBIT 2.6 The Value Net

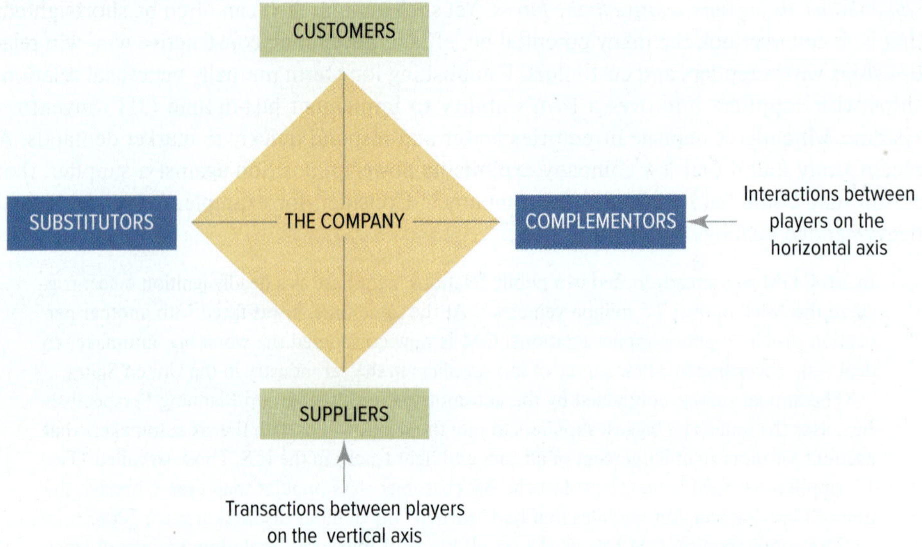

Source: Adapted from Brandenburger, A., and B. J. Nalebuff. 1995. The right game: Use game theory shape strategy. *Harvard Business Review,* July-August.

profitability: (1) choosing the appropriate time frame and (2) a rigorous quantification of the five forces.

- ***Good industry analysis looks rigorously at the structural underpinnings of profitability. A first step is to understand the time horizon.*** One of the essential tasks in industry analysis is to distinguish short-term fluctuations from structural changes. A good guideline for the appropriate time horizon is the full business cycle for the particular industry. For most industries, a three- to five-year horizon is appropriate. However, for some industries with long lead times, such as mining, the appropriate horizon may be a decade or more. It is average profitability over this period, not profitability in any particular year, which should be the focus of analysis.
- ***The point of industry analysis is not to declare the industry attractive or unattractive but to understand the underpinnings of competition and the root causes of profitability.*** As much as possible, analysts should look at industry structure quantitatively, rather than be satisfied with lists of qualitative factors. Many elements of five forces can be quantified: the percentage of the buyer's total cost accounted for by the industry's product (to understand buyer price sensitivity); the percentage of industry sales required to fill a plant or operate a logistical network to efficient scale (to help assess barriers to entry); and the buyer's switching cost (determining the inducement an entrant or rival must offer customers).

LO 2-7

Understand the concept of strategic groups and their strategy and performance implications.

strategic groups clusters of firms that share similar strategies.

Strategic Groups within Industries

In an industry analysis, two assumptions are unassailable: (1) No two firms are totally different, and (2) no two firms are exactly the same. The issue becomes one of identifying groups of firms that are more similar to each other than firms that are not, otherwise known as **strategic groups.**[87] This is important because rivalry tends to be greater among firms that are alike. Strategic groups are clusters of firms that share similar strategies. After all, is Target more concerned about Nordstrom or Walmart? Is Mercedes more concerned about Hyundai or BMW? The answers are straightforward.[88]

These examples are not meant to trivialize the strategic groups concept.[89] Classifying an industry into strategic groups involves judgment. If it is useful as an analytical tool, we must exercise caution in deciding what dimensions to use to map these firms. Dimensions include breadth of product and geographic scope, price/quality, degree of vertical integration, type of distribution (e.g., dealers, mass merchandisers, private label), and so on. Dimensions should also be selected to reflect the variety of strategic combinations in an industry. For example, if all firms in an industry have roughly the same level of product differentiation (or R&D intensity), this would not be a good dimension to select.

What value is the strategic groups concept as an analytical tool? *First, strategic groupings help a firm identify barriers to mobility that protect a group from attacks by other groups.*[90] Mobility barriers are factors that deter the movement of firms from one strategic position to another. For example, in the chainsaw industry, the major barriers protecting the high-quality/dealer-oriented group are technology, brand image, and an established network of servicing dealers.

The second value of strategic grouping is that it *helps a firm identify groups whose competitive position may be marginal or tenuous.* We may anticipate that these competitors may exit the industry or try to move into another group. In recent years in the retail department store industry, firms such as JCPenney and Sears have experienced extremely difficult times because they were stuck in the middle, neither an aggressive discount player like Walmart nor a prestigious upscale player like Neiman Marcus.

Third, strategic groupings *help chart the future directions of firms' strategies.* Arrows emanating from each strategic group can represent the direction in which the group (or a firm within the group) seems to be moving. If all strategic groups are moving in a similar direction, this could indicate a high degree of future volatility and intensity of competition. In the automobile industry, for example, the competition in the minivan and sport utility segments has intensified in recent years as many firms have entered those product segments.

Fourth, strategic groups are *helpful in thinking through the implications of each industry trend for the strategic group as a whole.* Is the trend decreasing the viability of a group? If so, in what direction should the strategic group move? Is the trend increasing or decreasing entry barriers? Will the trend decrease the ability of one group to separate itself from other groups? Such analysis can help in making predictions about industry evolution. A sharp increase in interest rates, for example, tends to have less impact on providers of higher-priced goods (e.g., Porsches) than on providers of lower-priced goods (e.g., Chevrolet Cobalt), whose customer base is much more price-sensitive.

Exhibit 2.7 provides a strategic grouping of the worldwide automobile industry.[91] The firms in each group are representative; not all firms are included in the mapping. We have identified five strategic groups. In the top left-hand corner are high-end luxury automakers that focus on a very narrow product market. Most of the cars produced by the members of this group cost well over $100,000. Some cost over twice that amount. The 2017 Ferrari California T starts at $210,843, and the 2017 Lamborghini Huracan will set you back $210,000 (in case you were wondering how to spend your employment signing bonus). Players in this market have a very exclusive clientele and face little rivalry from other strategic groups. Close to the bottom left-hand corner is a strategic group that has low-price/quality attributes and targets a narrow market. These players, Hyundai and Kia, limit competition from other strategic groups by pricing their products very low. The third group (near the middle) consists of firms such as Mercedes and BMW that are high in product pricing/quality and average in their product-line breadth. The fourth group (at the far right) consists of firms with a broad range of products and multiple price points. These firms have entries that compete at both the lower end of the market (e.g., the Ford Focus) and the higher end (e.g., Chevrolet Corvette).

EXHIBIT 2.7 The World Automobile Industry: Strategic Groups

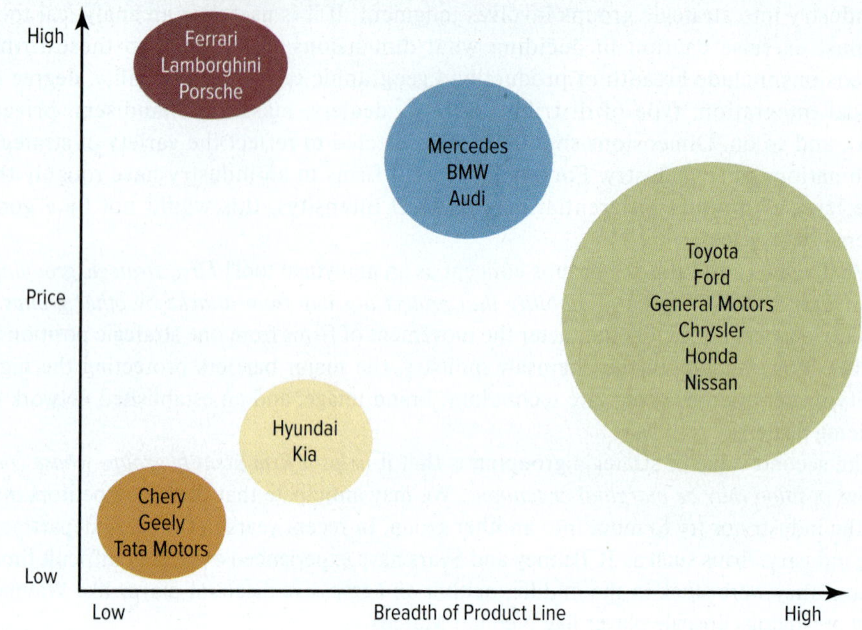

Note: Members of each strategic group are not exhaustive, only illustrative.

The auto market has been very dynamic and competition has intensified in recent years.[92] For example, some players are going more upscale with their product offerings. In 2009, Hyundai introduced its Genesis, starting at $33,000. This brings Hyundai into direct competition with entries from other strategic groups such as Toyota's Camry and Honda's Accord. And, in 2010, Hyundai introduced the Equus model. It was priced at about $60,000 to compete directly with the Lexus 460 on price. To further intensify competition, some upscale brands are increasingly entering lower-priced segments. In 2014, Audi introduced the Q3 SUV at a base price of only $32,500. And BMW, with its 1-series, is another well-known example. Such cars, priced in the low $30,000s, compete more directly with products from broad-line manufacturers like Ford, General Motors, and Toyota. This suggests that members of a strategic group can overcome mobility barriers and migrate to other groups that they find attractive if they are willing to commit time and resources.

Our discussion would not be complete, of course, without paying some attention to recent entries in the automobile industry that will likely lead to the formation of a new strategic group—placed at the bottom left corner of the grid in Exhibit 2.7. Three firms—China's Zhejiang Geely Holding Company, China's Chery Automobile Company, and India's Tata Motors—have introduced models that bring new meaning to the term "subcompact."[93] For example,

> Chery's 2013 QQ model sells for between $6,083 and $8,170 in the Chinese market and sports horsepower in the range of only 51 to 74. Geely's best-selling four-door sedan, the Free Cruiser, retails from $5,440 to $7,046. The firm has gone more upscale with some offerings, such as the GX7, a sports utility vehicle with a price starting at $14,910. For low price-points, India's Tata Motors has everyone beat by the proverbial mile. In January 2008, it introduced the Nano as the "World's Cheapest Car," with an astonishing retail price of only $2,500. It is a four-door, five-seat hatchback that gets 54 miles to the gallon (but this economy originally came with a 30 horsepower motor).

ISSUE FOR DEBATE

Can The Commercial Use Of Drones Be Stopped?

Since the first hobbyist drone was introduced at the Consumer Electronics Show in Las Vegas in 2010, drones have become a common sight in the skies across the United States. The FAA estimates that the number of consumer drones will increase from 1.1 million in 2016 to more than 3.5 million in 2021. The growth in commercial drones may be even higher following the permission to use drones commercially in 2016. According to the FAA, only 42,000 commercial drones were in use in 2016, but this figure could skyrocket to 1.6 million by 2021.

One area of commercial drone use is in the home and building inspection sector. Building inspectors traditionally rely on binoculars, ladders, and scaffolding to check the exteriors of buildings for damage and signs of deterioration. This old-school inspection process is lengthy, dangerous, and ultimately costly. New York City alone has thousands of old skyscrapers and requires all buildings over five stories to be inspected regularly. Commercial drones may play an important role in improving and modernizing this inspection process.

Using drones for buildings inspections offers many benefits. Most importantly for cash-strapped city governments, drones substantially lower the costs of building inspections. Cities that allow drone inspections have found that inspection costs are 10 times lower. But drones are not only able to reduce costs, they can also create more value. For instance, drones may shorten week-long projects that normally would require road closures and erection of scaffolding to a single day, reducing traffic congestion, and other disturbances. New drone generations also come equipped with more sophisticated software allowing drones to build 3D models of buildings and issue inspection reports. These software models track energy losses and water intrusion in the exterior of buildings, which reduce the operating costs of new construction and make buildings more environmentally sustainable.

Another often overlooked benefit of using drones is improved safety for construction workers and building inspectors. Before the days of drones, construction workers seeking access to skyscraper exteriors used small swing stages often used by window cleaners. High winds can topple these swing stages and cause deadly falls, which account for almost 40 percent of the 991 deaths in the construction industry in 2016. The use of drones for inspections and quality control may reduce this number.

While drones have many benefits, state and local regulators often restrict their use. New York City for example largely prohibits them, even for commercial uses. Regulators in densely populated areas often cite security concerns because drones could be used to carry explosive devices or facilitate other unwanted activities such as planning or assisting burglaries. Additionally, drones may invade the privacy of city dwellers when they—typically equipped with cameras—spy into apartment or office windows. Additionally, federal regulators restrict drone use in airspace shared with airplanes. For instance, the airspace in close proximity to airports, at high altitudes, or around wildfire firefighting operations is off limits because drone collisions may be worse than bird hits for traditional airplanes. In the short time since drone use became commonplace, several drones have collided with aircrafts and many "near-misses" have been reported. Given the rapid growth of the drone market, regulators will face many more challenges in ensuring safe operations while allowing drones to revolutionize many commercial applications.

continued

continued

Discussion Questions

1. If you were a local regulator, would you permit the use of drones?
2. How should regulators respond to drone accidents?
3. Do you think drone use could be successful in other commercial applications such as package delivery?

Sources: Nonko, E. 2018. Drones hit a wall on inspections. *Wall Street Journal*, February 21: B6; Shepardson, D. 2017. U.S. commercial drone use to expand tenfold by 2021. *www.reuters.com*, March 22: np; Madigan, N. 2018. Need a quick inspection of a 58-story tower? Send a drone. *New York Times*, August 14: np; Cellan-Jones, R. 2017. Drone collisions 'worse than bird hits'. *bbc.com*, December 5: np.

Reflecting on Career Implications . . .

This chapter addresses the importance of the external environment for strategic managers. As a strategic manager, you should strive in your career to benefit from enhancing your awareness of your external environment. The issues below focus on these ideas.

- **Creating the Environmentally Aware Organization:** Advancing your career requires constant scanning, monitoring, and intelligence gathering not only to find future job opportunities but also to understand how employers' expectations are changing. Consider using websites such as LinkedIn to find opportunities. Merely posting your résumé on a site such as LinkedIn may not be enough. Instead, consider in what ways you can use such sites for scanning, monitoring, and intelligence gathering.
- **SWOT Analysis:** As an analytical method, SWOT analysis is applicable for individuals as it is for firms. It is important for you to periodically evaluate your strengths and weaknesses as well as potential opportunities and threats to your career. Such analysis should be followed by efforts to address your weaknesses by improving your skills and capabilities.
- **General Environment:** The general environment consists of several segments, such as the demographic, sociocultural, political/legal, technological, economic, and global environments. It would be useful to evaluate how each of these segments can affect your career opportunities. Identify two or three specific trends (e.g., rapid technological change, aging of the population, increase in minimum wages) and their impact on your choice of careers. These also provide possibilities for you to add value for your organization.
- **Five-Forces Analysis:** Before you go for a job interview, consider the five forces affecting the industry within which the firm competes. This will help you to appear knowledgeable about the industry and increase your odds of landing the job. It also can help you to decide if you want to work for that organization. If the "forces" are unfavorable, the long-term profit potential of the industry may be unattractive, leading to fewer resources available and—all other things being equal—fewer career opportunities.

key points

LO2-1 Understand the importance of developing forecasts of the business environment.

- Managers must analyze the external environment to minimize threats and exploit opportunities. Effective managers proactively anticipate and detect early warning signs, which may represent key threats or opportunities to their business model.

LO2-2 Explain why environmental scanning, environmental monitoring, and collecting competitive intelligence are critical inputs to forecasting.

- Enhancing awareness of the external environment depends on three important processes: environment scanning, environment monitoring, and gathering competitive intelligence.
- These processes are used to develop environmental forecasts. Environmental forecasting involves the development of plausible projections about environmental changes.

LO2-3 Explain why scenario planning is a useful technique for firms competing in industries characterized by unpredictability and change.

- Scenario analysis is a structured approach to environmental forecasting. It involves experts from various disciplines working together to create projections of future events.

LO2-4 Recognize the impact of the general environment on a firm's strategies and performance.

- The general environment is composed of factors external to an industry—and usually beyond a firm's control—that affect a firm's strategy. It can be divided into six segments: demographic, sociocultural, political/legal, technological, economic, and global.
- The demographic segment consists of observable characteristics of a population, such as age and race composition.
- The sociocultural segment describes the values, beliefs, and lifestyles of a society.
- The political/legal segment describes how a society creates and exercises power, including rules, laws, and taxation policies.
- The technological segment describes innovation and the state of knowledge in areas such as engineering, applied sciences, and pure science; and their interaction with society.
- The economic segment includes the characteristics of the economy, including national income and monetary conditions.
- The global segment includes influences from foreign countries, including foreign market opportunities, foreign-based competition, and expanded capital markets.

LO2-5 Explain how forces in the competitive environment can affect profitability, and how a firm can improve its competitive position by increasing its power vis-à-vis these forces.

- Managers must consider the competitive environment (also referred to as the industry environment). The nature of competition in an industry, as well as the profitability of a firm, is often directly influenced by developments in the competitive environment.
- The "five forces" model is used for examining the competitive environment. It describes the competitive environment in terms of five forces: (1) The threat of new entrants, (2) The bargaining power of buyers, (3) The bargaining power of suppliers, (4) The threat of substitute products/services, (5) The intensity of rivalry in an industry.
- The threat of new entrants captures the possibility that the profits of established firms in the industry may be eroded by new competitors.
- The bargaining power of buyers describes the threat that buyers may force down prices, bargain for higher quality or more services, and play competitors against each other.
- The bargaining power of suppliers captures the threat that suppliers may raise prices or reduce the quality of goods and services.
- The threat of substitute products/services describes the threat of limiting the potential returns of an industry by placing a ceiling on the prices that firms in that industry can profitably charge without losing too many customers to substitute products.
- The intensity of rivalry in an industry captures the threat that customers will switch their business to competitors within the industry.

LO2-6 Explain how the Internet and digitally based capabilities are affecting the five competitive forces and industry profitability.

- The Internet has a significant impact on nearly every industry. In most cases, these changes have affected industry forces in ways that have created new strategic challenges. The five forces model can help to identify these strategic challenges.

LO2-7 Understand the concept of strategic groups and their strategy and performance implications.

- Two assumptions are unassailable: (1) No two firms are totally different, and (2) no two firms are exactly the same. Strategic groups help identify groups of firms that are similar to each other, resulting in groups of firms that share similar strategies. Strategic groups are important because rivalry tends to be greater among firms that are alike.

SUMMARY REVIEW QUESTIONS

1. Why must managers be aware of a firm's external environment?
2. What is gathering and analyzing competitive intelligence, and why is it important for firms to engage in it?
3. Discuss and describe the six elements of the external environment.
4. Select one of these elements and describe some changes relating to it in an industry that interests you.
5. Describe how the five forces can be used to determine the average expected profitability in an industry.
6. What are some of the limitations (or caveats) in using five-forces analysis?
7. Explain how the general environment and industry environment are highly related. How can such interrelationships affect the profitability of a firm or industry?
8. Explain the concept of strategic groups. What are the performance implications?

key terms

perceptual acuity 38
environmental scanning 39
environmental monitoring 39
competitive intelligence 40
environmental forecasting 41
scenario analysis 42
SWOT analysis 42
general environment 43
demographic segment of the general environment 45
sociocultural segment of the general environment 45
political/legal segment of the general environment 45
technological segment of the general environment 47
economic segment of the general environment 48
global segment of the general environment 48
Digital Economy 50
data analytics 51
industry 52
competitive environment 52
Porter's five forces model of industry competition 52
threat of new entrants 53
economies of scale 53
product differentiation 53
switching costs 53
bargaining power of buyers 54
bargaining power of suppliers 55
threat of substitute products and services 55
substitute products and services 55
intensity of rivalry among competitors in an industry 56
zero-sum game 61
complements 61
strategic groups 62

EXPERIENTIAL EXERCISES AND APPLICATION QUESTIONS

1. Strategy Spotlight 2.2 discusses the growing importance of environmental concerns and illustrates how companies in different industries deal with plastic waste issues. Many other environmental problems such as greenhouse gas emissions and the resulting climate change issues are major concerns for today's businesses and governments. Pick an industry with high greenhouse gas emissions such as electric utilities, air transportation, or livestock agriculture and identify the threats and opportunities facing the industries. Do you think companies with substantial greenhouse gas emissions should proactively address their environmental impact?
2. Select one of the following industries: personal computers, airlines, or automobiles. For this industry, evaluate the strength of each of Porter's five forces as well as complementors.

Industry Force	High? Medium? Low?	Why?
1. Threat of new entrants		
2. Power of buyers		
3. Power of suppliers		
4. Power of substitutes		
5. Rivalry among competitors		
6. Complementors		

3. Imagine yourself as the CEO of a large firm in an industry in which you are interested. Please (1) identify major trends in the general environment, (2) analyze their impact on the firm, and (3) identify major sources of information to monitor these trends. (Use Internet and library resources.)
4. Analyze movements across the strategic groups in the U.S. retail industry. How do these movements within this industry change the nature of competition?
5. What are the major trends in the general environment that have impacted the U.S. pharmaceutical industry?
6. Go to *www.kroger.com*. What are some of the five forces driving industry competition that are affecting the profitability of this firm?

ETHICS QUESTIONS

1. What are some of the legal and ethical issues involved in collecting competitor intelligence in the following situations?
   a. Hotel A sends an employee posing as a potential client to Hotel B to find out who Hotel B's major corporate customers are.
   b. A firm hires an MBA student to collect information directly from a competitor while claiming the information is for a course project.
   c. A firm advertises a nonexistent position and interviews a rival's employees with the intention of obtaining competitor information.
2. What are some of the ethical implications that arise when a firm tries to exploit its power over a supplier?

REFERENCES

1. Weber, G. W. 1995. A new paint job at PPG. *BusinessWeek.* November 13: 74-75.
2. Hamel, G. & Prahalad, C. K. 1994. *Competing for the future.* Boston: Harvard Business School Press.
3. Drucker, P. F. 1994. Theory of the business. *Harvard Business Review,* 72: 95-104.
4. For an insightful discussion on managers' assessment of the external environment, refer to Sutcliffe, K. M. & Weber, K. 2003. The high cost of accurate knowledge. *Harvard Business Review,* 81(5): 74-86.
5. Merino, M. 2013. You can't be a wimp: Making the tough calls. *Harvard Business Review,* 91(11): 73-78.

6. For insights on recognizing and acting on environmental opportunities, refer to Alvarez, S. A. & Barney, J. B. 2008. Opportunities, organizations, and entrepreneurship: Theory and debate. *Strategic Entrepreneurship Journal,* 2(3): entire issue.
7. Charitou, C. D. & Markides, C. C. 2003. Responses to disruptive strategic innovation. *MIT Sloan Management Review,* 44(2): 55–64.
8. Our discussion of scanning, monitoring, competitive intelligence, and forecasting concepts draws on several sources. These include Fahey, L. & Narayanan, V. K. 1983. *Macroenvironmental analysis for strategic management.* St. Paul, MN: West; Lorange, P., Scott, F. S., & Ghoshal, S. 1986. *Strategic control.* St. Paul, MN: West; Ansoff, H. I. 1984. *Implementing strategic management.* Englewood Cliffs, NJ: Prentice Hall; and Schreyogg, G. & Stienmann, H. 1987. Strategic control: A new perspective. *Academy of Management Review,* 12: 91–103.
9. An insightful discussion on how leaders can develop "peripheral vision" in environmental scanning is found in Day, G. S. & Schoemaker, P. J. H. 2008. Are you a "vigilant leader"? *MIT Sloan Management Review,* 49(3): 43–51.
10. Elenkov, D. S. 1997. Strategic uncertainty and environmental scanning: The case for institutional influences on scanning behavior. *Strategic Management Journal,* 18: 287–302.
11. For an interesting perspective on environmental scanning in emerging economies, see May, R. C., Stewart, W. H., & Sweo, R. 2000. Environmental scanning behavior in a transitional economy, Evidence from Russia. *Academy of Management Journal,* 43(3): 403–427.
12. Bryon, E. 2010. For insight into P&G, check Olay numbers. *Wall Street Journal,* October 27: C1.
13. Tang, J. 2010. How entrepreneurs discover opportunities in China: An institutional view. *Asia Pacific Journal of Management,* 27(3): 461–480.
14. Walters, B. A. & Priem, R. L. 1999. Business strategy and CEO intelligence acquisition. *Competitive Intelligence Review,* 10(2): 15–22.
15. Prior, V. 1999. The language of competitive intelligence, Part 4. *Competitive Intelligence Review,* 10(1): 84–87.
16. Hill, K. 2011. The spy who liked me. *Forbes,* November 21: 56–57.
17. Wolfenson, J. 1999. The world in 1999: A battle for corporate honesty. *The Economist,* 38: 13–30.
18. Drucker, P. F. 1997. The future that has already happened. *Harvard Business Review,* 75(6): 22.
19. Downes, L. & Nunes, P. 2014. *Big bang disruption.* New York: Penguin.
20. Fahey & Narayanan, op. cit., p. 41.
21. Insights on how to improve predictions can be found in Cross, R., Thomas, R. J., & Light, D. A. 2009. The prediction lover's handbook. *MIT Sloan Management Review,* 50(2): 32–34.
22. Courtney, H., Kirkland, J., & Viguerie, p. 1997. Strategy under uncertainty. *Harvard Business Review,* 75(6): 66–79.
23. Odlyzko, A. 2003. False hopes. *Red Herring,* March: 31.
24. Szczerba, R. J. 2015. 15 Worst tech predictions of all time. *www.forbes.com.* January 5: np; and, Dunn, M. 2016. Here are 20 of the worst predictions ever made about the future of tech. *www.news.com.au.* March 8: np.
25. Zweig, J. 2014. Lessons Learned from the year of shock. *The Wall Street Journal,* December 30: C1–C2.
26. For an interesting perspective on how Accenture practices and has developed its approach to scenario planning, refer to Ferguson, G., Mathur, S., & Shah, B. 2005. Evolving from information to insight. *MIT Sloan Management Review,* 46(2): 51–58.
27. The PPG example draws on: Camillus, J. C. 2008. Strategy as a wicked problem. *Harvard Business Review,* 86(5): 98-106; *www.ppg.com;* and, *finance.yahoo.com.*
28. Byrne, J. A. 2012. The 12 greatest entrepreneurs of our time. *Fortune,* April 9.
29. Dean, T. J., Brown, R. L., & Bamford, C. E. 1998. Differences in large and small firm responses to environmental context: Strategic implications from a comparative analysis of business formations. *Strategic Management Journal,* 19: 709–728.
30. Colvin, G. 2014. Q&A: McKinsey's Dom Barton on the four things that worry business. *Fortune*, October 9.
31. Colvin, G. 1997. How to beat the boomer rush. *Fortune,* August 18: 59–63.
32. Porter, M. E. 2010. Discovering–and lowering–the real costs of health care. *Harvard Business Review,* 89(1/2): 49–50.
33. Farrell, C. 2014. Baby boomers' latest revolution: Unretirement. *Dallas Morning News,* October 19: 4P.
34. Farrell, C. 2014. Chris Farrell: Baby boomers' latest revolution is unretirement. *The Dallas Morning News*, October 19.
35. Challenger, J. 2000. Women's corporate rise has reduced relocations. *Lexington* (KY) *Herald-Leader,* October 29: D1.
36. Anonymous. 2018. The 2018 state of women-owned businesses report. *American Express.*
37. Watkins, M. D. 2003. Government games. *MIT Sloan Management Review,* 44(2): 91–95.
38. A discussion of the political issues surrounding caloric content on meals is in Orey, M. 2008. A food fight over calorie counts. *BusinessWeek,* February 11: 36.
39. For a discussion of the linkage between copyright law and innovation, read Guterman, J. 2009. Does copyright law hinder innovation? *MIT Sloan Management Review,* 50(2): 14–15.
40. Davies, A. 2000. The welcome mat is out for nerds. *BusinessWeek,* May 21: 17; Broache, A. 2007. Annual H-1B visa cap met–already. *news.cnet.com,* April 3: np; and Anonymous. Undated. Cap count for H-1B and H-2B workers for fiscal year 2009. *www.uscis.gov* : np.
41. Weise, K. 2014. How to hack the visa limit. *Bloomberg Businessweek,* May 26–June 1: 39–40.
42. Hout, T. M. & Ghemawat, p. 2010. China vs. the world: Whose technology is it? *Harvard Business Review,* 88(12): 94–103.
43. Business ready for Internet revolution. 1999. *Financial Times,* May 21: 17.
44. A discussion of an alternate energy–marine energy–is the topic of Boyle, M. 2008. Scottish power. *Fortune,* March 17: 28.
45. Baker, S. & Aston, A. 2005. The business of nanotech. *BusinessWeek,* February 14: 64–71.
46. Wilson, H. J. 2013. Wearables in the workplace. *Harvard Business Review,* 91(9): 22–25.
47. Chen, A. 2018. Why an Apple Watch with EKG matters. *The Verge,* September 12: np.
48. For an insightful discussion of the causes of the global financial crisis, read Johnson, S. 2009. The global financial crisis–What really precipitated it? *MIT Sloan Management Review,* 50(2): 16–18.

49. Tyson, L. D. 2011. A better stimulus for the U.S. economy. *Harvard Business Review,* 89(1/2): 53.
50. An interesting and balanced discussion on the merits of multinationals to the U.S. economy is found in Mandel, M. 2008. Multinationals: Are they good for America? *BusinessWeek,* March 10: 41-64.
51. Insights on risk perception across countries are addressed in Purda, L. D. 2008. Risk perception and the financial system. *Journal of International Business Studies,* 39(7): 1178-1196.
52. Goll, I. & Rasheed, M. A. 1997. Rational decision-making and firm performance: The moderating role of environment. *Strategic Management Journal,* 18: 583-591.
53. Deloitte. 2018. What is digital economy? Unicorns, transformation and the Internet of things.
54. Gada, K. 2016. The digital economy in 5 minutes. *forbes.com,* June 16: np.
55. Anderson, L, & Wladawsky-Berger, I. 2016. The 4 things it takes to succeed in the digital economy. *hbr.org,* March 24: np.
56. Kapner, S. 2019. How Sears lost the American shopper. *The Wall Street Journal,* March 16.
57. This discussion draws heavily on Porter, M. E. 1980. *Competitive strategy:* chap. 1. New York: Free Press.
58. Ibid.
59. Rivalry in the airline industry is discussed in Foust, D. 2009. Which airlines will disappear in 2009? *BusinessWeek,* January 19: 46-47.
60. Fryer, B. 2001. Leading through rough times: An interview with Novell's Eric Schmidt. *Harvard Business Review,* 78(5): 117-123.
61. Anonymous. 2015. No reservations. *The Economist.* November 21: 63. Johnson, M. 2018. Strong growth in room supply puts a dent in hotel sector. *bizjournals.com.* December 17: np.
62. For a discussion on the importance of barriers to entry within industries, read Greenwald, B. & Kahn, J. 2005. *Competition demystified: A radically simplified approach to business strategy.* East Rutherford, NJ: Portfolio.
63. A discussion of how the medical industry has erected entry barriers that have resulted in lawsuits is found in Whelan, D. 2008. Bad medicine. *BusinessWeek,* March 10: 86-98.
64. Colvin, G. 2014. Welcome to the era of Lego innovations (some assembly required). *Fortune,* April 14: 52.
65. Wise, R. & Baumgarter, p. 1999. Go downstream: The new profit imperative in manufacturing. *Harvard Business Review,* 77(5): 133-141.
66. Salman, W. A. 2000. The new economy is stronger than you think. *Harvard Business Review,* 77(6): 99-106.
67. Mudambi, R. & Helper, S. 1998. The "close but adversarial" model of supplier relations in the U.S. auto industry. *Strategic Management Journal,* 19: 775-792.
68. Stevens, D. (vice president of Delta Pride Catfish, Inc.). 2014. *personal communication:* October 16; and Fritz, M. 1988. Agribusiness: Catfish story. *Forbes,* December 12: 37.
69. Trends in the solar industry are discussed in Carey, J. 2009. Solar: The sun will come out tomorrow. *BusinessWeek,* January 12: 51.
70. An interesting analysis of self-regulation in an industry (chemical) is in Barnett, M. L. & King, A. A. 2008. Good fences make good neighbors: A longitudinal analysis of an industry self-regulatory institution. *Academy of Management Journal,* 51(6): 1053-1078.
71. For an interesting perspective on the intensity of competition in the supermarket industry, refer to Anonymous. 2005. Warfare in the aisles. *The Economist,* April 2: 6-8.
72. For an interesting perspective on changing features of firm boundaries, refer to Afuah, A. 2003. Redefining firm boundaries in the face of the Internet: Are firms really shrinking? *Academy of Management Review,* 28(1): 34-53.
73. Time to rebuild. 2001. *The Economist,* May 19: 55-56.
74. *www.amazon.com.*
75. For more on the role of the Internet as an electronic intermediary, refer to Carr, N. G. 2000. Hypermediation: Commerce as clickstream. *Harvard Business Review,* 78(1): 46-48.
76. *www.mysimon.com;* and *www.pricescan.com.*
77. *www.cnet.com;* and *www.bizrate.com.*
78. For insights into strategies in a low-profit industry, refer to Hopkins, M. S. 2008. The management lessons of a beleaguered industry. *MIT Sloan Management Review,* 50(1): 25-31.
79. Foust, D. 2007. The best performers. *BusinessWeek,* March 26: 58-95; Rosenblum, D., Tomlinson, D., & Scott, L. 2003. Bottom-feeding for blockbuster businesses. *Harvard Business Review,* 81(3): 52-59; Paychex 2006 Annual Report; and WellPoint Health Network 2005 Annual Report.
80. Kumar, N. 1996. The power of trust in manufacturer-retailer relationship. *Harvard Business Review,* 74(6): 92-110.
81. Welch, D. 2006. Renault-Nissan: Say hello to Bo. *BusinessWeek,* July 31: 56-57.
82. Kelleher, J. B. 2014. GM ranked worst automaker by U.S. suppliers—survey. *finance.yahoo.com,* May 12: np; and Welch, D. 2006. Renault-Nissan: Say hello to Bo. *BusinessWeek,* July 31: 56-57.
83. Brandenburger, A. & Nalebuff, B. J. 1995. The right game: Use game theory to shape strategy. *Harvard Business Review,* 73(4): 57-71.
84. For a scholarly discussion of complementary assets and their relationship to competitive advantage, refer to Stieglitz, N. & Heine, K. 2007. Innovations and the role of complementarities in a strategic theory of the firm. *Strategic Management Journal,* 28(1): 1-15.
85. A useful framework for the analysis of industry evolution has been proposed by Professor Anita McGahan of Boston University. Her analysis is based on the identification of the core activities and the core assets of an industry and the threats they face. She suggests that an industry may follow one of four possible evolutionary trajectories—radical change, creative change, intermediating change, or progressive change—based on these two types of threats of obsolescence. Refer to McGahan, A. M. 2004. How industries change. *Harvard Business Review,* 82(10): 87-94.
86. Porter, M. I. 2008. The five competitive forces that shape strategy. *Harvard Business Review,* 86(1): 79-93.
87. Peteraf, M. & Shanley, M. 1997. Getting to know you: A theory of strategic group identity. *Strategic Management Journal,* 18 (Special Issue): 165-186.
88. An interesting scholarly perspective on strategic groups may be found in Dranove, D., Perteraf, M., & Shanley, M. 1998. Do strategic groups exist? An economic framework for analysis. *Strategic Management Journal,* 19(11): 1029-1044.
89. For an empirical study on strategic groups and predictors of performance, refer to Short, J. C.,

Ketchen, D. J., Jr., Palmer, T. B., & Hult, T. M. 2007. Firm, strategic group, and industry influences on performance. *Strategic Management Journal,* 28(2): 147–167.

90. This section draws on several sources, including Kerwin, K. R. & Haughton, K. 1997. Can Detroit make cars that baby boomers like? *BusinessWeek,* December 1: 134–148; and Taylor, A., III. 1994. The new golden age of autos. *Fortune,* April 4: 50–66.

91. Csere, C. 2001. Supercar supermarket. *Car and Driver,* January: 118–127.

92. For a discussion of the extent of overcapacity in the worldwide automobile industry, read Roberts, D., Matlack, C., Busyh, J., & Rowley, I. 2009. A hundred factories too many. *BusinessWeek,* January 19: 42–43.

93. McLain, S. 2014. India's middle class embraces minicars. *The Wall Street Journal,* October 9: B2; Anonymous. 2014. Geely GX7 launched after upgrading: Making versatile and comfortable SUV. *www.globaltimes.ch,* April 18: np; Anonymous. 2014. Adequate Guiyang Geely Free Cruiser higher offer 1,000 yuan now. *www.wantinews.com,* February 20: np; Anonymous. 2013. Restyled Chery QQ hit showrooms with a US$6,083 starting price. *www.chinaautoweb.com,* March 4: np; and Doval, p. 2014. Cheapest car tag hit Tata Nano: Creator. *economictimes.indiatimes.com,* August 21: np.

CHAPTER

3

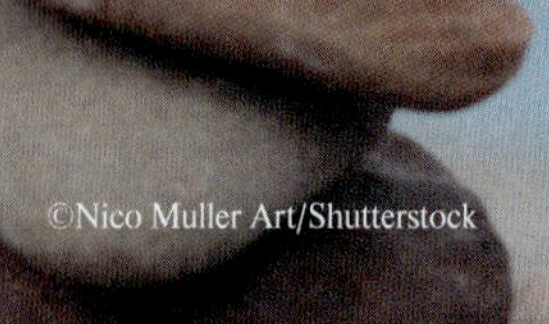

©Nico Muller Art/Shutterstock

Assessing the Internal Environment of the Firm

Learning Objectives

LO3-1 Identify the primary and support activities of a firm's value chain.

LO3-2 Understand how value-chain analysis can help managers create value by investigating relationships among activities within the firm and between the firm and its customers and suppliers.

LO3-3 Describe the resource-based view of the firm and the different types of tangible and intangible resources, as well as organizational capabilities.

LO3-4 Explain the four criteria that a firm's resources must possess to maintain a sustainable advantage and how value created can be appropriated by employees and managers.

LO3-5 Explain the usefulness of financial ratio analysis, its inherent limitations, and how to make meaningful comparisons of performance across firms.

LO3-6 Identify the value of the "balanced scorecard" in recognizing how the interests of a variety of stakeholders can be interrelated.

We encourage you to reflect on how the concepts presented in this chapter can enhance your career success (see "Reflecting on Career Implications..." at the end of the chapter).

LEARNING FROM MISTAKES

In early 2018, KFC made a major change in its supply chain system in the United Kingdom. The firm acted to "revolutionize the UK food service supply chain" by partnering with DHL to streamline its supply network to improve its efficiency. Previously, KFC had worked with a different logistics service provider, Bidvest, to supply its restaurants with fresh chicken. In going with DHL, the chain moved from a regional distribution system that used five distribution sites to a single, national distribution center. DHL applied experience it had delivering durable products, such as auto parts, and found that managing the logistics of fresh chicken was very different and challenging. Delays and bottlenecks at the distribution center in Rugby, England led to the spoiling of tons of chicken and, more dramatically, the closing of about two-thirds of KFC outlets across the UK for several days. The company found that its new supply system couldn't get chicken to all of its restaurants.[1]

The experience reminded the firm that inbound logistics is a key link in the firm's value chain. When they switched logistics service providers, the firm saw its entire operation get bogged down, resulting in lost sales and a public relations black eye. The mistake that the firm made was to focus on the cost-saving opportunity it saw in nationalizing its supply system. KFC had put the management of their supply chain system out to bid in 2017 and had picked DHL largely due to the cost savings DHL promised. As Kevin O'Marah, a supply chain consultant, stated, "too many business leaders still think of logistics and transportation simply in terms of cost."

KFC's solution was to bring its old partner, Bidvest, back into the game. To help build a more capable supply chain system, KFC signed a long-term contract with Bidvest to supply around a third of KFCs outlets in northern England. DHL's centralized warehouse continues to supply the remaining set of restaurants. Having a capable inbound logistics system is critical for the firm. As Ruari Lee, one of KFC's customers who was left unable to get lunch at his local KFC, warned "There's always a McDonald's down the road."

Discussion Questions

1. Why do firms like KFC get so focused on efficiency that they take actions that weaken their value chain?
2. What additional actions can the firm take to overcome this failure?

In this chapter we will place heavy emphasis on the value-chain concept. That is, we focus on the key value-creating activities (e.g., operations, marketing and sales, and procurement) that a firm must effectively manage and integrate in order to attain competitive advantages in the marketplace. However, firms not only must pay close attention to their own value-creating activities but also must maintain close and effective relationships with key organizations outside the firm boundaries, such as suppliers, customers, and alliance partners.

KFC was reminded that although streamlining its supply chain offered the opportunity to reduce cost, the firm needed to emphasize the effectiveness of its inbound logistics, a key link in its value chain. Its supply chain struggles threatened the ability of KFC to meet customers' needs and sustain the firm's reputation in the market.

We will begin our discussion of the firm's internal environment by looking at a value-chain analysis. This analysis gives us insight into a firm's operations and how the firm creates economic value.

VALUE-CHAIN ANALYSIS

value-chain analysis
a strategic analysis of an organization that uses value-creating activities.

primary activities
sequential activities of the value chain that refer to the physical creation of the product or service, its sale and transfer to the buyer, and its service after sale, including inbound logistics, operations, outbound logistics, marketing and sales, and service.

support activities
activities of the value chain that either add value by themselves or add value through important relationships with both primary activities and other support activities, including procurement, technology development, human resource management, and general administration.

Value-chain analysis views the organization as a sequential process of value-creating activities. The approach is useful for understanding the building blocks of competitive advantage and was described in Michael Porter's seminal book *Competitive Advantage.*[2] Value is the amount that buyers are willing to pay for what a firm provides them and is measured by total revenue, a reflection of the price a firm's product commands and the quantity it can sell. A firm is profitable when the value it receives exceeds the total costs involved in creating its product or service. Creating value for buyers that exceeds the costs of production (i.e., margin) is a key concept used in analyzing a firm's competitive position.

Porter described two different categories of activities. First, five **primary activities**–inbound logistics, operations, outbound logistics, marketing and sales, and service–contribute to the physical creation of the product or service, its sale and transfer to the buyer, and its service after the sale. Second, **support activities**–procurement, technology development, human resource management, and general administration–either add value by themselves or add value through important relationships with both primary activities and other support activities. Exhibit 3.1 illustrates Porter's value chain.

To get the most out of value-chain analysis, view the concept in its broadest context, without regard to the boundaries of your own organization. That is, place your organization within a more encompassing value chain that includes your firm's suppliers, customers, and alliance partners. Thus, in addition to thoroughly understanding how value is created within the organization, be aware of how value is created for other organizations in the overall supply chain or distribution channel.[3]

Next, we'll describe and provide examples of each of the primary and support activities. Then we'll provide examples of how companies add value by means of relationships among activities within the organization as well as activities outside the organization, such as those activities associated with customers and suppliers.[4]

LO 3-1

Identify the primary and support activities of a firm's value chain.

Primary Activities

Five generic categories of primary activities are involved in competing in any industry, as shown in Exhibit 3.2. Each category is divisible into a number of distinct activities that depend on the particular industry and the firm's strategy.[5]

inbound logistics
receiving, storing, and distributing inputs of a product.

Inbound Logistics **Inbound logistics** is primarily associated with receiving, storing, and distributing inputs to the product. It includes material handling, warehousing, inventory control, vehicle scheduling, and returns to suppliers.

EXHIBIT 3.1 The Value Chain: Primary and Support Activities

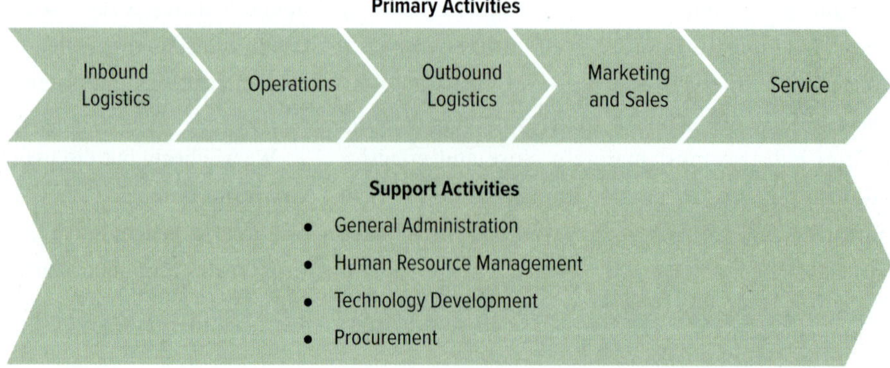

Source: Adapted from Porter, M. E. 1995, 1998. *Competitive Advantage: Creating and Sustaining Superior Performance.* New York: Free Press.

Inbound Logistics
• Location of distribution facilities to minimize shipping times. • Warehouse layout and designs to increase efficiency of operations for incoming materials.
Operations
• Efficient plant operations to minimize costs. • Efficient plant layout and workflow design. • Incorporation of appropriate process technology.
Outbound Logistics
• Effective shipping processes to provide quick delivery and minimize damages. • Shipping of goods in large lot sizes to minimize transportation costs.
Marketing and Sales
• Innovative approaches to promotion and advertising. • Proper identification of customer segments and needs.
Service
• Quick response to customer needs and emergencies. • Quality of service personnel and ongoing training.

Source: Adapted from Porter, M. E. 1985. *Competitive Advantage: Creating and Sustaining Superior Performance.* New York: Free Press.

EXHIBIT 3.2

The Value Chain: Some Factors to Consider in Assessing a Firm's Primary Activities

Just-in-time (JIT) inventory systems, for example, were designed to achieve efficient inbound logistics. In essence, Dell epitomizes JIT inventory systems, in which computer components arrive at the firm's assembly plants only hours before they are needed. JIT systems play a vital role in fulfilling Dell's commitment to fill a computer buyer's order in just a few days. Dell's operations are designed differently than traditional manufacturing systems that involve the ordering of components months before they are assembled into computers that are then sold through large chain retailers.

Operations **Operations** include all activities associated with transforming inputs into the final product form, such as machining, packaging, assembly, testing, printing, and facility operations.

operations
all activities associated with transforming inputs into the final product form.

Creating environmentally friendly manufacturing is one way to use operations to achieve competitive advantage. Shaw Industries (now part of Berkshire Hathaway), a world-class competitor in the floor-covering industry, is well known for its concern for the environment.[6] It has been successful in reducing the expenses associated with the disposal of dangerous chemicals and other waste products from its manufacturing operations. Its environmental endeavors have multiple payoffs. Shaw has received many awards for its recycling efforts–awards that enhance its reputation.

Outbound Logistics **Outbound logistics** is associated with collecting, storing, and distributing the product or service to buyers. These activities include finished goods, warehousing, material handling, delivery vehicle operation, order processing, and scheduling.

outbound logistics
collecting, storing, and distributing the product or service to buyers.

Campbell Soup uses an electronic network to facilitate its continuous-replenishment program with many of its retailers.[7] Each morning, retailers electronically inform Campbell of their product needs and of the level of inventories in their distribution centers. Campbell uses that information to forecast future demand and to determine which products require replenishment (based on the inventory limits previously established with each retailer). Trucks leave Campbell's shipping plant that afternoon and arrive at the retailers' distribution centers the same day. The program cuts the inventories of participating retailers from about a four- to a two-weeks' supply. Campbell Soup achieved this improvement because it slashed delivery time and because it knows the inventories of key retailers and can deploy supplies when they are most needed.

The Campbell Soup example also illustrates the win-win benefits of exemplary value-chain activities. Both the supplier (Campbell) and its buyers (retailers) come out ahead. Since the retailer makes more money on Campbell products delivered through continuous replenishment, it has an incentive to carry a broader line and give the company greater shelf space. After Campbell introduced the program, sales of its products grew twice as fast through participating retailers as through all other retailers. Not surprisingly, supermarket chains love such programs.

marketing and sales
activities associated with purchases of products and services by end users and the inducements used to get them to make purchases.

Marketing and Sales **Marketing and sales** activities are associated with purchases of products and services by end users and the inducements used to get them to make purchases.[8] They include advertising, promotion, sales force, quoting, channel selection, channel relations, and pricing.[9,10]

Consider product placement. This is a marketing strategy that many firms are increasingly adopting to reach customers without resorting to traditional advertising. For example, Anheuser-Busch InBev faced a challenge in reaching customers who watch commercial-free programs on Netflix. AB InBev struck a deal with the producers of House of Cards where they agreed to provide a stock of the firm's products–including Budweiser, Stella Artois, and Shock Top–to be used as props in the show.[11]

service
actions associated with providing service to enhance or maintain the value of the product.

Service The **service** primary activity includes all actions associated with providing service to enhance or maintain the value of the product, such as installation, repair, training, parts supply, and product adjustment.

Let's see how two retailers are providing exemplary customer service. At *Sephora.com,* a customer service representative taking a phone call from a repeat customer has instant access to what shade of lipstick she likes best. This will help the rep cross-sell by suggesting a matching shade of lip gloss. Such personalization is expected to build loyalty and boost sales per customer. Nordstrom, the Seattle-based department store chain, goes even a step further. It offers a cyber-assist: A service rep can take control of a customer's web browser and literally lead her to just the silk scarf that she is looking for. CEO Dan Nordstrom believes that such a capability will close enough additional purchases to pay for the $1 million investment in software.

Strategy Spotlight 3.1 discusses the costs of providing customer service and how retailers are putting in place policies to limit abuse by customers.

Support Activities

Support activities in the value chain can be divided into four generic categories, as shown in Exhibit 3.3. Each category of the support activity is divisible into a number of distinct value activities that are specific to a particular industry. For example, technology development's discrete activities may include component design, feature design, field testing, process engineering, and technology selection. Similarly, procurement may include activities such as qualifying new suppliers, purchasing different groups of inputs, and monitoring supplier performance.

procurement
the function of purchasing inputs used in the firm's value chain, including raw materials, supplies, and other consumable items as well as assets such as machinery, laboratory equipment, office equipment, and buildings.

Procurement **Procurement** refers to the function of purchasing inputs used in the firm's value chain, not to the purchased inputs themselves.[12] Purchased inputs include raw materials, supplies, and other consumable items as well as assets such as machinery, laboratory equipment, office equipment, and buildings.[13,14]

3.1 STRATEGY SPOTLIGHT — DIGITAL ECONOMY

RETAILERS REIN IN THEIR RETURN POLICIES

One of the most direct ways retailers can curry favor with customers is by offering generous return policies. Customers have grown accustomed to retailers offering the ability to return items with or without receipts for years after the product was purchased. This has often been seen as a hallmark for retailers wishing to be seen as providing a high level of customer service.

But retailers have found that this incurs significant cost for the firm, taking in used and out-of-date merchandise. For some large retailers, this results in billions of dollars of additional cost. Further, some of the returns are fraudulent. A 2017 survey found that retailers estimate that over 10 percent of their sales are returned with 11 percent of those returns being seen as likely fraudulent. For example, customers have brought in items they've purchased at other retailers, purchased at thrift stores, stolen, and even pulled out of trash bins and brought them to retailers for refunds.

In order to reduce costs and the potential for fraud, retailers have recently tightened their return policies. For example, L.L. Bean, long known for its generous return policies, has limited providing refunds on or replacement of products purchased within the last year and only if customers have a receipt. The company stated that their desire to meet the service expectations of customers has "been misinterpreted as a lifetime product replacement guarantee." Other retailers, including REI Inc. and Costco, have also instituted more restrictive return policies in recent years.

Some retailers are even leveraging the power of data analytics as they work to reduce return fraud. Retailers, including Best Buy, Home Depot, J.C. Penney, and Victoria's Secret, contract with Retail Equation, a data analytics firm. Retail Equation has developed customized algorithms for each retailer to track and score the return behavior of customers. This includes the frequency of returns, whether the customer has a receipt, whether the products have been used, whether the returned products are high-theft items, and other factors. When a customer makes a return, if their behavior has been flagged by Retail Equation's algorithm, the customer is warned that the retailer will not accept future returns from that customer. Retail Equation states that its systems are designed to identify the 1 percent of customers whose actions suggest fraud or abuse. Customers who receive a warning are then given information on how to contact Retail Equation to get information on their behavior that led to them being flagged for abuse.

While these actions allow retailers to lower their costs, they have also led to pushback from customers and online posting of complaints. Thus, retailers need to balance their desire to rein in costs and their desire to retain a high level of customer service.

Sources: Hufford, A. 2018. L.L. Bean to cap fabled return policy. *Wall Street Journal,* February 10: B1; and Safdar, K. 2018. Retailers crack down on serial returners. *Wall Street Journal,* March 14: A1.

EXHIBIT 3.3

The Value Chain: Some Factors to Consider in Assessing a Firm's Support Activities

General Administration

- Effective planning systems to attain overall goals and objectives.
- Excellent relationships with diverse stakeholder groups.
- Effective information technology to integrate value-creating activities.

Human Resource Management

- Effective recruiting, development, and retention mechanisms for employees.
- Quality relations with trade unions.
- Reward and incentive programs to motivate all employees.

Technology Development

- Effective R&D activities for process and product initiatives.
- Positive collaborative relationships between R&D and other departments.
- Excellent professional qualifications of personnel.
- Data analytics

Procurement

- Procurement of raw material inputs to optimize quality and speed and to minimize the associated costs.
- Development of collaborative win–win relationships with suppliers.
- Analysis and selection of alternative sources of inputs to minimize dependence on one supplier.

Source: Adapted from Porter, M.E. 1985. *Competitive Advantage: Creating and Sustaining Superior Performance.* New York: Free Press.

Microsoft has improved its procurement process (and the quality of its suppliers) by providing formal reviews of its suppliers. One of Microsoft's divisions has extended the review process used for employees to its outside suppliers.[15] The employee services group, which is responsible for everything from travel to 401(k) programs to the on-site library, outsources more than 60 percent of the services it provides. Unfortunately, the employee services group was not providing suppliers with enough feedback.

The evaluation system that Microsoft developed helped clarify its expectations to suppliers. An executive noted: "We had one supplier–this was before the new system–that would have scored a 1.2 out of 5. After we started giving this feedback, and the supplier understood our expectations, its performance improved dramatically. Within six months, it scored a 4. If you'd asked me before we began the feedback system, I would have said that was impossible."[16]

technology development
activities associated with the development of new knowledge that is applied to the firm's operations.

Technology Development Every value activity embodies technology.[17] The array of technologies employed in most firms is very broad, ranging from technologies used to prepare documents and transport goods to those embodied in processes and equipment or the product itself.[18] **Technology development** related to the product and its features supports the entire value chain, while other technology development is associated with particular primary or support activities.

human resource management
activities involved in the recruiting, hiring, training, development, and compensation of all types of personnel.

Human Resource Management **Human resource management** consists of activities involved in the recruiting, hiring, training, development, and compensation of all types of personnel.[19] It supports both individual primary and support activities (e.g., hiring of engineers and scientists) and the entire value chain (e.g., negotiations with labor unions).[20]

Like all great service companies, JetBlue Airways Corporation is obsessed with hiring superior employees.[21] But the company found it difficult to attract college graduates to commit to careers as flight attendants. JetBlue developed a highly innovative recruitment program for flight attendants–a one-year contract that gives them a chance to travel, meet lots of people, and then decide what else they might like to do. It also introduced the idea of training a friend and employee together so that they could share a job. With such employee-friendly initiatives, JetBlue has been very successful in attracting talent.

In their efforts to attract high-potential college graduates, some firms have turned to "program hiring." Facebook, Intuit, AB InBev, and others empower their recruiters to make offers on the spot when they interview college students, without knowing what specific position they will fill. These firms search for candidates with attributes such as being a self-starter and a problem-solver, and make quick offers to preempt the market. Later, the new employees have matching interviews with various units in the firm to find the right initial position. The firms may lose out with some candidates who dislike the uncertainty of what their role will be, but they believe the candidates who are open to this type of hiring will be a better fit in a dynamic, creative workplace.[22]

LO 3-2

Understand how value-chain analysis can help managers create value by investigating relationships among activities within the firm and between the firm and its customers and suppliers.

general administration
general management, planning, finance, accounting, legal and government affairs, quality management, and information systems; activities that support the entire value chain and not individual activities.

General Administration **General administration** consists of a number of activities, including general management, planning, finance, accounting, legal and government affairs, quality management, and information systems. Administration (unlike the other support activities) typically supports the entire value chain and not individual activities.[23]

Although general administration is sometimes viewed only as overhead, it can be a powerful source of competitive advantage. In a telephone operating company, for example, negotiating and maintaining ongoing relations with regulatory bodies can be among the most important activities for competitive advantage. Also, in some industries top management plays a vital role in dealing with important buyers.[24]

The strong and effective leadership of top executives can also make a significant contribution to an organization's success. For example, chief executive officers (CEOs) such as Jeff Bezos and Jack Ma have been credited with playing critical roles in the success of Amazon and Alibaba.

3.2 STRATEGY SPOTLIGHT

SCHMITZ CARGOBULL: ADDING VALUE TO CUSTOMERS VIA IT

Germany's truck and trailer manufacturer, Schmitz Cargobull, mainly serves customers that are operators of truck or trailer fleets. Like its rivals, the company derives a growing share of revenue from support services such as financing, full-service contracts for breakdowns and regular maintenance, and spare-parts supplies.

What sets the company apart is its expertise in telematics (the integrated application of telecommunications data) to monitor the current state of any Schmitz Cargobull–produced trailer. Through telematics, key information is continually available to the driver, the freight agent, and the customer. They can track, for instance, when maintenance is done, how much weight has been loaded, the current cargo temperature, and where the vehicle is on its route. Therefore, Schmitz Cargobull customers can better manage their trailer use and minimize the risk of breakdowns. The decision to introduce telematics, not surprisingly, derived from management's belief that real-time sharing of data would bind the company more closely to customers.

In applying its telematic tools in its products, Schmitz Cargobull is providing clear, tangible benefits. It uses information technology only where it makes sense. On the production line, for example, workers implement statistical quality controls manually, rather than rely on an automated system, because the company found manual control improves engagement and job performance.

That strategy has helped Schmitz Cargobull become an industry leader. The firm dominates the sales of semitrailer reefers (refrigerated trailers) in Germany and has the largest market share in all of Europe. Further, it has experienced strong growth, expanding sales by 27 percent from 2015 to 2018.

Sources: Anonymous. 2014. Schmitz Cargobull AG announces earnings and production results for the year ending March 2014. *www.investing.businessweek.com*, July 31: np; Anonymous. 2014. Premiere at the IAA Show 2014: Increased I-beam stability and payload. *www.cargobull.com*, September: np; Chick, S. E., Huchzermeier, A., and S. Netessine. 2014. Europe's solution factories. *Harvard Business Review*, 92(4): 11–115.; and *cargobull.com*.

Information technology (IT) can also play a key role in enhancing the value that a company can provide its customers and, in turn, increasing its own revenues and profits. Strategy Spotlight 3.2 describes how Schmitz Cargobull, a German truck and trailer manufacturer, uses IT to further its competitive position.

Interrelationships among Value-Chain Activities within and across Organizations

We have defined each of the value-chain activities separately for clarity of presentation. Managers must not ignore, however, the importance of relationships among value-chain activities.[25] There are two levels: (1) **interrelationships** among activities within the firm and (2) relationships among activities within the firm and with other stakeholders (e.g., customers and suppliers) that are part of the firm's expanded value chain.[26]

interrelationships collaborative and strategic exchange relationships between value-chain activities either (a) within firms or (b) between firms. Strategic exchange relationships involve exchange of resources such as information, people, technology, or money that contribute to the success of the firm.

With regard to the first level, Lise Saari, former Director of Global Employee Research at IBM, provided an example by commenting on how human resources needs to be integrated with the other functional areas of the firm. She put it this way: "HR [must be] a true partner of the business, with a deep and up-to-date understanding of business realities and objectives, and, in turn, [must ensure] HR initiatives fully support them at all points of the value chain."

With regard to the second level, Campbell Soup's use of electronic networks enabled it to improve the efficiency of outbound logistics.[27] However, it also helped Campbell manage the ordering of raw materials more effectively, improve its production scheduling, and help its customers better manage their inbound logistics operations.

Strategy Spotlight 3.3 discusses how firms have seen interrelationships both within and across organizational boundaries as they have worked to improve their sustainability efforts.

Applying the Value Chain to Service Organizations

The concepts of inbound logistics, operations, and outbound logistics suggest managing the raw materials that might be manufactured into finished products and delivered to customers. However, these three steps do not apply only to manufacturing. They correspond to any

3.3 STRATEGY SPOTLIGHT — ENVIRONMENTAL SUSTAINABILITY

SUSTAINABILITY ACROSS THE VALUE CHAIN

Corporations increasingly see the need for sustainability in their business operations. One survey indicates that 67 percent of firms have sustainability principles that they consider when evaluating the primary activities in their value chains. Still, many managers see sustainability as an initiative that is someone else's job and that the firm's responsibility for sustainability is limited to its own internal operations.

To make sustainability work, it is important to build it into all activities in the value chain. It starts with top management setting vision for and overarching goals associated with sustainability, but specific implementation and specific unit goals needs to be left to individual business units and departments. The following are some actions firms can take to build sustainability capabilities in both primary and support activities in the value chain.

- **Marketing:** Sustainability-focused firms look to marketing as a means not only to promote their products but also to promote movement on key issues for the firms. For example, Unilever brand managers are tasked with looking at the environmental and social impacts of their products and to come up with "brand purpose statements." The desire is to leverage the firm's marketing to inject a sense of social purpose for each of its brands.
- **Procurement:** Firms should train the procurement team on material sustainability goals and ways they can engage suppliers to improve sustainability. For example, IBM set goals and requirements for suppliers on eight different facets of sustainability and promised it would publicly share data on its improvements in these eight areas. However, the firm was not iron-fisted in its implementation. IBM gave suppliers advanced warning of the initiative and trained its procurement team on how to work with suppliers to achieve the targets.
- **Research & Development:** Firms should expand the purpose of R&D to include a focus on how innovation can improve the sustainability of their products. To accomplish this, firms can include sustainability assessments, such as eco-efficiency and life-cycle analyses, as part of product development processes and use product innovation efforts as ways to achieve sustainability goals. For example, Unilever has worked to address water conservation goals by both innovating to require less water in soap production and developing soaps that don't require water use by consumers.
- **Finance:** Given its focus on quantitative performance of the firm, many managers argue that typical decision-making processes do not effectively factor in sustainability elements. However, some leading firms, such as Dow Chemical, have factored sustainability criteria into economic value added analyses and other financial tools. SAP, a major enterprise application software firm, saw the demand for better reporting of sustainability performance and developed a reporting system that reports both financial and sustainability performance metrics.

Ultimately, the goal is to build sustainability considerations into all links in the value chain to ensure that managers across the firm consider sustainability as a core aspect of their responsibilities.

Sources: Anonymous. 2015. Chain reaction: Sustainability cascading through the value chain. *globalcompact15.org*; Bhattacharya, C. B., and P. Polman. 2017. Sustainability lessons from the front lines. *MIT Sloan Management Review,* 58(2): 71-78.

transformation process in which inputs are converted through a work process into outputs that add value. For example, accounting is a sort of transformation process that converts daily records of individual transactions into monthly financial reports. In this example, the transaction records are the inputs, accounting is the operation that adds value, and financial statements are the outputs.

What are the "operations," or transformation processes, of service organizations? At times, the difference between manufacturing and service is in providing a customized solution rather than mass production as is common in manufacturing. For example, a travel agent adds value by creating an itinerary that includes transportation, accommodations, and activities that are customized to your budget and travel dates. A law firm renders services that are specific to a client's needs and circumstances. In both cases, the work process (operation) involves the application of specialized knowledge based on the specifics of a situation (inputs) and the outcome that the client desires (outputs).

The application of the value chain to service organizations suggests that the value-adding process may be configured differently depending on the type of business a firm is engaged in. As the preceding discussion on support activities suggests, activities such as procurement and legal services are critical for adding value. Indeed, the activities that may provide

EXHIBIT 3.4 Some Examples of Value Chains in Service Industries

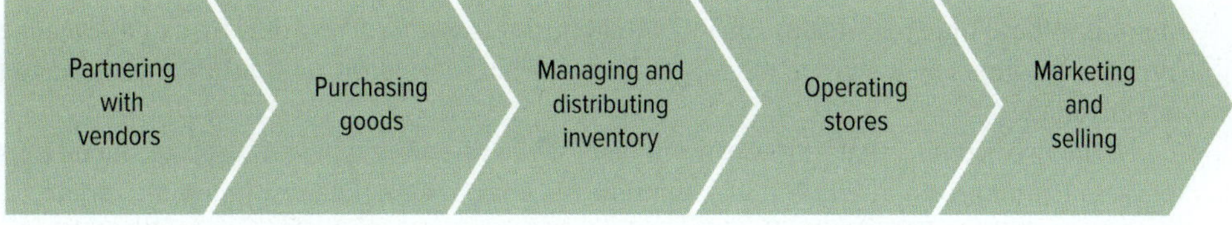

support only to one company may be critical to the primary value-adding activity of another firm.

Exhibit 3.4 provides two models of how the value chain might look in service industries. In the retail industry, there are no manufacturing operations. A firm such as Nordstrom adds value by developing expertise in the procurement of finished goods and by displaying them in its stores in a way that enhances sales. Thus, the value chain makes procurement activities (i.e., partnering with vendors and purchasing goods) a primary rather than a support activity. Operations refer to the task of operating Nordstrom's stores.

For an engineering services firm, research and development provides inputs, the transformation process is the engineering itself, and innovative designs and practical solutions are the outputs. The Beca Group, for example, is a large consulting firm with about 3,000 employees, based in 20 offices throughout the Asia Pacific region. In its technology and innovation management practice, Beca strives to make the best use of the science, technology, and knowledge resources available to create value for a wide range of industries and client sectors. This involves activities associated with research and development, engineering, and creating solutions as well as downstream activities such as marketing, sales, and service. How the primary and support activities of a given firm are configured and deployed will often depend on industry conditions and whether the company is service- and/or manufacturing-oriented.

LO 3-3

Describe the resource-based view of the firm and the different types of tangible and intangible resources, as well as organizational capabilities.

RESOURCE-BASED VIEW OF THE FIRM

resource-based view (RBV) of the firm perspective that firms' competitive advantages are due to their endowment of strategic resources that are valuable, rare, costly to imitate, and costly to substitute.

The **resource-based view (RBV) of the firm** combines two perspectives: (1) the internal analysis of phenomena within a company and (2) an external analysis of the industry and its competitive environment.[28] It goes beyond the traditional SWOT (strengths, weaknesses, opportunities, threats) analysis by integrating internal and external perspectives. The ability of a firm's resources to confer competitive advantage(s) cannot be determined without taking into consideration the broader competitive context. A firm's resources must be evaluated in terms of how valuable, rare, and hard they are for competitors to duplicate. Otherwise, the firm attains only competitive parity.

A firm's strengths and capabilities–no matter how unique or impressive–do not necessarily lead to competitive advantages in the marketplace. The criteria for whether advantages are created and whether or not they can be sustained over time will be addressed later in this section. Thus, the RBV is a very useful framework for gaining insights as to why some competitors are more profitable than others. As we will see later in the book, the RBV is also helpful in developing strategies for individual businesses and diversified firms by revealing how core competencies embedded in a firm can help it exploit new product and market opportunities.

In the two sections that follow, we will discuss the three key types of resources that firms possess (summarized in Exhibit 3.5): tangible resources, intangible resources, and organizational capabilities. Then we will address the conditions under which such assets and capabilities can enable a firm to attain a sustainable competitive advantage.[29]

EXHIBIT 3.5

The Resource-Based View of the Firm: Resources and Capabilities

Tangible Resources	
Financial	• Firm's cash account and cash equivalents. • Firm's capacity to raise equity. • Firm's borrowing capacity.
Physical	• Modern plant and facilities. • Favorable manufacturing locations. • State-of-the-art machinery and equipment.
Technological	• Data analytic algorithms. • Patents, copyrights, trademarks.
Organizational	• Effective strategic planning processes. • Excellent evaluation and control systems.
Intangible Resources	
Human	• Experience and capabilities of employees. • Trust. • Managerial skills. • Firm-specific practices and procedures.
Innovation and creativity	• Technical and scientific skills. • Innovation capacities.
Reputation	• Brand name. • Reputation with customers for quality and reliability. • Reputation with suppliers for fairness, non–zero-sum relationships.
Organizational Capabilities	

- Firm competencies or skills the firm employs to transfer inputs to outputs.
- Capacity to combine tangible and intangible resources, using organizational processes to attain desired end.

  EXAMPLES:

  - Outstanding customer service.
  - Excellent product development capabilities.
  - Innovativeness of products and services.
  - Ability to hire, motivate, and retain human capital.

Sources: Adapted from Barney, J. B. 1991. Firm resources and sustained competitive advantage. *Journal of Management,* 17: 101; Grant, R. M. 1991. *Contemporary Strategy Analysis.* Cambridge, England: Blackwell Business, 100–102; and Hitt, M. A., Ireland, R. D., and R. E. Hoskisson. 2001. *Strategic Management: Competitiveness and Globalization* (4th ed.). Cincinnati: South-Western College Publishing.

Types of Firm Resources

Firm resources are all assets, capabilities, organizational processes, information, knowledge, and so forth, controlled by a firm that enable it to develop and implement value-creating strategies.

Tangible Resources **Tangible resources** are assets that are relatively easy to identify. They include the physical and financial assets that an organization uses to create value for its customers. Among them are financial resources (e.g., a firm's cash, accounts receivable, and its ability to borrow funds); physical resources (e.g., the company's plant, equipment, and machinery as well as its proximity to customers and suppliers); organizational resources (e.g., the company's strategic planning process and its employee development, evaluation, and reward systems); and technological resources (e.g., trade secrets, patents, and copyrights).

tangible resources
organizational assets that are relatively easy to identify, including physical assets, financial resources, organizational resources, and technological resources.

Many firms are finding that high-tech, computerized training has dual benefits: It develops more-effective employees and reduces costs at the same time. Employees at FedEx take computer-based job competency tests every 6 to 12 months.[30] The 90-minute computer-based tests identify areas of individual weakness and provide input to a computer database of employee skills–information the firm uses in promotion decisions.

Intangible Resources Much more difficult for competitors (and, for that matter, a firm's own managers) to account for or imitate are **intangible resources,** which are typically embedded in unique routines and practices that have evolved and accumulated over time. These include human resources (e.g., experience and capability of employees, trust, effectiveness of work teams, managerial skills), innovation resources (e.g., technical and scientific expertise, ideas), and reputation resources (e.g., brand name, reputation with suppliers for fairness and with customers for reliability and product quality).[31] A firm's culture may also be a resource that provides competitive advantage.[32]

intangible resources
organizational assets that are difficult to identify and account for and are typically embedded in unique routines and practices, including human resources, innovation resources, and reputation resources.

As an example of how a firm can leverage the value of intangible resources, we turn to Harley-Davidson. You might not think that motorcycles, clothes, toys, and restaurants have much in common. Yet Harley-Davidson has entered all of these product and service markets by capitalizing on its strong brand image–a valuable intangible resource.[33] It has used that image to sell accessories, clothing, and toys, and it has licensed the Harley-Davidson Café in New York City to provide further exposure for its brand name and products.

Social networking sites have the potential to play havoc with a firm's reputation. Consider the unfortunate situation Comcast faced when one of its repairmen fell asleep on the job–and it went viral:

> Ben Finkelstein, a law student, had trouble with the cable modem in his home. A Comcast cable repairman arrived to fix the problem. However, when the technician had to call the home office for a key piece of information, he was put on hold for so long that he fell asleep on Finkelstein's couch. Outraged, Finkelstein made a video of the sleeping technician and posted it on YouTube. The clip became a hit–with more than a million viewings. And, for a long time, it undermined Comcast's efforts to improve its reputation for customer service.[34]

Organizational Capabilities **Organizational capabilities** are not specific tangible or intangible assets, but rather the competencies or skills that a firm employs to transform inputs into outputs.[35] In short, they refer to an organization's capacity to deploy tangible and intangible resources over time and generally in combination and to leverage those capabilities to bring about a desired end.[36] Examples of organizational capabilities are outstanding customer service, excellent product development capabilities, superb innovation processes, and flexibility in manufacturing processes.[37]

organizational capabilities
the competencies and skills that a firm employs to transform inputs into outputs.

In Strategy Spotlight 3.4, we see how Zara is incorporating new technologies and processes to enhance its capability to meet evolving customer needs.

3.4 STRATEGY SPOTLIGHT — DIGITAL ECONOMY

ZARA EMBRACES TECHNOLOGY TO MEET THE ONLINE RETAILER CHALLENGE

In the retailing business, the big threat to physical stores is the online retailers taking their customers. This includes highly diversified online retailers, such as Amazon, and specialty online retailers, Blue Nile, an online jewelry retailer. For Zara, the global clothing retailer, the threat comes from a number of online clothing retailers, such as Zalando, a German online apparel retailer, and ASOS, a British online competitor.

Brick and mortar retailers, such as Zara, are responding by offering both online and in-store experiences. A key challenge for these firms is to combine these operations to provide a seamless experience for customers. One of the services these firms can provide is "click and collect," where customers purchase online but pick up their orders in the store. Zara has been very successful in drawing its online customers into the store with one-third of its online orders being picked up at a Zara store.

Integrating this process into store operations is a major operational challenge that requires resource investments. Stores have to determine how they get products that are ordered online to the stores, where to store items ordered online, whether they will offer dedicated checkout lines to online customers, and whether the firm will rely on personal interactions or automated systems to serve online customers. Zara has developed strong competencies to get products from warehouses to the store, but it has struggled to provide effective in-store service to customers. For example, a customer going to a London Zara found that there was no signage directing him where to pick up his order. He was directed to wait in a regular checkout line only to be told, after a long wait in line, that he had to go to an upstairs counter to get his order. There, an attendant found his order form and retrieved his items by hand.

Zara's solution is to leverage automation to better serve customers. In outlets with large online business, Zara plans to create online kiosks where customers can enter or scan their order code from their online order. Behind-the-scenes robots would then retrieve the order from a small warehouse built into the store and deliver the order to a drop box where the customer would pick it up. Industry analysts note that this is a big change for a retailer since it requires the firm to reconfigure store and storeroom space and develop clear procedures. As Adam Silverman, SVP of marketing at Theatro stated, "throwing robots at the problem should only happen when the processes have been ironed out." Though challenging, Zara believes that the development of a resource set that meets the needs of both in-store and online customers best gives the firm the ability to fend off the online retailer challenge.

Sources: Neumann, J. 2018. Zara turns to robots for in-store pickup. *Wall Street Journal,* March 6: B4; and Anderson, G. 2018. Zara is 'throwing robots' at its click-and-collect problem. *forbes.com,* March 14: np.

LO 3-4

Explain the four criteria that a firm's resources must possess to maintain a sustainable advantage and how value created can be appropriated by employees and managers.

Firm Resources and Sustainable Competitive Advantages

As we have mentioned, resources alone are not a basis for competitive advantages, nor are advantages sustainable over time.[38] In some cases, a resource or capability helps a firm to increase its revenues or to lower costs but the firm derives only a temporary advantage because competitors quickly imitate or substitute for it.[39]

For a resource to provide a firm with the potential for a sustainable competitive advantage, it must have four attributes.[40] First, the resource must be valuable in the sense that it exploits opportunities and/or neutralizes threats in the firm's environment. Second, it must be rare among the firm's current and potential competitors. Third, the resource must be difficult for competitors to imitate. Fourth, the resource must have no strategically equivalent substitutes. These criteria are summarized in Exhibit 3.6. We will now discuss each of these criteria.

Is the Resource Valuable? Organizational resources can be a source of competitive advantage only when they are valuable. Resources are valuable when they enable a firm to formulate and implement strategies that improve its efficiency or effectiveness. The SWOT framework suggests that firms improve their performance only when they exploit opportunities or neutralize (or minimize) threats.

The fact that firm attributes must be valuable in order to be considered resources (as well as potential sources of competitive advantage) reveals an important complementary relationship among environmental models (e.g., SWOT and five-forces analyses) and the resource-based model. Environmental models isolate those firm attributes that exploit

Is the resource or capability . . .	Implications
Valuable?	• Neutralize threats and exploit opportunities
Rare?	• Not many firms possess
Difficult to imitate?	• Physically unique • Path dependency (how accumulated over time) • Causal ambiguity (difficult to disentangle what it is or how it could be re-created) • Social complexity (trust, interpersonal relationships, culture, reputation)
Difficult to substitute?	• No equivalent strategic resources or capabilities

EXHIBIT 3.6

Four Criteria for Assessing Sustainability of Resources and Capabilities

opportunities and/or neutralize threats. Thus, they specify what firm attributes may be considered as resources. The resource-based model then suggests what additional characteristics these resources must possess if they are to develop a sustained competitive advantage.

Is the Resource Rare? If competitors or potential competitors also possess the same valuable resource, it is not a source of a competitive advantage because all of these firms have the capability to exploit that resource in the same way. Common strategies based on such a resource would give no one firm an advantage. For a resource to provide competitive advantages, it must be uncommon, that is, rare relative to other competitors.

This argument can apply to bundles of valuable firm resources that are used to formulate and develop strategies. Some strategies require a mix of multiple types of resources–tangible assets, intangible assets, and organizational capabilities. If a particular bundle of firm resources is not rare, then relatively large numbers of firms will be able to conceive of and implement the strategies in question. Thus, such strategies will not be a source of competitive advantage, even if the resource in question is valuable.

Can the Resource Be Imitated Easily? Inimitability (difficulty in imitating) is a key to value creation because it constrains competition.[41] If a resource is inimitable, then any profits generated are more likely to be sustainable.[42] Having a resource that competitors can easily copy generates only temporary value.[43] This has important implications. Since managers often fail to apply this test, they tend to base long-term strategies on resources that are imitable. IBP (Iowa Beef Processors) became the first meatpacking company in the United States to modernize by building a set of assets (automated plants located in cattle-producing states) and capabilities (low-cost "disassembly" of carcasses) that earned returns on assets of 1.3 percent in the 1970s. By the late 1980s, however, ConAgra and Cargill had imitated these resources, and IBP's profitability fell by nearly 70 percent, to 0.4 percent.

Clearly, an advantage based on inimitability won't last forever. Competitors will eventually discover a way to copy most valuable resources. However, managers can forestall them and sustain profits for a while by developing strategies around resources that have at least one of the following four characteristics.[44]

Physical Uniqueness The first source of inimitability is physical uniqueness, which by definition is inherently difficult to copy. A beautiful resort location, mineral rights, or Pfizer's pharmaceutical patents simply cannot be imitated. Many managers believe that several of their resources may fall into this category, but on close inspection, few do.

Path Dependency A greater number of resources cannot be imitated because of what economists refer to as **path dependency.** This simply means that resources are unique and therefore scarce because of all that has happened along the path followed in their development

path dependency
a characteristic of resources that is developed and/or accumulated through a unique series of events.

and/or accumulation. Competitors cannot go out and buy these resources quickly and easily; they must be built up over time in ways that are difficult to accelerate.

The Gerber Products Co. brand name for baby food is an example of a resource that is potentially inimitable. Re-creating Gerber's brand loyalty would be a time-consuming process that competitors could not expedite, even with expensive marketing campaigns. Ashley furniture has found that controlling all steps of its distribution system has allowed it to develop specific competencies that are difficult to match. It has developed specially designed racks in its distribution centers and proprietary inventory management systems that would take time to match. It has also tasked its truck drivers to be "Ashley Ambassadors," building relationships with furniture store managers and employees. Both these operational and relational resources have built up over time and can't be imitated overnight.[45] Also, a crash R&D program generally cannot replicate a successful technology when research findings cumulate. Clearly, these path-dependent conditions build protection for the original resource. The benefits from experience and learning through trial and error cannot be duplicated overnight.

causal ambiguity
a characteristic of a firm's resources that is costly to imitate because a competitor cannot determine what the resource is and/or how it can be re-created.

Causal Ambiguity The third source of inimitability is termed **causal ambiguity.** This means that would-be competitors may be thwarted because it is impossible to disentangle the causes (or possible explanations) of either what the valuable resource is or how it can be re-created. What is the root of 3M's innovation process? You can study it and draw up a list of possible factors. But it is a complex, unfolding (or folding) process that is hard to understand and would be hard to imitate.

Often, causally ambiguous resources are organizational capabilities, involving a complex web of social interactions that may even depend on particular individuals. When trying to compete with Google, many competitors, such as Yahoo and Twitter, have found it hard to match Google's ability to innovate and launch new products. Most acknowledge this is tied to Google's ability to hire the best talent and the culture of creativity within the firm, but firms find it very challenging to identify the specific set of actions Google took to build its image and culture or how to match it.

social complexity
a characteristic of a firm's resources that is costly to imitate because the social engineering required is beyond the capability of competitors, including interpersonal relations among managers, organizational culture, and reputation with suppliers and customers.

Social Complexity A firm's resources may be imperfectly inimitable because they reflect a high level of **social complexity.** Such phenomena are typically beyond the ability of firms to systematically manage or influence. When competitive advantages are based on social complexity, it is difficult for other firms to imitate them.

A wide variety of firm resources may be considered socially complex. Examples include interpersonal relations among the managers in a firm, its culture, and its reputation with its suppliers and customers. In many of these cases, it is easy to specify how these socially complex resources add value to a firm. Hence, there is little or no causal ambiguity surrounding the link between them and competitive advantage.

The Edelman Trust Barometer, a comprehensive survey of public trust, has found that trust and transparency are more critical than ever.[46] In recent years, Edelman has found that impressions of openness, sincerity, and authenticity were more important to corporate reputation in the United States than the quality of products and services. This means trust affects tangible things such as supply chain partnerships and long-term customer loyalty. People want to partner with you because they have heard you are a credible company built through a culture of trust. In a sense, being a great company to work for also makes you a great company to work with.

Are Substitutes Readily Available? The fourth requirement for a firm resource to be a source of sustainable competitive advantage is that there must be no strategically equivalent valuable resources that are themselves not rare or inimitable. Two valuable firm resources (or two bundles of resources) are strategically equivalent when each one can be exploited separately to implement the same strategies.

Substitutability may take at least two forms. First, though it may be impossible for a firm to imitate exactly another firm's resource, it may be able to substitute a similar resource that enables it to develop and implement the same strategy. Clearly, a firm seeking to imitate another firm's high-quality top management team would be unable to copy the team exactly. However, it might be able to develop its own unique management team. Though these two teams would have different ages, functional backgrounds, experience, and so on, they could be strategically equivalent and thus substitutes for one another.

Second, very different firm resources can become strategic substitutes. For example, Internet retailers, such as Amazon.com, compete as substitutes for brick-and-mortar stores. The result is that resources such as premier retail locations become less valuable. In a similar vein, ride sharing services, such as Uber and Lyft, have undercut the value of the licenses held by traditional taxi service providers. For example, a New York City taxi medallion sold for a whopping $1.3 million in 2013. By 2018, prices had plunged to about $200,000.[47]

To recap this section, recall that resources and capabilities must be rare and valuable as well as difficult to imitate or substitute in order for a firm to attain competitive advantages that are sustainable over time.[48] Exhibit 3.7 illustrates the relationship among the four criteria of sustainability and shows the competitive implications.

In firms represented by the first row of Exhibit 3.7, managers are in a difficult situation. When their resources and capabilities do not meet any of the four criteria, it would be difficult to develop any type of competitive advantage, in the short or long term. The resources and capabilities they possess enable the firm neither to exploit environmental opportunities nor to neutralize environmental threats. In the second and third rows, firms have resources and capabilities that are valuable as well as rare, respectively. However, in both cases the resources and capabilities are not difficult for competitors to imitate or substitute. Here, the firms could attain some level of competitive parity. They could perform on par with equally endowed rivals or attain a temporary competitive advantage. But their advantages would be easy for competitors to match. It is only in the fourth row, where all four criteria are satisfied, that competitive advantages can be sustained over time.

Leveraging Artificial Intelligence to Increase the Sustainability of an Advantage Increasingly, firms are using artificial intelligence and leveraging data to better understand customer preferences, the use of products, and the operations of the firm to build a foundation for sustainable advantage. In effectively using data on customer preferences, efficient procedures, and other aspects of business, firms are able to build an understanding of markets and firm operations that existing competitors and new firms will find difficult to attack. Artificial intelligence, sometimes referred to as machine learning, involves the use of sophisticated programs that crunch vast volumes of data to find patterns and produce improved predictions or evaluations without the direct intervention of a human programmer or statistician.[49]

EXHIBIT 3.7
Criteria for Sustainable Competitive Advantage and Strategic Implications

Is a Resource or Capability...				
Valuable?	**Rare?**	**Difficult to Imitate?**	**Without Substitutes?**	**Implication for Competitiveness**
No	No	No	No	Competitive disadvantage
Yes	No	No	No	Competitive parity
Yes	Yes	No	No	Temporary competitive advantage
Yes	Yes	Yes	Yes	Sustainable competitive advantage

Source: Adapted from Barney, J. B. 1991. Firm resources and sustained competitive advantage. *Journal of Management,* 17: 99–120.

The advantages that these firms are building have a high degree of sustainability because they combine aspects of path dependence and social complexity that make imitation of their resource bases a challenge for later moving firms. These firms collect and analyze large reams of data in a real time basis to improve their efficiency and ability to meet customer needs. In doing so, the firm develops a path dependent advantage based on its superior understanding of its markets and firm operations. Newcomers to the market and slow moving rivals find it difficult to match or substitute for the leading firm's knowledge. These actions also allow these knowledge intensive firms to develop a reputation and brand identity as the most efficient and effective service provider.

Additionally, the advantages that these firms develop are difficult to imitate because the resource sets the firms develop are often socially complex. First, knowledge intensive firms typically tailor their entire value chain around the collection and leveraging of the data they collect, making it a challenge for later movers to match the leading firm unless the follower invests in a similar set of co-specialized resources. Second, these firms develop strong cultures emphasizing continuous improvement and communication patterns between managers that support their efforts to improve efficiencies and their ability to meet customer needs on an ongoing basis.

Together, the path dependent and socially complex resource sets these firms develop provide a basis for a sustainable advantage. The goal for these firms is to develop a virtuous cycle where their analytical models allow them to improve products and services which then stimulates greater demand. The firm's increased sales then provides more data on which to improve products and services even more, triggering increased sales once again, and so on. The following are some examples of firms that are exploiting the value of data and artificial intelligence to build a strong and sustainable advantage.

- While farming isn't the first industry that comes to mind when people think of the benefits of big data and analytical models, Monsanto is working to build a business in model-driven farming. The firm has invested over $1.5 billion to build a set of resources and capabilities that will allow it to identify optimal timing, location, and seed to optimize crop yields. Monsanto's models use data on historic yields, sensors built into tractors, other ground-based sensors, weather data, and field data collected in satellite imagery. As they build this business, they will be able to further optimize their models, further increasing the yields for farmers.
- inVia is taking the use of models into the warehouse. In major fulfillment centers, humans who compile products to fill orders can walk upward of 15 miles a day. inVia is building robots to replace human pickers in these centers. Their approach is to leverage the power of data to offer more efficient solutions for fulfillment centers. inVia uses data on the popularity and degree of association of products to optimally locate the shelving of all of the products in the fulfillment center. For example, data indicated that sunscreen and sunglasses should be located closely together since they are often ordered together. As a result, its robots can minimize the time spent zooming around the warehouse finding all of the products for an offer. Moving forward, every order provides additional information on more optimally structuring the layout of the fulfillment center. As customer demand changes, the system will aid in providing information on both warehouse layout and input on changes in the quantity and model of products needed in the warehouse.
- Ping An, a Chinese financial services company, is using artificial intelligence to spot dishonesty by potential borrowers. Customers wanting to borrow money answer questions about their income and repayment plans on a video application app. Ping An has developed an algorithm that monitors 50 facial expressions to assess borrower dishonesty. The company uses artificial intelligence to compile an overall score on a borrower based on his or her facial expressions and to regularly improve the predictive ability of the model by comparing the facial expressions of prior customers with their repayment behavior.

While these firms compete in very different markets, they show how leveraging the power of artificial intelligence opens up a powerful path for a firm to build a sustainable advantage.

The Generation and Distribution of a Firm's Profits: Extending the Resource-Based View of the Firm

The resource-based view of the firm is useful in determining when firms will create competitive advantages and enjoy high levels of profitability. However, it has not been developed to address how a firm's profits (often referred to as "rents" by economists) will be distributed to a firm's management and employees or other stakeholders such as customers, suppliers, or governments.[50] This is an important issue because firms may be successful in creating competitive advantages that can be sustainable for a period of time. However, much of the profits can be retained (or "appropriated") by a firm's employees and managers or other stakeholders instead of flowing to the firm's owners (i.e., the stockholders).*

Consider Viewpoint DataLabs, a subsidiary of software giant Computer Associates, that makes sophisticated three-dimensional models and textures for film production houses, video games, and car manufacturers. This example will help to show how employees are often able to obtain (or "appropriate") a high proportion of a firm's profits:

> Walter Noot, head of production, was having trouble keeping his highly skilled employees happy with their compensation. Each time one of them was lured away for more money, everyone would want a raise. "We were having to give out raises every six months–30 to 40 percent–then six months later they'd expect the same. It was a big struggle to keep people happy."[51]

Here, much of the profits is being generated by the highly skilled professionals working together. They are able to exercise their power by successfully demanding more financial compensation. In part, management has responded favorably because they are united in their demands and their work involves a certain amount of social complexity and causal ambiguity–given the complex, coordinated efforts that their work entails.

Four factors help explain the extent to which employees and managers will be able to obtain a proportionately high level of the profits that they generate:[52]

- ***Employee bargaining power.*** If employees are vital to forming a firm's unique capability, they will earn disproportionately high wages. For example, marketing professionals may have access to valuable information that helps them to understand the intricacies of customer demands and expectations, or engineers may understand unique technical aspects of the products or services. Additionally, in some industries such as consulting, advertising, and tax preparation, clients tend to be very loyal to individual professionals employed by the firm, instead of to the firm itself. This enables them to "take the clients with them" if they leave. This enhances their bargaining power.
- ***Employee replacement cost.*** If employees' skills are idiosyncratic and rare (a source of resource-based advantages), they should have high bargaining power based on the high cost required by the firm to replace them. For example, Jony Ive, Apple's iconic head of design, is seen as a critical player that the firm would find hard to replace. To keep him happy at the firm, Apple reportedly once gave him a $30 million bonus and $25 million in stock.[53]
- ***Employee exit costs.*** This factor may tend to reduce an employee's bargaining power. An individual may face high personal costs when leaving the organization. Thus, that individual's threat of leaving may not be credible. In addition, an employee's expertise may be firm-specific and of limited value to other firms.

---

*Economists define rents as profits (or prices) in excess of what is required to provide a normal return.

- ***Manager bargaining power.*** Managers' power is based on how well they create resource-based advantages. They are generally charged with creating value through the process of organizing, coordinating, and leveraging employees as well as other forms of capital such as plant, equipment, and financial capital (addressed further in Chapter 4). Such activities provide managers with sources of information that may not be readily available to others.

Chapter 9 addresses the conditions under which top-level managers (such as CEOs) of large corporations have been, at times, able to obtain levels of total compensation that would appear to be significantly disproportionate to their contributions to wealth generation as well as to top executives in peer organizations. Here, corporate governance becomes a critical control mechanism. Consider shareholders' reaction, in April 2012, to Citigroup's proposed $15 million pay package for then-CEO Vikram Pandit.[54] It was not positive, to say the least. After all, they had suffered a 92 percent decline in the stock's price under Pandit's five-year reign. They rejected the bank's compensation proposal. In October 2012, the board ousted Pandit after the New York-based firm failed to secure Federal Reserve approval to increase its shareholder payouts and Moody's Investors Service cut the bank's credit rating two levels.

Such diversion of profits from the owners of the business to top management is far less likely when the board members are truly independent outsiders (i.e., they do not have close ties to management). In general, given the external market for top talent, the level of compensation that executives receive is based on factors similar to the ones just discussed that determine the level of their bargaining power.[55]

In addition to employees and managers, other stakeholder groups can also appropriate a portion of the rents generated by a firm. If, for example, a critical input is controlled by a monopoly supplier or if a single buyer accounts for most of a firm's sales, this supplier's or buyer's bargaining power can greatly erode the potential profits of a firm. Similarly, excessive taxation by governments can also reduce what is available to a firm's stockholders.

EVALUATING FIRM PERFORMANCE: TWO APPROACHES

financial ratio analysis a method of evaluating a company's performance and financial well-being through ratios of accounting values, including short-term solvency, long-term solvency, asset utilization, profitability, and market value ratios.

This section addresses two approaches to use when evaluating a firm's performance. The first is **financial ratio analysis**, which, generally speaking, identifies how a firm is performing according to its balance sheet, income statement, and market valuation. As we will discuss, when performing a financial ratio analysis, you must take into account the firm's performance from a historical perspective (not just at one point in time) as well as how it compares with both industry norms and key competitors.[56]

The second perspective takes a broader stakeholder view. Firms must satisfy a broad range of stakeholders, including employees, customers, and owners, to ensure their long-term viability. Central to our discussion will be a well-known approach–the balanced scorecard–that has been popularized by Robert Kaplan and David Norton.[57]

Financial Ratio Analysis

The beginning point in analyzing the financial position of a firm is to compute and analyze five different types of financial ratios:

- Short-term solvency or liquidity
- Long-term solvency measures
- Asset management (or turnover)
- Profitability
- Market value

Exhibit 3.8 summarizes each of these five ratios.

EXHIBIT 3.8 A Summary of Five Types of Financial Ratios

I. Short-term solvency, or liquidity, ratios

$$\text{Current ratio} = \frac{\text{Current assets}}{\text{Current liabilities}}$$

$$\text{Quick ratio} = \frac{\text{Current assets} - \text{Inventory}}{\text{Current liabilities}}$$

$$\text{Cash ratio} = \frac{\text{Cash}}{\text{Current liabilities}}$$

II. Long-term solvency, or financial leverage, ratios

$$\text{Total debt ratio} = \frac{\text{Total assets} - \text{Total equity}}{\text{Total assets}}$$

$$\text{Debt-equity ratio} = \frac{\text{Total debt}}{\text{Total equity}}$$

$$\text{Equity multiplier} = \frac{\text{Total assets}}{\text{Total equity}}$$

$$\text{Times interest earned ratio} = \frac{\text{EBIT}}{\text{Interest}}$$

$$\text{Cash coverage ratio} = \frac{\text{EBIT} + \text{Depreciation}}{\text{Interest}}$$

III. Asset utilization, or turnover, ratios

$$\text{Inventory turnover} = \frac{\text{Cost of goods sold}}{\text{Inventory}}$$

$$\text{Days' sales in inventory} = \frac{\text{365 days}}{\text{Inventory turnover}}$$

$$\text{Receivables turnover} = \frac{\text{Sales}}{\text{Accounts receivable}}$$

$$\text{Days' sales in receivables} = \frac{\text{365 days}}{\text{Receivables turnover}}$$

$$\text{Total asset turnover} = \frac{\text{Sales}}{\text{Total assets}}$$

$$\text{Capital intensity} = \frac{\text{Total assets}}{\text{Sales}}$$

IV. Profitability ratios

$$\text{Profit margin} = \frac{\text{Net income}}{\text{Sales}}$$

$$\text{Return on assets (ROA)} = \frac{\text{Net income}}{\text{Total assets}}$$

$$\text{Return on equity (ROE)} = \frac{\text{Net income}}{\text{Total equity}}$$

$$\text{ROE} = \frac{\text{Net income}}{\text{Sales}} \times \frac{\text{Sales}}{\text{Assets}} \times \frac{\text{Assets}}{\text{Equity}}$$

V. Market value ratios

$$\text{Price-earnings ratio} = \frac{\text{Price per share}}{\text{Earnings per share}}$$

$$\text{Market-to-book ratio} = \frac{\text{Market value per share}}{\text{Book value per share}}$$

Appendix 1 to Chapter 13 (the Case Analysis chapter) provides detailed definitions for and discussions of each of these types of ratios as well as examples of how each is calculated. Refer to pages 414 to 423.

A meaningful ratio analysis must go beyond the calculation and interpretation of financial ratios.[58] It must include how ratios change over time as well as how they are interrelated. For example, a firm that takes on too much long-term debt to finance operations will see an immediate impact on its indicators of long-term financial leverage. The additional debt will negatively affect the firm's short-term liquidity ratio (i.e., current and quick ratios) since the firm must pay interest and principal on the additional debt each year until it is retired. Additionally, the interest expenses deducted from revenues reduce the firm's profitability.

LO 3-5

Explain the usefulness of financial ratio analysis, its inherent limitations, and how to make meaningful comparisons of performance across firms.

A firm's financial position should not be analyzed in isolation. Important reference points are needed. We will address some issues that must be taken into account to make financial analysis more meaningful: historical comparisons, comparisons with industry norms, and comparisons with key competitors.

Historical Comparisons When you evaluate a firm's financial performance, it is very useful to compare its financial position over time. This provides a means of evaluating trends. For example, Apple Inc. reported revenues of $266 billion and net income of $59 billion in 2018. Virtually all firms would be very happy with such remarkable financial success. These figures represent a stunning annual growth in revenue and net income of 16 percent and 23 percent, respectively, over Apple's 2017 figures. Had Apple's revenues and net income in

EXHIBIT 3.9 Historical Trends: Return on Sales (ROS) for a Hypothetical Company

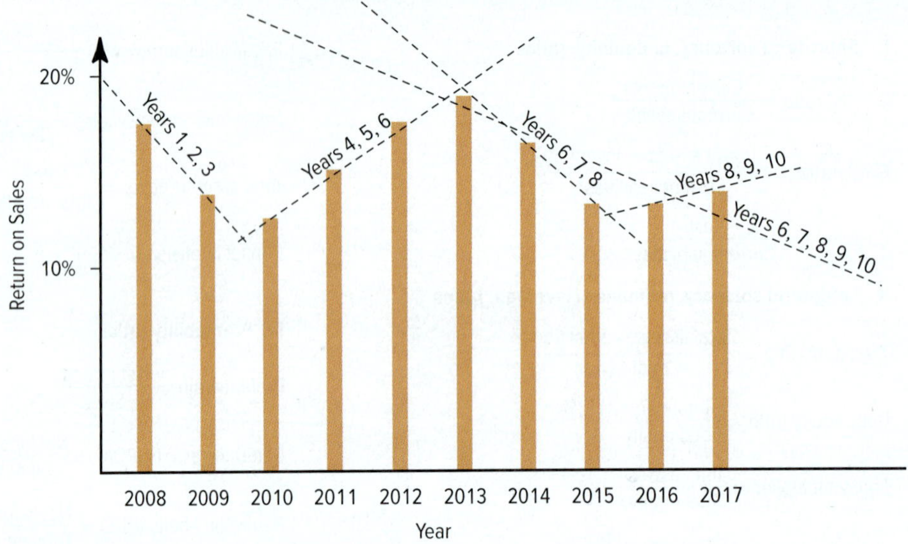

2018 been $200 billion and $40 billion, respectively, it would still be a very large and highly profitable enterprise. However, such performance would have significantly damaged Apple's market valuation and reputation as well as the careers of many of its executives.

Exhibit 3.9 illustrates a 10-year period of return on sales (ROS) for a hypothetical company. As indicated by the dotted trend lines, the rate of growth (or decline) differs substantially over time periods.

Comparison with Industry Norms When you are evaluating a firm's financial performance, remember also to compare it with industry norms. A firm's current ratio or profitability may appear impressive at first glance. However, it may pale when compared with industry standards or norms.

Comparing your firm with all other firms in your industry assesses relative performance. Banks often use such comparisons when evaluating a firm's creditworthiness. Exhibit 3.10 includes a variety of financial ratios for three industries: computers, grocery stores, and skilled-nursing facilities. Why is there such variation among the financial ratios for these three industries? There are several reasons. With regard to the collection period, grocery stores operate mostly on a cash basis, hence a very short collection period. Computer manufacturers sell their output to retailers and corporate customers on terms such as 2/15 net 45, which means they give a 2 percent discount on bills paid within 15 days and start charging interest after 45 days. Skilled-nursing facilities also have a longer collection period than grocery stores because they typically rely on payments from insurance companies.

The industry norms for return on assets also highlight differences among these industries. Health care facilities, in general, are limited in their pricing structures by Medicare/Medicaid regulations and by insurance reimbursement limits, resulting in very low profit ratios. Grocers operate with somewhat slim margins but can differentiate themselves to some degree to attract customers. Computer manufacturers have the ability to more substantially differentiate products and generate higher returns if their products have superior performance.

Comparison with Key Competitors Recall from Chapter 2 that firms with similar strategies are members of a strategic group in an industry. Furthermore, competition is more intense among competitors within groups than across groups. Thus, you can gain valuable insights

Financial Ratio	Computers	Grocery Stores	Skilled-Nursing Facilities
Quick ratio (times)	1.4	0.7	0.9
Current ratio (times)	2.3	1.8	1.2
Total liabilities to net worth (%)	67.2	69.7	162.3
Collection period (days)	54.0	4.0	38.5
Assets to sales (%)	46.6	24.0	56.6
Return on assets(%)	7.1	5.9	1.1

EXHIBIT 3.10
How Financial Ratios Differ across Industries

Source: Dun, Mergent and Bradstreet. 2017. Key Business Ratios, SIC 3571 (Computers); SIC 5411 (Grocery Stores); SIC 8051 (Skilled-Nursing Facilities). mergentkbr.com.

into a firm's financial and competitive position if you make comparisons between a firm and its most direct rivals. Consider a firm trying to diversify into the highly profitable pharmaceutical industry. Even if it was willing to invest several hundred million dollars, it would be virtually impossible to compete effectively against industry giants such as Pfizer and Merck. These two firms had 2018 revenues of $54 billion and $42 billion, respectively, and both had R&D budgets of over $8.0 billion.[59]

Integrating Financial Analysis and Stakeholder Perspectives: The Balanced Scorecard

LO 3-6
Identify the value of the "balanced scorecard" in recognizing how the interests of a variety of stakeholders can be interrelated.

It is useful to see how a firm performs over time in terms of several ratios. However, such traditional approaches can be a double-edged sword.[60] Many important transactions–investments in research and development, employee training and development, and advertising and promotion of key brands–may greatly expand a firm's market potential and create significant long-term shareholder value. But such critical investments are not reflected positively in short-term financial reports. Financial reports typically measure expenses, not the value created. Thus, managers may be penalized for spending money in the short term to improve their firm's long-term competitive viability!

Now consider the other side of the coin. A manager may destroy the firm's future value by dissatisfying customers, depleting the firm's stock of good products coming out of R&D, or damaging the morale of valued employees. Such budget cuts, however, may lead to very good short-term financials. The manager may look good in the short run and even receive credit for improving the firm's performance. In essence, such a manager has mastered "denominator management," whereby decreasing investments makes the return on investment (ROI) ratio larger, even though the actual return remains constant or shrinks.

The Balanced Scorecard: Description and Benefits To provide a meaningful integration of the many issues that come into evaluating a firm's performance, Kaplan and Norton developed a **"balanced scorecard."**[61] This provides top managers with a fast but comprehensive view of the business. In a nutshell, it includes financial measures that reflect the results of actions already taken, but it complements these indicators with measures of customer satisfaction, internal processes, and the organization's innovation and improvement activities–operational measures that drive future financial performance.

balanced scorecard
a method of evaluating a firm's performance using performance measures from the customer, internal, innovation and learning, and financial perspectives.

The balanced scorecard enables managers to consider their business from four key perspectives: customer, internal, innovation and learning, and financial. These are briefly described in Exhibit 3.11.

EXHIBIT 3.11 The Balanced Scorecard's Four Perspectives

- How do customers see us? (customer perspective)
- What must we excel at? (internal business perspective)
- Can we continue to improve and create value? (innovation and learning perspective)
- How do we look to shareholders? (financial perspective)

customer perspective measures of firm performance that indicate how well firms are satisfying customers' expectations.

Customer Perspective Clearly, how a company is performing from its customers' perspective is a top priority for management. The balanced scorecard requires that managers translate their general mission statements on customer service into specific measures that reflect the factors that really matter to customers. For the balanced scorecard to work, managers must articulate goals for four key categories of customer concerns: time, quality, performance and service, and cost.

internal business perspective measures of firm performance that indicate how well firms' internal processes, decisions, and actions are contributing to customer satisfaction.

Internal Business Perspective Customer-based measures are important. However, they must be translated into indicators of what the firm must do internally to meet customers' expectations. Excellent customer performance results from processes, decisions, and actions that occur throughout organizations in a coordinated fashion, and managers must focus on those critical internal operations that enable them to satisfy customer needs. The internal measures should reflect business processes that have the greatest impact on customer satisfaction. These include factors that affect cycle time, quality, employee skills, and productivity.

innovation and learning perspective measures of firm performance that indicate how well firms are changing their product and service offerings to adapt to changes in the internal and external environments.

Innovation and Learning Perspective Given the rapid rate of markets, technologies, and global competition, the criteria for success are constantly changing. To survive and prosper, managers must make frequent changes to existing products and services as well as introduce entirely new products with expanded capabilities. A firm's ability to do well from an innovation and learning perspective is more dependent on its intangible than tangible assets. Three categories of intangible assets are critically important: human capital (skills, talent, and knowledge), information capital (information systems, networks), and organization capital (culture, leadership).

financial perspective measures of firms' financial performance that indicate how well strategy, implementation, and execution are contributing to bottom-line improvement.

Financial Perspective Measures of financial performance indicate whether the company's strategy, implementation, and execution are indeed contributing to bottom-line improvement. Typical financial goals include profitability, growth, and shareholder value. Periodic financial statements remind managers that improved quality, response time, productivity, and innovative products benefit the firm only when they result in improved sales, increased market share, reduced operating expenses, or higher asset turnover.[62]

A key implication is that managers do not need to look at their job as balancing stakeholder demands. They must avoid the following mindset: "How many units in employee satisfaction do I have to give up to get some additional units of customer satisfaction or profits?" Instead, the balanced scorecard provides a win-win approach–increasing satisfaction among a wide variety of organizational stakeholders, including employees (at all levels), customers, and stockholders.

The Insights from Research discusses how balance in performance across a set of criteria leads to increased and more consistent future financial performance.

Limitations and Potential Downsides of the Balanced Scorecard There is general agreement that there is nothing inherently wrong with the concept of the balanced scorecard.[63] The key limitation is that some executives may view it as a "quick fix" that can be easily installed. If managers do not recognize this from the beginning and fail to commit to it long term, the organization will be disappointed. Poor execution becomes the cause of such performance

3.1 *INSIGHTS* from Research

THE BENEFITS OF BALANCE

Overview

Business leaders face strong pressures to produce financial results, but they also know that ignoring other areas of the firm can cause trouble down the line. This study speaks on that topic and shows that having balance in performance pays off for the firm financially.

What the Research Shows

Researchers from the Drucker Institute have compiled a dataset on 693 large, publicly-traded companies from 2012 to 2017. They collected information on 37 indicators of performance in five specific areas: customer satisfaction, employee engagement, innovation, social responsibility, and financial performance. Companies were scored on a range of 0 to 100 in each of these five areas. The scores were standardized so that the mean score on each scale was 50. The researchers were specifically focused on whether consistency in performance across the five areas would have an impact on the firm's future financial performance.

The results were very clear. The more a firm consistently performed across the five areas, the more the firm avoided major peaks and valleys, the better the firm's financial performance in the following year. For example, if a firm received an average score over the five areas of 70 (an above average score) and had a consistency score of 50 (right on the mean value), the predicted financial performance for the following year was 62. But if the firm's average score remained the same (70), but its consistency score was also well above average (70), it could anticipate the firm's performance in the following year would be 65. This three-point rise may not seem like much, but it moves the firm's anticipated financial performance from the top 12 percent into the top 7 percent of firms.

So, why is consistency beneficial? The researchers suggest that when a firm has uneven performance across these measures, there may be particular areas of weakness that could become major problems for the firm in coming years. The researchers use the metaphor of an elite athlete. If the athlete neglects endurance and focuses exclusively on strength and speed, she will not be able to sustain performance over time.

Key Takeaways

- Five key areas of performance for firms to focus on are customer satisfaction, employee engagement and development, innovation, social responsibility, and financial strength.
- Firms tend to perform better over time if they perform consistently across these five areas.
- Weakness on any of the five areas indicates an issue that could emerge into a crisis for the firm.

Questions

1. What are some examples of firms that have been strong performers but that faced struggles because of specific areas of weakness? How did these firms respond to these challenges?
2. Amazon is very highly ranked on a number of the dimensions examined, but the firm scored quite unevenly across the areas, scoring particularly low in social responsibility. Should Amazon see this as a potential threat? What actions, if any, should Amazon take moving forward?

Research Reviewed

Wartzman, R., and L. Crosby. 2018. The key to improving a firm's financial health. *The Wall Street Journal*, May 21: R6.

outcomes. And organizational scorecards must be aligned with individuals' scorecards to turn the balanced scorecards into a powerful tool for sustained performance.

In a study of 50 Canadian medium-size and large organizations, the number of users expressing skepticism about scorecard performance was much greater than the number claiming positive results. A large number of respondents agreed with the statement "Balanced scorecards don't really work." Some representative comments included: "It became just a number-crunching exercise by accountants after the first year," "It is just the latest management fad and is already dropping lower on management's list of priorities as all fads eventually do," and "If scorecards are supposed to be a measurement tool, why is it so hard to measure their results?" There is much work to do before scorecards can become a viable framework to measure sustained strategic performance.

Problems often occur in the balanced scorecard implementation efforts when the commitment to learning is insufficient and employees' personal ambitions are included. Without a set of rules for employees that address continuous process improvement and the personal improvement of individual employees, there will be limited employee buy-in and insufficient cultural change. Thus, many improvements may be temporary and superficial. Often, scorecards that failed to attain alignment and improvements dissipated very quickly. And, in many cases, management's efforts to improve performance were seen as divisive and were viewed by employees as aimed at benefiting senior management compensation. This fostered a "what's in it for me?" attitude.

ISSUE FOR DEBATE

One of the most difficult decisions firms in dynamic industries need to make is whether to invest primarily in one line of research and development or to spread its investments in multiple lines of research. Merck, a major pharmaceutical firm, faced this very choice recently. Up until recent years, Merck was a company that liked to spread its bets across a range of research directions and products. As Bernard Munos, a pharmaceutical R&D consultant stated, "Merck's R&D strategy was to bring as many drugs to market as they could."

Recently, the firm's focus shifted. Rather than developing a range of drugs, Merck has focused largely on one drug, Keytruda, a new type of cancer drug that leverages the patient's own immune system to fight cancer tumors. The drug is already marketed to treat skin, bladder, and other cancers, but the firm is looking for even more uses for it. Merck has expanded its oncology team, doctors who study and treat cancer, from 20 to 100 specialists. The firm has over 700 clinical trials examining how Keytruda could treat more than 30 types of cancer. Over half of Merck's budget for clinical trials is aimed at Keytruda. Merck's R&D head, Roger Perlmutter, put it bluntly to his staff when he said, "Whatever other projects you're working on, you can stop now, because we're doing this, and we're going to put a lot of muscle behind this."

Not all clinical trials have produced positive outcomes. The drug did not appear to extend the survival of gastric cancer patients. Still, the general news has been positive. Trials for kidney, brain, lung, and esophageal cancers have shown positive results. The sales of the drug have been growing rapidly, making up 9 percent of Merck's sales in 2017 and is projected to make up nearly 20 percent of the firm's sales in 2019, $8 billion in sales for the one drug alone. Even with its success, some wonder if Merck is investing too heavily in this one patented drug.

Discussion Questions

1. Why is Merck investing so heavily in this one drug? What are the risks and opportunities?
2. What are the long-term implications for Merck's culture, its human resources, and its knowledge base?
3. Is this a good "bet the company" decision? How do you think Merck should move forward from here?

Sources: Loftus, P. 2018. Why Merck is betting big on one cancer drug. *The Wall Street Journal*, April 15; Mishra, M. 2019. Merck's Keytruda tops $2 billion in quarterly sales, shares rise. *reuters.com*, February 1: np; and Gapper, J. 2019. Keytruda shows the high price of curing cancer. *ft.com*, February 13: np.

Reflecting on Career Implications . . .

This chapter addresses the importance of the internal environment for strategic managers. As a strategic manager, you should fully understand how you can leverage your competencies to both bring value to your firm and enhance your career opportunities.

- **The Value Chain:** It is important that you develop an understanding of your firm's value chain. What activities are most critical for attaining competitive advantage? Think of ways in which you can add value in your firm's value chain. How might your firm's support activities (e.g., information technology, human resource practices) help you accomplish your assigned tasks more effectively? How will you bring your value-added contribution to the attention of your superiors?
- **The Value Chain:** Consider the most important linkages between the activities you perform in your organization with other activities both within your firm and between your firm and its suppliers, customers, and alliance partners. Understanding and strengthening these linkages can contribute greatly to your career advancement within your current organization.
- **Resource-Based View of the Firm:** Are your skills and talents rare, valuable, and difficult to imitate, and do they have few substitutes? If so, you are in the better position to add value for your firm—and earn rewards and incentives. How can your skills and talents be enhanced to help satisfy these criteria to a greater extent? Get more training? Change positions within the firm? Consider career options at other organizations?
- **Balanced Scorecard:** Can you design a balanced scorecard for your life? What perspectives would you include in it? In what ways would such a balanced scorecard help you attain success in life?

key points

LO3-1 The primary and support activities of a firm's value chain.

- Primary activities include all parts of the organization that are involved in the direct physical creation, distribution, sale, or servicing of the firms products and services, including inbound logistics, operations, outbound logistics, marketing and sales, and service.
- Support activities either add value themselves or in combination with both primary and other support activities, including procurement, technology development, human resource management, and general administration.

LO3-2 How value-chain analysis can help managers create value by investigating relationships among activities within the firm and between the firm and its customers and suppliers.

- It is important to understand each of the firm's value-chain activities, but real firm value is generated when the firm leverages relationships among the different activities.
- This includes (1) interrelationships among activities within the firm and (2) relationships among activities within the firm and its suppliers and customers.
- Interrelationships improve overall firm value when they involve the effective coordination of actions and exchange of resources, such as information, technology, and people.

LO3-3 The resource-based view of the firm and the different types of tangible and intangible resources, as well as organizational capabilities.

- The resource-based view of the firm considers the firm as a bundle of resources: tangible resources, intangible resources, and organizational capabilities.
- Competitive advantages that are sustainable over time generally arise from the creation of bundles of resources and capabilities.

LO3-4 The four criteria that a firm's resources must possess to maintain a sustainable advantage and how value created can be appropriated by employees and managers.

- For advantages to be sustainable, four criteria must be satisfied: value, rarity, difficulty in imitation, and difficulty in substitution.
- The owners of a business may not capture all of the value created by the firm. The appropriation of value created by a firm between the owners and employees

is determined by four factors: employee bargaining power, replacement cost, employee exit costs, and manager bargaining power.

LO3-5 The usefulness of financial ratio analysis, its inherent limitations, and how to make meaningful comparisons of performance across firms.

- Financial ratio analysis involves identifying how a firm is performing according to its balance sheet, income statement, and market valuation.
- Common measures assessed include short-term solvency, long-term solvency, asset utilization, profitability, and market value ratios.
- Assessing the firm's performance is also more useful if it is evaluated in terms of how it changes over time, compares with industry norms, and compares with key competitors.

LO3-6 The value of the "balanced scorecard" in recognizing how the interests of a variety of stakeholders can be interrelated.

- Determining a firm's performance requires an analysis of its financial situation as well as a review of how well it is satisfying a broad range of stakeholders, including customers, employees, and stockholders.
- With the balanced scorecard, four perspectives are addressed: customer; internal business; innovation and learning; and financial factors.
- Central to this concept is the idea that the interests of various stakeholders can be interrelated. Thus, improving a firm's performance does not necessarily need to involve making trade-offs among different stakeholders.

SUMMARY REVIEW QUESTIONS

1. SWOT analysis is a technique to analyze the internal and external environments of a firm. What are its advantages and disadvantages?
2. Briefly describe the primary and support activities in a firm's value chain.
3. How can managers create value by establishing important relationships among the value-chain activities both within their firm and between the firm and its customers and suppliers?
4. Briefly explain the four criteria for sustainability of competitive advantages.
5. Under what conditions are employees and managers able to appropriate some of the value created by their firm?
6. What are the advantages and disadvantages of conducting a financial ratio analysis of a firm?
7. Summarize the concept of the balanced scorecard. What are its main advantages?

key terms

value-chain analysis 74
primary activities 74
support activities 74
inbound logistics 74
operations 75
outbound logistics 75
marketing and sales 76
service 76
procurement 76
technology development 78
human resource management 78
general administration 78
interrelationships 79
resource-based view (RBV) of the firm 81
tangible resources 83
intangible resources 83
organizational capabilities 83
path dependency 85
causal ambiguity 86
social complexity 86
financial ratio analysis 90
balanced scorecard 93
customer perspective 94
internal business perspective 94
innovation and learning perspective 94
financial perspective 94

EXPERIENTIAL EXERCISES AND APPLICATION QUESTIONS

1. In the Learning from Mistakes at the beginning of the chapter, we saw how KFC became too focused on cutting cost in their supply chain, and it hampered their ability to be able to serve customers effectively. Imagine you were advising KFC on how they need to emphasize the customer-orientation of every link in their value chain. To support this, lay out the key links in KFC's value chain and evaluate how each step is critical to creating customer value.
2. Caterpillar is a leading firm in the construction and mining equipment industry with extensive global operations. It has approximately 98,000 employees, and its revenues were $54 billion in 2018. In addition to its manufacturing and logistics operations, Caterpillar is well known for its superb service and parts supply, and it provides retail financing for its equipment. The following questions focus on Caterpillar's value-chain activities and the interrelationships among them as well as whether or not the firm is able to attain sustainable competitive advantage(s).

a. Where in Caterpillar's value chain is the firm creating value for its customers?

Value-Chain Activity	Yes/No	How Does Caterpillar Create Value for the Customer?
Primary:		
Inbound logistics		
Operations		
Outbound logistics		
Marketing and sales		
Service		
Support:		
Procurement		
Technology development		
Human resource management		
General administration		

b. What are the important relationships among Caterpillar's value-chain activities? What are the important interdependencies? For each activity, identify the relationships and interdependencies.

	Inbound logistics	Operations	Outbound logistics	Marketing and sales	Service	Procurement	Technology development	Human resource management	General administration
Inbound logistics									
Operations									
Outbound logistics									
Marketing and sales									
Service									
Procurement									
Technology development									
Human resource management									
General administration									

c. What resources, activities, and relationships enable Caterpillar to achieve a sustainable competitive advantage?

Resource/Activity	Is It Valuable?	Is It Rare?	Are There Few Substitutes?	Is It Difficult to Make?
Inbound logistics				
Operations				
Outbound logistics				
Marketing and sales				
Service				
Procurement				
Technology development				
Human resource management				
General administration				

3. Using published reports, select two CEOs who have recently made public statements regarding a major change in their firm's strategy. Discuss how the successful implementation of such strategies requires changes in the firm's primary and support activities.
4. Select a firm that competes in an industry in which you are interested. Drawing upon published financial reports, complete a financial ratio analysis. Based on changes over time and a comparison with industry norms, evaluate the firm's strengths and weaknesses in terms of its financial position.
5. How might exemplary human resource practices enhance and strengthen a firm's value-chain activities?
6. Using the Internet, look up your university or college. What are some of its key value-creating activities that provide competitive advantages? Why?

ETHICS QUESTIONS

1. What are some of the ethical issues that arise when a firm becomes overly zealous in advertising its products?
2. What are some of the ethical issues that may arise from a firm's procurement activities? Are you aware of any of these issues from your personal experience or businesses you are familiar with?

REFERENCES

1. Ellis, J, 2018. At KFC, a bucketful of trouble. *Bloomberg Businessweek*. March 5: 20-22.; Wood, Z. 2018. KFC returns to original supplier after chicken shortage fiasco. theguardian.com. March 8: np.; and O'Marah, K. 2018. 3 supply chain lessons from the KFC fowl-up. forbes.com. March 1: np.
2. Our discussion of the value chain will draw on Porter, M. E. 1985. *Competitive advantage:* chap. 2. New York: Free Press.
3. Dyer, J. H. 1996. Specialized supplier networks as a source of competitive advantage: Evidence from the auto industry. *Strategic Management Journal,* 17: 271-291.
4. For an insightful perspective on value-chain analysis, refer to Stabell, C. B. & Fjeldstad, O. D. 1998. Configuring value for competitive advantage: On chains, shops, and networks. *Strategic Management Journal,* 19: 413-437. The authors develop concepts of value chains, value shops, and value networks to extend the value-creation logic across a broad range of industries. Their work builds on the seminal contributions of Porter, 1985, op. cit., and others who have addressed how firms create value through key interrelationships among value-creating activities.
5. Ibid.
6. Shaw Industries. 1999. Annual report: 14-15.
7. Fisher, M. L. 1997. What is the right supply chain for your product? *Harvard Business Review,* 75(2): 105-116.
8. Jackson, M. 2001. Bringing a dying brand back to life. *Harvard Business Review,* 79(5): 53-61.
9. Anderson, J. C. & Nmarus, J. A. 2003. Selectively pursuing more of your customer's business. *MIT Sloan Management Review,* 44(3): 42-50.
10. Insights on advertising are addressed in Rayport, J. F. 2008. Where is advertising going? Into 'stitials. *Harvard Business Review,* 66(5): 18-20.
11. Fleck, A. 2018. 6 Product Placements on TV So Good You Didn't Realize You Were Being Sold Something. adweek.com. August 8: np.
12. For a scholarly discussion on the procurement of technology components, read Hoetker, G. 2005. How much you know versus how well I know you: Selecting a supplier for a technically innovative component. *Strategic Management Journal,* 26(1): 75-96.
13. For a discussion on criteria to use when screening suppliers for back-office functions, read Feeny, D., Lacity, M., & Willcocks, L. p. 2005. Taking the measure of outsourcing providers. *MIT Sloan Management Review,* 46(3): 41-48.
14. For a study investigating sourcing practices, refer to Safizadeh, M. H., Field, J. M., & Ritzman, L. P. 2008. Sourcing practices and boundaries of the firm in the financial services industry. *Strategic Management Journal,* 29(1): 79-92.
15. Imperato, G. 1998. How to give good feedback. *Fast Company,* September: 144-156.
16. Imperato, G. 1998. How Microsoft reviews suppliers. *Fast Company*.
17. Bensaou, B. M. & Earl, M. 1998. The right mindset for managing information technology. *Harvard Business Review,* 96(5): 118-128.
18. A discussion of R&D in the pharmaceutical industry is in Garnier, J-p. 2008. Rebuilding the R&D engine in big pharma. *Harvard Business Review,* 66(5): 68-76.
19. Ulrich, D. 1998. A new mandate for human resources. *Harvard Business Review,* 96(1): 124-134.
20. A study of human resource management in China is Li, J., Lam, K., Sun, J. J. M., & Liu, S. X. Y. 2008. Strategic resource management, institutionalization, and employment modes: An empirical study in China. *Strategic Management Journal,* 29(3): 337-342.
21. Wood, J. 2003. Sharing jobs and working from home: The new face of the airline industry. *AviationCareer.net:* February 21.
22. Gellman, L. 2015. When a job offer comes without a job. *Wall Street Journal.* December 2: B1, B7.
23. For insights on the role of information systems integration in fostering innovation, refer to Cash, J. I. Jr., Earl, M. J., & Morison, R. 2008. Teaming up to crack innovation and enterprise integration. *Harvard Business Review,* 66(11): 90-100.
24. For a cautionary note on the use of IT, refer to McAfee, A. 2003. When too much IT knowledge is a dangerous thing. *MIT Sloan Management Review,* 44(2): 83-90.
25. For an interesting perspective on some of the potential downsides of close customer and supplier relationships, refer to Anderson, E. & Jap, S. D. 2005. The dark side of close relationships. *MIT Sloan Management Review,* 46(3): 75-82.
26. Day, G. S. 2003. Creating a superior customer-relating capability. *MIT Sloan Management Review,* 44(3): 77-82.
27. To gain insights on the role of electronic technologies in enhancing a firm's connections to outside suppliers and customers, refer to Lawrence, T. B., Morse, E. A., &

Fowler, S. W. 2005. Managing your portfolio of connections. *MIT Sloan Management Review,* 46(2): 59-66.

28. Collis, D. J. & Montgomery, C. A. 1995. Competing on resources: Strategy in the 1990's. *Harvard Business Review,* 73(4): 119-128; and Barney, J. 1991. Firm resources and sustained competitive advantage. *Journal of Management,* 17(1): 99-120.
29. For critiques of the resource-based view of the firm, refer to Sirmon, D. G., Hitt, M. A., & Ireland, R. D. 2007. Managing firm resources in dynamic environments to create value: Looking inside the black box. *Academy of Management Review,* 32(1): 273-292; and Newbert, S. L. 2007. Empirical research on the resource-based view of the firm: An assessment and suggestions for future research. *Strategic Management Journal,* 28(2): 121-146.
30. Henkoff, R. 1993. Companies that train the best. *Fortune,* March 22: 83; and Dess & Picken, *Beyond productivity,* p. 98.
31. Gaines-Ross, L. 2010. Reputation warfare. *Harvard Business Review,* 88(12): 70-76.
32. Barney, J. B. 1986. Types of competition and the theory of strategy: Towards an integrative framework. *Academy of Management Review,* 11(4): 791-800.
33. Harley-Davidson. 1993. Annual report.
34. Stetler, B. 2008. Griping online? Comcast hears and talks back. *nytimes.com,* July 25: np.
35. For a rigorous, academic treatment of the origin of capabilities, refer to Ethiraj, S. K., Kale, P., Krishnan, M. S., & Singh, J. V. 2005. Where do capabilities come from and how do they matter? A study of the software services industry. *Strategic Management Journal,* 26(1): 25-46.
36. For an academic discussion on methods associated with organizational capabilities, refer to Dutta, S., Narasimhan, O., & Rajiv, S. 2005. Conceptualizing and measuring capabilities: Methodology and empirical application. *Strategic Management Journal,* 26(3): 277-286.
37. Lorenzoni, G. & Lipparini, A. 1999. The leveraging of interfirm relationships as a distinctive organizational capability: A longitudinal study. *Strategic Management Journal,* 20: 317-338.
38. A study investigating the sustainability of competitive advantage is Newbert, S. L. 2008. Value, rareness, competitive advantages, and performance: A conceptual-level empirical investigation of the resource-based view of the firm. *Strategic Management Journal,* 29(7): 745-768.
39. Arikan, A. M. & McGahan, A. M. 2010. The development of capabilities in new firms. *Strategic Management Journal,* 31(1): 1-18.
40. Barney, J. 1991. Firm resources and sustained competitive advantage. *Journal of Management,* 17(1): 99-120.
41. Barney, 1986, op. cit. Our discussion of inimitability and substitution draws upon this source.
42. A study that investigates the performance implications of imitation is Ethiraj, S. K. & Zhu, D. H. 2008. Performance effects of imitative entry. *Strategic Management Journal,* 29(8): 797-818.
43. Sirmon, D. G., Hitt, M. A., Arregale, J.-L. & Campbell, J. T. 2010. The dynamic interplay of capability strengths and weaknesses: Investigating the bases of temporary competitive advantage. *Strategic Management Journal,* 31(13): 1386-1409.
44. Deephouse, D. L. 1999. To be different, or to be the same? It's a question (and theory) of strategic balance. *Strategic Management Journal,* 20: 147-166.
45. Hagerty, J. 2015. A radical idea: Own your supply chain. *Wall Street Journal.* April 30: B1-B2.
46. Karlgaard, R. 2014. *The soft edge.* San Francisco: Jossey-Bass.
47. EN. Byrne, J. 2018. 139 taxi medallions will be offered at bankruptcy auction. nypost.com. June 9: np.
48. Robins, J. A. & Wiersema, M. F. 2000. Strategies for unstructured competitive environments: Using scarce resources to create new markets. In Bresser, R. F., et al. (Eds.), *Winning strategies in a deconstructing world:* 201-220. New York: Wiley.
49. Bass, A.S. 2018. GrAIt expectations. *The Economist.* March 31: 3-12. Cohen, S.A. & Granade, M.W. 2018. *wsj.com.* August 19: np.
50. Amit, R. & Schoemaker, J. H. 1993. Strategic assets and organizational rent. *Strategic Management Journal,* 14(1): 33-46; Collis, D. J. & Montgomery, C. A. 1995. Competing on resources: Strategy in the 1990's. *Harvard Business Review,* 73(4): 118-128; Coff, R. W. 1999. When competitive advantage doesn't lead to performance: The resource-based view and stakeholder bargaining power. *Organization Science,* 10(2): 119-133; and Blyler, M. & Coff, R. W. 2003. Dynamic capabilities, social capital, and rent appropriation: Ties that split pies. *Strategic Management Journal,* 24: 677-686.
51. Munk, N. 1998. The new organization man. *Fortune,* March 16: 62-74.
52. Coff, op. cit.
53. Elmer-Dewitt, P. 2016. How Much Does Apple Pay Jony Ive? fortune. com. January 7: np.
54. Anonymous. 2013. "All of them are overpaid": Bank CEOs got average 7.7% raise. *www.moneynews.com,* June 3: np.
55. We have focused our discussion on how internal stakeholders (e.g., employees, managers, and top executives) may appropriate a firm's profits (or rents). For an interesting discussion of how a firm's innovations may be appropriated by external stakeholders (e.g., customers, suppliers) as well as competitors, refer to Grant, R. M. 2002. *Contemporary strategy analysis* (4th ed.): 335-340. Malden, MA: Blackwell.
56. Luehrman, T. A. 1997. What's it worth? A general manager's guide to valuation. *Harvard Business Review,* 45(3): 132-142.
57. See, for example, Kaplan, R. S. & Norton, D. p. 1992. The balanced scorecard: Measures that drive performance. *Harvard Business Review,* 69(1): 71-79.
58. Hitt, M. A., Ireland, R. D., & Stadter, G. 1982. Functional importance of company performance: Moderating effects of grand strategy and industry type. *Strategic Management Journal,* 3: 315-330.
59. *finance.yahoo.com.*
60. Kaplan & Norton, op. cit.
61. Ibid.
62. For a discussion of the relative value of growth versus increasing margins, read Mass, N. J. 2005. The relative value of growth. *Harvard Business Review,* 83(4): 102-112.
63. Our discussion draws upon: Angel, R. & Rampersad, H. 2005. Do scorecards add up? *camagazine.com.* May: np.; and Niven, p. 2002. *Balanced scorecard step by step: Maximizing performance and maintaining results.* New York: John Wiley & Sons.

©Nico Muller Art/Shutterstock

CHAPTER

4

Recognizing a Firm's Intellectual Assets

Moving beyond a Firm's Tangible Resources

Learning Objectives

LO4-1 Explain why the management of knowledge professionals and knowledge itself is so critical in today's organizations.

LO4-2 Understand the importance of recognizing the interdependence of attracting, developing, and retaining human capital.

LO4-3 Describe the key role of social capital in leveraging human capital within and across the firm.

LO4-4 Explain the importance of social networks in knowledge management and in promoting career success.

LO4-5 Describe the vital role of technology in leveraging knowledge and human capital.

LO4-6 Explain why "electronic" or "virtual" teams are critical in combining and leveraging knowledge in organizations and how they can be made more effective.

LO4-7 Identify the challenge of protecting intellectual property and the importance of a firm's dynamic capabilities.

We encourage you to reflect on how the concepts presented in this chapter can enhance your career success (see "Reflecting on Career Implications..." at the end of the chapter).

LEARNING FROM MISTAKES

The 2012 bankruptcy of storied law firm Dewey & LeBoeuf LLP illustrates how even well-established firms can fail because of ineffective management of their talent. The failure of the firm is attributable to three major issues: a reliance on borrowed money, making large promises about compensation to incoming (called "lateral") partners, and a lack of transparency about the firm's financials.

Partnership in a major law firm, considered the brass ring in a legal career, once came with lifetime security, prestige, and entry into the 1 percent—and at times, the one-tenth of the 1 percent. However, the collapse of Dewey & LeBoeuf laid bare the increasingly Darwinian competition for lucrative clients that has afflicted even the highest ranks of the profession. Here was a firm that traced its roots to the 19th century and bore the name of a former Republican presidential candidate and New York governor, Thomas E. Dewey. The New York–based law firm once had 1,300 lawyers but filed for bankruptcy amid a huge exodus of talent and mounting debt. Few firms borrowed as much money as Dewey & LeBoeuf did—its credit line included a private bond placement of $125 million in 2010. And transparency did not seem to be one of Dewey's strengths: Some only learned about this transaction when it surfaced in a news report. One former partner said: "I read about it in the papers. And I certainly didn't sign off on it."

In 2007, Dewey & LeBoeuf was formed in a widely hailed merger of insurance-and-energy-focused LeBoeuf, Lamb, Greene & MacRae LLP, and Dewey Ballantine LLP. However, things soured quickly. The newly merged firm grew aggressively by making promises it ultimately couldn't honor—guaranteeing new partners huge salaries, sometimes over $5 million a year. Legacy partners were definitely not happy that new hires were being treated better than they were and, of course, demanded pay pacts of their own. By the fall of 2011, roughly a third of the firm's 300 partners had salary guarantees.

Large law firms sometimes woo big stars by promising to pay them a fixed amount for a year or two—regardless of the firm's or their own financial performance. But most firms use such guarantees very sparingly. By all accounts, Dewey took this practice to an extreme and made compensation guarantees for multiple years. To make matters worse, it offered guarantees to lawyers who did not prove to be rainmakers. News of the widespread guarantees angered the rank-and-file partners at Dewey, many of whom left the firm. Dewey's performance continued to suffer and after a round of failed merger attempts, the firm liquidated. This left thousands of staff and junior lawyers unemployed, and it became the largest law firm failure in U.S. history.

Elizabeth Sharrer, the chairwoman of 500-lawyer Holland and Hart LLP, said, "Leaders hopefully have learned a lesson that if you're making someone a compensation deal you have to hide from our partners, it's not a good deal." Law firms can dissolve within weeks if spooked partners bail. Sharrer notes, "You can circle the drain really, really quickly." Interviews with former partners, consultants, and others in the industry depict Dewey as a firm run by an insular coterie of attorneys and administrators who often withheld critical information from their partners, undermining their own credibility in the process. When the Great Recession of 2008 and 2009 hit and deep problems came to the surface, a sense of shared sacrifice and loyalty was in short supply!

Discussion Questions

1. How could these problems have been avoided at Dewey & LeBoeuf?
2. What practices should firms such as Dewey & LeBoeuf implement to attract and retain top talent?

Sources: Randazzo, S. 2015. Legal industry learns from Dewey's mistakes. *The Wall Street Journal*, October 19.; Stewart, J. B. 2014. The rise and fall of a rainmaker. *nytimes.com,* December 12: np; Longstreth, A., and N. Raymond. 2012. The Dewey chronicles: The rise and fall of a legal titan, *reuters.com,* May 11: np; and Frank, A. D. 2012. The end of an era. *fortune.com,* May 29: np.

Managers are always looking for stellar professionals who can take their organizations to the next level. However, attracting talent is a necessary but *not* sufficient condition for success. In today's knowledge economy, it does not matter how big your stock of resources is—whether it be top talent, physical resources, or financial capital. Rather, the question becomes: How good is the organization at attracting top talent and leveraging that talent to produce a stream of products and services valued by the marketplace?

Clearly, Dewey & LeBoeuf failed in retaining top talent. The firm lacked transparency and its partners were very resentful when they discovered that newly hired partners were provided with huge guaranteed pay packages. And, as noted, when major problems arose at the firm, there was very little goodwill among the legacy partners. Not surprisingly, many of them bolted and, as is frequently the case, took many of their clients with them.

In this chapter, we also address how human capital can be leveraged in an organization. We point out the important roles of social capital and technology.

LO 4-1

Explain why the management of knowledge professionals and knowledge itself is so critical in today's organizations.

THE CENTRAL ROLE OF KNOWLEDGE IN TODAY'S ECONOMY

Central to our discussion is an enormous change that has accelerated over the past few decades and its implications for the strategic management of organizations.[1] For most of the 20th century, managers focused on tangible resources such as land, equipment, and money as well as intangibles such as brands, image, and customer loyalty. Efforts were directed more toward the efficient allocation of labor and capital—the two traditional factors of production.

How times have changed. In the last quarter century, employment in the manufacturing sector declined at a significant rate. Today only 8.5 percent of the U.S. workforce is employed in this sector, compared to 21 percent in 1980. In contrast, the service sector grew from 73 percent of the workforce in 1980 to 79.5 percent by 2017.[2]

The knowledge-worker segment, in particular, is growing dramatically. Using a broad definition, it is estimated that knowledge workers currently outnumber other types of workers in the United States by at least four to one—they represent between a quarter and a half of all workers in advanced economies. Recent popular press has gone so far as to suggest that, due to the increased speed and competitiveness of modern business, all modern employees are knowledge workers.

knowledge economy
an economy where wealth is created through the effective management of knowledge workers instead of by the efficient control of physical and financial assets.

In the **knowledge economy,** wealth is increasingly created by effective management of knowledge workers instead of by the efficient control of physical and financial assets. The growing importance of knowledge, coupled with the move by labor markets to reward knowledge work, tells us that investing in a company is, in essence, buying a set of talents, capabilities, skills, and ideas—intellectual capital—not physical and financial resources.[3]

Human capital is growing more valuable in virtually every business.[4] This trend has been going on for decades as ever fewer workers function as low-maintenance machines—for example, turning a wrench in a factory—and more become thinkers and creators. Intangible assets, mostly derived from human capital, have soared from 17 percent of the S&P 500's market value in 1975 to 84 percent in 2015, according to the advisory firm Ocean Tomo. Even a manufacturer such as Stryker gets 70 percent of its value from intangibles; it makes replacement knees, hips, and other joints that are, in essence, loaded with intellectual capital.

To apply some numbers to our arguments, let's ask, What's a company worth?[5] Start with the "big three" financial statements: income statement, balance sheet, and statement of cash flow. If these statements tell a story that investors find useful, then a company's market

Company	Annual Sales ($ billions)	Market Value ($ billions)	Book Value ($ billions)	Ratio of Market to Book Value
Microsoft	110.4	798.2	82.7	9.5
Apple	266.0	720.3	107.1	6.7
Alphabet (parent of Google)	110.9	738.0	152.5	4.8
Intel	62.7	223.3	69.0	3.2
Nucor	20.3	17.7	9.1	1.9
General Motors	145.6	54.5	36.2	1.5

Note: The data on market valuations are as of January 13, 2019. All other financial data are based on the most recently available balance sheets and income statements.

Source: *finance.yahoo.com*.

EXHIBIT 4.1

Ratio of Market Value to Book Value for Selected Companies

value* should roughly (but not precisely, because the market looks forward and the books look backward) be the same as the value that accountants ascribe to it–the book value of the firm. However, this is not the case. A study compared the market value with the book value of 3,500 U.S. companies over a period of several decades. In 1978 the two were similar: Book value was 95 percent of market value. However, market values and book values have diverged significantly. By early 2019, the S&P industrials were–on average–trading at 3.10 times book value.[6] Robert A. Howell, an expert on the changing role of finance and accounting, muses, "The big three financial statements . . . are about as useful as an 80-year-old Los Angeles road map."

The gap between a firms market value and book value is far greater for knowledge-intensive corporations than for firms with strategies based primarily on tangible assets.[7] Exhibit 4.1 shows the ratio of market-to-book value for some well-known companies. In firms where knowledge and the management of knowledge workers are relatively important contributors to developing products and services–and physical resources are less critical–the ratio of market-to-book value tends to be much higher.

As shown in Exhibit 4.1, firms such as Microsoft, Apple, and Alphabet (parent of Google) have very high market value to book value ratios because of their high investment in knowledge resources and technological expertise. In contrast, firms in more traditional industry sectors such as Nucor and General Motors have relatively low market-to-book ratios. This reflects their greater investment in physical resources and lower investment in knowledge resources. A firm like Intel has a market-to-book value ratio that falls between the above two groups of firms. This is because its high level of investment in knowledge resources is matched by a correspondingly huge investment in plant and equipment. For example, Intel invested $3 billion to build a fabrication facility in Chandler, Arizona.[8]

intellectual capital the difference between the market value of the firm and the book value of the firm, including assets such as reputation, employee loyalty and commitment, customer relationships, company values, brand names, and the experience and skills of employees.

Many writers have defined **intellectual capital** as the difference between a firm's market value and book value–that is, a measure of the value of a firm's intangible assets.[9] This broad definition includes assets such as reputation, employee loyalty and commitment, customer relationships, company values, brand names, and the experience and skills of employees.[10] Thus, simplifying, we have:

$$\text{Intellectual capital} = \text{Market value of firm} - \text{Book value of firm}$$

*The market value of a firm is equal to the value of a share of its common stock times the number of shares outstanding. The book value of a firm is primarily a measure of the value of its tangible assets. It can be calculated by the formula Total assets - Total liabilities.

How do companies create value in the knowledge-intensive economy? The general answer is to attract and leverage human capital effectively through mechanisms that create products and services of value over time.

human capital
the individual capabilities, knowledge, skills, and experience of a company's employees and managers.

social capital
the network of friendships and working relationships between talented people both inside and outside the organization.

explicit knowledge
knowledge that is codified, documented, easily reproduced, and widely distributed.

tacit knowledge
knowledge that is in the minds of employees and is based on their experiences and backgrounds.

First, **human capital** is the "*individual* capabilities, knowledge, skills, and experience of the company's employees and managers."[11] This knowledge is relevant to the task at hand, as well as the capacity to add to this reservoir of knowledge, skills, and experience through learning.[12]

Second, **social capital** is "the network of relationships that individuals have throughout the organization." Relationships are critical in sharing and leveraging knowledge and in acquiring resources.[13] Social capital can extend beyond the organizational boundaries to include relationships between the firm and its suppliers, customers, and alliance partners.[14]

Third is the concept of "knowledge," which comes in two different forms. First, there is **explicit knowledge** that is codified, documented, easily reproduced, and widely distributed, such as engineering drawings, software code, and patents.[15] The other type of knowledge is **tacit knowledge** that is in the minds of employees and is based on their experiences and backgrounds.[16] Tacit knowledge is shared only with the consent and participation of the individual.

New knowledge is constantly created through the continual interaction of explicit and tacit knowledge. Consider two software engineers working together on a computer code. The computer code is the explicit knowledge. By sharing ideas based on each individual's experience—that is, their tacit knowledge—they create new knowledge when they modify the code. Another important issue is the role of "socially complex processes," which include leadership, culture, and trust.[17] These processes play a central role in the creation of knowledge.[18] They represent the "glue" that holds the organization together and helps to create a working environment where individuals are more willing to share their ideas, work in teams, and, in the end, create products and services of value.[19]

Numerous books have been written on the subject of knowledge management and the central role that it has played in creating wealth in organizations and countries throughout the developed world.[20] Here, we focus on some of the key issues that organizations must address to compete through knowledge.

We will now turn our discussion to the central resource itself—human capital—and some guidelines on how it can be attracted/selected, developed, and retained.[21] Tom Stewart, former editor of the *Harvard Business Review,* noted that organizations must also undergo significant efforts to protect their human capital. A firm may "diversify the ownership of vital knowledge by emphasizing teamwork, guard against obsolescence by developing learning programs, and shackle key people with golden handcuffs."[22] In addition, people are less likely to leave an organization if there are effective structures to promote teamwork and information sharing, strong leadership that encourages innovation, and cultures that demand excellence and ethical behavior. Such issues are central to this chapter. Although we touch on these issues throughout this chapter, we provide more detail in later chapters. We discuss organizational controls (culture, rewards, and boundaries) in Chapter 9, organization structure and design in Chapter 10, and a variety of leadership and entrepreneurship topics in Chapters 11 and 12.

LO 4-2

Understand the importance of recognizing the interdependence of attracting, developing, and retaining human capital.

HUMAN CAPITAL: THE FOUNDATION OF INTELLECTUAL CAPITAL

Take away my people, but leave my factories and soon grass will grow on the factory floors. . . . Take away my factories, but leave my people and soon we will have a new and better factory.[23]

—*Andrew Carnegie, Steel industry legend*

The importance of talent to organization success is hardly new. Organizations must recruit talented people—employees at all levels with the proper sets of skills and capabilities coupled with the right values and attitudes. Such skills and attitudes must be continually developed, strengthened, and reinforced, and each employee must be motivated and his or her efforts focused on the organization's goals and objectives.[24]

The rise to prominence of knowledge workers as a vital source of competitive advantage is changing the balance of power in today's organization.[25] Knowledge workers place professional development and personal enrichment (financial and otherwise) above company loyalty. Attracting, recruiting, and hiring the "best and the brightest" is a critical first step in the process of building intellectual capital. As noted by law professor Orly Lobel, in her book, *Talent Wants to be Free*:[26]

> Companies like Microsoft, Google, and Facebook are so hungry for talent that they acquire (or, as the tech-buzz is now calling it, acq-hire) entire start-ups only to discard the product and keep the teams, founders, and engineers.

Hiring is only the first of three processes in which all successful organizations must engage to build and leverage their human capital. Firms must also *develop* employees to fulfill their full potential to maximize their joint contributions.[27] Finally, the first two processes are for naught if firms can't provide the working environment and intrinsic and extrinsic rewards to *engage* their best and brightest.[28] Interestingly, a recent Gallup study showed that companies whose workers are the most engaged outperform those with the least engaged by a significant amount: 16 percent higher profitability, 18 percent higher productivity, and 25 to 49 percent lower turnover (depending on the industry).[29] The last benefit can really be significant: Software leader SAP calculated that "for each percentage point that our retention rate goes up or down, the impact on our operating profit is approximately $81 million."

These activities are highly interrelated. We would like to suggest the imagery of a three-legged stool (see Exhibit 4.2).[30] If one leg is weak or broken, the stool collapses.

To illustrate such interdependence, poor hiring impedes the effectiveness of development and retention processes. In a similar vein, ineffective retention efforts place additional burdens on hiring and development. Consider the following anecdote, provided by Jeffrey Pfeffer of the Stanford University Graduate School of Business:

> Not long ago, I went to a large, fancy San Francisco law firm—where they treat their associates like dog doo and where the turnover is very high. I asked the managing partner about the turnover rate. He said, "A few years ago, it was 25 percent, and now we're up to 30 percent." I asked him how the firm had responded to that trend. He said, "We increased our recruiting." So I asked him, "What kind of doctor would you be if your patient was bleeding faster and faster, and your only response was to increase the speed of the transfusion?"[31]

EXHIBIT 4.2 Human Capital: Three Interdependent Activities

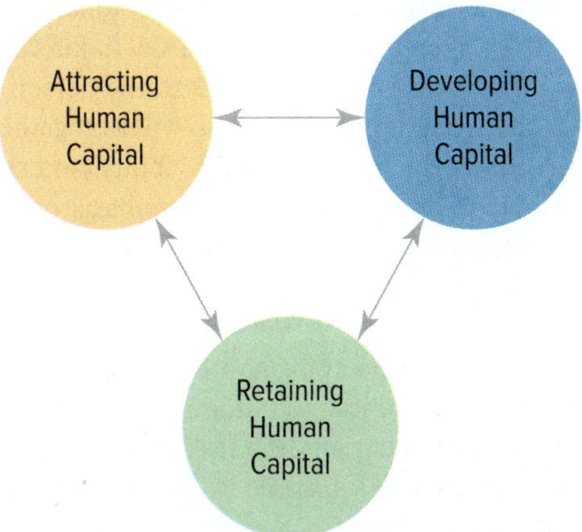

4.1 STRATEGY SPOTLIGHT — ENVIRONMENTAL SUSTAINABILITY

CAN GREEN STRATEGIES ATTRACT AND RETAIN TALENT?

Competing successfully for top talent and retaining high-performing employees are critical factors in an organization's success. Employee recruiting and turnover are, of course, very costly. Losing and replacing a top talent can cost companies up to 200 percent of an employee's annual salary, according to *Engaged! Outbehave Your Competition to Create Customers for Life*.

Today, some 40 percent of job seekers read a company's sustainability report, according to a survey commissioned by the Global Reporting Initiative (GRI). Prospective employees can also riffle through Google in seconds and unearth a myriad of sustainability news and accolades, including an Interbrand "Top 50 Global Green Brand" ranking. Further, a 2014 study by the nonprofit group Net Impact found that business school graduates would take a 15 percent pay cut to:

- Have a job that seeks to make a social or environmental difference in the world (83 percent)
- Have a job in a company committed to corporate and environmental responsibility (71 percent)

Below, we discuss an example of a green initiative by a well-known company that helps attract and retain talent:

- Intel's "Green Intel" intranet portal, environmental sustainability network, and environmental excellence awards are beginning to yield benefits for the company. "Intel's employee engagement has resulted in increased employee loyalty, more company pride, and improved morale," according to Carrie Freeman, a sustainability strategist at the firm. Intel managers expect the next organizational health survey will show increased levels of employee pride and satisfaction with their work, which are considered to be good predictors of employee retention.

Sources: Anonymous. 2015. Why a commitment to sustainability can attract and retain the best talent. *grantthornton.com,* April 30: np; Earley, K. 2014. Sustainabilty gives HR teams an edge in attracting and retaining talent. *www.theguardian.com,* February 20: np; Anonymous. 2010. The business case for environmental and sustainability employee education. *National Environmental Education Foundation,* November: np; Mattioli, D. 2007. How going green draws talent, cuts costs. *Wall Street Journal,* November 13: B10; and Lederman, G. 2013. *Engaged! Outbehave your competition to create customers for life.* Ashland, OR: Evolve.

Clearly, stepped-up recruiting is a poor substitute for weak retention.[32] Although there are no simple, easy-to-apply answers, we can learn from what leading-edge firms are doing to attract, develop, and retain human capital in today's highly competitive marketplace.[33] Before moving on, Strategy Spotlight 4.1 addresses the importance of a firm's "green" or environmental sustainability strategy in attracting young talent.

Attracting Human Capital

In today's world, talent is so critical to the success of what you're doing–their core competencies and how well they fit into your office culture. The combination can be, well, extraordinary. But only if you bring in the right people.[34]

–Mindy Grossman, CEO of WW International (Weight Watchers)

The first step in the process of building superior human capital is input control: attracting and selecting the right person.[35] Human resource professionals often approach employee selection from a "lock and key" mentality–that is, fit a key (a job candidate) into a lock (the job). Such an approach involves a thorough analysis of the person and the job. Only then can the right decision be made as to how well the two will fit together. How can you fail, the theory goes, if you get a precise match of knowledge, ability, and skill profiles? Frequently, however, the precise matching approach places its emphasis on task-specific skills (e.g., motor skills, specific information processing capabilities, and communication skills) and puts less emphasis on the broad general knowledge and experience, social skills, values, beliefs, and attitudes of employees.[36]

Many have questioned the precise matching approach. They argue that firms can identify top performers by focusing on key employee mind-sets, attitudes, social skills, and general orientations. If they get these elements right, the task-specific skills can be learned quickly. (This does not imply, however, that task-specific skills are unimportant; rather, it suggests that the requisite skill sets must be viewed as a necessary but not sufficient condition.)

4.1 *INSIGHTS* from Research

WELCOME BACK! RECRUITING BOOMERANG EMPLOYEES

Overview

The common assumption is that turnover creates vacancy problems and expenses to be avoided at all costs. However, sometimes turnover just can't be prevented. Employees who leave an organization aren't always unhappy–some might be willing to come back if given the opportunity. Consider "boomerang" employees as a key recruiting pool to save time and money.

What the Research Shows

Researchers at Texas Christian University, the University of Cincinnati, the University of Illinois, and the University of North Carolina recently published a study in *Personnel Psychology* that examines why employees leave an organization and why they may be willing to return. Using a sample of 452 employees who left and returned for employment, called "boomerangs," and 1,187 who left but had no desire to return, known as "alumni," the authors examined these employees' motives.

Traditional thinking about employment views employee turnover as an end state, where those who leave never want to return. However, this study suggests that this needn't be the case. There may be value in keeping in touch with employees who leave. These findings indicate that employees' willingness to return in the future is influenced by the reasons they left in the first place: Boomerangs were statistically more likely to leave initially for two main reasons. First, they experienced a negative life event, such as taking care of a sick parent that necessitated a change in employment. Second, they received an alternate job offer deemed too good to turn down. The research did find, however, that boomerangs are more likely to accept those alternate jobs in the same industry. Alumni, on the other hand, were statistically more likely to leave because they were dissatisfied with their jobs or because they wanted to change industries.

Not all employee turnover is bad. In fact, if business leaders understand the motivations for departures, turnover may create opportunities to bring valued employees back.

Key Takeaways

Understanding why employees leave is essential information for company recruiting strategies. Employees are more likely to return and be productive assets if they leave for reasons other than dissatisfaction. Because unhappy employees are more likely to leave and never return, you should monitor and address employee satisfaction levels on an ongoing basis.

Rehiring former employees can save money and time. Make sure your company has exit interviews and alumni programs that track potential boomerang employees.

Research Reviewed

Shipp, A. J., Furst-Holloway, S., Harris, T. B., and B. Rosen. 2014. Gone today but here tomorrow: Extending the unfolding model of turnover to consider boomerang employees. *Personnel Psychology,* 67(2): 421–462.

Discussion Questions

1. What do you think are the key reasons for an organization to rehire an employee? Avoid them?
2. What initiatives can an organization take to attract former employees who are willing to return?

Before we address some ideas about how to go about attracting talent, let's mention a source that is often ignored–former employees. Clearly, not everyone who leaves a company does so because they are unhappy and dissatisfied. Often, they might leave for a new and exciting opportunity. The accompanying *INSIGHTS* from Research 4.1 sidebar discusses the benefits of hiring former employees (often called "boomerangs") who are willing to come back.

"Hire for Attitude, Train for Skill" Organizations are increasingly emphasizing general knowledge and experience, social skills, values, beliefs, and attitudes of employees.[37] Consider Southwest Airlines' hiring practices, which focus on employee values and attitudes. Given its strong team orientation, Southwest uses an "indirect" approach. For example, the interviewing team asks a group of employees to prepare a five-minute presentation about themselves. During the presentations, interviewers observe which candidates enthusiastically support their peers and which candidates focus on polishing their own presentations while the others are presenting.[38] The former are, of course, favored.

Alan Cooper, president of Cooper Software, Inc., in Palo Alto, California, goes further. He cleverly *uses technology* to hone in on the problem-solving ability of his applicants and their attitudes before an interview even takes place. He has devised a "Bozo Filter," an online test that can be applied to any industry. Before you spend time on whether job candidates will work out satisfactorily, find out how their minds work. Cooper advised, "Hiring was a black hole. I don't talk to bozos anymore, because 90 percent of them turn away when they see our test. It's a self-administering bozo filter."[39] How does it work?

> The online test asks questions designed to see how prospective employees approach problem-solving tasks. For example, one key question asks software engineer applicants to design a table-creation software program for Microsoft Word. Candidates provide pencil sketches and a description of the new user interface. Another question used for design communicators asks them to develop a marketing strategy for a new touch-tone phone–directed at consumers in the year 1850. Candidates e-mail their answers back to the company, and the answers are circulated around the firm to solicit feedback. Only candidates with the highest marks get interviews.

Recognizing the Geographic Preferences of Talent The race for talent extends far beyond Silicon Valley.[40] Employers face many challenges: Cutting edge skills are evolving faster than universities can train people, the supply of talented young professionals entering areas such as software and advanced technologies isn't satisfying demand for them, and mobility–one's willingness to uproot their life for a job in a new location–has declined. That is, the odds of luring rare, coveted candidates away from their current position or city are long, according to Michael Brown, Vice President of Talent Acquisition for Siemens, the German industrial conglomerate.

Consider Toyota Motor Corporation. In 2016, it opened the Toyota Research Institute (TRI) with the goal of innovating in areas such as robotics and autonomous driving. The operation has grown to 300 people, half with PhDs, at three locations–Los Altos, California, Cambridge, Massachusetts, and Ann Arbor, Michigan, according to John Hanson, the Institute's spokesman. Why? The locations have developed close alliances with nearby schools–Stanford University, MIT, and the University of Michigan, respectively. This enables Toyota to attract talent who want to maintain formal relationships with their research institutions. For example, John Leonard, who heads TRI's autonomous driving research, continues to teach at MIT, where TRI has spent millions of dollars on research.

Attracting Millennials The Millennial generation has also been termed "Generation Y" or "Echo Boom" and includes people who were born after 1982. Many call them impatient, demanding, or entitled. However, if employers don't provide incentives to attract and retain young workers, somebody else will. Thus, they will be at a competitive disadvantage.[41]

Why? Demographics are on the Millennials' side–within a few years they will outnumber any other generation. The U.S. Bureau of Labor Statistics projects that by 2020 Millennials will make up 40 percent of the workforce. Baby boomers are retiring, and Millennials will be working for the next several decades. Additionally, they have many of the requisite skills to succeed in the future workplace–tech-savviness and the ability to innovate–and they are more racially diverse than any prior generation. Thus, they are better able to relate rapidly to different customs and cultures.

A study from the Center for Work-Life Policy sums this issue up rather well: Instead of the traditional plums of prestigious title, powerful position, and concomitant compensation, Millennials value challenging and diverse job opportunities, stimulating colleagues, a well-designed communal workspace, and flexible work options. In fact, 89 percent of Millennials say that flexible work options are an important consideration in choosing an employer.

Top talent will always be in high demand! At the same time, well-known and attractive employers typically receive thousands of applications each year. To determine who they

4.2 STRATEGY SPOTLIGHT — DIGITAL ECONOMY

UNILEVER'S USE OF ARTIFICIAL INTELLIGENCE TO HIRE THE BEST TALENT

In order to diversify its candidate pool for early-career roles that can be a fast track to management, Unilever PLC, the London-based maker of Dove soap, Axe deodorant, and many other well-known products, decided to do away with its traditional approach to campus recruiting. Instead, the firm has partnered with digital HR service providers Pymetrics and HireView to digitize the first steps in the process. Only after candidates pass the AI screening are they invited for in-person interviews.

Mike Clementi, a Unilever human resources executive explains: "With all the information readily available to us today about job candidates, why would we still choose to go to a small handful of campuses?" Unilever's process involves many steps:

- It places targeted advertisements on Facebook and career-advice sites such as WayUp and the Muse.
- Those who click on the ads are directed to a career site where they can apply for entry positions with just a few clicks (because Unilever can pull the needed information from the candidate's LinkedIn profile to complete the application). An algorithm then scans those applications—presently over 250,000—to select candidates who meet a given role's basic requirements.
- Candidates spend about 20 minutes on a set of 12 neuroscience-based games designed by Pymetrics to assess skills like concentration under pressure and short-term memory.
- The top third of candidates then submit video interviews on HireView, answering questions about how they would respond to business challenges they might face on the job.

During the online process, artificial intelligence can screen out 60 to 80 percent of the applicants. And to determine which candidates are most likely to be successful at Unilever, the AI uses data points such as how quick they respond to questions, as well as their facial expressions and vocabulary.

AI has definitely improved Unilever's hiring process. It is fast and accurate—about 80 percent of applicants who make it to the final round of job interviews get job offers—and a similar percentage accept them. In addition, Unilever was able to hire its "most diverse class to date," applications for jobs doubled, the average time for a candidate to be hired went from four months to four weeks, and recruiters' time spent reviewing applicants decreased by 75 percent. It is probably no surprise that this process that began in North America is now used by Unilever in 68 countries, conducted in 15 languages, and included 250,000 applicants.

Sources: Kelsey, G. 2017. Radical hiring experiment: Resumes are out. *wsj.com*, June 27: np; and Feloni, R. 2017. Consumer-goods giant Unilever has been hiring employees using brain games and artificial intelligence. *businessinsider.com*, June 28: np.

should pursue and hire, technology plays an increasingly important role. Strategy Spotlight 4.2 explains how Unilever is using artificial intelligence to help them make the right choice.

Developing Human Capital

> *CFO asks CEO: "What happens if we invest in developing our people and they leave?" CEO: "What happens if we don't and they stay?"*[42]
>
> *–Peter Baeklund*

It is not enough to hire top-level talent and expect that the skills and capabilities of those employees remain current throughout the duration of their employment. Rather, training and development must take place at all levels of the organization.[43] For example, Solectron assembles printed circuit boards and other components for its Silicon Valley clients.[44] Its employees receive an average of 95 hours of company-provided training each year. Chairman Winston Chen observed, "Technology changes so fast that we estimate 20 percent of an engineer's knowledge becomes obsolete each year. Training is an obligation we owe to our employees. If you want high growth and high quality, then training is a big part of the equation."

Leaders who are committed to developing the people who work for them in order to bring out their strengths and enhance their careers will have committed followers. According to James Rogers, CEO of Duke Energy: "One of the biggest things I find in organizations is that people tend to limit their perceptions of themselves and their capabilities, and one of my challenges is to open them up to the possibilities. I have this belief that anybody can do almost anything in the right context."[45]

In addition to training and developing human capital, firms must encourage widespread involvement, monitor and track employee development, and evaluate human capital.[46]

Encouraging Widespread Involvement Developing human capital requires the active involvement of leaders at all levels. It won't be successful if it is viewed only as the responsibility of the human resource department. Each year at General Electric, 200 facilitators, 30 officers, 30 human resource executives, and many young managers actively participate in GE's orientation program at Crotonville, its training center outside New York City. Topics include global competition, winning on the global playing field, and personal examination of the new employee's core values vis-à-vis GE's values. As a senior manager once commented, "There is nothing like teaching Sunday school to force you to confront your own values."

Similarly, A. G. Lafley, Procter & Gamble's former CEO, claimed that he spent 40 percent of his time on training and developing talent.[47] Andy Grove, who was previously Intel's CEO, required all senior people, including himself, to spend at least a week a year teaching high flyers. And Nitin Paranjpe, CEO of Hindustan Unilever, recruits people from campuses and regularly visits high-potential employees in their offices.

Mentoring Mentoring is most often a formal or informal relationship between two people—a senior mentor and a junior protégé.[48] Mentoring can potentially be a valuable influence in professional development in both the public and private sectors. The war for talent is creating challenges within organizations to recruit new talent as well as retain talent.

Mentoring can provide many benefits—to the organization as well as the individual.[49] For the organization, it can help to recruit qualified managers, decrease turnover, fill senior-level positions with qualified professionals, enhance diversity initiatives with senior-level management, and facilitate organizational change efforts. Individuals can also benefit from effective mentoring programs. These benefits include helping newer employees transition into the organization, helping developmental relationships for people who lack access to informal mentoring relationships, and providing support and challenge to people on an organization's "fast track" to positions of higher responsibility.

Mentoring is traditionally viewed as a program to transfer knowledge and experience from more senior managers to up-and-comers. However, many organizations have reinvented it to fit today's highly competitive, knowledge-intensive industries. For example, consider Intel:

> Intel matches people not by job title and years of experience but by specific skills that are in demand. Lory Lanese, Intel's mentor champion at its huge New Mexico plant (with 5,500 employees), states, "This is definitely not a special program for special people." Instead, Intel's program uses an intranet and e-mail to perform the matchmaking, creating relationships that stretch across state lines and national boundaries. Such an approach enables Intel to spread best practices quickly throughout the far-flung organization. Finally, Intel relies on written contracts and tight deadlines to make sure that its mentoring program gets results—and fast.[50]

Intel has also initiated a mentoring program involving its technical assistants (TAs) who work with senior executives. This concept is sometimes referred to as "reverse mentoring" because senior executives benefit from the insights of professionals who have more updated technical skills—but rank lower in the organizational hierarchy. And, not surprisingly, the TAs stand to benefit quite a bit as well. Here are some insights offered by Andy Grove (formerly Intel's CEO):[51]

> In the 1980s I had a marketing manager named Dennis Carter. I probably learned more from him than anyone in my career. He is a genius. He taught me what brands are. I had no idea—I thought a brand was the name on the box. He showed me the connection of brands to strategies. Dennis went on to be Chief Marketing Officer. He was the person responsible for the Pentium name, "Intel Inside"; he came up with all my good ideas.

Monitoring Progress and Tracking Development Whether a firm uses on-site formal training, off-site training (e.g., universities), or on-the-job training, tracking individual progress–and sharing this knowledge with both the employee and key managers–becomes essential. Like many leading-edge firms, GlaxoSmithKline (GSK) places strong emphasis on broader experiences over longer time periods. Dan Phelan, senior vice president and director of human resources, explained, "We ideally follow a two-plus-two-plus-two formula in developing people for top management positions." This reflects the belief that GSK's best people should gain experience in two business units, two functional units (such as finance and marketing), and two countries.

Other companies may take a less formal approach.[52] Former Alcoa CEO Klaus Kleinfeld says that he brings "the whole executive team into a room for two days to discuss succession planning and the talent that should be developed. We call it Talent Marketplace. In reality it is a fight for great talent."[53] Executives discuss the best employees and candidates for important positions and decide who goes where. "It is not rare that you say, 'Well, that person is ready to develop,' and people are scribbling it down," claims Kleinfeld. "You can bet that when you're not looking, they're already sending notes to the person: 'Hey, we need to talk.'"

Evaluating Human Capital In today's competitive environment, collaboration and interdependence are vital to organizational success. Individuals must share their knowledge and work constructively to achieve collective, not just individual, goals. However, traditional systems evaluate performance from a single perspective (i.e., "top down") and generally don't address the "softer" dimensions of communications and social skills, values, beliefs, and attitudes.[54]

To address the limitations of the traditional approach, many organizations use **360-degree evaluation and feedback systems.**[55] Here, superiors, direct reports, colleagues, and even internal and external customers rate a person's performance.[56] Managers rate themselves to have a personal benchmark. The 360-degree feedback system complements teamwork, employee involvement, and organizational flattening. As organizations continue to push responsibility downward, traditional top-down appraisal systems become insufficient.[57] For example, a manager who previously managed the performance of three supervisors might now be responsible for 10 and is less likely to have the in-depth knowledge needed to appraise and develop them adequately.

360-degree evaluation and feedback systems superiors, direct reports, colleagues, and even external and internal customers rate a person's performance.

At times, a firm's performance assessment methods may get in the way of team success.[58] Microsoft is an example. For many years, the software giant employed a "stack ranking" system as part of its performance evaluation model. With this system, a certain percentage of any team's members would be rated "top performers," "good," "average," "below average," and "poor," regardless of the team's overall performance. Perhaps, in some situations, this type of forced ranking works. However, in Microsoft's case, it had (not too surprisingly!) unintended consequences. Over time, according to inside reports, the stack ranking created a culture in which employees competed with one another rather than against the firm's rivals. And "A" players rarely liked to join groups with other "A" players, because they feared they might be seen as weaker members of the team.

Retaining Human Capital

> *"I like to say that recruiting without a focus on retention is like pouring water into a bucket full of holes."*[59]
>
> –*Josh Harley, CEO of Fathom Realty*

It has been said that talented employees are like "frogs in a wheelbarrow."[60] They can jump out at any time! By analogy, the organization can either try to force employees to stay in the firm or try to keep them from jumping out by creating incentives.[61] In other words, either today's leaders can provide the challenges, work environment, and incentives to keep productive employees and management from wanting to bail out, or they can use legal means such as employment contracts and noncompete clauses.[62] Firms must prevent the transfer of valuable and sensitive information outside the organization. Failure to do so would be the neglect of a leader's fiduciary responsibility to shareholders. However, greater efforts should be directed at the former (e.g., challenges, good work environment, and incentives), but, as we all know, the latter (e.g., employment contracts and noncompete clauses) have their place.[63]

Gary Burnison, CEO of Korn/Ferry International, the world's largest executive search firm, provides an insight on the importance of employee retention:[64]

> How do you extend the life of an employee? This is not an environment where you work for an organization for 20 years. But if you can extend it from three years to six years, that has an enormous impact. Turnover is a huge hidden cost in a profit-and-loss statement that nobody ever focuses on. If there was a line item that showed that, I guarantee you'd have the attention of a CEO.

Identifying with an Organization's Mission and Values People who identify with and are more committed to the core mission and values of the organization are less likely to stray or bolt to the competition. For example, take the perspective of the late Steve Jobs, Apple's widely admired former CEO:[65]

> When I hire somebody really senior, competence is the ante. They have to be really smart. But the real issue for me is: Are they going to fall in love with Apple? Because if they fall in love with Apple, everything else will take care of itself. They'll want to do what's best for Apple, not what's best for them, what's best for Steve, or anyone else.

"Tribal loyalty" is another key factor that links people to the organization.[66] A tribe is not the organization as a whole (unless it is very small). Rather, it is teams, communities of practice, and other groups within an organization or occupation.

Brian Hall, CEO of Values Technology in Santa Cruz, California, documented a shift in people's emotional expectations from work. From the 1950s on, a "task-first" relationship–"Tell me what the job is, and let's get on with it"–dominated employee attitudes. Emotions and personal life were checked at the door. In the past few years, a "relationship-first" set of values has challenged the task orientation. Hall believes that it will become dominant. Employees want to share attitudes and beliefs as well as workspace.

Challenging Work and a Stimulating Environment Arthur Schawlow, winner of the 1981 Nobel Prize in physics, was asked what made the difference between highly creative and less creative scientists. His reply: "The labor of love aspect is very important. The most successful scientists often are not the most talented.[67] But they are the ones impelled by curiosity. They've got to know what the answer is."[68] Such insights highlight the importance of intrinsic motivation: the motivation to work on something because it is exciting, satisfying, or personally challenging.[69] As noted by Jeff Immelt, former chairman and CEO of General Electric, "You want people with the self-confidence to leave, but you want them to stay. That puts pressure on you to keep work interesting."[70]

Lars Sorensen, CEO of Novo Nordisk, the huge Danish pharmaceutical firm, provides a poignant perspective on how to keep employees engaged: ". . . we bring patients to see employees. We illuminate the big difference we are making. Without our medication, 24 million people would suffer. There is nothing more motivating for people than to go to work and save people's lives."[71]

Firms can also keep highly mobile employees motivated and challenged through opportunities that lower barriers to an employee's mobility within a company. For example, Shell Oil Company has created an "open sourcing" model for talent. Jobs are listed on its intranet, and, with a two-month notice, employees can go to work on anything that interests them.

Financial and Nonfinancial Rewards and Incentives Financial rewards are a vital organizational control mechanism (as we will discuss in Chapter 9). Money—whether in the form of salary, bonus, stock options, and so forth—can mean many different things to people. It might mean security, recognition, or a sense of freedom and independence.

Paying people more is seldom the most important factor in attracting and retaining human capital.[72] Most surveys show that money is not the most important reason why people take or leave jobs and that money, in some surveys, is not even in the top 10. Consistent with these findings, Tandem Computers (part of Hewlett-Packard) typically doesn't tell people being recruited what their salaries would be. People who asked were told that Tandem's salaries were competitive. If they persisted along this line of questioning, they would not be offered a position. Why? Tandem realized a rather simple idea: People who come for money will leave for money.

Another nonfinancial reward is accommodating working families with children. Balancing demands of family and work is a problem at some point for virtually all employees.

Below we discuss how Google attracts and retains talent through financial and nonfinancial incentives. Its unique "Google culture," a huge attraction to potential employees, transforms a traditional workspace into a fun, feel-at-home, and flexible place to work.[73]

> Googlers do not merely work but have a great time doing it. The Mountain View, California, headquarters includes on-site medical and dental facilities, oil change and bike repair, foosball, pool tables, volleyball courts, and free breakfast, lunch, and dinner on a daily basis at 11 gourmet restaurants. Googlers have access to training programs and receive tuition reimbursement while they take a leave of absence to pursue higher education. Google states on its website, "Though Google has grown a lot since it opened in 1998, we still maintain a small company feel."

Enhancing Human Capital: Redefining Jobs and Managing Diversity

Before moving on to our discussion of social capital, it is important to point out that companies are increasingly realizing that the payoff from enhancing their human capital can be substantial. Firms have found that redefining jobs and leveraging the benefits of a diverse workforce can go a long way in improving their performance.

Enhancing Human Capital: Redefining Jobs Recent research by McKinsey Global Institute suggests that by 2020, the worldwide shortage of highly skilled, college-educated workers could reach 38 to 40 million, or about 13 percent of total demand.[74] In response, some firms are taking steps to expand their talent pool, for example, by investing in apprenticeships and other training programs. However, some are going further: They are redefining the jobs of their experts and transferring some of their tasks to lower-skilled people inside or outside their companies, as well as outsourcing work that requires less scarce skills and is not as strategically important. Redefining high-value knowledge jobs not only can help organizations address skill shortages but also can lower costs and enhance job satisfaction.

Consider the following examples:

- Orrick, Herrington & Sutcliffe, a San Francisco-based law firm with nine U.S. offices, shifted routine discovery work previously performed by partners and partner-tracked associates to a new service center in West Virginia staffed by lower-paid attorneys.
- In the United Kingdom, a growing number of public schools are relieving head teachers (or principals) of administrative tasks such as budgeting, facilities maintenance, human resources, and community relations so that they can devote more time to developing teachers.

- The Narayana Hrudayalaya Heart Hospital in Bangalore has junior surgeons, nurses, and technicians handle routine tasks such as preparing the patient for surgery and closing the chest after surgery. Senior cardiac surgeons arrive at the operating room only when the patient's chest is open and the heart is ready to be operated on. Such an approach helps the hospital lower the cost to a fraction of the cost of U.S. providers while maintaining U.S.-level mortality and infection rates.

Breaking high-end knowledge work into highly specialized pieces involves several processes. These include identifying the gap between the talent your firm has and what it requires; creating narrower, more-focused job descriptions in areas where talent is scarce; selecting from various options to fill the skills gap; and rewiring processes for talent and knowledge management.

Enhancing Human Capital: Managing Diversity A combination of demographic trends and accelerating globalization of business has made the management of cultural differences a critical issue.[75] Workforces, which reflect demographic changes in the overall population, will be increasingly heterogeneous along dimensions such as gender, race, ethnicity, and nationality.[76] Demographic trends in the United States indicate a growth in Hispanic Americans from 6.9 million in 1960 to over 35 million in 2000, with an expected increase to over 59 million by 2020 and 102 million by 2050. Similarly, the Asian American population should grow to 20 million in 2020 from 12 million in 2000 and only 1.5 million in 1970. And the African American population is expected to increase from 12.8 percent of the U.S. population in 2000 to 14.2 percent by 2025.[77]

Such demographic changes have implications not only for the labor pool but also for customer bases, which are also becoming more diverse.[78] This creates important organizational challenges and opportunities.

The effective management of diversity can enhance the social responsibility goals of an organization.[79] However, there are many other benefits as well. Six other areas where sound management of diverse workforces can improve an organization's effectiveness and competitive advantages are (1) cost, (2) resource acquisition, (3) marketing, (4) creativity, (5) problem solving, and (6) organizational flexibility.

- ***Cost argument.*** As organizations become more diverse, firms effective in managing diversity will have a cost advantage over those that are not.
- ***Resource acquisition argument.*** Firms with excellent reputations as prospective employers for women and ethnic minorities will have an advantage in the competition for top talent. As labor pools shrink and change in composition, such advantages will become even more important.
- ***Marketing argument.*** For multinational firms, the insight and cultural sensitivity that members with roots in other countries bring to marketing efforts will be very useful. A similar rationale applies to subpopulations within domestic operations.
- ***Creativity argument.*** Less emphasis on conformity to norms of the past and a diversity of perspectives will improve the level of creativity.
- ***Problem-solving argument.*** Heterogeneity in decision-making and problem-solving groups typically produces better decisions because of a wider range of perspectives as well as more thorough analysis. Jim Schiro, former CEO of PricewaterhouseCoopers, explains, "When you make a genuine commitment to diversity, you bring a greater diversity of ideas, approaches, and experiences and abilities that can be applied to client problems. After all, six people with different perspectives have a better shot at solving complex problems than sixty people who all think alike."[80]
- ***Organizational flexibility argument.*** With effective programs to enhance workplace diversity, systems become less determinant, less standardized, and therefore more fluid. Such fluidity should lead to greater flexibility to react to environmental changes. Reactions should be faster and less costly.

4.3 STRATEGY SPOTLIGHT

MILLENNIALS HAVE A DIFFERENT DEFINITION OF DIVERSITY AND INCLUSION THAN PRIOR GENERATIONS

A recent study by Deloitte and the Billie Jean King Leadership Initiative (BJKLI) shows that, in general, Millennials see the concepts of diversity and inclusion through a vastly different lens. The study analyzed the responses of 3,726 individuals who came from a wide variety of backgrounds with representation across gender, race/ethnicity, sexual orientation, national status, veteran status, disabilities, level within an organization, and tenure with an organization. The respondents were asked 62 questions about diversity and inclusion and the findings demonstrated a snapshot of shifting generational mindsets.

Millennials (born between 1977 to 1995) look upon diversity as the blending of different backgrounds, experiences, and perspectives within a team—which is known as cognitive diversity. They use this word to describe the mix of unique traits that help to overcome challenges and attain business objectives. For Millennials, inclusion is the support for a collaborative environment, and leadership at such an organization must be transparent, communicative, and engaging. According to the study, when defining diversity, Millennials are 35 percent more likely to focus on unique experiences, whereas 21 percent of non-Millennials are more likely to focus on representation.

The X-generation (born between 1965 and 1976) and Boomer generation (born between 1946 and 1964) have a different take. These generations view diversity as a representation of fairness and protection for all—regardless of gender, race, religion, ethnicity, or sexual orientation. Here, inclusion is the integration of individuals of all demographics into one workplace. It is the right thing to do, that is, a moral and legal imperative to achieve compliance and equality—regardless of whether it benefits the business. The study found that when asked about the business impact on diversity, Millennials are 71 percent more likely to focus on teamwork. In contrast, 28 percent of non-Millennials are more likely to focus on fairness of opportunity.

The study's authors contend that the disconnect between the traditional definitions of diversity and inclusion and those of Millennials can create problems for businesses. For example, clashes may occur when managers do not permit Millennials to express themselves freely. The study found that while 86 percent of Millennials feel that differences of opinion allow teams to excel, only 59 percent believe that their leaders share this perspective.

The study suggests that a company with an inclusive culture promotes innovation. And it cites research by IBM and Morgan Stanley that shows that companies with high levels of innovation achieve the quickest growth in profits and that radical innovation outstrips incremental change by generating 10 times more shareholder value.

Sources: Dishman, L. 2015. Millennials have a different definition of diversity and inclusion. *fastcompany*.com, May 18: np; and Anonymous. 2015. For millennials inclusion goes beyond checking traditional boxes, according to a new Deloitte-Billie Jean King Leadership Initiative Study. *prnewswire*.com, May 13: np.

Most managers accept that employers benefit from a diverse workforce. However, this notion can often be very difficult to prove or quantify, particularly when it comes to determining how diversity affects a firm's ability to innovate.[81]

New research provides compelling evidence that diversity enhances innovation and drives market growth. This finding should intensify efforts to ensure that organizations both embody and embrace the power of differences.

Strategy Spotlight 4.3 contrasts the views that Millennials have of diversity with those of other generations, and the implications of such differences for organizations.

THE VITAL ROLE OF SOCIAL CAPITAL

LO 4-3

Describe the key role of social capital in leveraging human capital within and across the firm.

Successful firms are well aware that the attraction, development, and retention of talent *is a necessary but not sufficient condition* for creating competitive advantages.[82] In the knowledge economy, it is not the stock of human capital that is important, but the extent to which it is combined and leveraged.[83] In a sense, developing and retaining human capital becomes less important as key players (talented professionals, in particular) take the role of "free agents" and bring with them the requisite skill in many cases. Rather, the development of **social capital** (that is, the friendships and working relationships among individuals within and outside the organization) gains importance, because it helps tie knowledge workers to a given firm.[84] Knowledge workers often exhibit greater loyalties to their colleagues and their profession than their employing organization, which may be "an amorphous, distant, and sometimes threatening entity."[85] Thus, a firm must find ways to create "ties" among its knowledge workers.

Let's look at a hypothetical example. Two pharmaceutical firms are fortunate enough to hire Nobel Prize-winning scientists.[86] In one case, the scientist is offered a very attractive salary, outstanding facilities and equipment, and told to "go to it!" In the second case, the scientist is offered approximately the same salary, facilities, and equipment plus one additional ingredient: working in a laboratory with 10 highly skilled and enthusiastic scientists. Part of the job is to collaborate with these peers and jointly develop promising drug compounds. There is little doubt as to which scenario will lead to a higher probability of retaining the scientist. The interaction, sharing, and collaboration will create a situation in which the scientist will develop firm-specific ties and be less likely to "bolt" for a higher salary offer. Such ties are critical because knowledge-based resources tend to be more tacit in nature, as we mentioned early in this chapter. Therefore, they are much more difficult to protect against loss (i.e., the individual quitting the organization) than other types of capital, such as equipment, machinery, and land.

Another way to view this situation is in terms of the resource-based view of the firm that we discussed in Chapter 3. That is, competitive advantages tend to be harder for competitors to copy if they are based on "unique bundles" of resources.[87] So, if employees are working effectively in teams and sharing their knowledge and learning from each other, not only will they be more likely to add value to the firm, but they also will be less likely to leave the organization, because of the loyalties and social ties that they develop over time.

How Social Capital Helps Attract and Retain Talent

The importance of social ties among talented professionals creates a significant challenge (and opportunity) for organizations. In *The Wall Street Journal,* Bernard Wysocki described the increase in a type of "Pied Piper effect," in which teams or networks of people are leaving one company for another.[88] The trend is to recruit job candidates at the crux of social relationships in organizations, particularly if they are seen as having the potential to bring with them valuable colleagues.[89] This is a process that is referred to as "hiring via personal networks." Let's look at one instance of this practice.

> Gerald Eickhoff, founder of an electronic commerce company called Third Millennium Communications, tried for 15 years to hire Michael Reene. Why? Mr. Eickhoff says that he has "these Pied Piper skills." Mr. Reene was a star at Andersen Consulting in the 1980s and at IBM in the 1990s. He built his businesses and kept turning down overtures from Mr. Eickhoff.
>
> However, later he joined Third Millennium as chief executive officer, with a salary of just $120,000 but with a 20 percent stake in the firm. Since then, he has brought in a raft of former IBM colleagues and Andersen subordinates. One protégé from his time at Andersen, Mary Goode, was brought on board as executive vice president. She promptly tapped her own network and brought along former colleagues.
>
> Wysocki considers the Pied Piper effect one of the underappreciated factors in the war for talent today. This is because one of the myths of the New Economy is rampant individualism, wherein individuals find jobs on the Internet career sites and go to work for complete strangers. Perhaps, instead of Me Inc., the truth is closer to We Inc.[90]

Another example of social relationships causing human capital mobility is the emigration of talent from an organization to form start-up ventures. Microsoft is perhaps the best-known example of this phenomenon.[91] Professionals frequently leave Microsoft en masse to form venture capital and technology start-ups, called "Baby Bills," built around teams of software developers. For example, Ignition Corporation, of Bellevue, Washington, was formed by Brad Silverberg, a former Microsoft senior vice president. Eight former Microsoft executives, among others, founded the company.

Social Networks: Implications for Knowledge Management and Career Success

LO 4-4

Explain the importance of social networks in knowledge management and in promoting career success.

Managers face many challenges driven by such factors as rapid changes in globalization and technology. Leading a successful company is more than a one-person job. As Tom Malone put it in *The Future of Work,* "As managers, we need to shift our thinking from command and control to coordinate and cultivate–the best way to gain power is sometimes to give it away."[92] The move away from top-down bureaucratic control to more open, decentralized network models makes it more difficult for managers to understand how work is actually getting done, who is interacting with whom both within and outside the organization, and the consequences of these interactions for the long-term health of the organization.[93]

Malcolm Gladwell, in his best-selling book *The Tipping Point,* used the term *connector* to describe people who have *used* many ties to different social worlds.[94] It's not the number of people that connectors know that makes them significant. Rather, it is their ability to link people, ideas, and resources that wouldn't normally bump into one another. In business, connectors are critical facilitators for collaboration and integration. David Kenny, president of Akamai Technologies, believes that being a connector is one of the most important ways in which he adds value:

> Kenny spends much of his time traveling around the world to meet with employees, partners, and customers. He states, "I spend time with media owners to hear what they think about digital platforms, Facebook, and new pricing models, and with Microsoft leaders to get their views on cloud computing. I'm interested in hearing how our clients feel about macroeconomic issues, the G20, and how debt will affect future generations." These conversations lead to new strategic insights and relationships and help Akamai develop critical external partnerships.

Social networks can also help one bring about important change in an organization–or simply get things done! Consider a change initiative undertaken at the United Kingdom's National Health Care Service–a huge, government-run institution that employs about a million people in hundreds of units and divisions with deeply rooted, bureaucratic, hierarchical systems. This is certainly an organization in which you can't rely solely on your "position power":[95]

> John wanted to set up a nurse-led preoperative assessment service intended to free up time for the doctors who previously led the assessments, reduce cancelled operations (and costs), and improve patient care. Sounds easy enough . . . after all, John was a senior doctor and near the top of the hospital's formal hierarchy. However, he had only recently joined the organization and was not well connected internally.
>
> As he began talking to other doctors and to nurses about the change, he was met with a lot of resistance. He was about to give up when Carol, a well-respected nurse, offered to help. She had even less seniority than John, but many colleagues relied on her advice about navigating hospital politics. She knew many of the people whose support John needed and she eventually converted them to the change.

social network analysis
analysis of the pattern of social interactions among individuals.

Social network analysis depicts the pattern of interactions among individuals and helps to diagnose effective and ineffective patterns.[96] It helps identify groups or clusters of individuals that comprise the network, individuals who link the clusters, and other network members. It helps diagnose communication patterns and, consequently, communication effectiveness.[97] Such analysis of communication patterns is helpful because the configuration of group members' social ties within and outside the group affects the extent to which members connect to individuals who:

- Convey needed resources.
- Have the opportunity to exchange information and support.
- Have the motivation to treat each other in positive ways.
- Have the time to develop trusting relationships that might improve the groups' effectiveness.

EXHIBIT 4.3 A Simplified Social Network

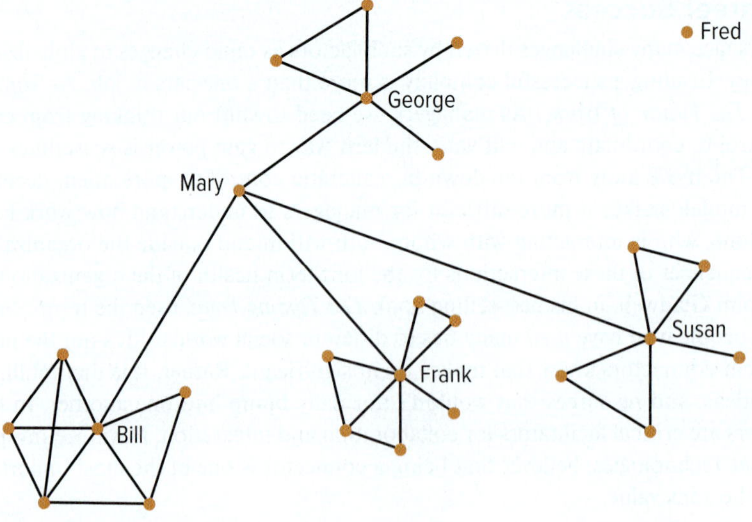

However, such relationships don't "just happen."[98] Developing social capital requires interdependence among group members. Social capital erodes when people in the network become independent. And increased interactions between members aid in the development and maintenance of mutual obligations in a social network.[99] Social networks such as Facebook may facilitate increased interactions between members in a social network via Internet-based communications.

Let's take a brief look at a simplified network analysis to get a grasp of the key ideas. In Exhibit 4.3, the links depict informal relationships among individuals, such as communication flows, personal support, and advice networks. There may be some individuals with literally no linkages, such as Fred. These individuals are typically labeled "isolates." However, most people do have some linkages with others.

To simplify, there are two primary types of mechanisms through which social capital will flow: *closure relationships* (depicted by Bill, Frank, George, and Susan) and *bridging relationships* (depicted by Mary). As we can see, in the former relationships one member is central to the communication flows in a group. In contrast, in the latter relationships, one person "bridges" or brings together groups that would have been otherwise unconnected.

Both closure and bridging relationships have important implications for the effective flow of information in organizations and for the management of knowledge. We will now briefly discuss each of these types of relationships. We will also address some of the implications that understanding social networks has for one's career success.

closure
the degree to which all members of a social network have relationships (or ties) with other group members.

Closure With **closure,** many members have relationships (or ties) with other members. As indicated in Exhibit 4.3, Bill's group would have a higher level of closure than Frank's Susan's, or George's groups because more group members are connected to each other. Through closure, group members develop strong relationships with each other, high levels of trust, and greater solidarity. High levels of trust help to ensure that informal norms in the group are easily enforced and there is less "free riding." Social pressure will prevent people from withholding effort or shirking their responsibilities. In addition, people in the network are more willing to extend favors and "go the extra mile" on a colleague's behalf because they are confident that their efforts will be reciprocated by another member in their group. Another benefit of a network with closure is the high level of emotional support. This becomes particularly valuable when setbacks occur that may destroy morale or an unexpected tragedy happens that might cause the group to lose its focus. Social support helps the group to rebound from misfortune and get back on track.

But high levels of closure often come with a price. Groups that become too closed can become insular. They cut themselves off from the rest of the organization and fail to share what they are learning from people outside their group. Research shows that while managers need to encourage closure up to a point, if there is too much closure, they need to encourage people to open up their groups and infuse new ideas through bridging relationships.[100]

Bridging Relationships The closure perspective rests on an assumption that there is a high level of similarity among group members. However, members can be quite heterogeneous with regard to their positions in either the formal or informal structures of the group or the organization. Such heterogeneity exists because of, for example, vertical boundaries (different levels in the hierarchy) and horizontal boundaries (different functional areas).

Bridging relationships, in contrast to closure, stress the importance of ties connecting people. Employees who bridge disconnected people tend to receive timely, diverse information because of their access to a wide range of heterogeneous information flows. Such bridging relationships span a number of different types of boundaries.

bridging relationships
relationships in a social network that connect otherwise disconnected people.

The University of Chicago's Ron Burt originally coined the term **"structural holes"** to refer to the social gap between two groups. Structural holes are common in organizations. When they occur in business, managers typically refer to them as "silos" or "stovepipes." Sales and engineering are a classic example of two groups whose members traditionally interact with their peers rather than across groups.

structural holes
social gaps between groups in a social network where there are few relationships bridging the groups.

A study that Burt conducted at Raytheon, a $25 billion U.S. electronics company and military contractor, provides further insight into the benefits of bridging.[101]

> Burt studied several hundred managers in Raytheon's supply chain group and asked them to write down ideas to improve the company's supply chain management. Then he asked two Raytheon executives to rate the ideas. The conclusion: *The best suggestions consistently came from managers who discussed ideas outside their regular work group.*
>
> Burt found that Raytheon managers were good at thinking of ideas but bad at developing them. Too often, Burt said, the managers discussed their ideas with colleagues already in their informal discussion network. Instead, he said, they should have had discussions outside their typical contacts, particularly with an informal boss, or someone with enough power to be an ally but not an actual supervisor.

Implications for Career Success Effective social networks provide many advantages for the firm.[102] They can also play a key role in an individual's career advancement and success. One's social network also potentially can provide three unique advantages: private information, access to diverse skill sets, and power.[103] Managers see these advantages at work every day but might not consider how their networks regulate them.

Private Information We make judgments using both public and private information. Today, public information is available from many sources, including the Internet. However, since it is so accessible, public information offers less competitive advantage than it used to.

In contrast, private information from personal contacts can offer something not found in publicly available sources, such as the release date of a new product or knowledge about what a particular interviewer looks for in candidates. Private information can give managers an edge, though it is more subjective than public information since it cannot be easily verified by independent sources, such as Dun & Bradstreet. Consequently the value of your private information to others–and the value of others' private information to you–depends on how much trust exists in the network of relationships.

Access to Diverse Skill Sets Linus Pauling, one of only two people to win a Nobel Prize in two different areas and considered one of the towering geniuses of the 20th century, attributed his creative success not to his immense brainpower or luck but to his diverse contacts. He said, "The best way to have a good idea is to have a lot of ideas."

While expertise has become more specialized during the past few decades, organizational, product, and marketing issues have become more interdisciplinary. This means that success is tied to the ability to transcend natural skill limitations through others. Highly diverse network relationships, therefore, can help you develop more complete, creative, and unbiased perspectives on issues. Trading information or skills with people whose experiences differ from your own provides you with unique, exceptionally valuable resources. It is common for people in relationships to share their problems. If you know enough people, you will begin to see how the problems that another person is struggling with can be solved by the solutions being developed by others. If you can bring together problems and solutions, it will greatly benefit your career.

Power Traditionally, a manager's power was embedded in a firm's hierarchy. But when corporate organizations became flatter, more like pancakes than pyramids, that power was repositioned in the network's brokers (people who bridged multiple networks), who could adapt to changes in the organization, develop clients, and synthesize opposing points of view. Such brokers weren't necessarily at the top of the hierarchy or experts in their fields, but they linked specialists in the firm with trustworthy and informative relationships.[104]

Most personal networks are highly clustered; that is, an individual's friends are likely to be friends with one another as well. Most corporate networks are made up of several clusters that have few links between them. Brokers are especially powerful because they connect separate clusters, thus stimulating collaboration among otherwise independent specialists.

Women and Networking Before moving on to a discussion of the downside of social capital, let's briefly discuss some of the challenges that women face when it comes to networking. Sheryl Sandberg, Chief Operating Officer of Facebook, Inc. and author of *Lean In*, notes that even though women are entering the U.S. workforce at the highest number in decades, gender parity in senior executive roles is still far off. That is, only about one in five senior leaders is a woman, and one in twenty-five is a woman of color–according to the fourth annual Women in the Workplace survey from LeanIn.org and McKinsey & Company. The survey was conducted in 2018 and the numbers are unchanged from the first survey that was taken in 2015.[105]

Although networking is vital for career advancement, such numbers become a central reason why women have a more difficult time than men when it comes to networking.[106] That is, if there are relatively few women in positions of leadership, it becomes more difficult for women to find sponsors to make introductions and referrals. And, models of effective leadership are typically geared toward men. Further, when an organization's senior ranks are heavily populated by men, the "likes attract" principle means that women have to work harder to build relationships with decision makers and influential stakeholders. Thus, they tend to become excluded from male-dominated social gatherings, wherein business professionals talk shop and bounce ideas around in an informal atmosphere that helps develop camaraderie and trust.

Strategy Spotlight 4.4 provides some suggestions on how women can more effectively engage in networking activities.

The Potential Downside of Social Capital

We'd like to close our discussion of social capital by addressing some of its limitations. First, some firms have been adversely affected by very high levels of social capital because it may breed **"groupthink"**–a tendency not to question shared beliefs.[107] Such thinking may occur in networks with high levels of closure where there is little input from people outside the network. In effect, too many warm and fuzzy feelings among group members prevent people from rigorously challenging each other. People are discouraged from engaging in the

groupthink
a tendency in an organization for individuals not to question shared beliefs.

4.4 STRATEGY SPOTLIGHT

HOW WOMEN CAN NETWORK MORE EFFECTIVELY

Herminia Ibarra is a leading scholar in organizational behavior who studies leadership and career development issues at the London Business School. She has suggested three tactics on how women can more successfully engage in networking activities.

Be a bridge. Women can improve their professional network by making connections across diverse circles that make up their network.

For example, a marketing executive for a large manufacturing firm realized that a lot of good ideas were being shared at events she attended that could help her colleagues. She began writing up what she was learning in a LinkedIn blog. This helped to increase her visibility in the firm. In addition, when she met the author of a book on agile working, she realized that his methodology could help transform her firm's operations. She was able to introduce him to a manager she had gotten to know through her LinkedIn column. Within five years, the methodology was widely used in her company and she earned a promotion.

Do it your way. To be an effective networker, one has to invest time in extracurricular activities. However, women may not be very interested in what would appear to be the limited choices, such as attending sporting events or playing golf. Thus, savvy networkers may consider leveraging a personal interest into something that may have strategic value for the organization.

Consider an investment banker who was passionate about the theatre. When she kept missing plays that she wanted to see, she decided to make it a core part of her business development. So, four times a year, she asked her secretary to book tickets, planned an informal buffet dinner at a restaurant, and invited prospective clients and other people she was interested in getting to know better. Her efforts provided a means to develop her business and made it easier to make strong connections among people in her network.

Join a women's professional network. Women are often unable to achieve their potential because their informal networks tend to have separate work and social spheres. The two spheres can be brought together by joining a women's network such as Wing. Such a network can be a supportive setting for women to compare notes and facilitate each other's learning. For example, one website founder from New Zealand stated, "Coming here, there is a sense of comfort, you can fully relax."

Source: Ibarra, H. 2018. C-Suite strategies (A special report)–What women need to do to network. *wsj.com*, May 21: np.

"creative abrasion" that Dorothy Leonard of Harvard University describes as a key source of innovation.[108] Two firms that were well known for their collegiality, strong sense of employee membership, and humane treatment–Digital Equipment (now part of Hewlett-Packard) and Polaroid–suffered greatly from market misjudgments and strategic errors. The aforementioned aspects of their culture contributed to their problems.

Second, if there are deep-rooted mindsets, there would be a tendency to develop dysfunctional human resource practices. That is, the organization (or group) would continue to hire, reward, and promote like-minded people who tend to further intensify organizational inertia and erode innovation. Such homogeneity would increase over time and decrease the effectiveness of decision-making processes.

Third, the socialization processes (orientation, training, etc.) can be expensive in terms of both financial resources and managerial commitment. Such investments can represent a significant opportunity cost that should be evaluated in terms of the intended benefits. If such expenses become excessive, profitability would be adversely affected.

Finally, individuals may use the contacts they develop to pursue their own interests and agendas, which may be inconsistent with the organization's goals and objectives. Thus, they may distort or selectively use information to favor their preferred courses of action or withhold information in their own self-interest to enhance their power to the detriment of the common good. Drawing on our discussion of social networks, this is particularly true in an organization that has too many bridging relationships but not enough closure relationships. In high-closure groups, it is easier to watch each other to ensure that illegal or unethical acts don't occur. By contrast, bridging relationships make it easier for a person to play one group or individual off another, with no one being the wiser.[109] We will discuss some behavioral control mechanisms in Chapter 9 (rewards, control, boundaries) that reduce such dysfunctional behaviors and actions.[110]

LO 4-5

Describe the vital role of technology in leveraging knowledge and human capital.

USING TECHNOLOGY TO LEVERAGE HUMAN CAPITAL AND KNOWLEDGE

Sharing knowledge and information throughout the organization can be a means of conserving resources, developing products and services, and creating new opportunities. In this section we will discuss how technology can be used to leverage human capital and knowledge within organizations as well as with customers and suppliers beyond their boundaries.

Using Networks to Share Information

As we all know, email is an effective means of communicating a wide variety of information. It is quick, easy, and almost costless. Of course, it can become a problem when employees use it extensively for personal reasons. And we all know how fast jokes or rumors can spread within and across organizations!

Email can also cause embarrassment, or worse, if one is not careful. Consider the plight of a potential CEO–as recalled by Marshall Goldsmith, a well-known executive coach:[111]

> I witnessed a series of e-mails between a potential CEO and a friend inside the company. The first e-mail to the friend provided an elaborate description of "why the current CEO is an idiot." The friend sent a reply. Several rounds of e-mails followed. Then the friend sent an e-mail containing a funny joke. The potential CEO decided that the current CEO would love this joke and forwarded it to him. You can guess what happened next. The CEO scrolled down the e-mail chain and found the "idiot" message. The heir apparent was gone in a week.

Email can, however, be a means for top executives to communicate information efficiently. For example, Martin Sorrell, former chairman of WPP Group PLC, the huge $15 billion advertising and public relations firm, was a strong believer in the use of email.[112] He emailed all of his employees once a month to discuss how the company was doing, addressed specific issues, and offered his perspectives on hot issues, such as new business models for the Internet. He believed that it kept people abreast of what he was working on.

Technology can also enable much more sophisticated forms of communication in addition to knowledge sharing. Cisco, for example, launched Integrated Workforce Experience (IWE) in 2010.[113] It is a social business platform designed to facilitate internal and external collaboration and decentralize decision making. It functions much like a Facebook "wall": A real-time news feed provides updates on employees' status and activities as well as information about relevant communities, business projects, and customer and partner interactions. One manager likens it to Amazon. "It makes recommendations based on what you are doing, the role you are in, and the choices of other people like you. We are taking that to the enterprise level and basically allowing appropriate information to find you," he says.

LO 4-6

Explain why "electronic" or "virtual" teams are critical in combining and leveraging knowledge in organizations and how they can be made more effective.

Electronic Teams: Using Technology to Enhance Collaboration

Technology enables professionals to work as part of electronic, or virtual, teams to enhance the speed and effectiveness with which products are developed. For example, Microsoft has concentrated much of its development on **electronic teams** (or e-teams) that are networked together.[114] This helps to accelerate design and testing of new software modules that use the Windows-based framework as their central architecture. Microsoft is able to foster specialized technical expertise while sharing knowledge rapidly throughout the firm. This helps the firm learn how its new technologies can be applied rapidly to new business ventures such as cable television, broadcasting, travel services, and financial services.

electronic teams a team of individuals that completes tasks primarily through email communication.

What are electronic teams (or e-teams)? There are two key differences between e-teams and more traditional teams:[115]

- E-team members either work in geographically separated workplaces or may work in the same space but at different times. E-teams may have members working in different spaces and time zones, as is the case with many multinational teams.

- Most of the interactions among members of e-teams occur through electronic communication channels such as fax machines and groupware tools such as email, bulletin boards, chat, and videoconferencing.

E-teams have expanded exponentially in recent years.[116] Organizations face increasingly high levels of complex and dynamic change. E-teams are also effective in helping businesses cope with global challenges. Most e-teams perform very complex tasks and most knowledge-based teams are charged with developing new products, improving organizational processes, and satisfying challenging customer problems. For example, Hewlett-Packard's e-teams solve clients' computing problems, and Sun Microsystems' (part of Oracle) e-teams generate new business models.

Advantages There are multiple advantages of e-teams.[117] In addition to the rather obvious use of technology to facilitate communications, the potential benefits parallel the other two major sections in this chapter—human capital and social capital.

First, e-teams are less restricted by the geographic constraints that are placed on face-to-face teams. Thus, e-teams have the potential to acquire a broader range of "human capital," or the skills and capacities that are necessary to complete complex assignments. So e-team leaders can draw upon a greater pool of talent to address a wider range of problems since they are not constrained by geographic space. Once formed, e-teams can be more flexible in responding to unanticipated work challenges and opportunities because team members can be rotated out of projects when demands and contingencies alter the team's objectives.

Second, e-teams can be very effective in generating "social capital"—the quality of relationships and networks that form. Such capital is a key lubricant in work transactions and operations. Given the broader boundaries associated with e-teams, members and leaders generally have access to a wider range of social contacts than would be typically available in more traditional face-to-face teams. Such contacts are often connected to a broader scope of clients, customers, constituents, and other key stakeholders.

Challenges However, there are challenges associated with making e-teams effective. Successful action by both traditional teams and e-teams requires that:

- Members *identify* who among them can provide the most appropriate knowledge and resources.
- E-team leaders and key members know how to *combine* individual contributions in the most effective manner for a coordinated and appropriate response.

Group psychologists have termed such activities "identification and combination" activities, and teams that fail to perform them face a "process loss."[118] Process losses prevent teams from reaching high levels of performance because of inefficient interaction dynamics among team members. Such poor dynamics require that some collective energy, time, and effort be devoted to dealing with team inefficiencies, thus diverting the team away from its objectives. For example, if a team member fails to communicate important information at critical phases of a project, other members may waste time and energy. This can lead to conflict and resentment as well as to decreased motivation to work hard to complete tasks.

The potential for process losses tends to be more prevalent in e-teams than in traditional teams because the geographic dispersion of members increases the complexity of establishing effective interaction and exchanges. Generally, teams suffer process loss because of low cohesion, low trust among members, a lack of appropriate norms or standard operating procedures, or a lack of shared understanding among team members about their tasks. With e-teams, members are more geographically or temporally dispersed, and the team becomes more susceptible to the risk factors that can create process loss. Such problems can be exacerbated when team members have less than ideal competencies and social skills. This can erode problem-solving capabilities as well as the effective functioning of the group as a social unit.

A variety of technologies, from email and Internet groups to Skype have facilitated the formation and effective functioning of e-teams as well as a wide range of collaborations within

4.5 STRATEGY SPOTLIGHT — DIGITAL ECONOMY

HOW SAP TAPS KNOWLEDGE WELL BEYOND ITS BOUNDARIES

Traditionally, organizations built and protected their knowledge stocks—proprietary resources that no one else could access. However, the more the business environment changes, the faster the value of what you know at any point in time diminishes. In today's world, success hinges on the ability to access a growing variety of knowledge flows in order to rapidly replenish the firm's knowledge stocks. For example, when an organization tries to improve cycle times in a manufacturing process, it finds far more value in problem solving shaped by the diverse experiences, perspectives, and learning of a tightly knit team (shared through knowledge flows) than in a training manual (knowledge stocks) alone.

Knowledge flows can help companies gain competitive advantage in an age of near-constant disruption. The software company SAP, for example, routinely taps the nearly 3 million participants in its Community Network, which extends well beyond the boundaries of the firm. This network includes a wide range of online forums. Here, users are able to post questions on a variety of topics that relate to the customization, implementation, and use of SAP's software. Peer members can then suggest potential solutions. The network also includes expert blogs, a technical library, e-learning catalogs, a code-sharing gallery, wikis, and other tools that support open communication between active members of the community.

According to Mark Yolton, senior vice president of SAP Communications and Social Media, "It's a very robust community with a great deal of activity. We see about 1.2 million unique visitors every month. Hundreds of millions of pages are viewed every year. There are 4,000 discussion forum posts every single day, 365 days a year, and about 115 blogs every day, 365 days a year, from any of the nearly 3 million members."

The site is open to everyone, regardless of whether you are a SAP customer, partner, or newcomer who needs to work with SAP technology. The site offers technical articles, web-based training, code samples, evaluation systems, discussion forums, and excellent blogs for community experts.

Sources: Huang, P., Tafti, A., and S. Mithas. 2018. The secret to successful knowledge seeding. *MIT Sloan Management Review*, 59(3): 10-11; Yolton, M. 2012. SAP: Using social media for building, selling and supporting. *MIT Sloan Management Review*, August 7: np; Hagel, J., III., Brown, J. S., and L. Davison. 2009. The big shift: Measuring the forces of change. *Harvard Business Review*, 87(4): 87; and Anonymous. Undated. SAP developer network. *sap.sys-con.com*: np.

companies. Such technologies greatly enhance the collaborative abilities of employees and managers within a company at a reasonable cost—despite the distances that separate them.

Codifying Knowledge for Competitive Advantage

There are two different kinds of knowledge. Tacit knowledge is embedded in personal experience and shared only with the consent and participation of the individual. Explicit (or codified) knowledge, on the other hand, is knowledge that can be documented, widely distributed, and easily replicated. One of the challenges of knowledge-intensive organizations is to capture and codify the knowledge and experience that, in effect, resides in the heads of its employees. Otherwise, they will have to constantly "reinvent the wheel," which is both expensive and inefficient. Also, the "new wheel" may not necessarily be superior to the "old wheel."[119]

Once a knowledge asset (e.g., a software code or a process) is developed and paid for, it can be reused many times at very low cost, assuming that it doesn't have to be substantially modified each time. For example, Access Health, a call-in medical center, uses technology to capture and share knowledge. When someone calls the center, a registered nurse uses the company's "clinical decision architecture" to assess the caller's symptoms, rule out possible conditions, and recommend a home remedy, doctor's visit, or trip to the emergency room. The company's knowledge repository contains algorithms of the symptoms of more than 500 illnesses. According to CEO Joseph Tallman, "We are not inventing a new way to cure disease. We are taking available knowledge and inventing processes to put it to better use."[120] The software algorithms were very expensive to develop, but the investment has been repaid many times over. The first 300 algorithms that Access Health developed have each been used an average of 8,000 times a year. Further, the company's paying customers—insurance companies and provider groups—save money because many callers would have made expensive trips to the emergency room or the doctor's office had they not been diagnosed over the phone.

The user community can be a major source of knowledge creation for a firm. Strategy Spotlight 4.5 highlights how SAP has been able to leverage the expertise and involvement of its users to develop new knowledge and transmit it to SAP's entire user community.

We close this section with a series of questions managers should consider in determining (1) how effective their organization is in attracting, developing, and retaining human capital and (2) how effective they are in leveraging human capital through social capital and technology. These questions, included in Exhibit 4.4, summarize some of the key issues addressed in this chapter.

EXHIBIT 4.4 Issues to Consider in Creating Value through Human Capital, Social Capital, and Technology

Human Capital

Recruiting "Top-Notch" Human Capital

- Does the organization assess attitude and "general makeup" instead of focusing primarily on skills and background in selecting employees at all levels?
- How important are creativity and problem-solving ability? Are they properly considered in hiring decisions?
- Do people throughout the organization engage in effective networking activities to obtain a broad pool of worthy potential employees? Is the organization creative in such endeavors?

Enhancing Human Capital through Employee Development

- Does the development and training process inculcate an "organizationwide" perspective?
- Is there widespread involvement, including top executives, in the preparation and delivery of training and development programs?
- Is the development of human capital effectively tracked and monitored?
- Are there effective programs for succession at all levels of the organization, especially at the topmost levels?
- Does the firm effectively evaluate its human capital? Is a 360-degree evaluation used? Why? Why not?
- Are mechanisms in place to ensure that a manager's success does not come at the cost of compromising the organization's core values?

Retaining the Best Employees

- Are there appropriate financial rewards to motivate employees at all levels?
- Do people throughout the organization strongly identify with the organization's mission?
- Are employees provided with a stimulating and challenging work environment that fosters professional growth?
- Are valued amenities provided (e.g., flextime, child care facilities, telecommuting) that are appropriate given the organization's mission, its strategy, and how work is accomplished?
- Is the organization continually devising strategies and mechanisms to retain top performers?

Social Capital

- Are there positive personal and professional relationships among employees?
- Is the organization benefiting (or being penalized) by hiring (or by voluntary turnover) en masse?
- Does an environment of caring and encouragement rather than competition enhance team performance?
- Do the social networks within the organization have the appropriate levels of closure and bridging relationships?
- Does the organization minimize the adverse effects of excessive social capital, such as excessive costs and "groupthink"?

Technology

- Has the organization used technologies such as e-mail and networks to develop products and services?
- Does the organization effectively use technology to transfer best practices across the organization?
- Does the organization use technology to leverage human capital and knowledge both within the boundaries of the organization and among its suppliers and customers?
- Has the organization effectively used technology to codify knowledge for competitive advantage?
- Does the organization try to retain some of the knowledge of employees when they decide to leave the firm?

Source: Adapted from Dess, G. G., and J. C. Picken. 1999. *Beyond Productivity*. New York: AMACON, 63–64.

LO 4-7

Identify the challenge of protecting intellectual property and the importance of a firm's dynamic capabilities.

PROTECTING THE INTELLECTUAL ASSETS OF THE ORGANIZATION: INTELLECTUAL PROPERTY AND DYNAMIC CAPABILITIES

In today's dynamic and turbulent world, unpredictability and fast change dominate the business environment. Firms can use technology, attract human capital, or tap into research and design networks to get access to pretty much the same information as their competitors. So what would give firms a sustainable competitive advantage?[121] Protecting a firm's intellectual property requires a concerted effort on the part of the company. After all, employees become disgruntled and patents expire. The management of intellectual property (IP) involves, besides patents, contracts with confidentiality and noncompete clauses, copyrights, and the development of trademarks. Moreover, developing dynamic capabilities is the only avenue providing firms with the ability to reconfigure their knowledge and activities to build and protect a sustainable competitive advantage.

Intellectual Property Rights

intellectual property rights
intangible property owned by a firm in the forms of patents, copyrights, trademarks, or trade secrets.

Intellectual property rights are more difficult to define and protect than property rights for physical assets (e.g., plant, equipment, and land). However, if intellectual property rights are not reliably protected by the state, there will be less incentive to develop new products and services. Property rights have been enshrined in constitutions and rules of law in many countries. In the information era, though, adjustments need to be made to accommodate the new realities of knowledge. Knowledge and information are fundamentally different assets from the physical ones that property rights have been designed to protect.

The protection of intellectual rights raises unique issues, compared to physical property rights. IP is characterized by significant development costs and very low marginal costs. Indeed, it may take a substantial investment to develop a software program, an idea, or a digital music tune. Once developed, though, its reproduction and distribution cost may be almost zero, especially if the Internet is used. Effective protection of intellectual property is necessary before any investor will finance such an undertaking. Appropriation of investors' returns is harder to police since possession and deployment are not as readily observable. Unlike physical assets, intellectual property can be stolen by simply broadcasting it. Recall Napster and MP3 as well as the debates about counterfeit software, music CDs, and DVDs coming from developing countries such as China. Part of the problem is that using an idea does not prevent others from simultaneously using it for their own benefit, which is typically impossible with physical assets. Moreover, new ideas are frequently built on old ideas and are not easily traceable.

Given these unique challenges in protecting IP, it comes as no surprise that legal battles over patents become commonplace in IP-heavy industries such as telecommunications and e-commerce. Consider what happened when Groupon refused to negotiate a licensing deal with IBM to use its IP.[122]

> Prodigy, an online service that prospered in the 1990s, quickly faded a decade later. But that wasn't the end of the story. It so happened that IBM was one of the original partners and it owns some patents on the foundations of e-commerce. You would be wrong to think that such IP wouldn't be worth much now. It turns out that several well-known companies have been paying fees to access some of these patents. These include Amazon.com ($49.8 million); Google ($35 million); and, Twitter ($36 million).
>
> IBM claimed that Groupon was violating some of their patents and offered to license its patents to them. Groupon refused. After IBM sued, Groupon's founder Andrew Mason rather facetiously said, "They finally got me—I stole the idea to sell goods and services at a discount from Prodigy." And, their lawyer claimed that IBM was a patent troll: "IBM uses its huge stock of patents as a club to get money from other companies."

In late July 2018—two years after the case was filed—the two companies faced off in a two-week trial. IBM's strongest argument was the precedent that was set wherein many other firms were already paying for access to the same patents, as noted above. IBM's lawyer told the jury that Groupon, "the new kid on the block," was refusing to "take responsibility for the technology that it is using." After deliberating only six hours, the jury reached its verdict: IBM was awarded $83.5 million—half of the damages that it had claimed.

Perhaps, the trial was as much about sending a message as reaping a financial reward. IBM has 45,000 patents, which generated $1.19 billion of its $79.1 billion of revenues in 2017. A concluding point: If you don't pay up when IBM comes calling, you will likely wind up in court

Countries are attempting to pass new legislation to cope with developments in new pharmaceutical compounds, stem cell research, and biotechnology. However, a firm that is faced with this challenge today cannot wait for the legislation to catch up. New technological developments, software solutions, electronic games, online services, and other products and services contribute to our economic prosperity and the creation of wealth for those entrepreneurs who have the idea first and risk bringing it to the market.

Dynamic Capabilities

Dynamic capabilities helps to explain competitive advantage in volatile industries.[123] In the past few decades, Internet-based technologies have altered the competitive landscape across a broad range of industries, raising new challenges to the conventional views of competitive advantage. Companies such as Apple, Alphabet (parent of Google), and Facebook have developed a capacity to sense, shape, and seize opportunities; revolutionize industries; and, transform national and global economies.

dynamic capabilities a firm's capacity to build and protect a competitive advantage, which rests on knowledge, assets, competencies, complementary assets, and technologies. Dynamic capabilities include the ability to sense and seize new opportunities, generate new knowledge, and reconfigure existing assets and capabilities.

In ever-changing markets, the functional and operational routines that drive competitive success in stable conditions, i.e., "baseline" capabilities such as supply chain management and access to distribution channels, can quickly become obsolete. Even if a firm's advantages are difficult to imitate due to experience or proprietary knowledge, disruptive technologies can undermine the key drivers of industry advantage, erode conventional advantages, and become out of step with market conditions and consumer demands.

The dynamic capabilities view maintains that success in volatile industries requires capabilities that enable companies to anticipate, shape, and adapt to shifting competitive landscapes. Although it accepts the importance of capabilities such as product design and manufacturing, it argues that success in volatile industries requires something more than baseline capabilities; namely, adaptive processes and structures that enable firms to change baseline capabilities, predict shifts in consumer demand, develop and integrate new technologies, learn from market events, and predict and capture new market opportunities.

Dynamic capabilities, therefore, defines the firm's ability to innovate, adapt, and foster change that is favorable to customers and unfavorable to competitors.[124] Dynamic capabilities can be viewed as consisting of three primary activities:

- Identifying, developing, and assessing technological opportunities (and threats) that relate to customer needs (the "sensing" of uncertain futures);
- Mobilizing resources to focus on needs and opportunities in order to capture value from doing so ("seizing"); and
- Continuing the ongoing process of renewal ("transforming" or "shifting").

These three activities—sensing, seizing, and transforming—are essential if organizations want to sustain themselves in the longer term as customers, competitors, and technologies change.

To illustrate, consider Amazon's launch of the Kindle in 2006.[125] This involved sensing the impending threat to its core book-selling business, seizing the opportunity through rapid development of a first-generation e-book reader, and then gradually transforming its internal activities to ensure that the Kindle became an integrated part of its overall market offering.

Dynamic capabilities can include many different activities that a firm might undertake to create competitive advantages such as product development, strategic decision making, and acquisitions.[126] Cisco Systems has made numerous acquisitions over the years. Cisco appears to have developed the capability to identify and evaluate potential acquisition candidates and seamlessly integrate them once the acquisition is completed. Other organizations can try to copy Cisco's practices. However, Cisco's combination of the resources of acquired companies and the configuration that Cisco has already achieved places it well ahead of its competitors. As markets become increasingly volatile, traditional sources of long-term competitive advantage become less relevant. In such markets, all that a firm can strive for is a series of temporary advantages. Dynamic capabilities enable a firm to create a series of temporary advantages through new resource configurations.

ISSUE FOR DEBATE

Does Providing Financial Incentives to Employees to Lose Weight Actually Work?

Assume your employer offered each of its staff $550 to lose weight, an amount that would be subtracted from their health insurance premiums the following year. Do you think it would work? Would it provide enough incentive for some of the employees to shed the pounds?

Approximately four out of five large employers in the United States now offer some type of financial incentive for employees to improve their health. And the Affordable Care Act has encouraged such programs by significantly increasing the amount of money, in the form of a percentage of insurance premiums, that employers can reward (or take away) to improve health factors such as body mass index, blood pressure and cholesterol, as well as for ending the use of tobacco.

Several professors and medical professionals decided to test whether or not incentives actually work. Employees were randomly assigned to two conditions: one group in which employees were offered the $550 incentive and another group–the control group–in which no incentive was offered. After one year the results were reported in the journal *Health Affairs*. The result: Employees assigned to the control group that received no financial incentive had no change in their weight. However, employees who were offered the $550 incentive also didn't lose weight.

Discussion Questions

1. Why do you think the $550 incentive did not result in people losing weight?
2. Can you think of how incentives could have been structured to be more successful?

Source: Patel, M. S., Asch, D. A., and K. G. Volpp. 2016. Does paying employees to lose weight work? *Dallas Morning News*, March 20: 1P, 5P.

Reflecting on Career Implications . . .

This chapter focuses on the growing importance of intellectual assets in the valuation of firms. Since improved organizational performance occurs when firms effectively combine human capital, social capital, and technology, the following issues help students to consider how they can leverage their talents though relationships and technology.

- **Human Capital:** Identify specific steps taken by your organization to effectively attract, develop, and retain talent. If you cannot identify such steps, you may have fewer career opportunities to develop your human capital at your organization. Do you take advantage of your organization's human resource programs, such as tuition reimbursement, mentoring, and so forth?
- **Human Capital:** As workplaces become more diverse, it is important to reflect on whether your organization values diversity. What kinds of diversity seem to be encouraged (e.g., age-based or ethnicity-based)? In what ways are your colleagues different from and similar to you? If your firm has a homogeneous workforce, there may be limited perspectives on strategic and operational issues and a career at this organization may be less attractive to you.
- **Social Capital:** Does your organization have strong social capital? What is the basis of your conclusion that it has strong or weak social capital? What specific programs are in place to build and develop social capital? What is the impact of social capital on employee turnover in your organization? Alternatively, is social capital so strong that you see effects such as "groupthink"? From your perspective, how might you better leverage social capital toward pursuing other career opportunities?
- **Social Capital:** Are you actively working to build a strong social network at your work organization? To advance your career, strive to build a broad network that gives you access to diverse information.
- **Technology:** Does your organization provide and effectively use technology (e.g., groupware, knowledge management systems) to help you leverage your talents and expand your knowledge base? If your organization does a poor job in this regard, what can you do on your own to expand your knowledge base using technology available outside the organization?

key points

LO 4-1 Why the management of knowledge professionals and knowledge itself is so critical to today's organizations.

- In the knowledge economy, wealth is increasingly created by the effective management of knowledge workers instead of by the efficient control of physical and financial assets.
- The growing importance of knowledge means that investing in a company is, in essence, buying a set of talents, capabilities, skills, and ideas—intellectual capital—not physical and financial resources.
- In firms where knowledge and the management of knowledge workers are relatively important contributors to developing products and services—and physical resources are less critical—the ratio of market-to-book value tends to be higher.
- Some have defined intellectual capital as the difference between a firm's market value and book value.

LO 4-2 The importance of recognizing the interdependence of attracting, developing, and retaining human capital.

- It is helpful to view the three activities—attracting, developing, and retaining human capital—as a "three-legged stool." That is, it is difficult for firms to be successful if they ignore or are ineffective in any one of these activities. For example, poor hiring practices can impede the effectiveness of development and retention processes.
- It is important to attract employees who can collaborate with others, given the importance of collective efforts such as teams and task forces.
- To develop human capital, firms need to encourage widespread involvement throughout the organization, monitor progress and track the development of human capital, and effectively evaluate human capital.
- To retain human capital, firms need to increase employees' identification with the organization's mission and values, ensure challenging work and a stimulating environment, and provide competitive financial and nonfinancial rewards.
- Organizations have found that redefining jobs and leveraging the benefits of a diverse workforce can go a long way in enhancing their performance.

LO 4-3 The key role of social capital in leveraging human capital within and across the firm.

- Social capital refers to the network of relationships that individuals have throughout the organization as well as with other stakeholders such as suppliers and customers. Such ties can be critical in obtaining both resources and information.

- Social ties among talented professionals can also help to attract and retain talent.
- Four potential downsides of very high levels of social capital in an organization are: (1) a tendency toward "groupthink"—that reinforces shared beliefs, (2) a potential for dysfunctional human resource practices, e.g., hire and employ like-minded people, (3) socialization processes may be expensive in terms of managerial commitment and financial resources, and (4) individuals may use their influence from social networks to pursue their own interests—which may conflict with those of the organization.

LO 4-4 The importance of social networks in knowledge management and in promoting career success.

- Social network analysis depicts the pattern of interactions among individuals and helps to improve communication effectiveness.
- Effective social networks can play a key role in an individual's career advancement and success. Three unique advantages are: access to private information, access to diverse skill sets, and greater power and influence.

LO 4-5 The vital role of technology in leveraging knowledge and human capital.

- Sharing information and knowledge throughout the organization can be a means of conserving resources, developing products and services, and creating new opportunities.
- Technology can be used to leverage human capital and knowledge within the organization as well as with customers and suppliers beyond their boundaries.
- Technology can also provide more sophisticated forms of communication. For example, it can be used to facilitate internal and external collaboration and decentralize decision making.

LO 4-6 Why "electronic" or "virtual" teams are critical in combining and leveraging knowledge in organizations and how they can be made more effective.

- Technology enables professionals to work as part of electronic, or virtual, teams to enhance the speed and effectiveness with which products and services are developed.
- The two primary advantages of e-teams are: (1) they are less restricted by the geographic constraints that are placed on face-to-face teams, and (2) they can be very effective in generating "social capital"—the quality of relationships and networks that form.
- The two primary challenges of e-teams are: (1) the members need to identify who among them can provide the most appropriate knowledge and resources, and (2) e-team leaders and key members must know how to combine individual contributions in the most effective manner for a coordinated and appropriate response.

LO 4-7 The challenge of protecting intellectual property and the importance of a firm's dynamic capabilities.

- Intellectual property are resources owned by the firm in the forms of patents, copyrights, trademarks, and trade secrets.
- If property rights are not reliably protected by the state, there will be less incentive to develop new products and services.
- Dynamic capabilities include the ability to sense and seize new opportunities, generate new knowledge, and reconfigure existing assets and capabilities.
- Dynamic capabilities, therefore, define a firm's ability to innovate, adapt, and foster change that is favorable to customers and unfavorable to rivals.
- Dynamic capabilities can include many different activities that a firm might undertake to create competitive advantages such as product development, strategic decision making, and acquisitions.

SUMMARY REVIEW QUESTIONS

1. Explain the role of knowledge in today's competitive environment.
2. Why is it important for managers to recognize the interdependence in the attraction, development, and retention of talented professionals?
3. What are some of the potential downsides for firms that engage in a "war for talent"?
4. Discuss the need for managers to use social capital in leveraging their human capital both within and across their firm.
5. Discuss the key role of technology in leveraging knowledge and human capital.

key terms

knowledge economy 104
intellectual capital 105
human capital 106
social capital 106
explicit knowledge 106
tacit knowledge 106
360-degree evaluation and feedback systems 113
social network analysis 119
closure 120
bridging relationships 121
structural holes 121
groupthink 122
electronic teams 124
intellectual property rights 128
dynamic capabilities 129

EXPERIENTIAL EXERCISES AND APPLICATION QUESTIONS

1. Electronic teams, which we address in the section entitled "Electronic Teams: Using Technology to Enhance Collaboration," are becoming widely used in all types of organizations. We address key differences between e-teams and more traditional teams, the advantages associated with e-teams, as well as the challenges associated with making them effective. Conduct an interview with two managers in different types of organizations who work in e-teams as part of their job. Ask them what they believe are the key advantages as well as the major challenges associated with using e-teams. Then ask them how they believe e-teams can be made more effective in their organizations. (Note: Try to get the respondents to be as specific as they can in answering your questions.)
2. Pfizer, a leading healthcare firm with $53 billion in revenues, is often rated as one of *Fortune*'s "Most Admired Firms." It is also considered an excellent place to work and has generated high return to shareholders. Clearly, Pfizer values its human capital. Using the Internet and/or library resources, identify some of the actions/strategies Pfizer has taken to attract, develop, and retain human capital. What are their implications? (Fill in the following table.)
3. Look up successful firms in a high-technology industry as well as two successful firms in more traditional industries such as automobile manufacturing and retailing. Compare their market values and book values. What are some implications of these differences?
4. Select a firm for which you believe its social capital—both within the firm and among its suppliers and customers—is vital to its competitive advantage. Support your arguments.
5. Choose a company with which you are familiar. What are some of the ways in which it uses technology to leverage its human capital?
6. Using the Internet, look up a company with which you are familiar. What are some of the policies and procedures that it uses to enhance the firm's human and social capital?

ETHICS QUESTIONS

1. Recall an example of a firm that recently faced an ethical crisis. How do you feel the crisis and management's handling of it affected the firm's human capital and social capital?
2. Based on your experiences or what you have learned in your previous classes, are you familiar with any companies that used unethical practices to attract talented professionals? What do you feel were the short-term and long-term consequences of such practices?

Activity	Actions/Strategies	Implications
Attracting human capital		
Developing human capital		
Retaining human capital		

REFERENCES

1. Parts of this chapter draw upon some of the ideas and examples from Dess, G. G. & Picken, J. C. 1999. *Beyond productivity.* New York: AMACOM.
2. Amadeo, K. 2018. US manufacturing statistics, and outlook. the balance. com. July 21: np; Anonymous. 2018. Distribution of the workforce across economic sectors in the United States from 2007 to 2017. statistica.com: np; and, Dekas, K.H. et al. 2013. Organizational citizenship behavior, version 2.0: A review and qualitative investigation of OCB's for knowledge workers at Google and beyond. *Academy of Management Perspectives*, 27(3): 219-237.
3. Stewart, T. A. 1997. *Intellectual capital: The new wealth of organizations.* New York: Doubleday/Currency.
4. Colvin, G. 2015. The 100 best companies to work for. *Fortune.* March 15: 109.
5. Stewart, T. A. 2001. Accounting gets radical. *Fortune,* April 16: 184-194.
6. Adams, S. & Kichen, S. 2008. Ben Graham then and now. *Forbes, www.multpl.com/s-p-500-price-to-book,* November 10: 56.
7. An interesting discussion of Steve Jobs's impact on Apple's valuation is in Lashinsky, A. 2009. Steve's leave—what does it really mean? *Fortune,* February 2: 96-102.
8. Anonymous. 2007. Intel opens first high volume 45 nm microprocessor manufacturing factory. *www.intel.com,* October 25: np.
9. Thomas Stewart has suggested this formula in his book *Intellectual capital.* He provides an insightful discussion on pages 224-225, including some of the limitations of this approach to measuring intellectual capital. We recognize, of course, that during the late 1990s and in early 2000, there were some excessive market valuations of high-technology and Internet firms. For an interesting discussion of the extraordinary market valuation of Yahoo!, an Internet company, refer to Perkins, A. B. 2001. The Internet bubble encapsulated: Yahoo! *Red Herring,* April 15: 17-18.
10. Roberts, P. W. & Dowling, G. R. 2002. Corporate reputation and sustained superior financial

performance. *Strategic Management Journal,* 23(12): 1077–1095.

11. For a study on the relationships between human capital, learning, and sustainable competitive advantage, read Hatch, N. W. & Dyer, J. H. 2005. Human capital and learning as a source of sustainable competitive advantage. *Strategic Management Journal,* 25: 1155–1178.
12. One of the seminal contributions on knowledge management is Becker, G. S. 1993. *Human capital: A theoretical and empirical analysis with special reference to education* (3rd ed.). Chicago: University of Chicago Press.
13. For an excellent overview of the topic of social capital, read Baron, R. A. 2005. Social capital. In Hitt, M. A. & Ireland, R. D. (Eds.), *The Blackwell encyclopedia of management* (2nd ed.): 224–226. Malden, MA: Blackwell.
14. For an excellent discussion of social capital and its impact on organizational performance, refer to Nahapiet, J. & Ghoshal, S. 1998. Social capital, intellectual capital, and the organizational advantage. *Academy of Management Review,* 23: 242–266.
15. An interesting discussion of how knowledge management (patents) can enhance organizational performance can be found in Bogner, W. C. & Bansal, p. 2007. Knowledge management as the basis of sustained high performance. *Journal of Management Studies,* 44(1): 165–188.
16. Polanyi, M. 1967. *The tacit dimension.* Garden City, NY: Anchor.
17. Barney, J. B. 1991. Firm resources and sustained competitive advantage. *Journal of Management,* 17: 99–120.
18. For an interesting perspective of empirical research on how knowledge can adversely affect performance, read Haas, M. R. & Hansen, M. T. 2005. When using knowledge can hurt performance: The value of organizational capabilities in a management consulting company. *Strategic Management Journal,* 26(1): 1–24.
19. New insights on managing talent are provided in Cappelli, p. 2008. Talent management for the twenty-first century. *Harvard Business Review,* 66(3): 74–81.
20. Some of the notable books on this topic include Edvisson & Malone, op. cit.; Stewart, op. cit.; and Nonaka, I. & Takeuchi, I. 1995. *The knowledge creating company.* New York: Oxford University Press.
21. Segalla, M. & Felton, N. 2010. Find the real power in your organization. *Harvard Business Review,* 88(5): 34–35.
22. Stewart, T. A. 2000. Taking risk to the marketplace. *Fortune,* March 6: 424.
23. Lobel, O. 2013.*Talent Wants to Be Free: Why We Should Learn to Love Leaks, Raids, and Free Riding.* New Haven, CT: Yale University Press.
24. Insights on Generation X's perspective on the workplace are in Erickson, T. J. 2008. Task, not time: Profile of a Gen Y job. *Harvard Business Review,* 86(2): 19.
25. Pfeffer, J. 2010. Building sustainable organizations: The human factor. *Academy of Management Perspectives,* 24(1): 34–45.
26. Lobel, op. cit.
27. Some workplace implications for the aging workforce are addressed in Strack, R., Baier, J., & Fahlander, A. 2008. Managing demographic risk. *Harvard Business Review,* 66(2): 119–128.
28. For a discussion of attracting, developing, and retaining top talent, refer to Goffee, R. & Jones, G. 2007. Leading clever people. *Harvard Business Review,* 85(3): 72–89.
29. Winston, A. S. 2014. *The big pivot.* Boston: Harvard Business Review Press.
30. Dess & Picken, op. cit., p. 34.
31. Webber, A. M. 1998. Danger: Toxic company. *Fast Company,* November: 152–161.
32. Martin, J. & Schmidt, C. 2010. How to keep your top talent. *Harvard Business Review,* 88(5): 54–61.
33. Some interesting insights on why home-grown American talent is going abroad are found in Saffo, P. 2009. A looming American diaspora. *Harvard Business Review,* 87(2): 27.
34. Grossman, M. 2012. The best advice I ever got. *Fortune,* May 12: 119.
35. Davenport, T. H., Harris, J., & Shapiro, J. 2010. Competing on talent analytics. *Harvard Business Review,* 88(10): 62–69.
36. Ployhart, R. E. & Moliterno, T. P. 2011. Emergence of the human capital resource: A multilevel model. *Academy of Management Review,* 36(1): 127–150.
37. For insights on management development and firm performance in several countries, refer to Mabey, C. 2008. Management development and firm performance in Germany, Norway, Spain, and the UK. *Journal of International Business Studies,* 39(8): 1327–1342.
38. Martin, J. 1998. So, you want to work for the best.... *Fortune,* January 12: 77.
39. Cardin, R. 1997. Make your own Bozo Filter. *Fast Company,* October-November: 56.
40. The next two paragraphs draw upon: Weber, L. 2018. Now fighting for top tech talent: Makers of turbines, tools, and Toyotas,*wsj.com.* May 31: np. 40. Anonymous. 100 best companies to work for. *money.cnn.com,* undated: np.
41. Martin, op. cit.; Henkoff, R. 1993. Companies that train best. *Fortune,* March 22: 53–60.
42. This section draws on: Garg, V. 2012. Here's why companies should give Millennial workers everything they ask for. *buisnessinsider.com,* August 23: np; *worklifepolicy.com;* and Gerdes, L. 2006. The top 50 employers for new college grads. *BusinessWeek,* September 18: 64–81.
43. An interesting perspective on developing new talent rapidly when they join an organization can be found in Rollag, K., Parise, S., & Cross, R. 2005. Getting new hires up to speed quickly. *MIT Sloan Management Review,* 46(2): 35–41.
44. Stewart, T. A. 1998. Gray flannel suit? Moi? *Fortune,* March 18: 80–82.
45. Bryant, A. 2011.*The Corner Office: Indispensable and Unexpected Lessons from CEOs on How to Lead and Succeed.* New York: Macmillan Publishers.
46. An interesting perspective on how Cisco Systems develops its talent can be found in Chatman, J., O'Reilly, C., & Chang, V. 2005. Cisco Systems: Developing a human capital strategy. *California Management Review,* 47(2): 137–166.
47. Anonymous. 2011. Schumpeter: The tussle for talent. *The Economist,* January 8: 68.
48. Training and development policy: Mentoring. *opm.gov:* undated, np.
49. Douglas, C. A. 1997. Formal mentoring programs in organizations. *centerforcreativeleadership.org:* np.
50. Warner, F. 2002. Inside Intel's mentoring movement.*Fast Company,* March 31.
51. Grove, A. 2011. Be a mentor. *Bloomberg Businessweek,* September 21: 80.
52. Colvin, G. 2016. Developing an internal market for talent. *Fortune.* March 1: 22.
53. Colvin, G. 1997. Developing an internal market for talent. *Fortune,* October 31: 56.
54. For an innovative perspective on the appropriateness of alternate approaches to evaluation and rewards, refer to Seijts, G. H. & Lathan, G. p. 2005. Learning versus performance goals: When should each be used? *Academy of Management Executive,* 19(1): 124–132.

55. The discussion of the 360-degree feedback system draws on the article UPS. 1997. 360-degree feedback: Coming from all sides. *Vision* (a UPS Corporation internal company publication), March: 3; Slater, R. 1994. *Get better or get beaten: Thirty-one leadership secrets from Jack Welch.* Burr Ridge, IL: Irwin; Nexon, M. 1997. General Electric: The secrets of the finest company in the world. *L'Expansion,* July 23: 18-30; and Smith, D. 1996. Bold new directions for human resources. *Merck World* (internal company publication), October: 8.
56. Interesting insights on 360-degree evaluation systems are discussed in Barwise, P. & Meehan, Sean. 2008. So you think you're a good listener. *Harvard Business Review,* 66(4): 22-23.
57. Insights into the use of 360-degree evaluation are in Kaplan, R. E. & Kaiser, R. B. 2009. Stop overdoing your strengths. *Harvard Business Review,* 87(2): 100-103.
58. Mankins, M., Bird, A., & Root, J. 2013. Making star teams out of star players. *Harvard Business Review,* 91(1/2): 74-78.
59. Harley, J. Fathom Realty gives agents stock, and they buy into purpose. *Dallas Morning News.*
60. Kets de Vries, M. F. R. 1998. Charisma in action: The transformational abilities of Virgin's Richard Branson and ABB's Percy Barnevik. *Organizational Dynamics,* Winter: 20.
61. We have only to consider the most celebrated case of industrial espionage in recent years, wherein José Ignacio Lopez was indicted in a German court for stealing sensitive product planning documents from his former employer, General Motors, and sharing them with his executive colleagues at Volkswagen. The lawsuit was dismissed by the German courts, but Lopez and his colleagues were investigated by the U.S. Justice Department. Also consider the recent litigation involving noncompete employment contracts and confidentiality clauses of *International Paper v. Louisiana-Pacific, Campbell Soup v. H. J. Heinz Co.,* and *PepsiCo v. Quaker Oats's Gatorade.* In addition to retaining valuable human resources and often their valuable network of customers, firms must also protect proprietary information and knowledge. For interesting insights, refer to Carley, W. M. 1998. CEO gets hard lesson in how not to keep his lieutenants. *The Wall Street Journal,* February 11: A1, A10; and Lenzner, R. & Shook, C. 1998. Whose Rolodex is it, anyway? *Forbes,* February 23: 100-103.
62. We have only to consider the most celebrated case of industrial espionage in recent years, wherein José Ignacio Lopez was indicted in a German court for stealing sensitive product planning documents from his former employer, General Motors, and sharing them with his executive colleagues at Volkswagen. The lawsuit was dismissed by the German courts, but Lopez and his colleagues were investigated by the U.S. Justice Department. Also consider the recent litigation involving noncompete employment contracts and confidentiality clauses of *International Paper v. Louisiana-Pacific, Campbell Soup v. H. J. Heinz Co.,* and *PepsiCo v. Quaker Oats's Gatorade.* In addition to retaining valuable human resources and often their valuable network of customers, firms must also protect proprietary information and knowledge. For interesting insights, refer to Carley, W. M. 1998. CEO gets hard lesson in how not to keep his lieutenants. *The Wall Street Journal,* February 11: A1, A10; and Lenzner, R. & Shook, C. 1998. Whose Rolodex is it, anyway? *Forbes,* February 23: 100-103.
63. For an insightful discussion of retention of knowledge workers in today's economy, read Davenport, T. H. 2005. *The care and feeding of the knowledge worker.* Boston, MA: Harvard Business School Press.
64. Weber, L. 2014. Korn/Ferry's CEO: What boards want in executives.*The Wall Street Journal,* December 21.
65. Fisher, A. 2008. America's most admired companies. *Fortune,* March 17: 74.
66. Stewart, T. A. 2001. *The wealth of knowledge,* New York: Currency.
67. For insights on fulfilling one's potential, refer to Kaplan, R. S. 2008. Reaching your potential. *Harvard Business Review,* 66(7/8): 45-57.
68. Amabile, T. M. 1997. Motivating creativity in organizations: On doing what you love and loving what you do. *California Management Review,* 40(1): 39-58.
69. For an insightful perspective on alternate types of employee-employer relationships, read Erickson, T. J. & Gratton, L. 2007. What it means to work here. *Harvard Business Review,* 85(3): 104-112.
70. Little, L. 2016. Leadership innovation. *Baylor Magazine.* Winter: 31.
71. Ignatius, A., and D. McGinn. 2015. Novo Nordisk CEO Lars Sorensen on what propelled him to the top. *Harvard Business Review,*93(11): 50-63.
72. Pfeffer, J. 2001. Fighting the war for talent is hazardous to your organization's health. *Organizational Dynamics,* 29(4): 248-259.
73. Best companies to work for 2011. 2011. *finance.yahoo.com,* January 20: np.
74. This section draws on Dewhurst, M., Hancock, B., & Ellsworth, D. 2013. Redesigning knowledge work. *Harvard Business Review,* 91 (1/2): 58-64.
75. Cox, T. L. 1991. The multinational organization. *Academy of Management Executive,* 5(2): 34-47. Without doubt, a great deal has been written on the topic of creating and maintaining an effective diverse workforce. Some excellent, recent books include Harvey, C. P. & Allard, M. J. 2005. *Understanding and managing diversity: Readings, cases, and exercises* (3rd ed.). Upper Saddle River, NJ: Pearson Prentice-Hall; Miller, F. A. & Katz, J. H. 2002. *The inclusion breakthrough: Unleashing the real power of diversity.* San Francisco: Berrett Koehler; and Williams, M. A. 2001. *The 10 lenses: Your guide to living and working in a multicultural world.* Sterling, VA: Capital Books.
76. For an interesting perspective on benefits and downsides of diversity in global consulting firms, refer to Mors, M. L. 2010. Innovation in a global consulting firm: When the problem is too much diversity. *Strategic Management Journal,* 31(8): 841-872.
77. Day, J. C. Undated. National population projections. *cps.ipums.org:* np.
78. Hewlett, S. A. & Rashid, R. 2010. The battle for female talent in emerging markets. *Harvard Business Review,* 88(5): 101-107.
79. This section, including the six potential benefits of a diverse workforce, draws on Cox, T. H. & Blake, S. 1991. Managing cultural diversity: Implications for organizational competitiveness. *Academy of Management Executive,* 5(3): 45-56.
80. *www.pwcglobal.com/us/eng/careers/diversity/index.html.*
81. Hewlett, S. A., Marshall, M., & Sherbin, L. 2013. How diversity can drive innovation. *Harvard Business Review,* 91(12): 30.
82. This discussion draws on Dess, G. G. & Lumpkin, G. T. 2001. Emerging issues in strategy process research. In Hitt, M. A., Freeman, R. E., & Harrison, J. S. (Eds.), *Handbook of strategic management:* 3-34. Malden, MA: Blackwell.

83. Wong, S.-S. & Boh, W. F. 2010. Leveraging the ties of others to build a reputation for trustworthiness among peers. *Academy of Management Journal,* 53(1): 129-148.

84. Adler, P. S. & Kwon, S. W. 2002. Social capital: Prospects for a new concept. *Academy of Management Review,* 27(1): 17-40.

85. Capelli, p. 2000. A market-driven approach to retaining talent. *Harvard Business Review,* 78(1): 103-113.

86. This hypothetical example draws on Peteraf, M. 1993. The cornerstones of competitive advantage. *Strategic Management Journal,* 14: 179-191.

87. Wernerfelt, B. 1984. A resource-based view of the firm. *Strategic Management Journal,* 5: 171-180.

88. Wysocki, B., Jr. 2000. Yet another hazard of the new economy: The Pied Piper effect. *The Wall Street Journal,* March 20: A1-A16.

89. Ideas on how managers can more effectively use their social network are addressed in McGrath, C. & Zell, D. 2009. Profiles of trust: Who to turn to, and for what. *MIT Sloan Management Review,* 50(2): 75-80.

90. Ibid.

91. Buckman, R. C. 2000. Tech defectors from Microsoft resettle together. *The Wall Street Journal,* October: B1-B6.

92. Malone, T. W. 2004.*The Future of Work: How the New Order of Business Will Shape Your Organization, Your Management Style, and Your Life.* Brighton, MA: Harvard Business School Publishing.

93. Aime, F., Johnson, S., Ridge, J. W., & Hill, A. D. 2010. The routine may be stable but the advantage is not: Competitive implications of key employee mobility. *Strategic Management Journal,* 31(1): 75-87.

94. Ibarra, H., and M. T. Hansen. 2011. Are you a collaborative leader? *Harvard Business Review,* 89(7/8): 68-74.

95. Battilana, J., and T. Casciaro. 2013. The network secrets of great change agents. *Harvard Business Review,* 91(7/8): 62-68.

96. There has been a tremendous amount of theory building and empirical research in recent years in the area of social network analysis. Unquestionably, two of the major contributors to this domain have been Ronald Burt and J. S. Coleman. For excellent background discussions, refer to Burt, R. S. 1992. *Structural holes: The social structure of competition.* Cambridge, MA: Harvard University Press; Coleman, J. S. 1990. *Foundations of social theory.* Cambridge, MA: Harvard University Press; and Coleman, J. S. 1988. Social capital in the creation of human capital. *American Journal of Sociology,* 94: S95-S120. For a more recent review and integration of current thought on social network theory, consider Burt, R. S. 2005. *Brokerage & closure: An introduction to social capital.* New York: Oxford Press.

97. Our discussion draws on the concepts developed by Burt, 1992, op. cit.; Coleman, 1990, op. cit.; Coleman, 1988, op. cit.; and Oh, H., Chung, M., & Labianca, G. 2004. Group social capital and group effectiveness: The role of informal socializing ties. *Academy of Management Journal,* 47(6): 860-875. We would like to thank Joe Labianca (University of Kentucky) for his helpful feedback and ideas in our discussion of social networks.

98. Arregle, J. L., Hitt, M. A., Sirmon, D. G., & Very, p. 2007. The development of organizational social capital: Attributes of family firms. *Journal of Management Studies,* 44(1): 73-95.

99. A novel perspective on social networks is in Pentland, A. 2009. How social networks network best. *Harvard Business Review,* 87(2): 37.

100. Oh et al., op. cit.

101. Hoppe, B. 2004. Good ideas at Raytheon and big holes in our own backyard. *connectedness.blogspot.com,* July 8: np.

102. Perspectives on how to use and develop decision networks are discussed in Cross, R., Thomas, R. J., & Light, D. A. 2009. How "who you know" affects what you decide. *MIT Sloan Management Review,* 50(2): 35-42.

103. Our discussion of the three advantages of social networks draws on Uzzi, B. & Dunlap. S. 2005. How to build your network. *Harvard Business Review,* 83(12): 53-60. For an excellent review on the research exploring the relationship between social capital and managerial performance, read Moran, p. 2005. Structural vs. relational embeddedness: Social capital and managerial performance. *Strategic Management Journal,* 26(12): 1129-1151.

104. EN. Setharaman, D. & Glazer, E. 2018. Sandberg assesses gender equality. *The Wall Street Journal.* October 25: B5.

105. Setharaman, D. & Glazer, E. 2018. Sandberg assesses gender equality. The Wall Street Journal. October 25: B5.

106. Ibarra, H. 2018. C-Suite strategies (A special report) - What women need to do to network. wsj.com. May 21: np; and, Hyder, S. 2017. Why do professional women need networking more than men? inc.com. August 27: np.

107. Prusak, L. & Cohen, D. 2001. How to invest in social capital. *Harvard Business Review,* 79(6): 86-93.

108. Leonard, D. & Straus, S. 1997. Putting your company's whole brain to work. *Harvard Business Review,* 75(4): 110-122.

109. For an excellent discussion of public (i.e., the organization) versus private (i.e., the individual manager) benefits of social capital, refer to Leana, C. R. & Van Buren, H. J. 1999. Organizational social capital and employment practices. *Academy of Management Review,* 24(3): 538-555.

110. The authors would like to thank Joe Labianca, University of Kentucky, and John Lin, University of Texas at Dallas, for their very helpful input in our discussion of social network theory and its practical implications.

111. Goldsmith, M. 2009. How not to lose the top job. *Harvard Business Review,* 87(1): 74.

112. Taylor, W. C. 1999. Whatever happened to globalization? *Fast Company,* December: 228-236.

113. Wilson, H. J., Guinan, P. J., Parise, S., and B. D. Weinberg. 2011. What's your social media strategy? Harvard Business Review, 89(7/8): 23-25.

114. Lei, D., Slocum, J., & Pitts, R. A. 1999. Designing organizations for competitive advantage: The power of unlearning and learning. *Organizational Dynamics,* Winter: 24-38.

115. This section draws upon Zaccaro, S. J. & Bader, p. 2002. E-leadership and the challenges of leading e-teams: Minimizing the bad and maximizing the good. *Organizational Dynamics,* 31(4): 377-387.

116. Kirkman, B. L., Rosen, B., Tesluk, P. E., & Gibson, C. B. 2004. The impact of team empowerment on virtual team performance: The moderating role of face-to-face interaction. *Academy of Management Journal,* 47(2): 175-192.

117. The discussion of the advantages and challenges associated with e-teams draws on Zaccaro & Bader, op. cit.

118. For a study exploring the relationship between team empowerment, face-to-face interaction, and performance in virtual teams, read Kirkman, Rosen, Tesluk, & Gibson, op. cit.

119. For an innovative study on how firms share knowledge with competitors and the performance implications, read Spencer, J. W. 2003. Firms'

knowledge sharing strategies in the global innovation system: Empirical evidence from the flat panel display industry. *Strategic Management Journal,* 24(3): 217–235.

120. Hansen, M. T., Nohria, N., and T. J. Tierney. 2011. What's your strategy for managing knowledge? *Harvard Business Review.*

121. This discussion draws on Conley, J. G. 2005. *Intellectual capital management.* Kellogg School of Management and Schulich School of Business, York University, Toronto, ON; Conley, J. G. & Szobocsan, J. 2001. Snow White shows the way. *Managing Intellectual Property,* June: 15–25; Greenspan, A. 2004. Intellectual property rights. Federal Reserve Board, Remarks by the chairman, February 27; and Teece, D. J. 1998. Capturing value from knowledge assets. *California Management Review,* 40(3): 54–79. The authors would like to thank Professor Theo Peridis, York University, for his contribution to this section.

122. This example draws on: Nocera, J. 2018. IBM's got patents and isn't afraid to enforce them. *Bloomberg Businessweek.* August 20: 64; and, Wolfe, J. 2018. IBM seeks $167 million from Groupon in dispute over early internet patents. *reuters.com.* July 18: np.

123. The first three brief paragraphs in this section draw on: Felin, T. & Powell, T. C. 2016. Designing organizations for dynamic capabilities.*California Management Review,* 58 (4): 78-96.

124. Teece, D., Peteraf, M., & Leih, S. 2016. Dynamic capabilities and organizational agility: Risk, uncertainty, and strategy in the innovation economy. *California Management Review,* 58 (4): 13-35.

125. Birkinshaw, J., Zimmerman, A., & Raisch, S. 2016. How do firms adapt to discontinuous change? Bridging the dynamic capabilities with ambidexterity perspectives. *California Management Review,* 58 (4): 36-58

126. Lee, G. K. 2008. Relevance of organizational capabilities and its dynamics: What to learn from entrants' product portfolios about the determinants of entry timing. *Strategic Management Journal,* 29 (12): 1257-1280; and, Eisenhardt, K. M. & Martin, J. E. 2000. Dynamic capabilities: What are they? *Strategic Management Journal,* 21: 1105-1121.

Nico Muller Art/Shutterstock

Business-Level Strategy

Creating and Sustaining Competitive Advantages

Learning Objectives

LO5-1 Describe the central role of competitive advantage in the study of strategic management and the three generic strategies: overall cost leadership, differentiation, and focus.

LO5-2 Explain how the successful attainment of generic strategies can improve a firm's relative power vis-à-vis the five forces that determine an industry's average profitability.

LO5-3 Identify the pitfalls managers must avoid in striving to attain generic strategies.

LO5-4 Explain how firms can effectively combine the generic strategies of overall cost leadership and differentiation.

LO5-5 Identify which factors determine the sustainability of a firm's competitive advantage.

LO5-6 Understand the importance of considering the industry life cycle to determine a firm's **business-level strategy** and its relative emphasis on functional area strategies and value-creating activities.

LO5-7 Understand the need for turnaround strategies that enable a firm to reposition its competitive position in an industry.

business-level strategy
a strategy designed for a firm or a division of a firm that competes within a single business.

We encourage you to reflect on how the concepts presented in this chapter can enhance your career success (see "Reflecting on Career Implications..." at the end of the chapter).

LEARNING FROM MISTAKES

A&P was the first traditional supermarket operator in the United States, with its roots going back to 1859. In its heyday, the firm operated over 4,200 stores. During the period from 1915 to 1975, A&P was the largest grocery retailer in the country. However it suffered a long, painful decline that led to multiple reorganization efforts as well as bankruptcies. In 2015, the long struggle to revive the firm came to an end when, as part of a bankruptcy filing, A&P sold off or closed its final 256 stores.[1]

What happened to this retailing icon? They were simply stuck in the middle. When it was on top, A&P provided a clear value proposition for its customers. It was one of the most cost-efficient retailers in the market while providing a wide array of products for its customers. As a result, it had both cost and differentiation advantages over its rivals. However, things started to turn in the 1950s. Rather than invest in, expand, and modernize its stores, its controlling owners distributed most of its profits to shareholders through large dividends. At the same time, new and aggressive competitors started to enter the market, and these competitors eroded A&P's distinctive positioning. In the battle to win the business of cost-conscious customers, A&P faced stiff competition from massive general market retailers, most notably Walmart, as well as focused discounters, such as dollar stores and discount grocers, including Aldi. Customers looking for a higher level of service and specialty foods gravitated to grocery retailers that offered a higher level of service in larger stores, such as Wegmans, and newer high-end providers, such as Whole Foods, that offered gourmet foods and wider organic food product lines.

A&P was initially slow to respond to these challenges. When they finally did respond, as Jim Hertel, a grocery industry consultant stated, "They got caught in a downward spiral of sales declines that forced them to cut costs." This resulted in challenges of hiring enough qualified staff and limited funds to update or upgrade stores. Even so, they were still at a cost disadvantage to both Walmart and Aldi. This left A&P with both higher prices than Walmart and other discounters and stores that felt old and dirty. In other words, the firm offered little in terms of value for its customers. After its initial bankruptcy, A&P attempted to modernize its stores and rebrand itself as a more upscale grocery retailer but lacked the financial resources to follow through on the change.

Discussion Questions

1. What decisions did A&P make when it was successful that led to its later failure?
2. How should the firm have responded to the new competitive challenges it faced?
3. What firm do you see today that faces similar challenges? How should this firm respond and act to reinforce its strategic position?

In order to create and sustain a competitive advantage, companies need to stay focused on their customers' evolving wants and needs and not sacrifice their strategic position as they mature and the market around them evolves. Since A&P failed to invest in and reinforce its market position as the grocery industry matured and new entrants came into the market, it is not surprising that its market leadership eroded, and it was forced out of the market.

LO 5-1

Describe the central role of competitive advantage in the study of strategic management and the three generic strategies: overall cost leadership, differentiation, and focus.

TYPES OF COMPETITIVE ADVANTAGE AND SUSTAINABILITY

generic strategies basic types of business-level strategies based on breadth of target market (industrywide versus narrow market segment) and type of competitive advantage (low cost versus uniqueness).

Michael Porter presented three **generic strategies** that a firm can use to overcome the five forces and achieve competitive advantage.[2] Each of Porter's generic strategies has the potential to allow a firm to outperform rivals in their industry. The first, *overall cost leadership,* is based on creating a low-cost position. Here, a firm must manage the relationships throughout the value chain and lower costs throughout the entire chain. Second, *differentiation* requires a firm to create products and/or services that are unique and valued. Here, the primary emphasis is on "nonprice" attributes for which customers will gladly pay a premium.[3] Third, a *focus* strategy directs attention (or "focus") toward narrow product lines, buyer segments, or targeted geographic markets, and they must attain advantages through either differentiation or cost leadership.[4] Whereas the overall cost leadership and differentiation strategies strive to attain advantages industrywide, focusers have a narrow target market in mind. Exhibit 5.1 illustrates these three strategies on two dimensions: competitive advantage and markets served.

Both casual observation and research support the notion that firms that identify with one or more of the forms of competitive advantage outperform those that do not.[5] There has been a rich history of strategic management research addressing this topic. One study analyzed 1,789 strategic business units and found that businesses combining multiple forms of competitive advantage (differentiation and overall cost leadership) outperformed businesses that used only a single form. The lowest performers were those that did not identify with any type of advantage. They were classified as "stuck in the middle." Results of this study are presented in Exhibit 5.2.[6]

For an example of the dangers of being stuck in the middle, consider department stores. Chains, such as J.C. Penney and Sears, used to be the main retailers consumers would shop at for clothes and housewares. However, they find themselves in a situation today where affluent customers are going upmarket to retailers like Saks Fifth Avenue for exclusive designer clothes while budget-conscious consumers are drifting to discount chains such as TJ Maxx and Ross Stores.

EXHIBIT 5.1 Three Generic Strategies

Markets Served	Competitive Advantage: Low Cost Position	Competitive Advantage: Superior Perceived Value by Customer
Broad Target Market	Overall Cost Leadership	Broad Differentiation
Narrow Target Markets	Cost Focus	Differentiation Focus

Source: Adapted from Porter, M. E. 1980, 1998. *Competitive Strategy: Techniques for Analyzing Industries and Competitors*. Free Press.

EXHIBIT 5.2 Competitive Advantage and Business Performance

	Competitive Advantage					
	Differentiation and Cost	Differentiation	Cost	Differentiation and Focus	Cost and Focus	Stuck in the Middle
Performance						
Return on investment (%)	35.5	32.9	30.2	17.0	23.7	17.8
Sales growth (%)	15.1	13.5	13.5	16.4	17.5	12.2
Gain in market share (%)	5.3	5.3	5.5	6.1	6.3	4.4
Sample size	123	160	100	141	86	105

Overall Cost Leadership

The first generic strategy is **overall cost leadership**. Overall cost leadership requires a tight set of interrelated tactics that include:

overall cost leadership
a firm's generic strategy based on appeal to the industrywide market using a competitive advantage based on low cost.

- Aggressive construction of efficient-scale facilities.
- Vigorous pursuit of cost reductions from experience.
- Tight cost and overhead control.
- Avoidance of marginal customer accounts.
- Cost minimization in all activities in the firm's value chain, such as R&D, service, sales force, and advertising.

Exhibit 5.3 draws on the value-chain concept (see Chapter 3) to provide examples of how a firm can attain an overall cost leadership strategy in its primary and support activities.

One factor often central to an overall cost leadership strategy is the **experience curve,** which refers to how business "learns" to lower costs as it gains experience with production processes. With experience, unit costs of production decline as output increases in most industries. The experience curve, developed by the Boston Consulting Group in 1968, is a way of looking at efficiency gains that come with experience. For a range of products, as cumulative experience doubles, costs and labor hours needed to produce a unit of product decline by 10 to 30 percent. There are a number of reasons why we find this effect. Among the most common factors are workers getting better at what they do, product designs being simplified as the product matures, and production processes being automated and streamlined. However, experience curve gains will be the foundation for a cost advantage only if the firm knows the source of the cost reduction and can keep these gains proprietary.

experience curve
the decline in unit costs of production as cumulative output increases.

To generate above-average performance, a firm following an overall cost leadership position must attain **competitive parity** on the basis of differentiation relative to competitors.[7] In other words, a firm achieving parity is similar to its competitors, or "on par," with respect to differentiated products.[8] Competitive parity on the basis of differentiation permits a cost leader to translate cost advantages directly into higher profits than competitors. Thus, the cost leader earns above-average returns.[9]

competitive parity
a firm's achievement of similarity, or being "on par," with competitors with respect to low cost, differentiation, or other strategic product characteristic.

The failure to attain parity on the basis of differentiation can be illustrated with an example from the automobile industry–the Tata Nano. Tata, an Indian conglomerate, developed the Nano to be the cheapest car in the world. At a price of about $2,000, the Nano was expected to draw in middle-class customers in India and developing markets as well as budget conscious customers in Europe and North America. However, it hasn't caught on in either market. The Nano doesn't have some of the basic features expected with cars, such as

EXHIBIT 5.3

Value-Chain Activities: Examples of Overall Cost Leadership

Support Activities

Firm Infrastructure

- Few management layers to reduce overhead costs.
- Standardized accounting practices to minimize personnel required.

Human Resource Management

- Minimize costs associated with employee turnover through effective policies.
- Effective orientation and training programs to maximize employee productivity.

Technology Development

- Effective use of automated technology to reduce scrappage rates.
- Expertise in process engineering to reduce manufacturing costs.

Procurement

- Effective policy guidelines to ensure low-cost raw materials (with acceptable quality levels).
- Shared purchasing operations with other business units.

Primary Activities

Inbound Logistics

- Effective layout of receiving dock operations.

Operations

- Effective use of quality control inspectors to minimize rework.

Outbound Logistics

- Effective utilization of delivery fleets.

Marketing and Sales

- Purchase of media in large blocks.
- Sales force utilization is maximized by territory management.

Service

- Thorough service repair guidelines to minimize repeat maintenance calls.
- Use of single type of vehicle to minimize repair costs.

Source: Adapted from Porter, M. E. 1985. *Competitive Advantage: Creating and Sustaining Superior Performance.* New York: Free Press.

power steering and a passenger side mirror. It also faces concerns about safety. In crash tests, the Nano received zero stars for adult protection and didn't meet basic UN safety requirements. Also, there were numerous reports of Nanos catching fire. Due to all of these factors, the Nano has simply been seen by customers as offering a lousy value proposition.[10]

The lesson is simple. Price is just one component of value. No matter how good the price, the most cost-sensitive consumer won't buy a bad product.

Gordon Bethune, the former CEO of Continental Airlines, summed up the need to provide good products or services when employing a low-cost strategy this way: "You can make a pizza so cheap, nobody will buy it."[11]

Next, we discuss two examples of firms that have built a cost leadership position.

Aldi, a discount supermarket retailer, has grown from its German base to the rest of Europe, Australia, and the United States by replicating a simple business format. Aldi limits the number of products (SKUs in the grocery business) in each category to ensure

5.1 STRATEGY SPOTLIGHT — ENVIRONMENTAL SUSTAINABILITY

PRIMARK STRIVES TO BALANCE LOW COSTS WITH ENVIRONMENTAL SUSTAINABILITY

Primark may be the most successful brand most Americans have never heard of. Though it didn't open its first U.S. store until 2015, it has been one of the fastest growing fashion retailers in the world over the last fifteen years, growing 286 percent between 2004 and 2018. The Irish-based retailer focuses on selling trendy clothes at astonishingly low prices. It emphasizes keeping its cost structure lower than any of its rivals by leveraging streamlined logistics, a very low marketing budget, and its large scale that helps it get bargain prices from its suppliers. It also marks its prices up above cost less than its major rivals. As a result, the average selling price of an article of women's clothing at Primark was 60 percent less than H&M, one of its major rivals, in Britain. It aims to make up for low margins by selling at a higher volume than its rivals. For example, for every square foot, Primark generates 55 percent greater sales annually than H&M. Primark's customers often buy a series of outfits, wear them a few times, and then come back for a fresh set of outfits. Primark appears to be benefiting from the "Instagram effect," where young fashion-conscious consumers feel the need to regularly post selfies of new outfits they just bought.

While it strives for low costs, the firm also tries to balance this with the need for sustainability. Primark developed the Primark Sustainable Cotton Program in partnership with the Self-Employed Women's Association (SEWA) and social business CottonConnect. In this effort, they promote sustainable farming methods to female smallholder cotton farmers in India that provide economic opportunities for women; reduce the use of fertilizer, pesticides and water; and improve cotton yields. As a result of its efforts, Primark has been honored by Greenpeace with a Detox Leader Award and by the Chartered Institute of Procurement with a Best Contribution to Corporate Responsibility Award.

Sources: Anonymous, 2015. Faster, cheaper fashion. *economist.com,* September 5: np; Doshi, V. 2016. Primark tackles fast fashion critics with cotton farmer project in India. *theguardian.com,* September 30: np; McGregor, L. 2016. Can Primark really claim to be sustainable? *sourcingjournalonline.com,* October 17: np; Percival, G. 2016. Irish arm helps to drive 9% sales growth at Primark. *irishexaminer.com,* September 13: np. statista.com

product turn, to ease stocking shelves, and to increase its power over suppliers. It also sells mostly private-label products to minimize cost. It has small, efficient, and simply designed stores. It offers limited services and expects customers to bring their own bags and bag their own groceries. As a result, Aldi can offer its products at prices 40 percent lower than competing supermarkets.[12]

Zulily, an online retailer, has built its business model around lower-cost operations in order to carve out a unique position relative to Amazon and other online retailers. Zulily keeps very little inventory and typically orders products from vendors only when customers purchase the product. It also has developed a bare-bones distribution system. Together, these actions result in deliveries that take an average of 11.5 days to get to customers and can sometimes stretch out to several weeks. Due to its reduced operational costs, Zulily is able to offer attractive prices to customers who are willing to wait.[13]

A business that strives for a low-cost advantage must attain an absolute cost advantage relative to its rivals.[14] This is typically accomplished by offering a no-frills product or service to a broad target market using standardization to derive the greatest benefits from economies of scale and experience. However, such a strategy may fail if a firm is unable to attain parity on important dimensions of differentiation such as quick responses to customer requests for services or design changes. Strategy Spotlight 5.1 discusses how Primark, an Irish clothing retailer, has built a low-cost strategy while also being seen as effectively addressing concerns about environmental sustainability.

LO 5-2

Explain how the successful attainment of generic strategies can improve a firm's relative power vis-à-vis the five forces that determine an industry's average profitability.

Overall Cost Leadership: Improving Competitive Position vis-à-vis the Five Forces An overall low-cost position enables a firm to achieve above-average returns despite strong competition. It protects a firm against rivalry from competitors, because lower costs allow a firm to earn returns even if its competitors eroded their profits through intense rivalry. A low-cost position also protects firms against powerful buyers. Buyers can exert power to drive down prices only to the level of the next most efficient producer. Also, a low-cost position provides more flexibility to cope with demands from powerful suppliers for input cost increases. The factors that lead to a low-cost position also provide a substantial entry barriers position with respect to substitute products introduced by new and existing competitors.[15]

A few examples will illustrate these points. Zulily's close attention to costs helps to protect the company from buyer power and intense rivalry from competitors. Thus, Zulily is able to drive down costs and reduce the bargaining power of its customers. By cutting costs lower than other discount clothing retailers, Primark both lessens the degree of rivalry it faces and increases entry barriers for new entrants. Aldi's extreme focus on minimizing costs across its operations makes it less vulnerable to substitutes, such as discount retailers like Walmart and dollar stores.

LO 5-3

Identify the pitfalls managers must avoid in striving to attain generic strategies.

Potential Pitfalls of Overall Cost Leadership Strategies Potential pitfalls of an overall cost leadership strategy include:

- ***Too much focus on one or a few value-chain activities.*** Would you consider a person to be astute if he canceled his newspaper subscription and quit eating out to save money but then "maxed out" several credit cards, requiring him to pay hundreds of dollars a month in interest charges? Of course not. Similarly, firms need to pay attention to all activities in the value chain.[16] Too often managers make big cuts in operating expenses but don't question year-to-year spending on capital projects. Or managers may decide to cut selling and marketing expenses but ignore manufacturing expenses. Managers should explore *all* value-chain activities, including relationships among them, as candidates for cost reductions.
- ***Increase in the cost of the inputs on which the advantage is based.*** Firms can be vulnerable to price increases in the factors of production. For example, consider manufacturing firms based in China that rely on low labor costs. Due to demographic factors, the supply of workers 16 to 24 years old has peaked and will drop by a third in the next 12 years, thanks to stringent family-planning policies that have sharply reduced China's population growth.[17] This is leading to upward pressure on labor costs in Chinese factories, undercutting the cost advantage of firms producing there.
- ***A strategy that can be imitated too easily.*** One of the common pitfalls of a cost leadership strategy is that a firm's strategy may consist of value-creating activities that are easy to imitate.[18] Such has been the case with online brokers in recent years.[19] As of early 2019, there were over 200 online brokers listed on allstocks.com, hardly symbolic of an industry where imitation is extremely difficult. And according to Henry McVey, financial services analyst at Morgan Stanley, "We think you need five to ten" online brokers.
- ***A lack of parity on differentiation.*** As noted earlier, firms striving to attain cost leadership advantages must obtain a level of parity on differentiation.[20] Firms providing online degree programs may offer low prices. However, they may not be successful unless they can offer instruction that is perceived as comparable to traditional providers. For them, parity can be achieved on differentiation dimensions such as reputation and quality and through signaling mechanisms such as accreditation agencies.
- ***Reduced flexibility.*** Building up a low-cost advantage often requires significant investments in plant and equipment, distribution systems, and large, economically scaled operations. As a result, firms often find that these investments limit their flexibility, leading to great difficulty responding to changes in the environment. For example, Coors Brewing developed a highly efficient, large-scale brewery in Golden, Colorado. Coors was one of the most efficient brewers in the world, but its plant was designed to mass-produce one or two types of beer. When the craft brewing craze started to grow, the plant was not well equipped to produce smaller batches of craft beer, and Coors found it difficult to meet this opportunity. Ultimately, Coors had to buy its way into this movement by acquiring small craft breweries.[21]

- ***Obsolescence of the basis of cost advantage.*** Ultimately, the foundation of a firm's cost advantage may become obsolete. In such circumstances, other firms develop new ways of cutting costs, leaving the old cost leaders at a significant disadvantage. The older cost leaders are often locked into their way of competing and are unable to respond to the newer, lower-cost means of competing. This is the position that discount investment advisors now find themselves. Charles Schwab and TD Ameritrade challenged traditional brokers with lower cost business models. Now, they find themselves having to respond to a new class of robo-advisor firms, such as Betterment, that offer even lower cost investment advice using automated data analytic-based computer systems.

Differentiation

As the name implies, a **differentiation strategy** consists of creating differences in the firm's product or service offering by creating something that is perceived *industrywide* as unique and valued by customers.[22] Differentiation can take many forms:

differentiation strategy
a firm's generic strategy based on creating differences in the firm's product or service offering by creating something that is perceived *industrywide* as unique and valued by customers.

- Prestige or brand image (Hotel Monaco, BMW automobiles).[23]
- Quality (Apple, Ruth's Chris steak houses, Michelin tires).
- Technology (Martin guitars, North Face camping equipment).
- Innovation (Medtronic medical equipment, Tesla Motors).
- Features (Cannondale mountain bikes, Ducati motorcycles).
- Customer service (Nordstrom department stores, USAA financial services).
- Dealer network (Lexus automobiles, Caterpillar earthmoving equipment).

Exhibit 5.4 draws on the concept of the value chain as an example of how firms may differentiate themselves in primary and support activities.

Firms may differentiate themselves along several different dimensions at once.[24] For example, the Cheesecake Factory, an upscale casual restaurant, differentiates itself by offering high-quality food, the widest and deepest menu in its class of restaurants, and premium locations.[25]

Firms achieve and sustain differentiation advantages and attain above-average performance when their price premiums exceed the extra costs incurred in being unique.[26] For example, the Cheesecake Factory must increase consumer prices to offset the higher cost of premium real estate and producing such a wide menu. Thus, a differentiator will always seek out ways of distinguishing itself from similar competitors to justify price premiums greater than the costs incurred by differentiating.[27] Clearly, a differentiator cannot ignore costs. After all, its premium prices would be eroded by a markedly inferior cost position. Therefore, it must attain a level of cost *parity* relative to competitors. Differentiators can do this by reducing costs in all areas that do not affect differentiation. Porsche, for example, invests heavily in engine design—an area in which its customers demand excellence—but it is less concerned and spends fewer resources in the design of the instrument panel or the arrangement of switches on the radio.[28] Although a differentiation firm needs to be mindful of costs, it must also regularly and consistently reinforce the foundations of its differentiation advantage. In doing so, the firm builds a stronger reputation for differentiation, and this reputation can be an enduring source of advantage in its market.[29]

Many companies successfully follow a differentiation strategy. For example, Zappos may sell shoes, but it sees the core element of its differentiation advantage as service. Zappos CEO Tony Hsieh puts it this way:[30]

> We hope that 10 years from now people won't even realize that we started out selling shoes online, and that when you say "Zappos," they'll think, "Oh, that's the place with the absolute best customer service." And that doesn't even have to be limited to being an online experience. We've had customers email us and ask us if we would please start an airline, or run the IRS.

EXHIBIT 5.4

Value-Chain Activities: Examples of Differentiation

Support Activities

Firm Infrastructure

- Superior MIS—to integrate value-creating activities to improve quality.
- Facilities that promote firm image.
- Widely respected CEO who enhances firm reputation.

Human Resource Management

- Programs to attract talented engineers and scientists.
- Provision of training and incentives to ensure a strong customer service orientation.

Technology Development

- Superior material handling and sorting technology.
- Excellent applications engineering support.

Procurement

- Purchase of high-quality components to enhance product image.
- Use of most-prestigious outlets.

Primary Activities

Inbound Logistics

- Superior material handling operations to minimize damage.
- Quick transfer of inputs to manufacturing process.

Operations

- Flexibility and speed in responding to changes in manufacturing specifications.
- Low defect rates to improve quality.

Outbound Logistics

- Accurate and responsive order processing.
- Effective product replenishment to reduce customer inventory.

Marketing and Sales

- Creative and innovative advertising programs.
- Fostering of personal relationship with key customers.

Service

- Rapid response to customer service requests.
- Complete inventory of replacement parts and supplies.

Source: Adapted from Porter, M. E. 1985. *Competitive Advantage: Creating and Sustaining Superior Performance.* New York: Free Press.

This emphasis on service has led to great success. Growing from an idea to a billion-dollar company in only a dozen years, Zappos is seeing the benefits of providing exemplary service.

Strategy Spotlight 5.2 discusses how video game developers design games to differentiate the experience and lock players in to playing more frequently and for longer periods of time.

5.2 STRATEGY SPOTLIGHT

ETHICS

THE NAME OF THE GAME IS TO MAKE IT HARDER TO STOP PLAYING

Debbie Vitany could not get her 17-year-old son, Carson, to stop playing Fortnite. He'd play the game 12 hours a day. His teachers complained he was falling asleep in class, and his grades were in free fall. Debbie and Carson's experience is not an isolated experience. The Vancouver Canucks NHL team banned the playing of Fortnite when the team was on the road because they had difficulty getting players to show up for team meetings.

Epic Games, the creator of Fortnite, and other video game developers have worked to increasingly differentiate their product, making it ever harder for players to put the games down. They use a combination of technology and features to draw in and hold player's attention. First, game developers have leveraged technology to allow the users to play the game almost seamlessly across multiple platforms, including gaming consoles, PCs, tablets, and smartphones. Second, they offer new content, often for a limited period of time, to keep players checking in regularly so they don't miss out. Third, they've made games a social experience so players become locked into playing a particular game because it is the game all of their friends are playing. Fourth, they offer virtual goods and features to allow players to customize their characters. Finally, many of the games offer rewards for logging in and completing tasks daily. All of this increases the perception that each game offers a different experience than other games and drives users to play more regularly and for longer periods.

As a result, the video game industry has grown rapidly, doubling in revenue from 2013 to 2018, and is now larger than the entire box-office and home-view revenue stream for the movie industry. For Epic Games, it has resulted in an epic valuation for the firm. Private investors made a $1.25 billion investment in the firm, suggesting that the overall value of the firm has soared to $15 billion.

But video game developers also face significant criticism for how they lock players into playing ever more. Douglas Gentile, a research scientist who examines the impact of media on users, states the games are "designed to hit the pleasure centers of the brain in some of the same ways that gambling can." Lorrine Marer, a British behavioral specialist puts it more starkly, commenting on Fortnite that "this game is like heroin. Once you are hooked, it's hard to get unhooked." Thus, while they have been able to generate growth and profits, the actions of video game developers have triggered criticism that they are acting in a socially irresponsible way.

Sources: Needleman, S.E. 2018. Video game developers are making it harder to stop playing. *wsj.com,* August 205: np; and Palmeri, C., and J. Feeley. 2018. Fortnite addiction is forcing kids into video-game rehab. *washingtonpost.com,* December 2: np.

Differentiation: Improving Competitive Position vis-à-vis the Five Forces Differentiation provides protection against rivalry since brand loyalty lowers customer sensitivity to price and raises customer switching costs.[31] By increasing a firm's margins, differentiation also avoids the need for a low-cost position. Higher entry barriers result because of customer loyalty and the firm's ability to provide uniqueness in its products or services.[32] Differentiation also provides higher margins that enable a firm to deal with supplier power. And it reduces buyer power, because buyers lack comparable alternatives and are therefore less price-sensitive.[33] Supplier power is also decreased because there is a certain amount of prestige associated with being the supplier to a producer of highly differentiated products and services. Last, differentiation enhances customer loyalty, thus reducing the threat from substitutes.[34]

Our examples illustrate these points. Porsche has enjoyed enhanced power over buyers because its strong reputation makes buyers more willing to pay a premium price. This lessens rivalry, since buyers become less price-sensitive. The prestige associated with its brand name also lowers supplier power since margins are high. Suppliers would probably desire to be associated with prestige brands, thus lessening their incentives to drive up prices. Finally, the loyalty and "peace of mind" associated with a service provider such as Zappos makes such firms less vulnerable to rivalry or substitute products and services.

Potential Pitfalls of Differentiation Strategies Potential pitfalls of a differentiation strategy include:

- ***Uniqueness that is not valuable.*** A differentiation strategy must provide unique bundles of products and/or services that customers value highly. It's not enough just to be "different." An example is Gibson's Dobro bass guitar. Gibson came up with a unique idea: Design and build an acoustic bass guitar with sufficient sound volume so that amplification wasn't necessary. The problem with other acoustic bass guitars was that they did not project enough volume because of the low-frequency bass notes. By adding a resonator plate on the body of the traditional acoustic bass, Gibson increased the sound volume. Gibson believed this product would serve a particular niche market—bluegrass and folk artists who played in small group "jams" with other acoustic musicians. Unfortunately, Gibson soon discovered that its targeted market was content with the existing options: an upright bass amplified with a microphone or an acoustic electric guitar. Thus, Gibson developed a unique product, but it was not perceived as valuable by its potential customers.[35]

- ***Too much differentiation.*** Firms may strive for quality or service that is higher than customers desire.[36] Thus, they become vulnerable to competitors that provide an appropriate level of quality at a lower price. For example, consider the expensive Mercedes-Benz S-Class, which ranged in price between $93,650 and $138,000 for the 2011 models.[37] *Consumer Reports* described it as "sumptuous," "quiet and luxurious," and a "delight to drive." The magazine also considered it to be the least reliable sedan available in the United States. According to David Champion, who runs the testing program, the problems are electronic. "The engineers have gone a little wild," he says. "They've put in every bell and whistle that they think of, and sometimes they don't have the attention to detail to make these systems work."[38] Some features include a computer-driven suspension that reduces body roll as the vehicle whips around a corner; cruise control that automatically slows the car down if it gets too close to another car; and seats that are adjustable 14 ways and are ventilated by a system that uses eight fans.
- ***Too high a price premium.*** This pitfall is quite similar to too much differentiation. Customers may desire the product, but they are repelled by the price premium. For example, Apple, a firm that has successfully differentiated itself and built strong customer loyalty, has appeared to hit a limit in pricing with the iPhone XS. This model of iPhone can cost as much as $1,500, but at that price, Apple found demand very weak. This led Apple to reduce the price of the phone in some markets to drum up sales.[39]
- ***Differentiation that is easily imitated.*** As we noted in Chapter 3, resources that are easily imitated cannot lead to sustainable advantages. Similarly, firms may strive for, and even attain, a differentiation strategy that is successful for a time. However, the advantages are eroded through imitation. Consider Cereality's innovative differentiation strategy of stores that offer a wide variety of cereals and toppings for around $4.[40] As one would expect, once the idea proved successful, competitors entered the market because much of the initial risk had already been taken. These new competitors included stores with the following names: the Cereal Cabinet, The Cereal Bowl, and Bowls: A Cereal Joint. Says David Roth, one of Cereality's founders: "With any good business idea, you're faced with people who see you've cracked the code and who try to cash in on it."[41]
- ***Dilution of brand identification through product-line extensions.*** Firms may erode their quality brand image by adding products or services with lower prices and less quality. Although this can increase short-term revenues, it may be detrimental in the long run. Consider Gucci.[42] In the 1980s Gucci wanted to capitalize on its prestigious brand name by launching an aggressive strategy of revenue growth. It added a set of lower-priced canvas goods to its product line. It also pushed goods heavily into department stores and duty-free channels and allowed its name to appear on a host of licensed items such as watches, eyeglasses, and perfumes. In the short term, this strategy worked. Sales soared. However, the strategy carried a high price. Gucci's indiscriminate approach to expanding its products and channels tarnished its sterling brand. Sales of its high-end goods (with higher profit margins) fell, causing profits to decline.

- ***Perceptions of differentiation that vary between buyers and sellers.*** The issue here is that "beauty is in the eye of the beholder." Companies must realize that although they may perceive their products and services as differentiated, their customers may view them as commodities. Indeed, in today's marketplace, many products and services have been reduced to commodities.[43] Thus, a firm could overprice its offerings and lose margins altogether if it has to lower prices to reflect market realities.

Overall Cost Leadership

- Too much focus on one or a few value-chain activities.
- Increase in the cost of the inputs on which the advantage is based.
- A strategy that can be imitated too easily.
- A lack of parity on differentiation.
- Reduced flexibility.
- Obsolescence of the basis of cost advantage.

Differentiation

- Uniqueness that is not valuable.
- Too much differentiation.
- A price premium that is too high.
- Differentiation that is easily imitated.
- Dilution of brand identification through product-line extensions.
- Perceptions of differentiation that vary between buyers and sellers.

EXHIBIT 5.5 Potential Pitfalls of Overall Cost Leadership and Differentiation Strategies

Exhibit 5.5 summarizes the pitfalls of overall cost leadership and differentiation strategies. In addressing the pitfalls associated with these two generic strategies, there is one common, underlying theme: Managers must be aware of the dangers associated with concentrating so much on one strategy that they fail to attain parity on the other.

Focus

A **focus strategy** is based on the choice of a narrow competitive scope within an industry. A firm following this strategy selects a segment or group of segments and tailors its strategy to serve them. The essence of focus is the exploitation of a particular market niche. As you might expect, narrow focus itself (like merely "being different" as a differentiator) is simply not sufficient for above-average performance.

focus strategy a firm's generic strategy based on appeal to a narrow market segment within an industry.

The focus strategy, as indicated in Exhibit 5.1, has two variants. In a cost focus, a firm strives to create a cost advantage in its target segment. In a differentiation focus, a firm seeks to differentiate in its target market. Both variants of the focus strategy rely on providing better service than broad-based competitors that are trying to serve the focuser's target segment. Cost focus exploits differences in cost behavior in some segments, while differentiation focus exploits the special needs of buyers in other segments.

Let's look at examples of two firms that have successfully implemented focus strategies. LinkedIn has staked out a position as the business social media site of choice. Rather than compete with Facebook head on, LinkedIn created a strategy that focuses on individuals who wish to share their business experience and make connections with individuals with whom they share or could potentially share business ties. In doing so, it has created an extremely strong business model. LinkedIn monetizes its user information in three ways: subscription fees from some users, advertising fees, and recruiter fees. The first two are fairly standard for social media sites, but the advertising fees are higher for LinkedIn since the ads can be more effectively targeted as a result of LinkedIn's focus. The third income source is fairly unique for LinkedIn. Headhunters and human resource departments pay significant user fees, up to $8,200 a year, to have access to LinkedIn's recruiting search engine, which can sift through LinkedIn profiles to identify individuals with desired skills and experiences. The power of this business model can be seen in the difference in user value for LinkedIn when compared to Facebook. For every hour that a user spends on the site, LinkedIn generates $1.30 in income. For Facebook, it is a paltry 6.2 cents.[44]

Marlin Steel Wire Products, a Baltimore-based manufacturing company, has also seen great benefit from developing a niche-differentiator strategy. Marlin, a manufacturer of commodity wire products, faced stiff and ever-increasing competition from rivals based in China and other emerging markets. These rivals had labor-based cost advantages that Marlin found hard to

5.3 STRATEGY SPOTLIGHT

EXTREME DIFFERENTIATION: THE ASTON MARTIN VALKYRIE

Even if you had $2.6 million burning a hole in your pocket, you wouldn't be able to buy an Aston Martin Valkyrie. All 150 of the hypercars that Aston Martin will build at this extraordinary price over the next few years have already been purchased. The Valkyrie is the ultimate play toy for auto enthusiasts and collectors.

Aston Martin partnered with the chief technical officer at Red Bull Racing Formula One racing team to develop a hypercar that included technology and design elements not yet used in Formula One cars to develop the ultimate street legal race car. Its sleek, carbon fiber body is powered by the combination of a 1130 horsepower engine and an electric motor charged by a hybrid system. The car can reach a top speed of 250 mph and is nimble enough to move around a racing circuit in a time that rivals a Formula One race car.

The car is customized to the needs of each customer. The buyer meets with Aston Martin and is measured so that the seat and interior can be customized to fit the customer. The seat is fixed in place and can't be adjusted. Thus, it must be designed and built to match the measurements of the driver. Customers also choose nearly every aspect of the car, including seat materials; the design of the dashboard and other trim elements; the color, finish, and reflectivity of body panels; and the look of the wheel coverings. Once customers have made these choices, they are sent a one-eighteenth scale replica of their car. They can then note any changes in color or look of the car, and they will be sent a revised model. Only when they are perfectly happy with the car will Aston Martin build their actual cars.

But one element you can't customize is the car radio. This hypercar doesn't need one. The only music the driver can listen to is the roar of the 1,000 horsepower symphony under the hood. If you have a few million waiting to be used, you may want to get on the waitlist now for the next hypercar Aston Martin builds.

Sources: Berk, B. 2017. A hypercar made to measure. *bloombergbusinessweek.com,* September 25: np.; and Lopez, J. 2018. Reaching for the next level in street-legal performance. *topspeed.com,* May 17: np.

counter. Marlin responded by changing the game it played. Drew Greenblatt, Marlin's president, decided to go upmarket, automating his production and specializing in high-end products. For example, Marlin produces antimicrobial baskets for restaurant kitchens and exports its products globally. Marlin provides products to customers in 36 countries and, in 2012, was listed as the 162nd fastest-growing private manufacturing company in the United States.[45]

Strategy Spotlight 5.3 illustrates how Aston Martin pursued an extreme focus positioning by developing a hypercar for the super rich.

Focus: Improving Competitive Position vis-à-vis the Five Forces Focus requires that a firm have either a low-cost position with its strategic target, high differentiation, or both. As we discussed with regard to cost and differentiation strategies, these positions provide defenses against each competitive force. Focus is also used to select niches that are least vulnerable to substitutes or where competitors are weakest.

Let's look at our examples to illustrate some of these points. First, by providing a platform for a targeted customer group, businesspeople, to share key work information, LinkedIn insulated itself from rivalrous pressure from existing social networks, such as Facebook. It also felt little threat from new generalist social networks, such as Google +. Similarly, the new focus of Marlin Steel lessened the power of buyers since the company provides specialized products. Also, it is insulated from competitors, which manufacture the commodity products Marlin used to produce.

Potential Pitfalls of Focus Strategies Potential pitfalls of focus strategies include:

- ***Cost advantages may erode within the narrow segment.*** The advantages of a cost focus strategy may be fleeting if the cost advantages are eroded over time. For example, early pioneers in online education, such as the University of Phoenix, have faced increasing challenges as traditional universities have entered with their own online programs that allow them to match the cost benefits associated with online delivery systems. Similarly, other firms have seen their profit margins drop as competitors enter their product segment.

- ***Even product and service offerings that are highly focused are subject to competition from new entrants and from imitation.*** Some firms adopting a focus strategy may enjoy temporary advantages because they select a small niche with few rivals. However, their advantages may be short-lived. A notable example is the multitude of dot-com firms that specialize in very narrow segments such as pet supplies, ethnic foods, and vintage automobile accessories. The entry barriers tend to be low, there is little buyer loyalty, and competition becomes intense. And since the marketing strategies and technologies employed by most rivals are largely nonproprietary, imitation is easy. Over time, revenues fall, profits margins are squeezed, and only the strongest players survive the shakeout.
- ***Focusers can become too focused to satisfy buyer needs.*** Some firms attempting to attain advantages through a focus strategy may have too narrow a product or service. Consider many retail firms. Hardware chains such as Ace and True Value are losing market share to rivals such as Lowe's and Home Depot that offer a full line of home and garden equipment and accessories. And given the enormous purchasing power of the national chains, it would be difficult for such specialty retailers to attain parity on costs.

Combination Strategies: Integrating Overall Low Cost and Differentiation

LO 5-4

Explain how firms can effectively combine the generic strategies of overall cost leadership and differentiation.

Perhaps the primary benefit to firms that integrate low-cost and differentiation strategies is the difficulty for rivals to duplicate or imitate.[46] This strategy enables a firm to provide two types of value to customers: differentiated attributes (e.g., high quality, brand identification, reputation) and lower prices (because of the firm's lower costs in value-creating activities). The goal is thus to provide unique value to customers in an efficient manner.[47] Some firms are able to attain both types of advantages simultaneously.[48] For example, superior quality can lead to lower costs because of less need for rework in manufacturing, fewer warranty claims, a reduced need for customer service personnel to resolve customer complaints, and so forth. Thus, the benefits of combining advantages can be additive, instead of merely involving trade-offs. Next, we consider four approaches to combining overall low cost and differentiation.

Adopting Automated and Flexible Manufacturing Systems Given the advances in manufacturing technologies such as CAD/CAM (computer aided design and computer aided manufacturing) as well as information technologies, many firms have been able to manufacture unique products in relatively small quantities at lower costs—a concept known as **mass customization.**[49]

mass customization
a firm's ability to manufacture unique products in small quantities at low cost.

Using Data Analytics Corporations are increasingly collecting and analyzing data on their customers, including data on customer characteristics, purchasing patterns, employee productivity, and physical asset utilization. These efforts have the potential to allow firms to better customize their product and service offerings to customers while more efficiently and fully using the resources of the company. For example, Caterpillar collects and analyzes large volumes of data about how customers use their tractors. Since this data helps Caterpillar better assess the uses and limitations of their current tractors, the firm can use data analytics to employ more focused and timely product improvement efforts. This allows the firm to simultaneously reduce the cost of new product development efforts and better differentiate their products.[50]

Exploiting the Profit Pool Concept for Competitive Advantage A **profit pool** is defined as the total profits in an industry at all points along the industry's value chain.[51] Although the concept is relatively straightforward, the structure of the profit pool can be complex.[52] The potential pool of profits will be deeper in some segments of the value chain than in others, and the depths will vary within an individual segment. Segment profitability may vary

profit pool
the total profits in an industry at all points along the industry's value chain.

widely by customer group, product category, geographic market, or distribution channel. Additionally, the pattern of profit concentration in an industry is very often different from the pattern of revenue generation. For example, with airlines squeezing aircraft manufacturers on the prices of planes the airlines are ordering, Boeing has made a big push into providing maintenance and repair services to airlines, business segments that are potentially more profitable than aircraft manufacturing.[53]

combination strategies
firms' integrations of various strategies to provide multiple types of value to customers.

Unscaling to Create a Combination Strategy For decades, firms built large-scaled operations to run as efficiently as possible in order to dominate markets. Doing so allowed the firm to build cost advantages over rivals, but this large scale also led them to be slow to responding to market changes and limited in their ability to customize their products to specific customer needs. Unscaling turns this logic on its head. Rather than building scaled operations to meet general customer needs, unscaled firms look to build small scale operations that meet the needs of particular customers as efficiently or possible, at times even more efficiently than scaled competitors.

Unscaling involves both the leveraging of technology, such as artificial intelligence, and the reliance on suppliers or customers to provide critical inputs to the process. For example, Waze, a GPS Navigation app, relies on inputs from users to provide information on traffic conditions and uses artificial intelligence to develop algorithms for each user, tailoring the route map for that user at that particular moment.

Larger firms that have previously relied on scale are also employing elements of unscaling. Proctor & Gamble (P&G) faces a slew of unscaled competitors, such as the Dollar Shave Club's subscription model and The Honest Co's environmentally friendly diapers. P&G has responded with its Connect + Develop initiative. After relying on internal development of products for 175 years, P&G now invites outside inventors to submit development proposals to the company. If their proposals are approved, these inventors can effectively "rent" P&G's distribution and marketing to get their products to market. Doing so allows P&G to be more nimble in meeting the needs of different customers in an efficient way since the firm doesn't bear the entire cost of product development. In essence, P&G is slowly translating itself into becoming a consumer product platform rented by an ever-changing set of small, focused product developers.[54]

Strategy Spotlight 5.4 discusses how one men's clothing retailer, Indochino, is leveraging the power of unscaled operations to outcompete traditional retailers.

Integrated Overall Low-Cost and Differentiation Strategies: Improving Competitive Position vis-à-vis the Five Forces Firms that successfully integrate both differentiation and cost advantages create an enviable position. For example, Walmart's integration of information systems, logistics, and transportation helps it to drive down costs and provide outstanding product selection. This dominant competitive position serves to erect high entry barriers to potential competitors that have neither the financial nor physical resources to compete head-to-head. Walmart's size—with over $482 million in sales in 2016—provides the chain with enormous bargaining power over suppliers. Its low pricing and wide selection reduce the power of buyers (its customers), because there are relatively few competitors that can provide a comparable cost/value proposition. This reduces the possibility of intense head-to-head rivalry, such as protracted price wars. Finally, Walmart's overall value proposition makes potential substitute products (e.g., Internet competitors) a less viable threat.

Pitfalls of Integrated Overall Cost Leadership and Differentiation Strategies The pitfalls of integrated overall cost leadership and differentiation include:

- ***Failing to attain both strategies and possibly ending up with neither, leaving the firm "stuck in the middle."*** A key issue in strategic management is the creation of competitive advantages that enable a firm to enjoy above-average returns. Some firms may

5.4 STRATEGY SPOTLIGHT — DIGITAL ECONOMY

MASS CUSTOMIZED MENSWEAR

Indochino, a men's retailer is looking to change the game for buying a suit. The firm started in 2007 selling custom-made suits online for prices much lower than those available in traditional men's clothing retailers and department stores. Customers who order online follow detailed video instructions to take their own measurements. Once they have their measurements down, they can customize the fabric they want to use as well as details such as the look of the lapels, linings used, pocket placement, and even monograms. Suit prices start at about $400, and once the order is complete, the customized suit shows up in a FedEx package within four weeks.

Indochino has also begun opening retail outlets to better serve customers. Many suit buyers are more comfortable having one of Indochino's salespeople, called style guides, measure them and walk them through their options. The firm also finds that these stores allow it to build brand awareness and drive online shopping as well. Peter Housley, Indochino's chief revenue officer says "After we open a store, sales at first shift from online to offline, but by the time the store is a year old, we see our online sales recover and the overall pie within the market grow."

To succeed, Indochino leverages the benefits of unscaling. Its basic business model is based on mass customization. The firm is able to be more efficient than its scaled competitors because it carries no finished inventory of products. Drew Green, Indochino's CEO explains it this way, "It's a virtual inventory model. We can open a showroom without spending hundreds of thousands of dollars on inventory, at a fraction of the cost at which our competition opens their stores. That's provided a really efficient way to grow."

Also, the firm uses sophisticated technology to improve the efficiency of its operations and boost its sales. It collects information on an ongoing basis on sales trends to optimize the selections of cloth it purchases and the promotions it offers on its website and in its stores. It also uses online sales data to optimally predict where to open new stores. When a customer comes into the store, it collects "dwell time" within the store to identify the potential to make a sale and the type of product to promote to the customer. It also uses sophisticated location logistics to identify consumer's mobile devices that use Wi-Fi within or near a store. It then pairs that data with databases managed by outside service providers to determine which consumers it wants to advertise to and what type of promotions to offer.

Altogether, these actions are allowing Indochino to grow rapidly and efficiently, but the firm sees great potential to grow further since it currently has less than 1 percent of the overall suit business.

Sources: Marikar, S. 2017. Made to measure. *Fortune*. September 15: 55-57; and Stambor, Z. 2019. Indochino plans to open 20 showrooms this year: Here's why. Vertical Web Media LLC, January 15: np.

become stuck in the middle if they try to attain both cost and differentiation advantages. As mentioned earlier in this chapter, mainline supermarket chains find themselves stuck in the middle as their cost structure is higher than discount retailers offering groceries and their products and services are not seen by consumers as being as valuable as those of high-end grocery chains, such as Whole Foods.

- ***Underestimating the challenges and expenses associated with coordinating value-creating activities in the extended value chain.*** Integrating activities across a firm's value chain with the value chain of suppliers and customers involves a significant investment in financial and human resources. Firms must consider the expenses linked to technology investment, managerial time and commitment, and the involvement and investment required by the firm's customers and suppliers. The firm must be confident that it can generate a sufficient scale of operations and revenues to justify all associated expenses.
- ***Miscalculating sources of revenue and profit pools in the firm's industry.*** Firms may fail to accurately assess sources of revenue and profits in their value chain. This can occur for several reasons. For example, a manager may be biased due to his or her functional area background, work experiences, and educational background. If the manager's background is in engineering, he or she might perceive that proportionately greater revenue and margins were being created in manufacturing, product, and process design than a person whose background is in a "downstream" value-chain activity such as marketing and sales. Or politics could make managers "fudge" the numbers to favor their area of operations. This would make them responsible for a greater proportion of the firm's profits, thus improving their bargaining position.

A related problem is directing an overwhelming amount of managerial time, attention, and resources to value-creating activities that produce the greatest margins—to the detriment of other important, albeit less profitable, activities. For example, a car manufacturer may focus too much on downstream activities, such as warranty fulfillment and financing operations, to the detriment of differentiation and cost of the cars themselves.

LO 5-5

Identify which factors determine the sustainability of a firm's competitive advantage.

CAN COMPETITIVE STRATEGIES BE SUSTAINED? INTEGRATING AND APPLYING STRATEGIC MANAGEMENT CONCEPTS

Thus far this chapter has addressed how firms can attain competitive advantages in the marketplace. We discussed the three generic strategies—overall cost leadership, differentiation, and focus—as well as combination strategies. Next we discussed the importance of linking value-chain activities (both those within the firm and those linkages between the firm's suppliers and customers) to attain such advantages. We also showed how successful competitive strategies enable firms to strengthen their position vis-à-vis the five forces of industry competition as well as how to avoid the pitfalls associated with the strategies.

Competitive advantages are, however, often short-lived. As we discussed in the beginning of Chapter 1, the composition of the firms that constitute the Fortune 500 list has experienced significant turnover in its membership over the years—reflecting the temporary nature of competitive advantages. Consider BlackBerry's fall from grace. BlackBerry initially dominated the smartphone market. BlackBerry held 20 percent of the cell phone market in 2009, and its users were addicted to BlackBerry's products, leading some to refer to them as crackberrys. However, the firm's market share quickly eroded with the introduction of touch screen smartphones from Apple, Samsung, and others. BlackBerry was slow to move away from its physical keyboards and saw its market share fall to 0.1 percent by 2016.[55]

Clearly, "nothing is forever" when it comes to competitive advantages. Rapid changes in technology, globalization, and actions by rivals from within—as well as outside—the industry can quickly erode a firm's advantages. It is becoming increasingly important to recognize that the duration of competitive advantages is declining, especially in technology-intensive industries.[56] Even in industries that are normally viewed as "low tech," the increasing use of technology has suddenly made competitive advantages less sustainable.[57] Amazon's success in book retailing at the cost of Barnes & Noble, the former industry leader, as well as cable TV's difficulties in responding to streaming services providers like Netflix and Hulu, serve to illustrate how difficult it has become for industry leaders to sustain competitive advantages that they once thought would last forever.

In this section, we will discuss some factors that help determine whether a strategy is sustainable over a long period of time. We will draw on some strategic management concepts from the first five chapters. To illustrate our points, we will look at a company, Atlas Door, which created an innovative strategy in its industry and enjoyed superior performance for several years. Our discussion of Atlas Door draws on a *Harvard Business Review* article by George Stalk, Jr.[58] It was published some time ago (1988), which provides us the benefit of hindsight to make our points about the sustainability of competitive advantage. After all, the strategic management concepts we have been addressing in the text are quite timeless in their relevance to practice. A brief summary follows.

Atlas Door: A Case Example

Atlas Door, a U.S.-based company, has enjoyed remarkable success. It has grown at an average annual rate of 15 percent in an industry with an overall annual growth rate of less than 5 percent. Recently, its pretax earnings were 20 percent of sales—about five times the industry average. Atlas is debt-free, and by its 10th year, the company had achieved the number-one competitive position in its industry.

Atlas produces industrial doors—a product with almost infinite variety, involving limitless choices of width and height and material. Given the importance of product variety, inventory is almost useless in meeting customer orders. Instead, most doors can be manufactured only after the order has been placed.

How Did Atlas Door Create Its Competitive Advantages in the Marketplace? *First,* Atlas built just-in-time factories. Although simple in concept, they require extra tooling and machinery to reduce changeover times. Further, the manufacturing process must be organized by product and scheduled to start and complete with all of the parts available at the same time.

Second, Atlas reduced the time to receive and process an order. Traditionally, when customers, distributors, or salespeople called a door manufacturer with a request for price and delivery, they would have to wait more than one week for a response. In contrast, Atlas first streamlined and then automated its entire order-entry, engineering, pricing, and scheduling process. Atlas can price and schedule 95 percent of its incoming orders while the callers are still on the telephone. It can quickly engineer new special orders because it has preserved on computer the design and production data of all previous special orders—which drastically reduces the amount of reengineering necessary.

Third, Atlas tightly controlled logistics so that it always shipped only fully complete orders to construction sites. Orders require many components, and gathering all of them at the factory and making sure that they are with the correct order can be a time-consuming task. Of course, it is even more time-consuming to get the correct parts to the job site after the order has been shipped! Atlas developed a system to track the parts in production and the purchased parts for each order. This helped to ensure the arrival of all necessary parts at the shipping dock in time—a just-in-time logistics operation.

The Result? When Atlas began operations, distributors had little interest in its product. The established distributors already carried the door line of a much larger competitor and saw little to no reason to switch suppliers except, perhaps, for a major price concession. But as a start-up, Atlas was too small to compete on price alone. Instead, it positioned itself as the door supplier of last resort—the company people came to if the established supplier could not deliver or missed a key date.

Of course, with an average industry order-fulfillment time of almost four months, some calls inevitably came to Atlas. And when it did get the call, Atlas commanded a higher price because of its faster delivery. Atlas not only got a higher price, but its effective integration of value-creating activities saved time and lowered costs. Thus, it enjoyed the best of both worlds.

In 10 short years, the company replaced the leading door suppliers in 80 percent of the distributors in the United States. With its strategic advantage, the company could be selective—becoming the supplier for only the strongest distributors.

Are Atlas Door's Competitive Advantages Sustainable?

We will now take both the "pro" and "con" positions as to whether or not Atlas Door's competitive advantages will be sustainable for a very long time. It is important, of course, to assume that Atlas Door's strategy is unique in the industry, and the central issue becomes whether or not rivals will be able to easily imitate its strategy or create a viable substitute strategy.

"Pro" Position: The Strategy Is Highly Sustainable Drawing on Chapter 2, it is quite evident that Atlas Door has attained a very favorable position vis-à-vis the five forces of industry competition. For example, it is able to exert power over its customers (distributors) because of its ability to deliver a quality product in a short period of time. Also, its dominance in the industry creates high entry barriers for new entrants. It is also quite evident that Atlas Door has been able to successfully integrate many value-chain activities within the firm—a fact that is integral to its just-in-time strategy. As noted in Chapter 3, such integration of activities provides a strong basis for sustainability, because rivals would have difficulty in imitating this strategy due to causal ambiguity and path dependency (i.e., it is difficult to build up in a short period of time the resources that Atlas Door has accumulated and developed as well as disentangle the causes of what the valuable resources are or how they can be re-created). Further, as noted in Chapter 4, Atlas Door benefits from the social capital that it has developed with a wide range of key stakeholders (Chapter 1). These would include customers, employees, and managers (a reasonable assumption, given how smoothly the internal operations flow and the company's long-term relationships with distributors). It would be very difficult for a rival to replace Atlas Door as the supplier of last resort—given the reputation that it has earned over time for "coming through in the clutch" on time-sensitive orders. Finally, we can conclude that Atlas Door has created competitive advantages in both overall low cost and differentiation (Chapter 5). Its strong linkages among value-chain activities—a requirement for its just-in-time operations—not only lower costs but enable the company to respond quickly to customer orders. As noted in Exhibit 5.4, many of the value-chain activities associated with a differentiation strategy reflect the element of speed or quick response.

"Con" Position: The Strategy Can Be Easily Imitated or Substituted An argument could be made that much of Atlas Door's strategy relies on technologies that are rather well known and nonproprietary. Over time, a well-financed rival could imitate its strategy (via trial and error), achieve a tight integration among its value-creating activities, and implement a just-in-time manufacturing process. Because human capital is highly mobile (Chapter 4), a rival could hire away Atlas Door's talent, and these individuals could aid the rival in transferring Atlas Door's best practices. A new rival could also enter the industry with a large resource base, which might enable it to price its doors well under Atlas Door to build market share (but this would likely involve pricing below cost and would be a risky and nonsustainable strategy). Finally, a rival could potentially "leapfrog" the technologies and processes that Atlas Door has employed and achieve competitive superiority. With the benefit of hindsight, it could use the Internet to further speed up the linkages among its value-creating activities and the order-entry processes with its customers and suppliers. (But even this could prove to be a temporary advantage, since rivals could relatively easily do the same thing.)

What Is the Verdict? Both positions have merit. Over time, it would be rather easy to see how a new rival could achieve parity with Atlas Door—or even create a superior competitive position with new technologies or innovative processes. However, two factors make it extremely difficult for a rival to challenge Atlas Door in the short term: (1) The success that Atlas Door has enjoyed with its just-in-time scheduling and production systems—which involve the successful integration of many value-creating activities—helps the firm not only lower costs but also respond quickly to customer needs, and (2) the strong, positive reputational effects that it has earned with its customers increases their loyalty and would take significant time for rivals to match.

Finally, it is important to also understand that it is Atlas Door's ability to appropriate most of the profits generated by its competitive advantages that make it a highly successful company. As we discussed in Chapter 3, profits generated by resources can be appropriated by a number of stakeholders such as suppliers, customers, employees, or rivals. The structure of the industrial door industry makes such value appropriation difficult: The suppliers provide generic parts, no one buyer is big enough to dictate prices, the tacit nature of the knowledge makes imitation difficult, and individual employees may be easily replaceable. Still, even with the advantages that Atlas Door enjoys, it needs to avoid becoming complacent or it will suffer the same fate as the dominant firm it replaced.

Strategies for Platform Markets

Before moving on to our discussion of industry life-cycle stages and competitive strategy, we introduce and discuss an emerging trend: two-sided or platform markets. In these markets, firms act as intermediaries between two sets of platform users: buyers and sellers. Firms that thrive in these markets often do not produce a product themselves. Instead, successful platform firms create a business that attracts a large range of suppliers and a wide population of customers, becoming the go-to clearinghouse that both suppliers and customers turn to in order to facilitate a transaction. In doing so, they typically successfully combine elements of both cost and differentiation advantages.

These types of markets have been in existence for a long period of time. For example, VISA became the largest credit card company by signing up both the most merchants and the most customers in their card network. Retailers and restaurants now perceive the need to accept VISA credit and debit cards because millions of customers carry them. On the other side, when considering which credit card(s) to carry, most customers feel the need to carry a VISA card since it is accepted by so many merchants. As the VISA example illustrates, the sheer number of buyers and sellers using a given platform provides the platform firm with a differentiated market position while simultaneously allowing it to become a cost leader due to the economies of scale it accrues as it becomes the largest platform.

While these types of markets have existed for decades, they have become increasingly common in the 21st century. Whether it is Amazon in retailing, Facebook in social networks, Airbnb in short-term housing rentals, Uber in driver services, Spotify in streaming services, or Etsy in craft products, platform businesses have taken on increasing prominence in the economy.

But how do firms position themselves to succeed in these two-sided markets? It involves a combination of actions to build a strong position and facilitate optimal interactions between suppliers and users. In doing so, these firms strive to simultaneously limit costs to users and also provide differentiated service. The issues platform businesses need to master to succeed include the following.[59]

- **Draw in users.** The key to success in platform models is to generate the best (and often biggest) base of suppliers and customers. Thus, firms must develop effective pricing and incentives for users to attract and retain them. This typically involves subsidizing early and price-sensitive users. For example, Adobe was able to emerge as the dominant pdf software partly because it allowed users to read and print documents for free. As it established itself as "the" pdf reader software, producers of documents and those who wished to edit documents became increasingly willing to purchase software from Adobe. Thus, Adobe provided the product at no cost to some users while differentiating itself in the eyes of other users. Successful platform providers also find ways to attract and retain "marquee" users. YouTube has done this by allowing users to set up their own channel and compensate them for the volume of traffic they bring in.
- **Create easy and informative customer interfaces.** Platform business providers need to make it easy for users to plug into the platform. For example, Quicken Loans strives to differentiate itself with its Rocket Mortgage product, arguing it is the easiest and quickest system for applying for a home mortgage–typically taking less than 10 minutes to complete the application. By developing an easy to use app that requires no lending officer interaction, Quicken Loans was also able to build a more cost-efficient lending system than traditional loan brokers. Uber similarly worked to differentiate itself with a simple app for users to connect with a driver and by providing updated information on the expected arrival time of the driver. On the supplier side, Apple strives to ease the process for software developers by providing the operating system and underlying library codes needed to develop new software.

- **Facilitate the best connections between suppliers and customers.** Platform businesses can learn a great deal about their suppliers and customers by observing their search and usage patterns. Successful platform firms leverage this data to figure out how to best fill their matchmaking role in bringing together suppliers and users. Google is notable in its ability to tailor advertising to the search patterns of its users in order to increase the success rates for its advertising. Similarly, Airbnb has worked to create systems that increase the likelihood that hosts will agree to offers from potential renters. The firm realizes that renters get frustrated if their rental offers are declined. Additionally, hosts will be dissatisfied if offers come from undesirable renters. Using data analytics, Airbnb analyzed when specific hosts accepted and declined offers and their satisfaction ratings of renters to develop profiles of preferred renter characteristics. Using the resulting algorithm for matching renter characteristics and host preferences, the company saw a 4 percent increase in its rate of converting offers into accepted rental matches.
- **Sequencing the growth of the business.** To maximize the chance of success, platform firms must consciously plan out the sequence of their businesses. This involves thinking in terms of both geographic and product market expansion. In planning out its geographic market expansion, Uber analyzed the supply and demand of the taxi markets in cities across the country and first entered cities with the greatest shortage of taxis. Since it started in markets with unmet demand, Uber was able to expand quickly in these markets to be as cost efficient as possible. It also heavily advertised its business in settings where taxis were likely to be in short supply, such as sporting events and concerts. Once Uber established itself in these markets and developed a brand image, it expanded into other markets. Platform firms also need to consider both the need and opportunity of expanding their product scope. For example, Facebook has looked to continually extend its differentiation by expanding the range of services it offers, and as a result, has been able to put the squeeze on narrow platform providers, such as Twitter. Similarly, Spotify expanded from music to video streaming services in a quest to be a more complete service provider.

If successful, a platform provider becomes the dominant player linking suppliers and customers. This success offers the firm great flexibility in pricing its services as the firm gains a near monopoly in its market.

LO 5-6

Understand the importance of considering the industry life cycle to determine a firm's business-level strategy and its relative emphasis on functional area strategies and value-creating activities.

INDUSTRY LIFE-CYCLE STAGES: STRATEGIC IMPLICATIONS

industry life cycle the stages of introduction, growth, maturity, and decline that typically occur over the life of an industry.

The **industry life cycle** refers to the stages of introduction, growth, maturity, and decline that occur over the life of an industry. In considering the industry life cycle, it is useful to think in terms of broad product lines such as personal computers, photocopiers, or long-distance telephone service. Yet the industry life-cycle concept can be explored from several levels, from the life cycle of an entire industry to the life cycle of a single variation or model of a specific product or service.

Why are industry life cycles important?[60] The emphasis on various generic strategies, functional areas, value-creating activities, and overall objectives varies over the course of an industry life cycle. Managers must become even more aware of their firm's strengths and weaknesses in many areas to attain competitive advantages. For example, firms depend on their research and development (R&D) activities in the introductory stage. R&D is the source of new products and features that everyone hopes will appeal to customers. Firms develop products and services to stimulate consumer demand. Later, during the maturity phase, the functions of the product have been defined, more competitors have entered the market, and competition is intense. Managers then place greater emphasis on production

G. 2010. The age of temporary advantage. *Strategic Management Journal,* 31(13): 1371-1385. This is the lead article in a special issue of this journal that provides many ideas that are useful to both academics and practicing managers. For an additional examination of declining advantage in technologically intensive industries, see Vaaler, P. M. & McNamara, G. 2010. Are technology-intensive industries more dynamically competitive? No and yes. *Organization Science,* 21: 271-289.

57. Rita McGrath provides some interesting ideas on possible strategies for firms facing highly uncertain competitive environments: McGrath, R. G. 2011. When your business model is in trouble. *Harvard Business Review,* 89(1/2): 96-98.
58. The Atlas Door example draws on Stalk, G., Jr. 1988. Time–the next source of competitive advantage. *Harvard Business Review,* 66(4): 41-51.
59. Eisenmann, T., Parker, G., & Van Alstyne, M. 2006. Strategies for two-sided markets. *hbr.org.* October: np; Bonchek, M. & Choudary, S. 2013. Three elements of a successful platform strategy. *hbr.org.* January 31: np; Anonymous. 2016. How Uber, Airbnb and Etsy attracted their first 1,000 customers. *horbes.com.* July 13: np; Ifrach, B. 2015. How Airbnb uses machine learning to detect host preferences. *nerds.airbnb.com.* April 14: np.
60. For an interesting perspective on the influence of the product life cycle and rate of technological change on competitive strategy, refer to Lei, D. & Slocum, J. W., Jr. 2005. Strategic and organizational requirements for competitive advantage. *Academy of Management Executive,* 19(1): 31-45.
61. Dickson, P. R. 1994. *Marketing management:* 293. Fort Worth, TX: Dryden Press; Day, G. S. 1981. The product life cycle: Analysis and application. *Journal of Marketing Research,* 45: 60-67.
62. Bearden, W. O., Ingram, T. N., & LaForge, R. W. 1995. *Marketing principles and practices.* Burr Ridge, IL: Irwin.
63. MacMillan, I. C. 1985. Preemptive strategies. In Guth, W. D. (Ed.), *Handbook of business strategy:* 9-1-9-22. Boston: Warren, Gorham & Lamont; Pearce, J. A. & Robinson, R. B. 2000. *Strategic management* (7th ed.). New York: McGraw-Hill; and Dickson, op. cit., pp. 295-296.
64. Bartlett, C. A. & Ghoshal, S. 2000. Going global: Lessons for late movers. *Harvard Business Review,* 78(2): 132-142.
65. Neuborne, E. 2000. E-tailers hit the relaunch key. *BusinessWeek,* October 17: 62.
66. Berkowitz, E. N., Kerin, R. A., & Hartley, S. W. 2000. *Marketing* (6th ed.). New York: McGraw-Hill.
67. MacMillan, op. cit.
68. Our discussion of reverse and breakaway positioning draws on Moon, Y. 2005. Break free from the product life cycle. *Harvard Business Review,* 83(5): 87-94. This article also discusses stealth positioning as a means of overcoming consumer resistance and advancing a product from the introduction to the growth phase.
69. MacMillan, op. cit.
70. Berkowitz et al., op. cit.
71. Bearden et al., op. cit.
72. The discussion of these four strategies draws on MacMillan, op. cit.; Berkowitz et al., op. cit.; and Bearden et al., op. cit.
73. Augustine, N. R. 1997. Reshaping an industry: Lockheed Martin's survival story. *Harvard Business Review,* 75(3): 83-94.
74. Snow, D. C. 2008. Beware of old technologies' last gasps. *Harvard Business Review,* January: 17-18; Lohr, S. 2008. Why old technologies are still kicking. *New York Times,* March 23: np; and McGrath, R. G. 2008. Innovation and the last gasps of dying technologies. ritamcgrath.com, March 18: np.
75. Coyne, K. P., Coyne, S. T., & Coyne, E. J., Sr. 2010. When you've got to cut costs–now. *Harvard Business Review,* 88(5): 74-83.
76. A study that draws on the resource-based view of the firm to investigate successful turnaround strategies is Morrow, J. S., Sirmon, D. G., Hitt, M. A., & Holcomb, T. R. 2007. Creating value in the face of declining performance: Firm strategies and organizational recovery. *Strategic Management Journal,* 28(3): 271-284.
77. For a study investigating the relationship between organizational restructuring and acquisition performance, refer to Barkema, H. G. & Schijven, M. Toward unlocking the full potential of acquisitions: The role of organizational restructuring. *Academy of Management Journal,* 51(4): 696-722.
78. For some useful ideas on effective turnarounds and handling downsizings, refer to Marks, M. S. & De Meuse, K. p. 2005. Resizing the organization: Maximizing the gain while minimizing the pain of layoffs, divestitures and closings. *Organizational Dynamics,* 34(1): 19-36.
79. Hambrick, D. C. & Schecter, S. M. 1983. Turnaround strategies for mature industrial product business units. *Academy of Management Journal,* 26(2): 231-248.

12. Corstjens, M. & Lal, R. 2012. Retail doesn't cross borders. *Harvard Business Review,* April: 104-110.
13. Ng, S. 2014. Zulily customers play the waiting game. *wsj.com,* May 4: np.
14. Interesting insights on Walmart's effective cost leadership strategy are found in Palmeri, C. 2008. Wal-Mart is up for this downturn. *BusinessWeek,* November 6: 34.
15. An interesting perspective on the dangers of price discounting is Mohammed, R. 2011. Ditch the discounts. *Harvard Business Review,* 89(1/2): 23-25.
16. Dholakia, U. M. 2011. Why employees can wreck promotional offers. *Harvard Business Review,* 89(1/2): 28.
17. Jacobs, A. 2010. Workers in China voting with their feet. *International Herald Tribune,* July 13: 1, 14.
18. For a perspective on the sustainability of competitive advantages, refer to Barney, J. 1995. Looking inside for competitive advantage. *Academy of Management Executive,* 9(4): 49-61.
19. Thornton, E. 2001. Why e-brokers are broker and broker. *BusinessWeek,* January 22: 94.
20. Mohammed, R. 2011. Ditch the discounts. *Harvard Business Review,* 89(1/2): 23-25.
21. Wilson, D. 2012. Big Beer dresses up in craft brewers' clothing. *Fortune.com,* November 15: np.
22. For an "ultimate" in differentiated services, consider time-shares in exotic automobiles such as Lamborghinis and Bentleys. Refer to Stead, D. 2008. My Lamborghini—today, anyway. *BusinessWeek,* January 18:17.
23. For an interesting perspective on the value of corporate brands and how they may be leveraged, refer to Aaker, D. A. 2004, *California Management Review,* 46(3): 6-18.
24. A unique perspective on differentiation strategies is Austin, R. D. 2008. High margins and the quest for aesthetic coherence. *Harvard Business Review,* 86(1): 18-19.
25. Eng, D. 2011. Cheesecake Factory's winning formula. *Fortune,* May 2: 19-20.
26. For a discussion on quality in terms of a company's software and information systems, refer to Prahalad, C. K. & Krishnan, M. S. 1999. The new meaning of quality in the information age. *Harvard Business Review,* 77(5): 109-118.
27. The role of design in achieving differentiation is addressed in Brown, T. 2008. Design thinking. *Harvard Business Review,* 86(6): 84-92.
28. Taylor, A., III. 2001. Can you believe Porsche is putting its badge on this car? *Fortune,* February 19: 168-172.
29. Roberts, P. & Dowling, G. 2008. Corporate reputation and sustained superior financial performance. *Strategic Management Journal,* 23: 1077-1093.
30. Mann, J. D. 2010. The best service in the world. *Networking Times,* January: np.
31. Bonnabeau, E., Bodick, N., & Armstrong, R. W. 2008. A more rational approach to new-product development. *Harvard Business Review,* 66(3): 96-102.
32. Insights on Google's innovation are in Iyer, B. & Davenport, T. H. 2008. Reverse engineering Google's innovation machine. *Harvard Business Review,* 66(4): 58-68.
33. A discussion of how a firm used technology to create product differentiation is in Mehta, S. N. 2009. Under Armour reboots. *Fortune,* February 2: 29-33 (5).
34. Bertini, M. & Wathieu, L. 2010. How to stop customers from fixating on price. *Harvard Business Review,* 88(5): 84-91.
35. The authors would like to thank Scott Droege, a faculty member at Western Kentucky University, for providing this example.
36. Dixon, M., Freeman, K., & Toman, N. 2010. Stop trying to delight your customers. *Harvard Business Review,* 88(7/8).
37. Flint, J. 2004. Stop the nerds. *Forbes,* July 5: 80; and Fahey, E. 2004. Over-engineering 101. *Forbes,* December 13: 62.
38. Fahey, J. 2004. Over-engineering 101. Forbes, December 20.
39. Kelly, G. 2019. Apple Warned iPhones Sales Are In Trouble. forbes. com. January 1: np.
40. Caplan, J. 2006. In a real crunch. *Inside Business,* July: A37-A38.
41. Caplan, J. 2006. In a real crunch. Inside Business, July: A37-A38.
42. Gadiesh, O. & Gilbert, J. L. 1998. Profit pools: A fresh look at strategy. *Harvard Business Review,* 76(3): 139-158.
43. Colvin, G. 2000. Beware: You could soon be selling soybeans. *Fortune,* November 13: 80.
44. Anders, G. 2012. How LinkedIn has turned your resume into a cash machine. *Forbes.com,* July 16: np.
45. Burrus, D. 2011. *Flash foresight: How to see the invisible and do the impossible.* New York: HarperCollins.
46. Hall, W. K. 1980. Survival strategies in a hostile environment, *Harvard Business Review,* 58: 75-87; on the paint and allied products industry, see Dess, G. G. & Davis, P. S. 1984. Porter's (1980) generic strategies as determinants of strategic group membership and organizational performance. *Academy of Management Journal,* 27: 467-488; for the Korean electronics industry, see Kim, L. & Lim, Y. 1988. Environment, generic strategies, and performance in a rapidly developing country: A taxonomic approach. *Academy of Management Journal,* 31: 802-827; Wright, P., Hotard, D., Kroll, M., Chan, P., & Tanner, J. 1990. Performance and multiple strategies in a firm: Evidence from the apparel industry. In Dean, B. V. & Cassidy, J. C. (Eds.), *Strategic management: Methods and studies:* 93-110. Amsterdam: Elsevier-North Holland; and Wright, P., Kroll, M., Tu, H., & Helms, M. 1991. Generic strategies and business performance: An empirical study of the screw machine products industry. *British Journal of Management,* 2: 1-9.
47. Gilmore, J. H. & Pine, B. J., II. 1997. The four faces of customization. *Harvard Business Review,* 75(1): 91-101.
48. Heracleous, L. & Wirtz, J. 2010. Singapore Airlines' balancing act. *Harvard Business Review,* 88(7/8): 145-149.
49. Gilmore & Pine, op. cit. For interesting insights on mass customization, refer to Cattani, K., Dahan, E., & Schmidt, G. 2005. Offshoring versus "spackling." *MIT Sloan Management Review,* 46(3): 6-7.
50. Kiron, D. 2013. From value to vision: Reimagining the possible with data analytics. *MIT Sloan Management Review Research Report,* Spring: 1-19.
51. Gadiesh & Gilbert, op. cit., pp. 139-158.
52. Insights on the profit pool concept are addressed in Reinartz, W. & Ulaga, W. 2008. How to sell services more profitably. *Harvard Business Review,* 66(5): 90-96.
53. Cameron, D. and Wall, R. 2018. Boeing swoops in on plane-parts specialist KLX. wsj.com. May 1; np.
54. Taneja, H., Maney, K. 2018. The end of scale.*MIT Sloan Management Review*. Spring: 67-72.
55. *statista.com/statistics/263439/global-market-share-held-by-rim-smartphones/.*
56. For an insightful, recent discussion on the difficulties and challenges associated with creating advantages that are sustainable for any reasonable period of time and suggested strategies, refer to D'Aveni, R. A., Dagnino, G. B., & Smith, K.

Nico Muller Art/Shutterstock

Corporate-Level Strategy

Creating Value through Diversification

Learning Objectives

LO6-1 Identify the reasons for the failure of many diversification efforts.

LO6-2 Explain how managers can create value through diversification initiatives.

LO6-3 Explain how corporations can use related diversification to achieve synergistic benefits through economies of scope and market power.

LO6-4 Explain how corporations can use unrelated diversification to attain synergistic benefits through corporate restructuring, parenting, and portfolio analysis.

LO6-5 Describe various means of engaging in diversification—mergers and acquisitions, joint ventures/strategic alliances, and internal development.

LO6-6 Identify managerial behaviors that can erode the creation of value.

We encourage you to reflect on how the concepts presented in this chapter can enhance your career success (see "Reflecting on Career Implications..." at the end of the chapter).

LEARNING FROM MISTAKES

The merger of Newell and Jarden seemed to make perfect sense. Newell, the maker of a range of household and office products including Graco strollers, Sharpie markers, Calphalon cookware, and Rubbermaid containers, had for years grown through the acquisition of other manufacturers. The firm had a long success of improving the operational efficiency of firms it acquired and dominating product segments. Jarden looked like a great target for Rubbermaid to continue this pattern. It made a range of similar household products, including Ball glass jars, First Alert fire detectors, and Sunbeam small appliances.

Michael Polk, the CEO of Newell, saw great value potential in the combination of the two firms. Jarden had allowed its business units to run autonomously. Newell could gain efficiencies by integrating the Jarden businesses into Newell's business model. By combining research and development, supply chains, and back office operations, the firm could reap $500M in savings annually. Newell could also leverage the power of some businesses to help others. For example, in the infant business, Newell's Graco was a major player. Newell could leverage the relationships Graco has built with major retailers to convince them to carry Jarden's Nuk line of pacifiers and bottles.[1]

It all seemed rational with strong potential for clear value creation. The stock of Newell was trading at $45 a share when it announced the $15B acquisition of Jarden in late 2015. The deal closed in April 2016, and the stock of Newell continued to rise as investors expected to see the success of the merger. The stock hit a peak of nearly $54 a share in June 2017, but then the tide turned dramatically. The firm reported disappointing sales and earnings. In early 2018, Newell managers decided to cancel paying $35M in employee bonuses. Activist investor funds pressured the firm for governance changes, including changing the makeup of the firm's board of directors, giving the activist investors majority control of the board. But the bad news kept coming for Newell. Sales declined by over 40 percent in 2018, and operating income dropped by over 50 percent. As of early 2019, the stock was down to $17 a share. At the time of the merger announcement, Newell and Jarden were worth $12B and $10B, respectively. As of February 2019, the combined firm was worth $8B. Thus, the acquisition arguably destroyed $14B of shareholder value.

Why did this merger fail? Problems arose both inside and outside the firm. The integration of Jarden into the Newell way of operating was not smooth. There were culture clashes and fights over the future structure of the firm. When Newell tried to combine units and centralize staff, many of Jarden's product experts were either shifted to support products they didn't know well or were laid off. For example, salespeople who specialized in a single product, such as fishing equipment, were forced into a generalist sales team for outdoor equipment in general. The combined sales teams generated disappointing sales with major retailers in 2017. In response, Newell undid many of these organizational changes. As a result, the firm found it had overstated the cost efficiencies that would come from the combination.

There were also difficult strategic differences. For example, Newell's sales tactics appeared out of place for some of Jarden's products that were more highly differentiated than most of Newell's products. Newell responded to sales shortfalls at Yankee Candle by ramping up sales of the candles at discount retailers, such as Walmart, at dramatically reduced prices. Martin Franklin, the former CEO of Jarden, complained this cheapened the brand image of Yankee Candle, which had been positioned as a premium brand.

The firm also faced external challenges. Hurricanes in the southeast in 2017 shut down a number of Newell's suppliers of resin, the core material used to make plastics. This resulted in an increase in cost for the firm as it had to seek out new suppliers. Also, the struggles of key retailers, most notably with the bankruptcy of Toys R Us, reduced demand for Newell's products. The firm also found itself relying more on retailers, such as Amazon and Walmart, who regularly pressure the firm on product pricing.

Newell has responded to these pressures by announcing that the firm would sell off a number of its businesses, accounting for over 30 percent of the firm's sales, and focus on nine core consumer product areas. But it is fairly clear that the combination of Newell and Jarden has failed to generate and will likely never generate any of the shareholder value projected when the deal was conceived.

Discussion Questions

1. In what ways did Newell expect to generate value by acquiring Jarden?
2. Why was Newell so overly optimistic about the value it could generate?
3. What mistakes did Newell make in its pursuit and post-merger integration of Jarden?

LO 6-1

Identify the reasons for the failure of many diversification efforts.

Newell and Jarden's experience is consistent with a large proportion of corporate mergers. Research shows that a majority of acquisitions of public corporations result in value destruction rather than value creation. Many other large multinational firms have also failed to effectively integrate their acquisitions, paid too high a premium for the target's common stock, or were unable to understand how the acquired firm's assets would fit with their own lines of business.[2] And, at times, top executives may not have acted in the best interests of shareholders. That is, the motive for the acquisition may have been to enhance the executives' power and prestige rather than to improve shareholder returns. At times, the only other people who may have benefited were the shareholders of the *acquired* firms—or the investment bankers who advise the acquiring firm, because they collect huge fees up front regardless of what happens afterward![3]

Academic research has found that acquisitions, in general, do not lead to benefits for shareholders. A review paper that looked at over 100 studies on mergers and acquisitions concluded that research has found that acquisitions, on average, do not create shareholder value.[4]

Exhibit 6.1 lists some well-known examples of failed acquisitions and mergers.

Many acquisitions ultimately result in divestiture—an admission that things didn't work out as planned. In fact, some years ago, a writer for *Fortune* magazine lamented, "Studies show that 33 percent to 50 percent of acquisitions are later divested, giving corporate marriages a divorce rate roughly comparable to that of men and women."[5]

EXHIBIT 6.1

Some Well-Known M&A Blunders

Examples of Some Very Expensive Blunders

- Sprint and Nextel merged in 2005. On January 31, 2008, the firm announced a merger-related charge of $31 billion. Its stock had lost 76 percent of its value by late 2012 when it was announced that Sprint Nextel would be purchased by SoftBank, a Japanese telecommunications and Internet firm. SoftBank's stock price dropped 20 percent in the week after announcing it would acquire Sprint.
- Newell and Jarden were worth a combined $22 billion when they merged in 2016. Three years later, the combined firm was worth only $8 billion.
- In 2012, Hewlett-Packard wrote off $9 billion of the $11 billion it paid for Autonomy, a software company that it purchased one year earlier. After the purchase, HP realized that Autonomy's accounting statements were not accurate, resulting in a nearly 80 percent drop in the value of Autonomy once those accounting irregularities were corrected.
- Similarly, in 2012, Microsoft admitted to a major acquisition mistake when it wrote off essentially the entire $6.2 billion it paid for a digital advertising firm, aQuantive, that it purchased in 2007.
- Yahoo purchased Tumblr for $1.1 billion in 2013 but had written off over 80 percent of this value by the middle of 2016. Commentators have noted that Yahoo's repeated failures to extract value from acquisitions is one of the key reasons it was unable to survive as an independent firm.

Sources: Ante, S. E. 2008. Sprint's wake-up call. *businessweek.com,* February 21: np; Tully, S. 2006. The (second) worst deal ever. *Fortune,* October 16: 102–119; Wakabayashi, D., Troianovski, A., and S. Ante. 2012. Bravado behind Softbank's Sprint deal. *wsj.com,* October 16: np; and Kim, E. 2016. Yahoo just wrote down another $482 million from Tumblr, the company it bought for $1 billion. *businessinsider.com,* July 18: np.

Admittedly, we have been rather pessimistic so far.[6] Clearly, many diversification efforts have worked out very well—whether through mergers and acquisitions, strategic alliances and joint ventures, or internal development. We will discuss many success stories throughout this chapter. Next, we will discuss the primary rationales for diversification.

MAKING DIVERSIFICATION WORK: AN OVERVIEW

LO 6-2

Explain how managers can create value through diversification initiatives.

diversification the process of firms expanding their operations by entering new businesses.

Clearly, not all **diversification** moves, including those involving mergers and acquisitions, erode performance. For example, acquisitions in the oil industry, such as British Petroleum's purchases of Amoco and Arco, performed well, as did the Exxon-Mobil merger. MetLife was able to dramatically expand its global footprint by acquiring Alico, a global player in the insurance business, from AIG in 2010 when AIG was in financial distress. Since AIG was desperate to sell assets, MetLife was able to acquire this business at an attractive price. With this acquisition, MetLife expanded its global reach from 17 to 64 countries and increased its non-U.S. revenue from 15 to 40 percent.[7] Many leading high-tech firms such as Google, Apple, and Intel have dramatically enhanced their revenues, profits, and market values through a wide variety of diversification initiatives, including acquisitions, strategic alliances, and joint ventures, as well as internal development.

So the question becomes: Why do some diversification efforts pay off and others produce poor results? This chapter addresses two related issues: (1) What businesses should a corporation compete in? and (2) How should these businesses be managed to jointly create more value than if they were freestanding units?

Diversification initiatives—whether through mergers and acquisitions, strategic alliances and joint ventures, or internal development—must be justified by the creation of value for shareholders.[8] But this is not always the case.[9] Acquiring firms typically pay high premiums when they acquire a target firm. For example, in 2016, Microsoft offered to buy LinkedIn for $26.2 billion, 50 percent higher than LinkedIn's value the day before. In contrast, you and I, as private investors, can diversify our portfolio of stocks very cheaply. With an intensely competitive online brokerage industry, we can acquire hundreds (or thousands) of shares for a transaction fee of as little as $10 or less—a far cry from the 30 to 40 percent (or higher) premiums that corporations typically must pay to acquire companies.

Given the seemingly high inherent downside risks and uncertainties, one might ask: Why should companies even bother with diversification initiatives? The answer, in a word, is *synergy*, derived from the Greek word *synergos,* which means "working together." This can have two different, but not mutually exclusive, meanings.

First, a firm may diversify into *related* businesses. Here, the primary potential benefits to be derived come from *horizontal relationships,* that is, businesses sharing intangible resources (e.g., core competencies such as marketing) and tangible resources (e.g., production facilities, distribution channels).[10] Firms can also enhance their market power via pooled negotiating power and vertical integration. For example, Procter & Gamble enjoys many synergies from having businesses that share distribution resources.

The degree of relatedness of business units can vary widely. A firm's diversification is *related linked* when the business units only share a few resources. For example, Nike shares the Nike brand and the swoosh logo across a number of its businesses but few other resources. In contrast, a firm's diversification is *related constrained* when there are a large number of resource links between the business units. The larger number of resource links in related constrained diversification means there is greater potential value to extract from the diversification, but it also means that the member businesses are constrained in the actions they can take to win in each of their markets since any action one business unit takes affects the other business units in the firm. For example, Polaris uses shared components, designs, production facilities, and distribution systems for its snowmobiles, ATVs, and electric vehicles.

EXHIBIT 6.2

Creating Value through Related and Unrelated Diversification

Related Diversification: Economies of Scope

Leveraging core competencies

- 3M leverages its competencies in adhesives technologies to many industries, including automotive, construction, and telecommunications.

Sharing activities

- Polaris, a manufacturer of snowmobiles, motorcycles, and off-road vehicles, shares manufacturing operations across its businesses. It also has a corporate R&D facility and staff departments that support all of Polaris's operating divisions.

Related Diversification: Market Power

Pooled negotiating power

- ConAgra, a diversified food producer, increases its power over suppliers by centrally purchasing huge quantities of packaging materials for all of its food divisions.

Vertical integration

- Shaw Industries, a giant carpet manufacturer, increases its control over raw materials by producing much of its own polypropylene fiber, a key input to its manufacturing process.

Unrelated Diversification: Parenting, Restructuring, and Financial Synergies

Corporate restructuring and parenting

- The corporate office of Cooper Industries adds value to its acquired businesses by performing such activities as auditing their manufacturing operations, improving their accounting activities, and centralizing union negotiations.

Portfolio management

- Novartis, formerly Ciba-Geigy, uses portfolio management to improve many key activities, including resource allocation and reward and evaluation systems.

As a result, the firm benefits by sharing resources and leveraging market power with suppliers, but it also means that any changes in production design, components, or manufacturing schedules needs to be done through a negotiation among the business units.

Second, a corporation may diversify into unrelated businesses.[11] Here, the primary potential benefits are derived largely from *hierarchical relationships,* that is, value creation derived from the corporate office. Examples of the latter would include leveraging some of the support activities in the value chain that we discussed in Chapter 3, such as information systems or human resource practices.

Please note that such benefits derived from horizontal (related diversification) and hierarchical (unrelated diversification) relationships are not mutually exclusive. Many firms that diversify into related areas benefit from information technology expertise in the corporate office. Similarly, unrelated diversifiers often benefit from the "best practices" of sister businesses even though their products, markets, and technologies may differ dramatically.

Exhibit 6.2 provides an overview of how we will address the various means by which firms create value through both related and unrelated diversification and also includes a summary of some examples that we will address in this chapter.[12]

LO 6-3

Explain how corporations can use related diversification to achieve synergistic benefits through economies of scope and market power.

RELATED DIVERSIFICATION: ECONOMIES OF SCOPE AND REVENUE ENHANCEMENT

related diversification a firm entering a different business in which it can benefit from leveraging core competencies, sharing activities, or building market power.

Related diversification enables a firm to benefit from horizontal relationships across different businesses in the diversified corporation by leveraging core competencies and sharing activities (e.g., production and distribution facilities). This enables a corporation to benefit from economies of scope. **Economies of scope** refers to cost savings from leveraging core competencies or sharing related activities among businesses in the corporation. A firm can also enjoy greater revenues if two businesses attain higher levels of sales growth combined than either company could attain independently.

economies of scope cost savings from leveraging core competencies or sharing related activities among businesses in a corporation.

Leveraging Core Competencies

The concept of core competencies can be illustrated by the imagery of the diversified corporation as a tree.[13] The trunk and major limbs represent core products; the smaller branches are business units; and the leaves, flowers, and fruit are end products. The core competencies are represented by the root system, which provides nourishment, sustenance, and stability. Managers often misread the strength of competitors by looking only at their end products, just as we can fail to appreciate the strength of a tree by looking only at its leaves. Core competencies may also be viewed as the "glue" that binds existing businesses together or as the engine that fuels new business growth.

Core competencies reflect the collective learning in organizations–how to coordinate diverse production skills, integrate multiple streams of technologies, and market diverse products and services.[14] Casio, a giant electronic products producer, synthesizes its abilities in miniaturization, microprocessor design, material science, and ultrathin precision castings to produce digital watches. These are the same skills it applies to design and produce its miniature card calculators, digital cameras, pocket electronic dictionaries, and other small electronics.

core competencies a firm's strategic resources that reflect the collective learning in the organization.

For a core competence to create value and provide a viable basis for synergy among the businesses in a corporation, it must meet three criteria:[15]

- ***The core competence must enhance competitive advantage(s) by creating superior customer value.*** Every value-chain activity has the potential to provide a viable basis for building on a core competence.[16] At Gillette, for example, scientists have developed a series of successful new razors, including the Sensor, Fusion, Mach 3, and ProGlide, building on a thorough understanding of several phenomena that underlie shaving. These include the physiology of facial hair and skin, the metallurgy of blade strength and sharpness, the dynamics of a cartridge moving across skin, and the physics of a razor blade severing hair. Such innovations are possible only with an understanding of such phenomena and the ability to combine such technologies into innovative products. Customers are willing to pay more for such technologically differentiated products.
- ***Different businesses in the corporation must be similar in at least one important way related to the core competence.*** It is not essential that the products or services themselves be similar. Rather, at least one element in the value chain must require similar skills in creating competitive advantage if the corporation is to capitalize on its core competence. For example, while we might think that film technology and beauty products have little in common, Fujifilm has found a link it could exploit. Fuji took expertise it had developed with collagen, a major component of both photo film and human skin, and used it to develop a new skin care product line, Astalift–a product line that produces over $3 billion in sales.[17] Similarly, IBM is combining its competencies in computing technology with crowdsourced medical research knowledge to provide healthcare services.
- ***The core competencies must be difficult for competitors to imitate or find substitutes for.*** As we discussed in Chapter 5, competitive advantages will not be sustainable if the competition can easily imitate or substitute them. Similarly, if the skills associated with a firm's core competencies are easily imitated or replicated, they are not a sound basis for sustainable advantages.

6.1 STRATEGY SPOTLIGHT

LEVERAGING VOLVO'S COMPETENCIES TO TRANSFORM GEELY

At the 2006 Detroit Auto Show, Geely was intent on staking its claim as a player in the global auto market. The Chinese auto manufacturer wanted to branch out and compete in the North American auto market. Geely displayed a compact car, the 7151CK, it intended to sell in the United States. However, the reaction Geely received was not what the firm had hoped for. Car and Driver magazine called its design "hopelessly outdated."

Geely knew it needed to improve its designs to compete on the global stage. Though its primary business was in bargain-priced cars, the firm realized it needed to build better cars and began focusing on quality. But Li Shufu, the firm's founder, concluded that he also wanted to try acquire capabilities that would help Geely compete on the global stage. His opportunity came when Ford decided to focus primarily on its Ford brand. Geely jumped in and acquired Volvo from Ford for $1.8B in 2010, quite a bit less than the $6B Ford had paid for the brand when it acquired it in 1999.

Many thought the acquisition would fail. The firms were located thousands of miles apart. Geely had no experience in the markets in which Volvo competed. Volvo was an upmarket brand while Geely was a discount brand. The CEOs of the two companies did not even speak a common language. Also, managers and workers at Volvo feared that Geely would try to combine the two firms and take away the autonomy of the Swedish firm, possibly even moving production out of Sweden. Li responded by signing a letter asserting that Volvo would remain Swedish; it would retain its autonomy.

With the two firms, he saw complementary strengths that would allow the combined firm to thrive. Geely had hard drive and access to financial resources. Volvo had a strong reputation for quality and safety, strong technology abilities, and strong engineering and design staffs capable of developing desirable new models. Geely invested $11B in Volvo allowing the firm to develop new models, technology, and factories. Geely also invited Volvo executives in to help make Geely more globally competitive. Peter Horbury, a former head of design for Volvo, came in and likened "Geely's cars to different animals in a zoo with nothing in common. He then projected another slide showing different types of cats. Like the cats, Geely cars needed to become recognizable as members of the same species." Geely took guidance from Volvo on design, technology, and safety and developed a line of cars that are competitive in the Chinese market, growing from sales of just over 400,000 in 2010 to nearly 1.4 million in 2018. As a representative from a Taiwanese investment firm said, with the changes it has been able to make, Geely has "elevated its brand image."

Sources: Moss, T., and W. Boston. 2018. How China's Geely turned a disassembled Mercedes into a global car company. *wsj.com,* March 4: np; Spring, J., and N. Shirouzu. 2017. China's Geely doubles earnings as Volvo tech boosts sales. *reuters.com,* March 22: np; and *carsalesbase.com.*

Consider Amazon's retailing operations. Amazon developed strong competencies in Internet retailing, website infrastructure, warehousing, and order fulfillment to dominate the online book industry. It used these competencies along with its brand name to expand into a range of online retail businesses. Competitors in these other market areas have had great difficulty imitating Amazon's competencies, and many have simply stopped trying. Instead, they have partnered with Amazon and contracted with Amazon to provide these services for them.[18]

Strategy Spotlight 6.1 outlines how Geely leveraged Volvo's core competencies to become a world class automaker.

Sharing Activities

sharing activities having activities of two or more businesses' value chains done by one of the businesses.

As we saw previously, leveraging core competencies involves transferring accumulated skills and expertise across business units in a corporation. Corporations also can achieve synergy by **sharing activities** across their business units. These include value-creating activities such as common manufacturing facilities, distribution channels, and sales forces. As we will see, sharing activities can potentially provide two primary payoffs: cost savings and revenue enhancements.

Deriving Cost Savings Typically, this is the most common type of synergy and the easiest to estimate. Peter Shaw, head of mergers and acquisitions at the British chemical and pharmaceutical company ICI, refers to cost savings as "hard synergies" and contends that the level of certainty of their achievement is quite high. Cost savings come from many sources, including from the elimination of jobs, facilities, and related expenses that are no longer needed when functions are consolidated and from economies of scale in purchasing. Cost savings are generally highest when one company acquires another from the same industry in the same country. Shaw Industries, a division of Berkshire Hathaway, is the nation's largest carpet producer. Over the years, it has dominated the competition through a strategy of acquisition that has enabled Shaw, among other things, to consolidate its manufacturing operations in a few, highly efficient plants and to lower costs through higher capacity utilization. Honda benefits by sharing small engine development and manufacturing across the more than 15 different types of power equipment it produces. Similarly, General Motors uses a shared engineering group and shared vehicle platforms across its Chevrolet, Buick, and GMC brands.

Sharing activities inevitably involve costs that the benefits must outweigh such as the greater coordination required to manage a shared activity. Even more important is the need to compromise on the design or performance of an activity so that it can be shared. For example, a salesperson handling the products of two business units must operate in a way that is usually not what either unit would choose if it were independent. If the compromise erodes the unit's effectiveness, then sharing may reduce rather than enhance competitive advantage.

ENHANCING REVENUE AND DIFFERENTIATION

Often an acquiring firm and its target may achieve a higher level of sales growth together than either company could on its own. For example, Starbucks has acquired a number of small firms, including La Boulange, a small bakery chain; Teavana, a tea producer; and Evolution Fresh, a juice company. Starbucks can add value to all of these firms by expanding their market exposure as Starbucks offers these products for sale in its national retail chain.[19]

Firms also can enhance the effectiveness of their differentiation strategies by means of sharing activities among business units. A shared order-processing system, for example, may permit new features and services that a buyer will value. As another example, financial service providers strive to provide differentiated bundles of services to customers. By having a single point of contact where customers can manage their checking accounts, investment accounts, insurance policies, bill-payment services, mortgages, and many other services, they create value for their customers.

As a cautionary note, managers must keep in mind that sharing activities among businesses in a corporation can have a negative effect on a given business's differentiation. For example, when Ford owned Jaguar, customers had lower perceived value of Jaguar automobiles when they learned that the entry-level Jaguar shared its basic design with and was manufactured in the same production plant as the Ford Mondeo, a European midsize car. Perhaps it is not too surprising that Jaguar was divested by Ford in 2008.

RELATED DIVERSIFICATION: MARKET POWER

We now discuss how companies achieve related diversification through **market power**. We also address the two principal means by which firms achieve synergy through market power: *pooled negotiating power* and *vertical integration.* Managers do, however, have limits on their ability to use market power for diversification, because government regulations can sometimes restrict the ability of a business to gain very large shares of a particular market. For example, in 2015, Walgreens announced a deal to acquire Rite Aid, but federal regulators blocked the deal arguing that a combined firm would dominate the drugstore market. After intense negotiations Walgreens agreed to dramatically scale back the deal in 2017 and ended up acquiring only 1,900 of Rite Aid's 4,500 stores.

market power
firms' abilities to profit through restricting or controlling supply to a market or coordinating with other firms to reduce investment.

6.2 STRATEGY SPOTLIGHT — ENVIRONMENTAL SUSTAINABILITY

TESLA BREAKS INDUSTRY NORMS BY VERTICALLY INTEGRATING

For decades, auto manufacturers vertically integrated and controlled all stages of the manufacturing process. By manufacturing their own components, the auto firms could coordinate design of parts, ensure the quality of components, and also ensure that there was adequate production of the parts they needed. However, in recent decades, auto firms have sold off most of their suppliers. By allowing outside suppliers to compete for contracts, the auto firms found they were able to buy components for lower cost than if they had built them in-house.

In contrast to the direction the major auto firms have gone, Tesla is going all in on building a vertically integrated business model. In 2015, Tesla announced that it was building a "gigafactory" to supply all of the batteries they will need for their cars. Tesla sees at least three benefits from making its own batteries. First, by taking on the $5 billion cost to build the factory, it is maximizing scale efficiencies in battery manufacturing that could result in a per unit cost reduction of 30 percent. Second, Tesla believes it will be able to better coordinate battery technology development as a vertically integrated firm. Third, if demand for electric vehicles takes off as Tesla expects, it will benefit from having an in-house supplier that can provide a steady supply of batteries rather than having to compete to buy batteries from outside suppliers. There simply isn't enough battery production capacity in the world to provide the batteries needed for Tesla to hit its goal of selling 500,000 vehicles per year. But it is a big bet that will be very costly to Tesla if demand doesn't grow as it expects or if new battery technology makes Tesla's lithium-ion batteries obsolete.

Sources: Gorzelany, J. 2014. Why Tesla's vertical manufacturing move could prove essential to its success. *forbes.com,* February 27: np; and Randall, T. 2017. Tesla flips the switch on the gigafactory. *bloomberg.com,* January 4.

Pooled Negotiating Power

Similar businesses working together or the affiliation of a business with a strong parent can strengthen an organization's bargaining position relative to suppliers and customers and enhance its position vis-à-vis competitors. Compare, for example, the position of an independent food manufacturer with that of the same business within Nestlé. Being part of Nestlé provides the business with significant clout–greater bargaining power with suppliers and customers–since it is part of a firm that makes large purchases from suppliers and provides a wide variety of products. Access to the parent's deep pockets increases the business's strength, and the Nestlé unit enjoys greater protection from substitutes and new entrants. Not only would rivals perceive the unit as a more formidable opponent, but the unit's association with Nestlé would also provide greater visibility and improved image.

pooled negotiating power
the improvement in bargaining position relative to suppliers and customers.

When acquiring related businesses, a firm's potential for **pooled negotiating power** vis-à-vis its customers and suppliers can be very enticing. However, managers must carefully evaluate how the combined businesses may affect relationships with actual and potential customers, suppliers, and competitors. For example, when Netflix diversified into developing its own shows and movies, competitors, such as Disney and Warner Brothers, decided to stop distributing their own shows and movies through Netflix's distribution system.

Vertical Integration

vertical integration
an expansion or extension of the firm by integrating preceding or successive production processes.

Vertical integration occurs when a firm becomes its own supplier or distributor. That is, it represents an expansion or extension of the firm by integrating preceding or successive production processes.[20] The firm incorporates more processes toward the original source of raw materials (backward integration) or toward the ultimate consumer (forward integration). For example, an oil refinery might secure land leases and develop its own drilling capacity to ensure a constant supply of crude oil. Or it could expand into retail operations by owning or licensing gasoline stations to guarantee customers for its petroleum products.

Vertical integration can be a viable strategy for many firms. Strategy Spotlight 6.2 discusses how Tesla is vertically integrating into battery production to ensure it has an adequate supply of batteries as it expands its production of vehicles.

EXHIBIT 6.3

Benefits and Risks of Vertical Integration

Benefits
• A secure source of raw materials or distribution channels.
• Protection of and control over valuable assets.
• Proprietary access to new technologies developed by the unit.
• Simplified procurement and administrative procedures.
Risks
• Costs and expenses associated with increased overhead and capital expenditures.
• Loss of flexibility resulting from large investments.
• Problems associated with unbalanced capacities along the value chain. (For example, the in-house supplier has to be larger than your needs in order to benefit from economies of scale in that market.)
• Additional administrative costs associated with managing a more complex set of activities.

Benefits and Risks of Vertical Integration Vertical integration is a means for an organization to reduce its dependence on suppliers or its channels of distribution to end users. However, the benefits associated with vertical integration—backward or forward—must be carefully weighed against the risks.[21] The primary benefits and risks of vertical integration are listed in Exhibit 6.3.

Winnebago, the leader in the market for drivable recreational vehicles, with a 33.9 percent market share, illustrates some of vertical integration's benefits.[22] The word *Winnebago* means "big RV" to most Americans. And the firm has a sterling reputation for great quality. The firm's huge northern Iowa factories do everything from extruding aluminum for body parts to molding plastics for water and holding tanks to dashboards. Such vertical integration at the factory may appear to be outdated and expensive, but it has allowed Winnebago to maintain their product quality.

In making vertical integration decisions, five issues should be considered:[23]

1. ***Is the company satisfied with the quality of the value that its present suppliers and distributors are providing?*** If the performance of organizations in the vertical chain—both suppliers and distributors—is satisfactory, it may not, in general, be appropriate for a company to perform these activities itself. But if firms are not happy with their current suppliers, they may want to backward integrate. For example, Kaiser Permanente, a health provider with 10.6 million subscribers, launched its own medical school to better train physicians to provide the integrated style of care Kaiser is striving to provide.[24]
2. ***Are there activities in the industry value chain presently being outsourced or performed independently by others that are a viable source of future profits?*** Even if a firm is outsourcing value-chain activities to companies that are doing a credible job, it may be missing out on substantial profit opportunities. Consider Best Buy. When it realized that the profit potential of providing installation and service was substantial, Best Buy forward integrated into this area by acquiring Geek Squad.
3. ***Is there a high level of stability in the demand for the organization's products?*** High demand or sales volatility is not conducive to vertical integration. With the high level of fixed costs in plant and equipment as well as operating costs that accompany endeavors toward vertical integration, widely fluctuating sales demand can either strain resources (in times of high demand) or result in unused capacity (in times of low demand). The cycles of "boom and bust" in the automobile industry are a key reason why the manufacturers have increased the amount of outsourced inputs.
4. ***Does the company have the necessary competencies to execute the vertical integration strategies?*** As many companies would attest, successfully executing strategies of vertical integration can be very difficult. For example, Boise Cascade, a lumber firm,

once forward integrated into the home-building industry but found that it didn't have the design and marketing competencies needed to compete in this market.

5. **Will the vertical integration initiative have potential negative impacts on the firm's stakeholders?** Managers must carefully consider the impact that vertical integration may have on existing and future customers, suppliers, and competitors. After Lockheed Martin, a dominant defense contractor, acquired electronics supplier Loral Corporation for $9.1 billion, it had an unpleasant and unanticipated surprise. Loral, as a subsidiary of Lockheed, was viewed as a rival by many of its previous customers. Thus, while Lockheed Martin may have seen benefits by being able to coordinate operations with Loral as a captive supplier, it also saw a decline in business for Loral with other defense contractors.

transaction cost perspective
a perspective that the choice of a transaction's governance structure, such as vertical integration or market transaction, is influenced by transaction costs, including search, negotiating, contracting, monitoring, and enforcement costs associated with each choice.

Analyzing Vertical Integration: The Transaction Cost Perspective Another approach that has proved very useful in understanding vertical integration is the **transaction cost perspective.**[25] According to this perspective, every market transaction involves some *transaction costs*. First, a decision to purchase an input from an outside source leads to *search* costs (i.e., the cost to find where it is available, the level of quality, etc.). Second, there are costs associated with *negotiating*. Third, a *contract* needs to be written spelling out future possible contingencies. Fourth, parties in a contract have to *monitor* each other. Finally, if a party does not comply with the terms of the contract, there are *enforcement* costs. Transaction costs are thus the sum of search costs, negotiation costs, contracting costs, monitoring costs, and enforcement costs. These transaction costs can be avoided by internalizing the activity, in other words, by producing the input in-house.

A related problem with purchasing a specialized input from outside is the issue of *transaction-specific investments*. For example, when an automobile company needs an input specifically designed for a particular car model, the supplier may be unwilling to make the investments in plant and machinery necessary to produce that component for two reasons. First, the investment may take many years to recover but there is no guarantee the automobile company will continue to buy from the supplier after the contract expires, typically in one year. Second, once the investment is made, the supplier has no bargaining power. That is, the buyer knows that the supplier has no option but to supply at ever-lower prices because the investments were so specific that they cannot be used to produce alternative products. In such circumstances, again, vertical integration may be the only option.

Vertical integration, however, gives rise to a different set of costs. These costs are referred to as *administrative costs*. Coordinating different stages of the value chain now internalized within the firm causes administrative costs to go up. Decisions about vertical integration are, therefore, based on a comparison of transaction costs and administrative costs. If transaction costs are lower than administrative costs, it is best to resort to market transactions and avoid vertical integration. For example, McDonald's may be the world's biggest buyer of beef, but it does not raise cattle. The market for beef has low transaction costs and requires no transaction-specific investments. On the other hand, if transaction costs are higher than administrative costs, vertical integration becomes an attractive strategy. Most automobile manufacturers produce their own engines because the market for engines involves high transaction costs and transaction-specific investments.

unrelated diversification
a firm entering a different business that has little horizontal interaction with other businesses of a firm.

LO 6-4

Explain how corporations can use unrelated diversification to attain synergistic benefits through corporate restructuring, parenting, and portfolio analysis.

UNRELATED DIVERSIFICATION: FINANCIAL SYNERGIES AND PARENTING

With **unrelated diversification,** unlike related diversification, few benefits are derived from horizontal relationships—that is, the leveraging of core competencies or the sharing of activities across business units within a corporation. Instead, potential benefits can be gained from *vertical* (or *hierarchical) relationships*–the creation of synergies from the interaction of the corporate office with the individual business units. There are two main sources of such synergies. First, the corporate office can contribute to "parenting" and restructuring of (often acquired) businesses. Second, the corporate office can add value by viewing the entire corporation as a family or "portfolio" of businesses and allocating resources to optimize corporate goals of profitability, cash flow, and growth. Additionally, the corporate office enhances value by establishing appropriate human resource practices and financial controls for each of its business units.

Corporate Parenting and Restructuring

We have discussed how firms can add value through related diversification by exploring sources of synergy *across* business units. Now, we discuss how value can be created *within* business units as a result of the expertise and support provided by the corporate office.

Parenting The positive contributions of the corporate office are called the **"parenting advantage."**[26] Many firms have successfully diversified their holdings without strong evidence of the more traditional sources of synergy (i.e., horizontally across business units). Diversified public corporations such as Berkshire Hathaway and Virgin Group and leveraged buyout firms such as KKR and Clayton, Dubilier & Rice are a few examples.[27] These parent companies create value through management expertise. How? They improve plans and budgets and provide especially competent central functions such as legal, financial, human resource management, procurement, and the like. They also help subsidiaries make wise choices in their own acquisitions, divestitures, and new internal development decisions. Such contributions often help business units to substantially increase their revenues and profits. For example, KKR, a private equity firm, has a team of parenting experts, called KKR Capstone, that works with newly acquired firms for 12 to 24 months to enhance the acquired firm's value. The team works to improve a range of operating activities, such as new product development processes, sales force activities, quality improvement, and supply chain management.

parenting advantage
the positive contributions of the corporate office to a new business as a result of expertise and support provided and not as a result of substantial changes in assets, capital structure, or management.

Restructuring **Restructuring** is another means by which the corporate office can add value to a business.[28] The central idea can be captured in the real estate phrase "Buy low and sell high." Here, the corporate office tries to find either poorly performing firms with unrealized potential or firms in industries on the threshold of significant, positive change. The parent intervenes, often selling off parts of the business; changing the management; reducing payroll and unnecessary sources of expenses; changing strategies; and infusing the company with new technologies, processes, reward systems, and so forth. When the restructuring is complete, the firm can either "sell high" and capture the added value or keep the business and enjoy financial and competitive benefits.

restructuring
the intervention of the corporate office in a new business that substantially changes the assets, capital structure, and/or management, including selling off parts of the business, changing the management, reducing payroll and unnecessary sources of expenses, changing strategies, and infusing the new business with new technologies, processes, and reward systems.

For the restructuring strategy to work, the corporate management must have the insight to detect undervalued companies (otherwise, the cost of acquisition would be too high) or businesses competing in industries with a high potential for transformation.[29] Additionally, of course, it must have the requisite skills and resources to turn the businesses around, even if they may be in new and unfamiliar industries.

Restructuring can involve changes in assets, capital structure, or management.

- ***Asset restructuring*** involves the sale of unproductive assets, or even whole lines of businesses, that are peripheral. In some cases, it may even involve acquisitions that strengthen the core business.
- ***Capital restructuring*** involves changing the debt-equity mix, or the mix between different classes of debt or equity. Although the substitution of equity with debt is more common in buyout situations, occasionally the parent may provide additional equity capital.

- ***Management restructuring*** typically involves changes in the composition of the top management team, organizational structure, and reporting relationships. Tight financial control, rewards based strictly on meeting short- to medium-term performance goals, and reduction in the number of middle-level managers are common steps in management restructuring. In some cases, parental intervention may even result in changes in strategy as well as infusion of new technologies and processes.

Portfolio Management

portfolio management a method of (a) assessing the competitive position of a portfolio of businesses within a corporation, (b) suggesting strategic alternatives for each business, and (c) identifying priorities for the allocation of resources across the businesses.

During the 1970s and early 1980s, several leading consulting firms developed the concept of **portfolio management** to achieve a better understanding of the competitive position of an overall portfolio (or family) of businesses, to suggest strategic alternatives for each of the businesses, and to identify priorities for the allocation of resources. Several studies have reported widespread use of these techniques among American firms.[30]

While portfolio management tools have been widely used in corporations, research on their use has offered mixed support. However, recent research has suggested that strategically channeling resources to units with the most promising prospects can lead to corporate advantage. Research suggests that many firms do not adjust their capital allocations in response to changes in the performance of units or the attractiveness of the markets in which units of the corporation compete. Instead, allocations are fairly consistent from year to year. However, firms that assess the attractiveness of markets in which the firm competes and the capabilities of each division and then choose allocations of corporate resources based on these assessments exhibit higher levels of corporate survival, overall corporate performance, stock market performance, and the performance of individual business units within the corporation. These effects have also been shown to be stronger when firms compete in more competitive markets and in times of economic distress.[31] These findings have shown that the ability to effectively allocate financial capital is a key competence of high-performance diversified firms.

Description and Potential Benefits The key purpose of portfolio models is to assist a firm in achieving a balanced portfolio of businesses.[32] This consists of businesses whose profitability, growth, and cash flow characteristics complement each other and adds up to a satisfactory overall corporate performance. Imbalance, for example, could be caused either by excessive cash generation with too few growth opportunities or by insufficient cash generation to fund the growth requirements in the portfolio.

The Boston Consulting Group's (BCG's) growth/share matrix is among the best known of these approaches.[33] In the BCG approach, each of the firm's strategic business units (SBUs) is plotted on a two-dimensional grid in which the axes are relative market share and industry growth rate. The grid is broken into four quadrants. Exhibit 6.4 depicts the BCG matrix. Following are a few clarifications:

1. Each circle represents one of the corporation's business units. The size of the circle represents the relative size of the business unit in terms of revenues.
2. Relative market share, measured by the ratio of the business unit's size to that of its largest competitor, is plotted along the horizontal axis.
3. Market share is central to the BCG matrix. This is because high relative market share leads to unit cost reduction due to experience and learning curve effects and, consequently, superior competitive position.

Each of the four quadrants of the grid has different implications for the SBUs that fall into the category:

- ***Stars*** are SBUs competing in high-growth industries with relatively high market shares. These firms have long-term growth potential and should continue to receive substantial investment funding.

EXHIBIT 6.4 The Boston Consulting Group (BCG) Portfolio Matrix

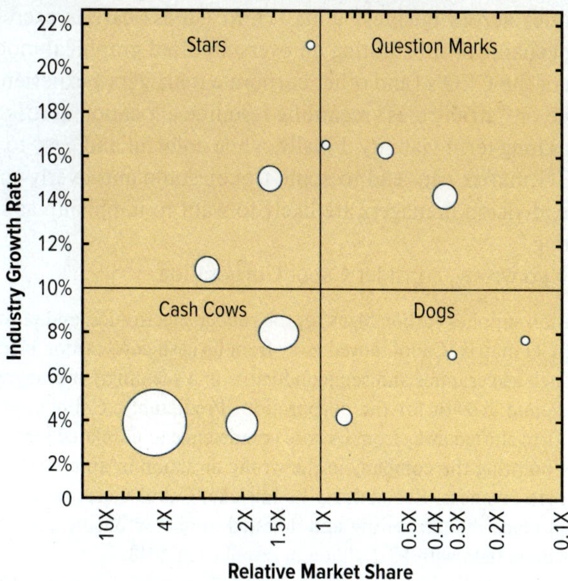

- ***Question marks*** are SBUs competing in high-growth industries but having relatively weak market shares. Resources should be invested in them to enhance their competitive positions.
- ***Cash cows*** are SBUs with high market shares in low-growth industries. These units have limited long-run potential but represent a source of current cash flows to fund investments in "stars" and "question marks."
- ***Dogs*** are SBUs with weak market shares in low-growth industries. Because they have weak positions and limited potential, most analysts recommend that they be divested.

In using portfolio strategy approaches, a corporation tries to create shareholder value in a number of ways.[34] First, portfolio analysis provides a snapshot of the businesses in a corporation's portfolio. Therefore, the corporation is in a better position to allocate resources among the business units according to prescribed criteria (e.g., use cash flows from the cash cows to fund promising stars). Second, the expertise and analytical resources in the corporate office provide guidance in determining what firms may be attractive (or unattractive) acquisitions. Third, the corporate office is able to provide financial resources to the business units on favorable terms that reflect the corporation's overall ability to raise funds. Fourth, the corporate office can provide high-quality review and coaching for the individual businesses. Fifth, portfolio analysis provides a basis for developing strategic goals and reward/evaluation systems for business managers. For example, managers of cash cows would have lower targets for revenue growth than managers of stars, but the former would have higher threshold levels of profit targets on proposed projects than the managers of star businesses. Compensation systems would also reflect such realities. Managers of cash cows understandably would be rewarded more on the basis of cash that their businesses generate than would managers of star businesses. Similarly, managers of star businesses would be held to higher standards for revenue growth than managers of cash cow businesses.

Limitations Despite the potential benefits of portfolio models, there are also some notable downsides. First, they compare SBUs on only two dimensions, making the implicit but erroneous assumption that (1) those are the only factors that really matter and (2) every unit can be accurately compared on that basis. Second, the approach views each SBU as a stand-alone entity, ignoring common core business practices and value-creating activities that may hold promise for synergies across business units. Third, unless care is exercised, the process becomes largely mechanical, substituting an oversimplified graphical model for the important contributions of the CEO's (and other corporate managers') experience and judgment. Fourth, the reliance on "strict rules" regarding resource allocation across SBUs can be detrimental to a firm's long-term viability. Finally, while colorful and easy to comprehend, the imagery of the BCG matrix can lead to some troublesome and overly simplistic prescriptions. For example, division managers are likely to want to jump ship as soon as their division is labeled a "dog."

To see what can go wrong, consider Cabot Corporation.

> Cabot Corporation supplies carbon black for the rubber, electronics, and plastics industries. Following the BCG matrix, Cabot moved away from its cash cow, carbon black, and diversified into stars such as ceramics and semiconductors in a seemingly overaggressive effort to create more revenue growth for the corporation. Predictably, Cabot's return on assets declined as the firm shifted away from its core competence to unrelated areas. The portfolio model failed by pointing the company in the wrong direction in an effort to spur growth—away from its core business. Recognizing its mistake, Cabot Corporation returned to its mainstay carbon black manufacturing and divested unrelated businesses. Today the company is a leader in its field with $3.2 billion in revenues in 2018.[35]

Caveat: Is Risk Reduction a Viable Goal of Diversification?

One of the purposes of diversification is to reduce the risk that is inherent in a firm's variability in revenues and profits over time. That is, if a firm enters new products or markets that are affected differently by seasonal or economic cycles, its performance over time will be more stable. For example, a firm manufacturing lawn mowers may diversify into snowblowers to even out its annual sales. Or a firm manufacturing a luxury line of household furniture may introduce a lower-priced line since affluent and lower-income customers are affected differently by economic cycles.

At first glance this reasoning may make sense, but there are some problems with it. First, a firm's stockholders can diversify their portfolios at a much lower cost than a corporation, and they don't have to worry about integrating the acquisition into their portfolio. Second, economic cycles as well as their impact on a given industry (or firm) are difficult to predict with any degree of accuracy.

Risk reduction in and of itself is rarely viable as a means to create shareholder value. It must be undertaken with a view of a firm's overall diversification strategy.

LO 6-5

Describe various means of engaging in diversification—mergers and acquisitions, joint ventures/strategic alliances, and internal development.

THE MEANS TO ACHIEVE DIVERSIFICATION

We have addressed the types of diversification (e.g., related and unrelated) that a firm may undertake to achieve synergies and create value for its shareholders. Now, we address the means by which a firm can go about achieving these desired benefits.

There are three basic means. First, through acquisitions or mergers, corporations can directly acquire a firm's assets and competencies. Although the terms *mergers* and *acquisitions* are used quite interchangeably, there are some key differences. With **acquisitions,** one firm buys another through a stock purchase, cash, or the issuance of debt.[36] **Mergers,** on the other hand, entail a combination or consolidation of two firms to form a new legal entity. Mergers are relatively rare and entail a transaction among two firms on a relatively equal basis. Despite such differences, we consider both mergers and acquisitions to be quite similar in terms of their implications for a firm's corporate-level strategy.[37]

acquisitions
the incorporation of one firm into another through purchase.

mergers
the combining of two or more firms into one new legal entity.

Second, corporations may agree to pool the resources of other companies with their resource base, commonly known as a joint venture or strategic alliance. Although these two forms of partnerships are similar in many ways, there is an important difference. Joint ventures involve the formation of a third-party legal entity where the two (or more) firms each contribute equity, whereas strategic alliances do not.

Third, corporations may diversify into new products, markets, and technologies through internal development. Called corporate entrepreneurship, it involves the leveraging and combining of a firm's own resources and competencies to create synergies and enhance shareholder value. We address this subject in greater length in Chapter 12.

Mergers and Acquisitions

The most visible and often costly means to diversify is through acquisitions. Over the past several years, several large acquisitions were announced. These include:[38]

- InBev's acquisition of Anheuser-Busch for $52 billion.
- AT&T's purchase of Time Warner for $85 billion.
- Facebook's acquisition of WhatsApp for $19.4 billion.
- Disney's purchase of 21st Century Fox for $71 billion.
- CVS's $67.5 billion acquisition of Aetna.

Exhibit 6.5 illustrates the volatility in worldwide M&A activity over the last several years. Several factors influence M&A activity. Julia Coronado, the chief economist at the investment bank BNP Paribas, highlights two of the key determinants, stating, "When mergers and acquisitions pick up, that's a good sign that businesses are feeling confident enough about the future that they're willing to become aggressive, look for deals, look for ways to grow and expand their operations. And it's also an indication that markets are willing to finance these transactions. So it's optimism from the markets and from the businesses themselves."[39] Thus, the general economic conditions and level of optimism about the future influence managers' willingness to take on the risk of acquisitions. Additionally, the availability of financing can influence acquisition activity. During boom periods, financing is typically widely available. In contrast, during recessionary periods, potential acquirers typically find it difficult to borrow money to finance acquisitions.

Governmental policies such as regulatory actions and tax policies can also make the M&A environment more or less favorable. For example, increased antitrust enforcement will decrease the ability of firms to acquire their competitors or possibly firms in closely related markets. In contrast, increased regulatory pressures for good corporate governance may leave boards of directors more open to acquisition offers.

EXHIBIT 6.5 Global Value of Mergers and Acquisitions ($ trillions)

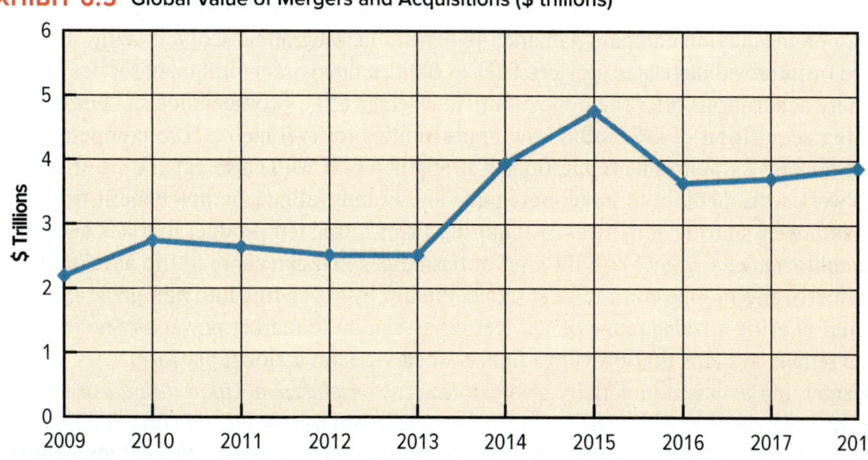

Source: Thomson Financial, Institute of Mergers, Acquisitions, and Alliances (IMAA) analysis.

Finally, currency fluctuations can influence the rate of cross-border acquisitions, with firms in countries with stronger currencies being in a stronger position to acquire. For example, the U.S. dollar has increased in value from .81 to .89 euro from early 2018 to early 2019, making it relatively cheaper for U.S. firms to acquire European firms.

Motives and Benefits Growth through mergers and acquisitions has played a critical role in the success of many corporations in a wide variety of high-technology and knowledge-intensive industries. Here, market and technology changes can occur very quickly and unpredictably.[40] Speed–speed to market, speed to positioning, and speed to becoming a viable company–is critical in such industries. For example, in 2010, Apple acquired Siri Inc. so that it could quickly fully integrate Siri's natural-language voice recognition software into iOS, Apple's operating system.

Mergers and acquisitions also can be a means of *obtaining valuable resources that can help an organization expand its product offerings and services.* Alphabet, Google's parent corporation, has undertaken over 170 acquisitions in the last decade. Google uses these acquisitions to quickly add new technology to its product offerings to meet changing customer needs.

Acquiring firms often use acquisitions to acquire critical human capital. These acquisitions have been referred to as *acq-hires*. In an acq-hire, the acquiring firm believes it needs the specific technical knowledge or the social network contacts of individuals in the target firm. This is especially important in settings where the technology or consumer preferences are highly dynamic. For example, in 2014, Apple purchased Beats Electronics for $3 billion. While Apple valued the product portfolio of Beats, its primary aim was to pull the founders of Beats, Jimmy Iovine and Dr. Dre (aka Andrew Young), into the Apple family. With Apple's iTunes business having hit a wall in growth, experiencing a 1 percent decline in 2013, Apple wanted to acquire new management talent to turn this business around. In addition to their experience at Beats, Iovine and Dr. Dre both have over 20 years of experience in the music industry, with Iovine founding and heading InterScope Records and Dr. Dre being a hip-hop pioneer and music producer. With this acquisition, Apple brought in a wealth of knowledge about the music business, the ability to identify music trends, up-and-coming talent, and industry contacts needed to rejuvenate Apple's music business. It seems to have worked. Apple's Services Division, which includes iTunes and Apple Music generated $10 billion in revenue in the fourth quarter of 2018, up nearly 60 percent from two years before.[41]

Mergers and acquisitions also can *provide the opportunity for firms to attain the three bases of synergy–leveraging core competencies, sharing activities, and building market power.* Consider some of eBay's acquisitions. eBay has purchased a range of businesses in related product markets, such as GSI Commerce, a company that designs and runs online shopping sites for brick-and-mortar retailers, and StubHub, an online ticket broker. Additionally, it has purchased Korean online auction company Gmarket to expand its geographic scope. Finally, it has purchased firms providing related services, such as Shutl, a rapid-order-fulfillment service provider.

These acquisitions offer the opportunity to leverage eBay's competencies.[42] For example, with the acquisition of GSI, eBay saw opportunities to leverage its core competencies in online systems as well as its reputation to strengthen GSI while also expanding eBay's ability to work with medium to large merchants and brands. eBay can also benefit from these acquisitions by sharing activities. In acquiring firms in related product markets and in new geographic markets, eBay has built a set of businesses that can share in the development of e-commerce and mobile commerce systems. Finally, by expanding into new geographic markets and offering a wider range of services, eBay can build market power as one of the few online retailer systems that provide a full set of services on a global platform.

Merger and acquisition activity also can *lead to consolidation within an industry and can force other players to merge.*[43] The airline industry has seen a great deal of consolidation in the last several years. With a number of large-scale acquisitions, including Delta's acquisition of Northwest Airlines in 2008, United's acquisition of Continental in 2010, and American's

6.3 STRATEGY SPOTLIGHT

A DIVERSIFIED FIRM USES ACQUISITIONS TO CHANGE ITS FOCUS

JAB Holding Co., a Luxembourg-based holding company, has long invested in a widely diversified set of companies ranging from RB, an industrial chemical firm, to luxury firms such as Bally International and Coty, a beauty products company. In recent years, JAB has reoriented its diversification strategy and has spent over $60 billion in acquiring firms. This acquisition frenzy has also brought a more refined focus to the firm's diversification strategy; coffee, bakeries, and soft drinks. In the coffee space, JAB has purchased Keurig Green Mountain Coffee, Caribou Coffee, Peet's Coffee and Tea, Espresso House, Stumptown Coffee Roasters, Revive Kombucha, D.E Master Blenders, Baresso Coffee A/S, Balzac Coffee, and Trade Coffee. In the bakery business, JAB has acquired Einstein Brothers Bagels, Bruegger's Bagels, Krispy Kreme, Panera Bread, Insomnia Cookies, and the British coffee and sandwich shop Pret A Manger. Its largest acquisition to date has been Dr. Pepper Snapple, which it acquired for $18.7 billion in early 2018.

In re-orienting from a diversified holding company to a more focused beverage and food firm, JAB is creating opportunities to extract value from its acquisition of these firms. Most notably, JAB has become the largest coffee purchaser in the world, giving it significant market power over its suppliers—coffee cooperatives and trading houses. In purchasing bakeries, it secures sources of distribution for its coffee and other drink products. While JAB allows the companies to operate fairly independently, over time, the businesses are beginning to identify areas in which they can share activities, such as in joint procurement of coffee beans. Finally, JAB has substantial financial resources and management expertise that can help acquired chains expand faster.

In short, JAB has leveraged acquisitions to remake the firm into a focused, related diversifier.

Sources: Almeida, I., and M. Perez. 2018. An empire fueled by caffeine and credit. *bloomberbbusinessweek.com,* February 5: np; Anonymous. This secretive German firm is consolidating the US Coffee Industry. *cbinsights.com,* May 30: np; and Nunes, K. JAB Holding to acquire Insomnia Cookies. *foodbuinessnews.net,* July 20: np.

purchase of US Airways in 2013, the U.S. airlines industry has been left with only four major players. By combining, these airlines have achieved both greater efficiencies by combining their networks and reduced rivalry within the industry. As a result of these benefits, the US Airline industry was profitable for the fifth consecutive year in 2017.[44]

Corporations can also *enter new market segments by way of acquisitions.* As mentioned previously, eBay–a firm that specialized in providing services to individuals and small businesses–moved into providing online retail systems for large merchants with its acquisition of GSI Commerce. Strategy Spotlight 6.3 discusses how JAB Holdings has used acquisitions to fundamentally change the set of markets in which it competes.

Exhibit 6.6 summarizes the benefits of mergers and acquisitions.

Potential Limitations As noted in the previous section, mergers and acquisitions provide a firm with many potential benefits. However, at the same time, there are many potential drawbacks or limitations to such corporate activity.[45]

First, *the takeover premium that is paid for an acquisition typically is very high.* Two times out of three, the stock price of the acquiring company falls once the deal is made public. Since the acquiring firm often pays a 30 percent or higher premium for the target company, the acquirer must create synergies and scale economies that result in sales and market gains exceeding the premium price. Firms paying higher premiums set the performance hurdle even higher. For example, Household International paid an 82 percent premium to buy Beneficial, and Conseco paid an 83 percent premium to acquire Green Tree Financial. Historically, paying a high premium over the stock price has been a poor strategy.

EXHIBIT 6.6
Benefits of Mergers and Acquisitions

- Obtain valuable resources, such as critical human capital, that can help an organization expand its product offerings.
- Provide the opportunity for firms to attain three bases of synergy: leveraging core competencies, sharing activities, and building market power.
- Lead to consolidation within an industry and force other players to merge.
- Enter new market segments.

EXHIBIT 6.7

Limitations of Mergers and Acquisitions

- Takeover premiums paid for acquisitions are typically very high.
- Competing firms often can imitate any advantages or copy synergies that result from the merger or acquisition.
- Managers' egos sometimes get in the way of sound business decisions.
- Cultural issues may doom the intended benefits from M&A endeavors.

Second, *competing firms often can imitate any advantages realized or copy synergies that result from the M&A.*[46] Thus, a firm can often see its advantages quickly erode. Unless the advantages are sustainable and difficult to copy, investors will not be willing to pay a high premium for the stock. Similarly, the time value of money must be factored into the stock price. M&A costs are paid up front. Conversely, firms pay for R&D, ongoing marketing, and capacity expansion over time. This stretches out the payments needed to gain new competencies. The M&A argument is that a large initial investment is worthwhile because it creates long-term advantages. However, stock analysts want to see immediate results from such a large cash outlay. If the acquired firm does not produce results quickly, investors often divest the stock, driving the price down.

Third, *managers' credibility and ego can sometimes get in the way of sound business decisions.* If the M&A does not perform as planned, managers who pushed for the deal find their reputation tarnished. This can lead them to protect their credibility by funneling more money, or escalating their commitment, into an inevitably doomed operation. Further, when a merger fails and a firm tries to unload the acquisition, the firm often must sell at a huge discount. These problems further compound the costs and erode the stock price. The accompanying Insights From Research outlines when and how managers respond to media evaluations of acquisitions they champion.

Fourth, *there can be many cultural issues that may doom the intended benefits from M&A endeavors.* Consider the insights of Joanne Lawrence, who played an important role in the merger between SmithKline and the Beecham Group.[47]

> The key to a strategic merger is to create a new culture. This was a mammoth challenge during the SmithKline Beecham merger. We were working at so many different cultural levels, it was dizzying. We had two national cultures to blend–American and British–that compounded the challenge of selling the merger in two different markets with two different shareholder bases. There were also two different business cultures: One was very strong, scientific, and academic; the other was much more commercially oriented. And then we had to consider within both companies the individual businesses, each of which has its own little culture.

Exhibit 6.7 summarizes the limitations of mergers and acquisitions.

Divestment: The Other Side of the "M&A Coin" When firms acquire other businesses, it typically generates quite a bit of "press" in business publications such as *The Wall Street Journal, Bloomberg Businessweek*, and *Fortune.* It makes for exciting news, and one thing is for sure–large acquiring firms automatically improve their standing in the Fortune 500 rankings (since it is based solely on total revenues). However, managers must also carefully consider the strategic implications of exiting businesses.

divestment
the exit of a business from a firm's portfolio.

Divestments, the exit of a business from a firm's portfolio, are quite common. One study found that large, prestigious U.S. companies divested more acquisitions than they kept.[48]

Divesting a business can accomplish many different objectives.* It can be used to help a firm reverse an earlier acquisition that didn't work out as planned. Often, this is simply to

---

* Firms can divest their businesses in a number of ways. Sell-offs, spin-offs, equity carve-outs, asset sales/dissolution, and split-ups are some such modes of divestment. In a sell-off, the divesting firm privately negotiates with a third party to divest a unit/subsidiary for cash/stock. In a spin-off, a parent company distributes shares of the unit/subsidiary being divested pro rata to its existing shareholders and a new company is formed. Equity carve-outs are similar to spin-offs except that shares in the unit/subsidiary being divested are offered to new shareholders. Dissolution involves sale of redundant assets, not necessarily as an entire unit/subsidiary as in sell-offs but a few bits at a time. A split-up, on the other hand, is an instance of divestiture whereby the parent company is split into two or more new companies and the parent ceases to exist. Shares in the parent company are exchanged for shares in new companies, and the exact distribution varies case by case.

6.1 *INSIGHTS* from Research

DO MANAGERS LEARN FROM MEDIA ASSESSMENTS OF ACQUISITIONS?

Overview

CEOs are often driven by ego and self-interest, but it is unclear how closely CEOs attend to media assessments of actions they take. This study examines that issue and shows that managers do pay attention to media evaluations of acquisitions, but the degree to which managers are future and past focused influences whether and how they learn from the media.

What the Research Shows

Acquisitions are high stake actions with uncertain benefits for corporations. Prior studies have shown that when investors give negative evaluations of acquisitions, firms are less likely to repeat those actions. But investors aren't the only ones who weigh in. The media also serve as prominent social evaluators of firms and their managers, but no research had examined whether and when negative media evaluations of acquisitions dampen firms' interest in undertaking additional acquisitions

Researchers from the University of Georgia and Michigan State University examined this question. Using a database on 745 large acquisitions undertaken by S&P 500 firms between 2006 and 2011, researchers examined the tone of stories on the acquisition announcement in major media outlets, such as the Wall Street Journal and Bloomberg BusinessWeek. They also assessed the temporal orientation of the firm's CEO, how focused the CEO is on the past and the future, using letters written by the CEO. The researchers were specifically focused on whether media evaluations influenced the firm's likelihood of making future acquisitions and if the CEO's temporal orientation influenced the effect of media evaluations.

The results were just as they had expected. Managers do appear to pay attention to media evaluations. Firms that received negative media evaluations spent less on acquisitions in the following year, 21 percent less in firms that had received fairly negative evaluations compared to those who received more typical evaluations. The effect was much stronger when the CEO was either high on past focus, the degree to which an individual dwells on and communicates about the past, or low on future focus, the degree to which an individual dwells on and communicates about the future

Interestingly, while these researchers also confirm prior findings that firms are less likely to pursue acquisitions when the stock market responded negatively to prior acquisitions, the CEO's temporal focus didn't influence that relationship. Thus, all managers appear to respond to the "hard" feedback provided by the stock market, but managers who are more attentive to the past are more influenced by the "soft" social evaluations provided by the media.

Key Takeaways

- In addition to feedback provided by investors, the top managers of firms appear to be sensitive to the evaluation of their decisions by the media.
- The temporal orientation of the CEOs, the degree to which they focus on the past and the future, influence how sensitive they are to media evaluations.
- But the temporal orientation of CEOs don't affect how they respond to stock market evaluations of his or her decisions.
- Stock market and media evaluations of acquisitions are largely independent of each other.

Questions

1. Why are managers sensitive to media evaluations?
2. What other types of evaluations are managers likely to attend to?
3. Are managers likely to look to media evaluations of other types of decisions? If so, what kind?

Research Reviewed

Gamache, D., and G. McNamara 2019. Responding to bad press: How CEO temporal focus influences the sensitivity to negative media coverage of acquisitions. *Academy of Management Journal*. Vol. 62, No. 3.

help "cut their losses." Other objectives include (1) enabling managers to focus their efforts more directly on the firm's core businesses,[49] (2) providing the firm with more resources to spend on more attractive alternatives, and (3) raising cash to help fund existing businesses.

Divesting can enhance a firm's competitive position only to the extent that it reduces its tangible (e.g., maintenance, investments, etc.) or intangible (e.g., opportunity costs, managerial attention) costs without sacrificing a current competitive advantage or the seeds of future advantages.[50] To be effective, divesting requires a thorough understanding of a business unit's current ability and future potential to contribute to a firm's value creation. However, since such decisions involve a great deal of uncertainty, it is very difficult to make such evaluations. In addition, because of managerial self-interests and organizational inertia, firms often delay divestments of underperforming businesses.

The Boston Consulting Group has identified seven principles for successful divestiture.[51]

1. ***Remove the emotion from the decision.*** Managers need to consider objectively the prospects for each unit in the firm and how this unit fits with the firm's overall strategy. Issues related to personal relationships with the managers of the unit, the length of time the unit has been part of the company, and other emotional elements should not be considered in the decision.[52]
2. ***Know the value of the business you are selling.*** Divesting firms can generate greater interest in and higher bids for units they are divesting if they can clearly articulate the strategic value of the unit.
3. ***Time the deal right.*** This involves both internal timing, whereby the firm regularly evaluates all its units so that it can divest units when they are no longer highly valued in the firm but will still be of value to the outside market, and external timing, being ready to sell when the market conditions are right.
4. ***Maintain a sizable pool of potential buyers.*** Divesting firms should not focus on a single potential buyer. Instead, they should discuss possible deals with several hand-picked potential bidders.
5. ***Tell a story about the deal.*** For each potential bidder it talks with, the divesting firm should develop a narrative about how the unit it is interested in selling will create value for that buyer.
6. ***Run divestitures systematically through a project office.*** Firms should look at developing the ability to divest units as a distinct form of corporate competencies. While many firms have acquisition units, they often don't have divesting units even though there is significant potential value in divestitures.
7. ***Communicate clearly and frequently.*** Corporate managers need to clearly communicate to internal stakeholders, such as employees, and external stakeholders, such as customers and stockholders, what their goals are with divestment activity, how it will create value, and how the firm is moving forward strategically with these decisions.

Strategic Alliances and Joint Ventures

strategic alliance
a cooperative relationship between two or more firms.

A **strategic alliance** is a cooperative relationship between two (or more) firms.[53] Alliances can exist in multiple forms. Contractual alliances are simply based on written contracts between firms. Contractual alliances are typically used for fairly simple alliance agreements, such as supplier, marketing, or distribution relationships that don't require a great deal of integration or technology sharing between firms and have a finite, identifiable end time period. If the terms of the agreement can be clearly laid out in contracts, then contracts can be a complete and effective basis for the agreement. However, when there is uncertainty about how the alliance will proceed and evolve over time or if one firm is much larger than the other, firms will often form equity alliances. In an equity alliance, at least one firm purchases a minority ownership stake in the other. Equity ownership in alliances helps align the interest of the two firms since the firm that buys the ownership stake benefits both from increases in its own value and the value of the partner it now owns a part of. This can reduce concerns that one firm will benefit more from the alliance than the partner firm or take advantage of the partner firm as the alliance evolves. This can be an especially large concern when a very large firm allies with a small firm. By taking an equity stake in the smaller firm, the larger firm signals that it is linking its own money into the success of the smaller firm. **Joint ventures** represent a special case of alliances, wherein two (or more) firms contribute equity to form a new legal entity.

joint ventures
new entities formed within a strategic alliance in which two or more firms, the parents, contribute equity to form the new legal entity.

Strategic alliances and joint ventures are assuming an increasingly prominent role in the strategy of leading firms, both large and small.[54] Such cooperative relationships have many potential advantages.[55] Among these are entering new markets, reducing manufacturing (or other) costs in the value chain, and developing and diffusing new technologies.[56]

Entering New Markets Often a company that has a successful product or service wants to introduce it into a new market. However, it may not have the financial resources or the requisite marketing expertise because it does not understand customer needs, know how to promote the product, or have access to the proper distribution channels.[57]

Zara, a Spanish clothing company, operates stores in over 70 countries. Still, when entering markets very distant from its home markets, Zara often uses local alliance partners to help it negotiate the different cultural and regulatory environments. For example, when Zara expanded into India in 2010, it did it in cooperation with Tata, an Indian conglomerate.[58]

Alliances can also be used to enter new product markets. For example, Lego has expanded its product portfolio by licensing the right to develop products built around characters and brands, such as Star Wars and Harry Potter. It also allied with the digital animation firm Animal Logic Pty Ltd and Warner Bros. to develop the Lego Movie and the Lego Movie 2.[59]

Reducing Manufacturing (or Other) Costs in the Value Chain Strategic alliances (or joint ventures) often enable firms to pool capital, value-creating activities, or facilities in order to reduce costs. For example, the PGA and LPGA tours joined together in a strategic alliance that allows them to save costs by jointly marketing golf, develop a shared digital media platform, and jointly negotiate domestic television contracts.[60]

Developing and Diffusing New Technologies Strategic alliances also may be used to build jointly on the technological expertise of two or more companies. This may enable them to develop products technologically beyond the capability of the companies acting independently.[61] For example, in 2019, Ford and VW signed a memorandum of understanding to work together to develop autonomous vehicles.

In Strategy Spotlight 6.5, we discuss how Honda, a firm that used to develop all technology in-house, is now leveraging multiple alliances to develop key technologies.

Potential Downsides Despite their promise, many alliances and joint ventures fail to meet expectations for a variety of reasons.[62] First, without the proper partner, a firm should never consider undertaking an alliance, even for the best of reasons.[63] Each partner should bring the desired complementary strengths to the partnership. Ideally, the strengths contributed by the partners are unique; thus synergies created can be more easily sustained and defended over the longer term. The goal must be to develop synergies between the contributions of the partners, resulting in a win–win situation. Moreover, the partners must be compatible and willing to trust each other.[64] Unfortunately, often little attention is given to nurturing the close working relationships and interpersonal connections that bring together the partnering organizations.[65]

Internal Development

Firms can also diversify by means of corporate entrepreneurship and new venture development. **In today's economy, internal development is such an important means by which companies expand their businesses that we have devoted a whole chapter to it (see Chapter 12).** Sony and the Minnesota Mining & Manufacturing Co. (3M), for example, are known for their dedication to innovation, R&D, and cutting-edge technologies. For example, 3M has developed its entire corporate culture to support its ongoing policy of generating at least 25 percent

internal development entering a new business through investment in new facilities, often called corporate entrepreneurship and new venture development.

6.4 STRATEGY SPOTLIGHT

HONDA LOOKS TO ALLIANCE PARTNERS TO MEET CHANGING MARKET NEEDS

Honda has always prided itself on developing and controlling the technology in its vehicles. Firm founder, Soichiro Honda put it bluntly when he once said, "We refuse to depend on anyone else." But times are changing in the auto market. With the push for electric and autonomous vehicles, the pace of technology change and the cost of developing new technologies is challenging any firm's ability to manage everything in-house.

For Honda, this became a stark reality in early 2017 when Honda took its autonomous SUV out on a test track for a government test. Its sensor technology was supposed to see and adjust to any events on the track. It failed miserably, including mowing down a child-sized test dummy that moved in the path of the SUV. In the end, Honda scored a 0.2 out of 25 points on the pedestrian-oriented part of the test, the lowest of any manufacturer tested. Honda realized it couldn't do it in-house. Honda decided to switch directions and allied with Bosch to gain access to a fully developed sensor system. The firm returned to the test track seven months later with an SUV that scored a 24.4 on the same test.

In contrast to Soichiro Honda's comment from five decades ago, Honda's current CEO, Takahiro Hachigo states, "We want to work with those that possess the best technology, regardless of whether they are Japanese suppliers or American ones or European ones." This significant change in perspective is evident in the range of Honda's alliances. In addition to working with Bosch on sensors, Honda is working with Baidu Inc., a large Chinese search engine company, on mapping technology and with SenseTime Co., a Chinese entrepreneurial firm, on camera software for its self-driving cars. It is also working with SoftBank Corp. on artificial intelligence that will read drivers' emotions to suggest music and other environmental elements for drivers. Even though Honda has always prided itself on its engine technology, it is working with Hitachi Ltd. to build motors for its electric cars. Looking further ahead, Honda is even collaborating with one of its largest rivals. In late 2018, Honda inked a 12-year alliance with Cruise Automation, a subsidiary of General Motors, to design and build a fully autonomous vehicle.

Thus, changes in the environment and the rapid pace of technological change have led Honda to abandon its long-held desire of internally developing key technologies. Instead, Honda now relies on a range of partners to bring key advanced technologies that Honda needs to design and sell the autos of tomorrow.

Sources: McLain, S. 2018. Honda took pride in doing everything itself. The cost of technology made that impossible. *The Wall Street Journal,* August 5: np; and Hawkins, A.J. 2018. GM's Cruise will get $2.75 billion from Honda to build a new self-driving car. *theverge.com,* October 3: np.

of total sales from products created within the most recent four-year period. While 3M exceeded this goal for decades, a push for improved efficiency that began in the early 2000s resulted in a drop to generating only 21 percent of sales from newer products in 2005. By refocusing on innovation, 3M raised that value back up to 33 percent in 2016. In 2018, 3M added an additional element to its new product development goals, that all new products also support sustainability.

Biocon, the largest Indian biotechnology firm, shows the power of internal development. Kiran Mazumdar-Shaw, the firm's founder, took the knowledge she learned while studying malting and brewing in college to start a small firm that produced enzymes for the beer industry in her Bangalore garage in 1978. The firm first expanded into providing enzymes for other food and textile industries. From there, Biocon expanded to producing generic drugs and is now the largest producer of insulin in Asia.[66]

Compared to mergers and acquisitions, firms that engage in internal development capture the value created by their own innovative activities without having to "share the wealth" with alliance partners or face the difficulties associated with combining activities across the value chains of several firms or merging corporate cultures.[67] Also, firms can often develop new products or services at a relatively lower cost and thus rely on their own resources rather than turning to external funding.[68]

There are also potential disadvantages. It may be time-consuming; thus, firms may forfeit the benefits of speed that growth through mergers or acquisitions can provide. This may be especially important among high-tech or knowledge-based organizations in fast-paced environments where being an early mover is critical. Thus, firms that choose to diversify through internal development must develop capabilities that allow them to move quickly from initial opportunity recognition to market introduction.

HOW MANAGERIAL MOTIVES CAN ERODE VALUE CREATION

LO 6-6

Identify managerial behaviors that can erode the creation of value.

Thus far in the chapter, we have implicitly assumed that CEOs and top executives are "rational beings"; that is, they act in the best interests of shareholders to maximize long-term shareholder value. In the real world, however, they may often act in their own self-interest. We now address some **managerial motives** that can serve to erode, rather than enhance, value creation. These include "**growth for growth's sake**," excessive egotism, and the creation of a wide variety of antitakeover tactics.

managerial motives managers acting in their own self-interest rather than to maximize long-term shareholder value.

growth for growth's sake managers' actions to grow the size of their firms not to increase long-term profitability but to serve managerial self-interest.

Growth for Growth's Sake

There are huge incentives for executives to increase the size of their firm. And these are not consistent with increasing shareholder wealth. Top managers, including the CEO, of larger firms typically enjoy more prestige, higher rankings for their firms on the Fortune 500 list (based on revenues, *not* profits), greater incomes, more job security, and so on. There is also the excitement and associated recognition of making a major acquisition. As noted by Harvard's Michael Porter, "There's a tremendous allure to mergers and acquisitions. It's the big play, the dramatic gesture. With one stroke of the pen you can add billions to size, get a front-page story, and create excitement in markets."[69]

Research suggests that underpaid CEOs are especially driven to pursue acquisitions in order to grow their firms. When CEOs receive less pay than peers running similar firms, they are more likely to acquire. Further, they more frequently use stock rather than cash to finance those acquisitions. When stock is used to finance an acquisition, the shareholders of the acquiring and target firms share both the gains that will occur if the acquisition generates value over time and losses if the acquisition destroys value. Thus, the use of stock indicates that managers see significant risk with the acquisition. This suggests that underpaid CEOs who undertake acquisitions to grow the firm understand that these acquisitions are risky for the acquiring firm. Still, these acquisitions serve their purpose for underpaid CEOs. The pay for underpaid acquiring CEOs typically rises substantially in the following year.[70]

At times, executives' overemphasis on growth can result in a plethora of ethical lapses, which can have disastrous outcomes for their companies. A good example (of bad practice) is Joseph Berardino's leadership at Andersen Worldwide. Berardino had a chance early on to take a hard line on ethics and quality in the wake of earlier scandals at clients such as Waste Management and Sunbeam. Instead, according to former executives, he put too much emphasis on revenue growth. Consequently, the firm's reputation quickly eroded when it audited and signed off on the highly flawed financial statements of such infamous firms as Enron, Global Crossing, and WorldCom. Berardino ultimately resigned in disgrace in March 2002, and his firm was dissolved later that year.[71]

Egotism

egotism managers' actions to shape their firms' strategies to serve their selfish interests rather than to maximize long-term shareholder value.

A healthy ego helps make a leader confident, clearheaded, and able to cope with change. CEOs, by their very nature, are intensely competitive people in the office as well as on the tennis court or golf course. But sometimes when pride is at stake, individuals will go to great lengths to win.

Egos can get in the way of a "synergistic" corporate marriage. Few executives (or lower-level managers) are exempt from the potential downside of excessive egos. Consider, for example, the reflections of General Electric's former CEO Jack Welch, considered by many to be the world's most admired executive. He admitted to a regrettable decision: "My hubris got in the way in the Kidder Peabody deal. [He was referring to GE's buyout of the soon-to-be-troubled Wall Street firm.] I got wise advice from Walter Wriston and other directors who said, 'Jack, don't do this.' But I was bully enough and on a run to do it. And I got whacked right in the head."[72] In addition to poor financial results, Kidder Peabody was wracked by a widely publicized trading scandal that tarnished the reputations of both GE and Kidder Peabody. Welch ended up selling Kidder.

antitakeover tactics
managers' actions to avoid losing wealth or power as a result of a hostile takeover.

greenmail
a payment by a firm to a hostile party for the firm's stock at a premium, made when the firm's management feels that the hostile party is about to make a tender offer.

golden parachute
a prearranged contract with managers specifying that, in the event of a hostile takeover, the target firm's managers will be paid a significant severance package.

poison pill
used by a company to give shareholders certain rights in the event of takeover by another firm.

Antitakeover Tactics

Unfriendly or hostile takeovers can occur when a company's stock becomes undervalued. A competing organization can buy the outstanding stock of a takeover candidate in sufficient quantity to become a large shareholder. Then it makes a tender offer to gain full control of the company. If the shareholders accept the offer, the hostile firm buys the target company and either fires the target firm's management team or strips the team members of their power. Thus, **antitakeover tactics** are common, including greenmail, golden parachutes, and poison pills.[73]

The first, **greenmail,** is an effort by the target firm to prevent an impending takeover. When a hostile firm buys a large block of outstanding target company stock and the target firm's management feels that a tender offer is impending, it offers to buy the stock back from the hostile company at a higher price than the unfriendly company paid for it. Although this often prevents a hostile takeover, the same price is not offered to preexisting shareholders. However, it protects the jobs of the target firm's management.

Second, a **golden parachute** is a prearranged contract with managers specifying that, in the event of a hostile takeover, the target firm's managers will be paid a significant severance package. Although top managers lose their jobs, the golden parachute provisions protect their income.

Third, **poison pills** are used by a company to give shareholders certain rights in the event of a takeover by another firm. They are also known as shareholder rights plans.

Clearly, antitakeover tactics can often raise some interesting ethical–and legal–issues.

ISSUE FOR DEBATE

Disney Diversifies to Take on Netflix

Disney is using a major acquisition and related actions to take on the new media challenge posed by Netflix, Amazon, and other streaming services. As cord-cutting consumers move away from traditional cable and satellite services, Netflix, Amazon, and others have built strong customer bases for their streaming services and become developers of media content themselves. Disney found itself in a weak position. It competes with Netflix and Amazon in developing movies and series, but it also had become increasingly reliant on these two firms to distribute its content to end consumers. Thus, Disney felt vulnerable in that Netflix and Amazon have limited incentive to push Disney content to end consumers and are not as reliant on Disney to provide content to pull in customers as cable providers have been.

Disney's solution is to diversify its operations in two key ways. First, it launched its own streaming service, Disney+, that carries Disney's own content, such as Star Wars and Marvel films as well as its classic films from Disney's archives and current Marvel series, such as "Daredevil," "Luke Cage," "Iron Fist," "Defenders," "Jessica Jones," and "The Punisher." Second, Disney acquired 21st Century Fox for $71.3 billion in March 2019. Disney saw acquisition as a means to bolster the amount of content it owns and controls. In addition, the acquisition gave Disney a controlling interest in Hulu, a firm partially owned by Fox. Thus, Disney is working to build a library of content that is broad enough to draw in customers and building streaming services to sell directly to those customers.

As it was taking these actions, Disney also announced that it was going to pull its shows and movies from Netflix. It is important to note that Disney is not alone in this action.

Warner Bros and Comcast announced a similar action. As a result, Netflix has lost about 20 percent of its total content library in terms of programming hours.

In taking charge of its own distribution and by purchasing 21st Century Fox, Disney has taken bold actions to become a broadly diversified, vertically integrated media player. What is unclear is whether customers will see enough value to sign up for Disney's services. Whether they do is critical to Disney since it will be the single distribution channel the firm will use to draw in viewers to its blockbuster releases after their theater runs are complete.

Discussion Questions

1. Is Disney making the right decision to develop its own exclusive streaming system rather than using Netflix and other streaming services to deliver its content?
2. Is the defection of Disney, Warner Bros, and Comcast from Netflix streaming services going to seriously harm Netflix?
3. What are the long-term consequences of these actions for Disney and Netflix? For consumers?

Sources: Mattioli, D. 2017. Fear of tech giants fuels deal boom. *Wall Street Journal,* November 21: A10; Lee, E., and B. Barnes. 2018. Disney and Fox shareholders approve deal, ending corporate duel. *nytimes.com,* July 27: np; and Whitten, S. 2019. Netflix can compete as Disney, Warner Bros. enter the streaming space, but it won't be cheap. *cnbc.com,* February 21: np.

Reflecting on Career Implications . . .

This chapter focuses on how firms can create value through diversification. The following questions lead you to consider how you can develop core competencies that apply in different settings and how you can leverage those skills in different value chain activities or units in your firms.

- **Corporate-Level Strategy:** Is your current employer a single business firm or a diversified firm? If it is diversified, does it pursue related or unrelated diversification? Does its diversification provide you with career opportunities, especially lateral moves? What organizational policies are in place to either encourage or discourage you from moving from one business unit to another?
- **Core Competencies:** What do you see as your core competencies? How can you leverage them within your business unit as well as across other business units?
- **Sharing Infrastructures:** Identify what infrastructure activities and resources (e.g., information systems, legal) are available in the corporate office that are shared by various business units in the firm. How often do you take advantage of these shared resources? Identify ways in which you can enhance your performance by taking advantage of these shared infrastructure resources.
- **Diversification:** From your career perspective, what actions can you take to diversify your employment risk (e.g., doing coursework at a local university, obtaining professional certification such as a CPA, networking through professional affiliation, etc.)? In periods of retrenchment, such actions will provide you with a greater number of career options.

key points

LO 6-1 The reasons for the failure of many diversification efforts.

- Paying an excessive premium for the target firm.
- Failing to integrate the activities of the newly acquired businesses into the corporate family.
- Undertaking diversification initiatives that are too easily imitated by the competition.

LO 6-2 How managers can create value through diversification initiatives.

- To create value with related diversification, managers can pursue two paths:
  - Economies of scope that are achieved from the leveraging of core competencies and the sharing of activities.
  - Market power that is attained from greater, or pooled, negotiating power and from vertical integration.

- To create value with unrelated diversification, the primary ways to create value are corporate restructuring and parenting, as well as the use of portfolio analysis techniques.

LO 6-3 How corporations can use related diversification to achieve synergistic benefits through economies of scope and market power.

- Economies of scope includes two elements, leveraging core competencies and sharing activities.
    - Core competencies reflect the collective learning in organizations, such as how to coordinate diverse production skills, integrate multiple streams of technology, and market diverse products and services.
    - Sharing activities involves the joint issues of value-creating activities, such as common manufacturing facilities, distribution systems, and sales forces by multiple business units in the corporation.
- Market power reflects the firm's ability to profit through restricting or controlling supply to a market or coordinating with other firms to reduce investment.
    - The two primary means to achieve market power are pooled negotiating power and vertical integration.

LO 6-4 How corporations can use unrelated diversification to attain synergistic benefits through corporate restructuring, parenting, and portfolio analysis.

- Parenting advantage involves the corporate office providing expertise and support to new business units to improve unit operations in areas such as in planning, financial management, procurement, and human resource management.
- Restructuring involves the intervention of the corporate office in a new business that substantially changes the assets, capital structure, and/or management, including selling off parts of the business, changing the management, reducing payroll and unnecessary sources of expenses, changing strategies, and infusing the new business with new technologies, processes, and reward systems.

LO 6-5 The various means of engaging in diversification—mergers and acquisitions, joint ventures/strategic alliances, and internal development.

- Mergers and acquisitions involve the purchasing of another organization and incorporating it into the parent firm. Acquisitions can help a firm:
    - Obtain valuable resources, such as critical human capital, that can help an organization expand its product offerings.
    - Provide the opportunity for firms to attain three bases of synergy: leveraging core competencies, sharing activities, and building market power.
    - Lead to consolidation within an industry and force other players to merge.
    - Enter new market segments.
- Strategic alliances are cooperative relationships between two or more firms.
    - Joint ventures are a specific form of strategic alliance where the partnering firms create a new legal entity that they jointly own.
    - Strategic alliances can be used to enter new markets, reduce costs in the value chain, or develop and diffuse new technologies.
- Internal development involves the entering of a new businesses or industry through the investment in new facilities, often referred to as corporate entrepreneurship and new venture development.

LO 6-6 Managerial behaviors that can erode the creation of value.

- While corporate actions should be aimed to enhance shareholder value, they are likely to erode value when they are driven by the following factors:
    - Growth for growth's sake.
    - Egotism.
    - Antitakeover tactics.

SUMMARY REVIEW QUESTIONS

1. Discuss how managers can create value for their firm through diversification efforts.
2. What are some of the reasons that many diversification efforts fail to achieve desired outcomes?
3. How can companies benefit from related diversification? Unrelated diversification? What are some of the key concepts that can explain such success?
4. What are some of the important ways in which a firm can restructure a business?
5. Discuss some of the various means that firms can use to diversify. What are the pros and cons associated with each of these?
6. Discuss some of the actions that managers may engage in to erode shareholder value.

key terms

diversification 175
related diversification 176
economies of scope 177
core competencies 177
sharing activities 178
market power 179
pooled negotiating power 180
vertical integration 180
transaction cost perspective 182
unrelated diversification 182
parenting advantage 183
restructuring 183
portfolio management 184
acquisitions 186
mergers 186

divestment 190
strategic alliance 192
joint ventures 192
internal development 193
managerial motives 195
growth for growth's sake 195
egotism 195
antitakeover tactics 196
greenmail 196
golden parachute 196
poison pill 196

EXPERIENTIAL EXERCISES AND APPLICATION QUESTIONS

1. What were some of the largest mergers and acquisitions over the last two years? What was the rationale for these actions? Do you think they will be successful? Explain.
2. Discuss some examples from business practice in which an executive's actions appear to be in his or her self-interest rather than the corporation's well-being.
3. Discuss some of the challenges that managers must overcome in making strategic alliances successful. What are some strategic alliances with which you are familiar? Were they successful or not? Explain.
4. Use the Internet and select a company that has recently undertaken diversification into new product markets. What do you feel were some of the reasons for this diversification (e.g., leveraging core competencies, sharing infrastructures)?
5. The Newell-Jarden merger has not generated value for shareholders. Imagine you were advising firm managers on how they could best leverage the businesses they have. Identify the key business units of the firm. Evaluate how the firm can leverage opportunities for (1) building on core competencies, (2) sharing infrastructures, and (3) increasing market power across business units. Also, evaluate if the firm should divest any of its remaining business units.
6. AT&T is a firm that follows a strategy of related diversification. Evaluate its success (or lack thereof) with regard to how well it has (1) built on core competencies, (2) shared infrastructures, and (3) increased market power. (Insert answers in the table that follows.)

Rationale for Related Diversification	Successful/Unsuccessful?	Why?
1. Build on core competencies		
2. Share infrastructures		
3. Increase market power		

ETHICS QUESTIONS

1. It is not uncommon for corporations to undertake downsizing and layoffs. Do you feel that such actions raise ethical considerations? Why or why not?
2. What are some of the ethical issues that arise when managers act in a manner that is counter to their firm's best interests? What are the long-term implications for both the firms and the managers themselves?

REFERENCES

1. Terlap, S. 2018. A Megadeal joined Sharpie Markers and Crock-Pots. What could go wrong? A lot. wsj.com. May 2: np.; Meyersohn, N. 2018. The fight for Sharpie and Yankee Candel. cnnmoney.com. February 22: np.; Terlep, S. & Lobardo, C. 2019. Newell CEO under pressure after disappointing sales. Wsj.com. February 21: np.; and finance.yahoo.com.
2. Insights on measuring M&A performance are addressed in Zollo, M. & Meier, D. 2008. What is M&A performance? *BusinessWeek,* 22(3): 55–77.
3. Insights on how and why firms may overpay for acquisitions are addressed in Malhotra, D., Ku, G., & Murnighan, J. K. 2008. When winning is everything. *Harvard Business Review,* 66(5): 78–86.
4. Haleblian, J., Devers, C., McNamara, G., Carpenter, M., & Davison, R. 2009. Taking stock of what we know about mergers and acquisitions: A review and research agenda. *Journal of Management,* 35: 469–502.
5. Pare, T. 1994. The new merger boom. *Fortune,* November 28: 96.
6. A discussion of the effects of director experience and acquisition performance is in McDonald, M. L. & Westphal, J. D. 2008. What do they know? The effects of outside director acquisition experience on firm acquisition performance. *Strategic Management Journal,* 29(11): 1155–1177.
7. Finance and economics: Snoopy sniffs an opportunity; MetLife buys Alico. 2010. *Economist.com,* March 13: np.
8. For a study that investigates several predictors of corporate diversification, read Wiersema, M. F. & Bowen, H. p. 2008. Corporate diversification: The impact of foreign competition, industry globalization, and product diversification. *Strategic Management Journal,* 29(2): 114–132.
9. Kumar, M. V. S. 2011. Are joint ventures positive sum games? The relative effects of cooperative and non-cooperative behavior. *Strategic Management Journal,* 32(1): 32–54.
10. Makri, M., Hitt, M. A., & Lane, P. J. 2010. Complementary technologies, knowledge relatedness, and invention outcomes in high technology mergers and acquisitions. *Strategic Management Journal,* 31(6): 602–628.
11. A discussion of Tyco's unrelated diversification strategy is in Hindo, B.

2008. Solving Tyco's identity crisis. *BusinessWeek,* February 18: 62.

12. Our framework draws upon a variety of sources, including Goold, M. & Campbell, A. 1998. Desperately seeking synergy. *Harvard Business Review,* 76(5): 131-143; Porter, M. E. 1987. From advantage to corporate strategy. *Harvard Business Review,* 65(3): 43-59; and Hitt, M. A., Ireland, R. D., & Hoskisson, R. E. 2001. *Strategic management: Competitiveness and globalization* (4th ed.). Cincinnati, OH: South-Western.
13. This imagery of the corporation as a tree and related discussion draws on Prahalad, C. K. & Hamel, G. 1990. The core competence of the corporation. *Harvard Business Review,* 68(3): 79-91. Parts of this section also draw on Picken, J. C. & Dess, G. G. 1997. *Mission critical:* chap. 5. Burr Ridge, IL: Irwin Professional.
14. Graebner, M. E., Eisenhardt, K. M., & Roundy, P. T. 2010. Success and failure in technology acquisitions: Lessons for buyers and sellers. *Academy of Management Perspectives,* 24(3): 73-92.
15. This section draws on Prahalad & Hamel, op. cit.; and Porter, op. cit.
16. A study that investigates the relationship between a firm's technology resources, diversification, and performance can be found in Miller, D. J. 2004. Firms' technological resources and the performance effects of diversification. A longitudinal study. *Strategic Management Journal,* 25: 1097-1119.
17. Khan, N. & Matsuda, K. 2015. Fujifilm shifts focus to stem cells and ebola drugs. *bloomberg.com,* August 17: np; and Flores, Y. 2018. 2 Japanese companies that you'd never expect to produce skincare products! *jpinfo.com,* March 7: np.
18. Chesbrough, H. 2011. Bringing open innovation to services. *MIT Sloan Management Review,* 52(2): 85-90.
19. Levine-Weinberg, A. 2014. Starbucks has decades of growth ahead. *money.cnn.com,* November 19: np.
20. This section draws on Hrebiniak, L. G. & Joyce, W. F. 1984. *Implementing strategy.* New York: Macmillan; and Oster, S. M. 1994. *Modern competitive analysis.* New York: Oxford University Press.
21. The discussion of the benefits and costs of vertical integration draws on Hax, A. C. & Majluf, N. S. 1991. *The strategy concept and process: A pragmatic approach:* 139. Englewood Cliffs, NJ: Prentice Hall.
22. Fahey, J. 2005. Gray winds. *Forbes,* January 10: 143.
23. This discussion draws on Oster, op. cit.; and Harrigan, K. 1986. Matching vertical integration strategies to competitive conditions. *Strategic Management Journal,* 7(6): 535-556.
24. Mathews, A. 2015. Kaiser Permanente to launch medical school. *wsj.com,* December 18: np.
25. For a scholarly explanation on how transaction costs determine the boundaries of a firm, see Oliver E. Williamson's pioneering books *Markets and hierarchies: Analysis and antitrust implications* (New York: Free Press, 1975) and *The economic institutions of capitalism* (New York: Free Press, 1985).
26. Campbell, A., Goold, M., & Alexander, M. 1995. Corporate strategy: The quest for parenting advantage. *Harvard Business Review,* 73(2): 120-132; and Picken & Dess, op. cit.
27. Anslinger, P. A. & Copeland, T. E. 1996. Growth through acquisition: A fresh look. *Harvard Business Review,* 74(1): 126-135.
28. This section draws on Porter, op. cit.; and Hambrick, D. C. 1985. Turnaround strategies. In Guth, W. D. (Ed.), *Handbook of business strategy:* 10-1-10-32. Boston: Warren, Gorham & Lamont.
29. Casico, W. F. 2002. Strategies for responsible restructuring. *Academy of Management Executive,* 16(3): 80-91; and Singh, H. 1993. Challenges in researching corporate restructuring. *Journal of Management Studies,* 30(1): 147-172.
30. Hax & Majluf, op. cit. By 1979, 45 percent of Fortune 500 companies employed some form of portfolio analysis, according to Haspelagh, p. 1982. Portfolio planning: Uses and limits. *Harvard Business Review,* 60: 58-73. A later study conducted in 1993 found that over 40 percent of the respondents used portfolio analysis techniques, but the level of usage was expected to increase to more than 60 percent in the near future: Rigby, D. K. 1994. Managing the management tools. *Planning Review,* September-October: 20-24.
31. Fruk, M., Hall, S., & Mittal, D. 2013. Never let a good crisis go to waste. *mckinsey.com,* October: np; and Arrfelt, M., Wiseman, R., McNamara, G., & Hult, T., 2015. Examining a key corporate role: The influence of capital allocation competency on business unit performance. *Strategic Management Journal,* in press.
32. Goold, M. & Luchs, K. 1993. Why diversify? Four decades of management thinking. *Academy of Management Executive,* 7(3): 7-25.
33. Other approaches include the industry attractiveness-business strength matrix developed jointly by General Electric and McKinsey and Company, the life-cycle matrix developed by Arthur D. Little, and the profitability matrix proposed by Marakon. For an extensive review, refer to Hax & Majluf, op. cit.: 182-194.
34. Porter, op. cit.: 49-52.
35. Picken & Dess, op. cit.; Cabot Corporation. 2001. 10-Q filing, Securities and Exchange Commission, May 14.
36. Insights on the performance of serial acquirers is found in Laamanen, T. & Keil, T. 2008. Performance of serial acquirers: Toward an acquisition program perspective. *Strategic Management Journal,* 29(6): 663-672.
37. Some insights from Lazard's CEO on mergers and acquisitions are addressed in Stewart, T. A. & Morse, G. 2008. Giving great advice. *Harvard Business Review,* 66(1): 106-113.
38. Coy, P., Thornton, E., Arndt, M., & Grow, B. 2005. Shake, rattle, and merge. *BusinessWeek,* January 10: 32-35; and Anonymous. 2005. Love is in the air. *The Economist,* February 5: 9.
39. Hill, A. 2011. Mergers indicate market optimism. *Market Place,* March 21: np.
40. For an interesting study of the relationship between mergers and a firm's product-market strategies, refer to Krishnan, R. A., Joshi, S., & Krishnan, H. 2004. The influence of mergers on firms' product-mix strategies. *Strategic Management Journal,* 25: 587-611.
41. Sisario, B. 2014. Jimmy Iovine, a master of Beats, lends Apple a skilled ear. *nytimes.com,* May 28: np; Dickey, M. 2014. Meet the executives Apple is paying $3 billion to get. *businessinsider.com,* May 28: np.; and Clover, J. 2018. Apple's Services revenue up 17% year-over-year in 4Q 2018, hits all time high of $10B. *macrumors.com.* November 1: np.
42. Ignatius, A. 2011. How eBay developed a culture of experimentation. *Harvard Business Review,* 89(3): 92-97.
43. For a discussion of the trend toward consolidation of the steel industry and how Lakshmi Mittal is becoming a dominant player, read Reed, S. & Arndt, M. 2004. The raja of steel. *BusinessWeek,* December 20: 50-52.
44. Colvin, G. 2011. Airline king. *Fortune,* May 2: 50-57; and Anonymous. 2018. 2017 Annual and 4th quarter U.S. airline financial data. *bts.gov.* May 9: np.

45. This discussion draws upon Rappaport, A. & Sirower, M. L. 1999. Stock or cash? The trade-offs for buyers and sellers in mergers and acquisitions. *Harvard Business Review,* 77(6): 147-158; and Lipin, S. & Deogun, N. 2000. Big mergers of 90s prove disappointing to shareholders. *The Wall Street Journal,* October 30: C1.
46. The downside of mergers in the airline industry is found in Gimbel, B. 2008. Why airline mergers don't fly. *BusinessWeek,* March 17: 26.
47. Muoio, A. 1998. Is bigger better? Unit of one. *Fast Company,* August 31.
48. Porter, M. E. 1987. From competitive advantage to corporate strategy. *Harvard Business Review,* 65(3): 43.
49. The divestiture of a business that is undertaken in order to enable managers to better focus on its core business has been termed "downscoping." Refer to Hitt, M. A., Harrison, J. S., & Ireland, R. D. 2001. *Mergers and acquisitions: A guide to creating value for stakeholders.* New York: Oxford University Press.
50. Sirmon, D. G., Hitt, M. A., & Ireland, R. D. 2007. Managing firm resources in dynamic environments to create value: Looking inside the black box. *Academy of Management Review,* 32(1): 273-292.
51. Kengelbach, J., Klemmer, D., & Roos, A. 2012. Plant and prune: How M&A can grow portfolio value. *BCG Report,* September: 1-38.
52. Berry, J., Brigham, B., Bynum, A., Leu, C., & McLaughlin, R. 2012. Creating value through divestitures—Deans Foods: Theory in practice. *Unpublished manuscript.*
53. This section draws on Hutt, M. D., Stafford, E. R., Walker, B. A., & Reingen, P. H. 2000. Case study: Defining the strategic alliance. *Sloan Management Review,* 41(2): 51-62; and Walters, B. A., Peters, S., & Dess, G. G. 1994. Strategic alliances and joint ventures: Making them work. *Business Horizons,* 4: 5-10.
54. For scholarly perspectives on the role of learning in creating value in strategic alliances, refer to Anard, B. N. & Khanna, T. 2000. Do firms learn to create value? *Strategic Management Journal,* 12(3): 295-317; and Vermeulen, F. & Barkema, H. p. 2001. Learning through acquisitions. *Academy of Management Journal,* 44(3): 457-476.
55. For a detailed discussion of transaction cost economics in strategic alliances, read Reuer, J. J. & Arno, A. 2007. Strategic alliance contracts: Dimensions and determinants of contractual complexity. *Strategic Management Journal,* 28(3): 313-330.
56. This section draws on Hutt, M. D., Stafford, E. R., Walker, B. A., & Reingen, P. H. 2000. Case study: Defining the strategic alliance. *Sloan Management Review,* 41(2): 51-62; and Walters, B. A., Peters, S., & Dess, G. G. 1994. Strategic alliances and joint ventures: Making them work. *Business Horizons,* 4: 5-10.
57. A study that investigates strategic alliances and networks is Tiwana, A. 2008. Do bridging ties complement strong ties? An empirical examination of alliance ambidexterity. *Strategic Management Journal,* 29(3): 251-272.
58. Fashion chain Zara opens its first Indian store. 2010. *bbc.co.uk/news/,* May 31: np.
59. Hoang, H. & Rothaermel, F. 2016. How to manage alliances strategically. *Sloan Management Review,* 76 (Fall): 69-73.
60. Anonymous. 2016. PGA TOUR and LPGA announce strategic alliance agreement. *lpga.com,* March 4: np.
61. Phelps, C. 2010. A longitudinal study of the influence of alliance network structure and composition on firm exploratory innovation. *Academy of Management Journal,* 53(4): 890-913.
62. For an institutional theory perspective on strategic alliances, read Dacin, M. T., Oliver, C., & Roy, J. p. 2007. The legitimacy of strategic alliances: An institutional perspective. *Strategic Management Journal,* 28(2): 169-187.
63. A study investigating factors that determine partner selection in strategic alliances is found in Shah, R. H. & Swaminathan, V. 2008. *Strategic Management Journal,* 29(5): 471-494.
64. Arino, A. & Ring, P. S. 2010. The role of fairness in alliance formation. *Strategic Management Journal,* 31(6): 1054-1087.
65. Greve, H. R., Baum, J. A. C., Mitsuhashi, H. & Rowley, T. J. 2010. Built to last but falling apart: Cohesion, friction, and withdrawal from interfirm alliances. *Academy of Management Journal,* 53(4): 302-322.
66. Narayan, A. 2011. From brewing, an Indian biotech is born. *Bloomberg Businessweek,* February 28: 19-20.
67. For an insightful perspective on how to manage conflict between innovation and ongoing operations in an organization, read Govindarajan, V. & Trimble, C. 2010. *The other side of innovation: Solving the execution challenge.* Boston: Harvard Business School Press.
68. Dunlap-Hinkler, D., Kotabe, M., & Mudambi, R. 2010. A story of breakthrough versus incremental innovation: Corporate entrepreneurship in the global pharmaceutical industry. *Strategic Entrepreneurship Journal,* 4(2): 106-127.
69. Porter, op. cit.: 43-59.
70. Seo, J., Gamache, D., Devers, C. & Carpenter, M. 2015. The role of CEO relative standing in acquisition behavior and CEO pay. *Strategic Management Journal.* 36: 1877-1894.
71. The fallen. 2003. *BusinessWeek,* January 13: 80-82.
72. Sellers, P. 2001. Get over yourself your ego is out of control. You're screwing up your career. Jack Welch, David Pottruck, and others can help you get control of your huge self. As if you care. *Fortune,* April 30: 76-88.
73. This section draws on Weston, J. F., Besley, S., & Brigham, E. F. 1996. *Essentials of managerial finance* (11th ed.): 18-20. Fort Worth, TX: Dryden Press, Harcourt Brace.

Nico Muller Art/Shutterstock

CHAPTER 7

International Strategy

Creating Value in Global Markets

Learning Objectives

LO7-1 Understand the importance of international expansion as a viable diversification strategy.

LO7-2 Identify the sources of national advantage; that is, why an industry in a given country is more (or less) successful than the same industry in another country.

LO7-3 Explain the motivations (or benefits) and the risks associated with international expansion, including the emerging trend for greater offshoring and outsourcing activity.

LO7-4 Explain the two opposing forces—cost reduction and adaptation to local markets—that firms face when entering international markets.

LO7-5 Identify the advantages and disadvantages associated with each of the four basic strategies: international, global, multidomestic, and transnational.

LO7-6 Understand the difference between regional companies and truly global companies.

LO7-7 Identify the four basic types of entry strategies and the relative benefits and risks associated with each of them.

We encourage you to reflect on how the concepts presented in this chapter can enhance your career success (see the "Reflecting on Career Implications..." sidebar at the end of the chapter).

LEARNING FROM MISTAKES

Since Ford entered the Chinese market in 2001, the U.S. automaker's strategic focus on China has yet to pay off. Ford had initial success in China, mostly based on a world car approach that aimed at selling similar cars around the world. This global approach took advantage of leveraging economies of scale in design and manufacturing to save costs. At its peak, Ford was the sixth-largest car company in China in 2014 with almost 5 percent of the Chinese car market. However, Ford's car sales have dwindled ever since. In early 2018, Ford plunged to 18th place among car manufacturers in China. To make matters worse, Ford posted a rare net financial loss in its China business in the first three months of that year.

The Chinese car market is now the largest in the world and Chinese customers demand different cars than North American and European customers. This change in demand has led to more market fragmentation, making global strategies less viable. Specifically, Chinese customers seek out cars with technological innovations such as Internet connectivity and best-in-class fuel economy. As a result of the increasing sophistication of Chinese customers, China is now home to the largest number of electric vehicles in the world.

Until recently, Ford's engineering and design work was located outside of China. This distance between the Chinese market and Ford's engineering and design prowess may have contributed to Ford's lack of appeal to Chinese customers. A Chinese proverb says that "distant water won't quench your thirst." In the same way, Ford's initial decision to locate key value chain activities outside of China may have caused issues with understanding the needs and wants of Chinese customers.

Ford responded to the recent challenges by separating the Chinese business from the broader Ford operation in the Asia Pacific region. The new China business will directly report to the Ford global headquarters in Dearborn, Michigan. Ford also named a new top executive to lead the China business, industry veteran Anning Chen, who brings ample local knowledge of the Chinese market from a previous position at Chery Jaguar Land Rover. Overall, Ford plans to address its recent challenges in China by launching 50 new vehicles for the Chinese market by 2025. While some analysts fear that the influx of new models will increase the complexity and cost of Ford cars, Ford's new China strategy finally pays greater attention to the local needs of the largest and most important car market in the world.

Discussion Questions

1. How should executives manage the tensions between attention to local tastes and the desire to cut costs in multinational companies?
2. How should Ford compete against local Chinese car manufacturers such as Geely who are uniquely positioned to understand and satisfy local customer tastes?

Sources: Rogers, C., and T. Moss. 2018. Why Ford's big China wager is faltering. *Wall Street Journal*, May 10: np; Choudhury, S. R. 2018. Ford sets up China business as a stand-alone unit. *cnbc.com*, October 24: np; Hoffman, B. 2017. Here's what's wrong with Ford's China plan–and what's right. *Forbes*, December 9: np; Hertzke P, Müller N, and S. Schenk. 2017. China's electric-vehicle market plugs in. *McKinsey Quarterly*, July: 1–3.

In this chapter we discuss how firms create value and achieve competitive advantage in the global marketplace. Multinational firms are constantly faced with many important decisions. These include entry strategies; the dilemma of choosing between local adaptation (in product offerings, locations, advertising, and pricing) and global integration; and others. We will address how firms can avoid pitfalls by developing a better understanding of the business environments of different countries as illustrated by the challenges Ford faced in China discussed previously. In addition, we address factors that can influence a nation's success in a particular industry. In our view, this is an important context in determining how well firms eventually do when they compete beyond their nation's boundaries.

LO 7-1

Understand the importance of international expansion as a viable diversification strategy.

THE GLOBAL ECONOMY: A BRIEF OVERVIEW

Managers face many opportunities and risks when they diversify abroad.[1] The trade among nations has increased dramatically in recent years, and it is estimated that recently the trade *across* nations exceeded the trade within nations. In a variety of industries such as semiconductors, automobiles, commercial aircraft, telecommunications, computers, and consumer electronics, it is almost impossible to survive unless firms scan the world for competitors, customers, human resources, suppliers, and technology.[2]

GE's wind energy business benefits by tapping into talent around the world. The firm has built research centers in China, Germany, India, and the United States. All four centers have played a key role in GE's development of huge 92-ton turbines:[3]

- Chinese researchers in Shanghai designed the microprocessors that control the pitch of the blade.
- Mechanical engineers from India (Bangalore) devised mathematical models to maximize the efficiency of materials in the turbine.
- Power-systems experts in the United States (Niskayuna, New York), which has researchers from 55 countries, do the design work.
- Technicians in Munich, Germany, have created a "smart" turbine that can calculate wind speeds and signal sensors in other turbines to produce maximum electricity.

globalization
a term that has two meanings: (1) the increase in international exchange, including trade in goods and services as well as exchange of money, ideas, and information; (2) the growing similarity of laws, rules, norms, values, and ideas across countries.

The rise of **globalization**–meaning the rise of market capitalism around the world–has undeniably created tremendous business opportunities for multinational corporations. For example, while smartphone sales declined in Western Europe in the third quarter of 2014, they grew at a 50 percent rate in Eastern Europe, the Middle East, and Africa.[4]

This rapid rise in global capitalism has had dramatic effects on the growth in different economic zones. For example, *Fortune* magazine's annual list of the world's 500 biggest companies included 156 firms from emerging markets in 2015, compared to only 18 in 1995.[5] McKinsey & Company predicts that by 2025 about 45 percent of the *Fortune* Global 500 will be based in emerging economies, which are now producing world-class companies with huge domestic markets and a commitment to invest in innovation.

Over half the world's output now comes from emerging markets. This is leading to a convergence of living standards across the globe and is changing the face of business. One example of this is the shift in the global automobile market. China supplanted the United States as the largest market for automobiles in 2009.

One of the challenges with globalization is determining how to meet the needs of customers at very different income levels. In many developing economies, distributions of income remain much wider than they do in the developed world, leaving many impoverished even as the economies grow. The challenge for multinational firms is to tailor their products and services to meet the needs of the "bottom of the pyramid." Global corporations are increasingly changing their product offerings to meet the needs of the nearly 5 billion poor people in the world who inhabit developing countries. Collectively, this represents a very large market with $14 trillion in purchasing power.

Next, we will address in more detail the question of why some nations and their industries are more competitive.[6] This establishes an important context or setting for the remainder of the chapter. After we discuss why some *nations and their industries* outperform others, we will be better able to address the various strategies that *firms* can take to create competitive advantage when they expand internationally.

FACTORS AFFECTING A NATION'S COMPETITIVENESS

Michael Porter of Harvard University conducted a four-year study in which he and a team of 30 researchers looked at the patterns of competitive success in 10 leading trading nations. He concluded that there are four broad attributes of nations that individually, and as a system, constitute what is termed the **diamond of national advantage.** In effect, these attributes jointly determine the playing field that each nation establishes and operates for its industries. These factors are:

- **Factor endowments.** The nation's position in factors of production, such as skilled labor or infrastructure, necessary to compete in a given industry.
- **Demand conditions.** The nature of home-market demand for the industry's product or service.
- **Related and supporting industries.** The presence or absence in the nation of supplier industries and other related industries that are internationally competitive.
- **Firm strategy, structure, and rivalry.** The conditions in the nation governing how companies are created, organized, and managed, as well as the nature of domestic rivalry.

diamond of national advantage
a framework for explaining why countries foster successful multinational corporations; consists of four factors—factor endowments; demand conditions; related and supporting industries; and firm strategy, structure, and rivalry.

factor endowments (national advantage)
a nation's position in factors of production.

demand conditions (national advantage)
the nature of home-market demand for the industry's product or service.

related and supporting industries (national advantage)
the presence, absence, and quality in the nation of supplier industries and other related industries that supply services, support, or technology to firms in the industry value chain.

firm strategy, structure, and rivalry (national advantage)
the conditions in the nation governing how companies are created, organized, and managed, as well as the nature of domestic rivalry.

Factor Endowments[7,8]

Classical economics suggests that factors of production such as land, labor, and capital are the building blocks that create usable consumer goods and services.[9] However, companies in advanced nations seeking competitive advantage over firms in other nations *create* many of the factors of production. For example, a country or industry dependent on scientific innovation must have a skilled human resource pool to draw upon. This resource pool is not inherited; it is created through investment in industry-specific knowledge and talent. The supporting infrastructure of a country—that is, its transportation and communication systems as well as its banking system—is also critical.

Factors of production must be developed that are industry- and firm-specific. In addition, the pool of resources is less important than the speed and efficiency with which these resources are deployed. Thus, firm-specific knowledge and skills created within a country that are rare, valuable, difficult to imitate, and rapidly and efficiently deployed are the factors of production that ultimately lead to a nation's competitive advantage.

For example, the island nation of Japan has little landmass, making the warehouse space needed to store inventory prohibitively expensive. But by pioneering just-in-time inventory management, Japanese companies managed to create a resource from which they gained advantage over companies in other nations that spent large sums to warehouse inventory.

LO 7-2

Identify the sources of national advantage; that is, why an industry in a given country is more (or less) successful than the same industry in another country.

Demand Conditions

Demand conditions refer to the demands that consumers place on an industry for goods and services. Consumers who demand highly specific, sophisticated products and services force firms to create innovative, advanced products and services to meet the demand. This consumer pressure presents challenges to a country's industries. But in response to these challenges, improvements to existing goods and services often result, creating conditions necessary for competitive advantage over firms in other countries.

Countries with demanding consumers drive firms in that country to meet high standards, upgrade existing products and services, and create innovative products and services. The conditions of consumer demand influence how firms view a market. This, in turn, helps a nation's industries to better anticipate future global demand conditions and proactively respond to product and service requirements.

Denmark, for instance, is known for its environmental awareness. Demand from consumers for environmentally safe products has spurred Danish manufacturers to become leaders in water pollution control equipment—products it has successfully exported.

Related and Supporting Industries

Related and supporting industries enable firms to manage inputs more effectively. For example, countries with a strong supplier base benefit by adding efficiency to downstream activities. A competitive supplier base helps a firm obtain inputs using cost-effective, timely methods, thus reducing manufacturing costs. Also, close working relationships with suppliers provide the potential to develop competitive advantages through joint research and development and the ongoing exchange of knowledge.

Related industries offer similar opportunities through joint efforts among firms. In addition, related industries create the probability that new companies will enter the market, increasing competition and forcing existing firms to become more competitive through efforts such as cost control, product innovation, and novel approaches to distribution. Combined, these give the home country's industries a source of competitive advantage.

In the Italian footwear industry the supporting industries enhance national competitive advantage. In Italy, shoe manufacturers are geographically located near their suppliers. The manufacturers have ongoing interactions with leather suppliers and learn about new textures, colors, and manufacturing techniques while a shoe is still in the prototype stage. The manufacturers are able to project future demand and gear their factories for new products long before companies in other nations become aware of the new styles.

Firm Strategy, Structure, and Rivalry

Rivalry is particularly intense in nations with conditions of strong consumer demand, strong supplier bases, and high new-entrant potential from related industries. This competitive rivalry in turn increases the efficiency with which firms develop, market, and distribute products and services within the home country. Domestic rivalry thus provides a strong impetus for firms to innovate and find new sources of competitive advantage.

This intense rivalry forces firms to look outside their national boundaries for new markets, setting up the conditions necessary for global competitiveness. Among all the points on Porter's diamond of national advantage, domestic rivalry is perhaps the strongest indicator of global competitive success. Firms that have experienced intense domestic competition are more likely to have designed strategies and structures that allow them to successfully compete in world markets.

In the European grocery retail industry, intense rivalry has led firms such as Aldi and Tesco to tighten their supply chains and improve store efficiency. Thus, it is no surprise that these firms are also strong global players.

The Indian software industry offers a clear example of how the attributes in Porter's "diamond" interact to lead to the conditions for a strong industry to grow. Exhibit 7.1 illustrates India's "software diamond," and Strategy Spotlight 7.1 further discusses the mutually reinforcing elements at work in this market.

Concluding Comment on Factors Affecting a Nation's Competitiveness

Porter drew his conclusions based on case histories of firms in more than 100 industries. Despite the differences in strategies employed by successful global competitors, a common theme emerged: Firms that succeeded in global markets had first succeeded in intensely competitive home markets. We can conclude that competitive advantage for global firms typically grows out of relentless, continuing improvement, and innovation.[10]

EXHIBIT 7.1 India's Software Diamond

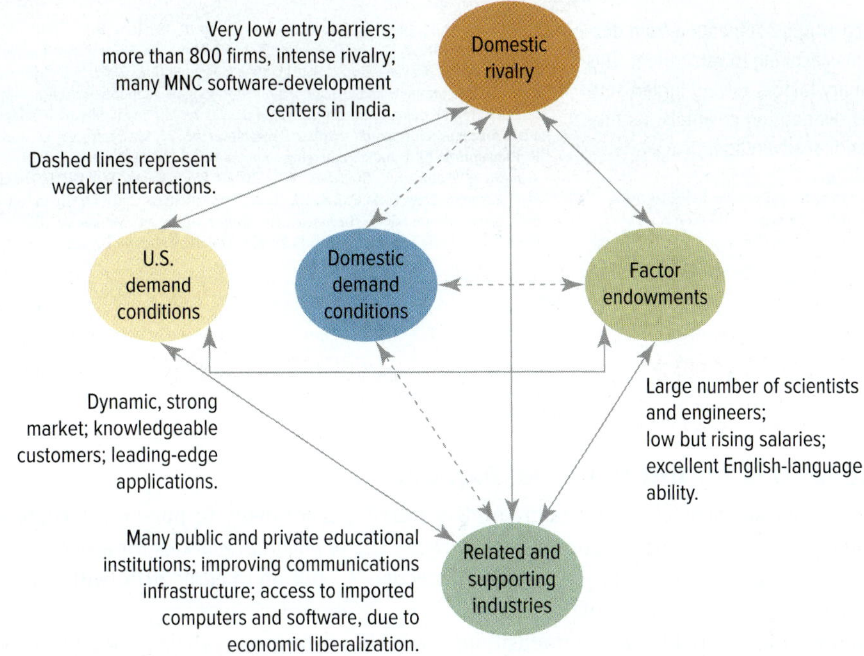

Source: Adapted from Kapur, D., and R. Ramamurti. 2001. India's emerging competitive advantage in services. *Academy of Management Perspectives*, 15(2): 20-33.

7.1 STRATEGY SPOTLIGHT

INDIA AND THE DIAMOND OF NATIONAL ADVANTAGE

The Indian software industry has become one of the leading global markets for software. The industry has grown to about $135 billion (in export) in 2018 and Indian IT firms provide software and services to over half the Fortune 500 firms. What are the factors driving this success? Porter's diamond of national advantage helps clarify this question. See Exhibit 7.1.

First, *factor endowments* are conducive to the rise of India's software industry. Through investment in human resource development with a focus on industry-specific knowledge, India's universities and software firms have literally created this essential factor of production. For example, India produces the second-largest annual output of scientists and engineers in the world, behind only the United States. In a knowledge-intensive industry such as software, development of human resources is fundamental to both domestic and global success.

Second, *demand conditions* require that software firms stay on the cutting edge of technological innovation. India has already moved toward globalization of its software industry; consumer demand conditions in developed nations such as Germany, Denmark, parts of Southeast Asia, and the United States created the consumer demand necessary to propel India's software makers toward sophisticated software solutions.*

Third, India has the *supplier base as well as the related industries* needed to drive competitive rivalry and enhance competitiveness. In particular, information technology (IT) hardware prices declined rapidly in the 1990s. Furthermore, rapid technological change in IT hardware meant that latecomers like India were not locked into older-generation technologies. Thus, both the IT hardware and software industries could "leapfrog" older technologies. In addition, relationships among knowledge workers in these IT hardware and software industries offer the social structure for ongoing knowledge exchange, promoting further enhancement of existing products. Further infrastructure improvements are occurring rapidly.

Fourth, with over 800 firms in the software services industry in India, *intense rivalry forces firms to develop competitive strategies and structures*. Although firms like TCS, Infosys, and Wipro

*Although India's success cannot be explained in terms of its home-market demand (according to Porter's model), the nature of the industry enables software to be transferred among different locations simultaneously by way of communications links. Thus, competitiveness of markets outside India can be enhanced without a physical presence in those markets.

continued

continued

have become large, they still face strong competition from dozens of small and midsize companies aspiring to catch them. This intense rivalry is one of the primary factors driving Indian software firms to develop overseas distribution channels, as predicted by Porter's diamond of national advantage.

Sources: Pai, M. 2016. No, India's software industry did not die on Friday. *www.ndtv.com,* October 16: np; Sachitanand, R. 2010. The new face of IT. *Business Today,* 19: 62; Anonymous. 2010. Training to lead. *www.Dqindia.com,* October 5: np; Nagaraju, B. 2011. India's software exports seen up 16–18 pct. in Fy12. *www.reuters.com,* February 2: np; Ghemawat, P., and T. Hout. 2008. Tomorrow's global giants. *Harvard Business Review,* 86(11): 80–88; Mathur, S. K. 2007. Indian IT industry: A performance analysis and a model for possible adoption. *ideas.repec.org,* January 1: np; Kripalani, M. 2002. Calling Bangalore: Multinationals are making it a hub for high-tech research. *BusinessWeek,* November 25: 52–54; Kapur, D., and R. Ramamurti. 2001. India's emerging competitive advantage in services. 2001. *Academy of Management Executive,* 15(2): 20–33; World Bank. 2001 *World Development Report:* 6. New York: Oxford University Press; Reuters. 2001. Oracle in India push, taps software talent. *Washington Post Online,* July 3; and Venkat, A. 2018. NASSCOM India Leadership Forum 2018. *CIO India,* February 20: np.

INTERNATIONAL EXPANSION: A COMPANY'S MOTIVATIONS AND RISKS

LO 7-3

Explain the motivations (or benefits) and the risks associated with international expansion, including the emerging trend for greater offshoring and outsourcing activity.

Motivations for International Expansion

Increase Market Size There are many motivations for a company to pursue international expansion. The most obvious one is to *increase the size of potential markets* for a firm's products and services.[11] The world's population exceeded 7.7 billion in early 2019, with the U.S. representing less than 5 percent.

multinational firms firms that manage operations in more than one country.

Many **multinational firms** are intensifying their efforts to market their products and services to countries such as India and China as the ranks of their middle class have increased over the past decade. The potential is great. An OECD study predicts that consumption by middle-class consumers in Asian markets will grow from $4.9 trillion in 2009 to over $30 trillion by 2020. At that point, Asia will make up 60 percent of global middle-class consumption, up from 20 percent in 2009.[12]

Expanding a firm's global presence also automatically increases its scale of operations, providing it with a larger revenue and asset base.[13] As we noted in Chapter 5 in discussing overall cost leadership strategies, such an increase in revenues and asset base potentially enables a firm to *attain economies of scale.* This provides multiple benefits. One advantage is the spreading of fixed costs such as R&D over a larger volume of production. Examples include the sale of Boeing's commercial aircraft and Microsoft's operating systems in many foreign countries.

Filmmaking is another industry in which international sales can help amortize huge developmental costs.[14] For example, 77 percent of the $1.1 billion box-office take for *Transformers: Age of Extinction* came from overseas moviegoers. Similarly, the market for kids' movies is largely outside the United States, with 70 percent of *Frozen*'s $1.3 billion in box-office take coming from overseas.

arbitrage opportunities an opportunity to profit by buying and selling the same good in different markets.

Take Advantage of Arbitrage *Taking advantage of* **arbitrage opportunities** is a second advantage of international expansion. In its simplest form, arbitrage involves buying something where it is cheap and selling it where it commands a higher price. A big part of Walmart's success can be attributed to the company's expertise in arbitrage. The possibilities for arbitrage are not necessarily confined to simple trading opportunities. It can be applied to virtually any factor of production and every stage of the value chain. For example, a firm may locate its call centers in India, its manufacturing plants in China or Vietnam, and its R&D in Europe, where the specific types of talented personnel may be available at the lowest possible cost. In today's integrated global financial markets, a firm can borrow anywhere in the world where capital is cheap and use it to fund a project in a country where capital is expensive.

Such arbitrage opportunities are even more attractive to global corporations because their larger size enables them to buy in huge volume, thus increasing their bargaining power with suppliers.

Enhancing a Product's Growth Potential *Enhancing the growth rate of a product* that is in its maturity stage in a firm's home country but that has greater demand potential elsewhere is another benefit of international expansion. As we noted in Chapter 5, products (and industries) generally go through a four-stage life cycle of introduction, growth, maturity, and decline. In recent decades, U.S. soft-drink producers such as Coca-Cola and PepsiCo have aggressively pursued international markets to attain levels of growth that simply would not be available in the United States. The differences in market growth potential have even led some firms to restructure their operations. For example, Procter & Gamble relocated its global skin, cosmetics, and personal care unit headquarters from Cincinnati to Singapore to be closer to the fast-growing Asian market.[15]

Optimize the Location of Value-Chain Activities *Optimizing the physical location for every activity in the firm's value chain* is another benefit. Recall from our discussions in Chapters 3 and 5 that the value chain represents the various activities in which all firms must engage to produce products and services. It includes primary activities, such as inbound logistics, operations, and marketing, as well as support activities, such as procurement, R&D, and human resource management. All firms have to make critical decisions as to where each activity will take place.[16] Optimizing the location for every activity in the value chain can yield one or more of three strategic advantages: performance enhancement, cost reduction, and risk reduction. We will now discuss each of these.

Performance Enhancement Microsoft's decision to establish a corporate research laboratory in Cambridge, England, is an example of a location decision that was guided mainly by the goal of building and sustaining world-class excellence in selected value-creating activities.[17] This strategic decision provided Microsoft with access to outstanding technical and professional talent. Location decisions can affect the quality with which any activity is performed in terms of the availability of needed talent, speed of learning, and the quality of external and internal coordination.

Strategy&, the consulting unit of PWC, the giant accounting firm, produces an annual survey of the world's 1,000 most innovative companies.[18] It found that in 2015, firms that spent 60 percent or more of their R&D budgets overseas enjoyed significantly higher operating margins and return on assets, as well as faster growth in operating income, than their more domestically oriented rivals.

Cost Reduction Two location decisions founded largely on cost-reduction considerations are (1) Nike's decision to source the manufacture of athletic shoes from Asian countries such as China, Vietnam, and Indonesia, and (2) the decision of Volkswagen to locate a new auto production plant in Chattanooga, Tennessee, to leverage the relatively low labor costs in the area as well as low shipping costs due to Chattanooga's close proximity to both rail and river transportation. Such location decisions can affect the cost structure in terms of local manpower and other resources, transportation and logistics, and government incentives and the local tax structure.

Performance enhancement and cost-reduction benefits parallel the business-level strategies (discussed in Chapter 5) of differentiation and overall cost leadership. They can at times be attained simultaneously. Consider our example in the previous section on the Indian software industry. When Oracle set up a development operation in that country, the company benefited both from lower labor costs and operational expenses and from performance enhancements realized through the hiring of superbly talented professionals.

Risk Reduction Given the erratic swings in the exchange ratios between the U.S. dollar and the Japanese yen (in relation to each other and to other major currencies), an important basis for cost competition between Ford and Toyota has been their relative ingenuity at managing currency risks. One way for such rivals to manage currency risks has been to spread the high-cost elements of their manufacturing operations across a few select and carefully chosen locations around the world. Location decisions such as these can affect the overall risk profile of the firm with respect to currency, economic, and political risks.[19]

Learning Opportunities By expanding into new markets, corporations expose themselves to differing market demands, R&D capabilities, functional skills, organizational processes, and managerial practices. This provides opportunities for managers to transfer the knowledge that results from these exposures back to their home office and to other divisions in the firm. Thus, expansion into new markets provides a range of learning opportunities. For example, when L'Oréal, a French personal care product manufacturer, acquired two U.S. firms that developed and sold hair care products to African-American customers, L'Oréal gained knowledge on what is referred to in the industry as "ethnic hair care." It then took this knowledge and built a new ethnic hair care division in Europe and later began making inroads in African markets. More generally, research suggests that overseas expansion leads to valuable learning at home. One study found that, rather than distracting the firm in its efforts in its home market, overseas acquisitions led to substantial performance improvements, an average of a 12 percent increase, in home markets.[20]

reverse innovation
new products developed by developed-country multinational firms for emerging markets that have adequate functionality at a low cost.

Explore Reverse Innovation Finally, *exploring possibilities for* **reverse innovation** has become a major motivation for international expansion. Many leading companies are discovering that developing products specifically for emerging markets can pay off in a big way. In the past, multinational companies typically developed products for their rich home markets and then tried to sell them in developing countries with minor adaptations. However, as growth slows in rich nations and demand grows rapidly in developing countries such as India and China, this approach becomes increasingly inadequate. Instead, companies like GE have committed significant resources to developing products that meet the needs of developing nations, products that deliver adequate functionality at a fraction of the cost. Interestingly, these products have subsequently found considerable success in value segments in wealthy countries as well. Hence, this process is referred to as reverse innovation, a new motivation for international expansion.

Reverse innovation becomes increasingly important because customers and governments in high-income countries are trying to reduce healthcare costs. Facing significant demographic changes such as an aging population and longer lifespans, high-income countries may be able to benefit tremendously from adopting process innovations invented in the healthcare delivery sector of emerging markets. Strategy Spotlight 7.2 describes how Indian hospital groups are able to provide high-quality medical procedures at a fraction of the costs of U.S. hospitals, and how hospitals in the United States may benefit from these process innovations.

Potential Risks of International Expansion

When a company expands its international operations, it does so to increase its profits or revenues. As with any other investment, however, there are also potential risks.[21] To help companies assess the risk of entering foreign markets, rating systems have been developed to evaluate political and economic, as well as financial and credit, risks.[22] *Euromoney* magazine publishes a semiannual "Country Risk Rating" that evaluates political, economic, and

7.2 STRATEGY SPOTLIGHT

REVERSE INNOVATION IN HEALTH CARE

Healthcare systems around the world are facing tremendous challenges. In 2017, the United States spent an astonishing $3.5 trillion, or 18 percent of GDP, on healthcare services. That is more than $10,500 per person and twice the amount of any other high-income nation. Healthcare costs are also bound to surge further. At the current pace, health-related expenses increase at twice the rate of the Consumer Price Index. By 2028, the federal government would need to subsidize healthcare spending at around 10 percent of GDP if current trends continue. Other industrialized countries face similar issues. In the UK, a high-ranking government official called the financial situation of the National Health Service (NHS) "a mess," and in France the healthcare system is at the brink of bankruptcy. An unconventional remedy to control costs in health care may come from reverse innovation efforts.

Reverse innovation refers to innovations that flow from low-income countries to high-income countries rather than the other way around. Innovations originating in low-income countries typically aim for value maximization. In other words, reverse innovations aim to provide products or services at low costs while producing high quality outcomes. An unexpected country for innovation in health care is India, featuring several successful hospital groups that deliver high quality health care at prices that are much lower than in the United States. Take Narayana Health as an example. Narayana Health was founded in 2000 and is specialized in cardiac care. While it received much praise for its high quality care, Narayana is able to offer various types of heart surgeries at a fraction of U.S. prices. A coronary bypass surgery, for instance, may only cost 1 to 3 percent of the U.S. price tag. How are Narayana Health and other Indian hospitals able to provide health care at such low prices while providing high quality care?

Many Indian hospitals reconfigured their healthcare delivery by creating a hub-and-spoke system. In this system, the most sophisticated equipment and specialized doctors are located in urban hubs. Smaller hospitals are arrayed around the hubs as spoke facilities to reach underserved patients in rural areas. However, spoke facilities neither duplicate the medical equipment of the hubs nor do they offer a full range of specialty services. Instead, these facilities focus on routine treatments, follow-up visits, and diagnosis, essentially acting as a gateway to the urban hubs should more sophisticated procedures or treatments become necessary. This hub-and-spoke approach is facilitated by the use of technologies. For instance, specialists at the hub use video conferencing technologies to connect with doctors and patients at the spokes. All these innovations are designed to lower costs, be it for the patients—who save transportation costs—or hospitals—which can use their facilities more efficiently due to higher volumes.

Reverse innovations inspired by Indian healthcare delivery have already influenced U.S. health care in regions that resemble the problems found in low-income countries. For instance, Mississippi is the U.S. state with the fewest doctors per capita. Patients must often travel several hours to reach the University of Mississippi Medical Center (UMMC)—the state's only academic medical center. It comes as little surprise that Mississippi was the first state in the United States to implement an Indian-style hub-and-spoke network. Doctors at community hospitals can videoconference with the specialists at UMMC. Today, 35 specialties at UMMC are connected with more than 200 rural community hospitals across the state, improving the quality of medical care while lowering healthcare delivery costs throughout Mississippi.

Sources: Govindarajan. V., and R. Ramamurti. 2018. *Reverse innovation in health care: How to make value-based delivery work*. Boston: Harvard Business Review Press; Govindarajan, V., and R. Ramamurti. 2013. Delivering world-class health care, affordably. *Harvard Business Review,* 91(11): 117–122; and Anonymous. 2018. American health care: Health spending and the federal budget. *Committee for a Responsible Federal Budget*, May 16: np.

other risks that entrants potentially face.[23] Exhibit 7.2 presents a sample of country risk ratings, published by AM Best. Note that the overall ratings range from 1 to 5, with higher risk receiving the higher score.

Next we will discuss the four main types of risk: political risk, economic risk, currency risk, and management risk.

Political and Economic Risk Generally speaking, the business climate in the United States is very favorable. However, some countries around the globe may be hazardous to the health of corporate initiatives because of **political risk.**[24] Forces such as social unrest, military turmoil, demonstrations, and even violent conflict and terrorism can pose serious threats.[25] Consider, for example, the ongoing tension and violence in the Middle East associated with the revolutions and civil wars in Egypt, Libya, Syria, and other countries. Such conditions increase the likelihood of destruction of property and disruption of operations as well as

political risk
potential threat to a firm's operations in a country due to ineffectiveness of the domestic political system.

EXHIBIT 7.2

A Sample of Country Risk Ratings, August 22, 2018

Country Score	Overall Country Rating	Economic Risk	Political Risk	Financial System Risk
Norway	1	2	1	1
Canada	1	1	1	1
United States	1	2	1	1
Singapore	1	2	1	1
Hong Kong	2	2	2	1
South Korea	2	2	2	2
South Africa	4	4	4	3
China	3	2	3	3
Bahrain	4	4	3	3
Kazakhstan	4	3	4	4
Colombia	4	3	4	4
Russia	4	3	4	4
Argentina	5	4	4	5
Libya	5	5	5	5

Source: Bests Country Risk Report. August 22, 2018.

nonpayment for goods and services. Thus, countries that are viewed as high risk are less attractive for most types of business.[26]

rule of law
a characteristic of legal systems whereby behavior is governed by rules that are uniformly enforced.

Another source of political risk in many countries is the absence of the **rule of law.** The absence of rules or the lack of uniform enforcement of existing rules leads to what might often seem to be arbitrary and inconsistent decisions by government officials. This can make it difficult for foreign firms to conduct business.

For example, consider Renault's experience in Russia. Renault paid $1 billion to acquire a 25 percent ownership stake in the Russian automaker AvtoVAZ in 2008. Just one year later, Russian Prime Minister Vladimir Putin threatened to dilute Renault's ownership stake unless it contributed more money to prop up AvtoVAZ, which was then experiencing a significant slide in sales. Renault realized its ownership claim may not have held up in the corrupt Russian court system. Therefore, it was forced to negotiate and eventually agreed to transfer over $300 million in technology and expertise to the Russian firm to ensure its ownership stake would stay at 25 percent.[27]

Interestingly, while corporations have historically been concerned about rule-of-law issues in developing markets, such issues have also become a significant concern in developed markets, most critically in the United States. In a 2012 World Economic Forum Global Competitive Report that examined the quality of governmental institutions and the rule of law, the United States fared poorly. Starkly, the United States was ranked among the top 20 countries on only 1 of the 22 measures of institutional quality the survey included. In line with these findings, the International Finance Corporation (IFC) found that governmental hurdles businesses face have become a greater challenge in the United States in recent years. The IFC compiles data annually on the burdens of doing business that are put in place by governments and found that the United States is one of only a few countries surveyed in which doing business has become more burdensome. In nearly 90 percent of countries, governmental burdens have eased since 2006, but the United States has bucked that trend and become a more difficult location in which to operate.

7.3 STRATEGY SPOTLIGHT — ETHICS

THE COUNTERFEIT CENTER ON THE U.S. BORDER? IT'S CANADA

Companies are typically concerned with counterfeit issues in developing countries such as India or China. Few would expect counterfeit issues in developed economies because high consumer incomes and effective institutions usually protect the intellectual property rights of companies. Not so in Canada in many cases. Canada stands out as a country with a history and reputation for mishandling intellectual property issues. In 2018, the Office of the United States Trade Representative (USTR) placed Canada—along with China, India, and Russia—on a priority watch list of countries that fail to effectively enforce intellectual property rights. Likewise, the U.S. Chamber of Commerce ranks Canada's intellectual property rights regime closer to economies such as Mexico and Malaysia than to the United States and the European Union.

The United States is particularly concerned that its neighbor to the north does not properly inspect and detain pirated goods shipped through Canada. The good news is that Canada has improved its laws and regulations, and even affords its customs officers ample rights to detain shipments if intellectual property theft is suspected. The bad news, however, is that Canada does not devote enough resources to the enforcement of its laws. Some recent numbers illustrate this predicament. While Canada had caught 50 suspected shipments between 2016 and 2017, U.S. customs had caught 30,000 shipments suspected of violating intellectual property rights. Even accounting for the larger size of the U.S. shipping sector, Canadian customs enforcement seems to work less effectively.

It is not just cross-border deals that concern companies from the United States and other parts of the world. Luxury brands such as Louis Vuitton and Rolex are concerned about counterfeit versions of their products being sold in Canada, specifically in the Pacific Mall near Toronto. The three-floor mall calls itself "the largest Chinese shopping mall in North America" and is often compared with notorious counterfeit markets such as the Silk Market in Beijing, China. The United States is concerned that Canada is too lax on enforcing the copyrights and trademarks of American firms. An important reason why Canada's enforcement of intellectual property rights is considered insufficient is the lack of a central law-enforcement unit responsible for counterfeit issues. Such policing units exist in the United States and the European Union, resulting in better enforcement of property rights issues in these countries.

Sources: Anonymous. 2018. Marked down in Markham. *The Economist*, February 24: 28; Anonymous. 2018. U.S. says Canada failing at enforcing intellectual property rights. *HuffPost Canada*, April 30: np; and Anonymous. 2017. U.S. Chamber international IP index. *U.S. Chamber of Commerce*, February: np.

As institutions deteriorate, the United States loses its luster as a place to base operations. This sentiment was reflected in a survey of business executives who are alumni of the Harvard Business School. When asked whether they had recently favored basing new operations in the United States or in a foreign location, an overwhelming majority, 84 percent, responded that they had chosen the foreign location. Thus, advanced economies, such as the United States, risk losing out to other countries if they fail to reinforce and strengthen their legal and political institutions.[28]

The laws, and the enforcement of laws, associated with the protection of intellectual property rights can be a major potential **economic risk** in entering new countries.[29] Microsoft, for example, has lost billions of dollars in potential revenue through piracy of its software products in many countries, including China. Other areas of the globe, such as the former Soviet Union and some eastern European nations, have piracy problems as well.[30] Firms rich in intellectual property have encountered financial losses as imitations of their products have grown due to a lack of law enforcement of intellectual property rights.[31]

economic risk
potential threat to a firm's operations in a country due to economic policies and conditions, including property rights laws and enforcement of those laws.

Counterfeiting, a direct form of theft of intellectual property rights, is a significant and growing problem. The International Chamber of Commerce estimated that the value of counterfeit goods could exceed $1.9 trillion in 2022, over 2 percent of the world's total economic output. "The whole business has just exploded," said Jeffrey Hardy, head of the anticounterfeiting program at ICC. "And it goes way beyond music and Gucci bags." Counterfeiting has moved well beyond handbags and shoes to include chemicals, pharmaceuticals, and aircraft parts. According to a University of Florida study, 25 percent of the pesticide market in some parts of Europe is estimated to be counterfeit. This is especially troubling since these chemicals are often toxic.[32] Strategy Spotlight 7.3 discusses how counterfeit issues are not only a problem in developing countries but also in developed economies such as Canada.

counterfeiting
selling of trademarked goods without the consent of the trademark holder.

Currency Risks Currency fluctuations can pose substantial risks. A company with operations in several countries must constantly monitor the exchange rate between its own currency and that of the host country to minimize **currency risks.** Even a small change in the exchange rate can result in a significant difference in the cost of production or net profit when doing business overseas. When the U.S. dollar appreciates against other currencies, for example, U.S. goods can be more expensive to consumers in foreign countries. At the same time, however, appreciation of the U.S. dollar can have negative implications for American companies that have branch operations overseas. The reason for this is that profits from abroad must be exchanged for dollars at a more expensive rate of exchange, reducing the amount of profit when measured in dollars. For example, consider an American firm doing business in Italy. If this firm had a 20 percent profit in euros at its Italian center of operations, this profit would be totally wiped out when converted into U.S. dollars if the euro had depreciated 20 percent against the U.S. dollar. (U.S. multinationals typically engage in sophisticated "hedging strategies" to minimize currency risk. The discussion of this is beyond the scope of this section.)

currency risk
potential threat to a firm's operations in a country due to fluctuations in the local currency's exchange rate.

Following, we discuss how Israel's strong currency–the shekel–forced a firm to reevaluate its strategy.

> For years O.R.T. Technologies resisted moving any operations outside Israel. However, when faced with a sharp rise in the value of the shekel, the maker of specialized software for managing gas stations froze all local hiring and decided to transfer some developmental work to Eastern Europe. Laments CEO Alex Milner, "I never thought I'd see the day when we would have to move R&D outside of Israel, but the strong shekel has forced us to do so."[33]

Management Risks **Management risks** may be considered the challenges and risks that managers face when they must respond to the inevitable differences that they encounter in foreign markets. These take a variety of forms: culture, customs, language, income levels, customer preferences, distribution systems, and so on.[34] As we will note later in the chapter, even in the case of apparently standard products, some degree of local adaptation will become necessary.[35]

management risk
potential threat to a firm's operations in a country due to the problems that managers have making decisions in the context of foreign markets.

Differences in cultures across countries can also pose unique challenges for managers.[36] Cultural symbols can evoke deep feelings.[37] For example, in a series of advertisements aimed at Italian vacationers, Coca-Cola executives turned the Eiffel Tower, Empire State Building, and Tower of Pisa into the familiar Coke bottle. So far, so good. However, when the white marble columns of the Parthenon that crowns the Acropolis in Athens were turned into Coke bottles, the Greeks became outraged. Why? Greeks refer to the Acropolis as the "holy rock," and a government official said the Parthenon is an "international symbol of excellence" and that "whoever insults the Parthenon insults international culture." Coca-Cola apologized.

Global Dispersion of Value Chains: Outsourcing and Offshoring

A major recent trend has been the dispersion of the value chains of multinational corporations across different countries; that is, the various activities that constitute the value chain of a firm are now spread across several countries and continents. Such dispersion of value occurs mainly through increasing offshoring and outsourcing.

A report issued by the World Trade Organization described the production of a particular U.S. car as follows: "30 percent of the car's value goes to Korea for assembly, 17.5 percent to Japan for components and advanced technology, 7.5 percent to Germany for design, 4 percent to Taiwan and Singapore for minor parts, 2.5 percent to UK for advertising and marketing services, and 1.5 percent to Ireland and Barbados for data processing. This means that only 37 percent of the production value is generated in the U.S."[38] In today's economy, we are increasingly witnessing two interrelated trends: outsourcing and offshoring.

Outsourcing occurs when a firm decides to utilize other firms to perform value-creating activities that were previously performed in-house.[39] It may be a new activity that the firm is perfectly capable of doing but chooses to have someone else perform for cost or quality reasons. Outsourcing can be to either a domestic or foreign firm.

outsourcing
using other firms to perform value-creating activities that were previously performed in-house.

Offshoring takes place when a firm decides to shift an activity that it was performing in a domestic location to a foreign location.[40] For example, both Microsoft and Intel now have R&D facilities in India, employing a large number of Indian scientists and engineers. Often, offshoring and outsourcing go together; that is, a firm may outsource an activity to a foreign supplier, thereby causing the work to be offshored as well.[41]

offshoring
shifting a value-creating activity from a domestic location to a foreign location.

The recent explosion in the volume of outsourcing and offshoring is due to a variety of factors. Up until the 1960s, for most companies, the entire value chain was in one location. Further, the production took place close to where the customers were in order to keep transportation costs under control. In the case of service industries, it was generally believed that offshoring was not possible because the producer and consumer had to be present at the same place at the same time. After all, a haircut could not be performed if the barber and the client were separated!

For manufacturing industries, the rapid decline in transportation and coordination costs has enabled firms to disperse their value chains over different locations. For example, Nike's R&D takes place in the United States, raw materials are procured from a multitude of countries, actual manufacturing takes place in China, Indonesia, or Vietnam, advertising is produced in the United States, and sales and service take place in practically all the countries. Each value-creating activity is performed in the location where the cost is the lowest or the quality is the best. Without finding optimal locations for each activity, Nike could not have attained its position as the world's largest shoe company.

The experience of the manufacturing sector was also repeated in the service sector by the mid-1990s. A trend that began with the outsourcing of low-level programming and data entry work to countries such as India and Ireland suddenly grew manyfold, encompassing a variety of white-collar and professional activities ranging from call centers to R&D.

Bangalore, India, in recent years, has emerged as a location where more and more U.S. tax returns are prepared. In India, U.S.-trained and licensed radiologists interpret chest x-rays and CT scans from U.S. hospitals for half the cost. The advantages from offshoring go beyond mere cost savings today. In many specialized occupations in science and engineering, there is a shortage of qualified professionals in developed countries, whereas countries like India, China, and Singapore have what seems like an inexhaustible supply.[42]

While offshoring offers the potential to cut costs in corporations across a wide range of industries, many firms are finding the benefits of offshoring to be more elusive and the costs greater than they anticipated.[43] A study by AMR Research found that 56 percent of companies moving production offshore experienced an increase in total costs, contrary to their expectations of cost savings. In a more focused study, 70 percent of managers said sourcing in China is more costly than they initially estimated.

The cause of this contrary outcome is actually not all that surprising. Common savings from offshoring, such as lower wages, benefits, energy costs, regulatory costs, and taxes, are all easily visible and immediate. In contrast, there are a host of hidden costs that arise over time and often overwhelm the cost savings of offshoring. These hidden costs include:

- ***Total wage costs.*** Labor cost per hour may be significantly lower in developing markets, but this may not translate into lower overall costs. If workers in these markets are less productive or less skilled, firms end up with a higher number of hours needed to produce the same quantity of product. This necessitates hiring more workers and having employees work longer hours.
- ***Indirect costs.*** In addition to higher labor costs, there are also a number of indirect costs that pop up. If there are problems with the skill level of workers, the firm will

find the need for more training and supervision of workers, more raw material and greater scrap due to the lower skill level, and greater rework to fix quality problems. The firm may also experience greater need for security staff in its facilities.

- ***Increased inventory.*** Due to the longer delivery times, firms often need to tie up more capital in work in progress and inventory.
- ***Reduced market responsiveness.*** The long supply lines from low-cost countries may leave firms less responsive to shifts in customer demands. This may damage their brand image and also increase product obsolescence costs, as they may have to scrap or sell at a steep discount products that fail to meet quickly changing technology standards or customer tastes.
- ***Coordination costs.*** Coordinating product development and manufacturing can be difficult with operations undertaking different tasks in different countries. This may hamper innovation. It may also trigger unexpected costs, such as paying overtime in some markets so that staff across multiple time zones can meet to coordinate their activities.
- ***Intellectual property rights.*** Firms operating in countries with weak IP protection can wind up losing their trade secrets or taking costly measures to protect these secrets.
- ***Wage inflation.*** In moving overseas, firms often assume some level of wage stability, but wages in developing markets can be volatile and spike dramatically. For example, the minimum wages set by provinces in China increased at an average of 13 percent per year in 2014.[44] As Roger Meiners, chairman of the Department of Economics at the University of Texas at Arlington, stated, "The U.S. is more competitive on a wage basis because average wages have come down, especially for entry-level workers, and wages in China have been increasing."

Firms need to take into account all of these costs in determining whether or not to move their operations offshore.

LO 7-4

Explain the two opposing forces—cost reduction and adaptation to local markets—that firms face when entering international markets.

ACHIEVING COMPETITIVE ADVANTAGE IN GLOBAL MARKETS

We now discuss the two opposing forces that firms face when they expand into global markets: cost reduction and adaptation to local markets. Then we address the four basic types of international strategies that they may pursue: international, global, multidomestic, and transnational. The selection of one of these four types of strategies is largely dependent on a firm's relative pressure to address each of the two forces.

Two Opposing Pressures: Reducing Costs and Adapting to Local Markets

Many years ago, the famed marketing strategist Theodore Levitt advocated strategies that favored global products and brands. He suggested that firms should standardize all of their products and services for all of their worldwide markets. Such an approach would help a firm lower its overall costs by spreading its investments over as large a market as possible. Levitt's approach rested on three key assumptions:

1. Customer needs and interests are becoming increasingly homogeneous worldwide.
2. People around the world are willing to sacrifice preferences in product features, functions, design, and the like for lower prices at high quality.
3. Substantial economies of scale in production and marketing can be achieved through supplying global markets.[45]

However, there is ample evidence to refute these assumptions.[46] Regarding the first assumption—the increasing worldwide homogeneity of customer needs and interests—consider the number of product markets, ranging from watches and handbags to soft drinks and fast foods. Companies have identified global customer segments and developed global products and brands targeted to those segments. Also, many other companies adapt lines to idiosyncratic country preferences and develop local brands targeted to local market segments. For example, Nestlé's line of pizzas marketed in the United Kingdom includes cheese with ham and pineapple topping on a French bread crust. Similarly, Coca-Cola in Japan markets Georgia (a tonic drink) as well as Classic Coke and Hi-C.

Consider the second assumption—the sacrifice of product attributes for lower prices. While there is invariably a price-sensitive segment in many product markets, there is no indication that this is increasing. In contrast, in many product and service markets—ranging from watches, personal computers, and household appliances to banking and insurance—there is a growing interest in multiple product features, product quality, and service.

Finally, the third assumption is that significant economies of scale in production and marketing could be achieved for global products and services. Although standardization may lower manufacturing costs, such a perspective does not consider three critical and interrelated points. First, as we discussed in Chapter 5, technological developments in flexible factory automation enable economies of scale to be attained at lower levels of output and do not require production of a single standardized product. Second, the cost of production is only one component, and often not the critical one, in determining the total cost of a product. Third, a firm's strategy should not be product-driven. It should also consider other activities in the firm's value chain, such as marketing, sales, and distribution.

Based on these assumptions, we would have a hard time arguing that it is wise to develop the same product or service for all markets throughout the world. While there are some exceptions, such as Boeing airplanes and some of Coca-Cola's soft-drink products, managers must also strive to tailor their products to the culture of the country in which they are attempting to do business. Few would argue that "one size fits all" generally applies.

The opposing pressures that managers face place conflicting demands on firms as they strive to be competitive.[47] On the one hand, competitive pressures require that firms do what they can to *lower unit costs* so that consumers will not perceive their product and service offerings as too expensive. This may lead them to consider locating manufacturing facilities where labor costs are low and developing products that are highly standardized across multiple countries.

In addition to responding to pressures to lower costs, managers must strive to be *responsive to local pressures* in order to tailor their products to the demand of the local market in which they do business. This requires differentiating their offerings and strategies from country to country to reflect consumer tastes and preferences and making changes to reflect differences in distribution channels, human resource practices, and governmental regulations. However, since the strategies and tactics to differentiate products and services to local markets can involve additional expenses, a firm's costs will tend to rise.

The two opposing pressures result in four different basic strategies that companies can use to compete in the global marketplace: international, global, multidomestic, and transnational. The strategy that a firm selects depends on the degree of pressure that it is facing for cost reductions and the importance of adapting to local markets. Exhibit 7.3 shows the conditions under which each of these strategies would be most appropriate.

LO 7-5

Identify the advantages and disadvantages associated with each of the four basic strategies: international, global, multidomestic, and transnational.

It is important to note that we consider these four strategies to be "basic" or "pure"; that is, in practice, all firms will tend to have some elements of each strategy.

International Strategy

There are a small number of industries in which pressures for both local adaptation and lowering costs are rather low. An extreme example of such an industry is the "orphan" drug industry. These are medicines for diseases that are severe but affect only a small number of

EXHIBIT 7.3 Opposing Pressures and Four Strategies

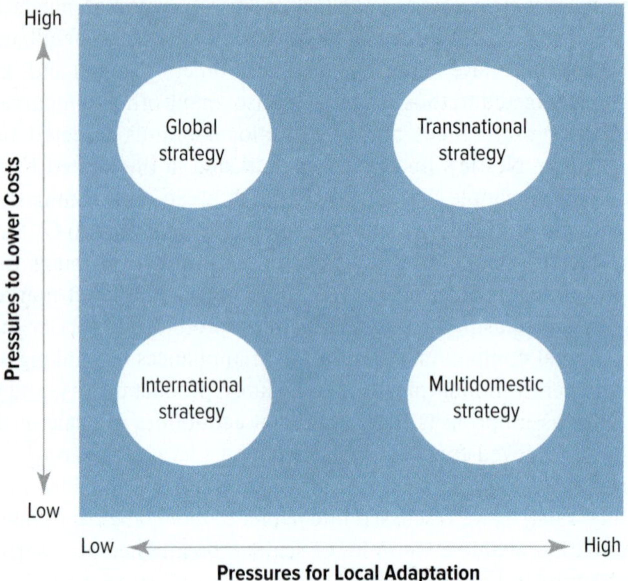

people. Diseases such as Gaucher disease and Fabry disease fit into this category. Companies such as Genzyme and Oxford GlycoSciences are active in this segment of the drug industry. There is virtually no need to adapt their products to the local markets. And the pressures to reduce costs are low; even though only a few thousand patients are affected, the revenues and margins are significant, because patients are charged up to $100,000 per year.

international strategy a strategy based on firms' diffusion and adaptation of the parent companies' knowledge and expertise to foreign markets; used in industries where the pressures for both local adaptation and lowering costs are low.

An **international strategy** is based on diffusion and adaptation of the parent company's knowledge and expertise to foreign markets. Country units are allowed to make some minor adaptations to products and ideas coming from the head office, but they have far less independence and autonomy compared to multidomestic companies. The primary goal of the strategy is worldwide exploitation of the parent firm's knowledge and capabilities. All sources of core competencies are centralized.

The majority of large U.S. multinationals pursued the international strategy in the decades following World War II. These companies centralized R&D and product development but established manufacturing facilities as well as marketing organizations abroad. Companies such as McDonald's and Kellogg are examples of firms following such a strategy. Although these companies do make some local adaptations, they are of a very limited nature. With increasing pressures to reduce costs due to global competition, especially from low-cost countries, opportunities to successfully employ an international strategy are becoming more limited. This strategy is most suitable in situations where a firm has distinctive competencies that local companies in foreign markets lack.

Risks and Challenges The following are some of the risks and challenges associated with an international strategy.

- Different activities in the value chain typically have different optimal locations. That is, R&D may be optimally located in a country with an abundant supply of scientists and engineers, whereas assembly may be better conducted in a low-cost location. Nike, for example, designs its shoes in the United States, but all the manufacturing is done in countries like China or Thailand. The international strategy, with its tendency to concentrate most of its activities in one location, fails to take advantage of the benefits of an optimally distributed value chain.

EXHIBIT 7.4 Strengths and Limitations of International Strategies in the Global Marketplace

Strengths	Limitations
• Leverage and diffusion of a parent firm's knowledge and core competencies. • Lower costs because of less need to tailor products and services.	• Limited ability to adapt to local markets. • Inability to take advantage of new ideas and innovations occurring in local markets.

- The lack of local responsiveness may result in the alienation of local customers. Worse still, the firm's inability to be receptive to new ideas and innovation from its foreign subsidiaries may lead to missed opportunities.

Exhibit 7.4 summarizes the strengths and limitations of international strategies in the global marketplace.

Global Strategy

As indicated in Exhibit 7.3, a firm whose emphasis is on lowering costs tends to follow a **global strategy.** Competitive strategy is centralized and controlled to a large extent by the corporate office. Since the primary emphasis is on controlling costs, the corporate office strives to achieve a strong level of coordination and integration across the various businesses.[48] Firms following a global strategy strive to offer standardized products and services as well as to locate manufacturing, R&D, and marketing activities in only a few locations.[49]

global strategy
a strategy based on firms' centralization and control by the corporate office, with the primary emphasis on controlling costs; used in industries where the pressure for local adaptation is low and the pressure for lowering costs is high.

A global strategy emphasizes economies of scale due to the standardization of products and services and the centralization of operations in a few locations. As such, one advantage may be that innovations that come about through efforts of either a business unit or the corporate office can be transferred more easily to other locations. Although costs may be lower, the firm following a global strategy may, in general, have to forgo opportunities for revenue growth since it does not invest extensive resources in adapting product offerings from one market to another.

A global strategy is most appropriate when there are strong pressures for reducing costs and comparatively weak pressures for adaptation to local markets. Economies of scale become an important consideration.[50] Advantages to increased volume may come from larger production plants or runs as well as from more efficient logistics and distribution networks. Worldwide volume is also especially important in supporting high levels of investment in research and development. As we would expect, many industries requiring high levels of R&D, such as pharmaceuticals, semiconductors, and jet aircraft, follow global strategies.

Another advantage of a global strategy is that it can enable a firm to create a standard level of quality throughout the world. Let's look at what Tom Siebel, former chairman of Siebel Systems (now part of Oracle), a developer of e-business application software, said about global standardization:

> Our customers—global companies like IBM, Zurich Financial Services, and Citicorp—expect the same high level of service and quality, and the same licensing policies, no matter where we do business with them around the world. Our human resources and legal departments help us create policies that respect local cultures and requirements worldwide, while at the same time maintaining the highest standards.[51]

Risks and Challenges There are, of course, some risks associated with a global strategy:[52]

- A firm can enjoy scale economies only by concentrating scale-sensitive resources and activities in one or few locations. Such concentration, however, becomes a "double-edged sword." For example, if a firm has only one manufacturing facility, it must export its output (e.g., components, subsystems, or finished products) to

EXHIBIT 7.5 Strengths and Limitations of Global Strategies

Strengths	Limitations
• Strong integration occurs across various businesses. • Standardization leads to higher economies of scale, which lower costs. • Creation of uniform standards of quality throughout the world is facilitated.	• Limited ability exists to adapt to local markets. • Concentration of activities may increase dependence on a single facility. • Single locations may lead to higher tariffs and transportation costs.

other markets, some of which may be a great distance from the operation. Thus, decisions about locating facilities must weigh the potential benefits from concentrating operations in a single location against the higher transportation and tariff costs that result from such concentration.

- The geographic concentration of any activity may also tend to isolate that activity from the targeted markets. Such isolation may be risky since it may hamper the facility's ability to quickly respond to changes in market conditions and needs.
- Concentrating an activity in a single location also makes the rest of the firm dependent on that location. Such dependency implies that, unless the location has world-class competencies, the firm's competitive position can be eroded if problems arise. A European Ford executive, reflecting on the firm's concentration of activities during a global integration program in the mid-1990s, lamented, "Now if you misjudge the market, you are wrong in 15 countries rather than only one."

Exhibit 7.5 summarizes the strengths and limitations of global strategies.

Multidomestic Strategy

multidomestic strategy
a strategy based on firms' differentiating their products and services to adapt to local markets; used in industries where the pressure for local adaptation is high and the pressure for lowering costs is low.

According to Exhibit 7.3, a firm whose emphasis is on differentiating its product and service offerings to adapt to local markets follows a **multidomestic strategy.**[53] Decisions evolving from a multidomestic strategy tend to be decentralized to permit the firm to tailor its products and respond rapidly to changes in demand. This enables a firm to expand its market and to charge different prices in different markets. For firms following this strategy, differences in language, culture, income levels, customer preferences, and distribution systems are only a few of the many factors that must be considered. Even in the case of relatively standardized products, at least some level of local adaptation is often necessary.

Consider, for example, the Oreo cookie.[54] Kraft Heinz has tailored the iconic cookie to better meet the tastes and preferences in different markets. For example, Kraft has created green tea Oreos in China, chocolate and peanut butter Oreos for Indonesia, and banana and dulce de leche Oreos for Argentina. Kraft has also lowered the sweetness of the cookie for China and reduced the bitterness of the cookie for India. The shape is also on the table for change. Kraft has even created wafer-stick-style Oreos.

To meet the needs of local markets, companies need to go beyond just product designs. One of the simple ways firms have worked to meet market needs is by finding appropriate names for their products. For example, in China, the names of products imbue them with strong meanings and can be significant drivers of their success. As a result, firms have been careful with how they translate their brands. For example, Reebok became *Rui bu,* which means "quick steps." Lay's snack foods became *Le shi,* which means "happy things." And Coca-Cola's Chinese name, *Ke Kou Ke Le,* translates to "tasty fun."

When companies enter foreign markets, they often face distinctly different consumer tastes. Strategy Spotlight 7.4 addresses some of the ways multinational companies such as Coca-Cola adapt their product offerings to foreign markets.

7.4 STRATEGY SPOTLIGHT

COCA-COLA DEVELOPS LOCAL DRINKS THAT TASTE NOTHING LIKE COKE

Entering foreign markets with standardized offerings can be tempting for companies with powerful global brands and well-known products. This may be particularly relevant for an iconic brand such as Coca-Cola, the sixth most valuable global brand according to a 2018 ranking released by Forbes Magazine. The potential benefits of global integration are substantial as the soft drink giant is able to leverage the Coke brand in foreign markets. In the past, Coca-Cola kept very tight control over its R&D and marketing processes to leverage its global appeal in foreign markets. More recently, however, Coca-Cola changed its international strategy.

When Coca-Cola CEO James Quincey was appointed in May 2017, he adopted elements of a multidomestic strategy to benefit from differentiating Coke's products in foreign markets. Quincey started by directing Coca-Cola's international subsidiaries to launch more local flavors. The results are nothing short of impressive. In 2017, Coca-Cola launched 500 drinks around the world, some of which are truly unique. The Indian Coke subsidiary, for instance, launched a "chunky mango" juice. Many Indians squeeze mangos and suck the pulp through a hole. The new drink, called Maaza Chunky, emulates this experience for the Indian market.

CEO Quincey hopes that the greater focus on the preferences of individual countries will introduce a new culture of entrepreneurship and risk-taking into the beverage company. Investors and analysts have long criticized Coca-Cola for betting too long on its globally well-known soft drinks and ignoring national differences in consumer tastes and health trends. As a result, international subsidiaries are now encouraged to experiment with new and innovative drink concepts. Naturally, this multidomestic focus comes with new risks. For instance, the new Maaza Chunky drink mentioned earlier must not only convince Indian consumers in terms of its taste but also requires new localized production techniques such as a modified filling process for the thick juice as well as newly designed cans.

However, Coke expects substantial benefits from the more localized approach. It allows Coca-Cola to test products in one market and then introduce the product to other foreign markets if proven successful. For instance, Coke launched "Coca-Cola Plus Coffee" in Australia before introducing a modified version with "dialed up coffee cues" in other coffee culture countries such as Turkey. Coke also experiments with novel ingredients. For instance, Coke is considering a new line of cannabis-infused beverages. While Coke is not planning to create drinks based on the psychoactive ingredient tetrahydrocannabinol (THC) in the foreseeable future, it considers new beverages that use the non-psychoactive marijuana component "cannabidiol" (CBD) to create wellness beverages. CBD is often used for medical purposes, such as easing pain and nausea. The obvious challenges with new ingredients, especially controversial ones such as cannabis, are the vastly different legal and social norms across countries, making Coke's newly found multidomestic strategy a challenging, but vital part of the soft drink giant's future.

Sources: Bellman, E., and J. Maloney. 2018. The many flavors of Coca-Cola. *Wall Street Journal*, August 24: B3; Gurdus, E. 2018. Coca-Cola CEO James Quincey talks coffee, cannabis strategy. *CNBC.com*, November 16: np; and Isidore, C. 2018. Coke could make a move into cannabis-infused drinks. *CNNMoney*, September 17: np.

Risks and Challenges As you might expect, there are some risks associated with a multidomestic strategy. Among these are the following:

- Typically, local adaptation of products and services will increase a company's cost structure. In many industries, competition is so intense that most firms can ill afford any competitive disadvantages on the dimension of cost. A key challenge of managers is to determine the trade-off between local adaptation and its cost structure. For example, cost considerations led Procter & Gamble to standardize its diaper design across all European markets. This was done despite research data indicating that Italian mothers, unlike those in other countries, preferred diapers that covered the baby's navel. Later, however, P&G recognized that this feature was critical to these mothers, so the company decided to incorporate this feature for the Italian market despite its adverse cost implications.
- At times, local adaptations, even when well intentioned, may backfire. When the American restaurant chain TGI Fridays entered the South Korean market, it purposely incorporated many local dishes, such as kimchi (hot, spicy cabbage), in its menu. This responsiveness, however, was not well received. Company analysis of the weak market acceptance indicated that Korean customers anticipated a visit to TGI Fridays as a visit to America. Thus, finding Korean dishes was inconsistent with their expectations.

EXHIBIT 7.6 Strengths and Limitations of Multidomestic Strategies

Strengths	Limitations
• Ability to adapt products and services to local market conditions. • Ability to detect potential opportunities for attractive niches in a given market, enhancing revenue.	• Decreased ability to realize cost savings through scale economies. • Greater difficulty in transferring knowledge across countries. • Possibility of leading to "overadaptation" as conditions change.

- The optimal degree of local adaptation evolves over time. In many industry segments, a variety of factors, such as the influence of global media, greater international travel, and declining income disparities across countries, may lead to increasing global standardization. On the other hand, in other industry segments, especially where the product or service can be delivered over the Internet (such as music), the need for even greater customization and local adaptation may increase over time. Firms must recalibrate the need for local adaptation on an ongoing basis; excessive adaptation extracts a price as surely as under adaptation.

Exhibit 7.6 summarizes the strengths and limitations of multidomestic strategies.

Transnational Strategy

transnational strategy
a strategy based on firms' optimizing the trade-offs associated with efficiency, local adaptation, and learning; used in industries where the pressures for both local adaptation and lowering costs are high.

A **transnational strategy** strives to optimize the trade-offs associated with efficiency, local adaptation, and learning.[55] It seeks efficiency not for its own sake but as a means to achieve global competitiveness.[56] It recognizes the importance of local responsiveness as a tool for flexibility in international operations.[57] Innovations are regarded as an outcome of a larger process of organizational learning that includes the contributions of everyone in the firm.[58] Also, a core tenet of the transnational model is that a firm's assets and capabilities are dispersed according to the most beneficial location for each activity. Thus, managers avoid the tendency to either concentrate activities in a central location (a global strategy) or disperse them across many locations to enhance adaptation (a multidomestic strategy). Peter Brabeck, former chairman of Nestlé, the giant food company, provides such a perspective:

> The closer we come to the consumer, in branding, pricing, communication, and product adaptation, the more we decentralize. The more we are dealing with production, logistics, and supply-chain management, the more centralized decision making becomes. After all, we want to leverage Nestlé's size, not be hampered by it.[59]

The Nestlé example illustrates a common approach in determining whether or not to centralize or decentralize a value-chain activity. Typically, primary activities that are "downstream" (e.g., marketing and sales, and service), or closer to the customer, tend to require more decentralization in order to adapt to local market conditions. On the other hand, primary activities that are "upstream" (e.g., logistics and operations), or further away from the customer, tend to be centralized. This is because there is less need for adapting these activities to local markets and the firm can benefit from economies of scale. Additionally, many support activities, such as information systems and procurement, tend to be centralized in order to increase the potential for economies of scale.

A central philosophy of the transnational organization is enhanced adaptation to all competitive situations as well as flexibility by capitalizing on communication and knowledge flows throughout the organization.[60] A principal characteristic is the integration of unique contributions of all units into worldwide operations. Thus, a joint innovation by headquarters and by one of the overseas units can lead potentially to the development of relatively standardized and yet flexible products and services that are suitable for multiple markets. Strategy Spotlight 7.5 discusses how Panasonic benefited from moving from a global to a transnational strategy.

7.5 STRATEGY SPOTLIGHT

PANASONIC'S CHINA EXPERIENCE SHOWS THE BENEFITS OF BEING A TRANSNATIONAL

Panasonic moved into China in the late 1980s, seeing it as a low-cost region in which to manufacture its products. Traditionally, Panasonic had used a global strategy in its operations. It designed standardized products in Japan, manufactured them in low-cost markets, and sold its products primarily in developed markets. China simply served as a manufacturing location.

This worked well until the Chinese economy started to grow and mature. As the Chinese middle class began to emerge, local competitors, such as Haier, quickly jumped in with products designed for the Chinese market and outcompeted Panasonic in the growing market. This led Panasonic to radically change its way of competing in the global market.

Panasonic embraced the need to balance global integration with local adaptation. It set up a Lifestyle Research Center in China. In this center, marketing and product development staff compiled and interpreted data on customer wants and needs. Their charge was to uncover hidden needs in the Chinese market and design products to meet those needs. At the same time, country managers emphasized the need for the center staff to design products that benefited from global integration. For example, staff members were told to regularly work with engineers in Japan to ensure that product designs used standard global parts in the Panasonic system and also leveraged technologies being developed in Japan. Over time, this built trust with the Japanese engineers, who began to discuss how to draw on their knowledge to help design products that could be sold in other markets. Thus, knowledge flowed in both directions: from Japan to China and from China to Japan and, by extension, the rest of the world. The system has worked so well in China that Panasonic has expanded its policies and built lifestyle research centers in Europe and India.

There are five key elements of Panasonic's transnational initiatives. Each allows Panasonic to manage the tension for global integration and local adaptation.

- ***Establish a dedicated unit.*** One organization should be devoted to embracing the tension. The aim of Panasonic's China Lifestyle Research Center was to both understand Chinese consumers and draw on Panasonic Japan's R&D capabilities.
- ***Create an on-the-ground mission.*** The unit's mission should state explicitly how local adaptation and cross-border integration support company strategy. The lifestyle center's mission was "data interpretation," not just data collection, to ensure that insights led to viable product proposals that leveraged Panasonic's technology assets.
- ***Develop core local staff.*** The unit should develop local staff who can engage in both localization and integration activities. At the lifestyle center, each staff member spent a year getting training and extensive coaching in fieldwork and proposal writing for products that leverage Panasonic's technology to meet local needs.
- ***Extend the reach.*** The unit must constantly push to expand its influence. The lifestyle center's leader ratcheted up communication and interaction between the center and engineers at Panasonic's headquarters to broaden the organization's scope and influence.
- ***Strengthen local authority.*** Sufficient authority should be given to overseas subsidiaries to enhance their autonomy while ensuring sound global integration. Seeing the early successes of the lifestyle center, Panasonic gave increasing authority to its Chinese operations for deeper local adaptation while also maintaining integrated working relationships between Japan and China.

Sources: Wakayama, T., Shintaku, J., and T. Amano. 2012. What Panasonic learned in China. *Harvard Business Review,* December: 109–113; and Osawa, J. 2012. Panasonic pins hopes on home appliances. *wsj.com*, March 25: np.

Risks and Challenges As with the other strategies, there are some unique risks and challenges associated with a transnational strategy:

- **The choice of a seemingly optimal location cannot guarantee that the quality and cost of factor inputs (i.e., labor, materials) will be optimal.** Managers must ensure that the relative advantage of a location is actually realized, not squandered because of weaknesses in productivity and the quality of internal operations. Ford Motor Co., for example, has benefited from having some of its manufacturing operations in Mexico. While some have argued that the benefits of lower wage rates will be partly offset by lower productivity, this does not always have to be the case. Since unemployment in Mexico is higher than in the United States, Ford can be more selective in its hiring practices for its Mexican operations. And given the lower turnover among its Mexican employees, Ford can justify a high level of investment in training and development. Thus, the net result can be not only lower wage rates but also higher productivity than in the United States.

EXHIBIT 7.7 Strengths and Limitations of Transnational Strategies

Strengths	Limitations
• Ability to attain economies of scale. • Ability to adapt to local markets. • Ability to locate activities in optimal locations. • Ability to increase knowledge flows and learning.	• Unique challenges in determining optimal locations of activities to ensure cost and quality. • Unique managerial challenges in fostering knowledge transfer.

- **Although knowledge transfer can be a key source of competitive advantage, it does not take place "automatically."** For knowledge transfer to take place from one subsidiary to another, it is important for the source of the knowledge, the target units, and the corporate headquarters to recognize the potential value of such unique know-how. Given that there can be significant geographic, linguistic, and cultural distances that typically separate subsidiaries, the potential for knowledge transfer can become very difficult to realize. Firms must create mechanisms to systematically and routinely uncover the opportunities for knowledge transfer.

Exhibit 7.7 summarizes the relative advantages and disadvantages of transnational strategies.

Global or Regional? A Second Look at Globalization

LO 7-6

Understand the difference between regional companies and truly global companies.

Thus far, we have suggested four possible strategies from which a firm must choose once it has decided to compete in the global marketplace. In recent years, many writers have asserted that the process of globalization has caused national borders to become increasingly irrelevant.[61] However, some scholars have questioned this perspective, and they have argued that it is unwise for companies to rush into full-scale globalization.[62]

Before answering questions about the extent of firms' globalization, let's try to clarify what "globalization" means. Traditionally, a firm's globalization is measured in terms of its foreign sales as a percentage of total sales. However, this measure can be misleading. For example, consider a U.S. firm that has expanded its activities into Canada. Clearly, this initiative is qualitatively different from achieving the same sales volume in a distant country such as China. Similarly, if a Malaysian firm expands into Singapore or a German firm starts selling its products in Austria, this would represent an expansion into a geographically adjacent country. Such nearby countries would often share many common characteristics in terms of language, culture, infrastructure, and customer preferences. In other words, this is more a case of regionalization than globalization.

Extensive analysis of the distribution data of sales across different countries and regions led Alan Rugman and Alain Verbeke to conclude that there is a stronger case to be made in favor of **regionalization** than globalization. According to their study, a company would have to have at least 20 percent of its sales in each of the three major economic regions–North America, Europe, and Asia–to be considered a global firm. However, they found that only 9 of the world's 500 largest firms met this standard! Even when they relaxed the criterion to 20 percent of sales each in at least two of the three regions, the number only increased to 25. *Thus, most companies are regional or, at best, biregional–not global–even today.*

regionalization
increasing international exchange of goods, services, money, people, ideas, and information; and the increasing similarity of culture, laws, rules, and norms within a region such as Europe, North America, or Asia.

In a world of instant communication, rapid transportation, and governments that are increasingly willing to open up their markets to trade and investment, why are so few firms "global"? The most obvious answer is that distance still matters. After all, it is easier to do business in a neighboring country than in a faraway country, all else being equal. Distance, in the final analysis, may be viewed as a concept with many dimensions, not just a measure of geographic distance. For example, both Canada and Mexico are the same distance from the United States. However, U.S. companies find it easier to expand operations into Canada than into Mexico. Why? Canada and the United States share many commonalities in terms of language, culture, economic development, legal and political systems, and infrastructure development. Thus, if we view distance as having many dimensions, the United States and Canada are very close, whereas there is greater distance between the United States and Mexico. Similarly, when we look at what we might call the "true" distance between the United States and China, the effects of geographic distance are multiplied by distance in terms of culture, language, religion, and legal and political systems between the two countries. On the other hand, although the United States and Australia are geographically distant, the "true" distance is somewhat less when one considers distance along the other dimensions.

Another reason for regional expansion is the rise of **trading blocs** and free trade zones. A number of regional agreements have been created that facilitate the growth of business within these regions by easing trade restrictions and taxes and tariffs. These have included the European Union (EU), North American Free Trade Agreement (NAFTA), Association of Southeast Asian Nations (ASEAN), and MERCOSUR (a South American trading block).

trading blocs
groups of countries agreeing to increase trade between them by lowering trade barriers.

Regional economic integration has progressed at a faster pace than global economic integration, and the trade and investment patterns of the largest companies reflect this reality. After all, regions represent the outcomes of centuries of political and cultural history that results in not only commonalities but also mutual affinity. For example, stretching from Algeria and Morocco in the West to Oman and Yemen in the East, more than 30 countries share the Arabic language and the Muslim religion, making these countries a natural regional bloc. Similarly, the countries of South and Central America share the Spanish language (except Brazil), the Catholic religion, and a history of Spanish colonialism. No wonder firms find it easier and less risky to expand within their region than to other regions.

ENTRY MODES OF INTERNATIONAL EXPANSION

LO 7-7

Identify the four basic types of entry strategies and the relative benefits and risks associated with each of them.

A firm has many options available to it when it decides to expand into international markets. Given the challenges associated with such entry, many firms first start on a small scale and then increase their level of investment and risk as they gain greater experience with the overseas market in question.[63]

Exhibit 7.8 illustrates a wide variety of modes of foreign entry, including exporting, licensing, franchising, joint ventures, strategic alliances, and wholly owned subsidiaries.[64] As the exhibit indicates, the various types of entry form a continuum ranging from exporting (low

EXHIBIT 7.8 Entry Modes for International Expansion

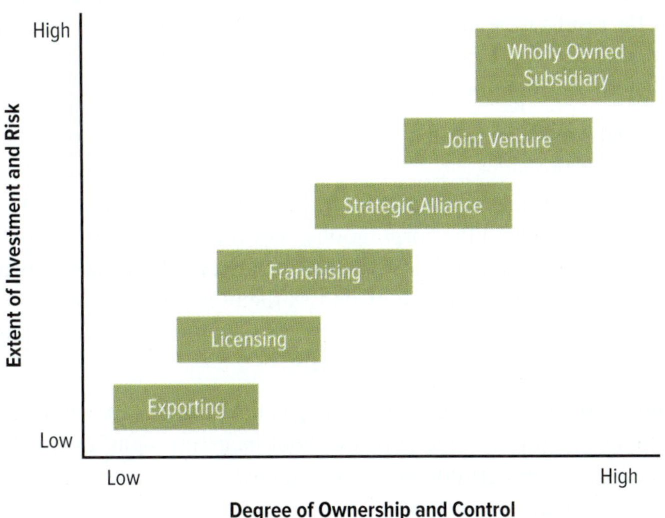

investment and risk, low control) to a wholly owned subsidiary (high investment and risk, high control).[65]

There can be frustrations and setbacks as a firm evolves its international entry strategy from exporting to more expensive types, including wholly owned subsidiaries. For example, according to the CEO of a large U.S. specialty chemical company:

> In the end, we always do a better job with our own subsidiaries; sales improve, and we have greater control over the business. But we still need local distributors for entry, and we are still searching for strategies to get us through the transitions without battles over control and performance.[66]

Exporting

exporting
producing goods in one country to sell to residents of another country.

Exporting consists of producing goods in one country to sell in another.[67] This entry strategy enables a firm to invest the least amount of resources in terms of its product, its organization, and its overall corporate strategy. Many host countries dislike this entry strategy because it provides less local employment than other modes of entry.[68]

Multinationals often stumble onto a stepwise strategy for penetrating markets, beginning with the exporting of products. This often results in a series of unplanned actions to increase sales revenues. As the pattern recurs with entries into subsequent markets, this approach, named a "beachhead strategy," often becomes official policy.[69]

Benefits Such an approach definitely has its advantages. After all, firms start from scratch in sales and distribution when they enter new markets. Because many foreign markets are nationally regulated and dominated by networks of local intermediaries, firms need to partner with local distributors to benefit from their valuable expertise and knowledge of their own markets. Multinationals, after all, recognize that they cannot master local business practices, meet regulatory requirements, hire and manage local personnel, or gain access to potential customers without some form of local partnership.

Multinationals also want to minimize their own risk. They do this by hiring local distributors and investing very little in the undertaking. In essence, the firm gives up control of strategic marketing decisions to the local partners–much more control than they would be willing to give up in their home market.

Risks and Limitations Exporting is a relatively inexpensive way to enter foreign markets. However, it can still have significant downsides. Most centrally, the ability to tailor the firm's products to meet local market needs is typically very limited. In a study of 250 instances in which multinational firms used local distributors to implement their exporting entry strategy, the results were dismal. In the vast majority of the cases, the distributors were bought (to increase control) by the multinational firm or were fired. In contrast, successful distributors shared two common characteristics:

- They carried product lines that complemented, rather than competed with, the multinational's products.
- They behaved as if they were business partners with the multinationals. They shared market information with the corporations, they initiated projects with distributors in neighboring countries, and they suggested initiatives in their own or nearby markets. Additionally, these distributors took on risk themselves by investing in areas such as training, information systems, and advertising and promotion in order to increase the business of their multinational partners.

The key point is the importance of developing collaborative, win-win relationships.

To ensure more control over operations without incurring significant risks, many firms have used licensing and franchising as a mode of entry. Let's now discuss these and their relative advantages and disadvantages.

Licensing and Franchising

Licensing and franchising are both forms of contractual arrangements. **Licensing** enables a company to receive a royalty or fee in exchange for the right to use its trademark, patent, trade secret, or other valuable item of intellectual property.[70]

Franchising contracts generally include a broader range of factors in an operation and have a longer time period during which the agreement is in effect. Franchising remains a primary form of American business. According to a survey, more than 400 U.S. franchisers have international exposure.[71] This is greater than the combined totals of the next four largest franchiser home countries–France, the United Kingdom, Mexico, and Austria.

licensing
a contractual arrangement in which a company receives a royalty or fee in exchange for the right to use its trademark, patent, trade secret, or other valuable intellectual property.

franchising
a contractual arrangement in which a company receives a royalty or fee in exchange for the right to use its intellectual property; franchising usually involves a longer time period than licensing and includes other factors, such as monitoring of operations, training, and advertising.

Benefits In international markets, an advantage of licensing is that the firm granting a license incurs little risk, since it does not have to invest any significant resources into the country itself. In turn, the licensee (the firm receiving the license) gains access to the trademark, patent, and so on, and is able to potentially create competitive advantages. In many cases, the country also benefits from the product being manufactured locally. For example, Yoplait yogurt is licensed by General Mills from Sodima, a French cooperative, for sale in the United States. The logos of college and professional athletic teams in the United States are another source of trademarks that generate significant royalty income domestically and internationally.

Franchising has the advantage of limiting the risk exposure that a firm has in overseas markets. At the same time, the firm is able to expand the revenue base of the company.

Risks and Limitations The licensor gives up control of its product and forgoes potential revenues and profits. Furthermore, the licensee may eventually become so familiar with the patent and trade secrets that it may become a competitor; that is, the licensee may make some modifications to the product and manufacture and sell it independently of the licensor without having to pay a royalty fee. This potential situation is aggravated in countries that have relatively weak laws to protect intellectual property. Additionally, if the licensee selected by the multinational firm turns out to be a poor choice, the brand name and reputation of the product may be tarnished.[72]

With franchising, the multinational firm receives only a portion of the revenues, in the form of franchise fees. Had the firm set up the operation itself (e.g., a restaurant through direct investment), it would have had the entire revenue to itself.

Companies often desire a closer collaboration with other firms in order to increase revenue, reduce costs, and enhance their learning–often through the diffusion of technology. To achieve such objectives, they enter into strategic alliances or joint ventures, two entry modes we will discuss next.

Strategic Alliances and Joint Ventures

Joint ventures and strategic alliances have recently become increasingly popular.[73] These two forms of partnership differ in that joint ventures entail the creation of a third-party legal entity, whereas strategic alliances do not. In addition, strategic alliances generally focus on initiatives that are smaller in scope than joint ventures.[74]

Benefits As we discussed in Chapter 6, these strategies have been effective in helping firms increase revenues and reduce costs as well as enhance learning and diffuse technologies.[75] These partnerships enable firms to share the risks as well as the potential revenues and profits. Also, by gaining exposure to new sources of knowledge and technologies, such partnerships can help firms develop core competencies that can lead to competitive advantages in the marketplace.[76] Finally, entering into partnerships with host-country firms can provide very useful information on local market tastes, competitive conditions, legal matters, and cultural nuances.[77]

Risks and Limitations Managers must be aware of the risks associated with strategic alliances and joint ventures and how they can be minimized.[78] First, there needs to be a clearly defined strategy that is strongly supported by the organizations that are party to the partnership. Otherwise, the firms may work at cross-purposes and not achieve any of their goals. Second, and closely allied to the first issue, there must be a clear understanding of capabilities and resources that will be central to the partnership. Without such clarification, there will be fewer opportunities for learning and developing competencies that could lead to competitive advantages. Third, trust is a vital element. Phasing in the relationship between alliance partners permits them to get to know each other better and develop trust. Without trust, one party may take advantage of the other by, for example, withholding its fair share of resources and gaining access to privileged information through unethical (or illegal) means. Fourth, cultural issues that can potentially lead to conflict and dysfunctional behaviors need to be addressed. An organization's culture is the set of values, beliefs, and attitudes that influence the behavior and goals of its employees.[79] Thus, recognizing cultural differences, as well as striving to develop elements of a "common culture" for the partnership, is vital. Without a unifying culture, it will become difficult to combine and leverage resources that are increasingly important in knowledge-intensive organizations (discussed in Chapter 4).[80]

Finally, the success of a firm's alliance should not be left to chance.[81] To improve their odds of success, many companies have carefully documented alliance-management knowledge by creating guidelines and manuals to help them manage specific aspects of the entire alliance life cycle (e.g., partner selection and alliance negotiation and contracting). For example, Hewlett-Packard developed 60 different tools and templates, which it placed in a 300-page manual for guiding decision making. The manual included such tools as a template for making the business case for an alliance, a partner evaluation form, a negotiation template outlining the roles and responsibilities of different departments, a list of the ways to measure alliance performance, and an alliance termination checklist.

When a firm desires the highest level of control, it develops wholly owned subsidiaries. Although wholly owned subsidiaries can generate the greatest returns, they also have the highest levels of investment and risk. We will now discuss them.

Wholly Owned Subsidiaries

wholly owned subsidiary
a business in which a multinational company owns 100 percent of the stock.

A **wholly owned subsidiary** is a business in which a multinational company owns 100 percent of the stock. Two ways a firm can establish a wholly owned subsidiary are to (1) acquire an existing company in the home country or (2) develop a totally new operation (often referred to as a "greenfield venture").

Benefits Establishing a wholly owned subsidiary is the most expensive and risky of the various entry modes. However, it can also yield the highest returns. In addition, it provides the multinational company with the greatest degree of control of all activities, including manufacturing, marketing, distribution, and technology development.[82]

Wholly owned subsidiaries are most appropriate where a firm already has the appropriate knowledge and capabilities that it can leverage rather easily through multiple locations. Examples range from restaurants to semiconductor manufacturers. To lower costs, for example, Intel Corporation builds semiconductor plants throughout the world—all of which use virtually the same blueprint. Knowledge can be further leveraged by hiring managers and professionals from the firm's home country, often through hiring talent from competitors.

Risks and Limitations As noted, wholly owned subsidiaries are typically the most expensive and risky entry mode. With franchising, joint ventures, or strategic alliances, the risk is shared with the firm's partners. With wholly owned subsidiaries, the entire risk is assumed by the parent company. The risks associated with doing business in a new country (e.g., political, cultural, and legal) can be lessened by hiring local talent.

For example, Wendy's avoided committing two blunders in Germany by hiring locals to its advertising staff.[83] In one case, the firm wanted to promote its "old-fashioned" qualities. However, a literal translation would have resulted in the company promoting itself as "outdated." In another situation, Wendy's wanted to emphasize that its hamburgers could be prepared 256 ways. The problem? The German word that Wendy's wanted to use for "ways" usually meant "highways" or "roads." Although such errors may sometimes be entertaining to the public, it is certainly preferable to catch these mistakes before they confuse the consumer or embarrass the company.

We have addressed entry strategies as a progression from exporting to the creation of wholly owned subsidiaries. However, we must point out that many firms do not follow such an evolutionary approach.

ISSUE FOR DEBATE

Should Airbus Invest For Political Favors?

Airbus has become a prime example of a sprawling multinational corporation. Founded in 1970 as a consortium consolidating the European aerospace industry, the company quickly became a world-leading commercial aircraft manufacturer competing eye-to-eye with its U.S. counterpart Boeing. Airbus's operations are spread across Europe, culminating in a complex web of 14 factories in a half-dozen European countries. In response to this unusual corporate structure, a company official noted, "If we had started with a blank sheet of paper, this is not how the company would have developed". This begs the question: Why does Airbus spread its production across so many countries?

Airbus's unusual corporate structure is the result of political interference. As a result, Airbus did not locate operations in countries that would maximize economic efficiency as a typical private sector company would, but in countries that would maximize political support. While political influence in corporations is a controversial topic, some positive aspects may result from it. Some even argue that Airbus's political roots are a core reason for its success.

When Airbus was formed by politicians from several European countries, they recognized that consolidating the European aerospace industry was the only way to compete against Boeing, which had a formidable first-mover advantage in the global aerospace sector. Political influence benefits Airbus in multiple ways, such as preferred access to bank loans and technology transfers from state-run universities and other European corporations. Airbus has also learned how to navigate complex political decision making processes, a skill that is useful when negotiating airplane orders with state-run airlines. In addition, Airbus built hard-to-replicate logistics capabilities emanating from the enormous challenges associated with transporting airplane components between dispersed production locations. For instance, Airbus developed the largest cargo airplanes in the world to facilitate the movement of airplane parts across its European manufacturing operations. This experience with large cargo aircrafts was instrumental in the development of the largest passenger aircraft in the world: the Airbus A380.

Naturally, political favors in exchange for influence may also pose challenges, especially when the political influence emanates from non-European governments. Not surprisingly, Airbus feels mounting pressure to set up production capacity outside of Europe because only one out of five Airbus airplane orders comes from Europe. One prominent and increasingly important customer for Airbus is China. Airbus has responded with its usual playbook and built a factory in China to garner political support for future airplane orders. However, instead of pacifying political demands, the Chinese government has ratcheted up its demands. In early 2018, China's aviation regulator delayed the airworthiness certification for several Airbus models, causing planes to pile up at Airbus factories in Europe. How did Airbus respond? It announced that it would increase the final assembly capacity of Airbus airplanes in its Chinese factory by 50 percent by 2020, bowing to political pressure from China.

Building production capacity in locations outside of Europe may also threaten intellectual property rights protection, an issue typically raised when investing in China. The Chinese government often forces foreign companies to share knowledge and transfer technologies to its State Owned Enterprises (SOEs). Airbus ultimately believes that some technology transfer is inevitable, but it wants to maintain its technology leadership for many years to come. For this purpose, Airbus does not partner directly with China's state-run aerospace company Commercial Aircraft Corporation of China (Comac) to minimize the risks of unwanted technology transfers to an emerging competitor in the global aerospace industry. However, Airbus does manufacturer airplanes in China and works with many Chinese suppliers. Merely investing and operating in China may lead to knowledge transfers that can help the Communist Party's goal of supplying 10 percent of China's airplane market with Chinese planes by 2025.

Discussion Questions

1. Should Airbus expand its investments and partnerships in China given the increasing competition from Chinese companies?
2. Can you think of other areas in which Airbus can leverage its expertise in navigating political forces?

Sources: Matlack, C., Katz, B., and A. Nussbaum. 2018. Airbus outgrows its European home. *Bloomberg BusinessWeek*, February 6: np; Gordon, S. 2014. Airbus–the European model. *Financial Times*, May 23: np; Ostrower, J. 2018. Airbus built a lot of planes for China last year–but can't deliver them. *CNNMoney*, January 12: np; Scheuer, S. 2016. Technology transfer: Airbus flying high in China–for now. *Handelsblatt*, March 3: np; Moss, T. 2017. China seeks foothold in aviation with flight of its first big passenger jet. *Wall Street Journal*, May 5: np.

Reflecting on Career Implications . . .

This chapter discusses the challenges and opportunities of international markets. The following issues ask students to consider how the globalization of business can create both opportunities and risks for their careers.

- **International Strategy:** Be aware of your organization's international strategy. What percentage of the total firm activity is international? What skills are needed to enhance your company's international efforts? How can you get more involved in your organization's international strategy? For your career, what conditions in your home country might cause you to seek a career abroad?
- **Outsourcing and Offshoring:** More and more organizations have resorted to outsourcing and offshoring in recent years. To what extent has your firm engaged in either? What activities in your organization can/should be outsourced or offshored? Be aware that you are competing in the global marketplace for employment and professional advancement. What is the likelihood that your own job may be outsourced or offshored? In what ways can you enhance your talents, skills, and competencies to reduce the odds that your job may be offshored or outsourced?
- **International Career Opportunities:** Taking on overseas assignments in other countries can often provide a career boost. There are a number of ways in which you can improve your odds of being selected for an overseas assignment. Studying abroad for a semester or doing an overseas internship are two obvious strategies. Learning a foreign language can also greatly help. Anticipate how such opportunities will advance your short- and long-term career aspirations.
- **Management Risks:** Explore ways in which you can develop cultural sensitivity. Interacting with people from other cultures, foreign travel, reading about foreign countries, watching foreign movies, and similar activities can increase your cultural sensitivity. Identify ways in which your perceptions and behaviors have changed as a result of increased cultural sensitivity.

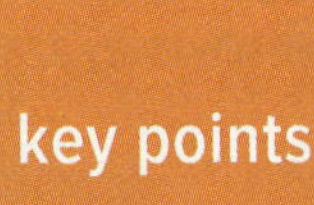

key points

LO 7-1 Understand the importance of international expansion as a viable diversification strategy.

- The trade among nations has increased dramatically in recent years. Specifically the rise of globalization—meaning the rise of market capitalism around the world—has created opportunities and threats for multinational corporations.

LO 7-2 Identify the sources of national advantage; that is, why an industry in a given country is more (or less) successful than the same industry in another country.

- The diamond of national advantage helps determine the sources of national competitive advantages along four attributes of nations.
- Factor endowments are the nation's position in factors of production, such as skilled labor or infrastructure, necessary to compete in a given industry.
- Demand conditions capture the nature of home-market demand for the industry's product or service.
- Related and supporting industries describe the presence or absence in the nation of supplier industries and other related industries that are internationally competitive.
- Firm strategy, structure, and rivalry capture the conditions in the nation governing how companies are created, organized, and managed, as well as the nature of domestic rivalry.

LO 7-3 Explain the motivations (or benefits) and the risks associated with international expansion, including the emerging trend for greater offshoring and outsourcing activity.

- Key motivations for international expansion include increasing the size of the potential market for products and services, achieving economies of scale, extending the life cycle of products, and optimizing the location for activities in the value chain.
- Key risks include political and economic risks, currency risks, and management risks.
- Managers should also consider the threats and opportunities associated with offshoring and outsourcing.

LO 7-4 Explain the two opposing forces—cost reduction and adaptation to local markets—that firms face when entering international markets.

- Firms can go about attaining competitive advantage in global markets by considering two opposing forces—cost reduction and adaptation to local markets.
- The relative importance of these two factors should guide which international strategies to select: international, global, multidomestic, or transnational.

LO 7-5 Identify the advantages and disadvantages associated with each of the four basic strategies: international, global, multidomestic, and transnational.

- Managers responsible for international expansion should consider the benefits and risks associated with each type of international strategy.

LO 7-6 Understand the difference between regional companies and truly global companies.

- Truly global companies have a significant presence in each major economic region around the world. However, many multinational companies follow a regionalization strategy by investing in countries that share characteristics in terms of language, culture, and customer preferences.
- Regionalization is often facilitated by trading blocs, defined as groups of countries that agree to trade among themselves by lowering trade barriers.

LO 7-7 Identify the four basic types of entry strategies and the relative benefits and risks associated with each of them.

- Managers may choose among four types of entry strategies when entering international markets: exporting, licensing/franchising, strategic alliances/joint ventures, and wholly owned subsidiaries.
- The key trade-off in each of these strategies is the level of investment or risk versus the level of control. Managers should carefully examine the relative benefits and risks associated with each of these market entry strategies.

SUMMARY REVIEW QUESTIONS

1. What are some of the advantages and disadvantages associated with a firm's expansion into international markets?
2. What are the four factors described in Porter's diamond of national advantage? How do the four factors explain why some industries in a given country are more successful than others?
3. Explain the two opposing forces—cost reduction and adaptation to local markets—that firms must deal with when they go global.
4. There are four basic strategies—international, global, multidomestic, and transnational. What are the advantages and disadvantages associated with each?

5. What is the basis of Alan Rugman's argument that most multinationals are still more regional than global? What factors inhibit firms from becoming truly global?
6. Describe the basic entry strategies that firms have available when they enter international markets. What are the relative advantages and disadvantages of each?

key terms

globalization 204
diamond of national advantage 205
factor endowments (national advantage) 205
demand conditions (national advantage) 205
related and supporting industries (national advantage) 205
firm strategy, structure, and rivalry (national advantage) 205
multinational firms 208
arbitrage opportunities 208
reverse innovation 210
political risk 211
rule of law 212
economic risk 213
counterfeiting 213
currency risk 214
management risk 214
outsourcing 215
offshoring 215
international strategy 218
global strategy 219
multidomestic strategy 220
transnational strategy 222
regionalization 224
trading blocs 225
exporting 226
licensing 227
franchising 227
wholly owned subsidiary 228

EXPERIENTIAL EXERCISES AND APPLICATION QUESTIONS

1. In this chapter, we discussed how several companies such as Ford (Learning from Mistakes opening incident) and Coca-Cola (Strategy Spotlight 7.4) adopted a localized international strategy. Interview a manager in an organization with foreign market exposure and ask the following questions: (1) What are the main benefits of localizing products or services in your industry?, (2) How do you manage the resulting complexity of localizing products or services?, and (3) Do you find it necessary to localize other value chain activities (such as HR management)? Then ask yourself this question: Do the responses indicate that the organization is guided by established industry best practices or systematic strategic analysis of the internal and external environment?
2. The United States is considered a world leader in the motion picture industry. Using Porter's diamond framework for national competitiveness, explain the success of this industry. (Fill in the following chart.)

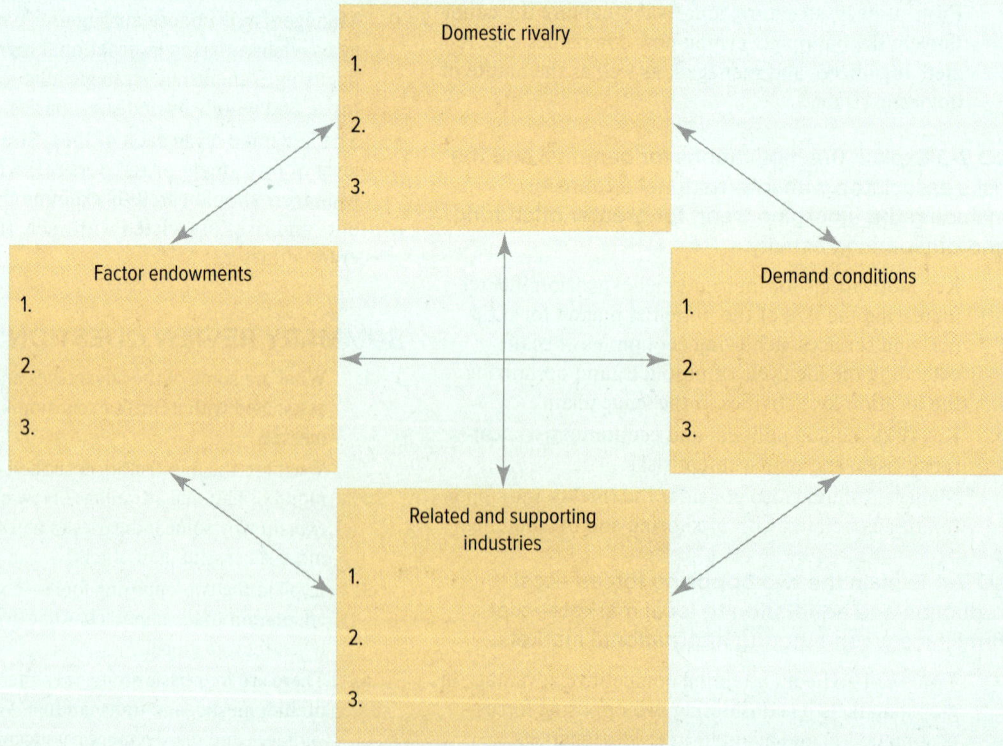

3. The Internet has lowered the entry barriers for smaller firms that wish to diversify into international markets. Why is this so? Provide an example.
4. Many firms fail when they enter into strategic alliances with firms that link up with companies based in other countries. What are some reasons for this failure? Provide an example.
5. Many large U.S.-based management consulting companies such as McKinsey and Company and the BCG Group have been very successful in the international marketplace. How can Porter's diamond explain their success?

ETHICS QUESTIONS

1. Over the past few decades, many American firms have relocated most or all of their operations from the United States to countries such as Mexico and China that pay lower wages. What are some of the ethical issues that such actions may raise?
2. Business practices and customs vary throughout the world. What are some of the ethical issues concerning payments that must be made in a foreign country to obtain business opportunities?

REFERENCES

1. For a discussion on globalization by one of international business's most respected authors, read Ohmae, K. 2005. *The next global stage: Challenges and opportunities in our borderless world.* Philadelphia: Wharton School.
2. Our discussion of globalization draws upon Engardio, P. & Belton, C. 2000. Global capitalism: Can it be made to work better? *BusinessWeek,* November 6: 72-98.
3. Sellers, p. 2005. Blowing in the wind. *Fortune,* July 25: 63.
4. Rivera, J. 2014. Gartner says sales of smartphones grew 20 percent in third quarter of 2014. *gartner.com,* December 15: np.
5. Anonymous. 2016. Why giants thrive. *The Economist.* September 17: 5-7.
6. Some insights into how winners are evolving in emerging markets are addressed in Ghemawat, P. & Hout, T. 2008. Tomorrow's global giants: Not the usual suspects. *Harvard Business Review,* 66(11): 80-88.
7. For another interesting discussion on a country perspective, refer to Makino, S. 1999. MITI Minister Kaora Yosano on reviving Japan's competitive advantages. *Academy of Management Executive,* 13(4): 8-28.
8. The following discussion draws heavily upon Porter, M. E. 1990. The competitive advantage of nations. *Harvard Business Review,* March-April: 73-93.
9. Landes, D. S. 1998. *The wealth and poverty of nations.* New York: W. W. Norton.
10. A study that investigates the relationship between international diversification and firm performance is Lu, J. W. & Beamish, P. W. 2004. International diversification and firm performance: The s-curve hypothesis. *Academy of Management Journal,* 47(4): 598-609.
11. Part of our discussion of the motivations and risks of international expansion draws upon Gregg, F. M. 1999. International strategy. In Helms, M. M. (Ed.), *Encyclopedia of management:* 434-438. Detroit: Gale Group.
12. Anthony, S. 2012. Singapore sessions. *Harvard Business Review,* 90(4): np.
13. Eyring, M. J., Johnson, M. W., & Nair, H. 2011. New business models in emerging markets. *Harvard Business Review,* 89 (1/2): 88-98.
14. Cieply, M. & Barnes, B. 2010. After rants, skepticism over Gibson bankability grows in non-U.S. markets. *International Herald Tribune,* July 23: 1.
15. Glazer, E. 2012. P&G unit bids goodbye to Cincinnati, hello to Asia. *wsj.com,* May 10: np.
16. This discussion draws upon Gupta, A. K. & Govindarajan, V. 2001. Converting global presence into global competitive advantage. *Academy of Management Executive,* 15(2): 45-56.
17. Stross, R. E. 1997. Mr. Gates builds his brain trust. *Fortune,* December 8: 84-98.
18. Anonymous. 2016. Why giants thrive. *The Economist.* September 17: 5-7.
19. For a good summary of the benefits and risks of international expansion, refer to Bartlett, C. A. & Ghoshal, S. 1987. Managing across borders: New strategic responses. *Sloan Management Review,* 28(5): 45-53; and Brown, R. H. 1994. *Competing to win in a global economy.* Washington, DC: U.S. Department of Commerce.
20. Capron, L. & Bertrand, O. 2014. Going abroad in search of higher productivity at home. *Harvard Business Review,* 92(6): 26.
21. For an interesting insight into rivalry in global markets, refer to MacMillan, I. C., van Putten, A. B., & McGrath, R. G. 2003. Global gamesmanship. *Harvard Business Review,* 81(5): 62-73.
22. It is important for firms to spread their foreign operations and outsourcing relationships with a broad, well-balanced mix of regions and countries to reduce risk and increase potential reward. For example, refer to Vestring, T., Rouse, T., & Reinert, U. 2005. Hedge your offshoring bets. *MIT Sloan Management Review,* 46(3): 27-29.
23. An interesting discussion of risks faced by Lukoil, Russia's largest oil firm, is in Gimbel, B. 2009. Russia's king of crude. *Fortune,* February 2: 88-92.
24. For a discussion of some of the challenges associated with government corruption regarding entry strategies in foreign markets, read Rodriguez, P., Uhlenbruck, K., & Eden, L. 2005. Government corruption and entry strategies of multinationals. *Academy of Management Review,* 30(2): 383-396.
25. For a discussion of the political risks in China for United States companies, refer to Garten, J. E. 1998. Opening the doors for business in China. *Harvard Business Review,* 76(3): 167-175.
26. Insights on how forensic economics can be used to investigate crimes and wrongdoing are in Fisman, R. 2009. The rise of forensic economics. *Harvard Business Review,* 87(2): 26.
27. Iosebashvili, I. 2012. Renault-Nissan buy into Russia's aged auto giant. *wsj.com,* May 3: np.

28. Ferguson, N. 2013. Is the business of America still business? *Harvard Business Review,* 91(6): 40.

29. For an interesting perspective on the relationship between diversification and the development of a nation's institutional environment, read Chakrabarti, A., Singh, K., & Mahmood, I. 2007. Diversification and performance: Evidence from East Asian firms. *Strategic Management Journal,* 28(2): 101-120.

30. A study looking into corruption and foreign direct investment is Brouthers, L. E., Gao, Y., & McNicol, J. P. 2008. *Strategic Management Journal,* 29(6): 673-680.

31. Gikkas, N. S. 1996. International licensing of intellectual property: The promise and the peril. *Journal of Technology Law & Policy,* 1(1): 1-26.

32. Hargreaves, S. 2012. Counterfeit goods becoming more dangerous. *cnnmoney.com,* September 27: np.

33. Sandler, N. 2008. Israel: Attack of the super-shekel.*Bloomberg Businessweek,* February 14: 38.

34. For an excellent theoretical discussion of how cultural factors can affect knowledge transfer across national boundaries, refer to Bhagat, R. S., Kedia, B. L., Harveston, P. D., & Triandis, H. C. 2002. Cultural variations in the cross-border transfer of organizational knowledge: An integrative framework. *Academy of Management Review,* 27(2): 204-221.

35. An interesting discussion on how local companies compete effectively with large multinationals is in Bhatacharya, A. K. & Michael, D. C. 2008. *Harvard Business Review,* 66(3): 84-95.

36. To gain insights on the role of national and regional cultures on knowledge management models and frameworks, read Pauleen, D. J. & Murphy, p. 2005. In praise of cultural bias. *MIT Sloan Management Review,* 46(2): 21-22.

37. Berkowitz, E. N. 2000. *Marketing* (6th ed.). New York: McGraw-Hill.

38. World Trade Organization. *Annual Report 1998.* Geneva: World Trade Organization.

39. Lei, D. 2005. Outsourcing. In Hitt, M. A. & Ireland, R. D. (Eds.), *The Blackwell encyclopedia of management,* Entrepreneurship: 196-199. Malden, MA: Blackwell.

40. Future trends in offshoring are addressed in Manning, S., Massini, S., & Lewin, A. Y. 2008. A dynamic perspective on next-generation offshoring: The global sourcing of science and engineering talent. *Academy of Management Perspectives,* 22(3): 35-54.

41. An interesting perspective on the controversial issue regarding the offshoring of airplane maintenance is in Smith, G. & Bachman, J. 2008. Flying in for a tune-up overseas. *BusinessWeek,* April 21: 26-27.

42. The discussion draws from Colvin, J. 2004. Think your job can't be sent to India? Just watch. *Fortune,* December 13: 80; Schwartz, N. D. 2004. Down and out in white collar America. *Fortune,* June 23: 321-325; and Hagel, J. 2004. Outsourcing is not just about cost cutting. *The Wall Street Journal,* March 18: A3.

43. Porter, M. & Rivkin, J. 2012 Choosing the United States. *Harvard Business Review,* 90(3): 80-93; Bussey, J. 2012. U.S. manufacturing, defying naysayers. *wsj.com,* April 19: np; and Jean, S. & Alcott, K. 2013. Manufacturing jobs have slid steadily as work has moved offshore. *Dallas Morning News,* January 14: 1D.

44. Wong, C. 2014. As China's economy slows, so too does growth in workers' wages. *blogs.wsj.com,* December 17: np.

45. Levitt, T. 1983. The globalization of markets. *Harvard Business Review,* 61(3): 92-102.

46. Our discussion of these assumptions draws upon Douglas, S. P. & Wind, Y. 1987. The myth of globalization. *Columbia Journal of World Business,* Winter: 19-29.

47. Ghoshal, S. 1987. Global strategy: An organizing framework. *Strategic Management Journal,* 8: 425-440.

48. For insights on global branding, refer to Aaker, D. A. & Joachimsthaler, E. 1999. The lure of global branding. *Harvard Business Review,* 77(6): 137-146.

49. Dawar, N. & Frost, T. 1999. Competing with Giants: Survival Strategies for Local Companies in Emerging Markets. *Harvard Business Review,* 77(3): 119-129.

50. Hout, T., Porter, M. E., & Rudden, E. 1982. How global companies win out. *Harvard Business Review,* 60(5): 98-107.

51. Fryer, B. 2001. Tom Siebel of Siebel Systems: High tech the old-fashioned way. *Harvard Business Review,* 79(3): 118-130.

52. The risks that are discussed for the global, multidomestic, and transnational strategies draw upon Gupta & Govindarajan, op. cit.

53. A discussion on how McDonald's adapts its products to overseas markets is in Gumbel, p. 2008. Big Mac's local flavor. *Fortune,* May 5: 115-121.

54. Einhorn, B. & Winter, C. 2012. Want some milk with your green tea Oreos? *Bloomberg Businessweek,* May 7: 25-26; Khosla, S. & Sawhney, M. 2012. Blank checks: Unleashing the potential of people and business. *Strategy-Business.com,* Autumn: np; and In China, brands more than symbolic. 2012. *Dallas Morning News,* November 27: 3D.

55. Prahalad, C. K. & Doz, Y. L. 1987. *The multinational mission: Balancing local demands and global vision.* New York: Free Press.

56. For an insightful discussion on knowledge flows in multinational corporations, refer to Yang, Q., Mudambi, R., & Meyer, K. E. 2008. Conventional and reverse knowledge flows in multinational corporations. *Journal of Management,* 34(5): 882-902.

57. Kidd, J. B. & Teramoto, Y. 1995. The learning organization: The case of Japanese RHQs in Europe. *Management International Review,* 35 (Special Issue): 39-56.

58. Gupta, A. K. & Govindarajan, V. 2000. Knowledge flows within multinational corporations. *Strategic Management Journal,* 21(4): 473-496.

59. Wetlaufer, S. 2001. The business case against revolution: An interview with Nestle's Peter Brabeck. *Harvard Business Review,* 79(2): 112-121.

60. Nobel, R. & Birkinshaw, J. 1998. Innovation in multinational corporations: Control and communication patterns in international R&D operations. *Strategic Management Journal,* 19(5): 461-478.

61. Chan, C. M., Makino, S., & Isobe, T. 2010. Does subnational region matter? Foreign affiliate performance in the United States and China. *Strategic Management Journal,* 31(11): 1226-1243.

62. This section draws upon Ghemawat, p. 2005. Regional strategies for global leadership. *Harvard Business Review,* 84(12): 98-108; Ghemawat, p. 2006. Apocalypse now? *Harvard Business Review,* 84(12): 32; Ghemawat, p. 2001. Distance still matters: The hard reality of global expansion. *Harvard Business Review,* 79(8): 137-147; Peng, M. W. 2006. *Global strategy:* 387. Mason, OH: Thomson South-Western; and Rugman, A. M. & Verbeke, A. 2004. A perspective on regional and global strategies of multinational enterprises. *Journal of International Business Studies,* 35: 3-18.

63. For a rigorous analysis of performance implications of entry strategies, refer to Zahra, S. A., Ireland, R. D., & Hitt, M. A. 2000. International expansion by new

venture firms: International diversity, modes of entry, technological learning, and performance. *Academy of Management Journal,* 43(6): 925–950.

64. Li, J. T. 1995. Foreign entry and survival: The effects of strategic choices on performance in international markets. *Strategic Management Journal,* 16: 333–351.
65. For a discussion of how home-country environments can affect diversification strategies, refer to Wan, W. P. & Hoskisson, R. E. 2003. Home country environments, corporate diversification strategies, and firm performance. *Academy of Management Journal,* 46(1): 27–45.
66. Arnold, D. 2000. Seven rules of international distribution. *Harvard Business Review,* 78(6): 131–137.
67. Sharma, A. 1998. Mode of entry and ex-post performance. *Strategic Management Journal,* 19(9): 879–900.
68. This section draws upon Arnold, op. cit., pp. 131–137; and Berkowitz, op. cit.
69. Salomon, R. & Jin, B. 2010. Do leading or lagging firms learn more from exporting? *Strategic Management Journal,* 31(6): 1088–1113.
70. Kline, D. 2003. Strategic licensing. *MIT Sloan Management Review,* 44(3): 89–93.
71. Martin, J. 1999. Franchising in the Middle East. *Management Review,* June: 38–42.
72. Arnold, op. cit.; and Berkowitz, op. cit.
73. An in-depth case study of alliance dynamics is found in Faems, D., Janssens, M., Madhok, A., & Van Looy, B. 2008. Toward an integrative perspective on alliance governance: Connecting contract design, trust dynamics, and contract application. *Academy of Management Journal,* 51(6): 1053–1078.
74. Knowledge transfer in international joint ventures is addressed in Inkpen, A. 2008. Knowledge transfer and international joint ventures. *Strategic Management Journal,* 29(4): 447–453.
75. Wen, S. H. & Chuang, C.-M. 2010. To teach or to compete? A strategic dilemma of knowledge owners in international alliances. *Asia Pacific Journal of Management,* 27(4): 697–726.
76. Manufacturer–supplier relationships can be very effective in global industries such as automobile manufacturing. Refer to Kotabe, M., Martin, X., & Domoto, H. 2003. Gaining from vertical partnerships: Knowledge transfer, relationship duration, and supplier performance improvement in the U.S. and Japanese automotive industries. *Strategic Management Journal,* 24(4): 293–316.
77. For a good discussion, refer to Merchant, H. & Schendel, D. 2000. How do international joint ventures create shareholder value? *Strategic Management Journal,* 21(7): 723–738.
78. This discussion draws upon Walters, B. A., Peters, S., & Dess, G. G. 1994. Strategic alliances and joint ventures: Making them work. *Business Horizons,* 37(4): 5–11.
79. Some insights on partnering in the global area are discussed in MacCormack, A. & Forbath, T. 2008. *Harvard Business Review,* 66(1): 24, 26.
80. For a rigorous discussion of the importance of information access in international joint ventures, refer to Reuer, J. J. & Koza, M. p. 2000. Asymmetric information and joint venture performance: Theory and evidence for domestic and international joint ventures. *Strategic Management Journal,* 21(1): 81–88.
81. Dyer, J. H., Kale, P., & Singh, H. 2001. How to make strategic alliances work. *MIT Sloan Management Review,* 42(4): 37–43.
82. For a discussion of some of the challenges in managing subsidiaries, refer to O'Donnell, S. W. 2000. Managing foreign subsidiaries: Agents of headquarters, or an independent network? *Strategic Management Journal,* 21(5): 525–548.
83. Ricks, D. 2006. *Blunders in international business* (4th ed.). Malden, MA: Blackwell.

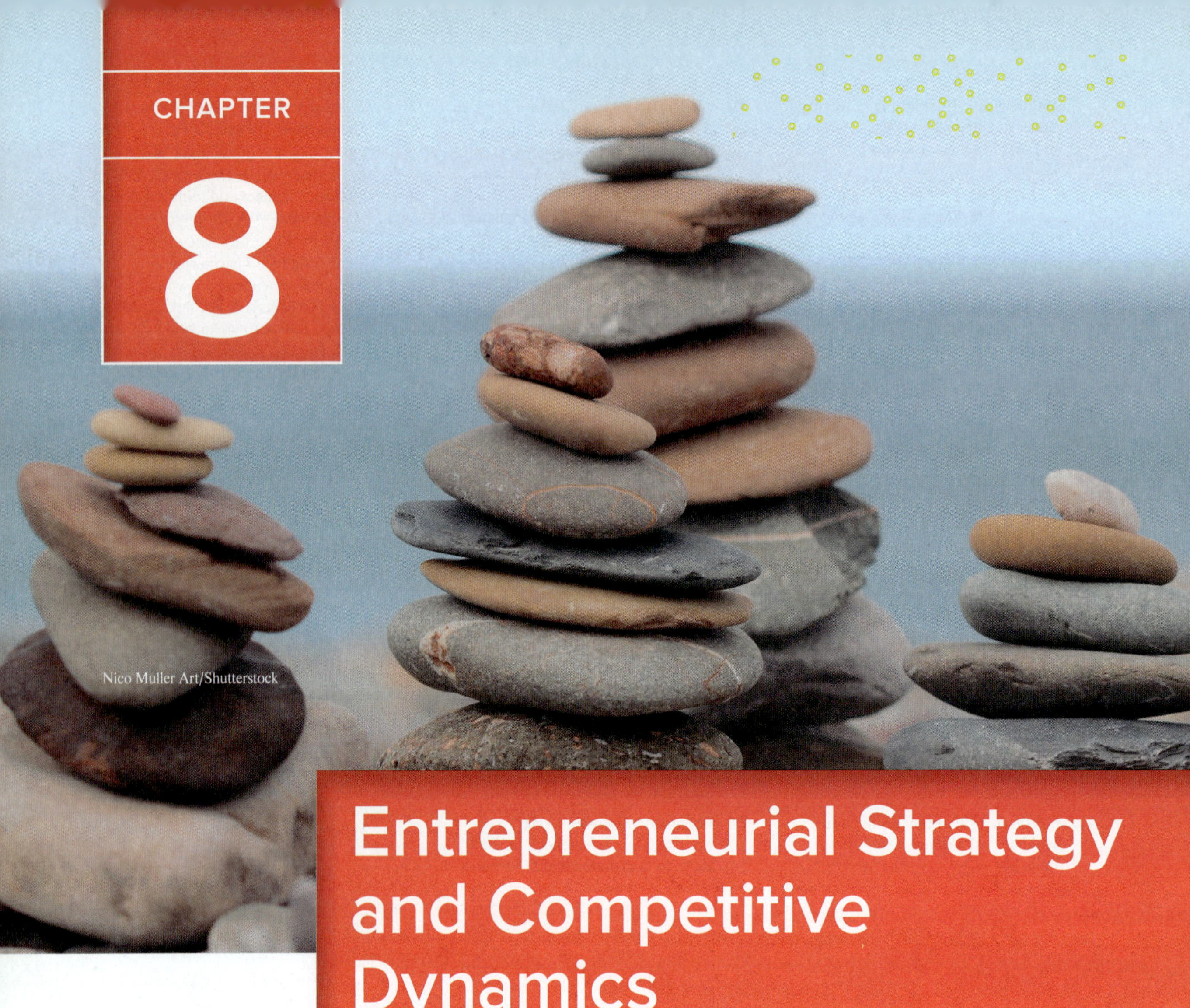

Entrepreneurial Strategy and Competitive Dynamics

Learning Objectives

LO8-1 Describe the role of opportunities, resources, and entrepreneurs in successfully pursuing new ventures.

LO8-2 Identify three types of entry strategies—pioneering, imitative, and adaptive—commonly used to launch a new venture.

LO8-3 Explain how the generic strategies of overall cost leadership, differentiation, and focus are used by new ventures and small businesses.

LO8-4 Explain how competitive actions, such as the entry of new competitors into a marketplace, may launch a cycle of actions and reactions among close competitors.

LO8-5 Identify the components of competitive dynamics analysis—new competitive action, threat analysis, motivation and capability to respond, types of competitive actions, and likelihood of competitive reaction.

We encourage you to reflect on how the concepts presented in this chapter can enhance your career success (see "Reflecting on Career Implications..." at the end of the chapter).

LEARNING FROM MISTAKES

The disappearing photo app, Snapchat, experienced a meteoric rise. Started by a set of Stanford undergraduate students in 2011, the app had a user base in excess of 150 million and had reached 10 billion daily video views by 2016. As the app grew in popularity, CEO Evan Spiegel and CTO Bobby Murphy found themselves in a long-term battle with Reggie Brown, a Kappa Sigma fraternity brother of theirs who claimed he was the original creator of Snapchat. According to Brown, he shared his idea for an app that would allow users to share photos that would quickly self-destruct with Spiegel. They then recruited Murphy to do computer programming for the app. That first app, Picaboo, evolved into the widely used Snapchat. While the app became a success, the collaboration did not. Spiegel apparently decided that Brown wasn't adding much to the team. He and Murphy locked Brown out of the company's system and disavowed any claims that Brown was one of the firm's founders or had any ownership rights to the company. In 2013, Brown sued, leading to an eventual confidential settlement in 2014. By that time, the overall firm was valued at about $20 billion. While the financial details of the settlement were never made public, Spiegel publicly admitted that Brown was central to the creation of the app, saying, "We acknowledge Reggie's contribution to the creation of Snapchat and appreciate his work in getting the application off the ground."

The Snapchat experience is not at all uncommon. Facebook, Twitter, Tinder, Beats Electronics, and others faced internal drama about who was responsible for the firms' start and who should reap the substantial financial rewards of their success. Why is this so common? Entrepreneurial teams are often composed of friends and family, leading the participants to expect that they can trust their partners and have no need for a written contract or statement of ownership. Luan Tran, the attorney for Brown, put it this way, "You don't think not to trust people you know a lot, and you don't think they are going to screw you. It's good to trust, but it's much better to memorialize your trust in a document." Amir Hassanabadi, another attorney who regularly works with start-up firms, recommends the following for founders on day one of their venture, "Go out to dinner. Settle who's who and what's what. Then put it in writing."[1]

Discussion Questions

1. Why do you think that so many start-up firms have these disputes?
2. Why do founders often fail to work up formal written contracts about ownership and credit?
3. Would you feel comfortable having that conversation early on with a partner in a new business? How would you initiate that conversation?

The Snapchat case illustrates how important it is for start-up firms to formalize the roles of founders and set up formal contracts that lay out responsibilities and ownership rights if they want to avoid later drama.

In this chapter we address entrepreneurial strategies. The previous three chapters have focused primarily on the business-level, corporate-level, and international strategies of incumbent firms. Here we ask: What about the strategies of those entering into a market or industry for the first time? In this chapter, we focus on strategic entrepreneurship—the actions firms take to create new ventures in markets. In Chapter 12, we focus on a related issue—how established firms can build or reinforce an entrepreneurial mindset as they strive to be innovative in markets in which the firm already competes.

Companies wishing to launch new ventures must also be aware that, consistent with the five-forces model in Chapter 2, new entrants are a threat to existing firms in an industry. Entry into a new market arena is intensely competitive from the perspective of incumbents in that arena. Therefore, new entrants can nearly always expect a competitive response from other companies in the industry they are entering. Knowledge of the competitive dynamics that are at work in the business environment is an aspect of entrepreneurial new entry that will be addressed later in this chapter.

Before moving on, it is important to highlight the role that entrepreneurial start-ups and small businesses play in entrepreneurial value creation. Small businesses, those defined as having 500 employees or fewer, have created about 62 percent of all new jobs in the United States since the end of the great recession.[2]

LO 8-1

Describe the role of opportunities, resources, and entrepreneurs in successfully pursuing new ventures.

RECOGNIZING ENTREPRENEURIAL OPPORTUNITIES

Defined broadly, **entrepreneurship** refers to new value creation. Even though entrepreneurial activity is usually associated with start-up companies, new value can be created in many different contexts, including:

- Start-up ventures
- Major corporations
- Family-owned businesses
- Nonprofit organizations
- Established institutions

entrepreneurship the creation of new value by an existing organization or new venture that involves the assumption of risk.

For an entrepreneurial venture to create new value, three factors must be present—an entrepreneurial opportunity, the resources to pursue the opportunity, and an entrepreneur or entrepreneurial team willing and able to undertake the opportunity.[3] The entrepreneurial strategy that an organization uses will depend on these three factors. Thus, beyond merely identifying a venture concept, the opportunity recognition process also involves organizing the key people and resources that are needed to go forward. Exhibit 8.1 depicts the three factors that are needed to successfully proceed—opportunity, resources, and entrepreneur(s). In the sections that follow, we address each of these factors.

Entrepreneurial Opportunities

The starting point for any new venture is the presence of an entrepreneurial opportunity. Where do opportunities come from? For new business start-ups, opportunities come from many sources—current or past work experiences, hobbies that grow into businesses or lead to inventions, suggestions by friends or family, or a chance event that makes an entrepreneur aware of an unmet need. Terry Tietzen, founder and CEO of Edatanetworks, puts it this way, "You get ideas through watching the world and through relationships. You get ideas

EXHIBIT 8.1 Opportunity Analysis Framework

Sources: Timmons, J. A., and S. Spinelli. 2004. *New Venture Creation* (6th ed.). New York: McGraw-Hill/Irwin; and Bygrave, W. D. 1997. The entrepreneurial process. In *The Portable MBA in Entrepreneurship* (2nd ed.). New York: Wiley.

from looking down the road."[4] For established firms, new business opportunities come from the needs of existing customers, suggestions by suppliers, or technological developments that lead to new advances.[5] For all firms, there is a major, overarching factor behind all viable opportunities that emerge in the business landscape: change. Change creates opportunities. Entrepreneurial firms make the most of changes brought about by new technology, sociocultural trends, and shifts in consumer demand.

How do changes in the external environment lead to new business creation? They spark creative new ideas and innovation. Businesspeople often have ideas for entrepreneurial ventures. However, not all such ideas are good ideas—that is, viable business opportunities. To determine which ideas are strong enough to become new ventures, entrepreneurs must go through a process of identifying, selecting, and developing potential opportunities. This is the process of **opportunity recognition.**[6]

opportunity recognition
the process of discovering and evaluating changes in the business environment, such as a new technology, sociocultural trends, or shifts in consumer demand, that can be exploited.

Opportunity recognition refers to more than just the "Eureka!" feeling that people sometimes experience at the moment they identify a new idea. Although such insights are often very important, the opportunity recognition process involves two phases of activity—discovery and evaluation—that lead to viable new venture opportunities.[7]

The discovery phase refers to the process of becoming aware of a new business concept.[8] Many entrepreneurs report that their idea for a new venture occurred to them in an instant, as a sort of "Aha!" experience—that is, they had some insight or epiphany, often based on their prior knowledge, that gave them an idea for a new business. The discovery of new opportunities is often spontaneous and unexpected. For example, Howard Schultz, CEO of Starbucks, was in Milan, Italy, when he suddenly realized that the coffee-and-conversation cafe model that was common in Europe would work in the United States as well. According to Schultz, he didn't need to do research to find out if Americans would pay $3 for a cup of coffee—he just *knew.* Starbucks was just a small business at the time but Schultz began literally shaking with excitement about growing it into a bigger business.[9]

Opportunity discovery also may occur as the result of a deliberate search for new venture opportunities or creative solutions to business problems. Viable opportunities often emerge only after a concerted effort. The search process is very similar to a creative process, which may be unstructured and "chaotic" at first but eventually leads to a practical solution or business innovation. To stimulate the discovery of new opportunities, companies often encourage creativity, out-of-the-box thinking, and brainstorming. While a deliberate search can aim to identify truly novel and creative entrepreneurial opportunities, it can also be more focused to look for "obvious" opportunities that others have failed to see. Experienced entrepreneurs discussing ways to look for new entrepreneurial opportunities identify several ways to undertake a structured search for entrepreneurial ideas:[10]

- ***Look at what's bugging you.*** What are the frustrations you have with current products or processes? Search for ideas on how to address these annoyances to identify entrepreneurial opportunities. For example, Jeannine Fradelizio noticed that at parties she hosted, guests would set down their wine glasses and forget which one was their glass. This would lead them to either abandon that glass and get another or end up drinking from someone else's glass which would sometimes lead to a minor dispute. In an effort to avoid these mix-ups Fradelizio tried having her friends write their names on their glasses with a marker but found that existing markers either didn't dry quickly enough or wouldn't wash off. She enlisted the help of a chemist and developed the Wine Glass Writer, a product now carried by Amazon, Walmart, Bed Bath & Beyond, and many other retailers.[11]

Strategy Spotlight 8.1 explores the frustrations that TJ Parker felt working at his father's pharmacy and how it led him to start a company that is now worth $1 billion.

8.1 STRATEGY SPOTLIGHT

MAKING IT EASIER TO TAKE YOUR PRESCRIPTIONS: A BILLION DOLLAR IDEA

As a youth, TJ Parker worked at his father's pharmacy. He saw how customers regularly struggled to keep track of what medicines they were supposed to take and when they were supposed to take them. He knew there had to be a better way, a way to keep patients on schedule with their medications, a key element of effectively treating medical conditions. Finding that way would allow him to make life much better for patients. Mr. Parker wrote the following in his blog, "For folks with chronic conditions, research shows that medication adherence goes a long way towards achieving health goals. It's a simple premise."

Parker went to pharmacy school, but he also took design classes at a nearby art college. He pulled together his training from these two lines of study to develop his solution. His idea is simple—sort all the pills patients are prescribed into "dose packets," small baggies marked with the date and time they are to be taken. The dose packets are then placed in a small box with each dose packet placed in the order they are to be taken.

Parker and his partner entered their idea in a venture funding pitch contest and won. Their firm, PillPack, was born. They received additional funding from venture capitalists and grew the business to about $100 million in sales. That's when Walmart and Amazon became interested. Eventually, Amazon offered a winning bid for the five-year-old firm, a bid that was reportedly nearly $1 billion in value.

Parker summed up his business in the following words. "PillPack makes it simple for any customer to take the right medication at the right time, and feel healthier." It's a simple concept but a very valuable concept.

Sources: Brown, E., and S. Terlep. 2018. Behind PillPack's $1 billion sale, a frustrated 32-year-old pharmacist. *wsj.com,* June 28: np; and Lunden, I. 2018. Amazon buys PillPack, an online pharmacy, for just under $1B. *techcrunch.com,* June 28: np.

- ***Talk to the people who know.*** If you have a general idea of the market you want to go into, talk to suppliers, customers, and front-line workers in this market. These discussions can lead to insights on how these stakeholders' needs aren't being met and can also open avenues to hear what they would like to see in new products and processes. For example, Precision Hawk, a company using drones to do aerial data analysis, reached out to Hahn Estate Winery so that Precision Hawk could better understand the needs of wineries in analyzing crop health and to develop the capabilities needed to meet those needs.[12]
- ***Look to other markets.*** One of the most powerful ways of finding new ideas is by borrowing ideas from other markets. This could involve looking at other industries or other geographic markets to identify new ideas. For example, in developing the idea for CarMax, the used-car superstore chain, Richard Sharp drew on his experience leading a major consumer electronics retailer to lay out the logic for his "big box" used-car lots, which allowed him to streamline operations and improve the efficiency of the used-car market. In essence, he decided to build the Best Buy or the Home Depot of the used-car market.
- ***Get inspired by history.*** Sometimes, the best ideas are not actually new ideas. Opportunities in industries can often be discovered by looking to the past to find good ideas that have slipped out of practice but might now be valued by the market again. For example, Sam Calagione, founder of Ancient Ales, developed an innovative line of craft beers by using ancient brewing techniques and ingredients that differ from modern brews.

Opportunity evaluation, which occurs after an opportunity has been identified, involves analyzing an opportunity to determine whether it is viable and strong enough to be developed into a full-fledged new venture. Ideas developed by new product groups or in brainstorming sessions are tested by various methods, including talking to potential target customers and discussing operational requirements with production or logistics managers. A technique known as feasibility analysis is used to evaluate these and other critical success factors. This type of analysis often leads to the decision that a new venture project should be

8.2 STRATEGY SPOTLIGHT — ENVIRONMENTAL SUSTAINABILITY

MOASIS LEVERAGES TECHNOLOGY TO IMPROVE WATER EFFICIENCY FOR FARMERS

The pervasive drought in California has had dire effects for farmers. At times, water usage restrictions have severely limited the water farmers can use. Even when they don't face difficult water restrictions, farmers have found their water bills go up by as much as 600 percent in recent years. This has led them to look to drought-resistant varieties, new fertilizers that reduce water demands, soil sensors that reduce the possibility of over-watering, and other actions to lower water needs.

A startup firm, mOasis, sees further opportunity with an environmentally friendly hydrogel. Farmers apply mOasis's gel polymer to soil when preparing the land for planting. The hydrogel particles are the size of a grain of sand but can soak up 250 times their weight in water. The hydrogel absorbs water during irrigation and releases it as the soil dries—ensuring the most efficient use of water possible. According to mOasis, farmers using the hydrogel can experience up to 25 percent higher crop yields with 20 percent lower water use. The gel stays effective for about a year but then breaks down into byproducts that are not environmentally damaging in any way.

Sources: Wang, U. 2013. For drought-plagued farmers: A gel that can suck up 250 times its weight in water. *gigaom.com,* October 29: np; Fehrenbacher, K. 2015. How water technology can help farmers survive California's drought. *fortune.com,* June 1: np; and Vekshin, A. 2014. California water prices soar for farmers as drought grows. *bloomberg.com,* July 24: np.

discontinued. If the venture concept continues to seem viable, a more formal business plan may be developed.[13]

Among the most important factors to evaluate is the market potential for the product or service. Established firms tend to operate in established markets. They have to adjust to market trends and to shifts in consumer demand, of course, but they usually have a customer base for which they are already filling a marketplace need. New ventures, in contrast, must first determine whether a market exists for the product or service they are contemplating. Thus, a critical element of opportunity recognition is assessing to what extent the opportunity is viable *in the marketplace.*

For an opportunity to be viable, it needs to have four qualities:[14]

- ***Attractive.*** The opportunity must be attractive in the marketplace; that is, there must be market demand for the new product or service.
- ***Achievable.*** The opportunity must be practical and physically possible.
- ***Durable.*** The opportunity must be attractive long enough for the development and deployment to be successful; that is, the window of opportunity must be open long enough for it to be worthwhile.
- ***Value creating.*** The opportunity must be potentially profitable; that is, the benefits must surpass the cost of development by a significant margin.

If a new business concept meets these criteria, two other factors must be considered before the opportunity is launched as a business: the resources available to undertake it and the characteristics of the entrepreneur(s) pursuing it. In the next section, we address the issue of entrepreneurial resources; following that, we address the importance of entrepreneurial leaders and teams. But first, consider the opportunities that have been created by the recent surge in interest in environmental sustainability. Strategy Spotlight 8.2 discusses how an entrepreneurial firm is responding to the California drought with an innovative, environmentally sustainable product that helps farmers use water more efficiently.

Entrepreneurial Resources

As Exhibit 8.1 indicates, resources are an essential component of a successful entrepreneurial launch. For start-ups, the most important resource is usually money because a new firm typically has to expend substantial sums just to start the business. However, financial resources are not the only kind of resource a new venture needs. Human capital and social capital are also important. Many firms also rely on government resources to help them thrive.[15]

Financial Resources Hand-in-hand with the importance of markets (and marketing) to new venture creation, entrepreneurial firms must also have financing. In fact, the level of available financing is often a strong determinant of how the business is launched and its eventual success. Cash finances are, of course, highly important. But access to capital, such as a line of credit or favorable payment terms with a supplier, can also help a new venture succeed.

The types of financial resources that may be needed depend on two factors: the stage of venture development and the scale of the venture.[16] Entrepreneurial firms that are starting from scratch—start-ups—are at the earliest stage of development. Most start-ups also begin on a relatively small scale. The funding available to young and small firms tends to be quite limited. In fact, the majority of new firms are low-budget start-ups launched with personal savings and the contributions of family and friends.[17] Among firms included in the *Entrepreneur* list of the 100 fastest-growing new businesses, 61 percent reported that their start-up funds came from personal savings.[18]

Although bank financing, public financing, and venture capital are important sources of small business finance, these types of financial support are typically available only after a company has started to conduct business and generate sales. Even **angel investors**—private individuals who provide equity investments for seed capital during the early stages of a new venture—favor companies that already have a winning business model and dominance in a market niche.[19] According to Cal Simmons, coauthor of *Every Business Needs an Angel,* "I would much rather talk to an entrepreneur who has already put his money and his effort into proving the concept."[20]

angel investors
private individuals who provide equity investments for seed capital during the early stages of a new venture.

Thus, while the press commonly talks about the role of **venture capitalists** and angel investors in start-up firms, the majority of external funding for young and small firms comes from informal sources such as family and friends. A Kauffman Foundation survey of entrepreneurial firms found that most start-up funding, about 70 percent, comes from either equity investments by the entrepreneur and the entrepreneur's family and friends or personal loans taken out by the entrepreneur. The leading source of business funding for more established firms, those in existence for five years, is loan financing from banks and other credit firms. At both stages, 5 percent or less of the funding comes from outside investors, such as angel investors or venture capitalists.

venture capitalists
companies organized to place their investors' funds in lucrative business opportunities.

In recent years, a new source of funding, **crowdfunding,** has emerged as a means for start-ups to amass significant pools of capital.[21] In these peer-to-peer investment systems, individuals striving to grow their business post their business ideas on a crowdfunding website. Potential investors who go to the site evaluate the proposals listed and decide which, if any, to fund. Typically, no individual makes a very sizable funding allotment. Most investors contribute up to a few hundred dollars to any investment, but the power of the crowd is at work. If a few thousand investors sign up for a venture, it can potentially raise over a million dollars. In addition to providing funding, Crowdfunding can also provide entrepreneurs with valuable feedback that can be used to refine or further innovate the firm's products. Investors often comment and offer suggestions. Some entrepreneurs take this further, responding to comments from investors, triggering a new round of feedback.[22]

crowdfunding
funding a venture by pooling small investments from a large number of investors; often raised on the Internet.

While crowdfunding offers a new avenue for corporations to raise funding, there are some potential downsides. First, the crowdfunding sites take a slice of the funds raised—typically 4 to 9 percent. Second, while crowdfunding offers a marketplace in which to raise funds, it also puts additional pressure on entrepreneurs. The social network-savvy investors who fund these ventures are quick to comment on their social media websites if the firm misses deadlines or falls short of its revenue projections. Finally, entrepreneurs can struggle with how much information to share about their business ideas. They want to share enough information without releasing critical information that competitors trolling these sites can benefit from. They also may be concerned about posting their financials, since these statements give their suppliers and customers access to sensitive information about margins and earnings.

Human Capital Bankers, venture capitalists, and angel investors agree that the most important asset an entrepreneurial firm can have is strong and skilled management.[23] According to Stephen Gaal, founding member of Walnut Venture Associates, venture investors do not invest in businesses; instead, "We invest in people . . . very smart people with very high integrity." Managers need to have a strong base of experience and extensive domain knowledge, as well as an ability to make rapid decisions and change direction as shifting circumstances may require. In the case of start-ups, more is better. New ventures that are started by teams of three, four, or five entrepreneurs are more likely to succeed in the long run than are ventures launched by "lone wolf" entrepreneurs.[24]

The ability of firms to extend their human capital base to outside partners is an especially important skill in the gig economy. Platform firms in this market will only succeed if they can deliver gig workers who deliver a high quality service. Urban professionals who go to Handy to find a contractor to do needed cleaning or painting will only return if the service provider follows through in a timely and professional way. Similarly, customers will only return to Fancy Hands for personal assistance if their first experience with a Fancy Hands assistant is good.[25] Thus, platform firms in these markets need to develop effective systems to recruit and evaluate potential service providers. On the positive side, firms that use a gig economy model greatly reduce the financial resources needed to expand their businesses.

Social Capital New ventures founded by entrepreneurs who have extensive social contacts are more likely to succeed than are ventures started without the support of a social network.[26] Even though a venture may be new, if the founders have contacts who will vouch for them, they gain exposure and build legitimacy faster.[27] This support can come from several sources: prior jobs, industry organizations, and local business groups such as the chamber of commerce. These contacts can all contribute to a growing network that provides support for the entrepreneurial firm. Janina Pawlowski, cofounder of the online lending company E-Loan, attributed part of her success to the strong advisers she persuaded to serve on her board of directors, including Tim Koogle, former CEO of Yahoo![28]

Strategic alliances represent a type of social capital that can be especially important to young and small firms.[29] Strategic alliances can provide a key avenue for growth by entrepreneurial firms.[30] By partnering with other companies, young or small firms can expand or give the appearance of entering numerous markets or handling a range of operations. According to the National Federation of Independent Business (NFIB), nearly two-thirds of small businesses currently hold or have held some type of alliance. Here are a few types of alliances that have been used to extend or strengthen entrepreneurial firms:

- ***Technology alliances.*** Tech-savvy entrepreneurial firms often benefit from forming alliances with older incumbents. The alliance allows the larger firm to enhance its technological capabilities and expands the revenue and reach of the smaller firm.
- ***Manufacturing alliances.*** The use of outsourcing and other manufacturing alliances by small firms has grown dramatically in recent years. Internet-enabled capabilities such as collaborating online about delivery and design specifications have greatly simplified doing business, even with foreign manufacturers.
- ***Retail alliances.*** Licensing agreements allow one company to sell the products and services of another in different markets, including overseas. Specialty products–the types sometimes made by entrepreneurial firms–often seem more exotic when sold in another country.

Although such alliances often sound good, there are also potential pitfalls. Lack of oversight and control is one danger of partnering with foreign firms. Problems with product quality, timely delivery, and receiving payments can also sour an alliance relationship if it is not carefully managed. With technology alliances, there is a risk that big firms may take advantage of the technological know-how of their entrepreneurial partners. However, even with these potential problems, strategic alliances provide a good means for entrepreneurial firms to develop and grow.

Government Resources In the United States, the federal government provides support for entrepreneurial firms in two key arenas–financing and government contracting. The Small Business Administration (SBA) has several loan guarantee programs designed to support the growth and development of entrepreneurial firms. The government itself does not typically lend money but underwrites loans made by banks to small businesses, thus reducing the risk associated with lending to firms with unproven records. The SBA also offers training, counseling, and support services through its local offices and Small Business Development Centers.[31] State and local governments also have hundreds of programs to provide funding, contracts, and other support for new ventures and small businesses. These programs are often designed to grow the economy of a region.

Another key area of support is government contracting. Programs sponsored by the SBA and other government agencies ensure that small businesses have the opportunity to bid on contracts to provide goods and services to the government. Although working with the government sometimes has its drawbacks in terms of issues of regulation and time-consuming decision making, programs to support small businesses and entrepreneurial activity constitute an important resource for entrepreneurial firms.

Entrepreneurial Leadership

Whether a venture is launched by an individual entrepreneur or an entrepreneurial team, effective leadership is needed. Launching a new venture requires a special kind of leadership. Research indicates that entrepreneurs tend to have characteristics that distinguish them from corporate managers. Differences include:

- ***Higher core self-evaluation.*** Successful entrepreneurs evidence higher levels of self-confidence and a higher assessment of the degree to which an individual controls his or her own destiny.[32]
- ***Higher conscientiousness.*** Entrepreneurs tend to have a higher degree of organization, persistence, hard work, and pursuit of goal accomplishment.
- ***Higher openness to experience.*** Entrepreneurs also tend to score higher on openness to experience, a personality trait associated with intellectual curiosity and a desire to explore novel ideas.
- ***Higher emotional stability.*** Entrepreneurs exhibit a higher ability to handle ambiguity and maintain even emotions during stressful periods, and they are less likely to be overcome by anxieties.
- ***Lower agreeableness.*** Finally, entrepreneurs tend to score lower on agreeableness. This suggests they typically look out primarily for their own self-interest and also are willing to influence or manipulate others for their own advantage.[33]

entrepreneurial leadership
leadership appropriate for new ventures that requires courage, belief in one's convictions, and the energy to work hard even in difficult circumstances; and that embodies vision, dedication and drive, and commitment to excellence.

These personality traits are embodied in the behavioral attributes necessary for successful **entrepreneurial leadership**–vision, dedication and drive, and commitment to excellence:

- ***Vision.*** This may be an entrepreneur's most important asset. Entrepreneurs envision realities that do not yet exist. But without a vision, most entrepreneurs would never even get their venture off the ground. With vision, entrepreneurs are able to exercise a kind of transformational leadership that creates something new and, in some way, changes the world. Just having a vision, however, is not enough. To develop support, get financial backing, and attract employees, entrepreneurial leaders must share their vision with others.

- ***Dedication and drive.*** Dedication and drive are reflected in hard work. Drive involves internal motivation; dedication calls for an intellectual commitment that keeps an entrepreneur going even in the face of bad news or poor luck. They both require patience, stamina, and a willingness to work long hours. However, a business built on the heroic efforts of one person may suffer in the long run. That's why the dedicated entrepreneur's enthusiasm is also important—like a magnet, it attracts others to the business to help with the work.[34]
- ***Commitment to excellence.*** Excellence requires entrepreneurs to commit to knowing the customer, providing quality goods and services, paying attention to details, and continuously learning. Entrepreneurs who achieve excellence are sensitive to how these factors work together. However, entrepreneurs may flounder if they think they are the only ones who can create excellent results. The most successful, by contrast, often report that they owe their success to hiring people smarter than themselves.

Successful entrepreneurs are often pictured as young. When Inc. magazine built a list of the fastest growing startups in 2015, the average age of the founders was 29. Iconic entrepreneurs Mark Zuckerberg, Steve Jobs, and Michael Dell were all in their early twenties when they started their firms. But research suggests that this common wisdom and these salient examples of successful entrepreneurs is wrong. The average age of entrepreneurs at the time of firm founding is 42. Even in the supposedly young IT industry, the average founder age for software startups is 40. More surprisingly, when researchers examined the fastest growing entrepreneurial firms, those in the top .1 percent of all startup firms, the average age of the founder is 49. In fact, looking at the fastest growing firms, the founder of the firm was almost three times more likely to be over 50 than under 30.

This research suggests that the experience of older entrepreneurs gives them an advantage in building a successful, fast-growing firm. Compared to founders who have no experience in an industry, founders with at least three years of work experience were 85 percent more likely to launch a highly successful startup. Even young founders often find their best success when they hit middle age. For example, Steve Jobs was 52 when Apple launched the iPhone, the firm's biggest hit product, and Amazon hit its peak growth period when Jeff Bezos was in his mid-40s.[35] Strategy Spotlight 8.3 discusses how Martin Roscheisen, a serial entrepreneur who is now in his 50s, is working to redefine the diamond business.

In his book *Good to Great,* Jim Collins makes another important point about entrepreneurial leadership: Ventures built on the charisma of a single person may have trouble growing "from good to great" once that person leaves.[36] Thus, the leadership that is needed to build a great organization is usually exercised by a team of dedicated people working together rather than a single leader. Another aspect of this team approach is attracting team members who fit with the company's culture, goals, and work ethic. Thus, for a venture's leadership to be a valuable resource and not a liability, it must be cohesive in its vision, drive and dedication, and commitment to excellence.

Once an opportunity has been recognized, and an entrepreneurial team and resources have been assembled, a new venture must craft a strategy. Prior chapters have addressed the strategies of incumbent firms. In the next section, we highlight the types of strategies and strategic considerations faced by new entrants.

8.3 STRATEGY SPOTLIGHT

THE DIAMOND FOUNDRY SHAKES UP THE DIAMOND BUSINESS NOW AND, POSSIBLY, THE COMPUTING INDUSTRY IN THE FUTURE

For decades, the diamond business has been controlled by a small set of firms that control the mining and wholesaling of the gems. However, Martin Roscheisen, the founder of Diamond Foundry has a vision to change the diamond business. Roscheisen, a Stanford University engineering graduate, has already built two entrepreneurial firms: an email messaging company he sold to Yahoo for $450 million and Nanosolar, a solar panel manufacturer. Now, he is taking on DeBeers and other diamond heavyweights. Rather than mine diamonds, Diamond Foundry uses plasma reactors to create large diamonds from tiny pieces of diamonds. Essentially, the reactors imitate, in a matter of weeks, what pressure does to carbon over millions of years in the ground.

Diamond Foundry has also allied with major jewelry brands including Swarovski and Vrai & Oro, a direct-to-consumer engagement ring retailer. Vrai & Oro and Diamond Foundry even offer the ability to customize diamonds to be the type, color, and shape that customers desire. In addition to winning customers, Diamond Foundry also won a fight with the traditional diamond firms when the Federal Trade Commission decided that a gem doesn't have to be mined to be called a diamond. The FTC ruled in 2018 that lab-grown diamonds are "real" diamonds. DeBeers must see Diamond Foundry as a threat since they've launched a competing lab-grown diamond brand, Lightbox Jewelry.

The interesting twist in this is that Roscheisen is not a gem man. He wears no jewelry, not even a watch. For him, the real future for diamonds is in quantum computing. He's just making diamond gems in order to perfect the ability to manufacture diamonds so that he will be well positioned when diamonds become the foundation for a future generation of semiconductors, something he predicts will happen in 5 to 10 years.

Sources: Marikar, S. 2018. Dirsupting De Beers. *Fortune,* April 1: 15-16; Friedman, J. 2018. A defining moment for lab-grown diamonds. *diamonds.net,* July 31: np; and Schieber, J. 2018. Diamond dynasty DeBeers stoops to conquer with new line of man-made diamond jewelry. *techcrunch.com,* May 29: np.

entrepreneurial strategy
a strategy that enables a skilled and dedicated entrepreneur, with a viable opportunity and access to sufficient resources, to successfully launch a new venture.

ENTREPRENEURIAL STRATEGY

Successfully creating new ventures requires several ingredients. As indicated in Exhibit 8.1, three factors are necessary–a viable opportunity, sufficient resources, and a skilled and dedicated entrepreneur or entrepreneurial team. Once these elements are in place, the new venture needs a strategy. In this section, we consider several different strategic factors that are unique to new ventures and also how the generic strategies introduced in Chapter 5 can be applied to entrepreneurial firms. We also indicate how combination strategies might benefit entrepreneurial firms and address the potential pitfalls associated with launching new venture strategies.

To be successful, new ventures must evaluate industry conditions, the competitive environment, and market opportunities in order to position themselves strategically. However, a traditional strategic analysis may have to be altered somewhat to fit the entrepreneurial situation. For example, five-forces analysis (as discussed in Chapter 2) is typically used by established firms. It can also be applied to the analysis of new ventures to assess the impact of industry and competitive forces. But you may ask: How does a new entrant evaluate the threat of other new entrants?

First, the new entrant needs to examine barriers to entry. If the barriers are too high, the potential entrant may decide not to enter or to gather more resources before attempting to do so. Compared to an older firm with an established reputation and available resources, the barriers to entry may be insurmountable for an entrepreneurial start-up. Therefore, understanding the force of these barriers is critical in making a decision to launch.

A second factor that may be especially important to a young venture is the threat of retaliation by incumbents. In many cases, entrepreneurial ventures *are* the new entrants that pose a threat to incumbent firms. Therefore, in applying the five-forces model to new ventures, the threat of retaliation by established firms needs to be considered.

Part of any decision about what opportunity to pursue is a consideration of how a new entrant will actually enter a new market. The concept of entry strategies provides a useful means of addressing the types of choices that new ventures have.

Entry Strategies

LO 8-2

Identify three types of entry strategies—pioneering, imitative, and adaptive—commonly used to launch a new venture.

One of the most challenging aspects of launching a new venture is finding a way to begin doing business that quickly generates cash flow, builds credibility, attracts good employees, and overcomes the liability of newness. The idea of an entry strategy or "entry wedge" describes several approaches that firms may take to get a foothold in a market.[37] Several factors will affect this decision:

- Is the product/service high-tech or low-tech?
- What resources are available for the initial launch?
- What are the industry and competitive conditions?
- What is the overall market potential?
- Does the venture founder prefer to control the business or to grow it?

In some respects, any type of entry into a market for the first time may be considered entrepreneurial. But the entry strategy will vary depending on how risky and innovative the new business concept is.[38] New-entry strategies typically fall into one of three categories—pioneering new entry, imitative new entry, or adaptive new entry.[39]

Pioneering New Entry New entrants with a radical new product or highly innovative service may change the way business is conducted in an industry. This kind of breakthrough—creating new ways to solve old problems or meeting customers' needs in a unique new way—is referred to as a **pioneering new entry.** If the product or service is unique enough, a pioneering new entrant may actually have little direct competition. The first personal computer was a pioneering product; there had never been anything quite like it, and it revolutionized computing. The first Internet browser provided a type of pioneering service. These breakthroughs created whole new industries and changed the competitive landscape. And breakthrough innovations continue to inspire pioneering entrepreneurial efforts.

pioneering new entry
a firm's entry into an industry with a radical new product or highly innovative service that changes the way business is conducted.

The pitfalls associated with a pioneering new entry are numerous. For one thing, there is a strong risk that the product or service will not be accepted by consumers. The history of entrepreneurship is littered with new ideas that never got off the launching pad. Take, for example, Smell-O-Vision, an invention designed to pump odors into movie theaters from the projection room at preestablished moments in a film. It was tried only once (for the film *Scent of a Mystery*) before it was declared a major flop. Innovative? Definitely. But hardly a good idea at the time.[40]

A pioneering new entry is disruptive to the status quo of an industry. It is likely based on a technological breakthrough. If it is successful, other competitors will rush in to copy it. This can create issues of sustainability for an entrepreneurial firm, especially if a larger company with greater resources introduces a similar product. For a new entrant to sustain its pioneering advantage, it may be necessary to protect its intellectual property, advertise heavily to build brand recognition, form alliances with businesses that will adopt its products or services, and offer exceptional customer service.

Imitative New Entry Whereas pioneers are often inventors or tinkerers with new technology, imitators usually have a strong marketing orientation. They look for opportunities to capitalize on proven market successes. An **imitative new entry** strategy is used by entrepreneurs who see products or business concepts that have been successful in one market niche or physical locale and introduce the same basic product or service in another segment of the market.

imitative new entry
a firm's entry into an industry with products or services that capitalize on proven market successes and that usually have a strong marketing orientation.

Sometimes the key to success with an imitative strategy is to fill a market space where the need had previously been filled inadequately. Entrepreneurs are also prompted to be imitators when they realize that they have the resources or skills to do a job better than an existing competitor. This can actually be a serious problem for entrepreneurial start-ups if the imitator is an established company. Consider the example of Square.[41] Founded in 2010, Square provides a means for small businesses to process credit and debit card sales without signing up for a traditional credit card arrangement that typically includes monthly fees and minimum charges. Square provides a small credit card reader that plugs into a smartphone to users who sign up for its service. Users swipe the card and input the charge amount. Square does the rest for a 2.75 percent transaction fee. As of 2016, Square was processing $46 billion in transactions annually. But success triggers imitation. A host of both upstart and established firms have moved into this new segment. While Square has quickly established itself in the market, it now faces strong competition from major competitors, including Apple, Google, and PayPal. With the strong competition it faces and the thin margins in its business, Square has never been able to turn a profit. As a result, the firm's value when the firm went public in November 2015 was only $2.9 billion, half of its estimated value only a year before.

Adaptive New Entry Most new entrants use a strategy somewhere between "pure" imitation and "pure" pioneering. That is, they offer a product or service that is somewhat new and sufficiently different to create new value for customers and capture market share. Such firms are adaptive in the sense that they are aware of marketplace conditions and conceive entry strategies to capitalize on current trends.

According to business creativity coach Tom Monahan, "Every new idea is merely a spin of an old idea. [Knowing that] takes the pressure off from thinking [you] have to be totally creative. You don't. Sometimes it's one slight twist to an old idea that makes all the difference."[42] An **adaptive new entry** approach does not involve "reinventing the wheel," nor is it merely imitative either. It involves taking an existing idea and adapting it to a particular situation. Exhibit 8.2 presents examples of four companies that successfully modified or adapted existing products to create new value.

adaptive new entry a firm's entry into an industry by offering a product or service that is somewhat new and sufficiently different to create value for customers by capitalizing on current market trends.

There are several pitfalls that might limit the success of an adaptive new entrant. First, the value proposition must be perceived as unique. Unless potential customers believe a new product or service does a superior job of meeting their needs, they will have little motivation to try it.

EXHIBIT 8.2 Examples of Adaptive New Entrants

Company Name	Product	Adaptation	Result
Under Armour, Inc. Founded in 1995	Undershirts and other athletic gear	Used moisture-wicking fabric to create better gear for sweaty sports.	Under Armour generated over $5.2 billion in 2018 and is now the number-two athletic-clothing firm in the United States after Nike.
Mint.com Founded in 2005	Comprehensive online money management	Created software that tells users what they are spending by aggregating financial information from online bank and credit card accounts.	Mint has over 20 million users and is helping them manage over $3 billion in assets.
Plum Organics Founded in 2005	Organic baby food and snack foods for children	Made convenient line of baby and toddler food using organic ingredients.	Plum now has over 20 products and had sales of in excess of $50 million in 2017.
Spanx Founded in 2000	Footless pantyhose and other undergarments for women	Combined nylon and Lycra to create a new type of undergarment that is comfortable and eliminates panty lines.	Spanx now produces over 200 products generating over $400 million in sales annually.

Sources: Bryan, M. 2007. Spanx me, baby! *www.observer.com*, December 10, np; Carey, J. 2006. Perspiration inspiration. *BusinessWeek*, June 4: 64; Palanjian, A. 2008. A planner plumbs for a niche. *The Wall Street Journal*, September 30, np; Worrell, D. 2008. Making mint. *Entrepreneur,* September: 55; *www.spanx.com*; *www.underarmour.com*; *plumorganics.com*; *forbes.com/companies/plum-organics/*; *blog.mint.com/credit/mint-by-the-numbers-which-user-are-you-040616/*; Berger, S. 2018. Self-made Spanx billionaire Sara Blakely has never had coffee. *cnbc.com,* June 30: np; *finance.yahoo.com*; and *statista.com*.

Second, there is nothing to prevent a close competitor from mimicking the new firm's adaptation as a way to hold on to its customers. Third, once an adaptive entrant achieves initial success, the challenge is to keep the idea fresh. If the attractive features of the new business are copied, the entrepreneurial firm must find ways to adapt and improve the product or service offering.

Considering these choices, an entrepreneur or entrepreneurial team might ask, Which new entry strategy is best? The choice depends on many competitive, financial, and marketplace considerations. Nevertheless, research indicates that the greatest opportunities may stem from being willing to enter new markets rather than seeking growth only in existing markets. One study found that companies that ventured into arenas that were new to the world or new to the company earned total profits of 61 percent. In contrast, companies that made only incremental improvements, such as extending an existing product line, grew total profits by only 39 percent.[43]

However, whether to be pioneering, imitative, or adaptive when entering markets is only one question the entrepreneur faces. A new entrant must also decide what type of strategic positioning will work best as the business goes forward. The strategic choices can be informed by the guidelines suggested for the generic strategies. We turn to that subject next.

Generic Strategies

Typically, a new entrant begins with a single business model that is equivalent in scope to a business-level strategy (Chapter 5). In this section we address how overall low cost, differentiation, and focus strategies can be used to achieve competitive advantages.

LO 8-3

Explain how the generic strategies of overall cost leadership, differentiation, and focus are used by new ventures and small businesses.

Overall Cost Leadership One of the ways entrepreneurial firms achieve success is by doing more with less. By holding down costs or making more efficient use of resources than larger competitors, new ventures are often able to offer lower prices and still be profitable. Thus, under the right circumstances, a low-cost leader strategy is a viable alternative for some new ventures. The way most companies achieve low-cost leadership, however, is typically different for young or small firms.

Recall from Chapter 5 that three of the features of a low-cost approach include operating at a large-enough scale to spread costs over many units of production (economies of scale), making substantial capital investments in order to increase scale economies, and using knowledge gained from experience to make cost-saving improvements. These elements of a cost-leadership strategy may be unavailable to new ventures. Because new ventures are typically small, they usually don't have high economies of scale relative to competitors. Because they are usually cash strapped, they can't make large capital investments to increase their scale advantages. And because many are young, they often don't have a wealth of accumulated experience to draw on to achieve cost reductions.

Given these constraints, how can new ventures successfully deploy cost-leader strategies? Compared to large firms, new ventures often have simple organizational structures that make decision making both easier and faster. The smaller size also helps young firms change more quickly when upgrades in technology or feedback from the marketplace indicate that improvements are needed. They are also able to make decisions at the time they are founded that help them deal with the issue of controlling costs. For example, they may source materials from a supplier that provides them more cheaply or set up manufacturing facilities in another country where labor costs are especially low. Thus, new firms have several avenues for achieving low-cost leadership.

Whatever methods young firms use to achieve a low-cost advantage, this has always been a way that entrepreneurial firms take business away from incumbents—by offering a comparable product or service at a lower price.

Differentiation Both pioneering and adaptive entry strategies involve some degree of differentiation. That is, the new entry is based on being able to offer a differentiated value proposition. In the case of pioneers, the new venture is attempting to do something strikingly different, either by using a new technology or by deploying resources in a way that radically alters the way business is conducted. Often, entrepreneurs do both. For example, Uber employed technology that effectively linked together passengers and drivers in a way that improved the use of driver time and offered passengers information on the progress of their trip. At the same time, the firm radically changed the resources needed to compete in the market, leveraging the private cars of drivers and lessening the cost of entry to any geographic market since the firm didn't have to buy a fleet of taxis.

There are several factors that make it more difficult for new ventures to be successful as differentiators. For one thing, the strategy is generally thought to be expensive to enact. Differentiation is often associated with strong brand identity, and establishing a brand is usually considered to be expensive because of the cost of advertising and promotion, paid endorsements, exceptional customer service, and so on. Differentiation successes are sometimes built on superior innovation or use of technology. These are also factors that might make it challenging for young firms to excel relative to established competitors.

Nevertheless, all of these areas–innovation, technology, customer service, distinctive branding–are also arenas where new ventures have sometimes made a name for themselves even though they must operate with limited resources and experience. To be successful, according to Garry Ridge, CEO of the WD-40 Company, "You need to have a great product, make the end user aware of it, and make it easy to buy."[44] It sounds simple, but it is a difficult challenge for new ventures with differentiation strategies.

Focus Focus strategies are often associated with small businesses because there is a natural fit between the narrow scope of the strategy and the small size of the firm. A focus strategy may include elements of differentiation and overall cost leadership, as well as combinations of these approaches. But to be successful within a market niche, the key strategic requirement is to stay focused. Let's consider why that is so.

Despite all the attention given to fast-growing new industries, most start-ups enter industries that are mature.[45] In mature industries, growth in demand tends to be slow and there are often many competitors. Therefore, if a start-up wants to get a piece of the action, it often has to take business away from an existing competitor. If a start-up enters a market with a broad or aggressive strategy, it is likely to evoke retaliation from a more powerful competitor. Young firms can often succeed best by finding a market niche where they can get a foothold and make small advances that erode the position of existing competitors.[46] From this position, they can build a name for themselves and grow.

Consider, for example, the "Miniature Editions" line of books launched by Running Press, a small Philadelphia publisher. The books are palm-size minibooks positioned at bookstore cash registers as point-of-sale impulse items costing about $4.95. Beginning with just 10 titles in 1993, Running Press grew rapidly and within 10 years had sold over 20 million copies. Even though these books represent just a tiny fraction of total sales in the $23 billion publishing industry, they have been a mainstay for Running Press.[47] As the Running Press example indicates, many new ventures are successful even though their share of the market is quite small.

Combination Strategies

One of the best ways for young and small businesses to achieve success is by pursuing combination strategies. By combining the best features of low-cost, differentiation, and focus strategies, new ventures can often achieve something truly distinctive.

Entrepreneurial firms are often in a strong position to offer a combination strategy because they have the flexibility to approach situations uniquely. For example, holding down expenses can be difficult for big firms because each layer of bureaucracy adds to the cost of doing business across the boundaries of a large organization.[48]

A similar argument could be made about entrepreneurial firms that differentiate. Large firms often find it difficult to offer highly specialized products or superior customer services. Entrepreneurial firms, by contrast, can often create high-value products and services through their unique differentiating efforts.

For nearly all new entrants, one of the major dangers is that a large firm with more resources will copy what they are doing. Well-established incumbents that observe the success of a new entrant's product or service will copy it and use their market power to overwhelm the smaller firm. The threat may be lessened for firms that use combination strategies. Because of the flexibility of entrepreneurial firms, they can often enact combination strategies in ways that the large firms cannot copy. This makes the new entrant's strategies much more sustainable.

Perhaps more threatening than large competitors are close competitors, because they have similar structural features that help them adjust quickly and be flexible in decision making. Here again, a carefully crafted and executed combination strategy may be the best way for an entrepreneurial firm to thrive in a competitive environment. Nevertheless, competition among rivals is a key determinant of new venture success. To address this, we turn next to the topic of competitive dynamics.

COMPETITIVE DYNAMICS

LO 8-4

Explain how competitive actions, such as the entry of new competitors into a marketplace, may launch a cycle of actions and reactions among close competitors.

New entry into markets, whether by start-ups or by incumbent firms, nearly always threatens existing competitors. This is true in part because, except in very new markets, nearly every market need is already being met, either directly or indirectly, by existing firms. As a result, the competitive actions of a new entrant are very likely to provoke a competitive response from companies that feel threatened. This, in turn, is likely to evoke a reaction to the response. As a result, a competitive dynamic—action and response—begins among the firms competing for the same customers in a given marketplace.

competitive dynamics intense rivalry, involving actions and responses, among similar competitors vying for the same customers in a marketplace.

Competitive dynamics—intense rivalry among similar competitors—has the potential to alter a company's strategy. New entrants may be forced to change their strategies or develop new ones to survive competitive challenges by incumbent rivals. New entry is among the most common reasons why a cycle of competitive actions and reactions gets started. It might also occur because of threatening actions among existing competitors, such as aggressive cost cutting. Thus, studying competitive dynamics helps explain why strategies evolve and reveals how, why, and when to respond to the actions of close competitors. Exhibit 8.3 identifies the factors that competitors need to consider when determining how to respond to a competitive act.

EXHIBIT 8.3 Model of Competitive Dynamics

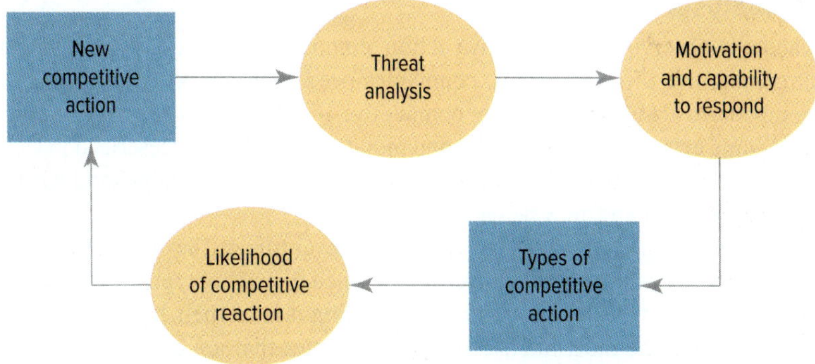

Sources: Adapted from Chen, M. J. 1996. Competitor analysis and interfirm rivalry: toward a theoretical integration. *Academy of Management Review,* 21(1): 100–134; Ketchen, D. J., Snow, C. C., and V. L. Hoover. 2004. Research on competitive dynamics: Recent accomplishments and future challenges. *Journal of Management,* 30(6): 779–804; and Smith, K. G., Ferrier, W. J., and C. M. Grimm. 2001. King of the hill: Dethroning the industry leader. *Academy of Management Executive,* 15(2): 59–70.

LO 8-5

Identify the components of competitive dynamics analysis—new competitive action, threat analysis, motivation and capability to respond, types of competitive actions, and likelihood of competitive reaction.

New Competitive Action

Entry into a market by a new competitor is a good starting point to begin describing the cycle of actions and responses characteristic of a competitive dynamic process.[49] However, new entry is only one type of competitive action. Price cutting, imitating successful products, and expanding production capacity are other examples of competitive acts that might provoke competitors to react.

Why do companies launch **new competitive actions**? There are several reasons:

- Improve market position
- Capitalize on growing demand
- Expand production capacity
- Provide an innovative new solution
- Obtain first-mover advantages

new competitive action
acts that might provoke competitors to react, such as new market entry, price cutting, imitating successful products, and expanding production capacity.

Underlying all of these reasons is a desire to strengthen financial outcomes, capture some of the extraordinary profits that industry leaders enjoy, and grow the business. Some companies are also motivated to launch competitive challenges because they want to build their reputation for innovativeness or efficiency. For example, Toyota's success with the Prius signaled to its competitors the potential value of high-fuel-economy cars, and these firms have responded with their own hybrids, electric cars, high-efficiency diesel engines, and even more fuel-efficient traditional gasoline engines. This is indicative of the competitive dynamic cycle. As former Intel chairman Andy Grove stated, "Business success contains the seeds of its own destruction. The more successful you are, the more people want a chunk of your business and then another chunk and then another until there is nothing left."[50]

When a company enters into a market for the first time, it is an attack on existing competitors. As indicated earlier in the chapter, any of the entry strategies can be used to take competitive action. But competitive attacks come from many sources besides new entrants. Some of the most intense competition is among incumbent rivals intent on gaining strategic advantages. "Winners in business play rough and don't apologize for it," according to Boston Consulting Group authors George Stalk, Jr., and Rob Lachenauer in their book *Hardball: Are You Playing to Play or Playing to Win?*[51] Exhibit 8.4 outlines their five strategies.

The likelihood that a competitor will launch an attack depends on many factors.[52] In the remaining sections, we discuss factors such as competitor analysis, market conditions, types of strategic actions, and the resource endowments and capabilities companies need to take competitive action.

Threat Analysis

threat analysis
a firm's awareness of its closest competitors and the kinds of competitive actions they might be planning.

Prior to actually observing a competitive action, companies may need to become aware of potential competitive threats. That is, companies need to have a keen sense of who their closest competitors are and the kinds of competitive actions they might be planning.[53] This may require some environmental scanning and monitoring of the sort described in Chapter 2. Awareness of the threats posed by industry rivals allows a firm to understand what type of competitive response, if any, may be necessary.

Being aware of competitors and cognizant of whatever threats they might pose is the first step in assessing the level of competitive threat. Once a new competitive action becomes apparent, companies must determine how threatening it is to their business. Competitive dynamics are likely to be most intense among companies that are competing for the same customers or that have highly similar sets of resources.[54] Two factors are used to assess whether or not companies are close competitors:

market commonality
the extent to which competitors are vying for the same customers in the same markets.

- **Market commonality.** Whether or not competitors are vying for the same customers and how many markets they share in common. For example, aircraft manufacturers

EXHIBIT 8.4 Five Ways to Aggressively Attack Your Rivals

Strategy	Description	Examples
Devastate rivals' profit sanctuaries	Not all business segments generate the same level of profits for a company. Through focused attacks on a rival's most profitable segments, a company can generate maximum leverage with relatively smaller-scale attacks. Recognize, however, that companies closely guard the information needed to determine just what their profit sanctuaries are.	In 2005, Walmart began offering low-priced extended warranties on home electronics after learning that its rivals such as Best Buy derived most of their profits from extended warranties.
Plagiarize with pride	Just because a close competitor comes up with an idea first does not mean it cannot be successfully imitated. Second movers, in fact, can see how customers respond, make improvements, and launch a better version without all the market development costs. Successful imitation is harder than it may appear and requires the imitating firm to keep its ego in check.	In designing its smartphones, Samsung copied the look, feel, and technological attributes of Apple's iPhone. Samsung lost a patent infringement lawsuit to Apple, but by copying Apple, Samsung was able to improve its market position.
Deceive the competition	A good gambit sends the competition off in the wrong direction. This may cause the rivals to miss strategic shifts, spend money pursuing dead ends, or slow their responses. Any of these outcomes support the deceiving firms' competitive advantage. Companies must be sure not to cross ethical lines during these actions.	Max Muir knew that Australian farmers liked to buy from family-firm suppliers but also wanted efficient suppliers. To meet both needs, he quietly bought a number of small firms to build economies of scale but didn't consolidate brands or his sales force so that, to his customers and rivals, they still looked like independent family firms.
Unleash massive and overwhelming force	While many hardball strategies are subtle and indirect, this one is not. This is a full-frontal attack whereby a firm commits significant resources to a major campaign to weaken rivals' positions in certain markets. Firms must be sure they have the mass and stamina required to win before they declare war against a rival.	Unilever took a dominant position, with 65 percent market share, in the Vietnamese laundry detergent market by employing a massive investment and marketing campaign. In doing so, it decimated the market position of the local, incumbent competitors.
Raise competitors' costs	If a company has superior insight into the complex cost and profit structure of the industry, it can compete in a way that steers its rivals into relatively higher cost/lower profit arenas. This strategy uses deception to make the rivals think they are winning, when in fact they are not. Again, companies using this strategy must be confident that they understand the industry better than their rivals.	Ecolab, a company that sells cleaning supplies to businesses, encouraged a leading competitor, Diversity, to adopt a strategy to go after the low-volume, high-margin customers. What Ecolab knew that Diversity didn't is that the high servicing costs involved with this segment make the segment unprofitable—a situation Ecolab ensured by bidding high enough to lose the contracts to Diversity but low enough to ensure the business lost money for Diversity.

Sources: Berner, R. 2005. Watch Out, Best Buy and Circuit City. *BusinessWeek,* November 10; Stalk, G., Jr. 2006. Curveball strategies to fool the competition. *Harvard Business Review,* 84(9): 114–121; and Stalk, G., Jr., and R. Lachenauer. 2004. *Hardball: Are You Playing to Play or Playing to Win?* Cambridge, MA: Harvard Business School Press; Lam, Y. 2013. FDI companies dominate Vietnam's detergent market. *www.saigon-gpdaily.com.vn,* January 22: np; Vascellaro, J. 2012. Apple wins big in patent case. *www.wsj.com,* August 25: np; and Pech, R., and G. Stamboulidis. 2010. How strategies of deception facilitate business growth. *Journal of Business Strategy,* 31(6): 37–45.

Boeing and Airbus have a high degree of market commonality because they make very similar products and have many buyers in common.

- **Resource similarity.** The degree to which rivals draw on the same types of resources to compete. For example, Huawei and Nokia are telecommunications equipment providers that are based in different continents and have different histories, but they have patent rights to similar technologies, high quality engineering staffs, and global sales forces.

resource similarity the extent to which rivals draw from the same types of strategic resources.

When any two firms have both a high degree of market commonality and highly similar resource bases, a stronger competitive threat is present. Such a threat, however, may not lead to competitive action. On the one hand, a market rival may be hesitant to attack a company that it shares a high degree of market commonality with because it could lead to an intense battle. On the other hand, once attacked, rivals with high market commonality will be much more motivated to launch a competitive response. This is especially true in cases where the shared market is an important part of a company's overall business.

How strong a response an attacked rival can mount will be determined by its strategic resource endowments. In general, the same set of conditions holds true with regard to resource similarity. Companies that have highly similar resource bases will be hesitant to launch an initial attack but pose a serious threat if required to mount a competitive response.[55] Greater strategic resources increase a firm's capability to respond.

Motivation and Capability to Respond

Once attacked, competitors are faced with deciding how to respond. Before deciding, however, they need to evaluate not only how they will respond but also their reasons for responding and their capability to respond. Companies need to be clear about what problems a competitive response is expected to address and what types of problems it might create.[56] There are several factors to consider.

First, how serious is the impact of the competitive attack to which they are responding? For example, a large company with a strong reputation that is challenged by a small or unknown company may elect to simply keep an eye on the new competitor rather than quickly react or overreact. Part of the story of online retailer Amazon's early success is attributed to Barnes & Noble's overreaction to Amazon's claim that it was "earth's biggest bookstore." Because Barnes & Noble was already using the phrase "world's largest bookstore," it sued Amazon, but lost. The confrontation made it to the front pages of *The Wall Street Journal,* and Amazon was on its way to becoming a household name.[57]

Companies planning to respond to a competitive challenge must also understand their motivation for responding. What is the intent of the competitive response? Is it merely to blunt the attack of the competitor, or is it an opportunity to enhance its competitive position? Sometimes the most a company can hope for is to minimize the damage caused by a competitive action.

A company that seeks to improve its competitive advantage may be motivated to launch an attack rather than merely respond to one. For example, a number of years ago, *The Wall Street Journal (WSJ)* attacked the *New York Times* by adding a local news section to the New York edition of the *WSJ.* Its aim was to become a more direct competitor of the *Times.* The publishers of the *WSJ* undertook this attack when they realized the *Times* was in a weakened financial condition and would be unable to respond to the attack.[58] A company must also assess its capability to respond. What strategic resources can be deployed to fend off a competitive attack? Does the company have an array of internal strengths it can draw on, or is it operating from a position of weakness?

Consider the role of firm age and size in calculating a company's ability to respond. Most entrepreneurial new ventures start out small. The smaller size makes them more nimble compared to large firms so they can respond quickly to competitive attacks. Because they are not well-known, start-ups also have the advantage of the element of surprise in how and when they attack. Innovative uses of technology, for example, allow small firms to deploy resources in unique ways.

Because they are young, however, start-ups may not have the financial resources needed to follow through with a competitive response.[59] In contrast, older and larger firms may have more resources and a repertoire of competitive techniques they can use in a counterattack. Large firms, however, tend to be slower to respond. Older firms tend to be predictable in their responses because they often lose touch with the competitive environment and rely on strategies and actions that have worked in the past.

Other resources may also play a role in whether a company is equipped to retaliate. For example, one avenue of counterattack may be launching product enhancements or new product/service innovations. For that approach to be successful, it requires a company to have both the intellectual capital to put forward viable innovations and the teamwork skills to prepare a new product or service and get it to market. Resources such as cross-functional teams and the social capital that makes teamwork production effective and efficient represent the type of human capital resources that enhance a company's capability to respond.

Types of Competitive Actions

Once an organization determines whether it is willing and able to launch a competitive action, it must determine what type of action is appropriate. The actions taken will be determined by both its resource capabilities and its motivation for responding. There are also marketplace considerations. What types of actions are likely to be most effective given a company's internal strengths and weaknesses as well as market conditions?

Two broadly defined types of competitive action include strategic actions and tactical actions. **Strategic actions** represent major commitments of distinctive and specific resources. Examples include launching a breakthrough innovation, building a new production facility, or merging with another company. Such actions require significant planning and resources and, once initiated, are difficult to reverse.

strategic actions major commitments of distinctive and specific resources to strategic initiatives.

Tactical actions include refinements or extensions of strategies. Examples of tactical actions include cutting prices, improving gaps in service, or strengthening marketing efforts. Such actions typically draw on general resources and can be implemented quickly. Exhibit 8.5 identifies several types of strategic and tactical competitive actions that illustrate the range of actions that can occur in a rivalrous relationship.

tactical actions refinements or extensions of strategies usually involving minor resource commitments.

Some competitive actions take the form of frontal assaults, that is, actions aimed directly at taking business from another company or capitalizing on industry weaknesses. This can be especially effective when firms use a low-cost strategy. The airline industry provides a good example of this head-on approach. When Southwest Airlines began its no-frills, no-meals strategy in the late 1960s, it represented a direct assault on the major carriers of the day. In Europe, Ryanair has similarly directly challenged the traditional carriers with an overall cost leadership strategy.

Guerrilla offensives and selective attacks provide an alternative for firms with fewer resources.[60] These draw attention to products or services by creating buzz or generating enough shock value to get some free publicity. TOMS Shoes has found a way to generate interest in its products without a large advertising budget to match Nike. Its policy of donating one pair of shoes to those in need for every pair of shoes purchased by customers has generated a lot of positive chatter about the firm.[61]

Some companies limit their competitive response to defensive actions. Such actions rarely improve a company's competitive advantage, but a credible defensive action can lower the risk of being attacked and deter new entry.

Several of the factors discussed earlier in the chapter, such as types of entry strategies and the use of cost leadership versus differentiation strategies, can guide the decision about what types of competitive actions to take. Before launching a given strategy, however, assessing the likely response of competitors is a vital step.[62]

Likelihood of Competitive Reaction

The final step before initiating a competitive response is to evaluate what a competitor's reaction is likely to be. The logic of competitive dynamics suggests that once competitive actions are initiated, it is likely they will be met with competitive responses.[63] The last step before mounting an attack is to evaluate how competitors are likely to respond. Evaluating

EXHIBIT 8.5 Strategic and Tactical Competitive Actions

	Actions	Examples
Strategic Actions	• Entering new markets	• Make geographical expansions • Expand into neglected markets • Target rivals' markets • Target new demographics
	• New product introductions	• Imitate rivals' products • Address gaps in quality • Leverage new technologies • Leverage brand name with related products • Protect innovation with patents
	• Changing production capacity	• Create overcapacity • Tie up raw materials sources • Tie up preferred suppliers and distributors • Stimulate demand by limiting capacity
	• Mergers/alliances	• Acquire/partner with competitors to reduce competition • Tie up key suppliers through alliances • Obtain new technology/intellectual property • Facilitate new market entry
Tactical Actions	• Price cutting (or increases)	• Maintain low-price dominance • Offer discounts and rebates • Offer incentives (e.g., frequent flyer miles) • Enhance offering to move upscale
	• Product/service enhancements	• Address gaps in service • Expand warranties • Make incremental product improvements
	• Increased marketing efforts	• Use guerrilla marketing • Conduct selective attacks • Change product packaging • Use new marketing channels
	• New distribution channels	• Access suppliers directly • Access customers directly • Develop multiple points of contact with customers • Expand Internet presence

Sources: Chen, M. J., and D. Hambrick. 1995. Speed, stealth, and selective attack: How small firms differ from large firms in competitive behavior. *Academy of Management Journal,* 38: 453–482; Davies, M. 1992. Sales promotions as a competitive strategy. *Management Decision,* 30(7): 5–10; Ferrier, W., Smith, K., and C. Grimm. 1999. The role of competitive action in market share erosion and industry dethronement: A study of industry leaders and challengers. *Academy of Management Journal,* 42(4): 372–388; and Garda, R. A. 1991. Use tactical pricing to uncover hidden profits. *Journal of Business Strategy,* 12(5): 17–23.

potential competitive reactions helps companies plan for future counterattacks. It may also lead to a decision to hold off—that is, not to take any competitive action at all because of the possibility that a misguided or poorly planned response will generate a devastating competitive reaction.

How a competitor is likely to respond will depend on three factors: market dependence, competitor's resources, and the reputation of the firm that initiates the action (actor's reputation). The implications of each of these are described briefly as follows.

Market Dependence If a company has a high concentration of its business in a particular industry, it has more at stake because it must depend on that industry's market for its sales. Single-industry businesses or those where one industry dominates are more likely to mount a competitive response. Young and small firms with a high degree of **market dependence** may be limited in how they respond due to resource constraints.

market dependence
degree of concentration of a firm's business in a particular industry.

Competitor's Resources Previously, we examined the internal resource endowments that a company must evaluate when assessing its capability to respond. Here, it is the competitor's resources that need to be considered. For example, a small firm may be unable to mount a serious attack due to lack of resources. As a result, it is more likely to react to tactical actions such as incentive pricing or enhanced service offerings because they are less costly to attack than large-scale strategic actions. In contrast, a firm with financial "deep pockets" may be able to mount and sustain a costly counterattack.

Actor's Reputation Whether a company should respond to a competitive challenge will also depend on who launched the attack against it. Compared to relatively smaller firms with less market power, competitors are more likely to respond to competitive moves by market leaders. Another consideration is how successful prior attacks have been. For example, price cutting by the big automakers usually has the desired result–increased sales to price-sensitive buyers–at least in the short run. Given that history, when GM offers discounts or incentives, rivals Ford and Chrysler cannot afford to ignore the challenge and quickly follow suit.

Choosing Not to React: Forbearance and Co-opetition

The previous discussion suggests that there may be many circumstances in which the best reaction is no reaction at all. This is known as **forbearance**–refraining from reacting at all as well as holding back from initiating an attack. The decision of whether a firm should respond or show forbearance is not always clear.

forbearance
a firm's choice of not reacting to a rival's new competitive action.

Related to forbearance is the concept of **co-opetition.** This is a term that was coined by network software company Novell's founder and former CEO Raymond Noorda to suggest that companies often benefit most from a combination of competing and cooperating.[64] Close competitors that differentiate themselves in the eyes of consumers may work together behind the scenes to achieve industrywide efficiencies.[65] For example, breweries in Sweden cooperate in recycling used bottles but still compete for customers on the basis of taste and variety. Similarly, several competing Hollywood studios came together and agreed to cooperate on buying movie film. They negotiated promises to buy certain quantities of film to keep Kodak from closing down its film manufacturing business.[66] As long as the benefits of cooperating are enjoyed by all participants in a co-opetition system, the practice can aid companies in avoiding intense and damaging competition.[67]

co-opetition
a firm's strategy of both cooperating and competing with rival firms.

Despite the potential benefits of co-opetition, companies need to guard against cooperating to such a great extent that their actions are perceived as collusion, a practice that has legal ramifications in the United States. In Strategy Spotlight 8.4, we see an example of crossing the line into illegal cooperation.

Once a company has evaluated a competitor's likelihood of responding to a competitive challenge, it can decide what type of action is most appropriate. Competitive actions can take many forms: the entry of a start-up into a market for the first time, an attack by a lower-ranked incumbent on an industry leader, or the launch of a breakthrough innovation that disrupts the industry structure. Such actions forever change the competitive dynamics of a marketplace. Thus, the cycle of actions and reactions that occur in business every day is a vital aspect of entrepreneurial strategy that leads to continual new value creation and the ongoing advancement of economic well-being.

8.4 STRATEGY SPOTLIGHT — ETHICS

SMOKING OUT COLLUSION AMONG THE GERMAN BIG THREE

Auto manufacturers face a challenge of trying to balance the desire to provide the best technology in their cars to win customers' business while also minimizing their cost to produce cars. European Commission investigators have alleged that the German Big Three auto manufacturers— Volkswagen, BMW, and Mercedes—found a way to reduce cost and guarantee that they wouldn't face a primary competitor with better technology. Investigators have concluded the three firms colluded to limit the emission reducing technology they would include in their cars.

The evidence suggests that the three auto firms met and "agreed not to use the best technology" in order to cut reduce costs. By agreement, they limited emission reducing components they would include in both diesel and gasoline models of their vehicles. In their diesel cars, the investigators concluded the firms agreed to limit the capabilities of Selective Catalytic Reduction (SCR) systems, which decrease the amount of nitrogen oxides (NO_x) released by the vehicle. In their gasoline vehicles, they agreed to not use "Otto" Particulate Filters (OPF), which capture small particulates emissions before they are emitted from the vehicle's tailpipe. While these actions cut the cost of the vehicles, they resulted in higher pollution from vehicles produced by the three manufacturers.

While these actions appear to have allowed the firms to reduce their costs in the short-run, they now face two major costs. First, their reputations are being hit hard. This is especially damaging to Volkswagen, a firm that had already recently faced a scandal about how it employed technology that allowed its diesel cars to cheat on emissions' tests. Second, anti-trust authorities plan to fine each of the three manufacturers $1.1 billion.

Sources: James, D. 2019. Volkswagen, BMW & Mercedes facing massive fines of €1 billion - noxious cartel caught? *Drivespark.com,* March 9: np; and Geuss, M. 2018. EU investigating German automakers, alleging collusion on emissions tech. *arstechnica.com,* September 19: np.

ISSUE FOR DEBATE

Where Have the Entrepreneurs Gone?

The United States has long been seen as the home of a vibrant entrepreneurial economy, but the statistics call this into question. From 1977 to 2011, the number of new start-up firms in the United States declined by 28 percent. More dramatically, relative to the size of the working population, the number of new start-ups has fallen by half. Even Silicon Valley has seen the rate of new business start-ups decline by 50 percent over the last three decades. Entrepreneurial actions have fallen most sharply among younger adults. People age 20 to 34 created only 22.7 percent of all new companies in 2013, down from 34.8 percent in 1996. This is an ironic change given that enrollment in college entrepreneurship programs has been growing.

This declining rate of entrepreneurship is setting off warning bells for many. It leads to less innovation in the economy and slower job opportunity growth. Over the long run, it would lead to lower living standards and stagnant economic growth.

Concerns on this issue have led to a discussion of the underlying causes of this change. The causes of this decline may be emotional or institutional. On the emotional level, it may be that the after-effects of the Great Recession have tilted society toward risk aversion. Additionally, many would-be entrepreneurs are saddled with significant student loan debt, leaving them less willing to take on the risk of entrepreneurship. Consistent with this view, Audrey Baxter, a woman who won a business proposal award as a student at UCLA, opted to take a corporate job when she graduated rather than pushing her small business forward. "Having a secure job with a really good salary was something to be considered carefully," Baxter said.

It may also be that institutional factors are reducing people's willingness or ability to start a business. Weakened antitrust enforcement may be playing a role. Firms have been able to grow and combine in a range of markets, leading to extremely large competitors that dominate markets, increasing the entry barriers for entrepreneurs. Also, lax antitrust enforcement has made it easier for large incumbent firms to respond very aggressively to newcomers, increasing the risk for entrepreneurs. Government red tape is another institutional barrier to entrepreneurs. For example, Celeste Kelly opened a business offering horse massage but had to shut down the business when the Arizona State Veterinary Medical Examining Board ordered her to "cease and desist" because it ruled she was practicing veterinary medicine without a license—even though no veterinarians in the area offered horse massage as a treatment. This may seem like an obscure example, but many businesses, including barbers, bartenders, cosmetologists, and even tour guides, are required to obtain licenses. Less than 5 percent of workers required licenses in the 1950s. That number is now 35 percent. According to economists Morris Kleiner and Alan Krueger, licenses increase the wage costs for a business by 18 percent.

Discussion Questions

1. How concerned are you about the drop in the rate of entrepreneurship?
2. What do you think are the primary causes of the decline?
3. What actions should be taken to increase the rate of new business start-ups? How effective will these actions be?
4. What factors influence your desire to work in an entrepreneurial firm versus an established firm?

Sources: Hamilton, W. 2014. A drop-off in start-ups: Where are all the entrepreneurs? *latimes.com*, September 7: np; Anonymous. 2014. Red tape blues: The best and worst states for small business. *The Economist*, July 5: 23–24; and Anonymous. 2014. Unshackle the entrepreneurs; America's license raj. *The Economist*, July 5: 14.

Reflecting on Career Implications . . .

This chapter focuses on the potential benefits and risks associated with entrepreneurial actions. You can enhance your career by looking for and leveraging entrepreneurial opportunities both in creating a start- up and in firms in which you work. The following questions allow you to explore these possibilities.

- **Opportunity Recognition:** What ideas for new business activities are actively discussed in your work environment? Could you apply the four characteristics of an opportunity to determine whether they are viable opportunities? If no one in your organization is excited about or even considering new opportunities, you may want to ask yourself if you want to continue with your current firm.
- **Entrepreneurial New Entry:** Are there opportunities to launch new products or services that might add value to the organization? What are the best ways for you to bring these opportunities to the attention of key managers? Or might this provide an opportunity for you to launch your own entrepreneurial venture?
- **Entrepreneurial Resources:** Evaluate your resources in terms of financial resources, human capital, and social capital. Are these enough to launch your own venture? If you are deficient in one area, are there ways to compensate for it? Even if you are not interested in starting a new venture, can you use your entrepreneurial resources to advance your career within your firm?
- **Competitive Dynamics:** There is always internal competition within organizations: among business units and sometimes even individuals within the same unit. What types of strategic and tactical actions are employed in these internal rivalries? What steps have you taken to strengthen your own position given the "competitive dynamics" within your organization?

key points

LO 8-1 The role of opportunities, resources, and entrepreneurs in successfully pursuing new ventures.

- Opportunity recognition is a process of determining which venture ideas are, in fact, promising business opportunities. These opportunities can occur as a result of emergence of new technologies, sociocultural trends, or shifts in consumer demand.
- The resources that start-ups need include financial resources as well as human and social capital. Many firms also benefit from government programs that support new venture development and growth.

- New ventures thrive best when they are led by founders or owners who have vision, drive and dedication, and a commitment to excellence.

LO 8-2 Three types of entry strategies—pioneering, imitative, and adaptive—commonly used to launch a new venture.

- Pioneering new entrants develop a radical new product or highly innovative service that may change the way business is conducted in an industry.
- Imitative new entrants see products or business concepts that have been successful in one market niche or physical locale and introduce the same basic product or service in another segment of the market.
- Adaptive new entrants neither pioneer radically new products or services nor do they merely imitate others. They take an existing idea and adapt it to a particular situation.

LO 8-3 How the generic strategies of overall cost leadership, differentiation, and focus are used by new ventures and small businesses.

- With an overall cost leadership strategy, entrepreneurial firms achieve success by doing more with less. It holds down costs or makes more efficient use of resources than larger competitors, allowing the entrepreneurial firm to offer lower prices and still be profitable.
- Both pioneering and adaptive entry strategies involve some degree of differentiation. In both cases, the new venture is attempting to do something different, either by using a new technology or by deploying resources in a way that alters the way business is conducted.
- Focus strategies are often associated with small businesses because there is a natural fit between the narrow scope of the strategy and the small size of the firm.

LO 8-4 How competitive actions, such as the entry of new competitors into a marketplace, may launch a cycle of actions and reactions among close competitors.

- The competitive actions of a new entrant are very likely to provoke a competitive response from companies that feel threatened. This, in turn, is likely to evoke a reaction to the response. As a result, a competitive dynamic–action and response–begins among the firms competing for the same customers in a given marketplace.

LO 8-5 The components of competitive dynamics analysis are new competitive action, threat analysis, motivation and capability to respond, types of competitive actions, and likelihood of competitive reaction.

- A new competitive action is an act that may provoke competitors to react, such as price cutting, new market entry, imitating successful products, and expanding production capacity.
- Threat analysis involves a firm's efforts to understand its closest competitors and the kinds of competitive actions they might be planning.
- Firms are more motivated to respond when a competitor's actions have a stronger impact on the firm's businesses.
- A firm's capability to respond is influenced by the resources the firm has and the flexibility of its culture and operations.
- Competitive actions include two primary types - strategic and tactical actions.
- The likelihood of a competitive reaction is driven by the degree of the competitor's market dependence, the competitor's resources, and the reputation of the firm initiating the competitive action.

SUMMARY REVIEW QUESTIONS

1. Explain how the combination of opportunities, resources, and entrepreneurs helps determine the character and strategic direction of an entrepreneurial firm.
2. What is the difference between discovery and evaluation in the process of opportunity recognition? Give an example of each.
3. Describe the three characteristics of entrepreneurial leadership: vision, dedication and drive, and commitment to excellence.
4. Briefly describe the three types of entrepreneurial entry strategies: pioneering, imitative, and adaptive.
5. Explain why entrepreneurial firms are often in a strong position to use combination strategies.
6. What does the term *competitive dynamics* mean?
7. Explain the difference between strategic actions and tactical actions and provide examples of each.

key terms

entrepreneurship 238
opportunity recognition 239
angel investors 242
venture capitalists 242
crowdfunding 242
entrepreneurial leadership 244
entrepreneurial strategy 246
pioneering new entry 247
imitative new entry 247
adaptive new entry 248
competitive dynamics 251
new competitive action 252
threat analysis 252
market commonality 252
resource similarity 253
strategic actions 255
tactical actions 255
market dependence 257
forbearance 257
co-opetition 257

EXPERIENTIAL EXERCISES AND APPLICATION QUESTIONS

1. In Strategy Spotlight 8.1, we saw how TJ Parker took something that bugged him and turned it into a very valuable business. Consider something that bugs or has bugged you and develop a business idea to address this issue. Discuss how this business creates value for customers and whether the idea is a pioneering, adaptive, or imitative entry into the market.
2. E-Loan and Lending Tree are two entrepreneurial firms that offer lending services over the Internet. Evaluate the features of these two companies. (Fill in the following table.)
   a. Evaluate their characteristics and assess the extent to which they are comparable in terms of market commonality and resource similarity.
   b. Based on your analysis, what strategic and/or tactical actions might these companies take to improve their competitive position? Could E-Loan and Lending Tree improve their performance more through co-opetition than competition? Explain your rationale.

Company	Market Commonality	Resource Similarity
E-Loan		
Lending Tree		

Company	Strategic Actions	Tactical Actions
E-Loan		
Lending Tree		

3. Using the Internet, research the Small Business Administration's website (*www.sba.gov*). What different types of financing are available to small firms? Besides financing, what other programs are available to support the growth and development of small businesses?
4. Think of an entrepreneurial firm that has been successfully launched in the last 10 years. What kind of entry strategy did it use–pioneering, imitative, or adaptive? Since the firm's initial entry, how has it used or combined overall low-cost, differentiation, and/or focus strategies?
5. Select an entrepreneurial firm you are familiar with in your local community. Research the company and discuss how it has positioned itself relative to its close competitors. Does it have a unique strategic advantage? Disadvantage? Explain.

ETHICS QUESTIONS

1. Imitation strategies are based on the idea of copying another firm's idea and using it for your own purposes. Is this unethical or simply a smart business practice? Discuss the ethical implications of this practice (if any).
2. Intense competition such as price wars are an accepted practice in the United States, but cooperation between companies has legal ramifications because of antitrust laws. Should price wars that drive small businesses or new entrants out of business be illegal? What ethical considerations are raised (if any)?

REFERENCES

1. Konrad, A. 2014. Snapchat billionaires protect their stakes by settling with ousted cofounder Reggie Brown. *Forbes,* September 29; Anonymous. 2015. Just getting started? Put it all in writing. *Dallas Morning News,* May 10: 4D; and *statista.com.*
2. McCracken, T. 2018. The Truth About How Small Businesses Create Jobs and Benefit the Economy. *inc.com.* April 17: np.
3. Combs, J. & Ketchen, D. 2017. The problem with independent boards. *Wall Street Journal.* May 17: R8; and Faleye, O. 2016. The downside to full board independence. sloanreview.mit.edu. November 29: np.
4. Bryant, A. 2012. Want to innovate? Feed a cookie to the monster. *The New York Times,* March 24.
5. Fromartz, S. 1998. How to get your first great idea. *Inc. Magazine,* April 1: 91–94; and Vesper, K. H. 1990. *New venture strategies* (2nd ed.). Englewood Cliffs, NJ: Prentice Hall.
6. For an interesting perspective on the nature of the opportunity recognition process, see Baron, R. A. 2006. Opportunity recognition as pattern recognition: How entrepreneurs "connect the dots" to identify new business opportunities. *Academy of Management Perspectives,* February: 104–119.
7. Gaglio, C. M. 1997. Opportunity identification: Review, critique and suggested research directions. In Katz, J. A. (Ed.), *Advances in entrepreneurship, firm emergence and growth,* vol. 3. Greenwich, CT: JAI Press: 139–202; Lumpkin, G. T., Hills, G. E., & Shrader, R. C. 2004. Opportunity recognition. In Welsch, H. L. (Ed.), *Entrepreneurship: The road ahead:* 73–90. London: Routledge; and Long, W. & McMullan, W. E. 1984. Mapping the new venture opportunity identification process. *Frontiers of entrepreneurship research, 1984:* 567–590. Wellesley, MA: Babson College.
8. For an interesting discussion of different aspects of opportunity discovery, see Shepherd, D. A. & De Tienne, D. R. 2005. Prior knowledge, potential financial reward, and opportunity identification. *Entrepreneurship Theory & Practice,* 29(1): 91–112; and Gaglio, C. M. 2004. The role of mental simulations and counterfactual thinking in the opportunity identification process. *Entrepreneurship Theory & Practice,* 28(6): 533–552.

9. Stewart, T. A. 2002. How to think with your gut. *Business 2.0,* November: 99-104.

10. Anonymous. 2013. How entrepreneurs come up with great ideas. *wsj.com,* April 29: np.

11. Garone, E. 2016. Whose glass is that? A startup has the answer. *wsj.com,* May 1: np.

12. Zaleski, A. 2016. Grapes of math. *fortune.com,* February 1: 28.

13. For more on the opportunity recognition process, see Smith, B. R., Matthews, C. H., & Schenkel, M. T. 2009. Differences in entrepreneurial opportunities: The role of tacitness and codification in opportunity identification. *Journal of Small Business Management,* 47(1): 38-57.

14. Timmons, J. A. 1997. Opportunity recognition. In Bygrave, W. D. (Ed.), *The portable MBA in entrepreneurship* (2nd ed.): 26-54. New York: Wiley.

15. Social networking is also proving to be an increasingly important type of entrepreneurial resource. For an interesting discussion, see Aldrich, H. E. & Kim, P. H. 2007. Small worlds, infinite possibilities? How social networks affect entrepreneurial team formation and search. *Strategic Entrepreneurship Journal,* 1(1): 147-166.

16. Bhide, A. V. 2000. *The origin and evolution of new businesses.* New York: Oxford University Press.

17. Small business 2001: Where are we now? 2001. *Inc.,* May 29: 18-19; and Zacharakis, A. L., Bygrave, W. D., & Shepherd, D. A. 2000. *Global entrepreneurship monitor–National entrepreneurship assessment: United States of America 2000 Executive Report.* Kansas City, MO: Kauffman Center for Entrepreneurial Leadership.

18. Cooper, S. 2003. Cash cows. *Entrepreneur,* June: 36.

19. Seglin, J. L. 1998. What angels want. *Inc.,* 20(7): 43-44.

20. Torres, N. L. 2002. Playing an angel. *Entrepreneur,* May 1: 130-138.

21. Our discussion of crowdfunding draws on Wasik, J. 2012. The brilliance (and madness) of crowdfunding. *Forbes,* June 25: 144-146; Anonymous. 2012. Why crowdfunding may not be path to riches. *Finance.yahoo.com,* October 23: np; and Espinoza, J. 2012. Doing equity crowd funding right. *The Wall Street Journal,* May 21: R3.

22. Stanko, M. & Henard, D. 2016. How crowdfunding influences innovation. *MIT Sloan Management Review,* Spring: 15-17.

23. Kroll, M., Walters, B., & Wright, P. 2010. The impact of insider control and environment on post-IPO performance. *Academy of Management Journal,* 53: 693-725.

24. Eisenhardt, K. M. & Schoonhoven, C. B. 1990. Organizational growth: Linking founding team, strategy, environment, and growth among U.S. semiconductor ventures, 1978-1988. *Administrative Science Quarterly,* 35: 504-529.

25. Anonymous. 2015. There's an app for that. *The Economist,* January 3: 17-20.

26. Dubini, P. & Aldrich, H. 1991. Personal and extended networks are central to the entrepreneurship process. *Journal of Business Venturing,* 6(5): 305-333.

27. For more on the role of social contacts in helping young firms build legitimacy, see Chrisman, J. J. & McMullan, W. E. 2004. Outside assistance as a knowledge resource for new venture survival. *Journal of Small Business Management,* 42(3): 229-244.

28. Vogel, C. 2000. Janina Pawlowski. *Working Woman,* June: 70.

29. For a recent perspective on entrepreneurship and strategic alliances, see Rothaermel, F. T. & Deeds, D. L. 2006. Alliance types, alliance experience and alliance management capability in high-technology ventures. *Journal of Business Venturing,* 21(4): 429-460; and Lu, J. W. & Beamish, P. W. 2006. Partnering strategies and performance of SMEs' international joint ventures. *Journal of Business Venturing,* 21(4): 461-486.

30. Monahan, J. 2005. All systems grow. *Entrepreneur,* March: 78-82; Weaver, K. M. & Dickson, p. 2004. Strategic alliances. In Dennis, W. J., Jr. (Ed.), *NFIB national small business poll.* Washington, DC: National Federation of Independent Business; and Copeland, M. V. & Tilin, A. 2005. Get someone to build it. *Business 2.0,* 6(5): 88.

31. For more information, go to the Small Business Administration website at *www.sba.gov.*

32. Simsek, Z., Heavey, C., & Veiga, J. 2009. The impact of CEO core self-evaluation on entrepreneurial orientation. *Strategic Management Journal,* 31: 110-119.

33. Zhao, H. & Seibert, S. 2006. The big five personality dimensions and entrepreneurial status: A meta-analytic review. *Journal of Applied Psychology,* 91: 259-271.

34. For an interesting study of the role of passion in entrepreneurial success, see Chen, X-P., Yao, X., & Kotha, S. 2009. Entrepreneur passion and preparedness in business plan presentations: A persuasion analysis of venture capitalists' funding decisions. *Academy of Management Journal,* 52(1): 101-120.

35. Azouley, P., Jones, B., Kim. J. & Miranda, J. 2018. Research: The average age of a successful startup founder is 45. hbr.org. July 11: np.; and Wilkinson, A. 2018. Think you're too old to found a startup? Think again. wsj.com. May 2: np.

36. Collins, J. 2001. *Good to great.* New York: HarperCollins.

37. The idea of entry wedges was discussed by Vesper, K. 1990. *New venture strategies* (2nd ed.). Englewood Cliffs, NJ: Prentice Hall; and Drucker, P. F. 1985. *Innovation and entrepreneurship.* New York: HarperBusiness.

38. See Dowell, G. & Swaminathan, A. 2006. Entry timing, exploration, and firm survival in the early U.S. bicycle industry. *Strategic Management Journal,* 27: 1159-1182, for a recent study of the timing of entrepreneurial new entry.

39. Dunlap-Hinkler, D., Kotabe, M., & Mudambi, R. 2010. A story of breakthrough vs. incremental innovation: Corporate entrepreneurship in the global pharmaceutical industry. *Strategic Entrepreneurship Journal,* 4: 106-127.

40. Maiello, M. 2002. They almost changed the world. *Forbes,* December 22: 217-220.

41. Pogue, D. 2012. Pay by app: No cash or card needed. *International Herald Tribune,* July 19: 18.

42. Williams, G. 2002. Looks like rain. *Entrepreneur,* September 1: 104-111.

43. Pedroza, G. M. 2002. Tech tutors. *Entrepreneur,* September: 120.

44. Romanelli, E. 1989. Environments and strategies of organization start-up: Effects on early survival. *Administrative Science Quarterly,* 34(3): 369-387.

45. Wallace, B. 2000. Brothers. *Philadelphia Magazine,* April: 66-75.

46. Buchanan, L. 2003. The innovation factor: A field guide to innovation. *www.forbes.com,* April 21.

47. Kim, W. C. & Mauborgne, R. 2005. *Blue ocean strategy.* Boston: Harvard Business School Press.

48. For more on how unique organizational combinations can contribute to competitive advantages of entrepreneurial firms, see Steffens,

P., Davidsson, P., & Fitzsimmons, J. Performance configurations over time: Implications for growth- and profit-oriented strategies. *Entrepreneurship Theory & Practice,* 33(1): 125–148.

49. Smith, K. G., Ferrier, W. J., & Grimm, C. M. 2001. King of the hill: Dethroning the industry leader. *Academy of Management Executive,* 15(2): 59–70.
50. Grove, A. S. 1999. *Only the Paranoid Survive: How to Exploit the Crisis Points that Challenge Every Company.* New York: Random House.
51. Stalk, G., Jr., & Lachenauer, R. 2004. *Hardball: Are you playing to play or playing to win?* Cambridge, MA: Harvard Business School Press.
52. Chen, M. J., Lin, H. C, & Michel, J. G. 2010. Navigating in a hypercompetitive environment: The roles of action aggressiveness and TMT integration. *Strategic Management Journal,* 31: 1410–1430.
53. Peteraf, M. A. & Bergen, M. A. 2003. Scanning competitive landscapes: A market-based and resource-based framework. *Strategic Management Journal,* 24: 1027–1045.
54. Chen, M. J. 1996. Competitor analysis and interfirm rivalry: Toward a theoretical integration. *Academy of Management Review,* 21(1): 100–134.
55. Chen, 1996, op. cit.
56. Chen, M. J., Su, K. H, & Tsai, W. 2007. Competitive tension: The awareness-motivation-capability perspective. *Academy of Management Journal,* 50(1): 101–118.
57. St. John, W. 1999. Barnes & Noble's epiphany. *www.wired.com,* June.
58. Anonymous. 2010. Is the *Times* ready for a newspaper war? *Bloomberg Businessweek,* April 26: 30–31.
59. Souder, D. & Shaver, J. M. 2010. Constraints and incentives for making long horizon corporate investments. *Strategic Management Journal,* 31: 1316–1336.
60. Chen, M. J. & Hambrick, D. 1995. Speed, stealth, and selective attack: How small firms differ from large firms in competitive behavior. *Academy of Management Journal,* 38: 453–482.
61. Fenner, L. 2009. TOMS Shoes donates one pair of shoes for every pair purchased. *America.gov,* October 19: np.
62. For a discussion of how the strategic actions of Apple Computer contribute to changes in the competitive dynamics in both the cellular phone and music industries, see Burgelman, R. A. & Grove, A. S. 2008. Cross-boundary disruptors: Powerful interindustry entrepreneurial change agents. *Strategic Entrepreneurship Journal,* 1(1): 315–327.
63. Smith, K. G., Ferrier, W. J., & Ndofor, H. 2001. Competitive dynamics research: Critique and future directions. In Hitt, M. A., Freeman, R. E., & Harrison, J. S. (Eds.), *The Blackwell handbook of strategic management:* 315–361. Oxford, UK: Blackwell.
64. Gee, p. 2000. Co-opetition: The new market milieu. *Journal of Healthcare Management,* 45: 359–363.
65. Ketchen, D. J., Snow, C. C., & Hoover, V. L. 2004. Research on competitive dynamics: Recent accomplishments and future challenges. *Journal of Management,* 30(6): 779–804.
66. Fritz, B. 2014. Movie film, at death's door, gets a reprieve. *wsj.com,* July 29: np.
67. Khanna, T., Gulati, R., & Nohria, N. 2000. The economic modeling of strategy process: Clean models and dirty hands. *Strategic Management Journal,* 21: 781–790.

Nico Muller Art/Shutterstock

Strategic Control and Corporate Governance

Learning Objectives

LO9-1 Understand the value of effective strategic control systems in strategy implementation.

LO9-2 Identify the key difference between "traditional" and "contemporary" control systems.

LO9-3 Explain the imperative for contemporary control systems in today's complex and rapidly changing competitive and general environments.

LO9-4 Identify the benefits of having the proper balance among the three levers of behavioral control: culture, rewards and incentives, and boundaries.

LO9-5 Identify the three key participants in corporate governance: shareholders, management (led by the CEO), and the board of directors.

LO9-6 Explain the role of corporate governance mechanisms in ensuring that the interests of managers are aligned with those of shareholders from both the United States and international perspectives.

We encourage you to reflect on how the concepts presented in this chapter can enhance your career success (see "Reflecting on Career Implications..." at the end of the chapter).

LEARNING FROM MISTAKES

When Charles Lazarus returned from serving in the U.S. Army during World War II, he had the drive and ambition to start his own business. He wasn't sure what type of business he should start until he realized what all his friends and colleagues were talking about—families and children. As Lazarus explained, "Everyone I talked to said they were going to go home, get married, have children, and live the American dream."[1] This sentiment led him to see opportunity. These young families would need toys for their children.

Drawing upon this insight, Lazarus opened his first big-box toy store outside Washington D.C. in 1957. By the early 2000s, his toy store chain, Toys R Us, had grown to over 1,500 stores across the globe. The mascot of the store, Geoffrey the Giraffe, became a cultural icon. The firm grew to become the largest toy retailer in the country, and investment bank Goldman Sachs once labeled the company "one of the outstanding companies in all of retailing." This success invited competitors into the market. Major retailers, including Walmart and Target, started emphasizing their toy departments and ate away at the market position of Toys R Us, with Walmart supplanting Toys R Us as the largest toy retailer in the country in 2008. Toys R Us also faced a growing threat from Amazon and other online retailers.

Fast forward to 2018. Toys R Us was forced into liquidation; all of its stores closed and the chain disappeared from the U.S. retailing landscape. Was this the result of the threat it faced from Walmart, Target, and Amazon? These rivals certainly offered a challenge for Toys R Us, but they do not appear to be the primary reason the firm failed. Instead, the firm was largely done in by decisions made by its owners. In 2005, Toys R Us was purchased by two private equity firms, Bain Capital LP and KKR & Co., and Vornado Realty Trust. The deal was a leveraged buyout, with the buyers primarily financing the deal by issuing $7.5 billion dollars in debt. With such a huge debt load, Toys R Us was required to pay interest of over $400 million a year, soaking up half of the firm's profits, even in good years. This limited the ability of the firm to invest in and improve their store operations. It also limited its ability to develop new systems to counter the threats the firm faced. For example, while Best Buy was able to invest in and build up Geek Squad to offer services online retailers couldn't, Toys R Us didn't have the capital to develop a strong online presence or services that would go beyond what Walmart or Amazon could offer.

With the retailing market struggling after the financial crisis of 2008, the firm wasn't generating the income necessary to keep up with its debt payments. When balloon payments on the debt came due, such as a $725 million payment the firm had to make in 2009, the firm took out more loans backed by the firm's real estate. It all became a vicious cycle of debt payments and more loans.

The end seemed to come in March 2018. Toy R Us had a very disappointing holiday season in 2017, with sales falling 15 percent from the year before. In crunching the numbers, the firm realized it was $250 million short of what it needed to survive until the next holiday buying season. And it had no remaining assets it could use to finance new loans. The decision was made to close all 735 remaining stores, sell off the firm's inventory, and look for buyers for its brand, mascot, and real estate leases.[2]

However, this does not quite appear to be the end for Toys R Us. The brand names associated with the Toys R Us (including Kids R Us and Babies R Us), its mascot, and its customer database have all been purchased out of bankruptcy by Tru Kids, a firm run by a former Toys R Us executive. Tru Kids' plan is to resurrect the brand both within and outside the United States.

Discussion Questions

1. Why did Bain Capital & KKR take on such a heavy debt burden when they took over Toys R Us?
2. What was the effect of the debt burden on Toys R Us?
3. Is there still value in Toys R Us' resources? How should Tru Kids go about bringing the brand back to compete in today's retail market?

strategic control the process of monitoring and correcting a firm's strategy and performance.

We first explore two central aspects of **strategic control:**[3] (1) *informational control,* which is the ability to respond effectively to environmental change, and (2) *behavioral control,* which is the appropriate balance and alignment among a firm's culture, rewards, and boundaries. In the final section of this chapter, we focus on strategic control from a much broader perspective—what is referred to as *corporate governance.*[4] Here, we direct our attention to the need for a firm's shareholders (the owners) and their elected representatives (the board of directors) to ensure that the firm's executives (the management team) strive to fulfill their fiduciary duty of maximizing long-term shareholder value. As we just saw in the Toys R Us example, poor decisions by owners can lead a firm on a path leading to organizational failure.

LO 9-1

Understand the value of effective strategic control systems in strategy implementation.

ENSURING INFORMATIONAL CONTROL: RESPONDING EFFECTIVELY TO ENVIRONMENTAL CHANGE

We discuss two broad types of control systems: "traditional" and "contemporary." As both general and competitive environments become more unpredictable and complex, the need for contemporary systems increases.

traditional approach to strategic control a sequential method of organizational control in which (1) strategies are formulated and top management sets goals, (2) strategies are implemented, and (3) performance is measured against the predetermined goal set.

A Traditional Approach to Strategic Control

The **traditional approach to strategic control** is sequential: (1) strategies are formulated and top management sets goals, (2) strategies are implemented, and (3) performance is measured against the predetermined goal set, as illustrated in Exhibit 9.1.

Control is based on a feedback loop from performance measurement to strategy formulation. This process typically involves lengthy time lags, often tied to a firm's annual planning cycle. Such traditional control systems, termed "single-loop" learning by Harvard's Chris Argyris, simply compare actual performance to a predetermined goal.[5] They are most appropriate when the environment is stable and relatively simple, goals and objectives can be measured with a high level of certainty, and there is little need for complex measures of performance. Sales quotas, operating budgets, production schedules, and similar quantitative control mechanisms are typical. The appropriateness of the business strategy or standards of performance is seldom questioned.[6]

LO 9-2

Identify the key difference between "traditional" and "contemporary" control systems.

James Brian Quinn of Dartmouth College has argued that grand designs with precise and carefully integrated plans seldom work.[7] Rather, most strategic change proceeds incrementally—one step at a time. Leaders should introduce some sense of direction, some logic in incremental steps.[8] Similarly, McGill University's Henry Mintzberg has written about leaders "crafting" a strategy.[9] Drawing on the parallel between the potter at her wheel and the strategist, Mintzberg pointed out that the potter begins work with some general idea of the artifact she wishes to create, but the details of design—even possibilities for a different design—emerge as the work progresses. For businesses facing complex and turbulent business environments, the craftsperson's method helps us deal with the uncertainty about how a design will work out in practice and allows for a creative element.

LO 9-3

Explain the imperative for contemporary control systems in today's complex and rapidly changing competitive and general environments.

Mintzberg's argument, like Quinn's, questions the value of rigid planning and goal-setting processes. Fixed strategic goals also become dysfunctional for firms competing in highly

EXHIBIT 9.1 Traditional Approach to Strategic Control

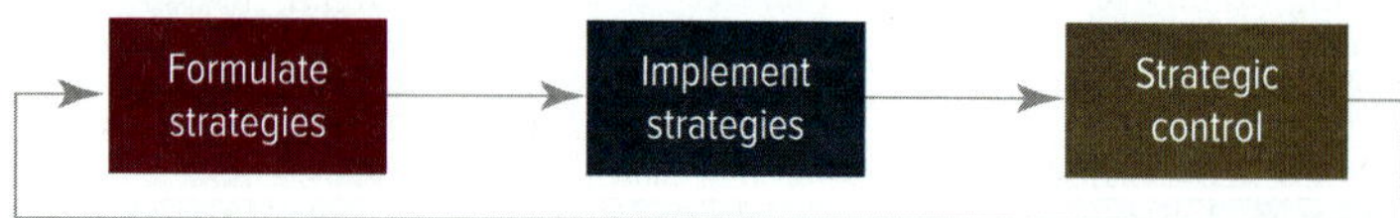

unpredictable competitive environments. Strategies need to change frequently and opportunistically. An inflexible commitment to predetermined goals and milestones can prevent the very adaptability that is required of a good strategy.

A Contemporary Approach to Strategic Control

Adapting to and anticipating both internal and external environmental change is an integral part of strategic control. The relationships between strategy formulation, implementation, and control are highly interactive, as suggested by Exhibit 9.2. The exhibit also illustrates two different types of strategic control: informational control and behavioral control.

informational control a method of organizational control in which a firm gathers and analyzes information from the internal and external environment in order to obtain the best fit between the organization's goals and strategies and the strategic environment.

Informational control is primarily concerned with whether or not the organization is "doing the right things." A key element of this is to allow organizational members to question whether there is a better path for the firm, even when objective measures say the firm is doing well. Alphabet, Google's parent, allows small self-identified teams to develop new products or processes that can change the direction of the firm. In one notable example, a team of three engineers saw machine learning technology as an emerging technology that would make key Google products more effective. Corporate managers initially encouraged the team to develop their ideas in GoogleX, the firm's incubator group. Eventually, the firm created a new business unit—Google Brain—and its engineers work with existing product teams to integrate machine technology into Google's products. This led to significant improvement in products, including reducing the error rates of voice-based search from 23 to 8 percent.[10]

behavioral control a method of organizational control in which a firm influences the actions of employees through culture, rewards, and boundaries.

Behavioral control, on the other hand, asks if the organization is "doing things right" in the implementation of its strategy. For example, even though it has an amazing track record of success, Pixar Animation Studios undertakes a review analysis after every movie it completes to assess how well each step of the process is working in the firm and makes adjustments for future films.

Both the informational and behavioral components of strategic control are necessary, but not sufficient, conditions for success. What good is a well-conceived strategy that cannot be implemented? Or what use is an energetic and committed workforce if it is focused on the wrong strategic target?

Informational control deals with the internal environment as well as the external strategic context. It addresses the assumptions and premises that provide the foundation for an organization's strategy. Do the organization's goals and strategies still "fit" within the context of the current strategic environment? Depending on the type of business, such assumptions may relate to changes in technology, customer tastes, government regulation, and industry competition.

This involves two key issues. First, managers must scan and monitor the external environment, as we discussed in Chapter 2. Also, conditions can change in the internal environment of the firm, as we discussed in Chapter 3, requiring changes in the strategic direction of the firm. These may include, for example, the resignation of key executives or delays in the completion of major production facilities.

EXHIBIT 9.2 Contemporary Approach to Strategic Control

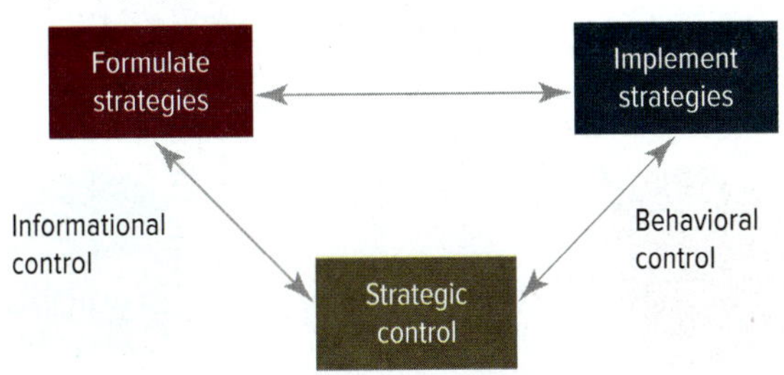

In the contemporary approach, information control is part of an ongoing process of organizational learning that continuously updates and challenges the assumptions that underlie the organization's strategy. In such double-loop learning, the organization's assumptions, premises, goals, and strategies are continuously monitored, tested, and reviewed. The benefits of continuous monitoring are evident—time lags are dramatically shortened, changes in the competitive environment are detected earlier, and the organization's ability to respond with speed and flexibility is enhanced.

Contemporary control systems must have four characteristics to be effective:[11]

1. The focus is on constantly changing information that has potential strategic importance.
2. The information is important enough to demand frequent and regular attention from all levels of the organization.
3. The data and information generated are best interpreted and discussed in face-to-face meetings.
4. The control system is a key catalyst for an ongoing debate about underlying data, assumptions, and action plans.

An executive's decision to use the control system interactively—in other words, to invest the time and attention to review and evaluate new information—sends a clear signal to the organization about what is important. The dialogue and debate that emerge from such an interactive process can often lead to new strategies and innovations.

LO 9-4

Identify the benefits of having the proper balance among the three levers of behavioral control: culture, rewards and incentives, and boundaries.

ATTAINING BEHAVIORAL CONTROL: BALANCING CULTURE, REWARDS, AND BOUNDARIES

Behavioral control is focused on implementation—doing things right. Effectively implementing strategy requires manipulating three key control "levers"—culture, rewards, and boundaries (see Exhibit 9.3). There are two compelling reasons for an increased emphasis on culture and rewards in a system of behavioral controls.[12]

First, the competitive environment is increasingly complex and unpredictable, demanding both flexibility and quick response to its challenges. As firms simultaneously downsize and face the need for increased coordination across organizational boundaries, a control system based primarily on rigid strategies, rules, and regulations is dysfunctional. The use of rewards and culture to align individual and organizational goals becomes increasingly important.

Second, the implicit long-term contract between the organization and its key employees has been eroded.[13] Today's younger managers have been conditioned to see themselves as

EXHIBIT 9.3 Essential Elements of Behavioral Control

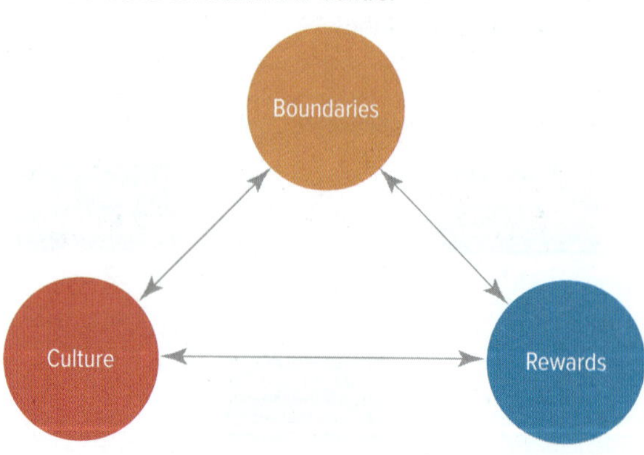

"free agents" and view a career as a series of opportunistic challenges. As managers are advised to "specialize, market yourself, and have work, if not a job," the importance of culture and rewards in building organizational loyalty claims greater importance.

Each of the three levers–culture, rewards, and boundaries–must work in a balanced and consistent manner. Let's consider the role of each.

Building a Strong and Effective Culture

Organizational culture is a system of shared values (what is important) and beliefs (how things work) that shape a company's people, organizational structures, and control systems to produce behavioral norms (the way we do things around here).[14] How important is culture? Very.

organizational culture a system of shared values and beliefs that shape a company's people, organizational structures, and control systems to produce behavioral norms.

Collins and Porras argued in *Built to Last* that the key factor in sustained exceptional performance is a cultlike culture.[15] You can't touch it or write it down, but it's there in every organization; its influence is pervasive; it can work for you or against you.[16] Effective leaders understand its importance and strive to shape and use it as one of their important levers of strategic control.[17]

The Role of Culture Culture wears many different hats, each woven from the fabric of those values that sustain the organization's primary source of competitive advantage. Some examples are:

- Zappos and Amazon focus on customer service.
- Lexus (a division of Toyota) and Apple emphasize product quality.
- Google and 3M place a high value on innovation.
- Nucor (steel) and Walmart are concerned, above all, with operational efficiency.

Culture sets implicit boundaries–unwritten standards of acceptable behavior–in dress, ethical matters, and the way an organization conducts its business.[18] By creating a framework of shared values, culture encourages individual identification with the organization and its objectives. Culture acts as a means of reducing monitoring costs.[19]

Strong culture can lead to greater employee engagement and provide a common purpose and identity. Firms have typically relied on economic incentives for workers, using a combination of rewards (carrots) and rules and threats (sticks) to get employees to act in desired ways. But these systems rely on the assumption that individuals are fundamentally self-interested and selfish. However, research suggests that this assumption is overstated.[20] When given a chance to act selfishly or cooperatively with others, over half of employees choose to cooperate, while only 30 percent consistently choose to act selfishly. Thus, cultural systems that build engagement, communication, and a sense of common purpose and identity would allow firms to leverage these collaborative workers.

While strong cultures can help a firm retain a common purpose and identity, it can also introduce core rigidities into the firm. Strategy Spotlight 9.1 outlines how General Electric (GE) suffered from a success-theater oriented culture.

Sustaining an Effective Culture Powerful organizational cultures just don't happen overnight, and they don't remain in place without a strong commitment–in terms of both words and deeds–by leaders throughout the organization.[21] A viable and productive organizational culture can be strengthened and sustained. However, it cannot be "built" or "assembled"; instead, it must be cultivated, encouraged, and "fertilized."[22]

Storytelling is one way effective cultures are maintained. 3M is a company that uses powerful stories to reinforce the culture of the firm. One of those is the story of Francis G. Okie.[23] In 1922, Okie came up with the idea of selling sandpaper to men as a replacement for razor blades. The idea obviously didn't pan out, but Okie was allowed to remain at 3M.

9.1 STRATEGY SPOTLIGHT

GE SHOWS ONE POTENTIAL DOWNSIDE OF A STRONG CULTURE

General Electric (GE) had long been one of the stalwart performers in the U.S. economy. For over 110 years, it had been a member of the elite Dow Jones Industrial Average, the set of 30 top U.S. firms used by Dow Jones to measure the health of the stock market. It was a true blue chip firm—large, successful financially, and very highly regarded. But the story for GE changed in 2017 and 2018. The firm's stock lost over 75 percent of its value over that two-year period, it was booted from the Dow Jones, and it replaced its CEO twice after having only two CEOs over the prior 36 years.

While a number of factors played into GE's struggles, its culture appears to have played a significant role. GE's culture and its management development program had long been seen very favorably. For decades, GE's strong performance-oriented culture was lauded in the business press and made GE managers attractive targets for other firms looking to recruit a new CEO or another top manager. But the dark side of its performance-oriented culture arose when the firm started to struggle.

The performance focus of GE matched up with its history of strong performance resulted in a culture that was overly confident about the future. As Peter Crist, an executive recruiter stated, "It's the mindset of invulnerability that iconic companies create—that we are a special entity. There was a time when GE players had a certain arrogance to them." With this dominant, confident culture, managers at all levels became very reluctant to pass along any bad news or concerns the managers had. Sandra Davis, the founder of MDA Leadership Consulting commented that "GE itself has never been a culture where people say, 'I can't.'" Former employees have commented that the firm developed a culture of "success theater," where being successful and projecting success was what was expected. As a result, employees were afraid to share information on the challenges they saw with their managers, division heads were reluctant to voice concerns to top management, and top managers kept the board of directors in the dark about the firm's struggles. As one former director of the firm stated, "many of us are in some level of shock" regarding GE's troubles.

So, how could GE have avoided the foibles of success theater? Ethan Burris, a professor at the University of Texas, argues that it starts at the top of the firm. Top managers have to model behavior that shows they want to constantly test assumptions and challenge projections. They need to be realistic about goals and forecasts and open digging into the causes when things go wrong. They should create venues, such as town halls where employees can voice their concerns or criticisms. Then, they should reward employees and managers who raise concerns. Kim Scott, a former senior executive at Google went so far as to use a crystal statue she called the "I was wrong, you were right" statue. She'd hand it out to colleagues and direct reports. "I was just letting people know I was happy to be wrong and I appreciated what I was told," she said.

The future will tell if GE will change its culture to foster greater discussion of and response to the challenges it faces. One indicator that the firm understands these challenges is it recruited H. Lawrence Culp as CEO in October 2018. Tellingly, he is the first outsider appointed as the firm's CEO in its long history.

Sources Gryta, T., Lublin, J.S., and D. Benoit. 2018. How Jeffrey Immelt's 'success theater' masked the rot at GE. *wsj.com,* February 21: np; McGregor, J. 2018. A lesson from GE: The power of telling hard truths - and the peril of avoiding them. *The Washington Post. washingtonpost.com,* February 26: np; and Egan, M. 2018. General Electric gets booted from the Dow. *cnn.com,* June 19: np.

Interestingly, the technology developed by Okie led 3M to develop its first blockbuster product: a waterproof sandpaper that became a staple of the automobile industry. Such stories foster the importance of risk taking, experimentation, freedom to fail, and innovation–all vital elements of 3M's culture. Strategy Spotlight 9.2 discusses the power of pictures and stories in building a customer-centric culture.

The actions of leaders and culture warriors can also play a critical role in reinforcing a firm's culture.[24] For example, the culture team at Warby Parker, an online eyewear retailer, is responsible for planning company outings and themed luncheons that reinforce company ideals and build a stronger sense of connectedness among workers. The culture team is also involved in screening potential new employees to ensure the firm's culture lives on as it grows. Corporate leaders can actively reinforce culture throughout the organization. Brent Beshore, CEO of adventur.es, a private investment firm, describes how he reinforces culture with personal contact:

> I make a point of walking around the office every day and thanking people for their contributions. It could be something as small as, "I really appreciated the email announcement you crafted," or something more substantive like, "Thanks for handling that tough situation a few days ago." Thanking them reminds them to thank others and be appreciative of what we have.[25]

9.2 STRATEGY SPOTLIGHT

USING PICTURES AND STORIES TO BUILD A CUSTOMER-ORIENTED CULTURE

Most firms tout that customers are their most important stakeholders. In firms that have value statements, these statements typically list the firms' responsibilities to their customers first. But it is hard to build and maintain a customer-centric culture. Using visual imagery and stories can help firms put customers at the center of their culture.

The old saying is that "a picture is worth a thousand words." This is certainly true when building a culture. A simple snapshot of a customer or end user can be a powerful motivating tool for workers to care about that customer. For example, radiologists rarely see patients. They look at X-rays from the files of patients, but these patients are typically faceless and anonymous to them. However, when pictures of the patients were added to their files, one study found that radiologists increased the length of their reports on the patients' X-rays by 29 percent and improved the accuracy of their diagnoses by 46 percent. Other firms have found the same effect. Microfinance provider Kiva includes pictures of the entrepreneurs whom it is trying to fund, believing that potential donors feel more of a connection with an entrepreneur when they have seen a picture of him or her.

Stories can also help build a customer-centric culture. Inside the firm, the stories that employees share with each other become imprinted on the organizational mind. Thus, as employees share their positive stories of experiences with customers, they not only provide encouragement for other employees to better meet the needs of customers but also reinforce the storytelling employee's desire to work hard to serve customers. For example, at Ritz-Carlton hotels, employees meet each day for 15 minutes to share stories about how they went the extra yard to meet customers' needs. These stories can even be more significant for new employees, helping them learn about the values of the firm. With outside stories, firms can draw on the accounts of customers to reinvigorate their employees. These can be based on personal statements from customers or even from news stories. To test these effects, one researcher gave lifeguards a few short news stories about swimmers who were saved by lifeguards on other beaches. The lifeguards who heard these stories reported that they found their job more meaningful, volunteered to work more hours, and were rated by their supervisors as being more vigilant in their work one month later.

Managers can help ensure that the stories told support the firm's customer-centric culture by taking the following steps:

- Tell positive stories about employees' interactions with customers.
- Share positive customer feedback with employees.
- Tie employee recognition to positive employee actions.
- Weave stories into the employee handbook and new employee orientation.
- Make sure that mentors in the firm know about the importance of using stories in their mentoring efforts.

The "short story" here is that firms can help build and reinforce a customer-centric culture if they just keep the customer in the center of the stories they tell and make the customer personally relevant to workers.

Sources: Grant, A. 2011. How customers rally your troops. *Harvard Business Review,* 89(6): 96–103; and Heathfield, S. 2014. How stories strengthen your work culture–or not. *humanresources.about.com*, December 29: np.

Motivating with Rewards and Incentives

Reward and incentive systems represent a powerful means of influencing an organization's culture, focusing efforts on high-priority tasks, and motivating individual and collective task performance.[26] Just as culture deals with influencing beliefs, behaviors, and attitudes of people within an organization, the **reward system**–by specifying who gets rewarded and why–is an effective motivator and control mechanism.[27] The managers at Not Your Average Joe's, a Massachusetts-based restaurant chain, changed their staffing procedures both to let their servers better understand their performance and to better motivate them.[28] The chain uses sophisticated software to track server performance–in both per customer sales and customer satisfaction as seen in tips. Highly rated servers are given more tables and preferred schedules. In shifting more work and better schedules to the best workers, the chain hopes to improve profitability and motivate all workers.

reward system policies that specify who gets rewarded and why.

The Potential Downside While they can be powerful motivators, reward and incentive policies can also result in undesirable outcomes in organizations. At the individual level, incentives can go wrong for multiple reasons. First, if individual workers don't see how their actions relate to how they are compensated, incentives can be demotivating. For example, if the rewards are related to the firm's stock price, workers may feel that their efforts have little if any impact and won't perceive any benefit from working harder. On the other hand, if the incentives are too closely tied to their individual work, they may lead to dysfunctional outcomes. For example, if a sales representative is rewarded for sales volume, she will be incentivized to sell at all costs. This may lead her to accept unprofitable sales or push sales through distribution channels the firm would rather avoid. Thus, the collective sum of individual behaviors of an organization's employees does not always result in what is best for the organization; individual rationality is no guarantee of organizational rationality.

Reward and incentive systems can also cause problems across organizational units. As corporations grow and evolve, they often develop different business units with multiple reward systems. These systems may differ based on industry contexts, business situations, stage of product life cycles, and so on. Subcultures within organizations may reflect differences among functional areas, products, services, and divisions. To the extent that reward systems reinforce such behavioral norms, attitudes, and belief systems, cohesiveness is reduced; important information is hoarded rather than shared, individuals begin working at cross-purposes, and they lose sight of overall goals.

Such conflicts are commonplace in many organizations. For example, sales and marketing personnel promise unrealistically quick delivery times to bring in business, much to the dismay of operations and logistics; overengineering by R&D creates headaches for manufacturing; and so on. Conflicts also arise across divisions when divisional profits become a key compensation criterion. As ill will and anger escalate, personal relationships and performance may suffer.

Creating Effective Reward and Incentive Programs To be effective, incentive and reward systems need to reinforce basic core values, enhance cohesion and commitment to goals and objectives, and meet with the organization's overall mission and purpose.[29] For example, Chesapeake Energy set a goal to improve workplace safety. To reinforce this, one year, it gave out over $8 million in "safety bonuses" to over 6,000 employees for following safe work practices.[30]

Effective reward and incentive systems share a number of common characteristics[31] (see Exhibit 9.4). The perception that a plan is "fair and equitable" is critically important. The firm must have the flexibility to respond to changing requirements as its direction and objectives change.

Recently, firms have emphasized agile compensation. The point of agile compensation is to spot and reward good performance at the moment it occurs. Research suggests that compensation is most effective in motivating behavior when the reward comes immediately after the desired behavior. Instant rewards reinforce the desired behavior, while annual raises are less effective in reinforcing behavior because there is too much time between the behavior and the reward. For example, Macy's uses spot bonuses supervisors can give out when they see exemplary behavior. Similarly, Patagonia makes monthly wage adjustments based on the difficulty of the projects on which employees are working or the degree to which they are going beyond expectations. The company retains a portion of its budget for individual awards and has developed a system in which supervisors can nominate top performers at any time.[32]

EXHIBIT 9.4

Characteristics of Effective Reward and Incentive Systems

- Objectives are clear, well understood, and broadly accepted.
- Rewards are clearly linked to performance and desired behaviors.
- Performance measures are clear and highly visible.
- Feedback is prompt, clear, and unambiguous.
- The compensation "system" is perceived as fair and equitable.
- The structure is flexible; it can adapt to changing circumstances.

However, incentive and reward systems don't have to be all about money. Employees respond not only to monetary compensation but also to softer forms of incentives and rewards. In fact, a number of studies have found that for employees who are satisfied with their base salary, nonfinancial motivators are more effective than cash incentives in building long-term employee motivation.[33] Three key reward systems appear to provide the greatest incentives. First, employees respond to managerial praise. This can include formal recognition policies and events. Employees also respond well to informal recognition rewards, such as personal praise, written praise, and public praise. This is especially effective when it includes small perks, such as a gift certificate for dinner, some scheduling flexibility, or even an extra day off. Positive words and actions are especially powerful since almost two-thirds of employees in one study said management was much more likely to criticize them for poor performance than praise them for good work. Second, employees feel rewarded when they receive attention from leaders and, as a result, feel valued and involved. One survey found that the number-one factor employees valued was "managerial support and involvement"—having their managers ask for their opinions, involve them in decisions, and give them authority to complete tasks. Third, managers can reward employees by giving them opportunities to lead projects or task forces. In sum, incentives and rewards can go well beyond simple pay to include formal recognition, praise, and the self-esteem that comes from feeling valued.

The Insights from Research box provides further evidence that employees are motivated more when they feel a sense of purpose in their work and feel valued by their employers than when they are only monetarily rewarded for their work.

Setting Boundaries and Constraints

In an ideal world, a strong culture and effective rewards should be sufficient to ensure that all individuals and subunits work toward the common goals and objectives of the whole organization.[34] However, this is not usually the case. Counterproductive behavior can arise because of motivated self-interest, lack of a clear understanding of goals and objectives, or outright malfeasance. **Boundaries and constraints** can serve many useful purposes for organizations, including:

boundaries and constraints rules that specify behaviors that are acceptable and unacceptable.

- Focusing individual efforts on strategic priorities.
- Providing short-term objectives and action plans to channel efforts.
- Improving efficiency and effectiveness.
- Minimizing improper and unethical conduct.

Focusing Efforts on Strategic Priorities Boundaries and constraints play a valuable role in focusing a company's strategic priorities. For example, in 2017, GM sold off its European operations so that it could better focus on the North American and Asian markets. Similarly, Pfizer sold its infant formula business as it refocused its attention on core pharmaceutical products.[35] This concentration of effort and resources provides the firm with greater strategic focus and the potential for stronger competitive advantages in the remaining areas.

Steve Jobs would use whiteboards to set priorities and focus attention at Apple. For example, he would take his "top 100" people on a retreat each year. One year, he asked the group what 10 things Apple should do next. The group identified ideas. Ideas went up on the board and then got erased or revised; new ones were added, revised, and erased. The group argued about it for a while and finally identified their list of top 10 initiatives. Jobs proceeded to slash the bottom seven, stating, "We can only do three."[36]

Boundaries also have a place in the nonprofit sector. For example, a British relief organization uses a system to monitor strategic boundaries by maintaining a list of companies whose contributions it will neither solicit nor accept. Such boundaries are essential for maintaining legitimacy with existing and potential benefactors.

9.1 *INSIGHTS* from Research

INSPIRE PASSION—MOTIVATE TOP PERFORMANCE

Overview

Often, managers approach and strive to motivate employees with extrinsic rewards. These produce some results; however, employees tend to perform best when their intrinsic needs are met. Think of ways to highlight the purpose of your employees' work. Allow employees to work on projects that ignite their passions.

What The Research Shows

Employees who are passionate about their jobs are more engaged in their jobs. And employees who are more engaged in their jobs perform them better, according to investigators from the University of Richmond, Nanyang Technological University, and Keppel Offshore and Marine Ltd. in Singapore. Their research, published in the *Journal of Management Studies,* utilized the performance appraisals of 509 headquarters employees of a large insurance company. The employees were given a survey to identify their attitudes toward their jobs. Using structural equations modeling, the researchers found a relationship between the employees' passion for their jobs and their performance of their jobs. However, the effect was significant only when mediated by the employees' absorption in their jobs.

Employees who had job passion identified with their jobs intrinsically and believed their work was meaningful. Therefore, they were able to feel passionate about their jobs while balancing that passion with other aspects of their lives that were also important to them. This resulted in an intensity of focus on and deep immersion in their tasks while they were working. When they were deeply engrossed in work, the employees were not distracted by other activities or roles in their lives. In turn, this job absorption resulted in superior performance on the job.

Key Takeaways

- Employees who are passionate about their jobs will be more engaged and absorbed in them and will perform better.
- When employees like their jobs and view them as important, they will be more passionate about their work.
- Employees whose jobs are significant to their personal identities–relative to the other roles they play in their lives–will be more passionate about their jobs.
- When employees are passionate about their jobs, they become deeply engrossed in their job tasks and aren't easily distracted by other activities.
- Although job passion must be voluntary and driven by employees' internal identities, managers can encourage it by helping employees see the significance of their work.

Questions

1. What types of jobs and industries are most appropriate for inspiring passion?
2. What are actions you can take to build passion in workers in lower skilled operational jobs?

Research Reviewed

Ho, V. T., Wong, S. S., and C. H. Lee. 2011. A tale of passion: Linking job passion and cognitive engagement to employee work performance. *Journal of Management Studies,* 48(1): 26–47.

Providing Short-Term Objectives and Action Plans In Chapter 1 we discussed the importance of a firm having a vision, mission, and strategic objectives that are internally consistent and that provide strategic direction. In addition, short-term objectives and action plans provide similar benefits. That is, they represent boundaries that help to allocate resources in an optimal manner and to channel the efforts of employees at all levels throughout the organization.[37] To be effective, short-term objectives must have several attributes. They should:

- Be specific and measurable.
- Include a specific time horizon for their attainment.
- Be achievable, yet challenging enough to motivate managers who must strive to accomplish them.

Research has found that performance is enhanced when individuals are encouraged to attain specific, difficult, yet achievable, goals (as opposed to vague "do your best" goals).[38]

Short-term objectives must provide proper direction and also provide enough flexibility for the firm to keep pace with and anticipate changes in the external environment, new government regulations, a competitor introducing a substitute product, or changes in consumer taste. Unexpected events within a firm may require a firm to make important adjustments in both strategic and short-term objectives. The emergence of new industries can have a drastic effect on the demand for products and services in more traditional industries.

Action plans are critical to the implementation of chosen strategies. Unless action plans are specific, there may be little assurance that managers have thought through all of the resource requirements for implementing their strategies. In addition, unless plans are specific, managers may not understand what needs to be implemented or have a clear time frame for completion. This is essential for the scheduling of key activities that must be implemented. Finally, individual managers must be held accountable for the implementation. This helps to provide the necessary motivation and "sense of ownership" to implement action plans on a timely basis.

Improving Operational Efficiency and Effectiveness Rule-based controls are most appropriate in organizations with the following characteristics:

- Environments are stable and predictable.
- Employees are largely unskilled and interchangeable.
- Consistency in product and service is critical.
- The risk of malfeasance is extremely high (e.g., in banking or casino operations).[39]

McDonald's Corp. has extensive rules and regulations that regulate the operation of its franchises.[40] Its policy manual from a number of years ago stated, "Cooks must turn, never flip, hamburgers. If they haven't been purchased, Big Macs must be discarded in 10 minutes after being cooked and French fries in 7 minutes. Cashiers must make eye contact with and smile at every customer."[41]

Guidelines can also be effective in setting spending limits and the range of discretion for employees and managers, such as the $2,500 limit that hotelier Ritz-Carlton uses to empower employees to placate dissatisfied customers.

Minimizing Improper and Unethical Conduct Guidelines can be useful in specifying proper relationships with a company's customers and suppliers.[42] Many companies have explicit rules regarding commercial practices, including the prohibition of any form of payment, bribe, or kickback. For example, Singapore Airlines has a three page policy outlining its ethical code of conduct.[43]

Behavioral Control in Organizations: Situational Factors

Here, the focus is on ensuring that the behavior of individuals at all levels of an organization is directed toward achieving organizational goals and objectives. The three fundamental types of control are culture, rewards and incentives, and boundaries and constraints. An organization may pursue one or a combination of them on the basis of a variety of internal and external factors.

Not all organizations place the same emphasis on each type of control.[44] In high-technology firms engaged in basic research, members may work under high levels of autonomy. An individual's performance is generally quite difficult to measure accurately because of the long lead times involved in R&D activities. Thus, internalized norms and values become very important.

When the measurement of an individual's output or performance is quite straightforward, control depends primarily on granting or withholding rewards. Frequently, a sales manager's compensation is in the form of a commission and bonus tied directly to his or her sales volume, which is relatively easy to determine. Here, behavior is influenced more

9.3 STRATEGY SPOTLIGHT — DATA ANALYTICS

USING DATA ANALYTICS TO ENHANCE ORGANIZATIONAL CONTROL

Tim Estes's goal was to develop cognitive computing as a useful business tool. Cognitive computing strives to integrate raw computing power with natural-language processing and pattern recognition to build powerful computer systems that mimic human problem solving and learning. He first found a ready home for his vision in national security. The U.S. Army's Ground Intelligence Center contracted with Digital Reasoning to develop systems to identify potential terrorists on the basis of analyses of large volumes of different sources of data, including emails, travel information, and other data.

More recently, Digital Reasoning has taken its expertise to the financial services industry and, in doing so, is providing a new type of control system to catch potential rogue traders and market manipulators within the firms. Digital Reasoning provides systems Estes refers to as "proactive compliance" to a number of major financial services providers, including Credit Suisse and Goldman Sachs. Digital Reasoning has developed software that looks for information in and patterns across billions of emails, instant messages, media reports, and memos that suggest an employee's intention to engage in illegal or prohibited behavior before the employee crosses the line. Rather than looking for evidence of actions already taken, Digital Reasoning's software looks into ongoing patterns of correspondence to search for evolving personal relationships within the company, putting up red flags when it sees unexpected patterns, such as people in different units of the firm suddenly communicating with unusual frequency or a heightened level of discussion on topics that may be tied to unethical or illegal behavior. Any unusual patterns are then investigated by analysts in each of the financial services' firms. The goal for the firms is to both control employee behavior to stay on the right side of the law and also to send signals to customers and regulators that they are taking steps to stay on the right side of legal and ethical boundaries.

Sources: McGee, J. 2014. When crisis strikes, Digital Reasoning takes action. *tennessean.com*, October 9: np; McGee, J. 2014. Digital reasoning gains $24M from Goldman, Credit Suisse. *tennessean.com*, October 9: np; and Dillow, C. 2014. Nothing to hide, everything to fear. *Fortune*, September 1: 45–48.

strongly by the attractiveness of the compensation than by the norms and values implicit in the organization's culture. The measurability of output precludes the need for an elaborate system of rules to control behavior.[45]

Control in bureaucratic organizations is dependent on members following a highly formalized set of rules and regulations. Most activities are routine, and the desired behavior can be specified in a detailed manner because there is generally little need for innovative or creative activity. Managing an assembly plant requires strict adherence to many rules as well as exacting sequences of assembly operations. In the public sector, the Department of Motor Vehicles in most states must follow clearly prescribed procedures when issuing or renewing driver licenses. Strategy Spotlight 9.2 highlights how Digital Reasoning is using data analytics to strengthen control in major financial firms.

Exhibit 9.5 provides alternative approaches to behavioral control and some of the situational factors associated with them.

EXHIBIT 9.5
Organizational Control: Alternative Approaches

Approach	Some Situational Factors
Culture: A system of unwritten rules that forms an internalized influence over behavior.	• Often found in professional organizations. • Associated with high autonomy. • Norms are the basis for behavior.
Rules: Written and explicit guidelines that provide external constraints on behavior.	• Associated with standardized output. • Most appropriate when tasks are generally repetitive and routine. • Little need for innovation or creative activity.
Rewards: The use of performance-based incentive systems to motivate.	• Measurement of output and performance is rather straightforward. • Most appropriate in organizations pursuing unrelated diversification strategies. • Rewards may be used to reinforce other means of control.

Evolving from Boundaries to Rewards and Culture

In most environments, organizations should strive to provide a system of rewards and incentives, coupled with a culture strong enough that boundaries become internalized. This reduces the need for external controls such as rules and regulations.

First, hire the right people–individuals who already identify with the organization's dominant values and have attributes consistent with them. Kroger, a supermarket chain, uses a preemployment test to assess the degree to which potential employees will be friendly and communicate well with customers.[46] Microsoft's David Pritchard is well aware of the consequences of failing to hire properly:

> If I hire a bunch of bozos, it will hurt us, because it takes time to get rid of them. They start infiltrating the organization and then they themselves start hiring people of lower quality. At Microsoft, we are always looking for people who are better than we are.[47]

Second, training plays a key role. For example, in elite military units such as the Green Berets and Navy SEALs, the training regimen so thoroughly internalizes the culture that individuals, in effect, lose their identity. The group becomes the overriding concern and focal point of their energies.

Third, managerial role models are vital. Andy Grove, former CEO and cofounder of Intel, didn't need (or want) a large number of bureaucratic rules to determine who is responsible for what, who is supposed to talk to whom, and who gets to fly first class (no one does). He encouraged openness by not having many of the trappings of success–he worked in a cubicle like all the other professionals. Can you imagine any new manager asking whether or not he can fly first class? Grove's personal example eliminated such a need.

Fourth, reward systems must be clearly aligned with the organizational goals and objectives. For example, as part of its efforts to drive sustainability efforts down through its suppliers, Marks and Spencer pushes the suppliers to develop employee reward systems that support a living wage and team collaboration.

THE ROLE OF CORPORATE GOVERNANCE

LO 9-5

Identify the three key participants in corporate governance: shareholders, management (led by the CEO), and the board of directors.

We now address the issue of strategic control in a broader perspective, typically referred to as "corporate governance." Here we focus on the need for both shareholders (the owners of the corporation) and their elected representatives, the board of directors, to actively ensure that management fulfills its overriding purpose of increasing long-term shareholder value.[48]

Robert Monks and Nell Minow, two leading scholars in **corporate governance,** define it as "the relationship among various participants in determining the direction and performance of corporations. The primary participants are (1) the shareholders, (2) the management (led by the CEO), and (3) the board of directors."[49] Our discussion will center on how corporations can succeed (or fail) in aligning managerial motives with the interests of the shareholders and their elected representatives, the board of directors.[50] As you will recall from Chapter 1, we discussed the important role of boards of directors and provided some examples of effective and ineffective boards.[51]

corporate governance
the relationship among various participants in determining the direction and performance of corporations. The primary participants are (1) the shareholders, (2) the management (led by the chief executive officer), and (3) the board of directors.

Good corporate governance plays an important role in the investment decisions of major institutions, and a premium is often reflected in the price of securities of companies that practice it. The corporate governance premium is larger for firms in countries with sound corporate governance practices compared to countries with weaker corporate governance standards.[52]

Sound governance practices often lead to superior financial performance. However, this is not always the case. For example, practices such as independent directors (directors who are not part of the firm's management) and stock options are generally assumed to result in better performance. But in many cases, independent directors may not have the necessary expertise or involvement, and the granting of stock options to the CEO may lead to decisions and actions calculated to prop up share price only in the short term.

At the same time, few topics in the business press are generating as much interest (and disdain!) as corporate governance.

Some recent notable examples of flawed corporate governance include:[53]

- In 2017, Lee Jae-yong, the heir apparent at the family run Samsung Corporation, was convicted of bribery of governmental officials. Though he was originally sentenced to five years in prison, an appeals court reduced his sentence and set him free. Though a convicted felon, he still serves as Vice-Chair of Samsung and is still considered "The Crown Prince of Samsung."[54]
- In 2016, John Stumpf, CEO of Wells Fargo, was forced to resign after both stakeholder and government scrutiny of the firm's practices. Firm management had instituted very aggressive sales goals for employees, leading employees to create sham accounts using the names and money of the bank's real customers.[55]
- In 2012 Japanese camera and medical equipment maker Olympus Corporation and three of its former executives pleaded guilty to charges that they falsified accounting records over a five-year period to inflate the financial performance of the firm. The total value of the accounting irregularities came to $1.7 billion.[56]

Because of the many lapses in corporate governance, we can see the benefits associated with effective practices.[57] However, corporate managers may behave in their own self-interest, often to the detriment of shareholders. Next we address the implications of the separation of ownership and management in the modern corporation, and some mechanisms that can be used to ensure consistency (or alignment) between the interests of shareholders and those of the managers to minimize potential conflicts.

The Modern Corporation: The Separation of Owners (Shareholders) and Management

Some of the proposed definitions for a *corporation* include:

- "The business corporation is an instrument through which capital is assembled for the activities of producing and distributing goods and services and making investments. Accordingly, a basic premise of corporation law is that a business corporation should have as its objective the conduct of such activities with a view to enhancing the corporation's profit and the gains of the corporation's owners, that is, the shareholders." (Melvin Aron Eisenberg, *The Structure of Corporation Law*)
- "An association of individuals, created by law or under authority of law, having a continuous existence independent of the existences of its members, and powers and liabilities distinct from those of its member." (dictionary.com)
- "An ingenious device for obtaining individual profit without individual responsibility." (Ambrose Bierce, *The Devil's Dictionary*)[58]

All of these definitions have some validity and each one reflects a key feature of the corporate form of business organization–its ability to draw resources from a variety of groups and establish and maintain its own persona that is separate from all of them. As Henry Ford once said, "A great business is really too big to be human."

corporation
a mechanism created to allow different parties to contribute capital, expertise, and labor for the maximum benefit of each party.

Simply put, a **corporation** is a mechanism created to allow different parties to contribute capital, expertise, and labor for the maximum benefit of each party.[59] The shareholders (investors) are able to participate in the profits of the enterprise without taking direct responsibility for the operations. The management can run the company without the responsibility of personally providing the funds. The shareholders have limited liability as well as rather limited involvement in the company's affairs. However, they reserve the right to elect directors who have the fiduciary obligation to protect their interests.

Over 80 years ago, Columbia University professors Adolf Berle and Gardiner C. Means addressed the divergence of the interests of the owners of the corporation from the professional managers who are hired to run it. They warned that widely dispersed ownership "released management from the overriding requirement that it serve stockholders." The separation of ownership from management has given rise to a set of ideas called "agency theory." Central to agency theory is the relationship between two primary players–the *principals,* who are the owners of the firm (stockholders), and the *agents,* who are the people paid by principals to perform a job on their behalf (management). The stockholders elect and are represented by a board of directors that has a fiduciary responsibility to ensure that management acts in the best interests of stockholders to ensure long-term financial returns for the firm.

Agency theory is concerned with resolving two problems that can occur in agency relationships.[60] *The first is the agency problem that arises (1) when the goals of the principals and agents conflict and (2) when it is difficult or expensive for the principal to verify what the agent is actually doing.*[61] The board of directors would be unable to confirm that the managers were actually acting in the shareholders' interests because managers are "insiders" with regard to the businesses they operate and thus are better informed than the principals. Thus, managers may act "opportunistically" in pursuing their own interests–to the detriment of the corporation.[62] Managers may spend corporate funds on expensive perquisites (e.g., company jets and expensive art), devote time and resources to pet projects (initiatives in which they have a personal interest but that have limited market potential), engage in power struggles (where they may fight over resources for their own betterment and to the detriment of the firm), and negate (or sabotage) attractive merger offers because they may result in increased employment risk.[63]

agency theory
a theory of the relationship between principals and their agents, with emphasis on two problems: (1) the conflicting goals of principals and agents, along with the difficulty of principals to monitor the agents, and (2) the different attitudes and preferences toward risk of principals and agents.

The second issue is the problem of risk sharing. This arises when the principal and the agent have different attitudes and preferences toward risk. The executives in a firm may favor additional diversification initiatives because, by their very nature, they increase the size of the firm and thus the level of executive compensation.[64] At the same time, such diversification initiatives may erode shareholder value because they fail to achieve some synergies that we discussed in Chapter 6 (e.g., building on core competencies, sharing activities, or enhancing market power). Agents (executives) may have a stronger preference toward diversification than shareholders because it reduces their personal level of risk from potential loss of employment. Executives who have large holdings of stock in their firms are more likely to have diversification strategies that are more consistent with shareholder interests–increasing long-term returns.[65]

Governance Mechanisms: Aligning the Interests of Owners and Managers

LO 9-6

Explain the role of corporate governance mechanisms in ensuring that the interests of managers are aligned with those of shareholders from both the United States and international perspectives.

As noted above, a key characteristic of the modern corporation is the separation of ownership from control. To minimize the potential for managers to act in their own self-interest, or "opportunistically," the owners can implement some governance mechanisms.[66] First, there are two primary means of monitoring the behavior of managers. These include (1) a committed and involved *board of directors* that acts in the best interests of the shareholders to create long-term value and (2) *shareholder activism,* wherein the owners view themselves as share*owners* instead of share*holders* and become actively engaged in the governance of the corporation. Finally, there are managerial incentives, sometimes called "contract-based outcomes," which consist of *reward and compensation agreements.* Here the goal is to carefully craft managerial incentive packages to align the interests of management with those of the stockholders.[67]

We close this section with a brief discussion of one of the most controversial issues in corporate governance–duality. Here, the question becomes: Should the CEO also be chairman of the board of directors? In many Fortune 500 firms, the same individual serves in both roles. However, in recent years, we have seen a trend toward separating these two positions. The key issue is what implications CEO duality has for firm governance and performance.

board of directors
a group that has a fiduciary duty to ensure that the company is run consistently with the long-term interests of the owners, or shareholders, of a corporation and that acts as an intermediary between the shareholders and management.

A Committed and Involved Board of Directors The **board of directors** acts as a fulcrum between the owners and controllers of a corporation. The directors are the intermediaries who provide a balance between a small group of key managers in the firm based at the corporate headquarters and a sometimes vast group of shareholders.[68] In the United States, the law imposes on the board a strict and absolute fiduciary duty to ensure that a company is run consistent with the long-term interests of the owners–the shareholders. The reality, as we have seen, is somewhat more ambiguous.[69]

The Business Roundtable, representing the largest U.S. corporations, describes the duties of the board as follows:

1. Making decisions regarding the selection, compensation and evaluation of a well-qualified and ethical CEO. The board also appoints or approves other members of the senior management team.
2. Directors monitor management on behalf of the corporation's shareholders. Exercise vigorous and diligent oversight of the corporation's affairs. This includes the following activities.
   a. Plan for senior management development and succession.
   b. Review, understand and monitor the implementation of the corporation's strategic plans.
   c. Review and understand the corporation's risk assessment and oversee the corporation's risk management processes.
   d. Review, understand and oversee annual operating plans and budgets.
   e. Ensure the integrity and clarity of the corporation's financial statements and financial reporting.
   f. Advise management on significant issues facing the corporation.
   g. Review and approve significant corporate actions.
   h. Nominate directors and committee members and oversee effective corporate governance.
   i Oversee legal and ethical compliance.
3. Represent the interests of all shareholders.[70]

While the roles of the board are fairly clear, following these guidelines does not guarantee that the board will be effective. To be effective, the board needs to allocate its scarce time to the most critical issues to which its members can add value. A survey of several hundred corporate board members revealed dramatic differences in how the most and least effective boards allocated their time. Boards that were seen as being ineffective, meaning they had limited impact on the direction and success of the firm, spent almost all of their time on the basic requirements of ensuring compliance, reviewing financial reports, assessing corporate diversification, and evaluating current performance metrics. Effective boards examined these issues but also expanded the range of issues they discussed to include more forward-looking strategic issues. Effective boards discussed potential performance synergies and the value of strategic alternatives open to the firm, assessed the firm's value drivers, and evaluated potential resource reallocation options. In the end, effective and ineffective boards spent about the same time on their basic board roles, but effective boards spent additional time together to discuss more forward-looking, strategic issues. As a result, board members of effective boards spent twice as many days, about 40 per year, in their role as a board member compared to only about 19 days per year for members of ineffective boards.[71]

To be more responsive to changing market demographics and market conditions, firms are pushing for younger and more diverse boards. This issue is discussed further in Strategy Spotlight 9.4.

9.4 STRATEGY SPOTLIGHT

A PUSH FOR YOUNGER AND MORE DIVERSE BOARDS

In 2017, 45 percent of the people who were appointed as new directors at S&P 500 companies had never been a board member before. This is the highest percentage recruiting firm Spencer Stuart had ever seen. Also, for the first time, a majority of new directors were female or minority candidates. These new directors are often also younger than prior typical board members, with 43% of S&P 500 firms now having at least one board member under the age of 50.

This push for younger, more diverse directors comes from external pressures from both government and activists as well as internal desires to make the board more reflective of the characteristics of customers and employees. Research by McKinsey consulting indicates that having a more diverse board helps attract and motivate talented employees, understand and voice the concerns of customers, and improve decision making quality. As Rodney McMullen, CEO of Kroger, stated "you get questions from perspectives that you hadn't thought of before, and I think this helps you avoid blind spots." Don Slager, CEO of Republic Services, a waste management company, expressed a similar view, saying "Change meant bringing people into the waste business who had other experiences. Prior . . . they were just a bunch of garbage men."

However, firms face challenges in how to identify these new directors and integrate them into the board. They are hard to identify because they haven't yet developed a profile or set of experiences that make them appear to be high potential board members. Boards historically have a tendency to look for individuals who are CEOs or have been board members of other firms since they have a track record in these other roles. Firms making a commitment to identify younger and diverse directors often include goals and policies to make sure the slate of candidates they consider are diverse. This could include a targeted percentage of board members in different categories. It could include policies to include younger, female, or ethnically diverse candidates in their pool. It could also include policies to recruit directors from industries that have a higher percentage of younger and diverse top managers. These firms sometimes even expand outside of business to find candidates in law firms, academia, and social sectors.

These younger, novice directors also typically require more training and coaching when they first join boards since they have no experience in that role. Firms, such as Tyson Foods, have developed crash courses on the meat industry since the new directors they are bringing in typically are from other industries. Firms often also pair the new directors up with established directors who provide one-on-one mentoring to help the new directors learn the ropes and start building social connections with the board.

The experiences of firms bringing on these novice directors show that it takes a conscious effort to seek out candidates with new and diverse perspectives and to bring them up to speed on the role of a board member. However, it appears to be worth the effort since it brings benefits in the form of better conversations within the board that allow the firm to be more effective in meeting the needs of its diverse stakeholders.

Sources: Green, J. 2018. New kids on the board. *Bloombergbusinessweek.com*. April 23: np.; Huber, C. & O'Rourke, S. 2017. How to accelerate gender diversity on boards. *Mckinsey.com*. January: np.; and Anonymous. 2017. Board composition: Consider the value of younger directors on your board. *Pwc.com*. December 29: np.

Although boards in the past were often dismissed as CEOs' rubber stamps, increasingly they are playing a more active role by forcing out CEOs who cannot deliver on performance.[72] Not only are they dismissing CEOs, but boards are more willing to make strong public statements about CEOs they dismissed. In the past, firms would often announce that a CEO was leaving the position to spend more time with family or pursue new opportunities. More frequently, boards are unambiguously labeling the action a dismissal to signal that they are active and engaged boards. For example, when the Lending Club removed CEO Renaud Laplanche in 2016, Hans Morris, the firm's Executive Chairman, lauded him, saying his "entrepreneurial spirit was critical to the success of the firm." But he also signaled the board was removing Mr. Laplanche since he had failed to build a strong control system and culture, stating "as a public company that provides a financial service, Lending Club must meet the industry's high standards of transparency and disclosure."[73] When Andrew Mason was ousted as head of Groupon, he released a humorous statement saying, "After four and a half intense and wonderful years as CEO of Groupon, I've decided to spend more time with my family. Just kidding–I was fired today."[74]

Another key trend found in corporate governance is a drive for director independence.[75] Some governance experts argue that a majority of directors should be free of all ties to either the CEO or the company.[76] This means that a minimum of "insiders" (past or present members of the management team) should serve on the board and that directors and their firms should be barred from doing consulting, legal, or other work for the company.[77] This has resulted in a dramatic rise in the proportion of boards dominated by outsiders (with over 84 percent now being outside board members).

This push for outsider dominance on boards has a number of benefits, including more independent oversight of the CEO and the firm's strategy, broader access to knowledge and resources in the broader business community, and a larger number of candidates for outsider-only board committees. At the same time, there are a number of disadvantages associated with outsider dominated boards.[78]

First, the board receives less information about the firm's operations since all information is filtered through the CEO. Even if non-board executives are invited to present to the board, the information shared is typically vetted by the CEO, and the board does not develop friendships with the executive. Thus, they are less likely to have informal interactions that allow them to learn about how things are really going. This deprives outside board members of insights on the day-to-day operations of the firm. At its worst, it gives CEOs the opportunity to blame shift when things go poorly.

Second, one of the most critical roles of the board is to undertake succession planning so that they can replace the CEO when necessary. But since the board does not interact regularly or build relationships with non-board member executives, they are less able to evaluate executives in regards to their capabilities of being a future CEO if no executives other than the CEO are on the board. As a result, the board may be more reluctant to replace an underperforming CEO since it won't have a clear idea of the right replacement candidate and will be less informed on who the best candidates are when they do have to make a change.

Third, non-CEO executives of the firm lose the opportunity to develop their strategic decision making skills. Members of the board are privy to the discussions about how to respond to environmental pressures, the logic for a firm's strategy, and the deployment of key resources to enact a strategy. Without having an opportunity to be a party to these discussions, executives outside of the CEO do not see how boards discuss firm strategy and evaluate the actions of the firm. Thus, they lose the opportunity to build strategic insights that they could both bring to their current positions and leverage if they are appointed as the CEO in the future.

Taking it one step further, research and simple observations of boards indicate that simple prescriptions, such as having a majority of outside directors, are insufficient to lead to effective board operations. Firms need to cultivate engaged and committed boards. There are several actions that can have a positive influence on board dynamics as the board works to both oversee and advise management.[79]

1. ***Build in the right expertise on the board.*** Outside directors can bring in experience that the management team is missing. For example, corporations that are considering expanding into a new region of the globe may want to add a board member who brings expertise on and connections in that region.
2. ***Keep your board size manageable.*** Small, focused boards, generally with 5 to 11 members, are preferable to larger ones. As boards grow in size, the ability for them to function as a team declines.
3. ***Choose directors who can participate fully.*** The time demands on directors have increased as their responsibilities have grown to include overseeing management, verifying the firm's financial statements, setting executive compensation, and advising on the strategic direction of the firm. Thus, firms should strive to include directors who are not currently overburdened by their core occupation or involvement on other boards.
4. ***Balance the need to focus on the past, the present, and the future.*** Boards have a three-tiered role. They need to focus on the recent performance of the firm, how the firm is meeting current milestones and operational targets, and what the strategic direction of the firm will be moving forward. Under current regulations, boards are

required to spend a great amount of time on the past as they vet the firm's financials. However, effective boards balance this time and ensure that they give adequate consideration to the present and the future.

5. ***Consider management talent development.*** As part of their future-oriented focus, effective boards develop succession plans for the CEO but also focus on talent development at other upper echelons of the organization.
6. ***Get a broad view.*** In order to better understand the firm and make contact with key managers, the meetings of the board should rotate to different operating units and sites of the firm.
7. ***Maintain norms of transparency and trust.*** Highly functioning boards maintain open, team-oriented dialogue wherein information flows freely and questions are asked openly. Directors respect each other and trust that they are all working in the best interests of the corporation.

Shareholder Activism As a practical matter, there are so many owners of the largest American corporations that it makes little sense to refer to them as "owners" in the sense of individuals becoming informed and involved in corporate affairs.[80] However, even an individual shareholder has several rights, including (1) the right to sell the stock, (2) the right to vote the proxy (which includes the election of board members), (3) the right to bring suit for damages if the corporation's directors or managers fail to meet their obligations, (4) the right to certain information from the company, and (5) certain residual rights following the company's liquidation (or its filing for reorganization under bankruptcy laws), once creditors and other claimants are paid off.[81]

Collectively, shareholders have the power to direct the course of corporations.[82] This may involve acts such as being party to shareholder action suits and demanding that key issues be brought up for proxy votes at annual board meetings.[83] The power of shareholders has intensified in recent years because of the increasing influence of large institutional investors such as asset managers (e.g., BlackRock), mutual funds (e.g., T. Rowe Price and Fidelity Investments), and retirement systems such as TIAA-CREF (for university faculty members and school administrative staff).[84] Institutional investors hold about 80 percent of the stock of the largest public firms in the United States.[85]

Shareholder activism refers to actions by large shareholders, both institutions and individuals, to protect their interests when they feel that managerial actions diverge from shareholder value maximization.

shareholder activism actions by large shareholders to protect their interests when they feel that managerial actions of a corporation diverge from shareholder value maximization.

Many institutional investors are aggressive in protecting and enhancing their investments. They are shifting from traders to owners. They are assuming the role of permanent shareholders and rigorously analyzing issues of corporate governance. In the process they are reinventing systems of corporate monitoring and accountability.[86]

Consider the proactive behavior of CalPERS, the California Public Employees' Retirement System, which manages over $350 billion in assets and is the third-largest pension fund in the world.[87] Every year CalPERS reviews the performance of the 1,000 firms in which it retains a sizable investment.[88] It reviews each firm's short- and long-term performance, governance characteristics, and financial status, as well as market expectations for the firm. CalPERS then meets with selected companies to better understand their governance and business strategy. If needed, CalPERS requests changes in the firm's governance structure and works to ensure shareholders' rights. If CalPERS does not believe that the firm is responsive to its concerns, it considers filing proxy actions at the firm's next shareholders meeting and possibly even court actions.

In addition to traditional institutional investors, a growing set of activist investors aggressively pressure firm managers for major changes.[89] These activist investors include individual investors, such as Carl Icahn, and activist investor funds, such as Pershing Square, ValuAct, and Trian. Activist investors typically purchase a small, but substantial stake in firms, often as little as 5 percent of the firm's stock, and then either pressure the firm to change its leadership or undertake strategic actions, typically a stock buy-back, selling parts of the firm off to focus on core operations, or the initiation of a search for a buyer to acquire the firm. In recent years, activist investors have played a role in the resignations of the CEOs of Darden Restaurants and pushed for a restructuring of Newell. Activist investors are often successful since many institutional investors, such as mutual funds, who have little interest in actively overseeing firm management, are willing to support activist investors in their efforts to push management to improve firm profitability and shareholder returns. As a result, when activist investors push for a proxy vote (a vote by firm shareholders), they win over 70 percent of the time. To keep things from coming to a vote, firm management is often willing to negotiate with activist investors to give them part of what they want.

Managerial Rewards and Incentives As we discussed earlier in the chapter, incentive systems must be designed to help a company achieve its goals.[90] From the perspective of governance, one of the most critical roles of the board of directors is to create incentives that align the interests of the CEO and top executives with the interests of owners of the corporation—long-term shareholder returns.[91] Shareholders rely on CEOs to adopt policies and strategies that maximize the value of their shares.[92] A combination of three basic policies may create the right monetary incentives for CEOs to maximize the value of their companies:[93]

1. Boards can require that the CEOs become substantial owners of company stock.
2. Salaries, bonuses, and stock options can be structured so as to provide rewards for superior performance and penalties for poor performance.
3. Dismissal for poor performance should be a realistic threat.

In recent years the granting of stock options has enabled top executives of publicly held corporations to earn enormous levels of compensation. In 2017, the average CEO in the Standard & Poor's 500 stock index took home 361 times the pay of the average worker—up from 40 times the average in 1980.[94]

Many boards have awarded huge option grants despite poor executive performance, and others have made performance goals easier to reach. However, stock options can be a valuable governance mechanism to align the CEO's interests with those of the shareholders. The extraordinarily high level of compensation can, at times, be grounded in sound governance principles.[95] Research by Steven Kaplan at the University of Chicago found that firms with CEOs in the top quintile of pay generated stock returns 60 percent higher than their direct competitors, while firms with CEOs in the bottom quintile of pay saw their stock underperform their rivals by almost 20 percent.[96]

CEO Duality: Is It Good or Bad?

CEO duality is one of the most controversial issues in corporate governance. It refers to the dual-leadership structure wherein the CEO acts simultaneously as the chair of the board of directors.[97] Scholars, consultants, and executives who are interested in determining the best way to manage a corporation are divided on the issue of the roles and responsibilities of a CEO. Two schools of thought represent the alternative positions.

Unity of Command Advocates of the unity-of-command perspective believe that when one person holds both roles, he or she is able to act more efficiently and effectively. CEO duality provides firms with a clear focus on both objectives and operations as well as eliminates confusion and conflict between the CEO and the chairman. Thus, it enables smoother, more effective strategic decision making. This perspective maintains that separating the two jobs—that of a CEO and that of the chairperson of the board of directors—may produce all types of undesirable consequences. CEOs may find it harder to make quick decisions. Companies like Cisco Systems, AT&T and Disney have not divided the CEO's and chairman's jobs.

Agency Theory Supporters of agency theory argue that the positions of CEO and chairman should be separate. The case for separation is based on the simple principle of the separation of power. How can a board discharge its basic duty–monitoring the boss–if the boss is chairing its meetings and setting its agenda? How can a board act as a safeguard against corruption or incompetence when the possible source of that corruption and incompetence is sitting at the head of the table? CEO duality can create a conflict of interest that could negatively affect the interests of the shareholders.

Duality also complicates the issue of CEO succession. In some cases, a CEO/chairman may choose to retire as CEO but keep his or her role as the chairman. Although this splits up the roles, which appeases an agency perspective, it nonetheless puts the new CEO in a difficult position. The chairman is bound to question some of the new changes put in place, and the board as a whole might take sides with the chairman they trust and with whom they have a history.[98]

A number of the largest corporations, including Ford Motor Company, General Motors, Citigroup, and Apple have divided the roles between the CEO and chairman and eliminated duality. Finally, more than 90 percent of S&P 500 companies with CEOs who also serve as chairman of the board have appointed "lead" or "presiding" directors to act as a counterweight to a combined chairman and chief executive.

External Governance Control Mechanisms

Thus far, we've discussed internal governance mechanisms. Internal controls, however, are not always enough to ensure good governance. The separation of ownership and control that we discussed earlier requires multiple control mechanisms, some internal and some external, to ensure that managerial actions lead to shareholder value maximization. Further, society-at-large wants some assurance that this goal is met without harming other stakeholder groups. Now we discuss several **external governance control mechanisms** that have developed in most modern economies. These include the market for corporate control, auditors, banks and analysts, governmental regulatory bodies, media, and public activists.

external governance control mechanisms
methods that ensure that managerial actions lead to shareholder value maximization and do not harm other stakeholder groups that are outside the control of the corporate governance system.

The Market for Corporate Control Let us assume for a moment that internal control mechanisms in a company are failing. This means that the board is ineffective in monitoring managers and is not exercising the oversight required of it and that shareholders are passive and are not taking any actions to monitor or discipline managers. Under these circumstances managers may behave opportunistically.[99] Opportunistic behavior can take many forms. First, managers can *shirk* their responsibilities. Shirking means that managers fail to exert themselves fully, as is required of them. Second, they can engage in *on-the-job consumption*. Examples of on-the-job consumption include private jets, club memberships, expensive artwork in the offices, and so on. Each of these represents consumption by managers that does not in any way increase shareholder value. Instead, they actually diminish shareholder value. Third, managers may engage in *excessive product-market diversification.*[100] As we discussed in Chapter 6, such diversification serves to reduce only the employment risk of the managers rather than the financial risk of the shareholders, who can more cheaply diversify their risk by owning a portfolio of investments. Is there any external mechanism to stop managers from shirking, consumption on the job, and excessive diversification?

The **market for corporate control** is one external mechanism that provides at least some partial solution to the problems described. If internal control mechanisms fail and the management is behaving opportunistically, the likely response of most shareholders will be to sell their stock rather than engage in activism.[101] As more stockholders vote with their feet, the value of the stock begins to decline. As the decline continues, at some point the market value of the firm becomes less than the book value. A corporate raider can take over the company for a price less than the book value of the assets of the company. The first thing that the raider may do on assuming control over the company is fire the underperforming management. The risk

market for corporate control
an external control mechanism in which shareholders dissatisfied with a firm's management sell their shares.

takeover constraint the risk to management of the firm being acquired by a hostile raider.

of being acquired by a hostile raider is often referred to as the **takeover constraint.** The takeover constraint deters management from engaging in opportunistic behavior.[102]

Although in theory the takeover constraint is supposed to limit managerial opportunism, in recent years its effectiveness has become diluted as a result of a number of defense tactics adopted by incumbent management (see Chapter 6). Foremost among them are poison pills, greenmail, and golden parachutes. Poison pills are provisions adopted by the company to reduce its worth to the acquirer. An example would be payment of a huge one-time dividend, typically financed by debt. Greenmail involves buying back the stock from the acquirer, usually at an attractive premium. Golden parachutes are employment contracts that cause the company to pay lucrative severance packages to top managers fired as a result of a takeover, often running to several million dollars.

Auditors Even when there are stringent disclosure requirements, there is no guarantee that the information disclosed will be accurate. Managers may deliberately disclose false information or withhold negative financial information as well as use accounting methods that distort results based on highly subjective interpretations. Therefore, all accounting statements are required to be audited and certified to be accurate by external auditors. These auditing firms are independent organizations staffed by certified professionals who verify the firm's books of accounts. Audits can unearth financial irregularities and ensure that financial reporting by the firm conforms to standard accounting practices.

However, these audits often fail to catch accounting irregularities. A study by the Public Company Accounting Oversight Board (PCAOB) found that audits conducted by the Big 4 accounting firms were often deficient. For example, 20 percent of the Ernst & Young audits examined by the PCAOB failed. And this was the best of the Big 4! The PCAOB found fault with 45 percent of the Deloitte audits it examined. Why do these reputable firms fail to find all of the issues in audits they conduct? First, auditors are appointed by the firm being audited. The desire to continue that business relationship sometimes makes them overlook financial irregularities. Second, most auditing firms also do consulting work and often have lucrative consulting contracts with the firms that they audit. Understandably, some of them tend not to ask too many difficult questions, because they fear jeopardizing the consulting business, which is often more profitable than the auditing work.

Banks and Analysts Commercial and investment banks have lent money to corporations and therefore have to ensure that the borrowing firm's finances are in order and that the loan covenants are being followed. Stock analysts conduct ongoing in-depth studies of the firms that they follow and make recommendations to their clients to buy, hold, or sell. Their rewards and reputation depend on the quality of these recommendations. Their access to information, their knowledge of the industry and the firm, and the insights they gain from interactions with the management of the company enable them to alert the investing community of both positive and negative developments relating to a company.

It is generally observed that analyst recommendations are often more optimistic than warranted by facts. "Sell" recommendations tend to be exceptions rather than the norm. Many analysts failed to grasp the gravity of the problems surrounding failed companies such as Lehman Brothers and Countrywide till the very end. Part of the explanation may lie in the fact that most analysts work for firms that also have investment banking relationships with the companies they follow. Negative recommendations by analysts can displease the management, who may decide to take their investment banking business to a rival firm. Otherwise independent and competent analysts may be pressured to overlook negative information or tone down their criticism.

Governmental Regulatory Bodies The extent of government regulation is often a function of the type of industry. Banks, utilities, and pharmaceuticals are subject to more regulatory

9.5 STRATEGY **SPOTLIGHT** ETHICS

JAPANESE GOVERNMENT PUSHES FOR GOVERNANCE REFORM

Corporate governance structures in Japan look very different than those found in the United States. Few members of boards of directors are independent of the firm. Instead, most are also firm managers, meaning they are unlikely to recommend the firm radically change its strategy even if such change may be warranted. Even though many Japanese firms have extensive global operations, only 274 of the approximately 40,000 director positions at Japanese firms were held by foreigners in 2015. Firms within business groups have cross-shareholding, where supplier firms own part of their customer firms and vice versa. Also, banks often own shares in the companies they lend to and, as a result, do not put strong public pressure on client firms to improve their operations or balance sheets. Government regulations do not require that accounting firms that serve as external auditors are independent of the firm. As a result, many firms use closely affiliated "outside" auditors, reducing the pressure the firm faces to accurately report earnings and file financial statements. Finally, top manager compensation is low compared to other countries and not closely tied to firm performance, reducing the incentive for management to take bold actions. These cozy governance systems fit the longstanding Japanese desire for economic stability and lifetime employment.

However, two decades of economic malaise has led Prime Minister Shinzo Abe and his government to push for governance reform. These cozy governance arrangements have resulted in firms that are slow to restructure, not very competitively aggressive, and unable to fully understand the different needs of the global markets in which they compete. One measure of the conservatism of firm management is that, in 2015, Japanese companies were hoarding $1.9 trillion in cash, an amount nearly half the size of the Japanese economy. This is cash firms could use to expand, develop new technologies, or acquire other firms, but these firms were choosing to sit on it instead. Abe and his government are trying to change things with a new corporate governance code. Rather than working up hard and fast rules, Abe's code lays out general principles and relies on social pressure to get firms to change. Companies are advised to improve communication with shareholders, to respond to large shareholder concerns, to focus more on increasing shareholder value, to remove anti-takeover provisions, to increase diversity and the promotion of women, and to use an independent auditor.

There is some evidence these social pressures are working. In 2016, firms distributed a record amount of cash to their stockholders. An increasing number of firms are introducing shareholder friendly measures, such as return on equity targets and regular earnings reports. Corporate boards are also becoming a bit more independent with the average number of outsiders on the boards of large Japanese firms rising from less than one to three members since 2012. Big banks have announced they will reduce their shareholding in customer firms by about 25 percent in the next five years. Cross-shareholdings between firms have reduced to 11 percent of market capitalization in 2016, compared to 34 percent in 1990. Finally, some major firms, such as Hitachi, are divesting unrelated and unprofitable business units and focusing on core, growing business operations.

Japan has no interest in fully incorporating American corporate governance practices. It sees the United States as too short term and shareholder focused. Instead, Abe wants to alter governance practices to push firms to be more aggressive and responsive while also maintaining a degree of stability and a longer term focus.

Sources: Anonymous. 2015. Meet Shinzo Abe, shareholder activist. *economist.com*. June 6: np; Smith, N. 2015. Japan flirts with governance reform. *bloomberg.com*. January 9: np; de Swaan, J. 2016. Abe must double down on Japan's corporate sector reforms. *ft.com*. September 28: np; and, Lewis, L. 2016. Abe's corporate governance reforms show signs of progress. *ft.com*. December 20: np.

oversight because of their importance to society. Public corporations are subject to more regulatory requirements than private corporations.[103]

All public corporations are required to disclose a substantial amount of financial information by bodies such as the Securities and Exchange Commission. These include quarterly and annual filings of financial performance, stock trading by insiders, and details of executive compensation packages. There are two primary reasons behind such requirements. First, markets can operate efficiently only when the investing public has faith in the market system. In the absence of disclosure requirements, the average investor suffers from a lack of reliable information and therefore may completely stay away from the capital market. This will negatively impact an economy's ability to grow. Second, disclosure of information such as insider trading protects the small investor to some extent from the negative consequences of information asymmetry. The insiders and large investors typically have more information than the small investor and can therefore use that information to buy or sell before the information becomes public knowledge.

Government pressures to improve corporate governance is not only found in the United States. Strategy Spotlight 9.5 discusses how Japanese regulators are pushing for governance reform in a country that has long resisted changes that would lead firms to focus more on shareholders.

Media and Public Activists The press is not usually recognized as an external control mechanism in the literature on corporate governance. There is no denying that in all developed capitalist economies, the financial press and media play an important indirect role in monitoring the management of public corporations. In the United States, business magazines such as *Bloomberg Businessweek* and *Fortune,* financial newspapers such as *The Wall Street Journal* and *Investor's Business Daily,* as well as television networks like Fox Business Network and CNBC are constantly reporting on companies. Public perceptions about a company's financial prospects and the quality of its management are greatly influenced by the media. For example, the business practices of Turing Pharmaceuticals were called into question in 2015, first on a health care news website, Healio, and then by *USA Today* and the *New York Times.*[104] The ensuing scrutiny resulted in Turing's CEO, Martin Shkreli, being described as "the most hated man in America" in a number of news articles. Shkreli resigned as firm CEO within a few months of the emergence of the scandal.

Similarly, consumer groups and activist individuals often take a crusading role in exposing corporate malfeasance.[105] For example, pressure from activists and consumers led firms that deal in diamonds, gold, and other precious minerals to change their sourcing behavior to ensure that their suppliers are legitimate operators, mines and dealers that provide appropriate wages for workers and safe working conditions as well as refuse to deal in "conflict minerals" (that rebel groups trade so that they can buy arms for military conflicts).

Corporate Governance: An International Perspective

The topic of corporate governance has long been dominated by agency theory and based on the explicit assumption of the separation of ownership and control.[106] The central conflicts are principal-agent conflicts between shareholders and management. However, such an underlying assumption seldom applies outside the United States and the United Kingdom. This is particularly true in emerging economies and continental Europe. Here, there is often concentrated ownership, along with extensive family ownership and control, business group structures, and weak legal protection for minority shareholders. Serious conflicts tend to exist between two classes of principals: controlling shareholders and minority shareholders. Such conflicts can be called **principal-principal (PP) conflicts,** as opposed to *principal-agent* conflicts (see Exhibits 9.6 and 9.7).

principal–principal conflicts
conflicts between two classes of principals—controlling shareholders and minority shareholders—within the context of a corporate governance system.

EXHIBIT 9.6 Traditional Principal–Agent Conflicts versus Principal–Principal Conflicts: How They Differ along Dimensions

	Principal–Agent Conflicts	Principal–Principal Conflicts
Goal incongruence	Between shareholders and professional managers who own a relatively small portion of the firm's equity.	Between controlling shareholders and minority shareholders.
Ownership pattern	Dispersed—5% to 20% is considered "concentrated ownership."	Concentrated—often greater than 50% of equity is controlled by controlling shareholders.
Manifestations	Strategies that benefit entrenched managers at the expense of shareholders in general (e.g., shirking, pet projects, excessive compensation, and empire building).	Strategies that benefit controlling shareholders at the expense of minority shareholders (e.g., minority shareholder expropriation, nepotism, and cronyism).
Institutional protection of minority shareholders	Formal constraints (e.g., judicial reviews and courts) set an upper boundary on potential expropriation by majority shareholders. Informal norms generally adhere to shareholder wealth maximization.	Formal institutional protection is often lacking, corrupted, or unenforced. Informal norms are typically in favor of the interests of controlling shareholders ahead of those of minority investors.

Source: Adapted from Young, M., Peng, M. W., Ahlstrom, D., & Bruton, G. 2002. Governing the Corporation in Emerging Economies: A Principal-Principal Perspective. *Academy of Management Best Papers Proceedings,* Denver.

EXHIBIT 9.7 Principal–Agent Conflicts and Principal–Principal Conflicts: A Diagram

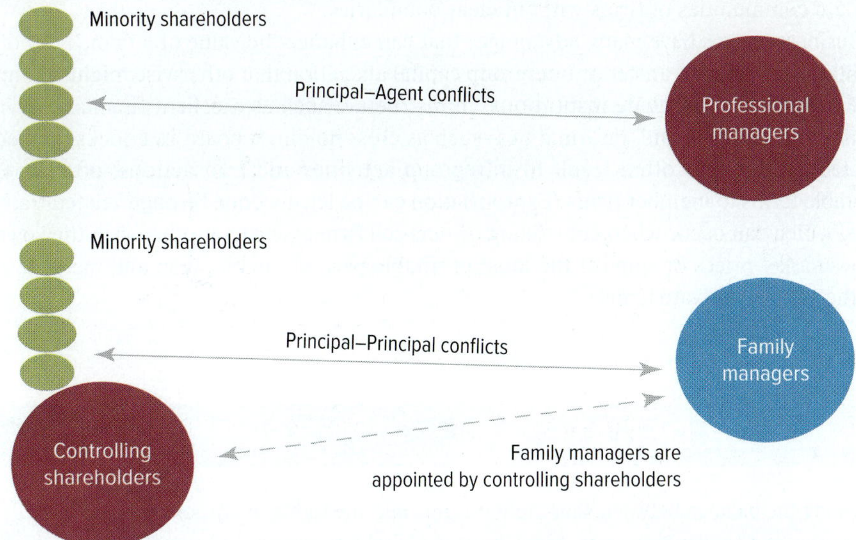

Source: Young, M. N., Peng, M. W., Ahlstrom, D., Bruton, G. D., & Jiang, 2008. Principal-Principal Conflicts in Corporate Governance. *Journal of Management Studies,* 45(1): 196–220; and Peng, M. V. 2006. *Global Strategy.* Cincinnati: Thomson South-Western. We are very appreciative of the helpful comments of Mike Young of Hong Kong Baptist University and Mike Peng of the University of Texas at Dallas.

Strong family control is one of the leading indicators of concentrated ownership. In East Asia (excluding China), approximately 57 percent of the corporations have board chairmen and CEOs from the controlling families. In continental Europe, this number is 68 percent. A very common practice is the appointment of family members as board chairmen, CEOs, and other top executives. This happens because the families are controlling (not necessarily majority) shareholders.

In general, three conditions must be met for PP conflicts to occur:

- A dominant owner or group of owners who have interests that are distinct from minority shareholders.
- Motivation for the controlling shareholders to exercise their dominant positions to their advantage.
- Few formal (such as legislation or regulatory bodies) or informal constraints that would discourage or prevent the controlling shareholders from exploiting their advantageous positions.

The result is often that family managers, who represent (or actually are) the controlling shareholders, engage in **expropriation of minority shareholders,** which is defined as activities that enrich the controlling shareholders at the expense of minority shareholders. What is their motive? After all, controlling shareholders have incentives to maintain firm value. But controlling shareholders may take actions that decrease aggregate firm performance if their personal gains from expropriation exceed their personal losses from their firm's lowered performance.

expropriation of minority shareholders
activities that enrich the controlling shareholders at the expense of the minority shareholders.

business group
a set of firms that, though legally independent, are bound together by a constellation of formal and informal ties and are accustomed to taking coordinated action.

Another ubiquitous feature of corporate life outside the United States and United Kingdom is *business groups* such as the keiretsus of Japan and the chaebols of South Korea. This is particularly dominant in emerging economies. A **business group** is "a set of firms that, though legally independent, are bound together by a constellation of formal and informal ties and are accustomed to taking coordinated action."[107] Business groups are especially common in emerging economies, and they differ from other organizational forms in that they are communities of firms without clear boundaries.

Business groups have many advantages that can enhance the value of a firm. They often facilitate technology transfer or intergroup capital allocation that otherwise might be impossible because of inadequate institutional infrastructure such as excellent financial services firms. On the other hand, informal ties–such as cross-holdings, board interlocks, and coordinated actions–can often result in intragroup activities and transactions, often at very favorable terms to member firms. Expropriation can be legally done through related transactions, which can occur when controlling owners sell firm assets to another firm they own at below-market prices or spin off the most profitable part of a public firm and merge it with another of their private firms.

ISSUE FOR DEBATE

Striking the balance between shareholder rights and the rights of corporate managers to run firms is a challenging issue. Since most shareholders, even institutional investors, own less than 5 percent of the stock in any one firm, there are typically no controlling shareholders who can, on their own, force management to make major changes or address the key concerns of the investors. To address this issue, U.S. regulators have created guidelines that make it easy for shareholders, even small shareholders, to initiate shareholder proposals at annual shareholder meetings. Shareholders who own $2,000 or 1 percent of a firm's stock, whichever is lower, have the right to submit a shareholder proposal. Once submitted, firm management must hold a vote, where all shareholders weigh in on whether they agree that the corporation should address the issues raised in the proposal. If the proposal gets support from at least 3 percent of shareholders, its sponsor can call for a vote on it again at the next shareholder meeting. Proponents of these rules believe that this is corporate democracy in action and keeps management from becoming tone deaf to the concerns of small shareholders.

However, these rules also allow small shareholders with personal concerns, sometimes called "corporate gadflies," to generate shareholder proposals that can potentially create unnecessary and costly work by firms. For example, Choice Hotels had to fight a shareholder proposal from one stockholder, who owned .001 percent of the firm's stock, which called for Choice to measure how much water flowed through every single showerhead in every bathroom in the 6,300 hotels the company owns. Some investors make it something of a career submitting these proposals. Three people, John Chevedden, William Steiner, and James McRitchie and their families, filed 70 percent of all of the shareholder proposals at Fortune 250 firms in 2013. Less than 5 percent of their proposals passed, but the cost to fight them was substantial. According to one estimate, the cost for firms to counter these proposals was $90 million.

Regulators struggle with how to deal with this issue. Making it harder to file shareholder proposals would reduce the cost to corporations, but it would also reduce the voice of shareholders to raise substantive issues.

Discussion Question

1. How would you strike a balance to ensure that shareholders have a voice while limiting the cost of unnecessary proposals? Are the current rules appropriate? If not, how would you change them?

Sources: Engler, J. 2016. How gadfly shareholders keep CEOs distracted. *Wall Street Journal*. May 27: A11; and Soloman, S. 2014. Grappling with the cost of corporate gadflies. *nytimes.com*. August 19: np.

Reflecting on Career Implications . . .

This chapter focuses on the varying means firms can use to control and direct behavior. The following questions ask you how you would respond to different control mechanisms and how you can construct monitoring and control systems to enhance you career.

- **Behavioral Control:** What types of behavioral control does your organization employ? Do you find these behavioral controls helping or hindering you from doing a good job? Some individuals are comfortable with and even desire rules and procedures for everything. Others find that they inhibit creativity and stifle initiative. Evaluate your own level of comfort with the level of behavioral control and then assess the match between your own optimum level of control and the level and type of control used by your organization. If the gap is significant, you might want to consider other career opportunities.
- **Setting Boundaries and Constraints:** Your career success depends to a great extent on you monitoring and regulating your own behavior. Setting boundaries and constraints on yourself can help you focus on strategic priorities, generate short-term objectives and action plans, improve efficiency and effectiveness, and minimize improper conduct. Identify the boundaries and constraints you have placed on yourself and evaluate how each of those contributes to your personal growth and career development. If you do not have boundaries and constraints, consider developing them.
- **Rewards and Incentives:** Is your organization's reward structure fair and equitable? On what criteria do you base your conclusions? How does the firm define outstanding performance and reward it? Are these financial or nonfinancial rewards? The absence of rewards that are seen as fair and equitable can result in the long-term erosion of morale, which may have long-term adverse career implications for you.
- **Culture:** Given your career goals, what type of organizational culture would provide the best work environment? How does your organization's culture deviate from this concept? Does your organization have a strong and effective culture? In the long run, how likely are you to internalize the culture of your organization? If you believe that there is a strong misfit between your values and the organization's culture, you may want to reconsider your relationship with the organization.

key points

LO 9-1 The value of effective strategic control systems in strategy implementation.

- Control systems provide the information necessary for firms to coordinate action and respond to environmental changes and feedback.

LO 9-2 The key difference between "traditional" and "contemporary" control systems.

- The traditional approach to strategic control is sequential: (1) strategies are formulated and top management sets goals, (2) strategies are implemented, and (3) performance is measured against the predetermined goal set.
- With contemporary control systems, the relationships between strategy formulation, implementation, and control are highly interactive.

LO 9-3 The imperative for contemporary control systems in today's complex and rapidly changing competitive and general environments.

- Fixed strategic goals and reactionary control systems become dysfunctional for firms competing in highly unpredictable competitive environments.
- In dynamic environments, an inflexible commitment to predetermined goals and milestones can prevent the very adaptability that is required of a good strategy.

LO 9-4 The benefits of having the proper balance among the three levers of behavioral control: culture, rewards and incentives, and boundaries.

- Organizational culture is a system of shared values (what is important) and beliefs (how things work) that shape a company's people, organizational structures, and control systems to produce behavioral norms (the way we do things around here).
- Reward and incentive systems represent a powerful means of influencing an organization's culture, focusing efforts on high-priority tasks, and motivating individual and collective task performance.
- Boundaries and constraints can serve many useful purposes for organizations, including:
  - Focusing individual efforts on strategic priorities.
  - Providing short-term objectives and action plans to channel efforts.
  - Improving efficiency and effectiveness.
  - Minimizing improper and unethical conduct.

LO 9-5 The three key participants in corporate governance: shareholders, management (led by the CEO), and the board of directors.

- The separation of ownership from management has led to a discussion of agency problems, where the stockholders (or principals) who own the firm work to ensure that management (or agents) act in the interests of the owners.
- Stockholders elect a board of directors to represent them and monitor management and make sure that management acts to generate value for the stockholders.

LO 9-6 The role of corporate governance mechanisms in ensuring that the interests of managers are aligned with those of shareholders from both the United States and international perspectives.

- There are two primary means for shareholders to monitor the behavior of managers.
  - A committed and involved board of directors that acts in the best interests of the shareholders to create long-term value.
  - Shareholder activism, wherein the owners become actively engaged in the governance of the corporation.
- Managerial incentives are powerful tools to align the interests of management with those of stockholders.
- In firms outside of the United States and the UK, governance challenges can even be greater.
  - In many countries, firms often have dominant shareholders, extensive family ownership and control, business group structures, and weak legal protection for minority shareholders.
  - Thus, serious conflicts can exist between two classes of principals: controlling shareholders and minority shareholders. Such conflicts can be called principal-principal (PP) conflicts, as opposed to the typical principal-agent conflicts discussed in the U.S. context.

SUMMARY REVIEW QUESTIONS

1. Why are effective strategic control systems so important in today's economy?
2. What are the main advantages of contemporary control systems over traditional control systems? What are the main differences between these two systems?
3. Why is it important to have a balance between the three elements of behavioral control–culture, rewards and incentives, and boundaries?
4. Discuss the relationship between types of organizations and their primary means of behavioral control.
5. Boundaries become less important as a firm develops a strong culture and reward system. Explain.
6. Why is it important to avoid a "one best way" mentality concerning control systems? What are the consequences of applying the same type of control system to all types of environments?
7. What is the role of effective corporate governance in improving a firm's performance? What are some of the key governance mechanisms that are used to ensure that managerial and shareholder interests are aligned?
8. Define principal-principal (PP) conflicts. What are the implications for corporate governance?

key terms

strategic control 266
traditional approach to strategic control 266
informational control 267
behavioral control 267
organizational culture 267
reward system 271
boundaries and constraints 273
corporate governance 277
corporation 278
agency theory 279
board of directors 280
shareholder activism 283
external governance control mechanisms 285
market for corporate control 285
takeover constraint 286
principal-principal conflicts 288
expropriation of minority shareholders 289
business group 289

EXPERIENTIAL EXERCISES AND APPLICATION QUESTIONS

1. In the Learning from Mistakes, we discussed how the decisions of owners led to the failure of the firm. Research the ownership and boards of directors of another major retailer and evaluate the degree to which the firm's corporate governance is likely to support the firm's success.
2. McDonald's Corporation is the world's largest fast-food restaurant chain. Using the online resources, evaluate the quality of the corporation in terms of management, the board of directors, and institutional owners. (Fill in the chart on the following page.) Are the issues you list favorable or unfavorable for sound corporate governance?
3. The problems of many firms may be attributed to a traditional control system that failed to continuously monitor the environment and make necessary changes in their strategy and objectives. What companies are you familiar with that responded appropriately (or inappropriately) to environmental change?
4. How can a strong, positive culture enhance a firm's competitive advantage? How can a weak, negative

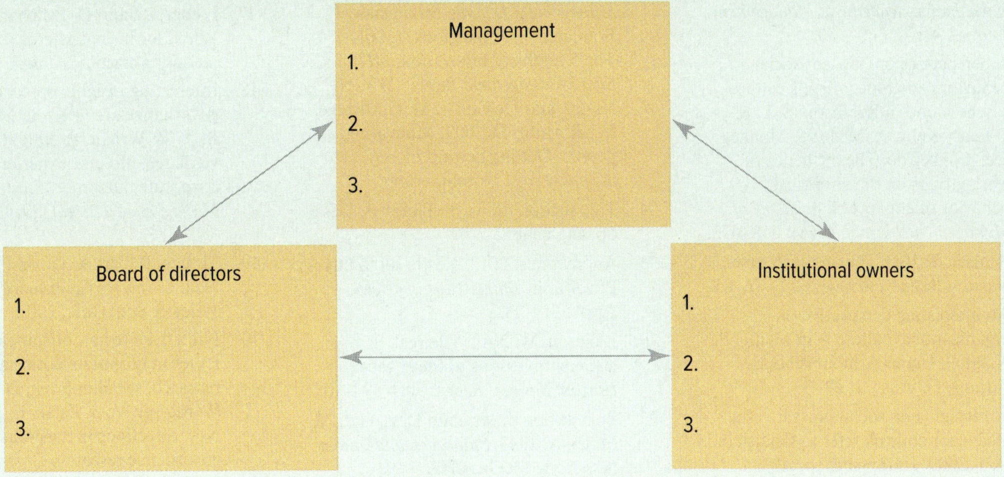

culture erode competitive advantages? Explain and provide examples.

5. Use the online resources to research a firm that has an excellent culture and/or reward and incentive system. What are this firm's main financial and nonfinancial benefits?
6. Go to the website of a large, publicly held corporation in which you are interested. What evidence do you see of effective (or ineffective) corporate governance?

ETHICS QUESTIONS

1. Strong cultures can have powerful effects on employee behavior. How does this create inadvertent control mechanisms? That is, are strong cultures an ethical way to control behavior?
2. Rules and regulations can help reduce unethical behavior in organizations. To be effective, however, what other systems, mechanisms, and processes are necessary?

REFERENCES

1. Lazarus, C. 2008. "Toy titan," *Entrepreneur,* October 10.
2. Berfield, S.; Ronalds-Hannon, E.; and Coleman-Lochner, L. 2018. How Toys R Us, once a mighty category killer, became an object lesson in financial mismanagement. *Bloomberg Businessweek*. June 11: 59-61.; and Blake, M. 2019. Toys R Us Is Making A Comeback As Tru Kids-With A Modern Customer Approach. forbes.com. February 12: np.
3. This chapter draws upon Picken, J. C. & Dess, G. G. 1997. *Mission critical.* Burr Ridge, IL: Irwin Professional.
4. For a unique perspective on governance, refer to Carmeli, A. & Markman, G. D. 2011. Capture, governance, and resilience: Strategy implications from the history of Rome. *Strategic Management Journal,* 32(3): 332-341.
5. Argyris, C. 1977. Double-loop learning in organizations. *Harvard Business Review,* 55: 115-125.
6. Simons, R. 1995. Control in an age of empowerment. *Harvard Business Review,* 73: 80-88. This chapter draws on this source in the discussion of informational control.
7. Goold, M. & Quinn, J. B. 1990. The paradox of strategic controls. *Strategic Management Journal,* 11: 43-57.
8. Quinn, J. B. 1980. *Strategies for change.* Homewood, IL: Irwin.
9. Mintzberg, H. 1987. Crafting strategy. *Harvard Business Review,* 65: 66-75.
10. Satell, G. 2017. How Google innovates. innovationexcellence.com. February 22: np.
11. This discussion of control systems draws upon Simons, op. cit.
12. Ryan, M. K., Haslam, S. A., & Renneboog, L. D. R. 2011. Who gets the carrot and who gets the stick? Evidence of gender discrimination in executive remuneration. *Strategic Management Journal,* 32(3): 301-321.
13. For an interesting perspective on this issue and how a downturn in the economy can reduce the tendency toward "free agency" by managers and professionals, refer to Morris, B. 2001. White collar blues. *Fortune,* July 23: 98-110.
14. For a colorful example of behavioral control in an organization, see Beller, P. C. 2009. Activision's unlikely hero. *Forbes,* February 2: 52-58.
15. Collins, J. C. & Porras, J. I. 1994. *Built to last: Successful habits of visionary companies.* New York: Harper Business.
16. Lee, J. & Miller, D. 1999. People matter: Commitment to employees, strategy, and performance in Korean firms. *Strategic Management Journal,* 6: 579-594.
17. For an insightful discussion of IKEA's unique culture, see Kling, K. & Goteman, I. 2003. IKEA CEO Anders Dahlvig on international growth and IKEA's unique corporate culture and brand identity. *Academy of Management Executive,* 17(1): 31-37.
18. For a discussion of how professionals inculcate values, refer to Uhl-Bien, M. & Graen, G. B. 1998. Individual self-management: Analysis of professionals' self-managing activities in functional and cross-functional

work teams. *Academy of Management Journal,* 41(3): 340-350.

19. A perspective on how antisocial behavior can erode a firm's culture can be found in Robinson, S. L. & O'Leary-Kelly, A. M. 1998. Monkey see, monkey do: The influence of work groups on the antisocial behavior of employees. *Academy of Management Journal,* 41(6): 658-672.
20. Benkler, Y. 2011. The unselfish gene. *Harvard Business Review,* 89(7): 76-85.
21. An interesting perspective on organizational culture is in Mehta, S. N. 2009. Under Armour reboots. *Fortune,* February 2: 29-33.
22. For insights on social pressure as a means for control, refer to Goldstein, N. J. 2009. Harnessing social pressure. *Harvard Business Review,* 87(2): 25.
23. Mitchell, R. 1989. Masters of innovation. *BusinessWeek,* April 10: 58-63.
24. *bigspaceship.com/warby-parker-culture; and businesscollective.com/12-ways-to-reinforce-your-company-culture.*
25. Beshore, B. 2014. 12 ways to reinforce your company culture. *Business Insider,* January 10.
26. Kerr, J. & Slocum, J. W., Jr. 1987. Managing corporate culture through reward systems. *Academy of Management Executive,* 1(2): 99-107.
27. For a unique perspective on leader challenges in managing wealthy professionals, refer to Wetlaufer, S. 2000. Who wants to manage a millionaire? *Harvard Business Review,* 78(4): 53-60.
28. Netessine, S. & Yakubovich, V. 2012. The Darwinian workplace. *Harvard Business Review,* 90(5): 25-28.
29. For a discussion of the benefits of stock options as executive compensation, refer to Hall, B. J. 2000. What you need to know about stock options. *Harvard Business Review,* 78(2): 121-129.
30. Anonymous. 2013. Rewarding your employees: 15 examples of successful incentives in the corporate world. *rrgexec.com.* June 20: np.
31. Carter, N. M. & Silva, C. 2010. Why men still get more promotions than women. *Harvard Business Review,* 88(9): 80-86.
32. Cappelli, P. & Tavis, A. 2018. HR goes agile. Harvard Business Review. 96(2): 47-52.
33. Sirota, D., Mischkind, L. & Meltzer, I. 2008. Stop demotivating your employees! *Harvard Management Update,* July: 3-5; Nelson, B. 2003. Five questions about employee recognition and reward. *Harvard Management Update;* Birkinshaw, J., Bouquet, C., & Barsaoux, J. 2011. The 5 myths of innovation. *MIT Sloan Management Review.* Winter, 43-50; and Dewhurst, M. Guthridge, M., & Mohr, E. 2009. Motivating people: Getting beyond money. *mckinsey.com.* November: np.
34. This section draws on Picken & Dess, op. cit., chap. 5.
35. Anonymous. 2012. Nestle set to buy Pfizer unit. *Dallas Morning News,* April 19: 10D.
36. Isaacson, W. 2012. The real leadership lessons of Steve Jobs. *Harvard Business Review,* 90(4): 93-101.
37. This section draws upon Dess, G. G. & Miller, A. 1993. *Strategic management.* New York: McGraw-Hill.
38. For a good review of the goal-setting literature, refer to Locke, E. A. & Latham, G. P. 1990. A *theory of goal setting and task performance.* Englewood Cliffs, NJ: Prentice Hall.
39. For an interesting perspective on the use of rules and regulations that is counter to this industry's (software) norms, refer to Fryer, B. 2001. Tom Siebel of Siebel Systems: High tech the old fashioned way. *Harvard Business Review,* 79(3): 118-130.
40. Thompson, A. A., Jr., & Strickland, A. J., III. 1998. *Strategic management: Concepts and cases* (10th ed.): 313. New York: McGraw-Hill.
41. Thompson, A. A., and A. J. Strickland. 1998. *Strategic Management: Concepts and Cases.* McGraw-Hill.
42. Weaver, G. R., Trevino, L. K., & Cochran, P. L. 1999. Corporate ethics programs as control systems: Influences of executive commitment and environmental factors. *Academy of Management Journal,* 42(1): 41-57.
43. https://www.singaporeair.com/en_UK/us/about-us/corporate-governance-policies/
44. William Ouchi has written extensively about the use of clan control (which is viewed as an alternative to bureaucratic or market control). Here, a powerful culture results in people aligning their individual interests with those of the firm. See Ouchi, W. 1981. *Theory Z.* Reading, MA: Addison-Wesley. This section also draws on Hall, R. H. 2002. *Organizations: Structures, processes, and outcomes* (8th ed.). Upper Saddle River, NJ: Prentice Hall.
45. Poundstone, W. 2003. *How would you move Mount Fuji?* New York: Little, Brown: 59.
46. Abby, E. 2012. Woman sues over personality test job rejection. *abcnews.go.com,* October 1: np.
47. Lieber, R., and D. Pritchard. 1996. Wired for hiring: Microsoft's slick recruiting machine.*Fortune,* February 5.
48. Interesting insights on corporate governance are in Kroll, M., Walters, B. A., & Wright, P. 2008. Board vigilance, director experience, and corporate outcomes. *Strategic Management Journal,* 29(4): 363-382.
49. Monks, Robert A. G., and Minow, Nell. *Corporate Governance,* 2e. John Wiley & Sons, Inc., 2001.
50. For a brief review of some central issues in corporate governance research, see Hambrick, D. C., Werder, A. V., & Zajac, E. J. 2008. New directions in corporate governance research. *Organization Science,* 19(3): 381-385.
51. Monks, R. & Minow, N. 2001. *Corporate governance* (2nd ed.). Malden, MA: Blackwell.
52. Pound, J. 1995. The promise of the governed corporation. *Harvard Business Review,* 73(2): 89-98.
53. Maurer, H. & Linblad, C. 2009. Scandal at Satyam. *BusinessWeek,* January 19: 8; Scheck, J. & Stecklow, S. 2008. Brocade ex-CEO gets 21 months in prison. *The Wall Street Journal,* January 17: A3; Levine, D. & Graybow, M. 2010. Mozilo to pay millions in Countrywide settlement. *finance.yahoo.com,* October 15: np; Ellis, B. 2010. Countrywide's Mozilo to pay $67.5 million settlement. *cnnmoney.com,* October 15: np; Frank, R., Efrati, A., Lucchetti, A., & Bray, C. 2009. Madoff jailed after admitting epic scam. *The Wall Street Journal,* March 13: A1; and Henriques, D. B. 2009. Madoff is sentenced to 150 years for Ponzi scheme. *www.nytimes.com,* June 29: np.
54. Shen, L. 2017. The 10 biggest business scandals of 2017. start.att.net. December 31: np.
55. Corkery, M. & Cowley, S. 2016. Wells Fargo CEO John Stumpf quits after scandal. *bostonglobe.com.* October 12: np.
56. Anonymous. 2012. Olympus and ex-executives plead guilty in accounting fraud. *nytimes.com,* September 25: np.
57. Corporate governance and social networks are discussed in McDonald, M. L., Khanna, P., & Westphal, J. D. 2008. *Academy of Management Journal,* 51(3): 453-475.
58. This discussion draws upon Monks & Minow, op. cit.
59. For an interesting perspective on the politicization of the corporation, read Palazzo, G. & Scherer, A. G. 2008. Corporate social responsibility, democracy, and the politicization of

the corporation. *Academy of Management Review,* 33(3): 773-774.

60. Eisenhardt, K. M. 1989. Agency theory: An assessment and review. *Academy of Management Review,* 14(1): 57-74. Some of the seminal contributions to agency theory include Jensen, M. & Meckling, W. 1976. Theory of the firm: Managerial behavior, agency costs, and ownership structure. *Journal of Financial Economics,* 3: 305-360; Fama, E. & Jensen, M. 1983. Separation of ownership and control. *Journal of Law and Economics,* 26: 301, 325; and Fama, E. 1980. Agency problems and the theory of the firm. *Journal of Political Economy,* 88: 288-307.
61. Nyberg, A. J., Fulmer, I. S., Gerhart, B., & Carpenter, M. 2010. Agency theory revisited: CEO return and shareholder interest alignment. *Academy of Management Journal,* 53(5): 1029-1049.
62. Managers may also engage in "shirking"—that is, reducing or withholding their efforts. See, for example, Kidwell, R. E., Jr. & Bennett, N. 1993. Employee propensity to withhold effort: A conceptual model to intersect three avenues of research. *Academy of Management Review,* 18(3): 429-456.
63. For an interesting perspective on agency and clarification of many related concepts and terms, visit *www.encycogov.com.*
64. The relationship between corporate ownership structure and export intensity in Chinese firms is discussed in Filatotchev, I., Stephan, J., & Jindra, B. 2008. Ownership structure, strategic controls and export intensity of foreign-invested firms in transition economies. *Journal of International Business,* 39(7): 1133-1148.
65. Argawal, A. & Mandelker, G. 1987. Managerial incentives and corporate investment and financing decisions. *Journal of Finance,* 42: 823-837.
66. For an insightful, recent discussion of the academic research on corporate governance, and in particular the role of boards of directors, refer to Chatterjee, S. & Harrison, J. S. 2001. Corporate governance. In Hitt, M. A., Freeman, R. E., & Harrison, J. S. (Eds.), *Handbook of strategic management:* 543-563. Malden, MA: Blackwell.
67. For an interesting theoretical discussion on corporate governance in Russia, see McCarthy, D. J. & Puffer, S. M. 2008. Interpreting the ethicality of corporate governance decisions in Russia: Utilizing integrative social contracts theory to evaluate the relevance of agency theory norms. *Academy of Management Review,* 33(1): 11-31.
68. Haynes, K. T. & Hillman, A. 2010. The effect of board capital and CEO power on strategic change. *Strategic Management Journal,* 31(110): 1145-1163.
69. This opening discussion draws on Monks & Minow, op. cit. pp. 164, 169; see also Pound, op. cit.
70. Business Roundtable. 2012. Principles of corporate governance.
71. Bhagat, C. & Kehoe, C. 2014. High performing boards: What's on their agenda? *mckinsey.com,* April: np.
72. The role of outside directors is discussed in Lester, R. H., Hillman, A., Zardkoohi, A., & Cannella, A. A., Jr. 2008. Former government officials as outside directors: The role of human and social capital. *Academy of Management Journal,* 51(5): 999-1013.
73. Rudegeair, P., and A. Andriotis. 2016. Inside the final days of Lending Club CEO Renaud Laplanche.*The Wall Street Journal,* May 16: np.
74. Feintzeig, R. 2014. You're fired! And we really mean it. *The Wall Street Journal,* November 5: B1, B6.
75. For an analysis of the effects of outside directors' compensation on acquisition decisions, refer to Deutsch, T., Keil, T., & Laamanen, T. 2007. Decision making in acquisitions: The effect of outside directors' compensation on acquisition patterns. *Journal of Management,* 33(1): 30-56.
76. Director interlocks are addressed in Kang, E. 2008. Director interlocks and spillover effects of reputational penalties from financial reporting fraud. *Academy of Management Journal,* 51(3): 537-556.
77. There are benefits, of course, to having some insiders on the board of directors. Inside directors would be more aware of the firm's strategies. Additionally, outsiders may rely too often on financial performance indicators because of information asymmetries. For an interesting discussion, see Baysinger, B. D. & Hoskisson, R. E. 1990. The composition of boards of directors and strategic control: Effects on corporate strategy. *Academy of Management Review,* 15: 72-87.
78. Combs, J. & Ketchen, D. 2017. The problem with independent boards. *Wall Street Journal.* May 17: R8; and Faleye, O. 2016. The downside to full board independence. sloanreview.mit.edu. November 29: np.
79. Corsi, C., Dale, G., Daum, J., Mumm, J., & Schoppen, W. 2010. 5 things board directors should be thinking about. *spencerstuart.com,* December: np; Evans, B. 2007. Six steps to building an effective board. *inc.com* : np; Beatty, D. 2009. New challenges for corporate governance. *Rotman Magazine,* Fall: 58-63; and Krause, R., Semadeni, M., & Cannella, A. 2013. External COO/presidents as expert directors: A new look at the service role of boards. *Strategic Management Journal,* 34(13): 1628-1641.
80. A discussion on the shareholder approval process in executive compensation is presented in Brandes, P., Goranova, M., & Hall, S. 2008. Navigating shareholder influence: Compensation plans and the shareholder approval process. *Academy of Management Perspectives,* 22(1): 41-57.
81. Monks and Minow, op. cit., p. 93.
82. A discussion of the factors that lead to shareholder activism is found in Ryan, L. V. & Schneider, M. 2002. The antecedents of institutional investor activism. *Academy of Management Review,* 27(4): 554-573.
83. For an insightful discussion of investor activism, refer to David, P., Bloom, M., & Hillman, A. 2007. Investor activism, managerial responsiveness, and corporate social performance. *Strategic Management Journal,* 28(1): 91-100.
84. There is strong research support for the idea that the presence of large-block shareholders is associated with value-maximizing decisions. For example, refer to Johnson, R. A., Hoskisson, R. E., & Hitt, M. A. 1993. Board of director involvement in restructuring: The effects of board versus managerial controls and characteristics. *Strategic Management Journal,* 14: 33-50.
85. McGrath, C. 2017. 80% of equity market cap held by institutions. *pionline.com.* April 25: np.
86. For an interesting perspective on the impact of institutional ownership on a firm's innovation strategies, see Hoskisson, R. E., Hitt, M. A., Johnson, R. A., & Grossman, W. 2002. *Academy of Management Journal,* 45(4): 697-716.
87. *calpers.ca.gov.*
88. *www.calpers-governance.org.*
89. Anonymous. 2011. Corporate boards now and then. *Harvard Business Review.* 89(11): 38-39.
90. For a study of the relationship between ownership and diversification, refer to Goranova, M.,

Alessandri, T. M., Brandes, P., & Dharwadkar, R. 2007. Managerial ownership and corporate diversification: A longitudinal view. *Strategic Management Journal,* 28(3): 211-226.

91. Jensen, M. C. & Murphy, K. J. 1990. CEO incentives—It's not how much you pay, but how. *Harvard Business Review,* 68(3): 138-149.
92. For a perspective on the relative advantages and disadvantages of "duality"—that is, one individual serving as both chief executive office and chairman of the board, see Lorsch, J. W. & Zelleke, A. 2005. Should the CEO be the chairman? *MIT Sloan Management Review,* 46(2): 71-74.
93. A discussion of knowledge sharing is addressed in Fey, C. F. & Furu, P. 2008. Top management incentive compensation and knowledge sharing in multinational corporations. *Strategic Management Journal,* 29(12): 1301-1324.
94. Hembree, D. 2018. CEO Pay Skyrockets To 361 Times That Of The Average Worker. *forbes.com.* May 22: np.
95. Research has found that executive compensation is more closely aligned with firm performance in companies with compensation committees and boards dominated by outside directors. See, for example, Conyon, M. J. & Peck, S. I. 1998. Board control, remuneration committees, and top management compensation. *Academy of Management Journal,* 41: 146-157.
96. Anonymous. 2012. American chief executives are not overpaid. *The Economist,* September 8: 67.
97. Chahine, S. & Tohme, N. S. 2009. Is CEO duality always negative? An exploration of CEO duality and ownership structure in the Arab IPO context. *Corporate Governance: An International Review,* 17(2): 123-141; and McGrath, J. 2009. How CEOs work. *HowStuffWorks.com.* January 28: np.
98. Tuggle, C. S., Sirmon, D. G., Reutzel, C. R., & Bierman, L. 2010. Commanding board of director attention: Investigating how organizational performance and CEO duality affect board members' attention to monitoring. *Strategic Management Journal,* 31: 946-968; Weinberg, N. 2010. No more lapdogs. *Forbes,* May 10: 34-36; and Anonymous. 2010. Corporate constitutions. *The Economist,* October 30: 74.
99. Such opportunistic behavior is common in all principal-agent relationships. For a description of agency problems, especially in the context of the relationship between shareholders and managers, see Jensen, M. C. & Meckling, W. H. 1976. Theory of the firm: Managerial behavior, agency costs, and ownership structure. *Journal of Financial Economics,* 3: 305-360.
100. Hoskisson, R. E. & Turk, T. A. 1990. Corporate restructuring: Governance and control limits of the internal market. *Academy of Management Review,* 15: 459-477.
101. For an insightful perspective on the market for corporate control and how it is influenced by knowledge intensity, see Coff, R. 2003. Bidding wars over R&D-intensive firms: Knowledge, opportunism, and the market for corporate control. *Academy of Management Journal,* 46(1): 74-85.
102. Walsh, J. P. & Kosnik, R. D. 1993. Corporate raiders and their disciplinary role in the market for corporate control. *Academy of Management Journal,* 36: 671-700.
103. The role of regulatory bodies in the banking industry is addressed in Bhide, A. 2009. Why bankers got so reckless. *BusinessWeek,* February 9: 30-31.
104. Timmerman, L. 2015. A timeline of the Turing Pharma controversy. *forbes.com.* September 23: np.
105. Swartz, J. 2010. Timberland's CEO on standing up to 65,000 angry activists. *Harvard Business Review,* 88(9): 39-43.
106. This section draws upon Young, M. N., Peng, M. W., Ahlstrom, D., Bruton, G. D., & Jiang, Y. 2005. Principal-principal conflicts in corporate governance (unpublished manuscript); and, Peng, M. W. 2006. *Global Strategy.* Cincinnati: Thomson South-Western. We appreciate the helpful comments of Mike Young of Hong Kong Baptist University and Mike Peng of the University of Texas at Dallas.
107. Khanna, T. and J. Rivkin. 2001. Estimating the performance effects of business groups in emerging markets. *Strategic Management Journal,* 22: 45-74.

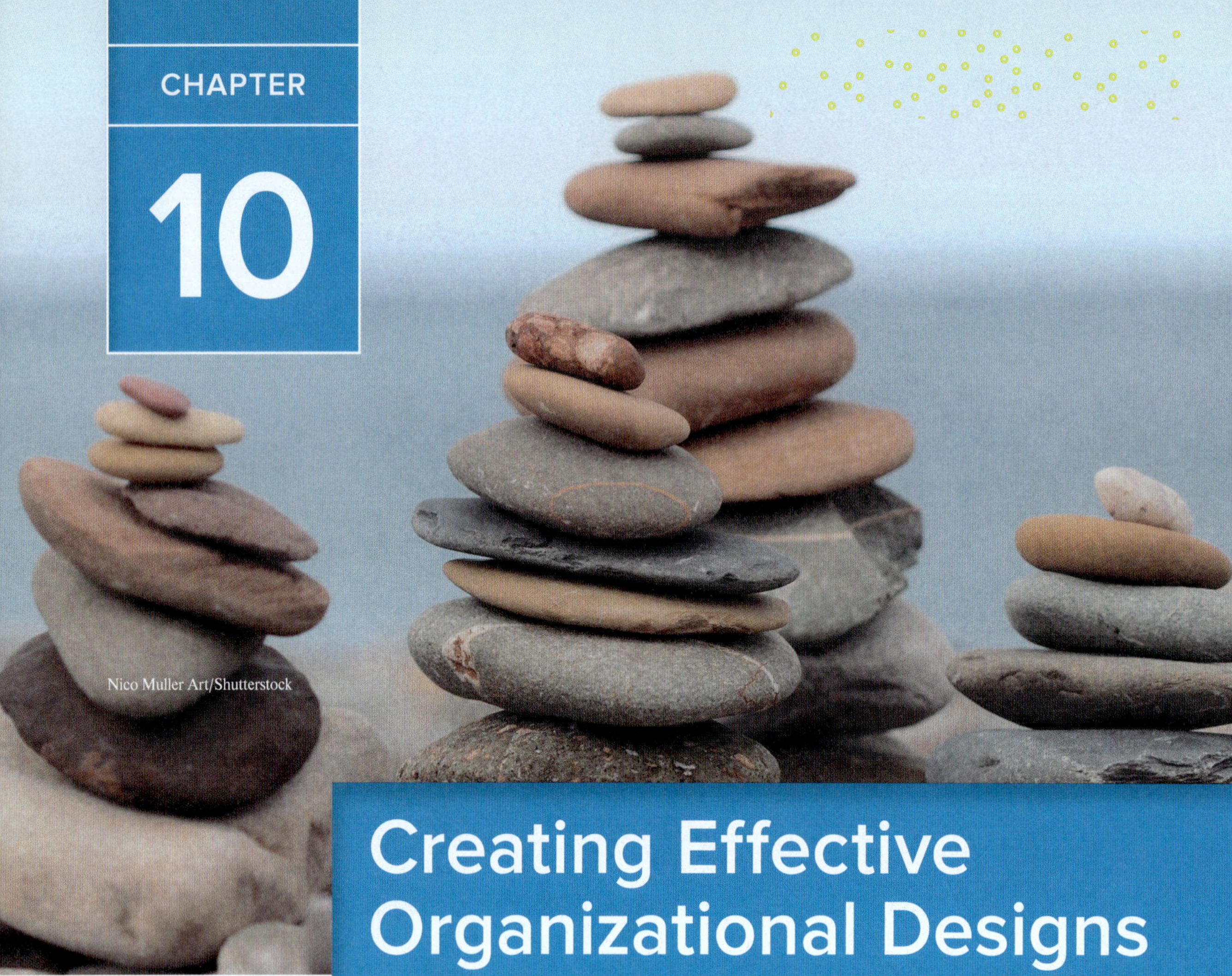

Nico Muller Art/Shutterstock

CHAPTER 10

Creating Effective Organizational Designs

Learning Objectives

LO10-1 Explain the growth patterns of major corporations and the relationship between a firm's strategy and its structure.

LO10-2 Identify each of the traditional types of organizational structure: simple, functional, divisional, and matrix.

LO10-3 Describe the implications of a firm's international operations for organizational structure.

LO10-4 Identify the different types of boundaryless organizations—barrier-free, modular, and virtual—and their relative advantages and disadvantages.

LO10-5 Explain the need for creating ambidextrous organizational designs that enable firms to explore new opportunities and effectively integrate existing operations.

We encourage you to reflect on how the concepts presented in this chapter can enhance your career success (see "Reflecting on Career Implications..." at the end of the chapter).

LEARNING FROM MISTAKES

The Boeing 787 Dreamliner is a game changer in the aircraft market.[1] It is the first commercial airliner that doesn't have an aluminum skin. Instead, Boeing designed it to have a composite exterior, which provides a weight savings that allows the plane to use 20 percent less fuel than the 767, the plane it is designed to replace. The increased fuel efficiency and other design advancements made the 787 very popular with airlines. Boeing received orders for over 900 Dreamliners before the first 787 ever took flight.

It was also a game changer for Boeing. In 2003, when Boeing announced the development of the new plane, it also decided to design and manufacture the 787 in a way that was different from what it had ever done before. In the past, Boeing had internally designed and engineered the major components of its planes. Boeing would then provide detailed engineering designs and specifications to its key suppliers. The suppliers would then build the components to Boeing's specifications. To limit the up-front investment it would need to make with the 787, Boeing moved to a modular structure and outsourced much of the engineering of the components to suppliers. Boeing provided them with basic specifications and left it to the suppliers to undertake the detailed design, engineering, and manufacturing of components and subsystems. Boeing's operations in Seattle were then responsible for assembling the pieces into a completed aircraft.

Working with about 50 suppliers on four continents, Boeing found the coordination and integration of the work of suppliers to be very challenging. Some of the contracted suppliers didn't have the engineering expertise needed to do the work and outsourced the engineering to subcontractors. This made it especially difficult to monitor the engineering work for the plane. Jim Albaugh, Boeing's commercial aviation chief, identified a core issue with this change in responsibility and stated, "We gave work to people that had never really done this kind of technology before, and we didn't provide the oversight that was necessary."[2] With the geographic stretch of the supplier set, Boeing also had difficulty monitoring the progress of the supplying firms. Boeing even ended up buying some of the suppliers once it became apparent they couldn't deliver the designs and products on schedule. For example, Boeing spent about $1 billion to acquire the Vought Aircraft Industries unit responsible for the plane's fuselage. When the suppliers finally delivered the parts, Boeing sometimes found they had difficulty assembling or combining the components. With its first 787, it found that the nose section and the fuselage didn't initially fit together, leaving a sizable gap between the two sections. To address these issues, Boeing was forced to co-locate many of its major suppliers together for six months to smooth out design and integration issues.

In the end, the decision to outsource cost Boeing dearly. The plane was three years behind schedule when the first 787 was delivered to a customer. The entire process took billions of dollars more than originally projected and also more than what it would have cost Boeing to design in-house. In early 2013, all 49 of the 787s that had been delivered to customers were grounded because of concerns about onboard fires in the lithium ion batteries used to power the plane—parts that were not designed by Boeing. As Boeing CEO Jim McNerney concluded, "In retrospect, our 787 game plan may have been overly ambitious, incorporating too many firsts all at once—in the application of new technologies, in revolutionary design and build processes, and in increased global sourcing of engineering and manufacturing content."[3]

Discussion Questions

1. A number of firms benefit from outsourcing design and manufacturing. What is different with Boeing that makes it so much harder to be successful?
2. What lessons does its experience with the 787 offer Boeing for its future plane development efforts?

One of the central concepts in this chapter is the importance of boundaryless organizations. Successful organizations create permeable boundaries among the internal activities as well as between the organization and its external customers, suppliers, and alliance partners. We introduced this idea in Chapter 3 in our discussion of the value-chain concept, which consisted of several primary (e.g., inbound logistics, marketing and sales) and support activities (e.g., procurement, human resource management). There are a number of possible benefits to outsourcing activities as part of becoming an effective boundaryless organization. However, outsourcing can also create challenges. As in the case of Boeing, the firm lost a large amount of control by using independent suppliers to design and manufacture key subsystems of the 787.

Today's managers are faced with two ongoing and vital activities in structuring and designing their organizations.[4] First, they must decide on the most appropriate type of organizational structure. Second, they need to assess what mechanisms, processes, and techniques are most helpful in enhancing the permeability of both internal and external boundaries.

TRADITIONAL FORMS OF ORGANIZATIONAL STRUCTURE

organizational structure the formalized patterns of interactions that link a firm's tasks, technologies, and people.

Organizational structure refers to the formalized patterns of interactions that link a firm's tasks, technologies, and people.[5] Structures help to ensure that resources are used effectively in accomplishing an organization's mission. Structure provides a means of balancing two conflicting forces: a need for the division of tasks into meaningful groupings and the need to integrate such groupings in order to ensure efficiency and effectiveness.[6] Structure identifies the executive, managerial, and administrative organization of a firm and indicates responsibilities and hierarchical relationships. It also influences the flow of information as well as the context and nature of human interactions.[7]

Most organizations begin very small and either die or remain small. Those that survive and prosper embark on strategies designed to increase the overall scope of operations and enable them to enter new product-market domains. Such growth places additional pressure on executives to control and coordinate the firm's increasing size and diversity. The most appropriate type of structure depends on the nature and magnitude of growth.

LO 10-1

Explain the growth patterns of major corporations and the relationship between a firm's strategy and its structure.

Patterns of Growth of Large Corporations: Strategy-Structure Relationships

A firm's strategy and structure change as it increases in size, diversifies into new product markets, and expands its geographic scope.[8] Exhibit 10.1 illustrates common growth patterns of firms.

A new firm with a *simple structure* typically increases its sales revenue and volume of outputs over time. It may also engage in some vertical integration to secure sources of supply (backward integration) as well as channels of distribution (forward integration). The simple-structure firm then implements a *functional structure* to concentrate efforts on both increasing efficiency and enhancing its operations and products. This structure enables the firm to group its operations into functions, departments, or geographic areas. As its initial markets mature, a firm looks beyond its present products and markets for possible expansion.

A strategy of related diversification requires a need to reorganize around product lines or geographic markets. This leads to a *divisional structure.* As the business expands in terms of sales revenues, and domestic growth opportunities become somewhat limited, a firm may seek opportunities in international markets. A firm has a wide variety of structures to choose from. These include *international division, geographic area, worldwide product division,*

EXHIBIT 10.1 Dominant Growth Patterns of Large Corporations

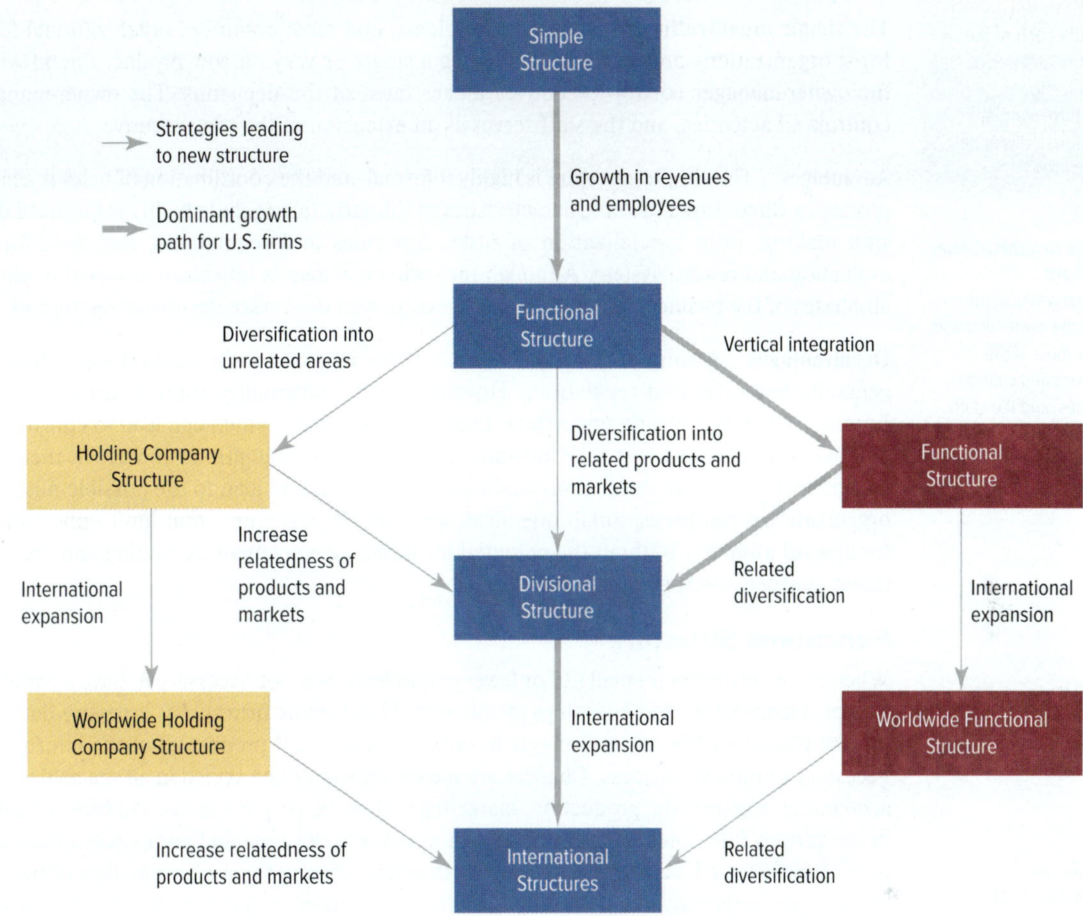

Source: Adapted from Galbraith, J. R., and R.K. Kazanjian. 1986. *Strategy Implementation: Structure, Systems and Process,* 2nd ed. St. Paul, MN: West Publishing Company.

worldwide functional, and *worldwide matrix.* Deciding upon the most appropriate structure when a firm has international operations depends on three primary factors: the extent of international expansion, type of strategy (global, multidomestic, or transnational), and degree of product diversity.[9]

Some firms may find it advantageous to diversify into several product lines rather than focus their efforts on strengthening distributor and supplier relationships through vertical integration. They would organize themselves according to product lines by implementing a divisional structure. Also, some firms may choose to move into unrelated product areas, typically by acquiring existing businesses. Frequently, their rationale is that acquiring assets and competencies is more economical or expedient than developing them internally. Such an unrelated, or conglomerate, strategy requires relatively little integration across businesses and sharing of resources. Thus, a *holding company structure* becomes appropriate. There are many other growth patterns, but these are the most common.

Now we will discuss some of the most common types of organizational structures–simple, functional, divisional (including two variants: *strategic business unit* and *holding company*), and matrix–and their advantages and disadvantages. We will close the section with a discussion of the structural implications when a firm expands its operations into international markets.[10]

LO 10-2

Identify each of the traditional types of organizational structure: simple, functional, divisional, and matrix.

Simple Structure

The **simple organizational structure** is the oldest, and most common, organizational form. Most organizations are very small and have a single or very narrow product line in which the owner-manager (or top executive) makes most of the decisions. The owner-manager controls all activities, and the staff serves as an extension of the top executive.

simple organizational structure
an organizational form in which the owner-manager makes most of the decisions and controls activities, and the staff serves as an extension of the top executive.

Advantages The simple structure is highly informal, and the coordination of tasks is accomplished by direct supervision. Characteristics of this structure include highly centralized decision making, little specialization of tasks, few rules and regulations, and an informal evaluation and reward system. Although the owner-manager is intimately involved in almost all phases of the business, a manager is often employed to oversee day-to-day operations.

Disadvantages A simple structure may foster creativity and individualism since there are generally few rules and regulations. However, such "informality" may lead to problems. Employees may not clearly understand their responsibilities, which can lead to conflict and confusion. Employees may take advantage of the lack of regulations and act in their own self-interest, which can erode motivation and satisfaction and lead to the possible misuse of organizational resources. Small organizations have flat structures that limit opportunities for upward mobility. Without the potential for future advancement, recruiting and retaining talent may become very difficult.

Functional Structure

When an organization is small (15 or fewer employees), it is not necessary to have a variety of formal arrangements and groupings of activities. However, as firms grow, excessive demands may be placed on the owner-manager in order to obtain and process all of the information necessary to run the business. Chances are the owner will not be skilled in all specialties (e.g., accounting, engineering, production, marketing). Thus, he or she will need to hire specialists in the various functional areas. Such growth in the overall scope and complexity of the business necessitates a **functional organizational structure** wherein the major functions of the firm are grouped internally. The coordination and integration of the functional areas become among the most important responsibilities of the chief executive of the firm (see Exhibit 10.2).

functional organizational structure
an organizational form in which the major functions of the firm, such as production, marketing, R&D, and accounting, are grouped internally.

Functional structures are generally found in organizations in which there is a single or closely related product or service, high production volume, and some vertical integration. Initially, firms tend to expand the overall scope of their operations by penetrating existing markets, introducing similar products in additional markets, or increasing the level of vertical integration. Such expansion activities clearly increase the scope and complexity of the operations. The functional structure provides for a high level of centralization that helps to ensure integration and control over the related product-market activities or multiple primary activities (from inbound logistics to operations to marketing, sales, and service) in the value chain (addressed in Chapters 3 and 4).

EXHIBIT 10.2 Functional Organizational Structure

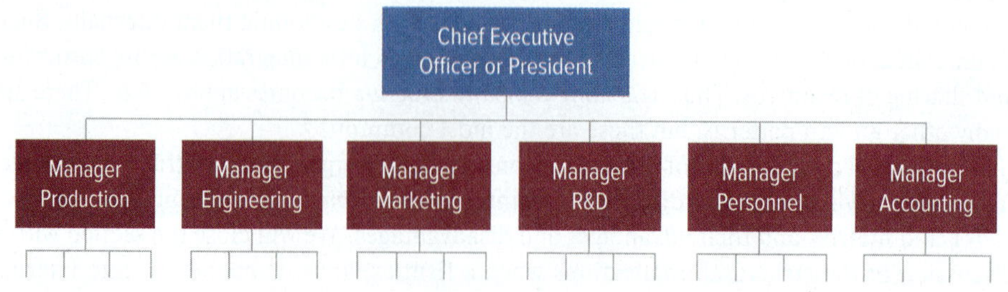

Advantages By bringing together specialists into functional departments, a firm is able to enhance its coordination and control within each of the functional areas. Decision making in the firm will be centralized at the top of the organization. This enhances the organizational-level (as opposed to functional area) perspective across the various functions in the organization. In addition, the functional structure provides for a more efficient use of managerial and technical talent since functional area expertise is pooled in a single department (e.g., marketing) instead of being spread across a variety of product-market areas. Finally, career paths and professional development in specialized areas are facilitated.

Disadvantages The differences in values and orientations among functional areas may impede communication and coordination. Edgar Schein, formerly a professor at MIT, argued that shared assumptions, often based on similar backgrounds and experiences of members, form around functional units in an organization. This leads to what are often called "stove pipes" or "silos," in which departments view themselves as isolated, self-contained units with little need for interaction and coordination with other departments. This erodes communication because functional groups may have not only different goals but also differing meanings of words and concepts. According to Schein:

> The word "marketing" will mean product development to the engineer, studying customers through market research to the product manager, merchandising to the salesperson, and constant change in design to the manufacturing manager. When they try to work together, they will often attribute disagreements to personalities and fail to notice the deeper, shared assumptions that color how each function thinks.[11]

Such narrow functional orientations also may lead to short-term thinking based largely upon what is best for the functional area, not the entire organization. In a manufacturing firm, sales may want to offer a wide range of customized products to appeal to the firm's customers; R&D may overdesign products and components to achieve technical elegance; and manufacturing may favor no-frills products that can be produced at low cost by means of long production runs. Functional structures may overburden the top executives in the firm because conflicts have a tendency to be "pushed up" to the top of the organization since there are no managers who are responsible for the specific product lines. Functional structures make it difficult to establish uniform performance standards across the entire organization. It may be relatively easy to evaluate production managers on the basis of production volume and cost control, but establishing performance measures for engineering, R&D, and accounting becomes more problematic.

Divisional Structure

The **divisional organizational structure** (sometimes called the multidivisional structure or M-Form) is organized around products, projects, or markets. Each of the divisions, in turn, includes its own functional specialists who are typically organized into departments.[12] A divisional structure encompasses a set of relatively autonomous units governed by a central corporate office. The operating divisions are relatively independent and consist of products and services that are different from those of the other divisions.[13] Operational decision making in a large business places excessive demands on the firm's top management. In order to attend to broader, longer-term organizational issues, top-level managers must delegate decision making to lower-level managers. Divisional executives play a key role: They help to determine the product-market and financial objectives for the division as well as their division's contribution to overall corporate performance.[14] The rewards are based largely on measures of financial performance such as net income and revenue. Exhibit 10.3 illustrates a divisional structure.

divisional organizational structure
an organizational form in which products, projects, or product markets are grouped internally.

General Motors was among the earliest firms to adopt the divisional organizational structure.[15] In the 1920s the company formed five major product divisions (Cadillac, Buick, Oldsmobile, Pontiac, and Chevrolet) as well as several industrial divisions. Since then, many

EXHIBIT 10.3 Divisional Organizational Structure

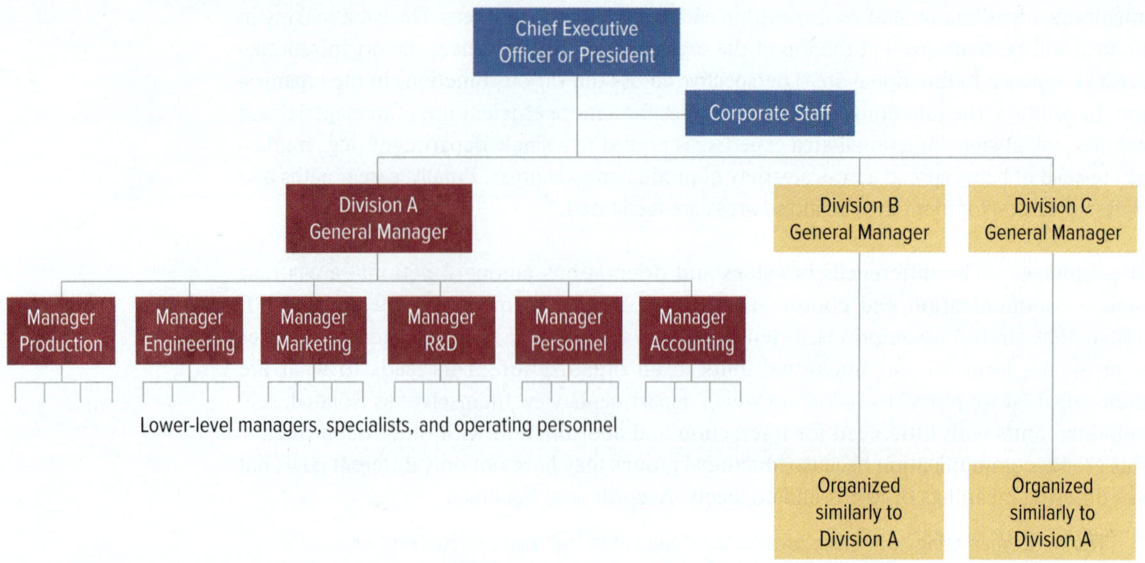

firms have discovered that as they diversified into new product-market activities, functional structures—with their emphasis on single functional departments—were unable to manage the increased complexity of the entire business.

Advantages By creating separate divisions to manage individual product markets, there is a separation of strategic and operating control. Divisional managers can focus their efforts on improving operations in the product markets for which they are responsible, and corporate officers can devote their time to overall strategic issues for the entire corporation. The focus on a division's products and markets—by the divisional executives—provides the corporation with an enhanced ability to respond quickly to important changes. Since there are functional departments within each division of the corporation, the problems associated with sharing resources across functional departments are minimized. Because there are multiple levels of general managers (executives responsible for integrating and coordinating all functional areas), the development of general management talent is enhanced.

Disadvantages It can be very expensive; there can be increased costs due to the duplication of personnel, operations, and investment since each division must staff multiple functional departments. There also can be dysfunctional competition among divisions since each division tends to become concerned solely about its own operations. Divisional managers are often evaluated on common measures such as return on assets and sales growth. If goals are conflicting, there can be a sense of a "zero-sum" game that would discourage sharing ideas and resources among the divisions for the common good of the corporation. In sum, divisional structures, by design, divide people, resources, and knowledge. They insulate divisional managers from other divisional managers, inhibiting their ability to coordinate activities, share resources, and learn from each other.

With many divisions providing different products and services, there is the chance that differences in image and quality may occur across divisions. One division may offer no-frills products of lower quality that may erode the brand reputation of another division that has top-quality, highly differentiated offerings. Since each division is evaluated in terms of financial measures such as return on investment and revenue growth, there is often an urge to focus on short-term performance. If corporate management uses quarterly profits as the key performance indicator, divisional management may tend to put significant emphasis on "making the numbers" and minimizing activities, such as advertising, maintenance, and capital investments, which would detract from short-term performance measures.

We now discuss two variations of the divisional form: the strategic business unit (SBU) and holding company structures.

Strategic Business Unit (SBU) Structure Highly diversified corporations such as ConAgra, a $8 billion food producer, may consist of dozens of different divisions.[16] If ConAgra were to use a purely divisional structure, it would be nearly impossible for the corporate office to plan and coordinate activities, because the span of control would be too large. To attain synergies, ConAgra has put its diverse businesses into two primary SBUs: commercial food service (restaurants), and consumer foods (grocery stores).

With an **SBU structure,** divisions with similar products, markets, and/or technologies are grouped into homogeneous units to achieve some synergies. These include those discussed in Chapter 6 for related diversification, such as leveraging core competencies, sharing infrastructures, and market power. Generally the more related businesses are within a corporation, the fewer SBUs will be required. Each of the SBUs in the corporation operates as a profit center.

strategic business unit (SBU) structure
an organizational form in which products, projects, or product-market divisions are grouped into homogeneous units.

Advantages The SBU structure makes the task of planning and control by the corporate office more manageable. Also, with greater decentralization of authority, individual businesses can react more quickly to important changes in the environment than if all divisions had to report directly to the corporate office.

Disadvantages Since the divisions are grouped into SBUs, it may become difficult to achieve synergies across SBUs. If divisions in different SBUs have potential sources of synergy, it may become difficult for them to be realized. The additional level of management increases the number of personnel and overhead expenses, while the additional hierarchical level removes the corporate office further from the individual divisions. The corporate office may become unaware of key developments that could have a major impact on the corporation.

Holding Company Structure The **holding company structure** (sometimes referred to as a *conglomerate*) is also a variation of the divisional structure. Whereas the SBU structure is often used when similarities exist between the individual businesses (or divisions), the holding company structure is appropriate when the businesses in a corporation's portfolio do not have much in common. Thus, the potential for synergies is limited.

holding company structure
an organizational form that is a variation of the divisional organizational structure in which the divisions have a high degree of autonomy both from other divisions and from corporate headquarters.

Holding company structures are most appropriate for firms with a strategy of unrelated diversification. Companies such as Berkshire Hathaway and Loews use a holding company structure to implement their unrelated diversification strategies. Since there are few similarities across the businesses, the corporate offices in these companies provide a great deal of autonomy to operating divisions and rely on financial controls and incentive programs to obtain high levels of performance from the individual businesses. Corporate staffs at these firms tend to be small because of their limited involvement in the overall operation of their various businesses.[17]

Advantages The holding company structure has the cost savings associated with fewer personnel and the lower overhead resulting from a small corporate office and fewer hierarchical levels. The autonomy of the holding company structure increases the motivational level of divisional executives and enables them to respond quickly to market opportunities and threats.

Disadvantages There is an inherent lack of control and dependence that corporate-level executives have on divisional executives. Major problems could arise if key divisional executives leave the firm, because the corporate office has very little "bench strength"—additional managerial talent ready to quickly fill key positions. If problems arise in a division, it may become very difficult to turn around individual businesses because of limited staff support in the corporate office.

Strategy Spotlight 10.1 discusses the prominent position of conglomerate firms in Asian countries.

10.1 STRATEGY SPOTLIGHT

WHERE CONGLOMERATES PROSPER

While conglomerates were numerous and well regarded in the United States and Western Europe in the 1960s and 1970s, firms that compete in a wide range of unrelated industries now are seen as being unfocused and unlikely to succeed. As a result, there are only about two dozen conglomerates still in existence in the United States and Europe.

The situation is quite different in much of the rest of the world, especially in Asia. For example, 45 of the largest 50 companies in India belong to a conglomerate business group. In South Korea, it is 40 of the largest 50. Additionally, in India, companies that belong to a conglomerate business group, on average, have outperformed independent companies. They also grow more rapidly than independent firms in their markets. For example, Indian conglomerates grew by more than 20 percent a year in the 2004 to 2013 period. Why is this the case? Some have argued that conglomerate business groups have thrived in developing markets because the social ties within conglomerate business groups serve as a substitute for weak governmental regulation and legal systems. The tightness of the group leads to social pressures that keep companies in line, and the head ownership group can settle disputes between companies. But these conglomerate groups have continued to grow even as the government and legal systems in these countries have modernized and become more westernized.

A second explanation is that the business groups in these countries are structured in a way that offers the benefits of being in a business with a vast range of competencies without some of the costs found in conglomerates in the United States, Canada, and Western Europe. A key difference is that while a conglomerate that is based in the United States, Canada, or Western Europe is a single corporation with a wide set of wholly owned subsidiaries, a conglomerate in Asia is actually made up of a set of legally separate corporations. Each of these corporations has its own board of directors and shareholders, but it is tied to the conglomerate since one of its major owners also owns part of the other corporations in the conglomerate. For example, the Tata group in India is comprised of over 100 separate companies. This type of structure allows the companies to have a degree of independence but also the benefits of size and power. This hybrid structure has a number of benefits.

- **Superior decision making.** The top managers of the affiliated firms have a great deal of autonomy to make decisions—meaning that key strategic decisions are made by managers who are close to the market. Thus, decisions can be quick and based on local market knowledge. In U.S. conglomerates, subsidiary managers typically have much less autonomy and have to get the approval of the corporate office.
- **Access to financial resources.** When affiliated units in business groups need financial capital to fund strategic investments, they can use funds within their own company, look to the central business group to provide funding, or look to outside investors to raise funds. Thus, they have great flexibility in raising capital. In contrast, the corporate offices of U.S. conglomerates typically accumulate financial resources and then allocate these funds to the business units. As a result, there is less funding available since units can't look to outside investors, and the process for allocating capital often becomes very political.
- **More effective managerial incentives.** Since the affiliated units are independent firms, the firm is able to set up evaluation and reward systems for managers that are tailored to the firm's distinctive needs and market position. In contrast, in U.S. conglomerates, the firms typically set up evaluation and rewards systems that are consistent across all of its units.
- **Resources and guidance from the group center.** These affiliated firms also have advantages over independent firms in their own market. These business groups have a center group that can provide strategic insight to the affiliated businesses. The center group will search for long-term business opportunities associated with emerging technologies or market changes and bring promising ideas to the affiliated businesses. This frees up the affiliated businesses to focus on current activities and allow the center group to do the longer term visioning. The center group is also responsible for linking together different businesses when cross-business opportunities arise. Finally, the center group ensures that all of the activities in the businesses align with the identity of the overall group. As a result, each of the businesses benefits from the strong and consistent image associated with the overall business group.

It is unclear if these conglomerates will continue to thrive in these markets, but their ability to sustain their dominance to date and their success in regularly moving into new markets suggest that they will continue to be major players for the foreseeable future.

Source: Hirt, M., Smit, S., and W. Yoo. 2013. Understanding Asia's conglomerates. *mckinsey.com,* February: np; and Ramachandran, J., Manikandan, K., and A. Pant. 2013. Why conglomerates thrive. *Harvard Business Review,* 91(2): 110–119.

Matrix Structure

One approach that tries to overcome the inadequacies inherent in the other structures is the **matrix organizational structure**. It is a combination of the functional and divisional structures. Most commonly, functional departments are combined with product groups on a project basis. For example, a product group may want to develop a new addition to its line; for this project, it obtains personnel from functional departments such as marketing, production, and engineering. These personnel work under the manager of the product group for the duration of the project, which can vary from a few weeks to an open-ended period of time. The individuals who work in a matrix organization become responsible to two managers: the project manager and the manager of their functional area. Exhibit 10.4 illustrates a matrix structure.

matrix organizational structure
an organizational form in which there are multiple lines of authority and some individuals report to at least two managers.

Some large multinational corporations rely on a matrix structure to combine product groups and geographic units. Product managers have global responsibility for the development, manufacturing, and distribution of their own line, while managers of geographic regions have responsibility for the profitability of the businesses in their regions. To manage its large global operations and expanding product scope, Starbucks uses a version of a matrix structure.[18]

Other organizations, such as Cisco, use a matrix structure to try to maintain flexibility. In these firms, individual workers have a permanent functional home but also are assigned to and work within temporary project teams.[19]

Advantages The matrix structure facilitates the use of specialized personnel, equipment, and facilities. Instead of duplicating functions, as would be the case in a divisional structure based on products, the resources are shared. Individuals with high expertise can divide their time among multiple projects. Such resource sharing and collaboration enable a firm to use resources more efficiently and to respond more quickly and effectively to changes in the competitive environment. The flexibility inherent in a matrix structure provides professionals with a broader range of responsibility. Such experience enables them to develop their skills and competencies.

Disadvantages The dual-reporting structures can result in uncertainty and lead to intense power struggles and conflict over the allocation of personnel and other resources. Working relationships

EXHIBIT 10.4 Matrix Organizational Structure

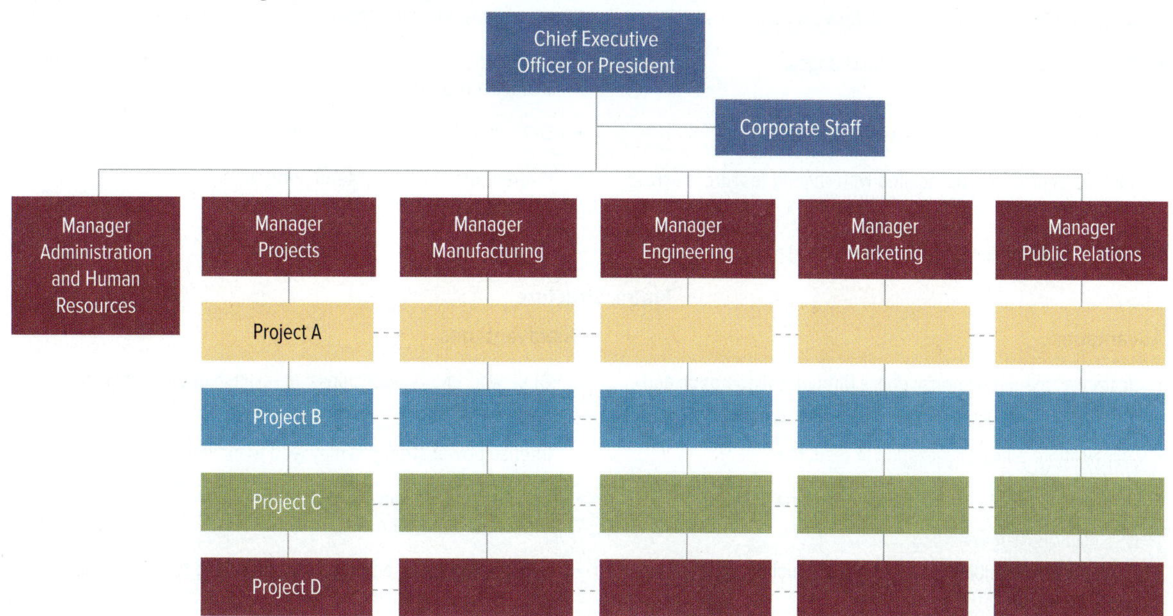

become more complicated. This may result in excessive reliance on group processes and teamwork, along with a diffusion of responsibility, which in turn may erode timely decision making.

Exhibit 10.5 briefly summarizes the advantages and disadvantages of the functional, divisional, and matrix organizational structures.

LO 10-3

Describe the implications of a firm's international operations for organizational structure.

International Operations: Implications for Organizational Structure

With increasing drive for globalization coupled with the rise of nationalist political policies, managers must maintain a global orientation toward their firm's businesses and competitive strategies. In the global marketplace, managers must ensure consistency between their strategies (at the business, corporate, and international levels) and the structure of their organization. As firms expand into foreign markets, they generally follow a pattern of change in structure that parallels the changes in their strategies.[20] Three major contingencies that influence the chosen structure are (1) the type of strategy that is driving a firm's foreign operations, (2) product diversity, and (3) the extent to which a firm is dependent on foreign sales.[21]

EXHIBIT 10.5 Functional, Divisional, and Matrix Organizational Structures: Advantages and Disadvantages

Functional Structure	
Advantages	**Disadvantages**
• Pooling of specialists enhances coordination and control.	• Differences in functional area orientation impede communication and coordination.
• Centralized decision making enhances an organizational perspective across functions.	• Tendency for specialists to develop short-term perspective and narrow functional orientation.
• Efficient use of managerial and technical talent.	• Functional area conflicts may overburden top-level decision makers.
• Facilitates career paths and professional development in specialized areas.	• Difficult to establish uniform performance standards.
Divisional Structure	
Advantages	**Disadvantages**
• Increases strategic and operational control, permitting corporate-level executives to address strategic issues.	• Increased costs incurred through duplication of personnel, operations, and investment.
• Quick response to environmental changes.	• Dysfunctional competition among divisions may detract from overall corporate performance.
• Increases focus on products and markets.	• Difficult to maintain uniform corporate image.
• Minimizes problems associated with sharing resources across functional areas.	• Overemphasis on short-term performance.
• Facilitates development of general managers.	
Matrix Structure	
Advantages	**Disadvantages**
• Increases market responsiveness through collaboration and synergies among professional colleagues.	• Dual-reporting relationships can result in uncertainty regarding accountability.
• Allows more efficient utilization of resources.	• Intense power struggles may lead to increased levels of conflict.
• Improves flexibility, coordination, and communication.	• Working relationships may be more complicated and human resources duplicated.
• Increases professional development through a broader range of responsibility.	• Excessive reliance on group processes and teamwork may impede timely decision making.

As international operations become an important part of a firm's overall operations, managers must make changes that are consistent with their firm's structure. The primary types of structures used to manage a firm's international operations are:[22]

- International division
- Geographic-area division
- Worldwide functional
- Worldwide product division
- Worldwide matrix

Multidomestic strategies are driven by political and cultural imperatives requiring managers within each country to respond to local conditions. The structures consistent with such a strategic orientation are the **international division** and **geographic-area division structures.** Here, local managers are provided with a high level of autonomy to manage their operations within the constraints and demands of their geographic market. As a firm's foreign sales increase as a percentage of its total sales, it will likely change from an international division to a geographic-area division structure. And, as a firm's product and/or market diversity becomes large, it is likely to benefit from a **worldwide matrix structure**.

international division structure
an organizational form in which international operations are in a separate, autonomous division. Most domestic operations are kept in other parts of the organization.

geographic-area division structure
a type of divisional organizational structure in which operations in geographic regions are grouped internally.

worldwide matrix structure
a type of matrix organizational structure that has one line of authority for geographic-area divisions and another line of authority for worldwide product divisions.

Global strategies are driven by economic pressures that require managers to view operations in different geographic areas to be managed for overall efficiency. The structures consistent with the efficiency perspective are the **worldwide functional** and **worldwide product division structures**. Here, division managers view the marketplace as homogeneous and devote relatively little attention to local market, political, and economic factors. The choice between these two types of structures is guided largely by the extent of product diversity. Firms with relatively low levels of product diversity may opt for a worldwide product division structure. However, if significant product-market diversity results from highly unrelated international acquisitions, a worldwide holding company structure should be implemented. Such firms have very little commonality among products, markets, or technologies and have little need for integration.

worldwide functional structure
a functional structure in which all departments have worldwide reponsibilities.

worldwide product division structure
a product division structure in which all divisions have worldwide responsibilities.

Global Start-Ups: A Recent Phenomenon

International expansion occurs rather late for most corporations, typically after possibilities of domestic growth are exhausted. Increasingly, we are seeing two interrelated phenomena. First, many firms now expand internationally relatively early in their history. Second, some firms are "born global"–that is, from the very beginning, many start-ups are global in their activities. For example, Logitech International, a leading producer of personal computer accessories, was global from day one. Founded in 1982 by a Swiss national and two Italians, the company was headquartered in both California and Switzerland. R&D and manufacturing were also conducted in both locations and, subsequently, in Taiwan and Ireland.[23]

The success of companies such as Logitech challenges the conventional wisdom that a company must first build up assets, internal processes, and experience before venturing into faraway lands. It also raises a number of questions: What exactly is a global start-up? Under what conditions should a company start out as a global start-up? What does it take to succeed as a global start-up?

A **global start-up** has been defined as a business organization that, from inception, seeks to derive significant competitive advantage from the use of resources and the sale of outputs in multiple countries. Right from the beginning, it uses inputs from around the world and sells its products and services to customers around the world. Geographic boundaries of nation-states are irrelevant for a global start-up.

global start-up
a business organization that, from inception, seeks to derive significant advantage from the use of resources and the sale of outputs in multiple countries.

There is no reason for every start-up to be global. Being global necessarily involves higher communication, coordination, and transportation costs. Therefore, it is important to identify the circumstances under which going global from the beginning is advantageous.[24] First, if the required human resources are globally dispersed, going global may be the best way to

10.2 STRATEGY SPOTLIGHT

GLOBAL START-UP, BRCK, WORKS TO BRING RELIABLE INTERNET CONNECTIVITY TO THE WORLD

BRCK is a notable technology pioneer. It's bringing a novel and potentially very valuable product to market, and it is doing so as a truly global start-up. BRCK's first product is a surge-resistant, battery-powered router to provide Internet service, which the firm is simply calling the BRCK. In many parts of the world, power systems are unreliable and offer only intermittent service. Additionally, they are prone to generate power surges that can fry many electronic products, including Internet routers. For example, in 2013, a single power-surge event in Nairobi, Kenya, blew out more than 3,000 routers. BRCK has developed a product to address these issues. Its router has a built-in battery that charges up whenever the power grid is operating and that runs off the battery for up to eight hours when the power grid goes down. It can also handle power surges up to 400 volts. The BRCK is also flexible as to how it connects to the Internet. It can connect directly to an ethernet line, can link up with a Wi-Fi network in its area, and can connect via a wireless phone connection. BRCK is aiming to sell its product to small and medium-size businesses, schools, and medical facilities. Its routers allow up to 20 users to simultaneously connect to the Internet. Its higher-end product, SupaBRCK, is water-resistant, can be mounted outside, and supports up to 100 users at a time, providing Wi-Fi in otherwise unserved areas. The technologies it uses are not cutting-edge, but the end product itself is innovative and meets a market need.

What really sets BRCK apart is that it is a global start-up that turns the table on typical global structures. Most tech-oriented global firms design their products in a technology center in the developed world and manufacture the products in a developing country. BRCK has flipped this model. BRCK designs its products in a developing country and manufactures in a developed country. Its corporate headquarters are in Nairobi, Kenya, at a technology center that houses a small group of entrepreneurs. The firm employs a dozen engineers to design its products in its corporate headquarters, and while its offices look a bit like those in Silicon Valley, the building has backup power for times when the Kenyan power grid inevitably goes down. The firm sources most of the components for its routers from Asia and manufactures its products in Austin, Texas. Even its sales are also going global right from the start. The firm has sold BRCKs to customers in over 50 countries. The firm has also received global acclaim, including winning Fast Company's 2016 Innovation by Design Award, the 2017 iF Design Award, and the Global SME Award at the 2016 ITU Global Telecom Conference.

Sources: Cary, J. 2014. Made in Kenya, assembled in America: This Internet-anywhere company innovates from silicon savannah. *fastcoexist.com*, September 4: np; Vogt, H. 2014. Made in Africa: A gadget startup. *wsj.com*, July 10: np; Hersman, E. 2017. The year at BRCK. *brck.com*, January 2: np; and Bright, J. 2017. Kenyan startup BRCK launches SupaBRCK device to solve Africa's Internet equation. *techcrunch.com*, March 8: np.

access those resources. For example, Italians are masters in fine leather and Swedes in ergonomics. Second, in many cases foreign financing may be easier to obtain and more suitable. Traditionally, U.S. venture capitalists have shown greater willingness to bear risk, but they have shorter time horizons in their expectations for return. If a U.S. start-up is looking for patient capital, it may be better off looking overseas. Third, the target customers in many specialized industries are located in other parts of the world. Fourth, in many industries a gradual move from domestic markets to foreign markets is no longer possible because if a product is successful foreign competitors may immediately imitate it. Therefore, preemptive entry into foreign markets may be the only option. Finally, because of high up-front development costs, a global market is often necessary to recover the costs. This is particularly true for start-ups from smaller nations that do not have access to large domestic markets.

Successful management of a global start-up presents many challenges. Communication and coordination across time zones and cultures are always problematic. Since most global start-ups have far less resources than well-established corporations, one key for success is to internalize few activities and outsource the rest. Managers of such firms must have considerable prior international experience so that they can successfully handle the inevitable communication problems and cultural conflicts. Another key for success is to keep the communication and coordination costs low. The only way to achieve this is by creating less costly administrative mechanisms. The boundaryless organizational designs that we discuss in the next section are particularly suitable for global start-ups because of their flexibility and low cost.

Strategy Spotlight 10.2 discusses a Kenyan technology start-up with a global vision and scope of operations.

How an Organization's Structure Can Influence Strategy Formulation

Discussions of the relationship between strategy and structure usually strongly imply that structure follows strategy. The strategy that a firm chooses (e.g., related diversification) dictates such structural elements as the division of tasks, the need for integration of activities, and authority relationships within the organization. However, an existing structure can influence strategy formulation. Once a firm's structure is in place, it is very difficult and expensive to change.[25] Executives may not be able to modify their duties and responsibilities greatly or may not welcome the disruption associated with a transfer to a new location. There are costs associated with hiring, training, and replacing executive, managerial, and operating personnel. Strategy cannot be formulated without considering structural elements.

An organization's structure can also have an important influence on how it competes in the marketplace. It can also strongly influence a firm's strategy, day-to-day operations, and performance.[26]

BOUNDARYLESS ORGANIZATIONAL DESIGNS

LO 10-4

Identify the different types of boundaryless organizations—barrier-free, modular, and virtual—and their relative advantages and disadvantages.

The term *boundaryless* may bring to mind a chaotic organizational reality in which "anything goes." This is not the case. Boundaryless does not imply that all internal and external boundaries vanish completely, but that they become more open and permeable.[27] We are not suggesting that **boundaryless organizational designs** replace the traditional forms of organizational structure, but they should complement them.

boundaryless organizational designs
organizations in which the boundaries, including vertical, horizontal, external, and geographic boundaries, are permeable.

We will discuss three approaches to making boundaries more permeable that help to facilitate the widespread sharing of knowledge and information across both the internal and external boundaries of the organization. The *barrier-free* type involves making all organizational boundaries–internal and external–more permeable. Teams are a central building block for implementing the boundaryless organization. The *modular* and *virtual* types of organizations focus on the need to create seamless relationships with external organizations such as customers or suppliers. While the modular type emphasizes the outsourcing of non-core activities, the virtual (or network) organization focuses on alliances among independent entities formed to exploit specific market opportunities.

The Barrier-Free Organization

The "boundary" mindset is ingrained deeply into bureaucracies. It is evidenced by such clichés as "That's not my job," or by endless battles over transfer pricing. In the traditional company, boundaries are clearly delineated in the design of an organization's structure. Their basic advantage is that the roles of managers and employees are simple, clear, well defined, and long lived. A major shortcoming was pointed out to the authors during an interview with a high-tech executive: "Structure tends to be divisive; it leads to territorial fights."

Such structures are being replaced by fluid, ambiguous, and deliberately ill-defined tasks and roles. Just because work roles are no longer clearly defined, however, does not mean that differences in skills, authority, and talent disappear. A **barrier-free organization** enables a firm to bridge real differences in culture, function, and goals to find common ground that facilitates information sharing and other forms of cooperative behavior. Eliminating the multiple boundaries that stifle productivity and innovation can enhance the potential of the entire organization.

barrier-free organization
an organizational design in which firms bridge real differences in culture, function, and goals to find common ground that facilitates information sharing and other forms of cooperative behavior.

We see how General Motors is striving to create a boundaryless organization in order to enhance its innovation in Strategy Spotlight 10.3.

Creating Permeable Internal Boundaries For barrier-free organizations to work effectively, the level of trust and shared interests among all parts of the organization must be raised.[29]

10.3 STRATEGY SPOTLIGHT

GM RESTRUCTURES FOR INNOVATION

For over one hundred years, General Motors (GM) has employed a formal structure to standardize procedures and bring operational efficiency to its automotive operations. However, it finds itself facing a rapidly changing environment and an uncertain future. The number of vehicles sold appears to have peaked in the United States, and younger generations are less committed to the auto than their parents. As evidence of this, 92 percent of young adults, 20 to 24 years old, had their driver's licenses in 1983, but this percentage dropped to 77 percent in 2014. More frequently, people are turning to ride sharing services to get themselves around, rather than using a personal car. Looking to the future, it is unclear if car ownership or car sharing will be the dominant model in 10 to 20 years. It is also unclear whether and how quickly electric motors will supplant internal combustion engines. Finally, it is uncertain how long your typical driver will actually drive his or her car in the future versus having the car drive itself.

In response to these changes and uncertainties, GM is striving to reinvent itself to retain its position of leadership in the rapidly evolving transportation industry. The key challenge for the firm is to be ambidextrous, both efficiently developing and producing autos to support its traditional business while also investing in and leveraging new technologies that will allow it to succeed in the future. To manage this balance, the firm is adding features of the boundaryless organization to its traditional formalized divisional structure.

First, the firm is working to break down internal boundaries. This is very evident in its Vehicle Engineering Center, where the firm has embraced the open, flexible atmosphere of a Silicon Valley tech firm. There are numerous open work spaces and informal areas to facilitate random interactions between engineers and designers. Mary Barra, GM's CEO, explains that the layout was designed to create "an environment for collaboration and giving people tools they need to work effectively. How can we make sure you really have a work environment that is enabling and empowering, instead of constricting?"[28] The goal is to facilitate creativity in how GM envisions and designs the auto of the future by getting personnel from engineering, design, operations, supply chain, and other functions to work together outside of their normal silos.

The firm is also forging relationships with external constituencies to facilitate creativity. This includes an alliance with Lyft, a major ride sharing service. It also involves purchasing Cruise Automation, a firm that makes autonomous systems; and Strobe, a firm that specializes in Lidar sensing systems which is a key component of autonomous vehicles. These firms are part of the GM family but have been given a degree of independence to retain their informal culture, drive, and innovativeness. Cruise Automation works on systems for autonomous vehicles independently but then coordinates with GM engineers and manufacturing plants to produce prototype autonomous cars.

To support these efforts, the firm has developed a long-term initiative, labeled Zero Zero Zero, which refers to zero accidents, zero emissions, and zero congestion. Barra has also backed up the initiative with training sessions for thousands of workers on task-oriented design thinking that emphasizes the need to work collaboratively and think innovatively. It isn't clear what the future holds for this industry, but GM is trying to build in flexibility to meet the emerging market conditions with its boundaryless organization.

Sources: Tetzeli, R. 2018. GM changes lanes. *Fortune,* June 1: 119-126; and Neiger, C. 2018. Why General Motors could win the driverless car race. *fool.com,* July 10: np.; LaReau, J. L. 2018. In auto talent war, GM hires 9,000, spends $1 billion on offices. *Detroit Free Press.*

The organization needs to develop among its employees the skill level needed to work in a more democratic organization. Barrier-free organizations also require a shift in the organization's philosophy from executive to organizational development and from investments in high-potential individuals to investments in leveraging the talents of all individuals.

Teams can be an important aspect of barrier-free structures.[30] Jeffrey Pfeffer, author of several insightful books, including *The Human Equation,* suggests that teams have three primary advantages.[31] First, teams substitute peer-based control for hierarchical control of work activities. Employees control themselves, reducing the time and energy management needs to devote to control. Second, teams frequently develop more creative solutions to problems because they encourage the sharing of the tacit knowledge held by individuals.[32] Brainstorming, or group problem solving, involves the pooling of ideas and expertise to enhance the chances that at least one group member will think of a way to solve the problems at hand. Third, by substituting peer control for hierarchical control, teams permit the removal of layers of hierarchy. This avoids the costs of having people whose sole job is to watch the people who watch other people do the work.

Research examining teams within innovative firms identifies several prescriptions for helping such teams succeed in being creative and agile. They include issues related to staffing the team, setting the charter for the team, fostering responsiveness on the team, and managing the team. Some specific recommendations include:[33]

- **Keep the size of the team small.** Small teams are able to more easily coordinate team activities and action plans. Something as simple as scheduling and coordinating meetings becomes difficult as the size of the team grows. Also, small team size lessens the chances that the team will break into factions that inhibit reaching and implementing decisions. Jeff Bezos' rule of thumb that if two pizzas isn't enough to feed a team, the team has gotten too big.
- **Staff the team with top performers.** Line managers often want to keep their best people close to them so that they can use them on projects the manager controls. However, to have effective cross-functional teams, these teams have to be staffed with the highest caliber employees and those with the most relevant knowledge. This also facilitates the building of experience by these top performers to help them build a broad, strategic view so that they will be more effective leaders in the future.
- **Fully funding the team up front.** Managers should create a budget up front for what they think the team will need. This includes funds to pay for internal staff support, hiring outside consultants, purchasing relevant data, and any other activities the team will likely undertake. This allows the team to act quickly and take action. Otherwise, the team would have to slow down each time it has to go back to corporate staff for additional funding.
- **Empower the team to spend the budget.** The team should have the authority to make key decisions, such as the ability to quickly hire new talent or contract with a supplier without going through standard human resource and procurement processes. By having the ability to act in a flexible and timely fashion, the team can sustain speed of action.
- **Hold the team accountable.** With the increased independence and flexibility given to the team, it is important that the team perceive a strong sense of accountability. This requires that the team, with the involvement of the responsible manager, identify the outcomes they are pursuing and identify the achievements they hope to achieve in clear, measurable terms. On an ongoing basis, the responsible manager, in consultation with the team, needs to assess progress toward those desired outcomes.
- **Have an engaged manager.** While teams should operate as independent entities, they should still work with managers on an ongoing basis. The manager should be there to provide support, guidance, and perspective to the team. An experienced manager can help facilitate communication with the rest of the organization, help the team see how their actions fit into the larger strategic goals of the organization, and can serve as a problem-solving expert. Some agile teams hold short, "stand-up" meetings in the morning to review processes, decisions, and difficulties. By attending these meetings regularly, the responsible manager can keep in touch with the team, provide advice, and undertake necessary actions to link the team's activities with the rest of the organization.

Developing Effective Relationships with External Constituencies In barrier-free organizations, managers must also create flexible, porous organizational boundaries and establish communication flows and mutually beneficial relationships with internal (e.g., employees) and external (e.g., customers) constituencies.[34] IBM has worked to develop a long-standing cooperative relationship with the Mayo Clinic. The clinic is a customer but more importantly a research partner. IBM has placed staff at the Mayo Clinic, and the two organizations have worked together on technology for the early identification of aneurysms, the

10.4 STRATEGY SPOTLIGHT **ENVIRONMENTAL SUSTAINABILITY**

THE BUSINESS ROUNDTABLE: A FORUM FOR SHARING BEST ENVIRONMENTAL SUSTAINABILITY PRACTICES

The Business Roundtable is a group of chief executive officers of major U.S. corporations that was created to promote pro-business public policy. It was formed in 1972 through the merger of three existing organizations: The March Group, the Construction Users Anti-Inflation Roundtable, and the Labor Law Study Committee. The group was called President Obama's "closest ally in the business community."

The Business Roundtable became the first broad-based business group to agree on the need to address climate change through collective action, and it remains committed to limiting greenhouse gas emissions and setting the United States on a more sustainable path. The organization considers that threats to water quality and quantity, rising greenhouse gas emissions, and the risk of climate change—along with increasing energy prices and growing demand—are of great concern.

Its report "Create, Grow, Sustain" provides best practices and metrics from Business Roundtable member companies that represent nearly all sectors of the economy with $6 trillion in annual revenues. CEOs from Walmart, FedEx, PepsiCo, Whirlpool, and Verizon are among the 126 executives from leading U.S. companies that shared some of their best sustainability initiatives in this report. These companies are committed to reducing emissions, increasing energy efficiency, and developing more sustainable business practices.

Let's look, for example, at some of Walmart's initiatives. The firm's former CEO, Mike Duke, emphasized the need to work with suppliers, partners, and consumers to drive its sustainability program. It has helped establish the Sustainability Consortium to drive metrics for measuring the environmental effects of consumer products across their life cycle. The retailer also helped lead the creation of a Sustainable Product Index to provide product information to consumers about the environmental impact of the products they purchase.

As part of its sustainability efforts, Walmart has over 335 renewable energy projects. Combined, these efforts have resulted in more than 2.2 billion kilowatt-hours of renewable energy production each year, providing one-quarter of Walmart's energy needs, with a goal of having 50 percent of its energy needs from renewable sources by 2025.

Walmart's renewable energy efforts have focused on three general initiatives:

- It has invested in developing distributed electrical generation systems on its property. As part of this effort, Walmart has installed solar panels on the roofs of over 500 of its stores and distribution centers.
- Expanding its contracts with suppliers for renewable energy has also been a focus of Walmart. Thus, Walmart bypasses the local utility to go directly to renewable energy suppliers to sign long-term contracts for renewable energy. With long-term contracts, Walmart has found that providers will give it more favorable terms. Walmart also believes that the long-term contracts give suppliers the incentive to invest in their generation systems, increasing the availability of renewable power for other users.
- In regions where going directly to renewable energy suppliers is difficult or impossible, Walmart has engaged the local utilities to increase their investment in renewable energy.

Sources: Helman, C. 2015. How Walmart became a green energy giant, using other people's money. *forbes.com*, November 4: np; Anonymous. 2010. Leading CEOs share best sustainability practices. *www.environmentalleader.com*, April 26: np; Hopkins, M. No date. Sustainable growth. *www.businessroundtable*, np; Anonymous. 2012. Create, grow, sustain. *www.businessroundtable.org*, April 18: 120; Rosalund, C. 2018. Walmart to host solar power on 130 more sites. *pv-magazine-use.com*, April 23: np; and *corporate.walmart.com/_news_/photos/renewable-energy-projects*.

mining of data in electronic health records to develop customized treatment plans for patients, and other medical issues.[35]

Barrier-free organizations create successful relationships between both internal and external constituencies, but there is one additional constituency—competitors—with whom some organizations have benefited as they developed cooperative relationships. For example, Coca-Cola and PepsiCo, often argued to be the most intense rivals in business, work together to develop new, environmentally conscious refrigerants for use in their vending machines.[36]

By joining and actively participating in the Business Roundtable—an organization consisting of CEOs of leading U.S. corporations—Walmart has been able to learn about cutting-edge sustainable initiatives of other major firms. This free flow of information has enabled Walmart to undertake a number of steps that have increased the energy efficiency of its operations. These are described in Strategy Spotlight 10.4.

The Insights from Research box offers evidence on how breaking down internal and external boundaries influences learning.

10.1 INSIGHTS from Research

WHERE EMPLOYEES LEARN AFFECTS FINANCIAL PERFORMANCE

Overview

What company wouldn't want to improve financial performance? Research suggests that when employees of innovative companies engage in learning activities both inside their companies, such as across functional areas, and outside their companies, such as via strategic alliances, they can achieve the best performance. This is particularly true for businesses operating in transitional economies.

What the Research Shows

Businesses are expanding into transitional economies, such as China and India, to capitalize on these large markets. But how can businesses operating in these economies improve their financial performance? Research in *Entrepreneurship, Theory, and Practice* from scholars at Xi'an Jiaotong University and Old Dominion University provides tips to enhance performance. The researchers conducted a study using face-to-face interviews with 607 top managers in manufacturing companies in China. They sought to understand how innovative companies with an "entrepreneurial orientation" could realize better performance when their employees learn about technology, markets, customers, and other important information from a range of sources.

In particular, the researchers examined whether it mattered if companies focused learning activities within their organizations–such as sharing information across functional areas or implementing technology to facilitate internal knowledge sharing–or outside the organization–such as studying competitors, learning from government sources, or engaging in strategic alliances with other companies. The results demonstrated that, in general:

- Companies with a high entrepreneurial orientation engage in more internal learning activities.
- Companies with a moderate entrepreneurial orientation engage in more external learning activities.
- Companies with a low entrepreneurial orientation engage in little external learning.
- When companies with a high entrepreneurial orientation engaged in more internal learning, performance improved.
- Learning from external sources enhanced financial performance but by a lesser amount than learning from internal sources.

Key Takeaways

- Entrepreneurial businesses operating in transition economies, such as China, can achieve the best performance when engaging in learning activities inside and outside the firm.
- When employees spend more time learning about internal company projects and activities, their companies are more innovative than when they try to learn from competitors in the industry.
- Companies whose employees have an innovative, entrepreneurial spirit and who spend time learning about internal company activities can improve their financial performance.
- Although learning through interactions with competitors or other external sources is valuable, businesses in transition economies can most improve their performance when employee learning is focused on internal company sources.

Questions

1. What are some ways firms can enhance internal learning?
2. This research examined learning in transition economies. Do you think these findings would translate to firms in developed economies? Why or why not?

Research Reviewed

Zhao, Y., Ly, Y., and L. Chen. 2011. Entrepreneurial orientation, organizational learning, and performance: Evidence from China. *Entrepreneurship, Theory and Practice,* 35: 293–317.

Risks, Challenges, and Potential Downsides Many firms find that creating and managing a barrier-free organization can be frustrating.[37] Puritan-Bennett Corporation, a manufacturer of respiratory equipment, found that its product development time more than doubled after it adopted team management. Roger J. Dolida, director of R&D, attributed this failure to a lack of top management commitment, high turnover among team members, and infrequent meetings. Often, managers trained in rigid hierarchies find it difficult to make the transition to the more democratic, participative style that teamwork requires.

The pros and cons of barrier-free structures are summarized in Exhibit 10.6.

EXHIBIT 10.6 Pros and Cons of Barrier-Free Structures

Pros	Cons
• Leverages the talents of all employees. • Enhances cooperation, coordination, and information sharing among functions, divisions, SBUs, and external constituencies. • Enables a quicker response to market changes through a single-goal focus. • Can lead to coordinated win–win initiatives with key suppliers, customers, and alliance partners.	• Difficult to overcome political and authority boundaries inside and outside the organization. • Lacks strong leadership and common vision, which can lead to coordination problems. • Time-consuming and difficult-to-manage democratic processes. • Lacks high levels of trust, which can impede performance.

The Modular Organization

modular organization an organization in which nonvital functions are outsourced, using the knowledge and expertise of outside suppliers while retaining strategic control.

The **modular organization** outsources non-vital functions, tapping into the knowledge and expertise of "best in class" suppliers, but retains strategic control. Outsiders may be used to manufacture parts, handle logistics, or perform accounting activities.[38] The value chain can be used to identify the key primary and support activities performed by a firm to create value: Which activities do we keep in-house and which activities do we outsource to suppliers?[39] The organization becomes a central hub surrounded by networks of outside suppliers and specialists, and parts can be added or taken away. Both manufacturing and service units may be modular.[40]

Apparel is an industry in which the modular type has been widely adopted. For example, adidas does little of its own manufacturing. Instead, it contracts with outside suppliers who run over 1,000 manufacturing plants in over 60 different countries. These production facilities are mostly located in low labor cost countries, including Cambodia, China, Egypt, Pakistan, and Turkey.[41] Avoiding large investments in fixed assets helps adidas derive large profits on minor sales increases. Adidas can also keep pace with changing tastes in the marketplace because its suppliers have become expert at rapidly retooling to produce new products.[42]

In a modular company, outsourcing the non-core functions offers three advantages:

1. A firm can decrease overall costs, stimulate new product development by hiring suppliers with talent superior to that of in-house personnel, avoid idle capacity, reduce inventories, and avoid being locked into a particular technology.
2. A company can focus scarce resources on the areas where it holds a competitive advantage. These benefits can translate into more funding for R&D to hire the best engineers and for sales and service to provide continuous training for staff.
3. An organization can tap into the knowledge and expertise of its specialized supply chain partners, adding critical skills and accelerating organizational learning.[43]

The modular type enables a company to leverage relatively small amounts of capital and a small management team to achieve seemingly unattainable strategic objectives.[44] Certain preconditions are necessary before the modular approach can be successful. First, the company must work closely with suppliers to ensure that the interests of each party are being fulfilled. Companies need to find loyal, reliable vendors who can be trusted with trade secrets. They also need assurances that suppliers will dedicate their financial, physical, and human resources to satisfy strategic objectives such as lowering costs or being first to market.

Second, the modular company must be sure that it selects the proper competencies to keep in-house. For adidas, its core competencies are design and marketing, not shoe manufacturing; for Honda, the core competence is engine technology. An organization must avoid outsourcing components that may compromise its long-term competitive advantages.

Strategic Risks of Outsourcing The main strategic concerns are (1) loss of critical skills or developing the wrong skills, (2) loss of cross-functional skills, and (3) loss of control over a supplier.[45]

Too much outsourcing can result in a firm "giving away" too much skill and control.[46] Outsourcing relieves companies of the requirement to maintain skill levels needed to manufacture essential components.[47] Firms can also lessen their ability to develop cross-functional skills, skills acquired through the interaction of individuals in various departments within a company.[48] Such interaction assists a department in solving problems as employees interface with others across functional units. However, if a firm outsources key functional responsibilities, such as manufacturing, communication across departments can become more difficult. The outsourced products may give suppliers too much power over the manufacturer. Suppliers that are key to a manufacturer's success can, in essence, hold the manufacturer "hostage."

Exhibit 10.7 summarizes the pros and cons of modular structures.[49]

The Virtual Organization

In contrast to the "self-reliant" thinking that guided traditional organizational designs, the strategic challenge today has become doing more with less and looking outside the firm for opportunities and solutions to problems. The virtual organization provides a means of leveraging resources and exploiting opportunities.[50]

The **virtual organization** can be viewed as a continually evolving network of independent companies—suppliers, customers, even competitors—linked together to share skills, costs, and access to one another's markets.[51] The members of a virtual organization, by pooling and sharing the knowledge and expertise of each of the component organizations, simultaneously "know" more and can "do" more than any one member of the group could do alone. By working closely together, each gains in the long run from individual and organizational learning.[52] The term *virtual* means "being in effect but not actually so." By assembling resources from a variety of entities, a virtual organization may seem to have more capabilities than it really possesses.[53]

virtual organization a continually evolving network of independent companies that are linked together to share skills, costs, and access to one another's markets.

Virtual organizations need not be permanent, and participating firms may be involved in multiple alliances. Virtual organizations may involve different firms performing complementary value activities or different firms involved jointly in the same value activities, such as production, R&D, and distribution. The percentage of activities that are jointly performed with partners may vary significantly from alliance to alliance.[54]

How does the virtual type of structure differ from the modular type? Unlike the modular type, in which the focal firm maintains full strategic control, the virtual organization is characterized by participating firms that give up part of their control and accept interdependent destinies. Participating firms pursue a collective strategy that enables them to cope with uncertainty through cooperative efforts. The benefit is that virtual organizations enhance the capacity or competitive advantage of participating firms.

Each company that links up with others to create a virtual organization contributes only what it considers its core competencies. It will mix and match what it does best with the

EXHIBIT 10.7 Pros and Cons of Modular Structures

Pros	Cons
• Directs a firm's managerial and technical talent to the most critical activities. • Maintains full strategic control over most critical activities—core competencies. • Achieves "best in class" performance at each link in the value chain. • Leverages core competencies by outsourcing with smaller capital commitment. • Encourages information sharing and accelerates organizational learning.	• Inhibits common vision through reliance on outsiders. • Diminishes future competitive advantages if critical technologies or other competencies are outsourced. • Increases the difficulty of bringing back into the firm activities that now add value due to market shifts. • Leads to an erosion of cross-functional skills. • Decreases operational control and potential loss of control over a supplier.

best of other firms by identifying its critical capabilities and the necessary links to other capabilities.[55]

In addition to linking a set of organizations in a virtual organization, firms can create internal virtual organizations, in which individuals who are not located together and may not even be in the same traditional organizational unit are joined together in virtual teams. These teams may be permanent but often are flexible, with changing membership as business needs evolve. For example, advertising agencies often create flexible membership teams for each client to provide the expertise that a firm's advertising program needs.

Challenges and Risks The virtual organization demands that managers build relationships both within the firm and with other companies, negotiate win–win deals for all parties, find the right partners with compatible goals and values, and provide the right balance of freedom and control. Information systems must be designed and integrated to facilitate communication with current and potential partners.

Managers must be clear about the strategic objectives while forming alliances. Some objectives are time-bound, and those alliances need to be dissolved once the objective is fulfilled. Some alliances may have relatively long-term objectives and will need to be clearly monitored and nurtured to produce mutual commitment and avoid bitter fights for control. The highly dynamic personal computer industry is characterized by multiple temporary alliances among hardware, operating system, and software producers.[56] But alliances in the more stable automobile industry have long-term objectives and tend to be relatively stable.

Planning for virtual organizations must address the diminished operational control and overwhelming need for trust and common vision among the partners. This new structure may be appropriate for firms whose strategies require merging technologies (e.g., computing and communication) or for firms exploiting shrinking product life cycles that require simultaneous entry into multiple geographic markets. For example, the profusion of alliances among airlines was primarily motivated by the need to provide seamless travel demanded by the full-fare-paying business traveler. Exhibit 10.8 summarizes the pros and cons of virtual structures.

Boundaryless Organizations: Making Them Work

Designing an organization that simultaneously supports the requirements of an organization's strategy, is consistent with the demands of the environment, and can be effectively implemented by the people around the manager is a tall order for any manager.[57] The most effective solution is usually a combination of organizational types. That is, a firm may outsource many parts of its value chain to reduce costs and increase quality, engage simultaneously in multiple alliances to take advantage of technological developments or penetrate new markets, and break down barriers within the organization to enhance flexibility.

EXHIBIT 10.8 Pros and Cons of Virtual Structures

Pros	Cons
• Enables the sharing of costs and skills. • Enhances access to global markets. • Increases market responsiveness. • Creates a "best of everything" organization since each partner brings core competencies to the alliance. • Encourages both individual and organizational knowledge sharing and accelerates organizational learning.	• Harder to determine where one company ends and another begins, due to close interdependencies among players. • Leads to potential loss of operational control among partners. • Results in loss of strategic control over emerging technology. • Requires new and difficult-to-acquire managerial skills.

Source: Miles, R. E., and C. C. Snow. 1986. Organizations: New concepts for new forms. *California Management Review,* Spring: 62–73; Miles and Snow. 1999. Causes of failure in network organizations. *California Management Review,* Summer: 53–72; and Bahrami, H. 1991. The emerging flexible organization: Perspectives from Silicon Valley. *California Management Review,* Summer: 33–52.

In this section, we will address two issues managers need to be aware of as they work to design an effective boundaryless organization. First, managers need to develop mechanisms to ensure effective coordination and integration. Second, managers need to be aware of the benefits and costs of developing strong and long-term relationships with both internal and external stakeholders.

Facilitating Coordination and Integration Achieving the coordination and integration necessary to maximize the potential of an organization's human capital involves much more than just creating a new structure. Techniques and processes to ensure the coordination and integration of an organization's key value-chain activities are critical.

Managers trained in rigid hierarchies may find it difficult to make the transition to the more democratic, participative style that teamwork requires. As Douglas K. Smith, co-author of *The Wisdom of Teams,* pointed out, "A completely diverse group must agree on a goal, put the notion of individual accountability aside and figure out how to work with each other. Most of all, they must learn that if the team fails, it's everyone's fault."[58] Within the framework of an appropriate organizational design, managers must select a mix and balance of tools and techniques to facilitate the effective coordination and integration of key activities. Some of the factors that must be considered include:

- Common culture and shared values.
- Horizontal organizational structures.
- Communications and information technologies.
- Human resource practices.

Common Culture and Shared Values Shared goals, mutual objectives, and a high degree of trust are essential to the success of boundaryless organizations. In the fluid and flexible environments of the new organizational architectures, common cultures, shared values, and carefully aligned incentives are often less expensive to implement and are often a more effective means of strategic control than rules, boundaries, and formal procedures. Tony Hsieh, the founder of Zappos, discussed the importance of culture and values this way: "We formalize the definition of our culture into . . . 10 core values at Zappos. And one of the really interesting things I found from the research is that it actually doesn't matter what your values are, what matters is that you have them and that you align the organization around them."[59]

Horizontal Organizational Structures These structures, which group similar or related business units under common management control, facilitate sharing resources and infrastructures to exploit synergies among operating units and help to create a sense of common purpose. Consistency in training and the development of similar structures across business units facilitates job rotation and cross-training and enhances understanding of common problems and opportunities. Cross-functional teams and interdivisional committees and task groups represent important opportunities to improve understanding and foster cooperation among operating units.

horizontal organizational structures
organizational forms that group similar or related business units under common management control and facilitate sharing resources and infrastructures to exploit synergies among operating units and help to create a sense of common purpose.

Communications and Information Technology (IT) The effective use of IT can play an important role in bridging gaps and breaking down barriers between organizations. This can include communication systems, such as internal social network systems, collaborative communication platforms, and other technology means to link people within an organization across regions and organizational units.

Human Resource Practices Change always involves and affects the human dimension of organizations. The attraction, development, and retention of human capital are vital to value creation. As boundaryless structures are implemented, processes are reengineered, and organizations become increasingly dependent on sophisticated ITs, the skills of workers and managers alike must be upgraded to realize the full benefits.

The Benefits and Costs of Developing Lasting Internal and External Relationships Successful boundaryless organizations rely heavily on the relational aspects of organizations. Rather than relying on strict hierarchical and bureaucratic systems, these firms are flexible and coordinate action by leveraging shared social norms and strong social relationships between both internal and external stakeholders.[60] At the same time, it is important to acknowledge that relying on relationships can have both positive and negative effects. To successfully move to a more boundaryless organization, managers need to acknowledge and attend to both the costs and benefits of relying on relationships and social norms to guide behavior.

There are three primary benefits that organizations accrue when relying on relationships:

- ***Agency costs within the firm can be dramatically cut through the use of relational systems.*** Managers and employees in relationship-oriented firms are guided by social norms and relationships they have with other managers and employees. As a result, the firm can reduce the degree to which it relies on monitoring, rules and regulations, and financial incentives to ensure that workers put in a strong effort and work in the firm's interests.
- ***There is also likely to be a reduction in the transaction costs between a firm and its suppliers and customers.*** If firms have built strong relationships with partnering firms, they are more likely to work cooperatively with these firms and build trust that their partners will work in the best interests of the alliance. This will reduce the need for the firms to write detailed contracts and set up strict bureaucratic rules to outline the responsibilities and define the behavior of each firm.
- ***Since they feel a sense of shared ownership and goals, individuals within the firm as well as partnering firms will be more likely to search for win-win rather than win-lose solutions.*** When taking a relational view, individuals and organizations are less likely to look out solely for their personal best interests. They will also be considerate of the benefits and costs to other individuals in the firm and to the overall firm.

While there are a number of benefits with using a relational view, there can also be some substantial costs:

- ***As the relationships between individuals and firms strengthen, they are also more likely to fall prey to suboptimal lock-in effects.*** The problem here is that as decisions become driven by concerns about relationships, economic factors become less important. As a result, firms become less likely to make decisions that could benefit the firm since those decisions may harm employees or partnering firms. This can be debilitating to firms in rapidly changing markets where successful firms add, reorganize, and sometimes exit operations and relationships regularly.
- ***Since there are no formal guidelines, conflicts between individuals and units within firms, as well as between partnering firms, are typically resolved through ad hoc negotiations and processes.*** In these circumstances, there are no legal means or bureaucratic rules to guide decision making. Thus, when firms face a difficult decision where there are differences of opinion about the best course of action, the ultimate choices made are often driven by the inherent power of the individuals or firms involved.
- ***The social capital of individuals and firms can drive their opportunities.*** Thus, rather than identifying the best person to put in a leadership role or the optimal supplier to contract with, these choices are more strongly driven by the level of social connection the person or supplier has. This may limit the likelihood that new partners and innovative ideas will enter into the considerations of the firm.

As mentioned earlier in the chapter, the solution may be to effectively integrate elements of formal structure and reward systems with stronger relationships. This may influence specific relationships so that a manager will want employees to build relationships while still maintaining some managerial oversight and reward systems that motivate the desired behavior. This may also result in different emphases with different relationships. For example, there may be some units, such as accounting, where a stronger role for traditional structures and forms of evaluation may be optimal. However, in new product development units, a greater emphasis on relational systems may be more appropriate.

CREATING AMBIDEXTROUS ORGANIZATIONAL DESIGNS

LO 10-5

Explain the need for creating ambidextrous organizational designs that enable firms to explore new opportunities and effectively integrate existing operations.

In Chapter 1, we introduced the concept of "ambidexterity," which incorporates two contradictory challenges faced by today's managers.[61] First, managers must explore new opportunities and adjust to volatile markets in order to avoid complacency. They must ensure that they maintain **adaptability** and remain proactive in expanding and/or modifying their product-market scope to anticipate and satisfy market conditions. Such competencies are especially challenging when change is rapid and unpredictable.

Second, managers must also effectively exploit the value of their existing assets and competencies. They need to have **alignment,** which is a clear sense of how value is being created in the short term and how activities are integrated and properly coordinated. Firms that achieve both adaptability and alignment are considered *ambidextrous organizations*—aligned and efficient in how they manage today's business but flexible enough to changes in the environment so that they will prosper tomorrow.

Handling such opposing demands is difficult because there will always be some degree of conflict. Firms often suffer when they place too strong a priority on either adaptability or alignment. If it places too much focus on adaptability, the firm will suffer low profitability in the short term. If managers direct their efforts primarily at alignment, they will likely miss out on promising business opportunities.

adaptibility managers' exploration of new opportunities and adjustment to volatile markets in order to avoid complacency.

alignment managers' clear sense of how value is being created in the short term and how activities are integrated and properly coordinated.

ambidextrous organizational designs organizational designs that attempt to simultaneously pursue modest, incremental innovations as well as more dramatic, breakthrough innovations.

Ambidextrous Organizations: Key Design Attributes

A study by Charles O'Reilly and Michael Tushman[62] provides some insights into how some firms were able to create successful **ambidextrous organizational designs**. They investigated companies that attempted to simultaneously pursue modest, incremental innovations as well as more dramatic, breakthrough innovations. The team investigated 35 attempts to launch breakthrough innovations undertaken by 15 business units in nine different industries. They studied the organizational designs and the processes, systems, and cultures associated with the breakthrough projects as well as their impact on the operations and performance of the traditional businesses.

Companies structured their breakthrough projects in one of four primary ways:

- Seven were carried out within existing *functional organizational structures.* The projects were completely integrated into the regular organizational and management structure.
- Nine were organized as *cross-functional teams.* The groups operated within the established organization but outside the existing management structure.
- Four were organized as *unsupported teams.* Here, they became independent units set up outside the established organization and management hierarchy.
- Fifteen were conducted within *ambidextrous organizations.* Here, the breakthrough efforts were organized within structurally independent units, each having its own

10.5 STRATEGY SPOTLIGHT

HOW INNOVATION BENEFITS FROM THE INVOLVEMENT OF ALL THE PLAYERS ON THE TEAM

A study by Great Places to Work, a research and consulting firm, highlights the benefits of breaking down boundaries to get all employees interested in innovative opportunities. Using data from surveys completed by over 500,000 employees at over 800 companies, the consulting firm assessed the degree to which the firms encouraged employees to provide input on new options for the firm and new approaches to their work.

The results were clear and supportive of these efforts. Compared to less open firms, employees at more inclusive firms were 14 percent more likely to stay and 32 percent more likely to put in extra effort at work. The results were more startling when looking at growth implications. Firms in the top quartile on the inclusiveness rankings had experienced growth, on average, five times greater than firms ranked in the bottom quartile.

Consider the following examples:

- Quicken Loans gives its employees "bullet time" of a few hours a week to develop new skills and new ideas. One employee took his "bullet time" to develop some app-building skills and then worked with a team to develop an Alexa-based app to interface with Quickens' Rocket Mortgage platform.
- Wegman's, a large grocery chain, builds formal "innovation teams" that involved store workers and corporate office employees. The new ideas the teams develop are then tested in select stores.
- At GoransonBain, a Dallas law firm, the firm uses a suggestion board. Once an idea is up on the board, other employees can sign on to support the idea. Once an idea has 10 supporting signatures, the idea is then forwarded to a committee to study implementation of the idea.

The specific processes at these firms may vary. However, the core elements are that the firms strive to both invite the involvement of workers and create connections within the firm to support the promotion and development of ideas.

Sources: Chada, J. 2018. Why innovation is a team sport. *wsj.com,* August 9: np; and Anonymous, 2018. Best places to work share best suggestions from employees. *bizjournal.com,* September 19: np.

processes, structures, and cultures. However, they were integrated into the existing senior management structure. In Strategy Spotlight 10.5, we discuss how innovative firms use teams that effectively draw on the contributions of individual team members.

The performance results of the 35 initiatives were tracked along two dimensions:

- Their success in creating desired innovations was measured by either the actual commercial results of the new product or the application of practical market or technical learning.
- The performance of the existing business was evaluated.

The study found that the organizational structure and management practices employed had a direct and significant impact on the performance of both the breakthrough initiative and the traditional business. The ambidextrous organizational designs were more effective than the other three designs on both dimensions: launching breakthrough products or services (i.e., adaptation) and improving the performance of the existing business (i.e., alignment).

Why Was the Ambidextrous Organization the Most Effective Structure?

The study found that there were many factors. A clear and compelling vision, consistently communicated by the company's senior management team, was critical in building the ambidextrous designs. The structure enabled cross-fertilization while avoiding cross-contamination. The tight coordination and integration at the managerial levels enabled the newer units to share important resources from the traditional units, such as cash, talent, and expertise. Such sharing was encouraged and facilitated by effective reward systems that emphasized overall company goals. The organizational separation ensured that the new units' distinctive processes, structures, and cultures were not overwhelmed by the forces of "business as usual." The established units were shielded from the distractions of launching new businesses, and they continued to focus all of their attention and energy on refining their operations, enhancing their products, and serving their customers.

ISSUE FOR DEBATE

Tata Motors and Tesla are two of a large number of firms that have taken steps to flatten their hierarchical structures. Tata, an India-based automaker, cut half of the levels in the organization, going from 12 to 6 levels of management, after the firm hired a consultant to help improve its structure. Similarly, Tesla announced in 2018 that it would flatten its structure "to improve communication." These firms are not alone in their drive to cut out layers of management. One survey concluded that 93 percent of polled firms indicated they intended to flatten their organization in the near future.

Proponents of flat leadership structures argue they offer cost, flexibility, and creativity benefits. First, flatter organizational structures are designed to be more responsive and faster acting. By cutting out layers of management that analyze and approve initiatives developed by lower level employees and teams, the firm empowers these teams to act quickly. Second, flatter organizations allow workers and teams to have autonomy, a desirable attribute for younger employees. Third, by cutting out layers of management, the firm reduces the cost of a large administrative task. Fourth, feedback loops through the organizational structure are quicker and shorter. Top level managers are closer to line employees and the market, allowing them to have better insight into the dynamics within the firm and the market.

However, critics have argued that flattening organizations face unintended negative consequences. First, management attention becomes stretched. With the expanding scope of their responsibilities, the remaining managers find that the bulk of their time is spent on communication. A number of studies have found that managers in flat organizations spent 80 to 90 percent of their day communicating, leaving little time for other tasks. This can lead to "interaction fatigue" on the part of managers. Second, middle-level managers often serve as critical negotiators between different units in the firm and between front-line employees and top managers. In cutting these managers, some firms have found that frictions between units have increased. Third, the removal of middle manager positions can be demotivating for some employees since there are reduced opportunities for advancement into the ranks of management. Echoing these concerns, Harvard researchers Thomas DeLong and Vineeta Vijayaraghavan argue that long serving middle managers are a competent and steadying influence in the firm. They are experts at how the firm operates and can insulate the firm from impulsive decisions that come from either the top or the bottom.

These conflicting perspectives suggest that organizations seeking to flatten their structures need to be aware of both the potential costs and benefits of the action. But the ultimate value of the action appears uncertain.

Discussion Questions

1. What are the benefits and the costs of flattening the organization? In your view, do the benefits generally outweigh the costs?
2. What industries or firms are most likely to benefit from flattening? In what situations does it not make sense?

Sources: Craig, W. 2018. What businesses need in order to develop a flat structure of leadership. *forbes.com,* February 6: np; Higgins, T. 2018. Tesla CEO Musk says company is 'flattening management structure' in reorganization. *wsj.com,* May 14: np; and Walker, S. 2018. There's a war on middle management and Tesla just joined it. *wsj.com,* May 18: np.

Reflecting on Career Implications . . .

This chapter discusses both organizational structures and the benefits of creating permeable boundaries across structural boundaries. You can enhance your value to your firms and career prospects by developing skills and abilities to span internal and external organizational boundaries. The questions that follow challenge you to consider ways you can build those skills.

- **Boundaryless Organizational Designs:** Does your firm have structural mechanisms (e.g., culture, human resource practices) that facilitate sharing information across boundaries? Regardless of the level of boundarylessness of your organization, a key issue for your career is the extent to which you are able to cut across boundaries within your organization. Such boundaryless behavior on your part will enable you to enhance and leverage your human capital. Evaluate how boundaryless you are within your organizational context. What actions can you take to become even more boundaryless?
- **Culture and Shared Values:** Does your firm or department have a strong or weak culture? Consider how your actions can help reinforce or build a strong culture. Also, think of the types of actions leaders in your group can take to strengthen the group's culture. Consider sharing these ideas with your leaders. Do you think they will be receptive to your suggestions? Their response likely gives you further insight into the group's culture.
- **Ambidextrous Organizations:** Firms that achieve *adaptability* and *alignment* are considered ambidextrous. As an individual, you can also strive to be ambidextrous. Evaluate your own ambidexterity by assessing your adaptability (your ability to change in response to changes around you) and alignment (how good you are at exploiting your existing competencies). What steps can you take to improve your ambidexterity?

LO 10-1 The growth patterns of major corporations and the relationship between a firm's strategy and its structure.

- A firm's strategy and structure typically changes as it increases in size, diversifies into new product markets, and expands its geographic scope.
- Firms often start with simple structures and move to functional structures as it grows. As firms expand their product and geographic scope, they often employ divisional or geographic-area structures.

LO 10-2 Each of the traditional types of organizational structure: simple, functional, divisional, and matrix.

- In a simple organizational structure, the owner-manager makes most of the decisions and controls major activities.
- In a functional structure, the firm creates functional departments in which the major functions of the firm, such as production, marketing, distribution, R&D, and accounting, are housed.
- In a divisional structure, the firm creates independent product divisions that are responsible for the firm's operations in a given industry or market.
- In a matrix structure, there are multiple lines of authority and employees often report to multiple managers, such as a functional and a divisional manager.

LO 10-3 The implications of a firm's international operations for organizational structure.

- In firms with international operations, three major contingencies influence the chosen structure:
  - the type of strategy that is driving a firm's foreign operations
  - the level of product diversity
  - the extent to which a firm is dependent on foreign sales

LO 10-4 The different types of boundaryless organizations—barrier-free, modular, and virtual.

- A barrier-free organization enables a firm to bridge real differences in culture, function, and goals to find common ground that facilitates information sharing and other forms of cooperative behavior.
- The modular organization outsources nonvital functions, tapping into the knowledge and expertise of "best in class" suppliers, but retains strategic control.
- The virtual organization can be viewed as a continually evolving network of independent companies–suppliers, customers, even competitors–linked together to share skills, costs, and access to one another's markets.

LO 10-5 The need for creating ambidextrous organizational designs that enable firms to explore new opportunities and effectively integrate existing operations.

- Ambidextrous organizational designs support the ability of the firm to pursue incremental innovations as well as more dramatic, breakthrough innovations.

- Typically, in ambidextrous organizations, breakthrough efforts are organized within structurally independent units, each having its own processes, structures, and cultures. However, these units are embedded within a more traditional organizational structure.

SUMMARY REVIEW QUESTIONS

1. Why is it important for managers to carefully consider the type of organizational structure that they use to implement their strategies?
2. Briefly trace the dominant growth pattern of major corporations from simple structure to functional structure to divisional structure. Discuss the relationship between a firm's strategy and its structure.
3. What are the relative advantages and disadvantages of the types of organizational structure–simple, functional, divisional, matrix–discussed in the chapter?
4. When a firm expands its operations into foreign markets, what are the three most important factors to take into account in deciding what type of structure is most appropriate? What are the types of international structures discussed in the text, and what are the relationships between strategy and structure?
5. Briefly describe the three different types of boundaryless organizations: barrier-free, modular, and virtual.
6. What are some of the key attributes of effective groups? Ineffective groups?
7. What are the advantages and disadvantages of the three types of boundaryless organizations: barrier-free, modular, and virtual?
8. When are ambidextrous organizational designs necessary? What are some of their key attributes?

key terms

organizational structure 300
simple organizational structure 302
functional organizational structure 302
divisional organizational structure 303
strategic business unit (SBU) structure 305
holding company structure 305
matrix organizational structure 307
international division structure 309
geographic-area division structure 309
worldwide matrix structure 309
worldwide functional structure 309
worldwide product division structure 309
global start-up 309
boundaryless organizational designs 311
barrier-free organization 311
modular organization 316
virtual organization 317
horizontal organizational structures 319
adaptability 321
alignment 321
ambidextrous organizational designs 321

EXPERIENTIAL EXERCISES AND APPLICATION QUESTIONS

1. Boeing has experienced another product crisis with its 737 Max aircraft. Investigate how the Boeing designed this plane, including the internal structure of the firm, the use of external partners, and the degree to which the firm employed a boundaryless design. In what ways might the structure used have played a part in the crisis with the 737 Max?
2. Many firms have recently moved toward a modular structure. For example, they have increasingly outsourced many of their information technology (IT) activities. Identify three such organizations. Using secondary sources, evaluate (1) the firm's rationale for IT outsourcing and (2) the implications for performance.

Firm	Rationale	Implication(s) for Performance
1.		
2.		
3.		

3. Select an organization that competes in an industry in which you are particularly interested. Use the Internet and determine what type of organizational structure this organization has. In your view, is it consistent with the strategy that it has chosen to implement? Why? Why not?
4. Choose an article from *Bloomberg Businessweek, Fortune, Forbes, Fast Company,* or any other well-known publication that deals with a corporation that has undergone a significant change in its strategic direction. What are the implications for the structure of this organization?
5. Use the Internet to look up some of the public statements or speeches of an executive in a major corporation about a significant initiative such as entering into a joint venture or launching a new product line. What do you feel are the implications for making the internal and external barriers of the firm more flexible and permeable? Does the executive discuss processes, procedures, integrating mechanisms, or cultural issues that should serve this purpose? Or are other issues discussed that enable a firm to become more boundaryless?
6. Look up a recent article in the publications listed in question 2 that addresses a firm's involvement in outsourcing (modular organization) or in strategic alliance or network organizations (virtual organization). Was the firm successful or unsuccessful in this endeavor? Why? Why not?

ETHICS QUESTIONS

1. If a firm has a divisional structure and places extreme pressures on its divisional executives to meet short-term profitability goals (e.g., quarterly income), could this raise some ethical considerations? Why? Why not?

2. If a firm enters into a strategic alliance but does not exercise appropriate behavioral control of its employees (in terms of culture, rewards and incentives, and boundaries–as discussed in Chapter 9) who are involved in the alliance, what ethical issues could arise? What could be the potential long-term and short-term downside for the firm?

REFERENCES

1. Wilson, K. & Doz, Y. 2012. 10 rules for managing global innovation. *Harvard Business Review,* 90(10): 84–92; Wallace, J. 2007. Update on problems joining 787 fuselage sections. *Seattlepi.com,* June 7: np; Peterson, K. 2011. Special report: A wing and a prayer: Outsourcing at Boeing. *Reuters.com,* January 20: np; Hiltzik, M. 2011. 787 Dreamliner teaches Boeing costly lesson on outsourcing. *Latimes.com,* February 15: np; Gates, D. 2013. Boeing 787's problems blamed on outsourcing, lack of oversight. *Seattletimes.com,* February 2: np; and Ostrower, J. 2014. Boeing's Key Mission: Cut Dreamliner cost. *wsj.com.* January 7: np.
2. Hiltzik, Michael, 2011. 787 Dreamliner teaches Boeing costly lesson on outsourcing. *Los Angeles Times,* February 15.
3. Peterson, Kyle, 2011. Special Report: A wing and a prayer: outsourcing at Boeing. *Reuters,* Januray 20.
4. For a unique perspective on organization design, see Rao, R. 2010. What 17th century pirates can teach us about job design. *Harvard Business Review,* 88(10): 44.
5. This introductory discussion draws upon Hall, R. H. 2002. *Organizations: Structures, processes, and outcomes* (8th ed.). Upper Saddle River, NJ: Prentice Hall; and Duncan, R. E. 1979. What is the right organization structure? Decision-tree analysis provides the right answer. *Organizational Dynamics,* 7(3): 59–80. For an insightful discussion of strategy-structure relationships in the organization theory and strategic management literatures, refer to Keats, B. & O'Neill, H. M. 2001. Organization structure: Looking through a strategy lens. In Hitt, M. A., Freeman, R. E., & Harrison, J. S. 2001. *The Blackwell handbook of strategic management:* 520–542. Malden, MA: Blackwell.
6. Gratton, L. 2011. The end of the middle manager. *Harvard Business Review,* 89(1/2): 36.
7. An interesting discussion on the role of organizational design in strategy execution is in Neilson, G. L., Martin, K. L., & Powers, E. 2009. The secrets to successful strategy execution. *Harvard Business Review,* 87(2): 60–70.
8. This discussion draws upon Chandler, A. D. 1962. *Strategy and structure.* Cambridge, MA: MIT Press; Galbraith J. R. & Kazanjian, R. K. 1986. *Strategy implementation: The role of structure and process.* St. Paul, MN: West; and Scott, B. R. 1971. Stages of corporate development. Intercollegiate Case Clearing House, 9-371-294, BP 998. Harvard Business School.
9. Our discussion of the different types of organizational structures draws on a variety of sources, including Galbraith & Kazanjian, op. cit.; Hrebiniak, L. G. & Joyce, W. F. 1984. *Implementing strategy.* New York: Macmillan; Distelzweig, H. 2000. Organizational structure. In Helms, M. M. (Ed.), *Encyclopedia of management:* 692–699. Farmington Hills, MI: Gale; and Dess, G. G. & Miller, A. 1993. *Strategic management.* New York: McGraw-Hill.
10. A discussion of an innovative organizational design is in Garvin, D. A. & Levesque, L. C. 2009. The multiunit enterprise. *Harvard Business Review,* 87(2): 106–117.
11. Schein, E. H. 1996. Three cultures of management: The key to organizational learning. *Sloan Management Review,* 38(1): 9–20.
12. Insights on governance implications for multidivisional forms are in Verbeke, A. & Kenworthy, T. p. 2008. Multidivisional vs. metanational governance. *Journal of International Business,* 39(6): 940–956.
13. Martin, J. A. & Eisenhardt, K. 2010. Rewiring: Cross-business-unit collaborations in multibusiness organizations. *Academy of Management Journal,* 53(2): 265–301.
14. For a discussion of performance implications, refer to Hoskisson, R. E. 1987. Multidivisional structure and performance: The contingency of diversification strategy. *Academy of Management Journal,* 29: 625–644.
15. For a thorough and seminal discussion of the evolution toward the divisional form of organizational structure in the United States, refer to Chandler, op. cit. A rigorous empirical study of the strategy and structure relationship is found in Rumelt, R. P. 1974. *Strategy, structure, and economic performance.* Cambridge, MA: Harvard Business School Press.
16. Koppel, B. 2000. Synergy in ketchup? *Forbes,* February 7: 68–69; and Hitt, M. A., Ireland, R. D., & Hoskisson, R. E. 2001. *Strategic management: Competitiveness and globalization* (4th ed.). Cincinnati, OH: South-Western.
17. Pitts, R. A. 1977. Strategies and structures for diversification. *Academy of Management Journal,* 20(2): 197–208.
18. Meyer, P. 2019. Starbucks coffee's organizational structure & its characteristics. panmore.com, February 14: np.
19. Silvestri, L. 2012. The evolution of organizational structure. *footnote1.com,* June 6: np.
20. Haas, M. R. 2010. The double-edged swords of autonomy and external knowledge: Analyzing team effectiveness in a multinational organization. *Academy of Management Journal,* 53(5): 989–1008.
21. Daniels, J. D., Pitts, R. A., & Tretter, M. J. 1984. Strategy and structure of U.S. multinationals: An exploratory study. *Academy of Management Journal,* 27(2): 292–307.
22. Habib, M. M. & Victor, B. 1991. Strategy, structure, and performance of U.S. manufacturing and service MNCs: A comparative analysis. *Strategic Management Journal,* 12(8): 589–606.
23. Our discussion of global start-ups draws from Oviatt, B. M. & McDougall, P. p. 2005. The internationalization of

entrepreneurship. *Journal of International Business Studies,* 36(1): 2-8; Oviatt, B. M. & McDougall, P. p. 1994. Toward a theory of international new ventures. *Journal of International Business Studies,* 25(1): 45-64; and Oviatt, B. M. & McDougall, P. P. 1995. Global start-ups: Entrepreneurs on a worldwide stage. *Academy of Management Executive,* 9(2): 30-43.

24. Some useful guidelines for global start-ups are provided in Kuemmerle, W. 2005. The entrepreneur's path for global expansion. *MIT Sloan Management Review,* 46(2): 42-50.

25. See, for example, Miller, D. & Friesen, P. H. 1980. Momentum and revolution in organizational structure. *Administrative Science Quarterly,* 13: 65-91.

26. Many authors have argued that a firm's structure can influence its strategy and performance. These include Amburgey, T. L. & Dacin, T. 1995. As the left foot follows the right? The dynamics of strategic and structural change. *Academy of Management Journal,* 37: 1427-1452; Dawn, K. & Amburgey, T. L. 1991. Organizational inertia and momentum: A dynamic model of strategic change. *Academy of Management Journal,* 34: 591-612; Fredrickson, J. W. 1986. The strategic decision process and organization structure. *Academy of Management Review,* 11: 280-297; Hall, D. J. & Saias, M. A. 1980. Strategy follows structure! *Strategic Management Journal,* 1: 149-164; and Burgelman, R. A. 1983. A model of the interaction of strategic behavior, corporate context, and the concept of strategy. *Academy of Management Review,* 8: 61-70.

27. An interesting discussion on how the Internet has affected the boundaries of firms can be found in Afuah, A. 2003. Redefining firm boundaries in the face of the Internet: Are firms really shrinking? *Academy of Management Review,* 28(1): 34-53.

28. LaReau, Jamie L. 2018. In auto talent war, GM hires 9,000, spends $1 billion on offices. *Detroit Free Press.*

29. Govindarajan, V. G. & Trimble, C. 2010. Stop the innovation wars. *Harvard Business Review,* 88(7/8): 76-83.

30. For a discussion of the role of coaching on developing high-performance teams, refer to Kets de Vries, M. F. R. 2005. Leadership group coaching in action: The zen of creating high performance teams. *Academy of Management Executive,* 19(1): 77-89.

31. Pfeffer, J. 1998. *The human equation: Building profits by putting people first.* Cambridge, MA: Harvard Business School Press.

32. For a discussion on how functional area diversity affects performance, see Bunderson, J. S. & Sutcliffe, K. M. 2002. Comparing alternative conceptualizations of functional diversity in management teams: Process and performance effects. *Academy of Management Journal,* 45(5): 875-893.

33. Bossert, O., Kretzberg, A., and J. Laartz. 2018. Unleashing the power of small, independent teams. mckinsey.com, July: np.

34. Public-private partnerships are addressed in Engardio, p. 2009. State capitalism. *BusinessWeek,* February 9: 38-43.

35. Aller, R., Weiner, H., & Weilart, M. 2005. IBM and Mayo collaborating to customize patient treatment plans. *cap.org,* January: np; and McGee, M. 2010. IBM, Mayo partner on aneurysm diagnostics. *informationweek.com,* January 25: np.

36. Winston, A. 2014: *The big pivot.* Boston: Harvard Business Review Press.

37. Dess, G. G., Rasheed, A. M. A., McLaughlin, K. J., & Priem, R. 1995. The new corporate architecture. *Academy of Management Executive,* 9(3): 7-20.

38. An original discussion on how open sourcing could help the Big 3 automobile companies is in Jarvis, J. 2009. How the Google model could help Detroit. *BusinessWeek,* February 9: 32-36.

39. For a discussion of some of the downsides of outsourcing, refer to Rossetti, C. & Choi, T. Y. 2005. On the dark side of strategic sourcing: Experiences from the aerospace industry. *Academy of Management Executive,* 19(1): 46-60.

40. Tully, S. 1993. The modular corporation. *Fortune,* February 8: 196.

41. *adidas-group.com/en/sustainability/compliance/supply-chain-structure/.*

42. Offshoring in manufacturing firms is addressed in Coucke, K. & Sleuwaegen, L. 2008. Offshoring as a survival strategy: Evidence from manufacturing firms in Belgium. *Journal of International Business Studies,* 39(8): 1261-1277.

43. Quinn, J. B. 1992. *Intelligent enterprise: A knowledge and service based paradigm for industry.* New York: Free Press.

44. For an insightful perspective on outsourcing and its role in developing capabilities, read Gottfredson, M., Puryear, R., & Phillips, C. 2005. Strategic sourcing: From periphery to the core. *Harvard Business Review,* 83(4): 132-139.

45. This discussion draws upon Quinn, J. B. & Hilmer, F. C. 1994. Strategic outsourcing. *Sloan Management Review,* 35(4): 43-55.

46. Reitzig, M. & Wagner, S. 2010. The hidden costs of outsourcing: Evidence from patent data. *Strategic Management Journal,* 31(11): 1183-1201.

47. Insights on outsourcing and private branding can be found in Cehn, S-F. S. 2009. A transaction cost rationale for private branding and its implications for the choice of domestic vs. offshore outsourcing. *Journal of International Business Strategy,* 40(1): 156-175.

48. For an insightful perspective on the use of outsourcing for decision analysis, read Davenport, T. H. & Iyer, B. 2009. Should you outsource your brain? *Harvard Business Review,* 87(2): 38.

49. See also Stuckey, J. & White, D. 1993. When and when not to vertically integrate. *Sloan Management Review,* Spring: 71-81; Harrar, G. 1993. Outsource tales. *Forbes ASAP,* June 7: 37-39, 42; and Davis, E. W. 1992. Global outsourcing: Have U.S. managers thrown the baby out with the bath water? *Business Horizons,* July-August: 58-64.

50. For a discussion of knowledge creation through alliances, refer to Inkpen, A. C. 1996. Creating knowledge through collaboration. *California Management Review,* 39(1): 123-140; and Mowery, D. C., Oxley, J. E., & Silverman, B. S. 1996. Strategic alliances and interfirm knowledge transfer. *Strategic Management Journal,* 17 (Special Issue, Winter): 77-92.

51. Doz, Y. & Hamel, G. 1998. *Alliance advantage: The art of creating value through partnering.* Boston: Harvard Business School Press.

52. DeSanctis, G., Glass, J. T., & Ensing, I. M. 2002. Organizational designs for R&D. *Academy of Management Executive,* 16(3): 55-66.

53. Barringer, B. R. & Harrison, J. S. 2000. Walking a tightrope: Creating value through interorganizational alliances. *Journal of Management,* 26: 367-403.

54. One contemporary example of virtual organizations is R&D consortia. For an insightful discussion, refer to Sakaibara, M. 2002. Formation of R&D consortia: Industry and company effects. *Strategic Management Journal,* 23(11): 1033-1050.

55. Bartness, A. & Cerny, K. 1993. Building competitive advantage through a global network of capabilities. *California Management Review,* Winter: 78–103. For an insightful historical discussion of the usefulness of alliances in the computer industry, see Moore, J. F. 1993. Predators and prey: A new ecology of competition. *Harvard Business Review,* 71(3): 75–86.

56. See Lorange, P. & Roos, J. 1991. Why some strategic alliances succeed and others fail. *Journal of Business Strategy,* January–February: 25–30; and Slowinski, G. 1992. The human touch in strategic alliances. *Mergers and Acquisitions,* July–August: 44–47. A compelling argument for strategic alliances is provided by Ohmae, K. 1989. The global logic of strategic alliances. *Harvard Business Review,* 67(2): 143–154.

57. This section draws upon Dess, G. G. & Picken, J. C. 1997. *Mission critical.* Burr Ridge, IL: Irwin Professional.

58. Katzenbach, J. R., and D. K. Smith. 1994. *The Wisdom of Teams: Creating the High-Performance Organization.* New York: HarperCollins.

59. Bulygo, Z. 2013. Tony Hsieh, Zappos, and the art of great company culture. *kissmetrics.com,* February 26: np.

60. Gupta, A. 2011. The relational perspective and east meets west. *Academy of Management Perspectives,* 25(3): 19–27.

61. This section draws on Birkinshaw, J. & Gibson, C. 2004. Building ambidexterity into an organization. *MIT Sloan Management Review,* 45(4): 47–55; and Gibson, C. B. & Birkinshaw, J. 2004. The antecedents, consequences, and mediating role of organizational ambidexterity. *Academy of Management Journal,* 47(2): 209–226. Robert Duncan is generally credited with being the first to coin the term "ambidextrous organizations" in his article entitled: Designing dual structures for innovation. In Kilmann, R. H., Pondy, L. R., & Slevin, D. (Eds.). 1976. *The management of organizations,* vol. 1: 167–188. For a seminal academic discussion of the concept of exploration and exploitation, which parallels adaptation and alignment, refer to March, J. G. 1991. Exploration and exploitation in organizational learning. *Organization Science,* 2: 71–86.

62. This section is based on O'Reilly, C. A. & Tushman, M. L. 2004. The ambidextrous organization. *Harvard Business Review,* 82(4): 74–81.

Nico Muller Art/Shutterstock

CHAPTER

11

Strategic Leadership

Creating a Learning Organization and an Ethical Organization

Learning Objectives

LO11-1 Explain the three key interdependent activities in which all successful leaders must be continually engaged.

LO11-2 Describe two elements of effective leadership: overcoming barriers to change and using power effectively.

LO11-3 Understand the crucial role of emotional intelligence (EI) in successful leadership, as well as its potential drawbacks.

LO11-4 Explain the importance of creating a learning organization.

LO11-5 Describe the leader's role in establishing an ethical organization.

LO11-6 Explain the difference between integrity-based and compliance-based approaches to organizational ethics.

LO11-7 Identify several key elements that organizations must have to become ethical organizations.

We encourage you to reflect on how the concepts presented in this chapter can enhance your career success (see "Reflecting on Career Implications..." at the end of the chapter).

LEARNING FROM MISTAKES

Carlos Ghosn was in a unique position. He was in charge of three major global car manufacturers: Renault, Nissan, and Mitsubishi. He was credited with turning around all three of the firms and was regarded as one of the most accomplished and ruthless business leaders in the world. He happily touted his accomplishments and accepted his nickname, "Le Cost Killer." His vast automotive empire led him to jet back and forth between Paris and Tokyo, but his world changed in late 2018 when he flew into Tokyo to meet with his youngest daughter and her boyfriend. When his private jet landed in Tokyo, it was surrounded by Japanese police and prosecutors who arrested Ghosn for failing to report millions of dollars of his pay in Nissan's financial statements.[1]

His journey at Nissan started very differently. In 1999, fresh from helping run a turnaround effort at the French carmaker, Renault, he arrived in Tokyo to restructure Nissan. The Japanese firm had accumulated a $35 billion dollar debt load, had a bloated employee base, and was losing market share. Renault had invested $5 billion in Nissan, taking a 37 percent ownership stake in the firm. Many in the industry questioned the move. One auto executive commented that Renault would have been better off "taking $5 billion, putting it on a barge, and sinking it in the middle of the ocean" than investing the money in Nissan.

Ghosn dove into the task. He reinforced his reputation as "Le Cost Killer" by laying off thousands of workers, closing plants, and cutting suppliers. But it wasn't all about cost cutting. He invested in design and reinvigorated the brand. He once commented on this combination of actions, saying "if a revival plan is only about cost-cutting, it will last two years; revival is when after 15 years, the company is still on the right track." Ghosn's revival succeeded. Nissan became Japan's #2 automaker and generated strong profits.

His business leadership of Nissan was celebrated, even receiving a Blue Medal Ribbon from Japan's emperor, the first foreign leader to win this accolade. At the same time, many in Japan's business and government eyed him with suspicion and distrust. He was seen as too western, flashy, and even imperialistic by many in Japan. His pay only reinforced these concerns. He pulled in pay of $17 million in 2017, nearly 11 times what the chairman of Toyota, the world's largest automaker made.

The concerns became something much more serious when a whistleblower came forward with charges that Ghosn and Greg Kelly, a Nissan board member, conspired to withhold Ghosn's deferred compensation from the firm's financial statements. In effect, his actions were seen as violating Japanese cultural norms. If executives take illegal actions to help the corporation, the Japanese public tends to be very forgiving. However, if the action is for personal gain, there is no grace. As Jesper Koll, an economist in Japan says, "the one thing that Japan does not want and would never tolerate is personal greed."

So, what led to Ghosn's downfall? When leaders get too much power, two problems often arise. First, those around them stop questioning their decisions. This allows leaders to make destructive choices without any real challenge. This appeared to happen at Nissan. As one firm manager stated, "no one dared to say anything that would confront his opinions." Second, leaders can make self-interested decisions. For years, Ghosn had, with the approval of the board of directors, used company resources to build a network of homes across the globe. It appears that the hiding of income was the next step in self-beneficial behavior.

His downfall also may have come from distrust and jealousy. Some in the firm and the government bristled at his pay and grandiosity. They may have found the complaints raised by the whistleblower as the evidence they needed to knock Ghosn off his perch. Hiroto Saikawa, was Ghosn's self-identified successor, but some had speculated that there had been rising tension between the two. Notably, Saikawa, who has taken control of Nissan, did not bow apologetically to the audience when he announced that Ghosn had been charged. Many saw this as an indication that Saikawa was distancing himself from Ghosn since bowing would have signaled that Saikawa was sharing the shame of Ghosn's actions.

For someone who navigated the cutthroat global auto market for decades, it was surprising that Ghosn was so surprised by the turn of events. As Shakespeare commented, "uneasy lies the head that wears a crown." It appears Ghosn should have been more aware of both how others assessed his actions and the extent to which his adversaries would use him as a poster child of corporate greed once he gave them the chance to do so.

Discussion Questions

1. What lessons can members of a board of directors take away from the Carlos Ghosn saga? What actions can boards take to limit the chance they will face a similar scandal?
2. What sort of punishment does Carlos Ghosn deserve for his actions?

Under Carlos Ghosn, Nissan went from a struggling to a very successful automaker. He was a strong leader, but his arrogance and self-interested behavior led to his downfall. While he set a clear direction for the firm and created and reinforced valuable strategies, he failed to maintain and reinforce an ethical culture and firm values that matched the national culture in which he operated.

This chapter provides insights into the role of strategic leadership in managing, adapting, and coping in the face of increased environmental complexity and uncertainty. First, we define leadership and its three interdependent activities–setting a direction, designing the organization, and nurturing a culture dedicated to excellence and ethical behavior. Then, we identify two elements of leadership that contribute to success–overcoming barriers to change and using power effectively. The third section focuses on emotional intelligence, a trait that is increasingly acknowledged to be critical to successful leadership. Next, we emphasize the importance of leaders developing competency companions and creating a learning organization. Here, we focus on empowerment wherein employees and managers throughout an organization develop a sense of self-determination, competence, meaning, and impact that is centrally important to learning. Finally, we address the leader's role in building an ethical organization and the elements of an ethical culture that contribute to firm effectiveness.

LEADERSHIP: THREE INTERDEPENDENT ACTIVITIES

leadership
the process of transforming organizations from what they are to what the leader would have them become.

In today's chaotic world, few would argue against the need for leadership, but how do we go about encouraging it? Is it enough to merely keep an organization afloat, or is it essential to make steady progress toward some well-defined objective? We believe custodial management is not leadership. Leadership is proactive, goal-oriented, and focused on the creation and implementation of a creative vision. **Leadership** is the process of transforming organizations from what they are to what the leader would have them become. This definition implies a lot: *dissatisfaction* with the status quo, a *vision* of what should be, and a *process* for bringing about change. An insurance company executive shared the following insight: "I lead by the Noah Principle: It's all right to know when it's going to rain, but, by God, you had better build the ark."

Doing the right thing is becoming increasingly important. Many industries are declining; the global village is becoming increasingly complex, interconnected, and unpredictable; and product and market life cycles are becoming increasingly compressed. When asked to describe the life cycle of his company's products, the CEO of a supplier of computer components replied, "Seven months from cradle to grave–and that includes three months to design the product and get it into production!"

Despite the importance of doing the "right thing," leaders must also be concerned about "doing things right." Charan and Colvin strongly believe that execution, that is, the implementation of strategy, is also essential to success:

> Mastering execution turns out to be the odds-on best way for a CEO to keep his job. So what's the right way to think about that sexier obsession, strategy? It's vitally important—obviously. The problem is that our age's fascination feeds the mistaken belief that developing exactly the right strategy will enable a company to rocket past competitors. In reality, that's less than half the battle.[2]

LO 11-1

Explain the three key interdependent activities in which all successful leaders must be continually engaged.

Thus, leaders are change agents whose success is measured by how effectively they formulate *and* implement a strategic vision and mission.[3]

Many authors contend that successful leaders must recognize three interdependent activities that must be continually reassessed for organizations to succeed. As shown in Exhibit 11.1, these are (1) setting a direction, (2) designing the organization, and (3) nurturing a culture dedicated to excellence and ethical behavior.[4]

The interdependent nature of these three activities is self-evident. Consider an organization with a great mission and a superb organizational structure but a culture that implicitly encourages shirking and unethical behavior. Or one with a sound direction and strong culture but counterproductive teams and a "zero-sum" reward system that leads to the dysfunctional situation in which one party's gain is viewed as another party's loss and collaboration and sharing are severely hampered. Clearly, such combinations would be ineffective.

Often, failure of today's organizations can be attributed to a lack of equal consideration of these three activities. The imagery of a three-legged stool is instructive: The stool will collapse if one leg is missing or broken. Let's briefly look at each of these activities as well as the value of an ambicultural approach to leadership.

Setting a Direction

A holistic understanding of an organization's stakeholders requires an ability to scan the environment to develop a knowledge of all of the company's stakeholders and other salient environmental trends and events. Managers must integrate this knowledge into a vision of what the organization could become.[5] This necessitates the capacity to solve increasingly complex problems, become proactive in approach, and develop viable strategic options. A strategic vision provides many benefits: a clear future direction; a framework for the organization's mission and goals; and enhanced employee communication, participation, and commitment.

EXHIBIT 11.1 Three Interdependent Leadership Activities

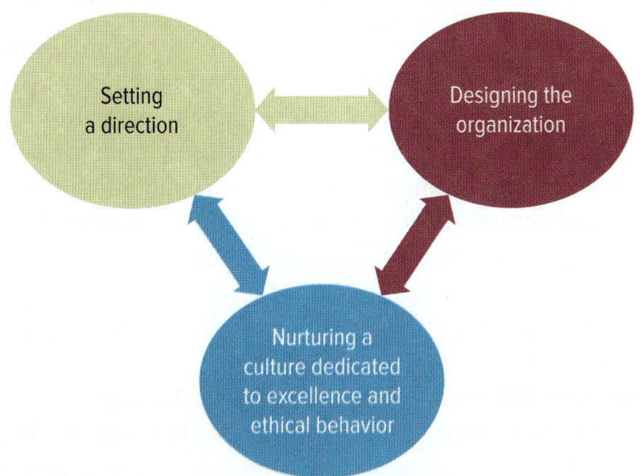

11.1 STRATEGY SPOTLIGHT

JOSH SILVERMAN LEADS A TURNAROUND AT ETSY

Etsy, an online platform that brings together providers of arts and crafts products with customers, was missing out on the exploding growth in online sales. Its sales growth was anemic. Its costs were rising. And its stock was tanking. This led the board of directors to fire the firm's CEO and bring in Josh Silverman to lead the firm in May 2017.

Silverman has initiated a dramatic turnaround in the firm. Drawing on experiences he had leading change efforts at American Express and eBay, Silverman reoriented the firm's focus in two key ways. First, he changed how the firm prioritized its stakeholders. The original vision of Etsy was oriented around serving the merchants who sold on Etsy's site. Silverman switched it around and made customers the primary stakeholder the firm would focus on. In Silverman's words, "the main thing is to keep the main thing the main thing." In his eyes, better serving customers to raise total merchant sales is the main thing. He started with customer's main complaint: it was difficult to find what they were looking for on Etsy's website. He tasked the engineers with redesigning the firm's search function to better serve customers.

Second, he narrowed down the projects the firm focused on. He saw that the firm had stretched itself way too thin by chasing after low revenue initiatives. He questioned "why are we launching brand-new businesses when the return on every hour we invest on the core marketplace is so enormous?" He was able to cut staff by 22 percent to reduce costs while redeploying the remaining staff to better serve customers in the firm's core market.

He also realized his changes were difficult for some workers. They had an emotional attachment to the firm and the way it had always been run. A few employees even tweeted that they thought the firm was moving away from its values. Silverman set up an all-employee meeting right after he was appointed to share his hopes for the firm, his desire to maintain its socially responsible mission, and he patiently answered questions from employees.

In sum, his key actions in initiating change brought greater strategic clarity to the firm, both in what the firm did and who the firm served. The results are dramatic. The firm's growth rate ramped up dramatically after Silverman took over, and its stock price jumped 600 percent from April 2017 to April 2019.

Sources: De Vynck, G. 2018. Investors love Etsy's CEO. The artists aren't so sure. *Bloomberg Businessweek*, June 21; and Rossolillo, N. 2018. What's behind Etsy's double so far in 2018? *fool.com*, July 11.

Strategy Spotlight 11.1 discusses how Josh Silverman led a dramatic turnaround at online marketplace Etsy.

Designing the Organization

At times, almost all leaders have difficulty implementing their vision and strategies.[6] Such problems may stem from a variety of sources:

- Lack of understanding of responsibility and accountability among managers.
- Reward systems that do not motivate individuals (or collectives such as groups and divisions) toward desired organizational goals.
- Inadequate or inappropriate budgeting and control systems.
- Insufficient mechanisms to integrate activities across the organization.

Successful leaders are actively involved in building structures, teams, systems, and organizational processes that facilitate the implementation of their vision and strategies. Without appropriately structuring organizational activities, a firm would generally be unable to attain an overall low-cost advantage by closely monitoring its costs through detailed and formalized cost and financial control procedures. With regard to corporate-level strategy, a related diversification strategy would necessitate reward systems that emphasize behavioral measures because interdependence among business units tends to be very important. In contrast, reward systems associated with an unrelated diversification strategy should rely more on financial indicators of performance because business units are relatively autonomous.

These examples illustrate the important role of leadership in creating systems and structures to achieve desired ends. As Jim Collins says about the importance of designing the organization, "Along with figuring out what the company stands for and pushing it to understand what it's really good at, building mechanisms is the CEO's role–the leader as architect."[7]

Nurturing a Culture Committed to Excellence and Ethical Behavior

Organizational culture can be an effective means of organizational control.[8] Leaders play a key role in changing, developing, and sustaining an organization's culture. Brian Chesky, cofounder and CEO of Airbnb, clearly understands the role of the leader in building and maintaining an organization's culture. In October 2013, as Airbnb was growing rapidly, Chesky sent out an email to his leadership team imploring the team members to be very conscious to maintain the culture of the firm. He stated, "The culture is what creates the foundation for all future innovation." He then went on to comment that they needed to uphold the firm's values in all they do: who they hire, how they work on a project, how they treat other employees in the hallway, and what they write in emails. Chesky then laid out the power of firm culture saying "When the culture is strong, you can trust everyone to do the right thing. People can be independent and autonomous. They can be entrepreneurial."[9]

In sharp contrast, leaders can also have a very detrimental effect on a firm's culture and ethics. Imagine the negative impact that Todd Berman's illegal activities have had on a firm that he cofounded–New York's private equity firm Chartwell Investments.[10] He stole more than $3.6 million from the firm and its investors. Berman pleaded guilty to fraud charges brought by the Justice Department. For 18 months he misled Chartwell's investors concerning the financial condition of one of the firm's portfolio companies by falsely claiming it needed to borrow funds to meet operating expenses. Instead, Berman transferred the money to his personal bank account, along with fees paid by portfolio companies.

Clearly, a leader's behavior and values can make a strong impact on an organization–for good or for bad. Strategy Spotlight 11.2 provides a positive example, with H. Fisk Johnson carrying on a legacy of maintaining a strong ethical culture at his family's firm.

11.2 STRATEGY SPOTLIGHT — ENVIRONMENTAL SUSTAINABILITY, ETHICS

FAMILY LEADERSHIP SUSTAINS THE CULTURE OF SC JOHNSON

SC Johnson, the maker of Windex, Ziploc bags, and Glade Air Fresheners, is known as one of the most environmentally conscious consumer products companies. The family-owned company is run by Fisk Johnson, the fifth generation of the family to serve as firm CEO. It is the 35th largest privately owned firm, with 13,000 employees and nearly $10 billion in sales. Over the decades, the firm has built and reinforced its reputation for environmental consciousness. Being privately owned by the Johnson family is part of it. Fisk Johnson lamented the short-term focus of Wall Street and commented that SC Johnson is fortunate to not have to worry about these short-term pressures. Instead, he asserted the value of the family-driven culture of the firm, stating "we're very fortunate that we have a family that is principled and has been very principled."

Fisk uses the benefits of dedicated family ownership to work in both substantive and symbolic ways. On the substantive side, he has implemented systems in place to improve its environmental performance. For example, with its Greenlist process, the firm rates the ingredients it uses or is considering using. It then rates each ingredient on several criteria, including biodegradability and human toxicity, and gives the ingredient a score ranging from 0 to 3, with 3 being the most environmentally friendly. The goal is to increase the percentage of ingredients rated a 2 or a 3 and eliminate those with a score of 0. With this system, the firm has increased the percentage of ingredients rated as a 2 or 3 (better or best) from about 20 percent to over 50 percent from 2001 to 2016.

Fisk uses stories from decisions in the past as he acts to sustain the firm's culture of environmental consciousness. In using stories to reinforce the environmental focus within the firm and to explain it to external stakeholders, Fisk Johnson draws on stories relating to decisions his father made as well as ones he's made. Most prominently, he uses a story about a decision his father made to stop using chlorofluorocarbons in the firm's aerosol products. "Our first decision to unilaterally remove a major chemical occurred in 1975, when research began suggesting that chlorofluorocarbons (CFCs) in aerosols might harm Earth's ozone layer. My father was CEO at the time, and he decided to ban them from all the company's aerosol products worldwide. He did so several years before the government played catch-up and banned the use of CFCs from everyone's

continued

continued

products." This decision was prescient and benefited the firm since it moved ahead of government pressures. This story is especially effective since it highlights his father's willingness and ability to take actions that can lead both the government and industry rivals to change.

A second story outlines the firm's decision to remove chlorine as an ingredient in its Saran Wrap. In the late 1990s, regulators and environmentalists were raising concerns that chlorine used in plastic released toxic chemicals when the plastic was burned. As Fisk Johnson explains, this was a difficult situation for him and the firm. "We set out to figure out an alternative for Saran that didn't contain chlorine, but that's just as good." In the end, they couldn't find such a product. Instead, they introduced a product that didn't cling as well, and they've steadily lost market share in this segment. This story demonstrates that he not only wants to lead the firm to be an agent of change, but he is also willing to sacrifice profits to do the right thing.

The combination of the firm's ownership structure, its strong leader, and its story-driven culture reinforce the firm's willingness to lead the market in environmental awareness. For example, in early 2016, Fisk decided that SC Johnson would be the first firm to list 100 percent of the fragrance ingredients it uses. He saw this decision as a means to push itself and its rivals to use more environmentally friendly fragrance ingredients.

SC Johnson is also striving to be a leader in energy efficiency in its operations. Most notably, the firm announced in early 2019 that it would reduce its non-renewable energy usage in its corporate headquarters by 62 percent. It plans to accomplish this using a combination of solar electric and geothermal heating and cooling. "Leading the industry in an environmentally responsible manner starts at home," Johnson said. "For us, that meant taking a look at our operations and finding where we can lessen our impact by reducing greenhouse gas emissions, addressing air quality and increasing the amount of energy offset from renewable resources. Transitioning to geothermal energy at our headquarters goes a long way toward accomplishing those goals."

Source: Kaufman, A. 2016. CEO admits that environmentalism does cost him profits. *huffingtonpost.com,* February 18: np; Johnson, F. 2015. SC Johnson's CEO on doing the right thing, even when it hurts business. *Harvard Business Review,* April; Byron, E. 2016. How Fisk Johnson works to keep the shine on the family business. *wsj.com,* March 11: np; and Thomas, A. 2019. SC Johnson targets 62% cut in Racine HQ energy use. *biztimes.com,* April 1: np.

Managers and top executives must accept personal responsibility for developing and strengthening ethical behavior throughout the organization. They must consistently demonstrate that such behavior is central to the vision and mission of the organization. Several elements must be present and reinforced for a firm to become highly ethical, including role models, corporate credos and codes of conduct, reward and evaluation systems, and policies and procedures. Given the importance of these elements, we address them in detail in the last section of this chapter.

LO 11-2

Describe two elements of effective leadership: overcoming barriers to change and using power effectively.

GETTING THINGS DONE: OVERCOMING BARRIERS AND USING POWER

The demands on leaders in today's business environment require them to perform a variety of functions. The success of their organizations often depends on how they, as individuals, meet challenges and deliver on promises. What practices and skills are needed to get the job done effectively? In this section, we focus on two capabilities that are marks of successful leadership—overcoming barriers to change and using power effectively. Then, in the next section, we will examine an important human trait that helps leaders be more effective—emotional intelligence.

barriers to change characteristics of individuals and organizations that prevent a leader from transforming an organization.

Overcoming Barriers to Change

What are the **barriers to change** that leaders often encounter, and how can leaders best bring about organizational change?[11] After all, people generally have some level of choice about how strongly they support or resist a leader's change initiatives. Why is there often so much resistance? Organizations at all levels are prone to inertia and are slow to learn, adapt, and change because:

1. Many people have **vested interests in the status quo.** People tend to be risk-averse and resistant to change. There is a broad stream of research on "escalation," wherein certain individuals continue to throw "good money at bad decisions" despite negative performance feedback.[12]
2. There are **systemic barriers.** The design of the organization's structure, information processing, reporting relationships, and so forth impedes the proper flow and evaluation of information. A bureaucratic structure with multiple layers, onerous requirements for documentation, and rigid rules and procedures will often "inoculate" the organization against change. For example, Tyson Foods found that its information systems didn't provide the information it needed to streamline its supply chain and become more flexible in meeting changing customers' tastes. To help overcome these challenges, the firm brought in Scott Spradley, a Silicon Valley executive as its Chief Technology Officer.[13]
3. **Behavioral barriers** cause managers to look at issues from a biased or limited perspective due to their education, training, work experiences, and so forth. Ian Read confronted this challenge as CEO of Pfizer, a global pharmaceutical firm. He found that managers in the firm had a paralyzing tendency to avoid responsibility, and this constrained the ability of the firm to learn and change. He gave a large coin stamped with the phrase "Own It" to all the firm's employees and told them to bring it out whenever other employees seemed reluctant to deal with tough issues.[14]
4. **Political barriers** refer to conflicts arising from power relationships. This can be the outcome of a myriad of symptoms such as vested interests, refusal to share information, conflicts over resources, conflicts between departments and divisions, and petty interpersonal differences.
5. **Personal time constraints** bring to mind the old saying about "not having enough time to drain the swamp when you are up to your neck in alligators." Gresham's law of planning states that operational decisions will drive out the time necessary for strategic thinking and reflection. This tendency is accentuated in organizations experiencing severe price competition or retrenchment wherein managers and employees are spread rather thin.

vested interest in the status quo
a barrier to change that stems from people's risk aversion.

systemic barriers
barriers to change that stem from an organizational design that impedes the proper flow and evaluation of information.

behavioral barriers
barriers to change associated with the tendency for managers to look at issues from a biased or limited perspective based on their prior education and experience.

political barriers
barriers to change related to conflicts arising from power relationships.

personal time constraints
a barrier to change that stems from people's not having sufficient time for strategic thinking and reflection.

Leaders must draw on a range of personal skills as well as organizational mechanisms to move their organizations forward in the face of such barriers. Two factors mentioned earlier—building a learning organization and building an ethical organization—provide the kind of climate within which a leader can advance the organization's aims and make progress toward its goals.

One of the most important tools a leader has for overcoming barriers to change is his or her personal and organizational power. On the one hand, good leaders must be on guard not to abuse power. On the other hand, successful leadership requires the measured exercise of power. We turn to that topic next.

Using Power Effectively

Successful leadership requires the effective use of power in overcoming barriers to change.[15] As humorously noted by Mark Twain, "I'm all for progress. It's change I object to." **Power** refers to a leader's ability to get things done in a way he or she wants them to be done. It is the ability to influence other people's behavior, to persuade them to do things that they

power
a leader's ability to get things done in a way he or she wants them to be done.

EXHIBIT 11.2 A Leader's Bases of Power

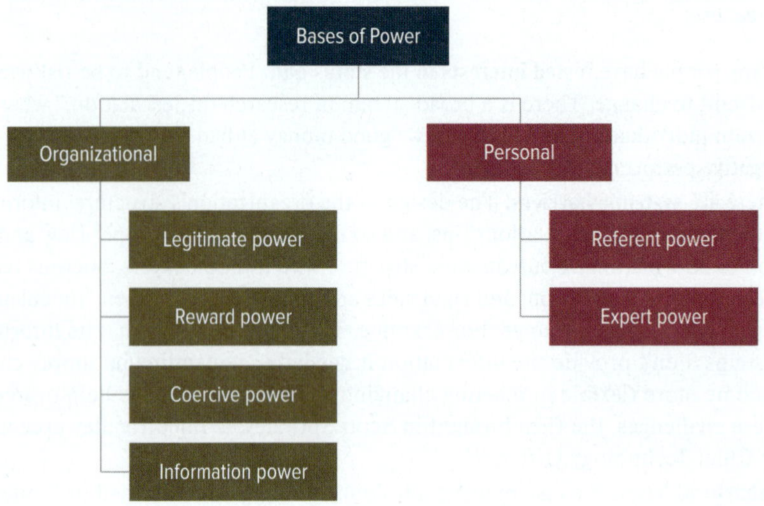

otherwise would not do, and to overcome resistance and opposition. Effective exercise of power is essential for successful leadership.[16]

A leader derives his or her power from several sources or bases. The simplest way to understand the bases of power is by classifying them as organizational and personal, as shown in Exhibit 11.2.

organizational bases of power
a formal management position that is the basis of a leader's power.

Organizational bases of power refer to the power that a person wields because of her formal management position.[17] These include legitimate, reward, coercive, and information power. *Legitimate power* is derived from organizationally conferred decision-making authority and is exercised by virtue of a manager's position in the organization. *Reward power* depends on the ability of the leader or manager to confer rewards for positive behaviors or outcomes. *Coercive power* is the power a manager exercises over employees using fear of punishment for errors of omission or commission. *Information power* arises from a manager's access, control, and distribution of information that is not freely available to everyone in an organization.

personal bases of power
a leader's personality characteristics and behavior that are the basis of the leader's power.

A leader might also be able to influence subordinates because of his or her personality characteristics and behavior. These would be considered the **personal bases of power,** including referent power and expert power. The source of *referent power* is a subordinate's identification with the leader. A leader's personal attributes or charisma might influence subordinates and make them devoted to that leader. The source of *expert power* is the leader's expertise and knowledge. The leader is the expert on whom subordinates depend for information that they need to do their jobs successfully.

Successful leaders use the different bases of power, and often a combination of them, as appropriate to meet the demands of a situation, such as the nature of the task, the personality characteristics of the subordinates, and the urgency of the issue.[18] Persuasion and developing consensus are often essential, but so is pressing for action. At some point stragglers must be prodded into line.[19] Peter Georgescu, former CEO of Young & Rubicam (an advertising and media subsidiary of the U.K.-based WPP Group), summarized a leader's dilemma brilliantly (and humorously), "I have knee pads and a .45. I get down and beg a lot, but I shoot people too."[20]

Strategy Spotlight 11.3 addresses how leaders can go beyond leveraging their power to produce short-term financial results. Instead, Dov Seidman argues great leaders implement moral leadership in their firms.

11.3 STRATEGY SPOTLIGHT

THE IMPORTANCE OF MORAL LEADERSHIP

Dov Seidman serves as CEO of LRN, an ethics and compliance management firm. He has an unusual background for a corporate CEO in that he has college degrees in philosophy, politics, economics, and law. He has taken this eclectic background and his experience as a CEO to build a position as a leading speaker and author on the ethics of leadership. From his perspective, it is the role of top management to set the moral tone for the organization, especially in times of crisis. He argues for four foundational elements for leaders to keep in mind as they strive to exhibit moral leadership.

1. **Moral leaders seek honorable missions**. Moral leaders strive to build a sense of purpose in their organizations. They lay out goals that are tied to human progress and prosperity. This generates a sense of drive, commitment, and hope in others in the organization. They accept that the path will not be easy or smooth and that the firm will at times stumble, but they emphasize the value of the journey as the firm works toward its mission.
2. **Moral leaders galvanize and uplift others in the organization**. Moral leaders cannot only be concerned about how and whether the actions they take are ethical. They also see the need to interact with others in a way that inspires others to act morally. To inspire morality in others, leaders must avoid enforcing personal loyalty from subordinates. Instead, they must see others they work with as fellow journeyers, invite their involvement in discussions and decisions, and treat them with full humanity as important and valuable partners.
3. **Moral leaders are motivated by strongly held ethical foundations**. Moral leaders develop and draw on core values and ethical beliefs. Moral leaders rely on these values and standards as they face difficult challenges, seeing the choices they make as being tied into issues larger than themselves and their current situation. This evidences itself as courage, the boldness to make the right decision when other courses may seem easier or more expedient. They also need to show patience with others, giving them the time and freedom to work through decisions and challenges so that others can consider and work toward the larger moral goals of the organization.
4. **Moral leaders work to build their moral judgment and intelligence**. Seidman refers to this as "building moral muscle." Just as an athlete works out to build physical strength, moral leaders continue to work out on ethical questions, considering questions of right and wrong, justice and injustice. They also set the environment within their team such that issues are debated, different perspectives are considered, and ethical elements are seen as central. In doing so, they build a practice in the team where the broad issues associated with a decision are seamlessly considered. When mistakes are made, moral leaders admit their fault and work to learn from the experience for future decisions. In humility, they look forward to working in a way that better matches their mission and values.

Seidman argues that moral leadership is increasingly important in our fast-paced, interconnected world. With the fast pace of life and business, it is increasingly challenging to take the time to consider the broader, moral elements of an organization's actions. But with the degree to which any failure is broadcast and shared, mistakes are that much more costly. As a result, authentic moral leadership is even more important for long-term organizational success. As leaders build in purpose and meaning and inspire others around them to do the same, organizations become better positioned to fully include ethical elements in their decision making and still meet the demands of the competitive environment.

Source: Seidman, D. 2017. The four pillars of moral leadership. *Fortune,* September 15: 90-92; Seidman, D. 2017. 4 pillars of moral leadership for navigating a crisis of trust. *lrn.com,* December 21.

EMOTIONAL INTELLIGENCE: A KEY LEADERSHIP TRAIT

LO 11-3

Understand the crucial role of emotional intelligence (EI) in successful leadership, as well as its potential drawbacks.

In the previous sections, we discussed skills and activities of strategic leadership. The focus was on "what leaders do and how they do it." Now the issue becomes "who leaders *are,*" that is, what leadership traits are the most important. Clearly, these two issues are related, because successful leaders possess the valuable traits that enable them to perform effectively in order to create value for their organization.[21]

There has been a vast amount of literature on the successful traits of leaders.[22] These traits include integrity, maturity, energy, judgment, motivation, intelligence, expertise, and so on. For simplicity, these traits may be grouped into three broad sets of capabilities:

- Purely technical skills (like accounting or operations research).
- Cognitive abilities (like analytical reasoning or quantitative analysis).
- Emotional intelligence (like self-management and managing relationships).

emotional intelligence (EI) an individual's capacity for recognizing his or her own emotions and those of others, including the five components of self-awareness, self-regulation, motivation, empathy, and social skills.

Emotional intelligence (EI) has been defined as the capacity for recognizing one's own emotions and those of others.[23]

Research suggests that effective leaders at all levels of organizations have high levels of EI.[24] After controlling for cognitive abilities and manager personality attributes, EI leads to stronger job performance across a wide range of professions, with stronger effects for professions that require a great deal of human interaction. Interestingly, there is only partial support for the catchy phrase "IQ gets you hired, but EQ (emotional quotient) gets you promoted." Evidence indicates that high levels of EI increase the likelihood of being promoted up to the middle-manager level. However, managers at high levels of the corporate hierarchy tend to evidence lower levels of EI, with the CEOs having, on average, lower levels of EI than managers at any other level. This is troubling given that firms led by CEOs high in EI outperform firms led by CEOs lower in EI. High-EI CEOs excel in managing relationships, influencing people, and forging alliances both inside and outside the firm. These CEOs can also benefit the firm since their ability to connect with and relate to outside stakeholders helps build the firm's reputation.

Exhibit 11.3 identifies the five components of EI: self-awareness, self-regulation, motivation, empathy, and social skill.

Self-Awareness

Self-awareness is the first component of EI and brings to mind that Delphic oracle that gave the advice "Know thyself" thousands of years ago. Self-awareness involves a person having a deep understanding of his or her emotions, strengths, weaknesses, and drives. People with strong self-awareness are neither overly critical nor unrealistically optimistic. Instead, they are honest with themselves and others.

Self-Regulation

Biological impulses drive our emotions. Although we cannot do away with them, we can strive to manage them. Self-regulation, which is akin to an ongoing inner conversation, frees us from being prisoners of our feelings.[25] People engaged in such conversation feel bad moods and emotional impulses just as everyone else does. However, they find ways to control them and even channel them in useful ways.

EXHIBIT 11.3 The Five Components of Emotional Intelligence at Work

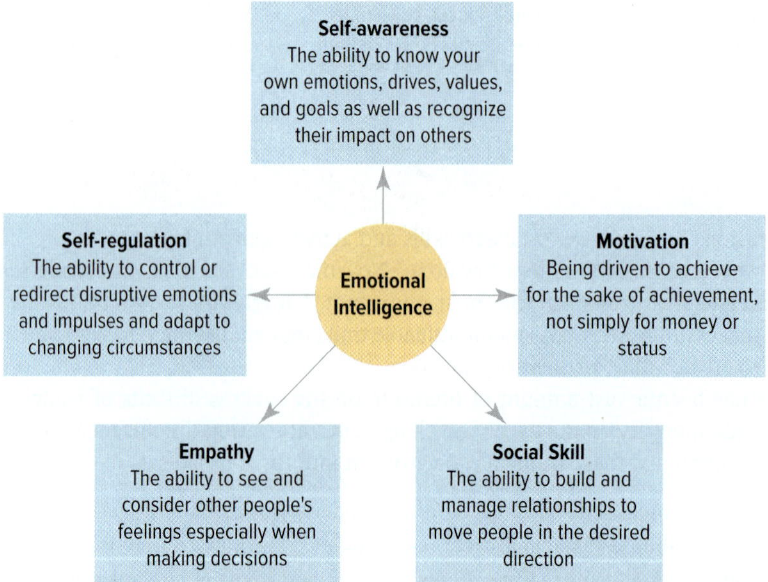

Self-regulated people are able to create an environment of trust and fairness where political behavior and infighting are sharply reduced and productivity tends to be high.

Motivation

Successful executives are driven to achieve beyond expectations–their own and everyone else's. Although many people are driven by external factors, such as money and prestige, those with leadership potential are driven by a deeply embedded desire to achieve for the sake of achievement. Motivated people show a passion for the work itself, such as seeking out creative challenges, a love of learning, and taking pride in a job well done.

Empathy

Empathy is probably the most easily recognized component of EI. Empathy means thoughtfully considering an employee's feelings, along with other factors, in the process of making intelligent decisions. Empathy is important for leading teams since it enables a manager to sense and understand the viewpoints of everyone around the table.

Empathy also plays a key role in retaining talent. Human capital is particularly important to a firm in the knowledge economy when it comes to creating advantages that are sustainable. Leaders need empathy to develop and keep top talent, because when high performers leave, they take their tacit knowledge with them.

Social Skill

Social skill may be viewed as friendliness with a purpose: moving people in the direction you desire, whether that's agreement on a new marketing strategy or enthusiasm about a new product.

Socially skilled people tend to have a wide circle of acquaintances as well as a knack for finding common ground and building rapport. They recognize that nothing gets done alone, and they have a network in place when the time for action comes.

A key to developing social skill is to become a good listener–a skill that many executives find to be quite challenging. Deborah Triant, former CEO of Check Point Software Technologies, says, "Debating is easy; listening with an open mind is not. The worst thing that you as a leader can do in the decision-making process is to voice your opinion before anyone else can."[26]

Emotional Intelligence: Some Potential Drawbacks and Cautionary Notes

Many great leaders have great reserves of empathy, interpersonal astuteness, awareness of their own feelings, and an awareness of their impact on others.[27] More importantly, they know how to apply these capabilities judiciously as best benefits the situation. Having some minimum level of EI will help a person be effective as a leader as long as it is channeled appropriately. However, if a person has a high level of these capabilities it may become "too much of a good thing" if he or she is allowed to drive inappropriate behaviors. Some additional potential drawbacks of EI can be gleaned by considering the flip side of its benefits.

Effective Leaders Have Empathy for Others However, they also must be able to make the "tough decisions." Leaders must be able to appeal to logic and reason and acknowledge others' feelings so that people feel the decisions are correct. However, it is easy to over-identify with others, making it more difficult to make tough decisions.

Effective Leaders Are Astute Judges of People A danger is that leaders may become judgmental and overly critical about the shortcomings they perceive in others.

Effective Leaders Are Passionate about What They Do, and They Show It However, there is a fine line between being excited about something and letting your passion close your mind to other possibilities or cause you to ignore realities that others may see.

Effective Leaders Create Personal Connections with Their People Most effective leaders take time to engage employees individually and in groups, listening to their ideas, suggestions, and concerns. However, if the leader makes too many unannounced visits, it may create a culture of fear and micromanagement. Clearly, striking a correct balance is essential.

LO 11-4

Explain the importance of creating a learning organization.

CREATING A LEARNING ORGANIZATION

To enhance the long-term viability of organizations, leaders also need to build a learning organization. Such an organization is capable of adapting to change, fostering creativity, and succeeding in highly competitive markets.

Successful, innovative organizations recognize the importance of having everyone involved in the process of actively learning and adapting. As noted by a leading expert on learning organizations, MIT's Peter Senge, the days when Henry Ford, Alfred Sloan, and Tom Watson *"learned for the organization"* are gone:

> In an increasingly dynamic, interdependent, and unpredictable world, it is simply no longer possible for anyone to "figure it all out at the top." The old model, "the top thinks and the local acts," must now give way to integrating thinking and acting at all levels. While the challenge is great, so is the potential payoff. "The person who figures out how to harness the collective genius of the people in his or her organization," according to former Citibank CEO Walter Wriston, "is going to blow the competition away."[28]

Learning and change typically involve the ongoing questioning of an organization's status quo or method of procedure. This means that all individuals throughout the organization must be reflective.[29] Many organizations get so caught up in carrying out their day-to-day work that they rarely, if ever, stop to think objectively about themselves and their businesses. They often fail to ask the probing questions that might lead them to call into question their basic assumptions, to refresh their strategies, or to reengineer their work processes.

To adapt to change, foster creativity, and remain competitive, leaders must build learning organizations. Exhibit 11.4 lists the five key elements of a learning organization.

learning organizations
organizations that create a proactive, creative approach to the unknown; characterized by (1) inspiring and motivating people with a mission and purpose, (2) empowering employees at all levels, (3) accumulating and sharing internal knowledge, (4) gathering and integrating external information, and (5) challenging the status quo and enabling creativity.

Inspiring and Motivating People with a Mission or Purpose

Successful **learning organizations** create a proactive, creative approach to the unknown, actively solicit the involvement of employees at all levels, and enable all employees to use their intelligence and apply their imagination. Higher-level skills are required of everyone, not just those at the top.[30] A learning environment involves organization-wide commitment to change, an action orientation, and applicable tools and methods.[31] It must be viewed by everyone as a guiding philosophy and not simply as another change program.

A critical requirement of all learning organizations is that everyone feels and supports a compelling purpose. In the words of William O'Brien, former CEO of Hanover Insurance, "Before there can be meaningful participation, people must share certain values and pictures about where we are trying to go. We discovered that people have a real need to feel that they're part of an enabling mission."[32] Medtronic, a medical products company, does this well. The company's motto is "restoring patients to full life," and it works to bring this to life

EXHIBIT 11.4 Key Elements of a Learning Organization

These are the five key elements of a learning organization. Each of these items should be viewed as necessary, *but not sufficient*. That is, successful learning organizations need all five elements.

1. Inspiring and motivating people with a mission or purpose.
2. Empowering employees at all levels.
3. Accumulating and sharing internal knowledge.
4. Gathering and integrating external information.
5. Challenging the status quo and enabling creativity.

for its employees. At the company's holiday party, patients, their families, and their doctors come and share their survival and recovery stories. The event inspires employees, who are moved to tears, are able to directly see the results of their work, and are motivated to do even more.

Inspiring and motivating people with a mission or purpose is a necessary but not sufficient condition for developing an organization that can learn and adapt to a rapidly changing, complex, and interconnected environment.

Empowering Employees at All Levels

"The great leader is a great servant," asserted Ken Melrose, former CEO and chairman of Toro Company and author of *Making the Grass Greener on Your Side.*[33] A manager's role becomes one of creating an environment where employees can achieve their potential as they help move the organization toward its goals. Instead of viewing themselves as resource controllers and power brokers, leaders must envision themselves as flexible resources willing to assume numerous roles as coaches, information providers, teachers, decision makers, facilitators, supporters, or listeners, depending on the needs of their employees.[34]

The central key to empowerment is effective leadership. Empowerment can't occur in a leadership vacuum. According to Melrose, "You best lead by serving the needs of your people. You don't do their jobs for them; you enable them to learn and progress on the job."

Leading-edge organizations recognize the need for trust, cultural control, and expertise at all levels instead of the extensive and cumbersome rules and regulations inherent in hierarchical control.[35] Some commentators have argued that too often organizations fall prey to the "heroes-and-drones syndrome," wherein the value of those in powerful positions is exalted and the value of those who fail to achieve top rank is diminished. Such an attitude is implicit in phrases such as "Lead, follow, or get out of the way" or, even less appealing, "Unless you're the lead horse, the view never changes." Few will ever reach the top hierarchical positions in organizations, but in the information economy, the strongest organizations are those that effectively use the talents of all the players on the team.

Empowering individuals by soliciting their input helps an organization to enjoy better employee morale. It also helps create a culture in which middle- and lower-level employees feel that their ideas and initiatives will be valued and enhance firm performance.

Accumulating and Sharing Internal Knowledge

Effective organizations must also *redistribute information, knowledge* (skills to act on the information), and *rewards.*[36] To do so, firms need to develop a culture that: (1) encourages employees to offer ideas, ask questions, and express concerns, (2) encourages widespread sharing of information from various sources, (3) identifies opportunities and makes it safe to experiment, (4) encourages collaborative decision making and the sharing of best practices, and (5) utilizes technology to facilitate both the gathering and sharing of information.

In addition to enhancing the sharing of company information both up and down as well as across the organization, leaders also have to develop means to tap into some of the more informal sources of internal information. In a survey of presidents, CEOs, board members, and top executives in a variety of nonprofit organizations, respondents were asked what differentiated the successful candidates for promotion. The consensus: The executive was seen as a person who listens. According to Peter Meyer, the author of the study, "The value of listening is clear: You cannot succeed in running a company if you do not hear what your people, customers, and suppliers are telling you. . . . Listening and understanding well are key to making good decisions."[37]

Gathering and Integrating External Information

Recognizing opportunities, as well as threats, in the external environment is vital to a firm's success. As organizations *and* environments become more complex and evolve rapidly, it is far more critical for employees and managers to become more aware of environmental trends and events—both general and industry-specific—and more knowledgeable about their firm's competitors and customers. Next, we will discuss some ideas on how to do it.

First, company employees at all levels can use a variety of sources to acquire external information. Firms can tap into knowledge from alliance partners, suppliers, competitors, and the scientific community. For example, in the pharmaceutical and biotechnology industries, participation in networks and alliances is increasingly common and critical to knowledge diffusion and learning. To gain up-to-date information on particular rivals, firms can monitor the direct communications from rival firms and their executives, such as press releases and quarterly-earnings calls. These communications can provide insight on the rival's actions and intended actions. It may also be valuable to follow rival-firm employees' online postings, on Twitter and other platforms, to gain insights on rivals' investments and actions.

benchmarking
managers seeking out best examples of a particular practice as part of an ongoing effort to improve the corresponding practice in their own organization.

competitive benchmarking
benchmarking in which the examples are drawn from competitors in the industry.

functional benchmarking
benchmarking in which the examples are drawn from any organization, even those outside the industry.

Second, **benchmarking** *can be a useful means of employing external information.* Here managers seek out the best examples of a particular practice as part of an ongoing effort to improve the corresponding practice in their own organization.[38] There are two primary types of benchmarking. **Competitive benchmarking** restricts the search for best practices to competitors, while **functional benchmarking** endeavors to determine best practices regardless of industry. Industry-specific standards (e.g., response times required to repair power outages in the electric utility industry) are typically best handled through competitive benchmarking, whereas more generic processes (e.g., answering 1-800 calls) lend themselves to functional benchmarking because the function is essentially the same in any industry.

Ford Motor Company works with its suppliers on benchmarking its competitors' products during product redesigns. At the launch of the redesign, Ford and its suppliers identify a few key components they want to focus on improving. They then do a "tear down" of Ford's components as well as matching components from three or four rivals. The idea is to get early input from suppliers so that Ford can design components that are best in class—lighter, cheaper, and more reliable.[39]

Third, focus directly on customers for information. For example, William McKnight, head of 3M's Chicago sales office, required that salesmen of abrasives products talk directly to the workers in their customers' shop floors to find out what they needed, instead of calling on only front-office executives.[40] This was very innovative at the time—1909! But it illustrates the need to get to the end user of a product or service. (McKnight went on to become 3M's president from 1929 to 1949 and chairman from 1949 to 1969.)

Challenging the Status Quo and Enabling Creativity

Earlier in this chapter we discussed some of the barriers that leaders face when trying to bring about change in an organization: vested interests in the status quo, systemic barriers, behavioral barriers, political barriers, and time constraints. For a firm to become a learning organization, it must overcome such barriers in order to foster creativity and enable it to permeate the firm. This becomes quite a challenge if the firm is entrenched in a status quo mentality.

Perhaps the best way to challenge the status quo is for the leader to forcefully create a sense of urgency. For example, when Tom Kasten was vice president of Levi Strauss, he had a direct approach to initiating change:

> You create a compelling picture of the risks of *not* changing. We let our people hear directly from customers. We videotaped interviews with customers and played excerpts. One big customer said, "We trust many of your competitors implicitly. We sample their deliveries. We open *all* Levi's deliveries." Another said, "Your lead times are the worst. If you weren't Levi's, you'd be gone." It was powerful. I wish we had done more of it.[41]

Such initiative, if sincere and credible, establishes a shared mission and the need for major transformations. It can channel energies to bring about both change and creative endeavors.

Establishing a "culture of dissent" can be another effective means of questioning the status quo and serving as a spur toward creativity. Here norms are established whereby dissenters can openly question a superior's perspective without fear of retaliation or retribution.

Closely related to the culture of dissent is the fostering of a culture that encourages risk taking. "If you're not making mistakes, you're not taking risks, and that means you're not going anywhere," claimed John Holt, coauthor of *Celebrate Your Mistakes*.[42] "The key is to make errors faster than the competition, so you have more chances to learn and win."

Companies that cultivate cultures of experimentation and curiosity make sure that *failure* is not, in essence, an obscene word. They encourage mistakes as a key part of their competitive advantage. It has been said that innovation has a great paradox: Success–that is, true breakthroughs–usually come through failure. The following are some approaches to encourage risk taking and learning from mistakes in an organization:[43]

- ***Formalize forums for failure.*** To keep failures and the important lessons that they offer from getting swept under the rug, carve out time for reflection. GE formalized the sharing of lessons from failure by bringing together managers whose "Imagination Breakthrough" efforts were put on the shelf.
- ***Move the goalposts.*** Innovation requires flexibility in meeting goals, since early predictions are often little more than educated guesses. Intuit's Scott Cook even goes so far as to suggest that teams developing new products ignore forecasts in the early days. "For every one of our failures, we had spreadsheets that looked awesome," he claims.
- ***Bring in outsiders.*** Outsiders can help neutralize the emotions and biases that prop up a flop. Customers can be the most valuable. After its DNA chip failed, Corning brought pharmaceutical companies in early to test its new drug-discovery technology, Epic.
- ***Prove yourself wrong, not right.*** Development teams tend to look for supporting, rather than countervailing, evidence. "You have to reframe what you're seeking in the early days," says Innosight's Scott Anthony. "You're not really seeking proof that you have the right answer. It's more about testing to prove yourself wrong."[44]

Finally, failure can play an important and positive role in one's professional development. Former Utah Governor Scott Matheson had strong views on the benefits of failure.

> You have to suffer failures occasionally in order to have successes. You've got to back up risk-takers in order to encourage people to try out new ideas that might succeed. . . . I never had much patience with the "play it safe" manager who attempted to minimize failures. Those people rarely have successes.[45]

The Attributes of Superbosses

Research on the most effective strategic leaders has identified key behaviors or "people strategies" that the most successful leaders use to build high performance organizations. These superbosses not only build strong firms but also help those around them accomplish more than they ever thought possible. How do they do it? First, they employ unconventional hiring. They strive to surround themselves with unusually gifted people. They have no desire to be the smartest person in the room. Instead, Lorne Michaels, the producer of Saturday Night Live, reflected the mindset of a superboss when he said, "If you look around the room and think, 'God, these people are amazing,' then you're probably in the right room." To identify and attract the most gifted people, these superbosses follow some simple rules:[46]

- **Focus on intelligence, creativity, and flexibility:** These leaders don't look to hire the best person for a specific task or role. They look for smart, flexible employees who can learn quickly and excel in different roles. In the words of one of his former subordinates, Norman Brinker, an innovator in the casual-dining market, "wasn't a fan of hiring people to play first base; he just wanted to hire a good baseball player."

- **Find unlikely winners:** Great leaders don't hire simply on the pedigree of one's degree or credentials. Instead, they look for people with something special and support them as they build the necessary skills to rise in the management ranks. In doing so, these superbosses are open to female and minority candidates. For example, Tommy Frist, the CEO of HCA a healthcare firm, was known to identify physical therapists or nurses that seemed to have something special and bring them into management ranks.
- **Look for novel ways to get to know employees:** Strong leaders often discard with typical interviews, and instead, observe employees in natural settings or ask them quirky questions. For example, real estate developer Bill Sanders would take both managers from his firm and potential employees up a hike on a 7,000 foot mountain on his ranch and observe how they interacted and handled the challenge of the hike. Managers would then share their impressions and decide who to hire. Designer Ralph Lauren used quirky questions to get insight on potential employees. For example, he would ask them to discuss why they chose what they wore to the interview to get a sense of how they saw themselves and how they defined and created a style.
- **Adapt the organization to fit the talent:** Superbosses look for the best way to use the talent around them rather than require that people fit into established roles. For example, iconic football coach Bill Walsh, faced a challenge when his starting quarterback was injured. The backup quarterback had a weak but accurate arm. To best use his talents, Walsh crafted a new offensive plan that emphasized quick, short passes, an offense that would become his famed West Coast offense that he used to win three Super Bowls.

Once in the firm, superbosses also figure out how to develop employees. To do so, they:

- **Set high expectations:** Superbosses are often seen as highly demanding. They set high expectations for those around them, but they also instill a sense of purpose and confidence in the team. One former employee of advertising executive Jay Chiat commented "Jay left something in people that made it hard to go back to being ordinary."
- **Help employees become a master:** Strong leaders create a balance in giving autonomy to employees while providing the mentoring needed to build skills. They trust their people to execute the firm's strategy and give them the opportunity to struggle and even fail. But they also look for opportunities to mentor. Tommy Frist, the HCA CEO, was also a licensed pilot. He would fly individual employees on his team to meetings in his private plane. As he flew the plane, Frist would strike up a conversation with the employee and look for opportunities to share wisdom that he had developed with the employee. As a skilled craftsman would do, these bosses give their apprentices plenty of experience doing their job, but they also provide a great deal of advice, and even work hand-in-hand with their apprentices on complex tasks that are new to employees.
- **Encourage continual growth:** Effective leaders look to give new challenges to their most promising employees. They don't rely solely on traditional promotion paths. They craft new roles and new paths to continually stretch their top performers. For example, Larry Ellison, CEO at Oracle, regularly looks to push his people into new roles. As one employee said, "One thing Oracle was incredibly good at was on a continual basis throwing new responsibility at people."
- **Maintain connection with their people:** As their top people rise in the firm and even after they leave the firm, strong leaders maintain relationships and continue to offer mentoring and a willingness to leverage their personal networks for the benefit of

their apprentices. For example, when former employees of Jay Chiat called on him when they faced new challenges or started new jobs, he would typically call back within hours and freely offer his advice. These connections often serve as opportunities to exploit new business relationships, such as strategic alliances. It also raises the opportunities for the former employees to build new skills and return to the superbosses' firm in new roles.

In attracting the best talent and relentlessly looking to build their skills, the most successful managers regularly expand the human and social capital around them. As their followers mimic this pattern of behavior, the firm is able to build a dynamic and sustainable business model.

CREATING AN ETHICAL ORGANIZATION

LO 11-5

Describe the leader's role in establishing an ethical organization.

Ethics may be defined as a system of right and wrong.[47] Ethics assists individuals in deciding when an act is moral or immoral, socially desirable or not. The sources for an individual's ethics include religious beliefs, national and ethnic heritage, family practices, community standards, educational experiences, and friends and neighbors. Business ethics is the application of ethical standards to commercial enterprise.

ethics
a system of right and wrong that assists individuals in deciding when an act is moral or immoral and/or socially desirable or not.

Individual Ethics versus Organizational Ethics

Many leaders think of ethics as a question of personal scruples, a confidential matter between employees and their consciences. Such leaders are quick to describe any wrongdoing as an isolated incident, the work of a rogue employee. They assume the company should not bear any responsibility for individual misdeeds. In their view, ethics has nothing to do with leadership.

Ethics has everything to do with leadership. Seldom does the character flaw of a lone actor completely explain corporate misconduct. Instead, unethical business practices typically involve the tacit, if not explicit, cooperation of others and reflect the values, attitudes, and behavior patterns that define an organization's operating culture. Ethics is as much an organizational as a personal issue. Leaders who fail to provide proper leadership to institute proper systems and controls that facilitate ethical conduct share responsibility with those who conceive, execute, and knowingly benefit from corporate misdeeds.[48]

The **ethical orientation** of a leader is a key factor in promoting ethical behavior. Ethical leaders must take personal, ethical responsibility for their actions and decision making. Leaders who exhibit high ethical standards become role models for others and raise an organization's overall level of ethical behavior. Ethical behavior must start with the leader before the employees can be expected to perform accordingly.

ethical orientation
the practices that firms use to promote an ethical business culture, including ethical role models, corporate credos and codes of conduct, ethically based reward and evaluation systems, and consistently enforced ethical policies and procedures.

There has been a growing interest in corporate ethical performance. Some reasons for this trend may be the increasing lack of confidence regarding corporate activities, the growing emphasis on quality-of-life issues, and a spate of recent corporate scandals. Without a strong ethical culture, the chance of ethical crises occurring is enhanced. Ethical crises can be very expensive—both in terms of financial costs and in the erosion of human capital and overall firm reputation. Merely adhering to the minimum regulatory standards may not be enough to remain competitive in a world that is becoming more socially conscious. Strategy Spotlight 11.4 highlights potential ethical problems at utility companies that were trying to capitalize on consumers' desire to participate in efforts to curb global warming.

The past two decades have been characterized by numerous examples of unethical and illegal behavior by many top-level corporate executives. These include executives of firms such as VW, Wells Fargo, Samsung, and Nissan who were all forced to resign and are facing (or have been convicted of) criminal charges. One of the most glaring examples is Elizabeth

11.4 STRATEGY SPOTLIGHT — ENVIRONMENTAL SUSTAINABILITY, ETHICS

GREEN ENERGY: REAL OR JUST A MARKETING PLOY?

Many consumers want to "go green" and are looking for opportunities to do so. Utility companies that provide heat and electricity are one of the most obvious places to turn, because they often use fossil fuels that could be saved through energy conservation or replaced by using alternative energy sources. In fact, some consumers are willing to pay a premium to contribute to environmental sustainability efforts if paying a little more will help curb global warming. Knowing this, many power companies in the United States have developed alternative energy programs and appealed to customers to help pay for them.

Unfortunately, many of the power companies that are offering eco-friendly options are falling short on delivering on them. Some utilities have simply gotten off to a slow start or found it difficult to profitably offer alternative power. Others, however, are suspected of committing a new type of fraud—"greenwashing." This refers to companies that make unsubstantiated claims about how environmentally friendly their products or services really are. In the case of many power companies, their claims of "green power" are empty promises. Instead of actually generating additional renewable energy, most of the premiums are going for marketing costs. "They are preying on people's goodwill," says Stephen Smith, executive director of the Southern Alliance for Clean Energy, an advocacy group in Knoxville, Tennessee.

Consider what two power companies offered and how the money was actually spent:

- Duke Power of Indiana created a program called "Go-Green Power." Customers were told that they could pay a green-energy premium and a specific amount of electricity would be obtained from renewable sources. What actually happened? Less than 18 percent of voluntary customer contributions in one year went to renewable energy development.
- Alliant Energy of Iowa established a program dubbed "Second Nature." Customers were told that they would "support the growth of earth-friendly 'green power' created by wind and biomass." What actually happened? More than 56 percent of expenditures went to marketing and administrative costs, not green-energy development.

Sources: Elgin, B., and D. Holden. 2008. Green power: Buyers beware. *BusinessWeek*, September 29: 68–70; *www.cleanenergy.org*; *duke-energy.com*; and *alliantenergy.com*.

Holmes, the founder and CEO of Theranos. Holmes claimed that the firm had a technology that would allow it to do a battery of blood tests using a single drop of blood. She further claimed the technology had been used in the battlefield by the U.S. military, was about to be rolled out in a major grocery chain, and had generated $100 million in sales for the firm. The value of the firm skyrocketed to $9 billion, but it all crashed down when all of Holmes' claims were found to be overstated or outright lies. Theranos went out of business. Holmes was charged with wire fraud and banned from being an officer in a public corporation for 10 years.[49]

The ethical organization is characterized by a conception of ethical values and integrity as a driving force of the enterprise.[50] Ethical values shape the search for opportunities, the design of organizational systems, and the decision-making process used by individuals and groups. They provide a common frame of reference that serves as a unifying force across different functions, lines of business, and employee groups. Organizational ethics helps to define what a company is and what it stands for.

There are many potential benefits of an ethical organization, but they are often indirect. Research has found somewhat inconsistent results concerning the overall relationship between ethical performance and measures of financial performance.[51] However, positive relationships have generally been found between ethical performance and strong organizational culture, increased employee efforts, lower turnover, higher organizational commitment, and enhanced social responsibility.

The advantages of a strong ethical orientation can have a positive effect on employee commitment and motivation to excel. This is particularly important in today's knowledge-intensive organizations, where human capital is critical in creating value and competitive advantages. Positive, constructive relationships among individuals (i.e., social capital) are vital in leveraging human capital and other resources in an organization. Drawing on the concept of stakeholder management, an ethically sound organization can also strengthen its bonds among its suppliers, customers, and governmental agencies.

LO 11-6

Explain the difference between integrity-based and compliance-based approaches to organizational ethics.

Integrity-Based versus Compliance-Based Approaches to Organizational Ethics

Before discussing the key elements of an ethical organization, one must understand the links between organizational integrity and the personal integrity of an organization's members.[52] There cannot be high-integrity organizations without high-integrity individuals. However, individual integrity is rarely self-sustaining. Even good people can lose their bearings when faced with pressures, temptations, and heightened performance expectations in the absence of organizational support systems and ethical boundaries. Organizational integrity rests on a concept of purpose, responsibility, and ideals for an organization as a whole. An important responsibility of leadership is to create this ethical framework and develop the organizational capabilities to make it operational.[53]

Lynn Paine, an ethics scholar at Harvard, identifies two approaches: the compliance-based approach and the integrity-based approach. (See Exhibit 11.5 for a comparison of compliance-based and integrity-based strategies.) Faced with the prospect of litigation, several organizations reactively implement **compliance-based ethics programs.** Such programs are typically designed by a corporate counsel with the goal of preventing, detecting, and punishing legal violations. But being ethical is much more than being legal, and an integrity-based approach addresses the issue of ethics in a more comprehensive manner.

compliance-based ethics programs programs for building ethical organizations that have the goal of preventing, detecting, and punishing legal violations.

integrity-based ethics programs programs for building ethical organizations that combine a concern for law with an emphasis on managerial responsibility for ethical behavior, including (1) enabling ethical conduct; (2) examining the organization's and members' core guiding values, thoughts, and actions; and (3) defining the responsibilities and aspirations that constitute an organization's ethical compass.

An **integrity-based ethics program** combines a concern for law with an emphasis on managerial responsibility for ethical behavior. It is broader, deeper, and more demanding than a legal compliance initiative. It is broader in that it seeks to enable responsible conduct. It is deeper in that it cuts to the ethos and operating systems of an organization and its members—their core guiding values, thoughts, and actions. It is more demanding because it requires an active effort to define the responsibilities that constitute an organization's ethical compass. Most importantly, organizational ethics is seen as the responsibility of management.

A corporate counsel may play a role in designing and implementing integrity strategies, but it is managers at all levels and across all functions who are involved in the process. Once integrated into the day-to-day operations, such strategies can prevent damaging ethical lapses, while tapping into powerful human impulses for moral thought and action. Ethics

EXHIBIT 11.5
Approaches to Ethics Management

Characteristics	Approach	Actions
Ethos	Compliance-based Integrity-based	Conformity with externally imposed standards Self-governance according to chosen standards
Objective	Compliance-based Integrity-based	Prevent criminal misconduct Enable responsible conduct
Leadership	Compliance-based Integrity-based	Driven by legal office Driven by management, with input from functional staff
Methods	Compliance-based Integrity-based	Reduced discretion, training, controls, audits, and penalties Education, leadership, accountability, decision processes, auditing, and penalties
Behavioral Assumptions	Compliance-based Integrity-based	Individualistic, self-interested actors Social actors, guided by a combination of self-interest, ideals, values, and social expectations

becomes the governing ethos of an organization and not burdensome constraints. Here is an example of an organization that goes beyond mere compliance to laws in building an ethical organization:

> In teaching ethics to its employees, Texas Instruments, the $16 billion chip and electronics manufacturer, asks them to run an issue through the following steps: Is it legal? Is it consistent with the company's stated values? Will the employee feel bad doing it? What will the public think if the action is reported in the press? Does the employee think it is wrong? If the employees are not sure of the ethicality of the issue, they are encouraged to ask someone until they are clear about it. In the process, employees can approach high-level personnel and even the company's lawyers. At TI, the question of ethics goes much beyond merely being legal. It is no surprise that this company is a benchmark for corporate ethics and has been honored as one of the World's Most Ethical Companies by the Ethisphere Institute every year since 2007.[54]

LO 11-7

Identify several key elements that organizations must have to become ethical organizations.

Compliance-based approaches are externally motivated—that is, based on the fear of punishment for doing something unlawful. On the other hand, integrity-based approaches are driven by a personal and organizational commitment to ethical behavior.

A firm must have several key elements to become a highly ethical organization:

- Role models.
- Corporate credos and codes of conduct.
- Reward and evaluation systems.
- Policies and procedures.

These elements are highly interrelated. Reward structures and policies will be useless if leaders are not sound role models. That is, leaders who implicitly say, "Do as I say, not as I do," will quickly have their credibility eroded and such actions will sabotage other elements that are essential to building an ethical organization.

Role Models

For good or for bad, leaders are role models in their organizations. Perhaps few executives can share an experience that better illustrates this than Linda Hudson, former president of General Dynamics.[55] Right after she was promoted to become the firm's first female president, she went to Nordstrom and bought some new suits to wear to work. A lady at the store showed her how to tie a scarf in a very unique way. The day after she wore it to work, guess what: No fewer than a dozen women in the organization were wearing scarves tied exactly the same way. She realized that people were watching everything she did and said. She became more aware of the example she offered, the tone she set for the organization, and the way she carried herself. As a leader, she was the role model for many others in the organization, especially for other female managers.

Clearly, leaders must "walk the talk"; they must be consistent in their words and deeds. The values as well as the character of leaders become transparent to an organization's employees through their behaviors. When leaders do not believe in the ethical standards that they are trying to inspire, they will not be effective as good role models. Being an effective leader often includes taking responsibility for ethical lapses within the organization—even though the executives themselves are not directly involved. Consider the actions of the senior executive team at AES, an $11 billion energy company. Several employees of the firm lied to the EPA about water quality at an AES-owned water treatment plant in Oklahoma. Although senior managers had no direct role in the scandal, they agreed to take pay cuts because they saw these employee actions as an indication that they hadn't done enough to communicate AES values.

Such action enhances the loyalty and commitment of employees throughout the organization. By sharing responsibility for misdeeds, top executives—through their highly visible action—make it clear that responsibility and penalties for ethical lapses go well beyond the "guilty" parties. Such courageous behavior by leaders helps to strengthen an organization's ethical environment.

Corporate Credos and Codes of Conduct

Corporate credos and codes of conduct are mechanisms that provide statements of norms and beliefs as well as guidelines for decision making. They provide employees with a clear understanding of the organization's policies and ethical position. Such guidelines also provide the basis for employees to refuse to commit unethical acts and help to make them aware of issues before they are faced with the situation. For such codes to be truly effective, organization members must be aware of them and what behavioral guidelines they contain.[56]

Large corporations are not the only ones to develop and use codes of conduct. For example, the Baylor College of Medicine, in Houston, has a short code of ethics that sets out basic rules. The code instructs all employees to follow Baylor's Mission Statement, Compliance Program, and Conflict of Interest policy. The code includes basic guidelines for how employees should handle business conduct; financial and medical records; confidentiality; Baylor property; the workplace environment; and contact with the government.[57]

Reward and Evaluation Systems

It is entirely possible for a highly ethical leader to preside over an organization that commits several unethical acts. How? A flaw in the organization's reward structure may inadvertently cause individuals to act in an inappropriate manner if rewards are seen as being distributed on the basis of outcomes rather than the means by which goals and objectives are achieved.[58]

Generally speaking, unethical (or illegal) behaviors are also more likely to take place when competition is intense. Some researchers have called this the "dark side of competition." Consider a couple of examples:[59]

- Competition among educational institutions for the best students is becoming stiffer. The Dean of the Fox School of Business was forced to resign after an investigation found that the school had falsified student data for its online programs in order to improve the ranking of its programs in the *U.S. News & World Report*'s annual listing of top b-schools. The school also settled a class action law suit with former students for $5 million to compensate for the devaluation of their degrees as a result of the scandals.[60]
- A study of 11,000 New York vehicle emission test facilities found that companies with a greater number of local competitors passed cars with considerably high emission rates and lost customers when they failed to pass the tests. The authors of the study concluded, "In contexts when pricing is restricted, firms use illicit quality as a business strategy."

Many companies have developed reward and evaluation systems that evaluate whether a manager is acting in an ethical manner. For example, Raytheon, a $27 billion defense contractor, incorporated the following items in its "Leadership Assessment Instrument":[61]

- Maintains unequivocal commitment to honesty, truth, and ethics in every facet of behavior.
- Conforms with the letter and intent of company policies while working to affect any necessary policy changes.

- Actions are consistent with words; follows through on commitments; readily admits mistakes.
- Is trusted and inspires others to be trusted.

As noted by Dan Burnham, Raytheon's former CEO: "What do we look for in a leadership candidate with respect to integrity? What we're really looking for are people who have developed an inner gyroscope of ethical principles. We look for people for whom ethical thinking is part of what they do—no different from 'strategic thinking' or 'tactical thinking.'"[62]

Policies and Procedures

Many situations that a firm faces have regular, identifiable patterns. Leaders tend to handle such routine by establishing a policy or procedure to be followed that can be applied uniformly to each occurrence. Such guidelines can be useful in specifying the proper relationships with a firm's customers and suppliers. For example, Levi Strauss has developed stringent global sourcing guidelines, and Chemical Bank (part of JPMorgan Chase Bank) has a policy of forbidding any review that would determine if suppliers are Chemical customers when the bank awards contracts.

Carefully developed policies and procedures guide behavior so that all employees will be encouraged to behave in an ethical manner. However, they must be reinforced with effective communication, enforcement, and monitoring, as well as sound corporate governance practices. In addition, the Sarbanes-Oxley Act of 2002 provides considerable legal protection to employees of publicly traded companies who report unethical or illegal practices. Provisions in the act:[63]

- Make it unlawful to "discharge, demote, suspend, threaten, harass, or in any manner discriminate against 'a whistleblower.'"
- Establish criminal penalties of up to 10 years in jail for executives who retaliate against whistleblowers.
- Require board audit committees to establish procedures for hearing whistleblower complaints.
- Allow the secretary of labor to order a company to rehire a terminated whistleblower with no court hearings whatsoever.
- Give a whistleblower the right to a jury trial, bypassing months or years of cumbersome administrative hearings.

ISSUE FOR DEBATE

Ben & Jerry's is an iconic producer of ice cream. Started by entrepreneurs Ben Cohen and Jerry Greenfield in 1978, the firm has always emphasized a business mission that goes beyond profit. The company has used a bakery that employs individuals who have faced employment barriers, suppliers who comply with fair trade policies, dairy farmers who emphasize sustainability, and ranches that produce free-range eggs. The firm also donates 7.5 percent of its pre-tax profits to a foundation that supports social initiatives. The firm has also used its brands to promote social causes, such as temporarily changing its Chocolate Chip Cookie Dough flavor to "I Dough, I Dough" to celebrate the Supreme Court decision guaranteeing the right for same-sex partners to marry.

This focus is especially notable since the firm is owned by Unilever, a global consumer products company. When Unilever purchased Ben & Jerry's in 2000, they promised to allow the firm to have its own CEO and board of directors. This is the only business in the Unilever portfolio that has such independent governance, but the firm saw it as important in maintaining the uniqueness of Ben & Jerry's.

Matthew McCarthy, who was appointed CEO of Ben & Jerry's in 2018, promised to reinforce the social activism orientation of the firm. He has a history of championing social causes within Unilever. For example, he led Unilever to move to 100 percent cage-free eggs in its Hellmann's mayonnaise. He also led Unilever's launch of Growing Roots, its first organic snack brand in the United States.

At Ben & Jerry's, McCarthy pledged to "double its social impact." In his early tenure, the firm sent a clear message that they were willing to take a clear stance on the U.S. political environment, when it launched "Pecan Resist" ice cream just before the 2018 elections. The firm stated they supported those "resisting the President's attack on our values, humanity, and environment." While he understands that this type of stance risks alienating conservative customers, McCarthy asserted it was important to stand for fighting racism and work for environmental and social justice. For example, McCarthy asserted the firm would continue to support the Black Lives Matter movement. Looking back to the mission laid out by the firm's founders, McCarthy states activism is "in the DNA of Ben & Jerry's, and why I'm excited to be part of the business."

Discussion Questions

1. Is it smart business for Ben & Jerry's to take a strong political stance, as Ben & Jerry's did with its Pecan Resist ice cream?
2. Is it important for companies to be socially active? If so, should they also be politically active?
3. If you were a competitor of Ben & Jerry's, how would you respond to its social and political activism? Would you try to match their actions? Would you take a different stance to differentiate yourself from Ben & Jerry's? Or would you avoid political issues all together?

Sources: Pfeffer, J. 2016. Why deception is probably the single most important leadership skill. *fortune.com,* June 2: np; and, Kerr, J. 2014. The trickle-down effect of deceptive leadership. *inc.com,* November 12: np.

Reflecting on Career Implications . . .

This chapter examines the skills and activities associated with effective organizational leadership. The following points challenge you to observe and learn from leaders of firms in which you work and outline issues to consider as you develop your own leadership skills.

- **Strategic Leadership:** The chapter identifies three interdependent activities that are central to strategic leadership; namely, setting direction, designing the organization, and nurturing a culture dedicated to excellence and ethical behavior. Both during your life as a student and in organizations at which you have worked, you have often assumed leadership positions. To what extent have you consciously and successfully engaged in each of these activities? Observe the leaders in your organization and assess to what extent you can learn from them the qualities of strategic leadership that you can use to advance your own career.
- **Power:** Identify the sources of power used by your superior at work. How do this person's primary source of power and the way he or she uses it affect your own creativity, morale, and willingness to stay with the organization? In addition, identify approaches you will use to enhance your power as you move up your career ladder. Explain why you chose these approaches.
- **Emotional Intelligence:** The chapter identifies the five components of emotional intelligence (self-awareness, self-regulation, motivation, empathy, and social skills). How do you rate yourself on each of these components? What steps can you take to improve your emotional intelligence and achieve greater career success?
- **Creating an Ethical Organization:** Identify an ethical dilemma that you personally faced in the course of your work. How did you respond to it? Was your response compliance-based, integrity-based, or even unethical? If your behavior was compliance-based, speculate on how it would have been different if it were integrity-based. What have you learned from your experience that would make you a more ethical leader in the future?

key points

LO 11-1 The three key interdependent activities in which all successful leaders must be continually engaged.

- Setting a direction: Managers need to develop a clear vision for the firm, including a clear future direction, a framework for the organization's mission and goals, and a clear communication strategy to share this vision.
- Designing the organization: Managers also need to build structures, teams, systems, and organizational processes to facilitate the implementation of their vision and strategies.
- Nurturing a culture dedicated to excellence and ethical behavior: Leaders play a key role in changing, developing, and sustaining an organization's culture.

LO 11-2 Two elements of effective leadership: overcoming barriers to change and using power effectively.

- To overcome barriers to change, leaders need to address issues that trigger organizational inertia, such as:
  - People's vested interest in the status quo.
  - Systemic barriers, such as established structures and information flows.
  - Behavioral barriers, such as biases, norms, or superstitions that have built up in the firm.
  - Political barriers.
  - Personal time constraints.
- To use power effectively, leaders need to leverage organizational and personal power bases.
  - Organizational power bases include legitimate, reward, coercive, and information power
  - Personal power bases include referent and expert power.

LO 11-3 The crucial role of emotional intelligence (EI) in successful leadership, as well as its potential drawbacks.

- Emotional intelligence is an individual's capacity for recognizing his or her own emotions and those of others.
- It has five components:
  1. Self-awareness
  2. Self-regulation
  3. Empathy
  4. Social skill
  5. Motivation
- However, high levels of EI can limit a leader's willingness to make tough decisions, result in leaders being seen as judgmental, becoming too passionate about causes, and lead to perceptions that the leader is too involved in decisions and micromanaging subordinates.

LO 11-4 The importance of creating a learning organization.

- Learning organizations are capable of adapting to change, fostering creativity, and succeeding in highly competitive markets.
- There are five key elements of a learning organization:
  1. Inspiring and motivating people with a mission or purpose.
  2. Empowering employees at all levels.
  3. Accumulating and sharing internal knowledge.
  4. Gathering and integrating external information.
  5. Challenging the status quo and enabling creativity.

LO 11-5 The leader's role in establishing an ethical organization.

- Managers should strive to provide proper leadership to institute systems and controls that facilitate ethical conduct.

LO 11-6 The difference between integrity-based and compliance-based approaches to organizational ethics.

- Compliance-based ethics programs are designed to prevent, detect, and punish ethical violations.
- Integrity-based ethics programs emphasize managerial responsibility for ethical behavior, including:
  - Enabling ethical conduct.
  - Examining the organization's and member's core guiding values.
  - Defining the responsibilities and aspirations that constitute an organization's ethical compass.

LO 11-7 Several key elements that organizations must have to become ethical organizations.

- Ethical orientations are embedded in the practices the firm uses to promote an ethical business culture, including ethical role models, corporate credos and codes of conduct, ethically-based reward and evaluation systems, and consistently enforced ethical policies and procedures.

SUMMARY REVIEW QUESTIONS

1. Three key activities—setting a direction, designing the organization, and nurturing a culture and ethics—are all part of what effective leaders do on a regular basis. Explain how these three activities are interrelated.
2. Define *emotional intelligence* (EI). What are the key elements of EI? Why is EI so important to successful strategic leadership? Address potential "downsides."
3. The knowledge a firm possesses can be a source of competitive advantage. Describe ways that a firm can continuously learn to maintain its competitive position.
4. How can the five central elements of "learning organizations" be incorporated into global companies?

5. What are the benefits to firms and their shareholders of conducting business in an ethical manner?
6. Firms that fail to behave in an ethical manner can incur high costs. What are these costs, and what is their source?
7. What are the most important differences between an "integrity organization" and a "compliance organization" in a firm's approach to organizational ethics?
8. What are some of the important mechanisms for promoting ethics in a firm?

key terms

leadership 332
barriers to change 336
vested interest in the status quo 337
systemic barriers 337
behavioral barriers 337
political barriers 337
personal time constraints 337
power 337
organizational bases of power 338
personal bases of power 338
emotional intelligence (EI) 340
learning organizations 342
benchmarking 344
competitive benchmarking 344
functional benchmarking 344
ethics • • •
ethical orientation 347
compliance-based ethics programs 349
integrity-based ethics programs 349

EXPERIENTIAL EXERCISES AND APPLICATION QUESTIONS

1. In the Issue for Debate, we discussed the socially active stance of Ben & Jerry's. Identify a company that is known for its conservative stances and evaluate whether stakeholders–including customers, governmental entities, and community activists–have responded similarly or differently to each of the firm's activism efforts.
2. Select two well-known business leaders–one you admire and one you do not. Evaluate each of them on the five characteristics of emotional intelligence in the following table.
3. Identify two CEOs whose leadership you admire. What is it about their skills, attributes, and effective use of power that causes you to admire them?
4. Founders have an important role in developing their organization's culture and values. At times, their influence persists for many years. Identify and describe two organizations in which the cultures and values established by the founder(s) continue to flourish. You may find research on the Internet helpful in answering this question.
5. Some leaders place a great emphasis on developing superior human capital. In what ways does this help a firm to develop and sustain competitive advantages?
6. In this chapter we discussed the five elements of a "learning organization." Select a firm with which you are familiar and discuss whether or not it epitomizes some (or all) of these elements.

ETHICS QUESTIONS

1. Sometimes organizations must go outside the firm to hire talent, thus bypassing employees already working for the firm. Are there conditions under which this might raise ethical considerations?
2. Ethical crises can occur in virtually any organization. Describe some of the systems, procedures, and processes that can help to prevent such crises.

Emotional Intelligence Characteristics	Admired Leader	Leader Not Admired
Self-awareness		
Self-regulation		
Motivation		
Empathy		
Social skills		

REFERENCES

1. Chozik, A, & Rich, M. 2018. The rise and fall of Carlos Ghosn. nytimes. com. December 30: np; McGrath, R. 2018. What happens when CEOs have too much power. cnn.com. November 29: np; and Khalaf, R. 2018. Le cost killer: The relentless drive of Carlos Ghosn. Wanted Online MMXIX.
2. Charan, R., and G. Colvin. 1999. Why CEOs fail: It's rarely for lack of smarts or vision. Most unsuccessful CEOs stumble because of one simple, fatal shortcoming. *Fortune,* June 21: 68-78.
3. Yukl, G. 2008. How leaders influence organizational effectiveness. *Leadership Quarterly,* 19(6): 708-722.
4. These three activities and our discussion draw from Kotter, J. P. 1990. What leaders really do. *Harvard Business Review,* 68(3): 103-111; Pearson, A. E. 1990. Six basics for general managers. *Harvard Business Review,* 67(4): 94-101; and Covey, S. R. 1996. Three roles of the leader in the new paradigm. In Hesselbein, F., Goldsmith, M., & Beckhard, R. (Eds.), *The leader of the future:* 149-160. San Francisco: Jossey-Bass. Some of the discussion of each of the three leadership activity concepts draws on Dess, G. G. & Miller, A. 1993. *Strategic management:* 320-325. New York: McGraw-Hill.
5. García-Morales, V. J., Lloréns-Montes, F. J., & Verdú-Jover, A. J. 2008. The effects of transformational leadership on organizational performance through knowledge and innovation. *British Journal of Management,* 19(4): 299-319.
6. Martin, R. 2010. The execution trap. *Harvard Business Review,* 88(7/8): 64-71.
7. Collins, J. 1997. What Comes Next? Mansueto Ventures LLC, October: 34-45.
8. Hsieh, T. 2010. Zappos's CEO on going to extremes for customers. *Harvard Business Review,* 88(7/8): 41-44.
9. Chesky, B. 2013. Don't f*ck up the culture. Medium.com (A Medium Corporation), October 21.
10. Anonymous. 2006. Looking out for number one. *BusinessWeek,* October 30: 66.
11. Schaffer, R. H. 2010. Mistakes leaders keep making. *Harvard Business Review,* 88(9): 86-91.
12. For insightful perspectives on escalation, refer to Brockner, J. 1992. The escalation of commitment to a failing course of action. *Academy of Management Review,* 17(1): 39-61; and Staw, B. M. 1976. Knee-deep in the big muddy: A study of commitment to a chosen course of action. *Organizational Behavior and Human Decision Processes,* 16: 27-44. The discussion of systemic, behavioral, and political barriers draws on Lorange, P. & Murphy, D. 1984. Considerations in implementing strategic control. *Journal of Business Strategy;* 5: 27-35. In a similar vein, Noel M. Tichy has addressed three types of resistance to change in the context of General Electric: technical resistance, political resistance, and cultural resistance. See Tichy, N. M. 1993. Revolutionalize your company. *Fortune,* December 13: 114-118. Examples draw from O'Reilly, B. 1997. The secrets of America's most admired corporations: New ideas and new products. *Fortune,* March 3: 60-64.
13. Norton, S. 2018. Tyson CTO brings silicon valley to Northwest Arkansas. wsj.com. April 11: np.
14. Rockoff, J. 2018. Pfizer CEO Read to step aside at year's end. wsj.com. October 1: np.
15. This section draws on Champoux, J. E. 2000. *Organizational behavior: Essential tenets for a new millennium.* London: South-Western; and The mature use of power in organizations. 2003. *RHR International-Executive Insights,* May 29, *12.19.168.197/execinsights/8-3.htm.*
16. An insightful perspective on the role of power and politics in organizations is provided in Ciampa, K. 2005. Almost ready: How leaders move up. *Harvard Business Review,* 83(1): 46-53.
17. Pfeffer, J. 2010. Power play. *Harvard Business Review,* 88(7/8): 84-92.
18. Westphal, J. D., & Graebner, M. E. 2010. A matter of appearances: How corporate leaders manage the impressions of financial analysts about the conduct of their boards. *Academy of Management Journal,* 53(4): 15-44.
19. A discussion of the importance of persuasion in bringing about change can be found in Garvin, D. A. & Roberto, M. A. 2005. Change through persuasion. *Harvard Business Review,* 83(4): 104-113.
20. Lorsch, J. W. & Tierney, T. J. 2002. *Aligning the stars: How to succeed when professionals drive results.* Boston: Harvard Business School Press.
21. Some consider EI to be a "trait," that is, an attribute that is stable over time. However, many authors, including Daniel Goleman, have argued that it can be developed through motivation, extended practice, and feedback. For example, in D. Goleman, 1998, What makes a leader? *Harvard Business Review,* 76(5): 97, Goleman addresses this issue in a sidebar: "Can emotional intelligence be learned?"
22. For a review of this literature, see Daft, R. 1999. *Leadership: Theory and practice.* Fort Worth, TX: Dryden Press.
23. EI has its roots in the concept of "social intelligence" that was first identified by E. L. Thorndike in 1920 (Intelligence and its uses. *Harper's Magazine,* 140: 227-235). Psychologists have been uncovering other intelligences for some time now and have grouped them into such clusters as abstract intelligence (the ability to understand and manipulate verbal and mathematical symbols), concrete intelligence (the ability to understand and manipulate objects), and social intelligence (the ability to understand and relate to people). See Ruisel, I. 1992. Social intelligence: Conception and methodological problems. *Studia Psychologica,* 34(4-5): 281-296. Refer to *trochim.human.cornell.edu/gallery.*
24. Joseph, D. & Newman, D. 2010. Emotional intelligence: An integrative meta-analysis and cascading model. *Journal of Applied Psychology,* 95(1): 54-78; Brusman, M. 2013. Leadership effectiveness through emotional intelligence. *workingresourcesblog.com,* September 18: np; and Bradberry, T. 2015. Why your boss lacks emotional intelligence. *forbes.com,* January 6: np.
25. Moss, S. A., Dowling, N., & Callanan, J. 2009. Towards an integrated model of leadership and self-regulation. *Leadership Quarterly,* 20(2): 162-176.
26. Muoio, A. 1998. Decisions, decisions. *fastcompany.com,* September 9: np.
27. This section draws upon Klemp. G. 2005. *Emotional intelligence and leadership: What really matters.* Cambria Consulting, Inc., *www.cambriaconsulting.com.*
28. Senge, P. M. 1990. The leader's new work: Building learning organizations. *Sloan Management Review,* 32(1): 7-23.
29. Bernoff, J. & Schandler, T. 2010. Empowered. *Harvard Business Review,* 88(7/8): 94-101.
30. Hannah, S. T. & Lester, P. B. 2009. A multilevel approach to building and

leading learning organizations. *Leadership Quarterly,* 20(1): 34-48.

31. For some guidance on how to effectively bring about change in organizations, refer to Wall, S. J. 2005. The protean organization: Learning to love change. *Organizational Dynamics,* 34(1): 37-46.
32. Covey, S. R. 1989. *The 7 Habits of Highly Effective People: Powerful Lessons in Personal Change.* New York: Simon & Schuster.
33. Melrose, K. 1995. *Making the Grass Greener on Your Side: A CEO's Journey to Leading by Serving.* San Francisco: Berrett-Koehler.
34. Tekleab, A. G., Sims, H. P., Jr., Yun, S., Tesluk, P. E., & Cox, J. 2008. Are we on the same page? Effects of self-awareness of empowering and transformational leadership. *Journal of Leadership & Organizational Studies,* 14(3): 185-201.
35. Helgesen, S. 1996. Leading from the grass roots. In Hesselbein et al., The *leader of the future:* 19-24. San Francisco: Jossey-Bass.
36. Bowen, D. E. & Lawler, E. E., III. 1995. Empowering service employees. *Sloan Management Review,* 37: 73-84.
37. Meyer, P. 1998 (January-February). So you want the president's job. *Business Horizons,* 41(1): 2-8.
38. The introductory discussion of benchmarking draws on Miller, A. 1998. *Strategic management:* 142-143. New York: McGraw-Hill.
39. Sedgwick, D. 2014. Ford and suppliers jointly benchmark competitors' vehicles. *automotivenews.com,* October 19: np.
40. Main, J. 1992. How to steal the best ideas around. *Fortune,* October 19: 102-106.
41. Sheff, D. 1996. Levi's changes everything. *Fast Company,* June-July: 65-74.
42. Holt, J. W. 1996. *Celebrate Your Mistakes: And 77 Other Risk-taking, Out-of-the-box Ideas from Our Best Companies.* New York: McGraw-Hill.
43. McGregor, J. 2006. How failure breeds success. *Bloomberg Businessweek,* July 10: 42-52.
44. McGregor, J. 2006. How failure breeds success. *Bloomberg Businessweek,* July 10.
45. Sitkin, S. 1992 (January 1). Learning through failure: The strategy of small losses. Research in Organizational Behavior, 14: 231-266.
46. Finkelstein, S. 2016. Managing yourself: Secrets of superbosses. *Harvard Business Review,* 94 (1/2): 104-107; Finkelstein, S. 2016. Three traits that will get you hired by the best bosses. bbc.com, May 5: np; McGregor, J. 2016. What makes a boss a 'Superboss.' washingtonpost.com, February 11: np; and Manciagli, D. 2016. 4 secrets of 'Superbosses.' bizjournals.com, September 28: np
47. This opening discussion draws upon Conley, J. H. 2000. Ethics in business. In Helms, M. M. (Ed.), *Encyclopedia of management* (4th ed.): 281-285. Farmington Hills, MI: Gale Group; Paine, L. S. 1994. Managing for organizational integrity. *Harvard Business Review,* 72(2): 106-117; and Carlson, D. S. & Perrewe, P. L. 1995. Institutionalization of organizational ethics through transformational leadership. *Journal of Business Ethics,* 14: 829-838.
48. Pinto, J., Leana, C. R., & Pil, F. K. 2008. Corrupt organizations or organizations of corrupt individuals? Two types of organization-level corruption. *Academy of Management Review,* 33(3): 685-709.
49. Anonymous. 2018. Theranos Bloodbath. *The Economist,* March 17: 64.
50. Soule, E. 2002. Managerial moral strategies—In search of a few good principles. *Academy of Management Review,* 27(1): 114-124.
51. Carlson & Perrewe, op. cit.
52. This discussion is based upon Paine, Managing for organizational integrity; Paine, L. S. 1997. *Cases in leadership, ethics, and organizational integrity: A Strategic approach.* Burr Ridge, IL: Irwin; and Fontrodona, J. 2002. Business ethics across the Atlantic. Business Ethics Direct, *www.ethicsa.org/BED_art_fontrodone.html.*
53. For more on operationalizing capabilities to sustain an ethical framework, see Largay, J. A., III, & Zhang, R. 2008. Do CEOs worry about being fired when making investment decisions? *Academy of Management Perspectives,* 22(1): 60-61.
54. See *www.ti.com/corp/docs/company/citizen/ethics/benchmark.shtml;* and *www.ti.com/corp/docs/company/citizen/ethics/quicktest.shtml.*
55. Bryant, A. 2011. *The corner office:* 91. New York: St. Martin's Griffin.
56. For an insightful, academic perspective on the impact of ethics codes on executive decision making, refer to Stevens, J. M., Steensma, H. K., Harrison, D. A., & Cochran, P. S. 2005. Symbolic or substantive document? The influence of ethics code on financial executives' decisions. *Strategic Management Journal,* 26(2): 181-195.
57. *media.bcm.edu/documents/2015/94/bcm-code-of-conduct-final-june-2015.pdf.*
58. For a study on the effects of goal setting on unethical behavior, read Schweitzer, M. E., Ordonez, L., & Douma, B. 2004. Goal setting as a motivator of unethical behavior. *Academy of Management Journal,* 47(3): 422-432.
59. Williams, R. 2012. How competition can encourage unethical business practices. *business.financialpost.com,* July 31: np.
60. Snyder, S. 2018. Temple pays more than $5 million to settle claims over false reporting by its business school. philly.com. December 21: np.
61. Fulmer, R. M. 2004. The challenge of ethical leadership. *Organizational Dynamics,* 33(3): 307-317.
62. Fulmer, R. M. 2004 (August). The challenge of ethical leadership. *Organizational Dynamics,* 33(3): 307-317.
63. *www.sarbanes-oxley.com.*

CHAPTER

12

Nico Muller Art/Shutterstock

Managing Innovation and Fostering Corporate Entrepreneurship

Learning Objectives

LO12-1 Understand the importance of implementing strategies and practices that foster innovation.

LO12-2 Identify the challenges and pitfalls of managing corporate innovation processes.

LO12-3 Explain how corporations use new venture teams, business incubators, and product champions to create an internal environment and culture that promote entrepreneurial development.

LO12-4 Explain how corporate entrepreneurship achieves both financial goals and strategic goals.

LO12-5 Identify the benefits and potential drawbacks of real options analysis in making resource deployment decisions in corporate entrepreneurship contexts.

LO12-6 Explain how an entrepreneurial orientation can enhance a firm's efforts to develop promising corporate venture initiatives.

We encourage you to reflect on how the concepts presented in this chapter can enhance your career success (see "Reflecting on Career Implications..." at the end of the chapter).

LEARNING FROM MISTAKES

If you ask a group of people to name a successful company, Google is likely to be one of the first firms mentioned. It dominates online search and advertising, has developed a successful browser, and developed the operating system that powers 75 percent of the smartphones in use in March 2019.[1] Its success is evident in its stock price, which rose from about $150 in early 2009 to over $1,220 a share in early 2019. But that doesn't mean that Google has been successful at all it has tried. One of Google's most notable failures occurred when it tried to venture outside the online and wireless markets. In 2006, Google decided to expand its advertising business to radio advertising. After spending several hundred million dollars on its entrepreneurial effort in the radio advertising market, Google pulled the plug on this business in 2009.

Google saw great potential in applying its business model to the radio advertising industry. In the traditional radio advertising model, companies that wished to advertise their products and services contracted with an advertising agency to develop a set of radio spots (commercials). They then bought blocks of advertising time from radio stations. Advertisers paid based on the number of listeners on each station. Google believed that it could develop a stronger model. Its design was to purchase large blocks of advertising time from stations. It would then sell the time in a competitive auction to companies that wished to advertise. Google believed it could sell ad time to advertisers at a higher rate if it could identify what ads on what stations had the greatest impact for advertisers. Thus, rather than charging based on audience size, Google would follow the model it used on the web and charge based on ad effectiveness. To develop the competency to measure ad effectiveness, Google purchased dMarc, a company that developed technology to manage and measure radio ads, for $102 million.

Google's overall vision was even broader. The company also planned to enter print and TV advertising. It could then provide a "dashboard" to marketing executives at firms that would provide information on the effectiveness of advertising on the web, on TV, in print, and on the radio. Google would then sell them a range of advertising space among all four to maximize a firm's ad expenditures.

However, Google found that its attempt to innovate the radio market bumped up against two core challenges. First, the radio advertising model was based much more on relationships than online advertising was. Radio stations, advertising firms, and advertising agencies had longstanding relationships that limited Google's ability to break into the market. In fact, few radio stations were willing to sell advertising time to Google. Also, advertising agencies saw Google as a threat to their business model and were unwilling to buy time from Google. Second, Google found that its ability to measure the effectiveness of radio ads was limited. Unlike the case with online markets, where it could measure whether people clicked on ads, the company found it difficult to measure whether listeners responded to ads. Google tried ads that mentioned specific websites that listeners could go to, but it found few people accessed these sites. In the end, Google was able to sell radio time at only a fraction of what radio stations could get from working their traditional advertising deals. This led stations to abandon Google's radio business.

Google found that it had the initiative to innovate the radio market but didn't have the knowledge, experience, or social connections needed to win in this market.

Discussion Questions

1. Why didn't the lessons Google learned in the online advertising market apply to the radio market?
2. Radio is increasingly moving to satellite and streaming systems. Is this a new opportunity for Google, or should it steer clear of radio altogether?

LO 12-1

Understand the importance of implementing strategies and practices that foster innovation.

Managing change is one of the most important functions performed by strategic leaders. There are two major avenues through which companies can expand or improve their business–innovation and corporate entrepreneurship. These two activities go hand in hand because they both have similar aims. The first is strategic renewal. Innovations help an organization stay fresh and reinvent itself as conditions in the business environment change. This is why managing innovation is such an important strategic implementation issue. The second is the pursuit of venture opportunities. Innovative breakthroughs, as well as new product concepts, evolving technologies, and shifting demand, create opportunities for corporate venturing. In this chapter we will explore these topics–how change and innovation can stimulate strategic renewal and foster corporate entrepreneurship.

MANAGING INNOVATION

innovation the use of new knowledge to transform organizational processes or create commercially viable products and services.

One of the most important sources of growth opportunities is innovation. **Innovation** involves using new knowledge to transform organizational processes or create commercially viable products and services. The sources of new knowledge may include the latest technology, the results of experiments, creative insights, or competitive information. However it comes about, innovation occurs when new combinations of ideas and information bring about positive change.

The emphasis on newness is a key point. For example, for a patent application to have any chance of success, one of the most important attributes it must possess is novelty. You can't patent an idea that has been copied. This is a central idea. In fact, the root of the word *innovation* is the Latin *novus,* which means "new." Innovation involves introducing or changing to something new.[2]

Among the most important sources of new ideas is new technology. Technology creates new possibilities. Technology provides the raw material that firms use to make innovative products and services. But technology is not the only source of innovations. There can be innovations in human resources, firm infrastructure, marketing, service, or many other value-adding areas that have little to do with anything "high-tech." Strategy Spotlight 12.1 highlights a simple but very successful innovation by Kraft Heinz with its MiO Drops.

12.1 STRATEGY SPOTLIGHT

MIO DROPS CHANGE THE BEVERAGE GAME

Sometimes relatively small innovations can create significant changes to markets. Kraft Heinz came up with such a change in 2011 when it introduced MiO drops. Kraft Heinz had long had a major stake in the drink mix market with its Crystal Light and Kool-Aid powdered beverage brands. Although the MiO product is a relatively incremental innovation, with it Kraft Heinz created an entirely new beverage category—liquid water enhancers. Within three years of its introduction, MiO was a $400 million dollar business for Kraft Heinz and was projected to grow to over $1 billion as Kraft Heinz expanded the product into global markets. Kraft Heinz called MiO "one of the most successful new product introductions" in its history. Kraft Heinz also received a number of innovation awards with MiO, including Walmart's Innovation of the Year Award in 2011 and a Gold Medal Edison Innovation Award in 2012. With MiO's commercial and critical success, it is not surprising to see a number of imitative products, such as Dasani Drops and Powerade Drops by Coke, Hawaiian Punch and Crush Drops from Dr Pepper, and Aquafina Splash from Pepsi. But MiO continues to be the market leader.

What insights led Kraft Heinz to develop this product? Kraft Heinz believed there was an opportunity with Millennial consumers who appeared to be more concerned with health and wellness than prior generations. They were moving away from traditional sweetened drinks and were open to alternative flavored beverages. Additionally, Kraft Heinz thought that a product that allowed customers to tailor the degree of flavoring and sweetening as well as a product that could easily be offered in a wide range of flavors would resonate with what Kraft Heinz saw as Millennials' desire for individual expression. Becky McAnich, MiO's marketing director, puts it this way: "Millennials really personalize every part of their life," and MiO "embraces their individuality, that customization."

Sources: Clements, M. 2013. Kraft's breakthrough innovation with MiO: Marketing to millennials. *chicagonow.com,* February 6: np; and Latif, R. 2014. Everyone's looking for the big squeeze. *bevnet.com,* March 28: np.

Types of Innovation

Although innovations are not always high-tech, changes in technology can be an important source of change and growth. When an innovation is based on a sweeping new technology, it often has a more far-reaching impact. Sometimes even a small innovation can add value and create competitive advantages. Innovation can and should occur throughout an organization—in every department and all aspects of the value chain.

One distinction that is often used when discussing innovation is between process innovation and product innovation.[3] **Product innovation** refers to efforts to create product designs and applications of technology to develop new products for end users. Recall from Chapter 5 how generic strategies were typically different depending on the stage of the industry life cycle. Product innovations tend to be more common during the earlier stages of an industry's life cycle. Product innovations are also commonly associated with a differentiation strategy. Firms that differentiate by providing customers with new products or services that offer unique features or quality enhancements often engage in product innovation.

product innovation efforts to create product designs and applications of technology to develop new products for end users.

Process innovation, by contrast, is typically associated with improving the efficiency of an organizational process, especially manufacturing systems and operations. By drawing on new technologies and an organization's accumulated experience (Chapter 5), firms can often improve materials utilization, shorten cycle time, and increase quality. Process innovations are more likely to occur in the later stages of an industry's life cycle as companies seek ways to remain viable in markets where demand has flattened out and competition is more intense. As a result, process innovations are often associated with overall cost leader strategies, because the aim of many process improvements is to lower the costs of operations.

process innovation efforts to improve the efficiency of organizational processes, especially manufacturing systems and operations.

Another way to view the impact of an innovation is in terms of its degree of innovativeness, which falls somewhere on a continuum that extends from incremental to radical.[4]

- **Radical innovations** produce fundamental changes by evoking major departures from existing practices. These breakthrough innovations usually occur because of technological change. They tend to be highly disruptive and can transform a company or even revolutionize a whole industry. They may lead to products or processes that can be patented, giving a firm a strong competitive advantage. Examples include electricity, the telephone, the transistor, desktop computers, fiber optics, artificial intelligence, and genetically engineered drugs.

radical innovation an innovation that fundamentally changes existing practices.

- **Incremental innovations** enhance existing practices or make small improvements in products and processes. They may represent evolutionary applications within existing paradigms of earlier, more radical innovations. Because they often sustain a company by extending or expanding its product line or manufacturing skills, incremental innovations can be a source of competitive advantage by providing new capabilities that minimize expenses or speed productivity. Examples include frozen food, sports drinks, steel-belted radial tires, electronic bookkeeping, shatterproof glass, and digital thermometers.

incremental innovation an innovation that enhances existing practices or makes small improvements in products and processes.

Some innovations are highly radical; others are only slightly incremental. But most innovations fall somewhere between these two extremes (see Exhibit 12.1).

Harvard Business School Professor Clayton M. Christensen identified another useful approach to characterize types of innovations.[5] Christensen draws a distinction between sustaining and disruptive innovations. *Sustaining innovations* are those that extend sales in an existing market, usually by enabling new products or services to be sold at higher margins. Such innovations may include either incremental or radical innovations. For example, smartphone technology was a breakthrough innovation that transformed how people access the Internet. But rather than disrupting the business of Google and Facebook, the rise of the smartphone offered these service providers new opportunities to extend their reach into users' lives.

EXHIBIT 12.1 Continuum of Radical and Incremental Innovations

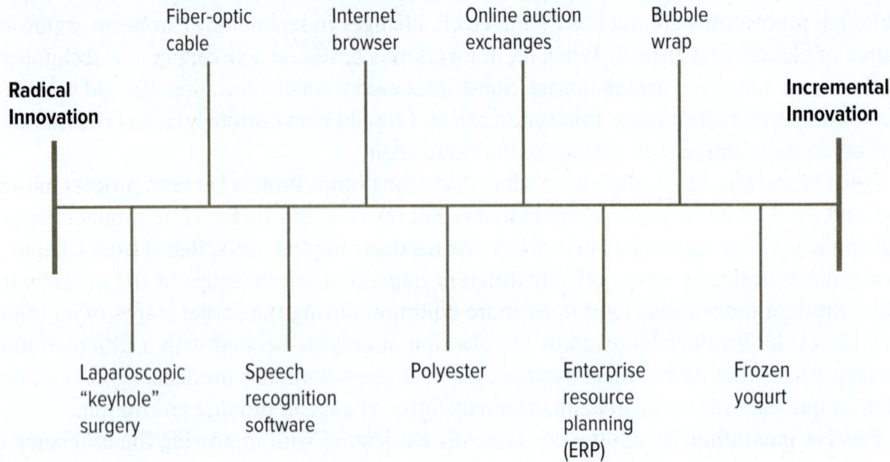

By contrast, *disruptive innovations* are those that overturn markets by providing an altogether new approach to meeting customer needs. The features of a disruptive innovation make it somewhat counterintuitive. Disruptive innovations:

- Are technologically simpler and less sophisticated than currently available products or services.
- Appeal to less demanding customers who are seeking more convenient, less expensive solutions.
- Take time to take effect and only become disruptive once they have taken root in a new market or low-end part of an existing market.

For example, streaming services, such as Hulu and Amazon Prime Video, have disrupted established cable and satellite systems by providing a more limited but more efficient distribution system for entertainment content. Similarly, sharing services in short-term housing, such as Airbnb, are offering a disruptive innovation that is a strong challenge to the hotel industry. "Instead of sustaining the trajectory of improvement that has been established in a market," says Christensen, a disruptive innovation "disrupts it and redefines it by bringing to the market something that is simpler."[6]

Innovation is both a force in the external environment (technology, competition) and a factor affecting a firm's internal choices (generic strategy, value-adding activities).[7] Nevertheless, innovation can be quite difficult for some firms to manage, especially those that have become comfortable with the status quo.

Challenges of Innovation

LO 12-2

Identify the challenges and pitfalls of managing corporate innovation processes.

Innovation is essential to sustaining competitive advantages. Recall from Chapter 3 that one of the four elements of the balanced scorecard is the innovation and learning perspective. The extent and success of a company's innovation efforts are indicators of its overall performance. As management guru Peter Drucker warned, "An established company which, in an age demanding innovation, is not capable of innovation is doomed to decline and extinction."[8] In today's competitive environment, most firms have only one choice: "Innovate or die."

As with change, however, firms are often resistant to innovation. Only those companies that actively pursue innovation, even though it is often difficult and uncertain, will get a payoff from their innovation efforts. But managing innovation is challenging.[9] As former Pfizer chairman and CEO William Steere puts it: "In some ways, managing innovation is analogous to breaking in a spirited horse. You are never sure of success until you achieve your goal. In the meantime, everyone takes a few lumps."[10]

What is it that makes innovation so difficult? The uncertainty about outcomes is one factor. Companies are often reluctant to invest time and resources in activities with an unknown future. Another factor is that the innovation process involves so many choices. These choices present five dilemmas that companies must wrestle with when pursuing innovation:[11]

- ***Seeds versus weeds.*** Most companies have an abundance of innovative ideas. They must decide which of these is most likely to bear fruit–the "seeds"–and which should be cast aside–the "weeds." This is complicated by the fact that some innovation projects require a considerable level of investment before a firm can fully evaluate whether they are worth pursuing. Firms need a mechanism with which they can choose among various innovation projects.
- ***Experience versus initiative.*** Companies must decide who will lead an innovation project. Senior managers may have experience and credibility but tend to be more risk-averse. Midlevel employees, who may be the innovators themselves, may have more enthusiasm because they can see firsthand how an innovation would address specific problems. Firms need to support and reward organizational members who bring new ideas to light.
- ***Internal versus external staffing.*** Innovation projects need competent staffs to succeed. People drawn from inside the company may have greater social capital and know the organization's culture and routines. But this knowledge may actually inhibit them from thinking outside the box. Staffing innovation projects with external personnel requires that project managers justify the hiring and spend time recruiting, training, and relationship building. Firms need to streamline and support the process of staffing innovation efforts.
- ***Building capabilities versus collaborating.*** Innovation projects often require new sets of skills. Firms can seek help from other departments and/or partner with other companies that bring resources and experience as well as share costs of development. However, such arrangements can create dependencies and inhibit internal skills development. Further, struggles over who contributed the most or how the benefits of the project are to be allocated may arise. Firms need a mechanism for forging links with outside parties to the innovation process.
- ***Incremental versus preemptive launch.*** Companies must manage the timing and scale of new innovation projects. An incremental launch is less risky because it requires fewer resources and serves as a market test. But a launch that is too tentative can undermine the project's credibility. It also opens the door for a competitive response. A large-scale launch requires more resources, but it can effectively preempt a competitive response. Firms need to make funding and management arrangements that allow for projects to hit the ground running, and they need to be responsive to market feedback.

These dilemmas highlight why the innovation process can be daunting. Strategy Spotlight 12.2 discusses the opportunities and challenges of leveraging a new technology, graphene, in batteries. Next, we consider five steps that firms can take to improve the innovation process within the firm.[12]

12.2 STRATEGY SPOTLIGHT

THE PROMISE AND PERIL OF GRAPHENE BATTERIES

A little over a decade ago, the innovation world was abuzz about a new component that was going to revolutionize a number of products. The component, graphene, is a nanomaterial that consists of thin sheets of carbon atoms, with the atoms arranged in a honeycomb lattice structure. It is light and strong and is an excellent conductor of both heat and electricity. Interest in the material, which was discovered in 2004, ramped up quickly. The scientists who discovered it won the Nobel Prize in Physics in 2010. Researchers looking at product applications for it identified a wide range of potential uses and filed over 200 graphene-focused patents in both 2010 and 2011. But the promise quickly fizzled out, with no blockbuster products launched and patent filings for the product dropping below ten per year in 2016 and 2017.

But interest in the product remains, and one product for which it has shown recent promise is in batteries. Manufacturers of batteries and products that rely heavily on batteries are always looking to find new and better batteries. The current dominant technology for batteries, lithium-ion, has a number of key weaknesses. The batteries rely on rare-earth metals that are expensive and on mining activities that are ecologically damaging. The batteries also generate heat, take a significant time to charge, decline in strength over time, and become a landfill problem when their lifespan is completed.

After 10 years of development, the question for firms is whether graphene-based batteries are a winning product innovation. The promise is substantial. Graphene batteries have the potential to charge up everything from cell phones to electric vehicles in as short as 10 to 15 minutes. The batteries do not lose charging capability over time. They could even be built into the covers of phones and body panels of cars. And once their usable life is completed, the batteries are much less troublesome as waste since they do not use toxic metals.

At the same time, there are still significant challenges. Most substantially, current graphene supercapacitor batteries typically lose their charge in a matter of hours. Also, producing high-quality graphene sheets is challenging, leading to quality problems in the components used in graphene batteries. Third, the productive capacity for graphene is limited and would likely fall short of demand if graphene batteries take off. It is unclear how long it would take to ramp up production. Finally, while the end product may be more ecologically friendly, the production process used to make graphene involves harsh chemicals and may not be sustainable if production ramps up significantly.

The development of graphene batteries shows both the potential value and challenges of substantial product innovations. Billions of dollars have been invested by firms, ranging from established major players like Samsung to firms like Earthdas, a Spanish entrepreneurial firm. Still, it is unclear after all this investment if graphene batteries will be a widely used battery technology and, if so, which firms will win the innovation contest.

Sources: Katwala, S. 2018. A graphene breakthrough hints at the future of battery power. *wired.com,* August 15: np; Loh, T. 2018. Once-hot material graphene could be next battery breakthrough. *bloomberg.com,* April 20: np; and Cuthberston, A. 2018. Graphene battery charges in just five minutes. *independent.co,* June 18: np.

Cultivating Innovation Skills

Some firms, such as Apple, Google, and Amazon, regularly produce innovative products and services, while other firms struggle to generate new, marketable products. What separates these innovative firms from the rest of the pack? Jeff Dyer, Hal Gregersen, and Clayton Christensen argue it is the innovative DNA of the leaders of these firms.[13] The leaders of these firms have exhibited "discovery skills" that allow them to see the potential in innovations and to move the organization forward in leveraging the value of those innovations.[14] These leaders spend 50 percent more time on these discovery activities than the leaders of less innovative firms. To improve their innovative processes, firms need to cultivate the innovation skills of their managers.

The key attribute that firms need to develop in their managers in order to improve their innovative potential is creative intelligence. Creative intelligence is driven by a core skill of associating–the ability to see patterns in data and integrate different questions, information, and insights–and four patterns of action: questioning, observing, experimenting, and networking. As managers practice the four patterns of action, they will begin to develop the skill of association.

The point is that by questioning, observing, experimenting, and networking as part of the innovative process, managers will not only make better innovation decisions now but, more importantly, start to build the innovative DNA needed to be more successful innovators in the future. As they get into the practice of these habits, decision makers will see opportunities and be more creative as they associate information from different parts of their life, different people they come in contact with, and different parts of their organizations. The five traits of the effective innovator are described and examples of each trait are presented in Exhibit 12.2.

To foster the ability to creatively respond to challenges and opportunities in the market, research also suggests that innovators would benefit from tapping into the knowledge of former friends and colleagues. Insights from Research 12.1 discusses the benefits of leveraging dormant ties.

In addition to individual behavior, organizational systems can also impact the degree to which a firm will be innovative. Strategy Spotlight 12.3 discusses the insights of Waguih Ishak, an innovative technology manager, on how firms can build an innovative corporate culture.

Defining the Scope of Innovation

Firms must have a means to focus their innovation efforts. By defining the "strategic envelope"–the scope of a firm's innovation efforts–firms ensure that their innovation efforts are not wasted on projects that are outside the firm's domain of interest. Strategic

EXHIBIT 12.2 The Innovator's DNA

Trait	Description	Example
Associating	Innovators have the ability to connect seemingly unrelated questions, problems, and ideas from different fields. This allows them to creatively see opportunities that others miss.	Pierre Omidyar saw the opportunity that led to eBay when he linked three items: (1) a personal fascination with creating more efficient markets, (2) his fiancee's desire to locate hard-to-find collectible Pez dispensers, and (3) the ineffectiveness of local classified ads in locating such items.
Questioning	Innovators constantly ask questions that challenge common wisdom. Rather than accept the status quo, they ask "Why not?" or "What if?" This gets others around them to challenge the assumptions that limit the possible range of actions the firm can take.	After witnessing the emergence of eBay and Amazon, Marc Benioff questioned why computer software was still sold in boxes rather than leased with a subscription and downloaded through the Internet. This was the genesis of Salesforce.com, a firm with over $4.1 billion in sales in 2014.
Observing	Discovery-driven executives produce innovative business ideas by observing regular behavior of individuals, especially customers and potential customers. Such observations often identify challenges customers face and previously unidentified opportunities.	From watching his wife struggle to keep track of the family's finances, Intuit founder Scott Cook identified the need for easy-to-use financial software that provided a single place for managing bills, bank accounts, and investments.
Experimenting	Thomas Edison once said, "I haven't failed. I've simply found 10,000 ways that do not work." Innovators regularly experiment with new possibilities, accepting that many of their ideas will fail. Experimentation can include new jobs, living in different countries, and new ideas for their businesses.	Founders Larry Page and Sergey Brin provide time and resources for Google employees to experiment. Some, such as the Android cell phone platform, have been big winners. Others, such as the Orkut and Buzz social networking systems, have failed. But Google will continue to experiment with new products and services.
Networking	Innovators develop broad personal networks. They use this diverse set of individuals to find and test radical ideas. This can be done by developing a diverse set of friends. It can also be done by attending idea conferences where individuals from a broad set of backgrounds come together to share their perspectives and ideas, such as the Technology, Entertainment, and Design (TED) Conference or the Aspen Ideas Festival.	Michael Lazaridis got the idea for a wireless email device that led him to found Research in Motion, now called BlackBerry, from a conference he attended. At the conference, a speaker was discussing a wireless system Coca-Cola was using that allowed vending machines to send a signal when they needed refilling. Lazaridis saw the opportunity to use the same concept with email communications, and the idea for the BlackBerry was hatched.

Source: Adapted from J.H. Dyer, Gregersen, H.G., and C.M. Christensen. 2009. The innovator's DNA. *Harvard Business Review,* December: 61–67.

12.1 *INSIGHTS* from Research

THE BENEFITS OF DORMANT TIES

Overview

Over the course of a career, individuals develop ties with thousands of other individuals, but most people only maintain 100 to 200 ties. As a result, most ties become dormant. Challenging the conventional view that these dormant ties are of little value, this study shows that reconnecting with dormant ties can efficiently provide novel insights into the innovation challenges managers face.

What the Research Shows

Researchers from Rutgers University, George Washington University, and Northwestern University had 224 students in Executive MBA classes reach out to someone with whom they once had a close relationship but hadn't interacted with for at least three years. They were instructed to pick someone whom they thought would have advice on how to deal with an issue the student was currently dealing with at work. They then measured how helpful the advice was that they received.

The results were quite striking. Study participants feared reaching out to dormant ties, thinking that they would be seen as a bother. They didn't want to be seen as being similar to an annoying telemarketer. However, the students found that people were very willing to provide their insights. More importantly, the advice they received was very helpful. The study found three key benefits of connecting with dormant ties.

1. The advice received was novel. While the study participant and the dormant tie may have shared a similar set of experiences when they were together, since separating, the dormant ties had a range of other experiences that helped them provide novel insights on the issue they were asked about. This is critical since novel insights are likely to be especially valuable in dealing with innovation-related challenges.
2. The exchange was efficient. Since the conversation had a specific purpose, study participants found that the interactions with dormant ties were quick, even shorter than everyday conversations with current ties.
3. The information shared was rich and was trusted by the students. The researchers found that when people reconnected, they still had strong feelings of trust between them. As a result, the dormant ties were willing to share meaningful and rich information, and the recipients of the advice valued the information shared.

The researchers conducted a second study with 116 students. They asked them to list 10 dormant ties the executives could reach out to, ranked from most to least promising. The researchers had them contact their highest ranked dormant tie and one of the nine others randomly chosen by the researchers. Interestingly, the value of the advice received did not vary across the highly ranked and lower ranked dormant ties. This finding suggests that the pool of potentially valuable dormant ties runs deep.

Key Takeaways

- Dormant ties offer the potential for novel information that could help decisions managers be more innovative in dealing with current challenges.
- Dormant ties are typically very willing to give their time and advice.
- It is not just the first dormant tie who comes to mind who can offer good advice. Former friends who were lower on the list of potential advisors offered advice that was just as valuable.

Questions:

1. Would you feel comfortable reaching out to a former friend or colleague to ask for advice or to help in another way? Why or why not?
2. How would you respond if someone you used to be close with reached out to you for advice or help?

Research Reviewed

Levin, D., Walter, J., and K. Murnighan. 2011. The power of reconnection—How dormant ties can surprise you. *MITSloan Management Review,* 52(3): 45–50; Levin, D., Walter, J., and K. Murnighan. 2011. Dormant ties: The value of reconnecting. *Organization Science,* 22: 923–939.

strategic envelope a firm-specific view of innovation that defines how a firm can create new knowledge and learn from an innovation initiative even if the project fails.

enveloping defines the range of acceptable projects. A **strategic envelope** creates a firm-specific view of innovation that defines how a firm can create new knowledge and learn from an innovation initiative even if the project fails. It also gives direction to a firm's innovation efforts, which helps separate seeds from weeds and builds internal capabilities.

One way to determine which projects to work on is to focus on a common technology. Then innovation efforts across the firm can aim at developing skills and expertise in a given technical area. Another potential focus is on a market theme.

12.3 STRATEGY SPOTLIGHT

BUILDING A CORPORATE CULTURE TO NURTURE INNOVATION

Waguih Ishak has worked in technology firms for over 40 years, including stints at HP Labs, Agilent Technologies, and Broadcom. He currently serves as chief technologist at Corning Research and Development Corporation. Based on his experience, he has developed six recommendations for building an innovative culture.

- **Practice "innovation parenting":** Ishak argues that leading an innovation team is much like parenting. You need to provide clear expectations and expect accountability, but you also need to give innovation workers discretion to conduct their work in their own way. He believes leaders need to be flexible in budgets and deadlines. But once scientists and engineers understand that they are accountable to deliver products and processes that meet the organization's objectives and serve the firm's stakeholders, they will typically work toward those and not waste the organization's resources.
- **Bust hierarchy:** Technology managers need to be flexible with how they put in place and apply rules and structure to the team. Ishak tells a story of a worker who was interested in attending a conference in Japan to learn about a new technology. Even though he was not eligible to travel to the conference, Ishak sent him anyway. Once he returned he convinced Ishak to go outside of the normal process and allowed him to construct a team of engineers and technicians and also recruit a couple of University of California professors. The result was a revolutionary low-cost computer product.
- **Encourage the unreasonable:** While most technology managers will employ brainstorming, telling employees to not limit themselves and to know that there are no bad ideas, Ishak recommends managers go one step further and encourage the unreasonable. Propose alternatives that seem impossible. Raise questions to challenge taken for granted assumptions. Propose unreasonable targets. For example, one scientist asked what would happen if a competitor figured out how to make a magnetic glass product that was a key Corning product without requiring extreme heat. Other scientists reacted at first that this was impossible, but the conversations then lead Corning to develop new insights on how they manufacture products.
- **Don't die of indigestion:** Ishak argues that many technologists get distracted by working on too many projects. If a scientist spends 25 percent of her time on one project, 15 percent on another, and 5 percent on each of 12 other projects, she's not invested enough in any single project. She feels no ownership of anything she works on. He argues scientists should stick to two to three projects at a time. As he sees it, one of the two key types of innovation team members are resource members. These are team members who have deep knowledge of projects and technology. They can only develop this deep knowledge by being heavily invested on the project.
- **Cultivate external relationships:** In addition to having deep knowledge, technology teams also need to have ties outside the team and the larger organization. This allows them to have access to a wider range of knowledge. For this reason, he argues the teams need a second type of team member, those he calls sources. Sources are team members who have wide but not deep knowledge. They are broad-thinking people who are connected to customers, suppliers, and the larger outside world.
- **Hire the best and do it quickly:** Ishak argues that technology managers need to develop connections with people outside the firm, such as university professors, and use these connections to find and recruit the best talent. Once they identify these individuals, they must be willing to move to hire them. Ishak once had a Stanford professor call to tell him that one of his best students was graduating. Even though she already had multiple offers, the professor thought she might best fit at Corning. Ishak agreed to meet her and immediately made her an offer even though he didn't have an opening on his team. When she said yes, he had to go to his boss to ask for the necessary funding. Rather than being angry, his boss simply asked if he had any other high potential scientists he wanted to hire.

Sources: Ishak, W. 2015. Waguih Ishak Fortune 500 intrapreneur on nurturing a culture of innovation. *uctv.tv,* February 16: np; and Ishak, W. 2017. Creating an innovation culture. *mckinsey.com,* September: np.

Companies must be clear about not only the kinds of innovation they are looking for but also the expected results. Each company needs to develop a set of questions to ask itself about its innovation efforts:

- How much will the innovation initiative cost?
- How likely is it to actually become commercially viable?
- How much value will it add; that is, what will it be worth if it works?
- What will be learned if it does not pan out?

However a firm envisions its innovation goals, it needs to develop a systematic approach to evaluating its results and learning from its innovation initiatives. Viewing innovation from this perspective helps firms manage the process.[15]

Managing the Pace of Innovation

Along with clarifying the scope of an innovation by defining a strategic envelope, firms also need to regulate the pace of innovation. How long will it take for an innovation initiative to realistically come to fruition? The project timeline of an incremental innovation may be 6 months to 2 years, whereas a more radical innovation is typically long term—10 years or more.[16] Radical innovations often begin with a long period of exploration in which experimentation makes strict timelines unrealistic. In contrast, firms that are innovating incrementally in order to exploit a window of opportunity may use a milestone approach that is more stringently driven by goals and deadlines. This kind of sensitivity to realistic time frames helps companies separate dilemmas temporally so they are easier to manage.

Time pacing can also be a source of competitive advantage because it helps a company manage transitions and develop an internal rhythm.[17] Time pacing does not mean the company ignores the demands of market timing; instead, companies have a sense of their own internal clock in a way that allows them to thwart competitors by controlling the innovation process. With time pacing, the firm works to develop an internal rhythm that matches the buying practices of customers. For example, for years, Intel worked to develop new microprocessor chips every 18 months. The company would have three chips in process at any point in time—one it was producing and selling, one it was currently developing, and one that was just on the drawing board. This pacing also matched the market, because most corporate customers bought new computers about every three years. Thus, customers were then two generations behind in their computing technology, leading them to feel the need to upgrade at the three-year point. In the post-PC era, Apple has developed a similar but faster internal cycle, allowing it to launch a new generation of the iPhone on an annual basis.

This doesn't mean the aim is always to be faster when innovating. Some projects can't be rushed. Companies that hurry their research efforts or go to market before they are ready can damage their ability to innovate—and their reputation. Thus, managing the pace of innovation can be an important factor in long-term success.

Staffing to Capture Value from Innovation

People are central to the processes of identifying, developing, and commercializing innovations effectively. They need broad sets of skills as well as experience—experience working with teams and experience working on successful innovation projects. To capture value from innovation activities, companies must provide strategic decision makers with staff members who make it possible.

This insight led strategy experts Rita Gunther McGrath and Thomas Keil to research the types of human resource management practices that effective firms use to capture value from their innovation efforts.[18] Four practices are especially important:

- Create innovation teams with experienced players who know what it is like to deal with uncertainty and can help new staff members learn venture management skills.
- Require that employees seeking to advance their career with the organization serve in the new venture group as part of their career climb.
- Once people have experience with the new venture group, transfer them to mainstream management positions where they can use their skills and knowledge to revitalize the company's core business.
- Separate the performance of individuals from the performance of the innovation. Otherwise, strong players may feel stigmatized if the innovation effort they worked on fails.

There are other staffing practices that may sound as if they would benefit a firm's innovation activities but may, in fact, be counterproductive:

- Creating a staff that consists only of strong players whose primary experience is related to the company's core business. This provides too few people to deal with the uncertainty of innovation projects and may cause good ideas to be dismissed because they do not appear to fit with the core business.
- Creating a staff that consists only of volunteers who want to work on projects they find interesting. Such players are often overzealous about new technologies or overly attached to product concepts, which can lead to poor decisions about which projects to pursue or drop.
- Creating a climate where innovation team members are considered second-class citizens. In companies where achievements are rewarded, the brightest and most ambitious players may avoid innovation projects with uncertain outcomes.

Unless an organization can align its key players into effective new venture teams, it is unlikely to create any differentiating advantages from its innovation efforts.[19] An enlightened approach to staffing a company's innovation efforts provides one of the best ways to ensure that the challenges of innovation will be effectively met.

Collaborating with Innovation Partners

It is rare for any one organization to have all the information it needs to carry an innovation from concept to commercialization. Even a company that is highly competent with its current operations usually needs new capabilities to achieve new results. Innovation partners provide the skills and insights that are needed to make innovation projects succeed.[20]

Innovation partners may come from many sources, including research universities and the federal government. Each year the federal government issues requests for proposals (RFPs) asking private companies for assistance in improving services or finding solutions to public problems. Universities are another type of innovation partner. Chip-maker Intel, for example, has benefited from underwriting substantial amounts of university research. Rather than hand universities a blank check, Intel bargains for rights to patents that emerge from Intel-sponsored research. The university retains ownership of the patent, but Intel gets royalty-free use of it.[21]

Strategic partnering requires firms to identify their strengths and weaknesses and make choices about which capabilities to leverage, which need further development, and which are outside the firm's current or projected scope of operations.

To choose partners, firms need to ask what competencies they are looking for and what the innovation partner will contribute.[22] These might include knowledge of markets, technology expertise, or contacts with key players in an industry. Innovation partnerships also typically need to specify how the rewards of the innovation will be shared and who will own the intellectual property that is developed.[23]

Innovation efforts that involve multiple partners and the speed and ease with which partners can network and collaborate are changing the way innovation is conducted.[24]

The Value of Unsuccessful Innovation

Companies are often reluctant to pursue innovations due to the high uncertainty associated with innovative efforts. They are torn about whether to invest in emerging technologies, wondering which, if any, will win in the market and offer the best payoff for the firm. Conventional wisdom suggests that firms pay dearly if they bet on the wrong technology or new product direction. However, research by NYU professor J. P. Eggers suggests that betting on a losing technology and then switching to the winner can position a company to come out ahead of competitors that were on the right track all along.[25]

His research shows that firms that initially invest in an unsuccessful innovative effort often end up dominating the market in the long run. The key is that the firm remains open to change and to learning from both its mistakes and the experience of the innovators that initially chose to pursue the winning technology. Eggers offers the following insights for companies competing in a dynamic market where it is uncertain which technology will emerge triumphant:

1. ***Avoid overcommitting.*** This can be difficult as the firm sees the need to build specific expertise and stake out a decisive position to be seen as a leader in the market. However, managers can become entrenched as confirmation bias leads them to focus only on data that suggest they've made the right choice. Eggers suggests firms consider joint ventures and other alliances to avoid overinvestments they may come to regret.
2. ***Don't let shame or despair knock you out of the game.*** Shame has been shown to be a particularly destructive reaction to failure. Remember that it is very likely no one could have had complete confidence regarding which technology would win. And try to avoid seeing things as worse than they are. Some companies that bet on the wrong technology decide, unnecessarily, to get out of the market entirely, missing out on any future market opportunities.
3. ***Pivot quickly.*** Once they realized they made a mistake, firms that were ultimately successful changed course and moved quickly. Studies have shown that the ideal moment to enter a high-tech industry is just as the dominant design emerges. So missing the target initially doesn't have to mean that a firm is doomed to failure if the firm moves swiftly as the dominant technology becomes clear.
4. ***Transfer knowledge.*** Successful firms use the information they gathered in a losing bet to exploit other market opportunities. For example, when flat-panel computer displays were first emerging, it was unclear if plasma or LCD technology would win. IBM initially invested heavily in plasma displays, a bet that turned out to be wrong when LCD technology won out. But IBM took away valuable knowledge from its plasma investments. For example, the heavy glass required by plasma technology forced IBM to become skilled at glass design, which helped it push glass technology in new directions in products such as the original ThinkPad laptop.
5. ***Be aware that it can be dangerous to be right at the outset.*** Managers in firms that initially select the winning technology have a tendency to interpret their ability to choose the most promising technology as an unconditional endorsement of everything they had been doing. As a result, they fail to recognize the need to rethink some details of their product and the underlying technology. Their complacency can give firms that initially chose the wrong technology the space to catch up and then pull ahead, since the later-moving firms are more open to see the need for improvements and are hungry and aggressive in their actions. The key to who wins typically isn't who is there first. Instead, the winning firm is the one that continuously incrementally innovates on the initial bold innovation to offer the best product at the best price.

Offering additional insight into the potential benefits of unsuccessful innovations, research by Julian Birkinshaw suggests that failure can be a great catalyst for learning.[26] He advises three key steps to ensure that firms can leverage the value of failures. First, firms should study individual projects that did not pan out and gather as many insights as possible from them. This should include what the failure can teach the firm about customers and market dynamics; the organization's culture, strategy, and processes; the decision team and firm leaders; and trends in the market and the larger environment.

Second, firms need to crystallize those insights and share them across the organization. This can involve regular meetings where firm leaders share their recent struggles and the lessons learned. It can also involve reports that are shared across the firm. For example, Engineers Without Borders, a global volunteer organization that strives to offer engineering solutions in underdeveloped countries, launched an annual "failure report" that discussed failures and their lessons.

Third, he advises that firm leaders take a step back and do overall corporate reviews occasionally to ensure that the overall approach to failure is yielding strong benefits. This can give insight into whether the organization is repeating the same pattern of failure or if it is learning and improving. It can also serve to identify the most widely applicable learning or the most critical areas needed for improvement. Finally, it can also help identify if the firm is being too conservative and failing too infrequently. One key takeaway is that highlighting the value of learning from failures can lessen the fear of failure by showing that it is not the end to an employee's career. Instead, it is the foundation for learning and something to accept as part of the process of innovation. As Sunil Sinha, an executive at Tata, stated: "We want people to be bold and not be afraid to fail."

CORPORATE ENTREPRENEURSHIP

Corporate entrepreneurship (CE) has two primary aims: the pursuit of new venture opportunities and strategic renewal.[27] The innovation process keeps firms alert by exposing them to new technologies, making them aware of marketplace trends, and helping them evaluate new possibilities. Corporate entrepreneurship uses the fruits of the innovation process to help firms build new sources of competitive advantage and renew their value propositions. Just as the innovation process helps firms to make positive improvements, CE helps firms identify opportunities and launch new ventures.

corporate entrepreneurship (CE) the creation of new value for a corporation through investments that create either new sources of competitive advantage or renewal of the value proposition.

Corporate new venture creation was labeled "intrapreneuring" by Gifford Pinchot because it refers to building entrepreneurial businesses within existing corporations.[28] However, to engage in corporate entrepreneurship that yields above-average returns and contributes to sustainable advantages, it must be done effectively. In this section we will examine the sources of entrepreneurial activity within established firms and the methods large corporations use to stimulate entrepreneurial behavior.

In a typical corporation, what determines how entrepreneurial projects will be pursued? The answer depends on many factors, including:

- Corporate culture.
- Leadership.
- Structural features that guide and constrain action.
- Organizational systems that foster learning and manage rewards.

All of the factors that influence the strategy implementation process will also shape how corporations engage in internal venturing.

Other factors will also affect how entrepreneurial ventures will be pursued:

- The use of teams in strategic decision making.
- Whether the company is product- or service-oriented.
- Whether its innovation efforts are aimed at product or process improvements.
- The extent to which it is high-tech or low-tech.

Because these factors are different in every organization, some companies may be more involved than others in identifying and developing new venture opportunities.[29] These factors will also influence the nature of the CE process.

Successful CE typically requires firms to reach beyond their current operations and markets in the pursuit of new opportunities, but firms often struggle in their efforts to leverage their existing technologies in new markets. Research suggests that firms are more likely to effectively leverage its technologies in new markets if they follow the following four steps.

1. **Redefine the technology or competency in general terms**. The goal is to de-link the technology from the specific products in which it is currently used and, instead, identify the more general applications of the technology. For example, SNI Inc. had

developed a technology to precisely place the heads of cutting tools in its grinding machines. To find broader applications for the technology, they redefined their technology in much broader terms. At its core, they realized their technology offered the ability to precisely place objects in space.

2. **Identify new applications of the technology.** Firms should consider a broad scope of potential markets. Two methods for identifying potential markets are desk research and field research. Desk research involves searching patent databases and more general web searches. Firms can search patent databases on key words related to the functions of their technology to identify arenas in which their technology may apply. Managers can also attend trade shows to look at current products in related markets to identify product areas to which their technology may apply. For example, Mario Cotta Zincometal Group, an Italian firm, had developed an innovative machine for cutting paper tissue. The firm sent three managers to Drupa, a printing and cutting technology trade show in Germany, to scour the booths at the conference to identify cutting product segments in which they could apply their technology.
3. **Select the most promising applications.** There are two key factors that help a firm select the right applications. First, firms need to assess whether their technology provides advantages over current products. Returning to SNI Inc., after redefining the technology broadly, they identified a range of markets where that is valuable and compared the strengths and weaknesses of their technology to current methods used in these markets to identify markets in which they could add the most value. Second, firms need to assess the practicality of their technology and take steps to identify the challenges they'll face. This can include computer simulations, prototyping products, and test marketing new products.
4. **Choose the best entry mode.** Firms need to identify the best mode to generate profits from new markets. At its core, this will involve the decision of whether the firm wants to enter the market on its own, do it through a strategic alliance with a partner, or license the technology to someone already in the market. This requires an honest assessment of the resources needed to win in the new market and an analysis of whether or not the firm has those resources.

In addition to identifying the right markets for a firm's CE efforts, the firm also needs to decide how it will organize for its CE efforts. In the sections that follow, we will address some of the strategic choice and implementation issues that influence the success or failure of CE activities.

focused approaches to corporate entrepreneurship corporate entrepreneurship in which the venturing entity is separated from the other ongoing operations of the firm.

Two distinct approaches to corporate venturing are found among firms that pursue entrepreneurial aims. The first is *focused* corporate venturing, in which CE activities are isolated from a firm's existing operations and worked on by independent work units. The second approach is *dispersed,* in which all parts of the organization and every organization member are engaged in intrapreneurial activities.

Focused Approaches to Corporate Entrepreneurship

LO 12-3

Explain how corporations use new venture teams, business incubators, and product champions to create an internal environment and culture that promote entrepreneurial development.

Firms using a **focused approach** typically separate the corporate venturing activity from the other ongoing operations of the firm. CE is usually the domain of autonomous work groups that pursue entrepreneurial aims independent of the rest of the firm. The advantage of this approach is that it frees entrepreneurial team members to think and act without the constraints imposed by existing organizational norms and routines. This independence is often necessary for the kind of open-minded creativity that leads to strategic breakthroughs. The disadvantage is that, because of their isolation from the corporate mainstream, the work groups that concentrate on internal ventures may fail to obtain the resources or support needed to carry an entrepreneurial project through to completion. Two forms—new venture groups (NVGs) and business incubators—are among the most common types of focused approaches.

New Venture Groups Corporations often form **new venture groups (NVGs)** whose goal is to identify, evaluate, and cultivate venture opportunities. These groups typically function as semiautonomous units with little formal structure. The NVG may simply be a committee that reports to the president on potential new ventures. Or it may be organized as a corporate division with its own staff and budget. The aims of the NVG may be open-ended in terms of what ventures it may consider. Alternatively, some corporations use an NVG to promote concentrated effort on a specific problem. In both cases, NVGs usually have a substantial amount of freedom to take risks and a supply of resources to do it with.[30]

new venture group (NVG)
a group of individuals, or a division within a corporation, that identifies, evaluates, and cultivates venture opportunities.

New venture groups usually have a larger mandate than a typical R&D department. Their involvement extends beyond innovation and experimentation to coordinating with other corporate divisions, identifying potential venture partners, gathering resources, and actually launching the venture. Taco Bell has leveraged the power of an NVG to generate innovations that keep the firm growing.

> Taco Bell employs a 40 member innovation center team that is tasked with coming up regularly with catchy, innovative food items. Its most notable innovation was Doritos Locos Tacos, which generated over $1 billion in sales in its first year. The group considers dozens of new ideas a week and aims to launch a new menu item every five weeks. These new items typically are only available for a limited time, but they generate 5 percent of sales. Notable products have included Cap'n Crunch Delights (cereal encrusted, icing filled doughnut holes) and DareDevil Loaded Grillers (burritos filled with a collection of hot peppers). This innovative effort has sparked nearly 10 percent annual growth in a mature market.

Business Incubators The term *incubator* was originally used to describe a device in which eggs are hatched. **Business incubators** are designed to "hatch" new businesses. They are a type of corporate NVG with a somewhat more specialized purpose–to support and nurture fledgling entrepreneurial ventures until they can thrive on their own as stand-alone businesses. Corporations use incubators as a way to grow businesses identified by the NVG. Although they often receive support from many parts of the corporation, they still operate independently until they are strong enough to go it alone. Depending on the type of business, they either are integrated into an existing corporate division or continue to operate as a subsidiary of the parent firm.

business incubator
a corporate new venture group that supports and nurtures fledgling entrepreneurial ventures until they can thrive on their own as stand-alone businesses.

Incubators typically provide some or all of the following five functions:[31]

- ***Funding.*** This includes capital investments as well as in-kind investments and loans.
- ***Physical space.*** Incubators in which several start-ups share space often provide fertile ground for new ideas and collaboration.
- ***Business services.*** Along with office space, young ventures need basic services and infrastructure, which may include anything from phone systems and computer networks to public relations and personnel management.
- ***Mentoring.*** Senior executives and skilled technical personnel often provide coaching and experience-based advice.
- ***Networking.*** Contact with other parts of the firm and external resources such as suppliers, industry experts, and potential customers facilitates problem solving and knowledge sharing.

To encourage entrepreneurship, corporations sometimes need to do more than create independent work groups or venture incubators to generate new enterprises. In some firms, the entrepreneurial spirit is spread throughout the organization.

Dispersed Approaches to Corporate Entrepreneurship

The second type of CE is dispersed. For some companies, a dedication to the principles and practices of entrepreneurship is spread throughout the organization. One advantage of this **dispersed approach** is that organizational members don't have to be reminded to think entrepreneurially or

dispersed approaches to corporate entrepreneurship
corporate entrepreunership in which a dedication to the principles and policies of entrepreneurship is spread throughout the organization.

be willing to change. The ability to change is considered to be a core capability. This leads to a second advantage: Because of the firm's entrepreneurial reputation, stakeholders such as vendors, customers, or alliance partners can bring new ideas or venture opportunities to anyone in the organization and expect them to be well received. Such opportunities make it possible for the firm to stay ahead of the competition. However, there are disadvantages as well. Firms that are overzealous about CE sometimes feel they must change for the sake of change, causing them to lose vital competencies or spend heavily on R&D and innovation to the detriment of the bottom line. Three related aspects of dispersed entrepreneurship include entrepreneurial cultures that have an overarching commitment to CE activities, resource allotments to support entrepreneurial actions, and the use of product champions in promoting entrepreneurial behaviors.

Entrepreneurial Culture In some large corporations, the corporate culture embodies the spirit of entrepreneurship. A culture of entrepreneurship is one in which the search for venture opportunities permeates every part of the organization. The key to creating value successfully is viewing every value-chain activity as a source of competitive advantage. The effect of CE on a firm's strategic success is strongest when it animates all parts of an organization. It is found in companies where the strategic leaders and the culture together generate a strong impetus to innovate, take risks, and seek out new venture opportunities.[32]

entrepreneurial culture
corporate culture in which change and renewal are a constant focus of attention.

In companies with an **entrepreneurial culture,** everyone in the organization is attuned to opportunities to help create new businesses. Many such firms use a top-down approach to stimulate entrepreneurial activity. The top leaders of the organization support programs and incentives that foster a climate of entrepreneurship. Many of the best ideas for new corporate ventures, however, come from the bottom up. Catherine Winder, former president of Rainmaker Entertainment, discussed how she welcomed any employee to generate and pitch innovative ideas this way:[33]

> We have an open-door policy for anyone in the company to pitch ideas . . . to describe their ideas in 15 to 30 seconds. If we like the core idea, we'll work with them. If you can be concise and come up with your idea in a really clear way, it means you're on to something.

An entrepreneurial culture is one in which change and renewal are on everybody's mind. Amazon, 3M, Intel, and Cisco are among the corporations best known for their corporate venturing activities. Many fast-growing young corporations also attribute much of their success to an entrepreneurial culture. But other successful firms struggle in their efforts to remain entrepreneurial.

Resource Allotments Corporate entrepreneurship requires the willingness of the firm to invest in the generation and execution of innovative ideas. On the generation side, employees are much more likely to develop these ideas if they have the time to do so. For decades, 3M allowed its engineers free time, up to 15 percent of their work schedule, to work on developing new products.[34] Intuit follows a similar model, offering employees the opportunity to spend 10 percent of their time on ideas that improve Intuit's processes or on products that address user problems. According to Brad Smith, Intuit's CEO, this time is critical for the future success of Intuit since "innovation is not going to come from me. It's going to come from challenging people to think about new and different ways of solving big, important problems."[35] In addition to time, firms can foster CE by providing monetary investment to fund entrepreneurial ideas. Johnson & Johnson (J&J) uses its Internal Ventures Group to support entrepreneurial ideas developed inside the firm. Entrepreneurs within J&J submit proposals to the group. The review board decides which proposals to fund and then solicits further investments from J&J's operating divisions. Nike's Sustainable Business and Innovation Lab and Google's Ventures Group have a similar charter to review and fund promising corporate entrepreneurship activities. The availability of these time and financing sources can enhance the likelihood of successful entrepreneurial activities within the firm.

Product Champions Corporate entrepreneurship does not always involve making large investments in start-ups or establishing incubators to spawn new divisions. Often, innovative ideas emerge in the normal course of business and are brought forth and become part of the way of doing business. Entrepreneurial champions are often needed to take charge of internally generated ventures. **Product champions** (or project champions) are those individuals working within a corporation who bring entrepreneurial ideas forward, identify what kind of market exists for the product or service, find resources to support the venture, and promote the venture concept to upper management.[36]

product champion an individual working within a corporation who brings entrepreneurial ideas forward, identifies what kind of market exists for the product or service, finds resources to support the venture, and promotes the venture concept to upper management.

When lower-level employees identify a product idea or novel solution, they will take it to their supervisor or someone in authority. A new idea that is generated in a technology lab may be introduced to others by its inventor. If the idea has merit, it gains support and builds momentum across the organization.[37] Even though the corporation may not be looking for new ideas or have a program for cultivating internal ventures, the independent behaviors of a few organizational members can have important strategic consequences.

No matter how an entrepreneurial idea comes to light, however, a new venture concept must pass through two critical stages or it may never get off the ground:

1. ***Project definition.*** An opportunity has to be justified in terms of its attractiveness in the marketplace and how well it fits with the corporation's other strategic objectives.
2. ***Project impetus.*** For a project to gain impetus, its strategic and economic impact must be supported by senior managers who have experience with similar projects. It then becomes an embryonic business with its own organization and budget.

For a project to advance through these stages of definition and impetus, a product champion is often needed to generate support and encouragement. Champions are especially important during the time after a new project has been defined but before it gains momentum. They form a link between the definition and impetus stages of internal development, which they do by procuring resources and stimulating interest for the product among potential customers.[38] Product champions play an important entrepreneurial role in a corporate setting by encouraging others to take a chance on promising new ideas.[39]

Measuring the Success of Corporate Entrepreneurship Activities

LO 12-4

Explain how corporate entrepreneurship achieves both financial goals and strategic goals.

At this point in the discussion, it is reasonable to ask whether CE is successful. Corporate venturing, like the innovation process, usually requires a tremendous effort. Is it worth it? We consider factors that corporations need to take into consideration when evaluating the success of CE programs. We also examine techniques that companies can use to limit the expense of venturing or to cut their losses when CE initiatives appear doomed.

Comparing Strategic and Financial CE Goals Not all corporate venturing efforts are financially rewarding. In terms of financial performance, slightly more than 50 percent of corporate venturing efforts reach profitability (measured by ROI) within six years of their launch.[40] If this were the only criterion for success, it would seem to be a rather poor return. On the one hand, these results should be expected, because CE is riskier than other investments such as expanding ongoing operations. On the other hand, corporations expect a higher return from corporate venturing projects than from normal operations. Thus, in terms of the risk-return trade-off, it seems that CE often falls short of expectations.[41]

There are several other important criteria, however, for judging the success of a corporate venture initiative. Most CE programs have strategic goals.[42] The strategic reasons for undertaking a corporate venture include strengthening competitive position, entering into new markets, expanding capabilities by learning and acquiring new knowledge, and building the corporation's base of resources and experience. Three questions should be used to assess the effectiveness of a corporation's venturing initiatives:[43]

1. ***Are the products or services offered by the venture accepted in the marketplace?*** Is the venture considered to be a market success? If so, the financial returns are likely to be

satisfactory. The venture may also open doors into other markets and suggest avenues for other venture projects.

2. ***Are the contributions of the venture to the corporation's internal competencies and experience valuable?*** Does the venture add to the worth of the firm internally? If so, strategic goals such as leveraging existing assets, building new knowledge, and enhancing firm capabilities are likely to be met.[44]
3. ***Is the venture able to sustain its basis of competitive advantage?*** Does the value proposition offered by the venture insulate it from competitive attack? If so, it is likely to place the corporation in a stronger position relative to competitors and provide a base from which to build other advantages.

These criteria include both strategic and financial goals of CE. Another way to evaluate a corporate venture is in terms of the four criteria from the balanced scorecard (Chapter 3). In a successful venture, not only are financial and market acceptance (customer) goals met but so are the internal business and innovation and learning goals. Thus, when assessing the success of corporate venturing, it is important to look beyond simple financial returns and consider a well-rounded set of criteria.[45]

Exit Champions Although a culture of championing venture projects is advantageous for stimulating an ongoing stream of entrepreneurial initiatives, many—in fact, most—of the ideas will not work out. At some point in the process, a majority of initiatives will be abandoned. Sometimes, however, companies wait too long to terminate a new venture and do so only after large sums of resources are used up or, worse, result in a marketplace failure. Motorola's costly global satellite telecom project known as Iridium provides a useful illustration. Even though problems with the project existed during the lengthy development process, Motorola refused to pull the plug. Only after investing $5 billion and years of effort was the project abandoned.[46]

exit champion
an individual working within a corporation who is willing to question the viability of a venture project by demanding hard evidence of venture success and challenging the belief system that carries a venture forward.

One way to avoid these costly and discouraging defeats is to support a key role in the CE process: **exit champions**. In contrast to product champions and other entrepreneurial enthusiasts within the corporation, exit champions are willing to question the viability of a venture project.[47] By demanding hard evidence and challenging the belief system that is carrying an idea forward, exit champions hold the line on ventures that appear shaky.

LO 12-5

Identify the benefits and potential drawbacks of real options analysis in making resource deployment decisions in corporate entrepreneurship contexts.

Both product champions and exit champions must be willing to energetically stand up for what they believe. Both put their reputations on the line. But they also differ in important ways.[48] Product champions deal in uncertainty and ambiguity. Exit champions reduce ambiguity by gathering hard data and developing a strong case for why a project should be killed. Product champions are often thought to be willing to violate procedures and operate outside normal channels. Exit champions often have to reinstate procedures and reassert the decision-making criteria that are supposed to guide venture decisions. Whereas product champions often emerge as heroes, exit champions run the risk of losing status by opposing popular projects.

The role of exit champion may seem unappealing. But it is one that could save a corporation both financially and in terms of its reputation in the marketplace. It is especially important because one measure of the success of a firm's CE efforts is the extent to which it knows when to cut its losses and move on.

real options analysis (ROA)
an investment analysis tool that looks at an investment or activity as a series of sequential steps, and for each step the investor has the option of (a) investing additional funds to grow or accelerate, (b) delaying, (c) shrinking the scale of, or (d) abandoning the activity.

REAL OPTIONS ANALYSIS: A USEFUL TOOL

One way firms can minimize failure and avoid losses from pursuing faulty ideas is to apply the logic of real options. **Real options analysis (ROA)** is an investment analysis tool from the field of finance. It has been slowly, but increasingly, adopted by consultants and executives to support strategic decision making in firms.

Applied to entrepreneurship, real options suggest a path that companies can use to manage the uncertainty associated with launching new ventures. Some of the most common applications of real options are with property and insurance. A real estate option grants the holder the right to buy or sell a piece of property at an established price some time in the future. The actual market price of the property may rise above the established (or strike) price—or the market value may sink below the strike price. If the price of the property goes up, the owner of the option is likely to buy it. If the market value of the property drops, the option holder is unlikely to execute the purchase. In the latter circumstance, the option holder has limited his or her loss to the cost of the option but during the life of the option retains the right to participate in whatever the upside potential might be.

Applications of Real Options Analysis to Strategic Decisions

The concept of options can also be applied to strategic decisions where management has flexibility. Situations arise where management must decide whether to invest additional funds to grow or accelerate the activity, perhaps delay in order to learn more, shrink the scale of the activity, or even abandon it. Decisions to invest in new ventures or other business activities such as R&D, motion pictures, exploration and production of oil wells, and the opening and closing of copper mines often have this flexibility.[49] Important issues to note are:

- ROA is appropriate to use when investments can be staged; a smaller investment up front can be followed by subsequent investments. Real options can be applied to an investment decision that gives the company the right, but not the obligation, to make follow-on investments.
- Strategic decision makers have "tollgates," or key points at which they can decide whether to continue, delay, or abandon the project. Executives have flexibility. There are opportunities to make other go or no-go decisions associated with each phase.
- It is expected that there will be increased knowledge about outcomes at the time of the next investment and that additional knowledge will help inform the decision makers about whether to make additional investments (i.e., whether the option is in the money or out of the money).

Consider the real options logic that Johnson Controls, a maker of car seats, instrument panels, and interior control systems, uses to advance or eliminate entrepreneurial ideas. Johnson options each new innovative idea by making a small investment in it. To receive additional funding, the idea must continue to prove itself at each stage of development. Here's how Jim Geschke, former vice president and general manager of electronics integration at Johnson, described the process:

> Think of Johnson as an innovation machine. The front end has a robust series of gates that each idea must pass through. Early on, we'll have many ideas and spend a little money on each of them. As they get more fleshed out, the ideas go through a gate where a go or no-go decision is made. A lot of ideas get filtered out, so there are far fewer items, and the spending on each goes up. . . . Several months later each idea will face another gate. If it passes, that means it's a serious idea that we are going to develop. Then the spending goes way up, and the number of ideas goes way down. By the time you reach the final gate, you need to have a credible business case in order to be accepted. At a certain point in the development process, we take our idea to customers and ask them what they think. Sometimes they say, "That's a terrible idea. Forget it." Other times they say, "That's fabulous. I want a million of them."[50]

This process of evaluating ideas by separating winning ideas from losing ones in a way that keeps investments low has helped Johnson Controls grow its revenues to over $38 billion a year. Using real options logic to advance the development process is a key way that firms reduce uncertainty and minimize innovation-related failures.[51] Real options logic can also be used with other types of strategic decisions. Strategy Spotlight 12.4 discusses how Intel uses real options logic in making capacity expansion decisions.

12.4 STRATEGY SPOTLIGHT

SAVING MILLIONS WITH REAL OPTIONS AT INTEL

The semiconductor business is complex and dynamic. This makes it a difficult one to manage. On the one hand, both the technology in the chips and the consumer demand for chips are highly volatile. This makes it difficult to plan for the future as far as the need for chip designs and production plants is concerned. On the other hand, it is incredibly expensive to build new chip plants, about $5 billion each, and chip manufacturing equipment needs to be ordered well ahead of when it is needed. The lead time for ordering new equipment can be up to three years. This creates a great challenge. Firms have to decide how much and what type of equipment to purchase long before they have a good handle on what the demand for semiconductor chips will be. Guessing wrong leaves the firm with too much or too little capacity.

Intel has figured out a way to limit the risk it faces by using option contracts. Intel pays an up-front fee for the right to purchase key pieces of equipment at a specific future date. At that point, Intel either purchases the equipment or releases the supplier from the contract. In these cases, the supplier is then free to sell the equipment to someone else. This all seems fairly simple. A number of commodities, such as wheat and sugar, have robust option markets. The challenge isn't in setting up the contracts. It is in pricing those contracts. Unlike wheat and sugar, where a large number of suppliers and buyers results in an efficient market that sets the prices of standard commodity products, there are few buyers and suppliers of chip manufacturing equipment. Further, the equipment is not a standard commodity. As a result, prices for equipment options are the outcome of difficult negotiations.

Karl Kempf, a mathematician with Intel, has figured out how to make this process smoother. Along with a group of mathematicians at Stanford, Kempf has developed a computing logic for calculating the price of options. He and his colleagues create a forecasting model for potential demand. They calculate the likelihood of a range of potential demand levels. They also set up a computer simulation of a production plant. They then use the possible demand levels to predict how many pieces of production equipment they will need in the plant to meet the demand. They run this over and over again, thousands of times, to generate predictions about the likelihood they will need to purchase a specific piece of equipment. They use this information to identify what equipment they definitely need to order. Where there is significant uncertainty about the need for equipment, they use the simulation results to identify the specific equipment for which they need option contracts and the value of those options to Intel. This helps with the pricing.

Intel estimates that in the five years from 2008 to 2012, the use of options in equipment purchases saved the firm in excess of $125 million and provided the firm with at least $2 billion in revenue upside for expansions it could have quickly made using optioned equipment.

Sources: Kempf, K., Erhun, F., Hertzler, E., Rosenberg, T., and C. Peng. 2013. Optimizing capital investment decisions at Intel Corporation. *Interfaces,* 43(1): 62–78; and King, I. 2012. A chipmaker's model mathematician. *Bloomberg Businessweek,* June 4: 35.

Potential Pitfalls of Real Options Analysis

Despite the many benefits that can be gained from using ROA, managers must be aware of its potential limitations or pitfalls. We will address three major issues, as follows.[52]

back-solver dilemma problem with investment decisions in which managers scheme to have a project meet investment approval criteria, even though the investment may not enhance firm value.

Agency Theory and the Back-Solver Dilemma Let's assume that companies adopting a real options perspective invest heavily in training and that their people understand how to effectively estimate variance–the amount of dispersion or range that is estimated for potential outcomes. Such training can help them use ROA. However, it does not solve another inherent problem: Managers may have an incentive and the know-how to "game the system." If managers know that a certain option value must be met in order for the proposal to get approved, they can back-solve the model to find a variance estimate needed to arrive at the answer that upper management desires.

Managerial Conceit: Overconfidence and the Illusion of Control Often, poor decisions are the result of such traps as biases, blind spots, and other human frailties. Much of this literature falls under the concept of **managerial conceit.**[53]

managerial conceit biases, blind spots, and other human frailties that lead to poor managerial decisions.

First, managerial conceit occurs when decision makers who have made successful choices in the past come to believe that they possess superior expertise for managing uncertainty. They believe that their abilities can reduce the risks inherent in decision making to a much greater extent than they actually can. Such managers are more likely to shift away from analysis to trusting their own judgment. In the case of real options, they can simply declare that any given decision is a real option and proceed as before.

Second, employing the real options perspective can encourage decision makers toward a bias for action. Such a bias may lead to carelessness. The cost to write the first stage of an option is much smaller than the cost of full commitment, and managers pay less attention to small decisions than to large ones. Because real options are designed to minimize potential losses while preserving potential gains, any problems that arise are likely to be smaller at first, causing less concern for the manager. Managerial conceit could suggest that managers will assume that those problems are the easiest to solve and control—a concern referred to as the illusion of control. Managers may fail to respond appropriately because they overlook the problem or believe that since it is small, they can easily resolve it. Thus, managers may approach each real option decision with less care and diligence than if they had made a full commitment to a larger investment.

Managerial Conceit: Irrational Escalation of Commitment A strength of a real options perspective is also one of its Achilles heels. Both real options and decisions involving **escalation of commitment** require specific environments with sequential decisions.[54]

escalation of commitment
the tendency for managers to irrationally stick with an investment, even one that is broken down into a sequential series of decisions, when investment criteria are not being met.

An option to exit requires reversing an initial decision made by someone in the organization. Organizations typically encourage managers to "own their decisions" in order to motivate them. As managers invest themselves in their decision, it proves harder for them to lose face by reversing course. For managers making the decision, it feels as if they made the wrong decision in the first place, even if it was initially a good decision. Thus, they are likely to continue an existing project even if it should perhaps be ended.[55]

Despite the potential pitfalls of a real options approach, many of the strategic decisions that product champions and top managers must make are enhanced when decision makers have an entrepreneurial mindset.

ENTREPRENEURIAL ORIENTATION

LO 12-6

Explain how an entrepreneurial orientation can enhance a firm's efforts to develop promising corporate venture initiatives.

Firms that want to engage in successful CE need to have an entrepreneurial orientation (EO).[56] **Entrepreneurial orientation** refers to the strategy-making practices that businesses use in identifying and launching corporate ventures. It represents a frame of mind and a perspective toward entrepreneurship that is reflected in a firm's ongoing processes and corporate culture.[57]

entrepreneurial orientation
the practices that businesses use in identifying and launching corporate ventures.

An EO has five dimensions that permeate the decision-making styles and practices of the firm's members: autonomy, innovativeness, proactiveness, competitive aggressiveness, and risk taking. These factors work together to enhance a firm's entrepreneurial performance. But even those firms that are strong in only a few aspects of EO can be very successful.[58] Exhibit 12.3 summarizes the dimensions of entrepreneurial orientation. We discuss the five dimensions of EO and how they have been used to enhance internal venture development.

Autonomy

Autonomy refers to a willingness to act independently in order to carry forward an entrepreneurial vision or opportunity. It applies to both individuals and teams that operate outside an organization's existing norms and strategies. In the context of corporate entrepreneurship, autonomous work units are often used to leverage existing strengths in new arenas, identify opportunities that are beyond the organization's current capabilities, and encourage development of new ventures or improved business practices.[59]

autonomy
independent action by an individual or a team aimed at bringing forth a business concept or vision and carrying it through to completion.

Autonomy represents a type of empowerment (see Chapter 11) that is directed at identifying and leveraging entrepreneurial opportunities. There are two common techniques firms can use to promote autonomy. First, they can create independent work groups, often called new venture groups or skunkworks, that are tasked with generating new ideas. Second, they can create organizational structures to foster creativity and flexibility, such as breaking large firms into smaller, decentralized entrepreneurial units.

EXHIBIT 12.3
Dimensions of Entrepreneurial Orientation

Dimension	Definition
Autonomy	Independent action by an individual or team aimed at bringing forth a business concept or vision and carrying it through to completion.
Innovativeness	A willingness to introduce novelty through experimentation and creative processes aimed at developing new products and services as well as new processes.
Proactiveness	A forward-looking perspective characteristic of a marketplace leader that has the foresight to seize opportunities in anticipation of future demand.
Competitive aggressiveness	An intense effort to outperform industry rivals characterized by a combative posture or an aggressive response aimed at improving position or overcoming a threat in a competitive marketplace.
Risk taking	Making decisions and taking action without certain knowledge of probable outcomes; some undertakings may also involve making substantial resource commitments in the process of venturing forward.

Sources: Dess, G. G., and Lumpkin, G. T. 2005. The role of entrepreneurial orientation in stimulating effective corporate entrepreneurship. *Academy of Management Executive*, 19(1): 147–156; Covin, J. G., and D. P. Slevin. 1991. A conceptual model of entrepreneurship as firm behavior. *Entrepreneurship Theory & Practice*, Fall: 7–25; Lumpkin, G. T., and G. G. Dess. 1996. Clarifying the entrepreneurial orientation construct and linking it to performance. *Academy of Management Review*, 21: 135–172; and Miller, D. 1983. The correlates of entrepreneurship in three types of firms. *Management Science*, 29: 770–791.

Creating autonomous work units and encouraging independent action may have pitfalls that can jeopardize their effectiveness. Autonomous teams often lack coordination. Excessive decentralization has a strong potential to create inefficiencies, such as duplicating effort and wasting resources on projects with questionable feasibility.

For autonomous work units and independent projects to be effective, such efforts have to be measured and monitored. This requires a delicate balance: Companies must have the patience and budget to tolerate the explorations of autonomous groups and the strength to cut back efforts that are not bearing fruit. Efforts must be undertaken with a clear sense of purpose–namely, to generate new sources of competitive advantage.

Innovativeness

innovativeness
a willingness to introduce novelty through experimentation and creative processes aimed at developing new products and services as well as new processes.

Innovativeness refers to a firm's efforts to find new opportunities and novel solutions. In the beginning of this chapter we discussed innovation; here the focus is on innovativeness–a firm's attitude toward innovation and willingness to innovate. It involves creativity and experimentation that result in new products, new services, or improved technological processes.[60] Innovativeness is one of the major components of an entrepreneurial strategy. As indicated at the beginning of the chapter, however, the job of managing innovativeness can be very challenging.

Innovativeness requires that firms depart from existing technologies and practices and venture beyond the current state of the art. Inventions and new ideas need to be nurtured even when their benefits are unclear. How firms invest their resources is often a powerful driver for innovativeness. Firms can do this by regularly budgeting significant resources in both product and process R&D to stay ahead of competitors. They can also do it in a more decentralized way by having internal competitions where employees can win funding to start internal new innovative businesses.

Innovativeness can be a source of great progress and strong corporate growth, but expenditures on R&D aimed at identifying new products or processes can be a waste of resources if the effort does not yield results.

Proactiveness

proactiveness
a forward-looking perspective characteristic of a marketplace leader that has the foresight to seize opportunities in anticipation of future demand.

Proactiveness refers to a firm's efforts to seize new opportunities. Proactive organizations monitor trends, identify the future needs of existing customers, and anticipate changes in demand or emerging problems that can lead to new venture opportunities. Proactiveness involves not only recognizing changes but also being willing to act on those insights ahead of the competition.[61] Such a forward-looking perspective is important for companies that seek to be industry leaders and also for firms that desire to change the very nature of competition in their industry.

Proactiveness puts competitors in the position of having to respond to successful initiatives. The benefit gained by firms that are the first to enter new markets, establish brand identity, implement administrative techniques, or adopt new operating technologies in an industry is called first-mover advantage.[62]

First movers are not always successful. The customers of companies that introduce novel products or embrace breakthrough technologies may be reluctant to commit to a new way of doing things.

Careful monitoring and scanning of the environment, as well as extensive feasibility research, are needed for a proactive strategy to lead to competitive advantages. Firms that do it well usually have substantial growth and internal development to show for it. Many of them have been able to sustain the advantages of proactiveness for years.

Competitive Aggressiveness

Competitive aggressiveness refers to a firm's efforts to outperform its industry rivals. Companies with an aggressive orientation are willing to "do battle" with competitors. They might slash prices and sacrifice profitability to gain market share or spend aggressively to obtain manufacturing capacity. As an avenue of firm development and growth, competitive aggressiveness may involve being very assertive in leveraging the results of other entrepreneurial activities such as innovativeness or proactiveness.

competitive aggressiveness
an intense effort to outperform industry rivals; characterized by a combative posture or an aggressive response aimed at improving position or overcoming a threat in a competitive marketplace.

Strategic managers can use competitive aggressiveness to combat industry trends that threaten their survival or market position. Sometimes firms need to be forceful in defending the competitive position that has made them an industry leader. Firms often need to be aggressive to ensure their advantage by capitalizing on new technologies or serving new market needs.

Competitive aggressiveness may not always lead to competitive advantages. Some companies (or their CEOs) have severely damaged their reputations by being overly aggressive. For example, Walmart's aggressive pricing structure has forced smaller, local retailers out of business in many markets. This has led a number of local communities, often at the urging of local retailers, to pass regulations that make it difficult for Walmart to move into or expand operations in these towns and cities.

Competitive aggressiveness is a strategy that is best used in moderation. Companies that aggressively establish their competitive position and vigorously exploit opportunities to achieve profitability may, over the long run, be better able to sustain their competitive advantages if their goal is to defeat, rather than decimate, their competitors.

Risk Taking

Risk taking refers to a firm's willingness to seize a venture opportunity even though it does not know whether the venture will be successful—to act boldly without knowing the consequences. To obtain high financial returns, firms take such risks as assuming high levels of debt, committing large amounts of firm resources, introducing new products into new markets, and investing in unexplored technologies.

risk taking
making decisions and taking action without certain knowledge of probable outcomes. Some undertakings may also involve making substantial resource commitments in the process of venturing forward.

All of the approaches to internal development that we have discussed are potentially risky. Whether they are being aggressive, proactive, or innovative, firms on the path of CE must act without knowing how their actions will turn out. Before launching their strategies, corporate entrepreneurs must know their firm's appetite for risk.[63]

Three types of risk that organizations and their executives face are business risk, financial risk, and personal risk:

- ***Business risk taking*** involves venturing into the unknown without knowing the probability of success. This is the risk associated with entering untested markets or committing to unproven technologies.

- ***Financial risk taking*** requires that a company borrow heavily or commit a large portion of its resources in order to grow. In this context, risk is used to refer to the risk-return trade-off that is familiar in financial analysis.
- ***Personal risk taking*** refers to the risks that an executive assumes in taking a stand in favor of a strategic course of action. Executives who take such risks stand to influence the course of their whole company, and their decisions also can have significant implications for their careers.

Even though risk taking involves taking chances, it is not gambling. The best-run companies investigate the consequences of various opportunities and create scenarios of likely outcomes. A key to managing entrepreneurial risks is to evaluate new venture opportunities thoroughly enough to reduce the uncertainty surrounding them.

Risk taking is a good place to close this chapter on corporate entrepreneurship. Companies that choose to grow through internal corporate venturing must remember that entrepreneurship always involves embracing what is new and uncertain.

ISSUE FOR DEBATE

Automakers across the globe are investing billions of dollars in investing in electric vehicle technology. Tesla has garnered a great deal of attention and investors by taking the lead in market share for electric cars. But a number of mainline auto makers are also fully committed to electric vehicles. General Motors has launched its Bolt EV, is adding an electric Buick SUV, and plans to make Cadillac its first all-electric brand. Looking further out, Mark Reuss, GMs' president said, "General Motors believes in an all-electric future." Similarly, Volvo plans to launch five all-electric vehicles by the end of 2022. Other automakers have similar plans.

One manufacturer who is taking a different path is Mazda. Instead of going full electric in the near term, Mazda is working to extend the life of the internal combustion engine. While the firm has signaled that they are working on an extended range electric car, they had not produced a prototype electric car as of early 2019. Instead, the firm has developed a new type of gasoline engine with an innovative technology that provides the efficiency of a diesel engine with the cleanliness of a gasoline engine. The Skyactiv-X engine that Mazda has developed uses a combination of compression ignition (a technology commonly used in diesel engines) and spark ignition (used in gasoline engines). This allows the engine to produce 10 to 30 percent more torque with 20 to 30 percent greater fuel efficiency than a prior similar sized engine. Mazda argues that when considering "wheel-to-wheel" carbon emission for a car, which includes carbon associated with fuel extraction, power generation, manufacturing, and shipping, a Mazda 3 with the Skyactiv-X engine produces only 10 percent more carbon dioxide than a similar-sized electric vehicle. And since it is based on established mass-manufacturing technologies and doesn't require the added cost of the large quantity of batteries needed in electric cars, Mazda's Skyactiv-X Model 3 is priced $13 to $15 thousand less than similar electric cars.

What is unknown is how the market will respond to Mazda's new technology. While Mazda argues this new engine puts it roughly on par with the environmental friendliness of an electric vehicle, it is not clear that consumers will see it the same way. Additionally, it may not meet regulatory pressures being put on automakers to manufacture products that meet zero emission standards.

Discussion Questions

1. Is Mazda's strategy to innovate to improve on internal combustion engine vehicles a valuable direction to go?

2. If you were choosing between a Mazda with their more efficient engine or a similar sized electric car, which would you select? Why?
3. What can Mazda do to have the best chance of succeeding with their more efficient gasoline engine vehicles?

Sources: Smith, L. 2018. Mazda could've just saved petrol–New engines so clean it could rival electric cars. *express.co.uk,* March 14: np; Carney, D. 2018. Mazda's new Skyactiv-X engine gives new life to internal combustion. *spectrum.ieee.org,* July 30: np; Valdes-Dapena, P. 2017. GM: The future is all-electric. *cnn.com,* October 2: np; and Calamur, K. 2017. Volvo's electric future. *theatlantic.com,* July 5: np.

Reflecting on Career Implications . . .

This chapter focuses on corporate entrepreneurship and innovation. You can provide greater value to your firm and build a higher impact career if you develop innovativeness skills and an entrepreneurial orientation. The following points identify issues to consider as you build these skills and orientation.

- **Innovation:** Identify the types of innovations being pursued by your company. Do they tend to be incremental or radical? Product-related or process-related? Are there ways in which you can add value to such innovations, no matter how minor your contributions are?
- **Cultivating Innovation Skills:** Exhibit 12.2 describes the five traits of an effective innovator (associating, questioning, observing, experimenting, and networking). Assess yourself on each of these traits. Practice the skills in your work and professional life to build your skills as an innovator. If you are interviewing for a job with an organization that is considered high on innovation, it might be in your interest to highlight these traits.
- **Real Options Analysis:** Success in your career often depends on creating and exercising career "options." However, creation of options involves costs as well, such as learning new skills, obtaining additional certifications, and so on. Consider what options you can create for yourself. Evaluate the cost of these options.
- **Entrepreneurial Orientation:** Consider the five dimensions of entrepreneurial orientation. Evaluate yourself on each of these dimensions (autonomy, innovativeness, proactiveness, competitive aggressiveness, and risk taking). If you are high on entrepreneurial orientation, you may have a future as an entrepreneur. Consider the ways in which you can use the experience and learning from your current job to become a successful entrepreneur in later years.

key points

LO 12-1 The importance of implementing strategies and practices that foster innovation.

- Innovation helps an organization stay fresh and reinvent itself as conditions in the business environment change.
- Product innovation refers to efforts to create product designs and applications of technology to develop new products for end users.
- Process innovation is associated with improving the efficiency of an organizational process, especially manufacturing systems and operations.
- Another important aspect is the degree of innovativeness of an action.
    - Radical innovations produce fundamental changes by evoking major departures from existing practices.
    - Incremental innovations enhance existing practices or make small improvements in products and processes.

LO 12-2 The challenges and pitfalls of managing corporate innovation processes.

- What is it that makes innovation so difficult?
    - The uncertainty about outcomes is one factor. Companies are often reluctant to invest time and resources in activities with an unknown future.
    - Another factor is that the innovation process involves so many choices, leading to five organizational trade-off decisions innovating organizations face:
        - Seeds vs. weeds.
        - Experience vs. initiatives.
        - Internal vs. external staffing.
        - Building capabilities vs. collaborating.
        - Incremental vs. preemptive launch.
- To be successful at innovating, firms need to develop the following key skills:
    - Cultivating the innovation skills of employees, including the innovative DNA of its leaders.
    - Defining the scope of innovation to ensure the firm's innovation efforts are not wasted on

projects that are outside the firm's domain of interest.
- Effectively manage the pace of innovation to match the type of innovative effort and the natural rhythm of the market.
- Staff innovation teams with the skill sets needed to capture the value from the innovation effort.
- Effectively collaborate with innovation partners.
- Appreciate the value of unsuccessful innovations.

LO 12-3 How corporations use new venture teams, business incubators, and product champions to create an internal environment and culture that promote entrepreneurial development.

- Firms using a focused approach typically separate the corporate venturing activity from the other ongoing operations of the firm.
    - New venture groups are teams within a corporation that are tasked with identifying, evaluating, and cultivating venture opportunities.
    - Business incubators are corporate new venture groups that support and nurture fledgling entrepreneurial ventures until they can thrive on their own as standalone businesses.
- Firms using a dispersed approach typically emphasize a broad focus on entrepreneurship spread throughout the entire organization.
    - With an entrepreneurial culture, everyone in the organization is attuned to opportunities to help create new businesses.
    - Firms using a dispersed approach often have competitions where internal entrepreneurs can have their projects funded using the firm's resource allotments.
    - Product champions are individuals who take the lead in bringing entrepreneurial ideas forward.

LO 12-4 How corporate entrepreneurship achieves both financial goals and strategic goals.

- In terms of financial performance, slightly more than 50 percent of corporate venturing efforts reach profitability (measured by ROI) within six years of their launch.
- The strategic reasons for undertaking a corporate venture include strengthening competitive position, entering into new markets, expanding capabilities by learning and acquiring new knowledge, and building the corporation's base of resources and experience.

LO 12-5 The benefits and potential drawbacks of real options analysis in making resource deployment decisions in corporate entrepreneurship contexts.

- Real options logic can help a firm to manage the uncertainty associated with launching new ventures. It provides a framework to decide whether to invest additional funds to grow or accelerate the activity, perhaps delay in order to learn more, shrink the scale of the activity, or even abandon it.
- Pitfalls of real options analysis include:
    - The back-solver dilemma—when firm managers scheme to have a project meet investment approval criteria even though the investment may not enhance firm value.
    - Managerial conceit—when biases, blind spots, and other human frailties weaken decision making.
    - Escalation of commitment—the tendency of managers to invest further in failing courses of action.

LO 12-6 How an entrepreneurial orientation can enhance a firm's efforts to develop promising corporate venture initiatives.

- Entrepreneurial orientation refers to the strategy-making practices that businesses use in identifying and launching corporate ventures. There are five dimensions of entrepreneurial orientation.
    - Autonomy refers to a willingness to act independently in order to carry forward an entrepreneurial vision or opportunity.
    - Innovativeness refers to a firm's efforts to find new opportunities and novel solutions.
    - Proactiveness refers to a firm's efforts to seize new opportunities.
    - Competitive aggressiveness refers to a firm's efforts to outperform its industry rivals.
    - Risk taking refers to a firm's willingness to seize a venture opportunity even though it does not know whether the venture will be successful—to act boldly without knowing the consequences.

SUMMARY REVIEW QUESTIONS

1. What is meant by the concept of a continuum of radical and incremental innovations?
2. What are the dilemmas that organizations face when deciding what innovation projects to pursue? What steps can organizations take to effectively manage the innovation process?
3. What is the difference between focused and dispersed approaches to corporate entrepreneurship?
4. How are business incubators used to foster internal corporate venturing?
5. What is the role of the product champion in bringing a new product or service into existence in a corporation? How can companies use product champions to enhance their venture development efforts?
6. Explain the difference between proactiveness and competitive aggressiveness in terms of achieving and sustaining competitive advantage.
7. Describe how the entrepreneurial orientation (EO) dimensions of innovativeness, proactiveness, and risk taking can be combined to create competitive advantages for entrepreneurial firms.

key terms

innovation 360
product innovation 361
process innovation 361
radical innovation 361
incremental innovation 361
strategic envelope 366
corporate entrepreneurship (CE) 371
focused approaches to corporate entrepreneurship 372
new venture group (NVG) 373
business incubator 373
dispersed approaches to corporate entrepreneurship 373
entrepreneurial culture 374
product champion 375
exit champion 376
real options analysis (ROA) 376
back-solver dilemma 378
managerial conceit 378
escalation of commitment 379
entrepreneurial orientation 379
autonomy 379
innovativeness 380
proactiveness 380
competitive aggressiveness 381
risk taking 381

EXPERIENTIAL EXERCISES AND APPLICATION QUESTIONS

1. Google has entered a number of markets since their radio debacle (discussed in the Learning from Mistakes in the opening section of the chapter). Pick two markets Google has entered and discuss the nature of the innovative effort it pursued, the actions the firm took to enter these markets, and the level of success the firm has experienced.
2. Select two different major corporations from two different industries (you might use Fortune 500 companies to make your selection). Compare and contrast these organizations in terms of their entrepreneurial orientation. (Fill in the table that follows.)

Based on your comparison:

1. How is the corporation's entrepreneurial orientation reflected in its strategy?
2. Which corporation would you say has the stronger entrepreneurial orientation?
3. Is the corporation with the stronger entrepreneurial orientation also stronger in terms of financial performance?

Entrepreneurial Orientation	Company A	Company B
Autonomy		
Innovativeness		
Proactiveness		
Competitive aggressiveness		
Risk taking		

4. Select a firm known for its corporate entrepreneurship activities. Research the company and discuss how it has positioned itself relative to its close competitors. Does it have a unique strategic advantage? Disadvantage? Explain.
5. Explain the difference between product innovations and process innovations. Provide examples of firms that have recently introduced each type of innovation. What are the types of innovations related to the strategies of each firm?
6. Using the Internet, select a company that is listed on the NASDAQ or New York Stock Exchange. Research the extent to which the company has an entrepreneurial culture. Does the company use product champions? Does it have a corporate venture capital fund? Do you believe its entrepreneurial efforts are sufficient to generate sustainable advantages?
7. How can an established firm use an entrepreneurial orientation to enhance its overall strategic position? Provide examples.

ETHICS QUESTIONS

1. Innovation activities are often aimed at making a discovery or commercializing a technology ahead of the competition. What are some of the unethical practices that companies could engage in during the innovation process? What are the potential long-term consequences of such actions?
2. Discuss the ethical implications of using entrepreneurial policies and practices to pursue corporate social responsibility goals. Are these efforts authentic and genuine or just an attempt to attract more customers?

REFERENCES

1. Eddy, N. 2014. Android captures 85 percent of smartphone market worldwide. *eweek.com,* August 8: np; Vascellaro, J. 2009. Radio tunes out Google in rare miss for web titan. *wsj.com,* May 12: np; and McGrath, R. 2011. Failing by design. *Harvard Business Review,* 89(4): 76–83; *statista.com.*
2. For an interesting discussion, see Johannessen, J. A., Olsen, B., & Lumpkin, G. T. 2001. Innovation as newness: What is new, how new, and new to whom? *European Journal of Innovation Management,* 4(1): 20–31.
3. The discussion of product and process innovation is based on Roberts, E. B. (Ed.). 2002. *Innovation: Driving product, process, and market change.* San Francisco: Jossey-Bass; Hayes, R. & Wheelwright, S. 1985. Competing through manufacturing. *Harvard Business Review,* 63(1): 99–109; and Hayes, R. & Wheelwright, S. 1979. Dynamics of product-process life cycles. *Harvard Business Review,* 57(2): 127–136.

4. The discussion of radical and incremental innovations draws from Leifer, R., McDermott, C. M., Colarelli, G., O'Connor, G. C., Peters, L. S., Rice, M. P., & Veryzer, R. W. 2000. *Radical innovation: How mature companies can outsmart upstarts.* Boston: Harvard Business School Press; Damanpour, F. 1996. Organizational complexity and innovation: Developing and testing multiple contingency models. *Management Science,* 42(5): 693–716; and Hage, J. 1980. *Theories of organizations.* New York: Wiley.
5. Christensen, C. M. & Raynor, M. E. 2003. *The innovator's solution.* Boston: Harvard Business School Press.
6. Dressner, H. 2004. The Gartner Fellows interview: Clayton M. Christensen. *www.gartner.com,* April 26.
7. For another perspective on how different types of innovation affect organizational choices, see Wolter, C. & Veloso, F. M. 2008. The effects of innovation on vertical structure: Perspectives on transactions costs and competences. *Academy of Management Review,* 33(3): 586–605.
8. Drucker, P. F. 1985. *Innovation and Entrepreneurship: Practice and Principles.* New York: Harper & Row.
9. Birkinshaw, J., Hamel, G., & Mol, M. J. 2008. Management innovation. *Academy of Management Review,* 33(4): 825–845.
10. Steere, W. C., Jr. and J. Niblack. 1997. Pfizer, Inc. In Kanter, R. M., Kao, J., & Wiersema, F. (Eds.), *Innovation: Breakthrough thinking at 3M, DuPont, GE, Pfizer, and Rubbermaid.* New York: HarperCollins, 123–145.
11. Morrissey, C. A. 2000. Managing innovation through corporate venturing. *Graziadio Business Report,* Spring, *gbr.pepperdine.edu;* and Sharma, A. 1999. Central dilemmas of managing innovation in large firms. *California Management Review,* 41(3): 147–164.
12. Sharma, op. cit.
13. Dyer, J. H., Gregersen, H. B., & Christensen, C. M. 2009. The innovator's DNA. *Harvard Business Review,* December: 61–67.
14. Eggers, J. P. & Kaplan, S. 2009. Cognition and renewal: Comparing CEO and organizational effects on incumbent adaptation to technical change. *Organization Science,* 20: 461–477.
15. For more on defining the scope of innovation, see Valikangas, L. & Gibbert, M. 2005. Boundary-setting strategies for escaping innovation traps. *MIT Sloan Management Review,* 46(3): 58–65.
16. Leifer et al., op. cit.
17. Bhide, A. V. 2000. *The origin and evolution of new businesses.* New York: Oxford University Press; Brown, S. L. & Eisenhardt, K. M. 1998. *Competing on the edge: Strategy as structured chaos.* Cambridge, MA: Harvard Business School Press.
18. McGrath, R. G. & Keil, T. 2007. The value captor's process: Getting the most out of your new business ventures. *Harvard Business Review,* May: 128–136.
19. For an interesting discussion of how sharing technology knowledge with different divisions in an organization can contribute to innovation processes, see Miller, D. J., Fern, M. J., & Cardinal, L. B. 2007. The use of knowledge for technological innovation within diversified firms. *Academy of Management Journal,* 50(2): 308–326.
20. Ketchen, D. J., Jr., Ireland, R. D., & Snow, C. C. 2007 Strategic entrepreneurship, collaborative innovation, and wealth creation. *Strategic Entrepreneurship Journal,* 1(3–4): 371–385.
21. Chesbrough, H. 2003. *Open innovation: The new imperative for creating and profiting from technology.* Boston: Harvard Business School Press.
22. For a study of what makes alliance partnerships successful, see Sampson, R. C. 2007. R&D alliances and firm performance: The impact of technological diversity and alliance organization on innovation. *Academy of Management Journal,* 50(2): 364–386.
23. For an interesting perspective on the role of collaboration among multinational corporations, see Hansen, M. T. & Nohria, N. 2004. How to build collaborative advantage. *MIT Sloan Management Review,* 46(1): 22–30.
24. Wells, R. M. J. 2008. The product innovation process: Are managing information flows and cross-functional collaboration key? *Academy of Management Perspectives,* 22(1): 58–60; Dougherty, D. & Dunne, D. D. 2011. Organizing ecologies of complex innovation. *Organization Science,* 22(5): 1214–1223; and Kim, H. E. & Pennings, J. M. 2009. Innovation and strategic renewal in mature markets: A study of the tennis racket industry. *Organization Science,* 20: 368–383.
25. Eggers, J. p. 2014. Get ahead by betting wrong. *Harvard Business Review,* 92(7/8): 26; and Lepore, J. 2014. The disruption machine. *newyorker.com,* June 23: np.
26. Birkinshaw, J. 2016. Increase your return on failure. *Harvard Business Review.* May: 89–93.
27. Guth, W. D. & Ginsberg, A. 1990. Guest editor's introduction: Corporate entrepreneurship. *Strategic Management Journal,* 11: 5–15.
28. Pinchot, G. 1985. *Intrapreneuring.* New York: Harper & Row.
29. For an interesting perspective on the role of context on the discovery and creation of opportunities, see Zahra, S. A. 2008. The virtuous cycle of discovery and creation of entrepreneurial opportunities. *Strategic Entrepreneurship Journal,* 2(3): 243–257.
30. Birkinshaw, J. 1997. Entrepreneurship in multinational corporations: The characteristics of subsidiary initiatives. *Strategic Management Journal,* 18(3): 207–229; and Kanter, R. M. 1985. *The change masters.* New York: Simon & Schuster.
31. Hansen, M. T., Chesbrough, H. W., Nohria, N., & Sull, D. 2000. Networked incubators: Hothouses of the new economy. *Harvard Business Review,* 78(5): 74–84.
32. For more on the importance of leadership in fostering a climate of entrepreneurship, see Ling, Y., Simsek, Z., Lubatkin, M. H., & Veiga, J. F. 2008. Transformational leadership's role in promoting corporate entrepreneurship: Examining the CEO-TMT interface. *Academy of Management Journal,* 51(3): 557–576.
33. Bryant, A. 2011. Got an idea? Sell it to me in 30 seconds. *The New York Times,* January 1: np.
34. Gunther, M. 2010. 3M's innovation revival. *cnnmoney.com,* September 24: np; Byrne, J. 2012. The 12 greatest entrepreneurs of our time. *Fortune,* April 9: 76; and Anonymous. 2007. Johnson & Johnson turns to internal venturing. *silico.wordpress.com,* July 16: np.
35. Colvin, G. 2014. Brad Smith: Getting rid of friction. *Fortune,* July 21: 24.
36. For an interesting discussion, see Davenport, T. H., Prusak, L., & Wilson, H. J. 2003. Who's bringing you hot ideas and how are you responding? *Harvard Business Review,* 80(1): 58–64.
37. Howell, J. M. 2005. The right stuff. Identifying and developing effective champions of innovation. *Academy of*

Management Executive, 19(2): 108-119. See also Greene, P., Brush, C., & Hart, M. 1999. The corporate venture champion: A resource-based approach to role and process. *Entrepreneurship Theory & Practice,* 23(3): 103-122; and Markham, S. K. & Aiman-Smith, L. 2001. Product champions: Truths, myths and management. *Research Technology Management,* May-June: 44-50.

38. Burgelman, R. A. 1983. A process model of internal corporate venturing in the diversified major firm. *Administrative Science Quarterly,* 28: 223-244.
39. Greene, Brush, & Hart, op. cit.; and Shane, S. 1994. Are champions different from non-champions? *Journal of Business Venturing,* 9(5): 397-421.
40. Block, Z. & MacMillan, I. C. 1993. *Corporate venturing–Creating new businesses with the firm.* Cambridge, MA: Harvard Business School Press.
41. For an interesting discussion of these trade-offs, see Stringer, R. 2000. How to manage radical innovation. *California Management Review,* 42(4): 70-88; and Gompers, P. A. & Lerner, J. 1999. *The venture capital cycle.* Cambridge, MA: MIT Press.
42. Cardinal, L. B., Turner, S. F., Fern, M. J., & Burton, R. M. 2011. Organizing for product development across technological environments: Performance trade-offs and priorities. *Organization Science,* 22: 1000-1025.
43. Albrinck, J., Hornery, J., Kletter, D., & Neilson, G. 2001. Adventures in corporate venturing. *Strategy + Business,* 22: 119-129; and McGrath, R. G. & MacMillan, I. C. 2000. *The entrepreneurial mind-set.* Cambridge, MA: Harvard Business School Press.
44. Kiel, T., McGrath, R. G., & Tukiainen, T. 2009. Gems from the ashes: Capability creation and transforming in internal corporate venturing. *Organization Science,* 20: 601-620.
45. For an interesting discussion of how different outcome goals affect organizational learning and employee motivation, see Seijts, G. H. & Latham, G. P. 2005. Learning versus performance goals: When should each be used? *Academy of Management Executive,* 19(1): 124-131.
46. Crockett, R. O. 2001. Motorola. *BusinessWeek,* July 15: 72-78.
47. The ideas in this section are drawn from Royer, I. 2003. Why bad projects are so hard to kill. *Harvard Business Review,* 80(1): 48-56.
48. For an interesting perspective on the different roles that individuals play in the entrepreneurial process, see Baron, R. A. 2008. The role of affect in the entrepreneurial process. *Academy of Management Review,* 33(2): 328-340.
49. For an interesting discussion on why it is difficult to "kill options," refer to Royer, I. 2003. Why bad projects are so hard to kill. *Harvard Business Review,* 81(2): 48-57.
50. Slywotzky, A. & Wise, R., 2003. *How to Grow When Markets Don't.* New York, NY: Warner Books; Slywotzky, A., and R. Wise. 2003. Double-digit growth in no-growth times. *Fast Company,* March 31; www.hoovers.com; and www.johnsoncontrols.com.
51. For more on the role of real options in entrepreneurial decision making, see Folta, T. B. & O'Brien, J. p. 2004. Entry in the presence of dueling options. *Strategic Management Journal,* 25: 121-138.
52. This section draws on Janney, J. J. & Dess, G. G. 2004. Can real options analysis improve decision-making? Promises and pitfalls. *Academy of Management Executive,* 18(4): 60-75. For additional insights on pitfalls of real options, consider McGrath, R. G. 1997. A real options logic for initiating technology positioning investment. *Academy of Management Review,* 22(4): 974-994; Coff, R. W. & Laverty, K. J. 2001. Real options on knowledge assets: Panacea or Pandora's box? *Business Horizons,* 73: 79; McGrath, R. G. 1999. Falling forward: Real options reasoning and entrepreneurial failure. *Academy of Management Review,* 24(1): 13-30; and Zardkoohi, A. 2004. Do real options lead to escalation of commitment? *Academy of Management Review,* 29(1): 111-119.
53. For an understanding of the differences between how managers say they approach decisions and how they actually do, March and Shapira's discussion is perhaps the best. March, J. G. & Shapira, Z. 1987. Managerial perspectives on risk and risk-taking. *Management Science,* 33(11): 1404-1418.
54. A discussion of some factors that may lead to escalation in decision making is included in Choo, C. W. 2005. Information failures and organizational disasters. *MIT Sloan Management Review,* 46(3): 8-10.
55. One very useful solution for reducing the effects of managerial conceit is to incorporate an exit champion into the decision process. Exit champions provide arguments for killing off the firm's commitment to a decision. For a very insightful discussion on exit champions, refer to Royer, I. 2003. Why bad projects are so hard to kill. *Harvard Business Review,* 81(2): 49-56.
56. For more on how entrepreneurial orientation influences organizational performance, see Wang, L. 2008. Entrepreneurial orientation, learning orientation, and firm performance. *Entrepreneurship Theory & Practice,* 32(4): 635-657; and Runyan, R., Droge, C., & Swinney, J. 2008. Entrepreneurial orientation versus small business orientation: What are their relationships to firm performance? *Journal of Small Business Management,* 46(4): 567-588.
57. Covin, J. G. & Slevin, D. p. 1991. A conceptual model of entrepreneurship as firm behavior. *Entrepreneurship Theory and Practice,* 16(1): 7-24; Lumpkin, G. T. & Dess, G. G. 1996. Clarifying the entrepreneurial orientation construct and linking it to performance. *Academy of Management Review,* 21(1): 135-172; and McGrath, R. G. & MacMillan, I. C. 2000. *The entrepreneurial mind-set.* Cambridge, MA: Harvard Business School Press.
58. Lumpkin, G. T. & Dess, G. G. 2001. Linking two dimensions of entrepreneurial orientation to firm performance: The moderating role of environment and life cycle. *Journal of Business Venturing,* 16: 429-451.
59. For an interesting discussion, see Day, J. D., Mang, P. Y., Richter, A., & Roberts, J. 2001. The innovative organization: Why new ventures need more than a room of their own. *McKinsey Quarterly,* 2: 21-31.
60. For insights into the role of information technology in innovativeness, see Dibrell, C., Davis, P. S., & Craig, J. 2008. Fueling innovation through information technology in SMEs. *Journal of Small Business Management,* 46(2): 203-218.
61. Danneels, E. & Sethi, R. 2011. New product exploration under environmental turbulence. *Organization Science,* 22(4): 1026-1039.
62. Lieberman, M. B. & Montgomery, D. B. 1988. First mover advantages. *Strategic Management Journal,* 9 (Special Issue): 41-58.
63. Miller, K. D. 2007. Risk and rationality in entrepreneurial processes. *Strategic Entrepreneurship Journal,* 1(1-2): 57-74.

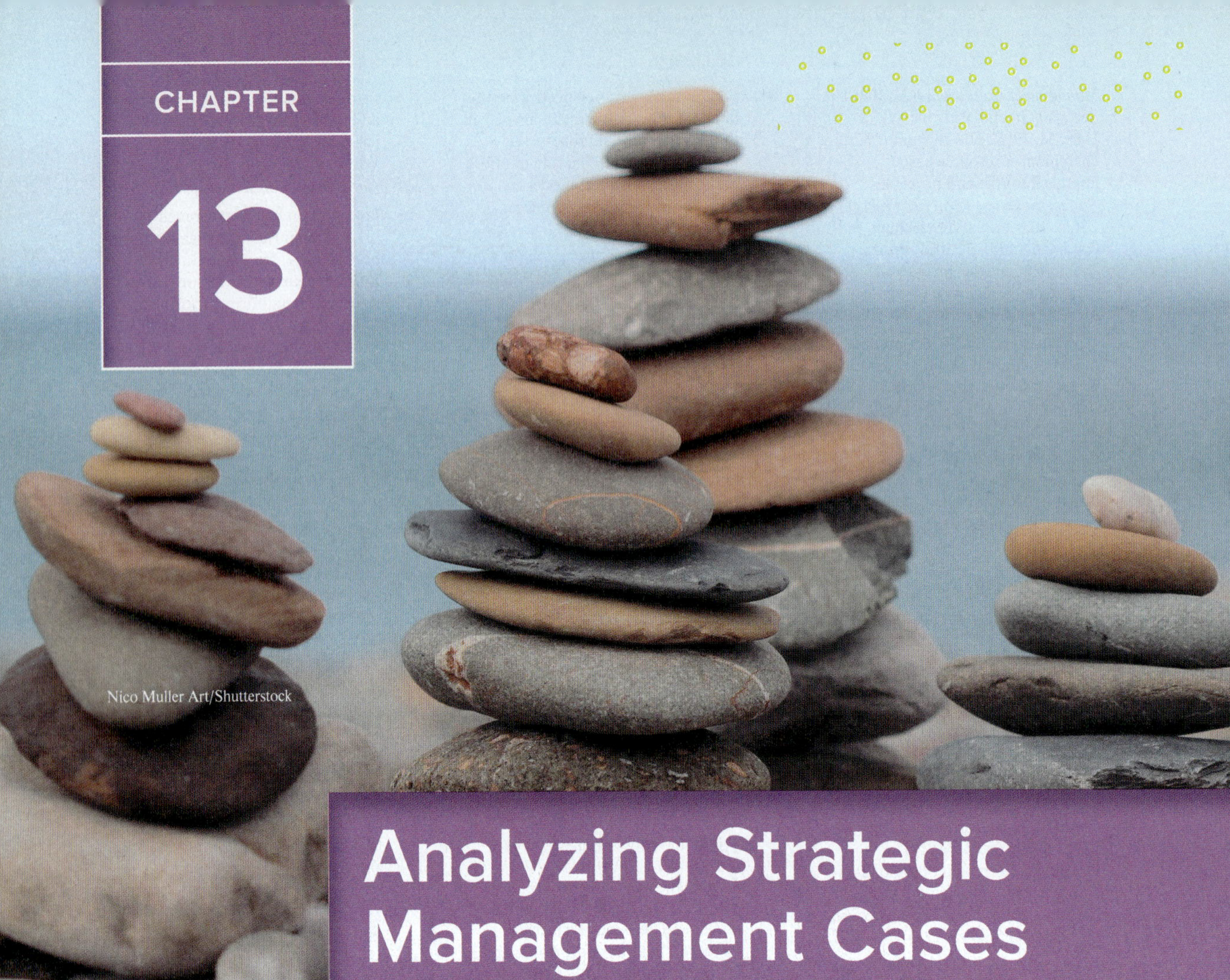

CHAPTER 13

Analyzing Strategic Management Cases

Learning Objectives

LO13-1 Understand how strategic case analysis is used to simulate real-world experiences.

LO13-2 Understand analyzing strategic management cases can help develop the ability to differentiate, speculate, and integrate when evaluating complex business problems.

LO13-3 Identify the steps involved in conducting a strategic management case analysis.

LO13-4 Understand how to get the most out of case analysis.

LO13-5 Understand how integrative thinking and conflict-inducing discussion techniques can lead to better decisions.

LO13-6 Understand how to use the strategic insights and material from each of the 12 previous chapters in the text to analyze issues posed by strategic management cases.

WHY ANALYZE STRATEGIC MANAGEMENT CASES?

If you don't ask the right questions, then you're never going to get the right solution. I spent too much of my career feeling like I'd done a really good job answering the wrong question. And that was because I was letting other people give me the question.[1]

–*Tim Brown, CEO of IDEO (a leading design consulting firm)*

It is often said that the key to finding good answers is to ask good questions. Strategic managers and business leaders are required to evaluate options, make choices, and find solutions to the challenges they face every day. To do so, they must learn to ask the right questions. The study of strategic management poses the same challenge. The process of analyzing, decision making, and implementing strategic actions raises many good questions:

- Why do some firms succeed and others fail?
- Why are some companies higher performers than others?
- What information is needed in the strategic planning process?
- How do competing values and beliefs affect strategic decision making?
- What skills and capabilities are needed to implement a strategy effectively?

How does a student of strategic management answer these questions? By strategic case analysis. **Case analysis** simulates the real-world experience that strategic managers and company leaders face as they try to determine how best to run their companies. It places students in the middle of an actual situation and challenges them to figure out what to do.[2]

Asking the right questions is just the beginning of case analysis. In the previous chapters we have discussed issues and challenges that managers face and provided analytical frameworks for understanding the situation. But once the analysis is complete, decisions have to be made. Case analysis forces you to choose among different options and set forth a plan of action based on your choices. But even then the job is not done. Strategic case analysis also requires that you address how you will implement the plan and the implications of choosing one course of action over another.

case analysis
a method of learning complex strategic management concepts—such as environmental analysis, the process of decision making, and implementing strategic actions—through placing students in the middle of an actual situation and challenging them to figure out what to do.

A strategic management case is a detailed description of a challenging situation faced by an organization.[3] It usually includes a chronology of events and extensive support materials, such as financial statements, product lists, and transcripts of interviews with employees. Although names or locations are sometimes changed to provide anonymity, cases usually report the facts of a situation as authentically as possible.

One of the main reasons to analyze strategic management cases is to develop an ability to evaluate business situations critically. In case analysis, memorizing key terms and conceptual frameworks is not enough. To analyze a case, it is important that you go beyond textbook prescriptions and quick answers. It requires you to look deeply into the information that is provided and root out the essential issues and causes of a company's problems.

LO 13-1
How strategic case analysis is used to simulate real-world experiences.

The types of skills that are required to prepare an effective strategic case analysis can benefit you in actual business situations. Case analysis adds to the overall learning experience by helping you acquire or improve skills that may not be taught in a typical lecture course. Three capabilities that can be learned by conducting case analysis are especially useful to strategic managers–the ability to differentiate, speculate, and integrate.[4] Here's how case analysis can enhance those skills:

LO 13-2
How analyzing strategic management cases can help develop the ability to differentiate, speculate, and integrate when evaluating complex business problems.

1. ***Differentiate.*** Effective strategic management requires that many different elements of a situation be evaluated at once. This is also true in case analysis. When analyzing cases, it is important to isolate critical facts, evaluate whether assumptions are useful or faulty, and distinguish between good and bad information. Differentiating between the factors that are influencing the situation presented by a case is necessary for making a good analysis. Strategic management also involves understanding that

problems are often complex and multilayered. This applies to case analysis as well. Ask whether the case deals with operational, business-level, or corporate issues. Do the problems stem from weaknesses in the internal value chain or threats in the external environment? Dig deep. Being too quick to accept the easiest or least controversial answer will usually fail to get to the heart of the problem.

2. ***Speculate.*** Strategic managers need to be able to use their imagination to envision an explanation or solution that might not readily be apparent. The same is true with case analysis. Being able to imagine different scenarios or contemplate the outcome of a decision can aid the analysis. Managers also have to deal with uncertainty since most decisions are made without complete knowledge of the circumstances. This is also true in case analysis. Case materials often seem to be missing data or the information provided is contradictory. The ability to speculate about details that are unknown or the consequences of an action can be helpful.
3. ***Integrate.*** Strategy involves looking at the big picture and having an organization-wide perspective. Strategic case analysis is no different. Even though the chapters in this textbook divide the material into various topics that may apply to different parts of an organization, all of this information must be integrated into one set of recommendations that will affect the whole company. A strategic manager needs to comprehend how all the factors that influence the organization will interact. This also applies to case analysis. Changes made in one part of the organization affect other parts. Thus, a holistic perspective that integrates the impact of various decisions and environmental influences on all parts of the organization is needed.

In business, these three activities sometimes "compete" with each other for your attention. For example, some decision makers may have a natural ability to differentiate among elements of a problem but are not able to integrate them very well. Others have enough innate creativity to imagine solutions or fill in the blanks when information is missing. But they may have a difficult time when faced with hard numbers or cold facts. Even so, each of these skills is important. The mark of a good strategic manager is the ability to simultaneously make distinctions and envision the whole, and to imagine a future scenario while staying focused on the present. Thus, another reason to conduct case analysis is to help you develop and exercise your ability to differentiate, speculate, and integrate. David C. Novak, the former chairman and CEO of Yum! Brands, provides a useful insight on this matter:[5]

> I think what we need in our leaders, the people who ultimately run our companies and run our functions, is whole-brained people—people who can be analytical but also have the creativity, the right-brain side of the equation.

Case analysis takes the student through the whole cycle of activity that a manager would face. Beyond the textbook descriptions of concepts and examples, case analysis asks you to "walk a mile in the shoes" of the strategic decision maker and learn to evaluate situations critically. Executives and owners must make decisions every day with limited information and a swirl of business activity going on around them. Consider the example of Sapient Health Network, an Internet start-up that had to undergo some analysis and problem solving just to survive. Strategy Spotlight 13.1 describes how this company transformed itself after a serious self-examination during a time of crisis.

As you can see from the experience of Sapient Health Network, businesses are often faced with immediate challenges that threaten their lives. The Sapient case illustrates how the strategic management process helped it survive. First, the company realistically assessed the environment, evaluated the marketplace, and analyzed its resources. Then it made tough decisions, which included shifting its market focus, hiring and firing, and redeploying its assets. Finally, it took action. The result was not only firm survival but also a quick turnaround leading to rapid success.

13.1 STRATEGY SPOTLIGHT

ANALYSIS, DECISION MAKING, AND CHANGE AT SAPIENT HEALTH NETWORK

Sapient Health Network (SHN) had gotten off to a good start. CEO Jim Kean and his two cofounders had raised $5 million in investor capital to launch their vision: an Internet-based healthcare information subscription service. The idea was to create an Internet community for people suffering from chronic diseases. It would provide members with expert information, resources, a message board, and chat rooms so that people suffering from the same ailments could provide each other with information and support. "Who would be more voracious consumers of information than people who are faced with life-changing, life-threatening illnesses?" thought Bill Kelly, one of SHN's cofounders. Initial market research and beta tests had supported that view.

During the beta tests, however, the service had been offered for free. The troubles began when SHN tried to convert its trial subscribers into paying ones. Fewer than 5 percent signed on, far less than the 15 percent the company had projected. Sapient hired a vice president of marketing who launched an aggressive promotion, but after three months of campaigning SHN still had only 500 members. SHN was now burning through $400,000 per month, with little revenue to show for it.

At that point, according to SHN board member Susan Clymer, "there was a lot of scrambling around trying to figure out how we could wring value out of what we'd already accomplished." One thing SHN had created was an expert software system that had two components: an "intelligent profile engine" (IPE) and an "intelligent query engine" (IQE). SHN used this system to collect detailed information from its subscribers.

SHN was sure that the expert system was its biggest selling point. But how could the company use it? Then the founders remembered that the original business plan had suggested there might be a market for aggregate data about patient populations gathered from the website. Could they turn the business around by selling patient data? To analyze the possibility, Kean tried out the idea on the market research arm of a huge east coast healthcare conglomerate. The officials were intrigued. SHN realized that its expert system could become a market research tool.

Once the analysis was completed, the founders made the decision: They would still create Internet communities for chronically ill patients, but the service would be free. And they would transform SHN from a company that processed subscriptions to one that sold market research.

Finally, they enacted the changes. Some of the changes were painful, including laying off 18 employees. However, SHN needed more healthcare industry expertise. It even hired an interim CEO, Craig Davenport, a 25-year veteran of the industry, to steer the company in its new direction. Finally, SHN had to communicate a new message to its members. It began by reimbursing the $10,000 of subscription fees they had paid.

All of this paid off dramatically in a matter of just two years. Revenues jumped to $1.9 million, and early in the third year SHN was purchased by WebMD. Less than a year after that, WebMD merged with Healtheon. And, in 2017, WebMD was acquired by private equity group KKR for $2.8 billion.

Sources: Ferguson, S. 2007. Health care gets a better IT prescription. *Baseline, www.baselinemag.com*, May 24; Brenneman, K. 2000. Healtheon/WebMD's local office is thriving. *Business Journal of Portland,* June 2; and Raths, D. 1998. Reversal of fortune. *Inc. Technology,* 2: 52–62.

HOW TO CONDUCT A CASE ANALYSIS

LO 13-3
The steps involved in conducting a strategic management case analysis.

The process of analyzing strategic management cases involves several steps. In this section we will review the mechanics of preparing a case analysis. Before beginning, there are two things to keep in mind that will clarify your understanding of the process and make the results of the process more meaningful.

First, unless you prepare for a case discussion, there is little you can gain from the discussion and even less that you can offer. Effective strategic managers don't enter into problem-solving situations without doing some homework–investigating the situation, analyzing and researching possible solutions, and sometimes gathering the advice of others. Good problem solving often requires that decision makers be immersed in the facts, options, and implications surrounding the problem. In case analysis, this means reading and thoroughly comprehending the case materials before trying to make an analysis.

The second point is related to the first. To get the most out of a case analysis, you must place yourself "inside" the case–that is, think like an actual participant in the case situation.

However, there are several positions you can take. These are discussed in the following paragraphs:

- ***Strategic decision maker.*** This is the position of the senior executive responsible for resolving the situation described in the case. It may be the CEO, the business owner, or a strategic manager in a key executive position.
- ***Board of directors.*** Since the board of directors represents the owners of a corporation, it has a responsibility to step in when a management crisis threatens the company. As a board member, you may be in a unique position to solve problems.
- ***Outside consultant.*** Either the board or top management may decide to bring in outsiders. Consultants often have an advantage because they can look at a situation objectively. But they also may be at a disadvantage since they have no power to enforce changes.

Before beginning the analysis, it may be helpful to envision yourself assuming one of these roles. Then, as you study and analyze the case materials, you can make a diagnosis and recommend solutions in a way that is consistent with your position. Try different perspectives. You may find that your view of the situation changes depending on the role you play. As an outside consultant, for example, it may be easy for you to conclude that certain individuals should be replaced in order to solve a problem presented in the case. However, if you take the role of the CEO who knows the individuals and the challenges they have been facing, you may be reluctant to fire them and will seek another solution instead.

The idea of assuming a particular role is similar to the real world in various ways. In your career, you may work in an organization where outside accountants, bankers, lawyers, or other professionals are advising you about how to resolve business situations or improve your practices. Their perspective will be different from yours, but it is useful to understand things from their point of view. Conversely, you may work as a member of the audit team of an accounting firm or the loan committee of a bank. In those situations, it would be helpful if you understood the situation from the perspective of the business leader who must weigh your views against all the other advice that he or she receives. Case analysis can help develop an ability to appreciate such multiple perspectives.

One of the most challenging roles to play in business is as a business founder or owner. For small businesses or entrepreneurial start-ups, the founder may wear all hats at once—key decision maker, primary stockholder, and CEO. Hiring an outside consultant may not be an option. However, the issues faced by young firms and established firms are often not that different, especially when it comes to formulating a plan of action. Business plans that entrepreneurial firms use to raise money or propose a business expansion typically revolve around a few key issues that must be addressed no matter what the size or age of the business. Strategy Spotlight 13.2 reviews business planning issues that are most important to consider when evaluating any case, especially from the perspective of the business founder or owner.

Next we will review five steps to follow when conducting a strategic management case analysis: becoming familiar with the material, identifying the problems, analyzing the strategic issues using the tools and insights of strategic management, proposing alternative solutions, and making recommendations.[6]

Become Familiar with the Material

Written cases often include a lot of material. They may be complex and include detailed financials or long passages. Even so, to understand a case and its implications, you must become familiar with its content. Sometimes key information is not immediately apparent. It may be contained in the footnotes to an exhibit or in an interview with a lower-level employee. In other cases the important points may be difficult to grasp because the subject

13.2 STRATEGY SPOTLIGHT

USING A BUSINESS PLAN FRAMEWORK TO ANALYZE STRATEGIC CASES

Established businesses often have to change what they are doing in order to improve their competitive position or sometimes simply to survive. To make the changes effectively, businesses usually need a plan. Business plans are no longer just for entrepreneurs. The kind of market analysis, decision making, and action planning that is considered standard practice among new ventures can also benefit going concerns that want to make changes, seize an opportunity, or head in a new direction.

The best business plans, however, are not those that are loaded with decades of month-by-month financial projections or that depend on rigid adherence to a schedule of events that is impossible to predict. The good ones are focused on four factors that are critical to new venture success. These same factors are important in case analysis as well because they get to the heart of many of the problems found in strategic cases.

1. **The people.** "When I receive a business plan, I always read the résumé section first," says Harvard Professor William Sahlman. The people questions that are critically important to investors include: What are their skills? How much experience do they have? What is their reputation? Have they worked together as a team? These same questions also may be used in case analysis to evaluate the role of individuals in the strategic case.
2. **The opportunity.** Business opportunities come in many forms. They are not limited to new ventures. The chance to enter new markets, introduce new products, or merge with a competitor provides many of the challenges that are found in strategic management cases. What are the consequences of such actions? Will the proposed changes affect the firm's business concept? What factors might stand in the way of success? The same issues are also present in most strategic cases.
3. **The context.** Things happen in contexts that cannot be controlled by a firm's managers. This is particularly true of the general environment, where social trends, economic changes, or events such as the September 11, 2001, terrorist attacks can change business overnight. When evaluating strategic cases, ask: Is the company aware of the impact of context on the business? What will it do if the context changes? Can it influence the context in a way that favors the company?
4. **Risk and reward.** With a new venture, the entrepreneurs and investors take the risks and get the rewards. In strategic cases, the risks and rewards often extend to many other stakeholders, such as employees, customers, and suppliers. When analyzing a case, ask: Are the managers making choices that will pay off in the future? Are the rewards evenly distributed? Will some stakeholders be put at risk if the situation in the case changes? What if the situation remains the same? Could that be even riskier?

Whether a business is growing or shrinking, large or small, industrial or service-oriented, the issues of people, opportunities, context, and risks and rewards will have a large impact on its performance. Therefore, you should always consider these four factors when evaluating strategic management cases.

Sources: Wasserman, E. 2003. A simple plan. *MBA Jungle,* February: 50–55; DeKluyver, C. A. 2000. *Strategic Thinking: An Executive Perspective.* Upper Saddle River, NJ: Prentice Hall; and Sahlman, W. A. 1997. How to write a great business plan. *Harvard Business Review,* 75(4): 98–108.

matter is so unfamiliar. When you approach a strategic case, try the following technique to enhance comprehension:

- Read quickly through the case one time to get an overall sense of the material.
- Use the initial read-through to assess possible links to strategic concepts.
- Read through the case again, in depth. Make written notes as you read.
- Evaluate how strategic concepts might inform key decisions or suggest alternative solutions.
- After formulating an initial recommendation, thumb through the case again quickly to help assess the consequences of the actions you propose.

Identify Problems

When conducting case analysis, one of your most important tasks is to identify the problem. Earlier we noted that one of the main reasons to conduct case analysis is to find solutions. But you cannot find a solution unless you know the problem. Another saying you may have heard is "A good diagnosis is half the cure." In other words, once you have determined what the problem is, you are well on your way to identifying a reasonable solution.

Some cases have more than one problem. But the problems are usually related. For a hypothetical example, consider the following: Company A was losing customers to a new competitor. Upon analysis, it was determined that the competitor had a 50 percent faster delivery time even though its product was of lower quality. The managers of company A could not understand why customers would settle for an inferior product. It turns out that no one was marketing to company A's customers that its product was superior. A second problem was that falling sales resulted in cuts in company A's sales force. Thus, there were two related problems: inferior delivery technology and insufficient sales effort.

When trying to determine the problem, avoid getting hung up on symptoms. Zero in on the problem. For example, in the company A example, the symptom was losing customers. But the problems were an underfunded, understaffed sales force combined with an outdated delivery technology. Try to see beyond the immediate symptoms to the more fundamental problems.

Another tip when preparing a case analysis is to articulate the problem.[7] Writing down a problem statement gives you a reference point to turn to as you proceed through the case analysis. This is important because the process of formulating strategies or evaluating implementation methods may lead you away from the initial problem. Make sure your recommendation actually addresses the problems you have identified.

One more thing about identifying problems: Sometimes problems are not apparent until *after* you do the analysis. In some cases the problem will be presented plainly, perhaps in the opening paragraph or on the last page of the case. But in other cases the problem does not emerge until after the issues in the case have been analyzed. We turn next to the subject of strategic case analysis.

Conduct Strategic Analyses

This textbook has presented numerous analytical tools (e.g., five-forces analysis and value-chain analysis), contingency frameworks (e.g., when to use related rather than unrelated diversification strategies), and other techniques that can be used to evaluate strategic situations. The previous 12 chapters have addressed practices that are common in strategic management, but only so much can be learned by studying the practices and concepts. The best way to understand these methods is to apply them by conducting analyses of specific cases.

The first step is to determine which strategic issues are involved. Is there a problem in the company's competitive environment? Or is it an internal problem? If it is internal, does it have to do with organizational structure? Strategic controls? Uses of technology? Or perhaps the company has overworked its employees or underutilized its intellectual capital. Has the company mishandled a merger? Chosen the wrong diversification strategy? Botched a new product introduction? Each of these issues is linked to one or more of the concepts discussed earlier in the text. Determine what strategic issues are associated with the problems you have identified. Remember also that most real-life case situations involve issues that are highly interrelated. Even in cases where there is only one major problem, the strategic processes required to solve it may involve several parts of the organization.

Once you have identified the issues that apply to the case, conduct the analysis. For example, you may need to conduct a five-forces analysis or dissect the company's competitive strategy. Perhaps you need to evaluate whether its resources are rare, valuable, difficult to imitate, or difficult to substitute. Financial analysis may be needed to assess the company's economic prospects. Perhaps the international entry mode needs to be reevaluated because of changing conditions in the host country. Employee empowerment techniques may need to be improved to enhance organizational learning. Whatever the case, all the strategic concepts introduced in the text include insights for assessing their effectiveness. Determining how well a company is doing these things is central to the case analysis process.

financial ratio analysis
a method of evaluating a company's performance and financial well-being through ratios of accounting values, including short-term solvency, long-term solvency, asset utilization, profitability, and market value ratios.

Financial ratio analysis is one of the primary tools used to conduct case analysis. Appendix 1 to Chapter 13 includes a discussion and examples of the financial ratios that are often used to evaluate a company's performance and financial well-being. Exhibit 13.1 provides a summary of the financial ratios presented in Appendix 1 to this chapter.

In this part of the overall strategic analysis process, it is also important to test your own assumptions about the case.[8] First, what assumptions are you making about the case materials? It may be that you have interpreted the case content differently than your team members or classmates. Being clear about these assumptions will be important in determining how to analyze the case. Second, what assumptions have you made about the best way to resolve the problems? Ask yourself why you have chosen one type of analysis over another. This process of assumption checking can also help determine if you have gotten to the heart of the problem or are still just dealing with symptoms.

As mentioned earlier, sometimes the critical diagnosis in a case can be made only after the analysis is conducted. However, by the end of this stage in the process, you should know

EXHIBIT 13.1 Summary of Financial Ratio Analysis Techniques

Ratio	What It Measures
Short-term solvency, or liquidity, ratios:	
Current ratio	Ability to use assets to pay off liabilities.
Quick ratio	Ability to use liquid assets to pay off liabilities quickly.
Cash ratio	Ability to pay off liabilities with cash on hand.
Long-term solvency, or financial leverage, ratios:	
Total debt ratio	How much of a company's total assets are financed by debt.
Debt-equity ratio	Compares how much a company is financed by debt with how much it is financed by equity.
Equity multiplier	How much debt is being used to finance assets.
Times interest earned ratio	How well a company has its interest obligations covered.
Cash coverage ratio	A company's ability to generate cash from operations.
Asset utilization, or turnover, ratios:	
Inventory turnover	How many times each year a company sells its entire inventory.
Days' sales in inventory	How many days on average inventory is on hand before it is sold.
Receivables turnover	How frequently each year a company collects on its credit sales.
Days' sales in receivables	How many days on average it takes to collect on credit sales (average collection period).
Total asset turnover	How much of sales is generated for every dollar in assets.
Capital intensity	The dollar investment in assets needed to generate $1 in sales.
Profitability ratios:	
Profit margin	How much profit is generated by every dollar of sales.
Return on assets (ROA)	How effectively assets are being used to generate a return.
Return on equity (ROE)	How effectively amounts invested in the business by its owners are being used to generate a return.
Market value ratios:	
Price-earnings ratio	How much investors are willing to pay per dollar of current earnings.
Market-to-book ratio	Compares market value of the company's investments to the cost of those investments.

the problems and have completed a thorough analysis of them. You can now move to the next step: finding solutions.

Propose Alternative Solutions

It is important to remember that in strategic management case analysis, there is rarely one right answer or one best way. Even when members of a class or a team agree on what the problem is, they may not agree upon how to solve the problem. Therefore, it is helpful to consider several different solutions.

After conducting strategic analysis and identifying the problem, develop a list of options. What are the possible solutions? What are the alternatives? First, generate a list of all the options you can think of without prejudging any one of them. Remember that not all cases call for dramatic decisions or sweeping changes. Some companies just need to make small adjustments. In fact, "Do nothing" may be a reasonable alternative in some cases. Although that is rare, it might be useful to consider what will happen if the company does nothing. This point illustrates the purpose of developing alternatives: to evaluate what will happen if a company chooses one solution over another.

Thus, during this step of a case analysis, you will evaluate choices and the implications of those choices. One aspect of any business that is likely to be highlighted in this part of the analysis is strategy implementation. Ask how the choices made will be implemented. It may be that what seems like an obvious choice for solving a problem creates an even bigger problem when implemented. But remember also that no strategy or strategic "fix" is going to work if it cannot be implemented. Once a list of alternatives is generated, ask:

- Can the company afford it? How will it affect the bottom line?
- Is the solution likely to evoke a competitive response?
- Will employees throughout the company accept the changes? What impact will the solution have on morale?
- How will the decision affect other stakeholders? Will customers, suppliers, and others buy into it?
- How does this solution fit with the company's vision, mission, and objectives?
- Will the culture or values of the company be changed by the solution? Is it a positive change?

The point of this step in the case analysis process is to find a solution that both solves the problem and is realistic. A consideration of the implications of various alternative solutions will generally lead you to a final recommendation that is more thoughtful and complete.

Make Recommendations

The basic aim of case analysis is to find solutions. Your analysis is not complete until you have recommended a course of action. In this step the task is to make a set of recommendations that your analysis supports. Describe exactly what needs to be done. Explain why this course of action will solve the problem. The recommendation should also include suggestions for how best to implement the proposed solution because the recommended actions and their implications for the performance and future of the firm are interrelated.

Recall that the solution you propose must solve the problem you identified. This point cannot be overemphasized; too often students make recommendations that treat only symptoms or fail to tackle the central problems in the case. Make a logical argument that shows how the problem led to the analysis and the analysis led to the recommendations you are proposing. Remember, an analysis is not an end in itself; it is useful only if it leads to a solution.

The actions you propose should describe the very next steps that the company needs to take. Don't say, for example, "If the company does more market research, then I would recommend the following course of action. . . ." Instead, make conducting the research part of

EXHIBIT 13.2 Preparing an Oral Case Presentation

Rule	Description
Organize your thoughts.	Begin by becoming familiar with the material. If you are working with a team, compare notes about the key points of the case and share insights that other team members may have gleaned from tables and exhibits. Then make an outline. This is one of the best ways to organize the flow and content of the presentation.
Emphasize strategic analysis.	The purpose of case analysis is to diagnose problems and find solutions. In the process, you may need to unravel the case material as presented and reconfigure it in a fashion that can be more effectively analyzed. Present the material in a way that lends itself to analysis—don't simply restate what is in the case. This involves three major categories with the following emphasis: Background/Problem Statement 10–20% Strategic Analysis/Options 60–75% Recommendations/Action Plan 10–20% As you can see, the emphasis of your presentation should be on analysis. This will probably require you to reorganize the material so that the tools of strategic analysis can be applied.
Be logical and consistent.	A presentation that is rambling and hard to follow may confuse the listener and fail to evoke a good discussion. Present your arguments and explanations in a logical sequence. Support your claims with facts. Include financial analysis where appropriate. Be sure that the solutions you recommend address the problems you have identified.
Defend your position.	Usually an oral presentation is followed by a class discussion. Anticipate what others might disagree with, and be prepared to defend your views. This means being aware of the choices you made and the implications of your recommendations. Be clear about your assumptions. Be able to expand on your analysis.
Share presentation responsibilities.	Strategic management case analyses are often conducted by teams. Each member of the team should have a clear role in the oral presentation, preferably a speaking role. It's also important to coordinate the different parts of the presentation into a logical, smooth-flowing whole. How well team members work together is usually very apparent during an oral presentation.

your recommendation. Taking the example a step further, if you also want to suggest subsequent actions that may be different *depending* on the outcome of the market research, that's OK. But don't make your initial recommendation conditional on actions the company may or may not take.

In summary, case analysis can be a very rewarding process but, as you might imagine, it can also be frustrating and challenging. If you follow the steps described, you will address the different elements of a thorough analysis. This approach can give your analysis a solid footing. Then, even if there are differences of opinion about how to interpret the facts, analyze the situation, or solve the problems, you can feel confident that you have not missed any important steps in finding the best course of action.

Students are often asked to prepare oral presentations of the information in a case and their analysis of the best remedies. This is frequently assigned as a group project. Or you may be called upon in class to present your ideas about the circumstances or solutions for a case the class is discussing. Exhibit 13.2 provides some tips for preparing an oral case presentation.

LO 13-4

Understand how to get the most out of case analysis.

HOW TO GET THE MOST FROM CASE ANALYSIS

One of the reasons case analysis is so enriching as a learning tool is that it draws on many resources and skills besides just what is in the textbook. This is especially true in the study of strategy. Why? Because strategic management itself is a highly integrative task that draws on many areas of specialization at several levels, from the individual to the whole of society. Therefore, to get the most out of case analysis, expand your horizons beyond the concepts in this text and seek insights from your own reservoir of knowledge. Here are some tips for how to do that:[9]

- ***Keep an open mind.*** Like any good discussion, a case analysis discussion often evokes strong opinions and high emotions. But it's the variety of perspectives that makes case analysis so valuable: Many viewpoints usually lead to a more complete analysis. Therefore, avoid letting an emotional response to another person's style or opinion keep you from hearing what he or she has to say. Once you evaluate what is said, you may disagree with it or dismiss it as faulty. But unless you keep an open mind in the first place, you may miss the importance of the other person's contribution. Also, people often place a higher value on the opinions of those they consider to be good listeners.
- ***Take a stand for what you believe.*** Although it is vital to keep an open mind, it is also important to state your views proactively. Don't try to figure out what your friends or the instructor wants to hear. Analyze the case from the perspective of your own background and belief system. For example, perhaps you feel that a decision is unethical or that the managers in a case have misinterpreted the facts. Don't be afraid to assert that in the discussion. For one thing, when a person takes a strong stand, it often encourages others to evaluate the issues more closely. This can lead to a more thorough investigation and a more meaningful class discussion.
- ***Draw on your personal experience.*** You may have experiences from work or as a customer that shed light on some of the issues in a case. Even though one of the purposes of case analysis is to apply the analytical tools from this text, you may be able to add to the discussion by drawing on your outside experiences and background. Of course, you need to guard against carrying that to extremes. In other words, don't think that your perspective is the only viewpoint that matters! Simply recognize that firsthand experience usually represents a welcome contribution to the overall quality of case discussions.
- ***Participate and persuade.*** Have you heard the phrase "Vote early . . . and often"? Among loyal members of certain political parties, it has become rather a joke. Why? Because a democratic system is built on the concept of one person, one vote. Even though some voters may want to vote often enough to get their candidate elected, doing so is against the law. Not so in a case discussion. People who are persuasive and speak their mind can often influence the views of others. But to do so, you have to be prepared and convincing. Being persuasive is more than being loud or long-winded. It involves understanding all sides of an argument and being able to overcome objections to your own point of view. These efforts can make a case discussion more lively. And they parallel what happens in the real world; in business, people frequently share their opinions and attempt to persuade others to see things their way.
- ***Be concise and to the point.*** In the previous point, we encouraged you to speak up and "sell" your ideas to others in a case discussion. But you must be clear about what you are selling. Make your arguments in a way that is explicit and direct. Zero in on the most important points. Be brief. Don't try to make a lot of points at once by jumping around between topics. Avoid trying to explain the whole case situation

at once. Remember, other students usually resent classmates who go on and on, take up a lot of "airtime," or repeat themselves unnecessarily. The best way to avoid this is to stay focused and be specific.

- ***Think out of the box.*** It's OK to be a little provocative; sometimes that is the consequence of taking a stand on issues. But it may be equally important to be imaginative and creative when making a recommendation or determining how to implement a solution. Albert Einstein once stated, "Imagination is more important than knowledge." The reason is that managing strategically requires more than memorizing concepts. Strategic management insights must be applied to each case differently–just knowing the principles is not enough. Imagination and out-of-the-box thinking help to apply strategic knowledge in novel and unique ways.
- ***Learn from the insights of others.*** Before you make up your mind about a case, hear what other students have to say. Get a second opinion, and a third, and so forth. Of course, in a situation where you have to put your analysis in writing, you may not be able to learn from others ahead of time. But in a case discussion, observe how various students attack the issues and engage in problem solving. Such observation skills also may be a key to finding answers within the case. For example, people tend to believe authority figures, so they would place a higher value on what a company president says. In some cases, however, the statements of middle managers may represent a point of view that is even more helpful for finding a solution to the problems presented by the case.
- ***Apply insights from other case analyses.*** Throughout the text, we have used examples of actual businesses to illustrate strategy concepts. The aim has been to show you how firms think about and deal with business problems. During the course, you may be asked to conduct several case analyses as part of the learning experience. Once you have performed a few case analyses, you will see how the concepts from the text apply in real-life business situations. Incorporate the insights learned from the text examples and your own previous case discussions into each new case that you analyze.
- ***Critically analyze your own performance.*** Performance appraisals are a standard part of many workplace situations. They are used to determine promotions, raises, and work assignments. In some organizations, everyone from the top executive down is subject to such reviews. Even in situations where the owner or CEO is not evaluated by others, top executives often find it useful to ask themselves regularly, Am I being effective? The same can be applied to your performance in a case analysis situation. Ask yourself, Were my comments insightful? Did I make a good contribution? How might I improve next time? Use the same criteria on yourself that you use to evaluate others. What grade would you give yourself? This technique not only will make you more fair in your assessment of others but also will indicate how your own performance can improve.
- ***Conduct outside research.*** Many times, you can enhance your understanding of a case situation by investigating sources outside the case materials. For example, you may want to study an industry more closely or research a company's close competitors. Recent moves such as mergers and acquisitions or product introductions may be reported in the business press. The company itself may provide useful information on its website or in its annual reports. Such information can usually spur additional discussion and enrich the case analysis. (*Caution:* It is best to check with your instructor in advance to be sure this kind of additional research is encouraged. Bringing in outside research may conflict with the instructor's learning objectives.)

Several of the points suggested for how to get the most out of case analysis apply only to an open discussion of a case, like that in a classroom setting. Exhibit 13.3 provides some additional guidelines for preparing a written case analysis.

EXHIBIT 13.3 Preparing a Written Case Analysis

Rule	Description
Be thorough.	Many of the ideas presented in Exhibit 13.2 about oral presentations also apply to written case analysis. However, a written analysis typically has to be more complete. This means writing out the problem statement and articulating assumptions. It is also important to provide support for your arguments and reference case materials or other facts more specifically.
Coordinate team efforts.	Written cases are often prepared by small groups. Within a group, just as in a class discussion, you may disagree about the diagnosis or the recommended plan of action. This can be healthy if it leads to a richer understanding of the case material. But before committing your ideas to writing, make sure you have coordinated your responses. Don't prepare a written analysis that appears contradictory or looks like a patchwork of disconnected thoughts.
Avoid restating the obvious.	There is no reason to restate material that everyone is familiar with already, namely, the case content. It is too easy for students to use up space in a written analysis with a recapitulation of the details of the case—this accomplishes very little. Stay focused on the key points. Restate only the information that is most central to your analysis.
Present information graphically.	Tables, graphs, and other exhibits are usually one of the best ways to present factual material that supports your arguments. For example, financial calculations such as break-even analysis, sensitivity analysis, or return on investment are best presented graphically. Even qualitative information such as product lists or rosters of employees can be summarized effectively and viewed quickly by using a table or graph.
Exercise quality control.	When presenting a case analysis in writing, it is especially important to use good grammar, avoid misspelling words, and eliminate typos and other visual distractions. Mistakes that can be glossed over in an oral presentation or class discussion are often highlighted when they appear in writing. Make your written presentation appear as professional as possible. Don't let the appearance of your written case keep the reader from recognizing the importance and quality of your analysis.

LO 13-5

Understand how integrative thinking and conflict-inducing discussion techniques can lead to better decisions.

USEFUL DECISION-MAKING TECHNIQUES IN CASE ANALYSIS

The demands on today's business leaders require them to perform a wide variety of functions. The success of their organizations often depends on how they as individuals—and as part of groups—meet the challenges and deliver on promises. In this section we address three different techniques that can help managers make better decisions and, in turn, enable their organizations to achieve higher performance.

First, we discuss integrative thinking, a technique that helps managers make better decisions through the resolution of competing demands on resources, multiple contingencies, and diverse opportunities. Second, we address the concept of "asking heretical questions." These are questions that challenge conventional wisdom and may even seem odd or unusual—but they can often lead to valuable innovations. Third, we introduce two approaches to decision making that involve the effective use of conflict in the decision-making process. These are devil's advocacy and dialectical inquiry.

Integrative Thinking

integrative thinking a process of reconciling opposing thoughts by generating new alternatives and creative solutions rather than rejecting one thought in favor of another.

How does a leader make good strategic decisions in the face of multiple contingencies and diverse opportunities? A study by Roger L. Martin reveals that executives who have a capability known as **integrative thinking** are among the most effective leaders. In his book *The Opposable Mind,* Martin contends that people who can consider two conflicting ideas simultaneously, without dismissing one of the ideas or becoming discouraged about reconciling them, often make the best problem solvers because of their ability to creatively synthesize the opposing thoughts. In explaining the source of his title, Martin quotes F. Scott Fitzgerald, who observed, "The test of a first-rate intelligence is the ability to hold two opposing ideas in mind at the same time and still retain the ability to function. One should, for example, be able to see that things are hopeless yet be determined to make them otherwise."[10]

In contrast to conventional thinking, which tends to focus on making choices between competing ideas from a limited set of alternatives, integrative thinking is the process by which people reconcile opposing thoughts to identify creative solutions that provide them with more options and new alternatives. Exhibit 13.4 outlines the four stages of the integrative thinking and deciding process. Martin uses the admittedly simple example of deciding where to go on vacation to illustrate the stages:

- ***Salience.*** Take stock of what features of the decision you consider relevant and important. For example: Where will you go? What will you see? Where will you stay? What will it cost? Is it safe? Other features may be less important, but try to think of everything that may matter.
- ***Causality.*** Make a mental map of the causal relationships between the features, that is, how the various features are related to one another. For example, is it worth it to invite friends to share expenses? Will an exotic destination be less safe?
- ***Architecture.*** Use the mental map to arrange a sequence of decisions that will lead to a specific outcome. For example, will you make the hotel and flight arrangements first, or focus on which sightseeing tours are available? No particular decision path is right or wrong, but considering multiple options simultaneously may lead to a better decision.

EXHIBIT 13.4 Integrative Thinking: The Process of Thinking and Deciding

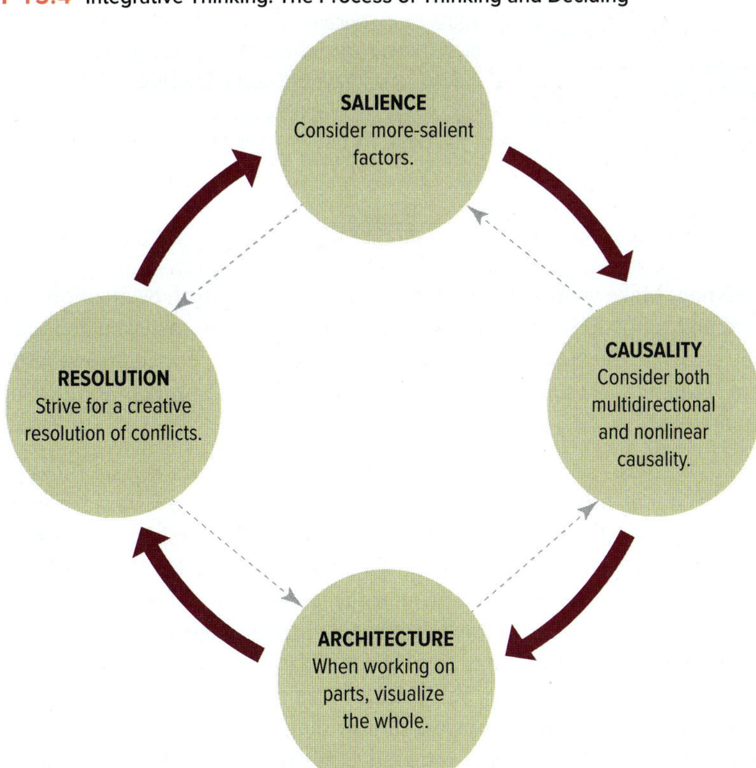

Source: Adapted from Martin, R. L. 2007. *The Opposable Mind: How Successful Leaders Win Through Integrative Thinking*. Boston: Harvard Business School Press.

13.3 STRATEGY SPOTLIGHT

INTEGRATIVE THINKING AT RED HAT, INC.

How can a software developer make money giving away free software? That was the dilemma Red Hat founder Bob Young was facing during the early days of the open-source software movement. A Finnish developer named Linus Torvalds, using freely available UNIX software, had developed an operating system dubbed "Linux" that was being widely circulated in the freeware community. The software was intended specifically as an alternative to the pricey proprietary systems sold by Microsoft and Oracle. To use proprietary software, corporations had to pay hefty installation fees and were required to call Microsoft or Oracle engineers to fix it when anything went wrong. In Young's view it was a flawed and unsustainable business model.

But the free model was flawed as well. Although several companies had sprung up to help companies use Linux, there were few opportunities to profit from using it. As Young said, "You couldn't make any money selling [the Linux] operating system because all this stuff was free, and if you started to charge money for it, someone else would come in and price it lower. It was a commodity in the truest sense of the word." To complicate matters, hundreds of developers were part of the software community that was constantly modifying and debugging Linux—at a rate equivalent to three updates per day. As a result, systems administrators at corporations that tried to adopt the software spent so much time keeping track of updates that they didn't enjoy the savings they expected from using free software.

Young saw the appeal of both approaches but also realized a new model was needed. While contemplating the dilemma, he realized a salient feature that others had overlooked—because most major corporations have to live with software decisions for at least 10 years, they will nearly always choose to do business with the industry leader. Young realized he had to position Red Hat as the top provider of Linux software. To do that, he proposed a radical solution: provide the authoritative version of Linux and deliver it in a new way—as a download rather than on CD. He hired programmers to create a downloadable version—still free—and promised, in essence, to maintain its quality (for a fee, of course) by dealing with all the open-source programmers who were continually suggesting changes. In the process, he created a product companies could trust and then profited by establishing ongoing service relationships with customers. Red Hat's version of Linux became the de facto standard. By 2000, Linux was installed in 25 percent of server operating systems worldwide and Red Hat had captured over 50 percent of the global market for Linux systems.

By recognizing that a synthesis of two flawed business models could provide the best of both worlds, Young exhibited the traits of integrative thinking. He pinpointed the causal relationships between the salient features of the marketplace and Red Hat's path to prosperity. He then crafted an approach that integrated aspects of the two existing approaches into a new alternative. By resolving to provide a free downloadable version, Young also took responsibility for creating his own path to success. The payoff was substantial: When Red Hat went public in 1999, Young became a billionaire on the first day of trading. And by 2015 Red Hat had over $1.5 billion in annual revenues and a market capitalization of nearly $13 billion.

Sources: Martin, R. L. 2007. *The Opposable Mind: How Successful Leaders Win Through Integrative Thinking*. Boston: Harvard Business School Press; and *finance.yahoo.com*; Martin, R. 2007. Bob Young and the rise of Red Hat software. *The Globe and Mail, November 20.*

- ***Resolution.*** Make your selection. For example, choose which destination, which flight, and so forth. Your final resolution is linked to how you evaluated the first three stages; if you are dissatisfied with your choices, the dotted arrows in the diagram (Exhibit 13.4) suggest you can go back through the process and revisit your assumptions.

Applied to business, an integrative thinking approach enables decision makers to consider situations not as forced trade-offs–either decrease costs or invest more; either satisfy shareholders or please the community–but as a method for synthesizing opposing ideas into a creative solution. The key is to think in terms of "both-and" rather than "either-or." "Integrative thinking," says Martin, "shows us that there's a way to integrate the advantages of one solution without canceling out the advantages of an alternative solution."[11]

Although Martin found that integrative thinking comes naturally to some people, he also believes it can be taught. But it may be difficult to learn, in part because it requires people to *un*learn old patterns and become aware of how they think. For executives willing to take a deep look at their habits of thought, integrative thinking can be developed into a valuable skill. Strategy Spotlight 13.3 tells how Red Hat Inc. cofounder Bob Young made his company a market leader by using integrative thinking to resolve a major problem in the domain of open-source software.

Asking Heretical Questions

In his recent book *The Big Pivot,* Andrew Winston introduced the concept of heretical innovation to help address the challenges associated with environmental sustainability in today's world.[12] He describes the need to pursue a deeper level of innovation that challenges long-held beliefs about how things work. Central to addressing these challenges is the need to pose "heretical questions"–those that challenge conventional wisdom. Typically, they may make us uncomfortable or may seem odd (or even impossible)–but they often become the means of coming up with major innovations. Although the context of Winston's discussion was environmental sustainability, we believe that his ideas have useful implications for major challenges faced by today's managers in a wide range of firms and industries.

Heretical questions can address issues that are both small and large–from redesigning a single process or product to rethinking the whole business model. One must not discount the value of the approach in considering small matters. After all, the vast majority of people in a company don't have the mandate to rethink strategy. However, anyone in an organization can ask disruptive questions that profoundly change one aspect of a business. What makes this heretical is how deeply it challenges the conventional wisdom.

Consider the fascinating story of UPS's "no left turns," a classic tale in the sustainability world that has become rather well known. The catchy phrase became a rallying cry for mapping out new delivery routes that avoided crossing traffic and idling at stoplights. UPS is saving time, money, and energy–about 85 million miles and 8 million gallons of fuel annually.

Also, take the example of dyeing clothing–a tremendously water-intensive process. Somebody at adidas asked a heretical question: Could we dye clothes with no water? The answer was yes. However, the company needed to partner with a small Thailand-based company, Yeh Group. The DryDye process adidas is now piloting uses heat and pressure to force pigment into the fibers. The process uses no water and also cuts energy and chemical use by 50 percent!

Finally, in 2010, Kimberly-Clark, the $21 billion firm that is behind such brands as Kleenex and Scott, questioned the simple assumption that toilet paper rolls must have cardboard tubes to hold their shape. It created the Scott Naturals Tube-Free line, which offers this household staple in the familiar cylindrical shape. But it comes with no cardboard core–just a hole the same size. It's been very successful–a key part of the now $100 million Scott Naturals brand. While this product may not save the world, if it became the industry standard, we could eliminate 17 billion tubes that are used in the United States every year and save fuel by shipping lighter rolls. This is a good example of heretical thinking. After all, the product doesn't incrementally use less cardboard–it uses none.

The concept of accepting failure and aiming for deep, heretical innovation is difficult for most organizations to embrace. Ed Catmull, the former president and cofounder of animation pioneer Pixar, claims that when you are doing something new, you are by definition doing something you don't know very well, and that means mistakes. However, if you don't encourage mistakes, he says, you won't encourage anything new: "We're very conscientious about making it so that mistakes really aren't thought of as bad . . . they're just learning."

Conflict-Inducing Techniques

Next we address some techniques often used to improve case analyses that involve the constructive use of conflict. In the classroom–as well as in the business world–you will frequently be analyzing cases or solving problems in groups. While the word *conflict* often has a negative connotation (e.g., rude behavior, personal affronts), it can be very helpful in arriving at better solutions to cases. It can provide an effective means for new insights as well as for rigorously questioning and analyzing assumptions and strategic alternatives. In fact, if you don't have constructive conflict, you may get only consensus. When this happens, decisions tend to be based on compromise rather than collaboration.

In your organizational behavior classes, you probably learned the concept of "groupthink."[13] *Groupthink,* a term coined by Irving Janis after he conducted numerous studies on executive decision making, is a condition in which group members strive to reach agreement or consensus without realistically considering other viable alternatives. In effect, group norms bolster morale at the expense of critical thinking, and decision making is impaired.[14]

Many of us have probably been "victims" of groupthink at one time or another in our life. We may be confronted with situations when social pressure, politics, or "not wanting to stand out" may prevent us from voicing our concerns about a chosen course of action. Nevertheless, decision making in groups is a common practice in the management of many businesses. Most companies, especially large ones, rely on input from various top managers to provide valuable information and experience from their specialty area as well as their unique perspectives. Organizations need to develop cultures and reward systems that encourage people to express their perspectives and create open dialogues. Constructive conflict can be very helpful in that it emphasizes the need for managers to consider other people's perspectives and not simply become a strong advocate for positions that they may prefer.

Chapter 11 emphasized the importance of empowering individuals at all levels to participate in decision-making processes. After all, many of us have experienced situations where there is not a perfect correlation between one's rank and the viability of one's ideas! In terms of this course, case analysis involves a type of decision making that is often conducted in groups. Strategy Spotlight 13.4 provides guidelines for making team-based approaches to case analysis more effective.

13.4 STRATEGY SPOTLIGHT

MAKING CASE ANALYSIS TEAMS MORE EFFECTIVE

Working in teams can be very challenging. Not all team members have the same skills, interests, or motivations. Some team members just want to get the work done. Others see teams as an opportunity to socialize. Occasionally, there are team members who think they should be in charge and make all the decisions; other teams have freeloaders—team members who don't want to do anything except get credit for the team's work.

One consequence of these various styles is that team meetings can become time wasters. Disagreements about how to proceed, how to share the work, or what to do at the next meeting tend to slow down teams and impede progress toward the goal. While the dynamics of case analysis teams are likely to always be challenging depending on the personalities involved, one thing nearly all members realize is that, ultimately, the team's work must be completed. Most team members also aim to do the highest-quality work possible. The following guidelines provide some useful insights about how to get the work of a team done more effectively.

Spend More Time Together

One of the factors that prevents teams from doing a good job with case analysis is their failure to put in the necessary time. Unless teams really tackle the issues surrounding case analysis—both the issues in the case itself and organizing how the work is to be conducted—the end result will probably be lacking because decisions that are made too quickly are unlikely to get to the heart of the problem(s) in the case. "Meetings should be a precious resource, but they're treated like a necessary evil," says Kenneth Sole, a consultant who specializes in organizational behavior. As a result, teams that care more about finishing the analysis than getting the analysis right often make poor decisions.

Therefore, expect to have a few meetings that run long, especially at the beginning of the project, when the work is being organized and the issues in the case are being sorted out, and again at the end, when the team must coordinate the components of the case analysis that will be presented. Without spending this kind of time together, it is doubtful that the analysis will be comprehensive and the presentation is likely to be choppy and incomplete.

Make a Focused and Disciplined Agenda

To complete tasks and avoid wasting time, meetings need to have a clear purpose. To accomplish this at Roche, the Swiss drug and diagnostic product maker, CEO Franz Humer implemented a "decision agenda." The agenda focuses only on Roche's highest-value issues, and discussions are limited to these major topics. In terms of case analysis, the major topics include sorting out the issues of the case, linking elements of the case to the strategic issues presented in class or the text, and assigning roles to various team members. Such objectives help keep team members on track.

Agendas also can be used to address issues such as the timeline for accomplishing work. Otherwise, the purpose of meetings may only be to manage the "crisis" of getting the case analysis finished on time. One solution is to assign a team member to manage the agenda. That person could make sure the team stays focused on the tasks at hand and remains mindful of time constraints. Another role could be to link the team's efforts to the steps presented in Exhibit 13.2 and Exhibit 13.3 on how to prepare a case analysis.

Pay More Attention to Strategy

Teams often waste time by focusing on unimportant aspects of a case. These may include details that are interesting but irrelevant or operational issues rather than strategic issues. It is true that useful clues to the issues in the case are sometimes embedded in the conversations of key managers or the trends evident in a financial statement. But once such insights are discovered, teams need to focus on the underlying strategic problems in the case. To solve such problems, major corporations such as Cadbury Schweppes and Boeing hold meetings just to generate strategic alternatives for solving their problems. This gives managers time to consider the implications of various courses of action. Separate meetings are held to evaluate alternatives, make strategic decisions, and approve an action plan.

Once the strategic solutions or "course corrections" are identified—as is common in most cases assigned—the operational implications and details of implementation will flow from the strategic decisions that companies make. Therefore, focusing primarily on strategic issues will provide teams with insights for making recommendations that are based on a deeper understanding of the issues in the case.

Produce Real Decisions

Too often, meetings are about discussing rather than deciding. Teams often spend a lot of time talking without reaching any conclusions. As Raymond Sanchez, CEO of Florida-based Security Mortgage Group, says, meetings are often used to "rehash the hash that's already been hashed." To be efficient and productive, team meetings need to be about more than just information sharing and group input. For example, an initial meeting may result in the team realizing that it needs to study the case in greater depth and examine links to strategic issues more carefully. Once more analysis is conducted, the team needs to reach a consensus so that the decisions that are made will last once the meeting is over. Lasting decisions are more actionable because they free team members to take the next steps.

One technique for making progress in this way is recapping each meeting with a five-minute synthesis report. According to Pamela Schindler, director of the Center for Applied Management at Wittenberg University, it's important to think through the implications of the meeting before ending it. "The real joy of synthesis," says Schindler, "is realizing how many meetings you won't need."

Not only are these guidelines useful for helping teams finish their work, but they can also help resolve some of the difficulties that teams often face. By involving every team member, using a meeting agenda, and focusing on the strategic issues that are critical to nearly every case, the discussion is limited and the criteria for making decisions become clearer. This allows the task to dominate rather than any one personality. And if the team finishes its work faster, this frees up time to focus on other projects or put the finishing touches on a case analysis presentation.

Sources: Mankins, M. C. 2004. Stop wasting valuable time. *Harvard Business Review,* September: 58–65; and Sauer, P. J. 2004. Escape from meeting hell. *Inc.,* May, *www.inc.com.*

Clearly, understanding how to work in groups and the potential problems associated with group decision processes can benefit the case analysis process. Therefore, let's first look at some of the symptoms of groupthink and suggest ways of preventing it. Then we will suggest some conflict-inducing decision-making techniques—devil's advocacy and dialectical inquiry—that can help to prevent groupthink and lead to better decisions.

Symptoms of Groupthink and How to Prevent It Irving Janis identified several symptoms of groupthink, including:

- ***An illusion of invulnerability.*** This reassures people about possible dangers and leads to overoptimism and failure to heed warnings of danger.
- ***A belief in the inherent morality of the group.*** Because individuals think that what they are doing is right, they tend to ignore ethical or moral consequences of their decisions.
- ***Stereotyped views of members of opposing groups.*** Members of other groups are viewed as weak or not intelligent.
- ***The application of pressure to members who express doubts about the group's shared illusions or question the validity of arguments proposed.***
- ***The practice of self-censorship.*** Members keep silent about their opposing views and downplay to themselves the value of their perspectives.

- ***An illusion of unanimity.*** People assume that judgments expressed by members are shared by all.
- ***The appointment of mindguards.*** People sometimes appoint themselves as mindguards to protect the group from adverse information that might break the climate of consensus (or agreement).

Clearly, groupthink is an undesirable and negative phenomenon that can lead to poor decisions. Irving Janis considers it to be a key contributor to such faulty decisions as the failure to prepare for the attack on Pearl Harbor, the escalation of the Vietnam conflict, and the failure to prepare for the consequences of the Iraqi invasion. Many of the same sorts of flawed decision making occur in business organizations. Janis has provided several suggestions for preventing groupthink that can be used as valuable guides in decision making and problem solving:

- Leaders must encourage group members to address their concerns and objectives.
- When higher-level managers assign a problem for a group to solve, they should adopt an impartial stance and not mention their preferences.
- Before a group reaches its final decision, the leader should encourage members to discuss their deliberations with trusted associates and then report the perspectives back to the group.
- The group should invite outside experts and encourage them to challenge the group's viewpoints and positions.
- The group should divide into subgroups, meet at various times under different chairpersons, and then get together to resolve differences.
- After reaching a preliminary agreement, the group should hold a "second chance" meeting that provides members a forum to express any remaining concerns and rethink the issue prior to making a final decision.

Using Conflict to Improve Decision Making In addition to the given suggestions, the effective use of conflict can be a means of improving decision making. Although conflict can have negative outcomes, such as ill will, anger, tension, and lowered motivation, both leaders and group members must strive to ensure that it is managed properly and used in a constructive manner.

Two conflict-inducing decision-making approaches that have become quite popular are *devil's advocacy* and *dialectical inquiry.* Both approaches incorporate conflict into the decision-making process through formalized debate. A group charged with making a decision or solving a problem is divided into two subgroups, and each will be involved in the analysis and solution.

devil's advocacy
a method of introducing conflict into a decision-making process by having specific individuals or groups act as a critic to an analysis or planned solution.

With **devil's advocacy,** one of the groups (or individuals) acts as a critic to the plan. The devil's advocate tries to come up with problems with the proposed alternative and suggest reasons why it should not be adopted. The role of the devil's advocate is to create dissonance. This ensures that the group will take a hard look at its original proposal or alternative. By having a group (or individual) assigned the role of devil's advocate, it becomes clear that such an adversarial stance is legitimized. It brings out criticisms that might otherwise not be made.

Some authors have suggested that the use of a devil's advocate can help boards of directors to ensure that decisions are addressed comprehensively and to avoid groupthink.[15] And Charles Elson, a director of Sunbeam Corporation, has argued:

> Devil's advocates are terrific in any situation because they help you to figure a decision's numerous implications. . . . The better you think out the implications prior to making the decision, the better the decision ultimately turns out to be. That's why a devil's advocate is always a great person, irritating sometimes, but a great person.

As one might expect, there can be some potential problems with using the devil's advocate approach. If one's views are constantly criticized, one may become demoralized. Thus, that person may come up with "safe solutions" in order to minimize embarrassment or personal risk and become less subject to criticism. Additionally, even if the devil's advocate is successful with finding problems with the proposed course of action, there may be no new ideas or counterproposals to take its place. Thus, the approach sometimes may simply focus on what is wrong without suggesting other ideas.

Dialectical inquiry attempts to accomplish the goals of the devil's advocate in a more constructive manner. It is a technique whereby a problem is approached from two alternative points of view. The idea is that out of a critique of the opposing perspectives–a thesis and an antithesis–a creative synthesis will occur. Dialectical inquiry involves the following steps:

dialectical inquiry a method of introducing conflict into a decision-making process by devising different proposals that are feasible, politically viable, and credible but rely on different assumptions and then debating the merits of each.

1. Identify a proposal and the information that was used to derive it.
2. State the underlying assumptions of the proposal.
3. Identify a counterplan (antithesis) that is believed to be feasible, politically viable, and generally credible. However, it rests on assumptions that are opposite to the original proposal.
4. Engage in a debate in which individuals favoring each plan provide their arguments and support.
5. Identify a synthesis which, hopefully, includes the best components of each alternative.

There are some potential downsides associated with dialectical inquiry. It can be quite time-consuming and involve a good deal of training. Further, it may result in a series of compromises between the initial proposal and the counterplan. In cases where the original proposal was the best approach, this would be unfortunate.

Despite some possible limitations associated with these conflict-inducing decision-making techniques, they have many benefits. Both techniques force debate about underlying assumptions, data, and recommendations between subgroups. Such debate tends to prevent the uncritical acceptance of a plan that may seem to be satisfactory after a cursory analysis. The approach serves to tap the knowledge and perspectives of group members and continues until group members agree on both assumptions and recommended actions. Given that both approaches serve to use, rather than minimize or suppress, conflict, higher-quality decisions should result. Exhibit 13.5 briefly summarizes these techniques.

EXHIBIT 13.5 Two Conflict-Inducing Decision-Making Processes

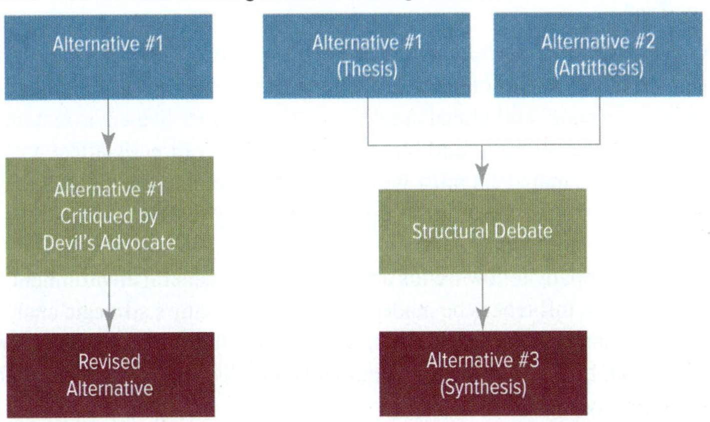

LO 13-6

Understand how to use the strategic insights and material from each of the 12 previous chapters in the text to analyze issues posed by strategic management cases.

FOLLOWING THE ANALYSIS-DECISION-ACTION CYCLE IN CASE ANALYSIS

In Chapter 1 we defined strategic management as the analyses, decisions, and actions that organizations undertake to create and sustain competitive advantages. It is no accident that we chose that sequence of words because it corresponds to the sequence of events that typically occurs in the strategic management process. In case analysis, as in the real world, this cycle of events can provide a useful framework. First, an analysis of the case in terms of the business environment and current events is needed. To make such an analysis, the case background must be considered. Next, based on that analysis, decisions must be made. This may involve formulating a strategy, choosing between difficult options, moving forward aggressively, or retreating from a bad situation. There are many possible decisions, depending on the case situation. Finally, action is required. Once decisions are made and plans are set, the action begins. The recommended action steps and the consequences of implementing these actions are the final stage.

Each of the previous 12 chapters of this book includes techniques and information that may be useful in a case analysis. However, not all of the issues presented will be important in every case. As noted earlier, one of the challenges of case analysis is to identify the most critical points and sort through material that may be ambiguous or seem unimportant.

In this section we draw on the material presented in each of the 12 chapters to show how it informs the case analysis process. The ideas are linked sequentially and in terms of an overarching strategic perspective. One of your jobs when conducting case analysis is to see how the parts of a case fit together and how the insights from the study of strategy can help you understand the case situation.

1. ***Analyzing organizational goals and objectives.*** A company's vision, mission, and objectives keep organization members focused on a common purpose. They also influence how an organization deploys its resources, relates to its stakeholders, and matches its short-term objectives with its long-term goals. The goals may even impact how a company formulates and implements strategies. When exploring issues of goals and objectives, you might ask:
   - Has the company developed short-term objectives that are inconsistent with its long-term mission? If so, how can management realign its vision, mission, and objectives?
   - Has the company considered all of its stakeholders equally in making critical decisions? If not, should the views of all stakeholders be treated the same or are some stakeholders more important than others?
   - Is the company being faced with an issue that conflicts with one of its longstanding policies? If so, how should it compare its existing policies to the potential new situation?
2. ***Analyzing the external environment.*** The business environment has two components. The general environment consists of demographic, sociocultural, political/legal, technological, economic, and global conditions. The competitive environment includes rivals, suppliers, customers, and other factors that may directly affect a company's success. Strategic managers must monitor the environment to identify opportunities and threats that may have an impact on performance. When investigating a firm's external environment, you might ask:
   - Does the company follow trends and events in the general environment? If not, how can these influences be made part of the company's strategic analysis process?
   - Is the company effectively scanning and monitoring the competitive environment? If so, how is it using the competitive intelligence it is gathering to enhance its competitive advantage?

- Has the company correctly analyzed the impact of the competitive forces in its industry on profitability? If so, how can it improve its competitive position relative to these forces?

3. ***Analyzing the internal environment.*** A firm's internal environment consists of its resources and other value-adding capabilities. Value-chain analysis and a resource-based approach to analysis can be used to identify a company's strengths and weaknesses and determine how they are contributing to its competitive advantages. Evaluating firm performance can also help make meaningful comparisons with competitors. When researching a company's internal analysis, you might ask:
   - Does the company know how the various components of its value chain are adding value to the firm? If not, what internal analysis is needed to determine its strengths and weakness?
   - Has the company accurately analyzed the source and vitality of its resources? If so, is it deploying its resources in a way that contributes to competitive advantages?
   - Is the company's financial performance as good as or better than that of its close competitors? If so, has it balanced its financial success with the performance criteria of other stakeholders such as customers and employees?
4. ***Assessing a firm's intellectual assets.*** Human capital is a major resource in today's knowledge economy. As a result, attracting, developing, and retaining talented workers is a key strategic challenge. Other assets such as patents and trademarks are also critical. How companies leverage their intellectual assets through social networks and strategic alliances, and how technology is used to manage knowledge, may be a major influence on a firm's competitive advantage. When analyzing a firm's intellectual assets, you might ask:
   - Does the company have underutilized human capital? If so, what steps are needed to develop and leverage its intellectual assets?
   - Is the company missing opportunities to forge strategic alliances? If so, how can it use its social capital to network more effectively?
   - Has the company developed knowledge-management systems that capture what it learns? If not, what technologies can it employ to retain new knowledge?
5. ***Formulating business-level strategies.*** Firms use the competitive strategies of differentiation, focus, and overall cost leadership as a basis for overcoming the five competitive forces and developing sustainable competitive advantages. Combinations of these strategies may work best in some competitive environments. Additionally, an industry's life cycle is an important contingency that may affect a company's choice of business-level strategies. When assessing business-level strategies, you might ask:
   - Has the company chosen the correct competitive strategy given its industry environment and competitive situation? If not, how should it use its strengths and resources to improve its performance?
   - Does the company use combination strategies effectively? If so, what capabilities can it cultivate to further enhance profitability?
   - Is the company using a strategy that is appropriate for the industry life cycle in which it is competing? If not, how can it realign itself to match its efforts to the current stage of industry growth?
6. ***Formulating corporate-level strategies.*** Large firms often own and manage portfolios of businesses. Corporate strategies address methods for achieving synergies among these businesses. Related and unrelated diversification techniques are alternative approaches to deciding which business should be added to or removed from a portfolio. Companies can diversify by means of mergers, acquisitions, joint ventures,

strategic alliances, and internal development. When analyzing corporate-level strategies, you might ask:

- Is the company competing in the right businesses given the opportunities and threats that are present in the environment? If not, how can it realign its diversification strategy to achieve competitive advantages?
- Is the corporation managing its portfolio of businesses in a way that creates synergies among the businesses? If so, what additional business should it consider adding to its portfolio?
- Are the motives of the top corporate executives who are pushing diversification strategies appropriate? If not, what action can be taken to curb their activities or align them with the best interests of all stakeholders?

7. ***Formulating international-level strategies.*** Foreign markets provide both opportunities and potential dangers for companies that want to expand globally. To decide which entry strategy is most appropriate, companies have to evaluate the trade-offs between two factors that firms face when entering foreign markets: cost reduction and local adaptation. To achieve competitive advantages, firms will typically choose one of three strategies: global, multidomestic, or transnational. When evaluating international-level strategies, you might ask:
   - Is the company's entry into an international marketplace threatened by the actions of local competitors? If so, how can cultural differences be minimized to give the firm a better chance of succeeding?
   - Has the company made the appropriate choices between cost reduction and local adaptation to foreign markets? If not, how can it adjust its strategy to achieve competitive advantages?
   - Can the company improve its effectiveness by embracing one international strategy over another? If so, how should it choose between a global, multidomestic, or transnational strategy?
8. ***Formulating entrepreneurial strategies.*** New ventures add jobs and create new wealth. To do so, they must identify opportunities that will be viable in the marketplace as well as gather resources and assemble an entrepreneurial team to enact the opportunity. New entrants often evoke a strong competitive response from incumbent firms in a given marketplace. When examining the role of strategic thinking on the success of entrepreneurial ventures and the role of competitive dynamics, you might ask:
   - Is the company engaged in an ongoing process of opportunity recognition? If not, how can it enhance its ability to recognize opportunities?
   - Do the entrepreneurs who are launching new ventures have vision, dedication and drive, and a commitment to excellence? If so, how have these affected the performance and dedication of other employees involved in the venture?
   - Have strategic principles been used in the process of developing strategies to pursue the entrepreneurial opportunity? If not, how can the venture apply tools such as five-forces analysis and value-chain analysis to improve its competitive position and performance?
9. ***Achieving effective strategic control.*** Strategic controls enable a firm to implement strategies effectively. Informational controls involve comparing performance to stated goals and scanning, monitoring, and being responsive to the environment. Behavioral controls emerge from a company's culture, reward systems, and organizational boundaries. When assessing the impact of strategic controls on implementation, you might ask:
   - Is the company employing the appropriate informational control systems? If not, how can it implement a more interactive approach to enhance learning and minimize response times?

- Does the company have a strong and effective culture? If not, what steps can it take to align its values and rewards system with its goals and objectives?
- Has the company implemented control systems that match its strategies? If so, what additional steps can be taken to improve performance?

10. ***Creating effective organizational designs.*** Organizational designs that align with competitive strategies can enhance performance. As companies grow and change, their structures must also evolve to meet new demands. In today's economy, firm boundaries must be flexible and permeable to facilitate smoother interactions with external parties such as customers, suppliers, and alliance partners. New forms of organizing are becoming more common. When evaluating the role of organizational structure on strategy implementation, you might ask:
    - Has the company implemented organizational structures that are suited to the type of business it is in? If not, how can it alter the design in ways that enhance its competitiveness?
    - Is the company employing boundaryless organizational designs where appropriate? If so, how are senior managers maintaining control of lower-level employees?
    - Does the company use outsourcing to achieve the best possible results? If not, what criteria should it use to decide which functions can be outsourced?
11. ***Creating a learning organization and an ethical organization.*** Strong leadership is essential for achieving competitive advantages. Two leadership roles are especially important. The first is creating a learning organization by harnessing talent and encouraging the development of new knowledge. Second, leaders play a vital role in motivating employees to excellence and inspiring ethical behavior. When exploring the impact of effective strategic leadership, you might ask:
    - Do company leaders promote excellence as part of the overall culture? If so, how has this influenced the performance of the firm and the individuals in it?
    - Is the company committed to being a learning organization? If not, what can it do to capitalize on the individual and collective talents of organizational members?
    - Have company leaders exhibited an ethical attitude in their own behavior? If not, how has their behavior influenced the actions of other employees?
12. ***Fostering corporate entrepreneurship.*** Many firms continually seek new growth opportunities and avenues for strategic renewal. In some corporations, autonomous work units such as business incubators and new venture groups are used to focus corporate venturing activities. In other corporate settings, product champions and other firm members provide companies with the impetus to expand into new areas. When investigating the impact of entrepreneurship on strategic effectiveness, you might ask:
    - Has the company resolved the dilemmas associated with managing innovation? If so, is it effectively defining and pacing its innovation efforts?
    - Has the company developed autonomous work units that have the freedom to bring forth new product ideas? If so, has it used product champions to implement new venture initiatives?
    - Does the company have an entrepreneurial orientation? If not, what can it do to encourage entrepreneurial attitudes in the strategic behavior of its organizational members?

We close this chapter with Strategy Spotlight 13.5—an example of how the College of Business and Economics at Towson University went about conducting a "live" business case competition across all of the strategic management sections. The "Description" and "Case Competition Checklist" includes many of the elements of the analysis-decision-action cycle in case analysis that we have discussed.

13.5 STRATEGY SPOTLIGHT

CASE COMPETITION ASSIGNMENT

Brief Description

The purpose of this assignment is to apply theory to a real-life strategic management case on Cintas Corporation (Baltimore). Your role is to analyze the case and recommend practical, innovative, and theoretically sound solutions. Participation in the competition will provide invaluable experience and the opportunity to interact with business executives in a meaningful activity. The executives will select the winning teams and identify Gold, Silver, and Bronze Team winners.

The case competition within each section will represent 25 percent of the grade for the course. The rubric for judging the winning team in each section will be standardized across all sections of the strategic management course to address conceptual skills in strategic analysis, strategy formulation, strategy implementation, and strategic control.

The case will be disseminated on the case competition Blackboard site. Each team must give a presentation as described below, turn in a hard copy of its multimedia presentation and any updated supplementary materials, and upload all relevant materials as specified by the instructor (presentation, supplements).

The team presentation may not exceed 15 minutes and will be graded based on coverage of all elements in the grading rubric. Approximately five additional minutes will be devoted to responding to questions and comments from the judges.

Case Competition Checklist

Be sure to address all of the following statements in order for your presentation to earn a positive evaluation.

To what extent do you agree with the following statements?

External Analysis

- Effectively uses an analysis of the general business environment to address all key general environment trends.
- Effectively uses Porter's Five Forces model to assess industry attractiveness.

Internal Analysis

- Identifies all key organization resources and capabilities.
- Appropriately discusses all key organization resources and capabilities and identifies the degree to which they serve as the foundation for a competitive advantage.
- Appropriately discusses Cintas Baltimore's strengths and weaknesses.
- Explains in depth all important implications for Cintas Baltimore.

Corporate Alignment

- Evaluates areas of alignment/misalignment (strategic fit) between the catalog line of business in the restaurant industry and the organization's overall corporate strategy.

Proposed Strategy and Resource Requirements

- Provides a comprehensive strategy for the catalog line of business that spans three years. This should include milestones that you hope to accomplish over that time period. Supplementary materials fully complement and support the presentation.
- Your plan's resource requirements are fully identified and explained.
- Your plan's resource needs are feasible with realistic costs.
- The total cost of your plan does not exceed $45,000 ($15,000 per year).
- All assumptions are clearly explained and logical.
- Strategic alternatives are fully explained in supporting supplementary materials.
- Recommendations address all major issues.
- Recommendations are explained in-depth.

Barriers to Imitation

- Obstacles for competitors to imitate the strategy are fully identified.
- Obstacles for competitors to imitate the strategy are justified with clear logic.

Tactics

- An appropriate number of milestones for the next three years is proposed.
- For each milestone, at least three tactics are proposed. All milestones and tactics clearly pertain to the strategy.

Writing and Presentation Criteria

- Written materials contain no technical/grammar/spelling errors.
- Writing is completely clear and well-organized.
- Writing uses appropriate word choice.
- All ideas not your own are appropriately referenced.
- Arguments are logically compelling.
- All exhibits are referenced.
- All exhibits' relevance is explained.
- Basic information that the business audience would know is not rehashed.
- The presentation is limited to 15 minutes.
- All members of the team present for at least one minute.
- All members are dressed professionally.
- All presenters are enthusiastic (eye contact, no filler words, posture).
- All presenters use proper diction and voice.
- All presenters clearly present the intended content (arguments are convincing).

- All presenters follow a group theme and structure.
- All presenters respond well to questions during the Q&A.
- All presenters show deep understanding of the analyses.
- All presenters are respectful and professional.

Note: We thank a team of contributors at Towson University for sharing this information with us, including Lori Kiyatkin, Doug Sanford, David Brannon, Shana Gass, Shohreh Kaynama, Don Kopka, Mariana Lebron, Jimmy Lien, Wayne Paul, Doug Ross, and Precha Thavikulwat. The information provided here is an abridged version of the materials actually used for the assignment, which would also include the grading rubric, etc.

key points

Strategic management case analysis provides an effective method of learning how companies analyze problems, make decisions, and resolve challenges. Strategic cases include detailed accounts of actual business situations. The purpose of analyzing such cases is to gain exposure to a wide variety of organizational and managerial situations. By putting yourself in the place of a strategic decision maker, you can gain an appreciation of the difficulty and complexity of many strategic situations. In the process you can learn how to ask good strategic questions and enhance your analytical skills. Presenting case analyses can also help develop oral and written communication skills.

In this chapter we have discussed the importance of strategic case analysis and described the five steps involved in conducting a case analysis: becoming familiar with the material, identifying problems, analyzing strategic issues, proposing alternative solutions, and making recommendations. We have also discussed how to get the most from case analysis. Finally, we have described how the case analysis process follows the analysis-decision-action cycle of strategic management and outlined issues and questions that are associated with each of the previous 12 chapters of the text.

key terms

case analysis 389
financial ratio analysis 394
integrative thinking 400
devil's advocacy 406
dialectical inquiry 407

REFERENCES

1. Bryant, A. 2011. *The Corner Office: Indispensable and Unexpected Lessons from CEOs on How to Lead and Succeed.* New York: Macmillan.
2. The material in this chapter is based on several sources, including Barnes, L. A., Nelson, A. J., & Christensen, C. R. 1994. *Teaching and the case method: Text, cases and readings.* Boston: Harvard Business School Press; Guth, W. D. 1985. Central concepts of business unit and corporate strategy. In Guth, W. D. (Ed.), *Handbook of business strategy:* 1-9. Boston: Warren, Gorham & Lamont; Lundberg, C. C., & Enz, C. 1993. A framework for student case preparation. *Case Research Journal,* 13 (Summer): 129-140; and Ronstadt, R. 1980. *The art of case analysis: A guide to the diagnosis of business situations.* Dover, MA: Lord.
3. Edge, A. G. & Coleman, D. R. 1986. *The guide to case analysis and reporting* (3rd ed.). Honolulu, HI: System Logistics.
4. Morris, E. 1987. Vision and strategy: A focus for the future. *Journal of Business Strategy,* 8: 51-58.
5. Bryant, A. 2011. *The Corner Office: Indispensable and Unexpected Lessons from CEOs on How to Lead and Succeed.* New York: Macmillan.
6. This section is based on Lundberg & Enz, op. cit., and Ronstadt, op. cit.
7. The importance of problem definition was emphasized in Mintzberg, H., Raisinghani, D., & Theoret, A. 1976. The structure of "unstructured" decision processes. *Administrative Science Quarterly,* 21(2): 246-275.
8. Drucker, P. F. 1994. The theory of the business. *Harvard Business Review,* 72(5): 95-104.
9. This section draws on Edge & Coleman, op. cit.
10. Evans, R. 2007. The either/or dilemma. *www.ft.com,* December 19: np; Martin, R. L. 2007. *The Opposable Mind: How Successful Leaders Win Through Integrative Thinking.* Boston: Harvard Business School Press; and Fitzgerald, F. S. 1965. *The Crack-up: With Other Pieces and Stories.* New York: Penguin Random House.
11. Martin, R. L. 2007. The Opposable Mind: How Successful Leaders Win Through Integrative Thinking. Boston: Harvard Business School Press.
12. This section draws on Winston, A. S. 2014. *The big pivot.* Boston: Harvard Business Review Press.
13. Irving Janis is credited with coining the term *groupthink,* and he applied it primarily to fiascos in government (such as the Bay of Pigs incident in 1961). Refer to Janis, I. L. 1982. *Victims of groupthink* (2nd ed.). Boston: Houghton Mifflin.
14. Much of our discussion is based upon Finkelstein, S. & Mooney, A. C. 2003. Not the usual suspects: How to use board process to make boards better. *Academy of Management Executive,* 17(2): 101-113; Schweiger, D. M., Sandberg, W. R., & Rechner, P. L. 1989. Experiential effects of dialectical inquiry, devil's advocacy, and consensus approaches to strategic decision making. *Academy of Management Journal,* 32(4): 745-772; and Aldag, R J. & Stearns, T. M. 1987. *Management.* Cincinnati: South-Western.
15. Finkelstein, S., and A. C. Mooney. 2005. Not the usual suspects: How to use board process to make boards better. *The Academy of Management Executive,* 17(2): 101-103.

FINANCIAL RATIO ANALYSIS*

Standard Financial Statements

One obvious thing we might want to do with a company's financial statements is to compare them to those of other, similar companies. We would immediately have a problem, however. It's almost impossible to directly compare the financial statements of two companies because of differences in size.

For example, Oracle and IBM are obviously serious rivals in the computer software market, but IBM is much larger (in terms of assets), so it is difficult to compare them directly. For that matter, it's difficult to even compare financial statements from different points in time for the same company if the company's size has changed. The size problem is compounded if we try to compare IBM and, say, SAP (of Germany). If SAP's financial statements are denominated in euros, then we have a size *and* a currency difference.

To start making comparisons, one obvious thing we might try to do is to somehow standardize the financial statements. One very common and useful way of doing this is to work with percentages instead of total dollars. The resulting financial statements are called *common-size statements*. We consider these next.

Common-Size Balance Sheets

For easy reference, Prufrock Corporation's 2018 and 2019 balance sheets are provided in Exhibit 13A.1. Using these, we construct common-size balance sheets by expressing each item as a percentage of total assets. Prufrock's 2018 and 2019 common-size balance sheets are shown in Exhibit 13A.2.

Notice that some of the totals don't check exactly because of rounding errors. Also notice that the total change has to be zero since the beginning and ending numbers must add up to 100 percent.

In this form, financial statements are relatively easy to read and compare. For example, just looking at the two balance sheets for Prufrock, we see that current assets were 19.7 percent of total assets in 2019, up from 19.1 percent in 2018. Current liabilities declined from 16 percent to 15.1 percent of total liabilities and equity over that same time. Similarly, total equity rose from 68.1 percent of total liabilities and equity to 72.2 percent.

Overall, Prufrock's liquidity, as measured by current assets compared to current liabilities, increased over the year. Simultaneously, Prufrock's indebtedness diminished as a percentage of total assets. We might be tempted to conclude that the balance sheet has grown "stronger."

Common-Size Income Statements

A useful way of standardizing the income statement, shown in Exhibit 13A.3, is to express each item as a percentage of total sales, as illustrated for Prufrock in Exhibit 13A.4.

This income statement tells us what happens to each dollar in sales. For Prufrock, interest expense eats up $.061 out of every sales dollar and taxes take another $.081. When all is said and done, $.157 of each dollar flows through to the bottom line (net income), and that amount is split into $.105 retained in the business and $.052 paid out in dividends.

These percentages are very useful in comparisons. For example, a relevant figure is the cost percentage. For Prufrock, $.582 of each $1 in sales goes to pay for goods sold. It would be interesting to compute the same percentage for Prufrock's main competitors to see how Prufrock stacks up in terms of cost control.

*This entire appendix is adapted from Rows, S. A., Westerfield, R. W., & Jordan, B. D. 1999. *Essentials of Corporate Finance* (2nd ed.), chap. 3. NewYork: McGraw-Hill.

EXHIBIT 13A.1

Prufrock Corporation

	2018	2019
Assets		
Current assets		
Cash	$ 84	$ 98
Accounts receivable	165	188
Inventory	393	422
Total	$ 642	$ 708
Fixed assets		
Net plant and equipment	$2,731	$2,880
Total assets	$3,373	$3,588
Liabilities and Owners' Equity		
Current liabilities		
Accounts payable	$ 312	$ 344
Notes payable	231	196
Total	$ 543	$ 540
Long-term debt	$ 531	$ 457
Owners' equity		
Common stock and paid-in surplus	$ 500	$ 550
Retained earnings	1,799	2,041
Total	$2,299	$2,591
Total liabilities and owners' equity	$3,373	$3,588

Balance sheets as of December 31, 2018 and 2019 ($ millions).

Ratio Analysis

Another way of avoiding the problems involved in comparing companies of different sizes is to calculate and compare *financial ratios.* Such ratios are ways of comparing and investigating the relationships between different pieces of financial information. We cover some of the more common ratios next, but there are many others that we don't touch on.

One problem with ratios is that different people and different sources frequently don't compute them in exactly the same way, and this leads to much confusion. The specific definitions we use here may or may not be the same as others you have seen or will see elsewhere. If you ever use ratios as a tool for analysis, you should be careful to document how you calculate each one, and, if you are comparing your numbers to those of another source, be sure you know how its numbers are computed.

For each of the ratios we discuss, several questions come to mind:

1. How is it computed?
2. What is it intended to measure, and why might we be interested?
3. What is the unit of measurement?
4. What might a high or low value be telling us? How might such values be misleading?
5. How could this measure be improved?

Financial ratios are traditionally grouped into the following categories:

1. Short-term solvency, or liquidity, ratios.
2. Long-term solvency, or financial leverage, ratios.
3. Asset management, or turnover, ratios.
4. Profitability ratios.
5. Market value ratios.

EXHIBIT 13A.2
Prufrock Corporation

	2018	2019	Change
Assets			
Current assets			
Cash	2.5%	2.7%	+ .2%
Accounts receivable	4.9	5.2	+ .3
Inventory	11.7	11.8	+ .1
Total	19.1	19.7	+ .6
Fixed assets			
Net plant and equipment	80.9	80.3	−.6
Total assets	100.0%	100.0%	.0%
Liabilities and Owners' Equity			
Current liabilities			
Accounts payable	9.2%	9.6%	+.4%
Notes payable	6.8	5.5	−1.3
Total	16.0	15.1	−.9
Long-term debt	15.7	12.7	− 3.0
Owners' equity			
Common stock and paid-in surplus	14.8	15.3	+.5
Retained earnings	53.3	56.9	+3.6
Total	68.1	72.2	+4.1
Total liabilities and owners' equities	100.0%	100.0%	.0%

Common-size balance sheets as of December 31, 2018 and 2019 (%).
Note: Numbers may not add up to 100.0% due to rounding.

EXHIBIT 13A.3
Prufrock Corporation

Sales		$2,311
Cost of goods sold		1,344
Depreciation		276
Earnings before interest and taxes		$ 691
Interest paid		141
Taxable income		$ 550
Taxes (34%)		187
Net income		$ 363
Dividends	$ 121	
Addition to retained earnings	242	

2019 income statement ($ millions).

EXHIBIT 13A.4
Prufrock Corporation

Sales		100.0%
Cost of goods sold		58.2
Depreciation		11.9
Earnings before interest and taxes		29.9
Interest paid		6.1
Taxable income		23.8
Taxes (34%)		8.1
Net income		15.7%
Dividends	5.2%	
Addition to retained earnings	10.5	

2019 Common-size income statement (%).

We will consider each of these in turn. In calculating these numbers for Prufrock, we will use the ending balance sheet (2019) figures unless we explicitly say otherwise. The numbers for the various ratios come from the income statement and the balance sheet.

Short-Term Solvency, or Liquidity, Measures

As the name suggests, short-term solvency ratios as a group are intended to provide information about a firm's liquidity, and these ratios are sometimes called *liquidity measures.* The primary concern is the firm's ability to pay its bills over the short run without undue stress. Consequently, these ratios focus on current assets and current liabilities.

For obvious reasons, liquidity ratios are particularly interesting to short-term creditors. Since financial managers are constantly working with banks and other short-term lenders, an understanding of these ratios is essential.

One advantage of looking at current assets and liabilities is that their book values and market values are likely to be similar. Often (though not always), these assets and liabilities just don't live long enough for the two to get seriously out of step. On the other hand, like any type of near cash, current assets and liabilities can and do change fairly rapidly, so today's amounts may not be a reliable guide to the future.

Current Ratio One of the best-known and most widely used ratios is the current ratio. As you might guess, the current ratio is defined as:

$$\text{Current ratio} = \frac{\text{Current assets}}{\text{Current liabilities}}$$

For Prufrock, the 2019 current ratio is:

$$\text{Current ratio} = \frac{\$708}{\$540} = 1.31 \text{ times}$$

Because current assets and liabilities are, in principle, converted to cash over the following 12 months, the current ratio is a measure of short-term liquidity. The unit of measurement is either dollars or times. So we could say Prufrock has \$1.31 in current assets for every \$1 in current liabilities, or we could say Prufrock has its current liabilities covered 1.31 times over.

To a creditor, particularly a short-term creditor such as a supplier, the higher the current ratio, the better. To the firm, a high current ratio indicates liquidity, but it also may indicate an inefficient use of cash and other short-term assets. Absent some extraordinary circumstances, we would expect to see a current ratio of at least 1, because a current ratio of less than 1 would mean that net working capital (current assets less current liabilities) is negative. This would be unusual in a healthy firm, at least for most types of businesses.

The current ratio, like any ratio, is affected by various types of transactions. For example, suppose the firm borrows over the long term to raise money. The short-run effect would be an increase in cash from the issue proceeds and an increase in long-term debt. Current liabilities would not be affected, so the current ratio would rise.

Finally, note that an apparently low current ratio may not be a bad sign for a company with a large reserve of untapped borrowing power.

Quick (or Acid-Test) Ratio Inventory is often the least liquid current asset. It's also the one for which the book values are least reliable as measures of market value, since the quality of the inventory isn't considered. Some of the inventory may later turn out to be damaged, obsolete, or lost.

More to the point, relatively large inventories are often a sign of short-term trouble. The firm may have overestimated sales and overbought or overproduced as a result. In this case, the firm may have a substantial portion of its liquidity tied up in slow-moving inventory.

To further evaluate liquidity, the *quick,* or *acid-test, ratio* is computed just like the current ratio, except inventory is omitted:

$$\text{Quick ratio} = \frac{\text{Current assets} - \text{Inventory}}{\text{Current liabilities}}$$

Notice that using cash to buy inventory does not affect the current ratio, but it reduces the quick ratio. Again, the idea is that inventory is relatively illiquid compared to cash.

For Prufrock, this ratio in 2019 was:

$$\text{Quick ratio} = \frac{\$708 - 422}{\$540} = .53 \text{ times}$$

The quick ratio here tells a somewhat different story than the current ratio, because inventory accounts for more than half of Prufrock's current assets. To exaggerate the point, if this inventory consisted of, say, unsold nuclear power plants, then this would be a cause for concern.

Cash Ratio A very short-term creditor might be interested in the *cash ratio:*

$$\text{Cash ratio} = \frac{\text{Cash}}{\text{Current liabilities}}$$

You can verify that this works out to be .18 times for Prufrock.

Long-Term Solvency Measures

Long-term solvency ratios are intended to address the firm's long-run ability to meet its obligations, or, more generally, its financial leverage. These ratios are sometimes called *financial leverage ratios* or just *leverage ratios.* We consider three commonly used measures and some variations.

Total Debt Ratio The *total debt ratio* takes into account all debts of all maturities to all creditors. It can be defined in several ways, the easiest of which is:

$$\text{Total debt ratio} = \frac{\text{Total assets} - \text{Total equity}}{\text{Total assets}}$$

$$= \frac{\$3{,}588 - 2{,}591}{\$3{,}588} = .28 \text{ times}$$

In this case, an analyst might say that Prufrock uses 28 percent debt.[1] Whether this is high or low or whether it even makes any difference depends on whether or not capital structure matters.

[1]Total equity here includes preferred stock, if there is any. An equivalent numerator in this ratio would be (Current liabilities + Long-term debt).

Prufrock has \$.28 in debt for every \$1 in assets. Therefore, there is \$.72 in equity (\$1 − .28) for every \$.28 in debt. With this in mind, we can define two useful variations on the total debt ratio, the *debt-equity ratio* and the *equity multiplier:*

$$\begin{aligned}\text{Debt-equity ratio} &= \text{Total debt/Total equity}\\ &= \$.28/\$.72 = .39 \text{ times}\\ \text{Equity multiplier} &= \text{Total assets/Total equity}\\ &= \$1/\$.72 = 1.39 \text{ times}\end{aligned}$$

The fact that the equity multiplier is 1 plus the debt-equity ratio is not a coincidence:

$$\begin{aligned}\text{Equity multiplier} &= \text{Total assets/Total equity} = \$1/\$.72 = 1.39\\ &= (\text{Total equity} + \text{Total debt})/\text{Total equity}\\ &= 1 + \text{Debt-equity ratio} = 1.39 \text{ times}\end{aligned}$$

The thing to notice here is that given any one of these three ratios, you can immediately calculate the other two, so they all say exactly the same thing.

Times Interest Earned Another common measure of long-term solvency is the *times interest earned* (TIE) *ratio.* Once again, there are several possible (and common) definitions, but we'll stick with the most traditional:

$$\begin{aligned}\text{Times interest earned ratio} &= \frac{\text{EBIT}}{\text{Interest paid}}\\ &= \frac{\$691}{\$141} = 4.9 \text{ times}\end{aligned}$$

As the name suggests, this ratio measures how well a company has its interest obligations covered, and it is often called the *interest coverage ratio.* For Prufrock, the interest bill is covered 4.9 times over.

Cash Coverage A problem with the TIE ratio is that it is based on earnings before interest and taxes (EBIT), which is not really a measure of cash available to pay interest. The reason is that depreciation, a noncash expense, has been deducted. Since interest is most definitely a cash outflow (to creditors), one way to define the *cash coverage ratio* is:

$$\begin{aligned}\text{Cash coverage ratio} &= \frac{\text{EBIT} + \text{Depreciation}}{\text{Interest paid}}\\ &= \frac{\$691 + 276}{\$141} = \frac{\$967}{\$141} = 6.9 \text{ times}\end{aligned}$$

The numerator here, EBIT plus depreciation, is often abbreviated EBDIT (earnings before depreciation, interest, and taxes). It is a basic measure of the firm's ability to generate cash from operations, and it is frequently used as a measure of cash flow available to meet financial obligations.

Asset Management, or Turnover Measures

We next turn our attention to the efficiency with which Prufrock uses its assets. The measures in this section are sometimes called *asset utilization ratios.* The specific ratios we discuss can all be interpreted as measures of turnover. What they are intended to describe is how efficiently, or intensively, a firm uses its assets to generate sales. We first look at two important current assets: inventory and receivables.

Inventory Turnover and Days' Sales in Inventory During the year, Prufrock had a cost of goods sold of $1,344. Inventory at the end of the year was $422. With these numbers, *inventory turnover* can be calculated as:

$$\text{Inventory turnover} = \frac{\text{Cost of goods sold}}{\text{Inventory}}$$

$$= \frac{\$1{,}344}{\$422} = 3.2 \text{ times}$$

In a sense, we sold off, or turned over, the entire inventory 3.2 times. As long as we are not running out of stock and thereby forgoing sales, the higher this ratio is, the more efficiently we are managing inventory.

If we know that we turned our inventory over 3.2 times during the year, then we can immediately figure out how long it took us to turn it over on average. The result is the average *days' sales in inventory:*

$$\text{Day's sales in inventory} = \frac{365 \text{ days}}{\text{Inventory turnover}}$$

$$= \frac{365}{3.2} = 114 \text{ days}$$

This tells us that, on average, inventory sits 114 days before it is sold. Alternatively, assuming we used the most recent inventory and cost figures, it will take about 114 days to work off our current inventory.

For example, we frequently hear things like "Majestic Motors has a 60 days' supply of cars." This means that, at current daily sales, it would take 60 days to deplete the available inventory. We could also say that Majestic has 60 days of sales in inventory.

Receivables Turnover and Days' Sales in Receivables Our inventory measures give some indication of how fast we can sell products. We now look at how fast we collect on those sales. The *receivables turnover* is defined in the same way as inventory turnover:

$$\text{Receivables turnover} = \frac{\text{Sales}}{\text{Accounts receivable}}$$

$$= \frac{\$2{,}311}{\$188} = 12.3 \text{ times}$$

Loosely speaking, we collected our outstanding credit accounts and reloaned the money 12.3 times during the year.[2]

This ratio makes more sense if we convert it to days, so the *days' sales in receivables* is:

$$\text{Day's sales in receivables} = \frac{365 \text{ days}}{\text{Receivables turnover}}$$

$$= \frac{365}{12.3} = 30 \text{ days}$$

Therefore, on average, we collect on our credit sales in 30 days. For obvious reasons, this ratio is very frequently called the *average collection period* (ACP).

Also note that if we are using the most recent figures, we can also say that we have 30 days' worth of sales currently uncollected.

Total Asset Turnover Moving away from specific accounts like inventory or receivables, we can consider an important "big picture" ratio, the *total asset turnover ratio.* As the name suggests, total asset turnover is:

[2]Here we have implicitly assumed that all sales are credit sales. If they were not, then we would simply use total credit sales in these calculations, not total sales.

$$\text{Total asset turnover} = \frac{\text{Sales}}{\text{Total assets}}$$

$$= \frac{\$2{,}311}{\$3{,}588} = .64 \text{ times}$$

In other words, for every dollar in assets, we generated $.64 in sales.

A closely related ratio, the *capital intensity ratio,* is simply the reciprocal of (i.e., 1 divided by) total asset turnover. It can be interpreted as the dollar investment in assets needed to generate $1 in sales. High values correspond to capital-intensive industries (e.g., public utilities). For Prufrock, total asset turnover is .64, so, if we flip this over, we get that capital intensity is $1/.64 = $1.56. That is, it takes Prufrock $1.56 in assets to create $1 in sales.

Profitability Measures

The three measures we discuss in this section are probably the best known and most widely used of all financial ratios. In one form or another, they are intended to measure how efficiently the firm uses its assets and how efficiently the firm manages its operations. The focus in this group is on the bottom line, net income.

Profit Margin Companies pay a great deal of attention to their *profit margin:*

$$\text{Profit margin} = \frac{\text{Net income}}{\text{Sales}}$$

$$= \frac{\$363}{\$2{,}311} = 15.7\%$$

This tells us that Prufrock, in an accounting sense, generates a little less than 16 cents in profit for every dollar in sales.

All other things being equal, a relatively high profit margin is obviously desirable. This situation corresponds to low expense ratios relative to sales. However, we hasten to add that other things are often not equal.

For example, lowering our sales price will usually increase unit volume, but will normally cause profit margins to shrink. Total profit (or, more importantly, operating cash flow) may go up or down; so the fact that margins are smaller isn't necessarily bad. After all, isn't it possible that, as the saying goes, "Our prices are so low that we lose money on everything we sell, but we make it up in volume!"[3]

Return on Assets *Return on assets* (ROA) is a measure of profit per dollar of assets. It can be defined several ways, but the most common is:

$$\text{Return on assets} = \frac{\text{Net income}}{\text{Total assets}}$$

$$= \frac{\$363}{\$3{,}588} = 10.12\%$$

Return on Equity *Return on equity* (ROE) is a measure of how the stockholders fared during the year. Since benefiting shareholders is our goal, ROE is, in an accounting sense, the true bottom-line measure of performance. ROE is usually measured as:

$$\text{Return on equity} = \frac{\text{Net income}}{\text{Total equity}}$$

$$= \frac{\$363}{\$2{,}591} = 14\%$$

[3]No, it's not; margins can be small, but they do need to be positive!

For every dollar in equity, therefore, Prufrock generated 14 cents in profit, but, again, this is only correct in accounting terms.

Because ROA and ROE are such commonly cited numbers, we stress that it is important to remember they are accounting rates of return. For this reason, these measures should properly be called *return on book assets* and *return on book equity.* In addition, ROE is sometimes called *return on net worth.* Whatever it's called, it would be inappropriate to compare the results to, for example, an interest rate observed in the financial markets.

The fact that ROE exceeds ROA reflects Prufrock's use of financial leverage. We will examine the relationship between these two measures in more detail as follows.

Market Value Measures

Our final group of measures is based, in part, on information not necessarily contained in financial statements–the market price per share of the stock. Obviously, these measures can be calculated directly only for publicly traded companies.

We assume that Prufrock has 33 million shares outstanding and the stock sold for \$88 per share at the end of the year. If we recall that Prufrock's net income was \$363 million, then we can calculate that its earnings per share were:

$$\text{EPS} = \frac{\text{Net income}}{\text{Shares outstanding}} = \frac{\$363}{33} = \$11$$

Price-Earnings Ratio The first of our market value measures, the *price-earnings,* or PE, *ratio* (or multiple), is defined as:

$$\text{PE ratio} = \frac{\text{Price per share}}{\text{Earning per share}}$$

$$= \frac{\$88}{\$11} = 8 \text{ times}$$

In the vernacular, we would say that Prufrock shares sell for eight times earnings, or we might say that Prufrock shares have, or "carry," a PE multiple of 8.

Since the PE ratio measures how much investors are willing to pay per dollar of current earnings, higher PEs are often taken to mean that the firm has significant prospects for future growth. Of course, if a firm had no or almost no earnings, its PE would probably be quite large; so, as always, be careful when interpreting this ratio.

Market-to-Book Ratio A second commonly quoted measure is the *market-to-book ratio:*

$$\text{Market-to-book ratio} = \frac{\text{Market value per share}}{\text{Book value per share}}$$

$$= \frac{\$88}{(\$2{,}591/33)} = \frac{\$88}{\$78.5} = 1.12 \text{ times}$$

Notice that book value per share is total equity (not just common stock) divided by the number of shares outstanding.

Since book value per share is an accounting number, it reflects historical costs. In a loose sense, the market-to-book ratio therefore compares the market value of the firm's investments to their cost. A value less than 1 could mean that the firm has not been successful overall in creating value for its stockholders.

Conclusion

This completes our definition of some common ratios. Exhibit 13A.5 summarizes the ratios we've discussed.

EXHIBIT 13A.5 A Summary of Five Types of Financial Ratios

1. Short-term solvency, or liquidity, ratios

$$\text{Current ratio} = \frac{\text{Current assets}}{\text{Current liabilities}}$$

$$\text{Quick ratio} = \frac{\text{Current assets} - \text{Inventory}}{\text{Current liabilities}}$$

$$\text{Cash ratio} = \frac{\text{Cash}}{\text{Current liabilities}}$$

2. Long-term solvency, or financial leverage, ratios

$$\text{Total debt ratio} = \frac{\text{Total assets} - \text{Total equity}}{\text{Total assets}}$$

Debt-equity ratio = Total debt/Total equity

Equity multiplier = Total assets/Total equity

$$\text{Times interest earned ratio} = \frac{\text{EBIT}}{\text{Interest paid}}$$

$$\text{Cash coverage ratio} = \frac{\text{EBIT} + \text{Depreciation}}{\text{Interest paid}}$$

3. Asset utilization, or turnover, ratios

$$\text{Inventory turnover} = \frac{\text{Cost of goods sold}}{\text{Inventory}}$$

$$\text{Days' sales in inventory} = \frac{\text{365 days}}{\text{Inventory turnover}}$$

$$\text{Receivables turnover} = \frac{\text{Sales}}{\text{Accounts receivable}}$$

$$\text{Days' sales in receivables} = \frac{\text{365 days}}{\text{Receivables turnover}}$$

$$\text{Total asset turnover} = \frac{\text{Sales}}{\text{Total assets}}$$

$$\text{Capital intensity} = \frac{\text{Total assets}}{\text{Sales}}$$

4. Profitability ratios

$$\text{Profit margin} = \frac{\text{Net income}}{\text{Sales}}$$

$$\text{Return on assets (ROA)} = \frac{\text{Net income}}{\text{Total assets}}$$

$$\text{Return on equity (ROE)} = \frac{\text{Net income}}{\text{Total equity}}$$

$$\text{ROE} = \frac{\text{Net income}}{\text{Sales}} \times \frac{\text{Sales}}{\text{Assets}} \times \frac{\text{Assets}}{\text{Equity}}$$

5. Market value ratios

$$\text{Price-earnings ratio} = \frac{\text{Price per share}}{\text{Earnings per share}}$$

$$\text{Market-to-book ratio} = \frac{\text{Market value per share}}{\text{Book value per share}}$$

APPENDIX 2 TO CHAPTER 13

SOURCES OF COMPANY AND INDUSTRY INFORMATION*

In order for business executives to make the best decisions when developing corporate strategy, it is critical for them to be knowledgeable about their competitors and about the industries in which they compete. The process used by corporations to learn as much as possible about competitors is often called "competitive intelligence." This appendix provides an overview of important and widely available sources of information that may be useful in conducting basic competitive intelligence. Much information of this nature is available in libraries in article databases and business reference books and on websites. This appendix will recommend a variety of them. Ask a librarian for assistance, because library collections and resources vary.

The information sources are organized into 10 categories:

Competitive Intelligence

Public or Private–Subsidiary or Division–U.S. or Foreign?

*This information was compiled by Ruthie Brock and Carol Byrne, business librarians at The University of Texas at Arlington. We greatly appreciate their valuable contribution.

Finding Public-Company Information
Guides and Tutorials
SEC Filings/EDGAR–Company Disclosure Reports
Company Rankings
Business Websites
Strategic and Competitive Analysis–Information Sources
Sources for Industry Research and Analysis
Search Engines

Competitive Intelligence

According to the Society of Competitive Intelligence Professionals (*http://www.scip.org*), "Competitive Intelligence is an ongoing process of developing a holistic analysis of your organizational environment. If used effectively, data and information can provide valuable insights and prepare companies to deal effectively with unexpected events."

Students and other researchers who want to learn more about the value and process of competitive intelligence should refer to recent articles or books on this subject. Ask a librarian about electronic (ebook) versions of the following titles. A few suggestions are provided as follows. Ask a librarian for assistance, if needed.

Clemons, Eriek. 2018. *New Patterns of Power and Profit: A Strategist's Guide to Competitive Analysis in the Age of Digital Transformation*. London: Palgrave Macmillan.

Heesen, Bernd. 2015. *Effective Strategy Execution: Improving Performance with Business Intelligence.* Berlin: Springer.

Maheshwari, Anil K. 2015. *Business Intelligence and Data Mining.* New York: Business Expert Press.

He, Wu, et al. 2015. Gaining competitive intelligence from social media data: Evidence from two largest retail chains in the world. *Industrial Management & Data Systems*, 115(9): 1622–1636. *http://dx.doi.org/10.1108/IMDS-03-2015-0098.*

Public or Private—Subsidiary or Division—U.S. or Foreign?

Companies traded on stock exchanges in the United States are required to file a variety of reports that disclose information about the company. This begins the process that produces a wealth of data on public companies and, at the same time, distinguishes them from private companies, which often lack available data. Similarly, financial data of subsidiaries and divisions are typically filed in a consolidated financial statement by the parent company, rather than treated independently, thus limiting the kind of data available on them. On the other hand, foreign companies that trade on U.S. stock exchanges are required to file 20F reports, similar to the 10-K for U.S. companies, the most comprehensive of the required reports. The following directories provide brief facts about companies, including whether they are public or private, subsidiary or division, U.S. or foreign.

Corporate Affiliations. New York, NY: RELX, Inc. (formerly Reed Elsevier), 2018.

This database of nearly 2 million corporate family relationships identifies ownership between entities such as ultimate parent, parent, subsidiary, joint venture, affiliate, division, factory or plant, branch, group, holding, and non-operating entities (shells). The database content includes both public and private companies, primarily large with U.S.-located headquarters. Detailed executive and board member profiles are provided. Mergers and acquisitions are tracked from announcement to post-merger organizational changes. Corporate Affiliations data is compiled by the LexisNexis Enterprise Entity Management Group. Downloading from multiple searches to one customized spreadsheet is a new feature. Some historical data is also available. Hard copy volumes can be purchased.

ReferenceUSA. Omaha, NE: Infogroup.Inc.

ReferenceUSA is an online directory of more than 15 million verified businesses located in the United States plus 30 million unverified. New businesses and closed businesses are searchable separately. This resource includes both public and private companies regardless of how small or large, as well as educational, medical, and nonprofit organizations. Job opportunities are provided by *Indeed.com* in search results when available. Specialized modules include consumer lifestyles, historical records, and health care. Check with a librarian regarding availability of specialized modules at your location.

Finding Public-Company Information

Most companies provide their annual report to shareholders and other financial reports are available on their corporate website usually listed under "Investor Relations" or similar headings. Searching Google with the company's name and annual report or 10K report finds most companies financials. Be aware that all company documents are by default told in the most positive language and images; therefore serious research should include analysts' assessments, SWOT analyses, and newspaper or magazine articles to get a complete and less biased view of the company's strengths and weaknesses.

Mergent Online. Fort Mill, SC: Mergent, Inc.
Mergent Online is a database that provides company reports and financial statements for both U.S. and foreign public companies. Mergent's database has up to 25 years of quarterly and annual financial data that can be downloaded into a spreadsheet for analysis across time or across companies. Tabs lead to other features for further analysis. Students should check with a librarian to determine the availability of this database at their college or university library.
http://mergentonline.com

Guides & Tutorials for Researching Companies and Industries

Researching Public Companies through EDGAR: A Guide for Investors. Washington DC: U.S. Securities and Exchange Commission.
This guide informs EDGAR database users about two different search interfaces: the EDGAR Full-Text Search which searches the full-text filings from the last four years only and the Historical EDGAR Archives Search which searches the headings information only (not full text) for a longer period, from 1994 to 2020 (up to yesterday's filings). Each version has some advantages and disadvantages for the user, depending on how exhaustive their research is.
https://www.sec.gov/oiea/Article/edgarguide.html

Ten Steps to Industry Intelligence Research. Industry Tutorial. George A. Smathers Libraries, University of Florida, Gainesville, FL.
This tutorial provides a step-by-step approach for finding information about industries, with embedded links to recommended sources.
http://businesslibrary.uflib.ufl.edu/industryresearch

Conducting Business Research. University of Texas at Austin Libraries, Austin, TX.
This tutorial provides a step-by-step process for business research. *https://legacy.lib.utexas.edu/services/instruction/learningmodules/businessresearch/intro.html*

Guide to Financial Statements. Armonk, NY: IBM.
International Business Machines (IBM) created an educational guide for beginners to learn how to understand and interpret a typical financial statement in a company's annual report.
http://www.ibm.com/investor/help/guide/index.html

How to Read Annual Reports. Armonk, NY: IBM.
An annual report is one of the most important documents a company produces and is often the first document someone consults when researching a company. Created by IBM, this guide explains the purpose of each of the elements that are included in annual reports or 10-K reports, so that novices who are not familiar with business terminology and financials are able to understand.
http://www.ibm.com/investor/help/reports/index.html

Ten Steps to Company Intelligence. Company Research Tutorial. William and Joan Schreyer Business Library, Penn State University, University Park, PA.
This tutorial provides a step-by-step approach to finding company intelligence information.
http://businesslibrary.uflib.ufl.edu/companyresearch

SEC Filings/EDGAR—Company Disclosure Reports

SEC Filings are the various reports that publicly traded companies must file with the Securities and Exchange Commission to disclose information about their corporation. These are often referred to as "EDGAR" filings, an acronym for the Electronic Data Gathering, Analysis and Retrieval System. Some websites and commercial databases improve access to these reports by offering additional retrieval features not available on the official *(www.sec.gov)* website.

EDGAR Database. U.S. Securities and Exchange Commission (SEC), Washington, DC.
Public companies are required to disclose financial information for the benefit of shareholders and other interested researchers and investors. The SEC is the agency which oversees the process and provides free access to more than 21 million filings in their EDGAR database. See also the guide described previously called: *Researching Public Companies through EDGAR. www.sec.gov/edgar/searchedgar/companysearch.html*

Nexis Uni. SEC Filings & Reports. Bethesda, MD: LexisNexis.
SEC filings are available in *Nexis Uni* by selecting "Search by Subject or Topic." Under the Companies category, select SEC Filings. A company-name search or an advanced search can be conducted at that point.

Mergent Online–Government Filings Search.
This database also provides an alternative search interface for SEC filings. *Mergent's Government Filings* search allows searching by company name, ticker, CIK (Central Index Key) number, or industry SIC number. The search can be limited by date and by type of SEC file. Ask a librarian whether your library subscribes to *Mergent Online* for this feature.

Company Rankings

Fortune 500. New York: Time Inc.
The *Fortune 500* list and other company rankings are published in the printed edition of *Fortune* magazine and are also available online.
http://fortune.com/fortune500

Forbes Global 2000. Forbes, Inc.
The companies listed on the Forbes Global 2000 are the biggest and most powerful in the world.
www.forbes.com/global2000/

Business Websites

Big Charts. San Francisco: MarketWatch, Inc.
BigCharts is an easy-to-use investment research website operated by and linked to *MarketWatch.com*. Research tools such as interactive charts, current and historical quotes, industry analysis, and intraday stock screeners, as well as market news and commentary are provided. Supported by site sponsors, it is free to self-directed investors.
http://bigcharts.marketwatch.com/

GlobalEdge. East Lansing, MI: Michigan State University.
GlobalEdge is a web portal providing a significant amount of information about international business, countries around the globe, the U.S. states, industries, and news.
http://globaledge.msu.edu/

Yahoo Finance. Sunnyvale, CA: Yahoo! Inc.
The finance section of Yahoo's website on U.S. world markets, financial news, and other information useful to investors.
http://finance.yahoo.com

Strategic and Competitive Analysis—Information Sources

Analyzing a company can take the form of examining its internal and external environments. In the process, it is useful to identify the company's strengths, weaknesses, opportunities, and threats (SWOT). Sources for this kind of analysis are varied, but perhaps the best would be articles from *The Wall Street Journal,* business magazines, and industry trade publications.

Publications such as these can be found in the following databases available at many public and academic libraries. When using a database that is structured to allow it, try searching the company name combined with one or more keywords, such as "IBM and competition" or "Microsoft and lawsuits" or "AMR and fuel costs" to retrieve articles relating to the external environment.

ABI/INFORM Complete. Ann Arbor, MI: ProQuest LLC.
ABI/INFORM Complete provides abstracts and full-text articles covering disciplines such as management, law, taxation, economics, health care, and information technology from more than 6,800 scholarly, business, and trade publications. Other types of resources include company and industry reports, case studies, market research reports, and a variety of downloadable economic data.

Business Insights: Essentials. Farmington Hills, MI: Gale CENGAGE Learning.
Business Insights provides company and industry intelligence for a selection of public and private companies. Company profiles include parent-subsidiary relationships, industry rankings, products and brands, industry statistics, and financial ratios. Selections of SWOT analysis reports are also available. The Company and Industry comparison tool allows a researcher to compare up to six companies' revenues, employees, and sales data over time. Results are available as an image, chart, or spreadsheet.

Business Source Complete. Ipswich, MA: EBSCO Industries.
Business Source Complete is a full-text database with over 3,800 scholarly business journals covering management, economics, finance, accounting, international business, and more. The database also includes detailed company profiles for more than one million public and private companies, as well as selected country economic reports provided by the Economist Intelligence Unit (EIU). The database includes case studies, investment and market research reports, SWOT analyses, and more. *Business Source Complete* contains over 2,400 peer-reviewed business journals.

IBISWorld. Los Angeles, CA: IBISWorld.
The database provides access to detailed industry reports for over 700-plus United States industries. Each report includes industry structure, market characteristics, product and customer segments, cost structure, industry conditions, major players, market share, supply chain structure, and 5-year revenue forecasts. Separate subscriptions are required for the Global and China industry reports.

Thomson ONE Research.
Thomson ONE Research offers full-text analytical reports on more than 65,000 companies worldwide. The research reports are excellent sources for strategic and financial profiles of a company and its competitors and of industry trends. Developed by a global roster of brokerage, investment banking, and research firms, these full-text investment reports include a wealth of current and historical information useful for evaluating a company or industry over time.

International Directory of Company Histories. Detroit, MI: St. James Press, 1988–present.
This directory covers more than 11,000 multinational companies, and the series is still adding volumes. Each company history is approximately three to five pages in length and provides a summary of the company's mission, goals, and ideals, followed by company milestones, principal subsidiaries, and competitors. Strategic decisions made during the company's period of existence are usually noted. This series covers public and private companies and nonprofit entities. Entry information includes a company's legal name, headquarters information, URL, incorporation date, ticker symbol, stock exchange listing, sales figures, and the primary North American Industry Classification System (NAICS) code. Further reading selections complete the entry information. Volumes 59 to the most recent are available electronically in the Gale Virtual Reference Library database from Gale CENGAGE Learning.

NexisUni Bethesda, MD: LexisNexis.
NexisUni provides access to legal, company, and industry information, news sources, and public records. Industry information is available through the Company Info tab or the "Search by content type" selection. The Company Dossier tool allows a researcher to compare up to five companies' financial statements at one time with download capabilities.

The Wall Street Journal. New York: Dow Jones & Co.

This respected business newspaper is available in searchable full text from 1984 to the present in the *Factiva* database. The "News Pages" link provides access to current articles and issues of *The Wall Street Journal.* Dow Jones, publisher of the print version of the *Wall Street Journal,* also has an online subscription available at *wsj.com*. Some libraries provide access to *The Wall Street Journal* through the ProQuest Newspapers database.

Sources for Industry Research and Analysis

Factiva. New York: Dow Jones & Co.

The *Factiva* database has several options for researching an industry. One would be to search the database for articles in the business magazines and industry trade publications. A second option in *Factiva* would be to search in the Companies/Markets category for company/industry comparison reports.

Mergent Online. New York: Mergent Inc.

Mergent Online is a searchable database of over 60,000 global public companies. The database offers worldwide industry reports, U.S. and global competitors, and executive biographical information. *Mergent's* Basic Search option permits searching by primary industry codes (either SIC or NAICS). Once the search is executed, companies in that industry should be listed. A comparison or standard peer-group analysis can be created to analyze companies in the same industry on various criteria. The Advanced Search allows the user to search a wider range of financial and textual information. Results, including ratios for a company and its competitors, can be downloaded to a spreadsheet.

North American Industry Classification System (NAICS)

The North American Industry Classification System has officially replaced the Standard Industrial Classification (SIC) as the numerical structure used to define and analyze industries, although some publications and databases offer both classification systems. The NAICS codes are used in Canada, the United States, and Mexico. In the United States, the NAICS codes are used to conduct an Economic Census every five years providing a snapshot of the U.S. economy at a given moment in time.

NAICS: *www.census.gov/eos/www/naics/*

Economic Census: *www.census.gov/programs-surveys/economic-census/year.html*

S&P Capital IQ Net Advantage. New York: S & P Capital IQ.

The database includes company, financial, and investment information as well as the well-known publication called *Industry Surveys.* Each industry report includes information on the current environment, industry trends, key industry ratios and statistics, and comparative company financial analysis. Available in HTML, PDF, or Excel formats.

Business Insights: Essentials. Farmington Hills, MI: Gale CENGAGE Learning.

Business Insights provides company and industry intelligence for a selection of public and private companies. Company profiles include parent-subsidiary relationships, industry rankings, products and brands, industry statistics, and financial ratios. Selections of SWOT analysis reports are also available. The Company and Industry comparison tool allows a researcher to compare up to six companies' revenues, employees, and sales data over time. Results are available as an image, chart, or spreadsheet.

Plunkett Research Online. Houston, TX: Plunkett Research, Ltd.

Plunkett's provides industry-specific market research, trends analysis, and business intelligence for 34 industries.

Search Engines

Bing. Redmond, WA: Microsoft Corporation.

Has easy to find licensing information for images.

DuckDuckGo. Paoli, PA: DuckDuckGo, Inc.

An internet search engine that became known primarily for protecting users' privacy.

Google. Mountain View, CA: Google, Inc.

Recognized for its advanced technology, quality of results, and simplicity, the search engine Google is highly recommended by librarians and other expert web surfers.

www.google.com

cases

CASE 1

ROBIN HOOD*

It was in the spring of the second year of his insurrection against the High Sheriff of Nottingham that Robin Hood took a walk in Sherwood Forest. As he walked he pondered the progress of the campaign, the disposition of his forces, the Sheriff's recent moves, and the options that confronted him.

The revolt against the Sheriff had begun as a personal crusade, erupting out of Robin's conflict with the Sheriff and his administration. Alone, however, Robin Hood could do little. He therefore sought allies, men with grievances and a deep sense of justice. Later he welcomed all who came, asking few questions, and only demanding a willingness to serve. Strength, he believed, lay in numbers.

He spent the first year forging the group into a disciplined band, united in enmity against the Sheriff, and willing to live outside the law. The band's organization was simple. Robin ruled supreme, making all important decisions. He delegated specific tasks to his lieutenants. Will Scarlett was in charge of intelligence and scouting. His main job was to shadow the Sheriff and his men, always alert to their next move. He also collected information on the travel plans of rich merchants and tax collectors. Little John kept discipline among the men, and saw to it that their archery was at the high peak that their profession demanded. Scarlock took care of the finances, converting loot into cash, paying shares of the take, and finding suitable hiding places for the surplus. Finally, Much the Miller's son had the difficult task of provisioning the ever-increasing band of Merrymen.

The increasing size of the band was a source of satisfaction for Robin, but also a source of concern. The fame of his Merrymen was spreading, and new recruits poured in from every corner of England. As the band grew larger, their small bivouac became a major encampment. Between raids the men milled about, talking and playing games. Vigilance was in decline, and discipline was becoming harder to enforce. "Why," Robin reflected, "I don't know half the men I run into these days."

The growing band was also beginning to exceed the food capacity of the forest. Game was becoming scarce, and supplies had to be obtained from outlying villages. The cost of buying food was beginning to drain the band's financial reserves at the very moment when revenues were in decline. Travelers, especially those with the most to lose, were now giving the forest a wide berth. This was costly and inconvenient to them, but it was preferable to having all their goods confiscated.

Robin believed that the time had come for the Merrymen to change their policy of outright confiscation of goods to one of a fixed transit tax. His lieutenants strongly resisted this idea. They were proud of the Merrymen's famous motto: "Rob the rich and give to the poor." "The farmers and the townspeople," they argued, "are our most important allies. How can we tax them, and still hope for their help in our fight against the Sheriff?"

Robin wondered how long the Merrymen could keep to the ways and methods of their early days. The Sheriff was growing stronger and better organized. He now had the money and the men, and was beginning to harass the band, probing for its weaknesses.

The tide of events was beginning to turn against the Merrymen. Robin felt that the campaign must be decisively concluded before the Sheriff had a chance to deliver a mortal blow. "But how," he wondered, "could this be done?"

Robin had often entertained the possibility of killing the Sheriff, but the chances for this seemed increasingly remote. Besides, while killing the Sheriff might satisfy his personal thirst for revenge, it would not improve the situation. Robin had hoped that the perpetual state of unrest, and the Sheriff's failure to collect taxes, would lead to his removal from office. Instead, the Sheriff used his political connections to obtain reinforcement. He had powerful friends at court, and was well regarded by the regent, Prince John.

Prince John was vicious and volatile. He was consumed by his unpopularity among the people, who wanted the imprisoned King Richard back. He also lived in constant fear of the barons, who had first given him the regency, but were now beginning to dispute his claim to the throne. Several of these barons had set out to collect the ransom that would release King Richard the Lionheart from his jail in Austria. Robin was invited to join the conspiracy in return for future amnesty. It was a dangerous proposition. Provincial banditry was one thing, court intrigue another. Prince John's spies were everywhere. If the plan failed, the pursuit would be relentless and retribution swift.

The sound of the supper horn startled Robin from his thoughts. There was the smell of roasting venison in the air. Nothing was resolved or settled. Robin headed for camp promising himself that he would give these problems his utmost attention after tomorrow's raid.

---

* Prepared by Joseph Lampel, City University, London. Copyright Joseph Lampel © 1985, revised 1991. Reprinted with permission.

CASE 2

THE GLOBAL CASINO INDUSTRY IN 2019*

For well over 50 years, the casino business has been on its way to becoming a $150 billion a year global industry. For much of that period, the United States has been leading the charge, accounting for nearly half the global gambling revenues as recently as 2010. Most of these revenues have come from Las Vegas and Atlantic City, magnets for gamblers from around the world. Over the last 20 years, these two locations have accounted for a large portion of the total revenues generated by all forms of casinos throughout the United States.

Over the past decade, however, Las Vegas and Atlantic City have had to deal with increased competition from other locales, as casinos opened all across the United States when other states legalized gambling in order to generate more tax revenues and promote tourism. Over a dozen states now generate substantial revenue from their casinos, many of which have opened on waterfronts such as rivers and lakes. When combined with Native American casinos, gambling revenues in other parts of the United States now exceed those generated by casinos in Las Vegas and Atlantic City (see Exhibit 1).

Casinos in Las Vegas and Atlantic City are able to rely upon gamblers who come from all over the world, as far away as China. Although casinos have operated for a long time in Europe and the Caribbean, no single location was ever able to compete with Las Vegas or Atlantic City. Las Vegas offers more than two dozen large casinos on its strip that have spent lavishly to differentiate themselves from all others. Luxor's pyramids and columns evoke ancient Egypt; Mandalay Bay borrows looks from the Pacific Rim; and the Venetian's plaza and canals re-create the Italian destination.

But more recently, the dominance of Las Vegas and Atlantic City in the global market has been challenged by the development of several casinos along a strip in the former Portuguese colony of Macau. Casinos have existed in Macau for decades, but basically served a local population. Since a monopoly on casinos by a single local tycoon was terminated in 2002, there has been a proliferation of mega-sized high-end casinos there, developed and managed by some of the world's largest casino operators, including those from Las Vegas. This has allowed Macau to grow from a tiny backwater territory to a booming center of gambling, with casinos generating almost $40 billion, more than six times that of the Las Vegas strip (see Exhibit 2).

EXHIBIT 1 Commercial Casino Revenues in the United States (in $ millions)

State	2016	2017	2018
Nevada	11,256	11,572	11,913
Pennsylvania	3,248	3,227	3,249
Louisiana	3,098	3,138	3,157
Illinois	2,523	2,700	2,875
New Jersey	2,519	2,647	2,845
Indiana	2,120	2,143	2,151
Mississippi	2,121	2,080	2,127
New York	2,013	2,015	2,064
Ohio	1,691	1,776	1,864
Missouri	1,715	1,738	1,754
Maryland	1,203	1,614	1,746
Iowa	1,446	1,463	1,467
Michigan	1,386	1,401	1,444
Colorado	811	828	842
Rhode Island	541	681	653
West Virginia	639	587	606
Florida	546	547	569
Delaware	398	418	419
Kansas	364	381	409
New Mexico	242	233	246
Maine	133	137	144
Oklahoma	113	125	140
South Dakota	99	100	100
Total USA	**40225**	**41551**	**42784**

Source: Center for Gaming Research, University Libraries Las Vegas, 2019.

Casinos have spread to other locations across the Asia-Pacific region. Singapore already has two casinos, while the Philippines is opening new ones and Japan just legalized them. Yet even as casinos are expanding into new locations, there are concerns about the potential for gaming revenues.

* Case prepared by Jamal Shamsie, Michigan State University, with the assistance of Professor Alan B. Eisner, Pace University. Material has been drawn from published sources to be used for purposes of class discussion. Copyright © 2019 Jamal Shamsie and Alan B. Eisner.

EXHIBIT 2 Top Casino Revenue Locations, 2018 ($ billions)

Location	Revenue
United States	42.8*
Macau	37.6
Singapore	6.0
Australia	4.0
South Korea	2.5
Malaysia	2.0
Philippines	2.0

*$6.9 billion comes from Las Vegas.

Source: Statista, author estimates.

Revenues from gaming have dipped considerably in locations like Macau and Atlantic City over the last three years, while they are still recovering in Las Vegas. Casino owners are trying to figure out how to draw in more gamblers by creating more interest among the younger generation.

Riding an American Wave

Although gambling has existed in the United States since colonial times, the recent advent of casinos can be traced back to the legalization of gaming in Nevada in 1931. For many years, this was the only state in which casinos were allowed. After New Jersey passed laws in 1976 to allow gambling in Atlantic City, the large population on the east coast acquired easier access to casinos. Since 1988, more and more states have begun to legalize the operation of casinos because of the tax revenues that they can generate.

As casinos spread across the United States, there has been a growing tendency to regard casino gambling as an acceptable form of entertainment for a night out. A large part of the growth in casino revenues has come from slot machines. These devices typically account for almost two-thirds of all casino gaming revenues (see Exhibit 3). A major reason for their popularity is that it is easier for prospective gamblers to feed a slot machine than to master the nuances of various table games.

EXHIBIT 3 Favorite U.S. Casino Games, 2018

Slot machines	61%
Blackjack	19
Roulette	8
Poker	4
Craps	4

Source: American Gaming Association, author estimates.

Over the years casinos in Las Vegas and Atlantic City have tried to draw gamblers by developing extravagant new properties. The most ambitious recent development in Las Vegas was the opening by MGM Mirage of its City Center, an $8.5 billion mini-city spread over 67 acres that includes luxury hotels, condominium units, restaurants, and shops. Even some of the older properties have undergone extensive renovation, such as Caesars Palace adding a new Colosseum and a new Roman Plaza. Atlantic City welcomed the much-ballyhooed opening of the $2.4 billion Revel Hotel built on 20 acres of beachfront, following the opening several years earlier of another lavish resort, the Borgata Hotel, which offered amenities such as penthouse spas and tropical indoor pools.

Aside from ramping up the appeal of their particular properties, most casinos have also offered incentives to keep their customers from moving over to competitors. These incentives can be particularly helpful in retaining those high rollers who come often and spend large amounts of money. Casinos try to maintain their business by providing complimentary rooms, food, beverages, shows, and other perks each year that are worth billions of dollars. Gamblers can also earn various types of rewards through the loyalty programs offered by the casinos, with the specific rewards being tied to the amount bet on the slot machines and at the tables.

Some of the larger casinos in the United States have also tried to fend off competition by growing through mergers and acquisitions. In 2004, Harrah's announced that it was buying casino rival Caesars, allowing it to become the nation's leading operator of casinos, with several properties in both Las Vegas and Atlantic City. This deal came just a month after MGM Mirage had stated that it was buying the Mandalay Resort Group, allowing it to double the number of casinos it held on the Las Vegas strip. Firms that own several casinos can pitch each of their properties to a different market and allow their customers to earn rewards on the firm's loyalty program by gambling at any of these properties.

Exploiting the Chinese Market

Though gambling has been legal for over a century in Macau, which was a former Portuguese territory, its casinos were typically small and seedy. This was partly because of the monopoly on gambling in the territory that was held by Stanley Ho, a local tycoon. However, this began to change in 2002, as the liberalization of casino licensing led to the development of new casinos by some of the world's largest casino operators, including many of the U.S. firms that wanted to find markets outside of Las Vegas. "The Las Vegas of the Far East" is how Sheldon Adelson, head of Las Vegas Sands, has described the recent development of Macau.

Macau has grown explosively with a tripling of casinos from the dozen or so that existed before 2002. Many are situated on the Cotai strip land that was once a stretch of water between the islands of Coloane and Taipa. Las Vegas-based

EXHIBIT 4 Financials of Macau Casinos, 2018

	Share of Revenues	Share of Profits
High rollers	63%	35%
Low rollers	34	52

Source: Deutsche Bank, author estimates.

firms such as Sands and Wynn have been investing billions of dollars into new casinos there. Sands, which already has a supersized version of the Venetian with a Grand Canal and a Rialto Bridge, has added a complex called the Parisian with an Eiffel Tower. Even locally based Sociedade de Jogos de Macau is opening a $3.9 billion complex that will feature three hotels, one modeled on the Palace of Versailles.

Macau's dramatic rise in the casino business owes much to a collision of geography and history. The Chinese love to gamble, but the leaders in Beijing have long forbidden casinos on the mainland. They did, however, let them continue to operate in Macau after the Portuguese handed over sovereignty in 1999. Like Hong Kong, Macau has retained a degree of legal autonomy and is also a few hours or less flying time from a billion potential gamblers in China. "We sit next to the biggest market in the world," said Edward M. Tracy, chief executive of the Hong Kong based subsidiary of Las Vegas Sands. "It's one billion more people than the U.S."[1]

Macau has been attracting a growing number of visitors from mainland China. Nearly 20 million people, or one in five Chinese who ventured outside mainland China last year, came to Macau to gamble. Many come from neighboring Guangdong province, usually on day trips. But bigger betters from as far away as Beijing have clearly played an important role in fueling Macau's growth. These high rollers will spend as much as $10 million on gambling in a single trip. They account for up to 65 percent of the revenues for the larger casinos (see Exhibit 4).

Even as Macau has shown remarkable growth over the last decade, its prospects for the future remain quite bright. Analysts at securities firms forecast that gambling revenue from Macau casinos could easily reach $40 billion by 2019. In part, this rise would be driven by an increase in visitors from mainland China because of rising affluence and improved transportation. China had increased the capacity of roads and high-speed trains to the territory, providing access for more visitors. Visitors from all over the world would also have better access because of a series of bridges that would connect Macau with Hong Kong's huge international airport.

Spreading across Asia

The growth of gambling revenues in Macau has led countries across the Asia-Pacific to abandon their hostilities to gambling and to encourage the development of casinos. Casinos have been opening in several countries, including Singapore, Philippines, Malaysia, South Korea, and Australia, and are likely to take off soon in other places such as Japan, Vietnam, Taiwan, and Sri Lanka. A group of investors have even made a deal to open a casino near Vladivostok in Russia's Far East. They claim that it takes less time for a high roller in Beijing to fly there than to steamy Macau.

Singapore, in particular, has been extremely successful with its two new upmarket casinos. In 2010, the island state issued permits to two large casino operators. The Marina Bay Sands is part of Las Vegas-based Sands casino operations and Resorts World Sentosa is run by Malaysia's Genting group. Even though Singapore has limited the size of its casinos and discourages locals from visiting them, they earn more than $6 billion annually, almost as much as all of the casinos on the Las Vegas strip. In 2019, Singapore's government agreed to extend the exclusivity period of the two casinos until the end of 2030. However, this came with a high price for both resorts, as they had to commit $9 billion in investments to expand their integrated resorts in non-gaming areas. At the same time, daily entry fees for Singapore citizens and permanent residents had been raised 50 percent, to $150.[2]

Among the other contenders, the Philippines looks like it is poised to claim a substantial share of global casino revenues. Malaysia-based casino giant Genting kickstarted Manila's casino craze when it opened Resorts World Manila opposite the capital's main airport in 2009. The opening of the new casino represented a departure from the older smoke-filled gambling dens and its success has lured other casinos. As many as four new casinos have been developed on a large plot overlooking Manila Bay. The first of these, Solaire Resort and Casino, is a sleek plate-glass building with a suitably flashy interior created by Paul Steelman, a casino designer from Las Vegas.

In 2018, Japan's parliament ended years of wrangling when it passed a bill allowing the establishment of casinos in three Japanese cities. A pet project of Shinzo Abe, the prime minister, the casinos will be embedded in family-friendly resorts, partly in a bid to counter their seedy image. Most Japanese have little enthusiasm for casinos, which they associate with gambling addiction and yakuza gangsters. Nearly two-thirds of the population oppose them.[3] Proponents of casinos argued that casinos will boost the country's earnings from foreign tourists and deliver a tax windfall to the heavily indebted government. A Japanese business magazine has argued that the country is being left behind as neighboring countries are rushing to build upscale casinos with luxury hotels, designer shops, and cultural attractions. The government wants to stick the casinos in new resorts alongside hotels, shops, and conference facilities. "Done well, the resorts will attract tourists and generate local wealth," says Toru Mihara, an academic who sat on a government panel last year.[4]

The casino operators that are developing casinos all over the region are hoping that they can lure Chinese high rollers away from Macau. A Chinese businessman who visits

Macau's casinos stated that the new Chinese leadership's crackdown on official corruption and flaunting of wealth will drive clients to other locations. "Beijing has too many cameras watching us in Macau," he explained.[5] Solaire, recently opened in Manila, is willing to send a private jet to pick up big spenders from all across China. "If we can get 7 percent of Macau business to come here," said the casino's chief operating officer, "then we all achieve our goals for the market."[6]

Moving beyond Gambling

Over the last couple of decades, Las Vegas has moved beyond gambling to offer visitors many choices for fine dining, great shopping, and top-notch entertainment. This has allowed most of its higher end casinos to generate revenues from offering a wide selection of activities apart from gambling. At MGM Mirage, for example, revenue from non-gaming activities has typically accounted for almost 60 percent of net revenue in recent years. During the 1990s, Las Vegas had tried to become more receptive to families, with attractions such as circus performances, animal reserves, and pirate battles. But the city has been very successful with its recent return to its sinful roots with a stronger focus on topless shows, hot night clubs, and other adult offerings that have been highlighted by the new advertising slogan "What happens in Vegas, stays in Vegas."

By comparison, visitors are drawn to Atlantic City mostly because of gambling. Although it does offer a beach and a boardwalk, along which its dozen large casino hotels are lined, the city has never been able to develop itself as a beach resort. The opening of the much-ballyhooed Revel a few years ago was part of a drive to make Atlantic City much more competitive with Las Vegas. But it failed to replicate the success of the Borgata Hotel, the major new resort that opened there in 2003. The failure to develop other forms of entertainment has led to the closing of several big casinos, including the Revel, as casinos that have opened in several neighboring states have drawn gamblers away from Atlantic City.

Macau has also been trying to reduce its dependence on gaming. By 2017, gambling revenues at its casinos were generating revenues that accounted for almost four-fifths of the territory's economy. But these revenues have begun to decline, in part because of the China's economic slowdown. Another factor has been that country's sweeping crackdown on corruption. Many of the high rollers from the mainland were gambling with the proceeds of shady deals, which are now subject to greater scrutiny. This is forcing the casinos to shift their focus away from the older, hardcore gamblers who come primarily to gamble toward younger, fun-loving gamblers who see gambling as only one part of their Macau experience.

The newer casinos are trying to offer more non-gambling activities by including restaurants, shops, cinemas, spas, and even concert arenas. The shops inside Sands casinos in Macau, for example, have been generating as much as $2 billion of revenues. Edward Tracy, the head of Sands China, is also bringing in shows ranging from boxing matches to Bollywood award ceremonies. One of the newly opened casinos has an enormous "fortune diamond" that emerges from a fountain every half-hour to the delight of photo-snapping onlookers. "There's an opportunity for Macau to attract a new breed of customer, one that is looking for a more holistic experience," said Aaron Fischer, a gambling analyst at a brokerage firm.[7]

In recent years, Macau started trying to overcome one of its most serious limitations—its small land area, just under 30 square kilometers—by expanding business on the thinly populated island of Hengqin. Three times the size of Macau, the island has been declared a special economic zone by Chinese officials. The idea is for it to develop accommodations and entertainment that can support Macau's aspirations for mass-market tourism. "Hengqin is the game changer for Macau," insists Sands China head Tracy.[8] In April 2019, China's State Council approved a proposal to turn Hengqin into an island of international tourism.[9] Analysts at Sanford C. Bernstein stated in a note that "future infrastructure development and non-gaming expansion in Hengqin will provide more hotel capacity for Macau, currently running at an average occupancy of about 95 percent."[10]

Gambling on the Future

In spite of growing competition from the many other U.S. and world locations, Las Vegas and Atlantic City continue fighting for visitors to come for various forms of entertainment—the clubs, stores, and concerts and shows—as well as gambling. "I think we're seeing a shift away from Las Vegas as the only gaming destination," said Stephen P. A. Brown from U.N.L.V. "But it is holding up as a tourist destination."[11] Genting, the Malaysian gaming group, has recently taken over the site of the Echelon, which was abandoned because of lack of funds during the recent recession. They intend to develop a stronger presence in the U.S. market by building one of the biggest new resorts in Las Vegas with a 3,500-room hotel and 175,000 feet of gambling space.

Casino operators in Macau are also continuing to make new bets, even as competition grows in neighboring countries. Eight new casino complexes, all of which will offer many forms of entertainment, are being added, promising to almost double the supply of hotel rooms on the strip. Galaxy Entertainment, a local casino firm, claims that with its $7.7 billion expansion its already huge Macau casino will be bigger even than the Pentagon. Another local operator, SJM, has developed a huge new resort on the Cotai strip to include a hotel designed by Versace, an Italian luxury fashion house.

As casinos' emphasis shifts from older high-stakes gamblers to younger customers who enjoy gambling but are interested in dining, drinking, shopping, and attending shows, casinos are also eager to embrace new types of gaming experiences that will attract Millennials who have grown up playing video and mobile phone games. "Gambling won't go out of fashion. It will just become part of a wider offering," says Ian M. Coughlan, president of Wynn Macau. "We've not really tapped all the demand that exists—we're far from it."[12]

ENDNOTES

1. Bettina Wassener. A hot streak for Macau. *New York Times,* March 26, 2014, p. B7.
2. Choo Yun Ting. 8 things to know about changes to Singapore's integrated. *The Straits Times,* April 3, 2019. https://www.straitstimes.com/singapore/8-things-to-know-about-changes-to-singapores-integrated-resorts.
3. Japan finally gets casinos. *The Economist,* July 26, 2018. https://www.economist.com/business/2018/07/26/japan-finally-gets-casinos.
4. Ibid.
5. The rise of the low rollers. *The Economist,* September 7, 2013, p. 63.
6. Ibid., p. 64.
7. Chris Horton. All in on gambling? Not for Macau. *International New York Times,* December 19, 2014, p. 1.
8. *The Economist,* p. 64.
9. Hengqin Island, adjacent to Macau, earmarked as an international tourist zone. *Macauhub,* April 3, 2019. https://macauhub.com.mo/2019/04/03/pt-ilha-de-hengqin-adjacente-a-macau-destinada-a-ser-zona-de-turismo-internacional/.
10. Nelson Moura. Hengqin to add hotel capacity to Macau - Brokerage. *Macaubusiness,* April 3, 2019. https://www.macaubusiness.com/hengqin-to-add-hotel-capacity-to-macau-brokerage/.
11. Adam Nagourney. Las Vegas bounces back, with caveats. *International New York Times,* August 2, 2013.
12. *New York Times,* March 26, 2014, p. B7.

CASE 3

SOUTHWEST AIRLINES: IS "LUV" AT THE LIMIT?*

At the beginning of 2019, Southwest Airlines fared third in the rankings of the best U.S. Airlines released by the Wall Street Journal. Delta Airlines ranked first and Alaska Airlines ranked second. These rankings were based on a composite set of parameters forming a scorecard. Southwest did best on two-hour tarmac delays and worst on mishandled baggage (see Exhibit 1). The Dallas-based airline, famously known for its highly efficient and successful "low-cost" operations, seemed to face other challenges as well. It paid millions over the past decade to settle safety violations. This included fines for flying planes that needed repairs. In the past nine years, there were at least two incidents where the roofs of Southwest planes opened up inflight.

The worst incident took place in April 2018. One of the engines on Southwest Flight 1380 blew apart at 32,000 feet over Pennsylvania. Jennifer Riordan, a 43-year-old mother of two, was blown partway out of a broken window. The National Transportation Safety Board (NTSB) said a fan blade that had snapped off the engine was showing signs of metal fatigue. Later, the NTSB chairman, Robert Sumwalt, said that the engine in the flight was missing a fan blade. This incident resulted in one fatality and seven others were also hurt. In another incident in 2016, an engine on a Southwest jet blew apart over Florida. This was also attributed to metal fatigue, or wear and tear, hurling debris that struck the fuselage and tail. No one was hurt in that incident.[1]

Further, the union that represented its mechanics accused Southwest Airlines of pressuring their maintenance workers to cut corners to keep planes flying. A Federal Aviation Administration (FAA) investigation of these whistleblower complaints found mistrust of management to the extent of hurting the airline's safety.[2]

Another development in the industry that also threatened the company's low-cost position was the advent of the "Ultra Low Cost Carriers" (ULCC). These carriers are even more bare-bones and keep their basic fares very low, thus eroding Southwest's low-price advantage. They, of course, charge extra for everything including baggage handling.[3]

As the investigation into the deadly engine failure continued, Southwest Chairman and CEO, Gary Kelly, was faced with several questions regarding its low-cost business model. Was the low-cost business model, which put its planes through frequent takeoffs and landings, putting the passengers at risk? Would Southwest withstand the onslaught of the ULCCs and continue to have its low-cost advantage to remain profitable in 2019 and beyond?

Emergence, Growth, and Transition[4]

Southwest Airlines began in response to an entrepreneurial opportunity that existed for low-cost, hassle-free travel

* This case study has been prepared by professors Naga Lakshmi Damaraju, Sonoma State University, Alan Eisner, Pace University, and Gregory Dess, The University of Texas at Dallas, to serve as a basis for classroom discussion. The case study is not intended to be an endorsement of effective or ineffective handling of administrative situations. Copyright © 2019 Damaraju and Eisner.

EXHIBIT 1 U.S. Airlines Rankings Released at the Beginning of January 2019

Rank number	Overall rank	On-time arrivals	Cancelled flights	Extreme delays	2-hour tarmac delays	Mishandled baggage	Involuntary bumping	Complaints
1	Delta	Delta	Delta	Alaska	Southwest	Spirit	Delta	Southwest
2	Alaska	Alaska	Spirit	Delta	Alaska	JetBlue	JetBlue	Alaska
3	Southwest	Spirit	Alaska	Southwest	Frontier	Delta	United	Delta
4	Spirit	Southwest	Southwest	Spirit	Spirit	United	American	JetBlue
5	JetBlue*	United	United	American	Delta	Alaska	Southwest	United
6	United*	American	Frontier	United	JetBlue	Frontier	Alaska	American
7	American	JetBlue	JetBlue	JetBlue	United	Southwest	Spirit	Spirit
8	Frontier	Frontier	American	Frontier	American	American	Frontier	Frontier

*JetBlue and United both ranked fifth in overall ranking.

Source: McCartney, S. The Best and Worst U.S. Airlines of 2018. *The Wall Street Journal*, January 16, 2019. https://www.wsj.com/articles/the-best-and-worst-u-s-airlines-of-2018-11547648032.

between the cities of Houston, Dallas, and San Antonio—the Golden Triangle that was experiencing rapid economic and population growth during the late 1960s. Rollin King, a San Antonio entrepreneur who owned a small commuter air service, and Herb Kelleher, a New Jersey-born, New York University Law School graduate who moved to San Antonio in 1967 to practice law, pooled the seed money to start Southwest Airlines in response to this opportunity. After an initial rough four years caused by the major airlines, Southwest got its flights to takeoff in 1971 with Dallas Love Field as its base and it crossed every major benchmark in the following years. It remained the consistently profitable discount carrier year after year and became a major airline in 1990 by crossing the $1 billion revenue mark. Focused on the business travelers who needed to be "on-time, every time," its business model had several intriguing elements. For example, by-passing the traditional "hub-and-spoke" configuration and offering short-haul, point-to-point airline service allowed savings on fundamentals such as gate fees because they could fly out of secondary airports; additional savings were through elimination of other fringe services like no assigned seats, no meals, no baggage transfers, or few or no reservations through travel agents. The choice of operating a new and uniform fleet of aircraft saved maintenance costs and facilitated optimum utilization of human resources. Brilliant fuel hedges resulted in huge cost savings for years. In addition, the charismatic leadership of Herb Kelleher, and a strong company culture and incentives focused on tight cost-control, made Southwest a legendary airline (see Exhibit 2 for Southwest's Mission Statement).

In 2004, the leadership transitioned to Gary Kelly, a long-term employee and the former Chief Financial Officer of Southwest Airlines. The same year, Kelly heralded a series of initiatives to put the airline on a high-growth trajectory. These included the code-sharing agreements beginning with ATA (in response to AirTran eyeing the Chicago market), a move into the Philadelphia market (a stronghold of USAir), and kicking off a campaign to repeal the Wright Amendment* that could boost Southwest's ability to fly uninterrupted services out of its traditional fort, Dallas Love Field airport.

EXHIBIT 2 Mission Statement

Mission Statement

The mission of Southwest Airlines is dedication to the highest quality of customer service delivered with a sense of warmth, friendliness, individual pride, and company spirit.

To Our Employees

We are committed to provide our Employees a stable work environment with equal opportunity for learning and personal growth. Creativity and innovation are encouraged for improving the effectiveness of Southwest Airlines. Above all, Employees will be provided the same concern, respect, and caring attitude within the organization that they are expected to share externally with every Southwest Customer.

Source: Mission statement of Southwest Airlines. Southwest Airlines Mission To Our Employees. Southwest website.

In 2007, a new fare structure was introduced that included Business Select, which gave customers the option of priority in boarding. With a new $40 fee that allowed customers to be among the first 15 passengers to board the plane, this new fare structure was definitely targeted at wooing some of the business travelers who wanted a little more than no frills. However, with this move, Southwest managed to irritate some of its most loyal customers. While Southwest continued its bags-fly-free policy, which had contributed to increasing its market share, Kelly declared "never say never" when probed about his company's plans to start charging baggage check-in fees in 2013. Southwest introduced an in-flight entertainment portal with free live and on-demand television, offering 20 live channels and 75 television episodes from popular series. It also introduced Internet access for $8 a day per device on Wi-Fi-enabled aircraft.

While all these were significant departures from the original Southwest business model, there were two other important strategic changes initiated in Kelly's regime. The first was expansion into the international markets that began in December 2008 when the company agreed to provide an online link to WestJet's booking portal to help its customers book flights to Canada. Later, Southwest formally filed an application with the Department of Transportation for the right to fly its own planes to Canada. As of January 2019, the company had operations to over 14 destinations internationally. A significant chunk of the company's revenues came from international operations—approximately $595 million of the operating revenues in 2017, $383 million in 2016, and $287 million in 2015, respectively, were attributable to foreign operations. The remainder of the operating revenues, approximately $20.6 billion in 2017, $20.0 billion in 2016, and $19.5 billion in 2015, respectively, were attributable to domestic operations.[5]

The second most significant departure was moving away from the organic growth strategy with the acquisition of AirTran Holdings Inc., the parent company of AirTran Airways (AirTran), for a combination of $1.4 billion cash and Southwest Airlines common stock. The acquisition, announced in September 2010, was only the third in Southwest's history. It gave the discounter its first service in Atlanta, a Delta Air Lines fortress for decades, and more flights from New York and Washington, DC.

Little more than a year after the transaction officially closed, Southwest was dehubbing AirTran's Atlanta hub and conceding markets to Delta. AirTran's Atlanta hub had been Southwest's motivation in acquiring AirTran, in addition to further pushing into international markets.[6] "To make

* The Wright amendment, signed into law by President Jimmy Carter on Feb. 15, 1980, restricted nonstop flights from Dallas Love Field to airports in Texas and four bordering states—Oklahoma, Louisiana, New Mexico, and Arkansas. Not only did the law bar flights beyond those states, but it also barred airlines from selling a ticket that would take a passenger to airports beyond those states even on a connecting or one-stop basis.

EXHIBIT 3
Cost Structure Information Available as of January 2019

Item description	Latest available information as of January 2019* (in cents)	Latest available information as of January 2018** (in cents)
Salaries, wages, and benefits	4.76	4.57
Fuel and oil	2.56	2.46
Maintenance materials and repairs	0.65	0.70
Aircraft rentals	0.13	0.15
Landing fees and other rentals	0.84	0.82
Depreciation and amortization	0.79	0.82
Other operating expenses	1.75	1.70
Total	11.48	11.22

*As of year ended December 2017

**As of year ended December 2016

Source: Southwest 10-k filings with SEC, 2018.

that shift in strategy has taken a huge effort, but as a leading domestic carrier, it was time 'that we think about stepping out,'" said Kelly.[7] Following what could possibly be the slowest merger in history, Southwest successfully completed it on December 28, 2014, when the last AirTran flight flew, retracing its original Atlanta-to-Tampa route of October 1993 (AirTran was called ValueJet at that time). "The company expected total acquisition and integration costs to be approximately $550 million (before profit sharing and taxes) upon completing the transition of AirTran 717-200s[†] out of the fleet in 2015," said company officials.[8]

The Triple-Pressure on Bottomline

Increasing Costs of Human Resources. At approximately 41 percent of total company operating expenses, salaries, wages, and benefits expenses were Southwest's largest operating costs. The terms of its collective-bargaining agreements limited the company's ability to reduce these costs.[9] Approximately 83 percent of its labor force was unionized. These employees had pay scale increases as a result of contractual rate increases. Additionally, there were new collective bargaining agreements ratified during 2016 with the majority of Southwest's unionized employees, including its pilots and flight attendants, among others. Meanwhile, other unionized employees, including its mechanics and material specialists were also in negotiations for labor agreements for the last six years. In September 2017, Southwest Airlines mechanics rejected a proposed contract offer that fell short of the pay rates they wanted. While Southwest described the pay rates and retirement benefits in the proposed contract as industry leading, union leaders had opinions otherwise. According to the union leaders, the contract did not measure up to the higher historical rates Southwest mechanics earned relative to the rest of the industry and it did not do enough to compensate members for their industry-leading productivity.[10] Any changes to the contract terms could put additional burden on the low-cost competitive position.

Increasing Fuel Costs.[11] Jet fuel and oil represented approximately 22 percent of the company's operating expenses as of the beginning of 2019 and represented the second largest operating cost (see Exhibit 3). The cost of fuel could be extremely volatile and unpredictable and fluctuated due to several factors beyond the company's control, for example, conflicts and hostilities in oil producing areas, problems in domestic refining or pipeline capacity due to adverse weather conditions and natural disasters, or changes in currency exchange rates. Southwest's ability to effectively address fuel price increases and pass them to the consumers could be limited by factors such as its historical low-fare reputation, the portion of its customer base purchasing travel for leisure purposes, and the risk that higher fares will drive a decrease in demand. This risk could partly be managed by utilizing over-the-counter fuel derivative instruments to hedge a portion of its future jet fuel purchases. However, energy prices could fluctuate significantly in a relatively short amount of time. Since the company used a variety of different derivative instruments at different price points, there was an inherent risk that the fuel derivatives it used would not provide adequate protection against significant increases in fuel prices and could in fact result in hedging losses. For a long time, the company also benefitted from accounting standards in the United States. It faced the risk that its fuel derivatives would not be effective or that they would no longer qualify for hedge accounting

[†] These are Boeing 717-200 aircrafts for which AirTran has been the first customer. Boeing 717 was different from Boeing 737 which has traditionally been the single aircraft type that Southwest operated and saved on training and maintenance costs. Therefore, this addition could have potentially increased some of these costs.

EXHIBIT 4
Southwest Airlines Firm Deliveries and Options for Boeing 737-700, 737-800, 737 MAX 7, and 737 MAX 8 Aircraft

Year	800 Firm orders	MAX 7 Firm orders	MAX 8 Firm orders	MAX 8 Options	Additional 700s	Total
2018	26	—	14	—	4	44
2019	—	7	15	—	—	22
2020	—	—	25	—	—	25
2021	—	—	34	—	—	34
2022	—	—	17	14	—	31
2023	—	12	22	23	—	57
2024	—	11	30	23	—	64
2025	—	—	40	36	—	76
2026	—	—	—	36	—	36
2027	—	—	—	23	—	23
Total	26	30	197 (a)	155	4 (b)	412

(a) The company has flexibility to substitute 737 MAX 7 in lieu of 737 MAX 8 firm orders beginning in 2019

(b) To be acquired in leases from various third parties

Source: Southwest 10-k filings with SEC, 2018.

under applicable accounting standards. This problem could have been severe without the recent increases in shale oil production in the United States.

Several efforts were underway to reduce fuel consumption and improve fuel efficiency. Southwest started modernizing its fleet and also initiated other fuel initiatives. It was the first airline company in North America to offer scheduled service utilizing Boeing's new 737 MAX 8 aircraft. This aircraft entered service in fourth quarter 2017. The Boeing 737 MAX 8 was expected to significantly reduce fuel use and CO_2 emissions. There were 13 Boeing 737 MAX 8 aircraft in its fleet by the end of 2017. Southwest was also the launch customer for the Boeing 737 MAX 7 series aircraft, with deliveries expected to begin in 2019. It had placed firm orders for 197 of 737 MAX 8 aircraft and 30 of 737 MAX 7 aircraft (see Exhibit 4). These aircrafts would also have lower maintenance costs since they are new and they are unlikely to increase training costs since they are all large Boeing 737 aircrafts, continuing the Boeing 737 tradition at Southwest.

Competition and the ULCC threat.[12] With moderate improvement in economic conditions over the last few years and an increased focus on costs by most airlines, competition has intensified in the airline industry. Southwest faced tough competition from major U.S. airlines, including American Airlines, Delta Air Lines, and United Airlines[‡] and other low-cost competitors, including JetBlue Airways (see Exhibits 5 and 6 for selected financial information). Southwest competed with these other airlines on virtually all of its scheduled routes. In addition, a new category of ultra-low cost carriers (ULCCs), for example, Frontier and Spirit Airlines, emerged as a credible threat (Refer to Exhibit 1).

The ULCCs represented a completely different approach to the traditional air travel model. While similar to the disruptive innovation like Southwest Airlines in its initial stages—when converting non-users to users of air travel—the ULCCs are yet significantly different in several ways. Allegiant Airlines perfected this model offering low-fare, high-value vacation packages from secondary airports to points in Florida and to Las Vegas.

The revenue stream for a ULCC was not based on air tickets, the core revenue for low-cost airlines like Southwest, but on purchase of ancillary products such as hotel and tour packages. The model evolved to be even less dependent on vacation/leisure travel. A ULCC aimed to stimulate travel decisions by offering very low fares and providing a nonstop routing where there was none, even if only for a few times a week. By offering a high value-to-cost equation for the consumer, these airlines aimed to divert discretionary dollars into air travel.

Unlike Southwest, the ULCCs were not in the business of connecting people and destinations. The stimulant of demand in the ULCC model was fares and not the need to get to a destination. Typically, a ULCC entered markets that it thought had latent potential, offered several flights, and then monitored the results. If the expectations about traffic materialized, it offered more services at that airport. If expectations did not materialize or the traffic was less productive than at other points, the ULCC moved out quickly. With the exception of some operations by Frontier

‡ Continental airline (another major airline in the United States) merged with UAL Corporation (parent company of United Airlines) in 2010. This stock is traded as United Continental Holdings Inc., (UAL).

EXHIBIT 5
Southwest Airlines Co. Consolidated Statements of Income (in millions except per share amount)

OPERATING REVENUES:	2018	2017 restated	2016 restated
Passenger	20,455	19,763	19,068
Freight	175	173	171
Other	1,335	1,210	1,050
Total operating revenues	**21,965**	**21,146**	**20,289**
OPERATING EXPENSES:			
Salaries, wages, and benefits	7,649	7,305	6,786
Fuel and oil	4,616	4,076	3,801
Maintenance materials and repairs	1,107	1,001	1,045
Landing fees and airport rentals	1,334	1,292	1,211
Depreciation and amortization	1,201	1,218	1,211
Other operating expenses	2,825	2,847	2,703
Total operating expenses	**18,759**	**17,739**	**16,767**
OPERATING INCOME	**3,206**	**3,407**	**3,522**
OTHER EXPENSES (INCOME):			
Interest expense	131	114	122
Capitalized interest	(38)	(49)	(47)
Interest income	(69)	(35)	(24)
Other (gains) losses, net	18	112	21
Total other expenses (income)	42	142	72
INCOME BEFORE INCOME TAXES	**3,164**	**3,265**	**3,450**
PROVISION FOR INCOME TAXES	699	(92)	1,267
NET INCOME	**2,465**	**3,357**	**2,183**
NET INCOME PER SHARE, BASIC ($)	4.30	5.58	3.48
NET INCOME PER SHARE, DILUTED ($)	4.29	5.57	3.45
Cash dividends declared per common share ($)	.6050	.4750	.3750

Source: Southwest 10-k filings with SEC, 2018.

at Denver, these airlines did not have their own turf nor did they operate connecting hubs. In this model, airplanes were moved around the country when opportunities were spotted. ULCC flight schedules fitted their fleet availability and not necessarily in timings that were most preferred by customers.

Alongside Allegiant, Frontier, Spirit, and Sun Country were the other prominent players in this genre. They represented about 7 percent of all U.S. airline departing seats by late 2018 and were expected to grow to over 12 percent by 2020.

Southwest in 2019

As of January 2019, Southwest Airlines offered services to over 100 destinations throughout the United States, Mexico, and the Caribbean. It operated more than 3,800 flights a day including more than 500 roundtrip markets.[13] Its international footprint expanded to over 14 destinations covered through 16 international gateway cities. The company remained profitable as of 2018. It made significant technology investments and completed its single largest technology project in its history in the recent years to completely transition its reservation system to the Amadeus Altéa Passenger Service System. The new reservation system was designed to improve flight scheduling and inventory management. It would enable operational enhancements to manage flight disruptions, such as those caused by extreme weather conditions. Additional international growth and other foundational

EXHIBIT 6 Selected Financial Information of Major Competitors of Southwest Airlines

Item	Southwest Airlines Co. (LUV)	American Airlines Group Inc., (AAL)	Delta Air Lines Inc., (DAL)	United Continental Holdings Inc., (UAL)	JetBlue Airlines (JBLU)
Enterprise value (bn)	32.1	46.54	50.2	35.17	6.11
Market capitalization (intraday) (bn)	32.39	16.93	34.51	24.45	5.53
Profit margin (%)	11.22	3.17	8.85	5.15	2.45
Operating margin (%)	14.42	7.73	11.73	9.15	9.44
Price-to-earnings ratio*	10.53	5.95	7.18	7.44	7.75
Net income (bn)	2.46	1.41	3.94	2.13	0.188
Gross profit (bn)	7.25	11.89	11.2	13.38	2.57
Revenue (bn)	21.97	44.54	44.44	41.3	7.66
Return on Assets (%)	7.71	3.84	5.74	5.42	N/A
Return on Equity (%)	24.31	75.17	28.53	22.65	4.07
Earnings before interest, tax, and depreciation (EBITDA) (bn)	4.37	5.61	7.58	6.02	1.2
Total debt (bn)	3.38	34.29	17.6	14.73	1.57
Book value per share	17.59	−0.37	20.11	36.65	14.48
Diluted EPS	4.29	3.03	5.67	7.69	0.6

*This is forward looking ratio.

Source: Yahoo finance: Thomson Reuters, EDGAR Online and Market Cap, January 15, 2019, EBITDA.

and operational capabilities were expected to get a boost.[14] The company continued to invest in technology to optimize other aspects of its operations. The progressive modernization of its fleet was also expected to facilitate cost control.

Nevertheless, the mid-seat rankings suggested Southwest faced stiff competition from both the traditional carriers and the ULCCs. The company's stock was down by 20 percent in 2018. The concerns about its planes and people continued. Amidst increasing fuel cost concerns, the company was expected to slow its expansion plans and capacity. Is Southwest on the gliding path to history?

ENDNOTES

1. McLaughlin, E.C., Todd, B., Jones, J. 2018. NTSB. Engine in deadly Southwest jet incident missing a fan blade. https://www.cnn.com/2018/04/17/us/philadelphia-southwest-flight-emergency-landing/index.html.
2. Koenig, D. 2018. Southwest Airlines has been faced with fines, union safety complaints. https://www.chicagotribune.com/business/ct-southwest-airlines-safety-investigation-20180424-story.html.
3. Boyd, M. 2018. Ultra-low cost are the new wildcatter airlines. https://www.forbes.com/sites/mikeboyd/2018/08/01/ultra-low-cost-carriers-are-the-new-wildcatter-airlines/#6372d0c46340.
4. This section draws heavily from the case study "Southwest Airlines: Is LUV soaring?" by Damaraju, N., Eisner, A., and Dess, G.G.. published in *Strategic Management: Text and Cases* by Dess, G.G., Lumpkin, T., Eisner, A. McNamara, G. 2014. McGraw-Hill Companies: NY.
5. Southwest Airlines, 10-k filings, 2018. https://www.sec.gov/Archives/edgar/data/92380/000009238018000031/luv-12312017x10k.htm.
6. Source: https://www.usatoday.com/story/todayinthesky/2013/05/08/southwest-de-hubbingatlanta-adds-more-airtran-cities/2144017/
7. Source: Jones, Charisse. Southwest announces first international flights. www.usatoday.com/story/travel/flights/2014/01/27/southwest-launches-internationalservices/4938011/.
8. Source: Maxon, T. Southwest Airlines tops $1 billion. https://www.dallasnews.com/business/airlines/2015/01/22/southwest-airlines-tops-1-billionin-annual-profits-for-first-time/
9. Southwest Airlines, 10-k filings, 2018. https://www.sec.gov/Archives/edgar/data/92380/000009238018000031/luv-12312017x10k.htm.
10. Shine, C. 2018. Southwest Airlines mechanics overwhelmingly reject proposed contract. *Dallas Morning News*. https://www.dallasnews.com/business/southwest-airlines/2018/09/18/southwest-airlines-mechanics-overwhelmingly-reject-proposed-contract.
11. This sub-section draws heavily from the company's 10-k filings with SEC for year 2018.
12. This sub-section draws heavily from the article mentioned in Endnote 3.
13. Company website.
14. Company's 10-k filing with SEC, 2018.

CASE 4

ZYNGA: IS THE GAME OVER?*

In 2019, Zynga was optimistic. In an interview, CEO Frank Gibeau, said, "We're set up for a really strong 2019. We have a good lineup of games to create the base for us, and then we have more than nine games being built right now that will come out over the next couple of years, with a bunch coming in soft launch."[1]

While battling some rough tides, the company had garnered its reputation as one with inconsistent leadership. In 2013, founder Mark Pincus stepped down and handed the charge to Don Mattrick, a 15-year employee of Electronic Arts expecting to turn the company around. In April 2015, Don Mattrick left the position, and Pincus returned as CEO for the second time. Just a year later in March 2016, Zynga announced the replacement of Pincus by the new CEO Frank Gibeau, another 20-year employee of Electronic Arts, again expecting to turn around the company. Zynga's lack of consistent leadership had been critical to not formulating an effective turnaround strategy that might have led to progress. Throughout the revolving door of CEO replacements, Zynga had not developed a substantially successful new game. Consequently, its revenues have been falling over the past years accompanied by consistent net losses.

The company eventually made a comeback under Gibeau's leadership with strong acquisitions. In less than two years, Zynga acquired Peak Games' casual card game studio, Gram Games and 80 percent of Small Giant Games, maker of Empires and Puzzles, for $560 million. Though Zynga's revenue rose by 5 percent to $670 million by the end of 2018, it still posted a net loss of $15 million for the year (see Exhibits 1 and 2). In 2018, their top three online game revenue-generating games were Zynga Poker, CSR Racing 2, and Hit It Rich! Slots.

In another attempt at innovation, Zynga launched Wonka's World of Candy in 2018. After years of struggling to introduce new hit games and failing to combat the decline of formerly blockbuster properties like FarmVille, the company has been focusing on getting the most out of evergreen franchises like Zynga Poker, Words with Friends, and CSR Racing 2 by keeping them alive with updates.[2] The fight to build new games that catch the audiences' attention might be hard, but Zynga's announcement of a multi-year agreement with Disney to develop a new Free-To-Play mobile Star Wars™ game brings an existing fandom as their audience.

* This case was developed by graduate students Eric S. Engelson, Professor Alan B. Eisner, Pace University and Professor Naga Lakshmi Damaraju, Sonoma State University. Material has been drawn from published sources to be used for class discussion. Copyright © 2019 Alan B. Eisner.

Zynga's Background

At the time it incorporated in October 2007, Zynga had become a dominant player in the online gaming field, almost entirely through the use of social media platforms. Located in San Francisco, the company was named by CEO Mark Pincus to pay tribute to his deceased beloved pet bulldog Zynga. Although this might have seemed whimsical, Zynga was actually a quite powerful company. Exemplifying Zynga's prominence, Facebook was reported to have earned roughly 12 percent of its revenue from the operations of Zynga's virtual merchandise sales.[3]

Zynga's collection of games continued to expand, with more and more success stories emerging. A relative newcomer to the market, its quick success was astonishing. However, Zynga's impressive financials were possibly at risk because of what some considered questionable decision making. Many of Zynga's competitors, and even some partners, were displeased with the company's actions and began to show it in the form of litigation. Agincourt, a plaintiff in a lawsuit brought against Zynga, stated, "Zynga's remarkable growth has not been driven by its own ingenuity. Rather it has been widely reported that Zynga's business model is to copy creative ideas and game designs from other game developers and then use its market power to bulldoze the games' originators."[4] If lawsuits and ethical issues continued to arise for Zynga, its powerful bulldog could start looking more like a poodle. In January 2019, Zynga received $12 million related to the settlement of the derivative litigation case for insider trading against the directors of the online gaming company.

The Products

With an abundance of software developers, the ability to create and distribute online games increases by the day, and the demand to play them is equally high. However, while many people find these online games fun and, better yet, therapeutic, others cannot understand the hype. The best way to understand the sudden infatuation is to view online gaming as simply a means of relaxation.

In the movies, at least, large executive offices are often shown with putting greens, dartboards, or even a bar full of alcoholic beverages. These amenities are all meant to serve the same purpose: to relieve stress during a hard day's work. We have all been there and looked for a way to cope. However, few of us have the opportunity to use such things as putting greens to unwind at the workplace. And even if we did, how long could we afford to engage in such an activity before being pulled back to our desks?

EXHIBIT 1 Zynga Consolidated Income Statements ($ thousands, except per-share data)

	Year Ended December 31		
	2018	2017	2016
Revenue:			
Online game	670,877	665,593	547,291
Advertising and other	236,331	195,797	194,129
Total revenue	907,208	861,390	741,420
Costs and expenses:			
Cost of revenue	304,658	258,971	238,546
Research and development	270,323	256,012	320,300
Sales and marketing	226,524	212,030	183,637
General and administrative	98,941	108,653	92,509
Impairment of intangible assets	—	—	20,677
Total costs and expenses	900,446	835,666	855,669
Income (loss) from operations	6,762	25,724	114,249
Interest income	6,549	5,309	3,057
Other income (expense), net	13,152	6,550	6,461
Income (loss) before income taxes	26,463	37,583	104,731
Provision for (benefit from) income taxes	11,006	10,944	3,442
Net income (loss)	15,457	26,639	108,173
Net income (loss) per share attributable to common stockholders			
Basic	0.02	0.03	0.12
Diluted	0.02	0.03	0.12
Weighted average common shares used to compute net income (loss) per share attributable to common stockholders:			
Basic	862,460	869,067	878,827
Diluted	889,584	897,165	878,827

Source: Zynga.

Stress reduction at work is one of the many purposes that virtual games fulfill–no need to leave our desks; no need to make others around us aware of our relaxation periods; and, better yet, no need to separate the task of relaxation from sitting at our computers while we work. The ability to play these games on office computers and relax now and then during the day makes online gaming enticing. This, of course, is just one of many uses for the games. Some people play them after work or at the end of a long day. With the onset of smartphones, people of all ages play these games on the go throughout the day sitting on the bus, in the waiting room of a doctor's office, or at the Department of Motor Vehicles. Diverting game play is readily available with the click of a button.

Market Size

Compared to other game developers with games present on the Facebook platform, Zynga had once been a dominant force, but by 2019, it ranked third after Miniclip's 8 Ball pool and King's Candy Crush Saga (see Exhibits 3 and 4). Miniclip, with its wildly popular 8 Ball Pool game, appeared to rule, making a reported $400 million with just in-app puchases.[5]

Zynga's virtual games provided the opportunity for constant buildup and improvements, offering users virtual goods and services to increase their gaming experience. These items could be purchased using a credit card and were often needed to accomplish fast progressions in the games. These goods were advertised throughout the

EXHIBIT 2
Zynga Balance Sheets ($ thousands, except par value)

	December 31, 2018	December 31, 2017
Assets		
Current assets:		
Cash and cash equivalents	544,990	372,870
Marketable securities	36,232	308,506
Accounts receivable	91,630	103,677
Income tax receivable	35,006	12,807
Restricted cash	26,914	24,253
Other current assets	12,505	8,837
Total current assets	747,277	830,950
Goodwill	934,187	730,464
Other intangible assets, net	118,600	64,258
Property and equipment, net	266,557	266,589
Restricted cash		20,000
Prepaid expenses	30,774	23,821
Other long-term assets	49,308	43,251
Total assets	2,146,703	1,979,333
Liabilities and stockholders' equity		
Current liabilities:		
Accounts payable	26,811	18,938
Income tax payable	4,895	6,677
Other current liabilities	156,829	123,089
Debt	100,000	—
Deferred revenue	191,299	134,007
Total current liabilities	479,834	282,711
Deferred revenue	1,586	568
Deferred tax liabilities	16,087	5,902
Other non-current liabilities	52,586	48,912
Total liabilities	550,093	338,093
Stockholders' equity:		
Common stock, $0.00000625 par value, and additional paid in capital - authorized shares: 2,020,517; shares outstanding: 886,850 shares (Class A, 770,269, Class B, 96,064, Class C, 20,517) as of December 31, 2016 and 903,617 (Class A, 769,533, Class B, 113,567, Class C, 20,517) as of December 31, 2015	3,504,713	3,426,505
Accumulated other comprehensive income (loss)	(118,439)	(93,4977)
Accumulated deficit	(1,789,664)	(1,691,768)
Total stockholders' equity	1,596,610	1,641,240
Total liabilities and stockholders' equity	2,146,703	1,979,333

Source: Zynga.

EXHIBIT 3 Most Popular Facebook Games as of April 2019, Based on Number of Daily Active Users (in millions)

Facebook Games	Number of Daily Active Users
8 Ball Pool	10
Candy Crush Saga	10
Texas HoldEm Poker	1
Farm Heroes Saga	1
Subway Surfers	1
Clash of Clans	1
Dragon City	1
Hay Day	1
Trivia Crack	1
Word with Friends	1

Source: GameHunters.Club. (n.d.). Most popular Facebook games as of April 2019, based on number of daily active users (in millions). Statista. https://www.statista.com/statistics/267003/most-popular-social-games-on-facebook-based-on-daily-active-users/.

EXHIBIT 4 Top 5 Virtual-Gaming Developers of 2018

Rank	Company	2018 Revenue ($ millions)	Key Games
1	Epic Games	Estimated $1,000	Fortnite
2	Tencent (mobile gaming division)	Estimated $11,960	Arena of Valor, QQ Speed Mobile, Clash Royale
3	NetEase	$1,793	Knives Out, Identity V, Onmyoji, Rules of Survival, Fantasy Westward Journey
4	King	$1,000	Candy Crush Saga, Candy Crush Soda Saga, Bubble Witch 3 Saga, Royal Charm Slots, Legend of Solgard
5	Netmarble	$1,780	Lineage 2: Revolution, Marvel Contest of Champions, Marvel Future Fight

Source: www.pocketgamer.biz, 2018 top developers list and author estimates.

games and the user was enticed by price cuts for larger purchases.

Zynga's virtual games could be played both remotely and through social media platforms, most commonly Facebook. Five of Zynga's games—FarmVille, CityVille, Empire and Allies, CastleVille, and Texas HoldEm Poker—were among the most popular games on Facebook.[6]

Of course, Zynga was not the only virtual-gaming company striving for this degree of success. In the past 10 years, many other gaming companies have grabbed the spotlight. The capability to create online games is widespread. Creativity and innovation are accepted to be the grounds on which competing companies challenge each other. With all competitors after the same audience, the industry is prone to a significant amount of head-butting rivalry.

Background of Competitors

Activision Blizzard is an interactive entertainment company that is based in Santa Monica, California. After acquiring King Digital for $5.9 Billion in 2016, Activision Blizzard had five business units including Activision Publishing, Blizzard Entertainment, Major League Gaming, Activision Blizzard Studios, and King. It is credited for some of the top games in history including Candy Crush Saga, World of Warcraft, and Call of Duty. In 2018, the company made a revenue of $7.5 billion, ranking fourth in video games after Sony, Microsoft, and Nintendo. In June 2017, alongside Electronic Arts and Atari, Activision Blizzard earned a spot on the Fortune 500 list.[7]

Activision has invested in careful strategic partnerships to enhance global growth. In 2019, Blizzard Entertainment and NetEase extended their China partnership until 2023. This partnership will enable Activision franchises to be available to Chinese users for the coming years. While Chinese revenues constitute only 5.2 percent of ATVI's top line, the market growth potential in China is astounding with Niko Partners projecting one billion Chinese gamers by 2019.[8]

NetEase, headquartered in Guangzhou, China, was founded in 2001 by Ding Lei. Some of NetEase's games include Knives Out, Identity V, Onmyoji, Rules of Survival, and Fantasy Westward Journey. In 2014, the company expanded into the west launching their U.S. headquarters. NetEase's revenue was $9.768 billion in 2018.[9] NetEase invested $100 million in the American video game developer Bungie for a minority stake in the company and a seat on the company's board of directors, Exploiting the demand for shooting games such as PUBG and Fortnite, NetEase announced the launch of its new shooter game Disorder. The company maintained its game Knives Out's position as China's top grossing mobile game in overseas markets for five consecutive months since August 2018.[10] Although NetEase is performing well with games, firm management is looking beyond video games for NetEase's future successes. CEO William Ding said it will focus on the promising e-commerce, music, and online education segments; the company intends to make substantial investments in those areas as part of its broader business strategy for 2019.[11]

Epic Games is the creator of Fortnite, Unreal, Gears of War, Shadow Complex, and the Infinity Blade series of games. Epic's Unreal Engine technology brings high-fidelity, interactive experiences to PC, console, mobile, AR, VR, and the Web. According to the Bloomberg Billionaires Index, Fortnight alone is on track to generate $2 billion this year, making Epic Games worth $5 billion to $8 billion.[12] Epic Games announced that it will launch its own digital storefront with "hand-curated" set of games, with the first wave rolling out on Mac and Windows before broadening to Android and other platforms later in 2019.[13]

With an estimated revenue of $1 billion in the previous year, Epic acquired 3Lateral in January 2019.[14] Known for its "digital human" creations, 3Lateral uses a combination of digital technology, motion capture, and other tools to create photo-realistic human subjects in real time.

Background of the Founder

Mark Jonathan Pincus was the entrepreneur behind Zynga. He was also the founder of Freeloader, Inc., Tribe Networks, and Support.com.[15] In prior years, Mark was named CEO of the Year in the Crunchies awards.[16] Prior to his entrepreneurial endeavors, Pincus worked in venture capital and financial services for several years. After graduating from Wharton, he went on to obtain his master's degree from Harvard Business School. Soon after graduating, Pincus launched his first start-up, Freeloader, Inc., a web-based push technology service. Individual, Inc., acquired the company only seven months later for $38 million.[17] Pincus later founded his third start-up, Tribe.net, one of the first social networks. Tribe.net focused on partnerships with major, yet local, newspapers and was supported by *The Washington Post,* Knight Ridder Digital, and Mayfield Fund.[18] Unfortunately for him, Pincus's resume did not impress his competitors, irritated by what they viewed as his questionable business tactics, nor did it dissuade them from making their feelings known via a lengthening laundry list of threats and lawsuits.

Intellectual Property and Ethical Issues

Nissan has claimed that its trademarks were used without consent in Zynga's game Street Racing. Zynga consequently changed the thumbnail images and renamed all the cars that were branded Nissan and Infiniti to "Sindats" and "Fujis."[19] Zynga was criticized on *Hacker News* as well as other social media sites for filing a patent application involving the ability to obtain virtual currency for cash on gambling and other gaming websites. Many said that the concept was not new and that, in fact, significant prior art for the concept already existed. The unveiling of the game Mafia Wars generated a lawsuit from the creators of Mob Wars. An attorney of the parent company of Mob Wars said that by making Mafia Wars, Zynga "copied virtually every important aspect of the game."[20] The lawsuit was later settled out of court for an amount between $7 million and $9 million.[21]

California-based web developer SocialApps brought Zynga to court seeking damages for alleged "copyright infringement, violation of trade secrets, breach of written contract, breach of implied-in-fact contract, and breach of confidence." SocialApps claimed to have entered into an agreement with Zynga, allowing Zynga access to the source code for SocialApps' Facebook game MyFarm in exchange for an undisclosed compensation. According to the suit, Zynga was given the code, but failed to pay SocialApps. SocialApps claimed that MyFarm's source code was the foundation of Farmville, as well as many of Zynga' s similar games.[22] Following Zynga' s release of the game Hidden Chronicles, *Forbes'* Paul Tassi wrote that Zynga "refuses to innovate in any way, and is merely a follower when it comes to ideas and game design."[23]

Ethical issues, though less tangible and definable than intellectual property, were equally troubling in assessments of Zynga' s operations. A former employee of the company revealed firsthand quotes from past CEO Mark Pincus, such as: "You're not smarter than your competitor. Just copy what they do and do it until you get their numbers." One contractor said he was presented with freelance work from Zynga related to imitating a competitor's application and was given precise instructions to "copy that game."[24] Other past employees, even those at the senior level, spoke out about the corrupt ways that Pincus had apparently decided to operate the business.

A former high-level Zynga employee provided an insight into the company's culture, as regarding any emphasis on creativity and originality. According to the employee, a group of designers brought a new and innovative idea to the table, only to have it turned down by Pincus because of his wariness toward a new idea that didn't fit the "tried-and-true" mold of other successes.[25]

Zynga was accused of taking advantage of its end customers, pertaining to a lack of security and safekeeping of consumer information. The Norwegian Consumer Council filed a complaint against Zynga to the Data Inspectorate concerning breaches of the Data Protection Act. According to the Consumer Council, Zynga's terms of use "do not offer a clear description of what is being collected in terms of information or what this information is being used for. Nor do they state how long the information is stored for or how it is protected against unauthorized access."

Zynga Going Forward

Although Zynga game users tend to be pleased with Zynga's games, many note there seem to be recurring obstacles that limit that pleasure. Many Zynga users complain of lag time while playing the games. Even more complain that when problems arise, Zynga support staff are nowhere to be found. The company has no customer service initiative and forces users to resort to sending their claims through e-mail, which many believed is ignored or never read. Further, many believe that the company makes it too difficult for users to make real strides in the games without spending ridiculous sums of money. Based on their experiences, many users believe that Zynga is all about revenue generation and that everything else comes second.

As Zynga looks to its optimistic future, where might its next big hit come from? With all the criticism aimed at Zynga' s past behavior, will the company continue on the path it has become notorious for and will the "more than nine games" that Zynga has lined up for the next few years get into trouble? With all eyes on the company as it recovers, it certainly will not be easy for Zynga to get away from its earlier reputation.

ENDNOTES

1. Takahashi, Dean. 2019. Zynga's turnaround: How one-beleaguered game company plans for 2019 growth. February 9, VentureBeat. https://venturebeat.com/2019/02/09/how-zynga-completed-its-turnaround-and-plans-for-39-growth-in-2019/.
2. Jordan, Jon. 2016. Top 50 mobile game developers of 2016. PocketGamer, May 3. https://www.pocketgamer.biz/list/62773/pocketgamerbiz-top-50-developer-of-2016/.
3. Zynga Inc, 2014. Earnings call transcripts.
4. Grigoriadis, Vanessa. 2011. Mark Pincus Farmville. June, 2011. https://www.vanityfair.com/news/2011/06/mark-pincus-farmville-201106.
5. King, Peter. 2018. Tech review: These apps feature some less common sports. *Newsday*. October 21. https://www.newsday.com/business/technology/tech-review-apps-to-access-less-popular-sports-1.22053288.
6. AppData. 2011. CityVille Application Metrics. March 16. http://www.appdata.com/apps/facebook/291549705119-cityville.
7. Lev-Ram, Michal. 2017. Activision Blizzard aims for the big leagues. *Fortune*. June 7. http://fortune.com/2017/06/07/fortune-500-activision-blizzard/.
8. Seeking Alpha. 2019. Activision Blizzard poised for success following 2019 transition. April 3. https://seekingalpha.com/article/4252595-activision-blizzard-poised-success-following-2019-transition-dcf-analysis.
9. NetEase. Fourth Quarter Results 2018.
10. Caplinger, Dan. 2019. NetEase fights rising competition. Feb 21. https://www.fool.com/investing/2019/02/21/netease-fights-rising-competition.aspx.
11. Epic Games. About. https://www.epicgames.com/site/en-US/about.
12. Pendleton, Devon; Pameri, Christopher. 2018. Fortnite mania fuels Epic growth to $8.5 billion. Bloomberg. July 24. https://www.bloomberg.com/news/features/2018-07-24/fortnite-phenomenon-turns-epic-game-developer-into-billionaire.
13. Frank, Allegra. 2018. Epic Games is launching its own store, and taking a smaller cut than Steam. Polygon. December 4. https://www.polygon.com/2018/12/4/18125498/epic-games-store-details-revenue-split-launch-date.
14. Takahasi, Dean. 2019. Epic Games acquires digital human 3Lateral, cuts ad deal with Appodeal. Venturebeat. January 23. https://venturebeat.com/2019/01/23/epic-games-acquires-digital-humans-tool-maker-3lateral-cuts-ad-deal-with-appodeal/.
15. Ha, Anthony. 2010. Congratulations to Facebook, Bing, and the other Crunchies winners. January 11. http://venturebeat.com/2010/01/11/crunchies-winners-facebook-bing/.
16. Rao, Leena. 2010. Congratulations Crunchies winners! Twitter takes best startup of 2010. http://techcrunch.com/2011/01/21/congratulations-crunchies-winners-twitter-takes-best-startup-of-2010/.
17. Merino, Faith. 2011. Zynga's IPO: made possible by the Zynga Dream Team. July 1. https://vator.tv/news/2011-07-01-zyngas-ipo-made-possible-by-the-zynga-dream-team.
18. Stone, Brad. 2007. Social networking's next phase. March 3. www.nytimes.com/2007/03/03/technology/03social.html?pagewanted51&_r51&ei55088&en5f718f182170673a4&ex51330578000.
19. Mafia Wars Wifi. Game Information. http://mafiawars.wikia.com/wiki/Zynga.
20. Hoge, Patrick. 2009. Game makers fight over proliferating lookalikes. July 12. BizJournal. https://www.bizjournals.com/sanfrancisco/stories/2009/07/13/story7.html.
21. Arrington, Michael. 2009. Zynga settles Mob Wars litigation as it settles in to Playdom war. http://techcrunch.com/2009/09/13/zynga-settles-mob-wars-litigation-as-it-settles-in-to-playdom-war/.
22. Joystiq. 2011. Lawsuit filed against Zynga over Farmville source code. www.joystiq.com/2011/07/18/lawsuit-filed-against-zynga-over-farmville-source-code/.
23. Tassi Paul. 2012. Zynga stocks falls as second post-IPO game fails to impress. Jan 6. *Forbes*. www.forbes.com/sites/insertcoin/2012/01/06/zynga-stock-falls-as-second-post-ipo-game-fails-to-impress/.
24. Blog.Games. 2010. Zynga CEO to employees: I don't f-ing want innovation. September 8. http://blog.games.com/2010/09/08/zynga-ceo-to-employees-i-dont-f-ing-want-innovation/.
25. Jamison, Peter. 2010. FarmVillains. September 8. *SF Weekly*. https://archives.sfweekly.com/sanfrancisco/farmvillains/Content?oid52178582.

CASE 5

WORLD WRESTLING ENTERTAINMENT 2019*

At its annual WrestleMania event in 2019, World Wrestling Entertainment will feature female wrestlers for the first time. WWE Chief Brand Officer Stephanie stated that the fans demanded the firm put women front and center. The move represented yet another attempt by WWE to deal with the growing competition from different forms of mixed martial arts, which represent a free-for-all of boxing, ju-jitsu, and wrestling, among other disciplines. Ultimate Fighting Championship has been expanding around the world, while ONE Championship has been stealing markets in Asia by building up local fighters in each of its markets.

WWE does not have much to worry about in the short run (see Exhibit 1). Its goal of coupling its live wrestling matches with programming on television, on the web and on mobile devices, has allowed it to become one of the world's most social brands. The firm recently announced a partnership with Roblox, a global platform that brings more than 80 million people together through play. It will allow players on Roblox to become one of their favorite WWE superstars by downloading their characters. "We are always looking for fun, imaginative ways to engage our fans across a variety of platforms," said Jayar Donlan, Executive Vice President of WWE Advanced Media.[1]

All of these achievements clearly indicate that WWE has moved out of a slump that it had endured between 2001 and 2005. During the 1990s, Vince McMahon had used a potent mix of shaved, pierced, and pumped-up muscled hunks; buxom, scantily-clad, and sometimes cosmetically enhanced beauties; and body-bashing clashes of good versus evil to build an empire that claimed over 35 million fans. Furthermore, the vast majority of these fans were males between the ages of 12 and 34, representing the demographic segment that makes most advertisers drool.

Just when it looked like everything was going well, WWE hit a rough patch. Its attempt to move beyond wrestling to other sports and entertainment was not successful. It failed with its launch of a football league during 2001, which folded after just one season. WWE has not done much better with its foray into movies that would use some of its wrestlers. The firm was also struggling with its efforts to build new wrestling stars and to introduce new characters into its shows. Some of its most valuable younger viewers were also turning to new reality-based shows on television such as *Survivor*, *Fear Factor*, and *Jackass*.

Since 2005, however, WWE has been turning pro wrestling into a perpetual road show that makes millions of fans pass through turnstiles in a growing number of locations around the globe. Its flagship television programs, *Raw* and *Smackdown!* are broadcast in over 30 languages in 150 countries reaching 36 million viewers around the world. WWE has also been signing pacts with dozens of licensees—including one with toymaker Mattel—to sell DVDs, video games, toys, and trading cards.

Developing a Wrestling Empire

Most of the success of the WWE can be attributed to the persistent efforts of Vince McMahon. He was a self-described juvenile delinquent who went to military school as a teenager to avoid being sent to a reformatory institution. Around 1970, Vince joined his father's wrestling company that operated in Northeastern cities such as New York, Philadelphia, and Washington, DC. He did on-air commentary, developed scripts, and otherwise promoted wrestling matches.

Vince bought the wrestling firm from his father in 1982, eventually renaming it World Wrestling Federation. At that time, wrestling was managed by regional fiefdoms where everyone avoided encroaching on anyone else's territory. Vince began to change all that by paying local television stations around the country to broadcast his matches. His aggressive pursuit of audiences across the country gradually squeezed out most of the other rivals. "I banked on the fact that they were behind the times, and they were," said Vince.[2]

* Case prepared by Jamal Shamsie, Michigan State University, with the assistance of Professor Alan B. Eisner, Pace University. Material has been drawn from published sources to be used for purposes of class discussion.

Copyright © 2019 Jamal Shamsie and Alan B. Eisner.

EXHIBIT 1
Income Statement ($ millions)

	2018	2017	2016	2015	2014
Net Revenues	$930.2	$801.0	$729.2	$658.8	$542.6
Operating Income	114.5	75.6	55.6	38.8	(42.2)
Net Income	99.6	32.6	33.8	24.1	(30.1)

Source: WWE Annual Report.

Soon after, Vince broke another taboo by admitting to the public that wrestling matches were scripted. Although he had made this admission in order to avoid the scrutiny of state athletic commissions, wrestling fans appreciated the honesty. The WWF began to draw in more fans through the elaborate story lines and the captivating characters of its wrestling matches. The firm turned wrestlers such as Hulk Hogan and Andre the Giant into mainstream icons of pop culture. By the late 1980s, the WWF's *Raw is War* had become a top-rated show on cable and the firm had also begun to offer pay-per-view shows.

Vince faced his most formidable competition after 1988, when Ted Turner brought out World Championship Wrestling, one of the few major rivals that was still operating. He spent millions luring away WWF stars such as Hulk Hogan and Macho Man Randy Savage. He used these stars to launch a show on his own TNT channel to go up against WWF's major show, *Raw is War*. Although Turner's new show caused a temporary dip in the ratings for WWF's shows, Vince fought back with pumped-up scripts, mouthy muscle-men, and lyca-clad women. "Ted Turner decided to come after me and all of my talent," growled Vince, "and now he's where he should be...."[3]

In 2001, Vince was finally able to acquire WCW from Turner's parent firm AOL Time Warner for a bargain price of $5 million. Because of the manner in which he eliminated most of his rivals, Vince has earned a reputation for being as aggressive and ambitious as any character in the ring. Paul MacArthur, publisher of the industry newsletter *Wrestling Perspective*, praised his accomplishments: "McMahon understands the wrestling business better than anyone else. He's considered by most in the business to be brilliant."[4]

In 2002, WWF was also hit by a ruling by a British court that their original WWF acronym belonged to the World Wildlife Fund. The firm had to undergo a major branding transition, changing its well-known name and triple logo from WWF to WWE. Although the change in name has been costly, it is not clear that this will hurt the firm in the long run. "Their product is really the entertainment. It's the stars. It's the bodies," said Larry McNaughton, managing director and principal of CoreBrand, a branding consultancy.[5] Vince's wife Linda stated that the new name might actually be beneficial for the firm. "Our new name puts the emphasis on the 'E' for entertainment," she commented.[6]

Creating a Script for Success

Since taking over the firm, Vince began to change the entire focus of the wrestling shows. He looked to television soap operas for enhancing the entertainment value of his live events. Vince reduced the amount of actual wrestling and replaced it with wacky yet somewhat compelling story lines. He began to develop interesting characters and create compelling story lines by employing techniques that were quite similar to those being used by many successful television shows. There was great deal of reliance on the "good versus evil" or the "settling the score" themes in the development of the plots for his wrestling matches. The plots and subplots ended up providing viewers with a mix of romance, sex, sports, comedy, and violence against a backdrop of pyrotechnics.

Over time, the scripts for the matches became tighter, with increasingly intricate story lines, plots, and dialogue. The details of every match were worked out well in advance, leaving the wrestlers themselves to decide only the manner in which they would dispatch their opponents to the mat. Vince's use of characters was well thought out and he began to refer to his wrestlers as "athletic performers" who were selected on the basis of their acting ability in addition to their physical stamina.

Vince also ensured that his firm owned the rights to the characters that were played by his wrestlers. This would allow him to continue to exploit the characters that he developed for his television shows, even after the wrestler who played that character had left his firm. By now, Vince holds the rights to many characters that have become familiar to audiences around the world.

By the late 1990s Vince had two weekly shows on television. Besides the original flagship program on the USA cable channel, WWE had added a *Smackdown!* show on the UPN broadcast channel. He developed a continuous story line using the same characters so that his audience would be driven to both the shows. But the acquisition of the WCW resulted in a significant increase in the number of wrestling stars under contract. Trying to incorporate almost 150 characters into the story lines for WWE's shows proved to be a challenging task. At the same time, the move of *Raw* to Spike TV channel resulted in a loss of viewers.

In October 2005, WWE signed a new agreement with NBC that moved *Raw* back to its USA channel. Its other show, *Smackdown,* is now carried by the Syfy channel, and has been climbing in the charts. Its newest show, *Total Divas,* has recently been launched on the E! Network. All of these programs have done well in ratings, particularly for male viewers because of the growth in popularity of a new breed of characters such as John Cena, Chris Benoit, Rey Mysterio, and Triple H. The visibility of these characters has also been enhanced through profiles on the WWE website and mobile apps.

Managing a Road Show

A typical workweek for the WWE can be grueling for the McMahons, for the talent and for the crew. The organization is now putting on almost 330 live shows a year requiring everyone to be on the road most days of the week. The touring crew includes over 200 crew members, including stage hands. All of WWE's live events, including those that are used for its two longstanding weekly shows *Raw* and *Smackdown!* as well as the newer ones, are held in different cities. Consequently, the crew is always packing up a dozen 18-wheelers and driving hundreds of miles to get from one performance to the other. Since there are no repeats of any WWE shows, the live performances must be held year round.

EXHIBIT 2
Principal Activities

MEDIA
Network: Subscriptions to WWE Network, fees for pay-per-view, video-on-demand
Television: Fees for television rights
Home Entertainment: Sales of WWE programs on various platforms, including DVDs and Blu-ray
Digital Media: Revenues from advertising on websites
LIVE EVENTS
Live Events: Revenues from ticket sales and travel packages for live events
CONSUMER PRODUCTS
Licensing: Revenues from royalties or license fees from video games, toys, or apparel
Venue Merchandise: Revenues from merchandise at live events
WWE Shop: Revenues from merchandise sales on websites
WWE STUDIOS
WWE Studios: Revenues from investing in, producing, and distributing films

Source: WWE Annual Report.

In fact, the live shows form the core of all of WWE's businesses (see Exhibit 2). They give the firm a big advantage in the entertainment world. Most of the crowd shows up wearing WWE merchandise and scream throughout the show. Vince and his crew pay special attention to the response of the audience to different parts of the show. The script for each performance is not set until the day of the show and sometimes changes are made in the middle of a show. This allows the crew some flexibility to respond to the emotions of the crowd as they witness the unfolding action. Vince boasted: "We're in contact with the public more than any entertainment company in the world."[7]

Although the live shows usually fill up, the tickets and merchandise sold at these shows manage to cover the cost of the production. But these live performances become a source for all the other revenue streams. They provide content for six hours of original television programming as well as for the growing list of pay-per-view and video-on-demand programming. These performances also create strong demand for WWE merchandise ranging from video games and toys to magazines and home videos. In fact, sales of merchandise have represented a significant and growing portion of the revenues from each of the live shows.

Much of the footage from these live shows is also being used on the WWE website, which is the growth engine for its new digital media business (see Exhibits 3 and 4). The firm even produces a show *WWE NXT* exclusively for the website. WWE offers content on the apps that it has launched for smartphones and tablets. Finally, fans can also follow programming on Hulu Plus, with which the

EXHIBIT 3
Breakdown of Revenues ($ millions)

	2018	2017	2016	2015	2014
Network	$270.8	$197.9	$180.9	$159.4	$114.9
Television	345.8	270.2	241.7	231.1	176.7
Home Entertainment	7.9	8.6	13.1	13.4	27.3
Digital Media	58.9	34.5	26.9	21.5	20.9
Live Events	144.2	151.7	144.4	124.7	110.7
Licensing	42.0	52.1	49.1	48.9	38.6
Venue Merchandise	18.7	23.8	24.2	22.4	19.3
WWE Shop	30.9	37.8	34.6	27.1	20.2
WWE Studios	11.0	18.6	10.1	7.1	10.9

Source: WWE Annual Report, author estimates.

EXHIBIT 4
Breakdown of Operating Income (OIBDA) ($ millions)

	2018	2017	2016	2015	2014
Network	$76.6	$64.2	$43.0	$48.4	$(1.8)
Television	147.9	139.4	119.8	97.0	61.9
Home Entertainment	1.1	1.6	5.3	4.6	15.0
Digital Media	16.9	10.2	4.6	4.4	0.3
Live Events	20.5	42.3	41.8	38.0	27.8
Licensing	23.9	31.1	27.4	28.8	20.9
Venue Merchandise	7.8	9.1	9.8	8.9	7.7
WWE Shop	7.7	8.3	7.3	5.1	3.5
WWE Studios	(5.4)	(3.6)	(0.2)	(1.5)	0.5

Source: WWE Annual Report, author estimates.

firm signed an exclusive multiyear contract in 2012. All of these channels promote the various offerings of the firm and carry many segments from its various other television programs.

The entire operations of WWE are overseen by Vince, along with some help from other members of his family. While the slick and highly toned Vince could be regarded as the creative muscle behind the growing sports entertainment empire, for many years his wife Linda had been quietly managing its day-to-day operations. Throughout its existence, she helped to balance the books, close the deals, and handle the details necessary for the growth and development of the WWE franchise. Their son and daughter have also been involved with various activities of the growing enterprise, with Stephanie McMahon holding an executive position in charge of creative development.

Searching for Growth

In 1999, shortly after going public, WWE launched an eight-team football league called the XFL. Promising a full competitive sport unlike the heavily scripted wrestling matches, Vince tried to make the XFL a faster-paced, more fan-friendly form of football than the NFL's brand. Vince was able to partner with NBC that was looking for a lower-priced alternative to the NFL televised games. The XFL kicked off with great fanfare in February 2001. Although the games drew good attendance, television ratings dropped steeply after the first week. The football venture ended after just one season, resulting in a $57 million loss for WWE. Both Vince and Linda insist that the venture could have paid off if it had been given enough time. Vince commented: "I think our pals at the NFL went out of their way to make sure this was not a successful venture."[8]

WWE has also tried to become involved with movie production using its wrestling stars, releasing a few films over the past decade such as Steve Austin's *The Condemned* and John Cena's *Legendary*. However, it is now largely involved with the development of smaller films that are designed for release in a few theatres and on television. Besides generating some box office revenues, these movies provide revenues from home video markets, distribution on premium channels, and offerings on pay-per-view.

Over the past few years, the firm has tried to seek growth opportunities that are driven by its core wrestling business. With more characters at their disposal and different characters being used in each of their shows, WWE has been ramping up the number of live shows, including more in overseas locations. By 2014, the firm was staging almost 70 shows in locations around the world and expanding its live performances, introducing them in six new countries such as UAE and Egypt. The company has opened offices in six cities around the world to manage its overseas operations. "While it is based in America, the themes are worldwide: sibling rivalry, jealousy. We have had no pushback on the fact it was an American product," said Linda.[9]

There has also been considerable excitement generated by the launch of WWE 24/7, a subscriber video-on-demand service. The new service allows the firm to distribute for a fee thousands of content hours consisting of highlights from old shows as well as exclusive new programming. Much of the firm's programming—both old and new—is also offered on its website, which has continued to show strong growth. By allowing audiences to watch WWE programming whenever they may want to, these new forms of distribution have allowed the firm to reach out to new audiences.

The new push for streaming on mobiles and through Hulu has provided even more opportunities for WWE to expand into digital media. The firm believes that offering their programming on smartphones and tablets will lead to a significant growth in revenues, in part from additional sales of their merchandise. "Our fans have proven that they want to consume WWE content day and night and now, through our new mobile app, they can stay completely connected to the action wherever they are," said Jason Hoch, WWE's recently appointed Senior Vice-President of Digital Operations.[10]

Reclaiming the Championship?

Although WWE may find it challenging to keep building on its already formidable fan base, there is no question that it continues to generate a lot of excitement. Most of this excitement is driven by the live shows in which they fill up the arenas. "They have the most excited fans that have come through our doors," said the director of sales and marketing at one of the arenas that holds WWE matches. "They make signs, dress up, and cheer constantly."[11] The interest in the live matches is most evident each year with the frenzy that is created by WrestleMania, the annual pop culture extravaganza that has become an almost weeklong celebration of everything wrestling. No wrestler becomes a true star until their performance is featured at WrestleMania and any true fan must make the pilgrimage at least once in their life.

WWE has begun to expand its audience by toning down its sex and violence during recent years to make their shows more family friendly. They no longer use fake prop blood and have toned down the use of abusive language in order to get a rating of TV-PG for their television programming. The use of new media like the launch of shows through streaming video is also expected to bring in younger viewers. "I think any good entertainment product has to change with the times," said McMahon. "You have to have your fingers on the pulse of the marketplace."[12]

McMahon is aware of the growing threat of mixed martial arts that started in Japan and Brazil and is spreading to more locations. Because of its similarity to wrestling, this new combat sport is likely to pull away some of WWE's fans. However, everyone at WWE is convinced that these real sports cannot match the drama and passion of the storylines and characters used to draw audiences to their matches. As Dana White, president of Ultimate Fighting Championship, has said: "People have been trying to count the WWE out for years. They are a powerhouse."[13]

There are some questions about the future of WWE after McMahon. The wrestling-based firm has relied on McMahon, now over 70, who single-handedly built his wrestling empire from his father's small regional business. Although it has branched out into other activities, the bulk of WWE's revenues and profits are tied to wrestling. Stephanie McMahon dismisses any possible doubts about the future of WWE. "All of our lines of business are more akin to Disney," she said. "We are a media property, with live shows, consumer products, television programs, and feature films. We have all the different aspects."[14]

Those who understand don't need an explanation. Those who need an explanation will never understand.

–Marty, a 19-year-old wrestling addict quoted in *Fortune*, October 6, 2000

ENDNOTES

1. Brett Hershman. Triple H, Stephanie McMahon talk WWE's future ahead of Wrestlemania 35. *Benzinga*, April 5, 2019.
2. Bethany McLean. Inside the world's weirdest family business. *Fortune*, October 16, 2000, p. 298.
3. Diane Bradley. Wrestling's real grudge match. *BusinessWeek*, January 24, 2000, p. 164.
4. Don Mooradian. WWF gets a grip after acquisition. *Amusement Business*, June 4, 2001, p. 20.
5 Dwight Oestricher & Brian Steinberg. WW . . . . E it is, after fight for F nets new name. *Wall Street Journal*, May 7, 2002, p. B2.
6. David Finnigan. Down but not out, WWE is using a rebranding effort to gain strength. *Brandweek*, June 3, 2002, p. 12.
7. Bethany McLean. Inside the world's weirdest family business. *Fortune*, October 16, 2000, p. 298.
8. Diane Bradley. Rousing itself off the mat? *BusinessWeek*, February 2, 2004, p. 73.
9. Brooke Masters. Wrestling's bottom line is no soap opera. *Financial Times*, August 25, 2008, p. 15.
10. *Business Wire*. WWE launches free mobile second screen app. August 17, 2012.
11. Brandi Ball. The face of the WWE. *McClatchy-Tribune Business News*, January 13, 2011.
12. Seth Berkman. The body slam is buffering. *New York Times*, March 31, 2014, p. B 7.
13. R.M. Schneiderman. Better days, and even the candidates, are coming to WWE. *New York Times*, April 28, 2008, p. B3.
14. Brett Hershman. Triple H, Stephanie McMahon talk WWE's future ahead of Wrestlemania 35.*Benzinga*, April 5, 2019.

CASE 6
MICROFINANCE: GOING GLOBAL . . . AND GOING PUBLIC?*

In the world of development, if one mixes the poor and nonpoor in a program, the nonpoor will always drive out the poor, and the less poor will drive out the more poor, unless protective measures are instituted right at the beginning.

–Dr. Muhammad Yunus, founder of Grameen Bank[1]

More than 2.5 billion people in the world earn less than $2.50 a day. None of the developmental economics theories have helped change this situation. Less than $2.50 a day means that these unfortunate people have been living without clean water, sanitation, sufficient food to eat, or a proper place to sleep. In Southeast Asia alone, more than 500 million people live under these circumstances. In the past, almost every effort to help the very poor has been either a complete failure or at best partially successful. As Dr. Yunus argues, in every one of these instances, the poor will push the very poor out!

In 1972, Dr. Muhammad Yunus, a young economics professor trained at Vanderbilt, returned home to Bangladesh to take a position at Chittagong University. Upon his arrival, he was struck by the stark contrast between the developmental economics he taught in the classroom and the abject poverty of the villages surrounding the university. Dr. Yunus witnessed more suffering of the poor when, in 1974, inclement weather wiped out food crops and resulted in a widespread and prolonged famine. The theories of developmental economics and the traditional banking institutions, he concluded, were completely ineffectual for lessening the hunger and homelessness among the very poor of that region.

In 1976, Dr. Yunus and his students were visiting the poorest people in the village of Jobra to see whether they could directly help them in any way. They met a group of craftswomen making simple bamboo stools. After paying for their raw materials and financing, the women were left with a profit of just two cents per day. From his own pocket, Dr. Yunus gave $27 to be distributed among 42 craftswomen and *rickshaw* (human-driven transport) drivers. Little did he know that this simple act of generosity was the beginning of a global revolution in microfinance that would eventually help millions of impoverished and poor begin a transition from destitution to economic self-sufficiency. Dr. Yunus was convinced that a nontraditional approach to financing is the only way to help the very poor to help themselves.

The Grameen Project would soon follow–it officially became a bank under the law in 1983. The poor borrowers own 95 percent of the bank, and the rest is owned by the Bangladeshi government. Loans are financed through deposits only, and there are 8.35 million borrowers, of which 97 percent are women. There are over 2,500 branches serving around 81,000 villages in Bangladesh with a staff of more than 22,000 people. Since its inception, the bank has dispersed more than $10 billion, with a cumulative loan recovery rate of 97.38 percent. The Grameen Bank has been profitable every year since 1976 except three years and pays returns on deposits up to 100 percent to its members.[2] In 2006, Dr. Yunus and the Grameen Bank shared the Nobel Peace Prize for the concept and methodology of microfinance, also known as micro-credit or microloans.[3]

What Is Microfinance?

Microfinance involves a small loan (US$20–$750) with a high rate of interest (0 to 200 percent), typically provided to poor or destitute entrepreneurs without collateral.[4] A traditional loan has two basic components captured by interest rates: (1) risk of future payment, and (2) present value (given the time value of money). Risk of future payments is particularly high when dealing with the poor, who are unlikely to have familiarity with credit. To reduce this uncertainty, many microfinance banks refuse to lend to individuals and only lend to groups. Groups have proven to be an effective source of "social collateral" in the microloan process.

In addition to the risk and time value of money, the value of a loan must also include the transaction costs associated with administering the loan. A transaction cost is the cost associated with an economic exchange and is often considered the cost of doing business. For banks like the Grameen Bank, the cost of administering ($125) a small loan may exceed the amount of the small loan itself ($120). These transaction costs have been one of the major deterrents for traditional banks.

Consider a bank with $10,000 to lend. If broken into small loans ($120), the available $10,000 can provide about 83 transactions. If the cost to administer a small loan ($120) is $125, its cost per unit is about 104 percent (!), while the cost of one $10,000 loan is only 1.25 percent. Because of the high cost per unit and the high risk of future payment, the rate of interest assigned to the smaller loan is much higher than the rate on the larger loan.

Finally, after these costs are accounted for, there must be some margin (or profit). In the case of microfinance

* This case was developed by Brian C. Pinkham, LL.M., and Dr. Padmakumar Nair, both from the University of Texas at Dallas. Material has been drawn from published sources to be used for class discussion. Copyright © 2011 Brian C. Pinkham and Padmakumar Nair.

banks, the margins are split between funding the growth of the bank (adding extra branches) and returns on deposits for bank members. This provides even the poorest bank member a feeling of "ownership."

Microfinance and Initial Public Offerings

With the global success of the microfinance concept, the number of private microfinance institutions exploded. Today there are more than 7,000 microfinance institutions, and their profitability has led many of the larger institutions to consider whether or not to "go public." Many microfinance banks redistribute profits to bank members (the poor) through returns on deposits. Once the bank goes public through an initial public offering (IPO), however, there is a transfer of control to public buyers (typically investors from developed economies). This transfer creates a fiduciary duty of the bank's management to maximize value for the shareholders.[5]

For example, Compartamos Banco (Banco) of Mexico raised $467 million in its IPO in 2007. The majority of buyers were leading investment companies from the United States and United Kingdom—the geographic breakdown of the investors was 52 percent United States, 33 percent Europe, 5 percent Mexico, and 10 percent other Latin American countries. Similarly, Bank Rakyat Indonesia (BRI) raised $480 million in its IPO by listing on multiple stock exchanges in 2003; the majority of investors who purchased the available 30 percent interest in the bank were from the United States and United Kingdom. The Indonesian government controls the remaining 70 percent stake in BRI. In Kenya, Equity Bank raised $88 million in its IPO in late 2006. Because of the small scale of Equity Bank's initial listing on the Nairobi Stock Exchange, the majority of the investors were from eastern Africa.[6] About one-third of the investors were from the European Union and United States."[7]

Compartamos Banco[8]

Banco started in 1990 as a nongovernmental organization (NGO). At the time, population growth in Latin America and Mexico outpaced job growth. This left few job opportunities within the largest population group in Mexico—the low-income. Banco recognized that the payoffs for high-income opportunities were much larger (dollars a day), relative to low-income opportunities that may return only pennies a day. Over the next 10 years, Banco offered larger loans to groups and individuals to help bridge the gap between these low-income and high-income opportunities. However, its focus is to serve low-income individuals and groups, particularly the women who make up 98 percent of Banco's members.

The bank offers two microfinance options available to women only. The first is the *crédito mujer* (women's credit). This loan ranges from $115 to $2,075, available to groups (12–50) of women. Maturity is four months, and payments are weekly or biweekly.

If a group of women demonstrates the ability to manage credit through the *crédito mujer,* they have access to *crédito mejora tu casa* (home-improvement loans). This loan ranges from $230 to $2,300 with a 6- to 24-month maturity. Payments are either biweekly or monthly.

The average interest rate on these loans is 80 percent. Banco focuses on loans to *groups* of women and requires the guarantee of the group—*every* individual in the group is held liable for the payment of the loan. This provides a social reinforcement mechanism for loan payments typically absent in traditional loans. The bank also prefers groups because they are more likely to take larger loans. This has proven effective even in times of economic downturn, when banks typically expect higher demand for loans and lower recovery of loans.

In 2009, with Mexico still reeling from the economic recession of 2008, Banco provided financing to 1.5 million Mexican households. This represented a growth of 30 percent from 2008. The core of the financing was *crédito mujer,* emphasizing the bank's focus on providing services for the low-income groups. The average loan was 4.6 percent of GDP per capita ($440), compared with an average loan of 54 percent of GDP per capita ($347) at the Grameen Bank in Bangladesh.[9] With pressure from the economic downturn, Banco also reduced its cost per client by more than 5 percent, and it continues (in late 2010) to have a cost per client under $125.

Consider two examples of how these microloans are used. Julia González Cueto, who started selling candy door-to-door in 1983, used her first loan to purchase accessories to broaden the image of her business. This provided a steppingstone for her decision to cultivate mushrooms and nopales (prickly pear leaves) to supplement her candy business. She now exports wild mushrooms to an Italian restaurant chain. Leocadia Cruz Gómez has had 16 loans, the first in April 2006. She invested in looms and thread to expand her textile business. Today, her workshop has grown, she is able to travel and give classes, and her work is widely recognized.

Beyond the Grameen Bank

These are just a few examples of how capitalistic free-market enterprises have helped the world to progress. It is generally accepted that charitable contributions and government programs alone cannot alleviate poverty. More resources and professional management are essential for microfinance institutions to grow further and sustain their mission. An IPO is one way to achieve this goal when deposits alone cannot sustain the demand for loans. At the same time, investors expect a decent return on their investment, and this expectation might work against the most important goal of microfinancing, namely, to help the very poor. Dr. Yunus has recently reemphasized his concern of the nonpoor driving out the poor, and he talks about microfinance institutions seeking investments from "social-objective-driven" investors with a need to create a separate "social stock market."[10]

The Grameen Bank story, and that of microfinancing, and the current enthusiasm in going public raise several concerns. Institutions like the Grameen Bank have to grow and sustain a long-run perspective. The Grameen Bank has not accepted donor money since 1998 and does not foresee a need for donor money or other sources of external capital. The Grameen Bank charges four interest rates, depending on who is borrowing and for what purpose the money is being used: 20 percent for income-generating loans, 8 percent for housing loans, 5 percent for student loans, and interest-free loans for struggling members (unsympathetically called beggars). (Although these rates would appear to be close to what U.S. banks charge, we must point out that the terms of these loans are typically three or four months. Thus, the annualized interest rates would be four or five times the aforementioned rates.)

The Grameen Bank's "Beggars-As-Members" program is a stark contrast to what has been theorized and practiced in contemporary financial markets—traditional banking would assign high-risk borrowers (like beggars) the highest interest rate compared to more reliable borrowers who are using the borrowed money for generating income. Interestingly, the loan recovery rate is 79 percent from the Beggars-As-Members program, and about 20,000 members (out of 110,000) have left begging completely.[11] However, it is difficult to predict the future, and it is possible that the Grameen Bank might consider expanding its capital base by going public just like its Mexican counterpart.

Most developmental economists question the wisdom of going public, because publicly traded enterprises are likely to struggle to find a balance between fiduciary responsibilities and social good.[12] The three large IPOs mentioned above (Banco, BRI, and Equity Bank) all resulted in improved transparency and reporting for stockholders. However, the profits, which were originally distributed to bank members as returns on deposits, are now split between bank members (poor) and stockholders (made up of mostly EU and U.S. investors). Many of these microfinance banks are feeling the pressure of NGOs and bank members requesting lower interest rates.[13] This trend could potentially erode the large profit margins these banks currently enjoy. When faced with falling profits, publicly traded microfinance institutions will have to decide how best to provide financial services for the very poor and struggling members of the society without undermining their fiduciary duties to stockholders.

ENDNOTES

1. Yunus, M. 2007. *Banker to the poor: Micro-lending and the battle against world poverty.* New York: PublicAffairs.
2. The Grameen Bank removes funding for administration and branch growth from the initial profits and redistributes the remaining profits to bank members. This means that a poor bank member who deposits $1 in January may receive up to $1 on December 31! Grameen Bank, www.grameen-info.org.
3. Grameen Bank, www.grameen-info.org.
4. Microfinance banks vary to the extent that the rates of interest are annualized or specified to the term. Grameen Bank, for instance, annualizes the interest on its microloans. However, many other banks set a periodic rate whereby, in extreme cases, interest may accrue daily. Grameen Bank, www.grameen-info.org.
5. Khavul, S. 2010. Microfinance: Creating opportunities for the poor? *Academy of Management Perspectives,* 24(3): 58–72.
6. Equity Bank, www.equitybank.co.ke.
7. Rhyne, E., & Guimon, A. 2007. The Banco Compartamos initial public offering. *Accion: InSight,* no. 23: 1–17, resources.centerforfinancialinclusion.org.
8. Unless otherwise noted, this section uses information from Banco Compartamos, www.compartamos.com.
9. We calculated all GDP per capita information as normalized to current (as of 2010) U.S. dollars using the International Monetary Fund (IMF) website, www.imf.org. The estimated percentages are from Banco Compartamos, www.compartamos.com.
10. Yunus. 2007. *Banker to the poor.*
11. Grameen Bank, www.grameen-info.org.
12. Khavul. 2010. Microfinance.
13. Rhyne & Guimon. 2007. The Banco Compartamos initial public offering.

CASE 7

FRESHDIRECT*

2019 started out difficult for FreshDirect. Although FreshDirect's website read, "We're on a mission to deliver quality beyond question and convenience that adds something great to your day," customers in its primary location–New York City–took it to the media the past year to report their dissatisfaction with the company. Due to persistent technical glitches, some customers in Manhattan received emails telling them none of the items they had ordered were available, a problem the company later attributed to a software upgrade gone awry. "I used to spend an average of $700 a month with you," wrote Ingrid Rose on the company's Facebook page. "But service has been so bad, I hardly ever order anymore. I used to be a super fan and I miss what you used to be."[1] These issues even caused longtime chief executive and co-founder, Jason Ackerman, to step down from his role. Following the opening of FreshDirect's new facility based in the South Bronx, New York City, co-founder David McInerney took over in September 2018 as CEO. "This is a very exciting time for the company as we settle into our new home. I look forward to working with the entire FreshDirect team as we usher the company into this next chapter of growth," said McInerney in an interview. Considering its current track and what its customers are saying, will the company be able to deliver quality beyond question without actually delivering its products?

Since 2001, operating out of its production center in Long Island City, Queens, FreshDirect had offered online grocery shopping and delivery service in Manhattan, Queens, Brooklyn, Nassau County, Riverdale, Westchester, select areas of Staten Island, the Bronx, the Hamptons, New Jersey including Jersey Shore, Philadelphia, Delaware, and parts of Connecticut. FreshDirect also offered pickup service at its Long Island City facility, as well as corporate service to select delivery zones in Manhattan and summer delivery service to the Hamptons on Long Island. In 2012, the company decided to move its facility from Long Island City, Queens, to a new 800,000-square-foot property in the Bronx, and received court clearance to do so. FreshDirect had threatened to relocate its operational hub and headquarters to New Jersey, but New York City and the state of New York offered close to a $130 million subsidy package, including tax breaks and abatements, to keep the online grocer in New York City. A petition by the community group South Bronx United had earlier challenged the move arguing that the city had failed to analyze properly the potential environmental impact (e.g., air and noise pollution) that would result from a "truck-intensive" business. However, the court ruled in FreshDirect's favor in 2013.[2]

During the early years of the company, FreshDirect had pronounced to the New York City market that it was "the new way to shop for food." This was a bold statement given that the previous decade had witnessed the demise of numerous online grocery ventures. However, the creators of FreshDirect were confident in the prospects for success of their business. Their entire operation had been designed to deliver on one simple promise to grocery shoppers– "higher quality at lower prices."

While this promise was an extremely common tagline used within and outside the grocery business, FreshDirect had integrated numerous components into its system to give real meaning to their words. Without a retail location, FreshDirect did not have to pay expensive rent for a retail space. To offer the highest-quality products to its customers, FreshDirect had designed a state-of-the-art production center and staffed it with expert personnel. The 600,000-square-foot production facility newly located in the Bronx opened in 2018. In each FreshDirect warehouse, 12 separate temperature zones ensured that each piece of produce, meat, and other food was kept at its optimal temperature for ripening and/or preservation. The company claimed the entire facility was kept colder and cleaner than any other retail environment.[3]

Further quality management was achieved by an SAP manufacturing software system that controlled every detail of the facility's operations. All of the thermometers, scales, and conveyor belts within the facility were connected to a central command center. Each specific setting was programmed into the system by an expert from the corresponding department of everything from the ideal temperature for ripening a cantaloupe to the amount of flour that went into the French bread. The system was equipped with a monitoring alarm that alerted staff to any deviation from the programmed settings.

FreshDirect maintained extremely high standards for cleanliness, health, and safety. The floor was immaculate. All food-preparation areas and equipment were bathed in antiseptic foam at the end of each day. Incoming and outgoing food was tested in FreshDirect's in-house laboratory, which ensured adherence to USDA guidelines and the Hazard Analysis and Critical Control Point food safety system. In all respects, food passing through the FreshDirect facility met the company's high health and safety standards.[4]

System efficiency was the key to FreshDirect's ability to offer its high-quality products at low prices. The middleman was completely eliminated. Instead of going through an intermediary, both fresh and dry products were ordered from individual growers and producers and shipped directly to

* This case was prepared by Professor Alan B. Eisner of Pace University as a basis for class discussion rather than to illustrate either effective or ineffective handling of an administrative situation. Thanks to graduate students Sushmitha Mudda, Saad Nazir, Dev Das, Rohit R. Phadtare, and Shruti Shrestha for research assistance. Copyright © 2019 Alan B. Eisner.

FreshDirect's production center, where its expert staff prepared them for purchase. In addition, FreshDirect did not accept any slotting allowances.[5] This unique relationship with growers and producers allowed FreshDirect to enjoy reduced purchase prices from its suppliers, passing the savings on to its customers.

Each department of the facility, including the coffee roaster, butcher, and bakery, was staffed by carefully selected experts. FreshDirect offered premium fresh coffees (roasted on site), pastries and breads (baked on site), deli, cheese, meats (roast beef dry-aged on site), and seafood. Perishable produce was FreshDirect's specialty by buying locally as much as possible and using the best sources of the season, it was able to bring food the shortest distance from farms, dairies, and fisheries to the customer's table.

FreshDirect catered to the tastes of its busy Manhattan clientele by offering a full line of heat-and-serve meals prepared in the FreshDirect kitchen by New York executive chef Michael Stark (formerly of Tribeca Grill) and his team. Another celebrity chef, Terrance Brennan of New York's French-Mediterranean restaurant Picholine, oversaw creation of "restaurant-worthy" four-minute meals. Made from raw ingredients delivered in a "steam valve system" package, these complete meals were not frozen but were delivered ready to cook in a microwave.

The proximity of FreshDirect's processing facility to its Manhattan customer base was a critical factor in its cost-effective operational design. The processing center's location in the South Bronx put approximately 4 million people within a 10-mile radius of FreshDirect, enabling the firm to quickly deliver a large volume of orders.[6] Further, cost controls had been implemented through FreshDirect's order and delivery protocols. Products in each individual order were packed in boxes, separated by type of item (meat, seafood, and produce packed together; dairy, deli, cheese, coffee, and tea packed together; grocery, specialty, and nonrefrigerated products packed together), and placed on a computerized conveyor system to be sorted, assembled, and loaded into a refrigerated truck for delivery.

Orders had to be a minimum of $40, with a delivery charge between $6.99 and $7.99 per order, depending on the order dollar amount and delivery location. Delivery was made by one of FreshDirect's own trucks and was available only during a prearranged two-hour window from 6:30 a.m. to 10 p.m. every day of the week. To attract more customers and to encourage repeat purchases, FreshDirect also offered DeliveryPass that enabled customers to get unlimited free deliveries by purchasing a free delivery subscription for 6 or 12 months. The DeliveryPass price for 6 months was $79 and for 12 months was $129.

Competing with other online grocers like AmazonFresh, specialty gourmet/gourmand stores in Manhattan, and high-end chain supermarkets like Whole Foods, Trader Joe's, and Fairway, FreshDirect was trying to woo the sophisticated grocery shopper with an offer of quality, delivered to the customer's door, at a price more attractive than others in the neighborhood. Operating in the black for the first time in 2005,[7] by choosing to remain a private company and expanding gradually, FreshDirect's owners hoped to turn a daily profit, steadily recovering the estimated $60 million start-up costs, silencing critics, and winning converts.[8]

An interesting idea for expansion was to cater to home cooks who liked to cook from scratch. FreshDirect teamed up with online recipe website Foodily to launch a new service called Popcart. Users could order deliveries of food ingredients directly applicable to online recipes. The Internet was a popular recipe source for home cooks, but shopping for ingredients was widely seen as an unpleasant chore. The new Popcart technology alleviated this burden by linking with the FreshDirect portal and providing next-day deliveries of whatever a recipe called for. This is really at the heart and soul of making food shopping easier for consumers. "About 70 percent of New Yorkers cook from scratch multiple times per week, and 30 percent cook multiple times per day. Think about that opportunity," said Jodi Kahn, chief consumer officer for FreshDirect.[9]

Founding Partners

Co-founder and its first chief executive officer Joseph Fedele was able to bring a wealth of experience in New York City's food industry to FreshDirect. In 1993 he had co-founded Fairway Uptown, a 35,000-square-foot supermarket on West 133 Street in Harlem. Many critics originally questioned the success of a store in that location, but Fairway's low prices and quality selection of produce and meats made it a hit with neighborhood residents, as well as many downtown and suburban commuters.

Co-founder Jason Ackerman, FreshDirect's vice chairman and chief financial officer, had gained exposure to the grocery industry as an investment banker with Donaldson Lufkin & Jenrette, where he specialized in supermarket mergers and acquisitions.

Fedele and Ackerman first explored the idea of starting a large chain of fresh-food stores, but they realized maintaining a high degree of quality would be impossible with a large enterprise. As an alternative, they elected to pursue a business that incorporated online shopping with central distribution. Using the failure of Webvan, the dot-com delivery service that ran through $830 million in five years of rapid expansion, as their example of what not to do, Fedele and Ackerman planned to start slowly, use off-the-shelf software and an automated delivery system, and pay attention to essentials such as forming relationships with key suppliers and micromanaging quality control.[10]

FreshDirect acquired the bulk of its $100 million investment from several private sources, along with the contribution that was expected to come from the state of New York in tax breaks. By locating FreshDirect's distribution center within the state border and promising to create at least 300 permanent, full-time, private-sector jobs in the state, FreshDirect became eligible for a $500,000 training grant from the Empire State Development Jobs Now Program. As its name implied, the purpose of the Jobs Now program was to create new, immediate job opportunities for New Yorkers.

CEO Successions

Although the press was mostly positive about FreshDirect's opportunities, growth and operational challenges remained. In the words of an ex-senior executive of FreshDirect, "The major problem seems to be constant change in Senior Management."[11] FreshDirect co-founder Joseph Fedele had remained CEO until January 2004, when co-founder Jason Ackerman succeeded him. Ackerman served as CEO of FreshDirect for a little over seven months; Dean Furbush succeeded him in September 2004. Ackerman remained vice chairman and chief financial officer. The tenure of Dean Furbush lasted a little over two years. Steve Michaelson, president since 2004, replaced Furbush as CEO of FreshDirect in early 2007.[12] In 2008, Michaelson left for another firm and FreshDirect's chairman of the board, Richard Braddock, expanded his role in the firm and took over as CEO. Braddock said, "I chose to increase my involvement with the company because I love the business and I think it has great growth potential." Braddock had previously worked at private equity firm MidOcean Partners and travel services retailer Priceline.com, where he'd also served as chairman and CEO.[13] Braddock wound up leaving the company in March 2011. Jason Ackerman returned to the role of CEO for a second time and stepped down in September 2018 and co-founder David McInerney took over.

Business Plan

While business started out relatively slowly, FreshDirect hoped to capture around 5 percent of the New York City grocery market. Availability citywide was originally slated for the end of 2002. However, to maintain its superior service and product quality, FreshDirect chose to expand its service area slowly. This business model seemed to be working well for FreshDirect, as the company continued to gradually expand successfully into new areas surrounding its Long Island City facility. With the success of its business model and its steady growth strategy, by the spring of 2011, FreshDirect had delivery available to select zip codes and neighborhoods throughout Manhattan and as far away as Westchester, Connecticut, New Jersey, and the Hamptons on Long Island (in the summer only).

By 2019, FreshDirect was serving Delaware, Jersey Shore, Hamptons, Connecticut, and some cities in Pennsylvania. They started serving in and around Center City in Philadelphia in 2017. The company employed a relatively low-cost marketing approach, which originally consisted mainly of billboards, public relations, and word of mouth to promote its products and services. FreshDirect hired Trumpet, an ad agency that promoted FreshDirect as a better way to shop by emphasizing the problems associated with traditional grocery shopping. For example, one commercial stressed the unsanitary conditions in a supermarket by showing a shopper bending over a barrel of olives as she sneezed, getting an olive stuck in her nose, and then blowing it back into the barrel. The advertisement ended with the question: "Where's your food been?" Another ad showed a checkout clerk morph into an armed robber, demand money from the customer, and then morph back into a friendly checkout clerk once the money was received. The ad urged viewers to "stop getting robbed at the grocery store."[14] FreshDirect enlisted celebrity endorsements from New York City personalities such as film director Spike Lee, actress Cynthia Nixon, former mayor Ed Koch, supermodel Paulina Porizkova, and chef Bobby Flay.[15] The company planned to change its marketing strategy by launching a new testimonial-based campaign using actual customers, rather than celebrities. FreshDirect was number 81 in the Internet Retailer Top 500 Guide of 2018.

Operating Strategy

Building on its efficient low-cost supply chain that eliminated the middleman and sourced direct from farms and fisheries, FreshDirect was able to pursue a make-to-order philosophy.[16] By focusing on providing produce, meat, seafood, baked goods, and coffees that were selected or made to the customer's specific order, FreshDirect offered its customers an alternative to the standardized cuts and choices available at most brick-and-mortar grocery stores. This strategy created a business model that was unique within the grocery business community.

A typical grocery store carried about 25,000 packaged goods, which accounted for approximately 50 percent of its sales, and about 2,200 perishable products, which accounted for the other 50 percent of sales. In contrast, FreshDirect offered about 5,000 perishable products, accounting for approximately 75 percent of its sales, but only about 3,000 packaged goods, which made up the remaining 25 percent of sales.[17]

While this stocking strategy enabled a greater array of fresh foods, it limited the brands and available sizes of packaged goods such as cereals, crackers, and laundry detergents. However, FreshDirect believed that customers would accept a more limited packaged-good selection in order to get lower prices, as evidenced in the success of wholesale grocery stores, which offered bulk sales of limited items. Jason Ackerman identified the ideal FreshDirect customers as those who bought their bulk staples from Costco on a monthly basis and bought everything else from FreshDirect on a weekly basis.[18]

FreshDirect's Website

FreshDirect's website not only offered an abundance of products to choose from but also provided a broad spectrum of information on the food that was sold and the manner in which it was sold (see Exhibit 1). Web surfers could take a pictorial tour of the FreshDirect facility; get background information on the experts who managed each department; get nutritional information on food items; compare produce or cheese on the basis of taste, price, and usage; specify the thickness of meat or seafood orders and opt for one of several marinades or rubs (see Exhibit 2); search for the right roast and variety of coffee according to taste preferences; and read nutritional information for fully prepared meals. A large selection of recipes was available depending on the items chosen.

For example, if you wanted to purchase chicken, you were first asked to choose from breasts and cutlets, cubes and

EXHIBIT 1 FreshDirect Website

Source: freshdirect.com

EXHIBIT 2 Example of FreshDirect Seafood Selection

Source: freshdirect.com

strips, ground, legs and thighs, specialty parts, split and quartered, whole, or wings. Once your selection was made – let's say you chose breasts and cutlets – you were given further options based on your preference for skin, bone, and thickness. The final selection step offered you a choice of rubs and marinades, including teriyaki, sweet and sour, garlic rosemary, poultry seasoning, lemon herb rub, and salt-and-pepper rub. Throughout, the pages offered nutritional profiles of each cut of meat as well as tips for preparation and storage.

As for FreshDirect's several delivery models, customers within the city were attracted to the FreshDirect service (prearranged two-hour delivery window) because it eliminated the need to carry groceries or park a car near their apartments to unload their purchases. Suburban customers were served in a slightly different manner. Many suburban customers worked at corporations in the tristate area that could arrange for depot drop-off in the office parking lot, creating a central delivery station. FreshDirect sent a refrigerated truck, large enough to hold 500 orders, to these key spots during designated times. Suburbanites, leaving their office building to go to their cars, swung by the FreshDirect truck, picked up their orders, and headed home. FreshDirect could also provide delivery to the parking lot of football or concert events for tailgate parties or picnics. Customers could also pick up their orders directly from the processing center. Orders were ready at the pickup desk 5 to 10 minutes after they were called in.

EXHIBIT 3 FreshDirect at the Office

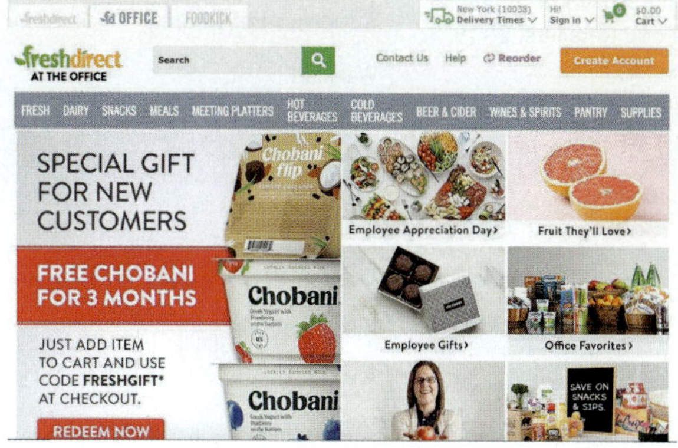

Source: freshdirect.com

For business customers in Manhattan, chef-prepared breakfast and luncheon platters and restaurant-quality individual meals were delivered right to the office. FreshDirect offered catering for business meetings and upscale events. FreshDirect provided dedicated corporate account managers and customer service representatives for corporate clients; however, FreshDirect provided only delivery, not setup and platter-arrangement services. The corporate delivery minimum order was $50, and delivery costs were $14.99 (see Exhibit 3).

The Retail Grocery Industry

In the United States, supermarket chains make over $632 billion in sales annually. The typical supermarket carries 39,500 items, averages about 42,800 square feet, and enjoys over $18 million in sales annually.[19] The top 10 supermarket chains in the United States command a large share of the total grocery industry business (see Exhibit 4).

The supermarket business is a low-margin business with net profits of only 1 to 2 percent of revenues. Store profits depend heavily on high customer traffic and rapid inventory turnover, especially for perishables such as produce and meat. Competitors must operate efficiently to make money, so tight control of labor costs and product spoilage is essential. Because of modest capital investment of mainly construction of distribution centers and stores, supermarket chains realize 15 to 20 percent returns on invested capital. Online grocery retailers, like FreshDirect—because of the flexibility of information control, automated order fulfillment, and reduced real estate costs—could potentially have operating margins up to 10 percent, rather than the 3 to 4 percent of traditional supermarkets.[20]

The Online Grocery Segment

Total online grocery shopping sales were estimated to be about $29.7 billion in 2021.[21] This accounted for about 4.4 percent of total grocery sales.

Online grocery shopping was slow to catch on in the 1990s, and industry newcomers had encountered high

EXHIBIT 4
Top 10 North American Food Retailers, 2018

Supermarket Chain	2018E*	Sales CAGR** 2013-2018E*	Sales CAGR 2018E-2023E*
Wal-Mart	$261,153.28	3.6%	2.3%
The Kroger Co.	$104,269.58	7.8%	2.7%
Walgreens Boots Alliance	602	118.72%	4.9%
CVS	$80,172.45	4.8%	2.9%
Costco Wholesale Club	$61,625.82	6.8%	5.2%
Albertsons Cos.	$54,291.08	24.6%	1.4%
Ahold Delhaize	$39,968.46	−0.3%	1.1%
Publix	$34,676.38	4.3%	1.6%
Target Corp.	$30,873.13	−1.0%	−2.9%
Aldi	$28,835.43	8.9%	6.6%

*Estimated

**Compound annual growth rate

Source: https://www.winsightgrocerybusiness.com/retailers/wgb-kantar-reveal-power-20-retailers.

start-up and operating costs. Sales volumes and profit margins remained too small to cover the high start-up costs. The problem, according to industry analysts, was that consumers had been disappointed in online service, selection, and prices. Coupled with the extensive investment needed in warehousing, fulfillment, and inventory control, this meant the "pure play" e-grocery models were risky. There was a belief then that better success would come from traditional grocery retailers that chose to venture online.[22]

However, some analysts expected online grocery sales to grow at a rapid pace as companies improved their service and selection, computer penetration of households rose, and consumers became more accustomed to making purchases online.[23] An article in *Computer Bits* examined the customer base for online grocers, looking specifically at the types of consumers who would be likely to shop online and the kinds of home computer systems that were required for online shopping. An Andersen Consulting report identified six major types of online shoppers (see Exhibit 5), and FreshDirect's Richard Braddock predicted that online grocery sales could account for as much as 20 percent or more of total grocery sales within the next 10 years.[24] A MARC Group study concluded, "Consumers who buy groceries online are likely to be more loyal to their electronic supermarkets, spend more per store 'visit,' and take greater advantage of coupons and premiums than traditional customers."[25]

A problem with online grocery shopping was that consumers were extremely price-sensitive when it came to buying groceries, and the prices of many online grocers at the outset were above those at supermarkets. Shoppers also were unwilling to pay extra to online grocers for home delivery. Consumer price sensitivity meant that online grocers had to achieve a cost structure that would allow them to (1) price competitively, (2) cover the cost of selecting items in the store

EXHIBIT 5
Types of Online Shoppers and Their Propensity to Be Attracted to Online Grocery Shopping

Types of Online Shoppers	Comments
Traditional	Might be older technology-avoiders or simply shoppers who like to sniff-test their own produce and eyeball the meat selection.
Responsible	Feed off the satisfaction of accomplishing this persistent to-do item.
Time-starved	Find the extra costs associated with delivery fees or other markups a small price to pay for saving time.
New technologists	Use the latest technology for any and every activity they can, because they can.
Necessity users	Have physical or circumstantial challenges that make grocery shopping difficult; likely to be the most loyal group of shoppers.
Avoiders	Dislike the grocery shopping experience for a variety of reasons.

Source: Andersen Consulting.

and delivering individual grocery orders, and (3) have sufficient margins to earn attractive returns on their investment. Some analysts estimated that to be successful, online grocers had to do 10 times the volume of a traditional grocer.[26]

Potential Competitors in the Online Grocery Segment

When online grocers started appearing within the industry, many established brick-and-mortar grocers began offering online shopping in an attempt to maintain and expand their customer base. Two basic models were used for online order fulfillment: (1) pick items from the shelves of existing stores within the grocer's chain, and (2) build special warehouses dedicated to online orders. The demand for home delivery of groceries had been increasing, but in many market areas the demand had not reached a level that would justify the high cost of warehouses dedicated to fulfilling online orders.[27]

Safeway began an ambitious online grocery venture, GroceryWorks, a shopping system that included warehouses dedicated to filling online orders. Unfavorable returns forced Safeway to reevaluate its system, and it eventually chose to form a partnership with Tesco, a U.K.-based grocer. Tesco filled its online orders from the shelves of local stores in close proximity to the customer's home. Safeway and Tesco worked together on GroceryWorks in Portland, Oregon, where they received a positive initial response from customers.[28]

The craze over health food had created room in the grocery industry for organic-food suppliers to enter as an attractive substitute to traditional groceries. When asked what kept him up at night, FreshDirect's former CEO Dean Furbush said that Whole Foods or Trader Joe's moving into a FreshDirect neighborhood was his biggest threat, as that hurt FreshDirect the most.

Whole Foods, the Austin, Texas-based supermarket chain subsidiary of Amazon with the organic-health-food focus, had already threatened FreshDirect's sales in Manhattan. Trader Joe's, another specialty food retailer, was opening a store in downtown Union Square, prime territory for FreshDirect.[29] Although commentators believed there was enough room for all, including even street farmers' markets, FreshDirect focused on organic foods to respond to the threats of Whole Foods and other specialty food stores.[30] With the shift among some customers to paying attention to local, sometimes organic, suppliers, FreshDirect highlighted its support of and partnership with the local companies that provided their produce, poultry, fish, cheese, milk, eggs, and specialties such as wine (see Exhibit 6). However, its efforts were inconsistent in this area. For example, to help shoppers and checkout operators distinguish between organic and nonorganic produce, FreshDirect wrapped organics in plastic, which in itself is not organic. FreshDirect chairman Jeff Turner recognized the incongruity.[31]

In 2019, FreshDirect saw four major players entering the online grocery market chipping into its NYC market share. With almost 9 million people packed into five boroughs of gridlocked traffic and subway chaos, no U.S. city is more suited to online grocery shopping than New York. Amazon Fresh, Walmart's Jet.com, Peapod, and YourGrocer.com were competing against FreshDirect in the NYC market.

EXHIBIT 6 FreshDirect Local Market Offerings

Source: FreshDirect Company Website

Rivals in the NYC Online Grocery Segment

Jet.com

After Acquiring Jet.com in 2016, Walmart's goal was to target urban areas like New York with high concentrations of affluent millennials, retailers' coveted demographic.[32] Jet.com was launched in 2014 by Marc Lore along with Mike Hanrahan and Nate Faust; It is headquartered in Hoboken, New Jersey. Walmart then acquired Jet.com in 2016 with a goal to revamp and rebrand Jet.com in an effort to "rehumanize" e-commerce (see Exhibit 7). Apart from offering groceries and perishable products in specific areas, Walmart has made several acquisitions of fashion and apparel brands including Bonobos, ModCloth, ShoeBuy, and Moosejaw, which will be sold on the Jet.com site. Jet, which continues to operates as a standalone site, gives Walmart the opportunity to sell upscale brands and reach higher-income customers who wouldn't normally consider shopping at Walmart.[33]

Most importantly, Walmart's acquisition of the same-day delivery start-up, Parcel gives Walmart a second front against Amazon. Jet.com, which had been offering only two-day free shipping, will allow most New York customers to schedule three-hour windows for same-day or next-day delivery.

EXHIBIT 7 Jet.com Website

Source: jet.com

Peapod

Founded in 1989 by brothers Andrew and Thomas Parkinson, Peapod was an early pioneer in e-commerce, inventing an online home-shopping service for grocery items years ahead of the commercial emergence of the Internet. With its tagline "Smart Shopping for Busy People," the company began providing consumers with a home-shopping experience in the early 1990s, going so far as to install modems in customer homes to provide an online connection.

From its founding in 1989 until 1998, the company's business model involved filling customer orders by forming alliances with traditional grocery retailers. The company chose a retail partner in each geographic area where it operated and used the partner's local network of retail stores to pick and pack orders for delivery to customers. Peapod personnel would cruise the aisles of a partner's stores, selecting the items each customer ordered, pack and load them into Peapod vehicles, and then deliver them to customers at prearranged times. Peapod charged customers a fee for its service and collected fees from its retail supply partners for using their products in its online service.

In 1997, faced with mounting losses despite growing revenues, Peapod management shifted to a new order-fulfillment business model utilizing a local company-owned central distribution warehouse to store, pick, and pack customer orders for delivery. By mid-1999 the company had opened new distribution centers in three of the eight markets it served–Chicago, Long Island, and Boston–and a fourth distribution center was under construction in San Francisco.

In late spring 2000, Peapod created a partnership with Royal Ahold, an international food provider based in the Netherlands. At the time, Ahold operated five supermarket companies in the United States: Stop & Shop, Tops Market, Giant-Landover, Giant-Carlisle, and BI-LO. In September 2000, Peapod acquired Streamline.com Inc.'s operations in Chicago and the Washington, DC, markets and announced that it planned to exit its markets in Columbus, Ohio, and in Houston, Dallas, and Austin, Texas. All of these moves were made as part of Peapod's strategic plan for growth and future profitability. Under Peapod's initial partnership agreement with Ahold, Peapod was to continue as a stand-alone company, with Ahold supplying Peapod's goods, services, and fast-pick fulfillment centers. However, in July 2001 Ahold acquired all the outstanding shares of Peapod and merged Peapod into one of Ahold's subsidiaries.

Peapod offered delivery services from its own warehouses to many areas, including Chicagoland, Milwaukee and southeast Wisconsin, and Indianapolis. Peapod by Stop & Shop provided delivery services in southern New Hampshire, Massachusetts, Rhode Island, Connecticut, New York, and New Jersey. And Peapod by Giant provided delivery services to Maryland, Virginia, Philadelphia and southeastern Pennsylvania, and Washington, DC.[34]

In large markets, orders were picked, packed, loaded, and delivered from a freestanding centralized fulfillment center; in smaller markets, Peapod established fast-pick centralized fulfillment centers adjacent to the facilities of retail partners.[35] Peapod's proprietary transportation routing system ensured on-time delivery and efficient truck and driver utilization.

AmazonFresh

AmazonFresh entered the grocery market in recent years by offering a wide range of dry goods. Amazon was always a threat to other online retailers because of its existing loyal customer base and legendary customer service. The selection of dry goods rather than perishables meant that Amazon, unlike FreshDirect and Peapod, did not have to worry about delivery costs on time- and climate-sensitive items.

AmazonFresh serviced residences in Boston, Baltimore, Dallas, Chicago, New York City, London, parts of California and New Jersey, and more. Recently, users in states like Pennsylvania, Maryland, Virginia, and California have reported that AmazonFresh no longer delivers to their zip code. AmazonFresh offered over 95,000 different items available for same day delivery if ordered before 10 a.m. and next day early morning delivery for items ordered between 10 a.m. and 10 p.m. The company had difficulty managing the economics of the grocery delivery business, and it kept membership prices considerably higher than competitors. To become an AmazonFresh member, a customer had to subscribe to Prime Fresh in addition to the subscription of Amazon Prime with a total annual cost of about $299. In contrast, FreshDirect and Peapod charged customers for delivery of the goods purchased, without requiring customers to pay subscription charges.

Still, AmazonFresh remains a vigorous competitor in the online grocery sector with a proven history of success in online retail. All the existing and rising competition amid growth in online grocery stores threatens FreshDirect's future profitability (see Exhibits 8 and 9).

Current Challenges

As the online grocery retailing business has matured, all players realize they must pay close attention to customer perception. Online grocery retailers need to "serve their online customers just like they would serve the customers who come into their physical stores."[36] Even mighty Amazon has suffered grocery delivery failures, from out-of-stock problems to delivery glitches and website crashes. Unique challenges confront the business model. Even though FreshDirect has been able to woo local New Yorkers, gaining a *Fast Company* "Local Hero" award, the company has had to absorb "hundreds of thousands of dollars in parking tickets to get its customers its orders within the delivery window."[37]

Some investors have shown confidence in FreshDirect's brand and its strategic approach to expanding outside the New York metro area. J.P. Morgan Asset Management group invested $189 million through its PEG Digital

EXHIBIT 8 Profiles of Select Online Grocers

Name	Minimum Area Covered	Delivery Order Minimum	Delivery Charge	Method	Specialization
FreshDirect	Manhattan, Queens, Brooklyn, Staten Island, the Bronx, Nassau County, Westchester County, Fairfield County, Hoboken, Philadelphia, Jersey City	$40	$6.99–$7.99, depending on order size and destination; tipping optional	Trucks; delivers every day 6:30 a.m. to 10 p.m. depending on location	• Mostly perishables: fresh produce, meats, baked goods • Low prices because there is no middleman
YourGrocer	Manhattan, the Bronx, Westchester, Greenwich, Brooklyn, Queens, Rockland	None	$9.95 for orders > $75; $14.95 for orders < $75	Rented vans; delivers 9 a.m. to 9 p.m. depending on location	• Bulk orders of packaged goods
Peapod	Chicago, Boston, Long Island, Connecticut, New Jersey, Rhode Island, Milwaukee, Wisconsin, Indiana, New Hampshire, Maryland, Virginia, Pennsylvania, Washington, DC	$60	$6.95	Trucks; delivery available 6 a.m. to 1 p.m. on Saturday and 6 a.m. to 10 p.m. every other day; pickup available as well	• Partner with Giant Foods and Stop & Shop; items picked from shelves of local warehouses near customer's home
AmazonFresh	Select cities in New York, Massachusetts, Maryland, Philadelphia, and California	None	$9.99 for orders under $40, in addition to 14.99 monthly membership	Order by 10 a.m. for delivery by 6 p.m. and order by 10 p.m. for delivery by 6 a.m.	• Nonperishables as well as packaged goods

Source: Company websites.

EXHIBIT 9 Comparison of Prices for Selected Online Grocers

	Prices			
	FreshDirect	Jet.com	Peapod	AmazonFresh
Chobani Non-Fat Greek Yogurt, Plain 5.3oz	$1.49/ea	$1.09/ea	$1.49/ea	$0.99/ea
Granny Smith apples	$4.99/ea (4ct)	$5.99 (6ct)	$3.99, 3lb bag | $0.08/oz	$5.99, 3lb bag
Ragu Old World Style Traditional Sauce, 24oz	$2.49/ea	$2.79/ea	$2.79/ea	$3.19 ($0.13/oz)
Hellmann's Real Mayonnaise 30 oz	$5.99/ea	$4.99/ea	$4.19/ea	$3.69/ea

Source: Company websites.

Growth Fund. However, expanding national operations is a challenge for FreshDirect's business model because most people residing outside metro areas own cars and prefer handpicked grocery shopping at nearby stores. According to research published by Morgan Stanley in 2016, about 67 percent of the consumers surveyed stated that they did not buy groceries online because they liked to select the fresh products themselves.[38] The study suggests that buying fresh products online remains an unwelcoming idea for most consumers.

Environmental concerns have started to creep in as a major issue for FreshDirect. First, because of the conveyor packing system at the processing facility, FreshDirect is forced to use lots of cardboard boxes to deliver groceries: Produce comes in one box, dry goods in another, and a single tube of toothpaste in its separate cardboard delivery container. Although FreshDirect has transitioned to the use of 100 percent post-consumer recycled paper,[39] the reusability of the cardboard boxes is limited and the general public is aware that its tax dollars are used to "collect and dispose of the huge stacks of cardboards that FreshDirect's customers leave in the trash."[40] As one environmentally conscious consumer observed, "I was baffled by the number of boxes they used to pack things. Groceries worth $40 came in five boxes. And after I unpacked, I had to discard the boxes. There was no system of returning them to FreshDirect to be recycled."[41]

A second environmental issue is the additional exhaust fumes FreshDirect trucks contribute to the urban atmosphere.[42] Issues of this nature were at the forefront of citizens' concerns regarding the environmental impact that FreshDirect's move into the South Bronx would have on their neighborhood. Third, FreshDirect trucks double-parking on busy city streets only makes traffic congestion worse. As one commentator stated, "It's probably no exaggeration to say that FreshDirect has built its financial success on its ability to fob off its social and environmental costs on the city as a whole."[43] Some city dwellers even express concern about FreshDirect's adverse effect on the overall makeup of their neighborhoods: "It is not just the impact they have on congestion, pollution, space, etc., but their very adverse impact on the best of businesses in neighborhoods that they can undersell because of their externalized costs. It is these small businesses, farmers markets and local grocery stores, that FreshDirect undercuts, that are some of the best businesses for supporting and preserving our walkable, diverse and safe neighborhoods."[44]

Another major issue for FreshDirect is its customers' concerns about how fresh the produce and meats really are. One of the biggest obstacles to the growth of online ordering of groceries is the inability to view and touch food, particularly fresh produce and meat. Online customers cannot pick up and thump a melon or peel back the leaves on a head of romaine lettuce to check for freshness the same way they could in the grocery store. FreshDirect has received numerous comments from consumers which basically state, "I can't see, touch, and smell the products. I have to rely on you." This lack of control over identifying the freshness of the food is a major concern for customers. The company has recognized the problem and spun this negative aspect of online shopping into a positive one by creating a food-quality rating system. Consumer feedback has jump-started a new way of doing business for FreshDirect.[45]

The company's Daily Produce Rating System ranks the quality of fruits and vegetables available for delivery the next day. The five-star rating system gives shoppers "a foolproof way to ensure that the ripest fruits and crunchiest veggies are consistently delivered to their doorsteps," as advertised at the company's website. The Daily Produce Rating System is based on a daily inspection of all produce in stock by a quality assurance team. Rating criteria include taste, color, firmness, and ripeness. Rankings are based on an easy ratings scale:

- Five stars: "never better, the best we've seen."
- Four stars: "great/delicious."
- Three stars: "good/reliably decent."
- Two stars: "average/inconsistent quality/generally OK."
- One star: "below average/expect wide inconsistency in quality/probably out of season."[46]

Results are updated each morning on FreshDirect's website to let customers know which fruits and veggies are the best bets for the following day. FreshDirect also offers the same five-star rating service for seafood; some 50 to 70 percent of its customers use this feature.[47] The system aims to simulate the in-store shopping experience, allowing the grocers to showcase their best stuff and customers to decide what looks good. "Not everyone is an expert on the seasonality of a fruit or vegetable, so this system takes the guesswork out of choosing the best available items," says FreshDirect's former chief marketing officer Steve Druckman. "Each of the buyers and managers who rate the produce have years on the job, so they have great expertise. I am not aware of any other online or conventional grocer that's developing a system such as this."[48]

However, the strategy comes with a big risk: To gain customers' trust, FreshDirect has had to acknowledge that not every item it stocks is picture-perfect every day. Before implementation not everyone at the company was enthusiastic about the idea. Many feared backlash from consumers about FreshDirect's products' not always being top quality. "Was it scary? Yeah!" recalls Glenn Walsh, the produce manager. "I thought it was insane in the beginning."[49]

Despite the risk, the company claims that the rating system has changed consumer buying patterns. Around 70 percent of customers say they have purchased something they wouldn't have if it weren't for the rating system. Druckman asserts, "One hundred percent of customers changed buying patterns. The rating system works. If we put something out like black seedless grapes or golden pineapples with four stars, we'll sell twice as many of those because of their rating than otherwise."[50]

In the recent months, however, New Yorkers have begun to lose trust in FreshDirect. Customers have found reason to go elsewhere. FreshDirect's expansion has been bumpy, with more than a few deliveries going astray and once-loyal customers griping on social media.[51] Meanwhile, companies like Amazon and Walmart have set their sights on New York. FreshDirect may be struggling with quality but wasn't standing still; it launched a same-day delivery service, branded "FoodKick" enabling customers who place an order before 10 a.m. to receive it that evening. The service was available throughout the New York City borough of Manhattan and was soon to be followed by rollouts to Brooklyn and Westchester County.[52] With the recent complaints of delivery from New York customers and the pressure of same day service, the question remains whether FreshDirect will be able to win back its reputation?

ENDNOTES

1. www.freshdirect.com.
2. Wall, Patrick. Judge tosses lawsuit meant to stop FreshDirect from moving to the Bronx. https://www.dnainfo.com/new-york/20130603/port-morris/judge-tosses-lawsuit-meant-stop-freshdirect-from-moving-bronx.
3. Clarke, E. Exclusive: A first look at FreshDirect's new Bronx home. SpectrumNews NY1, June 1, 2016, http://www.ny1.com/nyc/all-boroughs/news/2016/05/31/exclusive–a-first-look-at-freshdirect-s-new-bronx-home.html.
4. Dubbs, D. 2003. Catch of the day. *Multichannel Merchant,* July 1, multichannelmerchant.com/opsandfulfillment/orders/fulfillment_catch_day.
5. A slotting allowance is defined by the American Marketing Association as 1. (retailing definition) A fee paid by a vendor for space in a retail

store. 2. (sales promotion definition) The fee a manufacturer pays to a retailer in order to get distribution for a new product. It covers the costs of making room for the product in the warehouse and on the store shelf, reprogramming the computer system to recognize the product's UPC code, and including the product in the retailer's inventory system. www.marketingpower.com/mg-dictionary-view2910.php.

6. Laseter, T. et al. 2003. What FreshDirect learned from Dell. *Strategy Business,* 30 (Spring), www.strategy-business.com/article/8202.
7. Schoenberger, C. R. 2006. Will work with food. *Forbes,* September 18, members.forbes.com/global/2006/0918/041.html.
8. Smith, C. 2004. Splat: The supermarket battle between Fairway, FreshDirect, and Whole Foods. *New York: The Magazine,* May 24, nymag.com/nymetro/food/industry/n_10421.
9. Fahey, M. 2014. Foodily, FreshDirect start recipe delivery service. *Crains New York,* August 5.
10. Dignan, L. 2004. FreshDirect: Ready to deliver. *Baseline: The Project Management Center,* February 17, www. baselinemag.com/print_article2/0,1217,a5119342,00.asp.
11. *Chelsea-Wide Blogs.* 2006. chelsea.clickyourblock.com/bb/-archive/index.php?t-128.html.
12. *Supermarket News.* 2007. Michaelson named CEO at FreshDirect; Furbush resigns. January 9, supermarketnews.com/retail_financial/-michaelson_named_ceo_at_freshdirect_furbush_resigns_337/index.html.
13. *InternetRetailer.com.* 2008. FreshDirect's chairman hopes to deliver the goods in bigger role. July 14.
14. Elliot, S. 2003. A fresh and direct approach. *New York Times,* February 11.
15. Bosman, J. 2006. FreshDirect emphasizes its New York flavor. *New York Times,* January 31, www.nytimes.com/2006/01/31/business/media/31adco.html.
16. Laseter et al., op. cit.
17. Ibid.
18. Ibid.
19. Food Market Institute. Supermarket facts: Industry overview. www.fmi.org/facts_figs/superfact.htm.
20. Leonhardt, D. 2006. Filling pantries without a middleman. *New York Times,* November 22, www.nytimes.com/2006/11/22/business/22leonhardt.html?pagewanted51&_r52&adxnnlx51164556801-6ScpsMek8edyTRh8S2BWyA.
21. Statista. 2019. Online grocer shopping sales in the United States from 2012 to 2021 (in billion U.S. dollars). https://www.statista.com/statistics/293707/us-online-grocery-sales/.
22. Kempiak, M., & Fox, M. A. 2002. Online grocery shopping: Consumer motives, concerns and business models. *First Monday,* vol. 7, no. 9, www.firstmonday.org/issues/issue7_9/kempiak. and author estimates.
23. Machlis, S. 1998. Filling up grocery carts online. *Computerworld,* July 27: 4.
24. Hamstra, M. 2010. FreshDirect CEO predicts online gains in next decade. *Supermarket News,* March 1, supermarketnews.com/retail_financial/freshdirect-ceo-projects-online-gains-0301.
25. Woods, B. 1998. America Online goes grocery shopping for e-commerce bargains. *Computer News,* August 10: 42.
26. Fisher, L. M. 1999. Online grocer is setting up delivery system for $1 billion. *New York Times,* July 10: 1.
27. *Frontline Solutions.* 2002. Online supermarkets keep it simple. Vol. 3, no. 2: 46ñ49.
28. Ibid.
29. Smerd, J. 2005. Specialty foods stores will go head-to-head at Union Square. *New York Sun,* March 4, www.nysun.com/article/10058?page_no51.
30. *Progressive Grocer.* 2005. NYC's FreshDirect launches street fight against Whole Foods. March 3, www.allbusiness.com/retail-trade/food-stores/4258105-1.html.
31. *New Zealand Herald.* 2007. We don't have time to waste. February 3.
32. Cheng, Andria. 2018. Walmart's Jet.com is getting a makeover to try to win over New York's Millennials. *Forbes,* September 13.
33. Bowman, Jeremy. 2017. 1 year later, Wal-Mart's Jet.com acquisition is an undeniable success. *The Motley Fool,* Oct 3.
34. https://www.peapod.com/site/gateway/deliveryAreas.jsp.
35. Peapod Inc. Corporate fact sheet. www.peapod.com/corpinfo/peapodFacts.pdf.
36. Hamstra, M. 2007. Online stores may need to bone up on their execution. *Supermarket News,* January 29, supermarketnews.com/viewpoints/-online-stores-bone-up-execution/index.html.
37. Danigelis, A. 2006. Customers' first local hero: FreshDirect. *Fast Company,* September, www.fastcompany.com/customer/-2006/articles/local-fresh-direct.html.
38. Morgan Stanley. 2019. Are groceries the next big driver of global eCommerce? http://www.morganstanley.com/ideas/online-groceries-could-be-next-big-ecommerce-driver.
39. *Supermarket News.* 2007. FreshDirect transitions to eco-friendly boxes. May 11, supermarketnews.com/fresh_market/-freshdirect_eco_friendly/index.html.
40. *StreetsBlog.* 2006. FreshDirect builds a grocery empire on free street space. November 22, www.streetsblog.org/2006/11/22/fresh-direct-builds-a-grocery-empire-on-free-street-space.
41. Wadia, A. S. 2007. Is FreshDirect good for you? *Metroblogging NYC,* January 30, http://nyc.metblogs.com/2007/01/30/is-freshdirect-good-for-you/.
42. *StreetsBlog,* op. cit.
43. Ibid.
44. Ibid.
45. McConnon, Aili. 2009. The issue: FreshDirect focuses on customer service. *Bloomberg Businessweek,* July 1, www.businessweek.com/managing/content/jun2009/ca20090630_154481.htm.
46. FreshDirect. Undated. About our daily produce rating system. www.freshdirect.com/brandpop.jsp?brandId5fd_ratings.
47. Cohan, P. 2010. Growth matters: FreshDirect nudges its way to profits. *Dailyfinance,* March 23, www.dailyfinance.com/story/company-news/growth-matters-freshdirect-nudges-its-way-to-profits/19372267/.
48. Briggs, Bill. 2009. FreshDirect takes a new approach to customer service. *Internetretailer.com,* January 7, www.internetretailer.com/mobile/2009/01/07/freshdirect-takes-a-new-approach-to-customer-service.
49. Bruder, J. 2010. At FreshDirect, reinvention after a crisis. *New York Times,* August 12: B9.
50. *Perishable Pundit.* 2009. New York's FreshDirect succeeds when most online grocers have failed. May 22, www.perishablepundit.com/index.php?date505/22/09&pundit52.
51. Digital Commerce 360. 2018. Amazon and Walmart chip into FreshDirect's NYC market share. *Bloomberg News,* December 11, https://www.digitalcommerce360.com/2018/12/11/amazon-and-walmart-chip-into-freshdirects-nyc-market-share/.
52. Progressive Grocer. 2019. FreshDirect introduces same-day service, expands delivery. March 7, https://progressivegrocer.com/freshdirect-introduces-same-day-service-expands-delivery.

CASE 8

GREENWOOD RESOURCES: A GLOBAL SUSTAINABLE VENTURE IN THE MAKING*

"Money still grows on trees."

–Larry Light, Deputy Editor for Personal Finance, *Wall Street Journal*[1]

"The answer to some of the world's most pressing concerns (global warming, alternative energy, sustainable forestry) lies in one of the earth's most renewable resources–trees."

–GreenWood Resources, Inc.[2]

Jeff Nuss and other senior managers of GreenWood Resources, Inc., emerged after a long deliberation from the conference room in their headquarters in Portland, Oregon, in June 2010. On the one hand, they were inspired by their global vision to build "a resource that lasts forever" and their belief the company, with nearly 70 employees, was finally taking off after almost 10 years of persistent efforts in building the key elements (opportunity, people, resources, and business networks) for a successful tree plantation venture. On the other hand, they had just finished a grueling meeting during which they found it hard to reach a consensus on how to proceed with two strategic investment alternatives in rural China.

Since 2000, Jeff and several other senior managers had traveled to China on numerous occasions. The process of making a deal in the Chinese forest industry had proven to be more time-consuming than anticipated. Complex ownership structures, underdeveloped farming systems, and emerging, sometimes equivocal and unpredictable, government policies characterized the forest industry in China. Chinese farmers who embraced business models and management styles far different than those in the United States posed additional complications.

By March 2009, GreenWood had assessed some 20 potential investment projects in China. The Luxi and Dongji projects passed the initial phase of screening and became the company's top priorities. The due diligence on these two projects had been extensive, lasting over a year, but both projects still faced considerable obstacles and even potential deadlock. In June 2010, Jeff and his senior management team were still weighing the pros and cons of the two projects, which had been the subject of their last management meeting. They felt that GreenWood needed to proceed carefully to ensure the company's sustainable business criteria (rather than its financial return per se) were met in China but also realized the company needed to show some progress to its major investor in China, Oriental Timber Fund Limited. Jeff needed to bring a recommendation from his senior management team to the investment committee comprising himself and two representatives from Oriental. The decision deadline was approaching. Jeff anticipated that the next senior management meeting would result in a recommendation. Should GreenWood choose one of the two projects?

GreenWood Resources, Inc.

Founding of the Venture

In 1998, after 12 years of experience with CH2M Hill[3] as a bioresources engineer, Jeff Nuss, a native Oregonian, decided to start his own venture, GreenWood Resources, Inc., specializing in the development and management of high-yield, fast-growing tree plantations. Having looked into other potential businesses such as a golf course and a winery, he was eventually convinced, based on his education and years of experience working with poplar tree farms, that investments in tree plantations held great promise for the future (see Appendix 1 for background industry information).

Jeff's plan was to help institutional investors (pension funds, endowments, insurance companies, etc.) and wealthy individuals invest in professionally managed high-yield, short-rotation tree farms (Exhibit 1 illustrates tree rotation length and yield of several representative tree species). He wanted to operate farms in accordance with Forest Stewardship Council (FSC) certification. FSC's objective was to conserve biological diversity and enhance the long-term social and economic well-being of forest workers and local communities (see Exhibit 2).

Firms with FSC certificates were rare because the standards were stringent, often leading to higher operating costs. For example, FSC required the use of less toxic pesticides and herbicides, which were more expensive. It prohibited the use of genetically modified trees. It also demanded that 10 percent of tree farms be reserved for native habitats. At the same time, however, the economic benefits were uncertain because most end users of wood products were not necessarily willing to pay a premium price for FSC-certified products. Nevertheless, Jeff felt it

* Copyright © 2014 by the *Case Research Journal* and by Lei Li, Nottingham University Business School China; Howard Feldman, University of Portland; and Alan Eisner, Pace University. This case is developed solely as the basis for class discussion. It is not intended to serve as endorsements, sources of primary data, or illustrations of effective or ineffective management. The authors acknowledge the able assistance of Wendy Ye and Pratik Rachh in the process of developing the case.

EXHIBIT 1 Tree Rotation Length and Yield

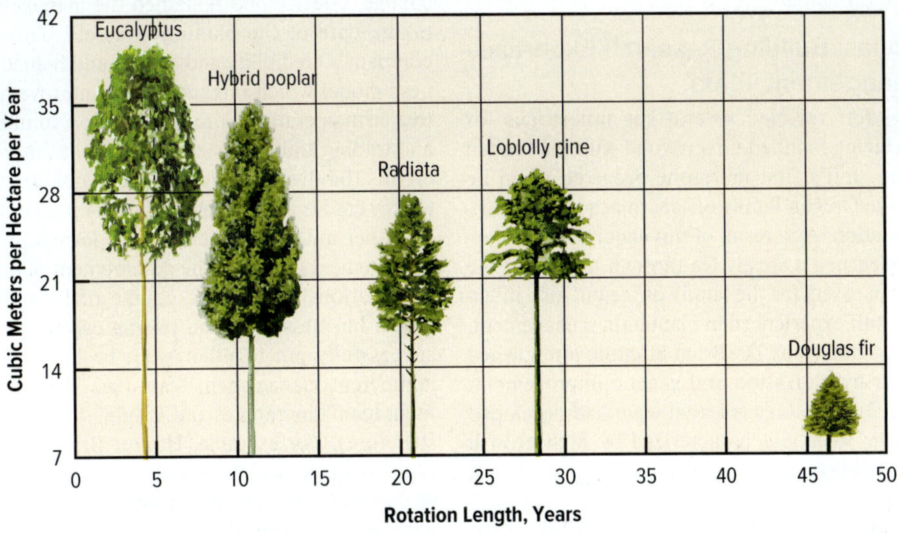

The figure shows that eucalyptus and hybrid poplar ripen for harvest much faster than other species.

Source: GreenWood's brochure.

EXHIBIT 2 Forest Stewardship Council (FSC) Principles and Criteria for Forest Management

1. **Compliance with laws and FSC principles and criteria.** Forest management shall respect all applicable laws of the country in which they occur, and international treaties and agreements to which the country is a signatory, and comply with all FSC principles and criteria.
2. **Tenure and use rights and responsibilities.** Long-term tenure and use rights to the land and forest resources shall be clearly defined, documented, and legally established.
3. **Indigenous people's rights.** The legal and customary rights of indigenous people to own, use, and manage their lands, territories, and resources shall be recognized and respected.
4. **Community relations and workers' rights.** Forest management operations shall maintain or enhance the long-term social and economic well-being of forest workers and local communities.
5. **Benefits from the forest.** Forest management operations shall encourage the efficient use of the forest's multiple products and services to ensure economic viability and a wide range of environmental and social benefits.
6. **Environmental impact.** Forest management shall conserve biological diversity and its associated value, water resources, soil, and unique and fragile ecosystems and landscapes, and, by so doing, maintain the ecological functions and the integrity of the forest.
7. **Management plan.** A management plan—appropriate to the scale and intensity of the operations—shall be written, implemented, and kept up to date. The long-term objectives of management, and the means of achieving them, shall be clearly stated.
8. **Monitoring and assessment.** Monitoring shall be conducted—appropriate to the scale and intensity of forest management—to assess the condition of the forest, yields of forest products, chain of custody, management activities, and their social and environmental impact.
9. **Maintenance of high-conservation-value forests.** Management activities in high-conservation-value forests shall maintain or enhance the attributes that define such forests. Decisions regarding high-conservation-value forests shall always be considered in the context of a precautionary approach.
10. **Plantations.** Plantations shall be planned and managed in accordance with Principles and Criteria 1–9, and Principle 10 and its Criteria. While plantations can provide an array of social and economic benefits, and can contribute to satisfying the world's needs for forest products, they should complement the management of, reduce pressures on, and promote the restoration and conservation of natural forests.

Austin, James E., and Reficco, Ezequiel. "Forest Stewardship Council." Harvard Business School Case 303-047, November 2002.[4]

was the right thing to do. "At the end of the day, we do what we believe (is right)."

Key Milestones: Building Research Expertise and the Management Team

Looking back, Jeff recalled several key milestones for GreenWood. Having founded GreenWood with his limited personal wealth, Jeff's first milestone occurred when he convinced a large Oregon family office[5] to acquire an existing poplar plantation. As a result of this acquisition, GreenWood not only earned a steady fee through managing the poplar plantation assets for the family office but also inherited a group of staff experienced in plantation management. The head of this group was Dr. Brian Stanton, a renowned expert in poplar hybridization and genetic improvement. Over the years, Dr. Stanton's research team had developed dozens of poplar varieties characterized by high growth rate, strong pest resistance, high wood density, and broad site adaptability.

The second milestone came in 2002. On behalf of the family office, GreenWood helped sell the poplar plantation to GMO Renewable Resources, a large timber investment management organization (TIMO). Despite the ownership change, GreenWood remained the management company, taking care of the plantation assets. This enhanced the company's credibility and stature and helped initiate a business model which integrated tree improvement, nurseries, tree farm operations, product (i.e., log, lumber, chips) sales, and trading and ecosystem services (i.e., monetizing carbon credits, biodiversity credits, water quality, and renewable energy credits and managing land for total ecosystem value).

Other milestones included the formation of a seasoned management team and the development of a series of strategic relationships. In the course of formulating a viable global business plan and raising capital, Jeff was able to successfully put together what he believed was a highly competent management team (see Exhibit 3 for management team biographies and Exhibit 4 for the organizational structure). For example, Hunter Brown, a veteran operational manager with experience in Asia, joined GreenWood as the chief operating officer. Brian Liu, a Chinese American with years of experience working for the Oregon State Department of Agriculture (responsible for the forest industry), was recruited to lead the company's China operations.

EXHIBIT 3 Executive Management Team Biographies, 2010

Jeff Nuss is the founder, chairman, and CEO of GreenWood Resources, Inc., and its subsidiaries and is directly responsible for the leadership and strategic direction of the company. He is a leading industry spokesman and advocate for novel methods of sustainable timber production and serves on the boards of the World Forestry Center, Agribusiness Council, and Western Hardwood Council. He received a BS in bioresource engineering and an MS in resource management and policy within the Civil Engineering Department of Oregon State University.

Hunter Brown is chief operating officer of GreenWood Resources, Inc. Prior to joining GreenWood, he was executive vice president for PACCESS, a global supply chain services management firm. He has extensive business experience in Asia. Hunter received a BS in forestry from the University of the South and an MS in forestry from Duke University, and he completed the Executive Program at the Darden School of Business at the University of Virginia.

Lincoln Bach is corporate controller of GreenWood Resources, Inc. Prior to joining GreenWood, he was corporate controller for an international family-wealth-management firm. He had previously served as an audit manager at Deloitte & Touche. He received a BS in accounting from Linfield College and is a CPA and CFP professional.

Brian Stanton is managing director of Tree Improvement Group & Nurseries at GreenWood Resources, Inc. For 20 years, he has overseen the technological developments for poplar on commercial tree farms in the United States where he has produced over 40,000 varieties of hybrid poplar that have been tested throughout Chile, China, Europe, and the United States. Brian is the chair of the Poplar and Willow Working Party for the International Union of Forest Research Organizations. He received a BS in biology from West Chester State College, an MS in forestry from the University of Maine, and a PhD in forest resources from Pennsylvania State University.

Don Rice is managing director of Resource Management Group at GreenWood Resources, Inc. Previously, Don was the Oregon poplar resource and manufacturing manager for Potlatch Corporation. Don has a degree in agricultural engineering from Washington State University.

Jake Eaton is managing director of resource planning and acquisitions at GreenWood Resources. He worked for 21 years with Potlatch Corporation. Jake has extensive global experience in short-rotation tree farm silviculture. He holds a BS in forest management from Oregon State University and an MS in silviculture and genetics from University of Montana.

Brian Liu is vice president and general manager of GreenWood Resources, Inc.'s China Operations. Previously, as an international trade representative for the State of Oregon Department of Agriculture, he successfully led the U.S. negotiation teams in opening the Chinese market for Oregon agricultural products. Brian was born and raised in Guangdong, China, and moved to the United States at the age of 14. He holds a BS in finance and an MBA in international management from Portland State University. He is fluent in English, Mandarin, and Cantonese.

Source: GreenWood Resources, Inc.

EXHIBIT 4 GreenWood Resources, Inc., Topline Organization Chart, 2010*

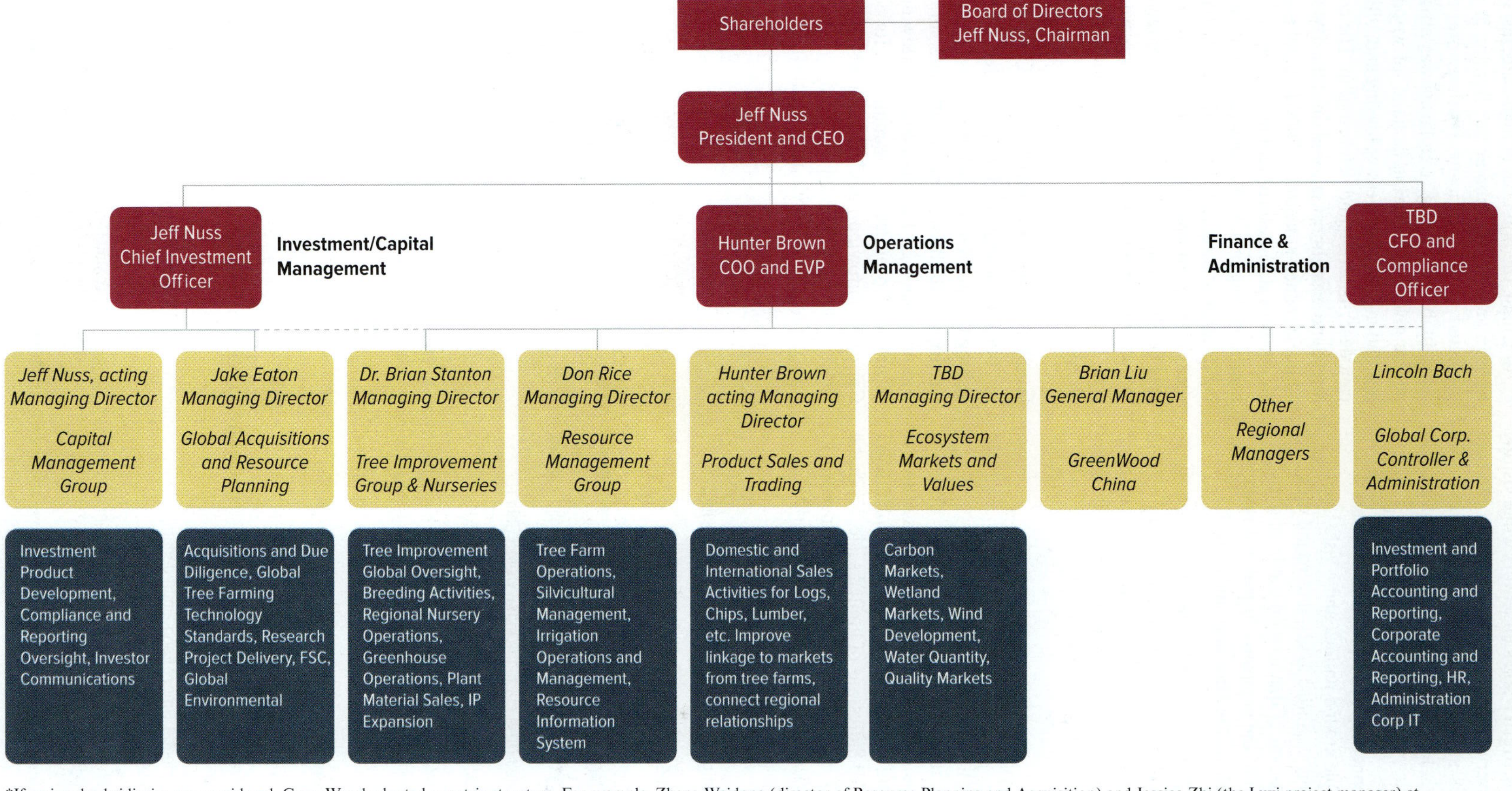

*If regional subsidiaries are considered, GreenWood adopted a matrix structure. For example, Zhang Weidong (director of Resource Planning and Acquisition) and Jessica Zhi (the Luxi project manager) at GreenWood China both reported to Brian Liu but also took professional advice from Jake Eaton, who was essentially the global functional manager of Resource Planning.

Source: GreenWood Resources, Inc.

Brian had supported GreenWood's endeavors while visiting China as a state government official, and he had been convinced to leave his stable government position to join GreenWood in 2005. In reflecting on his success in recruiting people, Jeff said:

> I am good at connecting to people. In that process, I am getting people around an idea and a vision and motivating (them). . . . I tried to first understand what is really their passion. If that passion can be aligned with (the vision of the company), it makes it really easy to get people on the same page and aboard.

Thanks to the dedication of its people as well as its growing business network, GreenWood looked to expand its operations to China and South America and launched two investment fund-raising campaigns to support its initiatives (see Exhibit 5).

Entering the Chinese Poplar Plantation Industry

Perhaps the most important entrepreneurial initiative for GreenWood was the decision to commit itself to the Chinese poplar plantation market. The poplar plantation industry in the United States was of limited scale. From the very beginning Jeff believed that GreenWood needed to consider opportunities in other regions of the world.

In China, the potential of high-yield, fast-growing plantations in general, and poplar tree farming in particular, was projected to be significant. Furthermore, the concept of "sustainably managing" tree farms was attractive to many people given that growing demand for wood products had resulted in years of excessive logging and, ultimately, significant desertification and deforestation. The country's loss of forestland was almost ignored until the 1990s. In response, China launched a project in 2000 to plant trees and grass in an effort to slow desertification in northern China, including the Beijing region. Nationwide, China set a goal of raising its afforestation (i.e., establishing forestland by planting seeds or trees in open land) rate to 26 percent of its land area by 2050, which would require an increase of forestland in excess of 65 million hectares.[6] To achieve this ambitious goal, high-yield, fast-growing plantations would have to play an important role.

GreenWood's Experience in China

In 2000, Jeff was invited to join a Mercy Corps task force visiting China. Mercy Corps was a Portland, Oregon–based charity whose mission was to alleviate suffering, poverty, and oppression by helping people worldwide to build just, secure, and productive communities. Its cofounder, Ells Culver, had grown up in China as a missionary's son in the 1940s and firmly believed tree farming could help Chinese rural communities develop and flourish. He convinced Jeff,

EXHIBIT 5 A Chronicle of GreenWood Resources, Inc.

Year	Event
1998	Jeff Nuss founded GreenWood with dedication to the innovative development and management of sustainable tree farms and their products.
1999	GreenWood started to manage poplar plantation assets on behalf of a large Oregonian family office.
2000	Jeff Nuss made the initial visit to China.
2001	Dr. Brian Stanton joined GreenWood.
2002	GreenWood helped sell the poplar plantation assets to GMO Renewable Resources on behalf of the Oregonian family office and consequently became a specialized poplar assets manager for GMO Renewable Resources.
2005	Hunter Brown and Brian Liu joined GreenWood.
2005	GreenWood established its Beijing office in China.
2006	GreenWood established its representative office in Chile.
2007	GreenWood raised $175 million through GreenWood Tree Farm Fund and acquired Potlatch's poplar plantation assets in Oregon.
2008	Oriental Timber Fund Limited made a capital commitment of $200 million for GreenWood to invest in tree plantation assets in China.
2009	Preliminary assessment of 20 potential investment projects was completed by March; the Luxi and Dongji projects became priorities.
2010	GreenWood was due to make an investment decision in China together with Oriental Timber Fund Limited.

Source: Interviews.

who had never thought about visiting China, to travel with him to explore the potential opportunities.

GreenWood's entry into China took part in two stages. The first took place in the five years following Jeff's initial trip, from 2000 to 2005. During this period, Jeff and his colleagues visited China three or four times every year with the express purpose of establishing relationships with academics, government agencies, and various businesses in the Chinese forest industry. Greenwood learned the market and local business practices. It also brought plant materials for site adaptability tests to one of the local tree-growing companies with which it planned to partner.

Establishing GreenWood Resources China, Ltd. (GreenWood China), a wholly owned subsidiary of GreenWood, based on greenfield investment,[7] and opening its Beijing office in 2005 highlighted the second stage of GreenWood's entry into China. Brian Liu, vice president and general manager in charge of GreenWood China, explained why it took the company five years before setting up its operating facility:

> Since the No. 9 state council decree was promulgated to encourage Chinese people to go out and grow trees in 2003, a lot of entrepreneurs jumped in. The market was overwhelmed. Some entrepreneurs were doing the wrong thing. For example, "Wanli Afforestation Group" and "Yilin Wood Industry Co., Ltd.," two large local private forestry companies, were involved in some sort of financial scheme. . . . I personally felt something was going wrong, but we didn't know what. It's not the correct way. It's not the Western way. It's just too chaotic for a Western company. In addition, we had financial and personnel constraints.

Jeff recalled the decision to enter China:

> We collectively looked at what we had been doing in China. We came to the conclusion that if we were going to do anything, we couldn't do it from afar . . . we knew that we wanted to go and put a nursery there. . . . China had two main hybrid varietals of poplar trees imported from Europe. We have many new hybrid varietals. We felt the best opportunity for us was that (China) needed more (plant) materials, better materials. . . . The (Chinese) government was issuing policies in the forestry sector that were all laser-driven to industry-based plantations, of which 45 percent were represented by poplar plantations.

Despite the potentially immense opportunities in the Chinese tree plantation market and Jeff's experience, passion, and business connections, raising institutional capital proved to be very challenging. Investors looked to historical performance and operating scale, which made it difficult for a relatively young venture like GreenWood to attract investment funds. GreenWood wanted to raise US$5 million (in the form of equity) to fund its entry but was able to raise only about US$1 million. Regardless, Jeff believed GreenWood's global vision, entrepreneurial spirit, and relationships with the right people at the right places would eventually lead the company to success.

Brian remembered the process involved in setting up GreenWood's subsidiary in China:

> Jeff got a vision. It's critical that a leader has that vision because a lot of times, people are uncertain when it's a good time to do that. At that time, the company was small with a very limited budget. But his vision was he could get more money. . . . We came to China pretty much with that US$1 million. We didn't know how long it would last. It was very scary. It was a classic example of entrepreneurship. Let's just do it and don't look back.

Fund-Raising Success!

While GreenWood was grappling with funding difficulties in China, an acquisition opportunity arose in the Pacific Northwest region in the United States. Potlatch, a large timber company, changed ownership and decided to sell its poplar plantation assets located in Oregon. Jeff had consulted with Potlatch while working with CH2M Hill. He knew that an acquisition of Potlatch's tree farms would expand GreenWood's scale to a point where the company would be really attractive to capital investors. With the help of his business connections, Jeff established GreenWood Tree Farm Fund L.P. (GTFF) and raised US$175 million of private equity funding. GTFF used the money to purchase 18,000 acres of poplar trees from Potlatch, Inc., as well as three other poplar tree farms totaling an additional 17,000 acres. According to Jeff, this was a breakthrough for the firm that was almost serendipitous in the way it happened.

The expanded scale and personnel resulting from the US$175 million investment in GTFF enabled GreenWood to become a much more visible player in the tree plantation industry. In February 2008, Oriental, a GTFF investor interested in emerging markets, made a commitment of US$200 million to GreenWood for use in the Chinese market.[8]

Brian relished the experience:

> We changed our strategy. A lesson we learned is that you should be able to change. You should have an entrepreneurial spirit. We wanted to raise US$5 million (of equity) but ended up raising US$200 million (of capital commitment).[9]

Risks and Challenges

China was an exploding timber market. The tree plantation industry, still in its nascent stage, was fragmented and lacked serious competition. GreenWood believed that abundant opportunities were available to it. For example, the company could use its elite plant materials and its sophisticated silvicultural (i.e., forest cultivation) management approach to substantially increase the annual growth of trees (quantity) in China as well as their quality.

GreenWood, however, faced a range of risks and challenges unique to China. First, there was a serious concern with the relatively weak intellectual property protection in the Chinese institutional system. Since plant materials existed in both tree nurseries and farms, it was hard to prevent people from "stealing" them. Elite plant materials were one of GreenWood's most valuable resources and were critical for developing its competitive advantages in China. GreenWood was confident, however, that it could capitalize on its years of experience to create increasingly better plant materials faster than any imitators could possibly copy them.

Second, there were political and social risks everywhere they turned. Chinese forestlands were owned either by the state or collectively. In practice, all kinds of government entities at different administrative levels (including small towns and villages) owned the lands, resulting in a very complex ownership structure. Many farmers worked small, government-allocated plots based on a lease contract of typically 20 to 30 years. GreenWood could negotiate long-term leases only with the local government, which either owned the lands and/or could represent farmers in striking a deal with foreign companies. A thorny issue was that "China's weak contract laws carried a risk for leaseholders. . . . In several instances, unhappy farmers waged protests against foreign companies when they felt they didn't get a fair share on the lease."[10] Thus, there was still a concern of potential expropriation for foreign investors.

Third, GreenWood needed to know where to find the most cost-effective tree farms and learn with whom to partner in acquiring and managing tree assets. The lack of proper documentation of plantation assets complicated this effort.

GreenWood also dealt with several other unique challenges. For example, the Chinese approach to silviculture was rudimentary compared to Western standards. There was a lack of knowledge in tree farm investment, plant materials development, and efficient irrigation, according to Zhang Weidong, director of the Resource Planning and Acquisition Group at GreenWood China.

The differences in silvicultural approaches presented the biggest challenge to Brian. In Western countries, long-term internal rate of return (IRR) was a prevalent business concept. This was at odds, however, with the mindset of Chinese farmers, who had a short-term focus and wanted to know only the "value" of their timber assets per *mu* (0.067 hectare),[11] which was either a historical price based on the booming market of previous years or a price determined by cumulative capital expenditures plus a desired surplus. Brian noted that his team often used both the Western method and the Chinese method to conduct side-by-side comparisons:

> I call myself a translator, translating Western concepts and applying them to China. . . . It's easier said than done. It took us two years to figure it out.

Another big challenge was cultural, especially the differences in business cultures. GreenWood followed a strict Western procedure when conducting environmental and tree asset evaluations (preliminary investigation, survey, inventory analysis, comprehensive due diligence, etc.), which its potential Chinese partners perceived as inefficient (because the procedure was time-consuming) or even inappropriate (because certain tree plantation data were not available in China). Hunter Brown, the COO of GreenWood, pointed out the key difference:

> The Chinese approach is an informal management style (as opposed to) the much more structured and organized contract-driven style in the United States.

Furthermore, during the global economic downturn of 2008–2009, there was a growing perception that GreenWood's market-based assessment and pricing were unfair to local farmers and communities.[12] Jake Eaton, director of GreenWood's Global Acquisitions and Resource Planning, acknowledged the disagreement with the company's potential Chinese partners regarding the valuation of existing tree plantation assets. For GreenWood, the valuation was based on current market prices, whereas its Chinese counterparts believed the market would quickly rebound and therefore the valuation should take into account the prices that prevailed prior to the economic downturn.

Business challenges in China notwithstanding, GreenWood grew its business steadily. In 2009, it had about 10 employees in China (out of 70 companywide) and operated five tree nurseries that were used to test GreenWood's elite plant materials for site adaptability.

Investment Opportunities in China

With the capital commitment of US$200 million for the Chinese market, GreenWood, in conjunction with Oriental, established Green China Forestry Company, Ltd. (GCFC). GCFC was essentially responsible for making investment decisions in China. An investment committee, comprising Jeff and two representatives from Oriental, made investment decisions while GreenWood China provided daily management services for a fee (see Exhibit 6 for an illustration of the management and investment relationship). The investment decision-making process consisted of two phases. First, GreenWood China conducted preliminary investigations to identify potential projects.[13] Some 20 potential investment projects had been reviewed by March 2009 (see Exhibit 7).

Marc Hiller, a specialist in Forest Stewardship Council (FSC) at GreenWood, commented on the phase one evaluation:

> In every project, we look at the quality of the (assets), the ability to sell the timber to the markets. . . . Can the tree farms (potentially) meet the FSC requirements? . . . Do the current owners have a lot of conflicts with the local communities? . . . Does the local company have problems with its employees? . . . Were the local farmers coerced to turn in their tree assets for the consolidation purpose?[14] . . . Can we acquire the assets at an attractive rate? . . . What are the financial and legal risks in acquiring the land?

Jeff also stressed the dual significance of financial viability and social responsibility:

> (The process) addresses the environmental and social issues. . . . The model (of sustainability) we hold ourselves to is FSC certification. . . . Of course, we've got to figure out how to become profitable. . . . Sustainability is not achieved unless you are economically sustainable.

Among the 20 potential projects, Luxi and Dongji were the most desirable based on preliminary analyses and thus entered phase two, which consisted of a more comprehensive due diligence analysis including economic, social, and environmental elements. The economic element was mainly reflected in the estimation of internal rate of return (IRR), net present value (NPV), and initial cash outlay. According to GreenWood, the investor's expected IRR was approximately 15 percent. The discount rate for NPV calculation was 10 percent.[15] The social and environmental due diligence analysis largely followed the FSC principles and criteria for forest management such as indigenous people's rights, community relations and workers' rights, compliance with laws and FSC principles, environmental impact, and so on, as described in Exhibit 2.

Both the Luxi and Dongji investments, if executed successfully, could achieve the investor's expected IRR, which was much higher than the approximate average return of 6 percent generated by timber investment in the United States. Moreover, it was anticipated that the investments would help improve the ecological environment in China and contribute to economic and social development in their respective local communities.

However, the two projects differed vastly in terms of physical locations, natural conditions, and partnership opportunities. The difference, as highlighted in GreenWood's detailed due diligence review, led to considerable discussion of the various pros and cons of the two projects.

Luxi Project[16]

Luxi County was located in Shandong, in east China. The county had fertile soil, sophisticated river and water irrigation networks, and other highly favorable natural conditions (ample sunlight, rain, and gentle slopes) for fast-growth, high-yield poplar plantations. Luxi had been making tremendous efforts in afforestation and sustainable economic development since 2002. A plan was executed to build a forestry park where tree plantation, landscaping, and tourism would be integrated to create an ecological system.

GreenWood explored investment opportunities in Luxi starting in late 2005. Since then, company personnel had visited Luxi many times surveying and analyzing tree farms and building *guanxi* (personal connections for mutual benefits)[17] with local government officials. The county government's support and coordination were critical for going forward with an investment since various local government agencies owned large parcels of poplar tree farms.

GreenWood was negotiating with the Luxi Forestry Bureau, a government agency with a mandate to implement government policies, regulate environmental construction, protect forest resources, and organize forestry development within Luxi County. Mr. Jiao, director of Luxi Forestry Bureau, indicated that he hoped GreenWood would help local farmers improve forestry management and facilitate local economic development by contributing capital and tree plantation know-how.

It was not, however, until December 2008 that GreenWood signed a nonbinding letter of intent (LOI) with the Luxi County government specifying the scope of the project. While commending GreenWood's meticulous style in dealing with the project, Jiao speculated that GreenWood's Portland headquarters had limited knowledge of the local situation and was not willing to delegate its responsibilities to the Beijing office. Consequently, the responses from GreenWood tended to be slow during the negotiation.

EXHIBIT 6 Relationships between GreenWood's Management and Investment Organizations

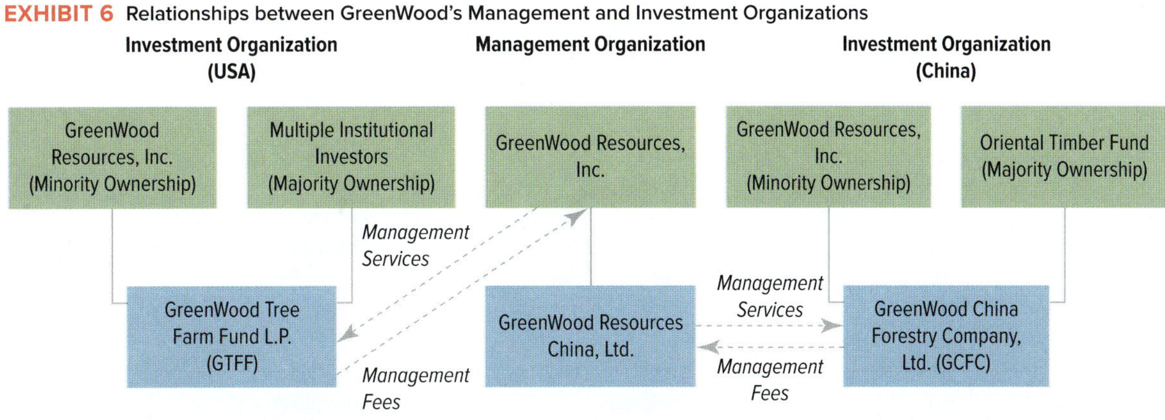

Source: GreenWood Internal Documents.

EXHIBIT 7 China Potential Investment Projects

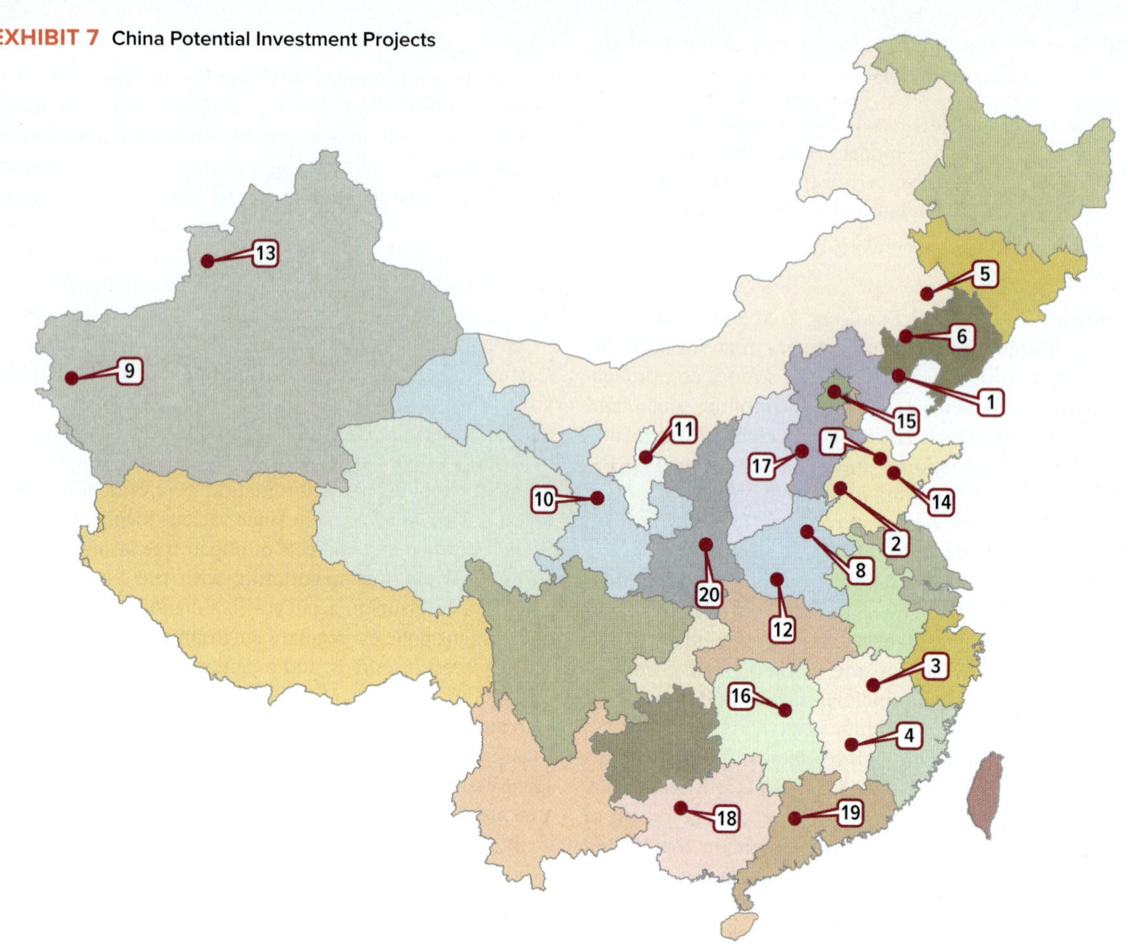

ID	Location	Province (area)
1	BSY	Hebei
2	**Luxi**	**Shandong**
3	Gengmin	Jiangxi
4	Zuheng	Jiangxi
5	**Dongji**	**Inner Mongolia**
6	Chaoyang	Liaoning
7	Dong Ying	Shandong
8	Kaifeng	Henan
9	Kashi	Xinjiang
10	Lanzhou	Gansu
11	Meili	NingXia
12	Nanyang	Henan
13	Yili	Xinjiang
14	Weifang	Shandong
15	Daxing	Beijing
16	AIC	Hunan
17	Jilin	Hebei
18	Nanning	Guangxi
19	Shaoguan	Guangdong
20	Zhongfu	Shaanxi

Source: GreenWood Internal Documents.

Jake Eaton agreed the process could have been faster. He pointed out that a major factor slowing down the negotiations was that GreenWood was often not talking to the real decision makers. Jessica Zhi, the Luxi project manager at GreenWood China, also mentioned the complexity of the Luxi project, in part because many local government bureaus were involved and at times leadership changes occurred.

If this project were selected, GreenWood planned to establish a wholly owned foreign enterprise in Luxi for acquiring and developing approximately 100,000 mu (6,667 hectares) of poplar tree plantations. The Luxi Forestry Bureau had been managing these tree plantations since 2002. It was expected to be a primary contractor for GreenWood, providing crop care activities at low labor costs and helping maintain the local relationships. The lease documents for the land were held by several government bureaus and were transferable. The land lease price was 300 to 400 renminbi (RMB), or US$43.90–58.60, per mu per year.[18] Typical lease length was 20 to 30 years, with some leases up to 70 years. GreenWood estimated that an investment of US$30–40 million was required in the first five years.

The high up-front fixed costs required by the Luxi project were a serious concern for the main investor, Oriental, as Jeff noted:

> If you look at the land (lease) pricing in China today, it would make more sense (for the investors) to buy (or lease) the land in another country (such as Australia, New Zealand, Poland and Romania).

As part of the negotiation process, the Luxi Forestry Bureau asked GreenWood to help set up a small wood-processing mill with an estimated investment of US$750,000. The mill, associated with high value-added activities, would provide employment opportunities to local residents. GreenWood, however, gave only a lukewarm response as the mill was not its essential business.

GreenWood planned to adopt a seven-year rotation strategy in Luxi (i.e., trees would be harvested at the age of seven for veneer log and pulpwood). It believed the locally tested GreenWood elite plant materials, coupled with favorable natural conditions and intensive management (e.g., site preparation, planting, spacing and thinning, weed and pest control, and fertilization) could readily enhance tree growth rate by 50 percent from 1.2 cubic meters (m^3) to 1.8m^3 per mu per year.

According to the data provided by the Luxi Forestry Bureau, GreenWood estimated the annual local timber demand within 100 kilometers (62 miles) of the project site was about 2.2 million m^3, which greatly exceeded the existing annual supply of 1 million m^3. As a result, local buyers looked to supplement their supply with imported timber. However, buyers found it increasingly difficult to depend on large volumes of imported timber because of high tariffs (e.g., for Russian logs) and high transportation costs required to bring logs into the area.

In addition to meeting the substantial demand in Luxi and its neighboring county, GreenWood was aiming at Linyi, a timber-processing hub and wood market about 300 kilometers (186.4 miles) from Luxi. There were about 2,600 mills in Linyi, and the largest 200 mills each needed more than 15,000 m^3 of timber annually. However, many of these mills were closing because their export-oriented businesses were seriously affected by the global financial crisis.

GreenWood tried to make an offer to the Luxi County government based on the local market prices of logs and its estimate of standing inventory volume. However, the county government argued that the assessment and subsequent offer would take unfair advantage of local entities and farmers, given the current economic meltdown in China due to the global financial crisis. Moreover, some government officials complained about GreenWood's slow pace in negotiating an agreement, which had resulted in the loss of seasonal planting and harvesting opportunities.

Dongji Project[19]

Dongji was located in the eastern part of the Inner Mongolia Autonomous Region in northeast China. The area suffered not only from a severe timber shortage but also from continued desertification. Although the area was semiarid and subject to windy weather all year, it was suitable for poplar cultivation due to its appropriate soil texture and access to the local river systems. The Dongji land was marginally fertile. It was estimated that the annual tree growth rate would not be much beyond 0.7 m^3 per mu even with GreenWood's elite plant materials and silvicultural management practices. One GreenWood analyst suggested that an annual rate of 0.9 m^3 per mu would be optimistic. Still, Dr. Stanton felt excited about the project because of the challenges it would bring to his research.

To combat desertification, the government of Dongji set up an ambitious goal of raising forest coverage from 22 to 30 percent from 2006 to 2010, resulting in a net increase of forestland by 10 million mu, of which 1.5 million mu was targeted for planting poplar trees.

Unlike the case in Luxi, private firms were essential in developing poplar tree plantations in Dongji. For example, Dongji Lideng Forestry Development Co., Ltd. (Lideng), a potential partner of GreenWood, held a 30-year lease on land totaling 126,600 mu planted with hybrid poplar, whereas 55 state-owned forest farms together had approximately 60,000 mu.

Lideng was a private forestry development company with activities in poplar plantation establishment, poplar nurseries, poplar stumpage, timber harvest rights transfer, and so on. To take advantage of the extensive land resources with large contiguous blocks and low land lease rates ranging from RMB15 to RMB25 per mu per year, the company planned to establish an additional 300,000 mu of poplar plantation within 3 to 5 years. This plan had already been approved by the State Forestry Administration, the central government agency for the forestry industry.

EXHIBIT 8 Estimated Investment Costs and Yields: Luxi versus Dongji[a]

	Total Existing Area[b] (mu)	Current Standing Inventory Volume (m^3)	Stumpage Price (2008) (weighted average, RMB/m^3)	Investment in Existing Plantation Assets (RMB)
Luxi	92,073	530,529	559	296,548,734
Dongji	202,650	225,391	445	100,298,995

	Land Lease and Related Expenses[c] (RMB/mu/year)	Crop Care Expenses (RMB/mu/year)	Planting Expenses (RMB/mu, 1st year)	Stumpage Volume at End of Each Rotation (m^3/mu)
Luxi	367	110	632	12.6 (year 7)
Dongji	87	45	255	7.0 (year 10)[d]

[a] 1 hectare = 15 mu; 1 U.S. dollar = 6.83 renminbi; the numbers are rounded.

[b] These total existing areas were used in GreenWood's investment feasibility reports.

[c] The related expenses include management fee, security fee, etc.

[d] The growth rate of 0.7 m^3 per mu per year for Dongji was deemed to be realistic, whereas the rate of 0.9 m^3 per mu per year was mentioned as an optimistic scenario.

Source: Adapted from GreenWood's investment feasibility reports.

Lideng had a trained professional poplar tree planting team equipped with a patented deep planting technique suited to the harsh environment of northern China. The planting technique and its accompanying machinery were the result of a 13-year forestry development research project, led by the United Nations Food and Agriculture Organization (FAO). The company had an annual planting capacity of 200,000 mu. Lideng also told GreenWood that it had the sole right to propagate commercially superior plant materials developed by the FAO project.

In response to GreenWood's interest in its poplar tree farm assets, Lideng offered 82,644 mu out of its existing total for GreenWood's purchase. The remaining 43,000-plus mu had already been bought by individual investors through a government-approved Dongji Stumpage Trading Center, in which Huang Jingbao, the CEO and president of Lideng, was a senior consultant.

GreenWood planned what it considered a prudent strategy for Dongji. First, it would focus on deploying local hybrid varietals while testing the suitability of its home-grown elite plant materials. Second, it would adopt a 10-year rotation scheme due to the low annual growth rate in Dongji. Third, it would capitalize on Lideng's expertise in planting and crop care activities.

In Dongji, timber was mainly consumed in the local market. A potential capacity of 2 million m^3 of annual wood consumption existed across 698 wood-processing mills. Though the local market experienced a limited impact from the economic meltdown, there was a concern that Russian timber could potentially flood the market due to Dongji's proximity to the Russian border. Moreover, the export market appeared to be relatively inaccessible for Dongji-based companies due to their inland locations.[20] Jeff and his senior management team also wondered whether there would be any reputational risks if GreenWood collaborated with Lideng. The latter had provided extensive silvicultural management services for Wanli Afforestation Group and Yilin Wood Industry Co., Ltd., the two large private forestry companies noted earlier that were currently under litigation for illegal fund-raising and the use of a pyramid scheme.

Huang believed Lideng and GreenWood would make a great partnership given the potential synergy between his company's local expertise and cost efficiency and GreenWood's sophisticated silvicultural management and leading poplar hybridization technology. However, he also believed his tree plantation assets had been undervalued by at least 20 percent based on GreenWood's assessment. Moreover, he had serious grievances with GreenWood's lengthy decision-making process. He considered dropping the deal if the negotiations continued to drag on for much longer.

What to Do?

Jeff and his senior management team knew expansion in China would help them achieve their vision of maximizing long-term returns for their investors and fulfilling the company's social and environmental responsibilities. They were also aware of potential business challenges as well as economic and political risks in an institutionally unique environment. After reading the two comprehensive due diligence reports, Jeff turned his attention to the financial data (see Exhibit 8) and a summarized assessment of economic, social, and environmental viability of the two

EXHIBIT 9 Assessment of Economic, Social, and Environmental Viability[a]

	Manager 1 (Beijing Office)[b]		Manager 2 (Beijing Office)		One Executive (Portland HQ)	
	Luxi	Dongji	Luxi	Dongji	Luxi	Dongji
Economic value	5	3–4	5	3	5	3
Social value	5	3–4	4	4	5	3
Environmental stewardship	1	5	3	5	3	5

[a] The scale is 1-5. (1 = very low potential value; 5 = very high potential value.)

[b] The manager pointed out that the ecological system had been considerably improved in Luxi in recent years. Thus, the potential value creation of environmental stewardship by GreenWood had declined.

Source: Interviews.

projects prepared by GreenWood staff (see Exhibit 9). Over a year had passed since the announcement of Oriental's capital commitment. Jeff understood that GreenWood needed to proceed with the investment with some sense of urgency, but he wanted to make sure that his team provided the best recommendations possible to the investment committee.

ENDNOTES

1. Light, L. (2009, May 6). "For Some, Sound of Profit Is 'Timber.'" *Wall Street Journal.*
2. See the company's website: www.greenwoodresources.com.
3. CH2M HILL provided a wide range of engineering and land development services including consulting, design, construction, procurement, operations and maintenance, and project management to federal, state, municipal, and local government entities as well as private industries in the U.S. and internationally.
4. Austin, J. and Reficco, E. (2006). Forest Stewardship Council. *Harvard Business School Case* (9-303-047).
5. A family office is a private company that manages investments and trusts for a single wealthy family.
6. Reporter (2009, May). "China to Fully Open Its Forestry Industry." *People's Daily* online, http://english.peopledaily.com.cn/200111/23/eng20011123_85194.html, accessed on May 14, 2009.
7. Greenfield investment is direct investment to build a new manufacturing, marketing, or administrative facility, as opposed to acquiring existing facilities.
8. The name of this investor was disguised as requested by GreenWood Resources, Inc.
9. GreenWood planned to recruit shareholders (i.e., equity owners) for its business expansion but ended up playing the role of investment (and assets) manager for large investors such as Oriental Timber Fund, Ltd.
10. Hsuan, A. (2009, Feb. 23). "See a Forest through the Trees." *The Oregonian.*
11. *Mu* is a common metric for land in China. 1 hectare = 15 mu, or 2.47 acres.
12. Interviews with GreenWood's two potential partners.
13. Although GreenWood China was responsible for the investigations, the parent company was supervising the relevant activities and controlling the process.
14. When business developers needed to lease a large piece of land for commercial purposes in China, they often tried to incentivize and/or at times coerce through the government agencies the current land users (e.g., farmers) to transfer their land lease contracts.
15. In the broadly defined forest industry, investors prefer long-term hold, good cash flows, and net value appreciation of tree assets resulting from biological growth. Tree plantation assets are also perceived as insurance against economic/financial crisis.
16. This section draws heavily upon Luxi Investment Feasibility Report by GreenWood Resources China, Ltd.
17. "Guanxi, as compared to social capital in the West, tends to be more personal and enduring, and involves more exchanges of favors. In general, relationships tend to precede business in China, whereas in the west it is usually the reverse, i.e., relationships follow as a result of the business." Tung, Worm, and Fang, 2008, *Organizational Dynamics,* 37(1): 69.
18. 1 U.S. dollar = 6.83 renminbi (the Chinese currency) in 2009; the land lease price does not include the price for the trees.
19. This section draws heavily upon Dongji Investment Feasibility Report by GreenWood Resources China, Ltd.
20. Interview with an industry expert on May 11, 2009.

APPENDIX 1

BACKGROUND—TIMBER INVESTMENTS AND TREE PLANTATION MANAGEMENT

Timber Investments

The United States had some of the most productive timberland (i.e., tree-growing land) in the world. Traditionally, timber investment was dominated by such large integrated forest product companies as Weyerhaeuser, International Paper Company, Plum Creek Timber Company, and James River Corporation, to name a few.

Since the mid-1990s, however, there had been a significant trend toward institutional ownership of timberlands. Institutional investors such as timber investment management organizations (TIMOs) and real estate investment trusts (REITs) purchased large tracts of land from the traditional forest product companies because of the potential to generate attractive long-term capital returns.[1] "Timber often is likened to high-grade bonds, meant to be held for 10 years or more. The average annual timber appreciation for the past decade was 4.1 percent versus minus 3.8 percent for the S&P-500 stock index."[2] Moreover, timber was not closely correlated with other asset classes. "Trees keep growing 4 percent per year, no matter what happens to inflation, interest rates or market trends."[3] In addition, potential federal and state tax benefits could be accrued from timber acquisitions.

Unfortunately, the downside of a timber investment was significant. It required a substantial amount of capital to be invested in a very illiquid asset with no quick payoff. For example, a minimum of $100,000 was required to participate in a TIMO.

Tree Plantations

U.S. commercial timberland was concentrated in the Northwest, Southeast, and Northeast regions of the country. The Northwest and Southeast were managed like farms, with landowners planting trees, allowing them to grow for a number of years, clear cutting the stand, and then planting again. Each cycle was a rotation. The Pacific Northwest contained 90 percent Western hemlock and Douglas fir with normal rotations of 45 to 60 years. In contrast, the Southeast United States was dominated by the Southern yellow pine species, with a typical rotation of 20 to 40 years. The Northeast United States had a diverse mix of trees, which were managed differently.

Plantation forests (as opposed to natural forests) were assuming a rapidly increasing role in commercial timber production. By 2005, the share of global timber production sourced from plantations was estimated as "approaching 50 percent." The largest plantation areas were located in Asia (China, India, and Japan), Europe (Russia, Scandinavia, and Eastern Europe), and the United States.[4]

The increasing importance of tree plantations was attributed to the fact that "less than half of the world's original forests remain, and ongoing deforestation is potentially devastating to the environment. Yet population growth and the increasing standard of living in many countries continue to drive the demand for timber products."[5]

High-yield, fast-growing tree farms lessen the pressure of deforestation by providing the type of timber products demanded by world markets. At the same time, tree farms are a sustainable environmental solution that can improve air and water quality, reclaim deforested land, and produce renewable energy in the form of biomass.[6]

Two popular, high-yield, and fast-growing tree species grown in plantation farms were eucalyptus and poplar. Eucalyptus was concentrated in tropical and subtropical regions of the world, while poplar was grown mainly in more temperate regions.

Hybrid Poplar Plantation Development[7]

Poplar was an important fiber resource for the global pulp and paper industry. In the United States, a number of prominent North American paper companies managed poplar plantations. Hybrid varieties, formed by crossing poplars, cottonwoods, and aspens, were among the first trees domesticated in North America by the pulp and paper industry. Several of these hybrid varieties were used to expand plantation development in the Pacific Northwest in the 1980s and 1990s.

As of 2009, hybrid poplars remained the best choice for hardwood plantation management for the manufacture of premium grades of communication papers throughout all of North America. There was also a growing trend to use hybrid poplars as a source for biomass feedstock for the emerging biofuels and composite-products industries and for hardwood lumber markets.

Key success factors for hybrid poplar plantations included (1) favorable natural site conditions (e.g., flat plain, river bottom), (2) elite plant materials (with high growth rate and strong pest resistance), and (3) sound silvicultural (forest cultivation) management, among others.[8]

Hybrid poplar plantations were tended throughout North America using cultivation methods that included mechanical and chemical methods of weed control, integrated pest management techniques, fertilization, and, in some cases, irrigation. Under competent management, hybrid poplar was the fastest-growing tree in the temperate zone.

APPENDIX ENDNOTES

1. Draffan, G. (2006, April). Notes on Institutional Ownership of Timber. www.endgame.org/timo.html, accessed on May 6, 2009.
2. Light, L. (2009, May 6). "For Some, Sound of Profit Is 'Timber.'" *Wall Street Journal.*
3. Ibid.
4. The Campbell Group. (2009, May 14). Global Supply. www.campbell-group.com/timberland/primer/global-supply.aspx, accessed on May 14, 2009.
5. GreenWood Resources, Inc., brochure.
6. Ibid.
7. This section draws heavily on an internal document of GreenWood Resources titled "Hybrid Poplar and the Pulp and Paper Industry in North America: Implications for a Secured Supply of Quality Fiber for Papermakers Worldwide."
8. *Silvicultural management* refers to integrated management of forestry, which includes land preparation, spacing and thinning, pruning, weed control, pest and disease control, fertilization, irrigation, and harvesting, among others.

CASE 9

KICKSTARTER AND CROWDFUNDING 2019*

In 2019, sixteen Kickstarter-funded films were heading to the SXSW Film Festival. Kickstarter had a record-breaking year for games and witnessed some changes in its management. Co-founder Perry Chen stepped down from his role as CEO, having taken over from co-founder, Yancey Strickler, only two years earlier. In March 2019, Aziz Hasan, the head of Kickstarter's design and product teams was made interim CEO.[1] While Chen had been at the helm, Kickstarter lost about 50 out of 120 Kickstarter employees. Among the departed were seven of the eight members of Strickler's executive team. [2] In interviews, employees said Chen strongly exerted his will on the company–making sudden changes to planned-out Kickstarter features, scrapping project timelines at the last minute, forcing out highly respected employees, and trying to shake up office culture in ways that struck the rank and file as simply bizarre.[3] Although Kickstarter is known to be Chen's brainchild, the future of the crowdfunding platform looks shaky with Chen's method of alienating and replacing the employees.

As a result of advancements in technology and worldwide adoption of media platforms, the concept of "crowdfunding" became a norm. According to Wharton School researcher Ethan Mollick, crowdfunding allowed "founders of for-profit, artistic, and cultural ventures to fund their efforts by drawing on relatively small contributions from a relatively large number of individuals using the Internet, without standard financial intermediaries."[4] It was considered "a novel method for funding a variety of new ventures," but it was not without its problems. Although billions of dollars had been raised for projects ranging from something as small as an artist's video diary to large endeavors, such as the development of a new product for accessing e-mail or an award-winning film documentary, very little was known about the kinds of mechanisms that made funding efforts successful or whether "existing projects ultimately deliver the products they promise."[5]

One example of this new phenomenon in entrepreneurship was the story of Kickstarter. As of March 2019, according to DigitalTrends.com, Kickstarter ranked first among the top 10 best crowdfunding sites, with over 159,246 successfully funded projects, over 15 million backers, and over $4 billion in pledged dollars; 340 projects had raised over $1 million each. Kickstarter also had a success rate of nearly 37 percent; however, 63 percent of the time the backers got nothing in return for their donations.[6] What was this crowdfunding thing all about, and was Kickstarter truly a boon for entrepreneurs, or a bust for backers?

"Kickstarter = Dumb people giving money to anonymous people in hope of some goodies in an unspecified amount of time."[7] So read a comment posted in response to a story about one nine-year-old girl's Kickstarter campaign. Mackenzie Wilson wanted to raise $829 so that she could go to computer camp and create her own video game. (She said her older brothers were making fun of her, and she wanted to prove that girls could do "tech stuff," too.) The trouble was that Kickstarter rules said someone had to be at least 18 years old in order to list a project, so Mackenzie's mom, Susan Wilson, created the information listing. Susan Wilson was a Harvard graduate, a known entrepreneur, and had allegedly promoted her daughter's Kickstarter campaign by tweeting celebrities like Lady Gaga and Ellen DeGeneres to elicit support.

Within 24 hours of the project launch, it not only had reached its $829 goal but was on its way to getting 1,247 backers and $22,562 in pledges.[8] Despite the success of a campaign that raised a lot of money, Wilson and her family received negative responses. The majority of the negative responses seemed to come from those who believed that Susan Wilson had misrepresented the nature of the project, that she had acted in bad faith–intending to profit from her daughter's story–and thereby had violated Kickstarter's project guidelines. It also received headlines because of the extreme public response–accusations of a scam and death threats against Wilson and her family.

Kickstarter clearly stated that its crowdfunding service could not be used for "charity or cause funding" such as an awareness campaign or scholarship; nor could a project be used to "fund my life"–for example, going on vacation, buying a new camera, or paying for tuition. And a project had to have a clear goal: "like making an album, a book, or a work of art. . . . A project is not open-ended. Starting a business, for example, does not qualify as a project." [9] In addition, for Kickstarter to maintain its reputation as one of the top crowdfunding services, it had to make sure it kept control of how the projects were promoted: "Sharing your project with friends, fans, and followers is one thing, but invading inboxes and social networks is another."[10]

* This case was prepared by graduate student Eric Engelson of Pace University, Professor Alan B. Eisner of Pace University, Professor Dan Baugher of Pace University, Associate Professor Pauline Assenza, Western Connecticut State University, and graduate student Sushmitha Mudda of Pace University. This case was solely based on library research and was developed for class discussion rather than to illustrate either effective or ineffective handling of an administrative situation. Copyright © 2019 Alan B. Eisner.

Kickstarter responded to comments on the Wilson project by affirming its support, saying, "Kickstarter is a funding platform for creative projects. The goal of this project is to create a video game, which backers are offered for a $10 pledge. On Kickstarter backers ultimately decide the validity and worthiness of a project by whether they decide to fund it."[11] However, backers and Kickstarter fans were concerned, with one user commenting, "It's all of our jobs to be on the lookout for shady Kickstarters and personally I don't want to see it devolve into a make-a-wish foundation for already privileged kids to learn how to sidestep rules of a website to profit."[12] And therein lies Kickstarter's dilemma—how to provide a service that allowed funding for obvious commercial ventures while also providing safeguards for backers.

Kickstarter remained a service business, collecting 5 percent of successfully funded projects as a fee for this service, and had kept itself hands-off otherwise. However, in addition to receiving comments such as the ones in response to the Wilsons' project, Kickstarter came under fire for providing no guarantees that funded projects would actually produce promised items or deliver on the project's goals. Kickstarter's three founders had to create a specific blog post titled "Kickstarter Is Not a Store"to remind backers that the ventures were *projects* and, as such, would be subject to delays, sometimes long ones, while in development.[13] Kickstarter made it clear that it was the project *creators*' responsibility to complete projects and that it would pull projects from its web pages if project promises were obviously unrealistic or violated copyright or patent law, but otherwise it gave no other protection to backers. And even if a project could not fully deliver, Kickstarter collected its fee. By keeping its business model as a fee-for-service commercial venture, was it in danger of losing its reputation and therefore its future business stream?

More competitors were entering the crowdfunding, crowd investing, or peer-to-peer lending space, partly because of the Jumpstart Our Business Startups (JOBS) Act passed by Congress in April 2012. The JOBS Act was designed to encourage small business and start-up funding by easing federal regulations, allowing individuals to become investors; and crowdfunding by the likes of Kickstarter was a "major catalyst in shifting the way small businesses" operated and found start-up capital.[14] Crowdsourcing had already changed the way businesses interacted with consumers; crowdfunding needed to figure out " how to build a community of supporters before, during, and after" a business launched.[15] But Kickstarter's founders seemed to believe "a big part of the value backers enjoy throughout the Kickstarter experience" was to get a closer look at the creative process as the project comes to life.[16] Kickstarter seemed to want to be a place where people could "participate in something," something they "held dear," and ultimately become a "cultural institution" that would outlive its founders.[17] Was that the vision of a commercial venture, or was it a wish to eventually become a not-for-profit legitimate cause-funding organization? What did Kickstarter want to be when it ultimately grew up?

The Kickstarter Business Model

By 2019, Kickstarter had become a popular middleman acting as a go-between, connecting the entrepreneur and the capital needed to turn an idea into a reality. The Kickstarter platform had launched on April 28, 2009, created by Perry Chen, Yancey Strickler, and Charles Adler, and was one of the first to introduce the new concept of crowdfunding: raising capital from the general public in small denominations. In a social media-filled world, an opportunity had been recognized—you could count on your peers to help you fund your big idea. Many creators, who were young, inexperienced, low on capital, or any combination of these, turned to websites such as Kickstarter for financial support for their projects. The site acted as a channel, enabling them to call on their friends, family, and other intrigued peers to help them raise money.

When establishing a listing on Kickstarter, the creator could place his or her project offering in one of 15 different categories: art, comics, crafts, dance, design, fashion, film & video, food, journalism, games, music, photography, publishing, technology, and theater. The project "owner" filled out some basic information, and the listing was on its way. However, certain standards had to be met before the listing could go live. If the project met those requirements, it was approved by the Kickstarter team and listed.

The guidelines were surprisingly basic and straightforward. First and foremost, the listing had to be for a project. As mentioned previously, it could not be for a charity or involve cause funding, nor could it be a "fund my life" kind of a project. The guidelines also disallowed prohibited content. Other than that, the project simply had to fit into one of the 15 designated categories. More recently, however, a few more cautious measures were added to ensure that only real and recognizable listings were created (see the section on rules and regulations later in this case). The project creator now had to set a deadline for the fund-raising, as well as a monetary goal, stating how much money he or she hoped to raise for the project. If that goal was met, the funds were then transferred to the project creator/owner. If the goal was not met, however, all donating parties were given refunds and the project was not funded. Additionally, the project owner could create rewards as incentives for different levels of donations, to be received by the donor if the project met its goal and was therefore funded. The more a donor pledged, the better the reward, which was usually related in some way to the project at hand, such as being the first backer to receive the finished product.

If the project succeeded in reaching its goal, payment was collected through Amazon. The project creator had to have an active Amazon Payments account when setting up his or her project. If a project was funded successfully, the money was transferred from the backers' credit cards to the creator's Amazon Payments account. If the project was not funded successfully, Amazon released the funds back to the backers' credit cards and no charges were issued; Kickstarter never actually possessed the funds at all. Once a project was funded successfully, Kickstarter took 5 percent of the total funds raised, while Amazon took around 3 to 5 percent for its services. [18] After both parties deducted their commissions, the project creator/owner could still expect a payout of about 90 percent of the total money that was raised. On January 6, 2015, Amazon decided to discontinue its payment service with Kickstarter. Kickstarter replaced Amazon with Stripe Payment, a service similar to PayPal.[19] For project creators, Stripe made it easier to collect the funds as it did not require setting up a separate account like Amazon did, and backers could check out faster using Stripe to pay directly via bank accounts or credit cards. It allowed Kickstarter to have a complete control on backers' checkout experience and access to raise funds anywhere in the world.

Kickstarter History

As previously mentioned, the company was launched in April 2009 by its three co-founders: Perry Chen, Yancey Strickler, and Charles Adler. Originally based in New York City, Kickstarter initially raised $10 million from Union Square Ventures and angel investors, including Jack Dorsey of Twitter, Zach Klein of Vimeo, Scott Heiferman of Meetup, and Caterina Fake of Flickr.[20] It all started with the hope of a musical success–a $20,000 late-night concert that Perry Chen was trying to organize at the 2002 New Orleans Jazz Fest. Chen had hopes of bringing a pair of DJs into town to perform. He had found a perfect venue for the concert and even gotten in touch with the DJs' management, yet the show never happened. The problem was the lack of capital, and, even if he had found willing backers, Chen had wondered what he would do if the show was unable to attract sufficient interest to pay back any investment.

This dilemma brought Chen to the realization that the world needed a better way to fund the arts. He thought to himself, "What if people could go to a site and pledge to buy tickets for a show? And if enough money was pledged they would be charged and the show would happen. If not, it wouldn't." [21] Although Chen loved this initial idea, he put it on the back burner, being more focused on making music and not on starting an Internet company. Three years later, in 2005, Chen moved back to New York and began to reconsider the potential for his business idea, but he was unsure how to go about building it. That fall, Chen met Yancey Strickler, the editor-in-chief of *eMusic*, through a mutual friend and approached him with the idea of Kickstarter. Strickler was intrigued, and the two began brainstorming. Then, about a year later, Chen was introduced to Charles Adler. Adler was also interested and began working with Chen and Strickler.[22] After months of work, the team had created specifications for an Internet site, yet one major problem remained–none of them knew HTML coding, so the project was put on hold. Adler moved to San Francisco to do some freelance work, and Strickler remained at his day job.

Finally, in the summer of 2008, Chen was introduced to Andy Baio, who joined the team remotely as an adviser, since he was living in Portland, Oregon, at the time. Soon after, Baio and Adler contacted some developers, including Lance Ivy in Walla Walla, Washington, and the site started to take shape. Although the team was scattered throughout the country, they were well connected through Skype and e-mail and finally began building the web portal. By April 28, 2009, Kickstarter had been created and was launched to the public. The idea for creating a new channel for artistic entrepreneurs of all kinds to explore their creativity was finally realized.[23]

Crowdfunding Competition

Although Kickstarter had become a well-known name in crowdfunding, many other companies had had the same idea. Not all of them had attracted as much media attention, but this meant that they had also avoided some of the negative press. Being a market follower rather than leader gave Kickstarter a prime opportunity to maintain a clean track record with the media because the company was able to avoid the mistakes made by other similar businesses.

One of the better-known Kickstarter competitors was Indiegogo, founded in January 2008 in San Francisco. Indiegogo was initially funded with $1.5 million from investors such as Zynga co-founder Steve Schoettler. By June 2012, the company had attracted over 100,000 projects from 196 countries. Aiming to "make an even bigger impact," in 2012 Indiegogo raised an additional $15 million in a "Series A" private equity stock offering.[24] CEO Slava Rubin said that the money was needed mostly to hire, build out, and increase resources to take on other crowdsourcing competitors such as Kickstarter. However, while Kickstarter focused on individuals' creative projects, Indiegogo was much more business-oriented. Projects on Indiegogo were not regulated as they were on Kickstarter. Indiegogo used an algorithm that decided which projects to promote on the basis of activity and engagement metrics like funding velocity.[25]

Additionally, Indiegogo projects followed the "keep it all" model–all funds collected were handed over to the project creator, regardless of any goal achievement. If the project fund-raising goal was never met, or the project's objectives were never achieved, it was up to the project creator to refund collected funds to the contributors. Indiegogo was also available for use internationally, while Kickstarter required backers to have either a U.S. or UK bank account.[26]

Other online crowdfunding companies, which raised funds for either charitable or creative projects, included ArtistShare for musicians[27] and Fundly for charitable projects and political campaigns. Meg Whitman used Fundly to raise $20 million for her 2010 campaign for governor of

California.[28] Illustrating the degree of competition, ArtistShare and Kickstarter had been in a patent dispute since 2011 over ownership of the "methods and apparatuses for financing and marketing a creative work," with ArtistShare claiming Kickstarter infringement.[29] Meanwhile, similar companies that created some buzz in the area of business investment were Crowdfunder and Grow VC. While only in start-up mode, Crowdfunder had made enough noise to grab some attention. This platform enabled funders to participate in three different ways: they could simply donate to a project, lend to a project and receive a return, or purchase equity. However, the third option–purchasing equity through crowdfunding–was still not allowed in the United States as of 2013.[30]

Grow VC, similar to Kickstarter, made funds accessible to the company or entrepreneur only when the goal had been reached. One important difference between the two was that Grow VC enabled companies to collect monthly installments from investors, allowing a growing business to collect a continuous influx of funds rather than just a one-time investment. The cap for funding was set at $1 million.[31] Other recognizable competitors were Rockethub, EarlyShares, and Bolstr in the United States; CrowdCube in the United Kingdom; and Symbid, based in the Netherlands. These were only a few of the more publicized newcomers to the industry–there were at least 50 legitimate crowdfunding platforms operating worldwide.[32]

Kickstarter Successes

By March 2019, Kickstarter had launched 437,085 projects, raising $4.16 billion, of which $3.70 billion was successfully collected by project owners, $429 million was unsuccessful, and $39 million was currently in "live" donation status on the site.[33] On February 8, 2012, the first project to ever get a million dollars funded from the site was a project in the design category, an iPod dock created by ElevationLab. Its goal was set at $75,000, and backers reached this goal almost instantly, raising a total of $1,464,706. However, as impressive as this feat was, its top-funding status was short-lived. Six hours later, in the game category, Double Fine beat that goal–receiving $3,336,371 to fund its new adventure game, far exceeding the initial request for $400,000.[34] On March 27, 2015, a California-based smartwatch company, Pebble Time, ran a record-breaking Kickstarter campaign by raising a total of $20,338,986.[35] The initial goal was to raise $500,000 yet Pebble Time was able to raise the first million dollars in less than an hour. Pebble Time was founded in 2012, and since then the company had been working to perfect its smartwatch that offered battery time of about 10 days and more than 6,500 applications via an open platform app store. However, one of the pioneers in the fitness tracker and smartwatch industry, Fitbit, acquired the intellectual property and hired key personnel from Pebble Technology Corp. in December 2016.

Other notable projects with over $1 million in funding included the TikTok and LunaTik multitouch watch kits and the Coolest Cooler in the design category; the OUYA TV console and Project Eternity in the games category; the FORM1 3-D printer and the Oculus Rift virtual reality headset in the technology category; and a new Amanda Palmer record, art book, and tour in the music category. Gustin premium menswear and Ministry of Supply men's dress shirts, in the fashion category, were notably successful offerings with over $400,000 in pledges.[36] In the movie category, in 2013, *Inocente* became the first Kickstarter crowdfunded film to win an Oscar-for Best Documentary (Short Subject)[37] and Kickstarter backers donated over $2 million in 12 hours to fund a movie based on the popular *Veronica Mars* franchise.[38] Kickstarter was becoming a source of major support for independent films. According to the company, as of 2013 it had facilitated over $100 million in donations to various "indie" films and had funded 10 percent of all the films shown at the 2013 Sundance Film Festival.[39]

These projects made contributions to Kickstarter's business model. Even with an office in New York City, large amounts of capital raised, and about 125 employees, Kickstarter had to have been profitable. Based on the 2018 statistics, Kickstarter took a 5 percent cut from the total money that was funded on the website.

Kickstarter Failures

However, as in all sectors of capital investment, some Kickstarter projects did not work out as planned. In the world of start-ups, many venture capitalists or angel investors made investments in projects that were inherently risky. Some were lucky and achieved their intended goals or did even better. Others fell short. There were many possible reasons for the failures, including lack of industry knowledge, unrealistic projections of cost, lack of managerial experience, manufacturing capabilities, or simply a lack of competence for the task at hand. These possibilities existed for Kickstarter projects as well, but in the Kickstarter model, investors/backers/donators did not "own" anything; project creators kept ownership of their work. As Kickstarter pointed out, "Backers are supporting projects to help them come to life, not to profit financially. "[40]

This disclaimer did not stop backers or the media from highlighting Kickstarter's risks. Eyez was one of the better-known project failures on Kickstarter. More than 2,000 backers collectively contributed more than $300,000 to the entrepreneurs developing the high-tech glasses, meant for recording live video. Eyez's product creators promised delivery of the glasses ahead of the fall 2011 goal, yet by 2013 Eyez glasses still were not being produced and none of the individual backers had received a pair. Meanwhile, the entrepreneurs had stopped providing online updates on the project and would not answer questions from backers.[41] Another prominent failed project was the Skarp campaign in 2015, which raised about $4 million. The project promised to develop and offer a razor that used a laser beam instead of a traditional blade. The Skarp campaign also showed a video demonstrating the procedure of laser razor to cut hair. However, in reality the prototype of the laser razor was far from a properly functioning product.[42] Others, such as the group behind MYTHIC, a nonexistent game from an imaginary team, continued to try to scam the crowdfunding scene.[43]

A major challenge to Kickstarter's business model was related to intellectual property rights. It was probable that anyone with a good idea trying to raise capital through Kickstarter would discover that his or her idea was already stolen by merchants in China. Yekutiel Sherman, an Israeli entrepreneur, spent years developing an innovative smartphone case that unfolded into a selfie stick. In December 2015, Sherman started a Kickstarter campaign, hoping to raise funds to capitalize on the new product. A week later, Sherman found that his designed selfie stick was already on sale by vendors across China. People around the world could buy the new selfie stick using online sites including eBay.

Ongoing Issues—Backers' Concerns and Rules and Regulations

Despite the success Kickstarter had achieved, the company was under fire for many things, particularly regarding false projects, the collection of funds with no end product, and the failure of backers to receive the stated rewards set by project creators. Kickstarter followed the "all or nothing" approach to funding—pledged dollars were collected only if the fund-raising goal was met. In the beginning, Kickstarter tried to explain that the company had no control over the donated funds once these funds were in the hands of the developer—there was no guarantee of product or project "delivery." Additionally, if the fund-raising goal was met but the project never made it to fruition, Kickstarter had no ability to issue refunds. These explanations did not keep backers from complaining of "delays, deception, and broken promises."[44]

In 2012, the Kickstarter founders felt it was necessary to reiterate "Kickstarter Is Not a Store" and point out, yet again, that "in addition to rewards, a big part of the value backers enjoy throughout the Kickstarter experience is getting a closer look at the creative process as the project comes to life."[45] Kickstarter then implemented a new set of rules, designed to prevent creators from promising a product they could not deliver. The goal, Kickstarter said, was to help prevent entrepreneurs from overpromising and disappointing backers by not delivering. By forcing creators to be transparent about their progress, Kickstarter hoped to discourage unrealistic projects and encourage the participation of more creative individuals who had the skills to ship products as promised.

These new rules required Kickstarter's project creators to list all potential problems involved in seeing their projects through to completion; to submit proper supporting materials—no simulations or "renderings," just technical drawings or photos of the actual current prototype; and to create a "reasonable" reward system in which backers received a reward based on their level of participation, which in most cases included a working version of the project in question. Kickstarter prohibited the use of multiple quantities at any reward level: Kickstarter was not a store, but an opportunity to invest in good ideas. The company also included the use of investors' funds in the project creator agreement. The regulations stated that if funds were collected, the creator was required to use those funds toward the creation of the project. If the funds were used for any other purpose, legal repercussions would follow.[46] In 2013 Kickstarter did a "major overhaul" on the set of tools project creators used to communicate with backers, including a "rewards sent" checklist, a tool to survey backers regarding rewards, and a project " dashboard" so that creators could track their progress.[47]

Even if Kickstarter was able to sustain its success with the implementation of tougher approval policies on its end, the future of the size and success of projects was also to be determined by the government and its ability to police the crowdfunding world through its own set of regulations. Recent federal legislation showed the government's intentions to do just that.

The JOBS Act

Signed into law in April 2012 by President Obama, the Jumpstart Our Business Startups (JOBS) Act supported entrepreneurship and the growth of small businesses in the United States and emphasized the new phenomenon of crowdfunding. The act eased federal regulations in regard to crowdfunding by allowing individuals to become investors in new business efforts. However, it also set out specific provisions to regulate just how much funding was acceptable, in order to ensure the financial safety and security of the investors. The new act stated that, as of January 2013, an equity-based company could raise no more than $1 million a year. Additionally, a company could sell to investors only through a middleman—a broker or website that was registered with the Securities and Exchange Commission (SEC). The middleman could sell only shares that had originated from the company.

The JOBS Act did not yet apply to Kickstarter, because there were no equity sales under its current business model—on its platform, the project creator maintained 100 percent ownership of the product or service.[48] With no cap to investments and minimal federal regulations, people could be more inclined to contribute to a Kickstarter project than invest in projects from an equity investment-based competitor.

The Future for Kickstarter

During the early days of Kickstarter, Perry Chen, the co-founder and person responsible for the idea behind Kickstarter, spoke about Kickstarter's optimistic future. Chen talked about funding business start-ups and stated that Kickstarter was not interested in that model: "We're going to keep funding creative projects in the way we currently do it. We're not gearing up for the equity wave if it comes. The real disruption is doing it without equity."[49]

In March 2019, Perry Chen stepped down from his role as CEO after two years and Aziz Hasan, the head of Kickstarter's design and product teams was made interim CEO. Chen only planned to return as CEO for six months to help with the transition in leadership. In a blog post on the company website, Chen wrote, "Those months quickly became two years dedicated to developing a better way to deliver on the core aspects of our service through a robust operating system, a strong product, and the team we have assembled at Kickstarter today."[50]

Chen's decision to resign followed the company staff's announcement to unionize with the Office and Professional Employees International Union (OPEIU) Local 153. Kickstarter staff said they were forming a union to promote "inclusion and solidarity, transparency and accountability," and gain "a seat at the table."[51] In April 2018, BuzzFeed News reported that the company was in turmoil under Chen's leadership. At the time of BuzzFeed's reporting, nearly 50 of the company's 120 staff had reportedly left, including seven out of eight members of the company's executive team.[52]

In April 2019, Kickstarter partnered with Kodansha, one of Japan's leading publishers, to support creators in Japan. Through the partnership, Kickstarter aims to provide Kodansha's team with the tools, knowledge, and resources to help creators in Japan bring projects to life on the Kickstarter platform.[53] The company also celebrated as backers had pledged more than $1 billion to Games projects on Kickstarter. Since launching in 2009, the Games category has grown steadily, helping titles like The Banner Saga, Exploding Kittens, Darkest Dungeon, Kingdom Death, Shovel Knight, and many more.[54]

Although its funded projects are heading to good places, what is Kickstarter heading toward? With disruptions from inside the company and outside, would it be able to optimize its business model for better? While it seemed to have a clear mission and was certainly profitable, as Wharton School researcher Mollick warned, "Crowdfunding represents a potentially disruptive change in the way that new ventures are funded."[55] Going forward, the Kickstarter founders needed to consider whether they had the right business model for the future.

ENDNOTES

1. Goggin, Benjamin. 2019. CEO and co-founder of crowdfunding giant Kickstarter resigns amid staff unionization effort. *Business Insider*, March 19, https://www.businessinsider.com/kickstarter-perry-chen-resigns-as-ceo-co-founder-2019-3.
2. Alba, Davey. 2018. Perry Chen says he wants to revitalize Kickstarter, employees say he's doing the opposite. BuzzFeed, April 17. https://www.buzzfeednews.com/article/daveyalba/kickstarter-perry-chen-founder-worship-turmoil.
3. Ibid.
4. Mollick, E. R. 2013. The dynamics of crowdfunding: Determinants of success and failure. University of Pennsylvania Wharton School, March 25, http://ssrn.com/abstract52088298 or http://dx.doi.org/10.2139/ssrn.2088298; from the abstract.
5. Ibid, p. 1.
6. From www.kickstarter.com/help/stats.
7. Reader comment by Devlin1776, attached to news story: Bindley, K. 2013. 9-year-old's $20,000 Kickstarter campaign draws scam accusations. *Huffington Post,* March 26, www.huffingtonpost.com/2013/03/26/9-year-old-kickstarter-campaign_n_2949294.html#slide51240691.
8. See the full Kickstarter project listing, plus current status, and both backer and general comments at www.kickstarter.com/projects/susanwilson/9-year-old-building-an-rpg-to-prove-her-brothers-w.
9. See Kickstarter funding guidelines at www.kickstarter.com/help/guidelines. See also comments on the Wilson project as a scam: Multi-millionaire scams Kickstarter for over $22,000 - sending daughter to game dev camp, http://imgur.com/zwyRWCa.
10. Ibid.
11. Bindley, K. 2013. 9-year-old's $20,000 Kickstarter campaign draws scam accusations. *Huffington Post,* March 26, www.huffingtonpost.com/2013/03/26/9-year-old-kickstarter-campaign_n_2949294.html#slide51240691.
12. Ibid.
13. See Chen, P., Strickler, Y., & Adler, C. 2012. Kickstarter is not a store. September 20, www.kickstarter.com/blog/kickstarter-is-not-a-store.
14. Farrell, J. 2012. The JOBS Act: What startups and small businesses need to know. *Forbes,* September 9, www.forbes.com/sites/work-in-progress/2012/09/21/the-jobs-act-what-startups-and-small-businesses-need-to-know-infographic/.
15. Ibid.
16. An, J. 2013. Dude, where's my Kickstarter stuff? Dealing with delays, deception and broken promises. *Digital Trends,* March 20, www.digitaltrends.com/social-media/dude-wheres-my-kickstarter-stuff/#ixzz2OmMqQ4dq.
17. From Strickler, Y. 2013. Talk given at Expand Engadget Conference, March 16, www.youtube.com/watch?v5thlaPwpobMk. Also see the conversation liveblog at www.engadget.com/2013/03/16/kickstarter-yancey-strickler-expand-liveblog/; and the interview with Myriam Joire, Engadget editor, linked at the *Huffington Post* story at www.huffingtonpost.com/2013/03/26/9-year-old-kickstarter-campaign_n_2949294.html#slide51240691.
18. Hess, K. 2013. Despite its popularity, I hate Kickstarter. *ZDnet,* November 22, https://www.zdnet.com/article/despite-its-popularity-i-hate-kickstarter/.
19. The Kickstarter Blog. 2015. Making payments easier for creators and backers. Jan 6, https://www.kickstarter.com/blog/making-payments-easier-for-creators-and-backers.
20. Kafka, P. 2011. Kickstarter fesses up: The crowdsourcing funding start-up has funding, too. *All Things* D, March 17, allthingsd.com/20110317/kickstarter-fesses-up-the-crowd-sourced-funding-startup-has-funding-too/.
21. See Kickstarter Pressroom at www.kickstarter.com/press.
22. Ibid.
23. Ibid.
24. Taylor, C. 2012. Indiegogo raises $15 million series A to make crowdfunding go mainstream. *TechCrunch.com,* June 6, techcrunch.com/2012/06/06/indiegogo-funding-15-million-crowdfunding/.
25. Jeffries, A. 2012. Kickstarter competitor Indiegogo raises $15M, staffing up in New York. *Observer,* June 6, observer.com/2012/06/kickstarter-competitor-indiegogo-raises-15-m-staffing-up-in-new-york/.
26. Taylor, C. 2011. Indiegogo wants to give Kickstarter a run for its money. *Gigaom.com,* August 5, gigaom.com/2011/08/05/indiegogo/.
27. See the *Wikipedia* entry at en.wikipedia.org/wiki/ArtistShare.
28. See the *Wikipedia* entry at en.wikipedia.org/wiki/Fundly.

29. Jeffries, A. 2012. Kickstarter wins small victory in patent lawsuit with 2000-era crowdfunding site. *BetaBeat,* May 14, betabeat.com/2012/05/kickstarter-artistshare-fan-funded-patent-lawsuit/.
30. See Crowdfunder: How it works, www.crowdfunder.com/how-it-works#a-1.
31. See Loikkanen, V. 2011. What is Grow VC? *GrowVC.com,* September 8, www.growvc.com/help/2011/09/08/what-is-grow-vc/.
32. See the list of crowdfunding services as of April 1, 2013, on *Wikipedia* at en.wikipedia.org/wiki/Comparison_of_crowd_funding_services; see also Fiegerman, S. 2012. 8 Kickstarter alternatives you should know about. *Mashable.com,* December 6, mashable.com/2012/12/06/kickstarter-alternatives/.
33. See current Kickstarter stats at www.kickstarter.com/help/stats.
34. See Strickler, Y. 2012. The history of #1. *Kickstarter Blog,* April 18, www.kickstarter.com/blog/the-history-of-1-0.
35. Etherington, D. 2015.Pebble Time's $20M Kickstarter Campaign By The Numbers. *TechCrunch.* March 29, https://techcrunch.com/2015/03/29/pebble-times-20m-kickstarter-campaign-by-the-numbers/
36. See "The most funded projects in Kickstarter history (since 2009!)," www.kickstarter.com/discover/most-funded.
37. Watercutter, A. 2013. The first Kickstarter film to win an Oscar takes home crowdsourced gold. *Wired,* February 15, www.wired.com/underwire/2013/02/kickstarter-first-oscar/.
38. McMillan, G. 2013. *Veronica Mars.* Kickstarter breaks records, raises over $2M in 12 hours. *Wired,* March 14, www.wired.com/underwire/2013/03/veronica-mars-kickstarter-record/.
39. Watercutter. 2013. The first Kickstarter film to win an Oscar takes home crowdsourced gold. *Wired,* February 15, www.wired.com/underwire/2013/02/kickstarter-first-oscar/.
40. See, what is Kickstarter? www.kickstarter.com/hello.
41. Krantz, M. 2012. Crowd-funding dark side: Sometimes investments go down drain. *USA Today,* August 14, usatoday30.usatoday.com/money/markets/story/2012-08-14/crowd-funding-raising-money/57058678/1.
42. Bershidsky, L. 2015. Failed inventions aren't scams. *Bloomberg,* October 15, https://www.bloomberg.com/view/articles/2015-10-15/failed-inventions-aren-t-scams.
43. Koetsler, J. 2012. Kickstarter dodges responsibility for failed projects. *Venture Beat,* September 4, venturebeat.com/2012/09/04/kickstarter-co-founder-failed-projects/.
44. An, J. 2013. Dude, where's my Kickstarter stuff? Dealing with delays, deception and broken promises. *Digital Trends,* March 20, www.digitaltrends.com/social-media/dude-wheres-my-kickstarter-stuff/#ixzz2OmMqQ4dq.
45. Ibid.
46. Boris, C. 2012. Kickstarter's new rules for entrepreneurs. *Entrepreneur,* September 28, www.entrepreneur.com/blog/224524.
47. See Better tools for project creators, www.kickstarter.com/blog/better-tools-for-project-creators.
48. Farrell. 2012. The JOBS Act: What startups and small businesses need to know. *Forbes,* September 9, www.forbes.com/sites/work-in-progress/2012/09/21/the-jobs-act-what-startups-and-small-businesses-need-to-know-infographic/.
49. Malik, O. 2012. Kickstarted: My conversation with Kickstarter co-founder Perry Chen. *Gigaom.com,* May 22, gigaom.com/2012/05/22/kickstarter-founder-perry-chen-intervie/#3.
50. Heater, B. 2019. Kickstarter CEO Perry Chen Steps Down. TechCrunch, March, https://techcrunch.com/2019/03/19/kickstarter-ceo-perry-chen-steps-down/.
51. Stephen, B. 2019. Kickstarter's CEO, Perry Chen, is resigning. The Verge, March 19, https://www.theverge.com/2019/3/19/18273318/kickstarter-ceo-resigning-perry-chen-chairman-board.
52. Goggin, B. 2019. CEO and co-founder of crowdfunding giant Kickstarter resigns amid staff unionization effort. *Business Insider,* March 19, https://www.businessinsider.com/kickstarter-perry-chen-resigns-as-ceo-co-founder-2019-3.
53. Kickstarter partners with Kodansha to support creators in Japan. Kickstarter, Company Blog, April 2019, https://www.kickstarter.com/blog/kickstarter-partners-with-kodansha-to-support-creators-in-japan.
54. $1 Billion (and Counting) pledged to games. Kickstarter, Company Blog, April 2019, https://www.kickstarter.com/blog/1-billion-and-counting-pledged-to-games.
55. Mollick, E. R. 2013. The dynamics of crowdfunding: Determinants of success and failure. University of Pennsylvania Wharton School, March 25, http://ssrn.com/abstract52088298 or http://dx.doi.org/10.2139/ssrn.2088298; from the abstract.

CASE 10

QVC IN 2019*

On April 1, 2019, QVC rebranded Beauty iQ, a female-oriented television channel as QVC3, airing rebroadcasts of previously recorded QVC and QVC2 programming 24 hours a day.[1] Since it was launched in 1986, QVC has rapidly grown to become the largest retail operation that uses broadcast networks, Internet websites, and mobile apps. Although it entered the market a couple of years after Home Shopping Network (HSN), the channel has managed to build a leading position. By 2018, its reach had extended to over 400 million households all over the world. It regularly features about 773 products on its sites each week, leading to over $9 million in sales (see Exhibit 1 and 2). Besides the United States, its presence has grown to the UK, Germany, France, Italy, Japan, and through a 49 percent interest to a joint venture in China (see Exhibit 3).[2]

The success of QVC is largely driven by its popular television home shopping shows that feature a wide variety of eye-catching products, many of which are unique to the channel. It organizes product searches in cities all over the United States in order to continuously find new offerings from entrepreneurs that can be pitched at customers. During these events, the firm has to screen hundreds of products in order to select those that it will offer. In one of its recent searches, QVC had to evaluate the appeal of products such as nail clippers that catch clippings, bicycle seats built for bigger bottoms, and novelty items shaped like coffins.

But QVC is also trying to entice new customers by battling a perception that direct-response TV retailers sell just hokey, flimsy, or kitschy goods. It has expanded its offerings in home, beauty, and apparel, reducing its sales of jewelry (see Exhibit 4). It has offered clothing from couture designers such as Marc Bouwer, who has made clothing for Angelina Jolie and Halle Berry. And it has recently added exclusive products from reality stars such as Kim Kardashian and Rachel Zoe. Such vendors have introduced thousands to QVC, often through social media like Facebook and Twitter. "Rachel Zoe brings so many new customers it's staggering," said CEO Michael George.[3]

In 2015, QVC expanded its offerings by acquiring the online retailer Zulily for $2.4 billion. Operated as a subsidiary, Zulily's target audience is mothers who have an interest in unique brands and products for their children. This audience has been described as "young, tech-savvy mothers." A majority of the firm's orders typically come from mobile devices. Although Zulily has managed to generate over $400 million in revenues, it is struggling to attain profitability. QVC has been relying on Zulily to develop a different customer base.

Furthermore, QVC has expanded its shopping experience to the Internet, attracting several million unique monthly visitors to its website. It has continued to direct customers from its television channel to its website, making it one of the leading multimedia retailers. Building on this, the firm has been creating a family of mobile shopping applications for smartphones and tablets. Although QVC is still developing this segment, mobile applications are already accounting for over a third of its sales.

Pursuing a Leading Position

QVC was founded by Joseph Segel in June 1986 and began broadcasting by November of the same year.

EXHIBIT 1 Annual Sales–QVC U.S. and International ($ billions)

2018	$9.1
2017	8.8
2016	8.7
2015	8.7
2014	8.8
2013	8.6
2012	8.5
2011	8.3
2010	7.8
2007	7.4
2004	5.7
2001	3.8
1998	2.4
1995	1.6
1992	0.9
1989	0.2

Source: QVC Inc. Annual Reports.

* Case prepared by Jamal Shamsie, Michigan State University, with the assistance of Professor Alan B. Eisner, Pace University. Material has been drawn from published sources to be used for purposes of class discussion. Copyright © 2019 Jamal Shamsie and Alan B. Eisner.

EXHIBIT 2 Consolidated Statement of Operations ($ millions)

	Year Ended December 31,			
	2018	2017	2016	2015
Net revenue	$11,282	8,771	8,682	8,743
Cost of goods sold	7,248	5,598	5,540	5,528
Gross profit	4,034	3,173	3,142	3,215
Operating expenses:				
Operating	881	601	606	607
Selling, general and administrative, including stock-based compensation	1,230	744	728	745
Depreciation	174	155	142	134
Amortization	237	364	463	454
	2,522	1,864	1,939	1,940
Operating income	1,512	1,309	1,203	1,275
Other (expense) income:				
Equity in losses of investee	(3)	(3)	(6)	(9)
Gains on financial instruments	(2)	—	2	—
Interest expense, net	(243)	(214)	(210)	(208)
Foreign currency gain	—	(6)	38	14
Loss on extinguishment of debt	(2)	—	—	(21)
	(250)	(223)	(176)	(224)
Income before income taxes	1,262	1,086	1,027	1,051
Income tax expense	(334)	(139)	(385)	(389)
Net income	928	947	642	662
Less net income attributable to the noncontrolling interest	(46)	(46)	(38)	(34)
Net income attributable to QVC, Inc. stockholder	882	910	604	628

Source: QVC Inc. Annual Reports.

EXHIBIT 3 Geographic Breakdown of Revenue ($ millions)

	Year Ended December 31,			
	2018	2017	2016	2015
United States	$ 8,544	6,140	$6,120	6,257
Japan	947	934	897	808
Germany	943	899	865	837
United Kingdom	679	640	654	718
Other countries	169	158	146	123
Consolidated QVC	11,282	8,771	8,682	8,743

Source: QVC Inc. Annual Reports.

EXHIBIT 4 Breakdown of Revenue by Product Category 2018 ($ million)

	QVC–U.S.	QVC–International	HSN
Home	2,265	1,023	910
Beauty	1,04	640	286
Apparel	1,14	453	183
Accessories	772	273	161
Electronics	674	119	455
Jewelry	324	213	149
Other revenue	134	17	58
Total net revenue	**6,349**	**2,738**	**2,202**

Source: QVC Inc. Annual Reports.

In early 1986, Segel had tuned into to the Home Shopping Network, which had been launched just two years earlier. He had not been particularly impressed with the crude programming and the down-market products of the firm. But Segel was convinced that another televised shopping network would have the potential to attract a large enough client base. He also felt that such an enterprise should be able to produce significant profits, because the operating expenses for a shopping network could be kept relatively low.

Over the next few months, Segel raised $30 million in start-up capital, hired several seasoned television executives, and launched his own shopping network. Operating out of headquarters that were located in West Chester, Pennsylvania, QVC offered 24-hour-a-day, seven-day-a-week television home shopping to consumers at home. By the end of its first year of operation, QVC had managed to extend its reach to 13 million homes by satellite and cable systems; 700,000 viewers had already become customers, resulting in the shipping of 3 million orders. Its sales had already topped $100 million and the firm was actually able to show a small profit.

Segel attributed the instant success of his company to the potential offered by television shopping. "Television's combination of sight, sound, and motion is the best way to sell a product. It is more effective than presenting a product in print or just putting the product on a store shelf," he stated. "The cost-efficiency comes from the cable distribution system. It is far more economical than direct mail, print advertising, or traditional retail store distribution."[4]

In the fall of 1988, Segel acquired the manufacturing facilities, proprietary technology, and trademark rights of the Diamonique Corporation, which produced a wide range of simulated gemstones and jewelry that could be sold on the QVC's shows. Over the next couple of years, Segel expanded QVC by acquiring its competitors such as the Cable Value Network Shopping channel.

By 1993, QVC had overtaken Home Shopping Network to become the leading televised shopping channel in terms of sales and profits. Its reach extended to over 80 percent of all cable homes and to 3 million satellite dishes. Segel retired during the same year, passing control of the company to Barry Diller. Since then, QVC's sales have continued to grow at a substantial rate. As a result, it has consistently widened the gap between its sales and those of Home Shopping Network, which had remained its closest competitor until 2018, when QVC's parent company Qurate Retail completed the acquisition of HSN and transferred the ownership to QVC (see Exhibit 5).

Striving for Retailing Excellence

Over the years, QVC had managed to establish itself as the world's preeminent virtual shopping mall that never closes. Its televised shopping channel has become a place where customers around the world can and do shop at any hour, at the rate of more than five customers per second. It sold a wide variety of products, using a combination of description and demonstration by live program hosts. QVC is extremely selective in choosing its hosts, screening as many as 3,000 applicants annually in order to pick three. New hosts are trained for at least six months before they are allowed to appear on a show. In addition, most of the products are offered on regularly scheduled shows, each of which is focused on a particular type of product and a well-defined market. Each of these shows typically lasts for one hour and is based on a theme such as Now You're Cooking or Cleaning Solutions.

QVC frequently entices celebrities such as clothing designers or book authors to appear live on special program segments in order to sell their own products. In order to prepare them to succeed, celebrities are given training on how to best pitch their offerings. On some occasions, customers are able to call in and have on-air conversations with

EXHIBIT 5 QVC Milestones

1986	Launched by Joseph Segel, broadcasting from studios in West Chester, PA
1987	Expands programming to 24 hours a day
1988	Acquires *Diamonique*, manufacturer of simulated gemstone jewelry
1993	Segel retires and Barry Diller is named Chairman and CEO. Launches channel in the UK
1995	Acquired by Comcast and Doug Briggs takes over as president and CEO
1996	Launches Internet site
2001	Launches channel in Japan
2003	Sold off to Liberty Media
2005	Michael George is named president
2006	George takes over as CEO with retirement of Briggs
2007	Ships its billionth package in the United States
2008	Launches QVCHD, a high definition simulcast in the United States
2009	Rolls out several mobile services
2010	Launches channel in Italy
2012	Acquires e-commerce shopping site Send the Trend. Launches joint venture in China
2013	Launches QVC PLUS as a second channel in the United States
2015	Launches channel in France
2016	Launches operations unit in Krakow, Poland, to streamline European business operation
2018	Parent company Qurate Retail acquires Home Shopping Network (HSN) and transfers ownership to QVC

Source: QVC.

program hosts and visiting celebrities. Celebrities are therefore often schooled in QVC's "backyard-fence" style, which means conversing with viewers the way they would chat with a friendly neighbor. "They're just so down-home, so it's like they're right in your living room demonstrating," said a long time QVC customer.[5]

In spite of the folksy presentation, the sales are minutely managed. Behind the scenes, a producer scans nine television and computer screens to track sales of each featured items. "We track new orders per minute in increments of six seconds; we can look backward in time and see what it was that drove that spike," said Doug Rose, who oversees programming and marketing.[6] Hosts and guests are prompted to make adjustments in their pitch that might increase sales. A beauty designer was recently asked to rub an eyeliner on her hand, which immediately led to a surge of new orders.

QVC's themed programs are telecast live 24 hours a day, seven days a week, to millions of households worldwide. The shopping channel transmits its programming live from its central production facilities in Pennsylvania through uplinks to a satellite. The representatives who staff QVC's four call centers, which handled more than 180 million calls last year, are well trained to take orders.

Of all the orders placed with QVC, more than 90 percent are shipped within 48 hours from one of their distribution centers. The distribution centers have a combined floor space that is equivalent to the size of over 100 football fields. Finally, everyone at QVC works hard to make sure that every item works as it should before it is shipped and that its packaging will protect it during the shipping process. "Nothing ships unless it is quality-inspected first," said one of the logistics managers for QVC. "Since our product is going business-to-consumer, there's no way to fix or change a product-related problem."[7]

Searching for Profitable Products

More than 100 experienced, informed buyers comb the world on a regular basis to search for new products to launch on QVC. The shopping channel concentrates on unique products that can be demonstrated on live television. Furthermore, the price of these products must be high enough for viewers to justify the additional shipping and handling charge. Over the course of a typical year, QVC carries more than 60,000 products. As many as 1,000 items are typically offered in any given week, of which about 20 percent are new products for the network. QVC's suppliers range from some of the world's biggest companies to small entrepreneurial enterprises.

All new products must, however, pass through stringent tests that are carried out by QVC's in-house Quality Assurance Lab. In many cases, this inspection process is carried out manually by the firm's employees. Only 15 percent of the products pass the firm's rigorous quality inspection on first try and as many as a third are never offered to the public because they fail altogether. In addition, Jeffrey Rayport, author of a book on customer service, states that "QVC staff look for a product that is complex enough–or interesting enough–that the host can talk about it on air."[8]

About a third of QVC's sales come from broadly available national brands. The firm has been able to build trust among its customers in large part through the offering of these well-known brands. QVC also relies upon promotional campaigns with a variety of existing firms for another third of its sales. It has made deals with firms ranging from Dell, Target, and Bath & Body Works for special limited time promotional offerings. But QVC has been most successful with products that are exclusively sold on QVC or not readily available through other distribution channels. Although such products account for another third of its sales, the firm has been able to earn higher margins with these proprietary products, many of which come from firms that are either start-ups or new entrants into the U.S. market.

Most vendors are attracted to QVC because they reap higher profits selling through their channel than they would make by selling through physical stores. Stores typically require vendors to help to train or pay the salesforce and participate in periodic sales where prices are discounted. QVC rarely sells products at discount prices. Maureen Kelly, founder of Tarte Cosmetics, said she typically makes more from an eight-minute segment on QVC than she used to make in a month at a high-end department store.

Apart from searching for exclusive products, QVC has also been trying to move away from some product categories, such as home appliances and electronic gadgets, which offer lower margins. It has been gradually expanding into many new product categories that have higher margins such as cosmetics, apparel, food, and toys. Several of these new categories have also displayed the strongest rates of growth in sales for the shopping channel over the past couple of years.

Expanding the Customer Base

Since its startup, QVC's shopping channel has managed to gradually penetrate almost all of the cable television and broadcast satellite homes in the United States. But only about 10 percent of the households that it reaches have actually brought anything from the network. However, QVC has developed a large customer base, many of whom make as many as 10 purchases in a year. QVC devotees readily call into the live segments to offer product testimonials, are up on the personal lives of their favorite program hosts, and generally view the channel as entertaining. "As weird as it may sound, for people who love the network, it's good company," said Rayport.[9]

QVC is also hoping to attract new customers on the basis of the reasonably strong reputation that surveys indicate that it has established among a large majority of its current buyers. By its initials alone, QVC had promised that it would deliver Quality, Value, and Convenience to its viewers. More than three-quarters of the shopping channel's customers have given it a score of 7 out of 7 for trustworthiness. This has led most of its customers to recommend it to their friends.

QVC has also benefited from the growing percentage of women entering the workforce, resulting in a significant increase in dual-income families. Although the firm's current customer base does span several socioeconomic groups, it is led by young professional families who have above average disposable income. They also enjoy various forms of "thrill-seeking" activities and rank shopping relatively higher as a leisure activity when compared to the typical consumer.

The firm is also trying to increase sales by making it easier for customers to buy its products by adding features such as an interactive service that would allow them to purchase whatever it is offering on its shopping channel with the single click of a remote. QVC also provides a credit program to allow customers to pay for goods over a period of several months. Everything it sells is also backed by a 30-day unconditional money-back guarantee. Furthermore, QVC does not impose any hidden charges, such as a "restocking fee," for any returned merchandise. These policies help the home shopping channel to attract customers for products that they can view but are not able to either touch or feel.

Over the years, QVC has also made acquisitions to add to its customer base. In 2012, it acquired Send the Trend, Inc., an e-commerce destination known for trendy fashion and beauty products. It uses proprietary technology to deliver monthly personalized recommendations that can easily be shared by customers over their social networks. Following this, QVC brought Zulily, an online retailer that targets mothers who look for unique items for their children. "We are interested in reaching out to new customers by adding more unique offerings," said a U.S.-based manager at QVC.[10]

Positioning for Future Growth

In spite of its success on television, QVC has been expanding to other forms of media. Since 1995, the firm has offered a website to complement its television channel, which has provided it with another form of access to customers. Initially, the site offered more detailed information about QVC offerings. Since then, it has branched out to develop its own customer base by featuring many products that have not been recently shown on its television channel. Over the last few years, QVC has been offering its products on mobile phone, interactive-television, and iPad apps.

QVC.com, a once-negligible part of the QVC empire, has grown to account for more than a third of the firm's domestic revenue. CEO Michael George recently stated that 60 percent of QVC's new customers in the United States buy on the Internet or on mobile devices. "The online business is becoming such a crucial part of the business for QVC," remarked Douglas Anmuth, an analyst at Barclay's Capital.[11] Furthermore, QVC.com is now more profitable than QVC's television operation. It needs fewer call-center workers, and while QVC must share profits with cable companies on TV orders, it does not have to pay them on online orders for products which have not been featured on the air for 24 hours.

Michael insists that QVC shoppers are less likely to drop cable services because they tend to be slightly older and more affluent. These customers tune in at different times of the day or night and are drawn to their offerings. "We're going to try and find 120 to 140 items every day where we think we can tell compelling stories and inspire you to consider it," said Michael.[12] Once viewers start buying from QVC, they tend to be loyal to the firm, buying around 24 items a year.

For many of its loyal consumers, nothing will ever replace the shopping on television. The website does not offer the hybrid of talk show and sales pitch that attracts audiences to the QVC shopping channel. Online shoppers also miss out on the interaction between hosts and shoppers and the continuous feedback about the time that they may have to order before an item is sold out. "You know, on Sundays I might find a program on Lifetime Movie Network, but whatever I'm watching, if it's not QVC, when the commercial comes on I'll flip it back to QVC," said one loyal QVC fan. "I'm just stuck on them."[13]

ENDNOTES

1. QVC. 2019. Introducing QVC3 and QVC's first digital-only network, Beauty iQ. April 23, https://corporate.qvc.com/newsroom/happenings/introducing-qvc3-and-qvcs-first-digital-only-network-beauty-iq/2019.
2. QVC, Inc. 10-K report 2018.
3. Clifford, Stephanie. 2010. Can QVC translate its pitch online? *New York Times,* November 21, p. B7.
4. QVC Annual Report, 1987–1988.
5. Clifford. op. cit.
6. Ibid.
7. Gilligan, Eugene. 2004. The show must go on. *Journal of Commerce,* April 12, p. 1.
8. Petrecca, Laura. 2008. QVC shops for ideas for future sales. *USA Today,* May 5, p. 2B.
9. Ibid.
10. Send the Trend relaunches with QVC to bring shoppers a more personalized e-commerce experience. *PR Newswire,* October 2, 2012.
11. Clifford. op. cit.
12. Ziobro, Paul. 2017. QVC's strength ebbs as web retail booms. *Wall Street Journal,* January 12, p. B6.
13. Clifford. op. cit.

CASE 11

CIRQUE DU SOLEIL IN 2019*

In 2019, Cirque du Soleil announced the acquisition of The Works Entertainment-the production firm behind the famous and highly successful magic show *The Illusionists* and other variety shows. "This transaction is a perfect example of how our group is diversifying through acquisitions, while always investing in our core activities," said Daniel Lamarre, president and CEO of Cirque du Soleil Entertainment Group.[1] It's the company's latest effort-after the acquisition of Blue Man Group in 2017 and VStar Entertainment in 2018-to regain its outstanding position in the live entertainment world.

For over three decades, Cirque du Soleil, led by the fire-eater-turned-billionaire Guy Laliberté, has reinvented and revolutionized the circus. From its beginning in 1984, the world's leading producer of high-quality live artistic entertainment has thrilled over 180 million spectators with a novel show concept that is an astonishing theatrical blend of circus acts and street entertainment, featuring spectacular costumes, fairyland sets, spellbinding music, and magical lighting. Cirque manages to run as many as 24 shows at a time and has played in 450 cities across 60 countries.

Cirque du Soleil's business triumphs have mirrored its high-flying aerial stunts, and it is a case study for business journal articles on carving out unique markets. In addition to a bleak outlook report from a consultant, a spate of poorly received shows over a couple of years, and a decline in revenue, in 2013 the company failed to generate a profit for the first time in recent history. In interviews with *The Wall Street Journal* at Cirque du Soleil's sleek headquarters in Montreal, top executives including founder and then 90 percent owner Laliberté talked about the firm's deteriorating finances and the need to restructure and refocus their business–shifting some of the attention away from their string of successful shows toward several other potential business ventures.

Starting a New Concept

Cirque du Soleil developed out of early efforts of Guy Laliberté, who left his Montreal home at the age of 14 with little more than an accordion. He traveled around, trying out different acts such as fire-eating for spare change in front of Centre Pompidou in Paris. When he returned home, he hooked up with another visionary street performer from Quebec, a stilt-walker named Gilles Ste-Croix. In 1982, Laliberté and Ste-Croix organized a street performance festival in the sleepy town of Baie St. Paul along the St. Lawrence valley.

In 1984, Cirque du Soleil was formed with financial support from the government of Quebec, as banks were reluctant to support the band of fire-eaters, stilt-walkers, and clowns. Its breakthrough 1987 show *We Reinvent the Circus* burst on the art scene in Montreal as an entirely new art form. No one had seen anything like it before. Laliberté and Ste-Croix had turned the whole concept of circus on its head. Using story lines, identifiable characters, and an emotional trajectory in the show, Cirque du Soleil embodied far more than a mere collection of disparate acts and feats.

Despite its early success, Cirque du Soleil struggled financially. They took a gamble on making their debut in the United States as the opening act of the 1987 Los Angeles Festival. They managed to sell out all of their performances, which were run in a tent on a lot adjacent to downtown's Little Tokyo. Its success in Los Angeles led to the troupe opening shows across the United States in cities such as Chicago, San Francisco, Miami, and Washington, DC. Soon after, Cirque du Soleil performed in Japan and Switzerland, introducing their concept to audiences outside North America.

In 1992, Cirque du Soleil took a show called *Nouvelle Experience* to Las Vegas for the first time. It was performed under the big top in the parking lot of the Mirage. The success of this show led to building a permanent theater at Treasure Island for a show called *Mystere,* a nonstop perpetual motion kaleidoscope of athleticism and raw emotion that thrilled audiences. It became the first of the troupe's permanent shows and led to several others that opened in other hotels along the Las Vegas strip. The most spectacular of these was *O* that included acts performed in a 25-foot-deep, 1.5-million-gallon pool of crystal clear water in a custom-built theater at Bellagio.

Growing with the Concept

Cirque du Soleil hired key people from the National Circus School in its formative years in order to develop its concept of the contemporary circus. Its first recruit was Guy Caron, the head of this school, to be the Cirque's artistic director. Shortly after, the troupe recruited Franco Dragone, another instructor from the National Circus School, who had been working in Belgium. Dragone brought with him his experience in commedia dell'arte techniques, which he imparted to the Cirque performers.

* Case prepared by Jamal Shamsie, Michigan State University, with the assistance of Professor Alan B. Eisner, Pace University. Material has been drawn from published sources to be used for purposes of class discussion.

Copyright © 2019 Jamal Shamsie and Alan B. Eisner.

Together, Caron and Dragone were behind the creation of all of the Cirque du Soleil shows during their formative years, including *Saltimbanco, Mystere, Algeria, Quidam,* and the extravagant *O.* Under the watchful eye of Laliberté, Cirque developed its unique formula that defined their shows. From the beginning, they promoted the whole show, rather than specific acts or performers. They eliminated spoken dialogue so that their show would not be culture bound, replacing this with a strong emotional soundtrack that was played from the beginning to the end by live musicians. Performers, rather than a technical crew, moved equipment and props on and off stage so that it did not disrupt the momentum as the show transitioned from one act to the next. Most important, the idea was to create a circus without a ring or animals, as Laliberté believed that the lack of these two elements would draw the audience more into the performance.

Even though Laliberté and his creative team were clearly innovative in their approach, they were not reluctant to obtain inspiration from outside sources. They drew on the tradition of pantomime and masks from circuses in Europe. They learned about blending presentational, musical, and choreographic elements from the Chinese. Caron readily admitted that Cirque took everything that had existed in the past and pulled it into the present, so that it would strike a chord with present day audiences.

All of Cirque du Soleil shows were originally developed to be performed under a Grand Chapiteau, or "big top," for an extended period of time before they were modified, if necessary, for touring in arenas and other venues. The troupe's grand chapiteau were easily recognizable by their blue and yellow coloring and could seat more than 2,600 spectators. However, after the contract to develop Mystere for Treasure Island in Las Vegas, Cirque also began to develop shows that were to be performed on a more permanent basis in specially designed auditoriums (see Exhibit 1).

From its small beginnings, Cirque du Soleil had grown to become an international entertainment conglomerate with 4,500 employees in offices all around the world. It had established its headquarters in a $40 million building in Montreal, where all of Cirque's shows are created and produced. Much of the building is devoted to practice studios for various types of performers and a costume department that outfits performers in fantastical hand-painted clothing. Cirque du Soleil has recruited many types of talent, among them acrobats, athletes, dancers, musicians, clowns, actors, and singers.

Losing Its Touch

Cirque du Soleil continued to expand even as the recent recession cut into demand. It had launched 20 shows in the 23 years from 1984 through 2006, none of which closed during that time, other than a couple of early failures. Over the next six years, however, Cirque opened 14 more shows, five of which flopped and closed early. The reasons for the failures differed. One show, *Zarkana,* could not make enough money to cover its production costs playing in New York City's 6,000-seat Radio City Music Hall. *Iris,* in Los Angeles, played in Hollywood, in a seedy neighborhood that despite heavy tourist traffic was commercially marginal. *Zaia,* in Macau, simply did not appeal to local audiences. Perhaps more troubling, the company's nearly perfect record of producing artistic successes began to waver. *Viva Elvis* and *Banana Shpeel* were among several Cirque shows that garnered terrible reviews. Both shows closed quickly. "Shows like that diluted the brand," said Patrick Leroux, a professor at Montreal's Concordia University who has closely studied Cirque du Soleil.[2]

One problem, say Cirque du Soleil executives, was that audiences did not understand the differences among various shows carrying the Cirque brand. As a result, many people would dismiss the opportunity to see, for instance, the show *Totem* thinking they had already seen something similar in the older *Varekai.* On the other hand, Cirque tried to move in different directions with each of the new shows that it developed. "We're constantly challenging ourselves," Laliberté said.[3] Audiences, however, complained that some newer shows were not as focused on the acrobatic feats that they had come to expect and enjoy from Cirque.

Debate has swirled over whether Cirque du Soleil should return to its roots or aim for constant reinvention. At the end of 2011, Bain & Co., contracted by Cirque, reported that its market had hit saturation and the company needed to be careful with how many new shows it added. Bain suggested Cirque seek growth by moving their concept to movies, television, and nightclubs. "Guy Laliberté always said we are a rarity–but the rarity was gone," said Marc Gagnon, a former top executive in charge of operations for Cirque du Soleil who left in 2012.[4]

By August 2012, Laliberté and Lamarre had become concerned and convened a five-day summit for executives at Laliberté's estate outside Montreal. There, the two and others drew up plans to lay off hundreds of executives and performers and pare the number of big new touring circus shows Cirque produced. The cuts began soon after and continued through 2013 and amounted to around $100 million of savings, according to Laliberté. The savings included everything from giving out fewer suede anniversary jackets to employees to cutting out child performers and tutors.

Laliberté also reexamined core production costs. The payroll for Cirque's show *O,* in Las Vegas, for instance, had ballooned thanks to a surge in contortionists. "I said, 'Why do we need six contortionists?'" Laliberté recalled while chain smoking inside his office.[5] In addition to the layoffs, Cirque also suffered a blow to morale when acrobat Sarah Guyard-Guillot was killed during a performance. The company overhauled the show's finale, a "battle" staged on a vertical wall, with performers suspended from motorized wire harnesses. Since the performer's death, Cirque has continued to stage the show, replacing the live finale with a videotape of the scene from a past performance.

EXHIBIT 1 Cirque du Soleil Shows

Grand Chapiteau & Arena Shows		Resident Shows	
1990	Nouvelle Experience	1993	Mystere* Treasure Island, Las Vegas
1992	Saltimbanco	1998	O* Bellagio, Las Vegas
1994	Alegria**	1998	La Nouba Downtown Disney, Lake Buena Vista
1996	Quidam	2003	Zumanity* New York New York, Las Vegas
1999	Dralion	2005	Ka* MGM Grand, Las Vegas
2002	Varekai	2006	Love* The Mirage, Las Vegas
2005	Corteo*	2008	Zaia The Venetian Macao
2006	Delirium	2008	Zed Tokyo Disney Resort, Tokyo
2007	Kooza*	2008	Criss Angel Believe Luxor, Las Vegas
2007	Wintuk	2009	Viva Elvis Aria Resort & Casino, Las Vegas
2009	Ovo*	2011	Iris Dolby Theatre, Los Angeles
2009	Banana Shpeel	2013	Michael Jackson: One* Mandalay Bay & Resort, Las Vegas
2010	Totem*	2014	JOYA* Riviera Maya, Mexico
2011	Michael Jackson: The Immortal World Tour	2016	PARAMOUR Lyric Theatre, Broadway, New York
2012	Amaluna*	2019	PARAMOUR* Stage Theater Neue Flora, Hamburg, Germany
2014	Kurios: Cabinet of Curiosities*	2019	X (The Land of Fantasy)* Hangzhou, China
2015	Toruk*		
2016	Luzia*		
2017	Séptimo Día – No Descansaré		
2017	Volta*		
2017	Crystal*		
2018	Bazzar*		
2019	Messi10*		

*Still in performance.

**Remake in 2019

Source: Cirque du Soleil.

Moving in New Directions

Laliberté had been working with his executive team to come up with a business restructuring plan to manage diversification through the creation of discrete business units under a central corporate entity to try to beef up the non-circus side of the business. *Paramour* was the first show to be launched by a new subsidiary for musical-theater production based in New York City. Another subsidiary of the firm–operating under the name of 45 Degrees–started to work on producing special events such as tourism events, dinner shows, sporting events, concerts, and corporate events. Other new areas that Cirque was venturing into included small cabaret shows at hotels, children's television programs, and theme parks. Analysts, however, believe that Cirque du Soleil has been trying to walk a fine line as it sought to expand into new ventures without damaging its central brand as a creative entity.

Despite all these efforts, Cirque du Soleil announced a change in ownership in April 2015. The company stated this step would strengthen the financial position and enable further growth. The majority share of 60 percent was going to the Texas-based private equity firm TPG Capital, 20 percent to China's Fosun Capital Group, and 10 percent to the Caisse de dépôt et placement du Québec, which manages public pensions plans in the Quebec province. The remaining 10 percent retained with Laliberté, who also remained as strategic and creative consultant (see Exhibit 2). "After 30 years building the Cirque du Soleil brand, we have now found the right partners in TPG, Fosun and the Caisse to take Cirque du Soleil forward to the next stage," said Laliberté. With the new investors the company hoped to expand its business to China and other Asian countries. "We are excited about the opportunity to bring our global platform of resources and know-how to propel the growth of Cirque's unique brand, content and capabilities around the world," said David Trujillo, partner at TPG.[6]

It took over two years under its new owners until Cirque announced further changes to the business. In July 2017, the company acquired the Blue Man Production LLC, best known for their pop-art shows performed by blue-painted bold men called *Blue Man Group*. "The acquisition of Blue Man, for us, is kind of a breakthrough to make clear to people that Cirque is going from a circus company to becoming a global leader of entertainment," said Daniel Lamarre.[7] The terms of the deal were not disclosed, however, Lamarre said the sale price was in the "tens of millions." Although being a multimillion dollar business, "we thought of some ways that the Blue Men and their performances could go on a bigger scale," said Blue Man Group co-founder Mr. Wink in a phone interview with the New York Times speaking about their intentions.[8]

It was one year later, in July 2018, when Cirque announced its acquisition of the Minnesota-based VStar Entertainment Group and its Florida-based circus arts subsidiary Cirque Dreams. The Group is specialized in live entertainment, theatrical shows, exhibits, cruise ship shows, and outdoor events. "VStar has a history of growing through partnerships with great entertainment brands and we are always on the lookout for the next transformative opportunity [. . .] and only a global producer like Cirque du Soleil could help us achieve our vision,"[9] said Eric Grilly, CEO of VStar Entertainment Group. Lamarre saw the acquisition as a good way to further diversify Cirque's business: "We firmly believe the knowledge transfer will help us develop our own capabilities in this type of entertainment and, therefore, contribute to growing our footprint in the live entertainment production industry."[10]

In February 2019, Cirque purchased The Works Entertainment from owners Simon Painter, Tim Lawson, and Kilburn Live. The production company is best known for their magic show *The Illusionists,* circus art shows such as *Circus 1903–The Golden Age of Circus,* as well as cabaret-style shows and musicals. "Like us, they have no stars, [. . .] the show is the star, and they're constantly using different magicians. The fact that they're not focused on stars gives you scalability," said Lamarre in a *New York Times* interview.[11] The acquisition was financed using a portion of a new US$120 million unsecured credit facility made available by the Fonds de Solidarité FTQ and the Caisse de dépôt et placement du Québec.

Building a Sustainable Future?

Over the years, Cirque du Soleil has managed to generate profits out of a business model that is quite challenging. Kenneth Feld, of Ringling Bros. and Barnum & Bailey circus, commented: "If you think about spending $165 million on a show that seats 1,900 people, the economics are just staggering."[12] But Laliberté's stroke of genius was to

EXHIBIT 2 Cirque du Soleil Ownership Structure

Owner Name	Type of Ownership	% Ownership Stake
TPG Capital LP	Private Equity	60%
Fosun International	Private Equity & Venture Captial	20%
Guy Laliberte	Inidvidual	10%
The Caisse de depot et placement du Quebec	Quais-Government Organization	10%

Source: PrivCo Media, LLC.

realize that Cirque never had to close. They could either keep touring or play in locations such as Las Vegas and Orlando that draw a lot of tourists.

By 2019, Cirque du Soleil had 24 shows, seven of them in Las Vegas. Over the last five years, the firm has launched seven new touring shows, six of which are still running. However, the rising costs of developing and operating so many shows has cut into the firm's revenues and profits, even with higher ticket prices. Recent efforts to trim costs and to branch out into new areas may help Cirque du Soleil to increase profitability. Furthermore, even though its acquisitions to move into new areas may greatly broaden the company's revenue base, with each new business still running quite independently it remains to be seen if Cirque can manage the challenges of its core show business.

ENDNOTES

1. Press Release. 2019. Cirque du Soleil Entertainment Group acquires the makers of 'The Illusionists' franchise. *Cirque du Soleil*, February 6, https://www.cirquedusoleil.com/press/news/2019/cirque-du-soleil-entertainment-group-acquires-the-works.
2. Alexandra Berzon. 2014. Cirque's next act: Rebalancing the business. *The Wall Street Journal*, December 2, p. B4.
3. Ibid.
4. Ibid, p. B1.
5. Christopher Palmeri. 2004. The $600 million circus maximus. *BusinessWeek*, December 13, p. 82.
6. Press Release. 2015. Cirque Du Soleil finds new strategic majority partner in TPG-led investor group. *Cirque du Soleil*, April 20, https://www.cirquedusoleil.com/press/news/2015/transaction-vente-20-avril-2015.
7. Sopan Deb. 2017. Blue Man Group is bought by Cirque du Soleil, with plans to expand. *New York Times*, July 6, https://www.nytimes.com/2017/07/06/theater/cirque-du-soleil-buys-blue-man-group.html.
8. Ibid.
9. Press Release. 2018. Cirque du Soleil Entertainment Group expands family offering with acquisition of Vstar Entertainment Group. *Cirque du Soleil*, July 5, https://www.cirquedusoleil.com/press/news/2018/acquisition-of-vstar-entertainment-group.
10. Ibid.
11. Sophie Haigney. 2019. Cirque du Soleil buys magic show company. *New York Times*, February 6, https://www.nytimes.com/2019/02/06/theater/cirque-du-soleil-buys-the-works-entertainment.html
12. Alexandra Berzon. 2014. Cirque's next act: Rebalancing the business. *The Wall Street Journal*, December 2, p. B4.

CASE 12

PIXAR*

In spite of its domination of Academy Awards for Best Animated Film since the category was introduced in 2001, Pixar has managed to win only once over the last three years. It was overlooked in 2018 for *Incredibles 2*, although the film broke all records for opening weekend box office revenue for an animated feature film. The $180 million that the film collected over three days was spectacular even by the standards that have been set by Pixar over the years (see Exhibit 1). But as with *Finding Dory*, the sequel to *Finding Nemo* that was released a couple of years earlier, the commercial success of the film failed to land the firm with an Academy Award.

This loss at the Academy Awards only added to the feelings within Pixar after the forced departure of John

* Case prepared by Jamal Shamsie, Michigan State University, with the assistance of Professor Alan B. Eisner, Pace University. Material has been drawn from published sources to be used for purposes of class discussion. Copyright © 2019 Jamal Shamsie and Alan B. Eisner.

EXHIBIT 1
Pixar Films Worldwide Rank 2018

All of Pixar's films released to date have ended up among the top animated films of all time based on worldwide box office revenues in millions of U.S. dollars.

Rank	Title	Year	Revenue ($US millions)
2	Incredibles 2*	2018	$1,243
4	Toy Story 3	2010	$1,065
6	Finding Dory	2016	$1,029
10	Finding Nemo	2003	$940
15	Inside Out	2015	$858
16	Coco	2017	$807
20	Monsters University	2013	$745
21	Up	2009	$735
27	The Incredibles	2005	$630
30	Ratatouille	2007	$620
34	Monsters, Inc	2002	$575
35	Cars 2	2011	$560
38	Brave	2012	$555
39	Wall-E	2009	$535
50	Toy Story 2	1999	$515
57	Cars	2006	$460
64	Cars 3	2017	$383
71	Toy Story	1995	$372
72	A Bug's Life	1998	$365
80	The Good Dinosaur	2015	$333

*Still playing in theatres around the world (03/2019)

Source: IMDB, Variety.

Lasseter, who had served as the firm's creative officer since its founding. Because of his influence on the firm, Lasseter had been heralded in the news media as a latter-day Walt Disney. A self-described Peter Pan, Lasseter had long been known for his jolly public persona and tendency to greet anyone in his proximity with lengthy bear hugs. He took a leave in 2017 following complaints about unwanted workplace hugging and then agreed to retire at the end of 2018. Some women had also complained that under Lasseter, Pixar had not offered much opportunity to women and minorities.

Despite the loss of Lasseter, Pixar is confident that it will continue to thrive as part of the Walt Disney Company. It was acquired by Disney in 2006 for the hefty sum of $7.4 billon. The deal had been finalized by the late Steve Jobs, the Apple Computer chief executive who had also served as the head of the computer animation firm. Disney CEO Bob Iger worked hard to acquire Pixar, whose track record has made it one of the world's most successful animation companies.

Both Jobs and Iger had been aware, however, that they must protect Pixar's creative culture while they also try to carry some of this over to Disney's animation efforts. In fact, Jobs had been convinced that Pixar's links with Disney would be mutually beneficial for both firms. In his own words: "Disney is the only company with animation in their DNA."[1] Lasseter, who had been overseeing all story development at Pixar had also denied any negative effects from Disney's acquisition of his firm. He had insisted that, in fact, Pixar's films were increasingly being subjected to higher standards because of its string of successes.

Ed Catmull, president of Pixar reiterated his firm's commitment to take whatever steps may be necessary in order to put out the best possible film. "Nobody ever remembers the fact that you slipped [up in] a film but they will remember a bad film" he said.[2] Catmull's remarks indicated that Pixar was dedicated to its lengthy process of playfully crafting a film to replace the standard production line approach that had been pursued by Disney. This contrast in culture is best reflected in the Oscars that the employees at Pixar have displayed proudly, but which have been painstaking dressed in Barbie doll clothing.

Pushing for Computer-Animated Films

The roots of Pixar stretch back to 1975 with the founding of a vocational school in Old Westbury, NY, called the New York Institute of Technology. It was there that Edwin E. Catmull, a straitlaced Mormon from Salt Lake City who loved animation but could not draw, teamed up with the people who would later form the core of Pixar. "It was artists and technologists from the very start," recalled Alvy Ray Smith, who worked with Catmull during those years. "It was like a fairy tale."[3]

By 1979, Catmull and his team decided to join forces with famous Hollywood director, George W. Lucas, Jr. They were hopeful that this would allow them to pursue their dream of making animated films. As part of Lucas's filmmaking facility in San Rafael, California, Catmull's group of aspiring animators made substantial progress in the art of computer animation. But the unit was not able to generate any profits and Lucas was not willing to let it grow beyond using computer animation for special effects.

In 1985 Catmull finally turned to Jobs, who had just been ousted from Apple. Jobs was reluctant to invest in a firm that wanted to make full-length feature films using computer animation. But a year later, Jobs decided to buy Catmull's unit for just $10 million, which represented a third of Lucas's asking price. While the newly named Pixar Animation Studios tried to push the boundaries of computer animation over the next five years, Jobs ended up having to invest an additional $50 million—more than 25 percent of his total wealth at the time. "There were times that we all despaired, but fortunately not all at the same time," said Jobs.[4]

Still, Catmull's team did continue to make substantial breakthroughs in the development of computer-generated full-length feature films (see Exhibit 2). In 1991, Disney gave Pixar a three-film contract that started with *Toy Story*. When the movie was finally released in 1995, its success surprised everyone in the film industry. Rather than the nice little film Disney had expected, *Toy Story* became the sensation of 1995. It rose to the rank of the highest grossing animated film for the year, earning $722 million in worldwide box office revenues.

Within days, Jobs had decided to take Pixar public. When the shares, priced at $22, shot past $33, Jobs called his best friend, Oracle CEO Lawrence J. Ellison, to tell him he had company in the billionaire's club. With Pixar's sudden success, Jobs returned to strike a new deal with Disney. Early in 1996, at a lunch with Walt Disney chief Michael D. Eisner, Jobs made his demands: an equal share of the profits, equal billing on merchandise and on-screen credits, and guarantees that Disney would market Pixar films as they did its own.

Boosting the Creative Component

With the success of *Toy Story*, Jobs realized that he had hit something big. He obviously had tapped into his Silicon Valley roots and turned to computers to forge a unique style of creative moviemaking. In each of their subsequent films, Pixar has continued to develop computer animation that has allowed for more lifelike backgrounds, texture, and movement than ever before. For example, since real leaves are translucent, Pixar's engineers developed special software algorithms that both reflect and absorb light, creating luminous scenes among jungles of clover.

In spite of the significance of these advancements in computer animation, Jobs was well aware that successful feature films would require a strong creative spark. He understood that it would be the marriage of technology with creativity that would allow Pixar to rise above most of its competition. To get that, Jobs fostered a campus-like environment within the newly formed outfit similar to the freewheeling, charged atmosphere in the early days of his

EXHIBIT 2 Milestones

1986	Steve Jobs buys Lucas's computer group and christens it Pixar. The firm completes a short film, *Luxo Jr.*, which is nominated for an Oscar.
1988	Pixar adds computer-animated ads to its repertoire, making spots for Listerine, Lifesavers, and Tropicana. Another short, *Tin Toy*, wins an Oscar.
1991	Pixar signs a production agreement with Disney. Disney is to invest $26 million; Pixar is to deliver at least three full-length, computer-animated feature films.
1995	Pixar releases *Toy Story*, the first fully digital feature film, which becomes the top-grossing movie of the year and wins an Oscar. A week after release, the company goes public.
1997	Pixar and Disney negotiate a new agreement: a 50-50 split of the development costs and profits of five feature-length movies. Short *Geri's Game* wins an Oscar.
1998–99	*A Bug's Life* and *Toy Story 2* are released, together pulling in $1.3 billion through box office and video.
2001–04	A string of hits from Pixar: *Monsters Inc., Finding Nemo*, and *The Incredibles*.
2006	Disney acquires Pixar and assigns responsibilities for its own animation unit to Pixar's creative brass. *Cars* is released and becomes another box office hit.
2008	*Wall-E* becomes the fourth film from Pixar to receive the Oscar for a feature-length animated film.
2009	*Up* becomes the Fifth film from Pixar to receive the Oscar for a feature-length animated film.
2011	*Toy Story 3* receives five Oscar nominations and wins two, including one for Best Animated Film.
2011	Steve Jobs dies, leaving Ed Catmull in charge.
2013	*Brave* becomes the seventh film from Pixar to receive an Oscar for Best Animated Film.
2015	*Inside Out* becomes the eighth film from Pixar to receive an Oscar for Best Animated Film.
2016	*Piper* received a nomination for an Oscar for Best Animated Short Film.
2017	*Coco* wins two Oscars in categories for Best Animated Film and Best Original Song—Pixar's ninth film to receive an Oscar for Best Animated Film.
2018	*Incredibles 2* sets the record for best debut for an animated film of all time, eventually grossing over $1.2 billion dollars worldwide. The film has also received a nomination for the Best Animated Feature.
2018–19	Lasseter steps down after accusations of sexual harassment toward employees; Ed Catmull and Lee Unkrich announce their retirements; Pete Docter and Jennifer Lee become new chief creative officers of Disney's animation divisions.

Source: Pixar.

beloved Apple, where he also returned as acting CEO. "It's not simply the technology that makes Pixar," said Dick Cook, former President of Walt Disney studios.[5]

Even though Jobs did play a crucial supportive role, it is Catmull that has been mainly responsible for insuring that the firm's technological achievements help to pump up the firm's creative efforts. He has been the keeper of the company's unique innovative culture, which has blended Silicon Valley techies, Hollywood production honchos, and artsy animation experts. In the pursuit of Catmull's vision, this eclectic group has transformed their office cubicles into tiki huts, circus tents, and cardboard castles with bookshelves that are stuffed with toys and desks that are adorned with colorful iMac computers.

One of Catmull's biggest achievements has been the creation of what is called the Pixar Braintrust (see Exhibit 3). This creative group of employees, which includes directors, meets on a regular basis to assess each movie that the firm is developing and offer their ideas for improvement. It is such an emphasis on creativity that has kept Pixar on the cutting edge. Each of their films has been innovative in many respects and has made the best possible use of computer animation. "They're absolute geniuses," gushed Jules Roman, co-founder and CEO of rival Tippett Studio. "They're the people who created computer animation really."[6]

Catmull has also been working hard to build upon this pursuit of creative innovation by creating programs to develop the employees. Employees are encouraged to devote up to four hours a week, every week, to further their education at Pixar University. The in-house training program offers 110 different courses that cover subjects such as live improvisation, creative writing, painting, drawing, sculpting,

EXHIBIT 3
Sample of Roles

Ed Catmull*	President, producer
Pete Docter	Chief creative officer, producer, director, writer
Jim Morris	Business manager
Brad Bird	Director, writer
Harley Jessup	Production designer
Bill Cone	Production designer
Ricky Nierva	Production designer, art director, character designer
Ralph Eggleston	Art director
Randy Barrett	Character designer, set designer, matte painter
Tia Kratter	Shading art director, digital painter
Bob Pauley	Character designer, sketch artist
Jay Shuster	Character and environment designer

*Retired 07/2019

Source: Pixar.

and cinematography. For many years, the school's dean was Randall E. Nelson, a former juggler who has been known to perform his act using chainsaws so students in animation classes have something compelling to draw.

Becoming Accomplished Storytellers

A considerable part of the creative energy goes into story development. Jobs had understood that a film works only if its story can move the hearts and minds of families around the world. His goal was to develop Pixar into an animated movie studio that becomes known for the quality of its storytelling above everything else. "We want to create some great stories and characters that endure with each generation," Jobs had stated.[7]

For story development, Pixar relied heavily on John Lasseter, who went by the title of vice-president of the creative. Known for his collection of 358 Hawaiian shirts and his irrepressible playfulness with toys, Lasseter had been the key to the appeal of all of Pixar's films. Lasseter would get very passionate about developing great stories and then harnessing computers to tell these stories. Most of Pixar's employees believed that it was this passion that allowed the studio to ensure that each of its films has been a commercial hit. In fact, Lasseter had been widely regarded as the Walt Disney for the 21st century.

When it was time to start a project, Lasseter would isolate a group of eight or so writers and direct them to forget about the constraints of technology. The group would bounce ideas off each other, taking collective responsibility for developing a story. While many studios try to rush from script to production, Lasseter took up to two years just to work out all the details. Once the script had been developed, artists created storyboards that connected the various characters to the developing plot. "No amount of great animation is going to save a bad story," he said. "That's why we go so far to make it right.[8]

Only after the basic story had been set would Lasseter begin to think about what was needed from Pixar's technologists. And it was always more than the computer animators expected. Lasseter, for example, demanded that the crowds of ants in *A Bug's Life* not be a single mass of lookalike faces. To solve the problem, computer expert William T. Reeves developed software that randomly applied physical and emotional characteristics to each ant. In another instance, writers brought a model of a butterfly named Gypsy to researchers, asking them to write code so that when she rubs her antennas, you can see the hairs press down and pop back up.

At any stage during the process, Lasseter would revisit potential problems that he might see with the story. In *A Bug's Life*, for example, the story was totally revamped after more than a year of work had been completed. Originally, it was about a troupe of circus bugs run by P.T. Flea that tries to rescue a colony of ants from marauding grasshoppers. But because of a flaw in the story–why would the circus bugs risk their lives to save stranger ants?–co-director Andrew Stanton recast the story to be about Flik, the heroic ant who recruits Flea's troupe to fight the grasshoppers. "You have to rework and rework it," explained Lasseter. "It is not rare for a scene to be rewritten as much as 30 times."[9]

Pumping Out the Hits

In spite of its formidable string of hits, Pixar has had difficulty in stepping up its pace of production. Although they may cost 30 percent less, computer-generated animated films do still take considerable time to develop. Furthermore, because of the emphasis on every single detail, Pixar used to complete most of the work on a film before moving on to the next one. Catmull and Lasseter then decided to work on several projects simultaneously, but the firm has not been able to release more than one movie in a year.

In order to push for an increase in production, Pixar has built up its workforce to well over 1,000 employees. It is also turning to a stable of directors to oversee its movies. Lasseter, who directed Pixar's first three films, supervised other directors who are taking helm of various films that the studio chooses to develop. *Monsters Inc.*, *Finding Nemo*, *The Incredibles*, *Ratatouille*, and *Brave* were directed by some of this new talent. But there are concerns about the number of directors that Pixar can rely upon to turn out high-quality animated films. Michael Savner of Banc of America Securities commented: "You can't simply double production. There is a finite amount of talent."[10]

To meet the faster production pace, Catmull has also added new divisions including one to help with the development of new movies and one to oversee movie development shot by shot. The eight-person development team has helped to generate more ideas for new films. "Once more ideas are percolating, we have more options to choose from so no one artist is feeling the weight of the world on their shoulders," said Sarah McArthur, who served as Pixar's vice president of production.[11]

Finally, Catmull has been overseeing the development of new animation software, called Luxo. Luxo has allowed him to use fewer people to address various challenges that must be faced. During the production of *Brave*, for example, the animators had to make the curly hair of the main character appear to be natural. Claudia Chung, who worked on the film, talked about their reaction to various methods they kept trying: "We'd kind of roll our eyes and say, 'I guess we can do that,' but inside we were all excited, because it's one more stretch we can do."[12]

At the same time, Catmull also understands that the high standards of the firm cannot be compromised for the sake of a steady flow of films. This was evident in their decision to delay the launch of *The Good Dinosaur* a few years ago because they wanted to rethink the film in order to ensure it would work well. Everyone at Pixar remains committed to the philosophy of Jobs that every one of Pixar's films should grow out of the best efforts of the firm's animators, storytellers, and technologists. "Quality is more important than quantity," he emphasized. "One home run is better than two doubles."[13]

In order to preserve its high standards, Catmull has been working hard to retain Pixar's commitment to quality even as it grows. He has been using Pixar University to encourage collaboration among all employees so that they can develop and retain the key values that are tied to their success. And he has helped devise ways to avoid collective burnout. A masseuse and a doctor now come by Pixar's campus each week, and animators must get permission from their supervisors if they want to work more than 50 hours a week.

To Infinity and Beyond?

As Pixar moves forward, it will do so without the guidance of John Lasseter. However, everyone at Pixar understands that a large part of their success can be attributed to the talent the firm is able to recruit and train to work together. This leads to a continuous exchange of ideas and fosters a collective sense of responsibility on all their projects. "We created the studio we want to work in," Lasseter had remarked. "We have an environment that's wacky. It's a creative brain trust: It's not a place where I make my movies–it's a place where a group of people make movies."[14]

Lasseter has been replaced by Pete Docter, a 28-year Pixar veteran who directed three of its most successful films–*Up*, *Inside Out*, and *Monsters, Inc.*–and helped write the screenplays for *Toy Story* and *Wall-E*. Docter expressed confidence in the future of Pixar, stating: "Together, we will keep pushing animation in new directions."[15] He will work alongside relative newcomer Jennifer Lee, who will take charge of the revered Walt Disney Animated Studios.

Under Docter's leadership, Pixar released *Toy Story 4*, one of its most anticipated films in the summer of 2019. It allowed the firm to show its stellar storytelling and dedication toward their work. The fourth installment of the world's first computer-animated feature film arrived after nearly a nine-year gap since *Toy Story 3* and more than two decades after the original. Its release was delayed by problems with its development, leading to changes among the individuals who were involved with its story and screenplay. Nevertheless, it received both critical acclaim and success at the box office, pulling in over $1 billion worldwide. [16]

However, Pixar now faces another transition since Ed Catmull, who spearheaded the firm's development, stepped down as president in July 2019. Catmull minimized the impact of his departure: "I have mixed emotions that come with the sadness that comes with stepping away from a group of people I love, but also with the utmost pride and pleasure that we now have at both Pixar and Disney the most dedicated and imaginative leaders that I have worked with."[17]

Think about how off-putting a movie about rats preparing food could be, or how risky it must've seemed to start a movie about robots with 39 dialogue-free minutes. We dare to attempt these stories, but we don't get them right on the first pass. This is as it should be.

-Ed Catmull from his book, *Creativity, Inc*, published in 2014

ENDNOTES

1. Soloman, C. 2006. Pixar creative chief to seek to restore the Disney magic. *New York Times*, January 25, p. C6.
2. Miller, D. 2013. Pixar film delay leads to layoffs. *Los Angeles Times*, November 23, p. B3.
3. Burrows, P. and R. Grover. 1998. Steve Jobs: movie mogul. *BusinessWeek*, November 23, p. 150.

4. Ibid.
5. Burrows, P. and R. Grover. 1998. Steve Jobs: movie mogul. *BusinessWeek*, November 23, p. 146.
6. Ibid.
7. Graser, M. 1999. Pixar run by focused group. *Variety*, December 20, p. 74.
8. Barnes, B. It Wasn't A Wreck, Not Really. *New York Times*, October 17, 2011, https://www.nytimes.com/2011/10/18/movies/john-lasseter-of-pixar-defends-cars-2.html
9. Burrows, P. and R. Grover. 1998. Steve Jobs: movie mogul. *BusinessWeek*, November 23, p. 146.
10. Bary, A. 2003. Coy story. Barron's, October 13, p. 21.
11. Tam, Pui-Wing. Pixar Bets It Can Boost Output To One Movie Feature a Year. The Wall Street Journal, February 15, 2001. https://www.wsj.com/articles/SB982187376277025044
12. Terdiman, D. 2012. Bravely going where Pixar animation tech has never gone. CNET News, June 16.
13. Burrows, P. and R. Grover. 2006. Steve Jobs' Magic Kingdom. *BusinessWeek*, February 6, p. 66.
14. Bary, A. 2003. Coy story. Barron's, October 13, p. 21.
15. Barnes, B. 2018. Disney picks new chiefs of animation. *New York Times*, June 20, p. B3.
16. https://www.the-numbers.com/movie/Toy-Story-4-(2019)#tab5summary
17. Kit, B. 2018. Pixar co-founder Ed Catmull to retire. *The Hollywood Reporter*, October 23.

CASE 13

HEINEKEN*

Dutch brewer Heineken was expanding its presence around the globe in response to the merger of Anheuser-Busch InBev with SABMiller, which would give the combined firm a commanding 30 percent of global beer sales. On March 19, 2019, it opened its first Mozambique brewery in the presence of His Excellency Filipe Nyusi, the President of the Republic of Mozambique. The new brewery, incorporating the latest technologies, represents a $100 million investment. Among its products will be Txilar, a local beer specifically made with a maize that is grown in the region. "The construction of Heineken's first brewery is a major step for the company's presence in the country," said Jean-Francois van Boxmeer, CEO of the firm.[1]

The move comes on the heels of acquisitions and capacity investments that Heineken has been making in other developing markets. In 2013, the firm had strengthened its position as the world's third largest brewer by taking full ownership of Asian Pacific Breweries, the owner of Tiger, Bintang, and other popular Asian beer brands. With this deal, Heineken added 30 breweries across several countries in the Asia Pacific region. A few years earlier, the firm had acquired Mexican brewer FEMSA Cervesa, producer of Dos Equis, Sol, and Tecate beers, to become a stronger, more competitive player in Latin America.

* Case prepared by Jamal Shamsie, Michigan State University, with the assistance of Professor Alan B. Eisner, Pace University. Material has been drawn from published sources to be used for purposes of class discussion. Copyright © 2019 Jamal Shamsie and Alan B. Eisner.

At the same time, Heineken has maintained its leading position across Europe. It had made a high-profile acquisition in 2008 of Scottish-based brewer Scottish & Newcastle, the brewer of well-known brands such as Newcastle Brown Ale and Kronenbourg 1664. Although the purchase had been made in partnership with Carlsberg, Heineken was able to gain control of the Scottish & Newcastle's operations in several crucial European markets such as the United Kingdom, Ireland, Portugal, Finland, and Belgium.

These decisions to acquire brewers that operate in different parts of the world have been a part of a series of changes that the Dutch brewer has been making to raise its stature in the various markets and respond to growing consolidation within the industry and changes occurring in the global market for beer. Even as sales of beer have stagnated in the United States and Europe, demand has been growing in other developing countries. This has led the largest brewers to expand across the globe through acquisitions of smaller regional and national players (see Exhibits 1 and 2).

The need for change was clearly reflected in the appointment in October 2005 of Jean-Francois van Boxmeer as Heineken's first non-Dutch CEO. He was brought in to replace Anthony Ruys, who had decided to resign because of his failure to improve performance. Prior to the appointment of Ruys in 2002, Heineken had been run by three generations of Heineken ancestors whose portraits still adorn the dark paneled office of the CEO in its Amsterdam headquarters. Like Ruys, van Boxmeer has tried to handle the

EXHIBIT 1
Income Statement (millions of euros)

	2018	2017	2016	2015
Total Revenue	22,471	21,888	20,792	20,511
Operating Profit	3,062	3,276	2,709	2,664
Net Income	1,903	1,935	1,540	1,892

Source: Heineken.

EXHIBIT 2
Balance Sheet (millions of euros)

	2018	2017	2016	2015
Assets	41,956	41,034	39,321	37,714
Liabilities	26,416	26,513	24,748	22,664
Equity	15,540	14,521	14,573	15,050

Source: Heineken.

challenge of preserving the firm's family-driven traditions, while addressing threats that have never been faced before.

Confronting a Globalizing Industry

Heineken was one of the pioneers of an international strategy, using cross-border deals to expand its distribution of its Heineken, Amstel, or about 300 other beer brands in more than 100 countries around the globe. For years, it has been picking up small brewers from several countries to add more brands and to obtain better access to new markets. From its roots on the outskirts of Amsterdam, the firm has evolved into one of the world's largest brewers, operating more than 190 breweries in over 70 countries in the world, claiming about 10 percent of the global market for beer (see Exhibits 3 & 4).

In fact, the firm's flagship Heineken brand ranked second only to Budweiser in a global brand survey jointly undertaken by BusinessWeek and Interbrand several years ago. The premier brand has achieved worldwide recognition according to Kevin Baker, director of alcoholic beverages at British market researcher Canadean Ltd. A U.S. wholesaler recently asked a group of marketing students to identify an

EXHIBIT 3
Geographical Breakdown of Sales (millions of euros)

	2018	2017	2016	2015
Western Europe	10,348	9,990	10,112	10,227
Americas	6,781	6,312	5,203	5,159
Africa, Middle East, & Eastern Europe	3,051	3,028	3,203	3,263
Asia Pacific	2,919	2,922	2,894	2,483

Source: Heineken.

EXHIBIT 4
Significant Heineken Brands In Various Markets

Markets	Brands
United States	Heineken, Amstel Light, Paulaner,[1] Moretti, Lagunitas
Netherlands	Heineken, Amstel, Lingen's Blond, Murphy's Irish Red
France	Heineken, Amstel, Buckler,[2] Desperados[3]
Italy	Heineken, Amstel, Birra Moretti
Spain	Heineken, Amstel, Cruzcampo, Buckler
Poland	Heineken, Krolewskie, Kujawiak, Zywiec
China	Heineken, Tiger, Reeb*
Singapore	Heineken, Tiger, Anchor, Baron's
India	Heineken, Arlem, Kingfisher
Indonesia	Heineken, Bintang, Guinness
Kazakhstan	Heineken, Amstel, Tian Shan
Egypt	Heineken, Birell, Meister, Fayrouz[2]
Israel	Heineken, Maccabee, Gold Star*
Nigeria	Heineken, Star, Maltina, Gulder
South Africa	Heineken, Amstel, Windhoek. Strongbow
Panama	Heineken, Soberana, Crystal, Panama
Chile	Heineken, Cristal, Escudo, Royal

*Minority interest

[1]Wheat beer

[2]Nonalcoholic beer

[3]Tequila-flavored beer

Source: Heineken.

EXHIBIT 5

Leading Global Brewers (2016 market share percentage based on annual sales, millions of U.S. dollars)

Brewers	Market Share
1. Anheuser-Busch InBev (ABI), Leuven, Belgium (incl. SABMiller)	27.3
2. Heineken, Amsterdam, Netherlands	9.7
3. China Resources Enterprise, China	6.1
4. Carlsberg, Copenhagen, Denmark	5.9
5. Molson Coors	4.9

Source: Statista.

assortment of beer bottles that had been stripped of their labels. The stubby green Heineken container was the only one that incited instant recognition among the group.

But the beer industry has been undergoing significant change due to a furious wave of consolidation. Most of the bigger brewers have begun to acquire or merge with their competitors in foreign markets in order to become global players. This has given them ownership of local brands, propelling them into a dominant position in various markets around the world. In addition, acquisitions of foreign brewers can provide the firm with the manufacturing and distribution capabilities they could use to develop a few global brands. "The era of global brands is coming," Alan Clark, a Budapest-based managing director of SABMiller Europe stated some years ago (see Exhibit 5).[2]

Since 2000, South African Breweries, Ltd, acquired U.S.-based Miller Brewing to become a major global brewer. They subsequently acquired Fosters, the largest Australian brewer. U.S.-based Coors linked with Canadian-based Molson in 2005, rising to a leading position among the world's biggest brewers with their combined operations. In 2008, Belgium's Interbrew, Brazil's AmBev, and U.S.-based Anheuser Busch all merged to become the largest global brewer with operations across most of the continents. Finally, Anheuser-Busch InBev made a move in 2016 to acquire SABMiller to become an even more dominant player in the industry.

Since its acquisition of Anheuser Busch, InBev has included Budweiser along with Stella Artois, Brahma, and Becks in its lineup of what it is promoting as its global flagship brands. Each of these brands originated in different locations, with Budweiser coming from the United States, Stella Artois coming from Belgium, Brahma from Brazil, and Becks from Germany. Similarly, SABMiller has been attempting to develop the Czech brand Pilsner Urquell into a global brand. Exports of this pilsner doubled shortly after SAB acquired it in 1999, but sales have since plateaued. John Brock, the CEO of InBev, commented: "Global brands sell at significantly higher prices, and the margins are much better than with local beers."[3]

Wrestling with Change

Although the management of Heineken has moved away from the family for the first time, they have been well aware of the longstanding and well-established family traditions that would be difficult to change. Even with the appointment of non-family members to manage the firm, a little over half of the shares of Heineken are still owned by a holding company that is controlled by the family. With the death of Freddy Heineken in 2002, the last family member to head the Dutch brewer, control has passed to his only child and heir, Charlene de Carvalho, who has insisted on having a say in all of the major decisions.

But the family members were behind some of changes that were announced at the time of van Boxmeer's appointment. These were intended to support Heineken's next phase of growth as a global organization. As part of the plan, dubbed Fit 2 Fight, the Executive Board was cut down from five members to CEO van Boxmeer and Chief Financial Officer Rene Hooft Graafland. The change was expected to centralize control at the top so that the firm can formulate a strategy that it should follow to win over younger customers across different markets whose tastes are still developing.

Heineken has also created management positions that would be responsible for five different operating regions and several different functional areas. These positions were created to define more clearly different spheres of responsibility. Van Boxmeer argued that the new structure also provides incentives for people to be accountable for their performance: "There is more pressure for results, for achievement."[4] He claimed the new structure has already encouraged more risk taking and boosted the level of energy within the firm.

The Executive Committee of Heineken was also cut down from 36 to 12 members in order to speed up the decision-making process. Besides the two members of the Executive Board, this management group consists of the managers who are responsible for the different operating regions and several of the key functional areas. Van Boxmeer has hoped that the reduction in the size of this group will allow the firm to combat the cumbersome consensus culture that has made it difficult for Heineken to respond swiftly to various challenges even as its industry has been experiencing considerable change.

Finally, all of the activities of Heineken have been overseen by a Supervisory Board, which currently consists of 10 members. Individuals that make up this board are drawn from different countries and cover a wide range of expertise and experience. They set up policies for the firm to use in making majors decisions in its overall operations. Members of the Supervisory Board are rotated on a regular basis.

Developing a Global Presence

Van Boxmeer has been well aware of the need for Heineken to use its brands to build upon its existing stature across global markets. In spite of its formidable presence in markets around the world with its flagship Heineken brand, the firm has been reluctant to match the recent moves of formidable competitors such as Belgium's InBev and the UK's SABMiller, which have grown significantly through mega-acquisitions. In large part, it is assumed that the firm has been reluctant to make such acquisitions because of the dilution of family control.

For many years, Heineken had limited itself to snapping up small national brewers such as Italy's Moretti to Spain's Cruzcampo that have provided it with small, but profitable avenues for growth. In 1996, for example, Heineken had acquired Fischer, a small French brewer, whose Desperados brand had been quite successful in niche markets. Similarly, Paulaner, a wheat beer that the firm picked up in Germany a few years ago, has been making inroads into the U.S. market.

But as other brewers have been reaching out to make acquisitions from all over the globe, Heineken has been running the risk of falling behind its more aggressive rivals. To deal with this growing challenge, the firm has broken out of its play-it-safe corporate culture to make a few big deals. In 2003, Heineken spent $2.1 billion to acquire BBAG, a family-owned company based in Linz, Austria. Because of BBAG's extensive presence in Central Europe, Heineken has become the biggest beer maker in seven countries across Eastern Europe. The acquisition of Scottish & Newcastle in 2008 similarly reinforced the firm's dominance in Western Europe.

At the same time, Heineken has been making a string of acquisitions in other parts of the world. Its recent acquisitions in Ethiopia, Singapore, and Mexico have allowed it to build its position in these growing markets. The firm has also made an aggressive push into Russia with the acquisition of mid-sized brewing concerns. Through several acquisitions since 2002, Russia has become one of Heineken's largest markets by volume. Heineken now ranks as the third-largest brewer in Russia, behind Sweden's Baltic Beverages Holding and InBev.

Rene Hooft Graafland, the company's Chief Financial Officer, has stated that Heineken will continue to participate in the consolidation of the $460 billion global retail beer industry, by targeting many different markets around the world. During the last decade, the firm has also added several labels to Heineken's shelf, pouncing on brewers in far flung places like Belarus, Panama, Egypt, and Kazakhstan. In Egypt, Ruys bought a majority stake in Al Ahram Beverages Co. and had been using the Cairo-based brewer's fruit-flavored, nonalcoholic malts as an avenue into other Muslim countries.

Maintaining a Premium Position

For decades, Heineken has been able to rely upon the success of its flagship Heineken brand, which has enjoyed a leading position among premium beers in many markets around the world. It had been the best-selling imported beer in the United States for several decades, giving it a steady source of revenues and profits from the world's biggest market. But by the late 1990s, Heineken had lost its 65-year-old leadership among imported beers in the United States to Group Modelo's Corona. The Mexican beer has been able to reach out to the growing Hispanic Americans who represent one of the fastest growing segments of beer drinkers.

Furthermore, the firm was also concerned that Heineken was being perceived as an obsolete brand by many young drinkers. John A. Quelch, a professor at Harvard Business School who has studied the beer industry said of Heineken: "It's in danger of becoming a tired, reliable, but unexciting brand."[5] Therefore, the firm has been working hard to increase awareness of their flagship brand among younger drinkers. Heineken also introduced a light beer, Heineken Premium Light, to target the growing market for such beers in the United States. Through such efforts, the firm has managed to reduce the average age of the Heineken drinker from about 40 years old to about 30 years old.

At the same time, Heineken has also been pushing other brands that would reduce its reliance on its core Heineken brand. It has already achieved considerable success with Amstel Light, which has become the leading imported light beer in the United States and has been selling well in many other countries. But many of the other brands that it carries are strong local brands added through its string of acquisitions of smaller breweries around the globe. It has managed to develop a relatively small but loyal base of consumers by promoting some of these as specialty brands, such as Murphy's Irish Red and Moretti.

Finally, Heineken has been stepping up its efforts to target Hispanics, who account for one-quarter of U.S. sales. Besides developing specific marketing campaigns for them, it added popular Mexican beers such as Tecate and Dos Equis to its line of offerings. For years, these had been marketed and distributed by Heineken in the United States under a license from FEMSA Cervesa. In 2010, the firm decided to acquire the firm, giving them full control over all of their brands. Benj Steinman, publisher and editor of Beer Marketer's Insight newsletter, believed their relationship with FEMSA had been quite beneficial: "This gives Heineken a commanding share of the U.S. import business and . . . gives them a bigger presence in the Southwest . . . and better access to Hispanic consumers," he stated.[6]

Above all, Heineken wants to maintain its leadership in the premium beer industry, which represents the most profitable segment of the beer business. In this category, the firm's brands face competition in the United States from domestic beers such as Anheuser's Budweiser Select and imported beers such as InBev's Stella Artois. Although premium brews often have slightly higher alcohol content than standard beers, they are developed through a more exclusive positioning of the brand. This allows the firm to charge a higher price for these brands. A six-pack of Heineken, for example, costs $9, versus around $6 for a six-pack of Budweiser. Furthermore, Just-drinks.com, a London-based online research service, estimates that the market for premium beer will continue to expand over the next decade.

Building on Its Past

The recent acquisitions in different parts of the world–Asia, Africa, Latin America and Europe–represent an important step in Heineken's quest to build upon its existing global stature. Van Boxmeer and his team have made an effort to enter new markets and build upon the firm's position in existing markets. In November 2018, Heineken signed an agreement with China Resources Enterprise and China Resources Beer to create a long-term strategic partnership for mainland China, Hong Kong, and Macau. The partnership will give the firm a 40 percent share in the Chinese firm that controls CR beer, the undisputed market leader in China, which represents the world's largest beer market.

In order to accompany this global expansion, van Boxmeer has also been committed to working on the company's culture in order to accelerate the speed of decision making. This led many people both inside and outside the firm to expect the new management to try and break loose from the conservative style that has resulted from the family's tight control. Instead, the affable 46-year-old Belgian indicated that he has been trying to focus on changes to the firm's decision-making process rather to make any drastic shifts in its existing culture. "Since 1952 history has proved it is the right concept," he stated about the Heineken's ownership structure. "The whole business about family restraint on us is absolutely untrue. Without its spirit and guidance, the company would not have been able to build a world leader."[7]

In fact, van Boxmeer's devotion to the firm is quite evident. Since he took over, Heineken has shown steady growth in revenues and profits, even with little growth in the global market for beer. Before he took over as Heineken's first non-Dutch CEO, van Boxmeer had spent 20 years working his way up within the firm. Even his cufflinks are silver miniatures of a Heineken bottle top and opener. "We are in the logical flow of history," he explained. "Every time you have a new leader you have a new kind of vision. It is not radically different, because you are defined by what your company is and what your brands are."[8]

ENDNOTES

1. GlobeNewswire. 2019. Heineken opens up first brewery in Mozambique, a US$100 million investment. March 13.
2. Ewing, J. and G. Khermouch. 2003. Waking up Heineken. *BusinessWeek,* September 8, p. 68.
3. Tomlinson, R. 2004. The new king of beers. *Fortune,* October 18, p. 238.
4. Bickerton, I. and J. Wiggins. 2006. Accelerated change is brewing at Heineken. *Financial Times,* May 8, p. 12.
5. Ewing, J. and G. Khermouch. 2003. Waking up Heineken. *BusinessWeek,* September 8, p. 69.
6. Kaplan, A. 2004. Border crossings. *Beverage World,* July 15, p. 6.
7. Bickerton, I. and J. Wiggins. 2006. Accelerated change is brewing at Heineken. *Financial Times,* May 8, p. 12.
8. Ibid.

CASE 14

eBAY: MISUNDERSTOOD?*

eBay's former CEO Devin Wenig said, "It's a real challenge for eBay as it one of the world's most iconic brands, but it is also one of the world's most misunderstood brands."[1] What did he mean by misunderstood and, as of 2019, what is eBay's position? Is it an auction website selling pre-owned products or an e-commerce platform with distinguished product quality and competitive delivery options?

eBay gained popularity in its initial years as an auction website, one where sellers had complete control of the products and shipping. In order to match its competitors such as Amazon, who offered new products faster with better control over their inventory, eBay tried to keep up and make a smooth transition from being just an auction website to an e-commerce one. While eBay's legacy is powerful, over the years it has discovered its limits. Amazon, not eBay, is what comes to a customer's mind when they think of shopping online. "I want eBay to be a place where people think of first for the things they love, not just the things they need," Wenig said as he stressed how he did not want eBay to be compared to Amazon.[2] But are the things we love different from the things we need? Or is eBay just trying emotional branding? "eBay: Electronics, Cars, Fashion, Collectibles, Coupons and More" is what the title tag reads when a customer googles eBay. Do these constitute the things we love, and how are they different from the things we need?

A need to re-establish what its brand meant to consumers resulted in an increased marketing investment by eBay to gain customers by 2019. The company tried getting its message across with ads through a number of marketing channels and, most importantly, social media. "Social media, both in terms of organic posts and ads, is a 'critical lever' for eBay's marketing and media strategies," said Suzy Deering, the online marketplace's chief marketing officer.[3] "At its core, we look to focus on creating quality interactions with the eBay brand, raising brand awareness and consideration, driving relevant traffic and, eventually, generating buyer growth and sales," she said.[4] eBay took on several initiatives to innovate and improve its offered services to combat the increasing competition. In January 2018, eBay partnered with the city of Akron, Ohio, to empower local entrepreneurs. They called the program "Retail Revival" through which the company and the city of Akron aimed to advance existing economic development efforts by harnessing the power of technology and eBay's global marketplace in support of the local business community.[5]

Moreover, in order to compete with popular two-day delivery services offered by many online retailers including Amazon and Walmart, eBay introduced a guaranteed rapid delivery service in summer 2017.[6] Guaranteed delivery service will enable the customers to buy more than 20 million eligible items with guaranteed delivery within two days. If a guaranteed item arrives later than two days, the company will refund the shipping cost to the customer in the form of store credit that can be used for future purchases. Brett Thome, Vice President of Business Development at Spreetail eBay store VM Innovations, said "We're very excited about eBay's Guaranteed Delivery. There are so many great sellers on eBay delivering an incredible shipping experience where they deliver in two days, and even next day, so the ability to highlight Guaranteed Delivery will further increase customer confidence and satisfaction.[7]

Apart from proving its brand value, the past few years were difficult for eBay's Marketplaces. A security-related password reset and web search engine optimization (SEO) changes heavily impacted customer traffic. The company publicly admitted that criminals were able to penetrate and steal certain data including usernames, encrypted user passwords, and other non-financial user data. eBay's loyal customers returned following the password changes, but the more occasional customers did not return as quickly as expected. Further, the SEO changes significantly diminished eBay's presence in natural search results, which impacted new-user growth.

eBay witnessed considerable pressure from Carl Icahn, an activist investor. Icahn had challenged the board by increasing his stake in the company and pressuring it to spin off its noncore businesses. The company finally agreed to spin off its PayPal and Enterprise businesses. In 2018, four years after his efforts to sever eBay's and PayPal's tie-up, the investor is reportedly dissolving his investments in the payment company.

A Successful Past

Since its inception in 1995, eBay had enjoyed strong revenue growth and been a dominant player in the online auction industry. Within two decades, the company had grown considerably, and it had a net revenue of $10.7 billion and an operating income of $2.2 billion in 2018 (see Exhibits 1 and 2).

---

* This case was prepared by Professor Alan B. Eisner and graduate students David J. Morates and Sushmitha Mudda of Pace University. This case was solely based on library research and was developed for class discussion rather than to illustrate either effective or ineffective handling of an administrative situation. Copyright ©2019 Alan B. Eisner.

EXHIBIT 1 Income Statement ($ millions)

	(in millions, except per share amounts)		
	2018	2017	2016
Net revenues	$10,746	$ 9,927	$ 9,298
Cost of net revenues	2,382	2,221	2,004
Gross profit	8,364	7,706	7,294
Operating expenses:			
Sales and marketing	3,391	2,878	2,691
Product development	1,285	1,224	1,114
General and administrative	1,131	1,030	899
Provision for transaction losses	286	272	231
Amortization of acquired intangible assets	49	38	34
Total operating expenses	6,142	5,442	4,969
Income from operations	2,222	2,264	2,325
Interest and other, net	496	11	1,326
Income from continuing operations before income taxes	2,718	2,275	3,651
Income tax benefit (provision)	(190)	(3,288)	3,634
Income (loss) from continuing operations	2,528	$(1,013)	$ 7,285
Income (loss) from discontinued operations, net of income taxes	2	(4)	(19)
Net income	$ 2,530	$(1,017)	$ 7,266
Income (loss) per share–basic:			
Continuing operations	$ 2.58	$ (0.95)	$ 6.43
Discontinued operations	–	–	(0.02)
Net income per share–basic	$ 2.58	$ (0.95)	$ 6.41
Income (loss) per share–diluted:			
Continuing operations	$ 2.55	$ (0.95)	$ 6.37
Discontinued operations	–	–	(0.02)
Net income(loss) per share–diluted	$ 2.58	$ (0.95)	$ 6.35
Weighted average shares:			
Basic	980	1,064	1,133
Diluted	991	1,064	1,144

Source: eBay SEC filings, 2018.

eBay's founder, Pierre Omidyar, had envisioned a community built on commerce, sustained by trust, and inspired by opportunity. The company's mission was to "enable individual self-empowerment on a global scale" and employ "business as a tool for social good." Omidyar cited "trust between strangers" as the social impact tied to eBay's ability to remain profitable.

The company's unique business model united buyers and sellers in an online marketplace. eBay enabled e-commerce at multiple levels (local, national, and international) through an array of websites, including eBay Marketplaces, PayPal, Rent.com, Shopping.com, and eBay Style.

EXHIBIT 2 Balance Sheet ($ millions)

	2018	2017
	(in millions, except per value)	
Assets		
Current assets:		
Cash and cash equivalents	$ 2,202	$ 2,120
Short-term investments	2,713	3,741
Accounts receivable, net	712	696
Other current assets	1,499	1,185
Total current assets	7,126	7,744
Long-term investments	3,778	6,331
Property and equipment, net	1,597	1,597
Goodwill	5,160	4,773
Intangible assets, net	92	69
Deferred tax asset, non-current	4,792	5,199
Other assets	274	273
Total assets	$22,819	$25,986
Liabilities and Stockholders' Equity		
Current liabilities:		
Short-term debt	$ 1,546	$ 781
Accounts payable	286	330
Accrued expenses and other current liabilities	2,335	2,134
Deferred revenue	170	137
Income taxes payable	117	177
Total current liabilities	4,454	3,559
Deferred and other tax liabilities, net	2,925	3,424
Long-term debt	7,685	9,234
Other liabilities	1,474	1,720
Total liabilities	16,538	17,937
Stockholders' equity:		
Common stock, $0.001 par value; 3,580 shares authorized; 1,087 and 1,184 shares outstanding	2	2
Additional paid-in capital	15,716	15,293
Treasury stock at cost, 557 and 443 shares	(26,394)	(21,892)
Retained earnings	16,459	13,929
Accumulated other comprehensive income	498	717
Total stockholders' equity	6,281	8,049
Total liabilities and stockholders' equity	**$22,819**	**$25,986**

Source: eBay SEC filings.

The company's range of products and services evolved from collectibles to household products, customer services, automobiles, and the mobile industry. The variety of products attracted a range of users that included students, small businesses, independent sellers, major corporations, and government agencies.

Despite eBay's outstanding growth performance, the company faced a number of challenges in both domestic and international markets. The low entry barriers in the online marketplace attracted a number of large dot-com competitors, including Amazon, Yahoo/Taobao, Google/Overstock, and Etsy. Historically, eBay had acquired other online competitors, such as StubHub (tickets), but established players such as Yahoo, Google, and Amazon posed a major threat to eBay's market share and ability to sustain profitability. Still, eBay's top management felt that the company would end up as a specialty business, an idea suggesting that it would face little threat from these major competitors. The company had no plans for further big acquisitions but intended to expand and identify synergies within existing business lines.

eBay acknowledged its inability to grow and compete in certain international markets. The company had created localized sites in 30 countries and established a presence in Latin America through its investment in Mercado Libre, a Latin American e-commerce company.[8] However, eBay sold a majority stake of the Latin American platform in 2016. eBay's numerous attempts to penetrate the Asia-Pacific market, specifically China and Japan, ended in failure, with the company pulling out of Japan and buying out Chinese start-up Eachnet, essentially canceling years of invested work. According to many analysts, the company's recent interest in its South Korean rival Gmarket Inc. and its joint venture with Beijing-based Tom Online were further indications that eBay could not compete in Asia-Pacific countries. eBay enjoyed financial benefits as a result of a tax provision that considerably improved the company's cash flow (see Exhibit 3). However, in order to remain successful and enjoy the same financial performance as it had in the past, eBay needed to develop an effective strategy to compete in major Asian markets and to mitigate the risk of existing local competitors.

eBay's overall strategy had traditionally comprised three primary components: products, sense of community, and aggressive expansion. All three components evolved around the various geographic and specialty platforms the company introduced.

Product Categories

eBay had an array of product categories and trading platforms that offered a range of pricing formats, such as fixed pricing. Relatively new for the company, the fixed-price format allowed eBay to compete directly with major competitors such as Amazon and penetrate new market space. Before fixed pricing, selling prices were solely determined by the highest auction bid, and this took days or weeks, depending on the length of the auction. eBay's different trading platforms also offered distinct services and target-specific market niches, which allowed eBay to broaden its customer base. The platforms included:

- *PayPal:* Founded in 1998 and acquired by eBay in 2002, PayPal enabled individuals to securely send payments quickly and easily online. PayPal was considered the global leader in online payments, with tens of millions of registered users. In 2011, PayPal's president, Scott Thompson, expected revenue to double, reaching $6 billion to $7 billion by 2013. He also predicted that 75 to 80 percent of eBay transactions would be done through PayPal by 2013, up from 69 percent in 2010.[9] However, in 2014 the company decided it was more prudent to spin off its PayPal business as a separate company. The spin-off occurred in 2015.[10]
- *Online classifieds:* By 2009, eBay had the world's leading portfolio of online classified sites, including Kijiji, Intoko, Gumtree, LoQUo.com, Marktplaats.nl, and mobile.de. CEO John Donahoe said, "We are the global leader in classifieds, with top positions in Canada, Australia, Germany, Japan, and the United Kingdom, and sites in more than 1,000 cities across 20 countries."[11]
- *Shopping.com:* With thousands of merchants and millions of products and reviews, Shopping.com empowered consumers to make informed choices, which drove value for merchants. In 2013, it was rebranded as the eBay Commerce Network.
- *Stubhub.com:* StubHub was an online marketplace for selling and purchasing tickets for sports events, concerts, and other live entertainment events.
- *eBay Express:* eBay Express behaved like a standard Internet shopping site but gave sellers access to over 200 million buyers worldwide. Sellers could design product categories within minutes, and buyers could purchase from multiple sellers by using a single shopping cart.
- *eBay Motors:* This specialty site was considered the largest marketplace for automobile buyers and sellers. Buyers could purchase anything from automobile parts to new or antique vehicles.
- *Skype:* Acquired by eBay in October 2005, Skype was the world's fastest-growing online communication solution, allowing free video and audio communication between users of Skype software. By November 2009, Skype connected more than 480 million registered users.[12] eBay's acquisition of Skype was expected to enhance the customer experience by improving communication between buyers and sellers. In November 2009, however, eBay sold Skype to a group led by Silver Lake Partners, a private equity firm in Silicon Valley, which eventually sold the entity to Microsoft.

EXHIBIT 3 Cash Flow Statement ($ millions)

eBay Inc. CONSOLIDATED STATEMENT OF CASH FLOWS			
	Year Ended December 31,		
	2018	2017	2016
		(In millions)	
Net income (loss)	2,530	(1,017)	7,266
(Income) loss from discontinued operations, net of income taxes	(2)	4	19
Provision for transaction losses	286	272	231
Depreciation and amortization	696	676	682
Stock-based compensation	538	483	416
(Gain) loss on investments, net	(572)	49	(1,236)
Gain on sale of business	–	(167)	–
Deferred income taxes	(153)	1,728	(4,556)
Change in fair value of warrant	(104)	–	–
Other	19	–	(15)
Accounts receivable	(98)	(195)	(48)
Other current assets	(143)	(148)	23
Other non-current assets	108	19	94
Accounts payable	(47)	19	(28)
Accrued expenses and other liabilities	(437)	206	(130)
Deferred revenue	33	8	4
Income taxes payable and other tax liabilities	7	1,209	105
Net income (loss)	2,530	(1,016)	7,266
Net cash provided by continuing operating activities	2,661	3,146	2,827
Net cash provided by (used in) discontinued operating activities	(3)	-	(1)
Net cash provided by operating activities	2,658	3,146	2,826
Cash flows from investing activities:			
Purchases of property and equipment	(651)	(666)	(626)
Purchases of investments	(28,115)	(14,599)	(11,212)
Maturities and sales of investments	30,901	14,520	10,063
Equity investment in Flipkart	–	(514)	–
Proceeds from sale of equity investment in Flipkart	1,029	–	–
Acquisitions, net of cash acquired	(302)	(34)	(212)
Changes in principal loans receivable, net	–	–	–
Other	32	(3)	(30)

continued

EXHIBIT 3 *Continued*

eBay Inc. CONSOLIDATED STATEMENT OF CASH FLOWS			
	Year Ended December 31,		
	2018	2017	2016
		(In millions)	
Net cash (used in) provided by investing activities	2,894	(1,295)	(2,017)
Proceeds from issuance of common stock	109	120	102
Repurchases of common stock	(4,502)	(2,746)	(2,943)
Tax withholdings related to net share settlements of restricted stock awards and units	(225)	(219)	(121)
Proceeds from issuance of long-term debt, net	–	2,484	2,216
Repayment of debt	(750)	(1,452)	(20)
Other	(30)	29	22
Net cash used in financing activities	(5,398)	(1,784)	(744)
Effect of exchange rate changes on cash, cash equivalents and restricted cash	(75)	238	(90)
Net increase (decrease) in cash, cash equivalents and restricted cash	79	305	(25)
Cash, cash equivalents and restricted cash at beginning of period	2,140	1,815	1,860
Cash, cash equivalents and restricted cash at end of period	2,219	2,140	1,835
Supplemental cash flow disclosures:			
Cash paid for:			
Interest	(75)	238	(90)
Income taxes	2,219	2,140	1,835

Source: eBay SEC filings.

- *Giosis*: Giosis, also known as Qoo10.jp platform is an online marketplace for Korean audience. eBay initially invested in Giosis in 2010 and Giosis progressed to establish dynamic marketplace businesses across Asia. With today's acquisition, eBay will build on Giosis' progress in Japan, enhancing the domestic customer experience and providing approximately two million Japanese buyers currently using the Qoo10.jp platform with a well-curated selection of merchandise sourced both locally and from across the globe.[13]

Sense of Community

The underlying key to all eBay sites and trading platforms was creating trust between sellers and buyers. The company created "community values," and this was why eBay users were willing to send money to strangers across the country. The Feedback Forum was created in February 1996 and encouraged users to post comments about trading partners. Originally, Omidyar had handled disputes between buyers and sellers via email by putting the disputing parties in touch with each other to resolve the issue themselves. He soon realized that an open forum in which users could post opinions and feedback about one another would create the trust and sense of community the site required. Buyers and sellers were encouraged to post comments (positive, negative, or neutral) about each other at the completion of each transaction. The individual feedback was recorded and amended to a user profile, which ultimately established a rating and reputation for each buyer and seller. eBay users could view this information before engaging in a transaction. The company believed that the Feedback Forum was critical for creating initial user acceptance for purchasing and selling over the Internet and that it contributed more than anything else to eBay's success.

Aggressive Expansion

To compete effectively and create a global trading platform, eBay continued to develop in U.S. and international markets that utilized the Internet. With intense competition in the online auction industry, eBay aimed to increase its market share and revenue through acquisitions and partnerships in related and unrelated businesses. For example:

- In June 2000, eBay acquired Half.com for $318 million.
- In August 2001, eBay acquired MercadoLibre, Lokau, and iBazar, Latin American auction sites.
- On August 13, 2004, eBay took a 25 percent stake in Craigslist, an online network of urban communities.
- In September 2005, eBay invested $2 million in the Meetup social networking site.
- In August 2006, eBay announced international cooperation with Google.
- In January 2007, eBay acquired online ticket marketplace StubHub for $310 million.
- In June 2010, eBay acquired RedLaser, a mobile application that let customers scan bar codes to list items faster on its online auction site and to compare prices.[14]
- In December 2010, eBay acquired Milo, a leading local shopping engine that provided consumers access to accurate, real-time, local-store inventory and pricing, giving them even more choices and flexibility when shopping online.[15]
- In December 2010, eBay acquired Critical Path Software Inc., a developer of smartphone applications, to accelerate its lead in mobile commerce.[16]
- In 2014, eBay announced its agreement to acquire Shutl, a UK-based marketplace that used a network of couriers to deliver local goods the same day.
- In July 2016, eBay completed the acquisition of SalesPredict, an artificial intelligence system that would help the company to effectively predict customer buying behavior, preferences, and machine learning.[17]
- In August 2016, eBay acquired Ticket Utils that became part of StubHub platform. Ticket Utils was a New Jersey-based software company that helped large ticket sellers organize and manage their tickets and distribution.[18]
- In February 2017, eBay announced its partnership agreement with Snupps, a social organizing app used to buy and sell online.[19]
- In March 2017, eBay announced an exclusive partnership with Flipkart, a popular e-commerce platform in India. eBay acquired a $500 million equity stake in exchange for eBay's India business.[20]
- In May 2018, eBay acquired Giosis, including the Qoo10.jp platform, which is an online marketplace for Korean audiences.

Evolution of the Auction Market

Traditional Auctions

According to Greek scribes, the first known auctions occurred in Babylon in 500 BC. At that time, women were sold on the condition of marriage, and it was considered illegal for daughters to be sold outside auctions. Auctions evolved during the French Revolution and throughout the American Civil War, where colonels auctioned goods that had been seized by armies.[21] Although there were various types of auctions, they all provided a forum at which sellers could find buyers. Auctions were considered one of the purest markets because buyers paid what they were willing to spend for an item, thereby determining the true market value of the item. Over time, auction formats evolved, and through technological advances and improved communication, they found a new home—the Internet.

Online Auctions

The primary difference between traditional and online auctions is that the online auction process occurs over the Internet rather than at a specific location where both buyers and sellers are present. Online auctions offer strategic advantages to both parties not typically available in traditional auctions. Buyers select from millions of products and engage in multiple auctions simultaneously. Given the massive inventory of an online auction market, items are usually available in multiple auctions, allowing buyers to compare starting-bid prices and search for better prices. Sellers are exposed to millions of buyers since more buyers have access to the Internet and feel comfortable making purchases online. Thus, the Internet gives buyers and sellers access to a marketplace that spans the world.

Online auctions also offer the following strategic advantages:

1. *No time constraints:* A bid can be placed at any time.
2. *No geographic constraints:* Sellers and buyers can participate from any location with Internet access.
3. *Network economies:* The large number of bidders attracts more sellers, which attracts more bidders, and so on. This creates a large system that has more value for both parties. Online auctions also allow businesses to easily sell off excess inventory or discontinued items.

This is done through either business-to-business (B2B) or business-to-consumer (B2C) auctions. Offering products and services in an online auction helps small businesses build their brand and reputation by establishing a devoted customer base. Finally, some businesses use the online marketplace as an inexpensive yet effective way to test-market upcoming products.

World of E-Commerce

Although Vannevar Bush originally conceived the idea of the Internet in 1945, it wasn't until the 1990s that the Internet became overwhelmingly popular. According to Internet World Stats, as of January 2019, there were about 4.4 billion active Internet users in over 150 countries. Exhibit 4 shows world Internet usage and population as of March 31, 2018, and Internet usage growth between 2000 and 2018.

EXHIBIT 4 World Internet Usage and Population Statistics, 2018

World Regions	Population (2018 Est.)	Population % of World	Internet Users June 30, 2018	Penetration Rate (% Pop.)	Growth 2000–2018	Users % Table
Africa	1,287,914,329	16.9	464,923,169	36.1	10,199	11.0
Asia	4,207,588,157	55.1	2,062,197,366	49.0	1,704	49.0
Europe	827,650,849	10.8	705,064,923	85.2	570	16.8
Latin America/ Caribbean	652,047,996	8.5	438,248,446	67.2	2,325	10.4
Middle East	254,438,981	3.3	164,037,259	64.5	4,894	3.9
North America	363,844,662	4.8	345,660,847	95.0	219	8.2
Oceania/Australia	41,273,454	0.6	28,439,277	68.9	273	0.7
WORLD TOTAL	7,634,758,428	100.0	4,208,571,287	55.1	1,066	100.0

Notes: (1) Internet Usage and World Population Statistics updated as of June 30, 2018. (2) Demographic (population) numbers are based on data from the United Nations Population Division. (3) Internet usage information comes from data published by Nielsen Online, by ITU, the International Telecommunications Union, by GfK, by local ICT Regulators, and other reliable sources.

Source: Internet World Stats 2018. Usage and Population Statistics, http://www.internetworldstats.com/stats.htm.

As of 2019, East Asia was the region most penetrated by the Internet, with approximately 1 billion Internet users. Although Asia constituted approximately 55 percent of the world's population, its penetration rate was only 47 percent. Compared to other regions with high usage growth rates, such as Africa and the Middle East, Asia invested more in its technology infrastructure and contained by far the most current Internet users, making it a more attractive market.

As the usage growth of the Internet increased, so did the popularity of e-commerce. E-commerce, or electronic commerce, was the concept of conducting business transactions over the Internet. Like online auctions, e-commerce eliminated boundaries such as time and geography, allowing businesses and customers to interact with one another constantly. As more users were exposed to the Internet, they became comfortable with the idea of conducting transactions online. In correlation with Internet growth usage, revenue generated through e-commerce increased dramatically after the 1990s.

In Asia, e-commerce had grown rapidly since China's admission into the World Trade Organization (WTO) on December 11, 2001. Induction into the WTO allowed China to conduct business with other nations more freely by reducing tariffs and eliminating market and government impediments.

Track Record of Proven Leadership

Computer programmer Pierre Omidyar founded the online auction website in San Jose, California, on September 3, 1995. Omidyar was born in Paris, France, and moved to Maryland with his family when his father took up a residency at Johns Hopkins University Medical Center. Omidyar became fascinated with computers and later graduated from Tufts University with a degree in computer science. While living and working in the San Francisco Bay area, he met his current wife, Pamela Wesley, a management consultant, who later became a driving force in launching the auction website. The couple's vision was to establish an online marketplace at which people could share the same passion and interest as Pamela had for her hobby of collecting and trading Pez candy dispensers.[22] Omidyar also envisioned an online auction format that would create a fair and open marketplace, where the market truly determined an item's value. To ensure trust in the open forum, Omidyar based the site on five main values:

1. People are basically good.
2. Everyone has something to contribute.
3. An honest, open environment can bring out the best in people.
4. Everyone deserves recognition and respect as a unique individual.
5. You should treat others the way you want to be treated.

On Labor Day weekend in 1995, Omidyar launched Auction Web, an online trading platform. After the business exploded, Omidyar decided to dedicate more attention to his new enterprise and work as a consultant under the name Echo Bay Technology Group. When he tried to register a website for his company, Omidyar discovered the name Echo Bay was unavailable, so he decided to use the abbreviated version eBay, which also stood for "electronic bay area." The company's name was also selected to attract San Francisco residents to the site and prompt them to buy and sell items.

EXHIBIT 5 Number of eBay Active Users from 2010 to 2018 (in millions)

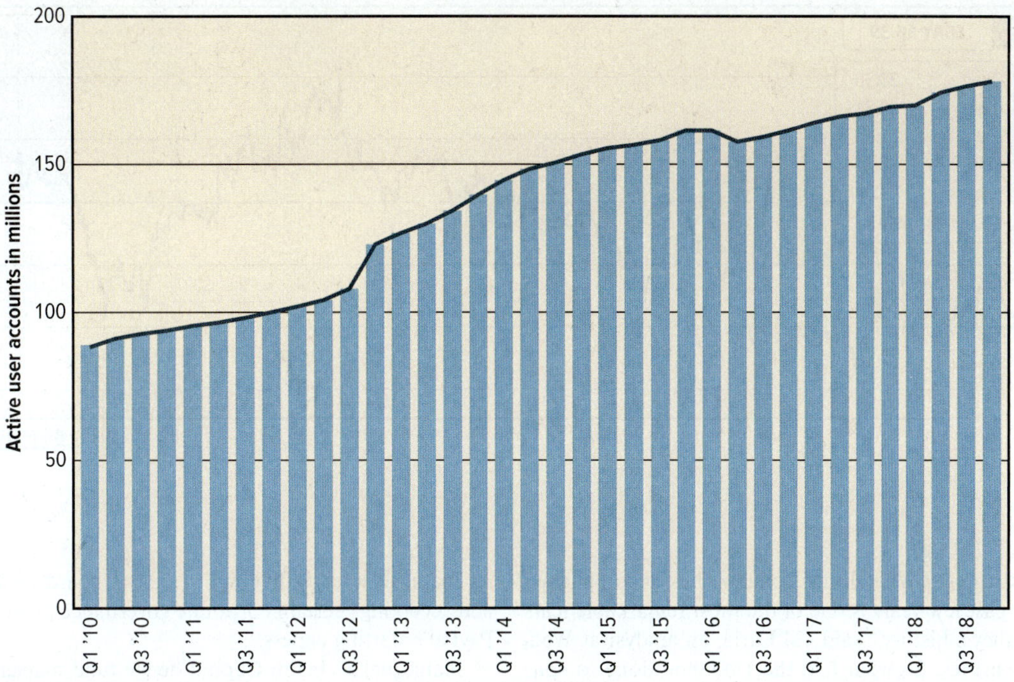

Source: Statista, 2018 https://www.statista.com/statistics/242235/number-of-ebays-total-active-users/.

Initially, the company did not charge fees to either buyers or sellers, but as traffic grew rapidly, Omidyar was forced to charge buyers a listing fee to cover Internet service provider costs. When Omidyar noticed that the fees had no effect on the level of bids, he realized the potential for profitability of his business. To handle and manage the company's day-to-day operations, Omidyar hired Jeffrey Skoll (BASc from University of Toronto and MBA from Stanford University). Skoll was hired as the company's first president, and he wrote the business plan that eBay later followed from its emergence as a start-up to its maturity as a financial success. The two worked out of Skoll's living room and various Silicon Valley facilities until they eventually settled in the company's current location in San Jose, California.

By the middle of 1997, after less than a year under the name eBay, the company was hosting nearly 800,000 auctions a day.[23] Although the rapid expansion of eBay's traffic caused the company to suffer a number of service interruptions, the site remained successful and continued to gain the confidence of its strong customer base. Skoll remained president until early 1998 when the company hired Meg Whitman as president and CEO. At the time, the company had only 30 employees and was solely located in the United States; in a decade the number of employees went up to over 15,000. In September 1998, eBay launched a successful public offering, making both Omidyar and Skoll instant billionaires. By the time eBay went public, less than three years after Omidyar had created the company, the site had more than 1 million registered users. The company grew exponentially in the late 1990s and, based on its 2013 performance, indicated no sign of stopping. Exhibit 5 highlights the company's recent growth performance in terms of active user accounts, in millions.

Whitman stepped down as the president and CEO of the company on March 31, 2008, but remained on the board of directors. Omidyar, the chairman of the board, said this about Whitman: "With humor, smarts, and unflappable determination, Meg took a small, barely known online auction site and helped it become an integral part of our lives."[24] Both Omidyar and Whitman were confident that the new CEO, John Donahoe, was a good choice to lead eBay. Donahoe had joined the company in 2005 as president of eBay's largest division, Marketplaces, and within three years managed to double the revenues and profits for this business unit. Before joining eBay, Donahoe served as the CEO of Bain & Company, an international consulting firm based in Boston.[25] "I'm extremely confident in John's skills and the abilities of John's veteran management team," Meg Whitman commented on the transition."[26]

Whitman's confidence appears to have been well founded. Donahoe helped eBay make impressive progress. Although eBay's financial outlook was not dreadful when Donahoe took over in March 2008, there was a growing perception that its growth was beginning to decline and that its run as the leader of the e-commerce industry was behind it, as Amazon began to make strides toward becoming the

EXHIBIT 6 eBay Stock Performance

Source: Yahoo Finance.

next best thing. "What John Donahoe has accomplished over the past few years is one of the most remarkable feats in the valley's history," said Gil Luria, an analyst at Wedbush Securities. So what had the Donahoe done to spur this turnaround? Luria noted that eBay began investing more in technology and was willing to take risks regarding altering the look and feel of the platform's shopping experience.[27] However, Donahoe stepped down from his role as CEO after the announcement of eBay's PayPal spinoff in 2015. Devin Wenig, the president of the eBay marketplace since 2011, took charge of the company as its new CEO in July 2015. eBay's stock price took a hit after the departure of Donahoe, perhaps because of investors' lack of confidence regarding changing leadership of eBay; however, the stock price rebounded after the third quarter of 2015. Under Wenig, eBay's stock price surged in the following years, and it was trading at about $38 per share by April 2019 (see Exhibit 6).

Board of Directors versus Activist Investor

During the previous few years, activist investor Carl Icahn had put together a 0.8 percent ownership stake in eBay and started pushing for strategy changes. The company refused to take his advice, so Icahn bought more shares and tried again. eBay had already decided to spin off its PayPal online payments service, but Icahn owned 2.5 percent of the company and insisted that management think about selling that operation to a cash-rich tech giant instead. eBay management still preferred the PayPal spin-off idea, much to Icahn's chagrin. Eventually, Ichan's eBay ownership expanded to 3.7 percent, and the company was pretty much doing what he wanted, or close to it.

eBay announced that it had reached a standstill agreement with Carl Icahn. The activist investor would not buy any more eBay stock in return for some concessions from eBay's active leadership. The concessions included adding an Icahn-selected individual to eBay's board of directors and accepting "certain corporate governance provisions" to PayPal's starting papers.

Icahn picked Icahn Capital hedge fund manager Jonathan Christodoro, who was a merger analyst and already served on four boards under Icahn's influence. eBay also gave Icahn the option of placing his candidate on either eBay's or PayPal's board when the two companies split later in the year. Given Christodoro's field of expertise, industry circles expected him to move on with PayPal and continue looking for buyout-style exit strategies.

Icahn, of course, was expected to use his large stock ownership and board representation to explore his favorite options for using surplus cash. He was known to like selling operations that no longer made sense, but he was not a big supporter of making acquisitions himself. Instead, he preferred enormous share buyback and dividend programs.

eBay had become a high-stakes games of chess. Icahn and his team wanted to monetize PayPal to the hilt before the service peaked, while eBay would rather hold on a little tighter and see where this train was headed. Industry analysts concluded that the arguments on both sides had merit but that the uncertainty of squabbling over the long-term strategy would hurt the company overall. Finally, eBay and PayPal split in July 2015 and PayPal's market value scaled around $49 billion as an independent publicly traded company, which had secured to achieve a bigger market cap than eBay.[28]

Company Business Model

eBay's business model is based on a person-to-person marketplace on the Internet, where sellers conveniently list items for sale and interested buyers bid on those items. The objective is to create a forum that allows buyers and sellers to come together in an efficient and effective manner. The business model overcame the inefficiencies of traditional fragmented marketplaces, which tended to offer a limited variety of goods. According to former CEO Meg Whitman, the company started with commerce and what grew out of that was a community, essentially creating a community-commerce model.[29] The company's success relied primarily on establishing a trustworthy environment that attracted a large number of buyers and sellers. As eBay's reputation grew, so did the number of buyers and sellers, keeping the company in line with Omidyar's original vision. However, as new competitors entered the online auction business and the popularity of the Internet increased, eBay tweaked its business model to accommodate changes in the fast-paced environment.

The company was aggressively expanding globally and looking for new products and services to offer to customers. It was also looking closely at the kind of merchants who sold on eBay. In the beginning, eBay focused on a consumer-to-consumer business model, but since some of the individuals became small dealers, the model changed to a mix of consumer-to-consumer and business-to-consumer. The sellers wanted to maintain their business on eBay since it was their most profitable distribution channel. eBay wanted new ways to generate revenue as a result of more small dealers and businesses selling their products through the company's website.

In addition to the primary revenue sources, there were specific elements of eBay's business model that made the company a success (see Exhibit 7). eBay's dominance of the online auction market and the large number of buyers, sellers, and listed items were primary reasons for eBay's tremendous growth. The trust and safety programs, such as the Feedback Forum, continued to attract and retain new and current eBay users. The cost-effective and convenient trading, coupled with the strong sense of community, added further value to the company's business model. However, as the company continued to grow and new trends evolved, eBay had to continue to adjust its model to remain competitive.

International Expansion

As competition intensified in the online auction industry, eBay expanded its international presence in an effort to create an online global marketplace. Gradually, eBay localized sites in the following countries:

- *Asia Pacific:* Australia, China, Hong Kong, Japan, India, Malaysia, New Zealand, Philippines, Singapore, South Korea, Taiwan, Thailand, and Vietnam
- *Europe:* Austria, Belgium, Denmark, France, Germany, Ireland, Italy, Netherlands, Poland, Spain, Sweden, Switzerland, United Kingdom, and Turkey
- *North America:* Canada and United States
- *Latin America:* Argentina, Brazil, Mexico[30]

EXHIBIT 7 Net Revenues by Type ($ millions, except percentage changes)

	Year Ended December 31,				
	2018	% Change	2017	% Change	2016
Net Revenues by Type:					
Net transaction revenues:					
Marketplace	$ 7,416	9%	$6,809	6%	$ 6,425
StubHub	1,068	6%	1,011	8%	938
Total net transaction revenues	8,484	8%	7,820	6%	7,363
Marketing services and other revenues:					
Marketplace	1,225	3%	1,192	5%	1,137
Classifieds	1,022	14%	897	13%	791
StubHub, Corporate and other	15		18		7
Total marketing services and other revenues	2,262	7%	2,107	9%	1,935
Total net revenues	$10,746	8%	$9,927	7%	$ 9,298
Net Revenues by Geography:					
U.S.	$ 4,373	4%	$4,187	6%	$ 3,967
International	6,373	11%	5,740	8%	5,331
Total net revenues	$10,746	8%	$9,927	7%	$ 9,298

Source: eBay SEC filings.

Intense Competitive Environment

As eBay's product offerings and pricing formats evolved, so did its range of competitors. Originally, the company faced competition from alternative auctions or other venues for collectors, such as flea markets and garage sales. However, as the company grew and introduced fixed pricing, the range of competitors included large retailers like Walmart and Kmart that also had online selling websites. eBay faced the harshest competition from major online companies, including Yahoo, Etsy, and Amazon, which also had online auctions that rivaled eBay's.

Yahoo!

eBay's largest online competitor was Yahoo, which had a strong global presence, particularly in Asian markets. Yahoo originally started as a search engine and quickly evolved to include additional products and services, such as Yahoo Mail, Yahoo Maps, and Yahoo Messenger. The company also offered e-commerce services through Yahoo Shopping, Yahoo Autos, Yahoo! Auctions, and Yahoo Travel. As with eBay, Yahoo's e-commerce sites allowed users to obtain relevant information and make transactions and purchases online. However, Yahoo's business model primarily focused on generating revenue through search advertising. In the United States, in response to potential threats from web giant Google, Yahoo and eBay formed an alliance in which Yahoo utilized eBay's payment system, PayPal, and eBay gained additional advertising through Yahoo searches. Still, Yahoo posed a major competitive threat in foreign markets, particularly the Asia-Pacific area, through its partnerships with Gmarket and Taobao.

Amazon

Despite not having a huge presence in the online auction industry, Amazon was still considered a fierce online global competitor. Amazon started as Earth's biggest bookstore and rapidly evolved to selling everything, including toys, electronics, home furnishings, apparel, health and beauty aids, groceries, and so on. Although Amazon had a large international presence, the company's linkage to brick-and-mortar shops in the United States made it a greater threat in local markets than in foreign markets. Amazon's international sites were in Canada, the United Kingdom, Germany, Japan, France, and China. Despite its large online presence, Amazon scaled back its online auction business, cutting staff and shutting down Livebid, as part of an overall corporate restructuring.

Google

Google started out as a browser much like Yahoo but ventured into the e-commerce space by acquiring Overstock.com. While it did not compete directly with eBay in the online auction market, it did compete with eBay in online retailing.

Etsy

As eBay tried to position itself as a trendy e-retailer, it directly competed with the trendy Etsy.com retailing site. The site was managed from an office in Brooklyn and had a strong and growing user base. Much like the customers of eBay, Etsy's customers went to its site for quaint collectible items.

Traditional Retailers

Given the trend toward e-commerce, many traditional brick-and-mortar companies like Walmart, Staples, and Home Depot were investing heavily in developing their online retail sites.

Facebook Marketplace

Considering eBay's original purpose as an auction site, Marketplace offers better deals between the buyer and seller based on their location. It is convenient for both the parties because there is a middle man involved.

Taobao

eBay faced unyielding competition in China from Alibaba Group's Taobao.com, the largest Chinese online retailer. Like eBay, Taobao strove to implement a more interactive and user-friendly customer service initiative. Taobao began using an instant communication tool called Aliwangwang to help buyers and sellers interact with one another. Alipay, an online payment system, was started soon after.

Interestingly, Taobao's parent company, Alibaba, seemed to be exploring expansion opportunities in the United States. It had a record-breaking IPO in the New York Stock Exchange in September 2014 and raised about $25 billion. U.S. retailers and industry analysts expected Alibaba would soon launch a service targeted at American consumers. Alibaba sold to American consumers through its global retail service AliExpress. But its core Taobao service, often likened to eBay's Marketplaces, was not yet available to U.S. customers in English.

Jack Ma, chairman of Alibaba, had apparently learned from the eBay playbook. At the IPO he repeatedly stressed the importance of trust in an e-commerce venture. "Today what we got is not money. What we got is the trust from the people," Ma said.[31] This had also been the mantra of Pierre Omidyar, founder of eBay.

The Future of eBay

Interested Bidders

As eBay prepares to hold a progressive position in a fiercely competitive market, the industry is rife with rumors about potential acquisitions of the remaining online auction business. "It would give a player like Alibaba a legitimate foothold into the American market," predicted Sean Udall, CIO of Quantum Trading Strategies and author of *The TechStrat Report*.[32]

Who exactly might acquire any of eBay's units, or the company itself someday, remains the speculation of analysts and the media. Amazon, Google, and Alibaba are each occasionally mentioned by Wall Street analysts.

Unhappy Customers

eBay's handling of the hacking incident created a number of disgruntled customers. The company had reset all customer passwords and adversely affected Internet browser search results. Further, a revision to the fee structure, with rates jumping to 9% of gross sales (up from 3–4%), displeased a number of small business owners. Fleur Filmer, a customer who ran a picnic gear business called Hanging Rock Picnics, was frustrated with the way changes were introduced at eBay, requiring circumnavigation of fine print to find fee updates:

> A lot of investment and resources have gone to their promotion of the majors online. They have actively gone after the big brands to establish eBay stores and haven't offered any new resources or assistance to small store owners.

New Competitors

eBay was once the go-to site for selling unwanted second-hand goods, but Facebook has now entered the fray. Millions of people have already conveniently bought and sold items using "For Sale" groups, and the social network is rolling out tools to make the process even easier. The new features are designed to regulate the process so buyers know exactly what is for sale, how much it costs, and where it is going to be sourced from. Users have said they prefer to trade on Facebook because the accounts show the names and details of the persons buying and selling. On sites such as eBay and Craigslist, members have a certain level of anonymity, and this makes resolving problems with transactions more difficult.

Moreover, smartphone apps like Offer-up are also posing additional competition for eBay in local neighborhoods. According to the founder of Offer-up, millions of Americans replace the old items with new ones that require a free or additional space. Offer-up provides a solution that frees up the space for new products by selling or tossing the used items through its platform. Offer-up provides an online platform for customers to buy and sell used items through a mobile app and a website. A customer can find used items for sale sorted by the zip code and specific neighborhoods. According to Offer-up, "The idea was a new kind of local marketplace to bring people together to get more value out of their used stuff that could start with something as simple as a photo from a smartphone."[33]

The years ahead are going to be challenging for eBay. Although the company has announced many initiatives that include exclusive partnerships and acquisitions, investors and shareholders will be watching keenly to see if management and the board can really fix things and chart a new course for the future. With senior management, an expanded board of directors, an activist investor, and potential acquirers in the mix, gaining alignment on the path forward will not be an easy task. Only time will tell which option proves right for the company to increase shareholder value over the long term. And the questions remain, will eBay be able to establish itself as a strong e-commerce business, or might eBay be better off offering itself for sale to a bidder?

ENDNOTES

1. GeekWire. October 30, 2018. Fireside chat: Devin Wenig, CEO, eBay. See also https://www.youtube.com/watch?v=GqLSBNC_nYQ
2. Levy, Nat. 2018. eBay sues Amazon, alleging tech giant illegally poached sellers from its platform. GeekWire, October 17, https://www.geekwire.com/2018/ebay-sues-amazon-alleging-tech-giant-illegally-poached-sellers-platform/
3. Stambor, Zak. 2018. How eBay plans to nearly triple its user base. Digital Commerce 360, August 24, https://www.digitalcommerce360.com/2018/08/24/how-ebay-plans-to-nearly-triple-its-active-user-base/
4. Ibid.
5. eBay Inc. 2018. eBay launches 'Retail Revival' program to boost small businesses. Press release, January 22.
6. eBay to Roll Out Guaranteed Delivery for 20 Million Items, Press relase, March 20 https://www.ebayinc.com/stories/news/ebay-to-roll-out-guaranteed-delivery-for-20-million-items/.
7. Ibid.
8. Soper, Spencer. 2016. EBay to Raise More Than $1 Billion Selling Stake in MercardoLibre. October 12,https://www.bloomberg.com/news/articles/2016-10-12/ebay-to-raise-more-than-1-billion-selling-stake-in-mercadolibre
9. Galante, J. 2011. PayPal's Revenue Will Double by 2013, Thompson Says. *Bloomberg News,* February 10, www.businessweek.com/news/2011-02-10/paypal-s-revenue-will-double-by-2013-thompson-says.html.
10. Bensinger, G. 2014. eBay to Split as Apple, Others Prepare to Challenge PayPal. *Wall Street Journal,* September 30.
11. eBay Inc. 2008. eBay Inc. Buys Leading Payments and Classifieds Businesses, Streamlines Existing Organization to Improve Growth. Press release, October 6, www.ebayinc.com/content/press_release/20081006005605.
12. Om, Malik. 2010. Skype By the Numbers: It's Really Big. April 20, https://gigaom.com/2010/04/20/skype-q4-2009-number/
13. eBay Inc.2018. eBay Completes Acquisition of Giosis' Japan Business
14. MacMillan, D. 2010. eBay Buys Bar-Code App. *Bloomberg Businessweek,* June 23, www.businessweek.com/technology/content/jun2010/tc20100623_901174.htm.
15. eBay Inc. 2010. eBay Acquires Milo, a Leading Local Shopping Engine. Press release, December 2, www.ebayinc.com/content/press_release/20101202006358.
16. eBay Inc. 2010. eBay Acquires Industry Leading Mobile Application Developer. Press release, December 15, www.ebayinc.com/content/press_release/20101215006520.
17. eBay Completes the Acquisition of SalesPredict, https://www.ebayinc.com/stories/news/ebay-acquires-salespredict/.
18. eBay Completes the Acquisition of Ticket Utils, https://www.ebayinc.com/stories/news/ebay-completes-the-acquisition-of-ticket-utils/.
19. eBay Partners with Snupps, A Social Organizing App, for Seamless Selling, https://www.ebayinc.com/stories/news/ebay-partners-with-snupps-a-social-organizing-app-for-seamless-selling/.
20. eBay and Flipkart Sign Exclusive Agreement to Jointly Address the eCommerce Market Opportunity in India, https://www.ebayinc.com/stories/news/ebay-and-flipkart-sign-exclusive-agreement-to-jointly-address-the-ecommerce-market-opportunity-in-india/.
21. Doyle, R. A. 2002. The History of Auctions. *Auctioneer,* November 1, www.absoluteauctionrealty.com/history_detail.php?id55094.
22. Internet Based Moms. 2007. Pierre Omidyaró The Man Behind eBay. April.
23. Academy of Achievement. 2005. BiographyóPierre Omidyar. www.achievement.org, November 9.
24. eBay Inc. 2008. Meg Whitman to Step Down.

25. eBay corporate website, ebayinc.com.
26. eBay Inc. 2008. Meg Whitman to Step Down.
27. O'Brien, Chris. 2012. Is eBay's John Donahoe the best CEO in Silicon Valley? *Mercurynews.com,* November 4, www.mercurynews.com/chris-obrien/ci_21908264/obrien-is-ebays-john-donahoe-best-ceo-silicon.
28. Rao, Leena. PayPal Makes Big Splash on First Day of Trading After eBay Spinoff, http://fortune.com/2015/07/20/paypal-ebay-split-valuation/.
29. Himelstein, L., & Whitman, M. 1999. Q&A with eBay's Meg Whitman. *BusinessWeek Online,* May 31, www.businessweek.com/1999/99_22/b3631008.htm.
30. ThaiPortal. eBay Regional Sites, https://thaiportal.ru/en/ebay-regional-sites/.
31. Kim, E. 2014. Alibaba CEO Jack Ma: 'We Earned The Trust Of People Today' *Business Insider,* September 20, https://www.businessinsider.com/alibaba-jack-ma-says-he-earned-the-trust-2014-9
32. Louis Bedigian. (February 10, 2015 Tuesday). Pro On Alibaba/eBay Merger Rumor: 'We've Seen Crazier Deals Done, Remember AOL/Time Warner?'. *Benzinga.com*
33. Offer-up website, https://offerup.com/about/.

CASE 15

WEIGHT WATCHERS IS NOW WW*

In April 2019, Weight Watchers (WW) launched a new marketing campaign called "It Works!" This promotional plan featured media mogul Oprah Winfrey encouraging WW members to celebrate their weight loss. The only problem was investors perceived this promotional push as too little, too late. WW had posted disappointing fiscal third- and fourth-quarter reports, missing estimates and reporting a decline in its subscriber base, which had fallen to 3.9 million from 4.2 million in the fall of 2018. In addition, WW saw expected 2019 revenue at $1.4 billion, down from the reported $1.5 billion in 2018, and projected earnings per share of $1.25 to $1.50, much worse than the $3.19 reported at year end.[1] Could the involvement of Oprah Winfrey turn this performance around?

Winfrey had started investing in Weight Watchers in October 2015, paying about $43 million to obtain an approximately 10 percent stake in the company. Three months later, in January 2016, she reported she was able to lose 26 pounds with the help of the program. Then in early 2017, the Weight Watchers "Beyond the Scale" advertising campaign featured Winfrey claiming that she had lost 40 pounds. Winfrey endorsed the Weight Watchers experience by emphasizing "It Works!"[2] However, investors did not buy it: just saying "it works" did not seem to be inspiring "increasingly distracted and skeptical customers."[3]

Winfrey's involvement, the advertising campaigns, and discount offers in 2018 were all part of a rebranding effort that ultimately had failed to impress investors. The price of Weight Watchers shares (ticker symbol: WTW) had been tumbling since its high point in 2011 and 2012.[4] This price decline echoed the financial reality: seven straight quarters of declining sales that had not started to reverse until mid-2018. What had gone wrong?

Weight Watchers had undergone some internal changes, starting with the resignation of CEO David Kirschoff in 2013. Kirschoff had presided over the firm during its most profitable years, yet his replacement, John Chambers, had been unable to reverse what appeared to be an inevitable decline and left WW in 2016. This left the firm without a full-time CEO until April 2017 when Weight Watchers named Mindy Grossman as President and CEO. One of Grossman's strategies was to rebrand the company–turning "Weight Watchers" into "WW" in an attempt to "embrace wellness," or encourage its customers to stay with the program long after they had achieved their target weight. However, this rebranding campaign, launched in the fall of 2018, only confused customers. The timing of this new message, just before the crucial holiday diet season, made it seem as if Weight Watchers was abandoning its core weight loss mission.[5] In her announcement of the disappointing fourth quarter and full year 2018 results, CEO Grossman said the following:

> While we are disappointed with our start to 2019, we are confident that our strategy to focus on providing holistic wellness solutions leveraging our best-in-class weight management program is the right path to support long-term sustainable growth. Looking ahead, I'm happy to say that Oprah Winfrey will play a central role in our upcoming TV and digital marketing campaign for spring, bringing to life a clear message on how WW is the program that works. Together with Oprah, we are also working on an initiative to galvanize and bring together communities through a series of digital and live experiences and events to accelerate WW's impact and allow us to reach new and diverse audiences. We will announce more details in the coming months, but anticipate the initiative will kick off later in 2019.[6]

Although Weight Watchers had been working to update its image and offerings and was still able to boast a high gross profit margin, it seemed revenue and cash generation as well as the firm's growth strategy had not been able to fully inspire either investor or customer confidence. Clearly, Weight Watchers was in trouble.

Company Story

Jean Nidetch began Weight Watchers in an unlikely, and unintended, way. In 1963, Jean invited six women into her home to help both herself and her neighbors and friends lose weight by communally discussing their weight-loss issues. Nidetch's belief, which became the core of the Weight Watchers philosophy, was that anyone could be given a diet but the group and social setting of "talk therapy" was the true secret not only to losing weight but also *to keeping it off.* She believed in fostering success through group support, and she created a simple reward system that included pins and tie bars to reward increments of weight loss. The idea was simple, yet very effective.[7] The basic concept of the Weight Watchers plan consisted of two components–the Weight Watchers program and the group support. The program was essentially a food plan and an activity plan. The food plan provided people with the educational tools they needed for weight loss and provided control mechanisms so that individuals could find their way to healthier

---

* This case was developed by Professor Alan B. Eisner, Pace University; Professor Helaine J. Korn, Baruch College–City University of New York; Professor Pauline Assenza, Western Connecticut State University; and graduate students Saad Nazir and Jennifer M. DiChiara, Pace University. Material has been drawn from published sources to be used for class discussion. Copyright © 2019 Alan B. Eisner.

food choices. This was supplemented with an activity plan tailored to their lifestyle.

Since its origins in 1963, Weight Watchers, originally targeting primarily women ages 25 to 55, had experienced growth into an iconic global brand. By 2019, Weight Watchers (now WW) provided weight-management services worldwide. Stating that it believed it was the leading global provider of paid digital subscription weight management products, the company had approximately 3.9 million subscribers, of which approximately 2.6 million were digital subscribers. Approximately 1.3 million subscribers had access weekly to in-person workshops or digital subscription product offerings and therefore could attend approximately 31,000 workshops each week around the world, run by approximately 8,300 coaches.[8]

What started in 1963 by Jean Nidetch as a women's support group in her home, had grown into a multibillion-dollar weight-loss goliath in five decades' time. By 2013, Weight Watchers International had fully evolved into a "points" system for food management that worked along with a weight management program, emphasizing weight loss by taking a holistic approach to a fit and healthy life style.[9] Customers could create their personal points "budget" according to their fitness goals and eat any type of food as long as it was within the consumption or calories limit allowed by their budget. Food with higher calories had higher points value as compared to the food with lower calories. With a counting system based on dietary guidelines, dieters were encouraged to maximize their points allowance by choosing more "Power Foods"—the healthiest, most filling foods, such as whole grains, lean meats, low-fat dairy, and unlimited quantities of fresh fruit and non-starchy vegetables. This system, along with optional in-person weekly group meetings, led by a role model who had seen success with the program, had helped millions of people lose weight.

Although doctors and nutritionists had given the points program a thumbs up, in 2012, Weight Watchers' then-CEO David Kirchhoff felt something was lacking. Citing evidence from behavioral scientists, Kirchhoff said he "realized that Weight Watchers needed to take into account social, environmental, and behavioral factors that led members to fail."[10] Weight Watchers had always believed in behavior change, encouraging people to be mindful of what they ate and just counting calories, as the points system did, was not enough.

In 2013, Weight Watchers created the "360-degree Program"—the "Points Plus program with a 21st-century makeover." By monitoring the amount of carbohydrates, fats, fiber, and proteins in the food choices people made on a daily basis, and using current scientific research on why people eat what they eat, Weight Watchers guided members toward making healthier eating decisions in all sorts of situations.[11] The 360-degree Program added two new components to tracking caloric intake: "spaces," which included tips for how to handle eating situations in the different environments members might encounter, and "routines," which encouraged members to create new habits—for instance, changing just three small behaviors a day, such as walking an extra five minutes, eating lunch at the same time, and drinking an additional glass of water. These 360-degree components—tracking, spaces, and routines—were even available as apps on the Weight Watchers website as well as on Apple and Android mobile devices. By adding the mobile apps and other online social networking support to the direct face-to-face support of the weekly meetings, Kirchhoff believed that Weight Watchers finally had a program that tied everything together.[12]

However, in August 2013, Kirchhoff resigned in order to "pursue other opportunities." This left the company facing a scenario where community social support for weight loss could be provided virtually rather than at a physical weekly meeting: the next generation of diet programs and online apps, like MyFitnessPal and the FitBit activity monitor, were providing this support basically for free, since the companies offering them did not need to charge meeting fees or employ trained support staff.[13] Former CEO Jim Chambers admitted, "The consumer has changed and we haven't kept pace. We need to turn this company inside out."[14]

The market for weight-loss products was growing, as obesity levels were on the rise in more and more parts of the world, and this made weight management an attractive industry, especially for deeply entrenched firms such as Weight Watchers. However, faced with competition from traditional rivals Nutrisystem and Medifast and other weight-loss programs such as Jenny Craig and the Biggest Loser franchise, Weight Watchers International had to monitor the larger environment and keep track of the major trends that could affect industry and firm profitability and revenues.

Those trends, as they related to Weight Watchers and the weight-loss industry as a whole, included the temporary emergence of fad diets; decreased effectiveness of marketing and advertising programs; the need for developing new and innovative products and services, many of which had to be delivered via online or mobile apps; the development of more favorably perceived or more effective weight-management methods (e.g., pharmaceuticals and surgical options such as the Lap-Band); and the threat of impairment of the Weight Watchers brand itself.[15] The challenge for Weight Watchers was repositioning itself and creating a forward-focused diet plan for the 21st century while staying true to the mission initially established by Jean Nidetch, its founder. The brand needed to remain relevant and, at the same time, pursue additional medium- to long-term initiatives, such as reaching out to new market segments.

In 2016, CEO Chambers resigned, and Weight Watchers' Board members, including Oprah Winfrey, began a search for his replacement. In April 2017, Weight Watchers named Mindy Grossman as President and CEO. Grossman had more than 38 years of experience in building and transforming consumer brands, including nine years as CEO of HSN, Home Shopping Network. Upon her arrival, Grossman began to map out a new direction, calling it an "Impact Manifesto," and calling out a goal of $2 billion in revenue and an overall customer base of 10 million people by 2020.[16] To move in that direction, WW implemented the "WW Freestyle" program as part of its mobile app–a new version of the points system that assigned a zero value to foods such as eggs or fish, encouraging members to eat more of these healthier options. Under Grossman's guidance, the company was also shifting its focus away from weight loss as a primary goal, and transitioning itself into a wellness brand. As an example of this, WW was collaborating with Headspace, the meditation app, to offer members "guided meditations in multiple languages to help transform their relationship with food and their body overall."[17]

In 2018, Grossman decided to modernize the brand. In keeping with the new focus on positive body image and overall health and wellness rather than weight loss through calorie counting, Weight Watchers changed its name and all its product marks to WW. As Grossman said, "Weight Watchers is now WW. We have a mission: to inspire healthy habits for real life–for everyone. We'll always be the global leader in weight loss. Now we're becoming the world's partner in wellness."[18] WW also implemented a "Wellness Wins" rewards program, a game-like app offering rewards for tracking and achieving activity and weight goals. The intent was to attract more men, who were still just 10 percent of WW's membership. Along with the new branding, in 2019 WW made the decision to remove artificial sweeteners, flavors, colors, and preservatives from all its food and related products. This product category included bars, snacks, and cookbooks, which made up 13 percent of revenue in 2018, and the hope was that this shift would help the category grow dramatically.

Industry and Competitive Environment

Weight Watchers had had over 55 years of success in helping people lose weight, and this success had come with some significant financial gains as well. However, Weight Watchers was also losing by 2018-year end; the company had missed both revenue and earnings per share targets by significant amounts, and had shed subscribers, sending the share price down over 58 percent for the year.[19]

Weight Watchers International had experienced stock price volatility in the past, as had the majority of its competitors, because of rival weight-management options–such as the over-the-counter weight-loss drug *Alli,* launched by GlaxoSmithKline in June 2006, and the development of Allergan's Lap-Band device. However, there had yet to be a widely supported "magic pill" or surgical option to weight management. In the absence of a safe and effective pharmaceutical or surgical alternative for weight loss, Weight Watchers and its competitors faced a weight-management industry characterized not only by competition and threats, but by opportunity as well.

Obesity was on the rise in the developed countries, especially in North America, and by 2018 weight loss, including the $70.3 billion weight loss industry[20] and the fitness industry constituted an $87.5 billion-a-year industry in the United States alone.[21] In addition, the obesity problem was not confined to the United States, and this made geographic expansion a possibility for weight-loss firms. Worldwide, the World Health Organization estimated 1.9 billion people to be overweight and more than 650 million to be obese.[22] Overall, the statistics proved there were still opportunities, and therefore competition, in the weight-loss industry.

Weight Watchers was attempting to reinvent itself while still paying close attention to the moves of its weight-loss rivals. Competition for Weight Watchers International included both price competition and competition from self-help, pharmaceutical, surgical, dietary supplement, and meal-replacement products, as well as other weight-management brands, diets, programs, and products.[23] Over the years, among the commercial plans, Weight Watchers had consistently earned among the highest overall ratings, according to various surveys, because of its nutritionally based diet, weekly meetings, and weigh-ins for behavioral support. In 2019, according to *U.S. News & World Report,* The Mediterranean Diet got top ranking, but Weight Watchers maintained its position in the top five. Other traditional competitors, Jenny Craig, Nutrisystem, and Medifast, came in further down the list. Going into 2019, top competitors included those listed in Exhibit 1.

One important factor in all these diets was the extent to which they were do-it-yourself efforts. Many of the successful diets, including the DASH and Mayo Clinic diets, required consistent self-control without any external support system. Obviously, Weight Watchers was different in this respect, as were best known competitors Jenny Craig and Nutrisystem.

Another differentiating factor was cost. The cost of plans in which people bought their own food depended, of course, on each person's food choices. The cost of the commercial plans also varied widely. Weight Watchers' cost depended on whether the member chose to attend weekly in-person meetings or use only the online tools. (Weight Watchers' membership costs ranged from about $3 per week for an online-only plan to $12 a week with personalized coaching.) None of the WW costs included food. With Jenny Craig, the initial registration fee could exceed $400, and a week's worth of Jenny's Cuisine might cost at least $100. Nutrisystem, which had basically fallen off the survey charts due to complaints about costs and the poor taste of the food, had a 28-day Select Plan, which included 10 days of frozen meals and 18 days of pantry food, and generally cost between $240 and $300. Packaged diets such as Slim-Fast did not have a personal support system, but food supplements could be customized to achieve a "satisfied feeling" that reduced regular food intake.

EXHIBIT 1 Top Competitors for Weight Watchers

Diet Plan	Diet Type	Good For	Ratings	Price	Comments
The Mediterranean Diet	Developed by Harvard School of Public Health	Overall healthy eating	Best diabetes and heart diet, easiest diet to follow, best diet overall	Buy-it-yourself food; fresh produce, olive oil, and nuts are expensive	Plant based, do it yourself, easy to follow
The DASH Diet	Government-developed suggested eating plan	Heart health, diabetes	*Second for diabetes control (tie);* second in best diets overall	Buy-it-yourself food	Stands for "Dietary Approaches to Stop Hypertension"
Flexitarian Diet	Developed by dietitian Dawn Jackson Blatner	Heart health, diabetes	*Second-best diabetes diet,* third in best diets overall	Buy-it-yourself food	Consists of plants, good for vegetarians
MIND Diet	Commercial diet	Enhances brain function	Fourth-best diet overall (tie), fourth best heart-healthy diet & easiest to follow (tie)	$10 for a pack	Contains 10 good for brain health foods
Weight Watchers	Commercial diet	Weight loss, heart health	First for weight loss; second in easiest diet to follow, tied for fourth as best diet overall	Membership costs less than $40/mo.; buy-it-yourself food is extra	Rated easy to follow
The TLC Diet	Developed by National Institutes of Health	Heart health	Fourth in heart health and healthy eating, eighth in best diet overall	Buy-it-yourself food	Stands for "Therapeutic Lifestyle Changes"
Mayo Clinic Diet	Nutritionist-developed, do-it-yourself plan	Diabetes	*Second-best for diabetes* control, sixth best diet overall (tie)	Buy-it-yourself food	Best for health, not necessarily weight control
Volumetrics Diet	Developed by Penn State University	Weight loss, diabetes	Second best weight loss diet, *second best for diabetes (tie)*	Buy-it-yourself food	Need to supplement with your own food
The Ornish Diet	Developed by Dr. Ornish for overall nutrition	Heart health, diabetes	First for heart health, sixth for diabetes control, ninth best overall diet (tie)	Buy-it-yourself food	Plant based, from book by Dean Ornish
Nordic Diet	From Denmark's University of Copenhagen	Weight loss, overall healthy eating	Third-best plant based diet, ninth in best diet overall (tie)	Buy-it-yourself food can be expensive	Not easy to follow, recipes hard to find

Source: "Best diets methodology: How we rated 41 eating plans," *U.S. News & World Report,* January 2, 2019

One major advantage Weight Watchers had was the extent of research done on its results. Two studies found that Weight Watchers was just as good as clinical weight-loss programs under a physician's control and that some Weight Watchers participants lost more than twice as much weight as individuals following clinical advice.[24] A physician from the Mayo Clinic said, "It's only natural that the weekly weigh-ins and 'group spirit' of programs such as Weight Watchers would prove more effective than occasional guidance from a doctor or nurse, since research has shown that dieters are more likely to stick with weight-loss programs that stress accountability."[25]

Business Model

Revenues for Weight Watchers International Inc., as shown in Exhibit 2, were principally gained from "service

EXHIBIT 2 Weight Watchers' Revenue Sources ($ millions)

	2018	2017	2016	2015	2014	2013	2012	2011
Service Revenues*	$1,273.2	$1,081.7	$ 949.1	$ 937.4	$1,181.9	$1,361	$1,425	$1,389
In-meeting product sales	240.9	137.9	125.5	127.3	169.1	212	253	281.8
Licensing, franchise royalties, and others	(included in above)	87.4	90.3	99.7	128.9	151	161	147.6
Total	$1,514.1	$1,306.9	$1,164.9	$1,164.4	$1,479.9	$1,724	$1,839	$1,819

*Includes Internet revenues

Source: WW International, Inc. Weight Watchers 10K Filings.

revenues" or meeting fees (members paid to attend weekly meetings), online revenues (from Internet subscription products), product sales (bars, cookbooks, and the like, sold as complements to weight-management plans), and revenues gained from licensing (the placement of the Weight Watchers logo on certain foods and other products) or franchising (franchisees typically paid a royalty fee of 10 percent of their meeting fee).[26] The costs of running meetings were low, with part-time class instructors paid on a commission basis, and many meeting locations were rented hourly in inexpensive local facilities such as churches. This lean organizational structure allowed wide profit margins.[27] Meeting fees were paid up front or at the time of the meeting by attendees, resulting in net negative working capital for Weight Watchers—an indication of cash-flow efficiency.

What was perhaps most important about Weight Watchers' business model was its flexibility. The number of meetings could be adjusted according to demand and seasonal fluctuations. The business model's reliance on a variable cost structure had enabled the company to maintain high margins even as the number of meetings over the same time period was expanded. When attendance growth outpaced meeting growth, the gross margins of Weight Watchers typically improved. Since fiscal year 2005, Weight Watchers International had maintained an annual gross margin in the operating segment of 50 percent or more.[28] Weight Watchers' business model yielded high profit margins as a result of the company's low variable expenses and low capital expenditure requirements. By allowing its meetings to be held anywhere, Weight Watchers kept its capital costs low—unlike Jenny Craig, which maintained its own centers with food inventories. This model also allowed Weight Watchers to gain entry into the workplace at wellness-minded companies via its Weight Watchers at Work Program.[29] Exhibits 3 to 5 show financial statements of the firm.

EXHIBIT 3 Income Statements ($ millions)

	2018	2017	2016	2015	2014
Total revenue	**$1,514**	**$1,307**	**$1,165**	**$1,164**	**$1,480**
Cost of goods sold	648	614	579	590	677
Gross profit	**866**	**693**	**586**	**574**	**803**
Operating expenses:	648	412	385	406	529
Operating income	**389**	**281**	**201**	**168**	**273**
Interest expense	142	123	115	122	123
Income before taxes	244	145	84	56	158
Provision for income taxes	20	−18	17	23	59
Net income from continuing operations	224	163	67	33	99
Net income	**$224**	**$163**	**$68**	**$33**	**$99**
Earnings per share	3.19	2.40	1.06	0.56	1.74

Source: WW International, Inc. Weight Watchers 10K Filings.

EXHIBIT 4 Balance Sheets ($ thousands)

	2018	2017	2016	2015	2014
Assets					
Current assets:					
Cash and cash equivalents	$237	$83	$109	$242	$301
Net receivables	27	24	28	29	32
Inventory	26	32	33	28	32
Other current assets	34	43	36	15	38
Total current assets	**366**	**209**	**235**	**351**	**428**
Gross property plant and equipment			205	202	204
Accumulated depreciation			(155)	(144)	(130)
Net property, plant and equipment	52	48	50	58	75
Goodwill	152	156	166	159	107
Intangible assets	808	801	807	814	868
Other long-term assets	35	32	13	32	38
Deferred LT asset charges	16	12			
Total assets	**1,415**	**1,246**	**1,271**	**1,422**	**1,515**
Current liabilities:					
Short/current debt	83	95	53	258	24
Accounts payable	27	24	41	38	54
Accrued liabilities	101	99	136	146	125
Deferred revenue	54	74	63	62	66
Other current liabilities	76	51			
Total current liabilities	**341**	**343**	**292**	**503**	**377**
Long-term debt	1,670	1,741	1,981	2,021	2,334
Deferred taxes			175	160	172
Other long-term liabilities	209	174	30	28	22
Total liabilities	**2,220**	**2,258**	**2,474**	**2,680**	**2,905**
Stockholders' equity:					
Retained earnings	2,382	2,203	2,057	1,995	1,883
Treasury stock	(3,191)	(3,219)	(3,237)	(3,247)	(3,254)
Other comprehensive income	(16)	(10)	(27)	(37)	(20)
Total shareholder's equity	**(1,770)**	**(1,973)**	**(1,208)**	**(1,290)**	**(1,390)**

Source: WW International, Inc. Weight Watchers 10K Filings.

EXHIBIT 5
Cash Flow Statements ($ millions)

	2018	2017	2016	2015	2014
Net income	**$224**	**$163**	**$67**	**$33**	**$99**
Depreciation	44	51	53	53	49
Amortization deferred financing costs	8	6	6	7	9
Impairment of assets	27	752	615	2	27
Share-based compensation expense	20	15	7	25	11
Deferred tax provision	(14)	(48)	11	–	22
Inventory	(1)	(5)	(10)	(3)	(3)
Prepaid expenses	(4)	(4)	(15)	(18)	(1)
Accounts payable	2	(15)	0	14	(10)
Accrued liabilities	17	4	(9)	31	10
Income taxes payable	27	4	–	–	1
Other working capital	–	–	0	(7)	(4)
Other non-cash items	–	–	18	8	(4)
Net cash provided by operating activities	**296**	**222**	**119**	**55**	**323**
Investment in property, equipment and plan	(46)	(41)	(34)	(36)	(52)
Acquisitions	(7)	0	(3)	(3)	(17)
Other investing activities	(10)	(1)	0	(1)	(1)
Net cash provided by investment activities	**(64)**	**(41)**	**(38)**	**(40)**	**(38)**
Debt issued	–	1,840	–	48	–
Debt repayment	(58)	(2,019)	(165)	(158)	(30)
Common stock issued	–	–	–	41	–
Common stock repurchased	–	–	–	–	–
Dividend paid	–	–	(0)	(0)	(0)
Other, financing activities	(17)	(32)	(47)	0	1
Net cash provided by financing activities	**(75)**	**(211)**	**(212)**	**(69)**	**(29)**
Effects of exchange rate	(4)	4	(2)	(6)	(7)
Net change in cash	154	(25)	(131)	(60)	127
Cash at beginning of period	83	109	242	301	175
Cash at end of period	**$237**	**$83**	**$109**	**$242**	**$301**

Source: WW International, Inc. Weight Watchers 10K Filings.

Innovation

Domestically and abroad, Weight Watchers was fortunate enough to build on a foundation of five decades of weight-management expertise that had allowed the company to become one of the most recognized and trusted brand names among weight-conscious consumers worldwide.[30]

The innovation initiatives at Weight Watchers were focused on three main objectives: (1) rejuvenating the brand through more effective marketing, (2) providing more customer value by introducing new products, and (3) broadening the customer mix by targeting new customer segments.

The Brand

With regard to its brand, Weight Watchers was fortunate that consumers considered its brand credible and effective. The brand image was reinforced by the involvement of celebrities such as Oprah Winfrey advocating the effectiveness of Weight Watchers diet programs. However, the company was always looking to differentiate its lifestyle-based approach from the strictly dieting orientation utilized by many of its competitors. In a focus group for Weight Watchers, a woman who had considered joining expressed concern that her weight would be called out in public and that she would have to tell her whole weight-loss struggle as if she were at an Alcoholics Anonymous meeting. Thus, one of the primary challenges for Weight Watchers was to correct such misperceptions as to what Weight Watchers actually was.[31] Weight Watchers had the challenge of dispelling concerns that the meeting experience was something akin to a *Biggest Loser* weigh-in and competition.

The second thing that Weight Watchers was trying to do was to reenergize the brand with more effective and differentiated marketing. Weight Watchers believed that its advertising needed to accomplish three basic tasks. First, it had to be noticed when it was seen. Second, on noticing it, people had to associate the advertising with the Weight Watchers brand. Third, it had to accomplish both the first and the second aims while communicating something new about Weight Watchers that would cause consumers to reconsider Weight Watchers as *their solution*—a plan at which they could be successful. Though the company had experienced success in the first two tasks, communicating something new to consumers still seemed difficult. Weight Watchers had to actively emphasize the innovative things that it was doing in order to overcome consumers' preconceived notions. The company needed to show its consumers that its approach was different from other weight management providers.

The brand, especially as Weight Watchers transitioned to the new WW, was focused on seven things: promoting mindfulness; continuing to recruit celebrity ambassadors; offering rewards of exclusive products and experiences for doing useful activities; personalizing the FitPoints system for each member based on height, weight, age, and sex; using Connect Groups to encourage members to connect online through shared interests; accessing SmartPoint values for food via smart devices such as Amazon's Alexa and Google's Assistant; and paying attention to the removal of artificial sweeteners, flavors, colors, or preservatives from all food products.[32] Weight Watchers also had to consider how to relay relevant information that would appeal to a wider net of demographic groups.

The Customer

Innovation at Weight Watchers also involved broadening the customer mix and targeting new customer segments. Weight Watchers was expanding beyond its target consumer market of women, ages 25 to 55. In an attempt to appeal to other demographic groups, such as men and the Hispanic community in the United States, Weight Watchers retooled its offerings and approach to appear more relevant to weight-loss consumers who sought different methods of weight management.

The company was committed to work to better serve the growing Hispanic population. For example, it had improved its Spanish-language meeting materials and increased the number of Spanish meetings offered.[33] Men, another attractive market segment, appeared to be more the self-help type and were not as much in favor of a group-support experience.[34] Weight Watchers meetings had been attended mostly by women, with men making up only 5 percent of meeting members, and thus WW was testing home-based weight-loss services for men.[35]

To attract this segment, Weight Watchers Online, the step-by-step online guide to following the Weight Watchers plan, had intentionally customized itself for men and their unique set of weight-loss challenges.[36] The weightwatchers.com for men customization was born of the realization that Weight Watchers needed to be more culturally relevant to more groups of people who wanted different things. For instance, according to research, about 70 percent of men were overweight and about 30 percent of men were obese. Yet, according to the study, only 28 percent of men were actively engaged in weight loss.[37] Weight Watchers sought to change this.

While the fundamental concepts of weight loss—eat less and exercise more—were the same for both genders, the approach to weight loss for each gender was different. As Chief Scientific Officer Miller-Kovach noted, "Men and women are biologically and emotionally different, and multiple variables factor into how each loses weight." However, the same underlying motivators for weight loss were shared between the genders: "appearance and health."[38] Thus, while the preferred means might be different, the desired end was the same. A dedicated page on weightwatchers.com allowed men to follow the Weight Watchers plan and get food and fitness ideas, as well as other content and resources, tailored specifically to them.[39] This afforded Weight Watchers a new opportunity to appeal to a large market segment that might not have otherwise considered giving the program a try.

Questions Remain

Weight Watchers had attempted to reinvent itself in several ways. It had looked beyond its core market of women to include men, and it had expanded its business model to include not only in-person meetings but also online weight-management tools. Weight Watchers was also exploring a business-to-business model by partnering with community centers, major health care plans, and large self-insured corporations that offered subsidized Weight Watchers memberships to eligible members and employees. Weight Watchers was actively promoting its larger health message.

In the announcement of the new WW and its focus on wellness, CEO Grossman said she considered Weight

Watchers an "aspirationally accessible brand" with programs and platforms that could span across a diverse subset, no matter what the income, race, or locale. As she said, "We are the brand that can bring health and wellness to everyone, and not just a certain few. I've met billionaires who are on Weight Watchers, and I've met people on food stamps that were on Weight Watchers. Wellness needs to be much more democratized and serve that many more people if we're really going to help solve the crisis that we're in right now."[40]

The question remains, would Weight Watchers be effective in staying true to the core of Jean Nidetch's goals, while still expanding to different target groups, different dieting or health wellness platforms, and different means of offering them? Only time will tell, but one thing is certain: The weight-loss and wellness industry is not going away, and members of Weight Watchers' senior management continue to have many tough decisions to make.

ENDNOTES

1. Bowman, J. 2019. Why Weight Watchers International stock tumbled today. *Motley Fool,* February 27, https://www.fool.com/investing/2019/02/27/why-weight-watchers-international-stock-tumbled-to.aspx.
2. Kilgore, T. 2016. Oprah Winfrey gained $3.6 million after saying she lost 40 pounds. http://www.marketwatch.com/story/oprah-winfrey-is-8-million-richer-after-saying-she-was-40-pounds-lighter-2016-12-22.
3. Brumley, J. 2019. Doubling down on misguided marketing isn't helping weight watchers stock. *Investor Place,* April 4, https://investorplace.com/2019/04/doubling-down-on-misguided-marketing-isnt-helping-weight-watchers-stock/.
4. Rupp, L., Coleman-Lochner, L., and Hwang, I. 2015. Weight Watchers tumbles as rebranding fails to wow investors. *BloombergBusiness,* January 2, www.bloomberg.com/news/articles/2015-01-02/weight-watchers-tumbles-as-rebranding-fails-to-impress-investors?cmpid5yhoo.
5. LaVito, A. 2019. Weight Watchers calls on Oprah to help sell wellness after abrupt name change to WW left people confused. *CNBC.com,* February 27, https://www.cnbc.com/2019/02/27/weight-watchers-calls-on-oprah-winfrey-to-help-sell-wellness.html.
6. Weight Watchers. 2019. WW announces fourth quarter and full year 2018 results. *WeightWatchers,* February 26, https://corporate.ww.com/file/Index?KeyFile5396885457.
7. Nidetch, J.T., and J. Rattner. 1979. *The Story of Weight Watchers.* New York: Penguin.
8. Weight Watchers. 2018 annual report.
9. Weight Watchers. 2010. Weight Watchers introduces revolutionary new program to help Americans improve their eating habits and successfully lose weight. November 29, https://www.prnewswire.com/news-releases/weight-watchers-introduces-revolutionary-new-program-to-help-americans-improve-their-eating-habits-and-successfully-lose-weight-110960109.html.
10. Kosner, A.W. 2012. Weight Watchers 360: Mobile apps can break hard habits with easy-to-follow steps. *Forbes,* December 17, www.forbes.com/sites/anthonykosner/2012/12/17/weight-watchers-360-mobile-apps-can-break-hard-habits-with-easy-to-follow-steps/.
11. Lane, C. 2013. Weight Watchers: 50 years of losing. *TimesUnion,* January 11, www.timesunion.com/living/article/Weight-Watchers-50-years-of-losing-4187277.php#page-1.
12. Ibid.
13. DePillis, L. 2013. Internet killed the dieting star: Why Weight Watchers is floundering. Washin*gton Post,* August 4, www.washingtonpost.com/blogs/wonkblog/wp/2013/08/04/internet-killed-the-dieting-star-why-weight-watchers-is-floundering/.
14. Berr, J. 2014. The Flabby business of shrinking waistlines. *The Fiscal Times,* February 3, www.thefiscaltimes.com/Articles/2014/02/03/Weight-Watchers-and-Flabby-Business-Shrinking-Waistlines.
15. Weight Watchers. 2011. Form 10-K, 2010 annual report.
16. Wahba, P. 2018. Weight Watchers changes name to 'WW' in big bet on wellness. *Fortune,* September 24, http://fortune.com/2018/09/24/weight-watchers-name-change/.
17. Burton, T.I. 2018. The rebranded Weight Watchers is bringing wellness to the masses. *Vox.com,* October 2, https://www.vox.com/2018/10/2/17923656/weight-watchers-ww-rebrand-wellness-culture-masses-trickle-down.
18. ww_us. (2018, September 24). Weight Watchers is now WW. We have a mission: to inspire healthy habits for real life—for everyone. We'll always be the global leader in weight loss. Now we're becoming the world's partner in wellness. Learn more: http://spr.ly/weareww #WeAreWW https://twitter.com/ww_us/status/1044201720639901697?lang5en
19. LaVie, A. 2019. Weight Watchers shares drop 30 percent Tuesday after company posts fourth-quarter results. *USA Today,* February 26, https://www.usatoday.com/story/money/2019/02/26/weight-watchers-stock-price-why-shares-dropped-tuesday/2997353002/.
20. LaRosa, J. 2018. U.S. weigh loss industry outlook strong for 2018 and beyond. https://blog.marketresearch.com/2018-outlook-strong-for-the-u.s.-weight-loss-market.
21. Wellness Creative Co. 2017. Fitness industry statistics [growth, trends, & resources 2018]. December 13, https://www.wellnesscreatives.com/fitness-industry-statistics-growth/.
22. Newman, T. 2017. The numbers behind obesity. *Medical News Today,* October 27, https://www.medicalnewstoday.com/articles/319902.php.
23. Weight Watchers, annual reports.
24. Salahi, L. 2012. Study: Weight Watchers as successful as clinical weight-loss programs. ABC News, October 9, http://abcnews.go.com/Health/w_DietAndFitness/study-weight-watchers-successful-clinical-weight-loss-programs/story?id517424647#.UOeEE6zNl8E.
25. MacMillan, A. 2012. Dieters in Weight Watchers study drop up to 15 pounds in a year. *Health.com,* January 4, www.cnn.com/2011/09/07/health/weight-watchers-lancet/index.html.
26. Weight Watchers. Form 10-K, annual reports.
27. Florian, E. 2002. When it comes to fat, they're huge. *Fortune,* October 14: 54.
28. Weight Watchers. Form 10-K, annual reports.
29. WW through your workplace. https://www.weightwatchers.com/us/work.
30. Weight Watchers. Form 10-K, annual reports.
31. Weight Watchers. 2007. Event brief of Q2 2007 Weight Watchers International, Inc. earnings conference call—final.
32. Kindelanvia, K. 2018. Weight Watchers rebrands as WW and puts focus on wellness, not just dieting. *ABCNews,* September 25, https://abcnews.go.com/GMA/Wellness/weight-watchers-rebrands-ww-puts-focus-wellness-dieting/story?id558065632.
33. Weight Watchers. 2006. Event brief of Q4 2006 Weight Watchers International, Inc. earnings conference call.
34. Ibid.
35. Marcial, G.G. 2002. Hefty gains for Weight Watchers? *BusinessWeek,* October 21: 168.
36. Weight Watchers. 2007. Weight loss: Announcing the launch of Weight Watchers Online for Men and Weight Watchers eTools for Men. *Women's Health Law Weekly,* April 22: 251.
37. See https://www.niddk.nih.gov/health-information/health-statistics/overweight-obesity
38. Weight Watchers. 2007. Weight loss: Announcing the launch of Weight Watchers Online for Men.
39. Weight Watchers Reimagined. 2019. A man's plan for weight-loss and healthy habits. https://www.weightwatchers.com/us/men.
40. Raphael, R. 2017. How Weight Watchers transformed itself into a lifestyle brand. *Fast Company,* December 4, https://www.fastcompany.com/40500280/how-weight-watchers-transformed-itself-into-a-lifestyle-brand.

CASE 16

DIPPIN' DOTS: IS THE FUTURE FROZEN?*

In 2019, Dippin' Dots had yet another flavor addition to its roster–Cool Mint Crunch. Dippin' Dots has produced and distributed its tiny flash-frozen beads of ice cream, yogurt, sherbet, and flavored-ice products since microbiologist Curt Jones invented the cryogenic ice cream process in 1988. Available in many tastes and types–Original Dots, Dots 'n Cream, Coffee, and Dot Treats–Dippin' Dots' innovative take on frozen food has changed some portion of the public's way of looking at ice cream. Made at the company's production facility in Paducah, Kentucky, Dippin' Dots' unique frozen products are distributed in all 50 states and 10 countries.

Whether consumers had tasted it in an amusement park, local mall, or a Chuck E Cheese, Dippin' Dots had pursued a multi-prolonged distribution strategy–since being acquired by Fischer Enterprises in 2012–of establishing partnerships with renowned amusement destinations. In 2019, Dippin' Dots planned to expand through China, including presence in several internationally branded amusement parks in China. The distribution strategy also included a partnership with Doc Popcorn, which increased the product presence in nearly 7,000 convenience stores around the United States. Many challenges remained, however, for the company to expand internationally and achieve organic growth instead of structuring partnership and co-branding contracts. But Dippin' Dots maintained a high profile, receiving the 2018 Martha Layne Collins Award given by World Trade Center Kentucky that recognizes companies that have shown exceptional progress and success internationally.

After being bailed out of bankruptcy in 2012, there seemed to be a lot of potential to grow Dippin' Dots at that time. The vision and creativity of the company founder and CEO, Curt Jones, appeared to perfectly align with the business acumen and experience of its president, Scott Fischer.[1] Since then, Fischer has guided the brand to a 2017 gross annual revenue of $120 million, with key acquisitions including Doc Popcorn, the largest franchised retailer of popcorn in the world, helping to fuel the turnaround. In 2018, Dippin' Dots celebrated its 30th anniversary, and summer sales were up 10 percent over the previous year.[2]

The company promoted the low cost of entry and flexibility of its franchising options. In an interview with *CNN Money,* Steve Rothenstein, Dippin' Dots director of franchising, said the company had a lot of opportunities to suit a variety of business models. With a franchise start-up fee of only $15,000, the company offered an economic option for budding entrepreneurs.

In 2018, the Food and Drug administration (FDA) issued a warning on consuming food processed with liquid nitrogen at the point of sale (where customers purchase and consume products). This provided a slight backlash for companies like Dippin' Dots, but the company assured their customers that Dippin' Dots are frozen using liquid nitrogen while they are made at the factory, and the liquid nitrogen would have completed dissipated by the time it reaches the customer.

Dippin' Dots was flexible with alternative delivery models in addition to its more traditional brick-and-mortar locations. These included kiosks at malls and carts at community events (e.g., fairs and festivals).

What remained to be seen was whether all these innovations and fixes would have a lasting impact on reversing the softness in company revenues and give the financials a much needed boost. Were these enhancements to the product portfolio, promotions, and business expansion efforts clever ways of growing the business, or just a last-ditch effort before the end? Despite the introduction of innovative new products, record-setting promotional events, and enticing franchise expansion opportunities, the future of the company remained uncertain.

Company Overview

In May 2012, Dippin' Dots LLC, a newly formed company based in Oklahoma and funded by private capital, acquired the Paducah, Kentucky-based Dippin' Dots Inc. A motion to approve the proposed sale was filed in April 2012 in the U.S. Bankruptcy Court in Louisville, Kentucky. In November 2011, Dippin' Dots Inc. had filed for Chapter 11 bankruptcy protection in federal court in Kentucky for a combination of reasons, including owing millions to lenders from costly patent litigation, as well as having increased operating costs and plummeting sales. Despite its unique twist on the classic frozen novelty, prior to the acquisition Dippin' Dots had been encountering abysmal revenues and having trouble maintaining attention in the market. Feeling the pressure, the company had looked to innovative new products, promotions, and business-expansion efforts as the hope for a turnaround. In the bankruptcy filing, the company listed about $20.2 million in assets and more than $12 million in liabilities.[3] The acquisition was approved shortly after.

* This case was prepared by Professor Alan B. Eisner of Pace University and graduate student Brian R. Callahan, Saad Nazir, and Sushmitha Mudda of Pace University as a basis for class discussion rather than to illustrate either effective or ineffective handling of an administrative situation. Copyright © 2019 Alan B. Eisner.

Dippin' Dots employed approximately 310 workers at its facility in Paducah, Kentucky, and Scott Fischer, president of Dippin' Dots LLC, had no particular plan to move the facility or let go any existing employees. Dippin' Dots LLC was unaffiliated with the existing Dippin' Dots Inc. entity. Fischer said:

> We are committed to ensuring that Dippin' Dots reclaims its status, not as a novelty of the past, but as the ice cream of the future.[4]

Fischer said they had taken the opportunity to acquire Dippin' Dots Inc. in a smooth and equitable transaction in order to rescue the frozen novelty and keep it afloat. Fischer added:

> We are looking forward to rolling up our sleeves and personally meeting with all of the employees, franchisees, and business associates of the company.[5]

In January 2013, showing their enthusiasm for growth, Fischer and the new executive team decided to invest over $3.1 million in the company's home facility in Kentucky, expanding operations and creating 30 new full-time jobs. Prior to the expansion, 60 of Dippin' Dots 170 workers lived in the Paducah area. Fischer stated, "This investment underscores our long-term commitment to market the wonderful Dippin' Dots brand, introduce new products to complement existing ones, and maintain the historic ties to Kentucky."[6] Other improvements were to include purchasing energy-efficient equipment, upgrading processes, and renovating the facility.

Earlier, Dippin' Dots had expanded its product line from ice creams to uniquely brewed coffees. Founder Curt Jones took a colder-than-cold instant-freezing process, similar to the one that made Dippin' Dots ice creams so delectable, and redirected that technology to fresh-brewed coffee. Just as he had dubbed Dippin' Dots the Ice Cream of the Future two decades earlier, he said the new "coffee dots" would adopt the slogan "Coffee of the Future." Real espresso was made from fresh, high-quality Arabica beans and then flash-frozen into dots immediately, capturing the flavor and aroma. Named "Forty Below Joe edible coffee," the coffee dots could be eaten with a spoon, heated with water and milk to make a hot "fresh-brewed" coffee without brewing, or blended with Frappe beads to make a Dippin' Dots Frappe. Jones' once kid-targeted dots now had a very adult twist.

For years Jones had been thinking of coming out with more kid-friendly treats—low-calorie, low-fat Dippin' Dots that could meet the nutrition requirements and regulations set by public schools and thus be sold at the schools. The result was "Chillz," a lower-calorie alternative to ice cream. Dippin' Dots Chillz was a low-fat frozen-beaded dessert made with Truvia, an all-natural sweetener. This healthier alternative to ice cream was also an excellent source of vitamin C. It was available in three flavors: Sour Blue Razz, Wango Rainbo, and Chocolate.[7] In the words of Dippin' Dots vice president of sales, Michael Barrette:

> We're starting to distribute Chillz through the vending channel. We already have two contracts underway and expect to get more. Vending companies know and love the Dippin' Dots brand. With Chillz and other products, it's a great opportunity for them. Schools need that revenue. They have thrown out a lot of products in recent times that have no nutritional value. So we feel bullish about Chillz.[8]

An Innovative Product

The company's chief operation was the sale of BB-sized pellets of flash-frozen ice cream in some two-dozen flavors to franchisees and national accounts throughout the world. As a Six Flags customer commented, "I gotta say, man, they're pretty darn good . . . starts off like a rock candy but ends up like ice cream."[9]

Dippin' Dots was the product of a marriage between old-fashioned handmade ice cream and space-age technology. Dippin' Dots were tiny round beads of ice cream made at super-cold temperatures, served at subzero temperatures in a soufflé cup, and eaten with a spoon. The super-cold freezing of Dippin' Dots ice cream by liquid nitrogen cryogenically locked in both flavor and freshness in a way that no other manufactured ice cream could offer. The process virtually eliminated the presence of trapped ice and air, giving the ice cream a fresh flavor and a hard texture. Not only had Jones discovered a new way of making ice cream, but many felt his product was more flavorful and richer than regular ice cream. According to Jones, "I created a way. . . [to] get a quicker freeze so the ice cream wouldn't get large ice crystals. . . . About six months later, I decided to quit my job and go into business."

Jones was a microbiologist by trade, with an area of expertise in cryogenics. His first job was researching and engineering as a microbiologist for ALLtech Inc., a bioengineering company based in Lexington, Kentucky. During his days at ALLtech, Jones worked with different types of bacteria to find new ways of preserving them so that they could be transported throughout the world. He applied a method of freezing using super-cold temperatures with substances such as liquid CO_2 and liquid nitrogen—the same method he later used to create Dippin' Dots.

One process Jones developed was "microencapsulating" the bacteria by freezing their medium with liquid nitrogen. Other scientists thought he was crazy, because nothing like that had ever been done before. Jones, however, was convinced his idea would work. He spent months trying to perfect the process and continued to make progress. While Jones was working over 80 hours a week in ALLtech's labs to perfect the microencapsulating process, he made the most influential decision of his life. He took a weekend off and attended a family barbeque at his parents' house. It just so happened that his mother was making ice cream the day of the barbeque. Jones began to reminisce about homemade ice cream prepared the slow, old-fashioned way. Then Jones wondered if it was possible to flash-freeze ice cream. Instead of using a bacteria medium, was it possible to microencapsulate ice cream?

The answer was yes. After virtually reinventing a frozen dessert that had been around since the second century BC,[10] Jones patented his idea to flash-freeze liquid cream, and he opened the first Dippin' Dots store.[11] Once franchising was offered in 2000, the "Ice Cream of the Future" could be found at thousands of shopping malls, amusement parks, water parks, fairs, and festivals worldwide. Dippin' Dots ice cream was transported coast to coast and around the world by truck, train, plane, and ship. In addition to being transported in specially designed cryogenic transport containers, the product was transported in refrigerated boxes known as pallet reefers. Both types of containers ensured fast and efficient delivery to franchisees around the world. The product was served in 4-, 5-, and 8-ounce cups and in 5-ounce vending prepacks.

Product Specifics

Dippin' Dots flash-frozen beads of ice cream typically are served in a cup or vending package. The ice cream averages 90 calories per serving, depending on the flavor, and has 9 grams of fat. The ice cream is produced by a patented process that introduces flavored liquid cream into a vat of negative 320-degree liquid nitrogen, where it is flash-frozen to produce the bead or dot shape. Once frozen, the dots are collected and either mixed with other flavors or packaged separately for delivery to retail locations. The product has to be stored at subzero temperatures to maintain the consistency of the dots. Subzero storage temperatures are achieved by utilizing special equipment and freezers supplemented with dry ice. Although storage is a challenge for international shipping, the beads can maintain their shape for up to 15 days in their special containers. To maintain product integrity and consistency, the ice cream has to be served at 10 to 20 degrees below zero. A retail location has to have special storage and serving freezers. Because the product has to be stored and served at such low temperatures, it is unavailable in regular frozen-food cases and cannot be stored in a typical household freezer. Therefore, it can be consumed only at or near a retail location, unless stored with dry ice to maintain the necessary storage temperature.

Industry Overview

The frozen dairy industry has traditionally been occupied by family-owned businesses such as Dippin' Dots, full-line dairies, and a couple of large international companies that focus on only a single sales region. The year 2018 was a relatively good year for Dippin' Dots. From bankruptcy in 2012 to annual sales of $300 million in 2017, the company had come a long way. CEO Scott Fischer said that the two important pieces of the puzzle were having a strong senior management team and knowing when to pivot out of the box. Fischer said:

> For a company like Dippin' Dots that has its core product which was selling bulk Dippin' Dots in national theme parks such as Universal Studios and Six Flags, which is good and that's one of the main veins of our revenue. But by pivoting outside of the box, we're able to go towards the impulse market with pre-packaged packages of Dippin' Dots. And that impulse market would be the consumers at the grocery store or a convenience store or any locations who see Dippin' Dots at the checkout lane, and they buy off of impulse. And that was one of our main segments of business that grew the fastest.

The ice cream segment in the United States is a battleground for two huge international consumer-product companies seeking to corner the ice cream market. Those two industry giants are Nestlé of Switzerland, the world's largest food company, with more than $90 billion in annual sales, and Unilever PLC of London and Rotterdam, with over $57 billion in annual revenues.[12] Both have been buying into U.S. firms for quite a while, but Nestlé, which already owned the Haagen-Dazs product line, upped the ante with its June 2003 merger with Dreyer's Grand/Edy's Ice Cream Inc. of Oakland, California. But even as the two giants dominate the U.S. ice cream industry, about 500 small businesses continue to produce and distribute frozen treats. As one commentator said, "Like microbrewers and small-scale chocolate makers, entrepreneurs are drawn to ice cream as a labor of love."[13] Some of the better-known brands are regional ones, such as Blue Bell, based in Brenham, Texas (see Exhibit 1).

A novelty product delivery system in the independent scoop shop is the "slab" concept. Employees at franchises such as Marble Slab Creamery and Cold Stone Creamery work ingredients on a cold granite or marble slab to blend premium ice cream with the customer's choice of tasty additives, such as crumbled cookies, fruits, and nuts, before serving it in a cup or cone. The novelty is the entertainment of watching the preparation. Both chains rank in *Entrepreneur's* list of the top 500 franchise opportunities, but commentators are skeptical of their sustainability once the novelty wears off, especially since the average price is $5 for a medium serving.[14]

Kona Ice, shaved ice with a wide range of flavors, was among the popular ice cream brands of 2019. The company's primary selling points are 814 decorated shaved ice cream trucks that entertain customers with colorful characters and tropical music while serving ice cream. Kona Ice franchisees own trucks that they bring to social events, schools, sports events, and other community groups. Interestingly, Kona Ice experienced steady growth from the start of the company in 2008 and ranked 67th on *Entrepreneur's* Franchise 500 list of 2019.[15]

Another prominent participant in the ice cream industry is Häagen-Dazs. Started in 1961, the New York-based company started with only three flavors: chocolate, vanilla, and coffee. As of 2019, the company has over 50 flavors which range from classic flavors, limited edition flavors, gelato flavors, sorbet flavors, frozen yogurt flavors, cup flavors, and Häagen-Dazs bars flavors. Häagen-Dazs has been

EXHIBIT 1 Top 10 Ice Cream Brands, 2018

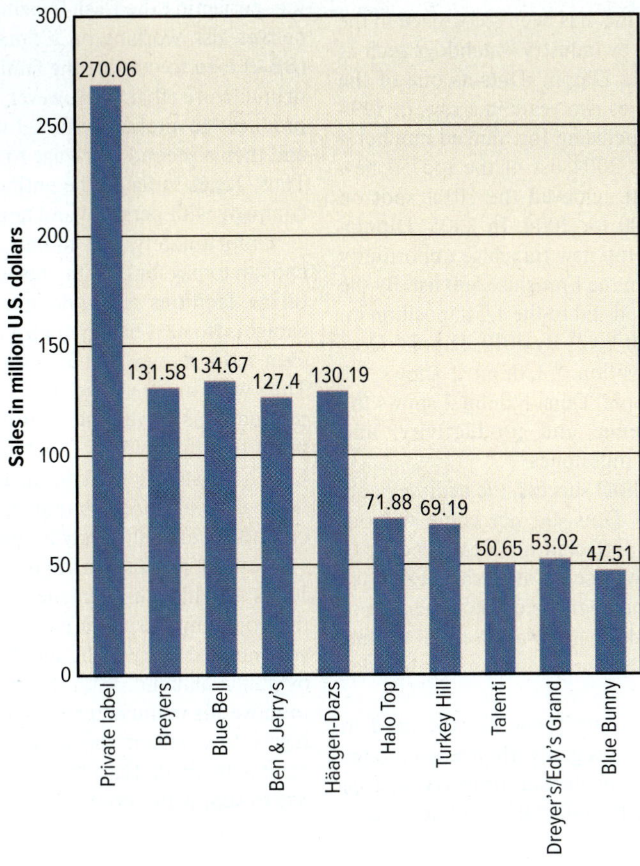

Source: Statista, 2019.

growing at a significant rate by expanding the number of franchises with over 900 shops in 54 countries worldwide. In 2001, Nestle SA agreed to pay $641 million to acquire General Mills Inc.'s 50 percent ownership stake in Ice Cream Partners USA, a U.S. premium ice-cream venture that includes the Haagen-Dazs brand.[16]

Industry Segmentation

Frozen desserts come in many forms. Each of the following foods has its own definition, and many are standardized by federal regulations.

- **Ice cream** consists of a mixture of dairy ingredients such as cream, milk, and nonfat milk, and ingredients for sweetening and flavoring such as fruits, nuts, and chocolate chips. Functional ingredients, such as stabilizers and emulsifiers, are often included in the product to promote proper texture and enhance the eating experience. By federal law, ice cream must contain at least 10 percent butterfat before the addition of bulky ingredients, and it must weigh a minimum of 4.5 pounds to the gallon.
- **Novelties** are separately packaged single servings of a frozen dessert, such as ice cream sandwiches, fudge sticks, and juice bars, which may or may not contain dairy ingredients.
- **Frozen custard** or **French ice cream** must also contain a minimum of 10 percent butterfat as well as at least 1.4 percent egg yolk solids.
- **Sherbets** have a butterfat content of between 1 and 2 percent and have a slightly higher sweetener content than ice cream. Sherbet weighs a minimum of 6 pounds to the gallon and is flavored with either fruit or other characterizing ingredients.
- **Gelato** is characterized by an intense flavor and is served in a semifrozen state. Gelato contains sweeteners, milk, cream, egg yolks, and flavoring.
- **Sorbet** and **water ices** are similar to sherbets, but they contain no dairy ingredients.
- A **quiescently frozen confection** is a frozen novelty such as a water-ice novelty on a stick.
- **Frozen yogurt** consists of a mixture of dairy ingredients, such as milk and nonfat milk, that have been cultured, as well as ingredients for sweetening and flavoring.[17]

Dippin' Dots' Growth from Its Origins[18]

The growth of Dippin' Dots Inc. has been recognized in the United States and the world by industry watchdogs such as *Inc.* magazine, which ranked Dippin' Dots as one of the 500 fastest-growing companies two years in a row, in 1996 and 1997. Dippin' Dots Franchising Inc. ranked number 4 on *Entrepreneur* magazine's 2004 list of the top 50 new franchise companies, and it achieved the 101st spot on *Entrepreneur's* Franchise 500 for 2004. In 2005, Dippin' Dots ranked number 2 as a top new franchise opportunity and climbed to number 93 on the Franchise 500 list. By the end of 2009, Dippin' Dots had slid to the 175th position on *Entrepreneur's* Franchise 500 list.[19] By 2019, Dippin' Dots had fallen to the 334th position.[20] Exhibit 2 shows the growth of franchises for Dippin' Dots. Exhibit 3 shows the growth trajectory of revenue and productivity; and Exhibit 4 lists key corporate milestones.

Despite the company's initial success, the achievements of Curt Jones and Dippin' Dots did not come without obstacles. Once Jones had perfected his idea, needing to start a company for the new process of flash-freezing ice cream, like many new entrepreneurs he enlisted the help of his family to support his endeavor. It was essential to start selling his product, and he had no protection for his idea from competitors.

The first obstacle confronting Jones was the need to locate funding to accomplish his goals. He needed money for the patent to protect his intellectual property, and he needed seed money to start manufacturing the ice cream once the patent was granted. At the same time that Jones was perfecting the flash-freezing process for his ice cream, he was also working on a Small Business Administration (SBA) loan to convert the family farm into one that would manufacture ethanol. However, instead of using the farm to produce the alternative fuel, Jones' parents took out a first and then a second mortgage to help fund Jones's endeavor. Thus, Jones initiated the entire venture by self-funding his company with personal and family assets.

Unfortunately, the money from Jones's parents was enough to pay for only the patent and some crude manufacturing facilities (a liquid nitrogen tank in his parents' garage). He next had to open a store, and doing so required even more money that Jones and his family did not have. They were unable to get the SBA loan because, while the product was novel and looked promising, there was no proof that it would sell. So Jones and his newly appointed CFO (his sister) went to an alternative lender who lent them cash at an exorbitant interest rate that was tacked onto the principal weekly if unpaid.

Now in possession of the seed money they needed, Jones and his family opened their first store. Its summertime opening created a buzz in the community. The store was mobbed every night, and Dippin' Dots was legitimized by public demand. With the influx of cash, Jones was able to move his manufacturing operation from his family's garage into a vacant warehouse. There he set up shop and personally made flash-frozen ice cream for 12 hours every day to supply the store.

EXHIBIT 2
Dippin' Dots Franchise Growth

Year	U.S. Franchises	Foreign Franchises	Company Owned
2018	208	11	1
2017	201	11	1
2016	120	14	1

Source: Entrepreneur Media, Inc.

EXHIBIT 3
Dippin' Dots Revenue

Year	Revenues (in millions)	Total Employees
2018	$120	310
2017	$120	310
2016	$130.9	220
2015	$ 34.80	170
2014	$ 32.85	170
2013	$ 31.26	170
2012	$ 29.87	165

Source: PrivCo

EXHIBIT 4 Dippin' Dots Milestones

1989	First amusement park account debuts at Opryland USA in Nashville.
1990	Production facility moves to Paducah, Kentucky.
1991	Dealer network is established for fair, festival, and commercial retail locations.
1994	First international licensee is set up (Japan).
1995	New 32,000-square-foot production facility opens in Paducah.
1997	Production facility expands by 20,000 square feet; company earns spot on *Inc.* 500 list of fastest-growing private companies in the United States.
2000	Dippin' Dots Franchising Inc. is established, and first franchise is offered; litigation against competitors is initiated to protect patent.
2001	Dippin' Dots enlists 30 new franchisees. *Franchise Times* magazine lists Dippin' Dots third in the United States in number of ice cream franchise locations, behind Baskin-Robbins and Dairy Queen.
2002	Dippin' Dots Franchising Inc. achieves 112th spot on *Entrepreneur* magazine's Franchise 500 list, ranks 69th on its list of the fastest-growing franchise companies, and is named the number 1 new franchise company. Dippin' Dots becomes a regular menu offering at McDonald's restaurants in the San Francisco Bay area.
2003	Dippin' Dots Franchising Inc. achieves 144th spot on *Entrepreneur* magazine's Franchise 500 list and number 4 on *Entrepreneur's* list of the top 50 new franchise companies. Dippin' Dots opens the Ansong manufacturing plant, 80 miles south of Seoul, South Korea.
2004	Dippin' Dots Franchising Inc. ranks number 4 on *Entrepreneur's* Top 50 New Franchise Companies list and achieves 101st spot on *Entrepreneur* magazine's Franchise 500 list. Curt Jones and Dippin' Dots are featured on a segment of the *Oprah Winfrey Show,* appearing in 110 countries. Dippin' Dots is featured among the top 10 ice cream palaces on the Travel Channel. Curt Jones is quoted in Donald Trump's best-selling *The Way to the Top* (p. 131).
2005	International Dairy Foods Association names Dippin' Dots Best in Show for Dot Delicacies. Dippin' Dots also wins three awards for package design. Dippin' Dots Franchising Inc. ranks number 1 on *Franchise Times* magazine's Fast 55 list of the fastest-growing young franchises in the nation. Ice cream cake and ice cream sandwiches (Dotwiches) are introduced to launch the Dot Delicacies program.
2006	Company leadership is restructured. Curt Jones becomes chairman of the board. Tom Leonard becomes president of Dippin' Dots Inc. Dots 'n Cream, conventional ice cream enhanced by beads of Dippin' Dots, is introduced for market testing in Kroger stores in the Midwest. The 200th franchisee begins operations.
2007	Dippin' Dots is available in Colombia, and *www.dippindots.com* V.5 is launched.
2008	Dippin' Dots Franchising Inc. ranks 112th on *Entrepreneur's* Franchise 500 list.
2009	Curt Jones returns to running the day-to-day operations of the firm. Dippin' Dots slides to 175th on *Entrepreneur's* Franchise 500 list.
2010	Dippin' Dots has 3 million Facebook fans.
2011	On November 4, 2011, Dippin' Dots files for chapter 11 bankruptcy.
2012	On May 18, 2012, the purchase of Dippin' Dots by Scott Fischer, president of Dippin' Dots LLC, is approved by U.S. Bankruptcy Court; Scott Fischer joins the team as president.
2013	Dippin' Dots begins distribution to pharmacies and convenience stores to increase access.
2014	Dippin' Dots enters *Guinness World Records* book for producing the largest number of ice cream cups with a team of five in 3 minutes.
2016	Dippin' Dots teams up with the singer/songwriter Dawin for exclusive remix dessert.
2018	Dippin' Dots received the Martha Layne Collins Award given by World Trade Center Kentucky, which recognizes companies that have shown exceptional progress and success internationally.

Source: Dippin' Dots, Inc.

After the store had been operating for a few months, the Joneses were able to secure small business loans from local banks to cover the expenses of a modest manufacturing plant and office. At the same time, Jones's sister made calls to fairs and other events to learn whether Dippin' Dots products could be sold at them. Luckily for the Joneses, the amusement park at Opryland in Nashville, Tennessee, was willing to have Dippin' Dots as a vendor. Unfortunately, the first Dippin' Dots stand was placed in front of a roller coaster, and people generally did not want ice cream before they went on a ride. After a few unsuccessful weeks, Jones moved the stand and business picked up considerably. Eventually, the Joneses were able to move to an inline location, which was similar to a store, where Dippin' Dots had its own personnel and sitting area to serve customers.

Through word of mouth, interest in Curt Jones and Dippin' Dots spread. Soon other entrepreneurs contacted Jones about opening up stores to sell Dippin' Dots. A dealership network was developed to sell ice cream to authorized vendors and provide support with equipment and marketing. During that time, Jones employed friends in corporate jobs. Dippin' Dots grew into a multimillion-dollar company with authorized dealers operating in all 50 states and internationally.

The result was a cash inflow for Dippin' Dots franchising. A franchise location was any mall, fair, national account, or large family entertainment center. According to the franchising information in 2016, the initial franchise fee was $15,000, with an estimated initial investment ranging from $112,204 to $376,950. In addition, franchisees are required to pay a variable royalty fee.

The Ice Cream of the Future

Dippin' Dots is counting on youthful exuberance to expand growth. "Our core demographic was pretty much 8- to 18-year-olds," said Terry Reeves, former corporate communications director. "On top of that, we're starting to see a generation of parents who grew up on Dippin' Dots and are starting to introduce the products to their kids." Although Dippin' Dots seems to appeal more to youngsters, the product still has to have stayed power as customers grow older. As one individual commented, "How can this stuff keep continuing to call itself the 'ice cream of the future'? Well, the future is now, folks, and they have been pushing this sorry excuse off on me at amusement parks and zoos since I was a little kid."[21]

In 2002, McDonald's reportedly spent $1.2 million on advertising to roll out Dippin' Dots in about 250 restaurants in the San Francisco area. Jones called the deal "open-ended" if it worked favorably for both firms. However, by 2007 Dippin' Dots was available only at a few McDonald's franchises in southern California. Storage and transportation issues were problematic, and the price of the product—5 ounces for $5—was too steep for all but the die-hard Dippin' Dots fans.

In other marketing efforts, Dippin' Dots ads were running in issues of *Seventeen* and *Nickelodeon* magazines. Additionally, Dippin' Dots hired a Hollywood firm to place its ice cream in the background of television and movie scenes, including the 2003 *Cheaper by the Dozen.* In 2002, the Food Network's *Summer Foods: Unwrapped* showcased Dippin' Dots as one of the most unique and coolest ice cream treats. 'NSync member Joey Fatone ordered a Dippin' Dots freezer for his home after seeing a Dots vending machine at a theater the band rented in Orlando. Caterers also sought Dippin' Dots for their star clients. A birthday party at the home of NBA star Shaquille O'Neal featured Dippin' Dots ice cream. Dippin' Dots continues to pursue the celebrity word-of-mouth route by serving its products at events such as the MTV awards and celebrity charity functions.

Dippin' Dots sales come from approximately 220 franchisees, 90 percent of which have multiple locations.[22] Dippin' Dots has met with increased competition in the out-of-home ice cream market. The major threats to Dippin' Dots are other franchise operations, such as Ben & Jerry's, Haagen-Dazs, Baskin-Robbins, Carvel, Dairy Queen, and newcomers such as Cold Stone Creamery and Marble Slab Creamery (see Exhibit 5).

EXHIBIT 5 Ice Cream Franchises, 2018

Franchise	Start-Up Costs	Number of Franchises
Abbott's Frozen Custard Frozen custard	$289K–406K	36
Baskin-Robbins Ice cream, frozen yogurt, frozen beverages	$94K–402K	8,041
Ben & Jerry's Ice cream, frozen yogurt, sorbet, smoothies	$149K–504K	593
Bruster's Real Ice Cream Ice cream, frozen yogurt, ices, sherbets	$270K–1.3M	198
Creamistry Franchise Inc. Liquid Nitrogen Ice cream	$225K–577K	62

Franchise	Start-Up Costs	Number of Franchises
Carvel Ice cream, ice cream cakes	$251K–416K	373
Cold Stone Creamery Ice cream, sorbet	$50K–468K	1,236
Culver Franchising System Inc. Frozen custard, specialty burgers	$2M–4.7M	667
Dairy Queen Ice cream, burgers, chicken	$1.1M–1.8M	7,068
Dippin' Dots Franchising LLC Specialty ice cream, frozen yogurt, ices, sorbet	$112K–367K	220
Freddy's Frozen Custard LLC Frozen custard, steakburgers, hot dogs	$578K–2M	311
The Haagen-Dazs Shoppe Co. Inc. Ice cream, frozen yogurt	$165K–543K	205
Happy Joe's Pizza, pasta, sandwiches, salads, frozen yogurt	$189K–1.1M	48
Kona Ice Shaved-ice truck	$125K–148K	1134
Marble Slab Creamery Ice cream, frozen yogurt, baked goods	$293K–376K	330
Menchie's Self-serve frozen yogurt	$218K–385K	496
Milani Gelateria Gelato	$176K–243K	1
Paciugo Gelato Caffé Gelato, beverages	$104K–455K	36
Popbar Gelato, sorbetto, and frozen yogurt on a stick	$217K–458K	28
Red Mango - Yogurt Cafe & Juice Bar Frozen yogurt, smoothies, juices, wraps	$194K–466K	315
Repicci's Italian Ice Italian ice and gelato	$152K–176K	47
Rita's Italian Ice Italian ice, frozen custard, gelato	$172K–431K	598
Ritter's Frozen Custard Frozen custard	$365K–1.1M	20
Sloan's Ice Cream Ice cream, candy, toys, novelty items	$588K–897K	10
Stricklands Frozen Custard Frozen custard, ice cream, yogurt, sorbet	$189K–315K	4
Sub Zero Ice Cream Ice cream, yogurt, custard, smoothies	$219K–476K	59
Yogurtland Franchising Inc. Self-serve frozen yogurt	$299K–693K	317

Source: Entrepreneur Media, Inc.

Meltdown?

Dippin' Dots has been around for 30 years, during which it has expanded internationally, filed for bankruptcy, sold to a new owner, and even found itself criticized by former White House Press Secretary Sean Spicer on Twitter.[23]

By 2019, Dippin' Dots had billed itself as the "Ice Cream of the Future" for over 30 years. However, Dippin' Dots was close to a meltdown. Founder Curt Jones said that Dippin' Dots "just got hit by a perfect storm" of soaring operating costs and plummeting sales. Jones resumed daily control over the troubled Dippin' Dots after a three-year break from operations. He let go President Tom Leonard, who had run Samsonite before joining Dippin' Dots, and Operations Vice President Dominic Fontana, who had earlier spent about 17 years with Haagen-Dazs. Jones described the separations as amicable and regrettable.

In spite of these challenges, Jones, always the inventor, invested in research and development to create a conventional ice cream product that has super-frozen dots embedded in it and withstands conventional freezers while preserving the super-frozen dots in the ice cream. Called Dots 'n Cream and available in berry crème, caramel cappuccino, mint chocolate, orange crème de la crème, vanilla bean, vanilla over the rainbow, wild about chocolate, and banana split, this product was introduced for market testing in Kroger stores in the Midwest in the early 2010s. Thus, Dippin' Dots was finally on the verge of having a take-home ice cream option. As of 2018, the Dots 'n Cream product was no longer available. The company has come a long way to market to its online audience. In August 2018, Dippin' Dots introduced Google Pay and Apple Pay as a payment method for online purchase and its kiosks.[24]

Along with the FDA issued warning on consuming food processed with liquid nitrogen at the point of sale, Dippin' Dots had another hurdle. In 2018, it issued a statement following the death of one of its employee's mother in Tacoma, Washington, due to dry ice. The company managed to escape the heat by issuing a statement saying, "Dry ice forms carbon dioxide gas, which displaces oxygen. This is particularly dangerous when dry ice is placed in an enclosed space, with lack of airflow. We take dry ice handling precautions and safety procedures very seriously, and this incident is a painful reminder for all of us who handle dry ice of the inherent dangers of working with the product."[25]

Despite the recent backlash of using liquid nitrogen and the incident with dry ice, the company has still managed to maintain an audience who are loyal to Dippin' Dots. Co-branding with its sister company Doc Popcorn, Dippin' Dots and Doc Popcorn expect to double year-over-year growth for each of the next five years in international markets.[26]

"We are proud that Dippin' Dots is an American brand that is shipped and sold across the world," said Dippin' Dots CEO Scott Fischer. "Our international growth has contributed significantly to our manufacturing facility production during our slower winter season." Fischer commented that this meant they could maintain more steadier opportunities year-round. Fischer said Dippin' Dots was expanding its production facility to be prepared for an uptick in business this season.[27]

Although optimistic about its future, with high competition, expenses and risks in the frozen novelty industry, will the once known "ice cream of the future" come to be the "ice cream of the past?"

ENDNOTES

1. Saving the ice cream of the future. *Profile Magazine*, http://profilemagazine.com/2013/dippin-dots/.
2. Gorman, Patrick. 2018. Dippin' Dots CEO Scott Fischer on manufacturing trends and managing growth. Chief Executive, September 27, https://chiefexecutive.net/dippin-dots-ceo-scott-fischer-on-manufacturing-trends-and-managing-growth/.
3. Associated Press. 2011. Dippin' Dots maker declares bankruptcy; 'Ice cream of the future' files for Chapter 11 reorganization. New York Daily News, November 7, www.nydailynews.com/life-style/eats/dippin-dots-maker-declares-bankruptcy-ice-cream-future-files-chapter-11-reorganization-article-1.973683.
4. Dippin' Dots News. 2012. See https://www.franchising.com/news/20120419_dippinrsquo_dots_signs_agreement_to_be_acquired_by.html for more information.
5. Ibid.
6. Dippin' Dots News. 2013.
7. Dippin' Dots Inc. 2010. Dippin' Dots Chillz frozen treat. *VendingMarketWatch.com*, January 7, www.vendingmarketwatch.com/product/10110602/dippin-dots-chillz-frozen-treat.
8. Perna, G. and B. Fairbanks. 2010. From the future to the present. *Food and Drink Digital*, March 24
9. Associated Press. 2006. Business blazing for supercold Dippin' Dots. July 23
10. Information from International Dairy Foods Association, Ice Cream Media Kit.
11. Gorman, Patrick. 2018. Dippin' Dots CEO Scott Fischer on manufacturing trends and managing growth. Chief Executive, September 27, https://chiefexecutive.net/dippin-dots-ceo-scott-fischer-on-manufacturing-trends-and-managing-growth/.
12. Annual Reports 2018. Nestle and Unilever.
13. Anderson, G. 2005. America's favorite ice cream. CNN/Money.com, July 29, money.cnn.com/2005/07/25/pf/goodlife/summer_ice_cream. 15. https://www.statista.com/statistics/326315/global-ice-cream-market-size/.
14. Murphy. 2006. Slabs are joining scoops in ice cream retailing. *New York Times*, October 26, www.nytimes.com/2006/10/26/business/26sbiz.html.
15. Entrepreneur. 2019. Kona Ice. https://www.entrepreneur.com/franchises/konaice/334197.
16. Merrick, Amy. 2001. Nestle acquires half of Haagen-Dazs unit that it doesn't own from General Mills. *Wall Street Journal*, December 27, https://www.wsj.com/articles/SB1009414941983387480.
17. All definitions are taken from International Dairy Foods Organization (IDFA). Undated. What's in the ice cream aisle? www.idfa.org/news–views/media-kits/ice-cream/whats-in-the-ice-cream-aisle/.
18. Dippin' Dots 10th anniversary promotional video.
19. Entrepreneur. 2015. 2015 Franchise 500 rankings, www.entrepreneur.com/franchises/rankings/franchise500-115608/2009,-4.html.
20. Dippin' Dots Franchising LLC, Franchise information.
21. Michelle, S. 2006. Review. Yelp Reviews–Chicago, November 17, www.yelp.com/biz/qnA4ml7Lu-9W4SDJOF1YPA.

22. Entrepreneur. Dippin' Dots Franchising LLC. 2019. https://www.entrepreneur.com/franchises/dippindotsfranchisingllc/289468.
23. Belanger, L. 2018. Ice cream company Dippin' Dots will use its freezing tech for cryogenics. Entrepreneur, January 5, https://www.entrepreneur.com/article/307046.
24. Dippin' Dots News. 2018. Dippin' Dots now accepts Google Pay & Apple Pay! August 21, https://www.dippindots.com/news/2018/08/Now-Accepting-Google-Pay–Apple-Pay-.html.
25. Dippin' Dots News. 2018. Dippin' Dots statement regarding dry ice incident. August 1, https://www.dippindots.com/news/2018/08/A-Statement-from-Dippin–Dots.html.
26. Prnewswire. 2018. Dippin' Dots continues China expansion, international growth fuels American-made brand. December 7, https://www.prnewswire.com/news-releases/dippin-dots-continues-china-expansion-international-growth-fuels-american-made-brand-300761915.html.
27. Ibid.

CASE 17

TATA STARBUCKS: A BREW FOR INDIA?*

In January 2019, Tata Starbucks appointed new CEO, Navin Gurnaney, who replaced Sumitro Ghosh who had been CEO for the previous three years. Speaking on the announcement, Ajoy Misra, Managing Director and CEO, Tata Global Beverages Limited praised Ghosh for establishing a strong foundation. Misra then shifted focus to the future saying, "We are pleased to bring on a seasoned leader like Navin, who is focused on operations excellence, relevant innovation and developing high-performing teams, and look forward to continued brand and business growth for Tata Starbucks in India."[1]

Ghosh replaced the menu-as-usual approach with his India-specific strategic vision.[2] As a result, Tata Starbucks narrowed its ongoing losses from above $7.51 million to $6.01 million, increasing sales by 39 percent. Ghosh said, "we are focused on a long-term, disciplined, and focused approach to building our brand in this dynamic market, earning the trust and respect of Indian consumers."[3]

Tata Starbucks Pvt. Ltd in India is a joint venture of U.S. beverage company, Starbucks, and Tata Global Beverages. Begun in October 2012, at first Tata Starbucks, under founding CEO Avani Davda, offered the usual Starbucks coffee menu in India, which was not successful. By early 2019, Tata Starbucks had refined the India-specific strategy, as a more promising path for future growth and success among Indian customers. One of the first things they did was to introduce Starbucks Teavana with 18 diverse varieties of tea to serve the Indian market.

Although the start of the venture had been disastrous, Tata Starbucks became EBITDA (earnings before interest, tax, depreciation, and amortization) positive this year after its sales doubled in fiscal year 2018. In the annual report of Tata Global Beverages, it said Tata Starbucks had boosted sales by 28 percent in FY18 and posted Rs. 272 crores[a] in sales during FY17.[4] Due to recent success, the company announced to open more than 25 stores across India in 2019.

Starbucks had had its eye on the large Indian market for some time before the joint venture was initiated. An attempt to enter the market several years earlier had failed due to complications with the Indian government and foreign direct investment (FDI) restrictions.[b] The company had withdrawn its application then, but when India's esteemed Tata Group knocked on its door with a partnership opportunity, Starbucks eagerly responded. A 50-50 joint venture was formed, and Starbucks coffee was introduced to the Indian market in October 2012 with a generous initial investment of $80 million.[5] The Tata Global Beverages board of directors expressed excitement about the potential of the newly formed joint venture between the company and Starbucks.[c] "Through Tata Starbucks, your company offers the legendary Starbucks coffee experience, backed by the trust of the Tata name, to the Indian consumer," announced Cyrus P. Mistry, chairman of Tata Global Beverages.[6]

The Indian cafe market certainly seemed to offer a lot of potential for the new Tata Starbucks alliance. While India was a nation known for tea drinkers, sipping coffee and socializing at coffee shops was becoming increasingly popular. Domestic consumption of coffee had risen 80 percent in the past decade. Given these encouraging trends, Starbucks CEO Howard Schultz believed that India could one day rival the company's successful venture in China.

In 2019, the Tata Starbucks joint venture had clearly come a long way since it was kicked off in 2012, but it was much too early to celebrate, since the company was just recovering from losses. Success in the Indian café market would require overcoming the usual two key challenges of competition and profitability. In July 2018, Starbucks recorded its first year of positive EBITDA. Its latest annual report said Tata Starbucks, improved sales by 28 percent in FY 2018 with robust in-store performance and new stores added during the year.

The market in India is intensely competitive, with multiple domestic and foreign players. The most formidable competitor of the Tata Starbucks venture is domestic giant Cafe Coffee Day (CCD), with its strategy of flooding the market with its cafés, closely mimicking what Starbucks has done in the United States. At the same time, high real estate costs and rental rates, along with competitive pricing pressures and India-specific cultural preferences, make it extremely difficult for new coffee companies in India to recover their initial investments.

Former Tata Starbucks CEO Avani Davda admits that the initial consumer experience was a humbling one. Tata Starbucks opened its first store with a lot of fanfare in the trendy Horniman Circle area of Mumbai. Despite having a high-profile local partner, Starbucks was unable to use its

* This case was developed by graduate students Dev Das and Saad Nazir, Sushmitha Mudda and Professor Alan B. Eisner, Pace University. Material has been drawn from published sources to be used for class discussion. Copyright © 2019 Alan B. Eisner.

[a] 1 crore = 10 million Rs, Exchange Rate: $1 USD = Rs.69.85 as of April, 2019. So, 1 crore Rs = $143,165 USD.

[b] The Government of India at the time permitted foreign retailers a maximum ownership stake of only 51 percent.

[c] Tata Global Beverages is the Tata Group subsidiary that manages coffee and tea sales.

name to secure any discounted rates in renting real estate. The first store was located in a Tata Group-owned 4,000-square-foot site that had been vacant for a while.

As of February 2019, Tata Starbucks had expanded to over 145 locations across the country in major metropolises such as Mumbai, Delhi, Pune, and Bengaluru.[7] Yet this was still well short of initial expectations. Clearly, something had changed in management's expectations of the size and pace of the venture's growth. Quarterly earnings presentations boasted of robust store profitability, but with no numbers provided, possibly pointing to a slower and more selective approach to expansion.[8] In its first full year in the Indian market (12 months ending March 2014), Tata Starbucks reported losses of $7.8 million more than half its total sales of $14.34 million during the same period.[9]

The joint venture appeared to be at the crossroads of an important strategic decision. It could revert to a plan to grow its store count aggressively, much like Starbucks did in the United States. It is possible that this was the original intent. After all, the initial launch pricing had been set to be competitive with CCD's pricing (coffee drinks available for as low as Rs 100). This approach would have put it in direct price competition with CCD, the domestic café market leader.

Gaining market share among the youth of the country was critical for Tata Starbucks to tap into a large demographic segment. India's population showed a pronounced skew to younger age brackets (see Exhibit 1) and lower incomes when compared to countries like Japan and the United States. Building a presence within these segments as CCD had done was critical for success in the long term.

Alternatively, instead of trying to saturate the country with stores at once, the venture could choose a premium-priced, niche approach similar to the one Starbucks had used successfully in other Asian countries, like Japan and China. The premium offering would cater to an older business elite with higher spending power. This would result in less rapid growth, with a cherry-picked list of high-profile, business-friendly locations, allowing the venture to build a premium brand with premium pricing.

Would Starbucks and Tata under Gurnaney's leadership be able to crack the code for sustained success in the competitive and complex Indian market? Though at first Starbucks appeared optimistic about the success of Teavana as the company focused on offering products exclusively according to the taste of the Indian customer, some critical strategic choices would need to be made to ensure the long-term success of Starbucks in India.

Schultz and Starbucks—Cultivating a Company from an Idea

Starbucks started out in 1971 with a single coffee roaster and retail store in the Pike Place Market in Seattle. Since then the company had expanded its global footprint mightily, with over 17,000 coffee stores in more than 50 countries.[10] The visionary behind this international success story was CEO Howard Schultz.

Schultz joined the company in 1981 and quickly assessed its growth potential after visiting coffeehouses in Italy. He envisioned his coffeehouses offering much more than just a cup of coffee. They were to become a third place, in addition to home and work, for people to meet and socialize. In addition to serving coffee, the coffeehouses would help people connect with other people and their local communities. Employees would be trained on coffee, company products, and customer service to deliver a positive "Starbucks Experience" to each and every customer.

EXHIBIT 1 Age Distribution by Country, 2018

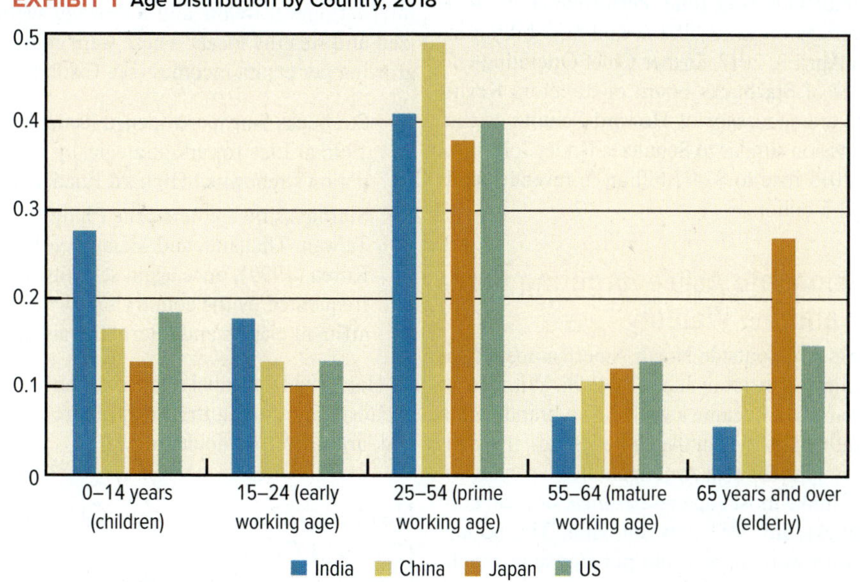

Source: CIA World Factbook.

Starbucks quickly acquired a reputation for being an employer of choice and a socially responsible player:

- When the company went public in 1992, all employees were made "partners" in the company and given a share of Starbucks equity (commonly known as "bean stock"). Comprehensive health care coverage was also provided to both full-time and part-time employees.
- Efforts were made to ethically source products and establish strong relationships with coffee-producing farmers all over the world. In later years, the company began to utilize reusable and recyclable cups in its stores. Its employee partners contributed many hours of volunteer work to help with community causes.
- After the 2008–2009 recession and the introduction of the Affordable Care Act in 2010, several companies began to cut employee benefits to manage costs. Schultz refused to reduce benefits for his partners, arguing that this was a short-term reaction and not in the interests of a company in the long term.
- In 2019, to help provide employment opportunities for refugees and military veterans in the United States, Starbucks announced a goal to hire 10,000 refugees by 2022, and 25,000 military veterans by 2025.

The company's mission was to inspire and nurture the human spirit, one person, one cup, and one neighborhood at a time. The company planned on doing this not just in the United States but across the globe. The Starbucks name had been taken from a character in Herman Melville's classic adventure novel *Moby Dick.* It was felt that the history of the coffee trade and Seattle had a strong association with the sea. In keeping with the sea theme, the image of a Norse twin-tailed siren was adopted as the company logo.[11]

The company under Schultz's leadership performed remarkably well financially over time. Performance in 2016 showed total revenues of $21.3 billion, and $2.8 billion in net earnings. On April 3, 2017, former Chief Operating Officer and member of Starbucks board of directors Kevin Johnson became the successor of Howard Schultz as the new CEO, with a vision similar to Schultz's. Under Johnson, performance in 2018 rose to $24.7 billion in revenues and net earnings of $4.5 billion.[12]

Initial Expansion into Asia—Targeting the Westernized and the Wealthy

The first Starbucks store outside North America opened in the fashionable Ginza district in Japan in 1996. Within the next few years, Starbucks became a well-known brand name in Japan. Like Starbucks shops in the United States, those in Japan featured comfy sofas with American music playing in the background. Unlike most Japanese *kisaten,* or local coffee shops, Starbucks did not allow smoking. The policy proved popular with women, who did not smoke as much as men in Japan. Men eventually followed the women to Starbucks locations, and business started humming. Given the strong performance, the stock of Starbucks Coffee Japan Ltd. made its debut on the NASDAQ Japan exchange and performed strongly. "Any way you measure it, we've exceeded our wildest expectations," CEO Howard Schultz announced jubilantly at the initial public offering in Tokyo, October 2001.

Tea-drinking Japan was not a total stranger to coffee. Dutch traders first brought coffee to Japan in the 17th century, but the shogun prohibited them from traveling freely in Japan, so very few Japanese were exposed to coffee and those who were lived mainly in port cities like Nagasaki. Coffee penetrated Japan further in the 1850s with the arrival of American ships. Soon after, Japanese started to travel overseas and brought back elements of the European coffee culture.

The first coffee shop opened in the 1880s in Tokyo's Ueno district, and drinking the brew became associated with the wealthy classes. Over the next few decades, coffee increased in popularity within Japan, and a number of coffee chains entered the market. As business flourished between the United States and Japan, many Japanese traveled to the United States. West Coast cities like Seattle were popular destinations. So when Starbucks finally entered Japan in 1996, many Japanese were already familiar with the brand. Starbucks soon cultivated a loyal clientele of wealthy Japanese, who considered it to be the original gourmet coffee shop and aspired to emulate the Western lifestyle.

Starbucks Coffee Japan turned its first profit in 2000, nearly four years after its initial launch. Clearly, Starbucks entered markets with a commitment to win them over the long haul. Starbucks grew to over 1,000 stores in the country. For a while, sales volume per store in Japan was twice as high as that in the United States.[13]

Between 1996 and 1999, Starbucks expanded to additional markets in other countries that had a high number of international travelers and a growing segment of westernized and wealthy locals. These were countries with high or growing per capita incomes (see Exhibit 2).

- Starbucks Singapore opened its first store in December 1996 at Liat Towers, strategically located along the nation's renowned Orchard Road shopping belt.
- Starbucks then entered the Philippines (1997), Taiwan, Thailand, and Malaysia (1998), and South Korea (1999), once again selecting premium locations frequented by the country's growing westernized, affluent classes and international travelers.[14]

Happy with its initial successes, Starbucks began planning expansions into countries with more entrenched cultures and large, diverse populations.

Next Expansion Wave—Cracking the Cultural Codes

Unlike Japan, tea-drinking China had little prior experience with coffee. In addition, the emerging superpower had

EXHIBIT 2 2019 Annual per Capita Income (in $USD)

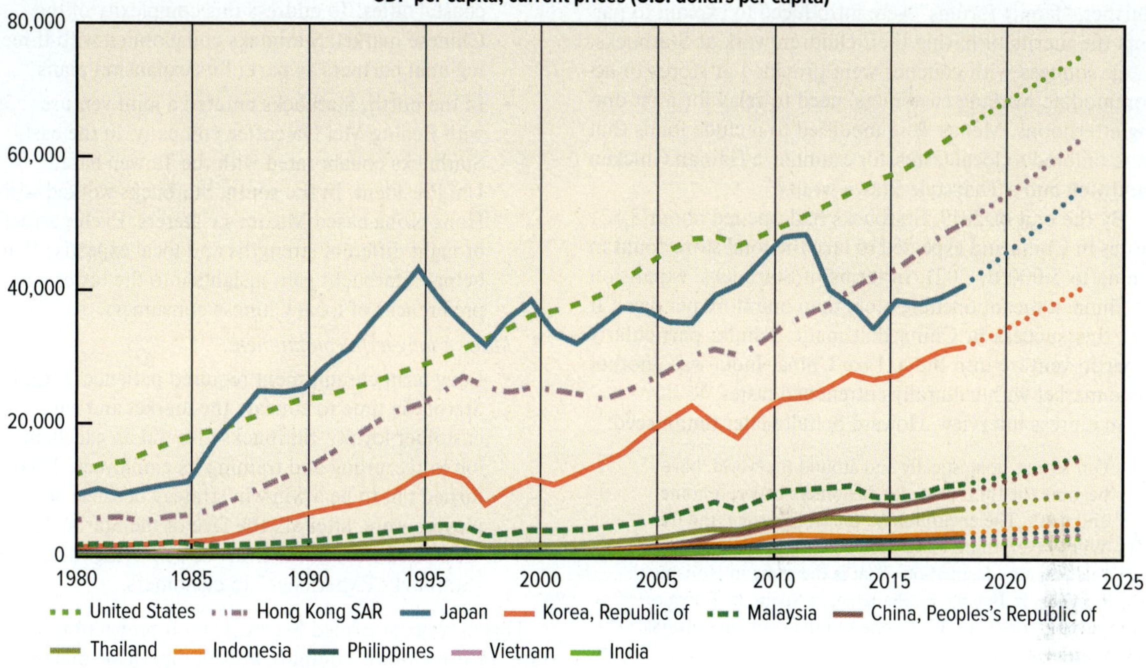

Source: IMF World Economic Outlook, 2019

deeply entrenched cultural traditions with regard to food and drink. Succeeding in China would be a critical challenge and opportunity for Starbucks. Cracking the cultural code there could facilitate conquering other emerging markets– like India.

Starbucks opened its first store in Beijing in 1999. The company recognized there was a universal need among individuals to be respected for their differences and to feel connected with others. Starbucks catered to this need by applying its own culture and values in a way that was yet conducive to local values and tastes.

In China, instant coffee accounted for upward of 80 percent of all coffee consumption. Given the average Chinese consumer's limited prior exposure to coffee, instant coffee had proved to be a highly effective and affordable way of expanding consumption. Starbucks took a different approach and targeted affluent Chinese consumers with beverages priced up to 50 percent higher than the prices at its U.S. stores. Most Starbucks beverages in China cost upward of 30 renminbi (RMB), or about US$5. In contrast, Nestlé's Nescafé instant coffee could cost as little as RMB1.5 (US$0.10) per packet.

Fueled by Starbucks, the wealthy commercial capital Shanghai quickly became the coffee culture capital of China. The owner of Shanghai-based Café del Volcan, one of Shanghai's popular coffee retail outlets, had noticed an interesting phenomenon in the initial days after opening his café. The prices had not yet been displayed, yet most customers ordered their beverages without inquiring about prices. Clearly, the Shanghai elite were not price-sensitive. Much like Starbucks, the café then began to focus primarily on achieving the highest level of quality and service.

In 2018, Starbucks generated an annual revenue of $4.5 billion from its business in China. Starbucks' Chinese outlets had become more profitable than those in the U.S. market. Although Starbucks' Americas revenue grew by 7 percent, its China/Asia Pacific revenue grew by 38 percent in 2018. To capitalize further on the Chinese market, Starbucks announced 1,400 additional stores in China to be built by 2019, bringing the total store count in China to 3,400.[15]

While Nestlé and Starbucks had radically different methods for getting the Chinese to drink coffee, both succeeded. This success in part can be attributed to segmenting the market and recognizing the Chinese as unique consumers with different tastes and habits than those of American consumers. For instance, Chinese consumers do not like the bitter taste associated with black coffee or espresso, so both players tailored their beverages accordingly. Nestlé's Nescafé packets included sugar and powdered milk, while Starbucks emphasized milk-based drinks like Frappuccinos, lattes, and mochas in its stores. Starbucks' Chinese menus also added some local flavor, with customized choices like green tea tiramisu and Chinese moon cakes.

In addition, Starbucks localized its outlets by offering large seating areas, since Chinese tend not to like to take their drinks off-site. Local Chinese customers began to enjoy the "Starbucks Experience" while sitting with friends and having something to munch on along with their coffee. Further, "family forums" were introduced to explain to parents the merits of having their children work at Starbucks. Large lounges with couches were provided at stores to accommodate working customers' need to relax for a bit during afternoons. Menus were modified to include foods that were tailored to local tastes, for example, a Hainan Chicken sandwich and a Thai-style Prawn wrap.[16]

By the end of 2019, Starbucks had opened about 3,521 stores in China and expected to take the total store count in China to 5,000 by 2021. In terms of Starbucks' expansion in China, it meant opening more than one store per day.[17] It was this success in China that made Schultz particularly eager to venture into India. Like China, India was another large market with culturally entrenched tastes.[18]

In a press interview, Howard Schultz later reminisced:

> Our stores, domestically and around the world, have become the third place for customers between home and work. The environment, the store design, the free Wi-Fi - everything we've been able to do has created this primary destination. That is the same in Honshu (China), in Beijing, in Shanghai, in Spain, in Tokyo or in New York City. We've cracked the code on universal relevance.[19]

Conquering Unfamiliar Markets—Seeking the Magic Formula

With Starbucks' stellar performance in its initial expansion into Asia, numerous industry analysts speculated on the best practices that could be used by the company to penetrate other markets, or that could be emulated by other companies.[20] Three key themes emerged:

1. *Be tactful in marketing the brand:*
    - Once Starbucks decided to enter China, it implemented a smart market-entry strategy. It did not use any advertising and promotions that could be perceived by the Chinese as an American intrusion into the local tea-drinking culture. It just quietly focused on carefully selecting premium locations to build its brand image.
    - Starbucks capitalized on the tea-drinking culture of Chinese consumers by introducing beverages using popular local ingredients such as green tea. It also added more milk-based beverages, such as Frappuccinos, since the Chinese did not like the taste of bitter coffee.
2. *Find a good local partner:*
    - Working with the right partners could be an effective way to reach local customers and expand quickly without going through a significant learning curve.
    - China was not one homogeneous market. There were many Chinas. The culture of northern China was very different from that of the east. Consumer spending power inland was not on par with that in coastal cities. To address this complexity of the Chinese market, Starbucks collaborated with three regional partners as part of its expansion plans.
    - In the north, Starbucks entered a joint venture with Beijing Mei Da coffee company. In the east, Starbucks collaborated with the Taiwan-based Uni-President. In the south, Starbucks worked with Hong Kong-based Maxim's Caterers. Each partner brought different strengths and local expertise that helped Starbucks gain insights into the tastes and preferences of local Chinese consumers.
3. *Make a long-term commitment:*
    - Long-term commitment required patience. It took Starbucks time to educate the market and gain customer loyalty. Starbucks also did an excellent job in recruiting and training its employees. This turned out to be a win-win strategy because employees were, after all, the face of the Starbucks brand and were at the heart of delivering the "Starbucks Experience" to customers.

This knowledge armed Starbucks as it prepared to penetrate an even more complex and competitive market of India.

Passage to India—Tata Group a Worthy Partner

Founded by Jamsetji Tata in 1868, Tata's early years were inspired by the spirit of nationalism. Tata pioneered several industries of national importance in India: steel, power, hospitality, and airlines. In more recent times, its pioneering spirit was showcased by companies such as TCS, India's first software company, and Tata Motors, which made India's first indigenously developed car, the Tata Indica, and the world's most affordable car, the Tata Nano.

The Tata Group comprised over 100 operating companies in seven business sectors–communications and information technology, engineering, materials, services, energy, consumer products, and chemicals. The group had operations in more than 100 countries across six continents, and its companies exported products and services to 150 countries.

Along with the increasing global footprint of Tata companies, the Tata brand was also gaining international recognition. Tata ranked 131st among *Forbes*' list of the Top Regarded companies, as of 2018.[21] Brand Finance, a UK-based consultancy firm, valued the Tata brand at $19.5 billion and ranked it 86th among the top 500 most valuable global brands in its Brand Finance Global 500 2019 report.

Like Starbucks, Tata had a strong belief in social responsibility. The company created national institutions for science and technology, medical research, social studies, and the performing arts. Its trusts provided aid and assistance to nongovernment organizations (NGOs) working in the areas of education, health care, and livelihoods. Individual Tata companies were known to extend social welfare activities to communities around their industrial units. The Tata name had been respected in India for more than 140 years because of the company's adherence to strong values and business ethics.

The total revenue of Tata companies was $110.7 billion in 2018, with nearly two-thirds coming from business outside India. Tata companies employed over half a million people worldwide. Every Tata company or enterprise operated independently. Each of these companies had its own board of directors and shareholders. The major Tata companies were Tata Steel, Tata Motors, Tata Consultancy Services (TCS), Tata Power, Tata Chemicals, Tata Teleservices, Titan Watches, Tata Communications, Indian Hotels, and Tata Global Beverages.

Much like Starbucks, the Tata Global Beverages unit was looking for a retail partner to sell its coffee products. Its broad product portfolio also included tea and bottled water. As with its Tata Group parents and Starbucks, Tata Global Beverages was proud of having strong values and purpose as a company. Thus, a promising partnership was formed, and Starbucks was ready to make a grand entry into the market.[22]

Coffee in India—An Existing but Lesser-Known Tradition

Unlike China, tea-drinking parts of south India did have some historical experience with coffee. The crop was first cultivated in Ethiopia, and by the 1600s, it was hugely popular throughout the Ottoman Empire. According to coffee historian and author Mark Pendergrast, the Turks boiled or roasted coffee beans before they left the Yemeni port of Mocha to keep them from being grown elsewhere. That is why, according to legend, a 17th-century Muslim pilgrim named Baba Budan taped seven coffee beans to his stomach and smuggled them to India. The hills where he planted those beans are now known as the Bababudan Giris.

When the British arrived in the 1600s, intending to break a Dutch monopoly on the spice trade, tea and coffee were "backyard crops" in India. Over the centuries, the British installed plantations and established more organized production processes. Tea, which was a much larger crop than coffee, was grown mostly in the north, while coffee was grown mostly in the south.

For decades, the Coorg (also called Kodavu) region in south India had been home to coffee plantations. The British began planting coffee there in the 19th century. When India gained independence in 1947, the original British planters sold their estates to the locals (known as Kodavas) and other southern Indians. Since the mid-1990s, when the Indian government changed its policies and allowed farmers to take control of their own sales, India's coffee industry has experienced a boost in quality and profits and taken a seat in gourmet coffee circles.[23]

With the Tata alliance, Starbucks gained access to locally produced premium-quality beans from Tata-owned plantations in the Coorg region. Tata Coffee, a unit of Tata Global Beverages, produced more than 10,000 metric tons of shade-grown Arabica and Robusta coffees at its 19 estates in south India.[24] This was a strategic asset for Starbucks as it prepared to do battle with the domestic giant, Café Coffee Day.

Indian Café Market—Dominated by Café Coffee Day

The Indian coffeehouse market was strong and growing at a robust rate of above 11 percent. While the market was crowded with international and domestic players, Starbucks main competition came from a domestic giant, Café Coffee Day (CCD). The presence of international coffee chains was significant, but the combined number of their outlets was only about one-third of the 1,600 outlets operated by home-grown CCD.[25]

CCD had been the market leader since its beginnings as a "cyber café" in 1996. As the retailing arm of the nearly 150-year-old Amalgamated Bean Coffee Trading Company Limited (ABCTCL), it had the benefit of sourcing its coffee locally from a network of ABCTCL-owned coffee plantations and using ABCTCL-manufactured coffee-roasting machines. This allowed CCD to insulate itself from global price fluctuations and serve coffee at lower prices than the competition. Most of the foreign competitors relied on imported coffee and foreign roasting machines.[26]

ABCTCL's charismatic CEO, V. G. Siddhartha, had rapidly expanded CCD stores across the country. The mission of the company was to provide a world-class coffeehouse experience at affordable prices. This made the stores ubiquitous, much like Starbucks stores in the United States. It also made CCD the destination of choice for the youth in the country who had limited money to spend and were looking for socially acceptable places to socialize. The majority of India still disapproved of socializing at bars, and cafés offered a respectable alternative. An industry study showed that the CCD brand was synonymous with coffee for most coffee drinkers in India.[27]

After CCD, the next-biggest player was the Barista chain, which started in 2000. From 2001 to 2004, Tata Global Beverages explored the option of partnering with Barista to sell its coffees but eventually sold its stake. In keeping with Barista's premium positioning, most of the company's products were imports and its coffee was roasted in Venice, Italy. In 2007, Barista was acquired by Italian coffee company Lavazza. However, profits proved elusive despite several years on the market and heavy investments. In 2014, Lavazza sold the Barista business to Carnation Hospitality Pvt. Ltd for an undisclosed amount.

Industry watchers said that the coffee business in India was becoming a difficult one to turn profitable even after years of operations. High rental expenses and intense competition had left most foreign players struggling to achieve profitability despite years of trying. According to industry estimates, rentals could account for 15 to 25 percent of the cost of running a café chain. Typical monthly rental market rates were 200 to 300 rupees (Rs) per square foot of real estate.[28] Then, there was the investment in making the stores appealing to customers, finding people to run them, and building a food and beverage menu that was hip enough to keep 18- to 24-year-olds-the target market for many coffee chains-coming back for more. CCD had found a way around this problem by entering into a revenue-sharing deal, paying 10 to 20 percent of a unit's proceeds as a fee. Coffee bars were a sit-in concept in India, where consumers generally hung around such outlets for hours, unlike the global phenomenon of grabbing coffee on the go from generally tiny outlets and kiosks.[29]

Café Coffee Day's vision was to become an "experience beyond a cup of coffee.". They wanted to become the premier destination for everyone who wanted to relax and socialize over a cup of coffee. The challenge that Café Coffee Day had in its initial years was that it was "just another expensive coffee shop." CCD's key strategic approach is based on the 3 As: Affordability, Accessibility, and Amazing Value. The brand caters as a youth meeting space with outlets near colleges and offices where people can unwind, relax, and rejuvenate over a cup of coffee.

Industry experts argued that coffee chains in India had to maintain elaborate and plush outlets–not kiosks–to give Indian consumers what they were looking for from a coffee chain even if the proposition turned out to be very expensive, and this concept made it difficult for many companies to stay in the business and made it hard to scale up. Unlike countries such as the United States, where purchasing coffee was often a quick transaction at a counter or kiosk for customers on the go, the culture in India was to sit down and socialize for hours over coffee or tea.[30] Some frustrated customers stopped frequenting stores because it was so hard to find a free table.[31] This made it much harder for coffee retailers to turn a profit. According to Manmeet Vohra, Tata Starbucks marketing and category chief, peak hours in India were 2 p.m. to 6 p.m. (compared to 5 a.m. to 11 a.m. in the United States) and takeout orders accounted for barely 20 percent of the business in India (compared to 80 percent in the United States).[32]

Other international entrants like the UK's Costa Coffee, the U.S.-based Coffee Bean and Tea Leaf Company, and Australia's Gloria Jean's Coffee experienced similar profitability challenges.[33] Costa Coffee entered the market in 2005 and soon found its stores were too small to handle the peak-time crowds. The Coffee Bean and Tea Leaf Company started out in 2007 and tried to entice customers by offering new menu items each month. Gloria Jean's Coffee entered the market in 2008 hoping it could crack the profitability code by serving coffee in more kiosks, which required a lower capital investment. However, achieving profitability continued to remain elusive for most international players.

Starbucks appeared to be doing well in its initial stores. As mentioned previously, in quarterly investor presentations, Tata Global Beverages reported robust profitability in its stores. While the company shared no numbers, industry experts corroborated the information. The 4,000-square-foot Horniman Circle store was estimated to be generating 8.5 lakh[d] in daily sales, which compared to 1 lakh rupees generated by the 400-square-foot CCD store at the Mumbai airport. Top Indian store revenues in U.S. dollars were comparable to those generated by the stores in China (about $600,000 per year). Since the real estate for the first store was obtained from the Tata Group, certainly that store, at least, was brewing a healthy profit.

Quick-Service Restaurant Chains—A Looming Threat

In addition to traditional coffee chains, the Indian café market was being encroached upon by other quick-service restaurant (QSR) options like McDonald's and Dunkin' Donuts. These players threatened to steal market share with lower-priced options for drinking coffee at existing quick-service establishments.

One of the major advantages for these chains over Starbucks and other competitors was the already-existing network of locations in the country that allowed ready access and brought down establishment costs. Further, this ubiquity and lower pricing would enable these players to tap into the larger demographic segments that made up a large section of the Indian population.

Amit Jatia, vice chairman and CEO of Hardcastle Restaurants, which is the McDonald's franchise for South Indian operations, stated: "McDonald's has the advantage as their ability to expand is better, considering that they have a larger footprint now."[34]

Price was another factor by which McDonald's McCafe expected to hold an edge over Starbucks. Getting a cappuccino for 90 rupees for a global brand like McCafe sounded more appealing than spending more than 110 rupees for the same drink at Starbucks. Like Starbucks, McCafe was sourcing its coffee locally from Chikmagalur in Karnataka.[35]

The Chai Revolution

India has traditionally been a tea-drinking nation. With a domestic consumption of over 1.8 billion pounds in 2013 and 2014, the market for chai by the year 2020 is expected to grow annually by 20 to 23 percent.[36] For every cup of coffee, an Indian drinks 30 cups of tea.[37] Indians are said to drink tea 66 percent in comparison to coffee that stands at 54 percent. However, in the last decade, coffee chains have increased with big players like Starbucks and Costa Coffee entering the Indian market.

[d] 1 lakh Rs = 100,000 Rs (Exchange Rate: $1 USD = Rs.69.85 as of April, 2019. So, 8.5 lakh Rs = $12,169 USD)

At Starbucks' inception, Howard Schultz had understood that the stores were more than just a cup of coffee. After walking the cobblestone streets of Milan for the first time in 1983, he returned with an idea that would change the trajectory of Starbucks Coffee Company. "The Italians had created the theatre, romance, art, and magic of experiencing espresso," Schultz recalled. "I was overwhelmed with a gut instinct that this is what we should be doing."[38] He wanted Starbucks to be an experience where people met and socialized, and returned to do the same again and again. Although this idea brought Starbucks to new heights in the 1980s, it is hard to say the company entered the Indian market with the same thought process.

In comparison to highly expensive bottled teas of Teavana, some tea startups in India explored the possibilities of sophisticated varieties of Indian chai for a fairly decent price. They realized the importance of tea more than that of coffee in the previous couple of years, and combined it with Schultz's initial idea of making the experience more than just a cup of chai. Chai Point is an Indian tea company and a cafe chain that focuses on tea-based beverages mostly popular in South India. Chai Point is revolutionizing the way chai is consumed in India. Beginning with the first pilot stores set up in Bangalore in April 2010, Chai Point has rapidly grown to become the go-to brand for a perfectly brewed cup of chai with over 300,000 cups sold every day.[39] Chai Point is present in eight cities—Bangalore, Delhi, Gurgaon, Noida, Mumbai, Pune, Hyderabad, and Chennai. Chai Point's offerings include varieties of hot chai, iced chai, shakes, and bite-sized Made-For-Chai snacks perfectly accompanying the morning and evening chai ritual. Chai Point retails its own brand of consumer-packaged goods, Made-For-Chai. These bite-sized snacks perfectly complement a cup of their chai. The recipes are developed after thorough research on the Indian palette.

It is tough to compete with Chai Point's reasonably priced flavored tea in the Indian tea market with consumption volume of more than $2 billion pounds in 2017. Their strategy revolves around catering tech parks and corporate professionals. Known to be the Silicon Valley of India, Bangalore has a large number of tech parks, and each of these hold multiple corporations with thousands of employees mostly comprised of individuals from middle-class backgrounds. A market that would be willing to spend more than 15 cents in Indian Rupees for a cup of tea, but not live a profligate lifestyle by spending up to $3 at a Starbucks. This is where the tea startups in India intervene. The Chai Point kiosks located in tech parks consist of numerous companies with professionals who prefer having a small affordable cup of chai with snacks during their lunch and breaks. This is in contrast to Starbucks Teavana that was launched in January 2017. Teavana is positioned as a premium offering competing against a slew of home-grown start-ups such as Chai Point that are willing to experiment with the Indian Chai at a reasonable price to give a branded experience. Is Teavana Starbucks the right answer to these home-grown start-ups? Or does Starbucks need to alter its strategy further to gain the trust of the Indian market?

Tata Starbucks—Challenging Decisions Ahead

In the words of John Culver, president of Starbucks Coffee China and Asia Pacific:

> We have studied and evaluated the market carefully to ensure we are entering India the most respectful way. We believe the size of the economy, the rising spending power and the growth of café culture hold strong potential for our growth and we are thrilled to be here and extend our high-quality coffee, handcrafted beverages, locally relevant food, legendary service, and the unique Starbucks Experience to customers here.[40]

The business looked simple—have a standardized decor, choose a suitable location, and offer good coffee and food—but ensuring that a customer's cappuccino tasted the same as it did yesterday and that the service did justice to the iconic Starbucks brand name every single day was far more complex. Doing so required carefully selected partners (store managers and stewards who went through intensive training) and an incredibly complex planning effort. For that reason, Starbucks had avoided the franchisee route, which could have seemed like the obvious choice for rapid expansion.

In addition, Starbucks had to meet the expectations of its world-traveled customers, who were aware of the "Starbucks Experience." Many of these customers would check whether the coffee tasted the same as it did abroad and whether the store ambience was equally comfortable. If the experiences matched up, they would become regulars.

Nevertheless, for sustained success, Starbucks needed to penetrate the domestic young and middle-income markets. Starbucks laid out plans for different formats, such as "abbreviated stores" that would be smaller in size, and stores at college and school campuses. The stores in India began experimenting with their food menu. While Starbucks globally offered blueberry and chocolate muffins, it wanted to serve local innovations at its Indian locations. Coinciding with its first anniversary in India, the company launched a new, local India Estates blend. This blend was Tata Starbucks' special country-specific coffee, developed thoughtfully with Tata for the Indian market, and it reflected the high-quality Arabica coffee available in India. The company also launched the Indian Espresso Roast, which was sourced locally through a coffee sourcing and roasting agreement between Starbucks and Tata. It was felt that the coffees captured the essence and rich heritage of the Indian coffee history. As already mentioned, to enrich the experience of Indian customers, Starbucks now unveiled a modern tea experience with 18 different varieties of premium tea in its stores.

The challenge facing CEO Gurnaney and Tata Starbucks was a difficult one. How could the company maximize the long-term success of the venture in India? Doing so would mean going beyond "the westernized and the wealthy" targeting that had worked so well in relatively older and more affluent Asian markets. Fomer CEO Ghosh had emphasized positioning the company to be socially responsible by promoting worker rights in India, saying, "We are proud to be a progressive workplace in India and will continue to engage in discussions with our partners to determine how to make their experience better and more valuable in line with the mission and values of both Tata Global Beverages and Starbucks."[41] While the partnership with Tata was occasionally helping in negotiating for good real estate, Starbucks still needed to figure out how to leverage the partnership to win over the larger young and middle-income demographic segments. Store financials needed to be managed to maintain profitability.

All these issues will need to be addressed quickly by Tata Starbucks as the company prepares to expand into the next tier of Indian cities. "As they move from high traffic and high spends locations, revenues, or productivity of the stores will come down. Hence, per store sales might come down over the years once they open stores in smaller locations," says Devangshu Dutta, chief executive at the Indian retail consultancy Third Eyesight.[42]

ENDNOTES

1. ETBrandEquity. 2018. Navin Gurnaney set to become Tata Starbucks' CEO on January 1, 2019. October 4, www.ETBrandEquity.com - https://brandequity.economictimes.indiatimes.com/news/the-people-report/navin-gurnaney-set-to-become-tata-starbucks-ceo-on-january-1-2019/66068894.
2. Malviya, S. 2015. Tata Starbucks' CEO Avani Davda quits, replaced by Sumi Ghosh. *The Economic Times*, December 18, http://economictimes.indiatimes.com/industry/services/retail/tata-starbucks-ceo-avani-davda-quits-replaced-by-sumi-ghosh/articleshow/50217972.cms.
3. Malviya, S. 2016. Starbucks' sales jump 39 per cent in FY16. The Economic Times, November 08, https://economictimes.indiatimes.com/industry/services/retail/starbucks-sales-jump-39-per-cent-in-fy16/articleshow/55301130.cms
4. ETBrandEquity. 2018. Navin Gurnaney set to become Tata Starbucks' CEO on January 1, 2019. October 4, www.ETBrandEquity.com - https://brandequity.economictimes.indiatimes.com/news/the-people-report/navin-gurnaney-set-to-become-tata-starbucks-ceo-on-january-1-2019/66068894.
4. Vijayaraghavan, K. 2015. Growth for now, but profits still need to come in, says Starbucks CEO Avani Saglani Davda. *Economic Times.*
5. Bahree, M. 2012. Starbucks will open cafes in India. *Wall Street Journal.*
6. Tata. 2012. Annual report.
7. Business Today. 2019. Starbucks to open 10 new stores in India within two months. February 10, https://www.businesstoday.in/current/corporate/starbucks-to-open-10-new-stores-in-india-within-two-months/story/318416.html.
8. Tata. 2014. Company website.
9. Special Correspondent. 2017. Tata Starbucks introduces Teavana to serve tea in India. The Hindu, January 18, http://www.thehindu.com/business/Tata-Starbucks-introduces-Teavana-to-serve-tea-in-India/article17055965.ece.
10. Starbucks. 2014. Company website.
11. Tata. 2012. Annual report; Starbucks 2012. Annual report.
12. Starbucks Annual report 2018.
13. Belson, K. 2001. As Starbucks grows, Japan too is awash. *New York Times.*
14. Tata. 2012. Annual report.
15. Starbucks. 2018. Annual report and author estimates.
16. Burkitt, L. 2012. Starbucks plays to local Chinese tastes. *Wall Street Journal.*
17. Levy, A. 2016. Starbucks will be bigger in China than in the U.S. The Motley Fool, December 31, https://www.fool.com/investing/2016/12/31/starbucks-will-be-bigger-in-china-than-the-us.aspx.
18. Barlow, N. 2013. China's coffee industry is booming. *China Briefing.*
19. Bartiromo, M. 2013. Starbucks' Schultz eyes global growth. *USA Today.*
20. Wang, H. 2012. Five things Starbucks did to get China right. *Forbes.*
21. Murphy, A. 2018. Global 2000: The world's best regarded companies 2018. *Forbes,* September 12, https://www.forbes.com/sites/andreamurphy/2018/09/12/global-2000-the-worlds-best-regarded-companies-2018/#62b113777e7b.
22. Bahree, M. 2012. Starbucks will open cafes in India. *Wall Street Journal.*
23. Allison, M. 2010. As India gains strength, so does its coffee. *Seattle Times.*
24. Tata Coffee. Corporate company profile. https://www.tatacoffee.com/corporate/company_profile.htm.
25. Karnik, M. 2015. The massive gap between Cafe Coffee Day and other coffee shops in India, charted. Quartz India, April 6, https://qz.com/377135/the-massive-gap-between-cafe-coffee-day-and-other-coffee-shops-in-india-charted.
26. CCD. 2014. Company website.
27. Kaushik, M. 2011. A stronger caffeine kick. *Business Today.*
28. Srivastava, S. 2012. Starbucks India isn't celebrating yet. *Forbes.*
29. Sachitanand, R. 2014. How Starbucks and Cafe Coffee Day are squaring up for control of India's coffee retailing market. *Economic Times.*
30. Bailay, R. 2014. Coffee chain Starbucks expanding aggressively in India. *Economic Times.*
31. Wang, H. 2012. Five things Starbucks did to get China right. *Forbes.*
32. Tata Coffee. Corporate company profile. https://www.tatacoffee.com/corporate/company_profile.htm.
33. Karnik, M. 2015. The massive gap between Cafe Coffee Day and other coffee shops in India, charted. Quartz India, April 6, https://qz.com/377135/the-massive-gap-between-cafe-coffee-day-and-other-coffee-shops-in-india-charted.
34. Staff, "Starbucks watch out: McCafe is coming for you with cheaper coffee" firstpost.com, Dec 20, 2014, https://www.firstpost.com/business/starbucks-watch-out-mccafe-is-coming-for-you-with-cheaper-coffee-1163753.html
35. Anonymous. 2013. Coffee war: McDonald's McCafe set to make its Indian debut, aims to wipe out Starbucks. *Daily Bhaskar.*
36. Kashyap, K. 2017. Starbucks is the company to beat in India's $30 billion tea market. *Forbes,* July 21, https://www.forbes.com/sites/krnkashyap/2017/07/21/starbucks-is-the-company-to-beat-in-indias-30-billion-tea-market/#54dc1f2137a5.
37. Tandon, S. 2018. Investors are pouring money into India's trendy new tea cafes. Quartz India, April 23, https://qz.com/india/1256617/chai-point-and-chaayos-investors-are-pouring-money-into-indias-tea-cafes/.
38. 2016. A Dream 33 Years in the Making, Starbucks to Open in Italy. Starbucks Stories, February 28, https://stories.starbucks.com/stories/2016/howard-schultz-dream-fulfilled-starbucks-to-open-in-italy/
39. Chai Point. 2019. https://chaipoint.com/about.html.
40. Bhattacharya, A. 2013. Pour out the coffee. *Financial Express.*
41. Nusra. 2016. Tata Starbucks to focus on progressive workplace in India, Restaurantindia.in, May 3, http://www.franchiseindia.com/restaurant/Tata-Starbucks-to-focus-on-progressive-workplace-in-India.8258.
42. Malviya, S. 2014. Starbucks outshines coffee chain rivals in first full year in India. *Economic Times.*

CASE 18

THE MOVIE EXHIBITION INDUSTRY: 2019*

The year 2018 saw a familiar cast battling seemingly invincible odds in a desperate bid for their very survival in an ongoing war. Is this the plot to the $2 billion global box office behemoth *Avengers: Infinity War* (see Exhibit 1)? Certainly, but it is analogous to the decades long fight facing domestic movie exhibitors–movie theaters–going into 2019. Consider the facts:

- As shown in Exhibit 2, 2018's $11.86 billion in domestic box office revenues[1] were a historical high, up 6.9 percent from 2017. The 1.3 billion tickets sold domestically in 2018 is impressive. However, 2018's attendance is still down from a high of 1.57 billion tickets sold in 2002, a 17 percent drop.
- The trend in per capita admissions is negative. In 2018, the average number of films seen per person was 3.97; in 2006, it was 4.7.[2] Both are well down from 1946's peak 4 billion tickets sold when the typical person attended 28 movies a year.
- In recent years ticket price increases have exceeded inflation indicating some recent pricing power. At $9.11, the average ticket price has risen 26.8 percent since 2008 (see Exhibit 3). Recent price increases, however, occur at the same time as attendance has declined, raising concerns that prices now exceed the value provided to a greater number of potential viewers.
- The demographic trends in exhibitor's core domestic market are changing. Studios target an audience of 12 to 24 year olds. While this demographic group will increase 15 percent by 2035, the fastest growing segment of the population is those 60 and older. This population segment will grow 36 percent by 2035. Unfortunately, at 2.5 visits per year, this audience currently attends the movies the least (see Exhibit 4).
- The industry's major initiative to lower costs and draw audiences fizzled out–investments of $2.6 billion since 2005 in digital projection (see Exhibit 5) have not reduced costs and yielded parity compared with home theaters. Audience interest in 3D movies, available with digitization, appears limited. 3D ticket sales peaked in 2010 at 17 percent of tickets and have since been in decline (see Exhibits 2 and 6).
- Exhibitors have little control over their largest cost: rental fees for motion pictures. Costs are high due to a small number of suppliers with high bargaining power due to highly differentiated content (see Exhibits 7, 10, and 12).
- The industry is increasingly bifurcated between two markets–domestic (clear signs of maturity such as a declining number of screens domestically, increasing threat of substitution, difficulty innovating, and signs of consolidation) and international (growth, rapidly expanding theater counts, rising attendance, and increasing revenues) (see Exhibits 1, 8, and 9).

Much like the Avengers in *Infinity War*, exhibitors are engaged in an epic struggle. Exhibitors, like the Avengers, have held a seemingly unquestionable place within society. Exhibitors have long held a position as *the* local face of the entertainment industry in communities. Are movie theaters still relevant? Will they survive? Might half or all movie theaters–warning, spoiler alert–disappear in a snap?

The Motion Picture Value Chain

The structure of the motion picture value chain has changed little since the 1920s. It consists of three stages: studio production, distribution, and exhibition–the theaters that show the films.

Studio Production

The studios produce the industry's life force: motion picture content. Studios are highly concentrated with the top six responsible for a minority of films, but the majority of domestic[3] film revenues (see Exhibit 7). Even within the top studios, concentration is increasing due to fewer films with larger budgets and global appeal. In 2018, the top six studios produced 114 major motion pictures (13.1 percent of films). Yet these films constitute 83.9 percent of all domestic box office receipts, up from 71 percent for the top six in 2000. Studios collectively released 873 films in 2018 compared to 738 in 2017, an average of 16.8 movies per week. The math for exhibitors is this: two of those movies are by Hollywood's major studios. Show those films or the audience will not attend. However, the combination of high studio concentration and highly differentiated content gives the studios considerable negotiating and pricing power over exhibitors, reducing exhibitor profits.

* This case was prepared by Professor Steve Gove of University of Vermont and Professor David Thornblad of Augustana College as a basis for class discussion rather than to illustrate either effective or ineffective handling of an administrative situation. Copyright © 2019 Steve Gove and David Thornblad.

EXHIBIT 1 Top 25 Motion Pictures Based on 2018 Domestic Box Office

							Domestic		International			Global			
Movie	2018 Dom. Gross	Dom. Rank	Studio	Genre	MPAA Rating	Prod. Budget (mil.)	Domestic Box Office to Budget Ratio	% Opening Weekend	Gross (mil.)	Rank	Intl. Box Office to Budget Ratio	Gross (mil.)	Rank	% Gross Outside U.S.	Global Box Office to Budget Ratio
Black Panther	$700	1	BV	Act Adv	PG-13	$200	3.5	29%	$647	5	3.2	$1,347	2	48%	6.7
Avengers: Infinity War	$679	2	BV	Act Adv	PG-13	$250	2.7	38%	$1,370	1	5.5	$2,048	1	67%	8.2
Incredibles 2	$609	3	BV	Anim	PG	$150	4.1	30%	$634	7	4.2	$1,243	4	51%	8.3
Jurassic World: Fallen Kingdom	$418	4	Uni.	Act Adv	PG-13	$170	2.5	35%	$892	2	5.2	$1,309	3	68%	7.7
Aquaman	$334	5	WB	Act Adv	PG-13	$200	1.7	20%	$808	3	4.0	$1,142	5	71%	5.7
Deadpool 2	$318	6	Fox	Act	R	$110	2.9	39%	$460	10	4.2	$785	9	59%	7.1
Dr. Seuss' The Grinch (2018)	$271	7	Uni.	Anim	PG	$75	3.6	25%	$240	17	3.2	$511	16	47%	6.8
Mission: Impossible - Fallout	$220	8	Par.	Act	PG-13	$178	1.2	28%	$571	8	3.2	$791	8	72%	4.4
Ant-Man and the Wasp	$217	9	BV	Act	PG-13	$175	1.2	35%	$406	12	2.3	$623	11	65%	3.6
Bohemian Rhapsody	$214	10	Fox	Dra	PG-13	$52	4.1	24%	$655	4	12.6	$870	6	75%	16.7
Solo: A Star Wars Story	$214	11	BV	Act Adv	PG-13	$275	0.8	39%	$179	19	0.7	$393	19	46%	1.4
Venom (2018)	$214	12	Sony	Act	PG-13	$100	2.1	38%	$641	6	6.4	$855	7	75%	8.6
A Star is Born (2018)	$213	13	WB	Mus Dra	R	$36	5.9	20%	$216	18	6.0	$429	18	50%	11.9
Ralph Breaks the Internet	$200	14	BV	Anim	PG	$175	1.1	28%	$320	16	1.8	$520	15	62%	3.0
A Quiet Place	$188	15	Par.	Horr Thr	PG-13	$17	11.1	27%	$153	23	9.0	$341	22	45%	20.1
Spider-Man: Into Spider-Verse	$187	16	Sony	Anim	PG	$90	2.1	19%	$175	21	1.9	$363	20	48%	4.0
Crazy Rich Asians	$175	17	WB	Rom Com	PG-13	$30	5.8	15%	$64	25	2.1	$239	25	27%	8.0
Mary Poppins Returns	$171	18	BV	Mus	PG	$130	1.3	14%	$176	20	1.4	$347	21	51%	2.7
Hotel Transylv. 3: Sum. Vacation	$168	19	Sony	Anim	PG	$80	2.1	26%	$361	14	4.5	$529	14	68%	6.6
Fantastic Beasts: The Crimes of Grindelwald	$160	20	WB	Fan	PG-13	$200	0.8	39%	$494	9	2.5	$653	10	76%	3.3
Halloween (2018)	$159	21	Uni.	Horr	R	$10	15.9	48%	$94	24	9.4	$254	24	37%	25.4
The Meg	$145	22	WB	S-F Thr	PG-13	$130	1.1	31%	$385	13	3.0	$530	13	73%	4.1
Ocean's 8	$140	23	WB	Act Adv	PG-13	$70	2.0	30%	$158	22	2.3	$298	23	53%	4.3
Ready Player One	$138	24	WB	S-F Act	PG-13	$175	0.8	30%	$445	11	2.5	$583	12	76%	3.3
Bumblebee	$127	25	Par.	S-F Act	PG-13	$135	0.9	17%	$332	15	2.5	$459	17	72%	3.4
Total for Top 25	$6,578					$3,213			$10,877			$17,461			
Average for Top 25	$263					$129	3.3	29%	$435		4.1	$698		59%	7.4

Notes: 2018 Gross is total domestic gross for all films originally released in 2018. Domestic, international, and total gross encompasses entire theatrical release.

Studios: BV = Disney/Buena Vista/Pixar/Marvel; Fox = 20th Century Fox; Para = Paramount, Sony = Sony: Univ = Universal: WB = Warner Bros.

Genres as follows: Act = Action, Adv = Adventure, Anim = Animation, Com = Comedy, Dra = Drama, Horr = Horror, Mus = Musical, Rom = Romantic, S-F = Science Fiction, Thr = Thriller

Some production budgets estimated.

Domestic = U.S. and Canada; International = Outside U.S. and Canada; Global = all locations

B:P Ratio = Total box office (domestic, international, and global) to Production Budget

% O.W. = percentage of total domestic box office from the opening weekend

Internal rank and global rank are based on international and global gross among the domestic top 25 motion pictures only.

Source: Boxofficemojo.com, MPAA, other sources and author estimates and calculations.

EXHIBIT 2 Domestic Box Office Receipts and Ticket Sales, 1980–2018

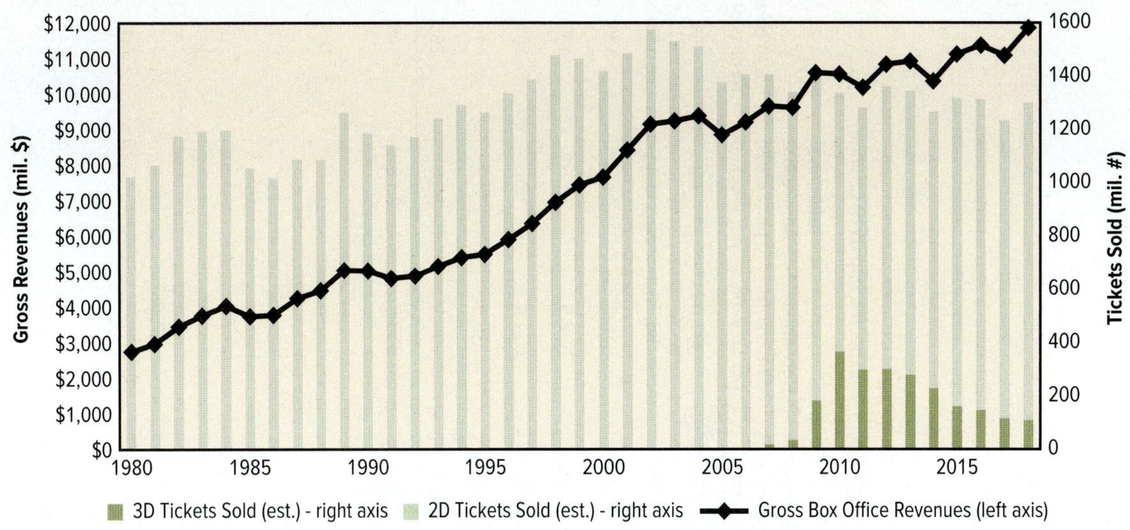

Source: National Association of Theater Owners (NATO), Boxofficemojo.com, MPAA Theatrical Statistics & Theatrical and Home Entertainment Market Environment (THEME) Reports, and author estimates.

EXHIBIT 3 Ticket Prices versus Inflation, 1988–2018

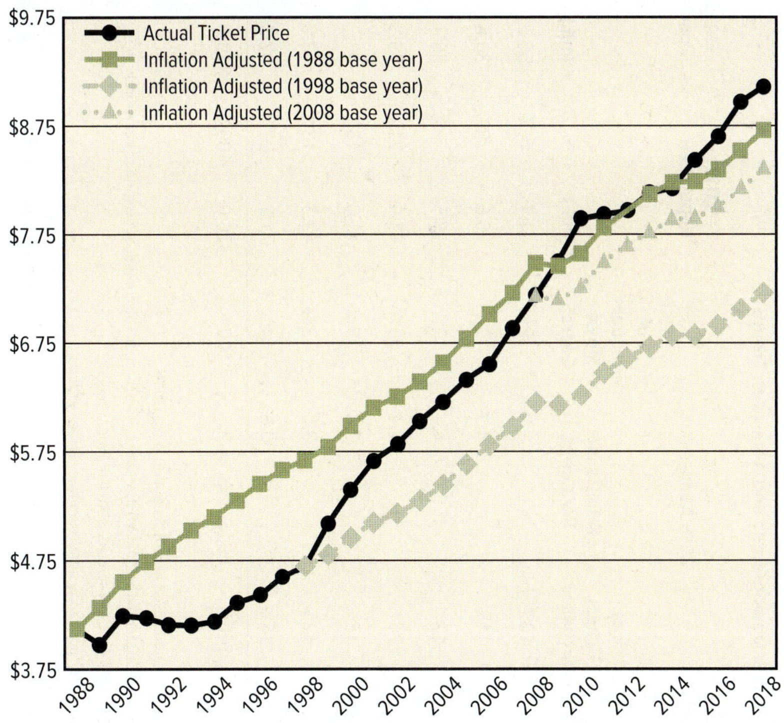

Notes: Inflation adjustments based on CPI values reported by Minneapolis Federal Reserve Bank.

Source: Consumer Price Index.

EXHIBIT 4 U.S. Demographic and Admission Trends

	2018 Admissions[1]			2018 Population		Est. 2035 Population		Change 2017–2035		Expected Impact of Change			
Age Segment	% of Tickets Purchased	Admissions Per Capita	% of Frequent Movie Goers[2]	# (mil.)	%	# (mil.)	%	# (mil.)	%	# Increase per existing screen[3]	New annual admissions per screen[4]	Additional Admissions per Screen per Weekend	% of New Admissions
2 to 11 yrs	10%	2.9	8%	44.7	14%	50.0	13%	5.3	12%	131.4	381.0	7.3	9%
12 to 17 yrs	11%	4.9	13%	26.6	8%	30.6	8%	4.0	15%	99.3	486.7	9.4	11%
18 to 24 yrs	12%	4.7	12%	30.5	9%	35.7	9%	5.2	17%	129.9	610.8	11.7	14%
25 to 39 yrs	26%	4.4	26%	67.9	21%	73.3	19%	5.5	8%	136.3	599.5	11.5	14%
40 to 49 yrs	13%	3.6	15%	41.3	13%	48.7	13%	7.3	18%	181.8	654.4	12.6	15%
50 to 59 yrs	12%	3.0	13%	43.3	13%	43.8	12%	0.5	1%	12.2	36.7	0.7	1%
60 yrs+	16%	2.5	14%	71.7	22%	97.3	26%	25.6	36%	635.7	1,589.3	30.6	36%
	100%	U.S. Avg. = 3.7	100%	326.0	100%	379.5	100%	53.5	15%	1,326.7	4,358.5	83.8	14%

Notes:

[1]Authors estimated based on 2017 admission statistics

[2]Frequent moviegoer defined by MPAA as one who attends the cinema at least once per month

[3]Based on 2018's 40,330 screens, actual # (not in mil.)

[4]Based on 2017 per capita admission rates by age group

Source: US Census (2014), Author estimates, MPAA Theatrical Statistics & Theatrical and Home Entertainment Market Environment (THEME) Reports.

EXHIBIT 5 U.S. Theaters Screens, 2000–2018

			Analog Screens			Digital Screens - Non-3D				Digital Screens - 3D					
Year	Total Screens	Change from Prior Year	#	Change from Prior Year	As % of Total Screens	#	Change from Prior Year	As % of Total Screen	Est. Digital Invest. ($ mil.)	#	Change from Prior Year	As % of Total Screens	As % of Digital Screens	Est. 3D Invest. ($ mil.)	Total Digital Investment ($ mil.)
2000	37,396		37,396		100.0%										
2001	36,764	−1.7%	36,764	−1.7%	100.0%										
2002	35,280	−4.0%	35,280	−4.0%	100.0%										
2003	36,146	2.5%	36,146	2.5%	100.0%										
2004	36,594	1.2%	36,594	1.2%	100.0%										
2005	38,852	6.2%	38,862	6.2%	100.0%	200		0.5%	$10						$10
2006	38,415	−1.1%	36,412	−6.3%	94.8%	2,003	901.5%	5.2%	$90						$90
2007	38,974	1.5%	34,342	−5.7%	88.1%	3,646	82.0%	9.4%	$82	986		2.5%	21.3%	$74	$156
2008	38,843	−0.3%	33,319	−3.0%	85.8%	4,088	12.1%	10.5%	$22	1,427	44.7%	3.7%	25.9%	$33	$55
2009	39,233	1.0%	31,815	−4.5%	81.1%	4,149	1.5%	10.6%	$3	3,269	129.1%	8.3%	44.1%	$138	$141
2010	39,547	0.8%	23,773	−25.3%	60.1%	7,937	91.3%	20.1%	$189	7,837	139.7%	19.8%	49.7%	$343	$532
2011	39,641	0.2%	14,020	−41.0%	35.4%	12,620	59.0%	31.8%	$234	13,001	65.9%	32.8%	50.7%	$387	$621
2012	42,803	8.0%	6,426	−54.2%	15.0%	21,643	71.5%	50.6%	$451	14,734	13.3%	34.4%	40.5%	$130	$581
2013	42,184	−1.4%	2,990	−53.5%	7.1%	24,042	11.1%	57.0%	$120	15,782	7.1%	37.4%	39.6%	$79	$199
2014	43,265	2.6%	1,747	−41.6%	4.0%	25,372	5.5%	58.6%	$67	16,146	2.3%	37.3%	38.9%	$27	$94
2016	43,531	−0.3%	872	−21.4%	2.0%	25,914	−0.8%	59.5%	$0	16,745	1.8%	38.5%	39.3%	$23	$23
2017	43,036	−1.1%	0	−100.0%	0.0%	26,238	1.3%	61.0%	$16	16,978	1.4%	39.5%	39.3%	$17	$34
2018	43,330	0.7%	0	NC	0.0%	26,325	0.3%	60.8%	$4	17,005	0.2%	39.2%	39.2%	$2	$6
									$1,326					$1,275	$2,601

Source: Author estimates, MPAA Theatrical Statistics & Theatrical and Home Entertainment Market Environment (THEME) Reports.

EXHIBIT 6 Domestic 3D – Screens, Revenues, and Releases

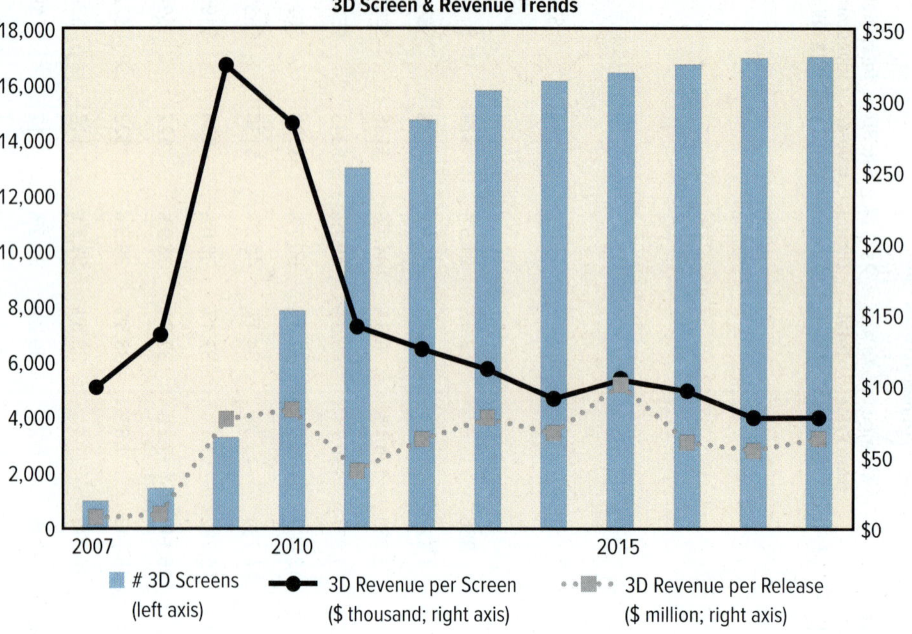

Source: MPAA Theatrical Statistics & Theatrical and Home Entertainment Market Environment (THEME) Reports, NATO, boxofficemojo, and author estimates.

The financial risk for studios is significant as production costs are considerable (Exhibit 1). Studios invested $3.2 billion for what became 2018's highest grossing 25 films ($129 million per film). Risks continue to increase as production budgets have skyrocketed. In 1980, the production budget for the highest grossing films averaged just $11 million. In the 1990s, films turned to special effects and costs reached $102 million (up 827 percent). Today, special effects alone can top $100 million for a major production. These investments, however, are no guarantee for success; a proven formula remains elusive. Many "sure things" flop at the box office while others surprise. For example, in 2018 Halloween cost $10 million to produce but brought in $159 million domestically; whereas *Solo: A Star Wars Story* had the largest budget of films released that year (est. $275 million), but brought in only $214 domestically.

Large hauls at the box office are a poor indication of wise production decisions; profitability is the ratio of box office receipts to production cost. While Hollywood has long made assessing profitability nearly impossible, at a box office, gross to production cost ratio of 2.0 a film has generally covered its costs. *Black Panther's* $1.3 billion global box office covered its estimated $200 million cost of production 2.6 times (a success), but not a smash. Meanwhile a largely unknown horror film, *A Quiet Place*, produced for just $17 million was an enormous critical and financial success. By the end of its theatrical run, the picture had grossed $188 million domestically, yielding a 11.1 ratio of domestic box office receipts to production cost. The level of investments and risk results in studios putting return on their investment ahead of all other parties, including exhibitors.

Studios focus on 12 to 24 year olds, consistently the largest audience for movies. At just 17 percent of the U.S. population, this group purchases 23 percent of all tickets (per capital attendance of 4.8 movies per year). More narrowly, 10 percent of the population are "frequent" moviegoers, those who attend more than one movie per month, and are responsible for half of all ticket sales. Thirty-five percent of these frequent moviegoers are 12 to 24 year olds.[4] Studios target this audience with PG and PG-13 fare including 22 of 2018's top 25 releases. However, more demographic trends are more favorable in other segments (Exhibit 4). While the U.S. population will increase 15 percent by 2035, this core audience will grow 16 percent, just 229 people per current theater screen or 21 additional attendees per screen on the typical weekend. The largest growth–in both percentage and number of individuals–is among 60+ year olds. This market currently has the lowest admissions per capita, just 2.5 annually, but represents a potentially lucrative market increasing by 25.6 million, up 36 percent. At current per capital attendance levels, the increased population in this segment adds more than 30 potential viewers per screen per weekend. Attracting this audience is largely outside of the control of the exhibitors, dependent instead on whether the studios produce films attractive to them.

Domestic exhibitors were once the sole distribution channel for films. This has changed dramatically. Within the top 25 domestic films, 59 percent of all box office revenue was from outside the domestic market (Exhibit 1).

EXHIBIT 7 Top 6 Studios / Distributors, 2000 versus 2018

	2000				2018				% Change 2000–2018	
Studio / Distributor	Rank	$ Share	Total Gross	# Films	Rank	$ Share	Total Gross	# Films	Total Gross	# Films
Buena Vista	1	15.5%	$1,176	21	1	26.0%	$3,092	10	163%	−52%
Warner Bros.	3	11.9%	$905	22	2	16.3%	$1,941	38	114%	73%
Universal	2	14.1%	$1,069	13	3	14.9%	$1,772	21	145%	62%
Paramount	4	10.4%	$791	12	6	6.4%	$757	10	−36%	−52%
Dreamworks SKG	5	10.3%	$777	10						
20th Century Fox	6	9.5%	$723	13	5	9.1%	$1,082	12	1%	−8%
Total for top 6			$5,441	91			$9,949	114	83%	25%
Top 6 as % of industry			71.0%	19.0%			83.9%	13.1%	18%	
All other studios			$2,220	387			$1,911	759	−14%	96%
All other studios as % of industry			29.0%	81.0%			16.1%	86.9%		
Industry Total			$7,661	478			$11,860	873	55%	83%

Source: MPAA Theatrical Statistics & Theatrical and Home Entertainment Market Environment (THEME) Reports, boxofficemojo, and author estimates.

EXHIBIT 8 Domestic versus International Box Office Receipts, 2000–2018

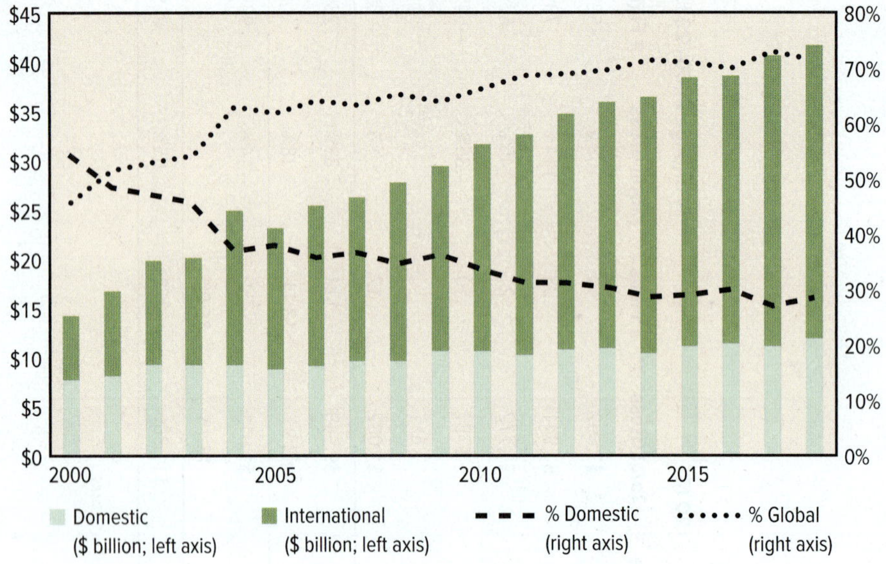

Source: MPAA Theatrical Statistics & Theatrical and Home Entertainment Market Environment (THEME) Reports, boxofficemojo, published reports and author estimates.

Overall, over 71 percent of the total global box office for U.S.-based studios are derived outside of the domestic market (Exhibit 8). Studios view this as their primary opportunity for growth as both ticket sales and dollar volume are rising rapidly. From 2000 to 2018, domestic receipts grew at a compounded annual rate of about 2.3 percent while international grew at 8.3 percent. Based on attendance, both India's 2.02 billion and China's 1.37 billion admissions in 2016 exceeded that of the United States. Unlike the domestic market, attendance in these markets is increasing each year. The studios are also changing their perspective on ticket prices in large population markets. In India, for example, attendees pay an average of just $0.72. In China, it is $4.98.[5]

This has led studios to internationalize their content. While horror films like *Halloween* and a musical dramas like *A Star is Born* require smaller production budgets than science fiction, action, and adventure films, they are riskier in international markets. The subtle nuances of a drama are easily lost across cultures and the appeal of horror films culturally dependent. Animated films targeting children, such as *The Incredibles 2,* and action-packed franchise films with known characters, little dialogue, made in 3D, and laden with special effects like *Avengers: Infinity War* have the greatest potential for cross-cultural appeal. Yet, these films carry two risks–lack of appeal to the 60+ demographic segment in the United States and larger budgets. Action-packed franchise films target the 12 to 24-year-old segment of the population, but are the least desirable domestically among the fastest growing segment of the domestic market, those 60 and older. Costs are also higher, increasing the risk if a movie bombs. Among the top 10 highest internationally grossing U.S. studio-produced films in 2017, the average production budget was $156 million–one quarter higher than the average for the top 25 and in the top 10 only one animated film, *Dr. Seuss' The Grinch*, had production under $100 million.

As studios shift their focus to the international market, they are increasingly less dependent on the domestic market, further increasing their bargaining power over exhibitors. The internationalization of the motion picture industry is starkly different for studios and exhibitors: Studios are seeking to increase revenues through product licensing, DVD and digital streaming sales, and international expansion. Domestic exhibitors, meanwhile, remain wholly reliant on charging an unchanging core market of viewers to see movies.

Distribution

Distributors are the intermediaries between the studios and exhibitors. Distribution entails all activities following artistic completion including marketing, logistics, and administration. Distributors negotiate a percentage of box office receipts for distribution services *or* purchase rights to films and profit directly from box office receipts. Distributors select and market films to exhibitors' booking agents, handle collections, audit reported attendance, and other administrative tasks. There are over 300 distributors, but the majority are performed by few majors, commonly a division of a studio. 2018's *Black Panther*, for example, was produced by Marvel Studios and distributed by Buena Vista. Both are owned by Disney.

EXHIBIT 9 Leading Domestic Circuits

Circuit & Headquarters Location	U.S. Theater Brands (Locations)	U.S. & Canada				Avg. Screens per Theater	Non-U.S. & Canada			Global		
		# Theaters	% of U.S. Theaters	# Screens	% of U.S. Screens		# Theaters	# Screens	% of Non-U.S. Screens	# Theaters	Screens	% Global Screens
AMC Theatres* Kansas City, KS	AMC & Carmike (national)	637	11.6%	8,114	20.1%	12.7	947	7,885	4.7%	1,584	15,999	9.3%
Regal Entertainment Group**Knoxville, TN	Regal, United Artists & Edwards (national)	547	10.0%	7,187	17.8%	13.1	235	2,240	1.3%	782	9,427	5.5%
Cinemark*** Plano, TX	Cinemark & Century (national)	341	6.2%	4,586	11.4%	13.4	205	1,462	0.9%	546	6,048	3.5%
Cineplex Entertainment Toronto, ON Canada	Cineplex Cinemas, VIP, Galaxy & Silver City	165	3.0%	1,683	4.2%	10.2	0	0	0.0%	165	1,683	1.0%
Marcus Theatres Milwaukee, WI	Marcus (WI, IL, IA, MN, MO, NE, ND, OH)	69	1.3%	889	2.2%	12.9	0	0	0.0%	69	889	0.5%
Harkins Theatres Scottsdale, AZ	Harkins (AZ, CA, CO, OK, TX)	34	0.6%	515	1.3%	15.1	0	0	0.0%	34	515	0.3%
Southern Theatres New Orleans, LA	The Grand Theaters, AmStar Cinemas & Movie Tavern (LA, MS, NC, TX, FL)	44	0.8%	499	1.2%	11.3	0	0	0.0%	44	499	0.3%
B&B Theatres Liberty, MO	B&B Theaters (MO, KS, OK, FL, TX, AR, MS)	50	0.9%	400	1.0%	8.0	0	0	0.0%	50	400	0.2%
National Amusements Norwood, MA	Showcase, Cinema de Lux, Multiplex, SuperLux and UCI (MA, NY, RI, CT, NJ, OH)	29	0.5%	392	1.0%	13.5	40	558	0.3%	69	950	0.6%
Malco Theatres Inc. Memphis, TN	Malco & local names (TN, MS, AR, LA, MO, KY)	34	0.6%	353	0.9%	10.4	0	0	0.0%	34	353	0.2%
Total for top four		1,690	30.8%	21,570	53.5%	12.8	1,387	11,587	7.0%	3,077	33,157	19.3%
Total for # 5-10		260	4.7%	3,048	7.6%	11.7	40	558	0.3%	300	3,606	2.1%
Total for top 10		1,950	35.6%	24,618	61.0%	12.6	1,427	12,145	7.3%	3,377	36,763	21.4%
All others		3,532	64.4%	15,712	39.0%	4.4		154,128	92.7%		134,992	78.6%
Industry total		5,482	100.0%	40,330	100.0%	7.4		166,273	100.0%		171,755	100.0%

*Under AMC: Odeon (Europe (UK, Spain, Italy, and Germany) and Nordic (Scandinavia) (369 theaters/2,977 screens). AMC consolidated financial statements reports 1,006 theaters/11,091 screens. Same common parent control of: Hoyts (Australia: 53/430), Wanda (China: 525/4,448).

**Under Regal: Guam, Saipan, and American Samoa (3 theaters/23 screens); Parent Company Cineworld Group Plc (232 theaters/2,217 screens) in UK, Ireland, Poland, Romania, Hungary, Czech Republic, Israel, Bulgaria, and Slovakia.

***Brazil (81 theaters/608 screens), Colombia (35/193), Argentina (21/184), Central America (includes Honduras, El Salvador, Nicaragua, Costa Rica, Panama, and Guatemala, 16/120), Chile (18/126), Peru (13/93), Ecuador (7/45), Bolivia (1/13), Paraguay (1/10), and Curacao (1/6).

Source: Domestic (US & Canadian) and global theaters and screens based on 2018 NATO data & MPAA Theatrical statistics, MPAA Theatrical and Home Entertainment Market Environment (THEME) Report, author estimates for international theaters and screens for some firms.

EXHIBIT 10 Typical Revenue and Expenses per Screen at an 8-Screen Theater

REVENUES	Annual	%	Avg. Weekend
Box Office Revenue	$293,652	63%	$5,647
Concessions	$160,847	33%	$3,093
Advertising	$ 22,886	4%	$ 440
Total Revenues ($13.34 per admission)	$477,385	100%	$9,180
EXPENSES			
Fixed			
Facility	$ 62,734	15%	$1,206
Labor	$ 63,468	9%	$1,220
Utilities	$ 74,085	11%	$1,424
Other SG&A	$ 27,310	18%	$ 525
Total Fixed Costs	$227,597	53%	$4,376
Variable			
Film Rental	$161,508	54%	$3,105
Concession Supplies	$ 23,322	14%	$ 448
Total Variable Costs	$184,830	36%	$3,553
Total Expenses	$412,427	89%	$7,931
OPERATING INCOME	$ 64,958	8.6%	$1,249

Notes:

Box Office Revenue: 1,310,000,000 attendees in 2018/40,246 screens = 32,234 attendees annually per screen X $9.11 per ticket = $293,652 annual box office revenue per screen. Data reported in Exhibits 2 and 9.

Concessions Revenue: 32,234 attendees annually per screen X $4.99/admission (avg. concessions sales per admission from Exhibit 12 (AMC, Regal, and Cinemark) = $160,847

Advertising Revenue: $920 million in 2018 (Exhibit 11)/1,310,000,000 attendees in 2018 = $0.71/admission X 32,234 attendees annually per screen = $22,886 annually

Fixed Expenses: Author estimates based on analysis of select large exhibitor SEC filings, MPAA, and NATO data; scaled to a single screen within an 8-theater multiplex; values may deviate from industry average and any individual firm. Facility expense averaged across AMC and Cinemark. Labor, Utilities, and Other scaled based on Cinemark's financials.

Variable Expenses: Film rental: 55% of Box Office Admission Revenue based on average for AMC and Cinemark in the domestic market.

Concession Supplies: 14.5% Percentage of Concession Revenue

Average weekend calculated as Annual/52

Source: Author estimates based on analysis of select large exhibitor SEC filings, MPAA and NATO data.

Until 2005, the distribution of motion pictures entailed the physical shipment of large reels of 35mm film. Each theater would receive a shipment of heavy physical canisters containing a "release print" of a film. These prints cost $20,000 to $30,000 up-front for each film plus $1,000 to $1,500 for each print. Print costs would total $3.50 to $5.25 million for a major picture opening on 3,500 screens. These costs were borne by the distributors, but paid for by movie attendees. Sequentially releasing films across markets reduced costs. It would premier domestically and phase across individual foreign markets as the transportation of the physical film allowed.

Beginning in 2006, distributors and studios encouraged exhibitors to transition to digital projection technology. Digital projection uses high-powered 4K LCD projectors to cast the movie onto a specialized screen. Distribution of encrypted files, to deter piracy, is via satellite, Internet, or reusable hard drive. This near instantaneous distribution allows a picture's release across multiple global markets. Additionally, digital projection allows for consistently high quality images, as there is no physical wear to the film, and enables the exhibition of "alternative content"–including sports, concerts, performance, and other events created and distributed outside of the motion picture studio value chain. This re-projecting of the domestic industry replaced film projection with digital. At the end of 2018, nearly 100 percent of commercial U.S. screens utilize digital projection, up from just five percent in 2006 (Exhibit 5). Each digital projection system serves a single screen and costs $50,000 to $75,000 including the projector, computers and hardware, and a specialized screen. This equates to a capital cumulative investment of approximately $2.6 billion in the United States alone. Virtual print fees, rebates from

EXHIBIT 11 Exhibitor Advertising Revenue (Total and Per Admission)

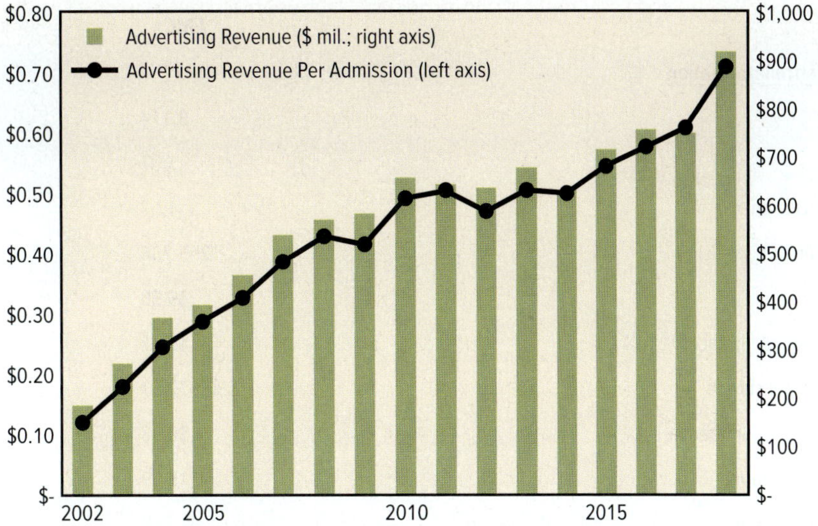

Source: Author calculations based on data from Cinema Advertising Council, 2017, MPAA Theatrical Statistics & Theatrical and Home Entertainment Market Environment (THEME) Report, boxofficemojo.com, and Marketing Charts.

distributors on each film distributed digitally, partially funded the conversion. These fees, as much as 17 percent of rental costs, expired in 2013. Despite the cost savings of digital distribution, film rental rates, which includes the cost of distribution, have averaged 50 to 55 percent of box office revenue for several decades. This suggests that the studios, not the exhibitors, benefit from the reduced cost of distribution.

Exhibition

An exhibitor, the local movie theater, provides a location where audiences can view a motion picture. The basic business model of exhibitors–using movies as the draw and selling concessions to make a profit–has changed little since the time of touring motion picture shows that would set up in town halls and churches. As attending movies became popular, permanent theaters were constructed. Studios recognized the potential profit in exhibition and vertically integrated, gaining control over the films shown and capturing downstream profits. This practice ended in 1948 with the Supreme Court's ruling against the studios in *United States v. Paramount Pictures*. Studios were forced to divest theaters, leaving the two to negotiate film access and rental fees. Single theater and single screen firms' exhibitors fared poorly as studios retained the upper hand in setting rental rates. Exhibitors sought to increase bargaining power and economies by consolidating, multiplying the bargaining power of individual theaters by the number of screens managed. This reached its zenith in the 1980s with the mass rollout of the multiplex concept. Maximizing both bargaining power based of multiple screens while minimizing labor and facility costs, exhibitors constructed large entertainment complexes, sometimes with dozens of screens. Most local single screen theaters have closed, unable to compete on cost or viewing experience.

Today, the 10 largest exhibitor "circuits" operate 35.6 percent of theaters, controlling a disproportionate 61 percent of screens (Exhibit 9). In many industries, this high concentration of industry outlets would provide the firms with significant buying power. Larger circuits benefit from some power as they can negotiate better prices on some concession supplies and access revenues from national advertisers. However, movie content is highly differentiated; theaters are not. An exhibitor trying to drive too hard of a bargain on rental rates may miss showing a film on opening weekend. Thus, the true power rests with the studios and distributors.

At the top of the circuits are the four largest of all national chains: AMC, Regal, and Cinemark serving the United States, and Cineplex, serving Canada. These chains operate large multiplexes, averaging 12 screens per location. These firms operate under one third of all U.S. and Canadian theater locations, but almost 54 percent of screens. The next tier of circuits consists of regional operators (Marcus, Harkins, Southern, B&B, National Amusements, and Malco). The regional operators control another 4.7 percent of theaters and 7.6 percent of screens. The remaining circuits, 64.4 percent of all theaters operating 39 percent of screens, range from smaller chains operating several miniplexes consisting of 2 to 7 screens down to single theater, single screen locations.

EXHIBIT 12 Select 2018 AMC and Cinemark Financials

	AMC*	Cinemark**
Theater and Attendance Information		
Screens (U.S. only)	8,114	4,586
Theaters (U.S. only)	637	341
Screens per Theater (U.S. only)	12.7	13.4
Total US Attendance (in thousands)	255,736	185,300
Avg. Ticket Price	$9.55	$7.89
Avg. Concessions per admittance	$5.17	$4.82
Avg. Other Revenue per screen	$30,872.57	$40,427.39
Avg. Other Revenue per admittance	$0.98	$1.00
Avg. Revenue per admittance	$15.69	$13.70
Avg. Attendance per screen	31,518	40,406
Avg. Admission revenue per screen	$300,900	$318,622
Income Statement ($ mil.)		
Revenues		
Admissions	$2,441.50	$1,461.20
Concessions	$1,321.20	$892.40
Other Income	$250.50	$185.40
Total Revenues	$4,013.20	$2,539.00
Admissions as % of Revenues	60.84%	57.55%
Concessions as % of Revenues	32.92%	35.15%
Other as % of Revenues	6.24%	7.30%
Expenses		
Film rental and advertising	$1,323.10	$822.60
Concessions	$190.20	$134.60
Building Rent	$584.40	$245.10
Salaries, Wages, Utilities, Depreciation, and Other	$1,683.70	$1,025.15
Total Cost of Operation	$3,781.40	$2,227.45
Operating Income	$231.80	$311.55
Operating Income per admission	$0.91	$1.68
Operating Income as % total revenue (Operating Margin)	5.78%	14.50%
Film rental and advertising expense as a % of Admission Revenue	54.19%	56.30%
Concessions Costs as % of Concession Revenues	14.40%	15.08%
Building Rent as a % of Admission Revenue	23.94%	16.77%

	AMC*	Cinemark**
Balance Sheet (Consolidated Domestic and International) ($ mil.)		
Current Assets	$781.30	$578.54
Property, Plant and Equipment	$3,039.60	$1,833.13
Other Assets (Goodwill, intangibles)	$5,674.90	$2,089.68
Total Assets	**$9,495.80**	**$4,501.35**
Current Liabilities	$1,328.10	$474.05
Long Term Liabilities	$6,769.70	$2,550.12
Total Liabilities	**$8,097.80**	**$3,024.17**
Equity	**$1,398.00**	**$1,477.18**
Current Ratio	0.59	1.22
Debt to Asset Ratio	0.85	0.67

*AMC's data was taken from their 2018 annual report.

** Cinemark's data was taken from their 2018 annual report. U.S. operating income is not reported. Number estimated based on the revenue splits between domestic and international revenues.

Source: AMC 2018 Annual Report and Cinemark 2018 Annual Report.

The Business of Exhibition

Exhibitors have three revenue sources: box office receipts, concessions, and advertising (see Exhibits 10 and 12). They have low discretion–their ability to influence revenues and expenses is limited. Exhibitor operating margins average a slim 10 percent; net income may fluctuate wildly based on the tax benefits of prior losses.

Box Office Revenues

Ticket sales constitute almost two thirds of exhibition business revenues. The return, however, is quite small due to the power of the studios. Among the largest exhibitors, film rental fees average 55 percent of box office receipts. These costs are typically higher for smaller circuits. The basis for rental rates are the size of the circuit and both the duration and seat commitment. While attendees may gripe about the average ticket price of $9.11, most do not realize that $5.01 (55 percent) goes to the studio. The exhibitor may not break even unless concessions are purchased.

The portion of box office revenues retained by the theater increases each week. On opening weekend, an exhibitor may pay the distributor 80 to 90 percent of the box office gross in rental fees, retaining only 10 to 20 percent. In subsequent weeks, the exhibitor's portion increases to as much as 80 to 90 percent. For truly event films, studios have considerable power and can capture a higher percentage of the box office. For 2017's *The Last Jedi*, the standard exhibition contract stipulated a rental rate of about 65 percent of the ticket price and required exhibitors to show the film on their largest screens for 4 weeks, or the rate increased to 70 percent.[6]

While non-opening weekends offer exhibitors larger margins, the studios focus on attracting audiences on opening weekend with well-funded publicity campaigns. Focusing on getting audiences to the theater on the opening weekend results in lower marketing expenses for each film, keeps the film pipeline flowing with releases, and avoids competition between films for a common audience (e.g., two R-rated comedies opening the same weekend). Among 2018's top 10 releases, an average of 30 percent of total domestic revenues were on the opening weekend. 2018's *Halloween* received 48 percent of their total domestic box office revenue in the opening weekend (Exhibit 1). While these films draw audiences, they are less lucrative for exhibitors than films staying in the theater for multiple weeks. Exhibitors can keep more of the box office receipts from films such as *Crazy Rich Asians* and *Mary Poppins Returns*, which respectively had only 14 percent and 15 percent of their sales opening weekend.

Such films are, however, the exception. A weak opening weekend typically results in a short run in theaters as attendance declines when studio-funded marketing campaigns shift toward the next film. In industry terminology, the "multiple" (the percentage coming after opening weekend) has been declining steadily, falling 25 percent since 2002.[7] This limits an exhibitors potential to save on film rental costs by skipping opening weekend. A theater will typically lose attendees as audiences seek another theater if one does not show a film on opening weekend.

Concessions

A frequent moviegoer lament is high concession prices. At an average of $4.99 per admission at AMC ($5.17 per admission) or Cinemark ($4.87 per admission), concessions constitute one third of exhibitor revenues (Exhibit 12). Direct costs of under 15 percent make concessions the primary source of exhibitor profit. Three factors drive concession profits: attendance, pricing, and material costs. The most important is attendance—more attendees yields more concession sales. Sales are also influenced by prices. The $5.00 and $9.00 price points for the large soda and popcorn are not accidental, but the result of considerable market research and profit maximization calculations. The inputs are largely commodities. Volume purchases reduce costs. Large circuits negotiate better prices on everything from popcorn and soda pop to cups and napkins.

Once consisting of only boxed candy, popcorn, and soft drinks purchased at the counter in the lobby, concessions now include a variety of food, drink, and location options. Concession options such as hamburgers, salads, hot appetizers, and alcoholic beverage sales increase average concession sales per patron. They must, however, be considered in conjunction with higher costs for kitchen facilities, labor, and food costs. A $15 burger has a lower gross margin percentage than a $9 tub of popcorn due to higher food costs, but may net the same profit in dollars. Patrons may skip one $5 soda for several rounds of $8 beer, wine, or bar sales.

Advertising

The low margins derived from ticket sales cause exhibitors to focus on other sources of revenue. The highest margin, and therefore the most attractive, is advertising, including pre-show and lobby advertising and previews. Advertising revenues have increased from $186 in 2002 to $920 million in 2018[8,9] (see Exhibit 11). More importantly, the time devoted to ads in each showing has increased. The number of previews has also increased from just three or four, ten years ago to six or seven, currently. This includes the two typically provided to the studio as part of the film rental agreement.[10] Though advertising constitutes just seven percent of exhibitor revenues, it is highly profitable and growing. Instead of paying for short films to show prior to the feature, exhibitors show ads, which they are paid to show. Advertising revenues for exhibitors averaged more than $21 thousand per screen and $0.71 per admission for the industry, but $30 and $40 thousand per screen for industry leaders AMC and Cinemark in 2018, $0.99 per admission (Exhibit 12).[11] Yet audiences express dislike for advertising at the theater and, if dissatisfaction increases, may opt to view movies at home. Balancing the lucrative revenues from ads with audience tolerance is an ongoing struggle for exhibitors.

The Major Exhibitor Circuits

Four exhibitor "circuits" dominate the domestic market, collectively controlling 30.8 percent of domestic theaters but a disproportionate 53.5 percent of screens. The four circuits serve different geographic areas and operate with different business-level strategies[12] (see Exhibit 9). AMC is the largest domestic exhibitor with 8,114 screens in 637 theaters. Domestically, the circuit uses the AMC and Loews chains to concentrate on urban areas near large population centers such as those in California, Florida, and Texas with megaplex theaters averaging 12.5 screens. By offering 3-D, IMAX, and other premium viewing experiences, at $9.55 AMCs average ticket price is consistently near the top of the market. Concession sales per attendee is also the highest among the majors at $5.17 per patron (see Exhibit 12).

Dalian Wanda Group, a Chinese conglomerate with commercial real estate and cultural holdings acquired AMC in 2012 for a reported $2.6 billion.[13] To many observers, the acquisition signaled the start of a wave of consolidation and globalization among exhibitors. At the time of the acquisition, Wanda operated some 150 theaters in China as well as significant studio production facilities. The acquisition resulted in Wanda becoming both the single largest and the most geographically diverse exhibitor globally. Since the acquisition of AMC, Wanda has continued its acquisition approach to expansion by purchasing European Odeon circuit and Australia's Hoyts. In 2017, Wanda/AMC announced the acquisition of Nordic, another European-based circuit with operations in Scandinavia. Wanda/AMC is the world's largest theater circuit with nearly 16,000 screens across more than 1,500 theaters. The scale and reach of the company is unprecedented—one company controlling nearly 10 percent of global screens across all of the major viewing markets. This scale could result in greater leverage negotiating rental rates.

Regal, unlike AMC, has historically focused almost exclusively on the domestic market. Regal operates 7,187 screens in 547 theaters in the United States with its namesake Regal as well as United Artists and Edwards Theaters and has long operated theaters in the U.S. territories of Guam, Saipan, and American Samoa. Continuing the consolidation wave, Regal was purchased by the UK-based Cineworld Group PLC in 2018 for $3.6 billion.[14] The combined company operates an additional 232 theaters with 2,217 screens in the UK, Ireland, Poland, Romania, Hungary, Czech Republic, Israel, Bulgaria, and Slovakia. Domestically, Regal focuses on mid-size markets using multi- and megaplexes with 13 screens per location, with an average ticket price of $10.20 and average concession sales of $4.72 per admission.

Cinemark, the #3 domestic circuit by size, operates 341 domestic locations with 4,586 screens under the Cinemark and Century brands. Cinemark serves smaller markets, operating as the sole theater in 90 percent of its markets. Their average ticket price is $7.89. Cinemark was the first domestic circuit to expand beyond the domestic market and currently operates 1,462 screens in 205 theaters across 15 Central and South American countries.

Canadian-based Cineplex Entertainment is the fourth largest domestic.[15] The result of several mergers and acquisitions, the circuit operates 165 theaters with 1,683 screens exclusively in Canada.

Major circuits compete based on geographic locations, not direct competition. The differentiators operate in higher cost locations near shopping and restaurants, within or in front of the mall. The cost leaders position theaters in less trafficked locations with lower rent such as in a strip mall or behind the shopping mall. Beyond location, there are more differences within each exhibitor's offerings than across circuits. The industry has a history of adding features to theaters to attract customers. These include being an early adopter of air conditioning, transitioning to digital projection, and using stadium seating among many others. Once introduced, competitors quickly adopt innovations as well as each one trying to lure customers to the theater and, to a lesser extent, away from competing theaters within a market. The result is that most theaters are indistinguishable from one another: a ticket booth, a lobby, snack bar, and multiple theaters each containing a projector, screen, sound system, and rows of seats. The same movies–produced, developed, and released by one of the major studios–with nearly identical same start times. Audiences pay, within a dollar or two within a local market, nearly the same price for admission in the low price versus differentiated theater.

Despite the apparent homogeneity, these innovations keep the movie exhibition industry relevant. What keeps customers returning to the theater? What attracts the audience?

Attracting the Audience

A recent CBS News poll indicates the movie theater is currently the *least* likely place for a viewer to watch a movie, well behind television and computer screens.[16] It is therefore important for exhibitors to understand why people choose to watch a movie in the theater as opposed to engaging one of a myriad of other viewing options. Traditionally, the draw of the theater may have been far more important than what film was showing. Moviegoers describe attending the theater as an experience, with the appeal owing to:

- Watching the giant theater screen
- Hearing a theatrical sound system
- The opportunity to be out of the house
- Not having to wait to see a particular movie
- The theater as a location option for a date[17]

The ability of theaters to provide these beyond what audiences can achieve at home is diminishing. Of the reasons why people go to the movies, the place aspects (i.e., the theater as a place to be out of house and as a place for a date), seem the most immune to substitution. While "third spaces"–places outside of the home where people can gather, meet, talk and linger–have become more common, theaters offer a unique opportunity for people to simultaneously be together while not talking. Few teenagers want movie and popcorn with their date at home with mom and dad.

The overall "experience" offered by theaters falls short for many. Marketing research firm, Mintel, reports the reasons for *not* attending the theater more frequently are largely the result of the declining experience. This is due to the overall cost, at home viewing options, interruptions such as cell phones in the theater, rude patrons, the overall hassle, and ads prior to the show.[18] The *Wall Street Journal* reported on the movie-going experience quite negatively, noting interruptions ranging from the intrusion of soundtracks in adjacent theaters to cell phones, out-of-order ticket kiosks, and a seemingly endless parade of preshow ads.[19]

The time allocated to pre-show ads has also inspired criticism, even by industry insiders. Toby Emmerich, New Line Cinema's head of production, faced a not-so-common choice: to attend opening night in a theater or in a private screening room at actor Jim Carrey's home. Because he generally enjoys the experience of watching a film among a large audience, he chose the theater. However, after sitting through 15 minutes of ads, he lamented to his wife that perhaps they should have attended the private screening after all.[20]

The Home Viewing Substitution

Rapid improvements and cost reductions in home viewing technology and the widespread availability of timely and inexpensive content are making home viewing a viable substitute to theater exhibition. The unique value proposition offered by movie theaters' large screens, the audio quality of a theatrical sound system, and avoiding the long wait for viewing the movie are fading.

Home Viewing Substitution: Screen & Sound

Televisions were historically small, expensive appliances with poor sound quality. These were inferior to the big screen and sound offered by theaters. This has changed dramatically in the last two decades as televisions have become larger, offer better picture and sound quality, and are cheaper. The average television is increasingly a large, high definition model coupled with inexpensive yet impressive audio system. Compared to home equipment options of the past, even modest in-home technology increasingly represents a viable visual substitute to the big screen at the theater.

In 1997, the average TV set was a 23" with a screen resolution of 480 horizontal lines. This increased to 32" in 2010 and to 39" in 2014.[21] In 2018, the purchase of sets 55" and larger is common and 75" and larger sets are available. Sharp, a leading TV manufacturer predicts the *average* screen will exceed 60" in the very near future.[22]

HD televisions became available in 2000, but were initially cost prohibitive. Wholesale prices for televisions fell 65 percent from the late 1990s to 2007[23] as manufacturing economies from the production of LCD screens emerged. In 2005, the average 32" TV set retailed for $1,566. By 2009, five years following mass adoption, the average price declined by 76 percent to $511. By 2016, the 10-year mark, the average price had fallen 84 percent to under $250. As of 2017, more than 83 percent of U.S. households have at least one HD television, most 32" or larger, allowing for very high quality images.

Bundled home theater systems include 65" 3D capable TV, surround sound audio, and Blu-ray player offer a movie experience that rivals many theaters, all for under $1,000. According to Mike Gabriel, Sharp's head of marketing and communications, the high-tech home theater that once seemed just the privilege of the wealthy has now become a staple among most average American homes.[24] Overall, home TVs are becoming larger and offer high-quality images that reduce the differentiated appeal of the "giant" screen offered by exhibitors.

If the size and resolution of today's home television screens are a problem for exhibitors, the next generation may be catastrophic, and the next-next generation apocalyptic. The next wave of televisions– "Ultra" HD (UHD) or 4K–is shifting from early adopters to mainstream purchasers. A 4K set has four times the resolution of a 1080 set. Despite an average sale price of $1,250 in 2018, sales of UHD TVs are the fastest growing category and constitute the majority of sets larger than 60". Of course, electronics companies are already working on the next-next thing–8K televisions.[25] The higher resolution will be most noticeable in very large TV sets, those 85" and up. The first commercially available 8K television, native 8K content is not yet available, is a 98" set by LG. The initial price? $55,000.[26] Potential purchasers should keep in mind that TV set prices drop dramatically. If 8K follows the price trend of LCD TV, look for that 98" LG 8K set at a cost approaching current sets in just a few years.

How large and how high a resolution a television must be to substitute for a theater screen is subjective. For many, a laptop screen is sufficient. While for others, only the true wall-size screen offered by the local exhibitor will do. What is clear, the unique value provided by home television and sound systems is rapidly eroding the unique value proposition offered by exhibitors. The most common projection standard in theaters, the one in which exhibitors just invested $2.6 billion during the conversion to digital, is 4K. The history of technology updates to compete on visual quality is as old as the exhibition business itself. To maintain an advantage in the visual experience provided at the theater, exhibitors must consider the next generation of 8K and 16K projectors or lose the visual quality advantage to home viewing.

Home Viewing Substitution: Content & Timing

Even the best home theater offers little value without content. Unfortunately, for exhibitors, home content is flourishing and goes well beyond movies. Consumer spending on home entertainment content including disk purchases, digital downloads, and streaming subscriptions exceeds $48 billion.[27] All companies serving this market–studios, exhibitors, rental and on-demand companies, networks, and streaming firms–are fighting to keep and grow their revenue stream.

Studios maximize profits by releasing motion pictures in a series of "windows" under which the sooner a motion picture is viewed following the theatrical release the costlier it is to see it. It begins with theatrical release, generating $5.01 per admission for the studio. The next window is consumer purchase of the motion picture: DVD or digital sales. Studios receive $12 to $15 per copy purchased. The purchaser is increasingly, to the detriment of exhibitors, a consumer who opted not to see the movie in a theater.[28] Studios once relied on DVD sales to fuel profits, but physical DVD sales declined from $13.7 billion in 2006 to $4 billion in 2018 (decline of 71 percent).[29,30] Digital sales of movies are on the rise, but 2018's $2.46 billion total sales suggests consumers are opting to stream or subscribe instead of purchasing movies.[31] To spur sales and capitalize on marketing expenditures from the theatrical release, studios have reduced the time between theatrical release and DVD availability. The window to DVD release has declined from 23.7 weeks in 2000 to 14 weeks in 2018. Movies become available for purchase approximately one week sooner every two years (see Exhibit 13).

EXHIBIT 13 DVD Announcement and Release Windows (in days)

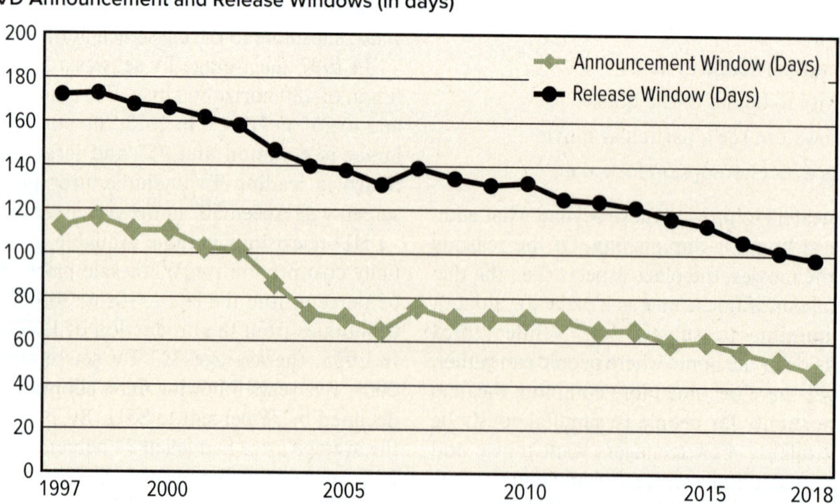

Source: National Association of Theater Owners (NATO) press releases on Average video release window and Average video announcement.

Digital video on demand (VOD) is the first in a series of rental options. VOD is provided by cable companies, iTunes, Amazon, among others and exceeded $2 billion in 2018.[32] VOD generates approximately $3.50 for the studio per purchase.[31] Releasing a motion picture shortly after it exits theaters, while it is still in the theater; even at the time of theatrical opening–"simultaneous release"–are all options. While premium VOD would have a negative impact on exhibitors, its potential revenue for studios–as much as $59.99 per purchase–is attractive. Exhibitors have previously banded together against premium VOD by threatening to boycott films by studios. Some studios, notably Disney, appear committed to the current theatrical release model.[32]

Physical rental, once the only rental option, is in rapid decline. Studios net approximately $1.25 per DVD sold to a physical rental company.[33] The dominant physical rental was store-based firms, such as Blockbuster Video, but is now a kiosk-based model, dominated by RedBox. From 2015 to 2016, the physical rental market declined by 19 percent to $2.5 billion.[34] RedBox, the industry leader, reported a same location rental decline of 4.9 percent in 2015 despite rentals costing as little as $1.75 per night.[35]

Streaming is the fastest growing portion of the rental market and among the most cost effective for viewers. Streaming services include Netflix, Amazon Prime Video, Hulu, HBONow, and others. License rates to streaming services vary considerably based on the popularity of the movie. Some estimates put the payment to studios below $0.50 per viewing.[36] The growth of streaming sufficiently cannibalized DVD and digital sales to the point that studios imposed a 28-day delay from DVD sales to the availability of streaming. Exhibitors expressed strong encouragement when several studios expressed a desire for a 56-day delay to increase DVD sales. Both Netflix and Amazon offer content in SD, HD, and 4K formats. The most distant from the theatrical release, and providing the least revenue to studios, is a showing on a subscription movie channel (e.g., HBO, Showtime, and Cinemax), a subscription cable television channel (e.g., TNT, FX, and AMC), or a major over-air broadcast network (e.g., ABC, CBS, NBC, and Fox).

Overall, the availability of quality content and the visual and audio experience available in the home is rapidly converging, some would argue, surpassing offerings available at the theater. The time viewing at home is time not spent at the theater. The average American spends 2.8 hours daily watching television.[37] Scaled differently, the time typically spent at the theater each *year* is equal to about *two days* of television viewing. For exhibitors, the time someone spends binge watching the last season of a show or just hanging out to "Netflix and chill" presents a lost revenue opportunity. Paul Dergarabedian, president of Hollywood.com's box-office division labels it a "cultural shift" in how people view entertainment.[38] People are more interested in content than ever before. Unfortunately, for movie exhibitors, there is more competition than ever in both the content worth viewing and ways to do so.

Recent Exhibitor Initiatives

With attending a movie costing nearly $20 a person including admission, a drink, and a snack versus the alternative of the sunk cost of an existing Netflix subscription at $13/month, how can exhibitors compete? In what areas should exhibitors be making their investments to continue to offer a unique theater-going experience? Exhibitors have historically been innovators. Exhibitors were among the first commercial adopters of air conditioning, which perhaps drew in as many customers as a refuge from summer heat as for entertainment. Advances in projection systems, screens, and sound systems all improve the experience. Others innovations increase experience quality while also lowering costs. The ubiquitous stadium-style seating was once an experience differentiator, but was equally beneficial as it reduced the square footage needed per seat. This reduced the size and cost of facilities. Exhibitors continue to pursue a number of strategic initiatives aimed at increasing attendance, increasing the viewer's willingness to pay, and lowering costs.

At no time in the movie exhibition industry's existence have the stakes seemed so high. Attendance has been in a slow decline since 2002. The wait needed to see a movie outside of the theater has never been shorter. Content other than motion pictures is increasingly popular. Impressive screens and sound systems are common in homes. Cell phones, ads, and sticky floors mar the overall experience at the theater. What will it take to bring audiences back to the theater?

Market research indicates that 80 to 90 percent of theater goers would pay a premium of $1 to $2 dollars each for a wide range of options to make the theater experience more luxurious or to decrease things which detract from the experience.[39] Improvements in video and sound quality, seating (including luxurious materials such as leather, sofa-style seating, footrests, along with more legroom), the ability to choose and reserve a seat location in advance, immersive viewing experiences such as 4D, higher-end food and drink options, the ability to order from your seat in the theater, and kid-free screens are among those desired. Exhibitors and their suppliers are developing, testing, and rolling out a range of options addressing these. Some are for individual screens, others for all screens within a theater complex. Theaters will invest in those strategic initiatives to draw audiences and produce revenue in excess of costs.

Projection Innovations

The conversion to digital projection and rollout of 3D are not the end of projection innovations. Some directors are opting to increase image quality through the number of frames per second (fps) of film from the long established standard of 24 to 48 and higher. Screeners of Ang Lee's *Billy Lynn's Long Halftime Walk* shown with 4K 3D laser projection at 120 frames per second used described the visual experience with terms like "impeccably bright" and "stunning detail and clarity."[40] Commercially, the film fared poorly in wide release, due in part, to a lack of theaters equipped with the required projection equipment. Thus, there exists something of a catch-22–some attendees will pay a premium for enhanced visual quality, but it requires both exhibitors and film producers to commit to making the investments needed. To date, few of either have.

Most large circuits offer some form of extra-large screens.[41] The original, IMAX, was traditionally restricted to specially constructed dome-shaped theaters in science museums. The IMAX format initially utilized film that was 10 times the size of that used in standard 35mm projectors. IMAX now operates more than 600 screens but with digital screens far smaller than the original. Action films, usually in 3D, are an IMAX staple. To capture more of this differentiated revenue, several circuits have begun creating their own super-size screens and formats. IMAX is typically a $3 to $7 premium per ticket. Revenues for IMAX Corporation grew approximately 30 percent from 2013 to 2017.[42]

Audio systems are being improved. In the 1980s, theaters impressed viewers with 7.1 sound systems–two rear channels (left and right), two channels mid screen, two near the screen, one under the screen, and a subwoofer channel for bass. Such systems have long been available for homes. To keep theater sound as a differentiator, Dolby® Laboratories has created Atmos™, a full surround system with up to 64 individual channels for speakers in a theater, including multiple ceiling speakers that can truly immerse the audience in sound.[43] While exhibitors may benefit, Dolby also offers a home version that emulates the experience in home theaters.

Alternative Content / Event Cinema

Exhibitors' transition to digital projection served as an enabling technology for alternative content, also called event cinema, a broad term encompassing virtually any content that is not a motion picture. This includes live concerts and theater, standup comedy, sporting events, television series premieres and finales, even virtual art gallery tours. Event cinema is the fastest growing segment at the box office, increasing from $112 million worldwide in 2010[44] to $277 million in 2014, and expected to reach $1 billion–about five percent of the box office–by 2019.[45] Ticket prices average $12.33 per event. Event cinema content can be singular events, such as recent concerts, or a series attracting repeat visits, such as *Metropolitan Opera Live* shown in 2,000 venues in 70 countries across six continents.[46] A typical season includes 10 live events on Saturday afternoons with an encore rebroadcast on Wednesdays, both historically slow times at the theater.

Alternative content is a supplement to motion picture content, typically shown during off-peak movie attendance times such as Monday through Thursday when less than five percent of theater seats are occupied.[47] The hurdle for success can be quite low. A "successful" event need only exceed the attendance for the least attended movie during these times. On average, event cinema draws 10 times the number of attendees than that of the lowest-grossing movie.[48] This can be a boon on otherwise slow nights. One theater's Wednesday night showing of Broadway's *West Side Story*, for example, had an average ticket price of $12.50 and grossed $2,425. In comparison, screens showing movies that night grossed just $56 to $73 each. The alternative content also brought in nearly 200 additional customers who may purchase concessions.[49]

The success of events rests heavily on having a built-in fan base or the ability to market individual events. Dan Diamond, VP of Fathom Events, reports that their most successful event came as a surprise: The November 25, 2013 showing of *Dr. Who: The Day of the Doctor* in celebration of the 50th Anniversary of *Dr. Who*, the popular BBC series. The box office gross was the largest on a per-screen basis for the day, raking in over $17,000 per location.[50] The challenge for exhibitors, accustomed to studio marketing campaigns promoting each week's box office release, is the development of capabilities in marketing single night events to niche audiences at low cost.

Luxury Theaters

Several chains and new entrants are trying to lure attendees with the promise of a luxury experience. Established players like AMC and Regal are reseating screens and entire theaters with premium seats. Smaller theater chain iPic, with 16 locations across the United States, offers perhaps the most luxurious theater available outside of a private screening room, complete with reclining leather chairs, pillows, and blankets. Lobbies resemble stylish high-end hotels and feature a cocktail lounge and full in-theater restaurant service. Complete with a membership program, the theaters operate more like social clubs than traditional theaters. Tickets purchases, $16 to $27 per seat without food, are made not at a ticket booth but rather with a concierge.[51]

Another chain, Cinépolis VIP, is a subsidiary of Mexican theater company Cinépolis. Cinépolis began with one location in San Diego in 2011 and has since expanded to 21 locations through development and acquisition.[52] Offerings differ by location, ranging from standard theaters with leather rocking seats to full service at-your-seat dining with bar service. Tickets for luxury screens average near $20. The company offers something for everyone: some showings are restricted to those 21 and older, while other theaters feature Cinépolis Junior with a children's in-theater playground available for use for 20 minutes before a movie starts.[53]

Immersion Experiences: 4D & Beyond

The first wave of immersive experiences was 3D technology. Ten years ago, 3D was to be *the* next great projection technology and revenue producer, but its appeal has peaked. 3D's share of domestic ticket sales peaked in 2010 at 27 percent of tickets and has since been in a steady decline to approximately 8 percent of tickets sold in 2018. It remains a draw in international markets.

The second wave of immersive experiences draws the viewer further into the action by combining 3D, off-screen special effects, and motion seating synchronized to the on-screen action into a "4D" experience.[54] Some theaters add additional immersive elements by introducing scents into the theater, using off-screen light effects, and even water sprayers to bring the action of the movie off the screen and into theater. An encounter with a dinosaur on a dark and stormy night is seen on the screen, heard through the sound system, and felt through a shaking seat. The encounter is even more real when water sprays and strobe lights flash. The whole experience can become a drink spilling experience. Liability wavers, minimum age requirements, and an abundance of caution are all standard. Wary of repeating the less-than expected results of 3D, 4D is being touted as occupying a niche within the broader theater experience. The 4D experience typically comes at a surcharge of $8 to $12 over standard tickets.

The third wave of immersion will merge movies with video games. Exhibitors, producers, and equipment companies are working on interaction elements ranging from simple interactions such as shooting on-screen targets with lasers to more complex bullet screens where you can text your thoughts about scenes and the movie and they are projected onto the screen in real time.[55] All are seeking to provide a more immersive and interactive experience than passive sitting and movie watching. Some industry observers anticipate that immersion technologies will include feedback systems and story forks where the actions and choices of the audience lead to plot twists and different story outcomes with each viewing. Horror audiences may be dismayed when a film's protagonist heeds the call to not go in there. Eventually, the line between what constitutes a movie versus a video game may blur.

Concession Initiatives

Expanding beyond the standard concession stand offers exhibitors opportunities to capture new revenue streams. Three main formats for concessions have emerged.

Expanded In-Lobby Many theaters have expanded in-lobby dining which causes many theater lobbies to resemble mall food courts. Taking a page from restaurants where a primary profit center is often the bar, some theaters now configure the lobby around a bar, with expanded and upscale fare, beer, and alcohol service.

In-Theater Dining Many theaters have adopted in-theater dining with orders placed from one's seat in the theater and delivered by waiters. Alamo Drafthouse Cinemas utilizes a single bar-style table in front of each row of seats that serves as a table for customer's orders. In comparison to traditional theaters, these formats see significant increases in food and beverage sales.

Upscale Within Theater Dining Several circuits are targeting the high end of the dining market, focusing on the experience of the theater with luxurious settings and upscale food. Customers purchase tickets for specific seats in smaller theaters equipped with reclining lounge chairs, complete with footrests, and order at their seat using a computerized system.

Advertising Initiatives

Exhibitors are keen to expand highly profitable advertising, but do so in ways that do not diminish the theater experience. On- and off-screen advertisements generate revenue. Off-screen advertising such as promotional videos, lobby events and sponsored concession promotions are nine percent of revenues. The majority, 91 percent, comes from on-screen ads for upcoming releases, companies, and products that play before the feature presentation.

Both exhibitors and advertisers seek ways to make on-screen ads more palatable to audiences. Many ads are in 3D with production quality rivaling a studio release. Theaters are also incorporating innovative technologies such as crowd gaming into ads where the movement or sound of the audience controls on-screen actions. Audiences in 100 Screenvision-equipped theaters selected the driving experience and virtually drove a XC90 as part of Volvo's re-launch of the vehicle. Attendees selected the scene, steered the car, and controlled the vehicles speed by waving.[56] The equipment required? A wireless video camera above the screen, a web-enabled laptop containing the game linked to the developer's website, and inexpensive motion-sensing technology all linked to the theater's digital projector.

Advertisers are keen on increasing the engagement of movie audiences to increase the return on ads.[57] From on-screen QR codes to Bluetooth devices that drop advertiser websites directly into the browser on attendees' phones, interactive is the next step in theater advertising. Making ads enjoyable and useful rather than loathed may create an opportunity to increase this small but high margin component of exhibitor revenues. Given all of these advertising initiatives, exhibitors may eventually draw from the pages of free software–the ability to pay a premium for an ad-free experience.

Seating

Movie theaters are among the minority of entertainment venues selling tickets without a commitment to the purchasers viewing experience. Sports and concertgoers, for example, always know where they will be seated in relation to a performance. Movie theaters have long been the province of a first-come, first-select seating model. However, all of the major exhibition chains have incorporated elements of reserved seating–purchasing a ticket tied to a specific seat during a specific showing–into their theaters. These take a variety of forms, ranging from theaters consisting entirely of reserved seat screens, to specific screens consisting exclusively of reserved seats, to screens with mixed open and reserved options. For the exhibitor, reserved seating requires a reservation and seat selection system and the ability to enforce seating disputes, but comes with additional revenues. Reserved seating, a common perk of luxury format, is typically built into ticket prices. Is it increasingly available in other theaters for a surcharge of $1 to $3 dollars per seat.

Dynamic Pricing

The technology needed for reserved seating is a gateway to dynamic pricing systems. Matinee, youth, and senior discounts are the primary pricing tiers. Most non-movie events have multiple pricing levels based on seating, show time, and weekday versus weekend. Movie theaters have limited flexibility due to the contract restrictions. "Dynamic pricing," which incorporates demand into pricing models, is the next generation of ticket pricing.[58] The simplest models involved surcharges for big-budget blockbusters films in their first few days of release.

A more advanced approach is to adjust prices for each movie, day of the week, show time, and even seat location based on demand tracked in real-time.[59] This could mean radical changes including lower ticket prices for off time and poorly attended movies and increased prices for prime seats at peak times and opening weekend. For the theater, dynamic pricing offers the opportunity to fill otherwise unsold seats and to move showings between screens based on demand. Australian chain Cineplex offers dynamic pricing, but studios are cautious. Disney, for example, has set and required payment of a minimum average ticket price for some films.[60] For customers, dynamic pricing offers the opportunity to reduce the cost of attending the theater. Do you not want to spend more than $5? Apps are on their way to find movies, locations, and showtimes matching your criteria.

Subscription Approaches

Subscription approaches are now being offered both by exhibitors and third-parties. Moviepass, founded in 2011, was the first to apply this approach to the mass audience. The idea is simple: subscribers pay a monthly fee that allows them to watch a large number of movies throughout that month. MoviePass started with pricing between $24.99 to $39.99 (dependent on the location with people in urban areas paying more) and the subscriber could see one 2D movie per day (no 3D or IMAX movies).[61] MoviePass dropped prices over the next few years in an attempt to gain subscribers. In August of 2017, the price for its unlimited plan (still restricted to one film per day) went to $9.95 per month.[62] Throughout all of the changes in pricing strategies, MoviePass was losing money rapidly because they paid full or near full ticket prices to the theaters. In the single month of May in 2018, MoviePass lost $40 million, and the next month the parent company of MoviePass raised $1.2 billion through the sale of equity to help keep MoviePass afloat.[63]

In July of 2018, AMC theaters, which long had a subscription program in the UK, announced its own subscription service called AMC Stubs A-List. For $19.95 a month, customers can see three movies a week (at most 13 movies a month at an average price of $1.53 per movie). This program has several other benefits beyond MoviePass: customers can see 3D and IMAX movies for no extra cost, there is no surge pricing, and the subscription includes a system in which subscribers get a $5 reward for every $50 spent on concessions or additional tickets.[64] Cinemark also has a subscription service, MovieClub. For $8.99 a month, subscribers can see one standard 2D movie a month, receive 20 percent off concessions, and if you do not see a movie one month, the free movie will roll over to the next month.[65] Both exhibitors emphasize the sustainability of their pricing at average viewing levels and benefit from increased concession sales. Meanwhile, MoviePass' economic model remains murky to many observers.

Beyond Content

Many smaller exhibitors are seeking increased profitability beyond movies by reimagining their theaters as multi-entertainment venues. By adding activities such as game rooms, bowling, even laser tag and at-table trivia, a theater becomes a one-stop location for family-friendly entertainment. Frank Theaters, for example, combines movies, bowling, and games for the whole family with dining in its locations, making it possible to spend an entertaining evening at the theater without ever seeing a movie.

Is Yours the Last Theater?

Thanos' finger snap at the end of *Avengers: Infinity War* resulted in the half of the population of the universe disappearing. Might local movie theaters soon see their numbers reduced too? While theaters experiment with a variety of initiatives to draw viewers, the clock is ticking. Prior initiatives, most recently 3D, have failed to live up to their potential as a durable and enduring way to attract audiences.

ENDNOTES

1. Ticket sales and box office data from www.boxofficemojo.com, MPAA Theatrical Statistics and THEME reports, UNESCO data, and other sources. Analysis by author.
2. MPAA 2017 THEME Report and U.S. census data.
3. North American Theater Owner Association (NATO), MPAA, and other industry groups collectively define the "domestic" market as including both the U.S. and Canadian markets.
4. MPAA Theatrical Statistics (2016 and earlier) and MPAA 2017 Theatrical and Home Entertainment Market Environment (THEME) report.
5. UNESCO. UNESCO Feature Films Dataset, http://data.uis.unesco.org/#.
6. Schwartzel, E. 2017. Disney lays down the law for theaters on 'Star Wars: The Last Jedi.' *Wall Street Journal*, November 1, https://www.wsj.com/articles/disney-lays-down-the-law-for-theaters-on-star-wars-the-last-jedi-1509528603?mg=prod/accounts-wsj.
7. Fritz, B. and A. Kaufman, 2011. Solid start, fast fade for movies. *LA Times*, December 30, latimes.com/entertainment/news/movies/la-fi-ct-box-office-wrap-20111230,0,2205189.story.
8. 2018 number of $920 million based on MarketingCharts.com citing PwC's Global Entertainment & Media Outlook report. 2018). US Online and Traditional Media Advertising Outlook, 2018-2022. https://www.marketingcharts.com/featured-104785.
9. Based on several press releases form the Cinema Advertising Council including: Council, C. A. 2018. Cinema advertising closes out 2017

with revenue topping $750 million for the second year running; Cinema Advertising Council 2017. Cinema advertising closes out record year with revenue topping $750 million for the first time. http://docs.wixstatic.com/ugd/eeeab3_ce921557d97d4e8986b21825c45bcf40.pdf.

10. Fritz, B. 2014. Movie theaters, studios in tiff over trailer lengths. *Wall Street Journal*, January 27.
11. Author calculations based on Cinema Advertising Council 2016 data, SEC filings, NATO press releases, and author estimates based on AMC and Cinemark data in Exhibit 12.
12. Data on the firms, theaters and screens, location, etc., from websites and SEC filings.
13. Kung, M. and A. Back. 2012. Chinese conglomerate buys AMC movie chain in U.S. *Wall Street Journal,* May 21, 2.
14. White, P. 2018. Cineworld's $3.6B acquisition of Regal cinemas approved by shareholders. *Deadline Hollywood*, February 2, https://deadline.com/2018/02/cineworlds-3-6b-acquisition-of-regal-cinemas-approved-by-shareholders-1202276987/.
15. Cineplex Entertainment. Cinemark 2016 Form 10-K. http://irfiles.cineplex.com/reportsandfilings/home/AIF_2017_03_27_final.pdf.
16. Survey: How do you watch movies? CBS News, Produced by CBS Sunday Morning, March 8, 2017.
17. Mintel Report, Movie Theaters - U.S. - February 2008 - Reasons to go to movies over watching a DVD.
18. Mintel Report, Movie Theaters - U.S. - February 2008 - Reasons why attendance is not higher.
19. Kelly, K., Orwall, B. and P. Sanders. 2005. The multiplex under siege. *Wall Street Journal*, December 24, P1.
20. Incident reported in Patrick Goldstein, "Now playing: A glut of ads," *Los Angeles Times*, July 12, 2005 in print edition E-1; http://articles.latimes.com/2005/jul/12/entertainment/et-goldstein12.
21. HIS Markit. 2014. LCD TV shipment forecast revised upward on strong consumer demand for larger sizes. DisplaySearch Reports his, December 31, http://news.ihsmarkit.com/press-release/design-supply-chain-media/lcd-tv-shipment-forecast-revised-upward-strong-consumer-dema.
22. Tech Digest. 2008. Average TV size up to 60-inch by 2015 says Sharp. *TechDigest,* January 2, http://www.techdigest.tv/2008/01/average_tv_size.html.
23. Ibid.
24. Price data on later years based on author analysis of retail LCD pricing of 32" sets on BestBuy.com, Amazon.com, and other sites. Early pricing data reported in *CNN Money* (Producer), 2010; CNN Holiday Money. 2010. 32-Inch LCD TV average prices. *CNN Holiday Money,* http://money.cnn.com/2010/11/24/technology/lcd_tv_deals/#.
25. Moynihan, T. 2016. 8K TVs are coming to market, and your eyeballs aren't ready. *Wired,* January 7, https://www.wired.com/2016/01/8k-tvs-coming-to-market/.
26. Wong, R. 2016. This $55,000 98-inch 8K TV is actually 'cheap'. September 3, http://mashable.com/2016/09/03/cheap-8k-tvs-are-coming-chinese-brands/#JzDkNbymamqT.
27. Motion Picture Association of America. 2017. 2017 THEME report: Theatrical and Home Entertainment Market Environment (THEME). MPAA.org.
28. Jannarone, J. 2012. As studios fight back, will Coinstar box itself into a corner? *Wall Street Journal,* February 6, p. C6.
29. Richter, F. "Streaming Dominates U.S. Home Entertainment Spending." *Statista*. Accessed March 2019. https://www.statista.com/chart/7654/home-entertainment-spending-in-the-us/
30. Kung, M. 2012. Movie magic to leave home for? *Wall Street Journal,* May 10, pp. D1–D2; Shepard, K. 2017. Streaming video outpaces DVD sales for first time in 2016: report. *The Washington Times,* January 6, http://www.washingtontimes.com/news/2017/jan/6/netflix-other-streaming-video-services-outpace-dvd/.
31. Jannarone, J. 2012. As studios fight back, will Coinstar box itself into a corner? *Wall Street Journal,* February 6, p. C6.
32. McNary, D. 2017. Disney's Bob Iger shuns early home movie releases. *Variety,* May 9, http://variety.com/2017/film/news/disneys-early-home-movie-releases-1202421565/.
33. Jannarone, J. 2012. As studios fight back, will Coinstar box itself into a corner? *Wall Street Journal,* February 6, p. C6.
34. Digital Home Entertainment Group. DEG report: U.S. consumer spending by format 2016 year end. https://www.degonline.org/wp-content/uploads/2017/05/2016-Q4-DEG-Home-Entertainment-Spending_Rev-3.0_01.04.17_-External_-Distribution_Final.pdf.
35. Outerwall Inc. Outerwall, Inc. (Redbox) SEC Form 10-K Filing. https://www.sec.gov/edgar/searchedgar/companysearch.html.
36. Jannarone, J. 2012. As studios fight back, will Coinstar box itself into a corner? *Wall Street Journal,* February 6, p. C6.
37. U.S. Bureau of Labor Statistics. 2017. American time use survey summary (USDL-16-1250*)*. June 27, https://www.bls.gov/news.release/atus.nr0.htm.
38. Verrier, R. 2011. U.S. theater owners get lump of coal at box office. *LA Times,* December 30, latimes.com/entertainment/news/movies/la-fi-ct-theaters-20111230,0,7228622.story.
39. Mintel report. Movie Theaters - US - November 2014.
40. Bishop, B. 2016. Ang Lee's new film shows the peril and incredible promise of high-frame rate movies. April 17, https://www.theverge.com/2016/4/17/11446020/ang-lee-billy-lynns-long-halftime-walk-hfr-nab.
41. Dodes, R. 2012. IMAX strikes back. *Wall Street Journal*. April 19, http://online.wsj.com/article/SB10001424052702304299304577347940832511540.html?KEYWORDS=IMAX+strikes+back.
42. IMAX 2017 10-K Filing. www.sec.gov.
43. Dolby Laboratories. Dolby Atmos cinema sound. https://www.dolby.com/us/en/index.html.
44. Sony. 2011. Alternative content for theatres. *Sony Digital Cinema 4K,* 1.
45. Ross, J. 2016. Making the case for event cinema. January 21, http://www.eventcinemaassociation.org/assets/eca-0000-asset-doc-making-the-case-for-event-cinema–jonathan-ross.pdf.
46. Metropolitan Opera. 2019. Metropolitan Opera: Our story. http://www.metopera.org/About/The-Met/.
47. Cinedigm. 2012 (May). Investor presentation: Jefferies 2012 Global Technology, Media & Telecom Conference. http://files.shareholder.com/downloads/AIXD/2302444840x0x567367/4a213e2c-11ae-4cdc-8dd1-970919ac80ac/CIDM%20IR%20deck%20050712%20Short.pdf.
48. Ellingson, A. 2012. Who's stressed about digital cinema? Not Digiplex's Bud Mayo. *The Business Journal - LA*, October 15.
49. Ibid.
50. Storm, A. 2014 (May). Alternative content takes center stage: Lessons in success from those who've made it work. *Film Journal International.*
51. iPic company website (www.ipictheaters.com) and iPic Theaters "iPic Theaters: Become an iPic Member." https://www.ipictheaters.com/#/createaccount/trial.
52. Cinépolis website (www.cinepolisusa.com/locations) and Winfrey, G. 2016. Why luxury theater chain Cinépolis is buying up movie houses all across the U.S. *IndieWire,* July 22, http://www.indiewire.com/2016/07/luxury-theater-chain-cinepolis-expanding-us-cinemas-1201707606/.
53. Holmes, A. 2017. A movie theater built a playground in front of the screen, and people are pissed. *Cinemablend.* http://www.cinemablend.com/news/1632940/a-movie-theater-built-a-playground-in-front-of-the-screen-and-people-are-pissed.
54. Kung, M. 2012. Movie magic to leave home for? *Wall Street Journal,* May 10, pp. D1–D2.
55. O'Connor, S. 2014. Chinese cinemas post text messages on-screen during movies. *TechDigest*, August 21, http://www.techdigest.tv/2014/08/chinese-cinemas-post-text-messages-on-screen-during-movies.html.
56. Tadena, N. 2015. Volvo puts moviegoers in driver's seat in new interactive ads. *Wall Street Journal,* August 15, https://blogs.wsj.com/cmo/2015/08/18/volvo-puts-moviegoers-in-drivers-seat-in-new-interactive-ads/.
57. Cooper, J. 2016. Going to the movies could be a fully interactive experience by 2020. *Adweek,* January 7, http://www.adweek.com/brand-marketing/why-going-movies-will-be-fully-interactive-experience-2020-168896/.

58. Lazarus, D. 2012. Movie tickets: Now how much would you pay? *LA Times*, April 26.

59. PRWeb. 2018. B&B Theatres and Dealflicks launch dynamic inventory of full-priced movie tickets and deals.

60. Verhoeven, D. and B. Coate. 2017. Coming soon to a cinema near you? Ticket prices shaped by demand. *The Conversation,* February 6, http://theconversation.com/coming-soon-to-a-cinema-near-you-ticket-prices-shaped-by-demand-72260.

61. Bishop, B. " MoviePass, take three: can a subscription service reignite the US box office?" *The Verge*. Accessed March 2019. https://www.theverge.com/2012/10/2/3438694/moviepass-movie-ticket-subscription-service-us-box-office

62. Plaugic, L. 2017. MoviePass is dropping subscription fees to $10 a month. *The Verge.* https://www.theverge.com/2017/8/15/16150628/moviepass-pricing-subscription-fee-theaters.

63. Amos, J. 2018. MoviePass' worst month ever (at least for now). *Forbes.* https://www.forbes.com/sites/jamos/2018/07/05/moviepass-worst-month-ever-at-least-for-now/#4bfa746d77f5

64. Reliford, A. 2018. I switched to AMC Stubs A-List – here's why it's better than MoviePass. *Business Insider.* https://www.businessinsider.com/amc-stubs-a-list-is-better-than-moviepass-2018-10.

65. Guerrasio, J. 2018. Why Cinemark's unsexy $8.99 movie-theater subscription plan may actually be the one that survives. *Business Insider.* https://www.businessinsider.com/cinemark-subscription-plan-may-be-best-business-model-for-movie-theaters-2018-8.

CASE 19

CAMPBELL: HOW TO KEEP THE SOUP SIMMERING*

In 2019, Campbell Soup was brimming with problems. In less than a year, the company had gone through three CEOs. The resignation of its long-term CEO Dennis Morrison proved to be a tough blow for Campbell, as its stocks had slumped from 2017. The company's interim CEO Keith R. McLoughlin, said, "Looking back at fiscal 2018, there is no question that Campbell had a difficult year."[1] Despite the challenges, the company added Pacific Foods, a leader in organic soups and broths, and Snyder's Lance–the second largest salty snack maker in the United States–to their portfolio.

Although one of their major challenges during 2018 was lackluster financial performance, net sales increased 10 percent from $7.89 billion to $8.685 billion in 2018, primarily due to an 11-point benefit from their acquisitions of Snyder's Lance and Pacific Foods. Denise Morrison, former CEO, had taken over the company several years prior. The change at the top of the company received a lukewarm response from investors, who were watching to see what drastic changes Morrison might have in store. By 2017, with Morrison at the helm, the Campbell Soup Company had launched more than 50 new products, including 32 new soups. This number was way up from previous years. One of its most important challenges was to remain attractive to health-conscious consumers. Morrison's vision to modernize Campbell and make it a major player in fresh foods turned out to be quite expensive for Campbell. The company made contrasting decisions to acquire Snyder's Lance, a salty snack maker, in 2018 while maintaining its position to venture into fresh foods. Morrison also shocked experts with the $1.55 billion buyout of California juice-and-carrot seller Bolthouse Farms, the largest acquisition in Campbell's history.[2] Despite the revitalization of its product line, however, the company failed to spark a financial turnaround.

Toward the end of 2018, the company announced Mark A. Clouse as the new Chief Executive Officer of Campbell, effective January 22, 2019. With more than 20 years of experience in the food industry, Clouse held senior management positions at popular brands such as Mondelēz International, Inc., Kraft Foods Inc., and Pinnacle Foods. Mark Clouse entered Campbell with an optimism duly needed at the company's historic crossroads. "I am honored to lead Campbell and its portfolio of iconic brands into the next chapter of the company's storied history," said Clouse. "I am committed to delivering Campbell's strategic objectives and look forward to partnering with the Board and working alongside the company's many talented employees to deliver sustainable, long-term growth. I am confident that together we can build a prosperous future for Campbell and all of its stakeholders."[3] The questions haunting investors today are: What is Clouse's revival strategy for Campbell? Will Campbell still try to build on its image as a fresh food company?

Company Background

Known for its red-and-white soup cans, the Campbell Soup Company was founded in 1869 by Abram Anderson and Joseph Campbell as a canning and preserving business. Over 140 years later, Campbell offered a whole lot more than just soup in a can.

In 2016, the company, headquartered in Camden, New Jersey, implemented a new product category structure by reducing from five categories to three: America's Simple Meals and Beverages, Global Biscuits and Snacks, and Campbell Fresh (see Exhibit 1). In 2018, Campbell's products were sold in over 100 countries around the world. The company had operations in the United States, Canada, Mexico, Australia, Belgium, China, France, Germany, Indonesia, Malaysia, and Sweden (see Exhibit 2).[4]

For a long time the company had been pursuing strategies designed to expand the availability of its products in existing markets and to capitalize on opportunities in emerging channels and markets around the globe. As an early step, in 1994, Campbell Soup Company, synonymous with the all-American kitchen for 125 years, had acquired Pace Foods Ltd., the world's largest producer of Mexican sauces. Frank Weise, CFO at that time, said that a major motivation for the purchase was to diversify Campbell and to extend the Pace brand to other products. In addition, he said the company saw a strong potential for Pace products internationally. Campbell also saw an overlap with its raw material purchasing operations, since peppers, onions, and tomatoes were already used in the company's soups, V8 juice, barbecue sauce, and pasta sauces.[5] To help reduce some of the price volatility for ingredients, the company used various commodity risk management tools for a number of its ingredients and commodities such as natural gas, heating oil, wheat, soybean oil, cocoa, aluminum, and corn.[6]

---

* This case study was prepared by Professors Alan B. Eisner and Dan Baugher of Pace University, Professor Helaine J. Korn of Baruch College, City University of New York, and graduate student Saad Nazir and Sushmitha Mudda of Pace University. The purpose of the case is to stimulate class discussion rather than to illustrate effective or ineffective handling of a business situation. Copyright © 2019 Alan B. Eisner.

EXHIBIT 1 Sales by Segment ($ millions)

	2018	2017	2016	% Change 2018/2017	% Change 2017/2016
America's Simple Meals and Beverages	**$4,213**	$4,256	$4,313	(1)%	(1)%
Global Biscuits and Snacks	**3,499**	2,667	2,631	(31)	(1)
Campbell Fresh	**970**	967	1,017	—	(5)
	$8,685	$7,890	$7,961	(10)%	(1)%

Source: The Campbell Soup Company, Annual Report, 2019.

EXHIBIT 2 Campbell's Principal Manufacturing Facilities

Inside the U.S.

Arizona
- Goodyear (GBS)

California
- Bakersfield (CF)
- Dixon (ASMB)
- Stockton (ASMB)

Connecticut
- Bloomfield (GBS)

Florida
- Lakeland (GBS)

Georgia
- Columbus (GBS)

Illinois
- Downers Grove (GBS)

Indiana
- Jeffersonville (GBS)

Massachusetts
- Hyannis (GBS)

Michigan
- Ferndale (CF)
- Grand Rapids (CF)

New Jersey
- East Brunswick (GBS)

North Carolina
- Charlotte (GBS)
- Maxton (ASMB)

Ohio
- Ashland (GBS)
- Napoleon (ASMB)
- Willard (GBS)

Oregon
- Salem (GBS)
- Tualatin (ASMB)

Pennsylvania
- Denver (GBS)
- Downingtown (GBS)
- Hanover (GBS)

Texas
- Paris (ASMB)

Utah
- Richmond (GBS)

Washington
- Everett (CF)
- Prosser (CF)

Wisconsin
- Beloit (GBS)
- Franklin (GBS)
- Milwaukee (ASMB)

Outside the U.S.

Australia
- Huntingwood (GBS)
- Marleston (GBS)
- Shepparton (GBS)
- Virginia (GBS)

Canada
- Toronto (ASMB)

Denmark
- Nørre Snede (GBS)
- Ribe (GBS)

England
- Norwich (GBS)
- Wednesbury (GBS)

Indonesia
- Bekasi (GBS)

Malaysia
- Selangor Darul Ehsan (GBS)

ASMB = Americas Simple Meals and Beverages
GBS = Global Biscuits and Snacks
CF = Campbell Fresh

Source: The Campbell Soup Company, Annual Report, 2019.

A leading food producer in the United States, Campbell Soup had some presence in approximately 9 out of 10 U.S. households. However, in recent years, the company faced a slowdown in its soup sales, as consumers were seeking more convenient meal options, such as ready meals and dining out. To compete more effectively, especially against General Mills' Progresso brand, Campbell had undertaken various efforts to improve the quality and convenience of its products.

China and Russia

Historically, consumption of soup in Russia and China has far exceeded that in the United States, but in both countries nearly all of the soup is homemade. With their launch of products tailored to local tastes, trends, and eating habits, Campbell presumed that it had a chance to lead in soup commercialization in Russia and China. According to Campbell, "We have an unrivaled understanding of consumers' soup consumption behavior and innovative technology capabilities within the Simple Meals category. The products we developed are designed to serve as a base for the soups and other meals Russian and Chinese consumers prepare at home."[7] For about three years, in both Russia and China, Campbell sent its marketing teams to study the local markets. The main focus was on how Russians and Chinese ate soup and how Campbell could offer something new. As a result, Campbell came up with a production line specifically created for the local Russian market. Called "Domashnaya Klassika," the line was a stock base for soups that contains pieces of mushrooms, beef, or chicken. Based on this broth, the main traditional Russian soup recipes could be prepared.

But after just four short years, Campbell pulled out of the Russian market that it had thought would be a simmering new location for its products. Campbell's chief operating officer and newly elected CEO Denise Morrison said results in Russia fell below what the company had expected. "We believe that opportunities currently under exploration in other emerging markets, notably China, offer stronger prospects for driving profitable growth within an acceptable time frame," Morrison said.[8]

When the company entered Russia, Campbell knew that it would be challenging to persuade a country of homemade-soup eaters to adopt ready-made soups. When Campbell initially researched the overseas markets, it learned that Russians eat soup more than five times a week, on average, compared with once a week among Americans.[9] This indicated that both the quality and sentiment of the soup meant a great deal to Russian consumers–something that, despite its research, Campbell may have underestimated.

As for China, a few years after Campbell infiltrated the market, CEO Denise Morrison was quoted by *Global Entrepreneur* as saying, "The Chinese market consumes roughly 300 billion servings of soup a year, compared with only 14 billion servings in the U.S."[10] When entering the Chinese market, Campbell had determined that if the company could capture at least 3 percent of the at-home consumption, the size of the business would equal that of its U.S. market share. "The numbers blow your hair back," said Larry S. McWilliams, president of Campbell's international group.[11] While the company did successfully enter the market, it remained to be seen whether Campbell had the right offerings in place to capture such a market share or whether China's homemade-soup culture would be as disinclined to change as Russia's was.

Industry Overview

The U.S. packaged-food industry had recorded faster current-value growth in recent years mainly due to a rise in commodity prices. In retail volume, however, many categories saw slower growth rates because Americans began to eat out more often again. This dynamic changed for a couple of years when cooking at home became a more popular alternative in response to the recession and the sharp rise in commodity prices.[12]

After years of expansions and acquisitions, U.S. packaged-food companies were beginning to downsize. In August 2011, Kraft Foods announced that it would split into two companies–a globally focused biscuits and confectionery enterprise and a domestically focused cheese, chilled processed-meats, and ready-meals firm. After purchasing Post cereals from Kraft, Ralcorp Holdings spun off its Post cereals business (Post Holdings Inc.) in February 2012.[13]

Though supermarkets were the main retail channel for buying packaged food, other competitors were gaining traction by offering lower prices or more convenience. The recession forced shoppers to consider alternative retail channels as they looked for ways to save money. A big beneficiary of this consumer trend was the discounters, which carried fewer items and national brands than supermarkets but offered lower prices in return. For example, dollar store chains Dollar General and Family Dollar expanded their food selections to increase their appeal. Drugstore chains CVS and Walgreens expanded their food selections as well, especially in urban areas, to leverage their locations as a factor of convenience. Mass merchandiser Target continued to expand its PFresh initiative, featuring fresh produce, frozen food, dairy products, and dry groceries.[14]

The increasing availability of refrigeration and other kinds of storage space in homes influenced the demand for packaged goods in emerging markets (see Exhibit 3). However, for consumers who lacked the ability to preserve and keep larger quantities, U.S. companies began selling smaller packages, with portions that could be consumed more quickly.[15]

Firm Structure and Management

Campbell Soup was controlled by the descendants of John T. Dorrance, the chemist who invented condensed soup

EXHIBIT 3 Leading U.S. Agricultural Export Destinations, by Value ($US)

FY 2018		FY 2017		FY 2016	
World Total	143,367,456,741	World Total	140,184,462,069	World Total	129,602,794,075
Canada	20,568,892,981	China	21,840,643,461	Canada	20,391,538,206
Mexico	18,844,622,947	Canada	20,442,051,832	China	19,167,801,194
China	16,308,626,015	Mexico	18,608,230,044	Mexico	17,617,874,494
European Union-28	12,724,435,619	Japan	11,829,920,119	European Union-28	11,664,769,077
Japan	12,604,512,527	European Union-28	11,551,590,231	Japan	10,600,812,208
South Korea	7,976,908,026	South Korea	6,846,960,804	South Korea	5,693,404,770
Hong Kong	4,200,037,770	Hong Kong	4,043,310,944	Hong Kong	3,504,490,432
Vietnam	3,896,838,657	Taiwan	3,398,029,805	Taiwan	3,072,322,755
Taiwan	3,793,241,456	Indonesia	2,967,819,632	Philippines	2,469,892,778
Indonesia	3,096,490,112	Philippines	2,627,753,477	Indonesia	2,375,719,583
Philippines	2,831,344,950	Vietnam	2,558,986,068	Vietnam	2,354,094,686
Colombia	2,757,403,699	Colombia	2,550,841,358	Colombia	2,257,243,101
Thailand	2,148,645,560	Thailand	1,781,611,046	Thailand	1,464,919,723
Egypt	1,695,419,327	Turkey	1,711,429,322	Turkey	1,384,109,233
Turkey	1,680,585,474	Saudi Arabia	1,588,478,200	Australia	1,304,323,652

Source: U.S. Economic Research Service, U.S. Department of Agriculture, 2018.

more than a century ago. In struggling times, the Dorrance family had faced agonizing decisions: Should they sell the Campbell Soup Company, which had been in the family's hands for three generations? Should they hire new management to revive flagging sales of its chicken noodle and tomato soups and Pepperidge Farm cookies? Or should Campbell perhaps become an acquirer itself? The company went public in 1954, when William Murphy was the president and CEO. Dorrance family members continued to hold a large portion of the shares. After CEO David Johnson left Campbell in 1998, the company weakened and lost customers,[16] until Douglas Conant became CEO and transformed Campbell into one of the food industry's best performers.

Conant became CEO and director of Campbell Soup Company in January 2001. He joined the Campbell's team with an extensive background in the processed- and packaged-food industry. He had spent 10 years with General Mills, filled top management positions in marketing and strategy at Kraft Foods, and served as president of Nabisco Foods. Conant worked toward the goal of implementing the Campbell's mission of "building the world's most extraordinary food company by nourishing people's lives everywhere, every day."[17] He was confident that the company had the people, the products, the capabilities, and the plans in place to actualize that mission.

Under Conant's direction, Campbell made many reforms through investments in improving product quality, packaging, and marketing. He worked to create a company characterized by innovation. During his tenure, the company improved its financial profile, upgraded its supply chain system, developed a more positive relationship with its customers, and enhanced employee engagement. Conant focused on winning in both the marketplace and the workplace. His efforts produced an increase in net sales from $7.1 billion in fiscal 2005 to $7.67 billion in fiscal 2010.[18]

For Conant, the main targets for investment, following the divestiture of many brands, included simple meals, baked snacks, and vegetable-based beverages. In 2010, the baking and snacking segments sales increased 7 percent, primarily due to currency conditions. Pepperidge Farm sales were comparable to those a year earlier, as the additional sales from the acquisition of Ecce Panis, Inc., and volume gains were offset by increased promotional spending. Some of the reasons for this growth were the brand's positioning, advertising investments, improvements and additions in the distribution system. Conant also secured an agreement with Coca-Cola North America and Coca-Cola Enterprises Inc. for distribution of Campbell's refrigerated single-serve beverages in the United States and Canada through the Coca-Cola bottler network.[19]

In fiscal year 2010, the company continued its focus on delivering superior long-term total shareowner returns by executing the following seven key strategies:

- Grow its icon brands within simple meals, baked snacks, and healthy beverages.
- Deliver higher levels of consumer satisfaction through superior innovation focused on wellness while providing good value, quality, and convenience.
- Make its products more broadly available and relevant in existing and new markets, consumer segments, and eating occasions.
- Strengthen its business through outside partnerships and acquisitions.
- Increase margins by improving price realization and companywide total cost management.
- Improve overall organizational excellence, diversity, and engagement.
- Advance a powerful commitment to sustainability and corporate social responsibility.[20]

Other major focuses for Conant and Campbell Soup were care for their customers' wellness needs, overall product quality, and product convenience. Some of the main considerations regarding wellness in the U.S. market were obesity and high blood pressure. For example, building on the success of the V8 V-Fusion juice offerings, the company planned to introduce a number of new V8 V-Fusion Plus Tea products. In the baked snacks category, the company planned to continue upgrading the health credentials of its cracker (or savory biscuit) offerings. Responding to consumers' value-oriented focus, Campbell's condensed soups were relaunched with a new contemporary packaging design and an upgrade to the company's gravity-fed shelving system.[21]

In 2011, after 10 years leading the company, Conant retired. His successor, Denise Morrison, had worked for Conant for quite some time, not just at Campbell but at Nabisco as well earlier in their careers. In August 2011, on her first day as CEO, she was set on employing a new vision for the company: stabilize the soup and simple meals businesses, expand internationally, grow faster in healthy beverages and baked snacks, and add back the salt.[22] With the younger generation now making up an increasingly large percentage of the population, Morrison knew that the company had to change in order to increase the appeal of its products. At that time, the U.S. population included 80 million people between the ages of 18 and 34, approximately 25 percent of the population. Early on in her role as chief executive, Morrison dispatched Campbell's employees to hipster hubs including Austin, Texas; Portland, Oregon; and London and Paris to find out what these potential customers wanted.[23]

To build employee engagement, Campbell provided manager training across the organization. This training was just one part of the curriculum at Campbell University, the company's internal employee learning and development program. Exemplary managers built strong engagement among their teams through consistent action planning. The company emphasized employees' innovation capabilities, leadership behavior, workplace flexibility, and wellness.

Challenges Ahead

Recognizing the need for significant change, in his role as interim CEO, Keith McLoughlin said that the company planned to return the company to long-term organic net sales and earnings growth. While *innovation* is not a term typically associated with the food-processing industry, Morrison said that innovation was a key to the company's future success. As an example, she cited Campbell's development of an iPhone application that provided consumers with Campbell's Kitchen recipes. According to Morrison, the company's marketing team devised the plan as a way to appeal to technologically savvy, millennial-generation consumers.[24]

In fiscal year 2018, under the leadership of Mcloughlin, the company had three actions that they planned to implement to return the company to long-term organic sales and earnings growth:

1. Become a more focused company in the core North American market;
2. Divest certain non-core businesses and use the proceeds to significantly pay down debt and strengthen the balance sheet; and,
3. Reduce costs and increase asset efficiency, to reflect the leaner, more focused and agile enterprise they are building. [25]

A few years into the former CEO Morrison's governance, analysts still had a lukewarm response about Morrison taking over. They still expressed their doubt about whether Morrison was the right choice, rather than some new blood as a CEO replacement. After Morrison's resignation, Campbell's Board of Directors engaged outside advisors in a rigorous and objective review of the company. The advisers helped provide the Board and management with a fresh, unbiased assessment of their strengths, weaknesses, strategy and execution.[26] Among these options were:

1. Optimizing the company's portfolio and divesting assets and businesses;
2. Splitting the company; or,
3. Selling the entire company.

To fasten their process, the company decided to divest two of their non-core businesses: Campbell International, which includes Arnott's, Kelsen, and their operations in Indonesia, Malaysia, Hong Kong and Japan; and Campbell Fresh, which includes Bolthouse Farms, Garden Fresh Gourmet, and their U.S. refrigerated soup business. The soup auction came to a boil when Kraft Heinz (KHC) and Mondelez (MDLZ) were both shortlisted to participate in the second round of bidding for the international assets of Campbell Soup.

Competition

Campbell operated in the highly competitive global food industry and experienced worldwide competition for all of its principal products. The principal areas of competition were brand recognition, quality, price, advertising, promotion, convenience, and service (see Exhibits 4 and 5).

Nestlé

Nestlé was the world's number-one food company in terms of sales, the world leader in coffee (Nescafé), one of the worlds' largest bottled-water (Perrier) makers, and a top player in the pet food business (Ralston Purina). Its most well-known global brands included Buitoni, Friskies, Maggi, Nescafé, Nestea, and Nestlé. The company-owned Gerber Products, Jenny Craig, about 75 percent of Alcon Inc. (ophthalmic drugs, contact-lens solutions, and equipment for ocular surgery), and almost 28 percent of L'Orèal.[27] In July 2007, it purchased Novartis Medical Nutrition, and in August 2007 it purchased the Gerber business from Sandoz Ltd., with the goal of becoming a nutritional powerhouse. Furthermore, by adding Gerber baby foods to its baby formula business, Nestlé became a major player in the U.S. baby food sector.

General Mills

General Mills was the U.S. number-one cereal maker, behind Kellogg, fighting for the top spot on a consistent basis. Its brands included Cheerios, Chex, Total, Kix, and Wheaties. General Mills was also a brand leader in flour (Gold Medal), baking mixes (Betty Crocker, Bisquick), dinner mixes (Hamburger Helper), fruit snacks (Fruit Roll-Ups), grain snacks (Chex Mix, Pop Secret), and yogurt (Colombo, Go-Gurt, and Yoplait). In 2001, it acquired Pillsbury from Diageo and doubled the company's size, making General Mills one of the world's largest food companies. Although most of its sales came from the United States, General Mills was trying to grow the reach and position of its brands around the world.[28]

The Kraft Heinz Company

The Kraft Foods Group and H. J. Heinz Company closed a merger deal in July 2015. The combined company was called The Kraft Heinz Company, and became the third largest food company in North America and fifth largest in the world. Its most popular brands included Kraft cheeses, beverages (Maxwell House coffee, Kool-Aid drinks), convenient meals (Oscar Mayer meats and Kraft Mac & Cheese), grocery fare (Cool Whip, Shake 'n Bake), and nuts (Planters). Kraft Foods Group was looking to resuscitate its business in North America.[29] H. J. Heinz had thousands of products. Even prior to the merger, Heinz products enjoyed first or second place by market share in more than 50 countries. One of the world's largest food producers, Heinz produced ketchup, condiments, sauces, frozen foods, beans, pasta meals, infant food, and other processed-food products. Its flagship product was ketchup, and the company dominated the U.S. ketchup market. Its leading brands included Heinz ketchup, Lea & Perrins sauces, Ore-Ida frozen potatoes, Boston Market, T.G.I. Friday's, and Weight Watchers foods. In 2013, Heinz agreed to be acquired by Berkshire Hathaway and 3G Capital.[30] The post-merger Kraft Heinz Company was also dedicated to offering healthy food products to its customers by adapting to changing tastes and consumer preferences.

Financials

In the 2018 fiscal year, Campbell's earnings from continuing operations decreased from $887 million to $261 million. Sales increased by 10 percent to $8.685 billion driven by an 11-point benefit from the acquisitions of Snyder's Lance and Pacific Foods. Adjusted earnings per share (EPS) from continuing operations decreased 6 percent to $2.87 per share, compared to $3.04 per share a year ago (see Exhibits 6, 7, and 8). With regard to financials, McLoughlin stated: "The results we delivered in fiscal 2018 reflect the need for the significant actions we are taking to turn the company around."[31]

Sustainability

Campbell Soup Company was named to the Dow Jones Sustainability Indexes (DJSI) repeatedly and to the DJSI World Index. This independent ranking recognized the company's strategic and management approach to delivering economic, environmental, and social performance. Launched in 1999, the DJSI tracked the financial performance of leading sustainability-driven companies worldwide. In selecting the top performers in each business sector, DJSI reviewed companies on several general and industry-specific topics related to economic, environmental, and social dimensions. These included corporate governance, environmental policy, climate strategy, human capital development, and labor practices. Campbell included sustainability and corporate social responsibility as one of its seven core business strategies.[32] Campbell's Napoleon, Ohio, plant had implemented a new renewable energy initiative, anchored by 24,000 new solar panels. The 60-acre, 9.8-megawatt solar power system was expected to supply 15 percent of the plant's electricity while reducing CO_2 emissions by 250,000 metric tons over 20 years.[33]

Additionally, Campbell employees volunteered an average of 20,000 hours annually at more than 200 nonprofit organizations. Supported by local farmers and Campbell, the Food Bank of South Jersey was earning revenue for hunger relief from sales of *Just Peachy* salsa. The salsa was created from excess peaches from New Jersey and was manufactured and labeled by employee volunteers at Campbell's plant in Camden.[34]

EXHIBIT 4 Campbell's Competitors, by Market Capitalization and Financials

	Morningstar Rating	Market Cap Mil	Net Income Mil	P/S	P/B	P/E	Dividend Yield%	5-Yr Rev CAGR%	Med Oper. Margin%	Interest Coverage	D/E
Campbell Soup Co	****	**11,496**	**−164**	**1.2**	**9.1**	**–**	**3.7**	**1.5**	**16.0**	**2.4**	**6.3**
Nestle SA (USD, CHF)	**	283,548	10,135	3.2	5.0	29.0	2.6	−0.1	15.8	13.9	0.4
Danone SA (USD, EUR)	***	51,586	2,349	1.9	2.8	19.6	2.8	3.0	13.9	7.1	0.9
The Kraft Heinz Co (USD)	*****	39,656	10,382	1.5	0.8	–	7.0	7.4	23.2	5.5	0.5
General Mills Inc (USD)	****	30,071	1,536	1.8	4.3	19.7	3.9	−2.4	16.4	6.5	1.7
Associated British Foods PLC (USD, GBP)		26,115	1,007	1.3	2.2	19.9	1.8	3.2	8.2	9.4	0.0
Hormel Foods Corp (USD)	**	21,244	950	2.3	3.7	22.8	2.0	1.8	12.1	45.6	0.0
McCormick & Co Inc (USD)	*	19,923	658	3.7	6.0	30.6	1.4	5.6	14.9	5.2	1.2
Kellogg Co (USD)	****	19,915	1,336	1.5	7.7	15.1	3.8	−1.7	10.8	5.6	3.2
Kerry Group PLC (USD, EUR)		19,244	540	2.6	4.2	31.4	0.7	2.5	11.2	10.1	0.5
WH Group Ltd (USD)		17,126	943	0.8	2.2	18.4	–	15.0	7.2	13.8	0.3
WH Group Ltd (USD)		17,126	943	0.8	2.2	18.2	3.0	15.0	7.2	13.8	0.3
Conagra Brands Inc (USD)	****	15,039	621	1.5	2.0	21.1	2.8	−12.5	10.1	6.4	1.5
China Mengniu Dairy Co Ltd (USD, CNY)		14,220	2,481	1.5	4.3	40.2	–	10.8	4.9	7.6	0.3
JM Smucker Co (USD)	**	13,788	628	1.8	1.7	22.0	2.8	4.5	16.8	5.9	0.7
Saputo Inc (USD, CAD)		13,195	761	1.4	3.2	23.4	1.1	9.6	8.9	29.1	0.4
JBS SA (USD, BRL)		12,695	25	0.3	2.1	2041.0	0.2	14.4	4.2	0.7	2.1
Meiji Holdings Co Ltd (USD, JPY)		11,246	72,451	1.1	2.8	22.4	0.8	2.0	6.7	121.6	0.2
Grupo Bimbo SAB de CV (USD, MXN)		10,139	3,719	0.7	2.7	53.8	0.8	9.1	8.0	3.0	–
Industry Average		**7,284**	**65,000**	**1.5**	**2.0**	**27.2**	**2.9**	**7.3**	**−72670.8**	**−40.9**	**0.9**

Source: Morningstar Inc., http://financials.morningstar.com/competitors/industry-peer.action?t=CPB.

EXHIBIT 5 Campbell Soup Top Competitors' Stock Prices

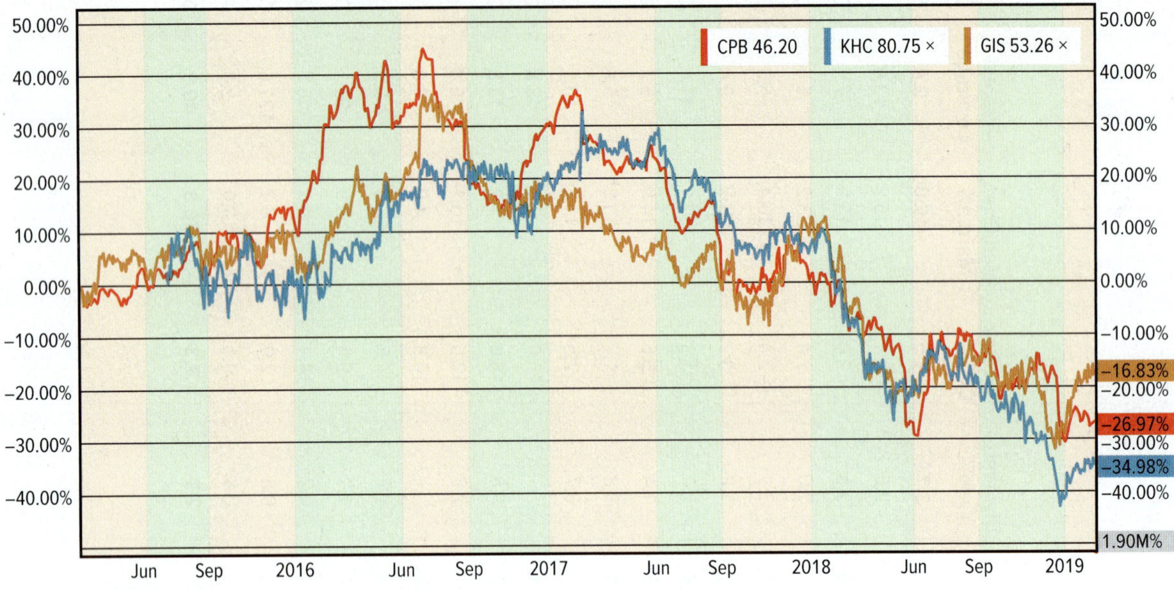

Source: finance.yahoo.com.

EXHIBIT 6 Campbell Income Statement

CAMPBELL SOUP COMPANY Consolidated Statements of Earnings (millions, except per share amounts)	2018 52 weeks	2017 52 weeks	2016 53 weeks
Net sales	$8685	$7,890	$7,961
Costs and expenses			
Cost of products sold	5,869	4,965	5,033
Marketing and selling expenses	902	855	852
Administrative expenses	654	550	575
Research and development expenses	110	111	105
Other expenses / (income)	619	(9)	405
Restructuring charges	62	18	31
Total costs and expenses	8,216	6,490	7,001
Earnings before interest and taxes	469	1,400	960
Interest expense	201	112	115
Interest income	4	5	4
Earnings before taxes	272	1,293	849
Taxes on earnings	11	406	286
Earnings from continuing operations	261	887	563
Net earnings	261	887	563
Net earnings attributable to Campbell Soup Company	$ 0.87	$ 2.91	$ 1.82
Per Share—Basic			
Earnings from continuing operations attributable to Campbell Soup Company	$ 0.86	$ 2.89	$ 1.81

Source: The Campbell Soup Company, Annual Report, 2018.

EXHIBIT 7 Campbell Balance Sheet

CAMPBELL SOUP COMPANY Consolidated Balance Sheets (millions, except per share amounts)		
	July 29, 2018	**July 30, 2017**
Current assets		
Cash and cash equivalents	$ 226	$ 319
Accounts receivable, net	785	605
Inventories	1,199	902
Other current assets	86	74
Total current assets	2,296	1,900
Plant assets, net of depreciation	3,233	2,454
Goodwill	4,580	2,115
Other intangible assets, net of amortization	4,196	1,118
Other assets ($77 as of 2018 and $51 as of 2017 attributable to variable interest entity)	224	139
Total assets	$ 14,529	$ 7,726
Current liabilities		
Short-term borrowings	$ 1,896	$ 1,037
Payable to suppliers and others	893	666
Accrued liabilities	676	561
Dividends payable	107	111
Accrued income taxes	22	20
Total current liabilities	3,594	2,395
Long-term debt	7,998	2,499
Deferred taxes	995	490
Other liabilities	569	697
Total liabilities	13,156	6,081
Commitments and contingencies		
Campbell Soup Company shareholders' equity		
Capital stock, $.0375 par value; authorized 560 shares; issued 323 shares	12	12
Additional paid-in capital	349	359
Earnings retained in the business	2,224	2,385
Capital stock in treasury, at cost	(1,103)	(1,066)
Accumulated other comprehensive loss	(118)	(53)
Total Campbell Soup Company shareholders' equity	1,364	1,637
Noncontrolling interests	9	8
Total equity	1,373	1,645
Total liabilities and equity	$ 14,529	$ 7,726

Source: The Campbell Soup Company, Annual Report, 2018.

EXHIBIT 8 Campbell's Key Ratios

Valuation	
P/E Current	45.35
P/E Ratio (with extraordinary items)	−71.58
P/E Ratio (without extraordinary items)	47.60
Price to Sales Ratio	1.42
Price to Book Ratio	9.03
Price to Cash Flow Ratio	9.47
Enterprise Value to EBITDA	12.67
Enterprise Value to Sales	2.22
Total Debt to Enterprise Value	0.45
Efficiency	
Revenue/Employee	377,609.00
Income Per Employee	11,348.00
Receivables Turnover	12.50
Total Asset Turnover	0.78
Liquidity	
Current Ratio	64%
Quick Ratio	31%
Cash Ratio	7%
Profitability Ratios	
Gross Margin	33.16
Operating Margin	15.14
Pre-tax Margin	3.13
Profit Margin	3.01
Pre-Tax ROE	2.35
After Tax ROE	17.39
Return on Total Capital	15.99
Valuation	
Return on Invested Capital	3.87
Capital Structure	
Total Debt to Total Equity	725.37
Total Debt to Total Capital	87.88
Total Debt to Total Assets	68.10
Long-Term Debt to Equity	586.36
Long-Term Debt to Total Capital	71.04

Source: MarketWatch Inc. 2019.

What's Next?

Through the tumultuous year, Campbell is looking forward to better days with a new CEO in place. The company sees a future opportunity to have additional cost savings, which will be driven by streamlining their organization, expanding their zero-based budgeting efforts and continuing to optimize the manufacturing network. In fiscal 2019, the company plans to rebase their soup business and strengthen their value proposition in the marketplace with a back-to-basics approach.[35] Will the new management prove more effective than the past couple of years? Will the company be able to resonate with the American consumer and increase their profits? Will Campbell's soup simmer toward a profitable future, or will the company boil over?

ENDNOTES

1. Campbell Soup Co. 2018 annual report.
2. Goudreau, J. 2012. Kicking the can: Campbell's CEO bets on soup-in-a-bag for 20-somethings. *Forbes.com*, December 6, www.forbes.com/sites/jennagoudreau/2012/12/06/kicking-the-can-campbells-ceo-bets-on-soup-in-a-bag-for-20-somethings.
3. Press release. 2018. Campbell names Mark A. Clouse President, Chief Executive Officer and a Director of the Board. https://www.campbellsoupcompany.com/newsroom/press-releases.
4. Campbells. Our company. www.campbellsoupcompany.com/around_the_world.asp.
5. Collins, G. 1994. Campbell Soup takes the big plunge into salsa. *New York Times*, November 29: D1.
6. Campbell Soup Co. 2010. 2009 annual report.
7. Campbell Soup Co. 2008. 2007 annual report.
8. Jargon, J. 2011. Campbell Soup to exit Russia. *Wall Street Journal*, June 29, online.wsj.com/article/SB10001424052702304447804576414202460491210.html.
9. Ibid.
10. *Want China Times*. 2013. Campbell Soup aims to break into Chinese market through chef endorsements. Posted on China Beverage News, March 10, http://www.chinabevnews.com/2013/03/campbell-soup-aims-to-break-into.html#!/2013/03/campbell-soup-aims-to-break-into.html
11. Boyle, M. 2009. Campbell's: Not about to let the soup cool. *BusinessWeek*, September 17.
12. PRNewswire. 2012. U.S. Packaged Food Market–Consumers seek out ethnic & bold flavours–new industry report. *PRNewswire*, March 12, www.prnewswire.com/news-releases/us-packaged-food-marketóconsumers-seek-out-ethnicñbold-flavoursónew-industry-report-142292805.html.
13. ReportsnReports. 2013. Packaged food in the US. April, www.reportsnreports.com/reports/150486-packaged-food-in-the-us.html.
14. Ibid.
15. Graves, T. and E.Y. Kwon. 2009. Standard and Poor's foods and nonalcoholic beverages industry report. July.
16. Abelson, R. 2000. The first family of soup, feeling the squeeze; Should it sell or try to go it alone? *New York Times*, July 30, www.nytimes.com/2000/07/30/business/first-family-soup-feeling-squeeze-should-it-sell-try-go-it-alone.html?pagewanted5all&src5pm.
17. Campbell Soup Co. 2008. 2007 annual report.
18. Campbell Soup Co. 2011. 2010 annual report.
19. Press release. 2007. The Coca-Cola Company, Campbell Soup Company and Coca-Cola Enterprises sign agreement for distribution of Campbell's beverage portfolio. investor.shareholder.com/campbell/releasedetail.cfm?ReleaseID5247903.
20. Campbell Soup Co. 2011. 2010 annual report.
21. Ibid.
22. Goudreau, J. 2012. Kicking the can: Campbell's CEO bets on soup-in-a-bag for 20-somethings. *Forbes.com*, December 6, www.forbes.com/sites/jennagoudreau/2012/12/06/kicking-the-can-campbells-ceo-bets-on-soup-in-a-bag-for-20-somethings.

23. Ibid.
24. Campbell Soup Co. 2017. 2018 annual report.
25. Campbell Soup Co. 2017. 2018 annual report.
26. Campbell Soup Co. 2018 annual report.
27. Hoovers. Undated. Company profiles: Nestlè. www.hoovers.com/company-information/cs/company-profile.Nestlè_SA.6a719827106be6ff.html.
28. Hoovers. Undated. Company profiles: General Mills. www.hoovers.com/company-information/cs/company-profile.General_Mills_Inc.a90ba57dc8f51a65.html.
29. Hoovers. Undated. Company profiles: Kraft Foods. www.hoovers.com/company-information/cs/company-profile.Kraft_Foods_Group_Inc.43af8ed4b4ae51f2.html.
30. Hoovers. Undated. Company profiles: H. J. Heinz Company. www.hoovers.com/company-information/cs/company-profile.H_J_Heinz_Company.1696a42275f81d38.html.
31. Campbell Soup Co. 2018 annual report.
32. News release. 2010. Campbell Soup company named to Dow Jones Sustainability Indexes. investor.campbellsoupcompany.com/phoenix.zhtml?c588650&p5irol-newsArticle&ID51471159.
33. Campbell Soup Co. 2013. 2012 annual report.
34. Ibid.
35. Campbell Soup Co. 2017. 2018 annual report.

CASE 20

NINTENDO: COULD THE SWITCH TURN ON GAMERS?*

The Nintendo Switch is a gaming console that comes with a pair of new and innovative controllers called Joy-Con Controllers, a hybrid of an attachable game pad and a controller that could be used separately for multiplayer game play. When it was introduced in 2017, Nintendo's management was highly optimistic about the Switch, and Nintendo believed that it could sell about 10 million units of Switch consoles within a year after the launch.[1] As of January 2019, Nintendo's latest gaming console Nintendo Switch had exceeded 32 million units sold, and software sales for the console had reached 163.61 million units.[2] A pair of Joy-Cons was included in the $299.99 price tag of the Switch console. The Joy-Con came in two color options for customers to choose from, one grey and red/blue and the other grey and black. A more innovative feature in the new gaming console was that it could be transformed into a 6.2-inch high-definition on-the-go gaming screen if a user decided to move away from the TV.

The Switch console also marked the release of Nintendo Switch's very first epic game called "The Legend of Zelda: Breadth of the Wild," which could be played both on Switch and Wii U consoles for a price of $59.99. Nintendo of America's COO and president, Reggie Fils-Aime, said, "Nintendo Switch makes it easy for anyone to enjoy their games in the living room and then quickly take them on the go."[3] The new gaming console design meant that console-gaming was not only limited to one stationary TV anymore and could be experienced anywhere anytime.

The launch of Nintendo's Switch caught the attention of consumers and mostly received a positive response, but apparently the news did not impress the investors, leaving the company's stock tumbling. This may have reflected concerns regarding the battery life of the portable console, its price, and third-party support. Nevertheless, a flood of customer orders led to stock shortages in stores like GameStop and Toys R Us, among others. Addressing the stock shortage, Reggie Fils-Aime said, "our focus is making sure that the consumer who wants to buy a Nintendo Switch can buy a Nintendo Switch."[4] The initial plan had been to ship 2 million consoles. Nintendo decided to double the production to deal with the shortage and meet the strong demand. The stocks had surged high by mid-2018, a year after Nintendo Switch's launch. According to *The Wall Street Journal,* to meet demand for one year out (ending April 2018), the company's management decided to manufacture 16 million Switch consoles–double the yearly quantity of 8 million units, Nintendo's traditional production target.[5]

One of the key topics of discussion in the popular press was whether or not the Switch console defined the "next generation" of gaming. This echoed similar press concerns after the launch of Nintendo's previous console, the Wii U. Prior to the launch of the Switch, its predecessor the Nintendo Wii U console had been on the market for only a short while, with the addition of innovative controls and new game titles. Then there had been uncertainty among industry experts, such as Gabrielle Shrager of Ubisoft and Mikael Haveri of Frozenbyte, as to whether or not the improved power and new controller interface justified that system's being considered a "new" generation.[6]

The Wii U initially was launched with 50 available games and a new controller interface, termed the GamePad. While the GamePad offered a new take on the Wii's controls, the new console was still compatible with the same motion-sensing controllers of the original Wii. However, the Wii U console was not sold with these controllers included. Instead, it came with just one of the new GamePads. Incorporating traits from tablet devices, the GamePad integrated both traditional input methods such as buttons, dual analog sticks, and a D-pad (directional pad) and a touchscreen. The touchscreen could be used to supplement a game by providing alternative functionality or an alternative view of a scenario in a game. With the Off-TV Play function, the screen could also be used to play a game strictly on the GamePad screen, without the use of a television display at all. With the Wii U console turned on, the GamePad could be used to display the same picture on its screen as would be seen using a TV display. There were also nongaming functions, such as the ability to use the GamePad as a television remote. While Nintendo was the first of the competitors to release its new gaming console, there was no doubt that both Sony's PlayStation and Microsoft's Xbox would be close behind in releasing their own upgraded systems.

Although Nintendo is slightly behind in comparison to competitors, the company saw a significant improvement in its net sales after Nintendo Switch (see Exhibits 1 and 2).

Background

Although Nintendo dated back to 1889 as a playing-card maker, Nintendo's first video-game systems were developed in 1979 and known as TV Game 15 and TV Game 6.[7]

* This case was prepared by Professor Alan B. Eisner and graduate students Sushmitha Mudda, Saad Nazir, Eshai J. Gorshein, and Eric S. Engelson of Pace University. This case is based solely on library research and was developed for class discussion rather than to illustrate either effective or ineffective handling of an administrative situation. Copyright © 2019 Alan B. Eisner.

EXHIBIT 1 Income Statement

	Year Ended March 31		
	2018	2019	
	(Millions of yen)	(Millions of yen)	(Millions of dollars)
Net sales	1,055,682	1,200,560	10,914
Cost of sales	652,141	699,370	6,357
Gross profit	403,540	501,189	4,556
Selling, general and administrative expenses	225,983	251,488	2,286
Operating income	177,557	249,701	2,270
Non-operating income			
Interest income	9,064	13,131	119
Foreign Exchange gains	–	5,426	49
Share of profit of entities accounted for using equity method	10,318	6,949	63
Other	4,126	2,807	25
Total non-operating income	23,509	28,315	257
Non-operating expenses			
Sales discounts	–	–	–
Foreign exchange losses	766	–	–
Loss on redemption of securities	794	440	4
Other	150	221	2
Total non-operating expenses	1,710	662	6
Ordinary income	199,356	277,355	2,521
Gain on sales of non-current assets	821	1	0
Gain on sales of investment securities	490	0	0
Reversal of loss on litigation	1,929	–	–
Total extraordinary income	3,240	1	0
Impairment loss	–	4,622	42
Loss on disposal of non-current assets	366	278	2
Loss on sales of investment securities	2	0	0
Loss on valuation of investment securities	–	682	6
Loss on litigation	1,138	–	–
Total extraordinary losses	1,507	5,584	50
Profit before income taxes	201,090	271,772	2,470
Income taxes - current	56,977	88,137	801
Income taxes - deferred	3,167	(10,932)	(99)
Total income taxes	60,144	77,204	701
Profit	140,945	194,568	1,768
Profit attributable to non-controlling interests	1,354	558	5
Profit attributable to owners of parent	139,590	194,009	1,763

*1 USD = 112.3095 JPY as of March 31, 2019

Source: Financial Morning Star.

EXHIBIT 2 Balance Sheet

	Year Ended March 31		
	2018	2019	
	(Millions of yen)	(Millions of yen)	(Millions of dollars*)
Assets			
Current assets			
Cash and deposits	744,555	844,550	7,677
Notes and accounts receivable - trade	69,829	78,169	710
Securities	243,431	238,410	2,167
Inventories	141,795	135,470	1,231
Other	66,405	48,453	440
Allowance for doubtful accounts	(87)	(82)	(0)
Total current assets	1,265,929	1,344,972	12,227
Non-current assets			
Property, plant and equipment			
Buildings and structures, net	36,094	37,592	341
Machinery, equipment and vehicles, net	1,450	1,575	14
Tools, furniture and fixtures, net	3,915	4,015	36
Land	41,812	38,223	347
Construction in progress	653	143	1
Total property, plant and equipment	83,926	81,550	741
Intangible assets			
Software	11,487	11,962	108
Other	2,533	2,128	19
Total intangible assets	14,020	14,090	128
Investments and other assets			
Investment securities	198,538	167,134	1,519
Deferred tax assets	37,094	57,992	527
Net defined benefit asset	7,931	7,056	64
Other	15,503	17,536	159
Allowance for doubtful accounts	(30)	(29)	(0)
Total investments and other assets	259,037	249,690	2,269
Total non-current assets	356,984	345,331	3,139
Total assets	1,633,748	1,690,304	15,366

	Year Ended March 31		
	2018	2019	
	(Millions of yen)	(Millions of yen)	(Millions of dollars*)
Liabilities			
Current liabilities			
Notes and accounts payable - trade	138,015	59,689	542
Income taxes payable	43,390	62,646	569
Provision for bonuses	3,217	3,891	35
Other	93,452	118,781	1,079
Total current liabilities	278,076	245,009	2,227
Non-current liabilities			
Net defined benefit liability	16,609	15,068	136
Other	15,487	15,427	140
Total non-current liabilities	32,097	30,496	277
Total liabilities	310,173	275,505	2,504
Net assets			
Shareholders' equity			
Capital stock	10,065	10,065	91
Capital surplus	13,742	12,069	109
Retained earnings	1,564,240	1,556,881	14,153
Treasury shares	(250,679)	(156,755)	(1,425)
Total shareholders' equity	1,337,369	1,422,260	12,929
Accumulated other comprehensive income			
Valuation difference on available-for-sale securities	16,402	17,665	160
Foreign currency translation adjustment	(34,736)	(30,214)	(274)
Total accumulated other comprehensive income	(18,334)	(12,548)	(114)
Non-controlling interests	4,540	5,086	46
Total net assets	1,323,574	1,414,798	12,861
Total liabilities and net assets	1,633,748	1,690,304	15,366

*1 USD = 112.3095 JPY as of March 31, 2019

Source: Nintendo Annual Report 2018.

In 1980, Nintendo developed the first portable LCD video game with a microprocessor. In 1985, Nintendo created the Nintendo Entertainment System (NES), an 8-bit video game console. The original NES was very successful, as its graphics were superior to any home-based console available at the time. As a result, more than 60 million units were sold worldwide.[8] The NES set the bar for subsequent consoles in platform design, as well as for accepting games that were manufactured by third-party developers.

When competitors began developing 16-bit devices, such as Sega's Genesis system and NEC's PC Engine, Nintendo responded with its own 16-bit system, the Super Nintendo Entertainment System (SNES). The Super Nintendo was released in 1991 and, when purchased, came with one game—Super Mario World. In 1996, Nintendo released Nintendo 64. The Nintendo 64 was the company's third-generation video game console and was named after the 64-bit processor. During its product lifetime, more than 30 million Nintendo 64 units were sold worldwide.[9]

The Nintendo 64, like its predecessors, used cartridges to play its games, but at the time the competing Sony and Sega systems were using CDs for game storage. Cartridges could store 64 megabytes of data, while CDs could store around 700 megabytes. Also, CDs were much cheaper to manufacture, distribute, and create; the average cost of producing a Nintendo 64 cartridge was $25, compared to 10 cents to produce a CD. Game producers passed the higher expense to the consumer, which explained why Nintendo 64 games tended to sell for higher prices than Sony PlayStation games. While most Sony PlayStation games rarely exceeded $50, Nintendo 64 titles could reach $70. To increase profits and to take advantage of the programming possibilities of the larger storage space, many third-party game developers that had traditionally supported Nintendo platforms began creating games for systems that used a CD platform (such as the PlayStation).[10]

In 2001, Nintendo released its GameCube, which was part of the sixth-generation era of video game systems. These systems included Sony's PlayStation 2, Microsoft's Xbox, and Sega's Dreamcast. Although the GameCube did not use cartridges, Nintendo began producing its games using a proprietary optical-disk technology. This technology, while similar in appearance to CDs, was actually smaller in diameter and could not be played using a standard CD player.

When Nintendo released the Wii video game console in 2006, it was already in the midst of a very competitive market. The previous generation of video game consoles consisted of the Sega Dreamcast, Sony PlayStation 2, Nintendo GameCube, and Microsoft Xbox. These systems were all released between 1999 and 2001 in the United States, and although the GameCube sold more systems than did the Sega Dreamcast, it fell into third place behind the PlayStation 2 and the Xbox. The PlayStation 2 sold more than 115 million units worldwide, more than twice the combined unit sales of the GameCube and Xbox (21 million and 24 million, respectively).

By 2019, Nintendo had gone beyond its Nintendo 3DS and Wii U, and was banking on Nintendo Switch to beat the competition. But it was accompanied by rumors of a PlayStation 5 that was set to release in 2021. In May 2018, Sony Interactive Entertainment CEO John Kodera told reporters, "We will use the next three years to prepare the next step, to crouch down so that we can jump higher into the future." This came shortly after he remarked that the PS4 was entering the "final phase of its life cycle."[11]

The Term *Wii*

In 2006, Nintendo released its direct successor to the GameCube, the Wii (pronounced "we"). There were many reasons cited as to why the name *Wii* was chosen, but perhaps the most compelling reason was that "'Wii' sounded like 'we,' which emphasized that the console was for everyone. Wii could be remembered easily by people around the world, no matter what language they spoke. No confusion."[12] Initially the system was known by its code name, Revolution, but later the name was changed to Wii. Nintendo stated that it wanted to make the Wii a system that would make anyone who tried it talk to his or her friends and neighbors about it.[13]

The Making of the Remote

The original Wii was created to establish a new standard in game control, using an innovative and unprecedented interface, the Wii Remote.[14] The Wii Remote was what made the Wii unique. The remote acted as the primary controller for the Wii. Its motion-sensor capabilities allowed the user to interact with and manipulate objects on the screen by moving and pointing the remote in various directions. The Wii Remote was the size of a traditional remote control, and it was "limited only by the game designer's imagination."[15] For example, in a game of tennis it served as the racket when the user swung his or her arm, while in a shooting game it served as the user's gun. Not only did the remote serve as a controller, but it also had a built-in speaker and a rumble feature for even greater tactile feedback and game involvement. Exhibit 3 shows the Wii and Wii Remote.

The second part of the Wii Remote innovation was the Wii Nunchuk. The Nunchuk was designed to perfectly fit the user's hand, and it connected to the remote at its expansion port. The Nunchuk had the same motion-sensing capabilities that the remote had, but it also had an analog stick to help the user move his or her characters. The ambidextrous nature of the Wii controllers was something seldom seen in other game controllers; the Wii controllers permitted the user to hold the remote and Nunchuk whichever way felt most comfortable.[16] In addition to the analog stick, the Nunchuk had two buttons that gave the user quick access to other game functions. Thus, the Nunchuk offered some of the benefits of a standard game controller coupled

EXHIBIT 3 Wii Console and Remote

Jill Braaten/McGraw-Hill Education

EXHIBIT 4 Wii U GamePad Controller

Stefano Tinti/Shutterstock

with the high-technology motion sensors of the remote. Users could hold a Nunchuk in one hand and the Wii Remote in the other while playing the Wii Sports boxing game and be transported into the boxing ring with on-screen opponents. The game controls were intuitive for jabs and punches. (However, a missed block did not hurt as much as if one were really in the boxing ring.)

While the Wii U was still compatible with the original Wii controllers, Nintendo revamped the controller usability when designing the Wii U. The new GamePad sold with the Wii U allowed the user to be more in touch with the game and provided more depth by offering multi-perspective capabilities on the Pad's screen. While using the TV display, players could now multitask within a game by using a variety of functions on their controller and could even play using solely the GamePad, with no TV display necessary. With the game console turned on, players had the option of using the GamePad as their main viewing screen, without the need for a TV monitor display (see Exhibit 4).

Nintendo Switch Features

Nintendo Switch came with a portable game console with a built-in screen, a pair of Joy-Con controllers, Joy-Con Straps, a Joy-Con grip, and a Nintendo Switch dock. The controllers' straps were detachable from the grip to be used with the portable screen to turn the Switch into a portable video game. The 6.2-inch detachable screen console came with a standard USB plug for charging. Along with the traditional method of playing games by using buttons, the Joy-Cons could also be used for motion-sensitive games just like their predecessors. Nintendo also offered an additional controller called Nintendo Switch ProController, which could be bought separately at a price of $69.99; it had the same features as Joy-Con, but looked like a traditional gaming controller. This was not the first time Nintendo had surprised the market with such a new design. For instance, the company had done it in the past when it introduced motion-sensitive controllers. However, this time, in a way, Nintendo had combined the GamePad controller with the Wii U console to design the Switch. Gamers could play games by attaching the Nintendo Switch dock with the TV or could convert it into a portable handheld game by attaching the controller straps with the 6.2-inch high-definition screen (720p), which also included a kick-stand to be placed on a flat surface and multi-touch features for various compatible games to enhance the gaming experience. The gamers could also take a screenshot of the game they played using a capture button on the left Joy-Con, which users could then share with their friends or put on social media. Similar to the past Nintendo controllers, both Joy-Cons included the motion controls (see Exhibit 5).

Switch supported the Nintendo eShop, an online game store that could be used to download games from different publishers and developers. Switch also supported the games by third-party publishers including Electronic Arts, Activision, and Ubisoft, among others. The user interface of the Switch software was a UI design. The home screen displayed several different icons, including icons for featured games, settings, controllers, albums (screenshots, videos), Nintendo eShop, and options. Users could make different player profiles to sign in to maintain exclusive game progress similar to what most people do using their personal computers. The top right corner of the screen showed battery status along with the time.

Prior to Nintendo Switch, the company had introduced Amiibo figurines that depicted popular Nintendo characters, and each contained a wireless antenna and flash memory. They allowed consumers to include digital versions of their favorite characters in compatible video games. Nintendo's first round of Amiibo characters were Mario, Peach, Yoshi, Donkey Kong, Link, Fox, Samus, Wii Fit Trainer, Villager, Pikachu, Kirby, and Marth. By 2019, the company had introduced a number of new games for Nintendo Switch including The Legend of Zelda: Breadth of the Wild, Super Mario Maker 2, Pokémon Quest, and a few others. In March 2019, it released the updated version of its latest game, Yoshi's Crafted World.

EXHIBIT 5 Switch Console and Joy-Con Controller

Dmitry Loshkin/123RF

In the past, Nintendo had hoped to penetrate the segment and boost sales of its Wii U console and 3DS handheld in the process. However, in 2017, the company combined both Wii U console and 3DS into a single gaming platform that was Nintendo Switch. The results for the fiscal year ended December 31, 2018 show a very positive trend in global hardware sales for Nintendo Switch, which sold a total of 32.27 million units during this fiscal year.[17]

Demographics

According to Nintendo, one of the key differences between the Switch and competitors' systems was the broad audience that the Switch targeted. Many of the Switch games could be played by people of all ages and experience, and the Switch's Joy-Cons were easier to use than the complicated controllers of the Sony PlayStation 4 or Microsoft's Xbox One. Nintendo's TV commercials for the Switch showed people playing the Switch at home by connecting the game console to TV and outdoors by connecting the Joy-Cons with the portable screen. According to the company, the Switch offered something for both the advanced gamer and the person who had never played a video game before. The advanced gamer would enjoy the remote's unique features, whereas the novice gamer could use the remote as his or her hand and would not need elaborate instructions on how to play a new game straight out of the box.

Although the Nintendo games were easily played by a greater range of ages and featured improved graphics, the company's competitors Xbox and Sony were offering 4K resolutions, best in the market at the time. While Nintendo hoped to target people of all ages, it had long been seen as a system that made video games for children, as evident from its Mario, Zelda, and Donkey Kong series. However, despite the limitation of this reputation, the innovation and uniqueness of its game play were enough to lure the masses, and sales were excellent.

Success, of course, bred competition. Upon seeing the success of the movement-sensing Switch, Microsoft and Sony moved quickly to release competing systems. Microsoft released its Kinect for the Xbox, while Sony released the Move for the PlayStation. Both the Move and Kinect used camera systems for their motion detectors, but in different ways. Move's camera sensed the movement of the light-up Move controller, whereas Microsoft's Kinect sensor tracked skeletal motion, eliminating the need for a controller.[18] While it was inevitable that gamers would have their favorite of the bunch, the relevant point was that it didn't take long for Microsoft and Sony to catch up to Nintendo. They moved forward to the new generation(s) of gaming quickly, maintaining an even playing field among competitors for gamer interaction and motion detection.

In the Game Developers Conference (GDC) 2019, Nintendo, along with its other competitors, witnessed another player in the market—Google. Google unveiled Stadia, a cloud gaming service that streams games from the cloud to all types of devices including the Chrome browser, Chromecast, and pixel devices.

Gaining the Interest of Game Developers

As evident from the history of game consoles, game developers had tried to make games more and more complex with each new generation of systems. This meant that more money was invested in the production of each subsequent generation of games. Because game developers were spending more money on developing games, they were at great financial risk if games did not succeed. Thus, many developers felt more secure in simply creating sequels to existing games, which restrained innovation. The Switch's innovative controller, the Joy-Cons, now required a rethinking and reengineering of the human interface by game developers and programmers. Another issue with developing games for the Switch was that its graphics were not quite as good as those of the PlayStation 4 and Xbox One, and therefore game developers had to be more creative and develop special Switch editions of their games.

Many game developers used virtual-machine software in developing new games. It was believed that game developers could develop games for the Switch and then make them for other platforms on the basis of the same programming, thereby reducing production costs. However, while the Joy-Con distinguished itself from its competitors, it created a hurdle for developers. When developers created a game for the PlayStation, they could create the same game for the Xbox and vice versa. When developers created a game for the Switch, however, it required significant rework to deploy the title for the other platforms. Converting a title from the Xbox or PlayStation also required significant work to modify the game to incorporate code for the Joy-Con's special features.

While this uniqueness had served Nintendo well in the past, the Joy-Con's incompatibility with the likes of Microsoft and Sony limited the selection of games immediately available to the Nintendo Switch's audience. The selection of games had to be fulfilling enough to keep Nintendo's audience happy, without leaving them feeling like they were missing out on games available only on the other platforms.

The Competition

If the launch of Nintendo's Switch was a foray into the fierce competition among such existing models as Xbox One and PS4, Switch's competitors were offering many features that Nintendo did not. The price of $299 for the basic Switch included a portable game console with a built-in screen, a pair of Joy-Con controllers, Joy-Con Straps, a Joy-Con grip, and a Nintendo Switch dock. The price of the PlayStation 4 was also $299 (500 GB edition), and the new Xbox One was $229. At a base price of $299 the Switch was intended to compete with the upper echelon of the next generation of gaming consoles unlike the low-cost position of the original Wii. Apart from pricing, there were many differences among the performance specifications of Switch in comparison to its fiercest competitors (for examples, see Exhibits 6 and 7).

EXHIBIT 6 Game Systems Comparison, 2019

Feature	Switch	Xbox One	PS4
CPU: Cores	4x ARM Cortex A57	8x AMD Jaguar	8x AMD Jaguar
CPU: Clock speed	1,020MHz	1,750MHz	1,600MHz
CPU: Cores	256 Nvidia CUDA	768x AMD Shaders	1152 AMD shaders
CPU: Docked speed	768MHz	853MHz	800MHz
CPU: Undocked speed	307.2MHz	N/A	N/A
HDR	No	Yes (One S)	Yes
Memory	4GB	8GB	8GB
Storage	32GB flash (microSD-expandable)	500GB HDD	500GB HDD
Physical game formats	Game Card	Disc	Disc
USB ports	2x USB2, 1x USB3.0	3x USB 3.0	2x USB 3.1 (gen1)
Video output	HDMI	HDMI	HDMI (HDR supported)
Audio ports	None	Optical	Optical
Networking ports	None	Gigabit Ethernet	Gigabit Ethernet
Power consumption	Unknown	~125W	~140W

Source: Passingham, Michael. Nintendo Switch vs Xbox One and PS4 - How do they compare? Trusted Reviews, December 17, 2018.

EXHIBIT 7 Game Controllers Comparison, 2019

Feature	Joy-Con pair	Switch Pro	Xbox One	PS4	PS4 Move pair
Control buttons	18 touchscreen	18	17	17 touch	18
Analogue sticks	2	2	2	2	2
Vibration	Yes	Yes	Yes	Yes	Yes
Wireless	Yes	Yes	Yes	Yes	Yes
Battery capacity	525mAh (each)	1300mAh	N/A	1000mAh	1520mAh (each)
Battery life	20h (official)	40h (official)	Variable	~7h	~10h
Motion controls	Yes	Yes	No	Yes	Yes
IR camera	Yes	No	No	No	No
Removable batteries***	No	No	Yes	No	No
Play and charge	Yes*	Yes	Yes**	Yes	Yes
Headphone jack	No	No	Yes	Yes	No

*With optional Charge Grip

**Play-and-charge kit available

***Without voiding warranty

Source: Passingham, Michael. Nintendo Switch vs Xbox One and PS4 - How do they compare? Trusted Reviews, December 17, 2018.

Microsoft Xbox One

In 2019, Microsoft was investing in new services like Mixer—which blurs the line between watching and playing—and Game Pass, a new unlimited subscription service.[19] The company released Xbox One S and Xbox One X in August 2016 and November 2017, and investing aggressively in content, community and cloud services across every endpoint to expand usage and deepen engagement with gamers. The latest Xbox One X was available at two different prices: $150 for the 500-GB model and $399 for the 1-TB model, as of 2019.

One of the important features of the Xbox One was Xbox Live. This feature allowed individuals to play online against other users around the world. Thus, Microsoft had created a community of individuals who were able to communicate with one another by voice chats and play against each other in a video game. In 2019, Xbox live had 57 million monthly users. Another service offered by Xbox Live was the Xbox Live Marketplace, which enabled users to download movies, game trailers, game demos, and arcade games. It was estimated that more than 70 percent of connected Xbox users were downloading content from the Xbox Live Marketplace, totaling more than 8 million members.

Microsoft introduced Kinect for Xbox One in 2014, which was based around a webcam-style add-on peripheral for the Xbox One console. It enabled users to control and interact with the Xbox One using gestures and spoken commands, without the need to touch a game controller. Kinect allowed the Xbox One to see the user and act according to the user's motions and gestures. This took the concept of the Wii and pursued it to its natural culmination, making the user the game controller. Kinect used software technology that enabled advanced gesture recognition, facial recognition, and voice recognition. Some critics believed that the concept used by Kinect had potential far beyond games and might even become a new way of controlling computers of all kinds. It automatically identified who one player was and paused when the player left its vicinity, so it was not hard to imagine this ingenuity controlling all kinds of devices, such as a PC, smartphone, or tablet.[20] Microsoft also released Xbox One S following the release of Xbox One. The Xbox One S was more compact in design, lighter in weight, had slight performance and graphic improvement, and supported better HDMI connectivity options. However, these changes were not so significant that critics would count Xbox One S as a next generation Xbox.

Sony PlayStation 4

In April 2019, Sony unveiled the details of its upcoming console—PlayStation 5. PlayStation lead system architect Mark Cerny spoke about the PS4's successor. While mentioning that the next-gen is backwards-compatible, Cerny also revealed that it is not an all-digital device, and will accept physical discs.[21] The last console, PlayStation 4 was released in November 2013. As of 2019, it is available at two different prices in two variations: PlayStation 4 Pro was priced at $400 with 4K resolution, and PlayStation 4 was priced at $300 with Blu-ray video quality. The PS4 included 8 GB of GDDR5 memory, which enabled rapid performance. Also, a player could use the loading power of this memory to power down the PS4 mid-game and then later turn it back on and within seconds be playing again right where he or she left off. The PS4 supported Blu-ray discs, DVDs, and HDMI output, as well as analog and optical digital output. In comparison to the PS4, the next console is set to house an AMD chip that has a CPU based on the third-generation Ryzen. It will have eight cores of the seven-nanometer Zen 2 microchip. Although the console will support 8K, displaying at this resolution will be dependent on TVs catching up.

Sony launched the PlayStation Virtual Reality headset in October 2016 that was developed by Sony Interactive Entertainment. Although PlayStation VR had a price tag of $400, it was the only one of its kind at the time of release, hence the company was able to charge the high price. It was a step up in gaming technology as PlayStation VR could be used with PS4 console that could mirror the television screen in a virtual reality view for the user. PlayStation VR could be used with PS4 DualShock controllers as well as with the PlayStation Move. PlayStation VR had an OLED panel that supported a 5.7-inch display with a full high-definition resolution of 1080p. As of February 19, 2019, PlayStation had sold about 4.2 million units of PlayStation VR.[22]

PS4 also launched with the ability to stream games directly to the PS Vita, Sony's handheld gaming device. As with the Switch, this allowed users to play on the tablet controller through a wireless connection, without the use of a TV display. A number of games were released for the PS4 including Onimusha: Warlords, Resident Evil 2, Over Watch, Mass Effect: Andromeda, and Battlefield One, among others. Part of the PlayStation Network's success was the ability to play games online. This allowed individuals to play with other players located in other parts of the world. The PlayStation Network allowed users to download games, view movie and game trailers, send text messages, and chat with friends, and these capabilities were sure to continue. As of January 9, 2019, Sony had sold over 91.6 million units of PS4 worldwide.[23]

Mobile Gaming

Recently, another form of competition in the gaming industry had become widely available. Mobile devices such as smartphones and tablets allowed casual gamers the ability to download and play a wide variety of free or low-priced games. The games could be seamlessly downloaded to the handheld device. While the interactivity on these devices was limited by a lack of controls and features, the convenience and price were something that console makers were starting to notice. In the span of a decade, mobile gaming will have grown from the smallest segment in 2012 to a 100-billion-dollar industry in 2021.[24] Mobile gaming companies like Super Cell and Machine Zone have crossed the billion-dollar threshold in annual revenues. Although these companies charge little per purchase, the huge number of worldwide users enables them to collect enormous total revenues. The number of smartphone users has grown dramatically during last decade, which automatically grows the potential users for mobile gaming companies without having to sell game consoles. Just having a smartphone opens the option of thousands of games for mobile gamers at a single platform for a minimal price. The growing trend and popularity of mobile gaming is definitely posing competition for gaming companies like Nintendo, among others.

Google Stadia

Google Stadia is looming on the gaming horizon, and not just on mobile phones. After its announcement in the Game Developers Conference 2019, a lot of gamers are anticipating its arrival. Stadia could be great for gamers who cannot afford the latest hardware. One of the features of Stadia is that it will let players view a game clip from the creator on YouTube and then hit "play now" to instantly stream a playable version of the title to any device that can run a Chrome browser. Google says it expects to support up to 4K at 60 fps at launch over an Internet connection with around 30Mbps of bandwidth, and it is planning to support up to 8K resolutions and 120 fps in the future.[25] To power all of this cloud streaming, Google is leveraging its global infrastructure of data centers to ensure servers are as close to players around the world as possible—a key part of Stadia, as lower latency is a necessity to stream games effectively across the Internet.[26] If it catches on, Stadia could be a significant player in gaming.

The Future of Switch

While Sony and Microsoft envision long-term profits on software sales for PlayStation 4 and Xbox One, both companies experience losses producing their consoles. Among the three rivals, Nintendo is the only one earning a significant profit margin on each Switch unit sold.

Sony's and Microsoft's gaming consoles are commonly thought of as superior to Nintendo's, however, perhaps the Switch's smaller processing unit and hardware but simplicity and family-friendly appeal have assisted it to become profitable. These traits attract not only end users but game developers as well, allowing the Nintendo to have the largest selection of games compared with its competitors. Although there was not enough data about the number of games for Switch at the time of writing this case, historically, the number of its games indicated that Switch's predecessor Wii was obviously a successful system one that has drawn a good amount of interest from game developers and gamers around the world.

Microsoft and Sony have started to invade the casual family-user market, a key market for Nintendo, expanding beyond their former customer base of mainly hardcore gamers. The Xbox and PS4 are becoming more like entertainment hubs for families. Now, with the Switch on the market, and introductions from competitors expected soon, the competition seems to be better positioned to combat Nintendo. As motion-sensing gaming the undisputed next best thing to come out of the gaming industry is a capability that all competitors now possess, it is a matter of whose system is most desirable to the gaming population, and whether or not sales volume solely will determine which system comes out on top. With similar technology being widespread across the industry, it may prove to be more difficult for Nintendo to set itself apart and portray itself as the family favorite, as it did in its early days of the Wii.

But the three rivals have another competition—Google. With Stadia, Google has placed itself against the industry's largest players: Microsoft, Sony, and Nintendo. While unveiling the service, Google CEO Sundar Pichai said, "We are starting our next big challenge: building a game platform for everyone. I think we can change the game by bringing together the power and creativity of the entire community, people who love to play games, people who love to watch games, and people who love to build games."[27] Sony's CEO Kenichiro Yoshida and Xbox boss Phil Spencer have said that both companies are working on hardware for the future, which many believe will be released next year. But does Nintendo have to worry about the new competition yet?

There is some concern for Nintendo with high competition in the market. Nintendo is known to be a unique brand with games that are limited to its platform. Its Mario and Zelda fans might not be incentivized easily to switch to multiple devices. In February 2019, Nintendo Switch outsold Xbox One and PS4, and generated its highest February-month hardware dollar sales since February 2011.[28] Having sold up to 32.27 million units by December 2018, Nintendo said that they expect there are still plenty of people who have played Nintendo games in the past but have not yet purchased Nintendo Switch.[29] Will Nintendo be able to communicate the appeal of Nintendo Switch to consumers? or Is Nintendo counting on power of nostalgia to maintain its consumer base?

ENDNOTES

1. Bankhurst, A. 2019. Nintendo Switch sales pass 32 million. IGN, January 31, https://www.ign.com/articles/2019/01/31/nintendo-switch-sales-pass-32-million.
2. Gurwin, G. 2017. Strong early sales reportedly making Nintendo double its Switch production. Digital trends, March 17, http://www.digitaltrends.com/gaming/nintendo-reportedly-doubles-switch-production/.
3. Nintendo, 2017. Nintendo Switch Ushers in a New Era of Console Gaming on the Go. Press Release found on Business Wire, March 3, https://www.businesswire.com/news/home/20170303005199/en/Nintendo-Switch-Ushers-New-Era-Console-Gaming.
4. Kohler, C. 2017. Nintendo's Boss Promises the Switch Won't Have the NES Classic's Supply Issues. Wired, January, 13, https://www.wired.com/2017/01/reggie-fils-aime-nintendo-interview/
5. Mochizuki, T. 2017. Nintendo to Double Production of Switch Console. *The Wall Street Journal*, March 17, https://www.wsj.com/articles/nintendo-to-double-production-of-switch-console-1489728545

6. Ba-Oh, J. 2013. Industry folk comment on Nintendo Wii U potential new or next generation? January 1, www.cubed3.com/news/17809/1/industry-folk-comment-on-wii-u-potential.html.
7. Nintendo. 2008. Annual report, March 31.
8. Nintendo. https://www.nintendo.com/corp/history.jsp
9. Nintendo. 2008. Annual report, March 31.
10. Bacani, C. and M. Mutsuko. 1997. Nintendo's new 64-bit platform sets off a scramble for market share. *AsiaWeek*, April 18, www.asiaweek.com/asiaweek/97/0418/cs1.html; GamePro. 2005. Biggest blunders. May: 45.
11. Gurwin, G. 2019. PlayStation 6 rumors: Everything you need to know. Digital Trends, April 17, https://www.digitaltrends.com/gaming/ps5-release-date-specs-price-news/.
12. Morris, C. 2006. Nintendo goes Wii . . . . *CNNMoney.com*, April 27, money.cnn.com/2006/04/27/commentary/game_over/nintendo/index.htm.
13. Surette, T. 2006. Nintendo exec talks Wii online, marketing. *GameSpot.com*, August 17, www.cnet.com.au/games/wii/0,239036428,240091920,00.htm.
14. Nintendo. 2006. Annual report.
15. Nintendo. wii.nintendo.com/controller.jsp.
16. Ibid.
17. Nintendo Website. 2018. Dedicated video game sales units. https://www.nintendo.co.jp/ir/en/finance/hard_soft/.
18. Greenwald, W. 2010. Kinect vs. PlayStation Move vs. Wii: Motion-control showdown. *PC Magazine*, November 6, www.pcmag.com/article2/0,2817,2372244,00.asp.
19. Microsoft. 2018. Annual Report.
20. Schiesel, S. 2010. A real threat now faces the Nintendo Wii. *New York Times*, December 2, www.nytimes.com/2010/12/03/technology/personaltech/03KINECT.html.
21. Hussain, T. 2019. PlayStation 5 details revealed: Specs, PS5 PSVR support, PS4 backwards compatibility, and more. Gamespot, April 23, https://www.gamespot.com/articles/playstation-5-details-revealed-specs-ps5-psvr-supp/1100-6466281/.
22. Grubb, J. 2019. Sony has sold 4.2 million PlayStation VR headsets. Venturbeat, March 25, https://venturebeat.com/2019/03/25/playstation-vr-sales/.
23. Kuchera, B. 2019. With 91.6M PS4s sold, Sony continues dominating console generation. Polygon, January 8, https://www.polygon.com/2019/1/8/18173711/ps4-hardware-sales-ces-2019.
24. Wijman, T. 2018. Mobile revenues account for more than 50% of the global games market as it reaches $137.9 billion in 2018. Newzoo, April 30, https://newzoo.com/insights/articles/global-games-market-reaches-137-9-billion-in-2018-mobile-games-take-half/.
25. Warren, T. 2019. Google unveils Stadia cloud gaming service, launches in 2019. The Verge, March 19, https://www.theverge.com/2019/3/19/18271702/google-stadia-cloud-gaming-service-announcement-gdc-2019.
26. Ibid.
27. Clark, P.A. 2019. Stadia, Google's big push into video games, could change everything about how we play. *Time*, March 19, http://time.com/5554601/google-stadia-video-games/.
28. Grubb, J. 2019. Nintendo Switch outsold Xbox One and PS4 in February 2019. Venture Beat, March 19, https://venturebeat.com/2019/03/19/switch-outsells-xbox-ps4/.
29. Nintendo Co., Ltd. 2019. Six Months Financial Results Briefing for Fiscal Year Ending March 2019.

CASE 21

SAMSUNG ELECTRONICS 2019*

In February 2019, Samsung Electronics celebrated the 10th anniversary of its introduction of the Galaxy S line of smartphones by introducing several new models. The Galaxy S10 models ranged in sizes and price from a more compact model with a 5.8-inch display to a full-size model with a 6.4-inch one. It even launched a souped-up model with a 6.7-inch screen that featured 5G technology. These new models also feature a "Infinity-O display," which cuts a hole for the front camera in the upper right corner to allow the display to maximize the entire front of the phone.

These anniversary models capped a period of two years during which Samsung Electronics had to cope with the conviction of its de facto leader, Lee Jae-yong, on charges of bribing South Korea's former president. Lee has been providing broad direction to the firm since his father, Lee Kun-hee, became incapacitated after suffering a heart attack in 2014. These troubles with its leadership have not diminished Samsung's status as an innovative–and highly profitable–powerhouse in the technology world (see Exhibits 1 and 2). It has gained in stature as the world's largest maker of memory chips, smartphones, and televisions among other electronic products (see Exhibit 3).

But the removal of Lee came at a tough time for Samsung, which has been seeking new avenues for growth as sales of its market-leading smartphones seem to be slowing down. A few months later, Samsung's chairman of the board, Kwon Oh-hyun, shocked everyone in the firm by suddenly announcing his resignation. Kwon claimed that the firm need to turn to a younger generation of leaders who could search for new growth engines by studying future trends. "I believe the time has now for the firm to start anew with a new spirit and young leadership" he said.[1] This led the firm to shake up its senior ranks in order to address concerns about a leadership vacuum. It replaced all three of its co-chief executives that were heading its main business lines–mobile, electronics components, and consumer electronics.

* Case prepared by Jamal Shamsie, Michigan State University, with the assistance of Professor Alan B. Eisner, Pace University. Material has been drawn from published sources to be used for purposes of class discussion.
Copyright © 2019 Jamal Shamsie and Alan B. Eisner.

EXHIBIT 1 Income Statement (billions of KRW)

	Years Ending December 31					
	2018	2017	2016	2015	2014	2013
Revenue	243,771	239,575	201,866	200,653	206,206	228,693
Gross Profit	111,377	110,284	81,589	77,171	77,927	90,996
Operating Profit	61,159	56,195	30,713	25,960	27,875	38,364
Net Income	43,890	41,344	22,415	18,694	23,082	29,821

Source: Samsung Financial Statements (2013–2018).

EXHIBIT 2 Balance Sheet (billions of KRW)

	Years Ending December 31					
	2018	2017	2016	2015	2014	2013
Total Assets	339,357	301,752	262,174	242,179	230,422	214,075
Total Liabilities	91,604	87,260	69,211	63,119	62,334	64,059
Total Shareholders Equity	240,068	207,213	186,424	172,876	162,181	144,442

Source: Samsung Financial Statements (2013–2018).

EXHIBIT 3 Smartphone Sales Worldwide

	Market Shares		
	2018	2017	2016
Samsung	19.0%	20.9%	18.1%
Apple	13.4%	14.0%	18.3%
Huawei	13.0%	9.8%	10.6%
Xiaomi	7.9%	5.8%	3.6%
OPPO	7.6%	7.3%	7.3%
Others	39.1%	42.2%	41.8%

Source: Gartner, 2019; Statista 2017.

EXHIBIT 4 Revenue by Division (trillions KRW)

Business Division	2018	2017	2016
Semiconductor	86.3	74.3	51.2
Display Panel	32.5	34.5	26.9
Consumer Electronics	42.1	44.6	45.1
IT & Mobile Communication	100.7	106.7	100.3

Source: Samsung Electronics Announces Fourth Quarter and FY 2018 Results. Samsung, January 31, 2019.

Everyone at Samsung has been hoping these new appointments will bring fresh blood in order to help revitalize the firm. Analysts claim that the firm faces strong pressures because of its heavy reliance on competing with its hardware while other competitors, ranging from Apple to Xiaomi, offer software and Internet services that set their products apart from all others because it runs only on their devices. Samsung did introduce its own operating system, Tizen, but this is unlikely to challenge existing systems such as Google's Android.

Executives at Samsung have claimed that the firm's strength lies in the diverse line of its products that include televisions, cameras, laptops, and even washing machines. Although smartphones have accounted for as much as two-thirds of their profits, they can also increase their revenues from their other offerings (see Exhibit 4). Furthermore, unlike their rivals, Samsung makes most of their own components that allow it to offer better products with lower costs. They can generate profits even if profit margins on some of these products continue to decline.

Discarding a Failing Strategy

Although Samsung chairman Lee Kun-hee had called for a shift in the firm's strategy, the transformation could not have been possible without the ceaseless efforts of Yun Jong Yong, who was appointed to the position of president and CEO in 1996. When Yun took charge, Samsung was still making most of its profits from lower-priced appliances that consumers were likely to pick up if they could not afford a higher-priced brand such as Sony or Mitsubishi. It had also become an established low cost supplier of various components to such larger and better-known manufacturers around the world.

Although they were making profits, Yun was concerned about the future prospects of a firm that was relying on a strategy of price competition with products based on technologies that had been developed by other firms. The success of this strategy was tied to the ability of Samsung to continually scout for locations that would allow it to keep its manufacturing costs down. At the same time, it would need to keep generating sufficient orders to maintain a high volume of production. In particular, he was concerned about the growing competition that the firm was likely to face from the many low-cost producers that were springing up in other countries such as China.

Yun's concerns were well founded. Within a year of his takeover, Samsung was facing serious financial problems that threatened its very survival. The company was left with huge debt as an economic crisis engulfed most of Asia in 1997, leading to a drop in demand and a crash in the prices of many electronic goods. In the face of such a deteriorating environment, Samsung continued to push for maintaining its production and sales records even as much of its output was ending up unsold in warehouses.

By July 1998, Samsung Electronics was losing millions of dollars each month. "If we continued, we would have gone belly-up within three or four years" Yun recalled.[2] He knew that he had to make some drastic moves in order to turn things around. Yun locked himself in hotel room for an entire day with nine other senior managers to try and find a way out. They all wrote resignation letters and pledged to resign if they failed.

After much deliberation, Yun and his management team decided to take several steps to try and push Samsung out of its precarious financial position. To start, they decided to lay off about 30,000 employees, representing well over a third of its entire workforce. They also closed down many of Samsung's factories for two months so that they could get rid of its large inventory. Finally, they sold off about $2 billion worth of businesses like pagers and electric coffeemakers perceived to be of marginal significance for the firm's future.

Developing a Premium Brand

Having managed to stem the losses, Yun decided to move Samsung away from its strategy of competition based largely on the lower price of its offerings. Consequently, he began to push the firm to develop its own products rather than to copy those that other firms had developed. In particular, Yun placed considerable emphasis on the development of products that would impress consumers with their attractive designs and their advanced technology. By focusing on such products, Yun hoped that he could develop

Samsung into a premium brand that would allow him to charge higher prices.

In order to achieve this, Yun had to reorient the firm and help it to develop new capabilities. He recruited new managers and engineers, many of whom had developed considerable experience in the United States. Once they had been recruited, Yun got them into shape by putting them through a four-week boot camp that consisted of martial drills at the crack of dawn and mountain hikes that would last all day. To create incentives for this new talent, Yun discarded Samsung's rigid seniority-based system and replaced it with a merit-based system for advancement.

As a result of these efforts, Samsung began to start launching an array of products that were designed to make a big impression on consumers. These included the largest flat-panel televisions, cell phones with a variety of features such as cameras and PDAs, ever-thinner notebook computers, and speedier and richer semiconductors. The firm calls them "wow products" and they are designed to elevate Samsung in the same way the Trinitron television and the Walkman helped to plant Sony in the minds of consumers.

Finally, to help Samsung change its image among consumers, Yun hired a marketing whiz, Eric Kim, who worked hard to create a more upscale image of the firm and its products. Kim moved Samsung's advertising away from 55 different advertising agencies around the world and placed them with one firm—Madison Avenues' Foote, Cone & Belding Worldwide—in order to create a consistent global brand image for its products. He also begun to pull Samsung out of big discount chains like Walmart and Kmart and place more of its products into more upscale specialty stores such as Best Buy and Circuit City.

Yun also began a practice of working closely with retailers to get more information about the specific needs of prospective consumers. Samsung teamed up with Best Buy to create the Samsung Experience Shop, a store-within-a-store that allows customers to test the company's newest products as well as receive training in mobile products they already own. This has allowed them to better understand existing markets and innovating inside them. "We get most of our ideas from the market," said Kim Hyun-Suk, an executive vice president at Samsung.[3]

Speeding Up New Product Development

Yun also took many steps to speed up Samsung's new product development process. He was well aware that he could only maintain the higher margins as long as his firm kept introducing new products into the market well ahead of its established rivals. Samsung managers who have worked for big competitors say they have to go through far fewer layers of bureaucracy than they had in the past to win approval for new products, budgets, and marketing plans, speeding up their ability to seize opportunities.

Apart from reducing the bureaucratic obstacles, Yun was able to take advantage of the emerging shift to digital technologies. He made heavy investments into key technologies ranging from semiconductors to LCD displays that could allow Samsung to push out a wide variety of revolutionary digital products. Samsung has continuously invested more in research and development than any of its rivals—almost $15 billion by 2018. It has a assembled a large force of designers and engineers that work in several research centers spread all around the world. More recently, Samsung has started a C-Lab at its headquarters—an in-house incubation center that encourages employees to build and develop their own ideas for growing a business.

Yun also forced its own units to compete with outsiders in order to speed up the process for developing innovative new products. In the liquid-crystal-display business, for example, Samsung bought half of its color filters from Sumitomo Chemical Company of Japan and sourced the other half internally, pitting the two teams against each other. "They really press these departments to compete," said Sumitomo President Hiromasa Yonekura.[4] As a result of these steps, Samsung claims that it has been able to reduce the time that it takes to go from new product concept to rollout to as little as five months, compared to over a year that it used to take the firm in 2000.

In large part, this has resulted from the effort of the firm's top managers, engineers, and designers who work relentlessly in the five-story VIP center nestled amid the firm's industrial complex in Suwon. They work day and night in the center, which includes dormitories and showers for brief rests to work out any problems that may hold back a product launch. This allows the firm to get its products to move quickly to manufacturing with minimal problems and at the lowest possible cost. Kyunghan Jung, a senior manager of the center explained: "Seventy to eighty percent of quality, cost, and delivery time is determined in the initial stages of product development."[5]

The speedier development process has allowed Samsung to introduce the first voice-activated phones, handsets with MP3 players, and digital camera phones that send photos over a global system for mobile communications networks. As an example of the firm's speed and agility, Charles Golvin of Forrester Research talked about its ability to create four different specifications of its Galaxy S smartphone for four varying wirelesss network types around the world and deliver them simultaneously. "They've had a long history of responding to market trends with a lot of alacrity," he remarked.[6]

Perfecting a Design Process

As Yun was building the Samsung brand, he was already trying to position the firm to compete with all others on the basis of the irresistible design of its wide range of products ranging from home appliances to handheld computers to flat-screen televisions that, eventually, would all be linked to each other. In fact, the firm does seem to be well placed to develop attractive gadgets that straddle traditional technology categories. "We have to combine computers, consumer electronics, and communications as Koreans mix their rice with vegetables and meats," said Dae Je Chin, the head of Samsung's digital media division.[7]

Although Samsung tries to pack its products with various attractive features, it draws on the knowledge of over 1,500 designers with backgrounds in disciplines as diverse as psychology, sociology, economics, and engineering. These designers in turn draw on information that is collected by over 60,000 staff members working in 35 research centers across the globe in cities such as San Francisco, London, Tokyo, Mumbai, and Shanghai. Inside these centers, designers observe the way that consumers actually use various products. The wide Galaxy Note phone, for example, resulted from the responses of focus groups who wanted a device that was good for handwriting, drawing, and sharing notes. Asian consumers said that they found it easier to write characters on a device using a pen than typing on a keyboard.

"The research process is unimaginable," said Chang Donghoon, an executive vice president of Samsung who has led the company's design efforts. "We go through all avenues to make sure we read the trends correctly."[8] Samsung has therefore been sending its growing group of designers to various locations to spend a few months at fashion houses, furniture designers, and cosmetic specialists to stay current with trends in other industries. Designers of the latest Galaxy smartphone said they drew inspiration from trips to ruins in Cambodia, vistas in Helsinki, a Salvador Dali art exhibit in London, and even a balloon ride in Africa.

Furthermore, Samsung appointed designers to management positions in order to make sure that they can get their ideas to top executives. In 2015, the firm managed to recruit Lee Don-Tae, who had been a top executive at a leading UK design agency. He joined Chang Don-Hoon, who was given charge of the firm's design strategy team, overseeing the design of products across all of the product lines. In the fall of 2014, Samsung unveiled a slick design website to shore up its self-proclaimed status as a design powerhouse. "Samsung strives to consistently lead the consumer electronics industry in product design and engineering innovation," an executive said.[9] As a result of these efforts, Samsung has managed to win several hundred design awards over the last years. In 2018 alone, the firm won 49 IDEA Design Awards, the most it has won in a single year thus far.[10]

Samsung has also been relying on the attractiveness of its products to make them the center piece of a digital home. In a showroom in the lobby of its headquarters in Seoul, the firm shows off many of its latest offerings ranging from tablet computers to digital cameras. Visitors can put on goggles to watch characters jump out on 3-D televisions or shuffle their feet on an interactive LED floor. Roger Entner, a wireless industry analyst at Neilson said about Samsung's efforts: "With its resources and experience, it's trying to capitalize on the emergence of smart connected devices. The question is, 'Can they be a cutting-edge trendsetter like Apple?'"[11]

Creating a Sustainable Model?

Samsung has been trying to deal with the setback that its de facto leader's arrest may have caused to its efforts to reassert its reputation for building innovative products. Although there are some doubts about its prospects for continued growth, the firm is confident in its savvy investments in chipmaking over the years. By 2017, Samsung had surpassed Intel to become the leading producer of semiconductors in the world.[12] This leadership will allow it to move into new growth areas such as artificial intelligence, autonomous driving, and growing Internet-based applications. "Samsung can actually advance into new areas leveraging its strength in the existing chip business, as we embrace a new era where memory capacity will be really important," said Marcello Ahn, a fund manager at Quad Investment.[13]

In the meantime, Samsung continues to invest into its existing businesses, such as its market-leading smartphone business. It has announced its plans to launch a smartphone with a foldable screen that folds like a book and opens to tablet size. The phone, whose screen would expand to 7.3 inches when opened, is expected to be launched in September 2019.[14] The hope is that the new offering will help Samsung compete with the growth of sales from lower-cost Chinese rivals. It could also lift sales, pushing consumers away from the recent trend of holding on to their handsets for longer periods of time.

At the same time, Samsung has been building a reputation for its efforts to advance the push for more sustainability. The firm has been making all of its products more energy efficient, allowing it to earn awards for some of its products. Its latest initiative, Galaxy Upcycling, allows consumers to transform the Galaxy phones that they no longer need into smart devices such as LCTVs, gaming consoles, and personal computers. This new approach is being gradually expanded to reach more and more consumers around the world.

Of all the new areas for growth of its chipmaking business, Samsung is most optimistic about the push for autonomous driving. According to Peter Yu, an analyst with BNP Paribas: "Autonomous driving will require huge data processing power, and Samsung can provide essential components such as sensors, storage chips, cameras, and display."[15] But in spite of the opportunities that can arise from such new developments as autonomous driving, the firm does face competition from several existing and potential entrants. Analysts therefore believe that Samsung's success with its movement into these new growth areas is likely to depend on its ability to convert its expertise of one sort of mobile technology to others.

Change everything except your wife and children.

–Address to employees from Samsung chairman Lee Kun-hee to push for its transformation to a leading electronics brand

ENDNOTES

1. Harris B. and Song Jung-A. Samsung record profits mask looming crisis. *Financial Times,* October 14-15, 2017, p. 15.
2. Gibney, Jr, F. Samsung moves upmarket. *Time,* March 25, 2002, p. 49.
3. Chen, B.X. Samsung's strategy to brake Apple juggernaut. *New York Times,* February 11, 2013, p. B1.

4. Lewis, P. A perpetual crisis machine. *Fortune,* September 19, 2005, p. 65.
5. Edwards, C., Ihlwan, M., and P. Engardio. The Samsung way. *BusinessWeek,* June 16, 2003, p. 61.
6. Yu, R. Samsung cranks up creativity. *USA Today,* November 16, 2010, p. 4B.
7. Rocks, D. and M. Ihlwan. Samsung design. *BusinessWeek,* December 6, 2004, p. 90.
8. Chen, B.X. Samsung's strategy to brake Apple juggernaut. *New York Times,* February 11, 2013, p. B1.
9. Anonymous. 2008. Samsung Electronics gets 46 CES innovations awards for 2009. *Wireless News,* November 24.
10. Samsung News. 2018. Samsung Electronics wins 49 IDEA Design Awards. September 20. https://news.samsung.com/global/samsung-electronics-wins-49-idea-design-awards.
11. Yu, R. Samsung cranks up creativity. *USA Today,* November 16, 2010, p. 4B.
12. Gartner. 2019. Market share held by semiconductor vendors worldwide from 2008 to 2018 [Graph]. In *Statista*. April 11, Retrieved from https://www-statista-com.rlib.pace.edu/statistics/266143/global-market-share-of-leading-semiconductor-vendors/
13. Harris B. and Song Jung-A. Samsung record profits mask looming crisis. *Financial Times,* October 14-15, 2017, p. 15.
14. The Associated Press. 2019. Samsung folding phone is different but also almost $2,000. WTHR, February 20. https://www.wthr.com/article/samsung-folding-phone-different-also-almost-2000-1.
15. Harris B. and Song Jung-A. Samsung record profits mask looming crisis. *Financial Times,* October 14-15, 2017, p. 15.

CASE 22

EMIRATES AIRLINE*

In 2019, Emirates Airline was rethinking its growth strategy that had propelled it from a small start-up to one of the world's biggest carriers measured by international passenger mileage. Started in 1985, the airline deviated from the strategy of most other airlines to use its position between the United States, Europe, Africa, and Asia to connect flights between distant pairs of cities such as New York and Shanghai or London and Nairobi. Tim Clark, the firm's president referred to these as "strange city pairs." No airline has grown like Emirates, whose expansion qualifies it to claim the crown of the freewheeling sultan of the skies.

Its strategy of flying large numbers of passengers around the would have been difficult without the introduction of Boeing 777 long-range planes and Airbus A380 superjumbos. In particular, Emirates has managed over the years to radically redraw the map of the world, transferring the hub of international travel from Europe to the Middle East. Dubai, the hub of Emirates, which currently handles over 80 million passengers each year, has become the world's busiest airport for international passengers. A new terminal, the largest in the world, was recently built at a cost of $4.5 billion just to accommodate the almost 265 Emirates aircraft that fly out to 155 destinations around the world (see Exhibit 1).[1]

Recent developments, however, such as the drop in oil prices and the growth in terrorist attacks have led to a decline in demand. Many companies, particularly in the Middle East, have been reducing travel for their employees, reducing the premium revenue that Emirates has been generating from first- and business-class passengers. Similarly, growing fears about terrorism has led passengers to cut back on international travel and to reduce connecting through the

* Case prepared by Jamal Shamsie, Michigan State University, with the assistance of Professor Alan B. Eisner, Pace University. Material has been drawn from published sources to be used for purposes of class discussion. Copyright © 2019 Jamal Shamsie and Alan B. Eisner.

EXHIBIT 1 Top Global Airlines

	Started	Main Hub	Fleet	Destinations
SINGAPORE	1972	Singapore	121	64
CATHAY PACIFIC	1946	Hong Kong	174	232
EMIRATES	1985	Dubai	265	155
THAI	1960	Bangkok	81	62
ASIANA	1988	Seoul	82	62
ETIHAD	2003	Abu Dhabi	110	91
EVA	1989	Taipei	79	63
AIR NEW ZEALAND	1940	Auckland	113	48
GARUDA	1949	Jakarta	90	102
QATAR	1994	Doha	146	146
ANA	1952	Tokyo	211	73
SOUTH AFRICAN	1934	Johannesburg	60	42
VIRGIN ATLANTIC	1984	London	40	30
QANTAS	1920	Sydney	137	42
LUFTHANSA	1953	Frankfurt	288	193

There are several rankings of the world's airlines, but a few have consistently been rated highest in service over the last five years. These are listed in no particular order.

Source: Skytrax.

EXHIBIT 2 Performance Highlights

Year Ended, 31 March	Passengers Flown (thousands)	Operating Profit or Loss (AEDm)
2019	58,601	2,647
2018	58,485	4,086
2017	56,076	2,435
2016	51,853	8,330
2015	49,292	5,893
2014	44,537	3,254
2013	39,391	2,839
2012	33,981	1,813
2011	31,422	5,443
2010	27,454	3,565
2009	22,731	2,278
2008	21,229	4,451

Source: Emirates Airline.

Middle East. The availability of Boeing's 787 long-range planes has also added to the problem by allowing passengers to fly directly from Europe to Asia.

Furthermore, the largest U.S. airlines alleged that Emirates, like others such as Etihad and Qatar, have received subsidies from their governments. It has, according to their claims, provided Emirates with an unfair advantage. Tim Clark, Emirates' president, responded to the charges in the report by insisting that his carrier has never received government subsidies or obtained free or cheap fuel. The airline has always disclosed its finances, used international auditors, and posted regular quarterly profits (see Exhibits 2 to 6). "We are confident that any allegation that Emirates has been subsidized is totally without grounds," Clark declared.[2] The dispute was finally settled with a deal between the United States and U.A.E. in May 2018.

In fact, Emirates claims that it has worked hard to achieve its leading position by offering onboard amenities, like bars and showers on its aircraft, which other carriers find frivolous (see Exhibit 7). Beyond this, it points to the high standards of service from its crew that speak many languages and come from many countries. Emirates service manager, Terry Daly, says that he uses a quote as an inspiring light: "I may not remember exactly what you said. I may not remember exactly what you did. I will always remember exactly how you made me feel."[3]

Launching a Dream

The roots of Emirates can be traced back to Gulf Air, which was a formidable airline owned by the governments of Bahrain, Abu Dhabi, Qatar, and Oman. In the early 1980s, the young sheikh of Dubai, Sheikh Mohammed bin Rashid al Maktoum, was upset by the decision of Gulf Air to cut flights into and out of Dubai. He responded by resolving to start his own airline that would help build Dubai into a center of business and tourism, given the emirates' lack of significant oil resources.

The sheikh recruited British Airways veteran Sir Maurice Flanagan to lay the groundwork for the new airline, which he bankrolled with $10 million in royal funding. He placed a member of his royal family, Sheikh Ahmed bin Saeed al Maktoum, to the top post. Just 26 years old, Ahmed bin Saeed had just graduated from the University of Denver in

EXHIBIT 3 Income Statement (in millions AED)

	Consolidated Income Statement for the year ended 31 March			
	2019	**2018**	**2017**	**2016**
Revenue	96,040	91,225	83,832	83,500
Other operating income	1,867	1,097	1,251	1,544
Operating costs	(95,260)	(88,236)	(82,648)	(76,714)
Operating profit	**2,647**	**4,086**	**2,435**	**8,330**
Finance income	497	375	281	220
Finance costs	(2,173)	(1,593)	(1,383)	(1,329)
Share of results of investments accounted for using the equity method	116	155	157	142
Profit before income tax	**1,087**	**3,023**	**1,490**	**7,363**
Income tax expense	(57)	(44)	(40)	(45)
Profit for the year	**1,030**	**2,979**	**1,450**	**7,318**
Profit attributable to non-controlling interests	159	183	200	193
Profit attributable to Emirates' owner	**871**	**2,796**	**1,250**	**7,125**

Source: Emirates Airline.

EXHIBIT 4 Balance Sheet (in millions of United Arab Emirates Dirham)

	2019	2018	2017	2016
ASSETS				
Non-current assets				
Property, plant and equipment	89,431	85,951	86,898	82,836
Intangible assets	1,574	1,496	1,441	1,317
Investments accounted for using the equity method	683	662	676	522
Advance lease rentals	4,619	5,065	4,421	2,580
Loans and other receivables	139	172	238	494
Derivative financial instruments	24	60	38	-
Deferred income tax asset	13	11	10	3
Total non-current assets	**96,483**	**93,417**	**93,722**	**87,752**
Current assets				
Inventories	2,525	2,387	2,238	2,106
Trade and other receivables	11,342	11,354	9,922	9,321
Derivative financial instruments	11	9	8	12
Short-term bank deposits	11,974	14,745	6,706	7,823
Cash and cash equivalents	5,063	5,675	8,962	12,165
Total current assets	**30,915**	**34,170**	**27,836**	**31,427**
Total assets	**127,398**	**127,587**	**121,558**	**119,179**
EQUITY AND LIABILITIES				
Capital and reserves				
Capital	801	801	801	801
Other reserves	(60)	15	(141)	
Retained earnings	36,408	35,638	33,848	32,287
Attributable to Emirates' Owner	**37,149**	**36,454**	**34,508**	**31,909**
Non-controlling interests	**594**	**592**	**586**	**496**
Total equity	**37,743**	**37,046**	**35,094**	**32,405**
Non-current liabilities				
Trade and other payables	155	123	683	513
Borrowings and lease liabilities	45,433	42,071	40,171	40,845
Deferred revenue	–	1,063	979	1,596
Deferred credits	2,437	2,621	2,227	1,090
Derivative financial instruments	81	26	192	440
Provisions	4,081	4,067	3,825	3,762
Deferred income tax liability	3	4	5	4
Total non-current liabilities	**52,190**	**49,975**	**48,082**	**48,250**
Current liabilities				
Trade and other payables	26,795	29,303	25,193	27,037
Income tax liabilities	35	18	19	35
Borrowings and lease liabilities	7,606	9,030	10,831	9,260

	2019	2018	2017	2016
Deferred revenue	2,009	1,180	1,486	1,316
Deferred credits	322	313	253	139
Derivative financial instruments	20	35	3	737
Provisions	678	687	597	-
Total current liabilities	**37,465**	**40,566**	**38,382**	**38,524**
Total liabilities	**89,655**	**90,541**	**86,464**	**86,774**
Total equity and liabilities	**127,398**	**127,587**	**121,558**	**119,179**

Source: Emirates Airline.

EXHIBIT 5 Revenue Breakdown (in millions AED)

	2019	2018
Passenger	78,562	73,963
Cargo	13,056	12,439
Consumer Goods	1,591	1,625
Food and Beverages	673	680
Hotel Operations	669	746
Catering Operations	654	677
Excess Baggage	444	433
Others	391	662
Total Revenue	**96,040**	**91,225**

Source: The Emirates Group, Annual Report 2017-2018.

EXHIBIT 6 Operating Costs (in millions AED)

	2019	2018
Jet Fuel	30,768	25,715
Employee (incl. retirement benefit obligations)	12,623	13,080
Aircraft operating leases	11,964	11,691
Depreciation and amortization	9,680	9,193
Sales and Marketing	6,137	6,404
Handling	5,544	5,335
In-flight catering and operating	3,519	3,323
Overflying	2,761	2,891
Facilities and IT related costs	2,626	2,485
Aircraft maintenance	2,413	2,364
Landing and parking	2,231	2,153
Cost of goods sold	1,588	1,575
Crew layover	1,094	1,125
Foreign exchange loss – net	333	-
Corporate overheads	1,979	1,902
Total operating costs	**95,260**	**88,236**

Source: The Emirates Group, Annual Report 2017-2018.

the United States. Since he had not held a job before, the young Sheikh looked to Flanagan in order to figure out how to run the airline.

However, the speculator growth of Emirates can be attributed to Sir Tim Clark, who was handed the critical task of route planning. He recognized that about two-thirds of the world's population was within eight hours of Dubai, but the firm lacked the aircraft to take advantage of its location. This began to change with the arrival of more advanced aircraft, beginning with the introduction of Boeing 777 in 1996 to the Airbus A380 in 2008. The long range of these aircraft allowed Emirates to develop routes that could link any two points in the world with one stop in Dubai.

From serving 12 destinations in 1988, Emirates was able to expand at an alarming rate, particularly after it started adding Boeing 777s to its fleet after 1996. The carrier continued to grow even through the recession that began in 2008, taking possession of more new aircraft than any other competitor. "We operated normally. We put on more aircraft. We carried more passengers," said Mohammed H. Mattar, senior vice president of the carrier's airport services.[4]

EXHIBIT 7 Service For Premium Passengers On Emirates A380

- Offer 4,000 channels of in-seat entertainment
- Offer unlimited free wi-fi throughout the flight
- Serve Cuvee Dom Perignon, 2000 champagne
- Serve Iranian caviar
- Serve gourmet cuisine prepared by chefs of 47 nationalities
- Offer largest selection of premium wines
- Use bone china by Royal Doulton
- Use specially made cutlery by British design house Robert Welch
- Provide Bulgari-designed amenity kits
- Feature a stand-up bar
- Offer two on-board walnut and marble design showers*

*Only for first-class passengers.

Source: Emirates Airline.

Providing the Ultimate Experience

Emirates strives to provide the best possible experience to its passengers in all sections of its aircraft. It was the first airline to offer in-flight viewing in the back of every seat. "That seems pretty normal for long haul airlines now, but it wasn't then," said Terry Daly, who is in charge of service at the carrier.[5] A caravan of flight attendants, who are fluent in a dozen languages, pass up and down the aisles, providing service with a smile. Daly, who maintains the highest standards for all in-flight services, is known for having once fired eight service supervisors on a single day when he discovered that the flight attendants they had supervised deviated from his precise instructions on how to respond to requests from passengers.

From its start, Emirates has also been known for the quality and selection of food that the airline provides, even to passengers in the back of the aircraft. The catering division is the world's biggest, a multi-floor maze of monorails and cameras, vast warehouses of wines and liquors, multinational chefs slaving over steaming pans, kettles, grills, stretching into eternity, along with the latest in robotics, all of which delivers 180,000 meal trays to Emirates planes each day. "It's about making sure the culinary offering is absolutely first class across the airplane," said Daly.[6]

But Emirates has always tried to push further and further on the service and amenities that it provides to its premium class passengers. Included with a business class ticket is a limousine ride to and from the airport, personal assistance with the check-in process, and use of one its 30 worldwide lounges. One of 600 multinational and multilingual members of a welcome team called Marhaba–Arabic for welcome–help all first- and business-class passengers clear all formalities upon departure and upon arrival.

Over the years, as Emirates has moved to larger and larger aircraft, it has found ways to enhance the experience of its premium passengers during flight. The airline had pioneered the concept of a suite in first class with its launch of A340 back in 2003. With its 50 A380s, the world's biggest jetliner, more than any other competitor, Emirates is able to offer 14 first class suites, each with a vanity table, closet, 23-inch TV screen, and electronic doors that seal shut for total seclusion.

First class passengers also have access to two enormous spa showers–a first in the industry. An event planner who flew first class said, "To walk onto the A380, to have an average-size bathroom, a seven minute shower, full-size bath towels, and your own attendant is pretty amazing."[7] All premium class passengers–both in first and business class–have access to a big and circular lounge, with a horseshoe-shaped stand-up bar in the center, for which Emirates forfeited a number of business-class seats.

Grooming a Special Employee

Each year, Emirates holds Open Days in more than 140 cities across 70 countries for the purpose of attracting new recruits to join its elite force of 23,135 flight attendants from 130 nationalities who speak more than 60 languages.[8]

They are not attracted to the starting salary–only about $30,000 per year–or to the free room and board that comes with it. They are excited about the possibility of joining an iconic brand that joins people around the world.

Once they have been recruited, Emirates uses a state-of-the-art facility to train its employees–from those who check in passengers to those who serve them on their planes. The exterior of the training facility resembles the fuselage of a jetliner. Inside, everyone pays particular attention to the flight attendants who must make sure that everyone on the aircraft receives the highest level of service on every single flight. This is particularly important for a carrier whose flights are of long duration because they serve destinations across all continents.

Catherine Baird is in charge of training the airline's new recruits who constitute only about 5 percent of the applications that make it through the selection process. The low acceptance rate pushes people with diverse backgrounds to compete in an American-Idol style brains-and-beauty contest for a chance to travel around the world as an Emirates cabin crew. According to a recent report, the crew has an average age of 26 years, compared to over age 40 at U.S. Airlines, and is 75 percent women. Their weight is carefully monitored, their makeup mandatorily reapplied regularly, and unwed pregnancy is not allowed.

The airline offers a vast no-expenses-spared crew training program, where each new recruit moves through different departments with specialists in different areas for seven weeks. By the end of their training, the newcomers have been instructed in aspects of posture, etiquette, safety, and evacuation. There are strict standards for the color of the lipstick, the shade of hair color, and even the style of lingerie. Everything must go well with the pinstripe khaki uniform, the color of sand, with white scarfs billowing like exotic sails. Women must adhere to certain hairstyles that the crowning blood red hat will work with. "When walking through an airport terminal, it's usually a *Catch Me If You Can* movie moment, with passengers all turning their heads," said one of the new recruits.[9]

Like everything else, Emirates is over the top in what it calls *Nujoum*, the Arabic word for stars, by including motivational team-building exercises in its training program. Travel writer Christine Negroni, who participated in one of these exercises, described the experience the new recruits typically go through: "It is a combination of a customer service experience and a come-to-Jesus rally, highly produced like a Hollywood spectacular. If you had told me that Disney produced it, I wouldn't doubt it. By the end of the day, they are whipped into a frenzy of feeling 'What can I do for Emirates?'"[10]

Communicating to the Masses

In spite of the extra touches that Emirates can provide to its passengers, the carrier discovered from focus groups they conducted that their name was not well known in many parts of the world to which they were expanding. They realized they needed to create a message used to develop their brand among consumers that would inform them what to expect from Emirates. This message could also be used to encourage existing and potential employees to rally behind the airline and work to deliver on its promise.

In its usual style of pushing for the best, Emirates summoned the world's top 10 advertising agencies to Dubai to compete for a massive international advertising campaign. StrawberryFrog, an advertising agency that had recently started operations in New York City, was one of the firms vying for the contract with the rapidly growing carrier. Its founder, Scott Goodson, had read an interview with Emirates president Tim Clark shortly before this gathering of advertising agencies. "And in that article, he was talking about his vision, that he wanted Emirates to be a global company and wanted to make the world a smaller place by bringing people together," said Goodson.[11]

These comments inspired Goodson to come up with the idea of "Hello Tomorrow," which allowed his firm to clinch the contract with Emirates. These words became not just the idea for an ad campaign but for a new way to think about an airline. Through the use of powerful storytelling, words, images, music, and film, this message portrayed Emirates not just as a carrier that delivered a superior experience, but as a catalyst for connecting a new global culture of shared aspirations, values, enthusiasm, and dreams. In his conversation with Tim Clark, Goodson said: "Ad campaigns are fleeting. The power of a movement is that it can change habits and rally millions."[12]

Immediately afterwards, the StrawberryFrog team spent 18 months at Emirates headquarters educating employees, making them foot soldiers in this campaign. In early spring 2012, the "Hello Tomorrow" brand was launched, a universal message in myriad languages in 150 countries. In television ads, an Emirates flight attendant pushes his drink cart as a mammoth A380 airplane seemed to be literally built around him, its various parts and personnel coming from countries spanning the globe, providing proof that the airline was truly a global enterprise.

Chasing Tomorrow?

Even as Emirates tries to set itself apart from other carriers by enhancing the customer experience, it is facing new challenges. It has found it difficult to fill its A380s, leading it to reduce its latest orders for the plane.[13] Emirates is also running out of room for further expansion at its hub in Dubai. The loss of orders from Emirates may have played a large part in the recent decision by Airbus to shut down production of the A380.[14]

At the same time, many of its competitors have also been trying to improve on their offerings, particularly for the passengers who are willing to pay a little more. Singapore Airlines, for example, has introduced a premium economy section that offers wider seats with more recline, a cocktail table, more storage space, and a sleek 13.3-inch high definition screen—the largest in its class. On it's A380 flights, Etihad has introduced, with grand bravado, a three-room, $21,000 one-way Residence and nine $16,000 one-way one-room First Apartments, complete with a Savoy Academy–trained butler and private chefs.

Rumors have circulated that Emirates might take over Etihad Airways, which has been losing money since it began service in 2003. A merger would create the world's largest airline, measured by available passenger seat kilometers. Both airlines rely on "super-connector" business models and serve many of the same markets. But several hurdles exist, since Emirates is nervous about taking on Etihad's liabilities, which include over 160 orders for planes worth tens of billions of dollars.

Some industry analysts have questioned the ability of Emirates to deal with these growing challenges. Joe Brancatelli, a business travel writer, recently stated: "I could make the case that Emirates' moment has passed. Emirates was the trendy airline three or four years ago."[15] In a recent meeting to announce the latest performance figures for the airline, Emirates chairman and CEO His Highness Sheikh Ahmed bin Saeed Al Maktoum brushed away these concerns. "Over the years, we have always managed to come up with new products," he responded to any concerns that were raised.[16]

ENDNOTES

1. Dubai Airport. 2019 (March). Fact Sheet. http://www.dubaiairports.ae/corporate/media-centre/fact-sheets/detail/dubai-airports.
2. Seal, M. 2014. Fly me to the moon . . . with a stop in Dubai. Departures.com., Summer, p. 276.
3. Departures.com, Summer 2014, p. 277.
4. Carey, S. 2015. U.S. carriers claim unfair practices. *Wall Street Journal*, March 6, p. B3.
5. Departures.com., Summer 2014, p. 276.
6. Ibid., p. 277.
7. Ibid., p. 277.
8. Emirates. 2019. The Emirates Service. https://www.emirates.com/english/experience/the-emirates-service/.
9. Departures.com, Summer 2014, p. 278.
10. Ibid., p. 277.
11. Ibid., p. 310.
12. Ibid., p. 278.
13. Press Release. 2019. Emirates signs deal for 40 A330-900s, 30 A350-900s. Emirates, February 14.
14. Tim Hepher & Alexander Cornwell. The future of the Airbus A380 is under threat as Emirates considered dumping the superjumbo for a smaller jet. Reuters, Jan. 31, 2019.
15. Departures.com, Summer 2014, p. 278.
16. Ibid., p. 275.

CASE 23

GENERAL MOTORS IN 2019*

In 2019, General Motors (GM) was in the midst of a great transformation. Mary T. Barra, the CEO of GM was moving the firm away from many of the passenger cars that it had sold to generations of consumers. It had also moved away from many overseas markets, knocking the leading U.S. automaker out of the chase to be the top seller globally, a spot it had owned until recently. A couple of years ago, GM had exited from the European market by selling its chronically unprofitable Opel unit to the French maker of Peugeot and Citroen cars. The sale had freed the firm from persistent losses in Europe and fulfilled pledges by Mary to improve overall profit margins and increase returns to shareholders (see Exhibits 1 and 2).

Industry analysts had expected that Barra, who had worked for GM her entire career, would let the firm relapse into the arrogance, complacency, and denial that had plunged it into bankruptcy in 2009. Instead, Barra has been preparing GM to be a formidable player in the future. She has pushed the firm to be more involved with new developments, such as electric vehicles, ride sharing, and driverless cars. When the firm launched its first hybrid car, the Volt, in 2010, it was significantly lagging behind all other competitors in terms of investing into emerging technologies. Nevertheless, Barra claimed that

* Case prepared by Jamal Shamsie, Michigan State University, with the assistance of Professor Alan B. Eisner, Pace University. Material has been drawn from published sources to be used for purposes of class discussion. Copyright © 2017 Jamal Shamsie and Alan B. Eisner.

EXHIBIT 1 Consolidated Income Statements (in millions of dollars)

	Years Ended December 31,		
	2018	2017	2016
Net sales and revenue			
Automotive	$133,045	$133,449	$140,205
GM Financial	14,004	12,139	8,979
Total net sales and revenue	147,049	145,588	149,184
Costs and expenses			
Automotive cost of sales	120,656	116,229	121,784
GM Financial interest, operating and other expenses	12,298	11,128	8,369
Automotive selling, general and administrative expense	9,650	9,570	10,345
Total costs and expenses	142,604	136,927	140,498
Operating income	4,445	8,661	8,686
Automotive interest expense	655	575	563
Interest income and other non-operating income, net	2,596	1,645	1,603
Equity income	2,163	2,132	2,282
Income before income taxes	8,549	11,863	12,008
Income tax expense	474	11,533	2,739
Loss from discontinued operations	70	4,212	1
Net income (loss)	8,005	(3,882)	9,268

Source: GM Annual Report 2018.

EXHIBIT 2

Consolidated Balance Sheets (in millions of dollars)

	December 31, 2018	December 31, 2017
ASSETS		
Current Assets		
Cash and cash equivalents	$ 20,844	$ 15,512
Marketable securities	5,966	8,313
Accounts and notes receivable (net of allowance of $211 and $278)	6,549	8,164
GM Financial receivables, net	26,850	20,521
Inventories	9,816	10,663
Equipment on operating leases, net	247	1,106
Other current assets	5,021	4,465
Total current assets	75,293	68,744
Non-current Assets		
GM Financial receivables, net	25,083	21,208
Equity in net assets of nonconsolidated affiliates	9,215	9,073
Property, net	38,758	36,253
Goodwill and intangible assets, net	5,579	5,849
GM Financial equipment on operating leases, net	43,559	42,882
Deferred income taxes	24,082	23,544
Other assets	5,770	4,929
Total non-current assets	152,046	143,738
Total Assets	227,339	212,482
LIABILITIES AND EQUITY		
Current Liabilities		
Accounts payable (principally trade)	$ 22,297	$23,929
Short-term debt and current portion of long-term debt		
Automotive	935	2,515
GM Financial	30,956	24,450
Accrued liabilities	28,049	25,996
Total current liabilities	82,237	76,890
Non-current Liabilities		
Long-term debt		
Automotive	13,028	10,987
GM Financial	60,032	56,267
Postretirement benefits other than pensions	5,370	5,998
Pensions	11,538	13,746

(continued)

EXHIBIT 2

(Continued)

	December 31, 2018	December 31, 2017
Other liabilities	12,357	12,394
Total non-current liabilities	102,325	99,392
Total Liabilities	184,562	176,282
Equity		
Common stock, $0.01 par value	14	14
Additional paid-in capital	25,563	25,371
Retained earnings	22,322	17,627
Accumulated other comprehensive loss	(9,039)	(8,011)
Total stockholders' equity	38,860	35,001
Noncontrolling interests	3,917	1,199
Total Equity	42,777	36,200
Total Liabilities and Equity	$ 227,399	$212,482

Source: GM Annual Report 2018

it was an important first step in acknowledging where GM needed to go.

Since then, GM has launched the new all-electric Bolt, which promises an almost 240-mile range between charges for a price of $30,000 after federal tax credits. It has moved quickly to beat Tesla's new budget-priced Model 3 to market. In January 2016, GM announced a $500 million investment in Lyft, the country's second largest ride-share service. It subsequently worked with Lyft to develop a program that allows Lyft drivers in seven big cities to rent GM cars at a discount. A few months later, the firm spent $1 billion acquiring Cruise Automation, which has built a complex array of software and hardware that uses artificial intelligence that can lead to driverless cars.

In order to shift its resources to fund these new initiatives, GM announced in November 2018 that it was halting operations at four plants in the United States and one in Canada, resulting in the loss of 6,000 factory jobs. All of these have been losing money because they have been producing small- and medium-sized cars such as the Chevrolet Cruze and Impala and the Buick LaCrosse. The firm also plans to trim its salaried staff by 8,000 representing over a third of its white-collar employees.

By making all of these moves, GM is, in fact, constructing a portfolio of assets that are dedicated to disrupting its own core business from within. Even as it lays off its older workforce, it has been recruiting younger employees with technology-heavy skills that go beyond traditional vehicle design and engineering. "The auto industry is on the cusp of change, and GM has to prove that a longtime established player is up to the task" said Michelle Krebs, a senior analyst for the car shopping site Autotrader.[1]

Moving through Bankruptcy

GM has witnessed a long decline from its dominant position in the 1950s when it held almost 50 percent of the U.S. market for automobiles. A succession of CEOs over the years failed to halt its decline in spite of their resolve to turn things around. When Richard Wagoner took over in 2000, he carried out three major restructurings, eliminating dozens of plants and tens of thousands of jobs, and jettisoning hundreds of dealers. In spite of these efforts, GM announced a loss of $30.9 billion dollars for 2008, amounting to a staggering $50 a share. The firm had not managed to post a profit since 2004, running up cumulative losses of over $82 billion between 2005 and 2009. Wagoner eventually began to run short of funds and turned to the U.S. government for loans in order to survive, but the Obama administration demanded his resignation for its support.

Wagoner was replaced on an interim basis by Frederick A. Henderson, who had been president and chief operating officer of the firm since 2008. Under Henderson, the firm was asked to negotiate with bondholders and the union for further concessions in order to reduce its bloated cost structure. Unable to reach any agreement, the firm announced in late July 2009 that it must seek Chapter 11 bankruptcy protection. Under the terms of the bankruptcy protection, GM was able to wipe out a big chunk of its debt, reducing this from over $46 billion before the filing to around $17 billion afterwards, saving about $1 billion a year in interest payments. The U.S. government agreed to invest another $30 billion into the firm, in addition to the $20 billion it had already contributed, in exchange for 61 percent of stock in the new GM.

Shortly after the bankruptcy filing, changes were made to the board of directors and there was a shake-up of the ranks of GM's senior management. The new board was determined to address problems that had been laid bare by the task force that had been assigned by the government to investigate GM in early 2009. They had been particularly astonished by the emphasis on past glories and the commitment to the status quo they had found to be quite widespread among the firm's management ranks. "Those values were driven from the top on down," said Rob Kleinbaum, a former GM executive and consultant. "And anybody inside who protested that attitude was buried."[2]

Over the following year, GM was led by two different board members. Edward E. Whitacre, Jr. ran the firm for about a year before being replaced by Dan Ackerson. Ackerson had been appointed by the U.S. government as a board member during GM's bankruptcy. A no-nonsense former navy officer, Ackerson began to address the various problems that continued to plague the firm. There was a strong consensus among the executives that the company was beginning to change its approach to its business. Shortly after he took over, Ackerson wrote in an internal memo: "Our results show that we are changing the company, so we never go down that path again."[3]

In January 2014, GM was finally able to move past the bankruptcy as the government-appointed Ackerson was replaced by Barra, who worked her way up within the firm and has become the first woman to ever run a big automobile company. She has been a rank-and-file engineer, a plant manager, the head of corporate human resources, and most recently the senior executive overseeing all of GM's global product development. Barra's appointment came on the heels of the sale of the last shares that the U.S. government had held of the firm, finally making it free of its bankruptcy obligations. "This is truly the next chapter in GM's recovery and turnaround history," Barra told employees upon her appointment. "And I am proud to be a part of it."[4]

Responding to Safety Concerns

Even as Barra was working on making GM more effective, GM executives decided that a recall of the 619,000 Chevrolet Cobalts and Pontiac G5s was necessary. Questions were raised about the delay of several years in recalling these vehicles in spite of knowledge of a faulty ignition switch that would cause these cars to shut off and disable its airbags. In 2004, engineers had suggested a fix, but executives decided against it because of potential delays and cost overruns in production. GM finally decided to move after the reports of accidents that had led to deaths and injuries could no longer be ignored. This was particularly embarrassing for the firm as GM had developed the Cobalt to show that it was no longer cutting corners and was capable of making competitive small cars.

In testimonies before a subcommittee of the House Committee on Energy and Commerce, Barra acknowledged that the safety problems had resulted from deep underlying problems with the GM culture. A report was released in June by Anton R. Valukas, a former U.S. attorney whom the firm hired to conduct a three-month investigation of the decision to ignore the problems with the ignition switch. Its findings indicated that all issues that arise are typically passed through a number of committees without being resolved. Furthermore, no minutes were taken of any of the meetings to indicate who was responsible or accountable for any decisions that were taken.

Valukas concluded that shifting responsibility for problems to others was deep in the firm's DNA. He referred to a GM salute that involved a crossing of arms and pointing outwards toward others, indicating that the responsibility belongs to someone else. In particular, Valukus found that employees at GM were given formal training about how to avoid accountability in documenting any safety issues. They were told to avoid using words such as *problem* or *defect* and replacing them with softer words such as *safety* or *condition*. "The story of the Cobalt is one of a series of individual and organizational failures that led to devasting consequences," Valukas stated to a committee hearing.[5]

Under Barra, GM executives did move quickly to respond to the safety problems. The firm ordered the dismissal of 15 employees, including a vice president for regulatory affairs and several corporate lawyers, and disciplined others. It appointed a new global head of vehicle safety and named a new vice president in charge of global product integrity. GM also decided to more than double to 55 a team of safety investigators that would work within engineering. Finally, it also hired a compensation expert to examine claims and make cash settlements for those that either died or were injured as a result of accidents caused by the defective ignition switch. "We are a good company," Barra insisted. "But we can and must be much better."[6]

Focusing on Fewer Brands

One of the issues that GM had wrestled with for years was the number of brands of vehicles that it offered. For years, the firm had built its position of dominance by offering cars that were designed for different customers by separate divisions. Each of these divisions came to represent a distinct nameplate or brand. Its extensive brand lineup had long been GM's primary weapon in beating back both domestic and foreign rivals. But as the firm's market share began to decline, it became difficult to design and market cars under several brands. In order to cut costs, GM began to share designs and parts across divisions, leading to some loss of distinctiveness between the different brands.

Analysts had been questioning for many years GM's decision to stick with as many as eight U.S. brands, with its final addition of Hummer. The decision to carry so many brands had placed considerable strain on GM's efforts to revamp its product line on a regular basis. However, the firm finally agreed to cut out four of its brands–Pontiac, Saturn, Saab, and Hummer–when it was forced to turn to the U.S. government for funding to stay afloat. A. Andrew Shapiro, an analyst, believes that GM should have started to think seriously about cutting back on its car divisions

EXHIBIT 3 Market Shares

	Years Ended December 31,								
	2018			2017			2016		
	Industry	GM	Market Share	Industry	GM	Market Share	Industry	GM	Market Share
North America									
United States	17,694	2,954	16.7%	17,570	3,002	17.1%	17,886	3,043	17.0%
Other	3,835	536	14.0%	3,986	574	14.4%	3,993	587	14.7%
Total North America	21,529	3,490	16.2%	21,556	3,576	16.6%	21,879	3,630	16.6%
Europe									
Total Europe	19,045	4	–%	19,190	685	3.6%	18,620	1,161	6.7%
Asia/Pacific, Middle East, and Africa									
China(a)	26,466	3,645	13.8%	28,231	4,041	14.3%	28,274	3,914	13.8%
Other	22,252	555	2.5%	21,287	629	3.0%	20,602	720	3.5%
Total Asia/Pacific, Middle East, and Africa	48,718	4,200	8.6%	49,518	4,670	9.4%	48,876	4,634	9.5%
South America									
Brazil	2,566	434	16.9%	2,239	394	17.6%	2,050	346	16.9%
Other	1,919	256	13.3%	1,928	275	14.3%	1,623	237	14.6%
Total South America	4,485	690	15.4%	4,167	669	16.1%	3,673	583	15.9%
Total Worldwide	93,777	8,384	8.9%	94,431	9,600	10.2%	93,048	10,008	10.8%
United States									
Cars	5,361	560	10.4%	6,145	709	11.5%	6,895	890	12.9%
Trucks	5,361	1,360	25.4%	5,041	1,328	26.3%	5,464	1,325	24.2%
Crossovers	6,972	1,034	14.8%	6,384	965	15.1%	5,523	828	15.0%
Total United States	17,694	2,954	16.7%	17,570	3,002	17.1%	17,882	3,043	17.0%
China(a)									
SGMS		1,749			1,906			1,806	
SGMW and FAW-GM		1,896			2,135			2,108	
Total China	26,466	3,645	13.8%	28,231	4,041	14.3%	28,270	3,914	13.8%

(a) Includes sales by the Automotive China JVs SAIC General Motors Sales Co., Ltd. (SGMS), SAIC GM Wuling Automobile Co., Ltd. (SGMW) and FAW-GM Light Duty Commercial Vehicle Co., Ltd. (FAW-GM). In the year ended December 31, 2016, wholesale volumes were used for Industry, GM, and Market Share. Our total vehicle sales in China were 3,871 in the year ended December 31, 2016.

Source: GM Annual Report 2018.

during the 1980s. "There are always short-term reasons for not doing something," explained Shapiro.[7]

Since it has cut down on its brands, GM has been working on revamping its remaining line-up of cars. The firm has been able to successfully reinvent Chevrolet as a global mass-market brand, with over 60 percent of its sales now coming from outside the United States (see Exhibits 3 and 4). Recent sales have been driven by the new pickup trucks and sport-utility vehicles such as the revamped heavy-duty Silverado capable of towing 35,000 pounds with a diesel engine. But GM is also

EXHIBIT 4
Vehicle Sales (deliveries in thousands)

	Years Ended	
	December 31, 2018	**December 31, 2017**
United States		
Chevrolet - Cars	476	617
Chevrolet - Trucks	969	926
Chevrolet - Crossovers	591	522
Cadillac	155	156
Buick	207	219
GMC	556	562
Total United States	2,954	3,002
Canada, Mexico, and Other	536	574
Total North America	3,490	3,576
Europe		
Opel/Vauxhall	1,159	1,113
Chevrolet(a)	48	63
Total Europe	1.207	1,176
Asia/Pacific, Middle East, and Africa		
Chevrolet	959	980
Wuling	1,071	1,141
Buick	1,020	1,183
Baojun	840	997
Cadillac	213	184
Other	97	185
Total Asia/Pacific, Middle East, and Africa(b)	4,200	4,670
South America	690	669
Total Europe	4	685
Total Worldwide	8,384	9,600

Source: GM Form 8-K, February 06, 2019.

expecting to be successful with its new Bolt all-electric subcompact car, which can run for almost 230 miles on a single charge. An executive explained the motivation behind pushing to develop cars that move away from a reliance on fuel: "We wanted to prove we could do it."[8]

GM has also been focusing on strengthening its more upscale brands such as Buick and Cadillac. Buick, the oldest active automobile brand in the United States, has been catering to a shrinking population of people over 65. Over the last couple of years, the firm worked on updating the brand by sticking to its image of "refined luxury" but moving away from being regarded as a living room on wheels. New models of the Enclave, Encore, and Envision have been designed to attract a younger, performance-oriented customer. In spite of these efforts, China alone has accounted for as much as 80 percent of its sales. Buick is no longer offered in most other markets other than the United States, Canada, and Mexico.

Finally, GM continues to struggle with its Cadillac luxury brand, which has had difficulty in competing with European automakers. It has slipped in quality, ranking 27th out of 31 brands in the J.D. Power 2018 U.S. Vehicle Dependability Study. The firm abruptly replaced four-year Cadillac chief Johan de Nysschen who was leading a $12 billion overhaul that was designed to make the brand more competitive. Steve Carlisle, who has taken over, realizes the challenges he faces in reviving the fortunes of the brand. He has focused on improving its quality, boosting its marketing, and better defining its identity. Cadillac has done better with its strong selling XT5, a midsized SUV and hopes to do well with its newer XT4 compact SUV. "There's no excuse to not be at the top of the pack in vehicle quality these days," said Maryann Keller of auto industry analyst firm Maryann Keller & Associates.[9]

Preparing for the Future

Even as GM is relying on pickup trucks and sport-utility vehicles to make profits in the short-run, it is banking on electric vehicles and self-driving cars for its future. In November 2018, Dan Ammann gave up his job as president of GM to become chief executive of Cruise, the division working on autonomous vehicles. The unit was formed when Ammann spearheaded GM's acquisition of Cruise Automation, a San Francisco start-up for more than $1 billion in 2016 (see Exhibit 5).

The appointment of Ammann has provided more management heft as it prepares to launch a driverless-ride service before the end of 2019. "This is technology that we wanted to develop and deploy in a massive scale," he stated about the commitment to self-driving vehicles in a recent interview.[10] In particular, GM is focused on a new technology known as lidar, which uses near-infrared light to detect the shape of objects around it. It has been making investments into advancements to lidar, which will reduce the costs of making cars and enable them to travel more safely at higher speeds.

In order to prepare for its launch, Cruise is already testing about 180 self-driving cars in San Francisco. Its vehicle, the Cruise AV, is a small electric car that has no steering wheel or pedals. It navigates streets using radar, cameras, and other sensors that allows the car's computer systems to identify pedestrians, intersections, other vehicles, and obstacles. With no steering wheel, it has two passenger seats in the front and a center console with a display screen, and also buttons and knobs for audio and climate control.

With Cruise, GM may be the first to rush into the field, but it faces plenty of competition from Ford, Uber, Lyft, and Waymo. However, Barra is confident that GM is well positioned to achieve success. "I do believe General Motors is a tech company," she recently stated. "We put these products on the road that integrate 30,000 parts and have hundreds of millions of lines of code in them already."[11] In fact, Cruise is well on its way to developing a potentially significant market value. GM has brought in SoftBank, the Japanese technology giant, and Honda Motor, the Japanese auto firm, as partners.

Firing on All Cylinders?

Barra felt quite confident that the investments GM has been making will yield results in the future. Although the firm is relying heavily on profits from its trucks and SUVs, it is banking on its new initiatives. Not only is the Bolt the first inexpensive long-range electric car on the road, it is also expected to function as the firm's platform for testing new models for ride sharing and autonomous driving. Soon after GM made an investment in Lyft, it also announced that it would launch a proprietary car-sharing service called Maven. A Zipcar-like offering, Maven taps into another possible future of mobility–replacing

EXHIBIT 5
Income by Operating Regions ($ millions)

	Years Ended	
	December 31, 2018	**December 31, 2017**
Operating segments		
GM North America (GMNA)	$10,769	$11,889
GM International (GMI)	423	1,300
GM Cruise	(728)	(613)
General Motors Financial Company, Inc. (GM Financial)	1,893	1,196
Total operating segments	12,357	13,772
Corporate and eliminations	(574)	(928)
EBIT-adjusted	11,783	12,844

Source: GM Form 8-K, February 06, 2019.

ownership with sharing. This startup within GM, which has features that are not available on Zipcar, lays the groundwork for a possible future when GM owns and operates a fleet of its own autonomous cars that could also be tapped for ride sharing.

GM realizes that it faces considerable competition in this new arena from other car firms as well as technology firms. However, product chief Mark Reuss believes that the firm has an advantage because with its acquisition of Cruise, it is well positioned to integrate self-driving technology into its own cars. Over the last couple of years, GM has already begun to incorporate aspects of self-driving technology into a few of its models, including software that alerts drivers if they veer out of their lane or that stops the car if it detects an imminent collision. Talking about the challenges about the use of this technology in cars, Reuss said: "The piece that is not well understood outside of the automotive industry is how hard it is to take technology and integrate it into a car. It seems like you should be able to layer it in and have it work and that would be great."[12]

In spite of this push into new technologies, sales for the Bolt have so far failed to exceed a few thousand cars a month, hardly enough to make a profit. Similarly, the profit potential is even less certain with GM's investments into self-driving technologies. It has been pouring billions into Cruise, its autonomous-driving unit, but even if its efforts are successful, it could be years before the firm may be able to earn back its investments. Nevertheless, in the words of Bill Rock, a 22-year veteran who has been working on the development of autonomous vehicles: "We're on the cutting edge here. It's a very complicated process, but it's the direction the company needs to go."[13]

ENDNOTES

1. Vlasic, B. 2017. G.M. Wants to Drive the Future of Cars That Drive Themselves. *New York Times*, June 04.
2. Vlasic, B. 2009. Culture shock: GM struggles to shed a legendry bureaucracy. *New York Times*, November 13, p. B4.
3. De La Merced, M.J., and B. Vlasic. 2012. U.S. to shed its stake in General Motors. *New York Times*, December 21, p. B3.
4. Vlasic, B. 2013. Company woman becomes new GM chief. *International New York Times*, December 12, p. 1.
5. Vlasic, B. and D. Ivory. 2014. Barra grilled over recall issue. June 18, *San Antonio Express-News*. https://www.expressnews.com/business/national/article/Barra-grilled-over-recall-issue-5562708.php
6. Ibid.
7. Maynard, M. 2009. A painful departure for some GM brands. *New York Times*, February 18, p. B 4.
8. Vlasic, B. 2011. To make tiny American car, GM also shrinks plant and wages. *New York Times*, July 13, p. A19.
9. LaReau, J. 2018. Cadillac hopes to get back on track with new models. *USA Today*, June 6, p.1B.
10. Boudette, N.E. 2018. GM chief to take helm of self-driving division. *New York Times*, November 30, p. B3.
11. Vlasic, B. 2017. G.M. Wants to Drive the Future of Cars That Drive Themselves. *New York Times*, June 04.
12. Tetzeli, R. 2016. Mary Barra Is Remaking GM's Culture-And The Company Itself. *Fast Company*, October 17.
13. Vlasic, B. 2017. G.M. Wants to Drive the Future of Cars That Drive Themselves. *New York Times*, June 04.

CASE 24

JOHNSON & JOHNSON*

On March 13, 2019, a California jury awarded $29 million to a woman who claimed that asbestos in Johnson & Johnson's (J&J) talcum-powder-based products caused her cancer.[1] The verdict marked the latest in a series of legal challenges that the world's largest healthcare company has faced about the quality of its products. In addition to having to settle misleading claims about its hip implants, J&J now faces more than 13,000 talc-related lawsuits across the United States—claims that some of its products, such as Johnson's Baby Powder, contain traces of asbestos that can cause cancer. Even though such talc-based products account for a very small share of J&J's overall sales, the firm's image has long been tied to the purity of these products.

These lawsuits have posed a serious problem for the well-established reputation of J&J that has been developed over many years. With 260 operating companies in virtually every country, J&J has managed to develop under its banner the world's largest medical device business, an even bigger pharmaceutical business and a consumer products division with a dozen megabrands from Neutrogena to Tylenol. The firm's reputation has been derived from its diversified businesses that have reflected its wide range of expertise and allowed it to develop a customer base spanning from consumers to hospitals to governments.

In fact, the financial stability that has resulted from its range of businesses has been J&J's calling card for decades. Its sales have risen on regular basis, although profits have dipped a bit in recent years (see Exhibit 1 and 2). The firm has raised its dividend for well over 50 years and it remains one of only two U.S. companies with an AAA credit rating from Standard and Poor's. "They're in a great position," said Kristen Stewart, an analyst at Deutsche Bank. "They have the luxury of time and the ability to look at different opportunities across different business units. That is what a diversified business platform affords them."[2]

However, even as it has grown and become more diversified, J&J has struggled to find a way to manage its vast portfolio of diversified businesses. Much of its growth has come from acquisitions and it has developed a culture of granting considerable autonomy to each of the firms that it has absorbed. Although this was intended to cultivate an entrepreneurial attitude among each of its units, this has prevented J&J from instilling a strong set of controls, such as for quality standards. It has also prevented the firm from pursuing opportunities on which its various units could combine their different areas of expertise.

Over the past decade, William C. Weldon, who spearheaded a period of dramatic growth at J&J, began to direct his efforts at trying to exert more control over its different businesses. After Alex Gorsky took over as CEO in 2012, he has pushed harder to try and weave together the operations of the different units. The need for greater oversight became more urgent after the firm ran into quality issues with some of its well-known products. But like Weldon, Gorsky realizes that it must try to find a balance between its new push for greater control with its traditional emphasis on autonomy throughout the organization.

EXHIBIT 1 Income Statement (in $ millions)

	Year Ending		
	2018	2017	2016
Total Revenue	$81,581	$76,450	$71,890
Gross Profit	54,490	51,011	51,101
Operating Income	20,049	18,489	20,862
Net Income	15,297	1,300	16,540

Source: Johnson & Johnson, Annual Report 2018.

EXHIBIT 2 Balance Sheet (in $ millions)

	Year Ending		
	2018	2017	2016
Current Assets	$ 46,033	$ 43,088	$ 65,032
Total Assets	152,954	157,303	141,208
Current Liabilities	31,230	30,537	26,287
Total Liabilities	93,202	97,143	70,790
Stockholder Equity	59,752	60,160	70,418

Source: Johnson & Johnson, Annual Report 2017-2018.

* Case prepared by Jamal Shamsie, Michigan State University, with the assistance of Professor Alan B. Eisner, Pace University. Material has been drawn from published sources to be used for purposes of class discussion. Copyright © 2019 Jamal Shamsie and Alan B. Eisner.

Cultivating Entrepreneurship

Johnson & Johnson was founded in 1886 by three brothers named Johnson. The company grew slowly for a generation before Robert Wood Johnson II decided reluctantly to take the family business public. He fretted about the effects that market pressures would have on the company's practices and values that led him to write a 307-word statement of corporate principles. This spelled out that J&J's primary responsibility was to patients and physicians, followed by employees, and then by communities. Shareholders were placed last on the list. This credo is inscribed in stone at the entrance of the firm's headquarters and is still routinely invoked around the company.

Over the years, as J&J has grown by acquisitions of firms engaged in some aspect of health care, it has been guided by its credo. The task has become more challenging as J&J has developed into an astonishingly complex enterprise, made up of over 260 different subsidiaries that have been broken down into three different divisions. The most widely known of these is the division that makes consumer products such as Johnson & Johnson baby care products, Band-Aid adhesive strips, and Visine eye drops. Its pharmaceuticals division sells several blockbuster drugs such as anemia drug Procrit and schizophrenia drug Risperdal. Its medical devices division is responsible for best-selling products such as Depuy orthopedic joint replacements and Cypher coronary stents.

In particular, J&J's credo has kept the firm focused on health care, even as it has expanded into several different business segments. Furthermore, it has pushed the company to adopt a decentralized approach in managing its different businesses. Most of its far-flung subsidiaries across its three divisions were acquired because of the potential demonstrated by some promising new products in its pipeline. Each of these units was therefore granted near-total autonomy to develop and expand upon their best-selling products in order to better serve their patients (see Exhibit 3).

It is widely believed that this independence has fostered an entrepreneurial attitude that has kept J&J intensely competitive as others around it have faltered. The relative autonomy that is accorded to the business units has also provided the firm with the ability to respond swiftly to emerging opportunities. A strong enough commitment from everyone throughout these units to the principles that have been laid out in the credo were considered to be sufficient to provide the necessary direction.

J&J has actually been quite proud of the considerable freedom it has given to its different subsidiaries in order to develop and execute their own strategies. Besides developing their strategies, these units have also been allowed to work with their own resources. Many of them have even been able to operate their own finance and human resources departments. While this degree of decentralization has led to relatively high overhead costs, none of the executives that have run J&J—Weldon included—had ever thought that this was too high a price to pay. "J&J is a huge company, but you didn't feel like you were in a big company," recalled a scientist who used to work there.[3]

Pushing for More Collaboration

The entrepreneurial culture that Johnson & Johnson developed over the years has clearly allowed it to show a consistent level of high performance. Indeed, J&J has top-notch products in each of the areas in which it operates. It has been spending heavily on research and development for many years, taking its position among the world's top spenders (see Exhibit 4). It has been spending about 12 percent of its sales on about 9,000 scientists working in research laboratories around the world. This allows each of the three divisions to continually introduce promising new products.

In spite of the benefits that J&J has derived from giving its various enterprises considerable autonomy, there have been growing concerns that they can no longer be allowed to operate in near isolation. Shortly after Weldon had taken charge of the firm, he realized that J&J was in a strong position to exploit new opportunities by drawing on the diverse skills of its various subsidiaries across the three divisions. In particular, he was aware that his firm may be able to derive more benefits from the combination of its knowledge in drugs, devices, and diagnostics, since few companies were able to match its reach and strength in these basic areas.

This had led Weldon to find ways to make its fiercely independent units to work together. In his own words: "There is a convergence that will allow us to do things we haven't done before."[4] Through pushing the various far-flung units of the firm to pool their resources, Weldon had believed that firm could become one of the few that may actually be able to attain that often-promised, rarely delivered idea of synergy. In order to pursue this, he created a corporate office that would get business units to work together on promising new opportunities. "It's a recognition that there's a way to treat disease that's not in silos," Weldon stated, referring to the need for collaboration between J&J's largely independent businesses.[5]

For the most part, however, Weldon confined himself to taking steps to foster better communication and more frequent collaboration among J&J's disparate operations. He was convinced that such a push for communication and coordination would allow the firm to develop the synergy he was seeking. But Weldon was also aware that any effort to get the different business units to collaborate must not quash the entrepreneurial spirit that had spearheaded most of the growth of the firm to date. Jerry Caccott, managing director of consulting firm Strategic Decisions Group, emphasized that cultivating those alliances "would be

EXHIBIT 3 Segment Information

Johnson & Johnson is made up of over 260 different companies, many of which it has acquired over the years. These individual companies have been assigned to three different divisions.

Geographic Areas			
	Sales to Customers		
(Dollars in Millions)	**2018**	**2017**	**2016**
Consumer—			
United States	$ 5,761	$ 5,565	$ 5,420
International	8,092	8,037	7,887
Total	13,853	13,602	13,307
Pharmaceutical —			
United States	23,286	21,474	20,125
International	17,448	14,782	13,339
Total	40,734	36,256	33,464
Medical Devices—			
United States	12,837	12,824	12,266
International	14,157	13,768	12,853
Total	26,994	26,592	25,119
Worldwide total	81,581	76,450	71,890

Business Segments					
	Income Before Tax			Identifiable Assets	
(Dollars in Millions)	**2018**	**2017**	**2016**	**2018**	**2017**
Consumer	$ 2,320	2,524	2,441	25,877	25,030
Pharmaceutical	12,568	11,083	12,827	56,636	59,450
Medical Devices	4,397	5,392	5,578	46,254	45,413
Total	19,285	18,999	20,846	128,767	129,893
Less: Expense not allocated to segments	1,286	1,326	1,043		
General corporate				24,187	27,410
Worldwide total	17,999	17,673	19,803	152,954	157,303

Source: Johnson & Johnson, Annual Report 2018.

challenging in any organization, but particularly in an organization that has been so successful because of its decentralized culture."[6]

These collaborative efforts did lead to the introduction of some highly successful products (see Exhibit 5). Even the company's fabled consumer brands have started to show growth as a result of increased collaboration between the consumer products and pharmaceutical divisions. Its new liquid Band-Aid is based on a material used in a wound-closing product sold by one of J&J's hospital-supply businesses. And J&J has used its prescription antifungal treatment, Nizoral, to develop a dandruff shampoo. In fact, products that have developed in large part out of such a form of cross-fertilization have allowed the firm's consumer business to experience considerable internal growth.

EXHIBIT 4 Research Expenditures (in $ millions)

2018	$10,775
2017	10,549
2016	9,095
2015	9,046
2014	8,494
2013	8,183
2012	7,665
2011	7,548
2010	6,864
2009	6,986
2008	7,577
2007	7,680

Source: Johnson & Johnson, Annual Report.

EXHIBIT 5 Significant Innovations

Antiseptic Surgery (1888)
Three brothers start up a firm based on antiseptics designed for modern surgical practices.
Band-Aids (1921)
Debuts the first commercial bandages that can be applied at home without oversight by a professional.
No More Tears (1954)
Introduces a soap-free shampoo that is gentle enough to clean babies' hair without irritating their eyes.
Acuvue Contact Lenses (1987)
Offers the first-ever disposable lenses that can be worn for up to a week and then thrown away.
Sirturo (2012)
Gets approval to launch a much-needed treatment for drug-resistant tuberculosis, the first new medication to fight this disease in more than 40 years.

Source: Bluestein, Will Johnson & Johnson's New Innovation Centers Point The Way Toward Its Future? *Fastcompany*, February 10, 2014.

Facing Quality Concerns

Even as Johnson & Johnson has been trying to get more involved with the efforts of its business units, it ran into problems with quality control with two of its divisions. Its medical devices division had run into problems with its newest artificial hip. Although it did eventually recall the device, it was not before rumors had begun to circulate that company executives may have concealed information out of concern for firm profits. The problems with the medical devices unit were compounded by serious issues that arose with the consumer products unit, which led it to recall many of its products–including the biggest children's drug recall of all time.

Quality problems have arisen before, but they were usually fixed on a regular basis. Analysts suggest that the problems at J&J's McNeil division may have exacerbated in 2006 when J&J decided to combine it with the newly acquired consumer health care unit from Pfizer. The firm believed that it could achieve $500 to $600 million in annual savings by merging the two units together. After the merger, McNeil was also transferred from the heavily regulated pharmaceutical division to the marketing driven consumer products division, which was not subjected to the same level of quality control.

Much of the blame for J&J's stumbles fell on William C. Weldon who stepped down as CEO in April 2012 after presiding over one of the most tumultuous decades in the firm's history. Critics said the company's once vaunted attention to quality had slipped under his watch. Weldon, who had started out as sales representative at the firm, was believed to have been obsessed with meeting tough performance targets, even by cutting costs that might affect quality. Erik Gordon, who teaches business at University of Michigan elaborated on this philosophy: "We will make our numbers for the analysts, period,"[7]

In April 2012, J&J appointed Gorsky to lead the healthcare conglomerate out of the difficulties with quality that it had faced over the past few years. He had been with the firm since 1988, holding positions in its pharmaceutical businesses across Europe, Africa, and the Middle East before leaving for a few years to work at Novartis. Shortly after his return to J&J in 2008, he took over its medical devices unit that made the problematic hip implants. Since he took over, Gorsky has been dealing with the various lawsuits the firm faced over the problems with its hip replacements, paying out over $2.5 billion in settlements.[8]

Even as J&J was trying to get over its problems with the hip implants, there were rising concerns about the asbestos that might have contaminated its talcum powder-based products. Memos that were obtained during the court cases revealed that the firm may have known about this problem for years, but it tried to deny the charge and downplay any possible health threats from the use of their Baby Powder and other similar products.[9] This ongoing problem with quality issues also forced Gorsky to find ways to gain more oversight over the firm's 260-odd units. As such, he wanted to push further than Weldon to work with the various units of the firm to establish standard practices that would allow the firm to pursue opportunities without posing risks to the firm's long-established reputation.

Pushing for Tighter Integration

In order to gain more oversight over all of its units, Gorsky lured Sandra Peterson from Bayer and gave her the position of group worldwide chairman. The newly created position gave Peterson sweeping responsibly to oversee technology across the entire firm. Gorsky believed that the very nature of the job required him to hire an outsider who had not had much exposure to J&J's existing culture. Because decentralization had allowed each of the business units to make all of their own decisions, there had been no consistency in their different practices. Gorsky wanted to bring order to this unwieldly machine. "Sometimes a customer doesn't want to deal with 250 J&J's" he said.[10]

Peterson worked feverishly to align everything from HR policy to procurement processes from the 250 business units that had been making their own decisions independently. She covered everything from the timing of financial forecasts to employee car policies. She also consolidated all of the firm's data–all of its 120,000 employees to a single HR database. Her efforts to process tons of data each day led to the creation of a warehouse, which contained upwards of 500 terabytes of data. By the time Peterson decided to leave J&J in October 2018, she claimed that her streamlining process would save the firm about $1 billion.

A far more significant effort had already been initiated by Paul Stoffels when he was appointed J&J's global head of pharmaceuticals a few years ago. All of the units that operated within the pharmaceutical division had also operated with complete autonomy. In particular, J&J's seven different drug R&D organizations had operated in completely siloed fashion. In some cases, multiple companies pursued the development of the same drugs and each had its own system for handling clinical or regulatory development. Stoffels began to merge all of the units under his purview into one group and organized it to target 11 different diseases. In the process, 12 of the division's 25 facilities were shuttered and nearly 200 projects were slashed.

This new integrated unit developed a streamlined development process, a highly coordinated system that Stoffels calls Accererando. Under this model, global teams–statisticians in China, data managers in India, regulatory folks in Europe–work 24/7 to speed drugs to market. The assembly-line approach has cut months and, in some cases, years off the development time. Its increase in drug approvals over the past decade have put J&J in a league of its own. "No other company has come close to that," said Bernard Munos, a pharmaceutical innovation consultant.[11]

Stoffels has accomplished more than just reducing the time needed to bring drugs to market. He has begun to look for ideas from all sources, whether it is from any of J&J's own business units or from entrepreneurs or scientists outside the firm. He has set up four innovation centers in biotech clusters–Cambridge, MA; Menlo Park, CA; London; and Shanghai–around the world, places where scientific entrepreneurs can interact with J&J's own drug and technology scouts. His flexible approach with these outsiders lets J&J work with them more casually and helps build stronger relationships. Since 2013, the firm has reviewed more than 3,400 opportunities through these centers, leading to 200 partnerships.

Is There a Cure Ahead?

Gorsky's biggest challenge came from a demand that Johnson & Johnson might be better off if it was broken off into smaller companies, perhaps along the lines of its different divisions. There were growing concerns about the ability of the conglomerate to provide sufficient supervision to all of its subsidiaries that were spread all over the globe. Gorsky dismissed the proposal, claiming that J&J drew substantial benefits from the diversified nature of its businesses. Given the enormous shifts in the healthcare industry and the large number of government and institutional customers and partners involved, he believes that the firm's huge scale could be a rare asset for negotiating deals.

In support of this belief, Gorsky has pointed to J&J's recent acquisition of Auris Health for approximately $3.4 billion in cash. The acquisition will accelerate the firm's entry into surgical robotics and other interventional applications that have shown considerable potential for growth. "We believe the combination of best-in-class robotics, advanced instrumentation, and unparalleled end-to-end connectivity will make a meaningful difference in patient outcomes," said Ashley McEvoy, executive vice president, who is in charge of J&J's medical devices division.[12] In another step, the firm has been working on an app in collaboration with Apple for its watch that can provide better data on cardiac issues.

Even as Gorsky plots a course for the future of J&J, he is aware that its stock has been struggling recently because of some slower-growing segments of its business. He realizes that it may not be possible to count on much growth from its existing model that grants considerable autonomy to each of its businesses. Above all, he feels strongly that he must provide more direction for these units, partly to encourage them to collaborate with each other in order to pursue emerging opportunities. He also understands that it is critical for J&J to take steps to develop sufficient controls that can minimize future problems with quality control.

Overall, it is clear that the healthcare giant has to rethink the process by which it manages its diversified portfolio of companies in order to ensure it can keep growing without creating issues that can pose further threats to its reputation. "This is a company that was purer than Caesar's wife, this was the gold standard, and all of a sudden it just seems like things are breaking down," said William Trombetta, a professor of pharmaceutical marketing at Saint Joseph's University in Philadelphia.[13]

ENDNOTES

1. Hsu, T. 2019. *Johnson & Johnson hit with $29 million verdict in case over talc and asbestos. New York Times*, March 14, https://www.nytimes.com/2019/03/14/business/johnson-johnson-powder-cancer.html.
2. Fry, E. 2016. Can big still be beautiful? *Fortune*, August 1, p.84.
3. Thomas, K. and R. Abelson. 2012. J&J chief to resign one role. *New York Times*, February 22, p. B8.

4. Thomas, K. 2012. J&J's next chief is steeped in sales culture. *New York Times*, February 24, p. B.1.
5. Loftus, P. and S.S. Wang. 2009. J&J sales show health care feels the pinch. *Wall Street Journal*, January 21, p. B1.
6. Johnson, A. 2007. J&J's consumer play paces growth. *Wall Street Journal*, January 24, p. A3.
7. Thomas, K. 2012. J&J's next chief is steeped in sales culture. *New York Times*, February 24, p. B.6.
8. Bellon, T. 2019. J&J, U.S. states settle hip implant claims for $120 million. Reuters, January 22, https://www.reuters.com/article/us-johnson-johnson-settlement/jj-u-s-states-settle-hip-implant-claims-for-120-million-idUSKCN1PG26K.
9. Girion, L. 2018. Powder keg. Reuters, December 14, https://www.reuters.com/investigates/special-report/johnsonandjohnson-cancer/
10. Fry, E. 2016. Can big still be beautiful? *Fortune*, August 1, p.86.
11. Ibid. p. 88.
12. Press Release. 2019 (February 13). Johnson & Johnson Announces Agreement to Acquire Auris Health, Inc.
13. Singer, N. 2010. Hip implants are recalled by J&J unit. *New York Times*, August 27, p. B1.

CASE 25

PROCTER & GAMBLE*

Procter & Gamble, a leading global consumer products firm announced a revamping of its management structure in July 2019 as part of an effort to streamline its operations. The firm had failed to show much growth over the last five years, resulting in pressure from activist Trian Fund Management, which waged a proxy fight in 2017 and whose co-founder, Nelson Peltz, now sits on P&G's board (see Exhibit 1 and 2). The firm said it would shrink the number of its business units from ten to six and give the heads of each of these control over the management of different products as well as over their regional sales teams. P&G will also reduce its corporate functions, with about 60 percent of corporate work shifting to the new business units. "There is a need for greater agility," said CEO David Taylor.[1]

Since its founding 175 years ago, P&G has risen to the status of an American icon with well-known consumer products such as *Pampers, Tide, Downy,* and *Crest* (see Exhibit 3). In fact, the firm has long been admired for its superior products, marketing brilliance, and the intense loyalty of its employees who have come to be known respectfully as Proctoids. In the 1990s, under Alan G. Lafley, P&G spent $70 billion scooping up brands such as *Gillette* razors, *Clairol* cosmetics, and *Iams* pet food. With 25 brands that generated more than $1 billion in sales, the firm claimed the status of the largest consumer products company in the world.

However, under Lafley's chosen successor, Bob McDonald, P&G's growth stalled as recession-battered consumers abandoned the firm's premium-priced products for cheaper alternatives. More significantly, the firm's vaunted innovation machine failed to achieve any major product success during his tenure. P&G's decline eroded morale among employees, with many managers taking early retirement or bolting to competitors. Says Ed Artzt, who was CEO from 1990 to 1995: "The most unfortunate aspect of this whole thing is the brain drain. The loss of good people is almost irreparable when you depend on promotion from within to continue building the company."[2]

Pressure from the board forced Lafley to back come out of retirement in May 2013 to make another attempt to pull P&G out of its doldrums. Soon after he took back the helm of the firm, Lafley announced that he would get rid of more

* Case prepared by Jamal Shamsie, Michigan State University, with the assistance of Professor Alan B. Eisner, Pace University. Material has been drawn from published sources to be used for purposes of class discussion. Copyright © 2019 Jamal Shamsie and Alan B. Eisner.

EXHIBIT 1
Income Statement (in millions of $)

	Year Ending			
	June 30, 2018	**June 30, 2017**	**June 30, 2016**	**June 30, 2015**
Revenue	$66,832	$65,058	$65,299	$70,749
Operating Income	13,711	13,955	13,441	11,049
EBIT	13,326	13,257	13,369	11,012
Net Income	9,861	15,411	10,604	7,144

Source: P&G Annual Report 2018.

EXHIBIT 2
Balance Sheet (in millions of $)

	Year Ending			
	June 30, 2018	**June 30, 2017**	**June 30, 2016**	**June 30, 2015**
Current Assets	$ 23,320	$ 26,494	$ 33,782	$ 29,646
Total Assets	118,310	120,406	127,136	129,495
Current Liabilities	28,237	30,210	30,770	29,790
Total Liabilities	65,427	64,628	69,153	66,445
Stockholder Equity	52,883	55,778	57,983	63,050

Source: P&G Annual Report(2018 and 2017)

EXHIBIT 3
Significant Innovations

- *Tide* was the first heavy-duty laundry detergent.
- *Crest* was the first fluoride toothpaste clinically proven to prevent tooth decay.
- *Downy* was the first ultra-concentrated rinse-add fabric softener.
- *Pert Plus* was the first 2-in-1 shampoo and conditioner.
- *Head & Shoulders* was the first pleasant-to-use shampoo effective against dandruff.
- *Pampers* was the first affordable, mass-marketed disposable diaper.
- *Bounty* was the first three-dimensional paper towel.
- *Always* was the first feminine protection pad with an innovative, dry-weave top sheet.
- *Febreze* was the first fabric and air care product that actually removed odors from fabrics and the air.
- *Crest White Strips* were the first patented in-home teeth whitening technology.

Source: P&G Innovations.

than half of its brands. Over the next three years, the firm sold off many of the brands it had acquired, capped by the $11.6 billion sale of dozens of beauty brands to Coty. He announced that the company would narrow its focus to 65 or 70 of its biggest brands such as *Tide, Crest,* and *Pampers.* "Less will be more," Lafley told analysts. "The objective is growth and much more reliable generation of cash and profit."[3]

David S. Taylor, who had spent years managing P&G's businesses finally took over as chairman and CEO of the firm in November 2015. He has made moves to resurrect the firm but has opted against launching new brands or making new acquisitions. "I understand the desire for faster growth and for a single-minded short-term objective, but we've seen this movie before" he said at a meeting with analysts soon after he had taken over.[4]

Fighting off a Decline

For most of its long history, P&G has been one of America's preeminent companies. The firm has developed several well known brands such as *Tide*, one of the pioneers in laundry detergents, which was launched in 1946; and *Pampers*, the first disposable diaper, which was introduced in 1961. P&G also built its brands through its innovative marketing techniques. But by the 1990s, P&G was in danger of becoming another Eastman Kodak or Xerox, a once-great company that might have lost its way. Sales on most of its 18 top brands were slowing as it was being outhustled by more focused rivals such as Kimberly-Clark and Colgate-Palmolive.

In 1999, P&G decided to bring in Durk I. Jager to try and make the big changes that were obviously needed to get P&G back on track. But the moves he made generally misfired, sinking the firm into deeper trouble. He introduced expensive new products that never caught on while letting existing brands drift. He also put in place a companywide reorganization that left many employees perplexed and preoccupied. During the fiscal year when he was in charge, earnings per share showed an anemic rise of just 3.5 percent, much lower than in previous years. And during that time, the share price slid 52 percent, cutting P&G's total market capitalization by $85 billion.

In 2000, the board of P&G asked Lafley to take charge of the troubled firm. He began his tenure by breaking down the walls between management and employees. Since the 1950s, all of the senior executives at P&G used to be located on the 11th floor at the firm's corporate headquarters. Lafley changed this setup, moving all five division presidents to the same floors as their staff. He replaced more than half of the company's top 30 managers, more than any P&G boss in memory, and trimmed its workforce by as many as 9,600 jobs. He also moved more women into senior positions. In fact, Lafley skipped over 78 general managers with more seniority to name 42-year-old Deborah A. Henretta to head P&G's then-troubled North American baby-care division.

Lafley was simply acknowledging the importance of developing people, particularly those in managerial roles at P&G. For years, the firm has been known to dispatch line managers rather than human resource staffers to do much of its recruiting. For the few that get hired, their work life becomes a career-long development process. At every level, P&G has a different "college" to train individuals and every department has its own "university." The general manager's college holds a week-long school term once a year when there are a handful of newly promoted managers.

Under Lafley, P&G also continued with its efforts to maintain a comprehensive database for all of its more than 130,000 employees, each of which is tracked carefully through monthly and annual talent reviews. All managers are reviewed not only by their bosses but also by lateral managers who have worked with them, as well as on their own direct reports. Every February, one entire board meeting is devoted to reviewing the high-level executives, with the goal of recommending at least three potential candidates for each of the 35 to 40 jobs at the top of the firm.

Gambling on its Brands

Above all, Lafley had been intent on shifting the focus of P&G back to its consumers. At every opportunity, he tried to drill his managers and employees to not lose sight of the consumer. He felt that P&G often let technology dictate its new products rather than consumer needs. He wanted to see the firm work more closely with retailers, the place where consumers first see the product on the shelf. And he placed a lot of emphasis on getting a better sense of the consumer's experience with P&G products when they actually use them at home.

Over the decade of Lafley's leadership, P&G managed to update all of its 200 brands by adding innovative new products. It began to offer devices that build on its core brands, such as *Tide StainBrush*, a battery-powered brush for removing stains, and *Mr. Clean AutoDry*, a water pressure-powered car cleaning system that dries without streaking. P&G also began to approach its brands more creatively. *Crest*, for example, which used to be marketed as a toothpaste brand, was redefined an oral care brand. The firm now sells *Crest*-branded toothbrushes and tooth whiteners.

In order to ensure that P&G continues to come up with innovative ideas, Lafley had also confronted head-on the stubbornly held notion that everything must be invented within P&G, asserting that half of its new products should come from the outside. Under the new "Connect and Develop" model of innovation, the firm pushed to get almost 50 percent of its new product ideas from outside the firm. This could be compared to the 10 percent figure that existed at P&G when Lafley had taken charge.

A key element of P&G's strategy, however, was to move the firm away from basic consumer products such as laundry detergents, which can be knocked off by private labels, to higher-margin products. Under Lafley, P&G made costly acquisitions of Clairol and Wella to complement its *Cover Girl* and *Oil of Olay* brands. The firm even moved into prestige fragrances through licenses with Hugo Boss, Gucci, and Dolce & Gabbana. When he stepped down, beauty products had risen to account for about a quarter of the firm's total revenues.

But P&G's riskiest moves had been its expansion into services, starting with car washes and dry cleaning. The car washes build on *Mr. Clean*, P&G's popular cleaning product. In expanding the brand to car washes, the firm expected to distinguish its outlets from others by offering additional services such as *Febreze* odor eliminators, lounges with Wi-Fi and big screen televisions, and spray guns that children can aim at cars passing through the wash. Similarly, P&G's dry cleaning outlets are named after *Tide*, its best selling laundry detergent. The stores will include drive-through services, 24-hour pickup, and environmentally benign cleaning methods.

Losing the Momentum

On July 1, 2009, Lafley passed the leadership of P&G to McDonald, who had joined the firm in 1980 and worked his way up through posts in Canada, Japan, the Philippines, and Belgium to become chief operating officer. McDonald took over after the start of a calamitous recession, and had to deal with various emerging problems. As consumers in the United States and Europe were not willing to pay premium prices, the firm's push to expand in emerging markets was also yielding few results in the face of stiff competition from Unilever and Colgate-Palmolive, who already had a strong presence. Furthermore, commodity prices were surging, even as P&G's products were already too expensive for the struggling middle class that it was targeting everywhere.

In order to deal with all of these challenges, McDonald replaced Lafley's clear motto of "the consumer is boss" with his own slogan of "purpose-inspired growth." In his own words, this meant that P&G was "touching and improving more consumers' lives, in more parts of the world, more completely."[5] "Purpose" was an undeniably laudable ambition, but many employees simply could not fathom how to translate this rhetoric into action. Dick Antoine, P&G's head of human resources from 1998 to 2008 commented: "'Purpose-inspired growth' is a wonderful slogan, but it doesn't help allocate assets."[6]

In part, P&G's troubles also stemmed from its inability to launch any major new products. As such, it was difficult for the firm to turn away from the pressure to cut back on the prices of its established brands. Given the wide range of problems that McDonald faced, in terms of pushing for growth across several different businesses across many markets, he made some effort to try and address all of them simultaneously. Ali Dibadj, a senior analyst at Sanford Bernstein commented on this multi-pronged effort by P&G: "The strategic problem was that they decided to go after everything. But they ran out of ammo too quickly."[7]

By the middle of 2012, it was becoming obvious that P&G was struggling under McDonald's leadership. Known for its reliable performance, the firm was forced to lower its profit guidelines three times in six months frustrating analysts and investors alike. Even within the firm, many executives realized that McDonald would not be able to take the bold moves that may allow the firm to recover from its slump. Activist investor Bill Ackerman commented: "We're delighted to see the company's made some progress. But P&G deserves to be led by one of the best CEO's in the world."[8]

Striving for Agility

Shareholder dissatisfaction with lack of improvement in performance led P&G to push McDonald out and bring back Lafley in May 2013. As soon as he stepped back in, Lafley was under pressure to respond to investor concerns that P&G had become too large and bloated to respond quickly to changing consumer demands. In April 2014, he began the process of streamlining the firm by selling off most of its pet food brands–including *Iams* and *Eukanuba* –to Mars for $2.9 billion.

A few months later, in August 2014, Lafley took a bolder step. He announced that the firm would unload as many as 100 of its brands in order to better focus on 60 to 70 of its biggest ones–such as *Tide* detergent and *Pampers* diapers–that generate about 90 percent of its $83 billion in annual sales and over 95 percent of its profit (see Exhibits 4 and 5). At the same time, Lafley insisted that sales will not be the only criteria for shedding brands. He stated that some large

EXHIBIT 4 Business Segments, 2018

Reportable Segments	% of Net Sales	% of Net Earnings	Product Categories (Sub-Categories)	Major Brands
Beauty	19%	23%	Hair Care	Head & Shoulders, Pantene, Rejoice
			Skin and Personal Care	Olay, Old Spice, Safeguard, SK-II
Grooming	10%	14%	Shave Care - *Female Blades & Razors, Male Blades & Razors, etc.*	Braun, Fusion, Gillette, Mach3, Prestobarba, Venus
Health Care	12%	13%	Oral Care	Crest, Oral-B
			Personal Health Care	Metamucil, Prilosec, Vicks
Fabric & Home Care	32%	27%	Laundry Products	Ariel, Downy, Gain, Tide
			Cleansers	Cascade, Dawn, Febreze, Mr. Clean, Swiffer
Baby, Feminine, & Family Care	27%	23%	Baby Care	Luvs, Pampers
			Feminine Care	Always, Tampax
			Paper Towels, Tissues, etc.	Bounty, Charmin, Puffs

Source: P&G Annual Report 2018.

brands will be jettisoned if they don't fit with the firm's core business: "If it's not a core brand–I don't care whether it's a $2 billion brand–it will be divested."[9]

Although analysts were receptive to the reduction of brands, they pointed out that P&G has already sold off more than 30 established brands over the past 15 years that were supposedly hindering growth. Many of these sold-off brands have been performing well with other firms. J.M. Smucker, for example, that bought *Crisco* shortening, *Folgers* coffee, and *Jif* peanut butter, has had 50 percent sales growth since 2009. Some critics charge that P&G, which was once was most successful in building and managing brands, has lost its touch.

In large part, the focus is on the cumbersome centralized and bureaucratic structure that has developed at P&G. Unlike many of its newer competitors, the firm still tends to rely less on working with outside partners. The Connect and Develop program that had been started by Lafley to bring in new ideas from outsiders has led to 50 percent of its new technologies coming from outside, but these are then reworked or modified by P&G's internal R&D group. This has stifled innovation, with most of the firm's growth coming from line extensions of existing brands or from costly acquisitions.

On November 1, 2015, Lafley stepped down, passing the reins to David Taylor, who had built his career at P&G. He had most recently been assigned to take over the firm's struggling beauty unit. Taylor continued with Lafley's strategy of cutting back on P&G's brands. The sale of 43 of the firm's beauty brands to Coty in a $12 billion deal was completed in October 2016. A few months earlier, P&G had completed the transfer of Duracell to Berkshire Hathaway through an exchange of shares.

Fighting for Its Iconic Status

Under Taylor, P&G has been trying to find ways to revive the prospects of its mostly aging brands. For years, P&G had spent heavily to build on its success with legacy soap and detergent brands to acquire hundreds of additional brands in new businesses that it hoped could also become part of consumers' daily routines. The latest effort to jettison over half of its brands indicated that the strategy was not working anymore. In particular, P&G has been struggling with its push to place more emphasis on products that carry higher margins in order to move it away from its dependence on household staples.

Above all, it is clear that the recent push to expand into new categories with acquired brands did not produce the desired results. The firm's aggressive push into beauty, for example, has struggled to show much growth. Lafley had tried to build the firm's presence in this business for years, regarding it as a high margin, faster growing complement to the firm's core household products. The firm has struggled to show growth in this business and it has been generating the lowest profit margins. Sales of *Olay* skin care products and *Pantene* hair care products have mostly sagged in recent years. Its efforts to build a line of perfumes around licenses with Dolce & Gabbana, Gucci, and Hugo Boss were also running into problems.

Analysts are hoping that the decision to restructure P&G will address long-standing problems that the firm has

EXHIBIT 5 Financial Breakdown 2018

Global Segment Results		Net Sales	Earnings/(Loss) from Continuing Operations Before Income Taxes	Net Earnings/ (Loss) from Continuing Operations	Depreciation and Amortization	Total Assets	Capital Expenditures
BEAUTY	**2018**	**$12,406**	**$ 3,042**	**$ 2,320**	**$ 236**	**$ 4,709**	**$ 766**
	2017	11,429	2,546	1,914	220	4,184	599
	2016	11,477	2,636	1,975	218	3,888	435
GROOMING	**2018**	**6,551**	**1,801**	**1,432**	**447**	**22,609**	**364**
	2017	6,642	1,985	1,537	433	22,759	341
	2016	6,815	2,009	1,548	451	22,819	383
HEALTH CARE	**2018**	**7,857**	**1,922**	**1,283**	**230**	**5,254**	**330**
	2017	7,513	1,898	1,898	209	5,194	283
	2016	7,350	1,812	1,250	204	5,139	240
FABRIC & HOME CARE	**2018**	**21,441**	**4,191**	**2,708**	**534**	**7,295**	**1,020**
	2017	20,171	4,249	2,713	513	6,886	797
	2016	20,730	4,249	2,778	531	6,919	672
BABY, FEMININE, & FAMILY CARE	**2018**	**18,080**	**3,527**	**2,251**	**899**	**9,682**	**1,016**
	2017	18,252	3,868	2,503	874	9,920	1,197
	2016	18,505	4,042	2,650	886	9,863	1,261
CORPORATE	**2018**	**497**	**(1,157)**	**(133)**	**488**	**68,761**	**221**
	2017	505	(1,289)	247	571	71,463	167
	2016	422	(1,379)	(174)	788	78,508	323
TOTAL COMPANY	**2018**	**$66,832**	**$13,326**	**$ 9,861**	**$2,834**	**$118,310**	**$3,717**
	2017	65,058	13,257	10,194	2,820	120,406	3,384
	2016	65,299	13,369	10,027	3,078	127,136	3,314

Source: P&G Annual Report 2018.

been facing. The new organization will give more responsibility for its different product categories to separate business units, giving them control over their sales for the largest 10 geographic markets, including the United States, China, Russia, and Germany. Such a push for decentralization would give these units more freedom to adjust their strategies to the needs of the different product categories in each of the markets. "We are accelerating the pace of change and stepping up execution to meet the challenges of today's dynamic world," said Taylor.[10]

ENDNOTES

1. Al-Muslim, A.2018. P&G streamlines its management. *Wall Street Journal*, November 9, p. B2.
2. Reingold, J. and D. Burke. 2013. Can P&G's CEO hang on? *Fortune*, February 25, p. 69.
3. Coolridge, A. 2014. P&G plans to unload more than its brands. *Cincinnati Enquirer*, August 2, p. 1.
4. Benoit, D. and S. Terlep. 2017. Activist builds $3 billion stake in P&G. *Wall Street Journal*, February 15, p. A1.
5. P&G Annual Report 2009.
6. Reingold, J. and D. Burke. 2013. Can P&G's CEO hang on? *Fortune*, February 25, p. 70.
7. Ibid.
8. Ibid. p. 75.
9. Ibid. p. 70.
10. Press Release. 2019 (January 23). P&G announces fiscal year 2019 second quarter results.

CASE 26

ASCENA: STILL STRUGGLING IN SPECIALTY RETAIL*

In the first quarter of 2019, nine retailers filed for bankruptcy, including teenage apparel retailer Charlotte Russe, kids clothing retailer Gymboree, and plus-size apparel brand FullBeauty Brands.[1] This was not unexpected. Certain firms in the retail sector had been struggling for several years, especially those dependent on mall traffic. Certainly competition from Amazon and other more nimble retailers with an online presence had put pressure on brick-and-mortar profit margins, but retailers could adapt if they paid attention. For those who did not adapt, reduced traffic, reduced revenue, and subsequent mounting debt would require difficult decisions.

It had been a tough few years. 2018 saw 17 bankruptcies, but 2017 had seen 21 closures, giving it the dubious distinction of being the worst year for retailing since the recession of 2008 when 20 entities closed shop.[2,3] Names of shuttered and at-risk stores included footwear and apparel retailers BCBG Max Azria, Eastern Outfitters, Wet Seal, Limited Stores, Payless, Bon-Ton, Claire's Stores, rue21, Nine West, and Diesel USA. Other chains such as the department stores J.C. Penney, Sears, and Kmart, and specialty retailers J.Crew, Land's End, Neiman Marcus, and Toms Shoes were closing stores, consolidating operations, searching for refinancing options and trying to figure out what to do when top-line growth inevitably slowed.[4] The sector was undergoing transformation and it was hard to find a way forward.

Although it was true that shoppers could be fickle, there was still room to create a loyal following, especially in markets where younger, wealthier consumers had the most disposable income.[5] Customers needed a reason to shop. Whether it be in a physical location or online, the shopping experience needed to be appealing, not only in quality and assortment of merchandise, but also in customer service and personalization options, including how browsing, ordering, and payment systems were integrated seamlessly across channels. Although analysts expected 2019 to be no worse for apparel retailers than 2018, and even expected single digit growth in some venues, the opinion was that the apparel sector would be "forced to evolve to meet the needs of aging baby boomers, casualization of the workforce and competition from fast-fashion and online retailers."[6] There was a need for innovative concepts in both the shopping experience and back-end operations, and those retailers who did not embrace change would suffer: "it will be mission-critical for brands to converge all their channels and touchpoints into single, seamless, branded shopping experiences."[7] When Ralph Lauren's New York City flagship store closed, one researcher noted, "at the end of the day, there is no natural law that suggests that an iconic brand, as iconic as his has been, is guaranteed to be successful forever and always."[8] This comment could also apply to other iconic retailers. Just having a powerful brand strategy might not be enough. There was a paradigm shift under way, and only those with results-oriented operations might be able to survive and thrive.

Going into 2019, Ascena Retail Group, Inc. (NASDAQ:ASNA), owners of a well-rounded portfolio of brands providing women's and girl's specialty apparel, was trying to position itself for this challenge. Ascena had made several moves to improve its portfolio, most recently with its acquisition of ANN INC., iconic specialty retailer of women's apparel provided under the Ann Taylor, LOFT, and Lou & Grey brands. As a standalone women's specialty retailer, ANN had missed earning projections, seen stagnant same-store sales, slow inventory turnover, and significant margin compression, with no fix in sight. ANN's activist investors had demanded action, which opened the door for Ascena's acquisition of ANN Inc. in August 2015.

With this acquisition, Ascena Retail Group had become the largest U.S. specialty retailer focused exclusively on women and girls. Only exceeded in net sales by L Brands, the owner of Victoria's Secret and Bath & Body Works, and by The Gap, Inc., Ascena offered apparel, shoes, and accessories for women and girls. Ascena operated four focused, branded retail options–the "Premium Fashion" segment with brands Ann Taylor, LOFT, and Lou & Grey; the "Value Fashion" segment, represented by the brands Maurices and Dressbarn; its "Plus Fashion" segment with Lane Bryant and Catherine's stores; and merchandise for tween girls via the Justice brand, under the "Kids Fashion" segment. Ascena also offered intimate apparel via Cacique and Catherine's Intimates. The ANN acquisition meant Ascena had expanded its brand profile even further across multiple segments, and would operate over 4,500 stores with annual projected sales of about $6.5 billion.

As a result of the ANN acquisition, Ascena not only gained a presence in the premium women's fashion market, but also hoped to realize $150 million in annualized run rate synergies through the integration of ANN's sourcing, procurement, distribution, and logistics operations. What might this mean for Ascena? Ascena had disappointing

---

* This case was prepared by Professor Pauline Assenza, Western Connecticut State University, and Professor Alan B. Eisner of Pace University. Special acknowledgment to Janelle T. Bennett, graduate student at Pace University, for research assistance. This case is solely based on library research and was developed for class discussion of strategies rather than to illustrate either effective or ineffective handling of the situation. Copyright © 2019 Pauline Assenza and Alan B. Eisner.

same-store sales in its previous portfolio for several years, and had boosted overall revenue primarily through acquisitions. Industrywide retail sales projections continued to be on the soft side, and many analysts worried that the increased debt Ascena now carried would need significant positive cash flow in order to provide adequate coverage. Given the uncertainty, analysts wondered if Ascena had pursued this growth strategy at the wrong time.[9] Although there were operational synergies Ascena could realize, it was still primarily reliant on store traffic, which was declining across many retailing categories.

December 2018 saw the worst overall holiday results in retail in nine years. Although some categories saw slight gains, such as the sporting goods and garden supply stores, others such as furniture and home goods did much worse. Clothing and accessories fell off the most.[10] It was hard to know what to do. In April 2019, Moody's, the credit rating agency, had downgraded Ascena stating that the company's rating is "constrained by company-specific execution missteps and the broader challenge of achieving material earnings improvement with a portfolio of primarily mature, mid- and value-priced brands amid a highly competitive apparel retail environment."[11] Ascena was relying on "streamlined operational efficiencies, improved IT capabilities, store-specific promotional activities and store closures" to continue its cost-cutting strategy, but still lacked a "meaningful eCommerce platform," making it difficult to adapt to the new consumer shopping preferences.[12] How had it come to this?

Ascena Retail Group Background

In 1962, there were few wear-to-work dresses and other clothing options for women entering the workforce, so Roslyn Jaffe and her husband Elliot opened the first Dressbarn in Stanford, Connecticut. By 1982 the company had become successful enough to go public as NASDAQ:DBRN and by 1985 they were operating 200 stores through the United States. Their vision of working women ages 35 to 55 expanded in 1989 with the opening of Dressbarn Woman, targeting plus-size individuals.

In the 1990s, trends in workplace fashion for women had shifted to a more casual look, and the company began to offer more sportswear, and expanded into shoes, petites, and jewelry. In 2002, Elliot and Roslyn's son David succeeded Elliot as CEO, while the elder Jaffe remained as chairman. Then, following the diversification trend, in 2005 Dressbarn Inc. acquired Maurices, a clothing chain from Duluth, Minnesota, that catered to women ages 17 to 34 who shopped primarily in the small-town strip malls of mid-America. Maurices was known for having sizing from 0 to 26 and employing "stylists" who could outfit customers for a reasonable price. In 2009, Dressbarn acquired Justice, the tween brand chain from New Albany, Ohio, that offered reasonably priced clothing and accessories to girls ages 7 to 14. Justice was formerly owned by Tween Brands, originally a subsidiary of The Limited.

In 2011, Dressbarn reorganized as Ascena Retail Group and changed its stock symbol to NASDAQ:ASNA. The following year Ascena acquired Charming Shoppes, adding the Lane Bryant and Catherine's plus-size brands to its portfolio. The Cacique line of intimates, sleepwear, and swimwear and Catherine's Intimates were added later to round out the offerings for full-sized women. The acquisition of ANN with its brands Ann Taylor, LOFT, and Lou & Grey in 2015 meant Ascena had 10 brands across four segments, a portfolio meant to serve the many wardrobing needs of women and tween girls, in all different ages, sizes, and demographics.

The Acquisition of Premium Brands

The ANN portfolio was intended to be a welcome addition to Ascena's portfolio. Founded in 1954, Ann Taylor had been the traditional wardrobe source for busy, socially upscale women, and the classic basic black dress and woman's power suit with pearls were Ann Taylor staples. The Ann Taylor client base consisted of fashion-conscious women from age 25 to 55. The overall Ann Taylor concept was designed to appeal to professional women who had limited time to shop and who were attracted to Ann Taylor stores by their total wardrobing strategy, personalized client service, efficient store layouts, and continual flow of new merchandise.

Ann Taylor had regularly appeared in the *Women's Wear Daily* Top 10 list of firms selling dresses, suits, and evening wear and ANN had three branded divisions focused on different segments of its customer base:

- Ann Taylor (AT), the company's original brand, provided sophisticated, versatile, and high-quality updated classics.
- Ann Taylor LOFT (LOFT), launched in 1998, was a newer brand concept that appealed to women who had a more relaxed lifestyle and work environment and who appreciated the more casual LOFT style and compelling value. Certain clients of Ann Taylor and LOFT cross-shopped both brands.
- Lou & Grey had evolved from the LOFT lounge collection in 2014 as a full lifestyle brand. Incorporating easygoing, texture-rich clothing with a selection of accessories, handcrafted by independent U.S. makers, Lou & Grey was for the woman on the go who did not want to have to choose between style and comfort.

The acquisition of these three brands had given Ascena a well-rounded portfolio for apparel shoppers.

Additional Ascena Portfolio Brands

In addition to the Premium Fashion brands Ann Taylor, LOFT, and Lou & Grey, the Ascena portfolio included the following:

Total Value Fashion

- Dressbarn—over 720 store locations throughout the United States with private label and contemporary fashions at great value to women in their mid-30s to mid-50s, including women's career, special occasion, casual, activewear, accessories, and footwear.

- Maurices–up-to-date casual, career/dressy, and athleisure fashion designed to appeal to middle-income females in their 20s and 30s in core and plus sizes who preferred a "hometown retailer." Over 40 percent of the over 970 stores were in the Midwest, with 37 stores in Canada.

Total Plus Fashion

- Lane Bryant–with over 740 locations, this was the most widely recognized brand name in plus-size fashion, catering to middle-income, female customers aged 25 to 45 in sizes 12 to 28 through private labels Lane Bryant, Cacique, and Livi Active. Products included intimate apparel, wear-to-work, casual sportswear, activewear, accessories, select footwear, and social occasion apparel.
- Catherine's–catered to women in U.S. sizes 16W to 34W and 0X to 5X. With over 340 stores nationwide, Catherine's had a competitive advantage with female consumers looking for hard-to-find extended sizes in clothing and intimates.

Total Kids Fashion

- Justice–offering fashionable apparel to 6- to 12-year-old tween girls in an energetic environment. In over 840 locations, products included apparel, activewear, footwear, intimates, accessories, and lifestyle products. The brand was positioned at the mid- to upper-end of pricing.

Heading into 2019, with this portfolio, Ascena appeared solidly positioned to serve the specialty apparel needs of women and girls from multiple consumer sectors. However, there were some significant challenges.

Apparel Retail Industry

Industry Sectors

To better appreciate the issues facing Ascena, it is helpful to understand the apparel retail industry. Several industry publications report data within the clothing sector. In addition to industry associations such as the National Retail Federation (NRF), the *Daily News Record* (DNR) reports on men's fashion news and business strategies, while *Women's Wear Daily* (WWD) reports on women's fashions and the apparel business. Practically speaking, industry watchers tend to recognize three categories of clothing retailers:

- *Discount mass merchandisers:* Chains such as Target, Walmart, TJX (T.J. Maxx, Marshall's, HomeGoods), and Costco.
- *Multitier department stores:* Those offering a large variety of goods, including clothing (full price examples like Macy's and JCPenney, lower price options like Ross Stores and Kohls), and the more luxury-goods-focused stores (for example, Nordstrom and Neiman Marcus).
- *Specialty store chains:* Those catering to a certain type of customer or carrying a certain type of goods (for example, Abercrombie & Fitch for casual apparel).

More specifically in the case of specialty retail, many primary categories existed, such as women's, men's, and children's clothing stores; for example, Victoria's Secret for women's undergarments,[13] Men's Wearhouse for men's suits, Abercrombie Kids for children ages 7 to 14.[14] Women's specialty stores were "establishments primarily engaged in retailing a specialized line of women's, juniors', and misses' clothing."[15]

Specialty Retailer Growth: Branding Challenges

Unlike department stores that sell many different types of products for many types of customers, specialty retailers focused on one type of product item and offered many varieties of that item. However, this single-product focus increased risk, as lost sales in one area could not be recouped by a shift of interest to another, entirely different product area. Therefore, many specialty retailers constantly sought new market segments (i.e., niches) that they could serve. However, this strategy created potential problems for branding.[16]

The Gap Inc. was an example of a specialty retailer that added several brand extensions to appeal to different customer segments. In addition to the original Gap line of casual clothing, the company offered the following: Old Navy with casual fashions at low prices; Banana Republic for more high-end casual items; Athleta with performance apparel and gear for active women; INTERMIX, an edited selection of clothing from coveted designers; Hill City, a high performance men's apparel brand established as B Corp certified brand, integrating sustainability throughout many of its products; and Janie and Jack, providing fashion for boys and girls up to age 12. Regarding other brand extensions, Gap had once spent $40 million to open a chain for upscale women's clothing called Forth & Towne, which closed after only 18 months. The store was supposed to appeal to upscale women over 35–the baby-boomer or "misses" segment–but, instead, the designers seemed "too focused on reproducing youthful fashions with a more generous cut" instead of finding an "interesting, affordable way" for middle-aged women to "dress like themselves."[17]

Gap had also acquired Weddington Way, a virtual showroom for bridesmaid dresses: customers could view the items online, discuss using social media, and then visit one of The Gap's other stores to try on and purchase their choices, but this operation was closed down in 2018. These acquisitions had been attempts to adapt to the new retail business models, providing personalization and the ability for customers to browse, order, and shop across what should be seamlessly integrated channels. It had not always worked, but even with these missteps, as of 2019 The Gap was still the apparel industry's leading specialty retailer.

In an attempt to remain in that position, The Gap had decided in early 2019 to spin off the Old Navy brand, and rename The Gap, which still included Banana Republic, Athleta, Hill City, and INTERMIX. The new company would be called "NewCo," and would help "refine the Gap brand store fleet," while a separate Old Navy would increase that brand's ability to be flexible in increasing customer access by "evolving its omni-channel model."[18] Some analysts were questioning the rationale of this move since, in fact, compared to the higher-end brands' choice to target more niche audiences, Old Navy was outperforming the rest of Gap's portfolio due to its focus on the off-price market segment.

Chico's FAS Inc. was another specialty retailer that had tried brand expansions. Chico's focused on private-label, casual-to-dressy clothing for women age 35 and older, with relaxed, figure-flattering styles constructed out of easy-care fabrics. An outgrowth of a Mexican folk art boutique, Chico's was originally a standalone entity, but made the decision to promote two new brands–White House/Black Market (WH/BM) and Soma by Chico's (Soma). Chico's WH/BM brand was based on the acquisition of an existing store chain, and it focused on women age 25 and older, offering fashion and merchandise in black-and-white and related shades. Soma was a brand offering intimate apparel, sleepwear, and active wear. Each brand had its own storefront, mainly in shopping malls, and was augmented by both mail-order catalog and Internet sales.

Similar to other women's specialty retailers, Chico's had seen increasing competition for its baby-boomer customers, and at one time had lost momentum, partly because of fashion missteps and lack of sufficiently new product designs. The company's response had been to create brand presidents for the different divisions to create more "excitement and differentiation."[19] Subsequently, Chico's FAS had been able to manage its market and by 2017, with a strong balance sheet and little debt, had become a specialty retailer focused on the omni-channel customer experience. This had not been enough, however, and in 2019 the company announced it would close at least 250 U.S. retail stores to better balance its mix between physical and online venues. Chico's FAS was also partnering with Amazon, ShopRunner, and QVC as well as thinking about implementing the buy-online-pick-up-in-store (BOPIS) model to drive traffic to the physical stores.[20]

In an attempt to better manage the proliferation of brands, many firms, similar to Chico's, created an organizational structure in which brands had their own dedicated managers, with titles such as executive vice president (EVP), general merchandise manager, chief merchandising officer, or outright "brand president."[21] With each brand supposedly unique, companies felt the person responsible for a brand's creative vision should be unique as well. Ascena was an example of how this structure worked: each of the segments was led by a CEO, CFO, or president with expertise in that area. For instance, the Premium Fashion segment, containing the ANN brands, had initially been run by Gary Muto, previously president of all ANN's brands, throughout all channels.

An alternative to brand extension was the divestiture of brands. In 1988, Limited Brands acquired Abercrombie and Fitch (A&F) and rebuilt A&F into what would become its current iconic representation of the "preppy" lifestyle of teenagers and college students ages 18 to 22. In 1996, Limited Brands spun A&F off as a separate public company, and by 2017 A&F was facing declining revenues, closing stores, and was rumored to be looking for a buyer.[22] Limited Brands had continued divesting:

- Teenage clothing and accessories brand The Limited TOO was divested in 1999, eventually became Justice, and was acquired by Ascena in 2009.
- Plus-size women's clothing brand Lane Bryant was sold to Charming Shoppes in 2001 and subsequently bought by Ascena in 2012.
- Professional women's clothing brand Lerner New York was divested in 2002, and in 2007 the casual women's clothing brands Express and The Limited were sold to Sun Capital Partners. Sun Capital ran these stores under The Limited brand until it filed for bankruptcy on January 7, 2017.

In 2013, Limited Brands renamed itself L Brands. Paring down in order to focus mostly on its key assets, Victoria's Secret and Bath & Body Works, the corporation had made a clear strategic decision to limit its exposure to changing clothing trends.[23] This strategy had been successful. In 2017, L Brands, at $12 billion net sales, with Pink, La Senza, and Henri Bendel in addition to its other two iconic brands, was the second largest specialty apparel retailer in the United States. However, by 2019 it had to consider the changing retail environment, and closed the Henri Bendel brand.[24] It had also sold off the Canadian lingerie brand La Senza in December 2018 and was planning to close over 50 Victoria's Secret stores in 2019 as it re-evaluated options. Victoria's Secret, the iconic brand known for its sexy lingerie and "angel" runway models, was no longer the brand of choice for those women seeking intimate apparel. The trend was to a more comfortable style and a shopping experience that was more inclusive of all body types and lifestyles.[25] Regardless, L Brands still secured the top revenue spot behind Gap and just ahead of Ascena. Gap had seven brands, L Brands had five, and Ascena had ten.

Ascena Retail Group Operations

According to Ascena's CEO David Jaffe, at the end of FY2018 Ascena was the largest specialty retailer focused exclusively on women and girls, and had a well-diversified portfolio of brands, covering multiple customer segments: Ascena served women and girls across generations, identities, affiliations, and body types.[26] Ascena had a revenue base spread across multiple real estate formats, and an efficient, scalable shared services platform. A $3001 million investment from FY13 to FY16 had consolidated corporate functions and created a global sourcing capability. An efficient distribution and fulfillment network fully supported an omni-channel platform, both online and in store. In 2018 Ascena's strong cash flow and liquidity appeared positioned to navigate industry change.

By 2019, Ascena had intended to evolve from the original seven $1 billion companies into one $7 billion powerhouse, using that "combined strength, expertise, and scale to exceed our customers' expectations and become a leader in specialty retail."[27] Ascena planned to do this via "centers of excellence" in procurement, global sourcing, real estate expertise, digital/customer platforms, supply chain optimization, and advanced analytics, with corporate oversight for human resources and finance. Refining the capabilities it had acquired with ANN, this would transform the enterprise through centralization, standardization, and using better methodologies and best practices. Through efficiency (reducing costs) and effectiveness (increasing capabilities) Ascena hoped to drive top line sales at profitable margins.

At the end of FY2018 Ascena had over 4,900 stores located throughout the United States in various real estate configurations. The majority of stores, especially the Maurices and Dressbarn stores that served the mid-America heartland, were located in strip malls, but the ANN properties were in downtown locations that attracted more affluent lifestyle customers. Acknowledging the challenges, Ascena had agreed it "probably" had too many stores, and was developing a "fleet optimization project" that would reduce the physical footprint as it transferred more business either to nearby stores or online.[28]

In addition to physical shopping locations, Ascena was investing in technology platforms to support the growth of its omni-channel strategy. ANN, Justice, and Maurices had all had e-commerce platforms, but the other brands needed to do the same. Retailers had to have an omni-channel strategy in order to compete. ANN had already brought Ascena the capability to ship from store, use an iPad app to shop an "endless aisle," do cross-channel returns, and use an "online find" app in the store. Going forward ANN and other Ascena brands would have to add the capability to buy online and pick up in the store, provide for alternative payments using a 1-click checkout, and allow enhanced site reviews.[29]

Ascena Retail Group Financial Profile

After the acquisition of ANN in 2015, sales at the Ascena Retail Group hit almost $7.0 billion. Growth had been the result of acquisitions and the expansion of technology platforms to augment e-commerce, but the trend over the next two years had been downward, and by 2019 the Acsena Retail Group had seen share prices drop, market capitalization decline, and comparable store sales in one of its four operating segments post a significant loss. Bloomberg noted that Ascena had over $1 billion in losses since 2015 and was more than $1.6 billion in debt.[30] Exhibit 1 represents a detailed income statement by segment for the last three fiscal years. Assets and liabilities, and a consolidated statement of operations and cash flows since 2015 are in Exhibit 2.

Commentary on Ascena's financials from Moody's in 2019 noted that even though the business had an uncertain future, as did so many other specialty retailers, so far its "conservative financial policies and good liquidity" boded well for the repayment of debt over the next few years.[31]

Odds of Survival in Specialty Retail?

In the 2018 Annual Report, CEO David Jaffee said:

> As we enter fiscal 2019, we are leveraging the foundation we've build over the past two years to pivot the organization toward the most critical pillar of our transformation program–reinvigorating growth from our core.[32]

Actions Ascena had taken toward this "reinvigoration" included closing underperforming stores across all segments, and addressing the "unacceptable level of profitability" in its value brands by offering up Maurices for acquisition by an affiliate of OpCapita LLP. The deal, which valued Maurices at an enterprise value of $300 million, was closed in May 2019. Ascena maintained a minority interest in the brand, and used the proceeds from this sale to pay down existing debt.[33] In the wake of this announcement, rumors were floated that Dressbarn was also up for grabs. This might fix the value segment's underperformance, but financial fixes would not help a company attract customers. Retailers needed to do something that would drive sales.

At the start of 2019 it appeared that the acquisition of the ANN portfolio had indeed helped Ascena–the premium brand segment was the best performing of the four–and moves were under way to fix the value brands, but things were still unresolved in the plus fashion segment. Although this was a sector of the apparel market Ascena had once dominated, both Lane Bryant and Catherines same store comparable sales had fallen eight and four percent in the second quarter, continuing a trend noted in 2018 and prompting a comment by Ascena Brand President Gary Muto that "Lane Bryant must enhance its emotional connection with its core customer."[34] But would that work when plus-size women could find fashionable items in stores like Target or even at Lou & Grey? In addition, sales in the Cacique intimates division were down as well. Just as Victoria's Secret had discovered, customers were looking for a more inclusive environment: "inclusivity is no mere fad . . . [retailers] should embrace different views, races, gender identifications, styles, along with sizes."[35]

In 2017 one fashion watcher had pointed out that customers wanted the opportunity to discover trends for themselves, openly seeking "self-expression through shopping," feeling that "they created the outfit, rather than it was created for them. . . The future success of fashion retailers will be found when they offer up the unexpected in interesting, stimulating and exciting ways."

EXHIBIT 1
Net Sales and Operating Income, 2016–2018

	Fiscal Years Ended		
	August 4, 2018	**July 29, 2017**	**July 30, 2016**
Net sales:		**(millions)**	
Premium Fashion[(a)]	$2,317.8	$ 2,322.6	$2,330.9
Value Fashion	1,820.5	1,950.2	2,094.6
Plus Fashion	1,340.0	1,353.9	1,463.6
Kids Fashion	1,100.0	1,023.1	1,106.3
Total net sales	$6,578.3	$6,649.8	$6,995.4
Operating income (loss):			
Premium Fashion[(a)(b)]	$ 135.2	$ 140.9	$ 13.3
Value Fashion	(83.2)	12.2	92.0
Plus Fashion	27.1	15.5	36.9
Kids Fashion	39.1	(36.7)	29.0
Unallocated acquisition and integration expenses	(5.4)	(39.4)	(77.4)
Unallocated restructuring and other related charges[(c)]	(78.5)	(81.9)	—
Unallocated impairment of goodwill (Note 6)	—	(596.3)	—
Unallocated impairment of intangible assets (Note 6)	—	(728.1)	—
Total operating income (loss)	$ 34.3	$(1,313.8)	$ 93.8

[(a)] The results of the **Premium Fashion** segment for the post-acquisition period from August 22, 2015 to July 30, 2016 are included within the Company's consolidated results of operations for Fiscal 2016.

[(b)] The results of the **Premium Fashion** segment for Fiscal 2016 include approximately $126.9 million of non-cash purchase accounting expense related to the amortization of the write-up of inventory to fair market value.

Source: Ascena 10K for the fiscal year ending August 4, 2018.

EXHIBIT 2
Consolidated Balance Sheet, Statement of Operations, Cash Flows

	August 4, 2018	**July 29, 2017**
	(millions, except per share data)	
ASSETS		
Current assets:		
Cash and cash equivalents	$ 238.9	$ 325.6
Inventories	622.9	639.3
Prepaid expenses and other current assets	248.5	157.4
Total current assets	1,110.3	1,122.3
Property and equipment, net	1,205.3	1,437.6
Goodwill	683.0	683.0
Other intangible assets, net	516.0	532.4
Other assets	55.9	96.2
Total assets	$3,570.5	$3,871.5

EXHIBIT 2
(Continued)

	August 4, 2018	July 29, 2017
	(millions, except per share data)	
LIABILITIES AND EQUITY		
Current liabilities:		
Accounts payable	$ 437.6	$ 411.6
Accrued expenses and other current liabilities	326.3	352.9
Deferred income	121.7	121.5
Income taxes payable	5.1	7.1
Current portion of long-term debt	—	44.0
Total current liabilities	890.7	937.1
Long-term debt	1,328.7	1,494.1
Lease-related liabilities	315.2	348.3
Deferred income taxes	29.6	79.3
Other non-current liabilities	207.8	191.7
Total liabilities	2,772.0	3,050.5
Commitments and contingencies (Note 15)		
Equity:		
Common stock, par value $0.01 per share; 196.3 and 195.1 million shares issued and outstanding	2.0	2.0
Additional paid-in capital	1,088.2	1,068.2
Accumulated deficit	(278.8)	(238.8)
Accumulated other comprehensive loss	(12.9)	(10.4)
Total equity	798.5	821.0
Total liabilities and equity	$3,570.5	$3,871.5

	Fiscal Years Ended		
	August 4, 2018	July 29, 2017	July 30, 2016
	(millions, except per share data)		
Net sales	$ 6,578.3	$ 6,649.8	$ 6,995.4
Cost of goods sold	(2,786.8)	(2,790.2)	(3,066.7)
Gross margin	3,791.5	3,859.6	3,928.7
Other operating expenses:			
Buying, distribution and occupancy expenses	(1,281.1)	(1,274.3)	(1,286.5)
Selling, general and administrative expenses	(2,036.7)	(2,068.5)	(2,112.3)
Acquisition and integration expenses	(5.4)	(39.4)	(77.4)
Restructuring and other related charges	(78.5)	(81.9)	—
Impairment of goodwill	—	(596.3)	—
Impairment of intangible assets	—	(728.1)	—
Depreciation and amortization expense	(355.5)	(384.9)	(358.7)
Total other operating expenses	(3,757.2)	(5,173.4)	(3,834.9)

EXHIBIT 2
(Continued)

	Fiscal Years Ended		
	August 4, 2018	July 29, 2017	July 30, 2016
	(millions, except per share data)		
Operating income (loss)	34.3	(1,313.8)	93.8
Interest expense	(113.0)	(102.2)	(103.3)
Interest and other income, net	2.2	1.8	0.4
(Loss) gain on extinguishment of debt	(5.0)	–	0.8
Loss before benefit (provision) for income taxes	(81.5)	(1,414.2)	(8.3)
Benefit (provision) for income taxes	41.8	346.9	(3.6)
Net loss	$ (39.7)	$(1,067.3)	$ (11.9)
Net loss per common share:			
Basic	$ (0.20)	$ (5.48)	$ (0.06)
Diluted	$ (0.20)	$ (5.48)	$ (0.06)
Weighted average common shares outstanding:			
Basic	196.0	194.8	192.2
Diluted	196.0	194.8	192.2

	Fiscal Years Ended		
	August 4, 2018	July 29, 2017	July 30, 2016
	(millions)		
Cash flows from operating activities:			
Net loss	$ (39.7)	$(1,067.3)	$ (11.9)
Adjustments to reconcile net loss to net cash provided by operating activities:			
Depreciation and amortization expense	355.5	384.9	358.7
Deferred income tax benefit	(47.1)	(371.3)	(26.8)
Deferred rent and other occupancy costs	(47.1)	(62.7)	(74.4)
Loss (gain) on extinguishment of debt	5.0	–	(0.8)
Gain on sale of fixed assets	(1.6)	–	–
Amortization of acquisition-related inventory write-up	–	–	126.9
Stock-based compensation expense	19.8	24.5	26.2
Impairment of tangible assets	49.2	35.6	13.3
Impairment of goodwill	–	596.3	–
Impairment of other intangible assets	–	728.1	–
Non-cash interest expense	11.9	12.1	11.3
Other non-cash expense (income), net	0.2	10.9	(0.9)
Excess tax benefits from stock-based compensation	–	–	(1.5)

EXHIBIT 2
(Continued)

	Fiscal Years Ended		
	August 4, 2018	July 29, 2017	July 30, 2016
		(millions)	
Changes in operating assets and liabilities:			
Inventories	16.4	10.0	111.4
Accounts payable, accrued liabilities and income taxes payable	(11.2)	(26.0)	(133.6)
Deferred income	13.0	15.6	7.8
Lease-related liabilities	20.9	31.4	52.5
Other balance sheet changes, net	(71.3)	21.5	(12.8)
Net cash provided by operating activities	273.9	343.6	445.4
Cash flows from investing activities:			
Cash paid for the acquisition of ANN INC., net of cash acquired	–	–	(1,494.6)
Capital expenditures	(186.3)	(258.1)	(366.5)
Acquisition of intangible assets	–	(11.6)	–
Proceeds from the sale of assets	14.6	–	–
Purchases of investments	–	–	(1.1)
Proceeds from the settlement of corporate-owned life insurance policies	37.5	–	–
Proceeds from sales and maturities of investments	–	0.8	26.5
Other investing activities	(0.2)	–	–
Net cash used in investing activities	(134.4)	(268.9)	(1,835.7)
Cash flows from financing activities:			
Proceeds from revolver borrowings	553.5	1,221.9	1,510.5
Repayments of revolver borrowings	(553.5)	(1,221.9)	(1,626.5)
Proceeds from term loan, net of original issue discount	–	–	1,764.0
Redemptions and repayments of term loan	(225.0)	(122.5)	(77.4)
Payment of deferred financing costs	(1.3)	–	(42.6)
Purchases and retirements of common stock	–	–	(18.6)
Proceeds from stock options exercised and employee stock purchases	0.4	1.6	10.6
Tax payments related to share-based awards	(0.3)	–	–
Excess tax benefits from stock-based compensation	–	–	1.5
Net cash (used in) provided by financing activities	(226.2)	(120.9)	1,521.5
Net (decrease) increase in cash and cash equivalents	(86.7)	(46.2)	131.2
Cash and cash equivalents at beginning of year	325.6	371.8	240.6
Cash and cash equivalents at end of year	$ 238.9	$ 325.6	$ 371.8

Source: Ascena 10K for the fiscal year ending August 4, 2018.

This commentator went on to say, "today the Ascena brands are a completely known quantity. And while they may be trusted and dependable, that also makes them boring."[36] In 2019, it was more apparent than ever that the changing consumer behavior was transforming retail. As The Gap, L Brands, and Ascena discovered, it appeared the odds of survival in specialty retail were not favorable, even for top companies.

ENDNOTES

1. Howland, D, Salpini, C. and K. Vembar. 2019. The running list of 2019 bankruptcy victims, *RetailDive,* March 13, https://www.retaildive.com/news/the-running-list-of-2019-bankruptcy-victims/545774/.
2. CB Insights. 2019. Here's a list of 68 bankruptcies in the retail apocalypse and why they failed. *CB Insights,* March 12, https://www.cbinsights.com/research/retail-apocalypse-timeline-infographic/.
3. Fader, P. and M.A. Cohen. 2017. Are retailers facing a coming "tsunami"? *Knowledge @* Wharton, April 6, http://knowledge.wharton.upenn.edu/article/are-retailers-facing-a-coming-tsunami/.
4. Thomas, L. 2018. Sears, Mattress Firm, and more: Here are the retailers that went bankrupt in 2018. *CNBC.com,* December 31, https://www.cnbc.com/2018/12/31/here-are-the-retailers-including-sears-that-went-bankrupt-in-2018.html.
5. Dunn, L. 2018. The Future of Women's Specialty Apparel, *The Robin Report,* August 13, https://www.therobinreport.com/the-future-of-womens-specialty-apparel/.
6. Ibid.
7. Ewen, L. 2017. The 7 trends that will shape apparel retail in 2017. *RetailDive.com,* January 4, http://www.retaildive.com/news/the-7-trends-that-will-shape-apparel-retail-in-2017/433249/.
8. Fader, P. and M.A. Cohen. 2017. Are retailers facing a coming "tsunami"? *Knowledge @* Wharton, April 6, http://knowledge.wharton.upenn.edu/article/are-retailers-facing-a-coming-tsunami/.
9. The Frugal Prof. 2017. Ascena: No end in sight for shareholder pain. *SeekingAlpha,* March 23, https://seekingalpha.com/article/4057390-ascena-end-sight-shareholder-pain; Longauer, P. 2017. Retail discount: Ascena. *SeekingAlpha,* February 13, https://seekingalpha.com/article/4045321-retail-discount-ascena; Arnold, J. 2016. Ascena retail group is an unmitigated disaster, *SeekingAlpha,* December 27, https://seekingalpha.com/article/4032967-ascena-retail-group-unmitigated-disaster.
10. Howland, D. 2019. January retail sales clouded by worst December in 9 years. *RetailDive,* March 12, https://www.retaildive.com/news/january-retail-sales-clouded-by-worst-december-in-9-years/550262/.
11. Whiteman, L. 2019. Here's why Ascena retail shares dropped on Tuesday. *Motley Fool,* March 19, https://www.fool.com/investing/2019/03/19/heres-why-ascena-retail-shares-dropped-on-tuesday.aspx.
12. Pinxter Analytics. 2019. Ascena retail: I just don't see a way forward. *SeekingAlpha,* March 12, https://seekingalpha.com/article/4248175-ascena-retail-just-see-way-forward.
13. Victoria's Secret is a division of L Brands (formerly Limited Brands), which also operates Pink (a subbrand of Victoria's Secret focused on sleepwear and intimate apparel for high school and college students), Bath & Body Works, C.O. Bigelow (personal beauty, body, and hair products), The White Barn Candle Co. (candles and home fragrances), Henri Bendel (high-fashion women's clothing), and La Senza (lingerie sold in Canada and worldwide). Reflecting challenges in the retail environment, Henri Bendel was closed down and La Senza was sold off in 2019.
14. Abercrombie & Fitch, as of 2015, had three brand divisions in addition to the flagship Abercrombie & Fitch stores–abercrombie (the brand name is purposely lowercase) for kids ages 7 to 14; Hollister Co. for southern California surf-lifestyle teens; and Gilly Hicks: Sydney, launched in 2008, specializing in women's intimate apparel. RUEHL No. 925, launched in 2004 with more sophisticated apparel for ages 22 to 35, closed in 2010.
15. U.S. Census Bureau. Monthly Retail Trade and Food Services NAICS Codes, Titles, and Descriptions, www.census.gov/svsd/www/artsnaics.html.
16. According to the American Marketing Association (AMA), a brand is a "name, term, sign, symbol or design, or a combination of them intended to identify the goods and services of one seller or group of sellers and to differentiate them from those of other sellers. . . . Branding is not about getting your target market to choose you over the competition, but it is about getting your prospects to see you as the only one that provides a solution to their problem." A good brand will communicate this message clearly and with credibility, motivating the buyer by eliciting some emotion that inspires future loyalty. From marketing.about.com/cs/brandmktg/a/whatisbranding.htm.
17. Turner, J. 2007. Go forth and go out of business. *Slate,* February 26, www.slate.com/id/2160668.
18. Duberstein, B. 2019. Here's why Gap is really spinning off Old Navy. *Motley Fool,* March 5, https://www.fool.com/investing/2019/03/05/heres-why-gap-is-really-spinning-off-old-navy.aspx.
19. Lee, G. 2007. Chico's outlines plan to improve results. *Women's Wear Daily,* March 8: 5.
20. Research in 2018 by Canadian firm OrderDynamics showed that North American consumers who participate in omni-channel retail environments made additional purchases when they came to pick up the item in the store, spending $40 more on additional unplanned purchases. This requires a seamless shopping integration by the retailer, however, because most of these consumers want to pick up their BOPIS orders within 24 hours. https://www.retaildive.com/press-release/20180725-more-than-half-of-most-active-click-and-collect-shoppers-made-additional-in/.
21. The responsibilities of these positions include "creative vision" for the brand–marketing materials, store design, and overall merchandising (developing product, ensuring production efficiency, monitoring store inventory turnover, and adjusting price points as needed).
22. LaMonica, P.R. 2017. Abercrombie & Fitch's latest sale may be itself. *Money.com,* May 10, http://money.cnn.com/2017/05/10/investing/abercrombie-fitch-takeover-rumors/index.html.
23. *Columbus Business First.* 2007. Limited Brands cutting 530 jobs. June 22, columbus.bizjournals.com/columbus/stories/2007/06/18/daily26.html.
24. Henri Bendel was an upscale retailer of handbags, accessories and gifts. Established in New York City in 1895, Bendel was the first retailer with an upper Fifth Avenue address. https://www.investopedia.com/articles/company-insights/090716/top-4-companies-owned-l-brands-including-victorias-secret-lb.asp.
25. Hirsch, L., and L. Thomas. 2019. L Brands to close 53 Victoria's Secret stores, says 'everything is on the table' for lingerie brand. *CNBC.com,* February 28, https://www.cnbc.com/2019/02/28/l-brands-plans-to-close-roughly-53-victorias-secret-stores-this-year.html.
26. Ascena Retail Group, Inc. 2019. Home page. https://www.ascenaretail.com/
27. See Slideshow Investor Presentation, January 18, 2017, https://seekingalpha.com/article/4038010-ascena-retail-group-asna-investor-presentation-slideshow.
28. Ascena Retail Group's Q2 2017 Results–Earnings Call Transcript, March 6, 2017, https://seekingalpha.com/article/4052526-ascena-retail-groups-asna-ceo-david-jaffe-q2-2017-results-earnings-call-transcript?part=single.
29. Slideshow Investor Presentation, January 18, 2017. https://seekingalpha.com/article/4038010-ascena-retail-group-asna-investor-presentation-slideshow.
30. Coleman-Lochner, L. and E. Ronalds-Hannon. 2019. Ascena is exploring the sale of its Dressbarn retail chain. *Bloomberg,* March 28, https://www.bnnbloomberg.ca/ascena-is-exploring-the-sale-of-its-dressbarn-retail-chain-1.1236446.
31. Whiteman, L. 2019. Here's why Ascena retail shares dropped on Tuesday. *Motley Fool,* March 19, https://www.fool.com/investing/2019/03/19/heres-why-ascena-retail-shares-dropped-on-tuesday.aspx.
32. Ascena 2018 Annual Report 10K.

33. Whiteman, L. 2019. Here's why Ascena retail shares dropped on Tuesday. *Motley Fool,* March 19, https://www.fool.com/investing/2019/03/19/heres-why-ascena-retail-shares-dropped-on-tuesday.aspx.
34. Ascena Retail Group's (ASNA) CEO David Jaffee on Q2 2019 Results – Earnings Call Transcript, March 14, 2019, https://seekingalpha.com/article/4248947-ascena-retail-groups-asna-ceo-david-jaffe-q2-2019-results-earnings-call-transcript?part=single.
35. Howland, D. 2019. The plus-size era is over before it began. *RetailDive,* February 11, https://www.retaildive.com/news/the-plus-size-era-is-over-before-it-began/547938/ .
36. Danziger, P.N. 2017. Why Ascena retail group is failing and what can be done about it. *Forbes,* June 15, https://www.forbes.com/sites/pamdanziger/2017/06/15/why-ascena-retail-group-is-failing-and-what-can-be-done-about-it/#a77670e35a4a.

CASE 27

THE BOSTON BEER COMPANY: BREWING UP SUCCESS?*

The Boston Beer Company, well known for its Samuel Adams brand, is the largest craft brewery in the United States. The past couple of years, the beer industry as a whole has been declining, and so was Boston Beer's revenue until a year ago. 2019 was a small relief for Boston Beer Company as it returned to volume sales growth in the last fiscal year. Jim Koch, the company's founder and chairman, stated:

> We are still seeing challenges across the industry, including a general softening of the craft beer category and retail shelves that offer an increasing number of options to drinkers. We continue to work hard on our Samuel Adams brand messaging . . . and we are planning to launch three new brands in 2019 that we believe will complement our current portfolio and help support our mission of long-term profitable growth.[1]

The company seemed fairly optimistic about its drinks in 2019 as the third CEO of Boston Beer, Dave Burwick, said, "Our overall plans for 2019 include significant investments in the second year of our successful 2018 innovations, which include Angry Orchard Rosé, Truly Berry Variety Pack, Truly Wild Berry, Sam '76, and Samuel Adams New England IPA."[2] He reaffirmed Koch's statement by saying:

> In 2019 we plan to build upon these successful innovations with three additional brands that address important health and wellness opportunities in our categories. These brands include 26.2 Brew from our wholly-owned affiliate Marathon Brewing Company, a thirst-quenching gose beer (top-fermented beer that originated in Goslar, Germany) made with sea salt to fit runners' active lifestyles; Wild Leaf Hard Tea, a craft hard tea with lower calories and sugar; and Tura Alcoholic Kombucha, an organic, light and refreshing shelf-stable alcoholic Kombucha with live probiotics and real fruit.[3]

The company saw a growth in the fourth quarter due to an increase in sales of Truly Hard Seltzer, Twisted Tea, and Angry Orchard brands. Along with challenges to remain a market leader for craft beers, the Boston Beer Company also aims to remain a market leader in the emerging segment of hard seltzer. The company faced immense competition from its four largest competitors, Molson Coors, Anheuser-Busch InBev, Heineken, and Constellation. These competitors aggressively acquired small- and medium-sized brewers and launched new domestic specialty brands to compete with the domestic market in various regions during the past couple of years. Boston Beer's focus remained on enhancing distribution, which perhaps cost the company missed acquisition opportunities taken by its competitors. The question remained that if customers had so many options to choose from, why should they buy Boston Beer? What was so special about it?

The Boston Beer Company, with its Samuel Adams brand, was the largest craft brewery in the United States, holding a 1 percent stake in the overall beer market.[4] In the past several years, the beer industry had declined, while sales of wines and spirits had increased. The Boston Beer Company competed within the premium-beer industry, which included craft beer and premium imported beers like Heineken and Corona. Although the beer industry had been on a decline, the premium-beer industry had seen a small amount of growth and the craft-beer industry had seen a surge in popularity. Because of the success of the craft breweries in particular, the major breweries had taken notice and many new craft breweries had sprung up.

Anheuser-Busch InBev and Molson Coors accounted for 68.8 percent of the beer market in 2019 in the United States.[5] They had caught on to the current trend in the beer industry toward higher-quality beers and started releasing their own. For example, Anheuser-Busch InBev released Bud Light Wheat and Bud Light Platinum in an effort to provide quality beers to its loyal customers. Molson Coors introduced Blue Moon beer, and Anheuser-Busch InBev released Shock Top to combat the popularity of Blue Moon. These companies also began to purchase smaller craft breweries, whose products had been rising in popularity. Anheuser-Busch Inbev acquired Pirate Life Brewing in November 2017. Similarly in 2017, Molson Coors acquired Le Trou du diable craft brewery in Quebec.

According to the Brewers Association, as of 2018, around 7,346 craft breweries and 7,450 total breweries operated in the United States (see Exhibit 1). While craft breweries accounted for over 98 percent of all the breweries in the United States, they produced only approximately 25 percent of all beer sold.[6] However, with the rise in popularity of premium beers, the craft breweries were expected to continue to grab more of the market. As the country's largest craft brewery, the Boston Beer Company had revenue of over $995.7 million in 2018 and sold over 4.2 million barrels of beer.[7] Other large craft breweries included D.G. Yuengling & Son, Inc., and Sierra Nevada Brewing Company. In addition, some smaller breweries had been merging to take advantage of economies of scale and enhance their competitive position.

* This case was developed by graduate students Peter J. Courtney, Eric S. Engelson, Dev Das, Saad Nazir, and Sushmitha Mudda and Professor Alan B. Eisner, Pace University. Material has been drawn from published sources to be used for class discussion. Copyright © 2019 Alan B. Eisner.

EXHIBIT 1
U.S. Brewery Count

U.S. Brewery Count					
	2014	**2015**	**2016**	**2017**	**2018**
CRAFT	**3,814**	**4,628**	**5,539**	**6,490**	**7,346**
Regional Craft Breweries	135	178	186	202	230
Microbreweries	2,076	2,626	3,251	3,933	4,522
Brewpubs	1,603	1,824	2,102	2,355	2,594
LARGE/NON-CRAFT	**46**	**44**	**67**	**106**	**104**
Total U.S. Breweries	**3,860**	**4,672**	**5,606**	**6,596**	**7,450**

Source: Number of Breweries. Brewers Association, 2018.

The biggest challenge for Boston Beer still remained the increasing competition as consumers had more variety of craft beers to choose from in the market. However, Boston Beer Company competed not only with domestic craft breweries but also with premium-beer imports, such as Heineken and Corona, which sold beer in a similar price range. Like Anheuser-Busch InBev and Molson Coors, Heineken and Corona had large financial resources and could influence the market.

The Brewers Association reported that in 2018, small and independent brewers collectively produced 25.9 million barrels and realized 4 percent total growth, increasing craft's overall beer market share by volume to 13.2 percent. Maintaining status as a craft brewery could be important for image and, therefore, sales. The size of the Boston Beer Company, however, was an issue. With continued growth, the brewery could potentially increase its volume output to more than 6 million barrels per year, thus losing its craft brewery status. Furthermore, with the size of the company and its ability to market nationwide, the company ran the risk of alienating itself from fans of craft brews that could come to believe Samuel Adams no longer fit the profile. Many such aficionados of craft breweries already believed that the company, which had been public since 1995, was more concerned with making money than with providing quality beer and educating the public on craft beers.

Size did have advantages, of course, providing more money for marketing and, especially in the beer business, facilitating distribution. A complaint heard from all craft breweries was the difficulty they had distributing their product in the current three-tier system (discussed later). The large breweries had power over the independent distributors because they accounted for most of their business. Thus, they could influence the distributors and make it difficult for craft breweries to sell their product. Because of its size, the Boston Beer Company had fewer problems with distributors than its smaller competitors did. Consequently, the company had less in common with other craft breweries and more in common with the major breweries in regard to distribution. This was good for Boston Beer Company's distribution but maybe bad for its image. One brewer from the Defiant Brewing Company in Pearl River, New York, said that the Boston Beer Company was becoming too large to be considered a craft brewery and that its substantial connections with distributors proved it.[8]

Clearly, the Boston Beer Company was facing a difficult competitive environment. It faced direct competition from both larger and smaller breweries and from premium imported beers. Some of the smaller craft breweries were growing quickly and wanted to be larger than the Boston Beer Company. Other craft breweries felt that the Boston Beer Company was too large already. Thus, while further growth would be beneficial in terms of revenue, growing too large could negatively affect the company's status as a craft brewery and the perceptions of its customers. Analyst, Pablo Zuanic, argues that Boston Beer's "fixation on justifying itself as a craft brewer is actually hindering success."[9] However, Jim Koch seems to disagree and claims that Boston Beer depended on its craft brewery status to justify premium pricing and its image.[10] The company had to pay close attention to maintaining its image among the growing customer base of premium-beer drinkers.

Company Background

Jim Koch started the Boston Beer Company in 1984 along with fellow Harvard MBA graduates Harry Rubin and Lorenzo Lamadrid. The company began with the sale of the now popular Samuel Adams Boston Lager, named after the famous American patriot who was known to have been a brewer himself. The recipe for the lager had actually been passed down from generation to generation in Koch's family, dating back to the 1860s. Koch began home brewing the beer in his own kitchen and soliciting local establishments in Boston to purchase and sell it. Just one year after its initial sales, Samuel Adams Boston Lager was voted Best Beer in America at the Great American Beer Festival in Denver, Colorado. In 1985, Samuel Adams grew immensely and sold 500 barrels of beer in Massachusetts, Connecticut, and West Germany.[11]

To avoid the high up-front capital costs of starting a brewery, Koch contracted with several existing breweries to make his beer. This allowed the production of Boston Lager to grow quickly from the relatively small quantities Koch could brew himself. Growth continued after that, and in 1988 the Boston Beer Company opened a brewery in Boston. By 1989 the Boston Beer Company produced 63,000 barrels of Samuel Adams beer annually.

The company went public in 1995, selling Class A common stock to potential investors. The stock was sold at two different prices–$15 to loyal customers and $20 through an IPO run by Goldman-Sachs. Koch decided to reward his loyal customers by advertising the stock offering on the packages of his six-packs, estimating that 30,000 buyers would be interested. He believed that those who enjoyed the beer and supported it should be the ones to have a stake in the company. After 100,000 potential investors sent checks in, Koch randomly chose 30,000.[12] Managers from Goldman-Sachs were upset that they did not receive the lowest-price offering. Koch owns 100 percent of the Class B common stock, which confers the right to make all major decisions for the company. This was seen as a risk to potential investors because Koch could make important decisions on the strategy of the company without receiving approval from them.

Continued success for the business led to the purchase of a large brewery in Cincinnati in 1997. Since 2000, Samuel Adams has won more awards in international beer-tasting competitions than any other brewery in the world. In 2008, the Boston Beer Company purchased a world-class brewery in Lehigh, Pennsylvania, to support growth.

As of 2018, in the craft brewery category, the Boston Beer Company was the second largest in craft brewery, after D. G. Yuengling and Son, in the United States. Boston Beer, brewing over 4 million barrels of Samuel Adams beer, still served only a fraction of the total U.S. beer market.[13] The company had expanded its selections to over 50 beer flavors, including seasonal and other flavorful beers, such as Samuel Adams Summer Ale, Samuel Adams Cherry Wheat, and Samuel Adams Octoberfest, as well as the non-beer brands Twisted Tea and HardCore Cider. The Boston Beer Company planned to use the profits gained from its non-beer brands to invest in Samuel Adams and build a stronger portfolio. Revenue for the company increased 15.4 percent from $862.9 million in 2017 to $995.7 million in 2018, while operating costs increased from $334.2 million to $396.3 million. Net income decreased slightly from $99 million to $92.6 million in the same period (see Exhibits 2 and 3). In March 2019, the company stock was selling at $266.97, nearly $127.97 above its low of $139 in April 2017.

The goal of the Boston Beer Company was to become the leading brewer in the premium-beer market. It was the second largest craft brewery, but it trailed Crown Imports, LLC, and Heineken USA in the premium-beer market. The company planned to surpass the large importers by increasing brand availability and awareness through advertising, drinker education, and the support of its over 300-member sales force. The salespeople for the company had a high level of product knowledge about beer and the brewing process and used this to educate distributors and the public on the benefits of Samuel Adams. The Boston Beer Company had formed a subsidiary called Alchemy & Science to seize new opportunities in the craft brewing industry. The purpose of this group was to identify better beer ingredients, methods for better brewing, and opportunities to purchase breweries that would help the business grow. One such opportunity, for instance, led to the group's purchase of Southern California Brewing.

Over the years, the company had continued to invest in efficiency initiatives to lower costs within its breweries and increase margins. One large program in late 2010 was its Freshest Beer Program. Typically, bottled and canned beer sat in a distributor's warehouse for three to five weeks, while kegs sat for three to four weeks. In an effort to reduce storage time in the distributor warehouses by approximately two weeks and consequently increase freshness of the beer at retailers, the company focused not only on better on-time service, forecasting, and production planning but also on great coordination and cooperation with distributors. By 2018, the company had 167 distributers participating in the Freshest Beer program, which accounted for 79 percent of its beer volume in the Freshest Beer Program, with the goal of expanding that number in the future.[14]

While expansion and growth are commonly deemed positive attributes, the Boston Beer Company was aware of the many other possible risks in the growth of its business, beyond the issue of being a craft beer or not. With the acquisition of the Lehigh brewery, Boston Beer Company now brewed over 90 percent of its beer at its own breweries. With capital tied up in large investments, there was a potential for the business to falter if an unexpected event affected one of the breweries and halted production at that facility. Additionally, the company had put forth a sizable investment to increase product offerings and another to keep its beer fresh during distribution. However, with its reliance on independent distributors, a mishap in its relationship with major distributors could lead to complications within its supply chain. Moreover, Boston Beer Company also depended on foreign suppliers of raw ingredients for its beer. An unexpected shortage of a crop might lead to a drop in production volume. In short, the company was still not large enough to be shielded from such risk and to be able to lean on suppliers and distributors like the largest breweries could. The image of the company would suffer if its products were not available to loyal fans whose enjoyment of the brand relied on the wide accessibility of its craft beer. Finally, with the surge of an enormous number of other craft-beer choices, customers increasingly had many options to choose from.

Industry

The U.S. beer market is known to be evergreen, but recently millennial consumers have come of age, and are demanding more options and upping their beer preferences. While the sales continue to increase, the rate of growth has dropped from 5 percent in 2015 to 1 percent in the first six months

EXHIBIT 2 Boston Beer Co., Inc., Income Statements ($ millions, except per-share)

(in thousands, except per share and net revenue per barrel data)	Dec. 29 2018	Dec. 30 2017	Year Ended Dec. 31 2016 (53 weeks)	Dec. 26 2015	Dec. 27 2014
Income Statement Data:					
Revenue	$1,057,495	$921,736	$968,994	$1,024,040	$966,478
Less excise taxes	61,846	58,744	62,548	64,106	63,471
Net revenue	995,649	862,992	906,446	959,934	903,007
Cost of goods sold	483,406	413,091	446,776	458,317	437,996
Gross profit	512,243	449,901	459,670	501,617	465,011
Operating expenses:					
Advertising, promotional and selling expenses	304,853	258,649	244,213	273,629	250,696
General and administrative expenses	90,857	73,126	78,033	71,556	65,971
Impairment (gain on sale) of assets, net	652	2,451	(235)	258	1,777
Total operating expenses	396,362	334,226	322,011	345,443	318,444
Operating income	115,881	115,675	137,659	156,174	146,567
Other income (expense), net	405	467	(538)	(1,164)	(973)
Income before provision for income taxes	116,286	116,142	137,121	155,010	145,594
Provision for income taxes	23,623	17,093	49,772	56,596	54,851
NET INCOME	**$ 92,663**	**$ 99,049**	**$ 87,349**	**$ 98,414**	**$ 90,743**
Net income per share—basic	$ 7.90	$ 8.18	$ 6.93	$ 7.46	$ 6.96
Net income per share—diluted	$ 7.82	$ 8.09	$ 6.79	$ 7.25	$ 6.69
Weighted average shares outstanding—basic	11,621	12,035	12,533	13,123	12,968
Weighted average shares outstanding—diluted	11,734	12,180	12,796	13,520	13,484

Source: The Boston Beer Company

of 2018 (see Exhibit 4). Among the five product segments, consumers' tastes are shifting to above-premium beers (which include craft beers), ciders, "sessionable" options (those with low alcohol levels), and emerging options like hard teas and seltzers[15] (see Exhibit 5).

Market dominance of industry stalwarts like Anheuser-Busch InBev, Molson Coors, and Heineken are being challenged by the others in the industry (Exhibit 6). While Anheuser-Busch InBev, Molson Coors, and Heineken all experienced a decline in sales in 2017 (by 0.7, 3.4, and 5.4 percent, respectively); Constellation Brands and Boston Beer achieved growth of 9.7 and 4.1 percent, respectively.[16] While Constellation Brands targeted growing consumer demand for imported beers, Boston Beer was growing their flavored malt beverages (FMB) and cider offerings.

The Three-Tier System

Seventy-five percent of the volume of beer sold in the United States was sold at off-trade value in supermarkets, beer distributors, and such, while the other 25 percent was sold in bars and restaurants. Despite the vast difference in the volumes sold, the values of beer sold at off-trade and on-trade sites were equal because of the premium charged for beer at a bar or a restaurant.

Breweries were not permitted to own either off-trade or on-trade establishments, so their beer had to be distributed. Before Prohibition, however, beer was sold in tavern-like establishments called "tied houses," which supplied and sold their own beer. There were no regulations regarding brewing companies owning all of the retail tied houses and selling only their own beer.

EXHIBIT 3 Boston Beer Co., Inc., Balance Sheets

THE BOSTON BEER COMPANY, INC. AND SUBSIDIARIES CONSOLIDATED BALANCE SHEETS		
(in thousands, except share data)	**December 29, 2018**	**December 30, 2017**
Assets		
Current Assets:		
Cash and cash equivalents	$ 108,399	$ 65,637
Accounts receivable	34,073	33,749
Inventories	70,249	50,651
Prepaid expenses and other current assets	13,136	10,695
Income tax receivable	5,714	7,616
Total current assets	231,571	168,348
Property, plant and equipment, net	389,789	384,280
Other assets	14,808	13,313
Goodwill	3,683	3,683
TOTAL ASSETS	**$639,851**	**$569,624**
Liabilities and Stockholders' Equity		
Current Liabilities:		
Accounts payable	$ 47,102	$ 38,141
Accrued expenses and other current liabilities	73,412	63,617
Total current liabilities	120,514	101,758
Deferred income taxes	49,169	34,819
Other liabilities	9,851	9,524
TOTAL LIABILITIES	**179,534**	**146,101**
Commitments and Contingencies		
Stockholders' Equity:		
Class A Common Stock, $.01 par value; 22,700,000 shares authorized; 8,580,593 and 8,603,152 shares issued and outstanding as of December 29, 2018 and December 30, 2017, respectively	86	86
Class B Common Stock, $.01 par value; 4,200,000 shares authorized; 2,917,983 and 3,017,983 shares issued and outstanding as of December 29, 2018 and December 30, 2017, respectively	29	30
Additional paid-in capital	405,711	372,590
Accumulated other comprehensive loss, net of tax	(1,197)	(1,288)
Retained earnings	55,688	52,105
Total stockholders' equity	460,317	423,523
TOTAL LIABILITIES AND STOCKHOLDERS' EQUITY	**$639,851**	**$569,624**

Source: The Boston Beer Company

EXHIBIT 4 Beer Trends: Year-over-Year Dollar Sales Growth

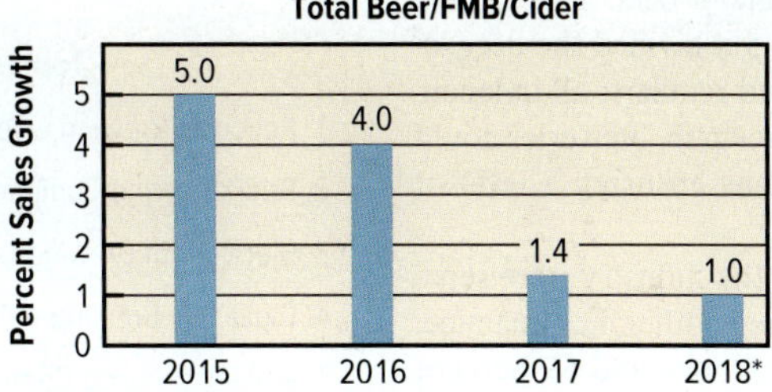

FMB: flavored malt beverages

*Estimated

Source: Nielsen Scantrack, Nielsen US xAOC.

EXHIBIT 5 Year-over-Year Dollar Sales Growth by Product Segment and Segment Definitions

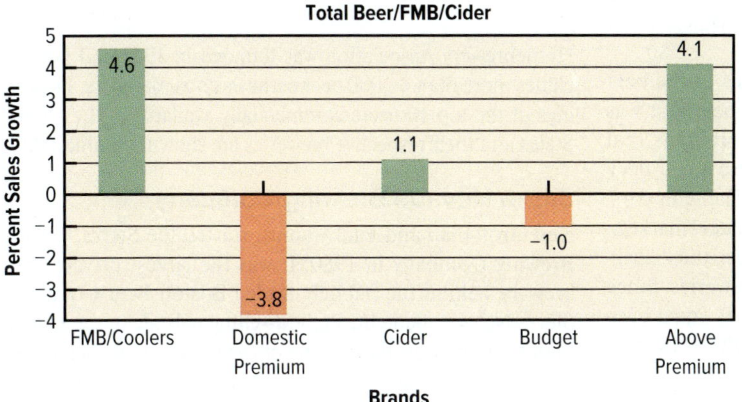

Segment definitions:

Segment	Sub-segment
Above premium	Import
	Craft
	Domestic super premium
Budget	Below premium
	Malt liquor
	Near beer
Cider	Cider
Domestic premium	Domestic premium
FMB/coolers	Flavored malt beverage
	Coolers

FMB: Flavored malt beverages

Source: Nielsen US xAOC.

EXHIBIT 6 Top Beer Manufacturers—Sales Growth 2017–2018

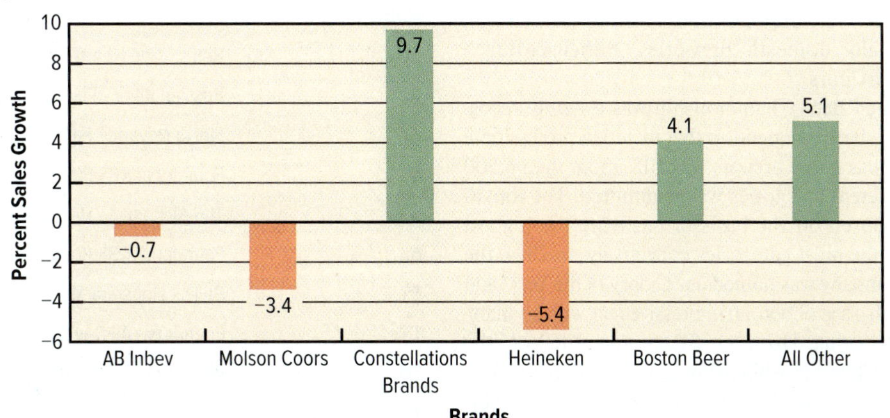

Source: Nielsen US xAOC.

After Prohibition, a system was put in place to discourage monopolies in the supply and sale of beer. This system was called the Three-Tier System, and it divided the beer industry into suppliers, distributors, and retailers, all independent of each other. Aside from the brewpub, breweries could not own retailers or distributors, thus ensuring a level of competition in the brewing industry.[17]

Although the three categories of the industry were separate, they had a large influence on one another. For instance, Anheuser-Busch InBev and Molson Coors sold 69 percent of the beer in the country. That meant that 69 percent of distributors' volume, and consequently revenue, was from these two companies. Hence, the distributors valued the business of Anheuser-Busch InBev and Molson Coors to a higher degree, in fear of losing their business. In an effort to maintain its dominant position in the industry, Anheuser-Busch InBev had contracted with several distributors on the condition that they would not work with any other breweries. Likewise, the other large breweries imposed restrictions on their distributors regarding which other breweries they could work with.

The distributors acted as the intermediary in the beer industry, providing the beer to retailers. The beer that was available from retailers was a result of the products that their distributors carried. The distributors were major decision makers for what beer taps would be available in bars, as well as the location of beer selections in supermarkets. Small breweries did not like the system because the distributors were heavily influenced by the major breweries. Since distributors had little incentive to treat them as equal business partners, small breweries found it difficult to compete and achieve growth. Consequently, it was a challenge for a small brewery to gain widespread recognition in the industry. Despite this challenge, the Boston Beer Company had made a name for itself and sold its beer to a network of approximately 350 distributors by 2019.

Competition

The Boston Beer Company mainly competed with other beers sold in the United States. The company faced competition from other craft brewers, premium import brewers, and the two major domestic breweries, Anheuser-Busch InBev and MillerCoors.

The U.S. Open Beer Championship was a highly recognized nationwide beer competition that included professional breweries as well as home brewers. In 2018, more than 6,300 beers in 110 different categories were submitted. The top 10 brewers were chosen on the basis of receiving the highest overall grade in the most categories collectively. In 2014, the Boston Beer Company was named as "Cidery of the Year" and received the fourth-place ribbon, an impressive feat with so many breweries participating. However, the company fell off the U.S. Open Beer Championship list in 2018 (see Exhibit 7).

Home brewing had become an extremely popular hobby, and in many instances it led home brewers to pursue their passion in the form of an actual brewery. The American Homebrewers Association was founded in 1978 and now includes more than 46,000 beer enthusiasts as members. Its rankings of the top 10 beers commercially available in the United States and their respective breweries are shown in Exhibit 8.[18]

EXHIBIT 7 Top 10 Brewers, U.S. Open Beer Championship, 2018

Top 10 Breweries 2018
1. Peticolas Brewing – Texas
2. Brink Brewing Company – Ohio
3. Black Tooth Brewing Co – Wyoming
4. Cigar City Brewing – Florida
5. Revelry Brewing Company – South Carolina
6. Garage Brewing Co – California
7. Atlanta Brewing – Georgia
8. Liquid Mechanics Brewing – Colorado
9. Motorworks Brewing – Florida
10. Reuben's Brews – Taproom – Washington

Source: U.S. Open Beer Championship 2018.

Sierra Nevada Brewing Company

Ken Grossman and Paul Camusi started the Sierra Nevada Brewing Company in 1980. It was the largest private craft brewery behind the publicly traded Boston Beer Company. Sierra Nevada made the highest-selling pale ale in the United States. Sierra Nevada was one of the earliest craft breweries, and its founders were consequently referred to as pioneers in the craft brewing industry. The company planned to open another brewing facility within the next few years to continue growth of the business. Sierra Nevada created goodwill by promoting the craft-beer industry and by striving to be

EXHIBIT 8 Top 10 U.S. Beers and Breweries, 2019

	Top Ranked Beers
Rank	
1.	Bell's - Two Hearted Ale
2.	Russian River - Pliny the Elder
3.	Sierra Nevada - Pale Ale
4.	Founders - KBS (Kentucky Breakfast Stout)
5.	The Alchemist - Heady Topper
6.	Founders - CBS (Canadian Breakfast Stout)
T7.	Bell's - Hopslam Ale
T7.	Founders - All Day IPA
T9.	WeldWerks - Juicy Bits
T9.	Founders - Breakfast Stout

Source: Home Brewers Association.

environmentally friendly in its beer's production. One of Sierra Nevada Brewing's goals was to overtake the Boston Beer Company as the largest craft brewery in the country.[19]

New Belgium Brewing Company

Jeff Lebesch founded the New Belgium Brewing Company in Fort Collins, Colorado, in 1991. New Belgium Brewing was the third-largest craft brewery in the United States, behind the Boston Beer Company and Sierra Nevada. The company's flagship beer was an amber ale called Fat Tire, but it had over 25 different beers in production. In recent years the company had sold over 800,000 barrels of beer, which were distributed in 29 states. Over the last several years, the company had growth of approximately 15 percent. New Belgium started building a $100 million brewery in North Carolina that was completed in May 2016 with capacity of brewing around 500,000 barrels per year. Like Sierra Nevada, New Belgium focused on energy-efficient practices. The company also hoped to become the largest craft brewery in the country. According to the Brewers association, New Belgium was the fourth-largest craft brewery as of 2018, whereas for overall breweries it stood at the 11th position in the United States.[20]

Crown Imports, LLC

Crown Imports, LLC, was a joint venture between Grupo Modelo and Constellation Brands. Crown Imports had a portfolio of beers that included Corona Extra, Corona Light, Modelo Especial, Pacifico, and others. Crown Imports had market share of approximately 9.6 percent, and its Corona was the leading imported beer in the United States in 2018.[21] Constellation owned over 200 brands of beer, wine, and spirits and had sales of above $4.6 billion as of 2018. With a large financial backing, Crown Imports wanted to remain the number-one import in the country and close the gap in market share between the company and the top two breweries in the U.S. market. In 2019, Constellation was betting big on marijuana legalization as it planned to enter into an agreement with Canopy Growth Corporation, a cannabis company based in Smith Falls, Ontario.[22]

Heineken

In 2018, Heineken was the third-largest import brewing company and the fourth-largest brewing company in the United States. As of 2017, the company had a market share of 9.6 percent in the United States.[23] The company was founded in 1873, and its beers were sold in 71 countries worldwide. Heineken imported popular brands such as Heineken, Amstel Light, Sol, Dos Equis, and Newcastle. The company had a revenue of about $25.2 billion in 2018.[24] With Heineken's large size and excellent reputation, it had the ability to advertise its products nationally. The Dos Equis brand had grown by over 10 percent since the popular "Most Interesting Man in the World" commercials began airing. Most of the brands offered by Heineken were in the price range of Samuel Adams, making them a close competitor.[25]

Anheuser-Busch InBev NV

Anheuser-Busch InBev was one of the largest beer companies in the world, with roughly $54.6 billion in revenue in 2018. The brewing portion of the company remained the largest brewery in the United States and had an approximately 45 percent stake in the U.S. beer industry.[26] It had the two best-selling beers in the country—Bud Light and Budweiser. However, the company had seen the sale of its products decline over the last several years. In an effort to combat the lower volume of sales, it had raised the prices of its beer products. Anheuser-Busch InBev reported 2018 global revenue growth of 4.8 percent—to more than $54.6 billion—despite continued declines in the United States.[27]

Additionally, the company had witnessed the explosive growth of the craft-beer industry. Although it could never be considered a craft brewery because of its size, Anheuser-Busch planned to make more craft-like beers, as it had done with its brand Shock Top. The company also planned to invest in and purchase small craft breweries, like Goose Island, which made the popular beer 312. Anheuser-Busch was not opposed to merging with other large breweries, and closed a merger deal of over $100 billion with SABMiller in 2016, creating the largest beer company in the world (the Miller and Coors brands were left to competitor Molson Coors following the merger). The company was reported to be in talks with the maker of Corona to purchase that company. The size and influence of the Anheuser-Busch InBev and SABMiller merger posed a threat to the Boston Beer Company because of its substantial lead in available capital and market share.

Molson Coors, Inc.

Molson Coors brands and its subsidiary MillerCoors, LLC, was the second-largest brewing company in the United States, accounting for approximately 30 percent of the market. It had two of the top five most popular beers, Miller Lite and Coors Light, and wanted to catch up with Anheuser-Busch InBev. The company traded publicly as Molson Coors Brewing Company. Molson Coors wanted to push its craft beers after witnessing the growth in the market. It had a popular craft-like beer called Blue Moon Belgian White. The company's group Tenth and Blake focused on the craft-beer industry and premium imports, and it planned to expand the group by 60 percent over the next few years. Some of its premium beers were Leinenkugel's Honey Weiss, George Killian's Irish Red, Batch 19, Henry Weinhard's IPA, Colorado Native, Pilsner Urquell, Peroni Nastro Azzurro, and Grolsch.[28]

Thinking about the Future of Beer

The Boston Beer Company created high-quality craft beers and sold them at higher prices than standard and economy lagers. It was the second-largest craft brewery in the United States and the ninth-largest overall brewery in terms of overall brewing companies. Boston Beer's goal was to become the third-largest overall brewery in the country in terms of dollar sales. Brand recognition is key to any business, and this is especially obvious in the beer industry. Anheuser-Busch InBev and Molson Coors spent enormous amounts of capital each year to advertise their products and the new merger would result in a substantial increase in competition for Boston Beer. Due in large part to Anheuser-Busch InBev and Molson Coors, beer has become synonymous with sports, and nowhere is this more apparent than the Super Bowl. Anheuser-Busch InBev was one of the main sponsors of the Super Bowl in 2019, and the world's largest brewer planned to run eight ads, totaling five minutes, 45 seconds.[29] The challenge for craft brewers is that they need to gain a bigger share of the attention of potential customers, while the large brewers have a great deal of money to spend vying for the same consumers. One might argue that the larger brewers' beers do not taste as good as the craft beers, but it is hard to be heard in a crowded space.

Jim Koch and the Samuel Adams team emphasized the number of hops and flavors that their products had, and they wanted to get "better beer" to potential customers. While evaluating hops with the mission of finding the perfect hops for the brewery's Boston Lager, Koch said, "The industrial brewers only buy alpha acids. They buy kids of alpha, they don't care about the aroma. When you're buying that way you don't evaluate."[30]

Over the last several years, the craft brewing industry has grown at the expense of standard and economy lagers. According to analysts, in 2019, craft beer is fetching higher sales than traditional beer due to endeavors from local and international brewers that are expanding their distribution network and at the same time offering exciting new flavors and tastes. The rising consumer preference for low alcohol by volume (ABV) beer is fueling the growth of the global craft beer market.[31] The major breweries have taken notice, and they have started to build up their craft-style beer portfolios. In the past, the Boston Beer Company had the advantage of being one of the only craft breweries that was nationally recognized. Exhibit 9 shows the pricing and alcohol by volume for popular U.S. beers.

EXHIBIT 9 Comparison of Domestic Beer Brands

Domestic Beers	Alcohol by Volume (%)	Average Price (six-pack)	Market Share (%)
Bud Light	4.20	$7.00	15.4
Coors Light	4.20	7.99	7.7
Miller Light	4.20	6.99	6.1
Budweiser	5.00	6.99	6.2
Michelob Ultra Light	4.60	6.99	3.6
Natural Light	4.20	3.49	3.0
Busch Light	4.10	7.99	3.0
Miller High Life	4.60	4.70	1.6
Busch	4.70	6.99	2.2
Keystone Light	4.13	5.99	1.6
Blue Moon Belgian White	5.36	8.49	1.0
Yuengling Traditional Lager	5.00	5.99	1.0
Bud Light Lime	4.90	8.49	1.2
Pabst Blue Ribbon	5.20	8.49	1.2
Coors	5.60	8.49	1.1
Natural Ice	5.20	8.99	1.1
Bud Light Platinum Lager	4.40	6.49	0.9
Samuel Adams Seasonal	5.00	8.99	0.9
Sierra Nevada Pale Ale	5.20	7.99	0.7
Leinenkugels Shandy	4.20	8.75	0.7

Sources: Efficientdrinker.com, 2018. Beer: Making Sense of All the Choices; Harrington, John 24/7 Wall Street, 2018. Which beer is loved most by consumers? 26 most popular U.S. beer brands. USA Today, May 3.; and author estimates.

Boston Beer had a sales growth of 4.1 percent from June 2017 to June 2018 (see Exhibit 6), and they plan on growing their flavored malt beverage and cider offerings to target the growing consumer demand. Although Boston Beer saw a growth in 2018, Boston Beer Company needs to up its game, as both the smaller craft breweries and the larger breweries plan to take over the craft beer industry.

ENDNOTES

1. The Boston Beer Company. 2019. Boston Beer reports fourth quarter 2018 results. Press Release. Feb 20.
2. Ibid.
3. Ibid.
4. Global Market Information Database. 2012. The Boston Beer Company, in alcoholic drinks (USA). February.
5. Euromonitor International from official statistics, trade associations, trade press, company research, store checks, trade interviews, trade sources.
6. Brewers Association, 2018. What is craft beer? https://www.craftbeer.com/beer/what-is-craft-beer.
7. The Boston Beer Company Annual Report 2018.
8. Personal interview with Woody from Defiant Brewery in Pearl River, NY, June 2012.
9. Kell, J. 2017. It's time for Sam Adams to admit it's no longer a craft brewer *Fortune*, February 23, http://fortune.com/2017/02/23/sam-adams-big-brewer/.
10. Ibid.
11. The Boston Beer Company. About Us - BBC HISTORY. Retrieved October 30, 2019, http://www.bostonbeer.com/about-us.
12. Sommer, J. 2012. An IPO that is customer-friendly. *New York Times*, February 18.
13. Press Release. 2019. Brewers Association releases 2018 top 50 brewing companies by sales volume. Brewers Association, March 12, https://www.brewersassociation.org/press-releases/brewers-association-releases-2018-top-50-brewing-companies-by-sales-volume/.
14. The Boston Beer Company Annual Report 2018.
15. CPG, FMCG, and Retail. 2019. In the crowded beer market, shelf space is key to maximizing sales. Nielsen, January 3, https://www.nielsen.com/us/en/insights/news/2019/in-the-crowded-us-beer-market–shelf-space-is-key-to-maximizing-sales.html.
16. Category Report. 2018. The changing face of beer retailing in the U.S. Nielsen.
17. Associated Beer Distributors of Illinois. The three-tier system. Retrieved October 30, 2019, http://www.abdi.org/the-three-tier-system.
18. American Homebrewers Association. Quick Facts. Retrieved October 30, 2019, https://www.homebrewersassociation.org/membership/american-homebrewers-association/
19. www.sierranevada.com; and Solomon, B. 2014. King of craft beer: How Sierra Nevada rules the hops world. *Forbes*, March 3.
20. Press Release. 2019. Brewers Association releases 2018 top 50 brewing companies by sales volume. Brewers Association, March 12, https://www.brewersassociation.org/press-releases/brewers-association-releases-2018-top-50-brewing-companies-by-sales-volume/.
21. Jacobsen, J. 2019. 2019 Beer Report: Imports continue to gain in US beer market. *Beverage Industry Magazine*, March.
22. Doorn, P.V. 2019. Corona and Canopy: A mix of beer and pot that could juice your stock portfolio. MarketWatch, April 19, https://www.marketwatch.com/story/corona-and-canopy-a-mix-of-beer-and-pot-that-could-juice-your-stock-portfolio-2019-04-18.
23. Euromonitor International from official statistics, trade associations, trade press, company research, store checks, trade interviews, trade sources.
24. Heineken Press Release. 2019. Heineken N.V. reports 2018 full year results. February 13, https://www.theheinekencompany.com/Media/Media-Releases/Press-releases/2019/02/2234675.
25. Heineken. 2019. Brands. Retrieved October 30, 2019, https://www.theheinekencompany.com/Brands.
26. Trefis. 2017. The year that was: Anheuser- Busch InBev. *Forbes*, January 26, https://www.forbes.com/sites/greatspeculations/2017/01/26/the-year-that-was-anheuser-busch-inbev/#a3cfb0115585.
27. Kendall, J. 2019. Anheuser-Busch InBev revenue tops $54.6 billion in 2018. BrewBound, February 28, https://www.brewbound.com/news/anheuser-busch-inbev-revenue-tops-54-6-billion-in-2018.
28. MillerCoors. 2019. Our Great Beers. Retrieved October 30, 2019, https://www.millercoors.com/beers/great-beers.
29. Ad Age. 2019. Who's buying ads in Super Bowl 2019. Ad Age, January 22, https://adage.com/article/super-bowl/2019-superbowl-liii-ad-chart/315605.
30. Price, E. 2019. What it's like to select hops with Jim Koch from Sam Adams. *Paste*, January 10, https://www.pastemagazine.com/articles/2019/01/what-its-like-to-do-hop-selection-with-the-brewers.html.
31. Industry Reports. 2019. Craft beer market 2019 worldwide demand, growth analysis and outlook. April 15, https://industryreports24.com/110359/craft-beer-market-2019-worldwide-demand-growth-analysis-and-outlook-budweiser-yuengling-the-boston-beer-company-sierra-nevada-new-belgium-brewing/.

CASE 28

McDONALD'S IN 2019*

On November 3, 2019, the McDonald's board of directors dismissed Steve Easterbrook over violations of company policy regarding a relationship with an employee and named Chris Kempczinski the new CEO. Kempczinski had experience at Kraft Foods and PepsiCo prior to joining McDonald's in 2015, most recently as president of the USA business unit.[1]

In March 2019, McDonald's, the largest restaurant chain, announced it will acquire artificial-intelligence startup Dynamic Yield, a company focused on personalization and decision logic technology. Access to this technology will allow the firm to update instantaneously its drive-through menus based on factors such as time of day, weather, and trending menu items. McDonald's plans to roll out the updated drive-through menus across the United States during the year. "With this acquisition, we're expanding both our ability to increase the role technology and data will play in our future and the speed with which we'll able to implement our vision of creating more personalized experiences for our customers," former CEO Steve Easterbrook said in a statement.[2]

McDonald's has been trying to attract more customers to its restaurants by offering more customized products that are also healthier. It has removed high fructose corn syrup from its buns, changed from the use of liquid margarine to real butter, decided to use chicken that has been raised without antibiotics, and to make use of cage-free eggs. Mike Andres, former president of McDonald's USA explained why the firm has decided to make these changes: "Why take a position to defend them if consumers are saying they don't want them?"[3]

These changes are expected to address some of challenges that McDonald's has been facing in many markets, including in the United States, where it has almost 15,000 of its 38,000 mostly franchised restaurants. It has lost a lot of ground with consumers, especially millennials, who are defecting to traditional competitors like Burger King and Wendy's as well as to new designer burger outlets such as Five Guys and Shake Shack. Changing tastes are also responsible for the loss of customers that are lining up at fast-casual chains such as Chipotle Mexican Grill and Panera Bread, which offer customized ordering and fresh ingredients (see Exhibits 1 to 4).

* Case prepared by Jamal Shamsie, Michigan State University, with the assistance of Professor Alan B. Eisner, Pace University. Material has been drawn from published sources to be used for purposes of class discussion. Copyright © 2019 Jamal Shamsie and Alan B. Eisner.

EXHIBIT 1
Income Statement ($ millions)

	Year Ending		
	Dec. 31, 2018	Dec. 31, 2017	Dec. 31, 2016
Total Revenue	$21,025	$22,820	$24,622
Operating Income	8,823	9,553	7,745
Net Income	5,924	5,192	4,687

Source: Annual Report of McDonald's Corporation, 2018.

EXHIBIT 2
Balance Sheet ($ millions)

	Year Ending		
	Dec. 31, 2018	Dec. 31, 2017	Dec. 31, 2016
Current Assets	$ 4,053	$ 5,327	$ 4,849
Total Assets	32,811	33,803	31,024
Current Liabilities	2,973	2,890	3,468
Total Liabilities	39,069	37,071	33,228
Shareholder Equity	(6,258)	(3,268)	(2,204)

Sources: Annual Report. McDonald's Corporation, 2018; Annual Report. McDonald's Corporation, 2019.

	2018	2017	2016
U.S.	$7,666	$8,006	$8,253
International Lead Markets	7,600	7,340	7,223
High Growth Markets	3,989	5,533	6,161
Foundational Markets & Corporate	1,770	1,941	2,985

EXHIBIT 3 Breakdown of Revenues ($ millions)

Source: Annual Report of McDonald's Corporation, 2018.

EXHIBIT 4 U.S. Customer Satisfaction Index for Selected Chains

Year	McDonald's	Burger King	Wendy's	KFC	Taco Bell	Chipotle Mexican Grill	Chick-fil-A	Panera Bread	Subway
2018	69	76	77	77	74	79	87	81	80
2017	69	77	76	78	76	79	87	82	81
2016	69	76	76	78	75	78	87	81	80
2015	67	72	73	73	72	83	86	80	77
2014	71	76	78	74	72	–	–	–	78
2013	73	76	79	81	74	–	–	–	83

Source: American Customer Satisfaction Index (ACSI).

Over the years, McDonald's response to this growing competition was to expand its menu with snacks, salads, and new drinks. From 33 basic items that the chain offered in 1990, the menu had grown by 2014 to 121 items. The greatly expanded menu led to a significant increase in costs and longer preparation times. This forced the firm to increase the prices of many of its items and to take more time to serve customers, moving it away from the attributes that it had built its reputation upon. "McDonald's stands for value, consistency, and convenience," said Darren Tristano, a restaurant industry consultant.[4]

The fast food chain has been through a similar crisis before. Back in 2002 and 2003, McDonald's had experienced a decline in performance because of quality problems as result of rapid expansion. At that time, the firm had brought James R. Cantalupo back out of retirement to turn things around. He formulated a "Plan to Win," which has been the basis of McDonald's strategy over the last decade. The core of the plan was to increase sales at existing locations by improving the menu, refurbishing the outlets, and extending hours. This time, however, such incremental steps might not be enough.

Pulling out of a Downward Spiral

Since it was founded more than 50 years ago, McDonald's has been defining the fast food business. It provided millions of Americans their first jobs even as it changed their eating habits. It rose from a single outlet in a nondescript San Bernardino, California to become one of the largest chain of outlets spread around the globe. But it gradually began to run into various problems that began to slow down its sales growth (see Exhibit 5).

This decline could be attributed in large part to a drop in McDonald's once-vaunted service and quality since its expansion in the 1990s, when headquarters stopped grading franchises for cleanliness, speed, and service. By the end of the decade, the chain ran into more problems because of the tighter labor market. McDonald's began to cut back on training as it struggled hard to find new recruits, leading to a dramatic falloff in the skills of its employees. According to a 2002 survey by market researcher Global Growth Group, McDonald's came in third in average service time behind Wendy's and sandwich shop Chick-fil-A Inc.

By the beginning of 2003, consumer surveys were indicating that McDonald's was headed for serious trouble. Measures for the service and quality of the chain were continuing to fall, dropping far behind those of its rivals. In order to deal with its deteriorating performance, the firm decided to bring back retired vice-chairman James R. Cantalupo, 59, who had overseen McDonald's successful international expansion in the 1980s and 1990s. Cantalupo, who had retired only a year earlier, was perceived to be the only candidate with the necessary qualifications, despite shareholder sentiment for an outsider. The board had felt that it needed someone who knew the company well and could move quickly to turn things around.

EXHIBIT 5 McDonald's Milestones

1948	Brothers Richard and Maurice McDonald open the first restaurant in San Bernadino, California, that sells hamburgers, fries, and milkshakes.
1955	Ray A. Kroc, 52, opens his first McDonald's in Des Plaines, Illinois. Kroc, a distributor of milkshake mixers, figures he can sell a bundle of them if he franchises the McDonald's business and install his mixers in the new stores.
1961	Six years later, Kroc buys out the McDonald brothers for $2.7 million.
1963	Ronald McDonald makes his debut as corporate spokesclown using future NBC-TV weatherman Willard Scott. During the year, the company also sells its 1 billionth burger.
1965	McDonald's stock goes public at $22.50 a share. It will split 12 times in the next 35 years.
1967	The first McDonald's restaurant outside the U.S. opens in Richmond, British Columbia. Today there are 31,108 McDonald's in 118 countries.
1968	The Big Mac, the first extension of McDonald's basic burger, makes its debut and is an immediate hit.
1972	McDonald's switches to the frozen variety for its successful French fries.
1974	Fred L. Turner succeeds Kroc as CEO. In the midst of a recession, the minimum wage rises to $2 per hour, a big cost increase for McDonald's, which is built around a model of young, low-wage workers.
1975	The first drive-through window is opened in Sierra Vista, Arizona.
1979	McDonald's responds to the needs of working women by introducing Happy Meals. A burger, some fries, a soda, and a toy give working moms a break.
1987	Michael R. Quinlan becomes chief executive.
1991	Responding to the public's desire for healthier foods, McDonald's introduces the low-fat McLean Deluxe burger. It flops and is withdrawn from the market. Over the next few years, the chain will stumble several times trying to spruce up its menu.
1992	The company sells its 90 billionth burger, and stops counting.
1996	In order to attract more adult customers, the company launches its Arch Deluxe, a "grown-up" burger with an idiosyncratic taste. Like the low-fat burger, it also falls flat.
1997	McDonald's launches Campaign 55, which cuts the cost of a Big Mac to $0.55. It is a response to discounting by Burger King and Taco Bell. The move, which prefigures similar price wars in 2002, is widely considered a failure.
1998	Jack M. Greenberg becomes McDonald's fourth chief executive. A 16-year company veteran, he vows to spruce up the restaurants and their menu.
1999	For the first time, sales from international operations outstrip domestic revenues. In search of other concepts, the company acquires Aroma Cafe, Chipotle, Donatos, and, later, Boston Market.
2000	McDonald's sales in the U.S. peak at an average of $1.6 million annually per restaurant. It is, however, still more than at any other fastfood chain.
2001	Subway surpasses McDonald's as the fastfood chain with the most U.S. outlets. At the end of the year it had 13,247 stores, 148 more than McDonald's.
2002	McDonald's posts its first-ever quarterly loss, of $343.8 million. The stock drops to around $13.50, down 40% from five years ago.
2003	James R. Cantalupo returns to McDonald's in January as CEO. He immediately pulls back from the company's 10–15% forecast for per-share earnings growth.
2004	Charles H. Bell takes over the firm after the sudden death of Cantalupo. He states he will continue with the strategies that have been developed by his predecessor.
2005	Jim Skinner takes over as CEO after Bell announces retirement for health reasons.
2006	McDonald's launches specialty beverages, including coffee-based drinks.
2008	McDonald's plans to add McCafés to each of its outlets.
2012	Don Thompson succeeds Skinner as CEO of the chain.
2015	Thompson resigns because of declining performance and is replaced by Steve Easterbrook, the firm's chief branding officer.
2016	McDonald's opens restaurant in the 120th country; the first McDonald's restaurant opens in Astana, Kazakhstan, on March 8, 2016.
2017	Global McDelivery Day is celebrated on July 26 to support the global launch of McDelivery with UberEATS.
2019	Steve Easterbrook is replaced due to poor judgement in a personal relationship with an employee and Chris Kempczinski, president of the USA business unit is named CEO.

Source: The McDonald's Story: Timeline; McDonald's Leadership. McDonald's Corporation.

Cantalupo realized that McDonald's often tended to miss the mark on delivering the critical aspects of consistent, fast, and friendly service and an all-around enjoyable experience for the whole family. He understood that its franchisees and employees alike needed to be inspired as well as retrained on their role in putting the smile back into McDonald's experience. When Cantalupo and his team laid out their turnaround plan in 2003, they stressed upon getting the basics of service and quality right, in part by reinstituting a tough "up or out" grading system that would kick out underperforming franchisees. "We have to rebuild the foundation. It's fruitless to add growth if the foundation is weak," said Cantalupo.[5]

In his effort to focus on its core business, Cantalupo sold off the non-burger chains that the firm had recently acquired. He also cut back on the opening of new outlets, focusing instead on generating more sales from its existing outlets. Cantalupo pushed McDonald's to try to draw more customers through the introduction of new products. The chain had a positive response to its increased emphasis on healthier foods, led by a revamped line of fancier salads. The revamped menu was promoted through a new world-wide ad slogan "I'm loving it," which was delivered by pop idol Justin Timberlake through a set of MTV style commercials.

Striving for a Healthier Image

When Jim Skinner took over from Cantalupo in 2004, he continued to push for McDonald's to change its image. Skinner felt that one of his top priorities was to deal with the growing concerns about the unhealthy image of McDonald's, given the rise of obesity in the United States. These concerns were highlighted in the popular documentary, *Super Size Me*, made by Morgan Spurlock. Spurlock vividly displayed the health risks that were posed by a steady diet of food from the fast food chain. With a rise in awareness of the high fat content of most of the products offered by McDonald's, the firm was also beginning to face lawsuits from some of its loyal customers.

In response to the growing health concerns, one of the first steps taken by McDonald's was to phase out supersizing by the end of 2004. The supersizing option allowed customers to get a larger order of French fries and a bigger soft drink by paying a little extra. McDonald's also announced that it intended to start providing nutrition information on the packaging of its products. The information was easy to read and would tell customers about the calories, fat, protein, carbohydrates, and sodium that are in each product. Finally, McDonald's also began to remove the artery-clogging trans fatty acids from the oil that it used to make its French fries and subsequently announced plans to reduce the sodium content in all of its products by 15 percent.

But Skinner was also trying to push out more offerings that are likely to be perceived by customers to be healthier. McDonald's has continued to build upon its chicken offerings using white meat with products such as Chicken Selects. It has also placed a great deal of emphasis upon its new salad offerings. McDonald's has carried out extensive experiments and tests with these, deciding to use higher quality ingredients, from a variety of lettuces and tasty cherry tomatoes to sharper cheeses and better cuts of meat. It offered a choice of *Newman's Own* dressings, a well-known higher-end brand. "Salads have changed the way people think of our brand," said Wade Thoma, vice president for menu development in the U.S. "It tells people that we are very serious about offering things people feel comfortable eating."[6]

McDonald's has also been trying to include more fruits and vegetables in its well-known and popular Happy Meals. It announced in 2011 that it would reduce the amount of French fries and phase out the caramel dipping sauce that accompanied the apple slices in these meals. The addition of fruits and vegetables has raised the firm's operating costs, because these are more expensive to ship and store because of their more perishable nature. "We are doing what we can," said Danya Proud, a spokesperson for the firm. "We have to evolve with the times."[7]

The rollout of new beverages, highlighted by new coffee-based drinks, represented the chain's biggest menu expansion in almost three decades. Under a plan to add a McCafé section to all of its nearly 14,000 U.S. outlets, McDonald's has been offering lattes, cappuccinos, ice-blended frappes, and fruit-based smoothies to its customers. "In many cases, they're now coming for the beverage, whereas before they were coming for the meal," said Lee Renz, an executive who was responsible for the rollout.[8]

Refurbishing the Outlets

As part of its turnaround strategy, McDonald's also been selling off the outlets that it owned. More than 80 percent of its outlets are now in the hands of franchisees and other affiliates. Skinner began working with the franchisees to address the look and feel of many of the chain's aging stores. Without any changes to their décor, the firm was likely to be left behind by other savvier fast food and drink retailers. The firm is in the midst of pushing harder to refurbish—or re-image—all of its outlets around the world. "People eat with their eyes first," said Thompson. "If you have a restaurant that is appealing, contemporary, and relevant both from the street and interior, the food tastes better."[9]

The re-imaging concept was first tried in France in 1996 by Dennis Hennequin, an executive in charge of the chain's European operations, who felt that the effort was essential to revive the firm's sagging sales. "We were hip 15 years ago, but I think we lost that," he said.[10] McDonald's has been applying the re-imaging concept to its outlets around the world, with a budget of more than half of its total annual capital expenditures. In the United States, the changes cost as much as $650,000 per restaurant, a cost that is shared with the franchisees when the outlet is not company owned.

One of the prototype interiors that was tested out by McDonald's has curved counters with surfaces painted in bright colors. In one corner, a touch-activated screen allows customers to punch in orders without queuing.

The interiors can feature armchairs and sofas, modern lighting, large television screens, and even wireless Internet access. The firm is also trying to develop new features for its drive-through customers, which account for 65 percent of all transactions in the United States. They include music aimed at queuing vehicles and a wall of windows on the drive-through side of the restaurant allowing customers to see meals being prepared from their cars.

The chain has even been developing McCafés inside its outlets next to the usual fast food counter. The McCafé concept originated in Australia in 1993 and has been rolled out in many restaurants around the world. McDonald's has been introducing the concept to the United States as part of the refurbishment of its outlets. In fact, part of the refurbishment has focused on the installation of a specialty beverage platform across all U.S. outlets. The cost of installing this equipment is running at about $100,000 per outlet, with McDonald's subsidizing part of this expense.

The firm has planned for all McCafés to offer espresso-based coffee, gourmet coffee blends, fresh baked muffins, and high-end desserts. Customers will be able to consume these while they relax in soft leather chairs listening to jazz, big band, or blues music. Commenting on this significant expansion of offerings, Marty Brochstein, executive editor of *The Licensing Letter* said: "McDonald's wants to be seen as a lifestyle brand, not just a place to go to have a burger."[11]

Rethinking the Business Model

In response to the decline in performance, McDonald's is testing a number of new concepts, including a kiosk in some locations that allows customers to skip the counter and head to tablet-like kiosks where they can customize everything about their burger, from the type of bun to the variety of cheese to the many, glossy toppings and sauces that can go on it. The firm has plans to gradually expand the concept to more locations, but franchises are concerned about the costs, which can run up to $125,000 per restaurant to make the required changes. "Customization is not McDonald's historic strength," said Mark Kalinowski, an analyst at Janney Montgomery Scott.[12]

Dubbed the "Create Your Taste" platform, McDonald's was hoping to attract more younger customers who may be moving away from frozen processed food that is loaded with preservatives. But it realized that there were considerable risks involved with making such a change. The burgers would be priced higher at $5.49, could take seven minutes to prepare, and could only be ordered from inside the store and eventually brought to your table. Franchises complained that this could not be offered to drive-through customers that make up about 70 percent of the chain's business.

Furthermore, such a change ran counter to the image for inexpensive and fast food that McDonald's has worked hard to build over the years. Easterbrook has subsequently shifted to a more efficient and less expensive format called "Signature Crafted Recipes" that would allow both in-store and drive-through customers to choose a bun and one of four sandwich types. McDonald's is hoping that such a push toward more customization would bring more customers into their outlets, bringing the U.S. counter/drive-through customer ratio closer to 50/50, up from the current 30/70.

McDonald's has also been working to simplify its menu, reducing the number of "value meal" promotions, groups of items that together cost less than ordering items individually. It has tweaked its "dollar menu" replacing it with "dollar value and more" raising the prices for many items as part of a bid to get each customer to spend more. But McDonald's had introduced these bargain menus because its prices had risen over the years, driving away customers to cheaper outlets. Consequently, as much as 15 percent of the chain's sales had been coming from its "dollar menu" where everything cost a dollar.

Over the past year, McDonald's saw a slight jump in U.S. sales after launching an all-day breakfast at most of its locations. The franchises had to be convinced to invest about $5,000 to add food preparation space in order to offer breakfast along with the regular lunch or dinner items. However, sales from the all-day breakfast have begun to flatten out, with a gradual decline in sales from customers who were coming in throughout the day to order breakfast.

More Gold in These Arches?

In spite of all the changes that have been made by Easterbrook, sales growth for McDonald's has continued to be sluggish. The firm does, however, believe that sales will rebound in the United States as well as in foreign markets. In order to provide a boost to its operations in China and Hong Kong, McDonald's announced a deal with Citic, a state-owned conglomerate and the Carlyle Group, a private equity firm. "China and Hong Kong represent an enormous growth opportunity for McDonald's," Easterbrook said in a recent news release. "The new partnership will combine one of the world's most powerful brands and our unparalleled quality standards with partners who have an unmatched understanding of the local markets."[13]

McDonald's has also been trying to grow by reaching out to different customer segments with different products at different times of the day. It has tried to target young adults for breakfast with its gourmet coffee, egg sandwiches, and fat-free muffins. It attracts working adults for lunch, particularly those who are squeezed for time, with its burgers and fries. And its introduction of wraps has drawn in teenagers late in the evening after they have been partying. Restaurant analyst Bryan Elliott commented: "They've tried to be all things to all people who walk in their door."[14]

Above all, McDonald's is concerned about the findings of a recent survey that showed only 20 percent of millennials had even tried a Big Mac. It is also aware that despite its efforts to diversify its menu, 30 percent of sales come from just five items: Big Macs, hamburgers, cheeseburgers, McNuggets, and fries. It has managed to increase traffic during the late-night hours, but this may be hurt by their recent announcement that they would offer a more limited sample of their full menu between midnight and 5 am.

Above all, the expansion of the menu beyond the staple of burgers and fries does raise some fundamental questions. Most significantly, it is not clear just how far McDonald's can stretch its brand while keeping all of its outlets under the traditional symbol of its golden arches. In fact, industry experts believe that the long-term success of the firm may well depend on its ability to compete with rival burger chains. "The burger category has great strength," added David C. Novak, chairman and CEO of Yum! Brands, parent of KFC and Taco Bell. "That's America's food. People love hamburgers."[15]

ENDNOTES

1. PRNewswire, 2019, McDonald's Corporation Announces Leadership Transition, https://www.prnewswire.com/news-releases/mcdonalds-corporation-announces-leadership-transition-300950405.html, November 3.; Grothhaus, M. 2019, Who is Chris Kempczinski Mcdonald's new CEO?, *Fastcompany*, https://www.fastcompany.com/90426246/who-is-chris-kempczinski-mcdonalds-new-ceo-5-things-you-need-to-know, November 4.
2. Taylor, K. 2019. McDonald's makes $300 million deal to sell things like Amazon does. *Business Insider*, March 30.
3. Strom, S. 2016. In a shift, McMuffins with real butter. *New York Times*, August 3, p. B2.
4. The Economist. 2015. When the chips are down. January 10, p. 53.
5. Pallavi, G. and M. Arndt. 2003. Hamburger hell. *BusinessWeek*, March 3, p. 105.
6. Warner, M. 2005. You want any fruit with that Big Mac? *New York Times*, February 20, p. 8.
7. Strom, S. 2011. McDonald's trims its Happy Meal. *New York Times*, July 26, p. B7.
8. Adamy, J. 2008. McDonald's coffee strategy is tough sell. *Wall Street Journal*, October 27, p. B3.
9. Paynter, B. 2010. Super style me. *Fast Company*, October, p. 107.
10. Grant, J. 2006. McDonald's to revamp UK outlets. *Financial Times*, February 2, p. 14
11. Horovitz, B. 2003. McDonald's ventures beyond burgers to duds, toys. *USA Today*, November 14, p. 6 B.
12. Tabuchi, H. 2015. McDonald's Chief Promises Turnaround in a Restructuring. *New York Times*, May 4.
13. Tsang, A. and W. Sui-Lee. 2017. McDonald's China operations to be sold to locally led consortium. *New York Times*, January 9, p. B1.
14. Kowitt, B. 2014. Fallen Arches: Can McDonald's get its mojo back? *Fortune*, December 1, p. 110.
15. Jargon, J. 2012. McDonald's is feeling fried. *Wall Street Journal*, November 9, p. B2.

CASE 29

LIME: IS BIKE SHARING THE NEXT UBER?*

It has been less than two years since Lime launched, and the bike-share company has managed to gain popularity among the rental transportation market with more than a thousand competitors around the globe. "If you ask me what the vision for the next 3 to 5 years will be, we want to become the default short-trip, on-demand service for getting people around cities" said Toby Sun, founder of Lime.[1] While Lime is one of the leading companies that created the market for cost-effective bike-sharing systems in the United States, it faces several hurdles with neck and neck competitors, municipal pushback, vandalism, and establishing a strong survival strategy for the long run.

Bike-share in the United States has continued its brisk growth, with around 35 million trips taken in 2017, a 25 percent increase from 2016.[2] Lime entered the marketplace with a goal of eliminating docking stations in order to make bikes more affordable in comparison to traditional bike-sharing models. The idea of saving millions per year for cities that invested in expensive stations and overpriced bikes appealed to both consumers and the government. The Lime dockless bike-share company operates in over 80 cities in the United States, 22 college campuses, and 7 countries. The mobile app charges $1 to unlock and 15 cents/min to ride after the user unlocks the bike (see Exhibits 1 and 2).

Lime was poised for another great year in 2019. It introduced dockless electric scooters in 2018 and was valued at a whopping $1.1 billion. The startup received a $335 million bid from Uber and Alphabet. In August 2018, Lime signed a deal with Uber to provide e-scooters as Uber planned to expand its service to bikes and scooters. Uber's partnership with Lime may surprise some close watchers of the brewing scooter wars, especially considering one of the company's main competitors in dockless scooter-sharing, Bird, was founded by a former Uber executive.[3] What is Lime's long-term strategy in a market with almost more rental business competitors than bikes or scooters to rent?

World of Bike Sharing

Bike sharing can be traced all the way back to 1965 when the White Bicycle Plan was launched in Amsterdam where free white bicycles were placed in various locations. This was introduced by Luud Schimmelpennink, a Dutch industrial designer, who intended to reduce air pollution in the city and facilitate public use of bicycles. While the idea was quite ahead of its time, it collapsed within days due to theft and damage of bikes. The problem of theft was only solved in 1996, when Bikeabout, a small bike-share system limited to students at Portsmouth University in the UK, introduced an individualized magnetic-stripe card to borrow a bike.[4] Over the next 15 years many of the major cities across the globe introduced bike-share systems with 2013 witnessing 65 new bike-share launches in China alone. By 2015, the number of bike-share bicycles had hit 1 million with China leading the bike-share market.[5]

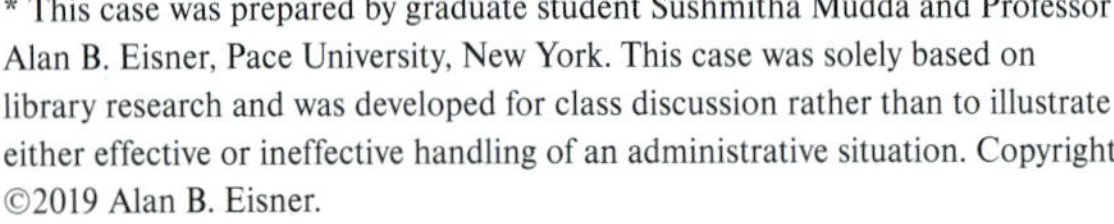

* This case was prepared by graduate student Sushmitha Mudda and Professor Alan B. Eisner, Pace University, New York. This case was solely based on library research and was developed for class discussion rather than to illustrate either effective or ineffective handling of an administrative situation. Copyright ©2019 Alan B. Eisner.

EXHIBIT 1 Lime Electric Bike

Alena Veasey/Shutterstock.

EXHIBIT 2 Lime App and Lime Electric Scooter

Vincent K Ho/Shutterstock.

Dockless bikes go back only a few years. The market for bike sharing had increased rapidly throughout the world by 2015. The third generation of bikes consisted of the automated station-based bikes, which could be borrowed from one docking station and returned at another station of the same system. With the automated biking stations, individuals could unlock their bikes with a smartcard or their phones. As of 2015, public bike-sharing programs existed on five continents, in 712 cities, operating approximately 806,200 bicycles at 37,500 stations.[6] This led companies to invest more time and effort into creating a more cost-effective system, which led to a dockless bike-sharing system. In the United States, during the second half of 2017, dockless bike-share companies introduced around 44,000 bikes in cities across the country. Station-based systems added approximately 14,000 bikes to their fleets, bringing the 2017 total to 54,000 station-based bikes. By the end of 2017, dockless bike-share bikes accounted for about 44 percent of all bike-share bikes in the United States[7] (see Exhibit 3).

Station-based to dockless bikes is the transition that keeps investors on their toes as companies are looking at higher revenues with lower expenses; the only downside of dockless bikes are expenses in theft, vandalism, and fines. The four major dockless bike-sharing companies in the United States include Lime, Jump, MoBike, and Spin. Ofo, a tough competitor, began to withdraw from many U.S. markets in 2018 as it plans to expand its global reach. Another company, Bluegogo, which was the first to introduce dockless bike-share bikes in the United States, declared bankruptcy during the summer of 2018.[8]

Lime Background

In 2015, Chinese startups like Ofo developed a new bike-sharing model without the need for docking stations.[9] This concept of dockless bikes led the San Mateo-based startup, Lime, to introduce dockless bikes in the United States in mid-2017. In March 2017, the company had managed to gather around $12 million of funding from investors such as Andreessen Horowitz and DCM. Lime launched its first market in Greensboro, North Carolina, in June 2017. By November 2017, it had reached over 300,000 users and penetrated 25 markets including 16 cities and 9 college campuses.

Lime was founded by Toby Sun, Brad Bao, and Adam Zang on the simple idea that all communities deserve access to smart, affordable mobility. Their initial belief that electric bikes are preferred over classic bikes and electric scooters for long-distance trips led Lime to surpass over 6 million rides in just over 12 months. Twenty-seven percent of riders in major urban markets reported using Lime to connect to or from public transit during their most recent trip; and 20 percent of riders in major urban markets reported using Lime to travel to or from a restaurant or shopping destination during their most recent trip.[10] In February 2018, with the recognition that there was market demand for scooters, Lime added electric scooters to its product mix. Riders can locate and unlock scooters using the company's smartphone app, and after paying the $1 unlocking fee riders are charged 15 cents per minute of use. By 2018, the company had $6 million in revenues with 400 total employees, up from just 50 employees in 2017.

Policies and Regulations

Over the past decade, shared active transportation systems in the United States have begun to thrive. These systems are highly dependent on the assistance and cooperation of the government and the public. In many places, coordination between cities, operators, and other community stakeholders has allowed bike-share practitioners to grapple with complex issues around access and equity, expanding transportation options for low-income individuals, and focusing investments among communities with history of chronic disinvestment.[11]

The National Association of City Transportation Officials (NACTO) is a non-profit coalition of 63 major North American cities and 10 transit agencies formed to exchange transportation ideas, insights, and practices to cooperatively approach national transportation issues. The NACTO

EXHIBIT 3 Percent of Total Bikes and Trips: Dockless vs Station-Based Bikes

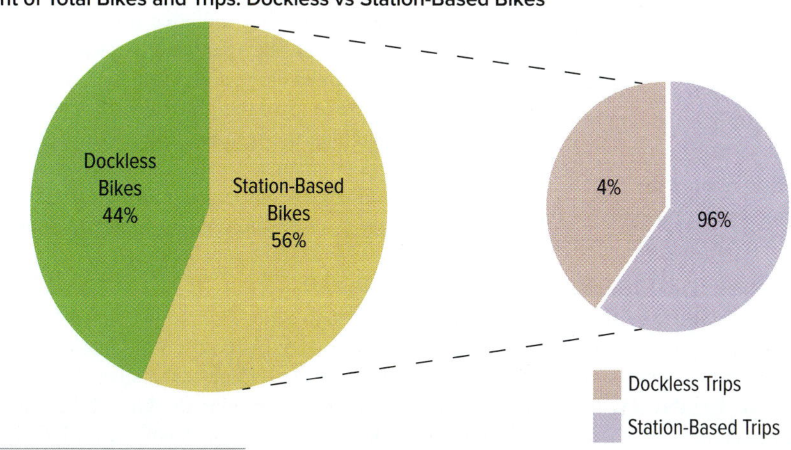

Source: Bike Share in the U.S.: 2017. National Association of City Transportation Officials. nacto.org.

EXHIBIT 4 Selected Permit Fees in the United States, June 2018

Permit Fees In the U.S. as of June 2018

City	Status	Permit/License Fee	Per Bike Fee	Performance Bond	Relocation/ Removal	Permit Duration
Boulder	Approved	$3,300 (Renewal: $1,800)	$100	$0	$80/bike	Annual
Charlotte	Approved (pilot)	$0	$0	$0	All costs	Pilot ended November 1, 2018
Dallas	Pending	$1,620 – $48,600 (Renewal Fee: $404)	$21	$10,000	All costs	6 months
Sacramento	Approved	$14,480 – $28,440 (Renewal Fee: $12,380 – $26,340)	$0	$0	All costs	Annual
St. Louis	Approved	$500	$10/bike	$0	All costs	Annual
Washington DC	Approved (pilot)	$0	$0	$0	$0	Pilot ended August 31, 2018

Source: NACTO Policy 2018: Guidelines for the Regulation and Management of Shared Active Transportation. NACTO, June 2018.

Policy 2018 states the guidelines for the regulation and management of shared active transportation. These guidelines include policies regarding small vehicle parking, community engagement, and equity programs.

Some of the general provisions include:

1. Relevant local government or city authorization is required for bike-share companies and other mobility service providers to operate in the public right-of-way.
2. Cities should reserve the right to limit the number of companies operating (e.g., cap the number of permits or licenses issued, issue exclusive contracts, permits, or licenses).
3. Cities should reserve the right to revoke permits, licenses, or contracts from specific companies (e.g., when a company fails to comply with permit, contract, or license terms, or fails to meet national accreditation standards if applicable).
4. Cities must reserve the right to prohibit specific companies from operating in the public-right-of way based on conduct or prior conduct (e.g., when a company deploys equipment prior to applying for a permit, license, or contract, or fails to comply with permit, contract, or license terms).
5. Cities are required to reserve the right to establish operating zones and fine companies for bikes and equipment found outside of those designated areas.

With regard to the Operations Oversight by NACTO, cities should require companies to remove small vehicles (e.g., damaged, abandoned, improperly placed, etc.) within contractually agreed-upon time frames and assess penalties for failure to do so (see Exhibit 4). Each city is also required to have a limited number of shared small vehicles allowed. Los Angeles allows a minimum of 500 bikes and a maximum of 500 bikes per company, while Washington, DC, which recently witnessed a few cases of vandalism, allows a minimum of 50 bikes and a maximum of 2,500 bikes per company.

Intense Competition

With 84 million trips in 2019 and strong year-on-year growth since 2010, bike share is gaining hold as a transportation option in cities across the United States. High venture capital funding, coupled with generally low ridership, raises questions regarding the overall sustainability and volatility of the dockless bike-share market. The big four dockless bikes in the United States are Lime, Jump, MoBike, and Spin. In less than a year of existence, one U.S.-focused company, Bluegogo, and a number of China-based companies have filed for bankruptcy, merged with other companies, or ceased operations.[12]

Lime believes it can fend off rivals with a city-friendly approach. That includes investing in higher-quality bikes (including safety features like solar-powered lights), sharing aggregated usage data with cities, and educating riders about where to leave their bikes.[13] Cities are proceeding cautiously, watching the results of pilot efforts, and encouraging dockless companies to share more data so that cities can better evaluate and understand how dockless bike share can further city goals of safety, equity, and sustainable mobility.

Mobike

Although taller riders may find Mobike's saddle does not go high enough to accommodate much more than a 30-inch inseam, the Beijing-based silver bike with orange wheels is among the popular dockless bikes in the United States. They started out of Washington, DC, in the United States and by 2018 had over 9 million bikes in some 200 cities in

14 countries around the world. In 2018, Mobike revealed an Apple Watch shortcut at the Apple Worldwide Developers Conference in San Jose.

Spin

Founded in 2016, Spin was presented with the idea of introducing Chinese dockless bikes to the United States. It first launched in Seattle, and further expanded to over 12 cities and 7 college campuses in the United States, and had over 1 million rides. In November 2018, Ford Motor Company acquired Spin for an estimated value of $80 to $90 million. With regard to the safety concerns of electric bikes, Spin offered an anonymous tip-line and promoted helmet usage in 2018. They also initiated pilot partnerships with safe street groups where Spin works with local community leaders who identify protected bike lane networks that are needed, and advocate for them to be built.

JUMP DC

JUMP's bikes have an electric motor in the front wheel with a battery in the frame. When a rider pedals a little, the bike senses the effort and adds some of its own. Jump's bikes are the only dockless entry in Washington, DC, that use pneumatic tires, so their ride is less harsh.[14] JUMP was originally founded as Social Bicycles and has been creating the hardware and software behind some of the greatest innovations in bike share since 2010.[15] The company soon partnered with Uber, and in 2018 was acquired by Uber Technologies Inc.

Electric Scooters

While many cities now have bike-sharing services, electric scooters, which cost less than $2 per ride, are the next innovation in mobility. Investors rooting for the next Uber Technologies, Inc. and Lyft, Inc.,[16] the app-based car-hailing services, are adding to the scooter-frenzy by pouring money into Bird and Lime, which are competing on a city-by-city basis to become the premier electric scooter brand.

Bird, started by a former executive of Lyft and Uber in September 2017 is limited to operating scooter services in about 40 U.S. cities, while Lime launched its scooters toward the end of 2018, and offers its services in 23 U.S. cities. Bird has reached 1 million total scooter rides in less than a year (see Exhibit 5). This year, Bird expanded to France and Israel. Lime has established a presence in France, Germany, and Spain. Scooters are even more prevalent in parts of China, an early pioneer of the market. No company has been able to break into the UK, however, because of strict laws that classify the electric scooters as motor vehicles requiring drivers' licenses and subject to tax and insurance. Even then, regulators will not allow scooters because they do not comply with "normal vehicle construction rules."

The scooter industry is experiencing some of the same problems as ride hailing, with aggressive startups butting heads with local governments. But there are key differences. With ride hailing, entrenched taxi industries argued that unregulated startups had an unfair advantage. There is no such incumbent industry opposing scooters. Urban congestion and climate change have also made alternatives to automobiles more popular with city governments.

Vandalism

There have been numerous cases of vandalism reported for shared bikes around the world. Dockless bike-sharing company Gobee bike had to pull out of Paris after 60 percent of

EXHIBIT 5 Growth of Bird and Lime Total Rides

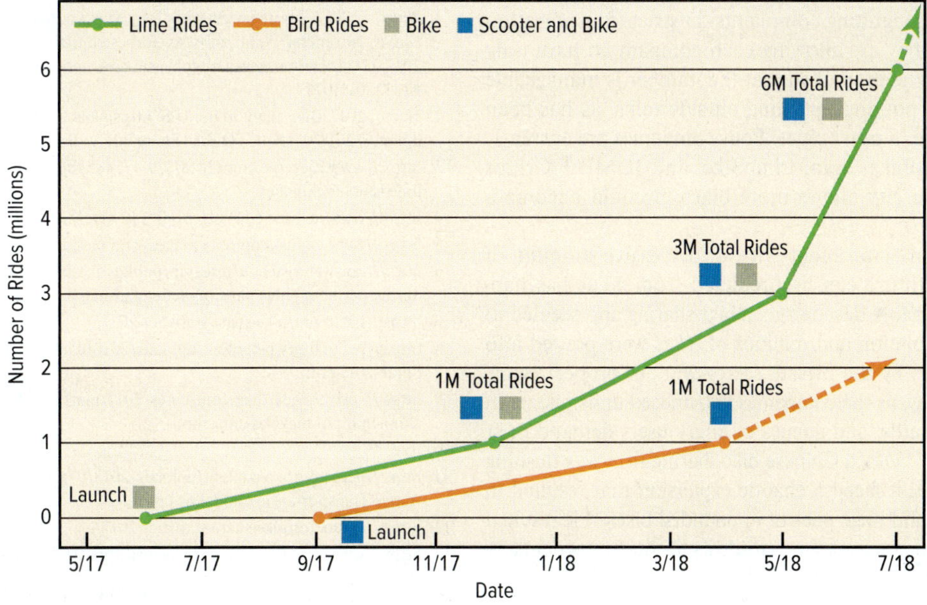

Source: Crunchbase news, company reports.

the bikes were stolen, vandalized, or "privatized" (the practice of renting the bike on a permanent basis, thereby removing it from the co-sharing space).[17] Not long after that, the Hong Kong–based company announced its closure due to losses and high maintenance costs.

In the United States, cases of vandalism have been on the rise since companies have been trying to introduce incentives to keep their bikes safe. Washington, DC, witnessed a couple of cases in 2019. Kimberly Lucas, the city's bike program specialist told a group of regional transportation officials at a dockless share workshop that companies have told city transportation officials that they have lost up to half of their fleets. This is significant because each company is allowed to operate a maximum of 400 bikes in the city.[18] In Arizona, dozens–if not hundreds–of Lime bikes were spotted last week at a scrapyard just northwest of Phoenix. A company spokesman said the bikes "were damaged beyond repair" and were being recycled. Mary Caroline Pruitt, a spokeswoman for Lime, said the company takes "meaningful steps" to prevent vandalism and theft. "All our bikes and scooters have anti-theft locks and audible alarms that sound if someone tries to tamper with them," she said. "If we find someone has vandalized one of our products, we do our best to make sure they are held responsible, including working with local authorities when appropriate."[19]

While Bird scooters have faced vandalism in San Francisco, Lime experienced trouble when they left several hundred of their scooters on the streets without the permission of municipal authorities. People started acting against the company when they figured out that the scooters were programmed to play the message "Unlock me to ride me, or I'll call the police" repeatedly, at a high volume, when their controls were touched.

These cases, documented on social media and neighborhood blogs, are igniting complaints. District transportation officials say they are allowing each company to have only 400 bikes on the ground so that the number is manageable and bikes do not end up piling on sidewalks, as has been the experience in other cities. Four companies are currently operating–Mobike, Spin, LimeBike, and JUMP.[20] Critics say that if the city allows more bikes, it could become a larger concern.[21]

The potential problem with an excessive amount of bikes in the future can be predicted from what has happened in China. A decade ago, a bike-sharing app seemed to be the ideal solution and millions of bikes were poured into China's streets by the private sector without proper regulations. But today, as the companies fail, unused units pile up in bicycle graveyards, and queues of angry users demand their deposits back.[22] Ofo, a Chinese bike-sharing firm was flushing with cash until it faced a chaotic expansion that resulted in bankruptcies and huge piles of impounded bikes.[23] It resulted in hordes of angry customers outside its headquarters demanding refunds.

The Future of Lime

Lime's multi-modal fleet has played an integral role in the international expansion of micro-mobility, with December's year-end report announcing that riders had already taken over 26 million rides on their bikes and scooters.[24] Equipped with a durable, all-aluminum frame and footboard, the new Lime-S promises to be the first shared scooter built for city streets in 2019. The senior director of policy and public affairs, Emily Warren, addressed the Consumer Electronics Show (CES) 2019 conference by saying, "We find that the majority of cities we speak to have spent years and taxpayer dollars trying to develop the mobility solution that Lime offers." Addressing Lime's future plans to work with the government, she added, "We want to work with governments and be transparent with our data to show them the benefits that Lime can have for their communities."[25] Although dockless bike-sharing sounds like a promising future for the rental transportation market, is it viable in huge cities and will Lime be able to penetrate the market?

The company expanded its senior leadership in 2018 by appointing Duke Stump and Li Fan as its Chief Marketing Officer and Chief Technology Officer. Although Lime is limitlessly taking on new initiatives to explore and innovate, and while some investors see a promising future for the bike-sharing business, analysts who witnessed the rise and fall of some of the Chinese bike-share companies disagree. These days, people want to use one app where "you can hail a scooter or a bike or a car," said Tu Le, founder of consulting firm Sino Auto Insights. "That's where the sweet spot's going to be."[26] With car-hailing services like Uber and Lyft entering the bike-share market, do startups like Lime and Bird have a future?

ENDNOTES

1. Beyer, S. 2017. An interview with Toby Sun, co-founder of LimeBike. *Forbes*, November 17, https://www.forbes.com/sites/scottbeyer/2017/11/17/an-interview-with-toby-sun-co-founder-of-limebike/#273230111075.
2. Nacto. 2017. Bike share in the U.S. https://nacto.org/wp-content/uploads/2018/05/NACTO-Bike-Share-2017.pdf.
3. https://www.theverge.com/2018/7/9/17548848/uber-investment-lime-scooter-alphabet.
4. https://www.nctr.usf.edu/jpt/pdf/JPT12-4DeMaio.pdf.
5. https://www.citylab.com/city-makers-connections/bike-share/.
6. http://transweb.sjsu.edu/research/public-bikesharing-north-america-during-period-rapid-expansion-understanding-business.
7. https://nacto.org/bike-share-statistics-2017/.
8. https://nacto.org/wp-content/uploads/2018/05/NACTO-Bike-Share-2017.pdf.
9. https://www.theguardian.com/cities/2017/mar/22/bike-wars-dockless-china-millions-bicycles-hangzhou.
10. Ibid.
11. https://nacto.org/wp-content/uploads/2018/07/NACTO-Shared-Active-Transportation-Guidelines.pdf.
12. https://nacto.org/bike-share-statistics-2017/.
13. https://www.wired.com/story/why-investors-are-betting-that-bike-sharing-is-the-next-uber/.

14. https://www.washingtonpost.com/news/dr-gridlock/wp/2017/09/22/we-rode-all-four-of-d-c-s-dockless-bike-share-so-you-wouldnt-have-to/?utm_term=.eefd7f2bc1e5.
15. https://jump.com/about/.
16. https://www.bloomberg.com/news/articles/2018-09-07/are-electric-scooters-the-future-of-urban-transport-quicktake.
17. https://www.treehugger.com/green-investments/can-lessons-be-learned-vandalism-dockless-bike-sharing-bicycles.html.
18. https://www.washingtonpost.com/news/dr-gridlock/wp/2018/07/01/theft-and-destruction-of-dockless-bikes-a-growing-problem/?noredirect=on&utm_term=.d3b92b0c9276.
19. Lazo, Luz. Theft and destruction of dockless bikes a growing problem. *The Washington Post,* July 01, 2018. https://www.washingtonpost.com/news/dr-gridlock/wp/2018/07/01/theft-and-destruction-of-dockless-bikes-a-growing-problem/?noredirect=on&utm_term=.d3b92b0c9276.
20. https://www.washingtonpost.com/news/dr-gridlock/wp/2017/10/05/abandoned-vandalized-and-illegally-parked-bike-share-bikes-now-a-d-c-problem/?utm_term=.c83071591d2f.
21. https://www.digitaltrends.com/cars/san-francisco-e-scooter-permit/.
22. https://foreignpolicy.com/2018/12/31/a-billion-bicyclists-can-be-wrong-china-business-bikeshare/.
23. https://www.cnn.com/2018/12/21/tech/ofo-china-bike-sharing-crisis/index.html.
24. https://www.li.me/blog/lime-honors-ces-2019-generation-gen-3-electric-scooter-lime-s-10m-riders.
25. Lime Takes Honors At CES 2019, Revealing New Gen 3 E-Scooter, 10M Riders And More. *Lime,* January 11, 2019. https://www.li.me/blog/lime-honors-ces-2019-generation-gen-3-electric-scooter-lime-s-10m-riders.
26. https://www.cnn.com/2018/12/21/tech/ofo-china-bike-sharing-crisis/index.html.

CASE 30

UNITED WAY WORLDWIDE*

In February 2019, United Way was named fifth on Fast Company's annual list of the World's Most Innovative Companies for 2019, and it remained America's largest charity organization.[1] As of 2019, there were nearly 1,800 communities around the world, in 40 countries and territories, with over 2.6 million volunteers. In the past decade, the concern that surrounded American donors was their ability to access information regarding how their donations were going to be used, what percentage of the charity's spending went toward actual current programs, how their privacy was going to be protected when giving via the Internet, and whether the charity met voluntary standards of conduct. It did not help that many nonprofits, including United Way of America, had suffered widely publicized scandals over misappropriation of funds.

Responding to all the challenges, United Way Worldwide's CEO, Brian Gallagher, formally initiated a shift in strategy. He established new membership standards to enhance the level of accountability and transparency in United Way affiliates' operations. He rebranded United Way as doing "what matters" in the communities it serves. In 2018, Brian Gallagher spoke about the digital transformation in United Way and how it had benefited the organization. He said, "In general, when people stop donating to United Way, it's not because they decided to do so; it's because they changed employers or we lost track of them and stopped asking. The digital strategy reduces instances of that, lowering churn rates and helping us recapture lapsed donors."[2] The company had established its digital service operating group in 2015, and worked closely with 11 of its local United Ways to create a website for donors. They eventually put together a donor database of more than a million people, who represented more than half a billion dollars in giving.

Adding to its digital innovation portfolio, United Way partnered with Salesforce.org, a non-profit social enterprise arm of Salesforce.com, to deliver Philanthropy Cloud. The first-of-its-kind network platform aims to transform the way corporations connect employees to engage and support the causes they care about. Talking about the partnership, Gallagher said, "United Way doesn't want to get into the technology business, so we needed a partner. Salesforce was perfect, because its software is already known and used by many of our corporate partners. By the end of 2017 we had signed up several companies to pilot the system, including Anheuser-Busch."[3]

As its latest bold step in its digital transformation, in 2019 the company launched UpPurpose, a cloud-based technology platform and creative agency designed to meet the unique content needs of nonprofits and the social good sector. Arlie Sisson, former Condé Nast and Starwood executive, will be heading UpPurpose. "The world needs cause-driven, social good companies and nonprofits more than ever," Sisson said. "We are built on the idea of crafting inspiring content, easy-to-use technology, insights that enable and hands-on support."[4]

Among its numerous campaigns, United Way Worldwide partnered with Valpak, one of North America's leading direct marketing companies to release a nationwide, multi-platform campaign called "United to Strengthen Our Local Communities." The campaign is intended to increase brand awareness, engagement, and fundraising for United Way through the integration of a robust direct mail and digital advertising campaign. The campaign will feature an integrated promotional package that will showcase United Way's 132-year-old brand on Valpak's iconic Blue Envelope of savings, reaching nearly 36 million households nationwide in September 2019.[5] Alongside Valpak, it teamed up with Chipotle to raise funds for United Way Nebraska and Iowa flood relief efforts in 2019, and The Asian Football Confederation to improve education and health in Asia in 2018.

A decade earlier, United Way of America (UWA) changed its name to United Way Worldwide (UWW) and merged with United Way International (UWI). UWW initiated a long-term program, "Live United," focused less on distribution of funds and more on advancing the common good by addressing underlying causes of problems in the core areas of education, financial stability, and health. Yet positive financial results were slow in coming.

Although it ranked #1 in the Forbes list of "100 Largest U.S. Charities" in 2018,[6] United Way saw a total revenue of $3.9 billion with charitable commitment at 86 percent.* United Way released an analysis suggesting further declines in middle- and lower-class giving. In the report, they noted a decline in the fraction of Americans giving to charity, especially among middle- and low-income families. The company stressed the need to rectify the declining behavior, and

* By Professor Alan B. Eisner of Pace University, Associate Professor Pauline Assenza of Western Connecticut State University, and graduate students Luz Barrera, Dev Das, and Saad Nazir of Pace University. This case is based upon public documents and was developed for class discussion rather than to illustrate either effective or ineffective handling of the situation. This research was supported in part by the Wilson Center for Social Entrepreneurship, Pace University.
Copyright © 2019 Alan B. Eisner.

* Charitable services as percent of total expenses.

said that "if these changes continue in the long term, it is unlikely that continued growth in philanthropic giving will be sustainable."[7]

The question remained, would donors finally become reenergized and create real change in the communities United Way served? Or had universal struggles weakened the ability and eagerness to donate of even those most able to do so? As it steps into the digital era, will United Way be able to retain and increase its donors by leveraging digital intelligence, or will its contributions ebb?

Overview and History of the United Way of America

United Way was founded in 1887 as the Charity Organizations Society of Denver, raising $21,700 for 22 local agencies in its second year of operation. In 1913, this model was expanded to become a "Community Chest" in Cleveland, and in 1918 a dozen fund-raising federations met in Chicago to form the American Association for Community Organizations. From 1919 to 1929, over 350 Community Chests were created, and by 1948 more than 1,000 communities had United Way Community Chests in operation. In 1973, the partnership between United Way and the National Football League began, with the goal to increase public awareness of social-service issues facing the country. Through the partnership, United Way public service announcements featured volunteer NFL players, coaches, and owners, and NFL players supported their local United Ways through personal appearances, special programs, and membership on United Way governing boards.

In 1974, United Ways in America and Canada raised $1,038,995,000, marking the first time in history that an annual campaign of a single organization raised more than $1 billion. In the same year, United Way International was formed to help nations around the world create United Way-type organizations. The 1981 to 1985 and 1997 and 1998 campaigns generated the greatest percentage increase in revenues, possibly driven by economic trends. Amounts raised since 2000 have generally failed to keep up with the rate of inflation (see Exhibit 1).[8]

The United Way is essentially a financial intermediary, providing fund-raising activities, primarily through donor organizations' employee payroll deductions, and then

EXHIBIT 1 United Way Campaign History

Year	Amount Raised ($ billions)	Change ($ billions)	%	CPI (1982 – 1984 = 100)*	Inflation Rate (%)	Amount Raised in Constant Dollars	Change ($ billions)	%
2000	3.912	0.14	3.8	172.2	3.4	2.272	0.095	0.4
2001	3.949	0.37	0.9	177.1	2.8	2.230	−0.042	−1.8
2002	3.709	−0.24	−6.1	179.9	1.6	2.062	−0.168	−7.5
2003	3.591	−0.11	−3.2	184.0	2.3	1.952	−0.110	−5.3
2004	3.606	0.15	0.4	188.9	2.7	1.909	−0.043	−2.2
2005	4.048	0.44	12.3	195.3	3.4	2.054	0.145	7.6
2006	4.143	0.95	2.3	201.6	3.2	2.043	−0.011	−0.5
2007	4.236	0.93	2.2	207.3	2.8	2.007	−0.036	−1.8
2008	4.023	−0.21	−5.0	215.3	3.8	1.919	−0.088	−4.4
2009	3.84	−0.18	−4.5	214.5	−0.4	1.795	−0.124	−6.5
2010	3.912	0.72	1.9	218.1	1.6	1.794	−0.001	−0.1
2011	3.927	0.15	0.4	224.9	3.2	1.746	−0.048	−2.7
2012	3.97	0.43	1.1	229.6	2.1	1.729	−0.017	−1.0
2013	3.939	−0.31	−0.8	233.0	1.5	1.691	−0.038	−2.2
2014	3.87	−0.69	−1.75	236.7	1.6	1.717	0.026	1.5
2015	3.71	−0.16	−4.13	237.0	0.1	1.719	0.002	0.1
2016	3.87	0.16	4.31	240.0	1.3	1.741	0.022	1.3
2017	3.54	−0.34	−8.5	244.7	2.1	1.775	.0034	2.0
2018	3.91	0.37	10.5	251.6	2.4	1.825	0.050	2.8

* CPI is the annualized rate for a calendar year.

Sources: United Way of America research services and author estimates.

EXHIBIT 2

Charity Report for United Way America, 2018

Governance

Chief Executive: Brian A. Gallagher, President and CEO
Total Compensation: $1,318,695
Chair of the Board: Neeraj Mehta
Board Size: 15

Uses of Funds as Percentage of Total Expenses for Year Ended December 31, 2018

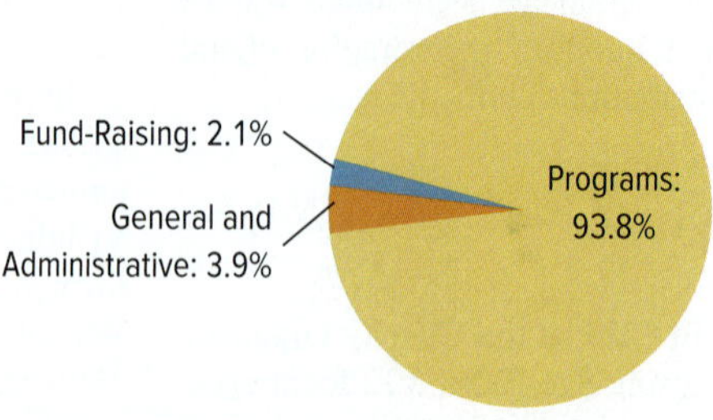

Sources: United Way Worldwide. Charity Navigator.

distributing those funds to agencies that can actually deliver services to clients in the target community. The parent organization, United Way Worldwide, services the local United Way chapters, which perform the bulk of the fund raising. Although there are other sources of revenue, including individual donations and government grants, around 70 percent of donations come from employees in local businesses; of the employee contributions, 75 percent are considered unrestricted dollars that the local United Ways put to use to address critical needs in their respective communities.

The parent organization, United Way Worldwide (UWW), is supported primarily by local United Way member organizations that pay annual membership fees based on an agreed-on formula, 1 percent of their communitywide campaign contributions. Trademark members, United Way member organizations raising less than $100,000, pay a fee of 0.3 percent of their total contributions. In addition to membership support, individual and corporate sponsorship, and federal grants, other sources for funds for the national umbrella organization are conferences, program service fees, promotional material sales, investment income, rental income, and service income (see Exhibits 2 and 3).

United Way is a system that operates as a federation—a network of local affiliates that share a mission, a brand, and a program model but are legally independent from one another and from the national office. Historically, United Way has been the loosest of federations, with almost all power residing at the local level. Each United Way chapter member is not only independent but also separately incorporated and governed by a local volunteer board. Through communitywide campaigns, each local United Way utilizes a network of local volunteers for raising funds to support a great variety of health and human services organizations.

Over the years, as United Way's local chapters grew bigger and more prosperous, they began to consider themselves more autonomous—gatekeepers, allocators, and managers of the local public trust—and began to question whether the seal of approval bestowed by United Way affiliation was worth it in light of the declining financial rewards. Therefore, some United Way agencies have considered forming their own member-oriented, self-governing federations.

Current Competition and Challenges

According to Giving USA, an annual report on Philanthropy that reports the sources and uses of charitable giving in the United States, there are more than 1.5 million charitable organizations in the United States.[9] The charitable-giving industry is massive, with $410.02 billion given away in 2017, up 5.2 percent from 2016.[10]

Donors have been concerned about the "impact" of their donations for a long time. In addition, because United Way's traditional function had been to parcel out the contributions it received to local charities, donors had begun to question the need for an organization that essentially just processed money. (A donor might ask, "Why not just give directly to the charity of my choice?") The perception was that the administrative function of United Way and other blanket charities added an additional level of overhead to organizational costs, with a smaller portion of the original donation actually reaching the intended target.

Donors were increasingly supporting specific causes and therefore were more attracted to alternative recipient organizations, those possibly more responsive to the idea of community based on gender, race, or sexual orientation, among other socially driven issues.[11] People were more inclined to support a cause that meant something to them. This increased the popularity of "donor-advised funds," which allows donors to establish and fund the account by making irrevocable, tax-deductible contributions to the charitable sponsor. According to the National

EXHIBIT 3 United Way of America Consolidated Financial Statements ($ thousands)

	Dec 31, 2018	Dec 31, 2017	Dec. 31, 2016	Dec. 31, 2015	Dec. 31, 2014	Dec. 31, 2013
Source of Funds						
Contributions	$173,557	$134,763	$67,729	$63,510	$53,599	$48,634
Membership support (net)	29,332	30,093	31,391	28,484	28,647	28,869
Campaign efforts (net)	—	—	—	—	(1,121)	(4,625)
Promotional material sales	455	487	489	608	725	694
Conferences	1,403	2,597	2,502	3,009	2,590	2,708
Program service fees	14,509	6,066	5,321	2,074	2,487	2,238
Investment return, net	(1,444)	(519)	681	190	610	1,099
Miscellaneous and other	1,403	1,402	1,413	1,124	983	1,044
Total Revenue	**219,460**	**174,891**	**109,526**	**98,999**	**88,521**	**80,661**
Program Expenses						
Brand strategy and marketing	5,937	10,447	9,800	7,164	5,376	6,929
Impact, strategy and innovation	623	15,412	14,199	10,702	9,170	8,757
Campaign and public relations	—	—	164	316	1,249	5,739
Other expenses, e.g., investor relations, international expenses	215,183		86,128	63,794	57,268	60,312
Total Program Expenses	**221,743**	**139,609**	**110,291**	**81,976**	**73,063**	**81,737**
Total Revenue	219,460	174,891	109,526	98,999	88,521	80,661
Program expenses	221,743	139,609	110,291	81,976	73,063	81,737
Fund-raising expenses	4,086	2,272	2,368	3,265	2,641	2,392
Administrative expenses	5,539	5,447	5,149	4,367	4,526	5,791
Total expenses	231,369	147,329	117,808	89,608	80,230	89,919
Income in excess of expenses	(11,908)	27,562	(8,282)	9,391	8,480	(9,258)
Beginning net assets	64,566	40,684	46,815	38,723	36,845	39,501
Changes in net assets	(13,947)	23,881	(6,131)	8,091	1,878	(2,656)
Ending net assets	50,620	64,566	40,684	46,815	38,724	36,845
Total liabilities	30,681	37,424	35,986	37,599	37,455	29,859
Total liabilities and net assets	81,301	101,991	76,670	84,414	76,178	66,704

Source: United Way Consolidated Financial Statements.

Philanthropic Trust, there was a 60.2 percent increase in the total number of DAF accounts from 2016 to 2017[12] (see Exhibit 4). This did not mean that traditional and venerable organizations like United Way, the Red Cross, the Salvation Army, and the American Cancer Society were necessarily in trouble; it just meant that they were perhaps in need of some strategic adjustment (see Exhibit 5).

With an emphasis on business models, Brian Gallagher, President and CEO of United Way Worldwide mentioned that the company is encouraged when they benchmark their approach against that of other nonprofits such as

EXHIBIT 4 Donor-Advised Fund Metric Overview ($ billions except as noted)

	2016	2017	2018
Charitable Assets	$86.45	$110.01	$121.42
Total Contributions	$25.09	$29.23	$37.12
Total Grant Dollars	$15.91	$19.08	$23.42
Grant Payout*	20.6%	22.1%	20.9%
Total # of DAF Accounts	289,478	463,622	728,563
Average Size of DAF** Account ($)	$298,628	$237,356	$166,653

* Grant Payout = Grant Dollars divided by Charitable Assets at end of prior year multiplied by 100 to get a percentage.
** Average size of a DAF Account = Total Assets Under Management divided by Total Number of DAF Accounts.

The DAF Report. National Philanthropic Trust, 2018, 2019.

EXHIBIT 5 Top 10 U.S. Charities, December 2018

Rank	Name	Private Support ($ millions)	Total Revenue ($ millions)	Fund-Raising Efficiency (%)	Charitable Commitment (%)	Donor Dependency (%)
1	United Way	3,471	3,919	91	86	100
2	Feeding America	2,654	2,718	99	99	99
3	Americares Foundation	2,379	2,381	100	99	81
4	Task Force for Global Health	2,161	2,197	100	100	100
5	Salvation Army	2,033	4,323	88	82	69
6	St. Jude Children's Research Hospital	1,511	2,086	84	71	57
7	Direct Relief	1,21	1,238	100	99	100
8	Habitat for Humanity Foundation	1,095	1,986	88	85	94
9	Boys & Girls Club of America	989	2,037	88	80	80
10	YMCA of the USA	974	7,402	85	85	55

The 100 Largest U.S. Charities. Forbes Media, 2018.

Greenpeace and AARP. "Not very many years ago, Greenpeace was best known for protesting at World Trade Organization events. It has shifted toward a direct-to-consumer advocacy model, creating an ecosystem that helps individuals find ways to make their voices heard . . . .We've adopted some of that thinking," he said.[13]

Complementing Gallagher's admiration of AARP's model of establishing commercial relationships to create real value for its members, AARP and United Way Worldwide announced the "Do You Care Challenge" in February 2018. It was an interactive online tool that let people get a sense of what "a day in the life" is like for a family caregiver. The tool was developed to help raise awareness about the surprising number of millennials ages 18 to 34 who are family caregivers and to encourage employers to create more caregiving-friendly workplaces.[14]

Scandals and Governance

As if the plateau in donations by the charitable-giving community were not enough, corporate scandals: Enron, ImClone, WorldCom, and Tyco all hit the headlines with examples of corporate greed and misappropriation of both funds and public trust. Given such egregious wrongdoing in publicly held organizations, the tolerance of the general population for similar activities in nonprofits was increasingly approaching zero, especially given the nature of the relationship—one based on donor trust.

The first major scandal at United Way had occurred in 1992, when William Aramony, president and CEO of United Way of America, and two other UWA executives, were convicted of fraud, conspiracy, and money laundering in a scheme that siphoned around $1 million from the organization. This event was perceived as a turning point in public perceptions of charitable organizations and was blamed for the first drop in United Way donations since World War II.[15]

In 2001, the United Way of the National Capital Area—the Washington, DC, chapter and the second-largest local United Way member in the country in donations—was in the news because of fraud. CEO Oral Suer had taken more than $500,000 from the charity to pay for personal expenses, annual leave, and an early pension payout he was not entitled to. Other employees had taken additional money for personal use, with the total fraud amounting to $1.6 million.

Then, in 2002, new United Way National Capital Area CEO Norman O. Taylor was asked to resign over misstated revenues and questionable overhead and credit card charges. In 2003, the CFO of the Michigan Capital Area United Way, Jacqueline Allen-MacGregor, was imprisoned for the theft of $1.9 million from the charity, which she had used to purchase racehorses for her personal farm. Also in 2003, Pipeline Inc., a spin-off from the California Bay Area United Way that was created to collect contributions, was investigated for losing $18 million when the financial records did not accurately reflect the amount owed by the charity.[16] In 2006, a former CEO of the United Way of New York City was investigated for diverting organizational assets valued at $227,000 for his own personal use.[17]

To be fair, United Way was not the only high-profile charity to experience these kinds of problems. After 9/11, Katrina, and Hurricane Sandy, the American Red Cross came under scrutiny for misdirection of disaster funds. In addition, the bookkeeper at Easter Seals of Iowa stole $230,000, the former president and seven others at Goodwill Industries of California embezzled $26 million, the financial administrator of the American Heart Association of New Jersey was convicted of theft of $186,000, and an executive at Goodwill Industries of Michigan was found guilty of stealing $750,000 from the agency over a 23-year period.[18]

The problem of official misconduct and lax oversight among the charitable organizations had reached alarming proportions. The picture it painted for the charitable giving community was not a cheerful one. What could be done to curtail this extremely disturbing trend?

The United Way of America's board during the Aramony scandal had consisted of many Fortune 500 CEOs who were, according to Aramony, fully informed about his compensation and perquisites.[19] Yet it appeared they still failed to exercise appropriate oversight, as did the boards at the DC and Michigan chapters. Finding committed and knowledgeable board members was critical to United Way's continued success. Given the federation model, each local chapter had its own board, recruited from community members who had not only fund-raising skills but also relationships with local leaders, politicians, and even regulators. Many local United Ways wanted to distance themselves from the scandals at UWA and high-profile chapters, and therefore they tried to stress local leadership and board autonomy. Serving on such a board required a commitment to the community and to the goals of the local United Way.

However, regardless of the degree of well-intentioned communication and disclosure, sometimes the goals of board members were in conflict. A 2004 survey by McKinsey & Company of executives and directors at 32 of *Worth* magazines' top 100 nonprofit performers found that many nonprofit boards had recurring problems, one of which was consensus over mission and goals: "Only 46 percent of the directors we surveyed thought that other directors on their boards could both summarize the mission of the organizations they serve and present a vision of where those organizations hope to be in five years' time."[20] In addition, for an organization such as United Way, the goals of the diverse stakeholders, both donors and recipients, might differ widely. This lack of consensus, coupled with the difficulty of measuring and evaluating performance, meant that nonprofit boards in general needed to practice serious self-scrutiny: "The time when nonprofit boards were populated by wealthy do-gooders who just raised money, hired CEOs, and reaffirmed board policy is over."[21]

Given the degree to which the public trust had been violated by nonprofits that were found to be acting irresponsibly, the U.S. Senate Finance Committee was considering tax-exempt reform containing provisions similar to those found in the Sarbanes-Oxley Act.[22] The 2008 scandal involving the Association of Community Organizations for Reform Now (ACORN), although focused on voter registration fraud, brought attention in Washington once again to the question of nonprofit legitimacy.[23]

This demand for greater accountability was not new. Nonprofits had sometimes been notoriously ineffective at accomplishing their social missions, inefficient at getting maximum return on the money they raised due to high administration costs, and willing to take on too much risk, either through inexperience or ignorance. Sometimes because of lax oversight procedures, individuals in control of the nonprofits were willing to engage in outright fraud, acquiring excessive benefits for themselves. These problems were enhanced by nonprofits' failure to provide extensive analysis, disclosure, and dissemination of relevant performance information and the lack of sanctions.[24] If nonprofit organizations would not police themselves, watchdog agencies would create external standards and provide public feedback, sometimes to the detriment of the organizations under scrutiny (see Exhibit 6).[25]

EXHIBIT 6 Watchdog Agencies—Information Resources about Nonprofits

- American Institute of Philanthropy
  www.charitywatch.org
- Better Business Bureau Wise Giving Alliance
  www.give.org
- Board Source
  www.boardsource.org
- Charity Navigator
  www.charitynavigator.org
- Governance Matters
  www.governancematters.com
- Guidestar
  www.guidestar.org
- Independent Sector
  www.independentsector.org
- Internet Nonprofit Center
  www.nonprofits.org
- IRS Exempt Organizations
  www.irs.gov/charities
- National Association of Attorneys General
  www.naag.org
- National Association of State Charity Officials
  www.nasconet.org
- National Council of Nonprofits
  www.councilofnonprofits.org
- Network for Good
  www1.networkforgood.org
- New York State Attorney General
  www.charitiesnys.com
- OMB Watch
  www.ombwatch.org
- Standards for Excellence Institute
  www.standardsforexcellenceinstitute.org

Source: Wasik, John F. "How to Choose a Charity Wisely." The New York Times Company, November 8, 2013. https://www.nytimes.com/2013/11/08/giving/how-to-choose-a-charity-wisely.html.

Gallagher's Response

In 2006, United Way of America CEO Brian Gallagher was invited by the U.S. Senate Finance Committee to participate in a roundtable discussion on needed reforms in nonprofit boards and governance. He was prepared to provide specific commentary. Since accepting the CEO position in 2001, Gallagher had been working to promote a change in the United Way strategy, including a change in mission, the creation of standards of performance excellence, and a requirement that local members certify their adherence to the membership standards.

Regarding the mission of United Way, Gallagher had worked to change the focus from fund raising to community impact—from "How much money did we raise?" to "How much impact did we have on our community?" In his initial statement to the Senate committee, Gallagher said:

> The ultimate measure of success is whether family violence rates have gone down and whether there is more affordable housing. And fund-raising is [just] part of making that happen. When you are asking people to contribute, you're asking for an investment in your mission. And like a for-profit business, you are then accountable to your investors, not just for keeping good books, but for creating value and offering a concrete return. For those of us in human development, that means efforts that lead to measurable improvements in people's lives. In other words, the organizations that produce the greatest results should grow and be rewarded. Those that do not should be forced to change or go out of business. The American public doesn't give us money just because our operations are clean. Why they really give us money is because they want to make a difference.[26]

As a result of the new mission, UWW required local affiliates to provide the national headquarters with annual financial reports with greater transparency and to embrace the revised standards of excellence developed by more than 200 United Way employees, volunteers, and consultants. Of interest is the fact that these standards were not mandatory but were presented as guidelines, giving chapters' suggestions for how they might revise their local strategies. The standards urged the affiliates to identify community problems, raise money to solve them, and demonstrate measurable progress toward their goals by adopting a code of ethics that included an annual independent financial audit. The hope was that by adopting these guidelines, the chapters would be able to provide tangible proof to donors, especially wealthy contributors, that the United Way chapters and the charities they support were making a difference (see Exhibit 7).[27]

In 2018, United Way had elected several new members to its board of trustees including the CEOs of Whirlpool Corporation and Western National Group, as well as senior executives from NBC Sports, Synchrony Financial, UPS, and Wells Fargo during the organization's annual meeting. Neeraj Mehta was elected chair of United Way's USA national board. "We are pleased to welcome the newest members to our board and appreciate the investment of their time and talent in United Way," said Brian Gallagher, President and CEO of United Way Worldwide. "I look

EXHIBIT 7 United Way New Standards of Excellence

Standards of Excellence, a comprehensive description of benchmark standards and best practices: Developed in conjunction with United Way executives, staff, and volunteers throughout the country, the standards are designed to enhance the effectiveness of the 1,350 United Way affiliates.

- **Introduction to the Standards of Excellence.** Spanning more than 100 pages, the new standards provide highly detailed descriptions regarding five key areas of operation.
- **Community Engagement and Vision.** Working with formal and informal leaders to develop a shared vision and goals for a community, including the identification of priority issues affecting the overall well-being of its citizens.
- **Impact Strategies, Resources, and Results.** Creating "impact strategies" that address the root causes and barriers of a community's priority issues; mobilizing essential assets such as people, knowledge, relationships, technology, and money; effectively implementing impact strategies; and evaluating the effectiveness of impact strategies in fostering continuous improvement.
- **Relationship Building and Brand Management.** Developing, maintaining, and growing relationships with individuals and organizations in order to attract and sustain essential assets.
- **Organizational Leadership and Governance.** Garnering trust, legitimacy, and support of the United Way in local communities through leadership and overall management.
- **Operations.** Providing efficient and cost-effective systems, policies, and processes that enable the fulfillment of the United Way's mission, while ensuring the highest levels of transparency and accountability.

Source: United Way of America.

forward to working with all of them as we fight for the health, education, and financial stability of every person in every community."[28]

As they moved into 2019, United Way's biggest challenge was the need to retain donors by leveraging digital strategy. Their new partnerships to establish the Salesforce Philanthropic Cloud and UpPurpose were in the limelight. When asked about these new technological tools, Gallagher was pretty optimistic, saying, "I'm really confident that it will. I say that because I've been doing this for a long time, and I've broken my pick on a lot of ideas or been disappointed by a lot of ideas. I just think that this one's it. Because it captures what we were just talking about."[29]

ENDNOTES

1. Press Release. 2019. United Way named to Fast Company's list of The World's Most Innovative Companies for 2019. United Way, February 20, https://www.unitedway.org/the-latest/press/united-way-worldwide-list-of-the-worlds-most-innovative.
2. Gallagher, B. 2018. United Way's CEO on shifting a century-old business model. *Harvard Business Review*, September-October issue, https://hbr.org/2018/09/united-ways-ceo-on-shifting-a-century-old-business-model.
3. Ibid.
4. Press Release. 2019. United Way launches UpPurpose amplifying stories of good. United Way, February 20, https://www.unitedway.org/the-latest/press/united-way-launches-uppurpose-amplifying-stories-of-good.
5. Press Release. 2019. Valpak and United Way launch "United to Strengthen Our Local Communities" campaign. United Way, April 23, https://www.unitedway.org/the-latest/press/valpak-and-united-way-launch-united-to-strengthen-our-local-communities-campaign.
6. Forbes. 2018. The 100 largest U.S. charities. United Way Worldwide, December 11, https://www.forbes.com/companies/united-way-worldwide/?list=top-charities#281688c0671a.
7. Research Brief. 2019. Weakening ties to charity: A smaller percentage of people giving to charity with greater declines among non-Itemizers than itemizers. United Way, Research and Publications.
8. From the United Way website, liveunited.org.
9. Giving USA. 2018. See the numbers–Giving USA 2018 infographic. June 14.
10. Ibid.
11. Ibid.
12. NPT. 2018. The 2018 DAF Report. National Philanthropic Trust, https://www.nptrust.org/reports/daf-report/.
13. Gallagher, B. 2018 United Way's CEO on shifting a century-old business model. *Harvard Business Review,* September-October issue, https://hbr.org/2018/09/united-ways-ceo-on-shifting-a-century-old-business-model.
14. Press Release 2018. AARP and United Way Worldwide team up to spotlight millennial family caregivers. United Way, February 7, https://www.unitedway.org/the-latest/press/aarp-and-united-way-worldwide-team-up-to-spotlight-millennial-family-caregi.
15. Gallagher, B. 2018 United Way's CEO on shifting a century-old business model. *Harvard Business Review,* September-October issue, https://hbr.org/2018/09/united-ways-ceo-on-shifting-a-century-old-business-model.
16. Gibelman, M. & Gelman, S. R. 2004. A loss of credibility: Patterns of wrongdoing among nongovernmental organizations. *International Journal of Voluntary and Nonprofit Organizations,* 15(4): 355–381.
17. Strom, S. 2006. United Way Says Ex-Leader took Assets. *The New York Times,* April 14, https://www.nytimes.com/2006/04/14/nyregion/united-way-says-exleader-took-assets.html
18. Gibelman & Gelman, op. cit.
19. Sinclair, M. 2002. William Aramony is back on the streets. *NonProfit Times,* March 1.

20. Jansen, P. and A. Kilpatrick. 2004. The dynamic nonprofit board. *McKinsey Quarterly,* 2: 72–81.
21. Ibid.
22. Kelley, C. and S. Anderson. 2006. Advising nonprofit organizations. *CPA Journal,* 76(8): 20–26.
23. McRay, G. 2009. Bad seeds: Why the ACORN scandal matters to other nonprofits. *Foundation Group,* September 16, www.501c3.org/blog/acorn-scandel-matters-to-nonprofits/.
24. Herzlinger, R. 1996. Can public trust in nonprofits and governments be restored? *Harvard Business Review,* March–April: 97–107.
25. Gibelman, & Gelman, op. cit.
26. Gallagher, B. 2005. Statement of Brian A. Gallagher, president and CEO United Way of America, before United States Senate Committee on Finance. *liveunited.org,* April 5:1.
27. Blum, D. E. 2005. Held to a new standard. *Chronicle of Philanthropy,* 17(13).
28. Press Release. 2018. United Way announces new appointments to its governing boards. United Way, July 16, https://www.unitedway.org/the-latest/press/united-way-announces-new-appointments-to-its-governing-boards.
29. Podcast. 2018. United Way's CEO on keeping an old nonprofit fresh. The Chronicle of Philanthropy, April 27, https://www.philanthropy.com/article/Podcast-United-Way-s-CEO-On/243242.

CASE 31

ALIBABA GROUP: RIVALS AT THE GATE?*

During a visit to the United States in 1995, Jack Ma, the founder of Alibaba, heard about the Internet for the first time. With his hands on the technology, he searched for the word beer on Yahoo. Ma was surprised to find that his Internet search came up with beers from Europe and America, but there was nothing from China. At that moment, he decided to build a business that could facilitate the buying and selling of Chinese products abroad. Even in the face of great scrutiny, he identified the great business potential of e-commerce and founded Alibaba in 1999.

Ma's once criticized vision for the Alibaba Group has now evolved into a thriving global operation, making it one of the most successful companies of the past decade. Alibaba's stock price has been one of the top performers among technology companies around the world. Its past year performance aggressively competed with one of its fiercest international competitors, Amazon (see Exhibit 1). However, Alibaba's continuously evolving business model, along with increasingly growing domestic competition from companies like Tencent Holdings, Baidu, and JD.com, create numerous challenges for the company to move forward and replicate that past performance record.

Intuitively, the meteoric rise of Alibaba has been accompanied by a number of direct and indirect challenges, which are consistently growing with the size of the company. From domestically-based pressures, such as increasing competition, to international obstacles involving new and unchartered U.S. market conditions, Ma's Alibaba Group has its work cut out. Additionally, the Chinese government tightened e-commerce regulation, which led to formal complaints aimed at Alibaba's practices regarding fraud protection. A great deal of debate is attempting to hash out the ambiguities associated with the determination of the company's future competitive sustainability and financial viability.[1]

* This case was developed by Professor Alan B. Eisner, Pace University; Professor Helaine J. Korn, Baruch College-City University of New York; and graduate student Saad Nazir, Pace University. Material has been drawn from published sources to be used for class discussion. Copyright © 2019 Alan B. Eisner.

Company History and Evolution

Ma Charm

Jack Ma did not benefit from any type of advantageous handicap. During a speech at Stanford University, Ma stated, "We are a very lucky company. . . There was no chance that we would survive. I don't have any background, rich father, or strong uncles."[2] Ma's success seems to be the outcome of his innovative vision and aggressive business savvy. Scott Kessler, an analyst from S&P Capital IQ, describes Ma as, "someone who thinks very long term–which is something

EXHIBIT 1 Alibaba Stock Price Performance vs. Amazon, JD.com, and Baidu

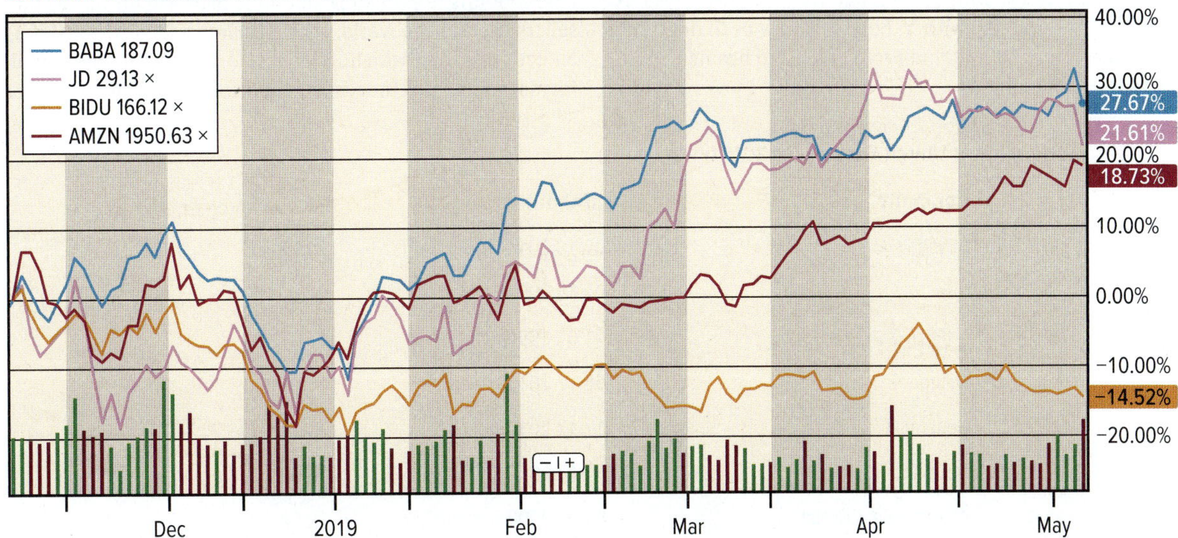

Source: Yahoo Finance, 2019.

that isn't very common these days."[3] Ma departs greatly from the typical Chinese personality archetype. Flamboyant style, forwardly opinionated demeanor, and unconventional business approach define the man known as Jack Ma.[4]

Ma first encountered the Internet during a business trip to the United States as a translator. While his initial goals pertaining to his travels failed, his introduction to the Internet surely made the endeavor worthwhile. After recognizing the Internet's potential, he headed back to China to pursue opportunities involving its application. Ma initially developed a Chinese listing website, which he eventually sold to the Chinese government. For some time, Ma worked with the Chinese Ministry of Commerce in Beijing. Finally, Ma decided to move back to his hometown, where he would discover something that would change everything.[5]

Alibaba Incorporated

In 1999, Jack Ma and his team of 17 co-founders officially established Alibaba Group out of his apartment in Hangzhou, Ma's hometown in Eastern China. Upon the company's commencement, a global wholesale business-to-business online marketplace, Alibaba.com was born.[6] From 1999 to 2000, Ma and his team worked to acquire venture capital funding. In January 2000, the company successfully signed a deal for US$20 million with a group of investors led by a Japanese multinational corporation, Softbank. Other financial institutions, such as Goldman Sachs and Fidelity, were also early investors in Alibaba Group. By 2001, the company surpassed one million users and operated with positive cash flow; this was Ma's first encounter with profitability.[7]

In 2005, U.S. corporation Yahoo and Alibaba.com formed an international strategic partnership. This partnership allowed the two companies to work together toward improving the Yahoo brand presence in China. Yahoo purchased US$1 billion of Alibaba.com shares, which, in agreement with Alibaba Group, provided Yahoo "40 percent economic interest with 35 percent voting rights."[8] Ma explained, "Teaming up with Yahoo will allow us to deliver an unmatched range of e-commerce services to businesses and consumers in China."[9]

In 2007, Alibaba began trading as a public company on the Hong Kong stock exchange as Alibaba.com Limited. The IPO raised $1.67 billion, which made Alibaba.com Limited the largest Internet IPO in Asia. The IPO share price opened at $1.73 and sharply rose 192.6 percent to $5.05 per share.[10] Ma stated, "We are pleased to welcome investors from Hong Kong and around the world to join us in building a world-class e-commerce company."[11] Major investors involved with the offering included Yahoo Inc., Foxconn Limited, the Industrial and Commercial Bank of China Limited, and AIG Global Investment Corporation Limited. David Wei, CEO of Alibaba.com, announced, "Our Hong Kong listing is an important milestone for our company . . . We will use the resources and brand exposure gathered from the listing to expand our community of members and add more value to their business."[12]

In 2014, Alibaba Group officially filed for an IPO in the United States.[13] After the international business community got the news that Alibaba Group would begin publicly trading in the United States, there was an uproar on Wall Street surrounding the monumental event. The tremendous growth trajectory of the company along with an increase in revenues provided promising evidence that Alibaba would not have a problem competing with American firms (see Exhibit 2).

Alibaba's revenue increased in 2018 but the marginal cost of revenue seems to be increasing. Over past few years, the quality of earnings declined compared to the quantity of earnings. Meaning, it seems that growth in the accounting revenue increased at the cost of operating performance. For past three years, while revenue increased sharply, most of the profitability ratios are in declining trend (see Exhibits 3, 9 and 10).

Company Philosophy

Alibaba Group participates in various markets through its different businesses. A central theme among Alibaba's businesses points to providing an online platform for buyers and sellers around the world. Alibaba Group identifies itself as an ecosystem, in which its diverse online marketplace platforms meet the needs of heterogeneous buyer-seller

EXHIBIT 2 **IPOs in the United States as of 2018 (in $ billions)**

Company	IPO date	IPO
Alibaba Group Holding	09.18.2014	21.77
Visa	03.18.2008	17.86
ENEL SpA	11.01.1999	16.45
Facebook	05.17.2012	16.01
General Motors	11.17.2010	15.77
Deutsche Telekom	11.17.1996	13.03
AT&T Wireless Group	04.26.2000	10.62

Source: Renaissance Capital, January 2018; Kiplinger.com October, 2018.

EXHIBIT 3 Alibaba Group Annual Revenue 2010–2018 in Millions of Chinese RMB

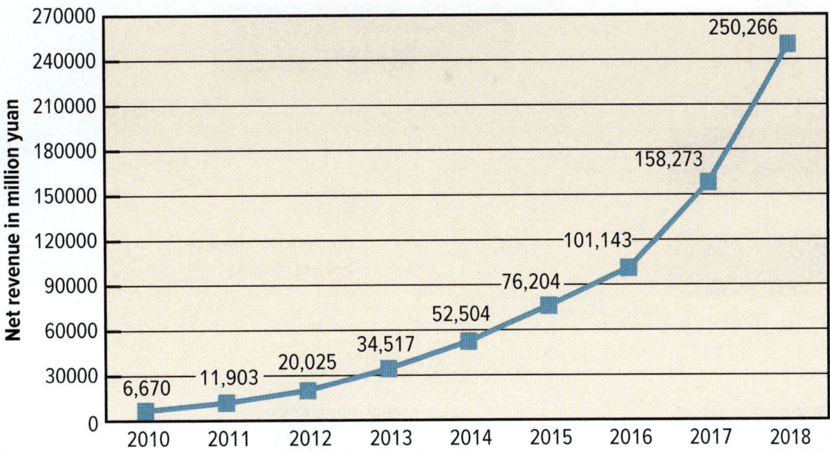

Note: $1 USD = 6.83 RMB

Source: Alibaba Annual Reports.

relationships throughout the world.[14] In a letter to investors, Ma states, "Alibaba is a value-based company driven by our mission to make it easy to do business anywhere. Our proposition is simple: we want to help small businesses grow by solving their problems through the Internet."[15] Alibaba Group is frequently compared to popular global e-commerce companies such as eBay, Amazon, and PayPal. Alibaba Group's multi-dimensional "open marketplace" is recognized as the largest global marketplace by volume.[16]

Business Model

Typically, e-commerce businesses maintain warehouses to store inventory. Engaging in direct selling is also a commonplace practice. In this effort, a company attempts to sell products directly to connected consumers through their e-commerce platform. Frequently, e-commerce businesses own or work in conjunction with committed distribution channels. The philosophy behind Alibaba's success strays from the classic e-commerce approach. Alibaba does not own any warehouses, does not oversee or corroborate with any distribution channels, and never engages in direct selling of goods. Alibaba aims to simply connect small businesses and manufacturers with a global pool of potential consumers.[17]

Alibaba's e-commerce revenue generation is acquired through variegated fees. Merchant fees are charged to users based on the number of units sold in retail centers. A fixed rate is required of members in the wholesale centers. Small businesses have the option to have their own storefronts for which there are special membership fees.[18] More than 50 percent of revenue is earned by online advertising efforts. Consumers use the Taobao Marketplace search engine to locate desired goods by entering phrases containing keywords. These keywords are auctioned–providing the highest bidders with advertising space for when a customer enters the specific keyword. Advertising revenue, a significant portion of revenues, comes through homepage advertising space. Taobao, Tmall.com, and Alibaba.com set aside areas on their respective homepages for merchants to purchase. Due to the shift from PC-based to mobile platform consumer preference, adjustments must be made to advertising efforts. Taobao and Baidu dominate the online advertising market in China.

Components of Alibaba

Alibaba's numerous businesses allow the company to accurately focus on divergent e-commerce trading relationships. While the company's original efforts to provide a global e-commerce platform still exist, the growth of the company led derivative businesses to be conceived in order to expand Alibaba's functionality and potential user base. The company provides its services to both large-scale and small-scale organizations alike. Additionally, some platforms are geared toward global e-commerce, while others primarily focus on domestic transactions within China (see Exhibit 4).

In 1999, Alibaba.com was created alongside the initial founding of Alibaba Group. The flagship business division is described as a "global wholesale marketplace online for international customers."[19] Globally, Alibaba.com is reported to be the largest online business-to-business platform. The e-commerce platform deals with buyers and sellers from over 240 countries.[20] The marketplace aims to connect international buyers with Chinese sellers. Nevertheless, Alibaba encourages vendors from anywhere in the world to utilize the global trading platform.[21]

1688.com, a business segment of Alibaba.com, was officially launched in March 2010. Like Alibaba.com, 1688.com is a business-to-business (B2B) online e-commerce platform. While Alibaba.com focuses on facilitating B2B trading transactions globally, 1688.com is specifically geared toward enabling B2B wholesale transactions within

EXHIBIT 4 Alibaba Group Organizational Structure

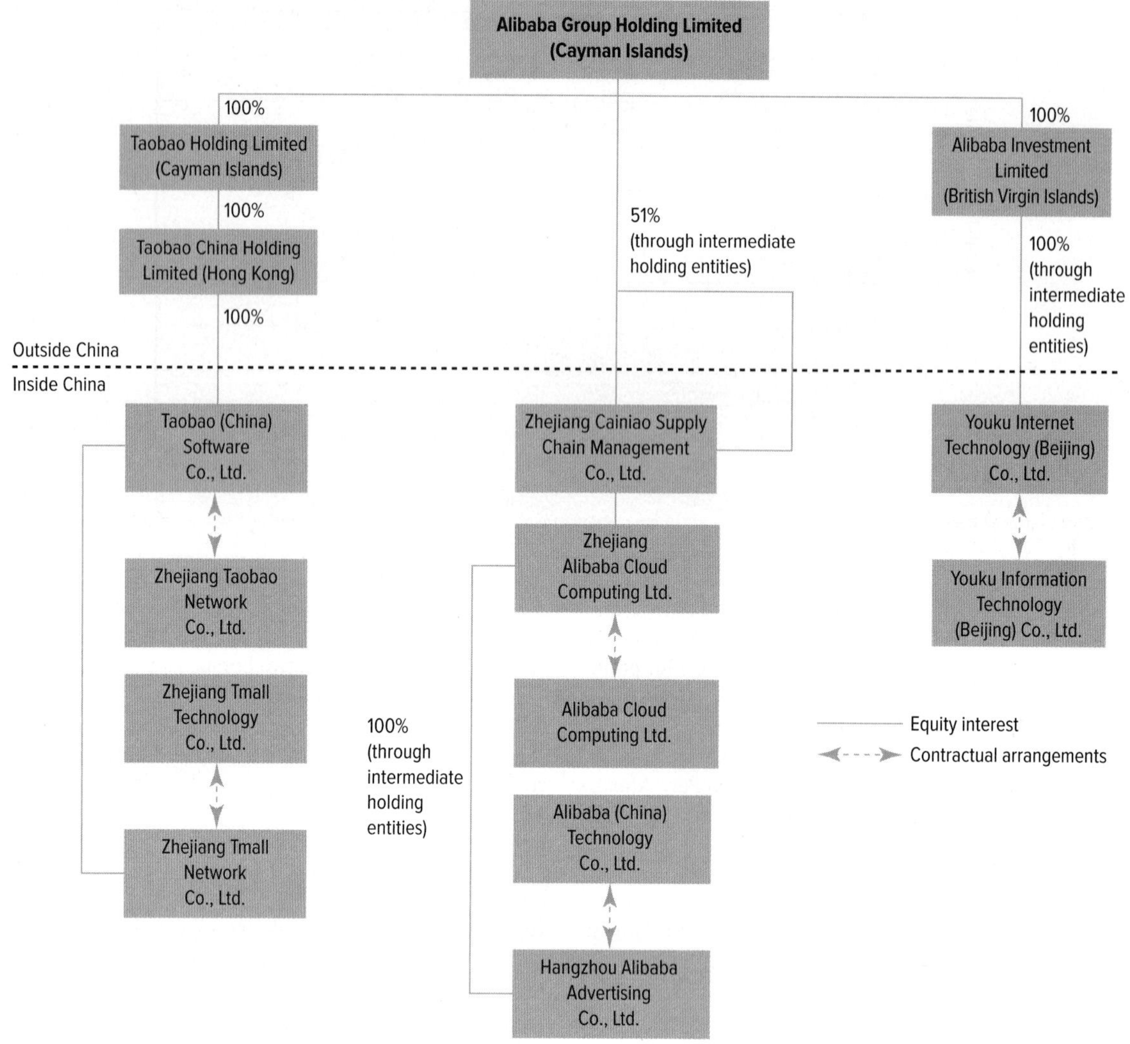

Source: Alibaba Annual Reports.

China domestically. As of 2013, 1688.com had acquired 100 million registered users.[22] AliExpress, one of Alibaba's businesses, was developed and released in April 2010. AliExpress's purpose, similar to Alibaba.com, focuses on smaller B2B interactions. AliExpress allows the targeted small businesses, internationally, to purchase goods in smaller quantities at wholesale prices (see Exhibit 5).[23]

The Taobao Marketplace, an alternative to Alibaba.com focusing on consumer-to-consumer trading transactions, was introduced in May 2003. With seven million registered merchants, Taobao Marketplace is the most preferred C2C online marketplace in China. Taobao marketplace attributes its growth to the incorporation of commission-less transaction platform Alipay. The majority of Taobao's revenue (85 percent) stems from advertising.

A Taobao Marketplace, including Tmall.com, was developed in April 2008, which eventually became a separate division of Alibaba Group in June 2011. Essentially, Tmall.com is a business-to-consumer retail online shopping mall. Vendors are permitted to register and open "storefronts" on the website and consumers can browse the different digital establishments. Tmall.com is the most popular B2C retail online web-platform, controlling approximately 50 percent of China's B2C market.[24] The Taobao and Tmall.com platforms have been aggressively adopted throughout China, so much so that remote townships completely rely on the e-commerce platforms. These "Taobao Villages" sustain themselves by using Taobao Marketplace and Tmall.com as their main sources of income.[25]

An initial issue that Alibaba Group faced was the absence of an online payment platform. In response, Alibaba Group developed its own online payment platform called Alipay. Originally, Alipay was considered a peripheral component of Alibaba.com, specifically on

EXHIBIT 5 The Networks Effect on and Across Alibaba Platforms

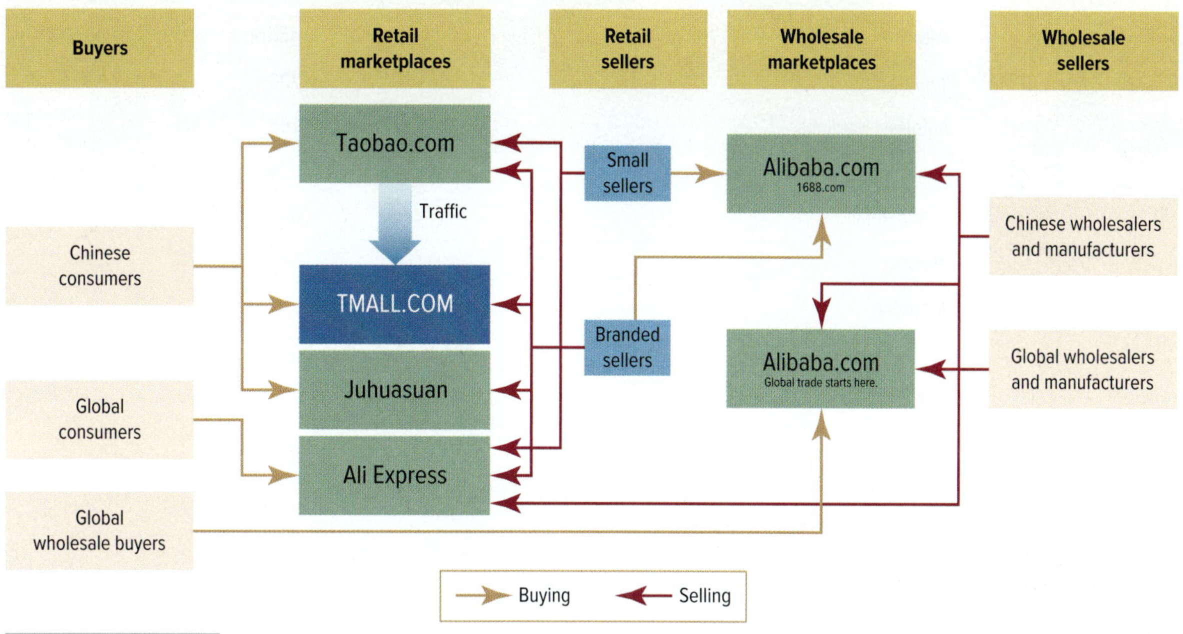

Source: Alibaba Annual Report.

the Taobao platform. In 2004, Alipay became a separate business. A valuable incorporated feature of Alipay is its escrow capabilities, which provides a buyer more security and more control over transactions. Alipay is the most used third-party online payment platform in China, which is responsible for approximately half of all electronic payments.[26]

Apart from the e-commerce businesses incorporated under Alibaba Group, many other businesses focus on adjacent markets. Aliyun.com, launched September 2009, is China's paramount cloud-computing platform. Alibaba Group shrewdly harmonizes Aliyun's cloud-computing capabilities with its other businesses. Aliyun's data mining, processing, and analytic capabilities can be applied to its e-commerce businesses, which provide massive amounts of raw data via buyer-seller transaction data.[27]

Alibaba Growth Strategy

Corporate Investments and Acquisitions

Alibaba Group's labyrinth-like internal structure is vast and complex compared to most traditional business models, yet its exceptionally constructed business architecture continues externally. Since its early years, the company has pursued acquisition and investment opportunities. Its first substantial external engagement dates back to 2005, when Yahoo China merged its China-based operations with the Alibaba Group business ecosystem.[28]

Upon the formal announcement of Alibaba's U.S. IPO, the company's acquisition and investment strategy continued to magnify. "We have made, and intend to continue to make, strategic investments and acquisitions to expand our user base, enhance our cloud computing business, add complementary products and technologies and further strengthen our ecosystem. For example, we expect to continue to make strategic investments and acquisitions relating to mobile, O2O services, digital media, category expansion, as well as logistics services."[29]

Alibaba has focused primarily on domestic investment endeavors, although the company has financially engaged some U.S. companies as well. Lyft, an American car service company, and Tango, an American messaging service, are two cases of Alibaba's investments in U.S. companies.[30]

Alibaba has penetrated various markets through acquisitions and investments (see Exhibit 6). At times, the decisions are perceived as ambiguous and unexpected. In 2013, a stake of 18 percent worth $586 million was acquired in Sina Weibo, which is a Chinese company analog of Twitter.[31] In April of 2014, Alibaba, along with Jack Ma's private equity company Yunfeng Capital, procured 18.5 percent of Youku Tudou, a popular Chinese Internet video company for a total of $1.2 billion. "We are excited to cooperate and work closely with Victor and his team to support their innovation in this key emerging space as well as accelerate our digital entertainment and video content strategy. This is an important strategic initiative that will further extend the Alibaba ecosystem and bring new products and services to Alibaba's customers."[32]

Additional investments focus on mobile applications and logistics. Umeng, a mobile analytics company, was purchased for US$80 million, and Alibaba invested US$50 million in Quixley–a mobile app search engine.

EXHIBIT 6 Alibaba's Investments as of 2018 (in $ millions)

Alibaba's Investments	in $ millions
Youku Tudou	1220
AutoNavi Holdings	1165
ChinaVision Media Group	829
Intime Retail	692
Weibo	586
TangoMe	280
Lyft	250
SingPost	249
Gooddaymart	240
Guangzhou Evergrande	194
CITIC 21CN	171
Kabam	120
TutorGroup	100
Beijing Byecity Technology Development	20

Source: The Economist.

EXHIBIT 7 Market Share of B2B E-Commerce Platforms in China

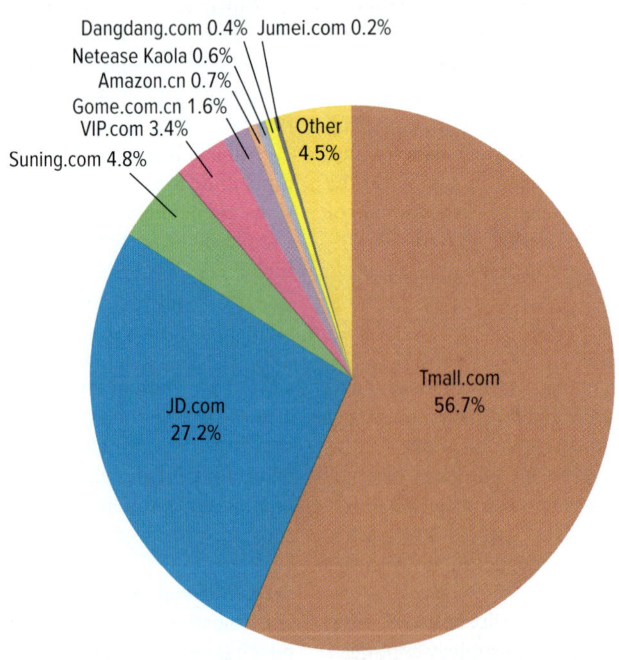

Source: China e-Business Research Center.

EXHIBIT 8 Market Share of B2C Online Shopping Websites in China

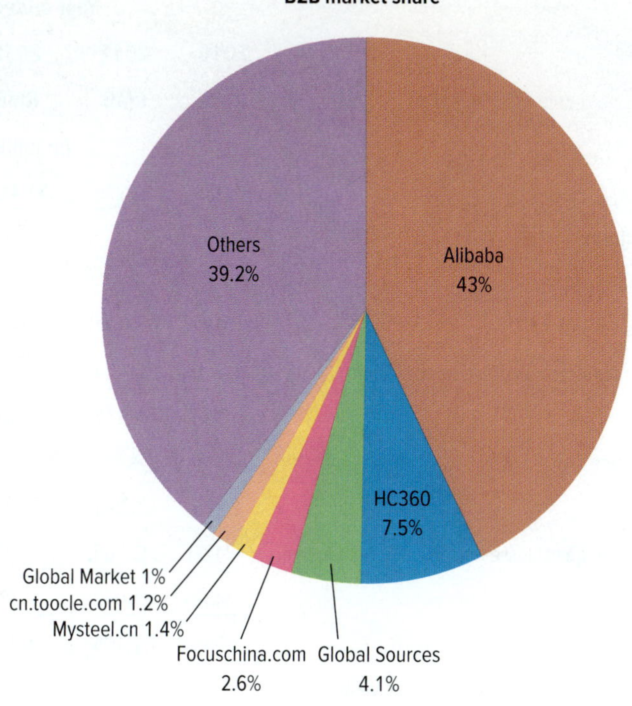

Source: iResearch.

The delivery service joint venture, China Smart Logistics, benefitted from an investment of US$269 million, which granted Alibaba 48 percent ownership. A more palpable investment took place in January 2014, when Alibaba invested US$15 million in a luxury e-commerce website called 1stdibs[33] Amid continuous investments and acquisitions, Alibaba has become a dominating force in the Chinese B2B and B2C markets (see Exhibits 7 and 8).

Brick and Mortar Retail Remains Strong in China

Annual retail revenue in China has increased from $370 billion to $2 trillion in the past 10 years.[34] In terms of consumption volume, China has become the largest food and grocery market in the world that is expected to grow at an increasing rate in the years to come. After experiencing success in the e-commerce market, Alibaba recently stepped into brick and mortar retail by introducing Hema Supermarkets in 2015. Over the past two years, the company invested about $8 billion on brick and mortar stores in China. In order to increase the speed of its brick and mortar retail market presence, Alibaba also announced an investment of $2.9 billion in Sun Art Retail Group.[35] Expanding physical presence in the retail market will challenge Alibaba in many ways, as the company has primarily been an Internet business. According to the National Bureau of Statistics in China, almost 100,000 retail companies are serving the Chinese people around the country. Competing with thousands of local grocery stores and vendors may not be the kind of competition that Alibaba had encountered so far.

The Competition

The Chinese digital market is expected to remain the world's largest as compared to the United States and Europe. Winning in China will translate into winning as a company for Alibaba as international competitors like Amazon will make it extremely challenging for Alibaba to dominate in the global e-commerce market. By 2018, the online population in China was around 700 million as compared to 265 million in the United States. Demographically, Alibaba is at an advantageous position in the world's largest digital market. However, the Chinese e-commerce market is also one of the toughest battleground territories for technology companies. Additionally, there are many untapped markets in the developing world when it comes to the e-commerce industry. Those potential markets include Africa, South Asia, Middle East, and South America.

Alibaba faces immense competition from two kinds of competitors, and both of those are squeezing the growth opportunities for Alibaba locally as well as internationally. Alibaba's top two global competitors include Amazon and eBay (see Exhibit 11), whereas the top homegrown competitors include JD.com and Baidu. Many U.S. companies, including Uber and Facebook, have failed to penetrate successfully in China. Nonetheless, achieving success in China as a domestic company is almost as difficult as it is for international companies.

EXHIBIT 9 Alibaba Consolidated Income Statement

	Year ended March 31,				
	2016	2017	2018	2019	
	RMB	RMB	RMB	RMB	US$
	(in millions)				
Net income	71,289	41,226	61,412	80,234	11,955
Other comprehensive income (loss):					
- Foreign currency translation:					
Change in unrealized gains (losses)	312	(2,191)	(805)	1,068	159
Reclassification adjustment for losses recorded in net income	21	44	—	—	—
Net change	333	(2,147)	(805)	1,068	159
- Available-for-sale securities:					
Change in unrealized gains	2,278	8,911	769	—	—
Reclassification adjustment for (gains) losses recorded in net income	(422)	(5,764)	57	—	—
Tax effect	(488)	(1,042)	385	—	—
Net change	1,368	2,105	1,211	—	—
- Share of other comprehensive income of equity method investees:					
Change in unrealized gains (losses)	65	780	(930)	582	87
- Interest rate swaps under hedge accounting:					
Change in unrealized gains	—	433	143	(295)	(44)
- Forward exchange contracts under hedge accounting:					
Change in unrealized (losses) gains	(168)	169	(85)	—	—
Other comprehensive income (loss)	1,598	1,340	(466)	1,355	202
Total comprehensive income	72,887	42,566	60,946	81,589	12,157
Total comprehensive loss attributable to noncontrolling interests	102	389	2,215	6,637	989
Total comprehensive income attributable to ordinary shareholders	72,989	42,955	63,161	88,226	13,146

Source: Alibaba Annual Reports.

Amazon

Jeff Bezos, the richest man in the world, founded Amazon in 1994 in Seattle, Washington. From an online bookstore to a world-class e-commerce company, Amazon's growth and success is a remarkable story. It has been a star among e-commerce companies in the recent past. The stock price performance topped all the Wall Street estimates and soared about 173 percent from January 2016 to January 2018.[36]

Amazon follows an operational style mirroring that of offline retailers. It engages in direct selling to customers, controls its own distribution-warehousing facilities, and engages in manufacturing its own brand of goods. In 2000, the company developed platform functionality that permitted individual sellers to connect with consumers through Amazon.com. The company's website boasts, "Over 2 million third-party sellers participate in Amazon where they offer new, used, and collectible selections at fixed prices to Amazon customers around the world."[37] Amazon is revered for its extremely effective logistics and customer service.[38]

Over the past decade, Amazon has become the largest e-commerce retailer in the world. The company dominates the U.S. online shopping industry and is consistently expanding around the world. Amazon achieved remarkable milestones in terms of growth and expansion. According to Gartner Research, Amazon's public cloud services are expected to grow at about 23 percent percent, whereas the total market in the same segment is expected to grow at about 13 percent.[39]

EXHIBIT 10 Alibaba Balance Sheet

	As of March 31,			
	2017	2018	2019	
	RMB	RMB	RMB	US$
	(in millions)			
Assets				
Current assets:				
Cash and cash equivalents	143,736	199,309	189,976	28,308
Short-term investments	3,011	6,086	3,262	486
Restricted cash and escrow receivables	2,655	3,417	8,518	1,269
Investment securities	4,054	4,815	9,927	1,479
Prepayments, receivables and other assets	28,408	43,228	58,590	8,730
Total current assets	181,864	256,855	270,273	40,272
Investment securities	31,452	38,192	157,090	23,407
Prepayments, receivables and other assets	8,703	16,897	28,018	4,175
Investments in equity investees	120,368	139,700	84,454	12,584
Property and equipment, net	20,206	66,489	92,030	13,713
Land use rights, net	4,691	9,377	—	—
Intangible assets, net	14,108	27,465	68,276	10,173
Goodwill	125,420	162,149	264,935	39,477
Total assets	506,812	717,124	965,076	143,801
Liabilities, mezzanine equity and shareholders' equity				
Current liabilities:				
Current bank borrowings	5,948	6,028	7,356	1,096
Current unsecured senior notes	8,949	—	15,110	2,251
Income tax payable	6,125	13,689	17,685	2,635
Escrow money payable	2,322	3,053	8,250	1,229
Accrued expenses, accounts, payable and other liabilities	46,979	81,165	117,711	17,540
Merchant deposits	8,189	9,578	10,762	1,604
Deferred revenue and customer advances	15,052	22,297	30,795	4,589
Total current liabilities	93,564	135,810	207,669	30,944
Deferred revenue	641	993	1,467	219
Deferred tax liabilities	10,361	19,312	22,517	3,355
Non-current bank borrowings	30,959	34,153	35,427	5,279
Non-current unsecured senior notes	45,876	85,372	76,407	11,385
Other liabilities	1,290	2,045	6,187	922
Total liabilities	182,691	277,685	349,674	52,104
Commitments and contingencies	—	—	—	—
Mezzanine equity	2,992	3,001	6,819	1,016

continued

EXHIBIT 10 *Continued*

	As of March 31,			
	2017	2018	2019	
	RMB	RMB	RMB	US$
	(in millions)			
Shareholders' equity				
Ordinary shares, US$0,000025 par value; 4,000,000,000 shares authorized as of March 31, 2017 and 2018; 2,529,364,189 and 2,571,929,843 shares issued and outstanding as of March 31, 2017 and 2018, respectively	1	1	1	—
Additional paid-in capital	164,585	186,764	231,783	34,537
Treasury shares, at cost	(2,823)	(2,233)	—	—
Restructuring reserve	(624)	(361)	(97)	(15)
Subscription receivables	(63)	(163)	(49)	(7)
Statutory reserves	4,080	4,378	5,068	755
Accumulated other comprehensive income				
Cumulative translation adjustments	(3,618)	(3,594)	(2,592)	(386)
Unrealized gains on available-for-sale securities, interest rate swaps and others	8,703	8,677	257	38
Retained earnings	108,558	172,353	257,886	38,426
Total shareholders' equity	278,799	365,822	492,257	73,348
Noncontrolling interests	42,330	70,616	116,326	17,333
Total equity	321,129	436,438	608,583	90,681
Total liabilities, mezzanine equity and equity	506,812	717,124	965,076	143,801

Source: Alibaba Annual Reports.

EXHIBIT 11 A Comparison of e-Commerce Platforms

	Amazon	Alibaba	eBay
Holds Inventory	Yes	No	No
Consumer Credit Services	Co-branded Credit Card	No	Bill Me Later
Advertising Services	Yes	Yes	Yes
Available Technology Platform	Yes (Amazon Web Services)	Yes	Yes (Open Source Platform)
E-Payment Service	No	Alipay	PayPal
Direct Sales	Yes	No	No
Matches Buyers and Sellers	Yes	Yes (via 1688.com)	Yes
Individual Storefronts	Yes	Yes	Yes
Manufactures Proprietary Goods	Yes (Kindle/Fire)	No	No
Content Provider	Yes (Streaming videos/e-books)	No	No
Publisher	Yes (Books/music/films/technology)	No	No
Membership Fees	Yes (Prime)	Yes	No

Sources: Investopedia, https://www.forbes.com/sites/hendriklaubscher/2018/07/12/the-prime-difference-between-amazon-alibaba/,https://revenuesandprofits.com/alibaba-vs-ebay-comparing-the-platforms-size-and-growth/,https://www.cnbc.com/2019/03/05/why-alibaba-isnt-competing-with-amazon-and-ebay-for-the-us-consumer.html.

Similar to Alibaba, Amazon's business model consists of many subcategories that include an online store, subscription services, third-party vendors, virtual assistant electronic devices, online advertising, online streaming services and many others. Amazon's annual growth rate averaged around approximately 50 percent over the past few years.[40] According to Jeff Bezos, Amazon achieved success due to its customer-focused business strategy. It allowed the company to amaze its customers by developing products and services based on their own ideas and preferences.

Despite Amazon's success in the United States and other parts of the world, China still remains a challenging market due to immense competition. China is one of the most lucrative markets for e-commerce companies in terms of an active number of online daily users, yet it remains one of the most challenging battlegrounds for domestic as well as international e-retailers such as Amazon. However, the most significant threat that Amazon poses to Alibaba is in the international territory.

eBay

eBay's auction-based platform aims to connect buyers and sellers. It originally provided its own payment system called PayPal.* The company claims, "We are primarily a transaction-based business that generates revenue from the transactions and payments that we successfully enable."[41] Similar to Alibaba, eBay does not partake in the holding of inventory. More recently, PayPal began offering credit services originally called "Bill Me Later" and eventually changed its title to PayPal Credit. eBay benefits from this development because now consumers can easily access a line of credit to help confidently engage in auctions. Another business under eBay is called eBay Enterprise, which deals with marketing, advertising, retail, and commerce. The company receives revenues streams from eBay Enterprise by storefronts such as StubHub.

eBay competes with Alibaba as both companies aim to bring buyers and sellers together. eBay's payment system, PayPal, competes with Alibaba's payment system called Alipay. Despite the success of Alibaba in the domestic market, it will be a challenge for the company to compete with eBay when it comes to offering an auction-based online platform to buyers and sellers in the United States and other markets outside China. eBay's brand recognition would make it difficult for Alibaba to take over eBay's customers outside China.

JD.com

JD.com, the homegrown archrival of Alibaba, offers a more traditional e-commerce experience. The company sells directly to its customers, actively holds inventory, and is responsible for taking care of its shipping and logistics. In China, JD.com is enjoying the largest volume of direct online sales transactions. JD.com is listed as JD on the NASDAQ in the United States. Although JD.com holds a comparatively smaller share of the Chinese e-commerce market, the company has the benefit of being a direct competitor of Alibaba. Therefore, JD.com is a likely ally of any company that wants to compete with Alibaba.

One of the allies of JD.com is Tencent, a Chinese Internet company founded in 1998. Tencent also stands as a competitive threat to Alibaba Group when it comes to Internet service portals and online payment systems. Tencent is one of the most used Internet service portals in China. WeChat, QQ.com, and Tenpay are some of the online destinations that Tencent operates. Originally, Tencent was involved with entertainment and social media, but its increased popularity caused the organization to pursue progressive growth opportunities. Tencent is listed as Tencent Holdings Limited (0700.HK) on the Hong Kong Stock Exchange.[42]

Baidu

The most popular Chinese Internet search engine, known as Baidu, was founded in the year 2000. Baidu's functionality and goals are parallel to that of Google. The company provides search engine capabilities along with other services such as maps and Internet TV. A unique and central component to Baidu's strategy revolves around the promotion of online-to-offline (O2O) services. O2O technology aims to promote consumer demand for physical business locations through mobile and Internet applications.[43] Baidu is traded on the U.S. NASDAQ as BIDU.[44]

Baidu is trying to eat Alibaba's lunch when it comes to digital advertising. Alibaba's online advertising revenue of about $16 billion has a market share of 31 percent in China.[45] Whereas Baidu, as a search engine, holds about 18 percent of the digital advertising market share in China. Baidu has also joined JD.com to compete with Alibaba, where JD.com benefits by having access to millions of Chinese shoppers. According to analyst estimates, such alliances are going to make it difficult for Alibaba to continue growing at a fast growth rate.

Alibaba's Challenges

Escalating Domestic Competition

Domestic competition in China, which once seemed futile to Alibaba, has begun consolidating and developing powerful strategic partnerships. Tencent has combated Alibaba's aggressive acquisition campaign by simultaneously pursuing acquisitions in the Chinese tech market. Chinese e-commerce has been ballooning and is experiencing a move from PC-based to mobile applications. This trend has made the mobile application market an area of interest for both Tencent and Alibaba.[46] Tencent developed its own messaging service called WeChat, which is widely used throughout China and has been adding e-commerce functionality to the mobile application.[47]

---

* eBay and PayPal are now separate companies. eBay still makes use of PayPal as its third party online payment system.

To compete more aggressively with Alibaba, Tencent invested US$215 million in JD.com for a 15 percent stake, effectively forming a significant partnership. According to Tencent's 2017 earnings report, its WeChat app has almost a billion active users in China. A partnership with Tencent gives a huge advantage to a competitor like JD.com by providing access to the largest group of consumers in the world. Tencent's competencies, in conjunction with JD.com's strong position in the e-commerce and excellent logistics infrastructure, furnish the cooperating organizations with a competitive advantage. Vice President of Forrester Research Bryan Wang elaborated, "JD was competing with Alibaba ... however, the scale was too small. But now with the WeChat platform that's a game changer."[48]

Aside from Tencent's collaboration with JD.com, the company is joining with Baidu and a property firm called Dalian Wanda Group to develop a massive e-commerce platform. Dalian Wanda owns 70 percent of the venture, while Tencent and Baidu hold 15 percent each. At the heart of the e-commerce venture is the dedicated integration of online-to-offline functionality. Dong Ce, the O2O venture's chief executive, declared, "by teaming up with Tencent and Baidu, Wanda will become the biggest online-to-offline e-commerce platform in the world." The joint venture's total investment sums up to $790 million. "The deal is structured over three years ... the initial investment by the three firms will amount to 1 billion [RMB]," said Tencent.[49]

Government Regulations In China

Recently, Alibaba ran into problems with China's State Administration for Industry and Commerce (SAIC). A scolding statement was publicly released haranguing Alibaba about the excessive presence of fraud on their e-commerce platforms. SAIC announced that in a sampling inspection, 63 percent of the products sold on Alibaba's online Taobao marketplace were found to be "unauthentic"–meaning they were fake, discredited, or came through unauthorized channels.[50] The SAIC statement also divulged that company employees were facilitating the illegal activity by partaking in commercial bribery. It was suggested that in exchange for financial compensation, employees, with the ability to control merchant placement, would ensure better platform placement. SAIC mysteriously retracted its formal accusation. "We feel vindicated," stated a spokesperson on behalf of Alibaba Group.

For some time Taobao Marketplace has dealt with grievances hinging on the alleged presence of counterfeit goods. This spat between a Chinese government agency and a Chinese-based corporation was distinctive. Xinhua News Agency described this event as "the most heated confrontation between the government and an enterprise in the era of the Internet economy."[51] Chinese bystanders hypothesized that this kind of government behavior could forecast further harassment for Alibaba. The source of heckling is postulated to arise from China's drill down "on intellectual-property protection in its effort to overhaul the economy, pumping up consumption and reducing reliance on cheap labor, exports, and big-ticket spending projects."[52]

While this was not the first instance of discord between a weighty corporation and the Chinese government, Alibaba's defensive positioning is unique. Alibaba drives Chinese e-commerce so significantly that any major persecution would lead to a setback to the Chinese economy. Alibaba maintains deep political connections in the Chinese government because government agencies have a vested interest in the firm's NYSE stock listing.[53]

Exposure to International Competition

In comparison to eBay and Amazon, Alibaba's volume of sales and global market share reign supreme. While impressive, and perhaps intimidating for U.S. firms, this does not mean that the company will easily penetrate U.S. e-commerce territories. Alibaba's brand recognition within the United States is relatively low in comparison to eBay and Amazon. Similarly, U.S. e-commerce and Internet companies find it extremely difficult to comfortably position themselves in Chinese markets. It is likely that the competing firms will dominate their respective domains. The competitive arena for Alibaba Group and U.S. brands, such as eBay and Amazon, is expected to take place outside their homelands. Foreign developing markets like Africa and South America will probably become the targeted untapped regions where these competitors will confront each other.[54]

Until an IPO on the U.S. NYSE, Alibaba Group had exclusively centralized its operations within China. The Chinese government acts as a supportive proponent to any domestic company that has potential to grow into a global player in the tech industry. The Chinese government has put certain policies in place to promote local firms, protecting them from foreign competition. Recently, Alibaba acquired Sina Weibo, a social platform like Twitter, as a move into Chinese social networking. Alibaba was able to move into the social media business because global leaders, such as Facebook, were not permitted in China. Alibaba was effectively given an advantageous handicap with the absence of outside competition. A parallel to this protective cultivation of the social media market lies in online video content as well. For instance, YouTube is banned in China, which might allow Alibaba to enter the market at its own leisure.[55]

The most important market incubation provided to Alibaba Group, naturally, lies in the e-commerce. While U.S. firms are not restricted from entering the Chinese e-commerce market, the Chinese government makes it difficult on purpose. eBay's operations were overshadowed by the growing success of Alibaba's Taobao Marketplace. Amazon is still persistently engaged in efforts to penetrate the Chinese market. The company has not faced much detrimental government attention, but it is hypothesized that this is due to its lack of success.[56]

Looking Ahead

Stemming from ambitious entrepreneurial dreams out of his modest Hangzhou apartment, Jack Ma's Alibaba was born. Through the evolution of its core businesses and bustling expansion into new, complementary markets via external acquisition, Alibaba Group commands a vast ecosystem of businesses. In the appraisal of Alibaba's performance, we see a company that expanded exponentially within 15 years–dominating the Chinese market and launching the biggest IPO in world history.

Currently, the company is facing a variety of pressures and threats. In the domestic domain, competition is mounting fast. Upon venturing outside China, Alibaba has increased its exposure to foreign competitors. Undoubtedly, the company's prosperous growth has been assisted by China's restrictive foreign policies. Alibaba's presence in the U.S. stock market and adherence to SEC standards inevitably leaves the company more transparent and vulnerable as compared to domestic Chinese companies as well as foreign competition. Despite the past success of Alibaba, the future of this Chinese e-commerce giant remains unpredictable. While Alibaba is equipped with many resources to pursue growth and success, increasing competition in the domestic and international markets will continue to make the company's growth more difficult. Time will tell whether Alibaba will be able to achieve success in the unique markets of the world. However, a closer look at global e-commerce infrastructure and players involved indicated that success will depend upon huge efforts and good luck.

ENDNOTES

1. 2015. How does 2015 look for Alibaba? *Forbes*, January 7.
2. Kopytoff, V. 2014. Who is Jack Ma? A profile of Alibaba's founder in the IPO spotlight. *Fortune*, May 6.
3. Ibid.
4. MacLeod, C. 2014. Alibaba's Jack Ma: From 'crazy' to China's richest man. *USA Today*, Gannett, September 19.
5. Ibid.
6. Ibid.
7. Alibaba Group History. Alibaba Group.
8. Alibaba Group. 2005. Press release, August 11.
9. Ibid.
10. Alibaba Group. 2007. Press release, November 6.
11. Ibid.
12. Ibid.
13. Alibaba Group. Wikipedia, the Free Encyclopedia. Wikimedia Foundation, Inc.
14. Barreiro, G. 2015. Alibaba: One of China's greatest innovators. IPWatchdog, April 7.
15. Sec.gov. 2014. Alibaba Group Holding Limited Prospectus. U.S. Securities and Exchange Commission, September 18.
16. Bajpai, P. 2014. Alibaba's Top Competitors. *Investopedia*, November 7.
17. Ibid.
18. Zucchi, K. 2014. Navigating e-commerce: Alibaba, eBay, and Amazon. *Investopedia*, October 28.
19. Kent, J.L. 2014. 5 things to know about the Alibaba IPO. *Investopedia*, September 3.
20. Ibid.
21. Walraven, P. 2009. A brief history (and future) of Alibaba.com. TechNode, January 22.
22. Roy, R. 2014. The Alibaba Group explained. *Slideshare*, April 24.
23. Ibid.
24. Ibid.
25. Ibid.
26. Ibid.
27. Ibid.
28. CIW Team. 2014. Alibaba investment timeline since 2005 before IPO. China Internet Watch, September 30.
29. De La Merced, M.J. 2014. Alibaba's acquisition strategy: Focused largely on China and mobile. *New York Times*, May 7.
30. Ibid.
31. Ibid.
32. Gough, N. 2014. Alibaba buys stake in Chinese Web TV Company for $1.2 billion. *New York Times*, April 28.
33. Ibid.
34. https://www-statista-com.rlib.pace.edu/statistics/277810/retail-revenue-in-china/.
35. https://www.forbes.com/sites/greatspeculations/2017/11/21/alibaba-takes-next-step-in-new-retail-with-2-9-billion-investment/#7e159a4e58b1.
36. https://finance.yahoo.com/quote/amzn?ltr=1.
37. Marketplace overview, https://www.wheretosellonline.com/marketplace-overviews/marketplace-overview-amazon/
38. Ibid.
39. https://www.statista.com/statistics/258718/market-growth-forecast-of-public-it-cloud-services-worldwide/.
40. Amazon Q4 2017 Press Release.
41. Ibid.
42. eBay Annual Report, 2014.
43. O2O commerce (Online to Offline). E-commerce Development–Mobile Development Company. TMO Group Shanghai, n.d.
44. Ibid.
45. eMarketer.https://www-statista-com.rlib.pace.edu/statistics/720478/china-market-share-of-online-ad-revenue-alibaba/.
46. Riddell, M. 2015. Alibaba maintains mobile e-commerce dominance through investments and acquisitions. *Stock Market Insights*, Seeking Alpha, April 9.
47. Ibid.
48. Carsten, P. 2014. Tencent-JD.com partnership goes straight for Alibaba's throat. *Reuters*, March 10.
49. Carsten, P. China's Wanda, Tencent, Baidu to set up $814 million e-commerce company. *Reuters*, August 29.
50. Shao, H. 2015. What happens when a Chinese tycoon stands up against the government? *Forbes*, January 29.
51. Ibid.
52. Burkitt, Laurie. January 30, 2015, "Alibaba Claims 'Vindication' in Dispute With Chinese Agency," *The Wall Street Journal*, https://www.wsj.com/articles/alibaba-chinas-saic-working-together-to-fight-counterfeits-1422631531
53. Ibid.
54. Einhorn, B. 2014. How China's government set up Alibaba's success. *Businessweek*. Businessweek.com, May 7.
55. Ibid.
56. Ibid.

CASE 32

APPLE INC.: WHERE'S THE NEXT INNOVATION?*

In April 2019, Apple CEO Tim Cook held the second quarter earnings presentation at the Apple Park corporate campus in the 1,000-seat auditorium named the Steve Jobs Theater. Part of a 175-acre campus developed in 2017, the ring-shaped 2.8-million-square-foot facility with walls of curved glass surrounding an inner greenspace courtyard was possibly the last evidence of the direct vision and innovation of Apple co-founder Steve Jobs. Originally envisioned by Jobs in 2011 as a center for creativity and collaboration, the building honored his legacy, memory, and enduring influence. Jobs, who died in 2011, would have turned 64 in February 2019. As Apple's current CEO Tim Cook said, "Steve's vision for Apple stretched far beyond his time with us. He intended Apple Park to be the home of innovation for generations to come."[1]

Yet the pace of innovation at Apple had slowed considerably. Since Steve Jobs's death, the only new physical product launched had been the Apple Watch in 2014. The iconic iPhone, in FY2018 representing 63 percent of total revenues, was over 10 years old, and even though upgrades kept customers coming back, competition had eroded Apple's smartphone market share such that second quarter 2019 iPhone revenues had declined by over 17 percent year over year. Mac computer and iPad sales had declined as well. Although Apple's FY2018 revenues were up by about 16 percent overall, the bulk of that increase came from services and other products such as the Apple Watch. In this environment, there was some concern that although research and development spending was up in FY2018, research output had not produced any recent meaningful breakthroughs. This posed yet again the unavoidable question that still seemed to haunt the 42-year-old Apple: What happens to a modern company whose innovations and inspirations are so closely tied to the vision of one leader when that leader's influence is no longer present?[2]

Tim Cook was considered a highly effective leader, yet had been criticized for "lack of ambition and vigor," for being perhaps too cautious about entering new product categories, pursuing acquisitions, or driving employees to achieve almost impossible stretch goals.[3] On the other hand, investors had been mostly very pleased with the stock performance under Cook. Since he was named CEO in August 2011, Apple share price had risen from an average of over $45 to a high of $230 in August 2018, and when the company reached a market capitalization of over $1 trillion in 2018, that made it the most valuable company in the world. In addition, Cook had instituted Apple's first dividend since 1995 in 2012, and bought back more than $200 billion of shares, producing strong free cash flows and an "impressive" balance sheet.[4] This had made investors happy.

Cook had done what CEOs of public companies are supposed to do–drive up value. But revenue from the flagship products–iMac, iPad and iPhone–was falling or stagnant, and only the services and other products sectors were seeing growth. In addition, operating margins were declining in products, indicating that high iPhone prices may have been the only thing keeping margins stable at around 30 percent. If iPhone sales were increasingly challenged by lower price competitors such as China's Xiaomi, and Huawei, something would have to change. Was Apple's recent shift into services and other products going to be the answer? (See Exhibits 1 to 3.) "Other products" included wearables such as the iWatch and the AirPod wireless earphones, and home products such as the HomePod voice-controlled smart speaker system. These were new, but perhaps not as innovative as Apple's other products. Were expectations of major breakthroughs unrealistic? As one analyst said, it is hard to find "ways to make the world's most valuable company even more valuable when it's already so big that conventional growth strategies–extending product lines, moving into new territories–would barely move the needle."[5]

Apple, *Fortune Magazine's* "world's most admired company" since 2008,[6] had distinguished itself by excelling over the years not only in product innovation but also in revenue and margins (since 2006 Apple had consistently reported gross margins of over 30 percent). By 2019, Apple Inc. was known for having top-selling products not only in desktop (iMac) and notebook (MacBook) personal computers but also in online music and "app" services (iTunes and App Store), mobile communication devices (iPhone), digital consumer entertainment (Apple TV), tablet computers (iPad), operating systems (macOS and iOS), software (Safari web browser) and online services (iCloud), as well as wearable technology (Apple Watch, AirPods) and home accessories (HomePod, Beats products), mobile payment systems (Apple Pay), and a subscription-based music streaming service (Apple Music). Additional services rolling out in 2019 included Apple TV+ original content, subscription services Apple Channels, Apple News+ and

* This case was prepared by Professor Alan B. Eisner of Pace University and Professor Pauline Assenza, Western Connecticut State University. This case is based solely on library research and was developed for class discussion rather than to illustrate either effective or ineffective handling of an administrative situation. Copyright © 2019 Alan B. Eisner.

EXHIBIT 1 **Apple Sales, 2015–2018 (dollars in millions and units in thousands)**

	2018	Change	2017	Change	2016	2015
Net Sales by Reportable Segment:						
Americas	$112,093	16%	$ 96,600	12%	$ 86,613	$ 93,864
Europe	62,420	14%	54,938	10%	49,952	50,337
Greater China	51,942	16%	44,764	(8)%	48,492	58,715
Japan	21,733	23%	17,733	5%	16,928	15,706
Rest of Asia Pacific	17,407	15%	15,199	11%	13,654	15,093
Total net sales	$265,595	16%	$229,234	6%	$215,639	$233,715
Net Sales by Product:						
iPhone (1)	$166,699	18%	$141,319	3%	$136,700	$155,041
iPad (1)	18,805	(2)%	19,222	(7)%	20,628	23,227
Mac (1)	25,484	(1)%	25,850	13%	22,831	25,471
Services (2)	37,190	24%	29,980	23%	24,348	19,909
Other Products (1)(3)	17,417	35%	12,863	16%	11,132	10,067
Total net sales	$265,595	16%	$229,234	6%	$215,639	$233,715
Unit Sales by Product:						
iPhone	217,722	—%	216,756	2%	211,884	231,218
iPad	43,535	—%	43,753	(4)%	45,590	54,856
Mac	18,209	(5)%	19,251	4%	18,484	20,587

(1) Includes deferrals and amortization of related software upgrade rights and non-software services.

(2) Includes revenue from Digital Content and Services, AppleCare, Apple Pay, licensing, and other services. Services net sales in 2018 included a favorable one-time item of $236 million in connection with the final resolution of various lawsuits. Services net sales in 2017 included a favorable one-time adjustment of $640 million due to a change in estimate based on the availability of additional supporting information.

(3) Includes sales of AirPods, Apple TV, Apple Watch, Beats products, HomePod, iPod touch, and other Apple-branded and third-party accessories.

Sources: Annual Report. Apple Inc. 2017.; Annual Report. Apple Inc. 2018.

EXHIBIT 2 **Apple Product Performance—Percentage of Total Sales**

Product	2018	2017	2016
iPhone	63%	62%	63%
iPad	7%	8%	10%
Mac	10%	11%	10%
Services	14%	13%	11%

Source: Annual Report. Apple Inc. 2018.

Apple Arcade for games, and Apple Card, a credit card stored in Apple Wallet. (see Exhibit 4).

As the time line shows, most of the product innovations occurred after 1998, when Apple was under Steve Jobs's leadership. However, there was also a 12-year period in which Jobs was not in charge. The company's ongoing stated strategy was to leverage "its unique ability to design and develop its own operations systems, hardware, application software and services to provide its customers products and solutions with innovative design, superior ease-of-use and seamless integration."[7] This strategy required not only product design and marketing expertise but also scrupulous attention to

EXHIBIT 3 **Apple Products and Services Revenue and Gross Margins**

Second Quarter Comparison 2018 to 2019						
	Three Months Ended			Six Months Ended		
	March 30, 2019	March 31, 2018	Change	March 30, 2019	March 31, 2018	Change
Net sales by category:						
iPhone (1)	$31,051	$37,559	(17)%	$ 83,033	$ 98,663	(16)%
Mac (1)	5,513	5,776	(5)%	12,929	12,600	3%
iPad (1)	4,872	4,008	22%	11,601	9,763	19%
Wearables, Home and Accessories (1)(2)	5,129	3,944	30%	12,437	9,425	32%
Services (3)	11,450	9,850	16%	22,325	18,979	18%
Total net sales	$58,015	$61,137	(5)%	$142,325	$149,430	(5)%

(1) Products net sales include amortization of the deferred value of unspecified software upgrade rights, which are bundled in the sales price of the respective product.

(2) Wearables, Home and Accessories net sales include sales of AirPods, Apple TV, Apple Watch, Beats products, HomePod, iPod touch, and Apple-branded and third-party accessories.

(3) Services net sales include sales from the company's digital content stores and streaming services, AppleCare, Apple Pay, licensing, and other services. Services net sales also include amortization of the deferred value of Maps, Siri, and free iCloud services, which are bundled in the sales price of certain products.

	Three Months Ended		Six Months Ended	
	March 30, 2019	March 31, 2018	March 30, 2019	March 31, 2018
Gross margin:				
Products	$14,518	$17,351	$39,715	$45,940
Services	7,303	6,071	14,137	11,394
Total gross margin	$21,821	$23,422	$53,852	$57,334
Gross margin percentage:				
Products	31.2%	33.8%	33.1%	35.2%
Services	63.8%	61.6%	63.3%	60.0%
Total gross margin percentage	37.6%	38.3%	37.8%	38.4%

Source: Quarterly Report Form 10-Q. Apple, March 30, 2019.

operational details. Given Apple's global growth in multiple product categories, and the associated complexity in strategic execution, CEO Tim Cook would be challenged to sustain the level of innovation for which the company was known.

Company Background

Founder Steve Jobs

Apple Computer was founded in Mountain View, California, on April 1, 1976, by Steve Jobs and Steve Wozniak. Jobs was the visionary and marketer, Wozniak was the technical genius, and A. C. "Mike" Markkula Jr., who had joined the team several months earlier, was the businessman. Jobs set the mission of empowering individuals, one person–one computer, and doing so with elegance of design and fierce attention to detail. In 1977, the first version of the Apple II became the first computer ordinary people could use right out of the box, and its instant success in the home market caused a computing revolution, essentially creating the personal computer industry. By 1980, Apple was the industry leader and went public in December of that year.

EXHIBIT 4 Apple Innovation Time Line

Date	Product	Events
1976	Apple I	Steve Jobs, Steve Wozniak, and Ronald Wayne found Apple Computer.
1977	Apple II	Apple logo first used.
1979	Apple II1	Apple employs 250 people; the first personal computer spreadsheet software, *VisiCalc*, is written by Dan Bricklin on an Apple II.
1980	Apple III	Apple goes public with 4.6 million shares; IBM personal computer announced.
1983	Lisa	John Sculley becomes CEO.
1984	Mac 128K, Apple IIc	Super Bowl ad introduces the Mac desktop computer.
1985		Jobs resigns and forms NeXT Software; Windows 1.01 released.
1986	Mac Plus	Jobs establishes Pixar.
1987	Mac II, Mac SE	Apple sues Microsoft over GUI.
1989	Mac Portable	Apple sued by Xerox over GUI.
1990	Mac LC	Apple listed on Tokyo Stock Exchange.
1991	PowerBook 100, System 7	System 7 operating-system upgrade released, the first Mac OS to support PowerPC-based computers.
1993	Newton Message Pad (one of the first PDAs)	Sculley resigns; Spindler becomes CEO; PowerBook sales reach 1 million units.
1996		Spindler is out; Amelio becomes CEO; Apple acquires NeXT Software, with Jobs as adviser.
1997		Amelio is out; Jobs returns as interim CEO; online retail Apple Store opened.
1998	iMac	iMac colorful design introduced, including USB interface; Newton scrapped.
1999	iMovie, Final Cut Pro (video editing software)	iBook (part of PowerBook line) becomes best-selling retail notebook in October; Apple has 11% share of notebook market.
2000	G4Cube	Jobs becomes permanent CEO.
2001	iPod, OS X, iTunes software, Apple Store	iTunes software is a mobile device management application. First physical retail store opens, in Virginia.
2002	iMac G4, iLife	Apple releases iLife software suite.
2003	iTunes Store	Apple reaches 25 million iTunes downloads.
2004	iMac G5	Jobs undergoes successful surgery for pancreatic cancer.
2005	iPod Nano, iPod Shuffle, Mac Mini	First video iPod released; video downloads available from iTunes.
2006	MacBook Pro	Apple computers use Intel's Core Duo CPU and can run Windows software; iWork software competes with Microsoft Office.
2007	iPhone, Apple TV, iPod Touch	Apple Computer changes name to Apple Inc.; Microsoft Vista released.
2008	iPhone 3G, MacBook Air, App Store	App Store launched for third-party applications for iPhone and iPod Touch and brings in $1 million in one day.
2009	17-inch MacBook Pro, iLife, iWork '09	iTunes Plus provides DRM-free music, with variable pricing; Jobs takes medical leave.
2010	iPad, iPhone 4, Mac App Store	iPhone 4 provides FaceTime feature; iTunes reaches 10 billion songs sold.
2011	iPad2, iPhone 4S, iCloud	iPhone available on Verizon Wireless; Jobs resigns as CEO, dies on October 5th. Tim Cook becomes CEO.

Continued

EXHIBIT 4 *Continued*

Date	Product	Events
2012	iBook Author, iPhone5, iPad Mini, Apple Wallet	iBook supports textbook creation on iPad. Retina displays, skinny Macs. Apple Wallet stores coupons, tickets. Apple becomes world's most valuable company by market capitalization.
2013	Mega Mac, iPad Air	Workstation in a small aluminum cylinder.
2014	iPhone 6 Plus, Apple Watch, Apple Pay	Biggest iPhone yet, Apple Watch = computer on your wrist introduced in 2014, actual delivery in 2015, Apple Pay mobile payment service, acquisition of Beats Electronic for headphones, streaming digital content.
2015	Apple Music	Streaming music subscription service, including Internet radio station Beats 1, blog platform Connect.
2016	iPhone 7, iPhone 7 Plus, iPad Pro, Apple AirPods, Apple Watch Series	Seventh generation iPhone, AirPods wireless earphones, Apple Watch multiple series included Nike and Hermes; over 1 billion Apple devices are in use worldwide.
2017	iPhone 8, iPhone 8 Plus, iPhone X	Fall 2017 release.
2018	HomePad, iPhone XS & XR, iPadPro with Face ID, iPad Air with Apple Pencil support	HomePad smart speaker with voice control; Apple reaches $1 trillion market value, becomes the largest publically traded corporation in the world by market capitalization.
2019	Apple TV+, Apple Channels, Apple News+, Apple Arcade, Apple Card	Apple TV+ will produce original content, Channels subscription gives access to premium network TV, News+ subscription gives access to digital magazines & newspapers, Apple Arcade gives access to games via the App Store, Apple Card is a credit card stored in Apple Wallet.

Sources: Timeline of Apple Inc. products. Wikipedia; author estimates.

In 1983, Wozniak left the firm and Jobs hired John Sculley away from PepsiCo to take the role of CEO at Apple, citing the need for someone to spearhead marketing and operations while Jobs worked on technology. The result of Jobs's creative focus on personal computing was the Macintosh. Introduced in 1984, with the now-famous Super Bowl television ad based on George Orwell's novel *Nineteen Eighty-Four*,[8] the Macintosh was a breakthrough in terms of elegant design and ease of use. Its ability to handle large graphic files quickly made it a favorite with graphic designers, but it had slow performance and limited compatible software was available. That meant the product as designed at that time was unable to help significantly Apple's failing bottom line. In addition, Jobs had given Bill Gates at Microsoft some Macintosh prototypes to use to develop software and, in 1985, Microsoft subsequently came out with the Windows operating system–a version of GUI for use on IBM PCs.

Steve Jobs's famous volatility led to his resignation from Apple in 1985. Jobs then founded NeXT Computer. The NeXT Cube computer proved too costly for the business to become commercially profitable, but its technological contributions could not be ignored. In 1997, then Apple CEO Gilbert Amelio bought out NeXT, hoping to use its Rhapsody–a version of the NeXTStep operating system–to jump-start the Mac OS development, and Jobs was brought back as a part-time adviser.

Under CEOs Sculley, Spindler, and Amelio

John Sculley had tried to take advantage of Apple's unique capabilities. Because of this, Macintosh computers became easy to use, with seamless integration (the original plug-and-play) and reliable performance. This premium performance meant Apple could charge a premium price. However, with the price of IBM compatibles dropping, and Apple's costs, especially research and development (R&D), way above industry averages, this was not a sustainable scenario.

Sculley's innovative efforts were not enough to substantially improve Apple's bottom line, and he was replaced as CEO in 1993 by company president Michael Spindler. Spindler continued the focus on innovation, producing the PowerMac in 1994. Even though this combination produced a significant price-performance edge over both previous Macs and Intel-based machines, the IBM clones continued to undercut Apple's prices. Spindler's response was to allow other companies to manufacture Mac clones, a strategy that ultimately led to clones stealing 20 percent of Macintosh unit sales.

Gilbert Amelio, an Apple director and former semiconductor turnaround expert, was asked to reverse the company's financial direction. Amelio intended to reposition Apple as a premium brand, but his extensive reorganizations and cost-cutting strategies could not prevent Apple's stock price from slipping to a new low. However, Amelio's decision to stop work on a brand-new operating system and jump-start development by using NeXTStep brought Steve Jobs back to Apple in 1997.

Steve Jobs's Return

One of Jobs's first strategies upon his return was to strengthen Apple's relationships with third-party software developers, including Microsoft. In 1997, Jobs announced an alliance with Microsoft that would allow for the creation of a Mac version of the popular Microsoft Office software. He also made a concerted effort to woo other developers, such as Adobe, to continue to produce Mac-compatible programs.

In late October 2001, Apple released its first major noncomputer product–the iPod. This device was an MP3 music player that packed up to 1,000 CD-quality songs into an ultraportable, 6.5-ounce design: "With iPod, Apple has invented a whole new category of digital music player that lets you put your entire music collection in your pocket and listen to it wherever you go," said Steve Jobs. "With iPod, listening to music will never be the same again."[9] This prediction became even truer in 2002, when Apple introduced an iPod that would download from Windows–its first product that did not require a Macintosh computer and thus opened up the Apple "magic" to everyone. In 2003, all iPod products were sold with a Windows version of iTunes, making it even easier to use the device regardless of computer platform.

In April 2003, Apple opened the online iTunes Music Store to everyone. This software, downloadable on any computer platform, sold individual songs through the iTunes application for 99 cents each. When announced, the iTunes Music Store already had the backing of five major record labels and a catalog of 200,000 songs. Later that year, the iTunes Music Store was selling roughly 500,000 songs a day. In 2003, the iPod was the only portable digital player that could play music purchased from iTunes, and this intended exclusivity helped both products become dominant.

After 30 years of carving a niche for itself as the premier provider of technology solutions for graphic artists, Web designers, and educators, Apple had reinvented itself as a digital entertainment company, moving beyond the personal computer industry. The announcement in 2007 of the iPhone, a product incorporating a wireless phone, a music and video player, and a mobile Internet browsing device, meant Apple was also competing in the cell phone/smartphone industry. That year, Apple changed its name from Apple Computer to Apple Inc.

Also introduced in 2007, the iPod Touch incorporated Wi-Fi connectivity, allowing users to purchase and download music directly from iTunes without a computer. Then, in 2008 Apple opened the App Store. Users could now purchase applications written by third-party developers specifically for the iPhone and iPod Touch.

In 2010, Apple launched the large-screen touch-based tablet called the iPad and sold over 2 million of these devices in the first two months.[10] That same year, Apple's stock value increased to the extent that the company's market cap exceeded Microsoft's, making it the biggest tech company in the world.[11] In 2011, Steve Jobs made his last product launch appearance to introduce iCloud, an online storage and syncing service. On October 4, 2011, Apple announced the iPhone 4S, which included "Siri," the "intelligent software assistant." The next day, on October 5, came the announcement that Steve Jobs had died.

Apple continued to innovate, however, and on September 21, 2012, Apple had its biggest iPhone launch ever with the iPhone 5.[12] On September 19, 2012, Apple stock reached $702.10, its highest level to date, which made Apple the most valuable company in the world. 2013 saw the iPhone5C and the high-range iPhone5S, which introduced the Touch ID fingerprint recognition system. The iPhone 6 and 6 Plus, with larger displays, faster processors, and support for mobile payments, were released in September 2014.[13] The prototype of the Apple Watch was unveiled in 2014. Also introduced in 2014 was Apple Pay, a mobile payment system meant to augment all Apple mobile products. February 2015 saw Apple reach the highest market cap of any U.S.-traded company. During 2016 Apple introduced Apple Music, a streaming music service meant to take advantage of its already strong relationship with artists and music publishers, and therefore positioned to successfully compete with Pandora and Spotify. In addition, iPhone 7 and 7 Plus and the Apple Watch Series 2 all had a positive response from customers. Apple products had more than 1 billion users worldwide by the end of 2017.

Apple had become a diversified digital entertainment corporation. Back in 2005 analysts believed Apple had "changed the rules of the game for three industries–PCs, consumer electronics, and music and appears to have nothing to fear from major rivals."[14] On top of steady sales of its computers, of the iPod, and of iTunes, the added categories of iPhone and iPad had shown substantial growth; but by 2013, Samsung had outperformed Apple in worldwide smartphone sales,[15] and Google's Android had captured the largest market share of cell phone operating systems. At the same time, both the Amazon Kindle Fire HD and Microsoft's Surface tablet had emerged to challenge the iPad. 2015 was marked by competition in the wearable tech space, and 2017 saw the Windows 10 operating system become four times more popular than the macOS, the Microsoft Surface defeating iPad in user satisfaction, and customers frustrated that the MacPro had not yet been redesigned to recover from its 2013 design misstep. Could Apple continue to grow, and, if so, in what categories?

Apple's Operations

Maintaining a competitive edge required more than innovative product design. Operational execution was also important. For instance, while trying to market its increasingly diverse product line, Apple believed that its own retail stores could serve customers better than any third-party retailers. By the beginning of 2019, Apple had 506 stores open, including 234 international locations.[16] Some of these stores worldwide were considered architectural wonders, including the iconic Fifth Avenue glass cube in New York City. Apple had even received trademark protection for its retail stores' "distinctive design and layout."[17] Partly due to the appealing design of both the shopping experience and the products being sold within, Apple retail stores had traditionally generated more sales per square foot than any other U.S. retailer, including its closest luxury rival Tiffany & Co.[18]

To solidify its supply chain, Apple had entered into multiyear agreements with suppliers of key components. Apple had had historically excellent margins, partly because of its simpler product line, leading to lower manufacturing costs.[19] Apple had outsourced almost all manufacturing and final assembly to its Asian partners, paying close attention to scheduling and quality issues. Outsourcing to Asian manufacturers was not without its problems, however. In 2012, headlines worldwide exposed China's Foxconn manufacturing facility for labor abuses that led to worker suicide threats. Apple, as well as most other technology companies, used Foxconn facilities to assemble products, including the iPad and iPhone. After the story broke, Apple CEO Tim Cook visited the Foxconn plant and reviewed an audit of working conditions that found violations in wages, overtime, and environmental standards. Apple stated that it remained "committed to the highest standards of social responsibility across our worldwide supply chain,"[20] and Cook announced that Apple would be bringing some of the production of Mac computers back to the United States, starting in 2013. They could do this without affecting the company's profitability, because of automation cost savings.[21]

Apple had also historically paid attention to research and development, increasing its R&D investment year after year. In the second quarter of 2019, Apple spent $3.9 billion on R&D, an increase of 1 percent from the previous year. As one of Steve Jobs's legacies, Apple had traditionally kept the specifics of its research and development a closely guarded secret and fiercely protected its innovative patents. For example, a well-publicized series of lawsuits in 2012 highlighted rifts between Apple and Samsung, who was both a rival and supplier. Samsung smartphones had captured more market share than Apple's iPhones in the beginning of 2012, and Apple argued that Samsung had succeeded with both its phones and tablets only by copying Apple's designs. Samsung replied by claiming that Apple had infringed on Samsung's patents.[22] U.S. intellectual property courts found in favor of Apple, but Japanese courts found in favor of Samsung. The threat of ongoing battle meant Apple needed to look for other suppliers of chips and displays. Supply chain watchers pointed out that Apple still had a major challenge finding reliable suppliers for increasingly scarce components, and that the continued reliance on Foxconn as the sole manufacturer of the iPhone meant that any disruption there could have major consequences for delivery.[23]

Status of Apple's Business Units in 2019

The Apple Computer Business

In the computer market, Apple had always refused to compete on price, relying instead on its reliability, design elegance, ease of use, and integrated features to win customers. An opportunity for increased market share was realized when Apple began using Intel processors in the iMac desktop and the MacBook portables, which allowed them to run Microsoft Office and other business software.

However, in FY2018 Apple's worldwide Mac computer sales decreased 5 percent over the previous year, continuing to signal the decline of this category since the introduction of the iPad in 2010. Overall it appeared that sales of desktop computers, especially, were slowing worldwide as the tablet and smartphone markets grew, and this was evident in the worldwide PC market share data from 2018, where only Dell saw any significant growth (see Exhibit 5). Apple

EXHIBIT 5 Worldwide PC Market Share, Calendar Year 2018 (units in thousands)

Company	2018 Shipments	2018 Market Share	2017 Shipments	2017 Market Share	2018/2017 Growth
1. HP	59,986	23.2%	58,809	22.6%	2.0%
2. Lenovo*	59,857	23.2%	58,049	22.4%	3.1%
3. Dell Inc	44,170	17.1%	41,822	16.1%	5.6%
4. Apple	18,021	7.0%	19,010	7.3%	−5.2%
5. Acer Group	17,841	6.9%	18,033	6.9%	−1.1%
Others	58,621	22.7%	63,925	24.6%	−8.3%
Total	**258,497**	**100.0%**	**259,647**	**100.0%**	**−0.4%**

Source: Inventory and Processor Supply Issues Weigh Against Holiday PC Shipments, According to IDC. IDC, January 10, 2019.

EXHIBIT 6 Worldwide SmartPhone Shipments, First Quarter 2019

Vendor	Q1 2019 shipments (million)	Q1 2019 Market share	Q1 2018 shipments (million)	Q1 2018 Market share	Annual growth
Samsung	71.5	22.8%	79.5	23.6%	−10.0%
Huawei	59.1	18.8%	39.3	11.7%	+50.2%
Apple	40.2	12.8%	52.2	15.5%	−23.2%
Xiaomi	27.8	8.9%	28.2	8.4%	−1.3%
Oppo	27.3	8.7%	25.7	7.6%	+6.4%
Others	88.0	28.0%	111.9	33.2%	−21.3%
Total	**313.9**	**100.0%**	**336.8**	**100.0%**	**−6.8%**

Source: Canalys: Apple iPhone shipments fall 23% as global smartphone market remains in freefall. Canalys, May 1, 2019.

saw the greatest decline amongst its rivals, a decline also evident in its own revenue profile, which had seen the Mac's share of Apple overall revenue drop from more than 40 percent in 2007 to about 11 percent in 2016, and slipping further to 9.5 percent in the first quarter of 2019.[24]

There had been rumors Apple was planning to refresh the iMac, and completely revamp the Mac Pro. Targeting professional users, and very expensive at around $3,000, the Mac Pro product had never had a large market share, but the creative professionals–the videographers, designers, and photographers–who embraced the original product were still waiting for a delayed redesign.[25] The iMac did see new processors and graphics in 2019, but the basic design remained the same.

Personal Digital Entertainment Devices: iPod

Although many analysts at the time felt the MP3 player market was oversaturated, Apple had introduced the iPod Touch in 2007, intending it to be an iPhone without the phone, a portable media player, and Wi-Fi Internet device without the AT&T phone bill. The iPod Touch borrowed most of its features from the iPhone, including the finger-touch interface, but it remained mainly an iPod, with a larger viewing area for videos. Apple released the fifth-generation iPod Touch in September 2012, and the sixth-generation version debuted in 2015. A seventh-generation was released in May, 2019.[26] The iPod Touch had sold well over 100 million units since its debut in 2007, and although it was no longer promoted on the Apple website, it was still for sale. The device was still a cheap way to get entertainment, and used for portable gaming, this device augmented with a cheap phone for calling and texting was still less expensive than an iPhone.

Mobile Communication Devices: iPhone

In 2007, Apple's iPhone combined an Internet-enabled smartphone and video iPod. The iPhone allowed users to access all iPod content and play music and video content purchased from iTunes. Subsequent smartphone models increased the quality of the photo and video components to make even the digital camera or camcorder appear obsolete. By the fourth quarter of 2015 Apple had achieved almost 19 percent market share, in a close tie with Samsung, and by July 2016 it had sold over 1 billion units, becoming "one of the most important, world-changing and successful products in history."[27] However, competition was fierce and by 2019 Apple's smartphone market share had dropped by over 23 percent. The main challenge was coming from Huawei (see Exhibit 6).

In addition, the smartphone market was increasingly turning into a battle between mobile operating systems. Apple's iPhone, running on iOS, had considerable competition from Samsung's line of smartphones. This was partly due to Samsung's use of Google's Android operating system. By 2018, the operating system map had Android devices capturing the majority of market share (see Exhibit 7).[28]

Over the years, in Asian markets especially, Apple's shares of mobile devices had lost considerable ground to Samsung, Huawei, and other smartphones produced by Asian manufacturers. Younger Asian users, the 20-something college students and fresh graduates, were looking for the next new thing, and that was increasingly an Android-driven device.[29]

In 2019, overall iPhone second quarter sales were down 17 percent from the previous year. The overall smartphone market was slowing down as mature markets were increasingly dependent on replacement purchases, and emerging markets appeared more interested in low-cost devices. Other than the removal of the headphone port, Apple had not made any significant technological changes to the iPhone lineup, so if Apple wanted to address its declining market share, it might have to lower prices, which, given the iPhone's major contribution to Apple's bottom line ($167B or 63 percent of total sales in 2018), would make it difficult for the company to maintain its profit margins or grow net income going forward. Even so, the iPhone was Apple's most important and potentially lucrative product.

Tablet Computer: iPad

In April 2010, Apple released the iPad, a tablet computer, as a platform for audio-visual media, including books, periodicals,

EXHIBIT 7 Smartphone Operating System Market Share, Fourth Quarter 2018

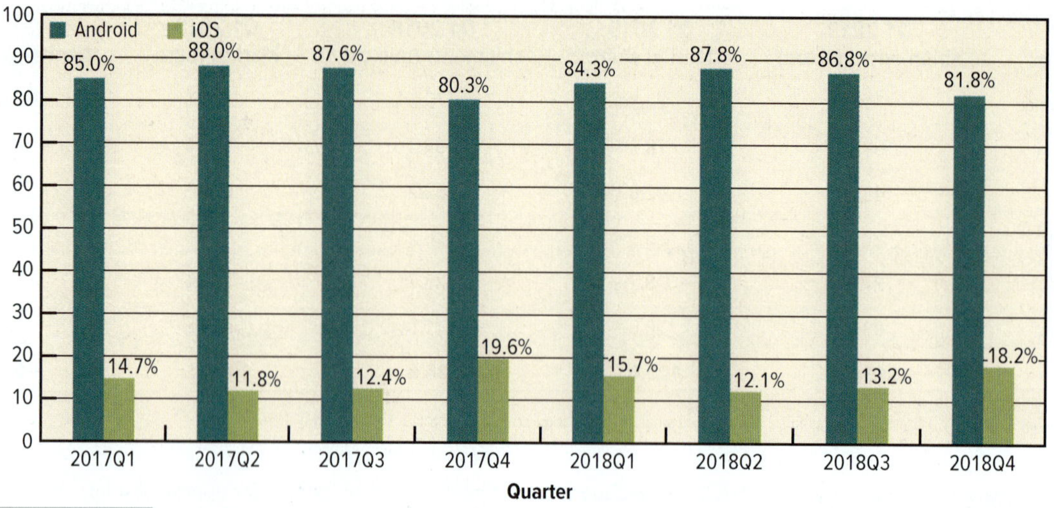

Source: Smartphone Market Share: OS Data Overview. IDC. https://www.idc.com/promo/smartphone-market-share/os

movies, music, games, and web content. More than 300,000 iPads were purchased by eager tech consumers during the device's first day on store shelves. Weighing only 1.5 pounds, this lightweight, portable, and touch-screen device was seen as a gigantic iPod Touch.[30] Features like the sleek design, touch screen, multiple apps, and fast and easy-to-navigate software made the iPad popular in business, education, and the entertainment industry. The iPad was selected by *Time* magazine as one of the 50 Best Inventions of the Year 2010.[31]

Up until September 2010, Apple iPads had accounted for 95 percent of tablet computer sales,[32] but by the end of 2012, that figure had fallen to 78.9 percent; and by the end of 2018 Apple held only about 26 percent of the market. The loss of share was partly due to tablet devices, such as Samsung's Galaxy, that were based on Google's open-source Android system. Other platforms and devices had also appeared, including Google's Chromebook, Amazon's Kindle Fire, and Microsoft Windows' Surface tablet.[33] Going into 2019 there were signs that the iPad models' sales–as well as the entire tablet industry–were in decline, perhaps due to the "jumbo" phones coming from the likes of Samsung (and Apple), and low-cost Google-based Chromebook laptops (see Exhibit 8).[34]

Apple finally redesigned the iPad lineup in 2019, providing a major upgrade in power with Apple's new A12 Bionic chip, and introducing a new iPad Mini and iPad Air, both ultra-portable with Apple Pencil support. The iPad Pro, although expensive, was redesigned to incorporate a full-screen Liquid Retina display, Face ID, as well as the powerful A12X Bionic chip with Neural Engine and support for the new Apple Pencil and Smart Keyboard. Even though the category had seen reduced activity as a whole,

EXHIBIT 8 Worldwide Quarterly Tablet Market Share, Third Quarter 2018

Company	3Q18 Unit Shipments	3Q18 Market Share	3Q17 Unit Shipments	3Q17 Market Share	Year-Over-Year Growth
1. Apple	9.7	26.6%	10.3	25.9%	−6.1%
2. Samsung	5.3	14.6%	6.0	15.0%	−11.4%
3. Amazon.com	4.4	12.0%	4.4	11.0%	−0.4%
4. Huawei	3.2	8.9%	3.0	7.6%	7.1%
5. Lenovo	2.3	6.3%	3.1	7.7%	−24.5%
Others	11.5	31.6%	13.1	32.9%	−12.1%
Total	**36.4**	**100.0%**	**39.9**	**100.0%**	**−8.6%**
Lenovo (excluding Fujitsu volume in 3Q17)	2.3	6.3%	3.0	7.4%	−22.1%

Source: Tablet Market Sees Modest Decline of 8.6% as Slate and Detachable Categories Continue to Struggle, According to IDC. IDC, November 2, 2018.

the iPad continued to perform for Apple, with 2018 seeing the strongest growth in years. Part of this growth was due to customer response to the iPad Pro and the adoption of the iPad in operational scenarios such as in airline pilots' flight bags and maintenance ground crews' service bays as an easy portable source for key information.

The Software Market

Although Apple had always created innovative hardware, software development also had been an important goal. Software had been Apple's core strength, especially in its computers, due to its reliability and resistance to virus infections and resulting crashes.[35] The premier piece of Apple software was the operating system. The iOS allowed Apple to develop software applications such as Final Cut Pro, a video-editing program for professionals' digital camcorders; GarageBand, for making and mixing personally created music; the iTunes digital music jukebox; and iWork, containing a PowerPoint-type program called Keynote and a word-processor/page-layout program called Pages.

Apple's Web browser, Safari, was upgraded in 2009 to compete with Windows Internet Explorer, Mozilla Firefox, and the new entrant, Chrome from Google. Apple announced, "Safari 4 is the world's fastest and most innovative browser,"[36] but analysts were quick to point out that Google's Chrome, which debuted six months earlier, was perhaps the first to take the browser interface in a new direction. One commentator called Chrome "a wake-up call for the Safari UI guys."[37] Browser market share data in 2019 showed Chrome in the top spot, with its various versions grabbing over 65 percent of global market share. Recent versions of Microsoft Internet Explorer and Edge held second place with 14 percent, and Firefox had 9.6 percent. Safari had 3.7 percent share.[38]

iCloud was introduced in 2011 during one of Steve Jobs's last public appearances. The web-based storage service initially struggled to get traction, but in 2014 was upgraded to iCloud Drive, allowing users to interoperate with Windows and connect all iOS devices. As an alternative to Google Drive and Dropbox, this gave Apple an intro into the enterprise/corporate user space, a market CEO Tim Cook had begun to successfully target.[39]

In other software development areas, Apple had not been that successful. In 2012, Apple stumbled badly with its Maps software. Released in iOS6, Apple Maps was meant to replace Google Maps on the iPhone, but instead produced distorted images and gave really bad directions. CEO Tim Cook had to apologize that Apple had fallen short of its commitment to making "world-class products," and suggested customers go back to using its competitor's mapping software.[40]

iTunes/Apple Music

Arguably, Apple's most innovative software product was iTunes, a free downloadable software program for consumers running on either Mac or Windows operating systems. It came bundled with all Mac computers and iPods and connected with the iTunes Music Store for purchasing digital music and movie files that could be downloaded and played by iPods, iPads, and the iPhone, and by iTunes on PCs.

Although the volume was there, iTunes had not necessarily been a profitable venture. Traditionally, out of the 99 cents Apple charged for a song, about 65 cents went to the music label; 25 cents for distribution costs, including credit card charges, servers, and bandwidth; and the balance to marketing, promotion, and the amortized cost of developing the iTunes software.[41] However, if not wildly profitable, iTunes was still considered a media giant—especially with its over 50 million songs, and 100,000 TV shows and movies available in its database as of 2019.[42]

Growth, however, was occurring in the streaming service market, especially with the rising popularity of online radio and Internet streaming providers Pandora and Spotify, and by 2015 music sales on iTunes had fallen by over 14 percent worldwide. This trend helped explain why Apple acquired the monthly subscription streaming service Beats Music in 2014. The $3 billion acquisition included headphone maker Beats Electronics,[43] and ultimately led to the development of Apple Music in 2015. By April 2019, Apple Music had over 28 million U.S. subscribers, beating out Spotify.[44] Worldwide, Spotify still had a lead, especially when factoring in non-paying users, but Apple was working to draw from its base of 900 million iPhone users to increase this.

The App Store – Apple Arcade, Apple News+

In March 2008, Apple announced that it was releasing the iPhone software development kit (SDK), allowing developers to create applications for the iPhone and iPod Touch and sell these third-party applications via the Apple App Store. The App Store was made available on iTunes, and it was directly available from the iPhone, iPad, and iPod Touch products. This opened the window for another group of Apple customers, the application developers, to collaborate with Apple. Developers could purchase the iPhone Developer Program from Apple for $99, create either free or commercial applications for the iPhone and iPod Touch, and then submit these applications to be sold in the App Store. Developers would be paid 70 percent of the download fee customers paid to the App Store, and Apple would get 30 percent of the revenue.

By 2019, over 180 billion apps had been downloaded from Apple's App Store,[45] but Google Play, the app store for Android users, had grabbed more of the download business. In the third quarter of 2018 the App Store saw 7.6 billion downloads, while Google Play had 19.5 billion. The most popular App Store downloads were games.[46] It was worth noting that the mobile app industry was large—in 2019 there were an estimated 2.7 billion smartphone users and 1.35 billion tablet users worldwide, and this number was expected to continue to grow. Data showed that 90 percent of mobile time was spent on apps, and this was a potentially lucrative business for both the app developer and the platform host. Apple was intending to capitalize on this by offering its new Apple Arcade, an ad-free subscription service, providing access to over 100 exclusive or new games. Apple was attracting game developers who appreciated the superior iPhone animation technology and, unlike on the Google Play platform, Apple had the ability to provide security and protection against malware, counterfeiting, and piracy. This meant high quality games would be available for Apple products exclusively.[47]

Also available in 2019 in the App Store was Apple News+, a $9.99 per month subscription to 300 magazines including *Time, Vogue, Popular Science, Sports Illustrated,* and *Fortune*. Premium digital content from *The Wall Street Journal, Los Angeles Times,* and *TechCrunch* made this an attractive offering.

Apple Pay/Apple Card

Introduced in late 2014, Apple Pay allowed iPhone users in the United States to make secure payments for goods and services using their phones. With over 1 million credit and debit card activations within the first 72 hours of its release, Apple Pay was intended to replace the user's wallet and, according to CEO Tim Cook, would "forever change the way all of us buy things," primarily because the process was more secure than a traditional card-based transaction. Major retailers such as Macy's, Walgreens, McDonald's, Whole Foods, and Disney had all agreed to accept Apple Pay. Apple reportedly received 0.15 percent of each purchase, making the service a potentially lucrative venture, but adoption had been poor, with only one-third of iPhone users trying it once or more. In 2019, Apple debuted the Apple Card in partnership with Mastercard and Goldman Sachs. This was both a digital and physical credit card option that provided better security in its physical form, since nothing was printed on the card. The digital card could be used anywhere Apple Pay was accepted, while the physical version could be used in other places. Apple was hoping this option would increase the use of Apple Pay.

Other Products: Apple Watch, AirPods, HomePod, Apple TV

Apple Watch was the first all-new product since the iPad, and therefore CEO Tim Cook's most ambitious gamble. Once again, Apple was not the first company to enter the wearable tech space, following the lead of Samsung, Sony, and Motorola, and competing against fitness trackers produced by Nike, FitBit, and others. However, Apple's preorders for the launch in 2015 indicated demand would run to a combined five to six million units of the three watch models.[48] This category was a bit of a departure for Apple as it had positioned the Watch as a personalized device, with the market segmented between mass market and luxury.[49] Although initial sales appeared disappointing, Apple continued to innovate the product, and by 2019 had sold over 46 million, making the Apple Watch the number one smartwatch in the world. Software improvements using HealthKit and ResearchKit had helped wearers monitor and improve their health and fitness, showing that this device was more than just an iPhone extension on the wrist.

Apple's AirPods, first released in 2016, were Apple's most popular accessory product, with over 35 million units sold in 2018. These wireless Bluetooth earphones not only played audio but could handle phone calls and receive assistance from Siri, Apple's digital assistant. AirPods had full functionality with all Apple products, including Apple Watch and Apple TV.

The Apple HomePod was another way to interact with Apple devices. This smart speaker introduced in early 2018 was intended to compete with Amazon's Echo and Google's Home device, and by 2019 the Apple device had captured a 6 percent share. Reviews had been mixed, however, especially since the HomePod version of Siri was not as helpful as Amazon's Alexa or Google's Assistant, so the initial price had been lowered, presumably to attract more Apple users.[50] Once again, the intention was to use the device for its high quality speaker capability, pairing it with AppleTV, Apple Music, and the iPhone, extending the reach of the Apple ecosystem.

Apple TV, around since 2007, had undergone four upgrades, and had partnered with NBC Universal to offer users access to seven of its networks' most popular series. Similar to rivals Roku, Amazon Fire, and Chromecast, Apple TV was a digital media player that could stream content to a compatible television. Unlike its rivals, Apple TV could play all the content from iTunes, apps, and games from the iPhone, and use Siri voice recognition software to search and recognize viewer choices. However, it was more expensive and did not provide easy access to Amazon Prime content, a popular destination for many viewers. 2019 saw the addition of new services Apple TV+ streaming service, designed to cement loyalty among Apple users.[51] Original content designed for Apple TV+ and access to streaming content from other providers may be a new and developing revenue source for Apple.[52]

Product Extensions, Growth of Services

Rumors surfaced in 2015 that Apple had acquired resources, primarily engineers and related technology, that would enable it to develop an automobile ready for market by 2020. Speculation was that the Apple would not do the actual assembly but, as with its other products, would use its sophisticated supply chain expertise to outsource manufacturing, focusing its considerable innovation skills on the design and sales of a product that incorporates Apple technology in multiple configurations.[53] By 2019, restructuring had led to the dismissal of over 200 employees from Apple's Project Titan autonomous driving unit. Rumors had spread that Apple would not pursue the actual automobile, but instead was investigating the development of self-driving car software, or the application of artificial intelligence in multiple products, using its available cash to acquire both businesses and people, making a "heavy investment in machine learning and autonomous systems."[54]

With the existing hardware products all appearing to stagnate, analysts were looking to Apple's services and "other products" for growth opportunities. While the "other" products such as Apple Watch, Apple TV, AirPods, and HomePod grew 35 percent in FY2018, the services category–which included Apple Pay, Apple Music, iCloud, iTunes, and the App Store–grew 24 percent to a record $37.2 billion and accounted for 14 percent of all revenues, beating every category except the iPhone. In addition, making this sector more attractive, profit margin estimates averaged almost 64 percent. In particular, the App Store, having tripled revenue between 2013 and 2016, was projected to produce about two-thirds of Apple's growth target for 2020.[55] In 2019, Apple reported over 390 million paid subscriptions across its services portfolio, an increase of 120 million since the previous year. Many analysts were wondering whether Apple could create "the world's greatest subscription model, where users can opt to have the latest iPhone and many services for a fixed fee. This would lock many into its ecosystem and create a constant stream of recurring revenues."[56] Others cautioned that Apple's strength is "using the services division to boost the sales of the iPhone and keep people locked into an ever-growing cycle of updated hardware."[57] This may be Apple's exact intention.

The Future of Apple

Under Cook, Apple had transitioned itself "from being a hypergrowth company to being a premium, branded consumer company."[58] Apple was a truly vertically integrated designer and marketer of products and services. If long-time Apple fans were not satisfied with the state of Apple's innovation today, they might have to realize, as former Apple marketing guru Guy Kawasaki did, that

> [It is] difficult for Apple to top itself. .... It would be foolish to bet against Apple based on my experience.... If nothing else, Apple will once again force everyone to improve their game.[59]

As CEO Tim Cook said during the second quarter earnings call of 2019:

> One of Apple's great strengths is our culture of flexibility, adaptability, and creativity. This quarter featured some important announcements that speak to the power of our commitment to innovation and long-term thinking... we previewed a game-changing array of new services, each of them rooted in principles that are fundamentally Apple.... These features aren't just nice to have. They actually help to eliminate the boundary between hardware, software, and service, creating a singularly exceptional experience for our users.[60]

It is entirely possible Apple is not done innovating.

ENDNOTES

1 Apple Press Release. 2017. Apple Park opens to employees in April. *Apple Newsroom*, February 22, http://www.apple.com/newsroom/2017/02/apple-park-opens-to-employees-in-april.html.

2 Stone, B. and P. Burrows. 2011. The essence of Apple. *Bloomberg Businessweek*, January 24–30; Kahney, L. 2019. The big question hanging over Tim Cook's tenure at Apple. *Yahoo! Finance*, April 15, https://finance.yahoo.com/news/tim-cook-leander-kahney-163732037.html.

3 Dudovskiy, J. 2017. Apple leadership–an effective leadership by Tim Cook that is difficult to sustain. *Research Methodology*, March 2, http://research-methodology.net/apple-leadership-and-apple-organizational-structure/.

4 Sure Dividend. 2017. Will Apple be the next AAA-rated company? *Seeking Alpha*, March 21, https://seekingalpha.com/article/4056857-will-apple-next-aaa-rated-company?app=1&auth_param=70583:1cd2qfc:b996ecb86441181f700647f3f12dfd52&uprof=14.

5 Colvin, G. 2016. Tim Cook's epic growth challenge at Apple. *Fortune*, January 7, http://fortune.com/2016/01/07/tim-cook-apple-growth-challenge/.

6 *Fortune*. 2018. World's most admired companies. http://fortune.com/worlds-most-admired-companies/.

7 Apple Inc. 2018. 2018 annual report, 10-K filing. www.apple.com/investor.

8 January 24, 2009, was the 25th anniversary of the Macintosh, unveiled by Apple in the "Big Brother" Super Bowl ad in 1984. www.youtube.com/watch?v5OYecfV3ubP8. See also the 1983 Apple keynote speech by a young Steve Jobs, introducing this ad: www.youtube.com/watch?v5lSiQA6KKyJo.

9 Apple Inc. 2001. Ultra-portable MP3 music player puts 1,000 songs in your pocket. October 23, www.apple.com/pr/library/2001/oct/23ipod.html.

10 Apple Inc. 2010. Apple sells two million iPads in less than 60 days. Press release. May 31, www.apple.com/pr/library/2010/05/31Apple-Sells-Two-Million-iPads-in-Less-Than-60-Days.html.

11 BBC News. 2010. Apple passes Microsoft to be biggest tech company. BBC News, May 27, www.bbc.co.uk/news/10168684.

12 Keizer, G. 2012. Apple drains iPhone5 pre-order supplies in an hour. *Computerworld*, September 14, www.computerworld.com/s/article/9231285/Apple_drains_iPhone_5_pre_order_supplies_in_an_hour.

13 IDC. 2015. In a near tie, Apple closes the gap on Samsung in the fourth quarter as worldwide smartphone shipments top 1.3 billion for 2014, according to IDC. *IDC*, January 29, http://www.idc.com/getdoc.jsp?containerId=prUS25407215.

14 Schlender, B. 2005. How big can Apple get? *Fortune*, February 21, money.cnn.com/magazines/fortune/-fortune_archive/2005/02/21/8251769/index.htm.

15 Tofel, K.C. 2012. Why only Samsung builds phones that outsell iPhones. *GigaOM*, November 9, www.businessweek.com/articles/2012-11-09/why-only-samsung-builds-phones-that-outsell-iphones.

16 MacRumors Staff. 2019. Apple stores: Keep track of Apple's retail stores worldwide. *MacRumors*, February 6, https://www.macrumors.com/roundup/apple-retail-stores/.

17 Apple Inc. 2012. 2012 Annual Report; Palladino, V. 2013. Apple Store receives trademark for "distinctive design and layout." *Wired*, January 30, www.wired.com/design/2013/01/apple-store-trademark/.

18 Wahba, P. 2015. Apple extends lead in U.S. top 10 retailers by sales per square foot. *Fortune*, March 13, http://fortune.com/2015/03/13/apples-holiday-top-10-retailers-iphone/.

19 Fox, F. 2008. Mac Pro beats HP and Dell at their own game: Price. *LowEndMac.com*, May 16, lowendmac.com/ed/fox/08ff/mac-pro-vs-dell-hp.html.

20 Lowensohn, J. 2012. Lingering issues found at Foxconn's iPhone factory. *CNET*, December 14, news.cnet.com/8301-13579_3-57559327-37/lingering-issues-found-at-foxconns-iphone-factory/.

21 Bennett, D. 2012. Apple's Cook says more Macs will be born in the U.S.A. *Bloomberg Businessweek*, December 10, www.businessweek.com/articles/2012-12-10/apples-cook-says-more-macs-will-be-born-in-the-u-dot-s-dot-a-dot.

22 Jones, A. and J.E. Vascellaro. 2012. Apple v. Samsung: The patent trial of the century. *Wall Street Journal*, July 24, online.wsj.com/

article/SB10000872396390443295404577543221814648592.
html?mod5wsj_streaming_apple-v-samsung-trial-over-patents.

23 Noel, P. 2014. iProblems: Learning from Apple's strained supply chain. *MBTMag*, November 11, http://www.mbtmag.com/articles/2014/11/iproblems-learning-apple%E2%80%99s-strained-supply-chain.

24 Rexaline, S. 2017. Amid reports of a revamp how much does the Mac mean to Apple? *Yahoo Finance*, April 7, https://finance.yahoo.com/news/amid-reports-revamp-much-does-180029678.html; Share of Apple's revenue by product category from the 1st quarter of 2012 to the 2nd quarter of 2019, https://www.statista.com/statistics/382260/segments-share-revenue-of-apple/.

25 Haslam, K. 2017. New Mac Pro 2018 latest rumours: Release date, UK price, features & specs. *Mac World*, April 10, http://www.macworld.co.uk/news/mac/new-mac-pro-2018-latest-rumours-release-date-uk-price-features-specs-3536364/.

26 MacRumors Staff. 2019. What's next for the iPod Touch? *MacRumors*, March 19, https://www.macrumors.com/roundup/ipod-touch/.

27 Apple Newsroom. 2016. Apple celebrates one billion iPhones. July 27, https://www.apple.com/newsroom/2016/07/apple-celebrates-one-billion-iphones.html.

28 IDC. 2012. Worldwide mobile phone growth expected to drop to 1.4 % in 2012 despite continued growth of smartphones, according to IDC. *IDC*, December 4, www.idc.com/getdoc.jsp?containerId5prUS23818212#.UQSn-_J5V8E.

29 Wagstaff, J. 2012. In Asia's trend-setting cities, iPhone fatigue sets in. Reuters, January 27, news.yahoo.com/asias-trend-setting-cities-iphone-fatigue-sets-212849658-finance.html.

30 Pogue, D. 2010. Looking at the iPad from two angles. *New York Times*, March 31, www.nytimes.com/2010/04/01/technology/personaltech/01pogue.html?_r51&pagewanted5all&partner5rss&emc5rss.

31 McCracken, H. 2010. iPad. *Time*, November 11, www.time.com/time/specials/packages/article/0,28804,2029497_2030652,00.html.

32 Cellan-Jones, R. 2011. iPad 2 tablet launched by Apple's Steve Jobs. BBC News, March 2, www.bbc.co.uk/news/technology-12620077.

33 Johnson, J. 2013. Kindle Fire, Android tablets chip away at iPad marketshare. *Inquisitr*, January 2, www.inquisitr.com/465784/kindle-fire-android-tablets-chip-away-at-ipad-marketshare/#Q2bAVTfXbEpu72tB.99.

34 Inquisitr. 2015. Galaxy Tab S2 tries to kill Apple's 'already dying' iPad Air. *Inquisitr*, February 18, http://www.inquisitr.com/1853887/samsung-galaxy-tab-s2-tries-to-kill-apples-already-dying-ipad-air/.

35 Schlender. 2005. How big can Apple get?

36 Apple Inc. 2009. Apple announces Safari 4—the world's fastest and most innovative browser. Press release. February 24, www.apple.com/pr/library/2009/02/24safari.html.

37 Siracusa, J. 2008. Straight out of Compton: Google Chrome as a paragon of ambition, if not necessarily execution. *ars technica*, September 2, arstechnica.com/staff/fatbits/2008/09/straight-out-of-compton.ars.

38 Widder, B. 2014. Battle of the best browsers. *Digital Trends*, November 25, http://www.digitaltrends.com/computing/the-best-browser-internet-explorer-vs-chrome-vs-firefox-vs-safari/; https://www.netmarketshare.com/browser-market-share.aspx?options.

39 Sanders, J. 2014. iCloud Drive: Apple's appealing recipe for cloud storage. *TechRepublic*, June 5, http://www.techrepublic.com/article/icloud-drive-apples-appealing-recipe-for-cloud-storage/.

40 Cheng, R. 2012. Apple CEO: We are "extremely sorry" for Maps flap. CNET, September 28, news.cnet.com/8301-13579_3-57522196-37/apple-ceo-we-are-extremely-sorry-for-maps-flap/.

41 Cherry, S. 2004. Selling music for a song. *Spectrum Online*, December, www.spectrum.ieee.org/dec04/3857.

42 https://www.apple.com/itunes/music/.

43 Karp, H. 2014. Apple iTunes sees big drop in music sales. *Wall Street Journal*, October 24, http://www.wsj.com/articles/itunes-music-sales-down-more-than-13-this-year-1414166672.

44 Aycock, J. 2019. WSJ: Apple Music passes Spotify in U.S. paying subscribers. *Seeking Alpha*, April 5, https://seekingalpha.com/news/3448760-wsj-apple-music-passes-spotify-u-s-paying-subscribers.

45 https://www.statista.com/statistics/263794/number-of-downloads-from-the-apple-app-store/.

46 Blair, I. 2019. Mobile app download and usage statistics (2019). https://buildfire.com/app-statistics/.

47 Dilger, D.E. Editorial: The new services–Apple Arcade plays to win, but what game? *Apple Insider*, May 3, https://appleinsider.com/articles/19/05/03/editorial-the-new-services---apple-arcade-plays-to-win-but-what-game.

48 Luk, L. and D. Wakabayashi. 2015. Apple orders more than 5 million watches for initial run. *Wall Street Journal*, February 17, http://blogs.wsj.com/digits/2015/02/17/apple-orders-more-than-5-million-watches-for-initial-run/?mod=rss_Technology.

49 Cybart, N. 2015. Don't focus on Apple Watch edition pricing. *SeekingAlpha*, February 25, http://seekingalpha.com/article/2950516-dont-focus-on-apple-watch-edition-pricing.

50 Sun, L. 2018. Apple gains a foothold in the smart speaker market: A foolish tale. *USAToday*, August 18, https://www.usatoday.com/story/tech/news/2018/08/18/apple-market-share-smart-speaker-google-amazon/37458353/.

51 https://www.macrumors.com/2019/11/01/hands-on-with-apple-tv-plus/

52 Dilger, D.E. 2019. Editorial: Apple's super obvious secret–Services is software. *Apple Insider*, May 1, https://appleinsider.com/articles/19/05/01/editorial-apples-super-obvious-secret---services-is-software.

53 DoctoRx. 2015. The real importance of the Apple car project. *SeekingAlpha*, February 20, http://seekingalpha.com/article/2935276-the-real-importance-of-the-apple-car-project?auth_param=70583:1aeel0c:036a6dfaf470ca644123bac661ffb276&uprof=14.

54 Painter, L. 2017. iCar release date rumours, features and images–Apple Car rumours. *MacWorld*, March 3, http://www.macworld.co.uk/news/apple/icar-apple-car-release-date-rumours-news-caros-evidence-patents-march-2017-3425394/; Betz, B. 2019. Apple increased autonomous testing in 2018 (update). *SeekingAlpha*, February 13, https://seekingalpha.com/news/3432866-apple-increased-autonomous-testing-2018-update.

55 D.M. Martins Research. 2017. App store: Key to apple's growth target. *Seeking Alpha*, March 29, https://seekingalpha.com/article/4058813-app-store-key-apples-growth-target?app=1&auth_param=70583:1cdnih0:243d936e23ab6d685e106ccb80db6615&uprof=14.

56 The Growth Guy. 2019. What is the next big phase in Apple's growth? Subscriptions. *SeekingAlpha*, March 28, https://seekingalpha.com/article/4251532-next-big-phase-apples-growth-subscriptions.

57 Spence, E. 2019. 2019 iPhone hints suggest a lack of innovation. *Forbes*, January 14, https://www.forbes.com/sites/ewanspence/2019/01/14/apple-iphone-new-leak-rumor-innovation-camera-boring-failure/#27e8c28b2315.

58 Russolillo, S. 2013. Apple losing luster: Is it now a value stock? *Wall Street Journal*, January 14, blogs.wsj.com/marketbeat/2013/01/14/apple-growth-or-value-stock/.

59 Clifford, C. 2019. Ex-Apple exec Guy Kawasaki: I want a product that will make me 'wait like a fool outside an Apple store.' *CNBC*, March 26, https://www.cnbc.com/2019/03/26/guy-kawasaki-on-the-state-of-innovation-at-apple.html.

60 Apple, Inc. Q2 2019 Earnings Conference Call April 30, 2019 5:00 PM ET. https://seekingalpha.com/article/4258275-apple-inc-aapl-ceo-tim-cook-q2-2019-results-earnings-call-transcript?part=single.

CASE 33

JETBLUE AIRWAYS CORPORATION: GETTING OVER THE "BLUES"?*

In March 2019, JetBlue's reputation was challenged by a lawsuit by two of its flight attendants claiming that they were raped by its pilots and accusing the airline of not taking sufficient corrective actions as an organizational response.[1] This crisis emerged over and above the operating challenges that JetBlue was already facing. JetBlue had been facing challenges that included rising fuel prices, troubling technical disruptions, and declining quality of the flying experience. Prior to that, for several years in a row, JetBlue had enjoyed low fuel prices that helped increase the company's earnings,[2] but the company experienced technical issues that caused booking problems and resulted in delays, as well as bad publicity. In order to cope with the likelihood of a rise in future fuel prices, JetBlue undertook massive cost reductions by investing in cabin restyling; for instance, adding more seats to JetBlue's A320 airplanes. However, the shrinking legroom that accompanied the cabin restyling was despised by passengers, which posed a problem for an airline that had once offered customers a captivating (as opposed to a captive) flying experience.

In February 2015, Robin Hayes took charge of the company as its third chief executive. Hayes was the executive vice president of British Airways for the Americas before joining JetBlue in August 2008. Having worked for about 25 years and having extensive experience in the airline industry, Hayes was considered an optimal choice to become the third chief executive of JetBlue.

To meet the challenges, CEO Robin Hayes orchestrated various initiatives that the company was planning. Those initiatives included wider fare options, enhanced Mint services, cabin restyling, new lines of JetBlue credit cards, and partnerships with other airlines.[3] In spite of these efforts, JetBlue faced substantial headwinds, and its operating margins declined precipitously.

In promoting Robin Hayes to be the airline's new CEO, JetBlue's board signaled its readiness to focus on investor-friendly changes. With news of his selection, the share price immediately soared by 5 percent. But JetBlue loyalists who loved the company for its customers-first policies were getting more and more uncomfortable (see Exhibit 1).[4] Would JetBlue soar into clearer skies, or would it sink into the "blues" again?

The U.S. Airline Industry[5]

The U.S. airline industry consists of three primary segments: major airlines, regional airlines, and low-fare airlines. Major U.S. airlines, as defined by the Department of Transportation, are those with annual revenues of over $1 billion. Most major airlines utilize the hub-and-spoke route system. In this system, the operations are concentrated in a limited number of hub cities, while other destinations are served by providing one-stop or connecting service through the hub. Scheduled flights serve most large cities within the United States and abroad and also serve numerous smaller cities.

* This case study was prepared by Professor Naga Lakshmi Damaraju of Sonoma State University, Professor Alan B. Eisner of Pace University, and Professor Noushi Rahman of Pace University. The purpose of the case is to stimulate class discussion rather than to illustrate effective or ineffective handling of a business situation. The authors thank Professor Michael Oliff at the University of Texas at Dallas for his valuable comments on an earlier version of this case. Copyright © 2019 Alan B. Eisner.

EXHIBIT 1 JetBlue's Stock Performance versus S&P 500

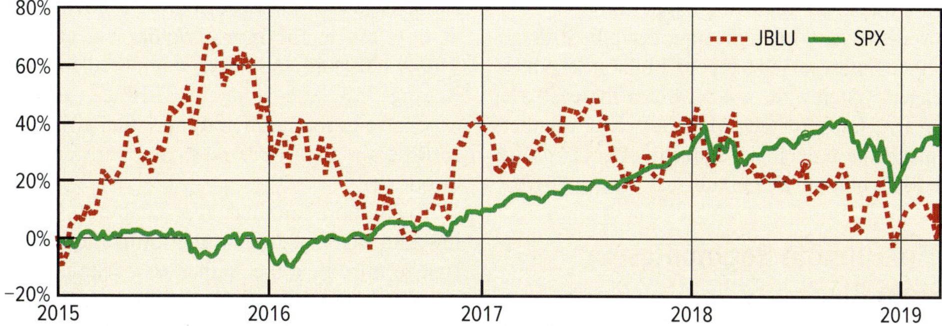

Source: Morningstar.com

Regional airlines typically operate smaller aircraft on lower-volume routes than do major airlines. They typically enter into relationships with major airlines and carry their passengers on the "spoke," that is, between a hub or larger city and a smaller city. Unlike the low-fare airlines, the regional airlines do not have an independent route system.

Deregulation of the U.S. airline industry in 1978 ushered in competition in the previously protected industry. Several low-cost, low-fare operators entered the competitive landscape that Southwest had pioneered. The low-fare airlines operate from point to point with their own route systems. The target segment of low-fare airlines is fare-conscious leisure and business travelers who might otherwise use alternative forms of transportation or not travel at all. Low-fare airlines have stimulated demand in this segment and have been successful in weaning business travelers from the major airlines. Southwest was the outstanding example; however, Southwest has since become a major airline, growing to a market capitalization of about $30 billion by 2019.

The main bases of competition in the airline industry are fare pricing, customer service, routes, flight schedules, types of aircraft, safety record and reputation, codesharing relationships, in-flight entertainment systems, and frequent-flier programs. The economic downturn in the late 1990s and the terrorist attacks on the World Trade Center and the Pentagon on September 11, 2001, severely affected the airline industry and changed the competitive relationships among carriers. The demand for air travel dropped significantly, leading to a reduction in traffic and revenue. Security concerns, security costs, and liquidity concerns increased. Lower fares and the increased capacity of the low-cost airlines created a very unprofitable environment for traditional networks. Since 2011, most of the traditional network, hub-and-spoke airlines have filed for bankruptcy or undergone financial restructuring, mergers, or consolidations.[6] With these restructurings, many of them have been able to significantly reduce labor costs, restructure debt, and generally gain a more competitive cost structure. This has enabled the major airlines to provide innovative offerings similar to those of low-cost airlines while still maintaining their alliances, frequent-flier programs, and expansive route networks. The gap between low-cost airlines and traditional network airlines has diminished drastically.

The improvements have not gone unnoticed. In 2018, airlines in the United States served a record 1 billion scheduled service passengers systemwide, a 4.8 percent increase over the previous year.[7] Unfortunately, while passenger numbers have grown, profits have declined. Industry after-tax profits for 2018 were $11.8 billion, $3.5 billion less than in 2017.[8]

JetBlue: The Humble Beginnings and the Great Rise[9]

Born in Sao Paulo, Brazil, and brought up in Salt Lake City, David Neeleman, along with June Morris, launched Utah-based Morris Air, a charter operation, in 1984. Morris Air was closely modeled after Southwest Airlines, the legendary discount airline. Neeleman considered Herb Kelleher, Southwest's founder, his idol.

While following the Southwest model, Neeleman brought his own innovations into the business. He pioneered the use of at-home reservation agents, routing calls to agents' homes to save money on office rent and infrastructure expense. He also developed the first electronic ticketing system in the airline industry. Impressed by Morris's low costs and high revenue, Southwest bought the company for $129 million in 1992. Neeleman became an executive vice president of Southwest; however, he could not adjust to Southwest's pace of doing things. By 1994, he was at odds with top executives, and he left after signing a five-year noncompete agreement.

After the noncompete agreement with Southwest Airlines ended in 1999, Neeleman launched his own airline. He raised about $130 million of capital in two weeks.[10] With such strong support from venture capitalists, JetBlue began as the highest-funded start-up airline in U.S. aviation history. JetBlue commenced operations in August 2000, with John F. Kennedy International Airport (JFK) as its primary base of operations. In 2001, JetBlue extended its operations to the West Coast with its base at Long Beach Municipal Airport, which served the Los Angeles area. In 2002, the company went public and was listed on NASDAQ as JBLU. JetBlue's stock offering was one of the hottest IPOs of the year.[11]

JetBlue had been established with the goal of being a leading low-fare passenger airline that offered customers a differentiated product and high-quality customer service on point-to-point routes. JetBlue had a geographically diversified flight schedule that included both short-haul and long-haul routes. The mission of the company, according to Neeleman, was "to bring humanity back to air travel." To stimulate demand, the airline focused on underserved markets and large metropolitan areas that had high average fares. These efforts have paid off: JetBlue now serves over 42 million customers, offering flights to over 100 cities in the United States, Caribbean, and Latin America.[12]

JetBlue was committed to keeping its costs low. To achieve this objective, the company originally operated a single-type aircraft fleet comprising Airbus A320 planes as opposed to the more popular but costly Boeing 737. The A320s had 162 seats, compared to 132 seats in the Boeing 737. According to JetBlue, the A320 was less expensive to maintain and more fuel-efficient. Since all of JetBlue's planes were new, the maintenance costs were also lower.

In addition, the single type of aircraft kept training costs low and increased personnel utilization. JetBlue was the first to introduce the "paperless cockpit," in which pilots, equipped with laptops, had ready access to flight manuals that were constantly updated at headquarters. As a result, pilots could quickly calculate the weight, balance, and takeoff performance of the aircraft instead of having to download and print the manuals to make the calculations. The paperless cockpit ensured faster takeoffs by reducing paperwork and thus helped the airline achieve quicker turnarounds and higher aircraft utilization.[13] No meals were served on the planes, and pilots had to be ready, if need be, to do cleanup work on the plane to minimize the time the aircraft was on the ground. Turnaround time was also reduced by the airline's choice of less congested airports.[14] Innovation was everywhere. For example, there were no paper tickets to lose and no mileage statements to mail to frequent fliers.

With friendly, customer service-oriented employees, new aircraft, roomier leather seats with 36 channels of free LiveTV, 100 channels of free XM satellite radio, movie channel offerings from FOXInflight, and more legroom (one row of seats was removed to create additional space), JetBlue promised its customers a distinctive flying experience, the "JetBlue experience." With virtually no incidents of passengers being denied boarding, high completion factors (99.6 percent as compared to 98.3 percent at other major airlines), the lowest incidence of delayed, mishandled, or lost bags, and the third-lowest number of customer complaints, the company was indeed setting higher standards for low-cost operations in the industry. JetBlue was voted the best domestic airline in the *Conde Nast Traveler*'s Readers' Choice Awards for five consecutive years. In addition, it earned the Passenger Service Award from *Air Transport World*.[15] In 2018, Alaska Airlines was voted the best domestic airline, pushing JetBlue to second position in the *Conde Nast Traveler's* Readers' Choice Awards.

Hitting Bumpy Air

High fuel prices, the competitive pricing environment, and other cost increases made it increasingly difficult to keep JetBlue growing and profitable. In 2005, the airline suffered its first-ever losses after its IPO. It posted net losses of $20 million and $1 million for 2005 and 2006, respectively.[16]

The ice storm on Valentine's Day of 2007 cost Neeleman his job, and it was a nightmare in JetBlue's hitherto high-flying history for more than one reason. Not only did the event destroy JetBlue's reputation for customer friendliness, but it also exposed critical weaknesses in the systems that had kept the airline's operations going. The airline's reputation hit rock bottom. To limit the damage, JetBlue announced huge compensations to customers (refunds and future flights) which were to cost the airline about $30 million. Neeleman quickly followed up with a new Customer Bill of Rights. The Customer Bill of Rights outlined self-imposed penalties for JetBlue and major rewards for its passengers if the airline experienced operational problems and could not adjust to weather-related cancelations within a "reasonable" amount of time. All these announcements and even a public apology could not restore things to normalcy. Neeleman was pushed out as CEO on May 10, 2007. Dave Barger, the president, assumed the position of chief executive officer.

Restoring JetBlue's Luster?

Under the second CEO, Dave Barger, JetBlue added several new services and embarked on capacity expansion to give the airline a new boost. In July 2007, it became the first U.S. carrier to let passengers send free email and text messages from wireless handheld devices, a technology developed through its LiveTV LLC subsidiary.[17] Later, in September 2007, it expanded to smaller cities that did not have sufficient demand for the larger planes flown by Southwest, Virgin America, and Skybus Airlines. It also introduced Embraer jets to its fleet.[18]

In 2007, JetBlue had its first full-year profit in three years as an increase in traffic and operational improvements helped compensate for skyrocketing fuel costs. However, as a result of global financial turmoil and skyrocketing fuel prices, JetBlue's profits tanked again in 2008, and the company reported a net loss of $85 million.[19] Nevertheless, the company returned to profitability in 2009. In April 2010, JetBlue successfully completed the International Air Transport Association's (IATA's) Operational Safety Audit (IOSA) and achieved IOSA registration, meeting the same highest industry benchmarks as other world-class airlines.[20]

Dave Barger was known for "being overly concerned" with customer service and comfort.[21] During Barger's tenure, JetBlue earned tributes for its customer service. However, its low-fare business model was being threatened as its costs kept going up. In April 2014, its pilots, long non-union, voted to join the Air Line Pilots Association.[22] In the wintertime the airline was again rocked by weather-driven flight cancelations. JetBlue's stock under Barger's leadership lagged behind big legacy carriers Delta Air Lines and fellow discounter Southwest Airlines. The shares were up just 9 percent since Barger had become CEO.[23] In the same period, Southwest's shares gained more than 140 percent, and the overall Bloomberg U.S. Airline index gained 49 percent.[24]

Current Leadership

The new CEO, Robin Hayes, unveiled a new pricing model that included four different pricing categories (see Exhibit 2). Under the new fare structure, passengers were able to choose which features they did or did not want included in the ticket price. At the low end of the pricing spectrum, tickets did not include a checked bag. Passengers who paid higher fares were entitled to checked bags (one bag at Blue-Plus level, two at the Blue-Flex and Mint levels) and got bonus loyalty points. At the high end of the pricing, the "Even More" seating option offered extra legroom (38 inches of pitch), expedited security clearance, and priority access to overhead bin space. With this fare structure, seats were subject to variable pricing not only by flight but also by their specific position in the aircraft. Hayes said that the airline was committed to delivering "the best travel experience for our customers. . . . JetBlue's core mission to Inspire Humanity and its differentiated model of serving underserved customers remain unchanged."[25]

EXHIBIT 2 JetBlue Fare Options

	Blue	Blue Plus	Blue Flex	Mint
Checked bags included	0	1	2	2
Carry-On (1 Bag + 1 Personal Item)	Included	Included	Included	Included
Base Trueblue points (per dollar)	3	3	3	3
Trueblue online booking bonus (per dollar)	3	4	5	3
Changes (plus any fare difference) or cancellations	$75 (fares up to $99) $100 (fares up to $149) $150 (fares up to $199) $200 (fares $200+)	$75 (fares up to $99) $100 (fares up to $149) $150 (fares up to $199) $200 (fares $200+)	Included	$200
Same-day changes	$75	$75	Included	$75
Revenue standby	$75	$75	Included	$75
Even More® Speed (expedited security)	$10/$15	$10/$15	Included	Included
Most legroom in coach	Included	Included	Included	Lie-flat seat
Free snacks and soft drinks	Included	Included	Included	Included
Fly-Fi® (broadband internet)	Included	Included	Included	Included
DIRECTV®	Included	Included	Included	Included
SiriusXM Radio®	Included	Included	Included	Included
JetBlue Features™ (movies)	Included	Included	Included	Included
Lie-flat seat, early boarding, dining options, dedicated check-in and more!	N/A	N/A	N/A	Included

Our Fare: Keep Your Options Opens. JetBlue Airways Corporation.

The substantial challenge regarding a trade-off between travel experience and profit margins remained. The question was, would JetBlue be able to hold onto its core mission and still be able to make its stakeholders happy? Investors wondered if JetBlue really had a strong and clear strategic position and coherent business model to support it. Were too many complexities being introduced into its simple model of success?

The "Interline" Model

Unlike many other carriers around the world, JetBlue chose to stay independent. The carrier relied on signing a series of "interline" agreements instead of joining an airline alliance. While the interline agreements do not fit into a strict hub-and-spoke model, they nearly amount to the same thing, allowing JetBlue passengers in New York, Boston, and San Juan to connect to destinations around the world.

In February 2007, under the leadership of Barger, JetBlue had announced its first codeshare agreement, with Cape Air. Under this agreement, JetBlue passengers from Boston's Logan Airport were carried to Cape Air's destinations throughout Cape Cod and the surrounding islands, and customers were able to purchase seats on both airlines under one reservation.[26] While Lufthansa's January 2008 acquisition of a minority equity stake (42.6 million shares of common stock, translating to 19 percent equity stake) in JetBlue did not automatically lead to any codeshare agreements, Lufthansa expected to have "operational cooperation" with JetBlue.[27]

JetBlue continued on the path of signing more interline agreements. In March 2011, it announced an interline agreement with Virgin Atlantic. Virgin Atlantic and Virgin America had some shared ownership, with Virgin Group owning 25 percent of Virgin America. Virgin America was a major competitor of JetBlue.[28] Virgin America was acquired by Alaska Airlines in 2016, with the FAA formally recognizing the two operating as one airline in January 2018.[29] In March 2013, JetBlue entered its 22nd codeshare agreement, with Qatar Airways, which followed its partnerships with the UAE-based Emirates airline, Korean Air, Air China, and the Indian carrier Jet Airways, allowing JetBlue to expand its reach far beyond the Americas, into India, China, the Middle East, and other parts of Asia.[30] Etihad Airways and El Al Israel joined this list in

January 2014 and November 2014, respectively.[31] After replacing the second CEO, Hayes continued expanding the partnership and codeshare agreements through 2018. JetBlue signed codeshare agreements with Seaborne Airlines and Azul Brazilian Airlines, and expanded the existing codeshare agreements with many airlines including Hawaiian Airlines, Cape Air, Icelandair, and AirBerlin, among others. In response to growing competition, JetBlue's expansion of codeshare agreements marked a departure from the company's initial strategy to stay strictly independent.

More Goodies for Customers

Over the years, JetBlue has constantly tried to maintain its customer-first attitude. It introduced its "Go Places" application on Facebook, which rewarded customers with TrueBlue points and special discounts so they could earn free trips faster. The "Even More" suite of products and services–including early boarding, early access, expedited security experience, and extra legroom–has been an interesting innovation. JetBlue has added more benefits for its frequent fliers through its "TrueBlue Mosaic" loyalty program. The services include a free second checked bag, a dedicated 24-hour customer service line, and bonus points, among many other offers.[32]

JetBlue became the first Federal Aviation Administration-certified carrier in the United States to utilize the new satellite-based Special Required Navigation Performance Authorization Required (RNP AR) approaches at its home base at New York's JFK airport. These unique procedures have resulted in stabilized approach paths and shorter flight times, as well as reduced noise levels, reduced greenhouse gas emissions, and increased fuel savings by as much as 18 gallons per flight.[33] Since 2017, JetBlue's operating margin has been steadily declining. More recently, the operating margins were sharply lower, hovering around 3.5 percent, by quarter three of 2018 and, notwithstanding optimistic outlooks provided by management, remained stagnant at that level in the first quarter of 2019 (see Exhibit 3).

In April 2019, JetBlue announced that it would begin offering services to London in 2021.[34] The jury is still out about whether this expansion plan will be a success story. On an immediate note, JetBlue has to weather the severe downward pressures that it is facing regarding its financial performance. First quarter 2019 results are not promising: GAAP pre-tax income plummeted to $58 million, down a staggering 48.5 percent from Q1 2018.[35]

Reinventing JetBlue

In October 2013, amid cost cutting, JetBlue had announced a fleet modernization program that included deferral of 24 Embraer aircraft from 2014-2018 to 2020-2022 so that capital expenditures could be reduced over the near term (see Exhibits 4 to 6). It also converted 18 orders with Airbus from A320 to A321 aircraft. It said its future focus would be on adding aircraft with more fuel-efficient engines. JetBlue also shrank legroom, adding 15 more seats to its Airbus A320 planes (see Exhibit 7).[36]

EXHIBIT 3 Jet Blue Operating Margin by Quarter-End

Quarter	Operating Margin
12/31/16 (end of Q4, 2016)	19.14%
03/31/17 (end of Q1, 2017)	16.03%
06/30/17 (end of Q2, 2017)	16.08%
09/30/17 (end of Q3, 2017)	15.29%
12/31/17 (end Q4, 2017)	14.16%
03/31/18 (end Q1, 2018)	13.32%
06/30/18 (end Q2, 2018)	6.68%
09/30/18 (end Q3, 2018)	3.41%
12/31/18 (end Q4, 2018)	3.76%
03/31/19 (end Q1, 2019)	3.07%

Source: JetBlue 10Q filings.

Under Hayes's leadership, JetBlue has gone through many changes to "reinvent" the company, including new interline agreements, new codesharing agreements, various strategic partnerships with other commercial airlines, launch of JetBlue credit cards, and creation of JetBlue Technology Ventures LLC to invest in emerging technologies related to the travel and hospitality industry.[37] However, the company has also faced challenges, including technical problems when customers were unable to book or modify their existing reservations amid an outage in computer systems.[38]

In May 2016, eight passengers were injured amid heavy turbulence on a JetBlue flight from San Juan to Orlando.[39] In August 2016, heavy turbulence on another JetBlue flight from Boston to Sacramento put 24 people in the hospital, including two crew members and 22 passengers.[40] By the middle of 2018, JetBlue reported a $120 million loss and provided a cautious outlook into the future. The company's stock plunged 9%.[41] More recently, in March 2019, two flight attendants formally filed a lawsuit against JetBlue, claiming that they were raped by JetBlue pilots and the airline failed to take sufficient corrective actions.[42]

Numerous factors will determine the future of JetBlue under Hayes's leadership. Will the company be able to maintain high operating margins as the fuel price starts to go up either for the depletion of existing oil supply glut or any artificial supply reduction due to emerging geo-political reasons? Will the lawsuit by the two flight attendants snowball and tarnish JetBlue's reputation in a way that customers may become less willing to fly on the airline? While JetBlue deals with these challenges, will the company be able to provide its customers a great travel experience by keeping low fares?

EXHIBIT 4 Statement of Operations

(in millions except per share data)	2018	2017	2016	2015	2014
Statements of Operations Data					
Operating revenues	$7,658	$ 7,012	$ 6,584	$ 6,416	$5,817
Operating expenses:					
Aircraft fuel and related taxes	1,899	1,363	1,074	1,348	1,912
Salaries, wages and benefits	2,044	1,887	1,698	1,540	1,294
Landing fees and other rents	420	397	357	342	321
Depreciation and amortization	491	446	393	345	320
Aircraft rent	103	100	110	122	124
Sales and marketing	294	271	263	264	231
Maintenance, materials and repairs	625	622	563	490	418
Other operating expenses	1,059	933	866	749	682
Special items	435	—	—	—	—
Total operating expenses	7,370	6,019	5,324	5,200	5,302
Operating income	288	993	1,260	1,216	515
Other income (expense)	(69)	(79)	(96)	(119)	108
Income before income taxes	219	914	1,164	1,097	623
Income tax expense (benefit)	31	(211)	437	420	222
NET INCOME	**$ 188**	**$1,125**	**$ 727**	**$ 677**	**$ 401**
Earnings per common share:					
Basic	$ 0.60	$ 3.42	$ 2.23	$ 2.15	$ 1.36
Diluted	$ 0.60	$ 3.41	$ 2.13	$ 1.98	$ 1.19
Other Financial Data:					
Operating margin	3.8%	14.2%	19.1%	19.0%	8.9%
Pre-tax margin	2.9%	13.0%	17.7%	17.1%	10.7%
Net cash provided by operating activities	$1,217	$ 1,396	$ 1,632	$ 1,598	$ 912
Net cash used in investing activities	(1,156)	(979)	(1,046)	(1,134)	(379)
Net cash provided by (used in) financing activities	113	(553)	(472)	(487)	(417)

Annual Report. JetBlue Airways Corporation, December 31, 2018.

EXHIBIT 5 Balance Sheet

(in millions, except per share data)	December 31, 2018	2017
ASSETS		
CURRENT ASSETS		
Cash and cash equivalents	$ 474	$ 303
Investment securities	413	390
Receivables, less allowance (2018-$1; 2017-$1)	211	245
Inventories, less allowance (2018-$18; 2017-$14)	78	55
Prepaid expenses and other	298	213
Total current assets	1,474	1,206
PROPERTY AND EQUIPMENT		
Flight equipment	9,525	8,980
Predelivery deposits for flight equipment	293	204
Total flight equipment and predelivery deposits, gross	9,818	9,184
Less accumulated depreciation	2,448	2,125
Total flight equipment and predelivery deposits, net	7,370	7,059
Other property and equipment	1,074	1,041
Less accumulated depreciation	461	405
Total other property and equipment, net	613	636
Assets constructed for others	561	561
Less accumulated depreciation	229	207
Total assets constructed for others, net	332	354
Total property and equipment, net	8,315	8,049
OTHER ASSETS		
Investment securities	3	2
Restricted cash	59	56
Other	575	468
Total other assets	637	526
TOTAL ASSETS	**$10,426**	**$ 9,781**

(Continued)

EXHIBIT 5 *(Continued)*

(in millions, except per share data)	December 31, 2018	2017
LIABILITIES AND STOCKHOLDERS' EQUITY		
CURRENT LIABILITIES		
Accounts payable	$ 437	$ 378
Air traffic liability	1,035	966
Accrued salaries, wages and benefits	313	313
Other accrued liabilities	324	293
Current maturities of long-term debt and capital leases	309	196
Total current liabilities	2,418	2,146
LONG-TERM DEBT AND CAPITAL LEASE OBLIGATIONS	1,361	1,003
CONSTRUCTION OBLIGATION	424	441
DEFERRED TAXES AND OTHER LIABILITIES		
Deferred income taxes	1,088	999
Air traffic liability—loyalty non-current	447	385
Other	77	75
Total deferred taxes and other liabilities	1,612	1,459
COMMITMENTS AND CONTINGENCIES		
STOCKHOLDERS' EQUITY		
Preferred stock, $0.01 par value; 25 shares authorized, none issued	—	—
Common stock, $0.01 par value; 900 shares authorized, 422 and 418 shares issued and 306 and 321 shares outstanding at 2018 and 2017, respectively	4	4
Treasury stock, at cost; 116 and 97 shares at 2018 and 2017, respectively	(1,272)	(890)
Additional paid-in capital	2,203	2,127
Retained earnings	3,679	3,491
Accumulated other comprehensive income	(3)	—
Total stockholders' equity	4,611	4,732
TOTAL LIABILITIES AND STOCKHOLDERS' EQUITY	**$10,426**	**$9,781**

Annual Report. JetBlue Airways Corporation, December 31, 2018.

EXHIBIT 6 Operating Statistics

	2018	2017	2016	2015	2014
Operating Statistics:					
Revenue passengers (thousands)	42,150	40,038	38,263	35,101	32,078
Revenue passenger miles (millions)	50,790	47,240	45,619	41,711	37,813
Available seat miles (ASMs) (millions)	59,881	56,007	53,620	49,258	44,994
Load factor	84.8%	84.3%	85.1%	84.7%	84.0%
Aircraft utilization (hours per day)	11.8	11.7	12.0	11.9	11.8
Average fare	$ 175.11	$ 168.88	$ 166.74	$ 167.89	$ 166.57
Yield per passenger mile (cents)	14.53	14.31	13.99	14.13	14.13
Passenger revenue per ASM (cents)	12.33	12.07	11.90	11.96	11.88
Operating revenue per ASM (cents)	12.79	12.52	12.28	13.03	12.93
Operating expense per ASM (cents)	12.31	10.75	9.93	10.56	11.78
Operating expense per ASM, excluding fuel	8.34	8.25	7.88	7.82	7.53
Departures	366,619	353,681	337,302	316,505	294,800
Average stage length (miles)	1,096	1,072	1,093	1,092	1,088
Average number of operating aircraft during period	246.8	233.5	218.9	207.9	196.2
Average fuel cost per gallon, including fuel taxes	$ 2.24	$ 1.72	$ 1.41	$ 1.93	$ 2.99
Fuel gallons consumed (millions)	849	792	760	700	639
Average number of full-time equivalent Crewmembers	17,766	17,118	15,696	14,537	13,280

Annual Report. JetBlue Airways Corporation, December 31, 2018.

EXHIBIT 7 Aircraft Inventory and Orders

Inventory

Aircraft	Seating Capacity	Owned	Capital Leased	Operating Leased	Total	Average Age in Years
Airbus A320	162/150[1][2]	115	4	11	130	13.3
Airbus A321	200/159[1][3]	60	2	1	63	2.5
Embraer E190	100	30	—	30	60	10.2
		205	**6**	**42**	**253**	9.8

(1) During 2018, we completed the buyout of two of our aircraft leases.
(2) Our Airbus A320 with a restyled cabin configuration has a seating capacity of 162 seats. Our Airbus A320 with a classic cabin configuration has a seating capacity of 150 seats.
(3) Our Airbus A321 with a single cabin layout has a seating capacity of 200 seats. Our Airbus A321 with our Mint® premium service has a seating capacity of 159 seats.

(Continued)

EXHIBIT 7 *(Continued)*

Orders

Year	Airbus A321neo	Airbus A220	Total
2019	13	—	13
2020	15	1	16
2021	16	6	22
2022	15	8	23
2023	14	19	33
2024	12	22	34
2025	—	4	4
TOTAL	**85**	**60**	**145**

Note: Airbus A220-300 aircraft was previously called the Bombardier CS300. JetBlue plans to phase in the A220-300 as a replacement for existing Embraer E190 aircraft from 2020 to 2025.

Annual Report. JetBlue Airways Corporation, December 31, 2018.

ENDNOTES

1. Stack, L. 2019. Lawsuit says JetBlue pilots raped 2 flight attendants. *New York Times*, March 23.
2. Stynes, T. 2016. Low fuel costs help JetBlue's profit rise. *Wall Street Journal* July 26. from www.wsj.com/articles/low-fuel-costs-help-jetblues-profit-rise-1469545330.
3. JetBlue. 2016. Jet Blue Investor Day Presentation, December 13, blueir.investproductions.com/~/media/Files/J/Jetblue-IR-V2/reports-and-presentations/2016-investor-day-12-12-2016.pdf.
4. Tuttle, B. 2014. A new era has begun for JetBlue, and travelers will hate it. *Time,* November 19, www.time.com/money/3595360/jetblue-fees-legroom-hates/.
5. This section draws heavily on the SEC filings of JetBlue for the years 2008 and 2009. Other sources include Zellner, W. 2003. Look who's buzzing the discounters. *BusinessWeek,* November 24; Zellner, W. 2004. Folks are finally packing their bags. *BusinessWeek,* January 12; and a joint study by A. T. Kearney and the Society of British Aerospace Companies, www.atkearney.com/shared_res/pdf/Emerging_Airline_Industry_S.pdf.6.
6. Peterson, K. and M. Daily. 2011. American Airlines files for bankruptcy. Reuters, November 29, www.reuters.com/article/2011/11/29/us-americanairlines-idUSTRE7AS0T220111129.
7. https://www.bts.gov/newsroom/2018-traffic-data-us-airlines-and-foreign-airlines-us-flights.
8. https://www.bts.gov/newsroom/2018-annual-and-4th-quarter-us-airline-financial-data.
9. This section draws heavily on Gajilan, A.T. 2004. The amazing JetBlue. *Fortune Small Business,* www.fortune/smallbusiness/articles/0.15114,444298-2,00.html.
10. Gale/Cengage Learning. n.d. JetBlue Airways Corporation. In International directory of company histories, galenet.galegroup.com.
11. CNNMoney. 2002. JetBlue IPO soars. April 12, money.cnn.com/2002/04/12/markets/ipo/jetblue.
12. http://blueir.investproductions.com/investor-relations/investor-overview.
13. BusinessWeek. 2003. WEBSMART50. November 24: 92.
14. Bay, W. and D. Neeleman. 2002. JetBlue reaches new heights in airline industry (interview with David Neeleman by Willow Bay of *CNN Business Unusual*). Aired June 23, www.cnn.com/TRANSCRIPTS/0206/23/bun.00.html.
15. JetBlue. SEC filings, 2006.
16. JetBlue. SEC filings, 2007 and 2008.
17. Associated Press. 2007. N.Y. discount carrier JetBlue to detail wireless email plans. *Toronto Star,* July 6.
18. Ray, S. 2007. Repaired planes boost JetBlue expansion plan. *Bloomberg News,* September 1.
19. JetBlue. SEC filings, 2008ñ2010.
20. From company press releases, 2010. JetBlue completes top international safety audit. April 19, www.jetblue.com.
21. Tuttle, B. 2014. A new era has begun for JetBlue, and travelers will hate it. *Time,* November 19, www.time.com/money/3595360/jetblue-fees-legroom-hates/.
22. Nicas, J. 2014. Jetblue's pilots vote to unionize. *Wall Street Journal,* April 22, www.wsj.com/articles/SB10001424052702304049904579517911131169286.
23. Carey, S. 2014. JetBlue CEO Barger to retire in February. *Wall Street Journal,* September 18, www.wsj.com/articles/jetblue-ceo-barger-to-retire-in-february-1411072958.
24. Schlangenstein & Sasso, https://www.bloomberg.com/news/articles/2016-09-07/airline-shares-jump-as-southwest-eases-fears-about-overcapacity.
25. Schaal, D. 2014. The new JetBlue will have more bag fees and less legroom. November 19, http://skift.com/2015/01/29/jetblue-to-unveil-bag-fees-and-new-types-of-fares-in-the-second-quarter/.
26. Compart, A. 2007. JetBlue's pact with Cape Air is airline's first codeshare deal. February 19, www.travelweekly.com/Travel-News/Airline-News/JetBlue-s-pact-with-Cape-Air-is-airline-s-first-codeshare-deal/.
27. Associated Press. 2007. Lufthansa pays $300 million for JetBlue stake.
28. Associated Press. 2011. JetBlue partners with Virgin Atlantic; and Blank, D. 2011. JetBlue and Virgin Atlantic (finally) announce interline agreement. *Online Travel Review,* March 22, www.onlinetravelreview.com/2011/03/22/jetblue-and-virgin-atlantic-finally-announce-interline-agreement/.
29. https://blog.alaskaair.com/alaska-airlines/company-news/virgin-america-alaska-single-operating-certificate/.
30. Unnikrishnan, M. 2012. JetBlue signs codeshare agreement with Air China. *Aviation Week,* June 12, www.aviationweek.com/Article.aspx?id=/article-xml/awx_06_12_2012_p0-467058.xml.
31. Associated Press. 2014. JetBlue, Etihad Airlines announce partnership. *New Zealand Herald,* January 22; and JetBlue Airways and El Al Israel Airlines sign codeshare agreement, November 21,

2014, www.heritagefl.com/story/2014/11/21/features/jetblue-airways-and-el-al-israel-airlines-sign-codeshare-agreement/3600.html.

32. JetBlue. Press releases.
33. Drum, B. 2012. JetBlue Airways becomes first FAA-certified carrier to fly special (non-public) RNP AR approaches with Airbus A320s at New York's JFK Airport. June 20, http://worldairlinenews.com/2012/06/20/jetblue-airways-becomes-first-faa-certified-carrier-to-fly-special-non-public-rnp-ar-approaches-with-airbus-a320s-at-new-yorks-jfk-airport/.
34. Wichter, Z. 2019. JetBlue plans service to London in 2021. *New York Times,* April 21.
35. Jet Blue Press Release. 2019. JetBlue announces first quarter 2019 results. April 23, http://blueir.investproductions.com/investor-relations/press-releases/2019/04-23-2019-120038557.
36. Tuttle, B. 2014. A new era has begun for JetBlue, and travelers will hate it. *Time,* November 19, www.time.com/money/3595360/jetblue-fees-legroom-hates/.
37. JetBlue Annual Report, 2015.
38. Reuters. 2016. Here's why Southwest and JetBlue were having booking problems. *Fortune,* October 17, http://fortune.com/2016/10/17/southwest-jetblue-booking-system/?iid=sr-link7.
39. Reuters. 2016. Heavy turbulence on a JetBlue flight put 24 people in the hospital. Fortune, August 12, http://fortune.com/2016/08/12/jetblue-turbulence-injuries/?iid=sr-link5.
40. Ibid.
41. Associated Press. 2018. JetBlue shares drop after airline reports $120 million loss. July 24.
42. Stack, L. 2019. Lawsuit says JetBlue pilots raped 2 flight attendants. *New York Times,* March 23.

APPENDIX A

GLOSSARY OF KEY TERMS USED

aircraft utilization The average number of block hours operated per day per aircraft for the total fleet of aircraft.

available seat-miles The number of seats available for passengers multiplied by the number of miles the seats are flown.

average fare The average one-way fare paid per flight segment by a revenue passenger.

average stage length The average number of miles flown per flight.

break-even load factor The passenger load factor that will result in operating revenues being equal to operating expenses, assuming constant revenue per passenger-mile and expenses.

load factor The percentage of aircraft seating capacity that is actually utilized (revenue passenger-miles divided by available seat-miles).

operating expense per available seat-mile Operating expenses divided by available seat-miles.

operating revenue per available seat-mile Operating revenues divided by available seat-miles.

passenger revenue per available seat-mile Passenger revenue divided by available seat-miles.

revenue passenger-miles The number of miles flown by revenue passengers.

revenue passengers The total number of paying passengers flown on all flight segments.

yield per passenger-mile The average amount one passenger pays to fly one mile.

CASE 34

FORD: AN AUTO COMPANY IN TRANSITION*

In January 2019, the Ford Motor Company celebrated as the F-Series line of pickups became the top-selling trucks in the United States for the 42nd consecutive year. This line of trucks also marked 37 years as the best-selling vehicle in the United States overall. In 2018, the F-Series, which included the Super Duty and the F-150 Raptor, sold 909,330 vehicles–just 30,181 units short of the all-time record set in 2004.[1] Jim Farley, Ford executive vice president and president, Global Markets, pointed to the F-Series as a "juggernaut" that "leads the world in sales, capability, and smart technology, setting the bar others follow."[2] But would truck sales alone help the increasingly depressed auto market, where the overall industry had already seen a drop in sales of 2.6 percent in the first months of 2019? This was the biggest decline since the recession of 2009, and there appeared to be no relief in sight.[3] Something would have to change. Bold leadership was needed.

The ability to anticipate customers' needs was crucial to any company's long-term success, but it was especially important in the capital-intensive, consumer-driven, globally competitive automobile industry. As the major players from Asia, Europe, and the United States jockeyed for position in the sales of traditional trucks and cars, smaller, more innovative companies such as Tesla, Elio Motors,[4] and start-up Faraday Futures were creating concept cars that addressed consumers' interests in alternative fuels, low operational costs, and self-driving autonomous designs that promised to leave the passenger free to use in-transit time for other more productive pursuits. The auto industry was going through a "significant secular change" that was hard to predict. The trend seemed to be going toward less car ownership and, as the industry became more niche focused, rapid technological changes meant it was essential to be able to refresh the product portfolio rapidly in order to maintain market share.[5]

Responding to this trend, Mark Fields, CEO of Ford from 2014 to 2017, had said Ford would be using innovation "not only to create advanced new vehicles but also to help change the way the world moves by solving today's growing global transportation challenges."[6] Self-driving cars were reported to be coming as early as 2019 to the global roadways; and Ford Motor Company had made a commitment to this business, testing its fleet of 100 autonomous cars in Florida, Pennsylvania, and Michigan.[7] But in 2019 Ford was still at least two years away from releasing a long-range electric vehicle while General Motors (GM) had already brought the Bolt to market.

Given the increasing disruption in the industry, and the obligation to return value to understandably concerned investors, Ford had some significant decisions to make, one of which was selecting the right leader for this business. Executive Chairman Bill Ford had said "this is a time of unprecedented change. And a time of great change, in my mind, requires a transformational leader."[8] Ford was feeling pressure from investors, who had seen the stock price steadily decline from a high of over 17.50 in 2014 to a low of under 10.00 in 2017. In 2017, Ford had asked Fields to resign and promoted Jim Hackett to the CEO position. Hackett, previously head of Ford Smart Mobility LLC–a subsidiary of Ford formed to accelerate the company's plans to design, build, grow, and invest in emerging mobility services such as autonomous vehicles–believed in the need for transformation. Hackett had said "breakthrough technologies are transforming nearly every aspect of the vehicles we build and how people use them, demanding a rethink of how we design transportation systems."[9] But Hackett was Ford's third CEO in five years. Why was this job so difficult?

Fields had gotten the CEO job in July 2014 after the retirement of Alan Mulally, widely hailed as one of the "five most significant corporate leaders of the last decade," and architect of Ford's eight-year turnaround from the brink of bankruptcy in 2006.[10] It was Mulally who had created the vision that drove Ford's revitalization–"ONE Ford." The ONE Ford message was intended to communicate consistency across all departments, all segments of the company, requiring people to work together as one team, with one plan, and one goal: "an exciting viable Ford delivering profitable growth for all."[11] Mulally worked to create a culture of accountability and collaboration across the company. His vision was to leverage Ford's unique automotive knowledge and assets to build cars and trucks that people wanted and valued, and he managed to arrange the financing necessary to pay for it all. The 2009 economic downturn that caused a financial catastrophe for U.S. automakers trapped General Motors and Chrysler in emergency government loans, but Ford was able to avoid bankruptcy because of Mulally's actions.

Mulally had groomed Mark Fields as his successor since 2012, instilling confidence among the company's stakeholders that Ford would be able to continue to be profitable

* This case study was prepared by Professor Pauline Assenza of Western Connecticut State University; Professor Helaine J. Korn of Baruch College, City University of New York; Professor Naga Lakshmi Damaraju of the Sonoma State University; and Professor Alan B. Eisner of Pace University. The purpose of the case is to stimulate class discussion rather than to illustrate effective or ineffective handling of a business situation. Copyright © 2019 Alan B. Eisner.

once Mulally stepped down. Even with this preparation, CEO Fields had faced an industry affected by general economic conditions over which he had little control and a changing technological and sociocultural environment where consumer preferences were difficult to predict. And rivals were coming from unexpected directions. Fields had to be able to anticipate and address numerous challenges as he tried to position the company for continued success. Ultimately, Fields was not able to do so.

Attempts at repositioning Ford had been under way for many years. In the 1990s, former CEO Jacques Nasser had emphasized acquisitions to reshape Ford, but day-to-day business activities were ignored in the process. When Nasser left in October 2001, Bill Ford, great-grandson of company founder Henry Ford, took over and emphasized innovation as a core strategy to reshape Ford. In an attempt to stem the downward slide at Ford, and perhaps to jump-start a turnaround, Bill Ford recruited industry outsider Alan Mulally, who was elected president and chief executive officer of Ford on September 5, 2006. Mulally, former head of commercial airplanes at Boeing, was expected to steer the struggling automaker out of the problems of falling market share and financial losses. Mulally created his vision of ONE Ford to reshape the company and in 2009 finally achieved profitability. Mulally was able to sustain this success past the initial stages of his tenure, and maintained profitability up until his retirement in June 2014.

CEO Mark Fields took over, but challenging global conditions meant 2014 year-end profit saw a 56 percent drop from 2013—meaning Fields had work to do. In 2015, Fields continued the focus on ONE Ford, highlighting the idea that Ford could achieve profitable growth for all. By successfully launching 16 new global products, opening the last of 10 new plants to support growth in Asia Pacific, and seeing profitable global business unit performance in every region except South America, Ford had the most profitable year ever in 2015, and 2016 was just slightly lower, and the second best ever.

But in 2016 CEO Mark Fields decided to restructure, creating a new focus and expanding the company's scope from vehicles to "mobility," through business model innovation. In the 2016 income statement, there appeared an "Other" revenue item for the first time, representing the newly operational Ford Smart Mobility LLC, a subsidiary formed to design, build, grow, and invest in emerging mobility services. Designed to compete like a start-up company, Ford Smart Mobility LLC was planning to focus solely on mobility services, and collaborate with start-ups and tech companies as needed to pursue opportunities. Jim Hackett was chosen to head up this new division. Hackett, formerly the CEO of Steelcase, a Michigan furniture company, had been credited with developing that business into a global leader, transitioning it from a traditional furniture manufacturer into an industry innovator.

CEO Fields reminded investors of the company's long-term legacy, pointing to a history going back to founder Henry Ford of "democratizing technology,"—not just making products for people who could afford luxury vehicles, but using technology to solve problems of mobility and access, and providing not only products but also transportation services that made people's lives better.[12] So, although Ford would always sell cars and trucks, it was also making big bets in autonomous technology (self-driving cars), electric vehicles, and other transportation services such as urban mobility solutions via ride-sharing, bike-sharing, and customized interior vehicle experiences serving multiple customer needs.

In 2019, CEO Hackett was sustaining this vision while migrating from a production line focus on multiple vehicle types to one where each team was dedicated to a specific product line and expected to "understand every small detail of the underlying product and customers they serve."[13] This was no longer ONE Ford. Under Hackett, Ford was planning to execute in four strategic areas:

- Develop a winning portfolio that provides products customers want in the markets where we know we can win.
- Make propulsion choices that create clean-running cars without sacrificing power, style, and performance by creating an entire portfolio of electric vehicles.
- Build a viable autonomous vehicle business by bringing components of autonomous technology together, designing products such as ride-hailing and delivery services that are centered on the needs of humans, providing solutions for city leaders and transportation planners, as well as vehicle owners.
- Create a set of mobility experiences that encourages freedom of movement—orchestrating millions of connections across a digital network accessible to all, equipping our vehicles with software and services that connect to the smart world around them, and addressing the problems of congested cities and roads.

This vision of a seismic shift in personal transportation was fully supported and even driven by Ford's executive chairman Bill Ford, who had championed the concept of increased mobility back when the only things to invest in were "parking and municipal ticketing solutions."[14] Now, in 2019, Bill Ford was supporting the company's movement beyond selling vehicles to investing heavily in mobility services. As the initial architect of this shift, Bill Ford predicted the company could make increased profit margins on new services, more than double what it had traditionally made selling cars and trucks, but the ultimate goal, beyond making money, was to improve people's lives. In doing so, Bill Ford would be protecting his great-grandfather's legacy.[15]

History of the Ford Motor Company

At the beginning of 2019, Ford Motor Company, based in Dearborn, Michigan, had about 199,000 employees and 61 plants worldwide. It manufactured or distributed the automotive brands Ford and Lincoln across six continents, and provided financial services via Ford Motor Credit. It was also aggressively pursuing emerging opportunities with investments in electrification, autonomous vehicles, and consumer mobility. It was the only company in the industry where the company name still honored the vision and innovative legacy of its founder, Henry Ford.

American engineer and industrial icon Henry Ford had been a true innovator. He did not invent the automobile or the assembly line, but through his ability to recognize opportunities, articulate a vision, and inspire others to join him in fulfilling that vision, he was responsible for making significant changes in the trajectory of the automobile industry and even in the history of manufacturing in America. Starting with the invention of the self-propelled Quadricycle in 1896, Ford had developed other vehicles—primarily racing cars—which attracted a series of interested investors. In 1903, 12 investors backed him in the creation of a company to build and sell horseless carriages, and Ford Motor Company was born.

Starting with the Model A, the company had produced a series of successful vehicles, but in 1908 Henry Ford wanted to create a better, cheaper "motorcar for the great multitude."[16] Working with a group of hand-picked employees, he designed the Model T. The design was so successful, and demand so great that Ford decided to investigate methods for increasing production and lowering costs. Borrowing concepts from other industries, by 1913 Ford had developed a moving assembly line for automobile manufacture. Although the work was so demanding that it created high employee turnover, the production process was significantly more efficient, reducing chassis assembly time from 12 ½ hours to 2 hours 40 minutes. In 1904, Ford expanded into Canada, and by 1925 Ford had assembly plants in Europe, Argentina, South Africa, and Australia. By the end of 1919, Ford was producing 50 percent of all the cars in the United States, and the assembly line disruption in the industry had led to the demise of most of Ford's rivals.[17]

The Automotive Industry and Ford Leadership Changes

The automotive industry in the United States had always been a highly competitive, cyclical business. By 2019 there was a wide variety of product offerings from a growing number of manufacturers, including the electric car lineup from Tesla Motors, self-styled as "not just an automaker, but also a technology and design company with a focus on energy innovation."[18] The total number of cars and trucks sold to retail buyers, or "industry demand," varied substantially from year to year depending on general economic situations, the cost of purchasing and operating cars and trucks, and the availability of credit and fuel. Because cars and trucks were durable items, consumers could wait to replace them and, based on the most recent report, the average age of light vehicles on U.S. roads was over 12 years, with domestic nameplate vehicles 3.6 years older than foreign ones.[19] Partly due to this, replacement demand was forecasted to stay fairly flat. Any increase in sales would be aided by an improvement in the general economic situation, reduced gasoline prices, and lower interest rates for car loans. However, sales in U.S. markets had not belonged only to U.S. manufacturers for some time.

In the United States, Ford's market share had dropped over time—from almost 25 percent in 1999 to 14.4 percent in 2018,[20] with major blows to market share in the light-vehicle segment. Going into 2019, Ford claimed the third spot in the U.S. market, just behind Toyota (see Exhibit 1).

Originally dominated by the "Big 3" Detroit-based car companies—Ford, General Motors, and Fiat/Chrysler—competition in the United States had intensified since the 1980s, when Japanese carmakers began gaining a foothold in the market. To counter the problem of being viewed as foreign, Japanese companies Nissan, Toyota, and Honda had set up production facilities in the United States and thus gained acceptance from American consumers. Production quality and lean production were judged to be the major weapons that Japanese carmakers used to gain an advantage over American carmakers. Starting in 2003, because of innovative production processes that yielded better quality for American consumers, Toyota vehicles had unquestionably become "a better value proposition" than Detroit's products.[21]

Back in 1999, Ford Motor Company had been in good shape, having attained a U.S. market share of 24.8 percent, and had seen profits reach a remarkable $7.2 billion ($5.86 per share) with pre-tax income of $11 billion. At that time people even speculated that Ford would soon overtake General Motors as the world's number-one automobile manufacturer.[22] But soon Toyota, through its innovative technology, management philosophy of continuous improvement, and cost arbitrage due to its presence in multiple geographic locations, was threatening to overtake GM and Ford.

In addition, unfortunately, the profits at Ford in 1999 had come at the expense of not investing in Ford's future. Jacques Nasser, the CEO at that time, had focused on corporate acquisition and diversification rather than new vehicle development. By the time Chairman Bill Ford had stepped in and fired Nasser in 2001, Ford was seeing decline in both market share and profitability. By 2005, market share had dropped to 18.6 percent and Ford had skidded out of control, losing $1.6 billion (pre-tax) in North American profits. It was obvious Ford needed a change in order to adapt and survive. Since taking the CEO position in 2001, Bill Ford had tried several times to find a qualified successor, claiming that to undertake major changes in Ford's dysfunctional culture, an outsider might be more qualified than even the most proficient auto industry insider.[23]

In 2006, Alan Mulally was selected as the new CEO and was expected to accomplish "nothing less than

EXHIBIT 1 Sales and Share of U.S. Total Market by Manufacturer, 2018

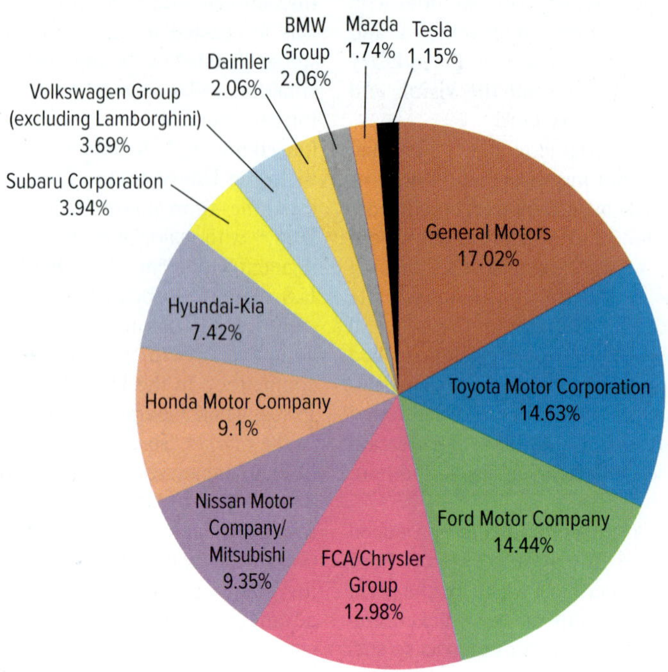

Source: statista.com

undoing a strongly entrenched management system put into place by Henry Ford II almost 40 years ago"–a system of regional fiefdoms around the world that had sapped the company's ability to compete in a global industry, a system that Chairman Bill Ford could not or would not unwind by himself.[24]

Mulally set his own priorities for fixing Ford: Ford needed to pay more attention to cutting costs and transforming the way it did business than to traditional measurements such as market share.[25] The vision was to have a smaller and more profitable Ford. The overall strategy was to use restructuring as a tool to obtain operating profitability at lower volume and create a mix of products that better appealed to the market.

By 2011, Ford had closed or sold a quarter of its plants and cut its global workforce by more than a third. It also slashed labor and healthcare costs, plowing the money back into the design of some well-received new products, like the Ford Fusion sedan and Ford Edge crossover. This put Ford in a better position to compete, especially taking into consideration that General Motors and Chrysler had filed for bankruptcy in 2009, and Toyota had recently announced a major recall of its vehicles for "unintended acceleration" problems.[26] Ford's sales grew at double the rate of the rest of the industry in 2010, but entering 2011 its rivals' problems seemed to be in the rearview mirror, and General Motors, especially, was on the rebound.

Mulally had set three priorities–first, to determine the brands Ford would offer; second to be "best in class for all its vehicles"; and third to make sure that those vehicles would be accepted and adapt[able] by consumers around the globe: "If a model was developed for the U.S. market, it needed to be adaptable to car buyers in other countries."[27] Mulally said that the "real opportunity going forward is to integrate and leverage our Ford assets around the world" and decide on the best mix of brands in the company's portfolio.[28] The "best mix of brands" was addressed going into 2011. Brands such as Jaguar, Land Rover, Aston Martin, and Volvo were all sold off, and the Mercury brand was discontinued. Ford also had an equity interest in Mazda Motor Corporation, which it reduced substantially in 2010, retaining only a 3.5 percent share of ownership; it was finally sold off in 2015. This left the company with only the Ford and Lincoln brands, but the Lincoln offerings had struggled against Cadillac and other rivals for the luxury car market.

In 2014, thanks to Mulally's vision and perseverance, Ford maintained its position. Ford had introduced 24 vehicles around the world, but although still profitable, net income was down $4 billion from 2013. Even though Ford maintained its number two position in Europe, behind Volkswagen, major losses had occurred in that sector, primarily due to Russian economic instabilities. South America had also seen losses due to currency devaluation and changing government rules. In addition, Ford's push into Asia-Pacific, specifically China, was behind schedule. North American sales, while still strong, had resulted in operating margin reductions due to recalls and costs associated with the relaunch of the F-150. The one bright spot was in financial services. Ford Motor Credit, the financing company that loans people money to buy new cars, saw its best results since 2011.[29]

Going into 2015 the financials, especially the balance sheet, appeared strong and because of this the company was able to reinstate and subsequently boost the dividend to shareholders, rewarding those investors who had stayed the course. However, this did not last. From 2016 into 2019, the financials began to falter. CEO Hackett admitted 2018 was a "disappointing year."[30] (see Exhibits 2 and 3.)

Starting in 2016, CEO Fields had begun restructuring, and the cash flow reflected this (see Exhibit 4). The forecast for 2017 had projected total automotive operating cash flow remaining positive through 2018, with the overall cash balance expected to stay at or above the company's minimum target of $20 billion.[31] This did not happen.

However, Ford had made good use of cash in the past, most recently acquiring the iconic Michigan Central Station in Detroit's historic Corktown neighborhood. Chairman Bill Ford planned to transform this former railroad station into the centerpiece of a vibrant new campus "where Ford and its partners will work on autonomous and electric vehicle businesses, and design solutions for a transportation operating system that makes mobility convenient and accessible."[32]

EXHIBIT 2 Ford Motor Company and Subsidiaries: Consolidated Income Statement

	For the years ended December 31,		
	2016	**2017**	**2018**
Revenues			
Automotive	$141,546	$145,653	**$148,294**
Ford Credit	10,253	11,113	**12,018**
Mobility	1	10	**26**
Total revenues	151,800	156,776	**160,338**
Costs and expenses			
Cost of sales	126,195	131,321	**136,269**
Selling, administrative, and other expenses	10,972	11,527	**11,403**
Ford Credit interest, operating, and other expenses	8,847	9,047	**9,463**
Total costs and expenses	146,014	151,895	**157,135**
Interest expense on Automotive debt	894	1,133	**1,171**
Interest expense on Other debt	57	57	**57**
Other income/(loss), net	169	3,267	**2,247**
Equity in net income of affiliated companies	1,780	1,201	**123**
Income before income taxes	6,784	8,159	**4,345**
Provision for/(Benefit from) income taxes	2,184	402	**650**
Net income	4,600	7,757	**3,695**
Less: Income/(Loss) attributable to noncontrolling interests	11	26	**18**
Net income attributable to Ford Motor Company	$ 4,589	$ 7,731	**$ 3,677**
EARNINGS PER SHARE ATTRIBUTABLE TO FORD MOTOR COMPANY COMMON AND CLASS B STOCK			
Basic income	$ 1.16	$ 1.94	$0.93
Diluted income	1.15	1.93	0.92

Note: Figures in millions, except per-share amounts; year-end December 31.

Source: Annual Report. Ford Motor Company, December 31, 2018.

EXHIBIT 3 Ford Motor Company and Subsidiaries: Sector Balance Sheets

	December 31, 2017	December 31, 2018
ASSETS		
Cash and cash equivalents	$ 18,492	**$ 16,718**
Marketable securities	20,435	**17,233**
Ford Credit finance receivables, net	52,210	**54,353**
Trade and other receivables, less allowances of $412 and $94	10,599	**11,195**
Inventories	11,176	**11,220**
Other assets	3,889	**3,930**
Total current assets	116,801	**114,649**
Ford Credit finance receivables, net	56,182	**55,544**
Net investment in operating leases	28,235	**29,119**
Net property	35,327	**36,178**
Equity in net assets of affiliated companies	3,085	**2,709**
Deferred income taxes	10,762	**10,412**
Other assets	8,104	**7,929**
Total assets	$258,496	**$256,540**
LIABILITIES		
Payables	$ 23,282	**$ 21,520**
Other liabilities and deferred revenue	19,697	**20,556**
Automotive debt payable within one year	3,356	**2,314**
Ford Credit debt payable within one year	48,265	**51,179**
Total current liabilities	94,600	**95,569**
Other liabilities and deferred revenue	24,711	**23,588**
Automotive long-term debt	12,575	**11,233**
Ford Credit long-term debt	89,492	**88,887**
Other long-term debt	599	**600**
Deferred income taxes	815	**597**
Total liabilities	222,792	**220,474**
Redeemable noncontrolling interest	98	**100**
EQUITY		
Common Stock, par value $.01 per share (4,000 million shares issued of 6 billion authorized)	40	**40**
Class B Stock, par value $.01 per share (71 million shares issued of 530 million authorized)	1	**1**
Capital in excess of par value of stock	21,843	**22,006**
Retained earnings	21,906	**22,668**
Accumulated other comprehensive income/(loss) (Note 21)	(6,959)	**(7,366)**
Treasury stock	(1,253)	**(1,417)**
Total equity attributable to Ford Motor Company	35,578	**35,932**
Equity attributable to non-controlling interests	28	**34**
Total equity	35,606	**35,966**
Total liabilities and equity	$258,496	**$256,540**

Note: Figures in millions.

Source: Annual Report. Ford Motor Company, December 31, 2018.

EXHIBIT 4 Ford Motor Company and Subsidiaries: Sector Statements of Cash Flows

	For the years ended December 31,		
	2016	**2017**	**2018**
Cash flows from operating activities			
Net income	$ 4,600	$ 7,757	**$ 3,695**
Depreciation and tooling amortization	9,023	9,122	**9,280**
Other amortization	(306)	(669)	**(972)**
Provision for credit and insurance losses	672	717	**609**
Pension and other postretirement employee benefits ("OPEB") expense/(income)	2,667	(608)	**400**
Equity investment (earnings)/losses in excess of dividends received	(178)	240	**206**
Foreign currency adjustments	283	(403)	**529**
Net (gain)/loss on changes in investments in affiliates	(139)	(7)	**(42)**
Stock compensation	210	246	**191**
Net change in wholesale and other receivables	(1,449)	(836)	**(2,408)**
Provision for deferred income taxes	1,473	(350)	**(197)**
Decrease/(Increase) in accounts receivable and other assets	(2,855)	(2,297)	**(2,239)**
Decrease/(Increase) in inventory	(803)	(970)	**(828)**
Increase/(Decrease) in accounts payable and accrued and other liabilities	6,595	6,089	**6,781**
Other	57	65	**17**
Net cash provided by/(used in) operating activities	19,850	18,096	**15,022**
Cash flows from investing activities			
Capital spending	(6,992)	(7,049)	**(7,785)**
Acquisitions of finance receivables and operating leases	(56,007)	(59,354)	**(62,924)**
Collections of finance receivables and operating leases	38,834	44,641	**50,880**
Purchases of marketable and other securities	(31,428)	(27,567)	**(17,140)**
Sales and maturities of marketable and other securities	29,354	29,898	**20,527**
Settlements of derivatives	825	100	**358**
Other	112	(29)	**(177)**
Net cash provided by/(used in) investing activities	(25,302)	(19,360)	**(16,261)**
Cash flows from financing activities			
Cash dividends	(3,376)	(2,584)	**(2,905)**
Purchases of common stock	(145)	(131)	**(164)**
Net changes in short-term debt	3,864	1,229	**(2,819)**
Proceeds from issuance of long-term debt	45,961	45,801	**50,130**
Principal payments on long-term debt	(38,797)	(40,770)	**(44,172)**
Other	(107)	(151)	**(192)**
Net cash provided by/(used in) financing activities	7,400	3,394	**(122)**
Effect of exchange rate changes on cash, cash equivalents, and restricted cash	(265)	489	**(370)**
Net increase/(decrease) in cash, cash equivalents, and restricted cash	$ 1,683	$ 2,619	**$ (1,731)**
Cash, cash equivalents, and restricted cash at January 1	$ 14,336	$ 16,019	**$ 18,638**
Net increase/(decrease) in cash, cash equivalents, and restricted cash	1,683	2,619	**(1,731)**
Cash, cash equivalents, and restricted cash at December 31	$ 16,019	$ 18,638	**$ 16,907**

Note: Figures in millions; year-end December 31.

Source: Annual Report. Ford Motor Company, December 31, 2018.

The hope was that Corktown would serve as a magnet for talent and a catalyst for change. However, CEO Hackett reminded investors the company would not meet its financial targets for 2018 and also would not be able to reach the proposed 8 percent profit margin goal set for 2020.

Ford and the Automobile Industry Changing Product Mix

Going into 2019, the entire automobile industry was facing disruption, but this was not unusual. For instance, the 2009 global economic downturn and financial crisis had had a significant impact on global sales volumes in the auto industry—the once-profitable business of manufacturing and selling trucks and SUVs was facing change. Especially in the United States, oil prices had been fluctuating, making it difficult to anticipate consumer demand. By 2010, this had caused a shift in consumers' car-buying habits, reducing the demand for large vehicles.

The core strategy at Ford at that time had centered on a change in products, shifting to smaller and more fuel-efficient cars. Ford had imported European-made small vehicles, the European Focus and Fiesta, into North America. It also converted three truck-manufacturing plants to small-car production.[33] The Ford and Lincoln lines were upgraded, emphasizing fuel-economy improvement and the introduction of hybrid cars. In 2012, Ford launched six new Ford hybrid cars in North America. In 2014, Ford began producing its first hybrid electric car in Europe. And by 2015, Ford was the world's second largest manufacturer of hybrids, after Toyota.[34]

By late 2015 gas prices had reduced enough to spur interest in SUVs once again. This trend should have been good for Ford, given their branding emphasis on the F-150, Edge, Escape, and Explorer, but Ford and other U.S. manufacturers still had large inventories of smaller vehicles on dealer lots. U.S. auto manufacturers, including Ford, had to adjust once again to meet the demand for crossover vehicles. The smaller crossovers and SUVs now had greatly improved fuel economy and were attractive to consumers due to their versatility, while the smaller sedan and compact owners were an older demographic, and less likely to be impulse buyers.

These kinds of fluctuations in the industry meant automobile executives had to keep close track of trends and maximize their ability to adjust to demand.[35] In 2015, Ford relaunched the F-150 and further developed 15 other global products. 2016 saw the launch of the F-150 Raptor high-performance off-road pickup truck, and a significant investment in Ford's hybrid fleet. By 2018, Ford had become the top-selling plug-in hybrid brand in the United States, and was second in overall U.S. electrified vehicle sales,[36] but the Ford F-Series pickup was still the best-selling vehicle in the United States.

By 2018 the demand for cars, especially the large sedans, had pretty much dried up, while crossovers and especially small SUVs had seen double-digit growth. But the light-duty trucks were still the best-selling vehicle, by far. See Exhibit 5 for shifting vehicle sales figures in the U.S. market.

In 2018, partly because of this change in consumer preference, CEO Hackett had decided to make some drastic changes in the Ford lineup. Ford would be exiting the car market, no longer selling any sedans, and offering only the Mustang and a redesigned Focus crossover that would not be available in the United States. In the United States, the Fiesta subcompact, the Fusion midsize sedan, and the C-Max van would be phased out in 2019 and 2020. The last Taurus large sedan rolled off the production line in March 2019.

Globalizing the Ford Brand

Under the ONE Ford vision, Mulally had globalized the Ford brand, meaning that all Ford vehicles competing in global segments would be the same in North America, Europe, and Asia.[37] The company had been looking for a reduction of complexity, and thus costs, in the purchasing and manufacturing processes. The idea was to deliver more vehicles worldwide from fewer platforms and to maximize the use of common parts and systems. However, each year posed new challenges.

Heading into 2019, the global marketplace for automobiles was uncertain for all manufacturers, and each geographical segment had its issues. Both North American and European auto sales were subject to political uncertainty, due to policy shifts in government, and Brexit issues in the UK. The Chinese and larger Asian market was still growing, although starting to slow, especially with questions of tariffs looming for U.S. manufacturers. For Ford, tariffs had cost more than $750 million in 2018. Eastern European economic concerns, especially in Russia, made this a difficult area to manage. South American government regulations and currency fluctuations impacted growth there.[38]

The need for a global strategy was driving all major auto manufacturers to reduce the number of vehicle platforms, while simultaneously adding models in response to consumer preferences. In addition, partnering with local producers and manufacturers made it easier to deal with local barriers to entry, as long as these relationships could be mutually managed. Although the increased complexity raised costs, this more flexible approach allowed for improved product commonality and increased volume. As components could be shared between cars and platforms, this also reduced the number of suppliers. Ford had reduced its supplier base from 1,150 to 750.[39] Although seemingly a positive, this could also prove costly if a major supplier had a problem, as had occurred with Japanese air bag manufacturer Takata.[40] Although many other manufacturers were similarly affected, Ford had had to recall 850,000 vehicles for airbag problems, at a cost of $500 million.[41]

For Ford, 2018 saw the worst global performance in 10 years, primarily driven by a drop of more than 40 percent in China. Only South America and Middle East and Africa regions saw better results than in the prior year (see Exhibit 6).

EXHIBIT 5 U.S. Vehicle Sales by Segment as of April 2018

Tuesday, April 03, 2018 Segment totals, ranked by Mar unit sales	Mar 2018	% Change from Mar'17	YTD	% Change from YTD
Cars	**555,625**	−9.2	1,374,507	−10.8
Midsize	**231,529**	−13.4	580,263	−14.5
Small	**238,056**	−7.7	579,198	−10.8
Luxury	**86,029**	−0.9	215,006	0.7
Large	**11**	−57.7	40	−64.0
Light-duty trucks	**1,097,904**	16.3	2,736,038	9.8
Pickup	**260,949**	7.9	653,891	2.8
Crossover	**572,829**	27.0	1,415,954	18.2
Minivan	**48,325**	5.2	126,145	2.7
Small Van	**6,984**	0.8	17,799	2.1
Large Van	**34,809**	0.1	85,662	0.4
Midsize SUV	**82,140**	−7.4	220,338	−6.6
Large SUV	**30,820**	7.3	78,730	−1.4
Small SUV	**35,107**	45.6	75,328	27.9
Luxury SUV	**25,941**	19.2	62,191	9.7
Total SUV/Crossover	**746,837**	21.6	1,852,541	13.7
Total SUV	**174,008**	6.6	436,587	1.2
Total Crossover	**572,829**	27.0	1,415,954	18.2

Source: The Wall Street Journal and www.motorintelligence.com, http://www.wsj.com/mdc/public/page/2_3022-autosales.html#autosalesD.

EXHIBIT 6 Ford Performance by Region, Earnings Before Interest and Taxes ($ millions)

	Earnings 2018	Change from 2017 to 2018
North America	$7,607	$ (450)
South America	(678)	75
Europe	(398)	(765)
Middle East & Africa	(7)	239
Asia Pacific	(1,102)	(1,761)
Total Automotive	$5,422	$(2,662)

Source: Ford 10K

Regarding global growth, in Asia Pacific, Ford had developed two car plants and had joint agreements with Mahindra in India, seeing a profit in that market for the first time in 2018, but Ford also knew it needed to address challenges in China.[42] Sales growth in this region was critical, given that Ford was late to the China market. For all manufacturers, growth in China was a challenge, but for U.S. automakers Chinese market share had dropped to just 10.7 percent, down from 12 percent in 2017. GM, who had abandoned India, had a higher brand penetration in China than Ford did, but Chinese manufacturers were continuing to offer consumers a lot of options. Ford had introduced the Mustang and Taurus in China during 2016, and saw strong sales of these performance vehicles. In 2017, Ford began exporting the all-new F-150 Raptor to China, making it the first high-performance off-road pickup truck to be offered there. Going into 2019, Ford was planning to produce some brands, especially the Ford Explorer and some Lincoln vehicles, using local Chinese supply chain and assembly partners. Ford had also created a new SUV, the Territory, specifically for this market.[43]

Ford was taking a new look at how to address global growth. Europe, once a good market for Ford, had seen market share drop from over 8 percent in 2010 to barely 6.5 percent in 2018. Although Europe was a strong market for commercial vehicles, the shift would be made from smaller cars to SUVs, crossovers, and electrified vehicles. In addition, CEO Hackett had made the decision to close factories in Europe, cutting thousands of jobs in Germany, Spain, and the UK, and would review its joint venture in Russia.[44]

Unlike its rival General Motors, Ford was addressing performance issues worldwide through cost-cutting strategies and changes to the product mix, while GM's CEO Mary Barra had abandoned the "growth-at-all-costs strategy," and closed money-losing operations in Russia and South Africa. In 2018, GM had exited Europe by selling off its German-based Open Vauxhall subsidiary to France's PSA Group. In North America, GM was shutting down three plants. And, just like Ford, GM was consolidating its car lineup, stopping production of the Chevrolet Cruze and Impala, and the Volt plug-in hybrid, and discontinuing the Buick LaCrosse, Cadillac XTS, and CT6.[45] Belt-tightening was occurring all over.

Looking Ahead

Ford Motor Company was the sixth-largest automobile manufacturer in the world, but like all others who produced a multi-vehicle lineup, Ford was facing considerable uncertainty. Global markets were hard to predict and countries were increasing regulatory requirements for safety and environmental impact. All vehicles were seeing an increase in the amount of onboard technology that required a shift in both engineering and manufacturing priorities. Worldwide manufacturers were making design changes that allowed more lean production and consolidation of suppliers, and consumers were changing how they purchased vehicles and rethinking what they wanted from the transportation experience overall.[46]

Several marked shifts in the overall landscape were occurring: the interest, worldwide, in electric or alternative-fueled vehicles; the development of autonomously controlled cars that were also personally connected to a user who might not be the driver; and the reduction in demand for actual automobile ownership in favor of rental or on-demand transportation options. These shifts created opportunities but also challenges for entrenched car manufacturers.

Partnerships were inevitable: GM was partnering with Lyft, and Ford with Uber, which had tried out the Ford Fusion autonomous vehicle. Ford had put Amazon's virtual digital assistant Alexa in its cars. Ford had invested in Velodyne, a company that developed lidar remote-sensing technology for self-driving cars, and in artificial intelligence software firm Argo AI. Ford had acquired an app-based, crowd-sourced, ride-sharing service, Chariot, but subsequently shut it down in 2019. Ford had teamed up with Motivate, the global leader in bike-sharing to include the FordPass mobility network in the Ford GoBike commuting transportation option. Through its innovation and research centers, Ford was also developing strategies in fleet and data management, route and journey planning, and telematics, using artificial intelligence and robotics, all in an effort to help solve congestion and help move people more efficiently in urban environments.[47] In an attempt to gain some competitive advantage, and adopt a leaner business model, Ford had also formed a strategic alliance with Volkswagon to jointly produce vans and pickup trucks, further developing electric and autonomous vehicles. This move by both global auto companies was seen as "a strategically defensive move to share vehicle architecture-related expenses in an attempt to offset the intensifying competitive pressures and escalating costs facing the auto industry over the next decade."[48]

These fundamental changes in the industry required leadership that could anticipate trends and allocate resources wisely, all while crafting a vision for the future that could inspire all relevant stakeholders to support and promote the company's success. Alan Mulally's ONE Ford slogan, focused on operational synergies, had helped the automaker avoid bankruptcy and return to a position of financial strength in the industry. Mark Fields's shift had seemed to be toward TWO Fords, refocusing the company into both an automaker and a transportation services provider. This included plans to offer electric vehicles and experiment with ways to provide innovative solutions to transportation and mobility problems in cities across the globe.[49] Hackett was continuing this dual approach, and restructured the company, promoting Joe Hinrichs to president of global automotive operations, while giving Jim Farley responsibility for Ford's self-driving unit as president of new business, technology, and strategy. This operational split confirmed that Mulally's original ONE Ford vision was no longer a good fit for current conditions, and would position either Hinrichs or Farley as a possible successor to Hackett.[50] Hackett had given leaders at various levels in the company the ability to choose how the work would get done, hoping to increase level of innovation and leverage talent.[51]

Unfortunately, investors were not sure about any of this: Ford's stock had fallen by about 40 percent since Mulally's departure. One analyst pointed out what others were saying: "They have a lot of the right initiatives; they're doing something in every box. The difference from the Mulally days is there isn't a single message that is more than just public-relations, tying it all together."[52] Fields had tried to position the company to take on rivals from other industries, and investors had wondered what bike-sharing and artificial intelligence had to do with the car business. As had most U.S. automobile manufacturers, Ford under Hackett had taken steps to remove sedans from the auto lineup, and invest in retooling to support SUVs and trucks. In 2019, Hackett was also proceeding with an $11 billion global restructuring effort in an attempt to reposition Ford for success once again, but at this point the industry was forcing all manufacturers to ask some basic questions: "Do people want to own their cars or share them? Drive them or have them driven?"[53]

Ford and other global automobile companies were betting on the "mobility" trend to bring new products and services to a depressed market, but how might this really work? Henry Ford had the initial vision of disruption in personal transportation. Would the 21st century version of Ford Motor Company be as successful?

ENDNOTES

1. Gastelu, G. 2019. The 10 best-selling vehicles in the United States in 2018 were mostly trucks and SUVs. *FoxNews*, January 4, https://www.foxnews.com/auto/the-10-best-selling-vehicles-in-the-united-states-in-2018-were-mostly-trucks-and-suvs.
2. Ford Media. 2019. Ford surpasses 1 million truck sales in 2018. *Ford Media*, January 12. https://media.ford.com/content/fordmedia/fna/us/en/news/2019/01/12/ford-surpasses-1-million-truck-sales-in-2018.html.
3. Muller, D. 2019. Sales off to weakest start in 5 years. *AutoNews*, March 4, https://www.autonews.com/sales/sales-weakest-start-5-years.
4. Elio Motors has focused on very small, economical concept cars, and even though they anticipate that by 2022 under 35 percent of new-car sales will be passenger vehicles and more than 65 percent will be trucks and SUVs, they still believe their three-wheeled safe, environmental-friendly vehicle will fill a useful niche. See https://www.eliomotors.com/about-elio/.
5. Neto, A. 2019. Ford is a truck company with a truck-sized dividend. *SeekingAlpha*, May 16, https://seekingalpha.com/article/4264507-ford-truck-company-truck-sized-dividend.
6. Ford Media. 2015. Ford at CES announces smart mobility plan and 25 global experiments designed to change the way the world moves. January 6, https://media.ford.com/content/fordmedia/fna/us/en/news/2015/01/06/ford-at-ces-announces-smart-mobility-plan.html.
7. Muoio, D. 2017. These 19 companies are racing to build self-driving cars in the next 5 years. *BusinessInsider*, January 12, http://www.businessinsider.com/companies-making-driverless-cars-by-2020-2017-1/#tesla-recently-made-a-big-move-to-meet-its-goal-of-having-a-fully-self-driving-car-ready-by-2018-1; Wiggers, K. 2019. Ford to deploy up to 100 autonomous cars by the end of 2019, expand testing to third city. venturebeat, April 26, https://venturebeat.com/2019/04/26/ford-plans-to-deploy-as-many-as-100-autonomous-vehicles-by-the-end-of-this-year-expand-testing-to-a-new-city/.
8. Kane, J., and M. Kennedy. 2017. Ford replaces CEO Mark Fields in management shake-up. *NPR.org*, May 22, https://www.npr.org/sections/thetwo-way/2017/05/22/529459034/ford-replacing-ceo-mark-fields-in-management-shakeup.
9. Staff, "Failing to take care of business today cost Mark Fields his future at Ford," Financial Post, https://business.financialpost.com/transportation/failing-to-take-care-of-business-today-cost-mark-fields-his-future-at-ford.
10. Caldicott, S.M. 2014. Why Ford's Alan Mulally is an innovation CEO for the record books. *Forbes*, June 25, http://www.forbes.com/sites/sarahcaldicott/2014/06/25/why-fords-alan-mulally-is-an-innovation-ceo-for-the-record-books/2/.
11. Ford Motor Company 2014 10K filing.
12. Thompson. C. 2017. Ford's CEO reveals his plan for the company's biggest transformation in history. *BusinessInsider*, January 15, http://www.businessinsider.com/ford-ceo-mark-fields-interview-2017-1.
13. Neto, A. 2019. Ford is a truck company with a truck-sized dividend. *SeekingAlpha*, May 16, https://seekingalpha.com/article/4264507-ford-truck-company-truck-sized-dividend.
14. Newcomb, D. 2016. Bill Ford on why the family business is betting on mobility. *Forbes*, September 15, https://www.forbes.com/sites/dougnewcomb/2016/09/15/bill-ford-on-why-the-family-business-is-betting-on-mobility/#321209bb659b.
15. Martinez, M. 2017. Bill Ford: Mobility can lift margins. *AutoNews*, January 16, http://www.autonews.com/article/20170116/OEM02/301169995/bill-ford%3A-mobility-can-lift-margins.
16. The Innovator and Ford Motor Company. *The Henry Ford Museum*, http://www.thehenryford.org/exhibits/hf/The_Innovator_and_Ford_Motor_Company.asp.
17. History of Ford Motor Company. 2019. In *Wikipedia*, The Free Encyclopedia, http://en.wikipedia.org/wiki/History_of_Ford_Motor_Company.
18. Tesla. (n.d.) About Tesla. http://www.teslamotors.com/about.
19. Lang, J. 2018. Average vehicle age in U.S. reaching record levels. *Ratchetandwrench.com*, April 12, https://www.ratchetandwrench.com/articles/6136-average-vehicle-age-in-us-reaching-record-levels.
20. *MotorIntelligence.com*. www.motorintelligence.com.
21. Maynard, M., and M. Fackler. 2006. Toyota is poised to supplant GM as world's largest carmaker. *New York Times*, December 23, http://www.nytimes.com/2006/12/23/business/worldbusiness/23toyota.html?_r=0.
22. Flint, J. 2006. Ford: Overhaul time–again. *Forbes*, January 23, http://www.forbes.com/2006/01/23/ford-restructuring-autos-cz_jf_0123flint.html.
23. Berfield, S. 2006. The best leaders. *BusinessWeek Online*, December 18.
24. Kiley, D. 2007. Mulally: Ford's most important new model. *BusinessWeek Online*, January 9, www.businessweek.com.
25. Maynard, M. 2006. Ford expects to fall soon to no. 3 spot. *New York Times*, December 21, www.nytimes.com.
26. Durbin, D.-A., and T. Krisher. 2011. Ford stock falls after company misses expectations. Associated Press, January 28, www.businessweek.com/ap/financialnews/archives/March2011/D9L1JHCO1.htm.
27. LaRocco, L. A. 2014. For Mulally, Ford's culture is job one. *The Street*, March 3, http://www.thestreet.com/story/1543980/1/for-mulally-fords-culture-is-job-one.html.
28. Bunkley, N., and M. Maynard. 2007. Ford breaks string of losing quarters, but says respite will be brief. *New York Times*, July 27: C3.
29. Geier, B. 2015. Ford's profit beats estimates, but its European outlook dims. *Fortune*, January 29, http://fortune.com/2015/01/29/fords-profit-beats-estimates-but-its-european-outlook-dims/.
30. Ford Motor Company Annual Report 2018.
31. Media Ford. 2016. Ford outlines growth plan. September 14, https://media.ford.com/content/fordmedia/fna/us/en/news/2016/09/14/ford-outlines-growth-plan.html.
32. Ford Motor Company Annual Report 2018.
33. Praet, N. V. 2008. US$8.7B loss turns Ford. *Financial Post*, July 25.
34. Crowe, P. 2014. Ford Mondeo Hybrid now in EU production. *Hybridcars*, November 28, http://www.hybridcars.com/ford-mondeo-hybrid-now-in-eu-production/.
35. DeBord, M. 2016. The US auto industry may surprise everyone in 2017. *BusinessInsider*, December 21, http://www.businessinsider.com/us-auto-industry-growth-in-2017-2016-12.
36. Ford Media. 2016. Ford finishes 2016 strong; fourth quarter and full-year profits in line with expectations. https://corporate.ford.com/content/dam/corporate/en/investors/investor-events/Quarterly%20Earnings/2017/4Q16-FINAL-Press-Release.pdf.
37. Ford Motor Company. 2009. Ford reports 4th quarter 2008. media.ford.com/images/10031/4Qfinancials.pdf.
38. *Business Wire*. 2017. Global auto sales set to reach 93.5 million in 2017, but risk is greater than ever, IHS Markit says. *Business Wire*,

February 21, http://finance.yahoo.com/news/global-auto-sales-set-reach-130000753.html.

39. Hirsh, E., Kakkar, A., Singh, A., and R. Wilk. 2015. Auto trends. Strategy+business, January, http://www.strategyand.pwc.com/perspectives/2015-auto-trends.
40. Ma, J., and C. Trudell. 2014. Air-Bag crisis seen spurring shift from Japan's Takata. *BloombergBusiness*, October 24, http://www.bloomberg.com/news/articles/2014-10-23/air-bag-crisis-seen-spurring-shift-from-japan-s-takata.
41. Shepardson, D. 2014. New Ford recall to cost $500M, stock falls 7.5%. *The Detroit News*, September 29, http://www.detroitnews.com/story/business/autos/ford/2014/09/29/ford-recall-will-cost-million/16441255/.
42. Shah, A. 2018. Ford goes local in India, aims for bigger slice of competitive market. *Reuters*, November 5, https://www.reuters.com/article/us-ford-motor-india-strategy-focus/ford-goes-local-in-india-aims-for-bigger-slice-of-competitive-market-idUSKCN1NB07P.
43. Ferris, R. 2019. Ford's 5 big fixes for its troubled international business. *CNBC.com*, January 24, https://www.cnbc.com/2019/01/24/fords-5-big-fixes-for-its-troubled-international-business.html.
44. Behrmann, E. 2019. Ford's global cost purge hits Europe with thousands of job cuts. *Bloomberg News*, January 10, https://www.ttnews.com/articles/fords-global-cost-purge-hits-europe-thousands-job-cuts.
45. Capparella, J. 2018. GM closing plants, ending production of multiple models; President Trump threatens retribution. *Car and Driver*, November 27, https://www.caranddriver.com/news/a25306076/gm-plant-closing-production-cars/.
46. Hirsh, E., Kakkar, A., Singh, A., and R. Wilk. 2015. 2015 auto industry trends. *Strategy+business*, January, http://www.strategyand.pwc.com/perspectives/2015-auto-trends.
47. Ford Media. 2016. Ford outlines growth plan. September 14, https://media.ford.com/content/fordmedia/fna/us/en/news/2016/09/14/ford-outlines-growth-plan.html.
48. Winton, N. 2019. Ford, VW alliance said to be disappointingly narrow and defensive. *Forbes*, January 23, https://www.forbes.com/sites/neilwinton/2019/01/23/ford-vw-alliance-said-to-be-disappointingly-narrow-and-defensive/#79a42e921534.
49. Rogers, C. 2016. CEO Mark Fields sets Ford on a dual track: Alongside core auto business, company eyes role as transportation-services provider. *Wall Street Journal* (Online), October 17.
50. Williams, J. 2019. Ford plots future with latest leadership shakup. *FoxBusiness*, April 10, https://www.foxbusiness.com/industrials/ford-plots-future-with-latest-leadership-shakeup.
51. Pascus, B. 2018. Ford to cut salaried jobs as the auto giant undergoes an $11 billion restructuring effort. *BusinessInsider*, October 10, https://www.businessinsider.com/ford-to-cut-jobs-as-part-of-global-restructuring-effort-2018-10.
52. Rogers, C. 2016. CEO Mark Fields sets Ford on a dual track: Alongside core auto business, company eyes role as transportation-services provider. *Wall Street Journal* (Online), October 17.
53. Useem, J. 2019. Why Ford hired a furniture maker as CEO. *The Atlantic*, March issue, https://www.theatlantic.com/magazine/archive/2019/03/ford-ceo-jim-hackett-ux-design-thinking/580438/.

CASE 35

JAMBA JUICE: FOCUS IS ON THE MENU*

On January 22, 2019, FOCUS Brands announced that the transition of the executive leadership team for its recently acquired Jamba Juice brand was now complete. Geoff Henry replaced Dave Pace, CEO of Jamba Juice since January of 2016. Coming in as Jamba President, Henry was previously responsible for growth in the water, tea, and coffee divisions of Coca Cola. Also new to the team was Shivram Vaideeswaran, most recently CMO of Blaze Pizza with experience building lifestyle food brands in the primarily franchised environments of Tender Greens and Taco Bell. Signaling the renewed emphasis on franchise growth, Steve DeSutter, CEO of FOCUS Brands, pointed out that the new additions to the Jamba Juice team brought both talent and industry experience, combined with a passion for health and wellness, that could become a "powerful combination in fueling Jamba's continued success," adding "leadership of our brands is critical to building guest-centered businesses."[1]

Jamba Juice, the lifestyle brand with a passion for making healthy living fun, had needed a refresh. Since 2015 the brand had been undergoing repositioning on multiple levels. Financial results for recent years had indicated a decrease in revenues and sluggish profits (see Exhibit 1). Although the company had tried to explain this by pointing to the non-recurring expenses of business model adjustment and corporate relocation, investors were wary as the stock price continued to slide.[2] The largest shareholder and activist investor, Engaged Capital, had called on the company to "slash costs and close unprofitable stores,"[3] which CEO Dave Pace proceeded to do.

Jamba Juice had made moves on many fronts: relocation of headquarters, reduction in corporate headcount, removal of self-serve kiosks in non-franchisee-operated locations, transition from company-owned and operated units to over 90 percent of its stores in franchisee hands, changes to menu offerings, and a shift in the quality of franchise operators with a move to attract multi-store franchising partners. Although the intent was to improve Jamba Juice's operational and revenue-producing opportunities, the significant changes to the company's business model, leadership, and key personnel resulted in a "significant increase in non-routine transactions and impacted certain routine processes needed to effectively accumulate and present consolidated financial results,"[4] which made it impossible for Jamba to produce audited financials from Q3-2016 until Q1-2018. This failure to file prompted NASDAQ to threaten delisting, and made the company un-investable for many market participants. Despite this, several analysts believed the transformation from an company operator to a franchisor model had "massively improved marginal profitability and reduced capital requirements," subsequently increasing the firm's "take-private potential," and noting even "franchisees think that the company would be more focused if it were not beholden to quarterly reporting demands."[5] Obviously, FOCUS Brands thought so as well.

FOCUS Brands was an Atlanta-based developer of global multichannel foodservice brands operating more than 5,000 locations around the world. With expertise in franchise operations, its brands included Carvel, Cinnabon, Schlotzsky's, Moe's Southwest Grill, Auntie Anne's, and McAlister's Deli. On August 2, 2018, FOCUS had agreed to buy Jamba Juice for $200 million, or $13 per share, which was 17 percent higher than Jamba's stock price that day, and the firm's highest share price point since 2015.[6] This made Jamba Juice a privately-held subsidiary of FOCUS Brands. The mutually beneficial merger took Jamba Juice out of the public eye, removing the necessity of meeting increasingly aggressive quarterly financial growth goals, and allowed Jamba Juice to utilize FOCUS's market experience to accelerate the growth of the brand. Jamba's common stock ceased trading on the NASDAQ after market close on September 13, 2018.

Now under private control, Jamba Juice had an opportunity to flourish. Could it achieve the potential many thought was there?

Company Background

Juice Club was founded by Kirk Perron and opened its first store in San Luis Obispo, California, in April 1990.[7] While many small health-food stores had juice bars offering fresh carrot juice, wheat germ, and protein powder, dedicated juice and smoothie bars did not gain widespread popularity until the mid- to late 1990s.

Juice Club began with a franchise strategy and opened its second and third stores in northern and southern California in 1993. In 1994, management decided that an expansion strategy focusing on company stores would provide a greater degree of quality and operating control. In 1995, the company changed its name to Jamba Juice Company to provide a point of differentiation as competitors began offering similar healthy juices and smoothies in the marketplace.

---

* This case was developed by Professor Alan B. Eisner, Pace University and Professor Pauline Assenza, Western Connecticut State University. Material has been drawn from published sources as a basis for class discussion rather than to illustrate either effective or ineffective handling of an administrative situation. Copyright © 2019 Alan B. Eisner.

In March 1999, Jamba Juice Company merged with Zuka Juice Inc., a smoothie retail chain with 98 smoothie retail units in the western United States. On March 13, 2006, Jamba Juice Company agreed to be acquired by Services Acquisition Corp. International (headed by Steven Berrard, former CEO of Blockbuster Inc.) for $265 million.[8] The company went public in November 2006 as Nasdaq-traded JMBA. Jamba Juice stores were owned and franchised by Jamba Juice Company, which was a wholly owned subsidiary of Jamba Inc.

In August 2008, Jamba Juice faced significant leadership changes. Steven Berrard agreed to assume the responsibilities of interim CEO, and in December 2008, James D. White was named CEO and president, while Berrard remained chairman of the board of directors. Prior to joining Jamba Juice, White had been senior vice president of consumer brands at Safeway, a publicly traded Fortune 100 food and drug retailer. During what CEO White called the turnaround years from 2009 to 2011, he worked to eliminate short-term debt, innovate, expand the menu, and change the business model by refranchising stores, growing internationally, and commercializing product lines.

Transition from Company-Owned to Franchise "Asset-light" Format

Originally, Jamba Juice Company had followed a strategy of expanding its store locations in existing markets and only opening stores in select new markets. Jamba soon began acquiring the assets of Jamba Juice franchised stores in an attempt to gain more control over growth direction. Under CEO Paul E. Clayton, Jamba acquired several franchise stores and expected to continue making additional franchise acquisitions as part of its ongoing growth strategy. However, the company-owned franchises were not as productive and accounted for a disproportionately low portion of company revenues.[9]

Clayton stepped down after eight years, and was ultimately replaced by James White. White reversed the trajectory of the company-owned growth strategy, focusing on the acceleration of franchise and nontraditional store growth. The more heavily franchised business model tended to require less capital investment and reduced the volatility of cash flow performance over time. However, revenue sources then came more from royalties and franchise fees rather than retail sales.

When Dave Pace, an industry veteran formerly with Bloomin' Brands, took over in 2016, he focused on improving franchisee relationships and continued the strategy of refranchising company-owned stores. The "asset-light" franchise model had several efficiencies that translated to increased profitability. When a company placed most of the risk for running a business in the hands of a franchisee, the franchisor—Jamba Juice in this case—did not have to pay for employees, rent, or upkeep on the store assets. The franchisee was expected to put his or her capital to work, running the business. In this case, store management was "more likely to act in the best interest of shareholders because the franchisee's net worth is more often directly correlated with the outcome of his or her store."[10] The incentives were clear. The franchisee took the risk and earned the profits, while the franchisor made 7.5 to 10 percent royalty on all sales, and collected a marketing fee.

In addition, Pace worked to achieve a cost reduction in both cost of goods sold, by leveraging national purchasing scale to renegotiate produce costs, and SG&A spending by reducing headcount and wages through the relocation of corporate headquarters from California to Texas. He also began to offer the drive-thru as a franchise option, and encouraged lower-quality operators to leave the system in favor of those franchisees who preferred to operate multi-unit locations.

Although it decreased the need for readily available capital to run the company, allowing Jamba Juice to hold onto more cash, the transition to a franchising model caused revenue and GAAP reported profitability to fall, resulting in less than ideal financials (see Exhibits 1 and 2). When Jamba Juice finally released financial results for the fiscal year ending January 2, 2018, total revenue had declined $8.7 million, but net income (loss) had improved $19.7 million, to a loss of $2.7 million. By the second quarter of 2018, although still a net loss, systemwide comparable store sales had increased by 2.2 percent. CEO Pace commented on the revitalization of the Jamba business, pointing out that "the announced transaction with FOCUS Brands was only possible due to the significant progress made in resetting the foundation of the business to materially improve performance over the past several quarters...I continue to be optimistic about the performance of the brand and look forward to seeing this progress continue under FOCUS Brands ownership."[11]

In March 2018, CEO Pace had announced Jamba Juice was actively seeking both single- and multi-unit franchise partners to more aggressively expand franchise locations on the east coast. These new partners would have a unique opportunity to be among the first to deploy the concept's new store design, characterized by new technology, digital menu boards, modern colors, and contemporary elements. In addition, franchise owners were also encouraged to consider Jamba Juice's new drive-thru format, which created greater accessibility and convenience, as well as an increase in customer traffic.[12] Although, including a franchise fee of $35,000, the initial investment for a Jamba Juice ranged between $236,100 and $501,800—lower than the average food franchise investment—this expansion had stalled going into 2019 because the Company did not have an active Franchise Disclosure Document (FDD) to solicit prospective franchisees through much of 2017, due to the delayed financial reporting. As a result, through 2019, Jamba Juice single store and drive-thru expansion had been led by existing franchisees.[13]

EXHIBIT 1 Income Statements

(Dollars in thousands, except share and per share amounts)	Fiscal Year Ended January 2, 2018	January 3, 2017	December 29, 2015	December 30, 2014
Revenue:				
Company stores	$ 44,673	$ 51,282	$ 137,025	$ 198,737
Franchise and other revenue	26,253	28,341	24,651	19,311
Total revenue	70,926	79,623	161,676	218,048
Costs and operating expenses (income):				
Cost of sales	10,231	12,601	33,737	52,236
Labor	15,653	17,872	44,732	61,749
Occupancy	6,487	7,659	18,951	27,630
Store operating	8,228	9,285	25,152	33,089
Depreciation and amortization	3,549	5,749	6,569	10,084
General and administrative	28,260	37,958	36,872	37,278
Gain on disposal of assets	688	790	(21,609)	(2,957)
Store pre-opening	711	1,224	1,031	763
impairment of long-lived assets	–	3,410	2,523	175
Store lease termination and closure	297	4,160	1,669	575
Other operating, net	15	1,083	1,795	726
Total costs, operating expenses, and gain	74,119	101,791	151,422	221,348
Income (loss) from operations	(3,193)	(22,168)	10,254	(3,300)
Other income (expense):				
Interest income	105	250	137	74
Interest expense	(325)	(439)	(220)	(195)
Total other expense, net	(220)	(189)	(83)	(121)
Income (loss) before income taxes	(3,413)	(22,357)	10,171	(3,421)
Income tax expense	671	(79)	(701)	(168)
Net income (loss)	(2,742)	(22,436)	9,470	(3,589)
Less: Net income attributable to noncontrolling interest	–	–	52	43
Net income (loss) attributable to Jamba, Inc.	$ (2,742)	$ (22,436)	$ 9,418	$ (3,632)
Weighted-average shares used in the computation of earnings (loss) per share attributable to Jamba, Inc.:				
Basic	15,513,028	15,229,102	15,787,806	17,197,904
Diluted	15,513,028	15,229,102	16,228,033	17,197,904
Earnings (loss) per share attributable to Jamba, Inc. common stockholders:				
Basic	$ (0.18)	$ (1.47)	$ 0.60	$ (0.21)
Tainted	$ (0.18)	$ (1.47)	$ 0.58	$ (0.21)

Source: Annual Report. Jamba, Inc, January 2, 2018.

EXHIBIT 2 Balance Sheet

(Dollars in thousands, except share and per share amounts)	January 2, 2018	January 3, 2017	December 29, 2015	December 30, 2014
Assets				
Current assets:				
Cash and cash equivalents	$ 10,030	$ 7,133	$ 19,730	$ 17,750
Receivables, net of allowances of $618 and $280	10,098	11,778	16,932	16,977
Inventories	465	534	818	2,300
Prepaid and refundable taxes	127	243	356	474
Prepaid rent	776	1,053	1,682	504
Assets held for sale	—	206	—	22,845
Prepaid expenses and other current assets	4,194	2,757	4,495	8,105
Total current assets	25,690	23,704	44,013	68,955
Property, fixtures and equipment, net	10,928	12,512	18,744	17,988
Goodwill	1,181	1,183	1,184	945
Trademarks and other intangible assets, net	1,211	1,327	1,464	2,360
Deferred tax asset	791	—	—	—
Notes receivable and other long-term assets	847	2,894	4,211	2,241
Total assets	$ 40,648	$ 41,620	$ 69,616	$ 92,489
Liabilities and stockholders' equity				
Current liabilities:				
Accounts payable	$ 3,279	$ 2,749	$ 3,815	$ 3,926
Accrued compensation and benefits	1,900	3,580	3,788	6,325
Workers' compensation and health insurance reserves	222	675	633	1,311
Accrued gift card liability	27,469	24,131	29,306	38,184
Accrued expenses	6,791	7,658	—	—
Other current liabilities	8,052	7,664	18,093	16,454
Total current liabilities	47,713	46,457	55,635	66,200
Deterred rent and other long-term liabilities	7,509	8,940	8,990	9,544
Total liabilities	55,222	55,397	64,625	75,744
Commitments and contingencies (Notes 8 and 17)				
Stockholders' equity:				
Common stock, $.001 par value, 30,000,000 shares authorized; 18,447,023 issued and 15,588,206 outstanding	18	18	18	17
Additional paid-in capital	409,518	407,273	403,605	396,629
Treasury shares, at cost, 1,948,004 and 910,813, respectively	(40,009)	(40,009)	(40,009)	(11,991)
Accumulated deficit	(384,101)	(381,059)	(358,623)	(368,041)
Total stockholders' (deficit) equity	(14,574)	(13,777)	4,991	16,745
Total liabilities and stockholders' equity	$ 40,648	$ 41,620	$ 69,616	$ 92,489

Sources: Annual Report. Jamba, Inc, 2015; Annual Report. Jamba Inc, 2018.

EXHIBIT 3 Store Type and Locations

	Fiscal Year Ended			
	January 2, 2018	January 3, 2017	December 30, 2015	December 31, 2014
Company Stores:				
Beginning of year	66	70	263	268
Company Stores opened	1	2	–	–
Company Stores acquired from franchisees	–	–	2	26
Company Stores closed	(1)	(5)	(16)	(13)
Company Stores sold to franchisees	(13)	(1)	(179)	(18)
Total Company Stores	53	66	70	263
Franchise Stores – Domestic:				
Beginning of year	726	706	504	535
Franchise Stores opened	39	44	44	43
Franchise Stores purchased by Company	–	–	(2)	(26)
Franchise Stores closed	(29)	(25)	(19)	(27)
Franchise Stores purchased from Company	13	1	179	18
Total Franchise Stores – Domestic	749	726	706	543
International Stores:				
Beginning of year	70	75	62	48
International Stores opened	10	19	22	24
International Stores closed	(9)	(24)	(9)	(10)
Total International Stores	71	70	75	62

Sources: Annual Report. Jamba, Inc, 2015; Annual Report. Jamba Inc, 2018.

Going into 2019, Jamba Juice had 908 locations, consisting of 51 company owned and operated stores and 737 franchise stores, with 60 licensed sites overseas. International growth was also part of the strategy (see Exhibit 3). Starting with the first South Korean location in January 2011, Jamba Juice had grown to 71 stores internationally by 2018, with outlets in Indonesia, South Korea, the Philippines, Taiwan, the Middle East, and Thailand. International stores were located in prominent locations like the Mall of Asia–the largest integrated shopping, dining, and leisure destination in the Philippines.[14]

Top-of-Mind Brand

By 2019, Jamba Juice was the smoothie brand leader and #1 retailer for fresh squeezed made-to-order juices.[15] Jamba also boasted over 1.8 million Facebook fans and over 100 million annual visits to its stores. The consumer messaging was centered on "Whole Food Nutrition," designed to focus consumers on the benefits of the fresh fruits and vegetables that were used to make Jamba's products. This campaign was executed over multiple media sources including digital, social, public relations, TV, radio, and print.

In 2014, the Jamba Insider Rewards (JJR) e-mail marketing program was introduced, and by 2017 it had over 2 million loyalty members who were rewarded with promotional offers such as discounts, free products, and advance notice of in-store events. In 2019, franchisees continued to be provided with tools and technologies that targeted their customers through e-mail, social media, radio, and out-of-home advertising, and Jamba had piloted a first-ever television ad campaign in key markets.

Regarding its marketing efforts, historically, Jamba had not engaged in any mass-media promotional programs, relying instead on word of mouth and in-store promotions to increase customer awareness. However, Jamba was featured in stories appearing in the *Wall Street Journal, New York Times, USA Today*, as well as profiled spots on TV news shows such as *Good Morning America.* Jamba had also run an "Ambassadors of WOW" contest nationwide, encouraging fans to nominate themselves or worthy friends or family members to be the new faces of Jamba Juice, creating "wow" through support and involvement within their communities. These ambassadors would have the opportunity to appear in Jamba Juice advertisements and promotional campaigns.[16]

Jamba also capitalized on the openings of new sites as opportunities to reach out to the media and secure live local television coverage, radio broadcasts, and articles in local print media. Openings were also frequently associated with a charitable event, thus serving to reinforce Jamba Juice Company's strong commitment to its communities. In addition, Jamba aligned itself with "active living" spokespeople, such as NFL players Vernon Davis, tight end for the Washington Redskins, and Mohamed Sanu, wide receiver for the New England Patriots. Davis and Sanu partnered up to develop six Jamba Juice stores in the Washington DC metro area, and Davis was franchise owner of five Jamba Juice locations in northern California.[17]

New Products, Category Leadership

Jamba sought "top-of-mind" leadership by creating innovative and "craveable" menu items they could offer throughout the day—for breakfast, lunch, afternoon, and dinner. Jamba Juice stores offered customers a range of fresh squeezed fruit juices, blended beverages, baked goods and meals, nutritional supplements, and healthy snacks. Jamba smoothie and juice options were made with real fruit and 100 percent fruit juices. Jamba smoothies were rich in vitamins, minerals, proteins, and fiber, were blended to order, and provided four to six servings of fruits and vegetables. In addition to the natural nutrients in Jamba smoothies, Jamba offered supplements in the form of Boosts and Shots. Boosts included 10 combinations of vitamins, minerals, proteins, and extracts designed to give the mind and body a nutritious boost. Shots included combinations of wheatgrass, orange, and lemon juice designed to give customers a natural concentrate of vitamins, minerals, and antioxidants.

As complements to its smoothie and boost offerings, Jamba also offered baked goods and other meal items. Called "tasty bites," each of these items was made with natural ingredients and was high in protein and fiber. One popular item was steel-cut hot oatmeal with fruit, a low-calorie organic product that captured a "best of" rating by nutritionists when compared against offerings from McDonald's, Starbucks, Au Bon Pain, and Cosi.[18] Jamba also offered a variety of grab-and-go wraps, sandwiches, and California flatbread food offerings, as well as "energy bowls" that incorporated whole fruit, fresh Greek yogurt and/or soy milk, and an assortment of dry toppings.

Jamba also transitioned existing stores in selected markets to a fresh-squeezed juice emphasis. This addressed competition from both Juice It Up! and Starbucks, who were expanding their premium juice bar businesses. But the big announcement was when Jamba introduced its Kids Meals. This new menu was targeted toward children ages 4 to 8, with a complete meal—a smoothie plus a food item—containing fewer than 500 calories. The items included whole grains, 2.5 servings of fruit or vegetables, and no added sugar.

One of the key objectives of Jamba's growth strategy was to increase sales year-round and significantly decrease weather and seasonal vulnerabilities. Seasonal issues were serious, since the traditional driver of Jamba's revenue and profit was the sale of smoothies during hot weather. In southern states (e.g., California), where the weather remained warm year-round, Jamba experienced fairly steady sales. However, in the northern states (e.g., New York), where there was a cold and fairly lengthy winter season, Jamba experienced severe seasonal variability. To counter the seasonal slump, Jamba pushed to increase the presence of nontraditional stores inside existing venues.

Nontraditional Locations

Jamba had generally characterized its stores as either traditional or nontraditional. Traditional locations included suburban strip malls and various retail locations in urban centers. Traditional stores averaged approximately 1,400 square feet in size and were designed to be fun, friendly, energetic, and colorful to represent the active, healthy lifestyle that Jamba Juice promoted.

Nontraditional stores were considered those located in areas that allowed Jamba to generate awareness and try out new products to fuel the core business. In 2019, and only available to existing franchisees, Jamba's nontraditional opportunities included store-within-a-store locations, an example of which was the 2016 opening of a combination Timothy's World Coffee and Jamba Juice franchise location within a Stop & Shop store in Long Island, New York.[19] Other nontraditional venues included airports and shopping malls, where the indoor setting helped to alleviate weather and seasonal vulnerabilities that challenged traditional locations, and colleges and universities.

Additional high-traffic, nontraditional locations existed. Many large health clubs included a juice and smoothie bar within their buildings. Jamba could partner with a major gym chain or individual private gyms with high membership rates. Another possibility was to partner with a large school district. Schools across the country were under increasing scrutiny to offer healthy alternatives to the traditional fat-, carbohydrate-, and preservative-rich foods served in cafeterias, especially as a number of states were prohibiting the sale of junk food on K–12 campuses.

Jamba had introduced self-service JambaGO automated drink stations in nontraditional locations, including schools. Taking roughly the space of a soda fountain beverage dispenser, the JambaGo format, which CEO White called a wellness center, included the chain's branded packaged products, as well as the option of several preblended smoothies. This licensed concept represented no capital investment for Jamba and used the razor/razor blade net profit model. White was hoping Jamba would become "the go-to resource for healthy solutions for school foodservice directors."[20] However, former CEO Dave Pace announced plans to exit the JambaGo platform in 2017, stating:

> After a detailed review, the company determined that the JambaGo platform does not align with these objectives and is not a viable option through which to drive long-term profitability and shareholder value.[21]

Interestingly, customer feedback had indicated that the quality of the JambaGo product was not up the standards that consumers expected from Jamba; therefore, Jamba management felt JambaGo would degrade the brand and impact the company's opportunity to grow the core business and brand over the long term.

Building a Global Consumer Packaged Goods Platform

Jamba Inc. was also aggressively pursuing licensing agreements for commercialized product lines in the areas of Jamba-branded make-at-home frozen smoothie kits, frozen yogurt novelty bars, all-natural energy drinks, coconut water fruit juice beverages, Brazilian super fruit shots, trail mixes, and fruit cups. The objective was to reinforce the Jamba better-for-you message with convenient and portable products available at multiple consumer locations.

For instance, Jamba promoted "At Home Smoothies," a kit containing fruit and yogurt with a healthy antioxidant boost, one full serving of fruit, and 100% daily value of vitamin C. Available in the local grocer's fruit aisle, the package made two eight-ounce servings by adding juice and blending. The blending was facilitated by Jamba's new appliance line, offering a juice extractor, manual juicer, professional blender, and a "quiet blend" blender for quick midnight meals.

Competition

Jamba was the smoothie industry leader and initially had several competitors with similar health and fitness focuses, such as Juice It Up!, Planet Smoothie, and Smoothie King, but over time that had changed. Starbucks and Panera Bread had entered the smoothie market, and McDonald's brought its marketing machine into the frozen drink category, launching its line of smoothies with a value pitch. A taste-test in 2019 of strawberry-banana smoothies from Auntie Anne's, McDonald's, Panera Bread, Planet Smoothie, and Jamba Juice found Panera Bread and Planet Smoothie both besting Jamba Juice in taste and texture.[22] This highlighted the ongoing competitive push in the smoothie category. Regarding the juice bar and other beverage categories, Starbucks, with its smoothies already in place, had acquired both Evolution Fresh, the premium juice bar operator, and Teavana Teas. This positioned Starbucks as another head-to-head competitor to Jamba Juice. In response, similar to Starbucks, Jamba had strengthened its customer reach by offering ready-to-drink products, and hot food and drink items to attract customers during the cold-weather months, plus a range of breakfast and lunch food items to complement its juice-based offerings and satisfy customer desires all day and all year-round.

The juice and smoothie bar industry had seen a reduction in growth since 2012 as competition increased from fast-food chains and yogurt shops. The category of smoothies and juices had seen increasing consumer acceptance as health claims become more commonplace, especially as the "cold press" juice option, yielding highly nutritious juice from chopped spinach, kale, and ginger gained in popularity. However, the juice category was still relatively expensive compared with other refreshment options, and more informed consumers became concerned about the high sugar content from natural fructose. This, combined with the fact that the regular quick-serve restaurants such as McDonald's were reported to make up nearly 40 percent of the juice and smoothie bar market, meant that the pure juice and smoothie providers such as Jamba Juice, Planet Smoothie, and Smoothie King were facing difficult growth options.[23] In addition, these smoothie providers were under increased scrutiny by health advocacy groups for misleading consumers into thinking their beverages were made from whole fruit and vegetables when, in reality, consumers were "paying premium prices for products that are primarily made of unadvertised, less nutritious, and cheap ingredients like pear and white grape juices from concentrate."[24] A class action lawsuit was filed against Jamba Juice in 2018 for making misleading claims about product ingredients. The message was "these drinks get an undeserving health halo. You're better off eating actual produce and considering Jamba Juice a treat instead of a regular meal."[25]

Acquisition and Consolidation Trends in the Restaurant Chain Industry

The quick-serve, fast-food industry was a lot more competitive than it was in 2008 when James White started the turnaround at Jamba Juice. Although there were "mega brands" such as McDonald's, Starbucks, and Chick-fil-A, the category was increasingly under consolidation. As of 2019, 10 companies controlled more than 50 of the biggest restaurant chains in the world. This included not only Yum! Brands' KFC, Taco Bell, and Pizza Hut, plus Restaurant Brands International's Tim Hortons, Popeyes and Burger King, but also included Roark Capital, the private-equity owner of Inspire Brands–Arby's, Buffalo Wild Wings, Rusty Tacos, and Sonic–plus FOCUS Brands, the new owner of Jamba Juice as well as Seattle's Best Coffee, Carvel, Cinnabon, Auntie Anne's, Schlotzsky's, McAlister's Deli, and Moe's Southwest Grill.[26] These acquisitions made sense, because, as costs rose, a standalone brand faced significant need for increased spending on corporate overhead, general and administrative structures, and scale became increasingly important. Bringing brands together allowed for the cost to be spread out among multiple acquisitions and to fine tune the operational model.[27] For instance, FOCUS Brands had developed a system for franchises that offered business consultants on call 24 hours a day, plus extensive training, marketing, and technological support. Roark Capital was reportedly considering an IPO for FOCUS Brands in 2019.[28]

CEO Dave Pace's remarks upon reaching the merger agreement with FOCUS Brands noted how FOCUS was known for overseeing the success of its franchisees. Pace's final remarks as CEO of Jamba were as follows: "Over the last few years, we have worked hard to strengthen our foundation and reposition this iconic brand for the future. Partnering with FOCUS Brands will allow us to build on this work and further accelerate the company's growth."[29] Would FOCUS Brands and Jamba be successful?

ENDNOTES

1. Jamba Juice. 2019. Jamba Juice rounds out top executive team with external hires and internal promotion. *PRNewswire*, January 22, https://www.prnewswire.com/news-releases/jamba-juice-rounds-out-top-executive-team-with-external-hires-and-internal-promotion-300782313.html.
2. Pines, L. 2016. Jamba Juice stock: 4 things to watch. *Investopedia*, August 31, http://www.investopedia.com/articles/company-insights/083116/jamba-juice-stock-4-things-watch-jmba.asp.
3. Bennett, J. 2016. Jamba Juice feels investors' heavy hand. *FranchiseTimes*, September 21, http://www.franchisetimes.com/October-2016/Jamba-Juice-feels-investors-heavy-hand/.
4. BusinessWire. 2017. Jamba, Inc. announces receipt of Nasdaq staff determination letter and intent to request hearing. *BusinessWire*, September 19, https://www.businesswire.com/news/home/20170919005556/en/Jamba-Announces-Receipt-Nasdaq-Staff-Determination-Letter.
5. Terk, B. 2018. Why Jamba Juice has a sweet 45% upside. *Barrons*, May 2, https://www.barrons.com/articles/stocks-with-big-dividend-yields-51553720912.
6. Maze, J. 2018. Cinnabon's owner to buy Jamba Juice for $200M. *Restaurant Business Online*, August 2, https://www.restaurantbusinessonline.com/financing/cinnabons-owner-buy-jamba-juice-200m.
7. FundingUniverse.com. n.d. Jamba Juice Company (company history). www.fundinguniverse.com/company-histories/Jamba-Juice-Company-Company-History.html.
8. Jamba Juice Company. 2006. Jamba Juice Company and Services Acquisition Corp. International announce merger. March 13, www.sec.gov/Archives/edgar/data/1316898/000110465906015960/a06-6826_1ex99d1.htm.
9. Lee, L. 2007. A smoothie you can chew on: To appeal to diners as well as drinkers, Jamba Juice is adding heft to its concoctions. *BusinessWeek*, June 11: 64.
10. Clayton, N. 2016. Jamba Juice's business transformation 7 years in the making is nearly complete. *Seeking Alpha*, March 8, http://seekingalpha.com/article/3956540-jamba-juice-business-transformation-7-years-making-nearly-complete.
11. BusinessWire. 2018. Jamba, Inc. reports results for the second quarter of fiscal 2018. *BusinessWire*, August 13, https://www.businesswire.com/news/home/20180813005156/en/.
12. QSR Magazine. 2018. Jamba Juice re-energizes franchise strategy. *QSRMagazine*, March 22, https://www.qsrmagazine.com/news/jamba-juice-re-energizes-franchise-strategy.
13. Business Wire, 2018. Jamba, Inc. reports results for fiscal 2017, provides Q1 business update, and nears return to a standard reporting cadence. *Business Wire*, May 11, https://www.businesswire.com/news/home/20180511005119/en/.
14. Jamba Inc. 2012. Jamba announces significant progress in international expansion. *Business Wire*, July 17, ir.jambajuice.com/phoenix.zhtml?c=192409&p=irol-newsArticle&ID=1715180.
15. Fernandez, C. 2018. Juice & smoothie bars in the US. *IBIS World*, December 2018, https://clients1-ibisworld-com.wcsu.idm.oclc.org/reports/us/industry/ataglance.aspx?entid=4325.
16. Jamba Inc. 2011. Jamba Juice announces two new "Ambassadors of WOW." *PRNewswire*, May 9, ir.jambajuice.com/phoenix.zhtml?c=192409&p=irol-newsArticle&id=1561602.
17. Parker, A. 2018. Catching the next thing. *Franchising World*, August 14, https://www.franchise.org/catching-the-next-thing.
18. Jamba Inc. 2011. Jamba Juice oatmeal favorite pick on Good Morning America today. *ABC News*, February 8, ir.jambajuice.com/phoenix.zhtml?c=192409&p=irol-news&nyo=0; video clip available at abcnews.go.com/GMA/video/fast-food-oatmeal-how-healthy-is-it-12865436.
19. Industry News. 2016. Timothy's World Coffee and Jamba Juice team up. https://www.qsrmagazine.com/news/.
20. Jennings, L. 2012. Jamba Juice launches next phase of growth. *Nation's Restaurant News*, January 10, nrn.com/archive/jamba-juice-launches-next-phase-growth.
21. *Business Wire*. 2016. Jamba, Inc. announces strategic exit from JambaGo Platform. *PR Newswire*, October 5. http://ir.jambajuice.com/phoenix.zhtml?c=192409&p=irol-newsArticle&ID=2209604.
22. Suknanan, J. 2019. We tried smoothies from 5 different chains and the winner tasted creamy and fresh. *This Is Insider*, January 8, https://www.thisisinsider.com/best-place-to-get-smoothies-2019-1.
23. Wolf, B. 2013. Bringing the juice. *QSR Magazin*, February, https://www.qsrmagazine.com/consumer-trends/bringing-juice.
24. D'Souza, K. 2018. What's really in your Jamba Juice? *Mercury News*, August 24, https://www.mercurynews.com/2018/08/24/whats-really-in-your-jamba-juice/.
25. London, J. 2018. Is Jamba Juice healthy? Smoothie fans might not like the answer. *Good Housekeeping*, August 29, https://www.goodhousekeeping.com/health/diet-nutrition/a22850252/is-jamba-juice-healthy/.
26. Yuan,Y & Taylor, K. 2019. 10 companies you've never heard of control more than 50 of the biggest restaurant chains in the world. *Business Insider*, March 30, https://www.businessinsider.com/who-owns-taco-bell-arbys-burger-king-2019-3#jollibee-foods-corporation-10.
27. Maze, J. 2019. Can the multiple brand approach turn struggling chains around? *Restaurant Business Online*, March 12, https://www.restaurantbusinessonline.com/financing/can-multiple-brand-approach-turn-struggling-chains-around.
28. Porter, K. 2018 Owner of Cinnabon and Auntie Anne's weighs IPO in 2019. *Bloomberg*, October 26, https://www.bloomberg.com/news/articles/2018-10-26/owner-of-cinnabon-and-auntie-anne-s-is-said-to-weigh-ipo-in-2019.
29. Jachec, H. 2018. Focus Brands to acquire Jamba Juice in a $200m deal. *FoodBev*, August 8, https://www.foodbev.com/news/focus-brands-to-acquire-jamba-juice-in-a-200m-deal/.

CASE 36

BLACKBERRY IN 2019*

Ten years ago, BlackBerry's annual report featured a picture of its phone followed by the statement, "Ask Someone Why They Love BlackBerry." The next page answered, "People love BlackBerry smartphones because they make life easier." Once a market leader in the smartphone industry, BlackBerry's all-time high share price of $144.56 in 2008 came crashing down to less than $7 by 2016. Over the last decade, BlackBerry has lost significant market share in the smartphone industry. Speculations began to rise among investors whether BlackBerry would ever recover. After experiencing severe losses in both hardware revenues and mobile subscribers, the company hired John Chen in 2013, a turnaround specialist, as its CEO to get the formerly dominant smartphone producer back to profitability. Soon after joining the company, Chen formulated a plan that emphasized a focus on corporate and government enterprises. This significantly reduced the company's operating costs. With Chen at the helm, BlackBerry appeared to be stabilizing, but would this strategy be sustainable?

"Everybody remembered BlackBerry as the handset company. But what is the essence of that handset? Security," said John Chen, Executive Chairman and CEO. "This is why President Obama uses it, you know. This is why a lot of politicians, bankers, all [use] it—because of security."[1] The realization that security has always been a company strength inspired a new direction. BlackBerry acquisitions from 2014 to 2016, Secusmart, WatchDox (now BlackBerry Workspaces), AtHoc, and Encription, highlight this shift of focus.[2]

In February 2019, BlackBerry became a billion-dollar cybersecurity company after acquiring Cylance, an Artificial Intelligence (AI) and cybersecurity company. "Today BlackBerry took a giant step forward towards our goal of being the world's largest and most trusted AI-cybersecurity company," said Chen. "Securing endpoints and the data that flows between them is absolutely critical in today's hyper-connected world. By adding Cylance's technology to our arsenal of cybersecurity solutions we will help enterprises intelligently connect, protect and build secure endpoints that users can trust."[3] Already considered a leader in the Global Automotive Infotainment OS market share by Strategy Analytics, BlackBerry Cylance's leadership was also recognized in five categories of the 2019 Cybersecurity Excellence Awards: Best Cybersecurity Company, Most Innovative Cybersecurity Company, Endpoint Detection and Response, Endpoint Security, and Best Cybersecurity Podcast.[4]

In the past three years, BlackBerry formed a number of corporate and government partnerships. The government of Canada will invest up to CAD $40 Million to support the development of BlackBerry QNX software for autonomous cars.[5] Along with its QNX software, the company's core end-to-end Internet of Things platform includes BlackBerry Dynamics, BlackBerry AtHoc, Secusmart, BlackBerry Workspaces, and the BlackBerry Unified Endpoint Management (UEM). The BlackBerry UEM offers a "single pane of glass," or unified console view, for managing and securing devices, applications, identity, content, and Internet of Things endpoints across all leading operating systems. BlackBerry UEM was ranked as a leader in the Forrester enterprise mobility management report,[6] alongside IBM, Microsoft, and VMware.[7]

But what about the BlackBerry devices? After realizing that they had fallen behind in the touchscreen game and reentering the smartphone industry seemed like a long shot, BlackBerry decided to stop making its own phones in 2016. As of February 2019, handheld devices resulted in only 1.4 percent of BlackBerry's revenue, while its enterprise software and services dominated with 40.1 percent (see Exhibit 1). Although we can confidently say BlackBerry, that just a couple of years ago was barely surviving, has made an impressive move from smartphones to software and security, investors are still a little doubtful about its future. "We don't own BlackBerry [stock] and we're not looking to add it," says Poole, CEO and Managing Director of GlobeInvest Capital. "I think that the CEO has made good moves to transition from hardware into software, but I think going forward there's still not a lot of visibility about how they're going to grow their top line."[8]

Research in Motion

Mihal "Mike" Lazaridis and his childhood friend Doug Fregin founded Research in Motion (RIM) in 1984. Lazaridis was born in Istanbul in 1960 and came from a Greek working-class family. His father's aspirations to become a tool-and-die maker led the family to relocate to Ontario, Canada. Lazaridis displayed remarkable intelligence at an early age and excelled in both reading and science. Lazaridis was frequently exposed to electrical engineering, sharpening his intuitive understanding of the basic science behind every electrical innovation. After graduating from high school,

* This case was prepared by Professor Alan B. Eisner and graduate student Saad Nazir of Pace University, and Professor Helaine J. Korn of Baruch College, City University of New York. This case was solely based on library research and was developed for class discussion rather than to illustrate either effective or ineffective handling of an administrative situation. Copyright © 2019 Alan B. Eisner.

EXHIBIT 1 RIM (BlackBerry) Revenue by Segments, 2019

	For the Years Ended (in millions)					
	February 28, 2019		February 28, 2018		Change	
Revenue by Product and Service						
Enterprise software and services (1*2)	$367	40.1%	$423	43.7%	$(56)	(13.2)%
BTS	204	22.3%	163	16.9%	41	25.2%
Licensing, IP and other	286	31.2%	196	20.3%	90	45.9%
Handheld ld devices	13	1.4%	64	6.6%	(51)	(79.7)%
SAF	46	5.0%	121	12.5%	(75)	(62.0)%
	$916	100.0%	$967	100.0%	$(51)	(5.3)%

Source: Annual Report. BlackBerry Limited, February 28, 2019.

Lazaridis attended the University of Waterloo, however, he dropped out before graduation and decided to try his luck in business at the age of 23. The Canadian government enabled the formation of RIM by granting Lazaridis and Fregin a $15,000 loan. The duo set up RIM headquarters in Waterloo, Canada, as an electronics and computer science consulting company. According to Lazaridis, the name Research in Motion meant, "we never stop, we never end," signaling innovation that would drive RIM forward.

During the company's early years, Lazaridis accepted all sorts of contracts, most of which entailed writing code or making small insignificant technological gadgets. None of the early projects proved to be a commercial success, but they generated enough revenue to keep the company viable for more than a decade.

The company's game changer was introduction of e-mail and data devices. Lazaridis was introduced to e-mail while in college, at a time when only professors and scientists were using the service. Lazaridis was convinced that data would become extremely important in the near future, but it was hard to find the funding for a project involving e-mail. In the early 1990s, major mobile carriers were focused on devices with voice capabilities and in selling as much as possible until the market became saturated. Reading e-mails on a handheld device was unheard of. Lack of demand for devices with e-mail support did not weaken Lazaridis's determination; he developed initial prototypes by writing gateway codes hooked up to an HP Palmtop, the company's first device with "e-mail on a belt." Although the device was not commercially applicable, it became extremely popular with RIM employees. Lazaridis recalls that "employees started taking these things home, and they wouldn't return them."[9] What he then understood was that the idea of "e-mail on a belt" had the potential to generate high demand, but the challenge lay in making such a product practical enough for consumers to use on a daily basis.

RIM had great technological potential; it needed strong business leadership. Enter Harvard graduate Jim Balsillie. In the 1990s, Balsillie was an employee of a small technology company called Sutherland and Schultz, which would become one of RIM's clients. Lazaridis and Balsillie first crossed paths when Sutherland and Schultz tried to acquire RIM. Lazaridis passed on the offer, but he got a chance to see Balsillie in action and was impressed. Lazaridis wanted someone to help out with the business aspect of his company. When a company from the Netherlands bought Sutherland and Schultz in 1992, Balsillie was left without a job. Lazaridis quickly picked up the phone and invited Balsillie to join his company. Due to RIM's small size and limited resources, Balsillie would have to accept a severe salary reduction and to spend $250,000 to acquire 33 percent of RIM. Balsillie believed in Lazaridis's abilities and the potential for the company, so he agreed to the terms. The two shared duties as co-CEOs and formed a powerful leadership team in which Lazaridis focused on product development, and Balsillie took responsibility for management of the company. With limited success up until 1992, RIM made a conscious decision to leave its comfort zone and pursue the brass ring: wireless data. Balsillie truly believed that the future could be great for RIM, and according to former Senior VP Patrick Spence, "Balsillie was really strategic in terms of how he was thinking and really ambitious in terms of what he wanted to do."[10] Introduced in 1996, the Interactive Pager 900 contained peer-to-peer messaging and also an e-mail gateway. Unfortunately, the device had several deficiencies and operating errors. It was also too big and bulky to gain commercial acceptance. Thinking of its size, Lazaridis nicknamed it "the Bullfrog."

After "the Bullfrog" came "the Leapfrog." The revolutionary component of "the Leapfrog" was its ability to send e-mails at any time from any place. A forerunner to the hugely popular signature product we know today as

BlackBerry, the Leapfrog was a success. BellSouth, which had spent over $300 million in building its mobile "Mobitex" network, ordered $60 million dollars' worth of Leapfrogs in 1997. In order to get the necessary funds to continue its product development, RIM went public at the Toronto Stock Exchange in 1997, and the IPO raised more than $115 million.[11]

The BlackBerry Smartphone and Its Success

Lazaridis was responsible for developing RIM's next version of a wireless data device that would have better parts, longer battery power, and a bigger screen. RIM hired Lexicon, the company credited for naming Apple's PowerBook and Intel's Premium brands, to come up with a name for the device. The buttons on the new device looked like tiny seeds. Lexicon played around with different fruit names such as strawberry and melon, before it eventually settled on BlackBerry. RIM now had a great product with a catchy name, and it became Balsillie's responsibility to spread the word on the new offering.

The BlackBerry 850 hit the market in 1999, with wireless data, e-mail, and a tiny QWERTY keyboard. Initially, the Leapfrog and the early BlackBerry device were mostly used by law enforcement, firefighters, and ambulance workers. One of the things that this niche group greatly valued was the product's extreme reliability and security features. Balsillie thought this would resonate well with corporations on Wall Street. He knew that corporate IT departments often made decisions regarding companywide hardware and purchased the same devices for all their employees. RIM next resorted to a guerilla marketing strategy, in which hundreds of devices were given away to ground-level employees on Wall Street. The strategy became an instant success; Wall Street employees got hooked on the device and subsequently pressured IT departments to make BlackBerry the official device for their companies. Big corporations like Credit Suisse and Merrill Lynch gave in to this pressure and ordered BlackBerrys by the thousands. The success led RIM to go public on the NASDAQ in 1999. RIM raised an additional $250 million to invest in the development of its technology.[12] Revenues exploded from $47.34 million in 1999 to $84.96 million in 2000, with BlackBerry accounting for 41 percent of the revenues.[13] RIM's management team then targeted the Capitol, where security and reliability are perhaps even more crucial than in the corporate world. Soon, a large number of politicians and congressional staffers were ordering BlackBerrys.

RIM's reputation was significantly bolstered by the tragic events that transpired on September 11, 2001. Instead of relying on cellular telephone systems, BlackBerry functioned on data systems that held up extraordinarily well. Data systems could be used exclusively to communicate data in the form of text messages or e-mails by using dedicated data networks that were abundant in lower Manhattan. Almost all cellular networks shut down during the terrorist attacks, which disabled both incoming and outgoing telephone calls. However, the BlackBerry and its network remained operational, enabling victims to call loved ones and keeping vital communication lines between law enforcement and rescue workers open. One of the victims of 9/11, Ms. Federman, recalled, "I had my cellphone in one hand, and it was useless, and my BlackBerry in the other, and it was my lifeline that day."[14] In the eyes of the government there was no doubt that BlackBerry's features were important for public servants. Almost immediately after the events on 9/11, the American government ordered 3,000 BlackBerrys for representatives, staffers, and senators.

Growth was rapid at RIM in this period, and it was enhanced by something that the company did not anticipate. All of a sudden, actors, athletes, and other high-profile individuals were spotted using BlackBerrys. Among other organizations, the BlackBerry became standard issue for 31 out of 32 teams in the NFL. This created a demand among the general public, who wanted to use the same device they saw their favorite celebrities using. This resulted in rapidly expanding sales and market share; RIM had more than 2 million users in 2004 and sold devices in 40 countries through 80 carriers. The massive popularity in the 2000s saw RIM emerge as a dominant producer of smartphones, and at its peak in 2009 it had acquired 20.1 percent market share and sold nearly 15 million devices per quarter.[15]

According to former account and carrier manager Chris Key, the BlackBerry became so popular with major companies that CTOs often referred to it as digital heroin, and many started calling it "CrackBerry." With competition from Google, Samsung, and Apple mounting in the mid-2000s, however, RIM decided to focus on its core competencies in security and reliability. By 2018, Blackberry's smartphone market share had gone below 0.1 percent, with Android holding an 88 percent market share and iPhone with an 11.9 percent market share. The era of the BlackBerry smartphones had come to an end (see Exhibit 2).

Industry Landscape

Internet of Things

The Internet of Things (IoT) is the interconnection via the Internet of computing devices embedded in everyday objects, enabling them to send and receive data. IoT has the potential to be the next great computing era overlapping and extending the mobile era and, of course, the PC era, which still clings to relevancy. BlackBerry's software aims to provide the embedded intelligence to secure the Enterprise of Things so that the Internet of Things can thrive.[16] 451 Research, a preeminent information technology research and advisory company, breaks IoT down into four subcategories: consumer, enterprise, government, and vertical-specific uses. The enterprise segment of the IoT concerns the integration of IoT with the full support of enterprise IT tools, platforms, processes, and organizational alignment. Some vendors have taken to branding this important

EXHIBIT 2 Global Smartphone Market Shares, 2014–2018

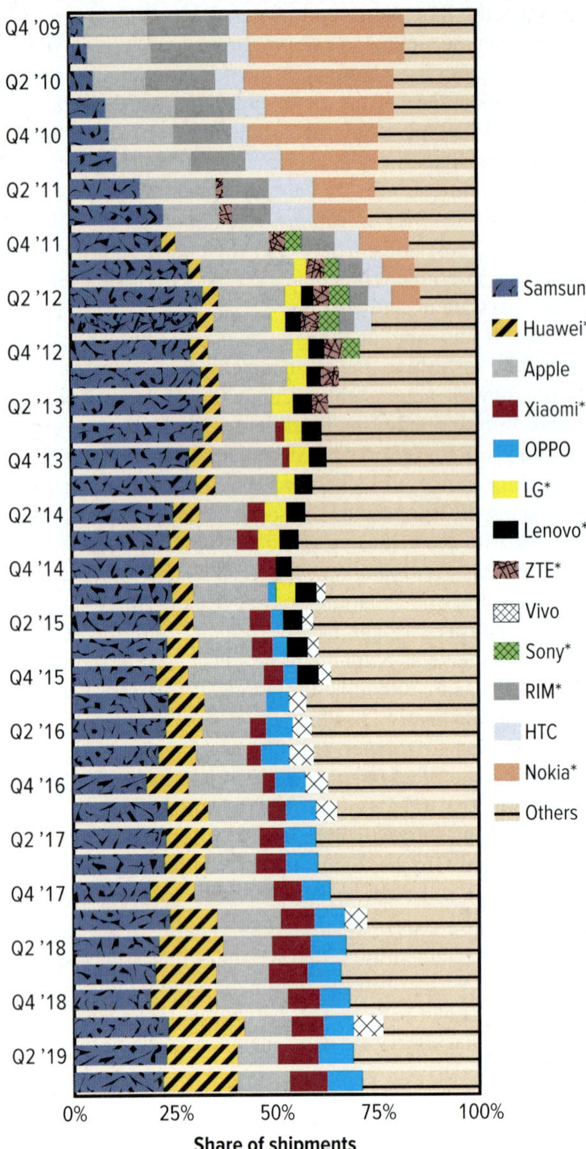

Source: Statista, 2018

submarket as "The Enterprise of Things."[17] BlackBerry defines the Enterprise of Things as the network of smartphones, computers, vehicles, sensors, equipment, and other online devices within the enterprise that communicate with each other to enable smart business processes that span across people, connected endpoints, and their data. The vulnerabilities in the Enterprise of Things has opened a plethora of cybercrimes and has given a way for hackers to access enterprise networks. This has resulted in an increased requirement in the Endpoint Security Software Industry. The Endpoint security market is projected to surpass $7.5 billion in 2025.[18] Some of the key players in the endpoint security market include McAfee, Microsoft, and Symantec. BlackBerry's enterprise software portfolio includes leading unified endpoint management, secure business productivity, application containerization, secure collaboration, and digital rights management capabilities.

Unified Endpoint Management (UEM) occupies a larger part of BlackBerry's portfolio. UEM revolves around securing and controlling computers, laptops, smartphones, and tablets in a connected manner from a single console. Quite popular in the industry today, many companies are opting for UEM. "We feel that UEM will be the best practice for organizations with diverse endpoints in their environment," said Jason Lendvay, Assistant Vice President of M&T Bank. "We are working towards our move to UEM in conjunction with our Windows 7 to Windows 10 migration. We see the Windows 10 OS and modern management capabilities are a key enabler for our move to UEM, which is a primary reason why we are looking to move towards UEM at this time."[19] In the Forrester Wave Report, they evaluated the 12 most significant UEM providers in the market. On a scale of 0 (weak) to 5 (strong), BlackBerry got a 4.32 in market presence, and 5 in both Application and Network security. One of the other leaders in the market, IBM, got a 3.68 in market presence, and 5 and 3 in Application and Network Security, respectively (see Exhibit 3). Customers frequently cite the security benefits of BlackBerry's Secure Connectivity service as well as the strong app and data-level security features included with the platform.[20]

Cylance, BlackBerry's recent acquisition, shifted the narrative from BlackBerry's homegrown services to those originally developed at Cylance. Cylance grew at a 92 percent year-over-year (YoY) rate during 2018 (see Exhibit 4). In its Q4 2019 Earnings report, Chen praised Cylance, stating that in joining forces with BlackBerry Spark, it "will make our endpoint management and embedded software products stronger and more essential for enterprises to generate value from the Internet of Things."[21] Cylance uses AI such as algorithmic science and machine learning to protect mobile devices, tablets and other Internet-connected devices from cyber-attacks. Over 20 percent of Fortune 500 companies use its solutions.[22]

BlackBerry's QNX real-time operating system enables automakers to build secure and scalable software solutions for connected and autonomous cars. Audi, BMW, Jaguar Land Rover, and Toyota use the software for infotainment systems, acoustics, and dashboard functions. QNX is embedded in 125 million vehicles today. The road ahead for BlackBerry in 2019 requires successful execution of strategies that support embedded operating systems, Internet of Things platforms, and security solutions.[23]

Smartphones

Apple, Inc. entered the smartphone industry in 2007 when its CEO, Steve Jobs, introduced the world to the company's newest innovation, the iPhone. Apple had a completely different strategy from that of BlackBerry; Apple's strategy was to cater to all the smartphone customers and not just the corporations.

EXHIBIT 3 Unified Endpoint Management Providers, Q4 2018

Vendor	Product and version evaluated	Product version evaluated
BlackBerry	BlackBerry UEM	V12.7.2
Cisco	Meraki Systems Manager	
Citrix Systems	Citrix Endpoint Management	10
IBM	IBM MaaS360	10.70
Ivanti	Ivanti Endpoint Manager (EPM)	2018 release
Jamf	Jamf Pro	10.7
Kaspersky Lab	Kaspersky Endpoint Security for Business	11
Matrix42	Matrix42 Unified Endpoint Management	2018 release
Microsoft	Enterprise Mobility + Security	
MobileIron	MobileIron	55 (Cloud) v10 (on-premises)
Sophos	Sophos Central (Mobile UEM)	8.5
VMware	Workspace One	9.6

Source: 2018 Forrester research, Inc. The Forrester WaveTM: Unified Endpoint Management, Q4 2018.

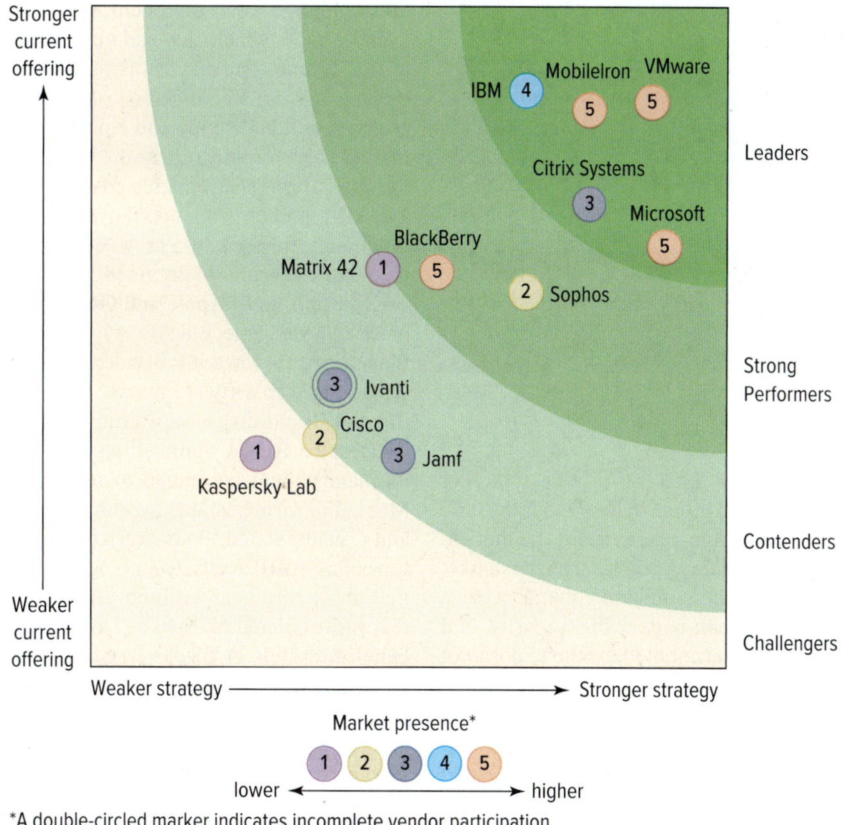

Source: 2018 Forrester research, Inc. 2018. The Forrester WaveTM: Unified Endpoint Management, Q4.

EXHIBIT 4 Cylance Inc. Consolidated Statement of Operations (in thousands)

CYLANCE INC. Consolidated Statements of Operations (in thousands)	Year Ended April 30,	
	2017	2018
Revenue:		
Subscription	$ 54,153	$105,207
Services	15,252	28,724
Total revenue	69,405	133,931
Cost of revenue:		
Subscription	15,333	27,095
Services	13,404	20,177
Total cost of revenue	28,737	47,272
Gross Profit	40,668	86,659
Operating Expenses:		
Sales and marketing	107,589	108,529
Research and development	48,793	64,747
General and administrative	24,862	26,343
Total operating expenses	181,244	199,619
Loss from operations	(140,576)	(112,960)
Other expenses, net	(331)	(625)
Loss before income taxes	(140,907)	(113,585)
Provision for income taxes	142	739
Net Loss	$(141,049)	$(114,324)

Source: Form 6-K. BlackBerry Limited, April 2019.

Steve Jobs and management at Apple believed that the individual consumer would drive the next surge in the market. Clearly, RIM's management did not believe that the market was shifting, and BlackBerry continued to enhance what it thought made its product great: battery life, security, and e-mail. In 2006, corporations accounted for the majority of RIM revenues, and the company intended to keep enterprises as its main target market. Lazaridis believed that the iPhone would be a fad and could not understand why anyone would want an iPhone, given its poor battery life and capacity. He was also extremely skeptical of the touchscreen keyboard. In an interview in 2007, Balsillie said, "As nice as the Apple iPhone is, it poses a real challenge to its users. Try typing a web key on a touchscreen on an Apple iPhone, that's a real challenge. You cannot see what you type."[24] BlackBerry's inventor believed that consumers preferred typing e-mails and messages using a physical keyboard rather than using a touchscreen. Co-CEO Balsillie declared that the iPhone was "not a sea-changer for BlackBerry."[25]

With further developments in touchscreen phones, consumers cared more about iPhone and Android phones' access to applications rather than battery life, security features, and QWERTY keyboards. The touchscreen smartphones also gained traction among suppliers. Software developers found it easier to work with Android and iPhone systems as compared to BlackBerry's complex Java-based system. Consequently, iPhone and Android phones experienced rapid growth and market acceptance, which created internal tensions within RIM.

When it was unable to acquire a license to sell iPhones, Verizon contacted RIM with an offer to collaborate on developing an "iPhone killer," which meant a smartphone with touchscreen capabilities and no QWERTY keyboard. The result of this partnership was the "BlackBerry Storm," which unfortunately did not gain popularity among consumers because the Storm's touchscreen was not easy to use, and the device was slow and full of bugs. RIM tried its luck with a touchscreen phone once again in 2010, when AT&T contracted with the company to make a competitor to the iPhone. This could help AT&T to differentiate itself from Verizon, which now had obtained licenses for the sale of the iPhone. The result was the "BlackBerry Torch," but this too was not a commercial success.

Even though iPhone and Android phones were gaining market share rapidly, Lazaridis remained optimistic about the BlackBerry's sustainable advantage. He warned his fellow RIM directors in a board meeting that trying to sell all-touch smartphones in a crowded market would be a huge mistake. Lazaridis maintained full confidence that RIM would catch up to Apple and Google (Android) with their newest device, the BlackBerry 10. While developing the BlackBerry 10, Lazaridis decided to acquire QNX Software, a leading-edge software maker. QNX had the technology that the BlackBerry 10 operating system needed.

Despite RIM's diminishing position in the industry, its management continued to remain optimistic. Andrew MacLeod, former managing director for the United States and Canada, stated, "I am heartened by the fact that we have tons of assets-IP assets, technology assets. We have a culture that at its core is about innovation and are in an industry that moves incredibly fast."[26] This signaled that there was a belief internally at BlackBerry that its core competencies could redefine the industry with new innovations. Lazaridis solidified this notion in an interview to the *Globe and Mail:* "Many companies go through cycles. Intel experienced it, IBM experienced it, and Apple experienced it." He went on to say, "People counted IBM, Apple, and other companies out only to be proven wrong. I am rooting that they are wrong on BlackBerry as well."[27]

To generate revenue for RIM, Balsillie saw great potential with the BBM messaging service as well. The BBM messenger was developed as an application for the BlackBerry in 2005, and it enabled users to communicate by using their devices' PIN numbers. The BBM was innovative and is credited with being the first instant messaging service on wireless devices. Among the BBM's key strengths were its reliability and the fact that users could send an unlimited number of messages without any extra cost, unlike standard SMS text messaging. Further, the messaging service was very secure and gave users the privacy they sought. With increasing competition and the decreasing sales and market share of BlackBerry, Balsillie wanted to make the BBM platform available on all devices. He envisioned that telecom carriers could integrate BBM as their own enhanced version of SMS text messaging. This could generate additional sales for the carriers, which would get RIM a percentage of the carriers' revenues.

In 2019, Emtek, the company that took over the BBM in 2016, announced that it would be shutting down the BBM consumer service on May 31, 2019. In a blog post they explained the unsuccessful efforts to revamp the once popular application: "The technology industry however, is very fluid, and in spite of our substantial efforts, users have moved on to other platforms, while new users proved difficult to sign on."[28]

Operations of BlackBerry

Under Chen's leadership, BlackBerry intended to return to its core strengths that catered to enterprises with security and efficiencies. Chen's first task as CEO was to restructure the operating units. By 2019, the company had four distinct operating segments from which it drew revenue: Enterprise Software and Services; BlackBerry Technology Solutions ("BTS"); Licensing, IP and Other, Handheld Devices; and Service Access Fees ("SAF").[29] Chen believed this structure would lead BlackBerry to an increased focus on software services. BlackBerry also continued to remain popular with governments; all seven G7 countries' governments were BlackBerry customers.

Chen is highly credited for his turnaround strategy involving BlackBerry. Prior to BlackBerry, he steered Sybase's trajectory toward financial gains. Chen pivoted the database and business services company into the emerging mobile information sector. The move proved brilliant. Mobile information generated hundreds of million dollars in annual revenue, returning Sybase to profitability.[30] Sybase was then sold to SAP for $5.8 billion. After he came to BlackBerry in 2013, his strategy to put aside the mobile hardware business and shift BlackBerry's focus to cybersecurity and embedded software has proven successful for the company, with the majority of its revenue and growth coming from its software and services.

Although BlackBerry's revenue had dropped from $19.9 billion in FY2011 to $904 million in FY2019, its stock began to climb out of a deep dive as revenue and profits beat expectations, in comparison to the past couple of years. CEO John Chen estimated that BlackBerry's current 2020 financial year would see a revenue growth of between 23 and 27 percent.[31] (see Exhibits 5 and 6 for detailed information regarding BlackBerry's financial situation).

Competition

BlackBerry's software security division consists of a long list of companies providing a wide range of different types of enterprise security. However, BlackBerry Limited specializes in Mobile and Data Security for Enterprises. Providers of enterprise software solutions that compete with BlackBerry's BlackBerry Enterprise Mobility Suite include VMware Inc., Microsoft Corporation ("Microsoft"), Citrix Systems, Inc. ("Citrix"), MobileIron Inc., SOTI Inc., Sophos Ltd., and IBM Corporation. Providers of endpoint security technologies that compete with the BlackBerry Cylance platform include McAfee, Microsoft, and Symantec. Providers of embedded software that compete with the Company's BlackBerry QNX automotive business include customized Linux open-source operating system providers, Wind River Systems, Green Hills Software, Mentor Graphics Corporation and SYSGO AG.[32] Although BlackBerry does not consider itself to be in the smartphone market anymore, BlackBerry's two most significant competitors in the smartphone industry were Apple and Samsung Electronics Co.

Microsoft Corporation

Established in 1975, Microsoft initially entered the Operating System (OS) business in 1980 with their own version of Unix, called Xenix. Enterprise Mobility + Security (EMS) is a bundle of Microsoft products that includes Advanced Threat Analytics, Azure Ad Premium, Azure information Protection, Cloud App Security, intune, and System Center Configuration Manager (ConfigMgr).[33] Although competitors in the Unified Endpoint Management market, in 2018, BlackBerry and Microsoft partnered to offer enterprises a solution that integrates BlackBerry's expertise in mobility and security with Microsoft's unmatched cloud and productivity products. Carl Wiese, president of Global Sales at BlackBerry explained the alliance: "We saw a need for a hyper-secure way for our joint customers to use native Office 365 mobile apps. BlackBerry Enterprise BRIDGE addresses this need and is a great example of how BlackBerry and Microsoft continue to securely enable workforces to be highly productive in today's connected world."[34]

VMware

VMware is a global leader in cloud infrastructure and digital workspace technology that accelerates digital transformation for evolving IT environments. Over the past year, VMware has invested heavily in helping customers embrace modern management with AirWatch, an enterprise mobility management (EMM) technology that powers VMware Workspace ONE. Workspace ONE provides unified endpoint management and a seamless user experience for accessing any app on any device, across knowledge worker, line of business (LOB), high security, and any other use

EXHIBIT 5 BlackBerry Consolidated Statement of Operations

BlackBerry Limited (United States dollars, in millions, except per share data) Consolidated Statements of Operations			
		For the Years Ended	
	February 28, 2019	February 29, 2017	February 28, 2016
Revenue	$904	$932	$1,309
Cost of sales	206	262	542
Inventory write-down	—	—	150
Gross margin	698	670	617
Operating expenses			
Research and development	219	239	306
Selling, marketing and administration	406	467	553
Amortization	136	153	186
Impairment of goodwill	—	—	57
Impairment of long-lived assets	—	11	501
Loss on sale, disposal and abandonment of long-lived assets	3	9	171
Debentures fair value adjustment	(117)	191	24
Arbitration awards and settlements, net	(9)	(683)	—
Operating income (loss)	60	283	(1,181)
Investment income (loss), net	17	123	(27)
Income (loss) before income taxes	77	406	(1,208)
Provision for (recovery of) income taxes	(16)	1	(2)
Net income (loss)	93	405	(1,206)
Earnings (loss) per share			
Basic	0.17	0.76	(2.30)
Diluted	0.00	0.74	2.30

Source: Annual Report. BlackBerry Limited, February 28, 2019.

case in organizations. In 2019, Dell introduced Unified Workspace, a comprehensive solution to help IT deploy, secure, manage, and support endpoints from the cloud. Dell teamed up with VMware; Workspace ONE transforms and automates every phase of PC management–from configuration to onboarding to pushing regular updates–and is the backbone of Dell Technologies Unified Workspace.[35]

McAfee

A familiar name that comes to mind when we think of cyber security is McAfee. Its products help secure computers, endpoints, networks, and cloud from viruses, malware, and other security threats. McAfee was purchased by Intel in February 2011 to build Intel's security division of online computing. "With the rapid expansion of growth across a vast array of Internet-connected devices, more and more of the elements of our lives have moved online," said Paul Otellini, former Intel president and CEO. "In the past, energy-efficient performance and connectivity have defined computing requirements. Looking forward, security will join those as a third pillar of what people demand from all computing experiences."[37]

EXHIBIT 6 BlackBerry Balance Sheet

BlackBerry Limited United States dollars, in millions) Consolidated Balance Sheets	As at	
	February 28, 2019	**February 29, 2018**
Assets		
Current		
Cash and cash equivalents	$ 48	$ 816
Short-term investments	368	1,443
Accounts receivable, net	194	151
Other receivables	19	71
Income taxes receivable	9	26
Other current assets	56	38
Total current assets	1,194	2,545
Restricted cash and cash equivalents	34	39
Long Term Investments	55	55
Other Long term investments	28	28
2	2	3
Property, plant and equipment, net	85	64
Goodwill	1,463	569
Intangible assets, net	1,068	477
Liabilities	**3,929**	**3,780**
Current		
Accounts payable	$ 48	$ 46
Accrued liabilities	192	205
Income taxes payable	17	18
Deferred revenue	214	142
Total current liabilities	471	411
Deferred revenue, non-current	136	53
Other long-term liabilities	19	23
Long-term debt	665	782
Deferred income tax liability	2	6
Total liabilities	**1,206**	**2,326**
Shareholders' equity	2,688	2,560
Capital stock and additional paid-in capital		
Issued - 530,497,193 voting common shares (February 29, 2016–521,172,271)	(20)	(10)
Retained earnings (deficit)	2,636	2,505
Accumulated other comprehensive loss	$3,929	$3,780

Sources: Annual Report. BlackBerry Limited, February 28, 2019.

In 2014, Intel announced the availability of a family of hardware and software products called Intel® In-Vehicle Solutions, which were paired with McAfee's whitelisting technology from Intel Security to fully secure the connected car. CRN, a brand of The Channel Company, added McAfee to its 100 Coolest Cloud Computing Companies of 2019 list, and its annual Security 100 list.[38]

Wind River Systems

Wind River is a world leader in embedded software for intelligent connected systems. In 2018, Wind River announced that it would be acquired by TPG, a global alternative asset firm. TPG was acquiring Wind River from Intel. Nehal Raj, Partner and Head of Technology investing at TPG said, "We see a tremendous market opportunity in industrial software driven by the convergence of the Internet of Things (IoT), intelligent devices, and edge computing."[39] In 2019, Wind River announced its achievement as the leader in continued embedded real-time operating system (RTOS) and commercial Linux revenues, according to VDC Research. The company also ranked as the leading commercial provider of both embedded hypervisors and safe and secure operating systems.[40]

Apple Inc.

A major player in the smartphone industry is iPhone by Apple Inc. The company has core competencies in product design, software development, application development, and hardware. Apple Inc. not only targets corporations and governments as potential customers but also targets general consumers, academic institutions, and small and medium-sized enterprises (SMEs). Most of the Apple products are sold through Apple's own retail and online stores; however, the company also utilizes indirect distribution channels such as telecom carriers, wholesalers, retailers, and value-added resellers. Another core competence for Apple is a continuous focus on research and development (R&D), in order to keep up with and lead technological advancements. Apple Inc.'s R&D expenditure was about $14 billion by March 2019,[41] which is more than most smartphone companies were worth. A significant source of Apple's competitive strength is its ecosystem. Apple's iCloud service enables users to sync a particular file or data on all Apple devices, so if one edits a photo on iPhone, the changes show up automatically on all other devices.[42] These features give Apple users an incentive to purchase other Apple products, because benefits and convenience of use bring value to the consumer.

Samsung Electronics Co.

The other major player in the smartphone industry is the South Korean tech giant Samsung Electronics Co. Samsung maintains its leadership status across multiple sectors by investing heavily in R&D. By 2019, Samsung was #1 in the world for R&D spending, with $15.2 billion, according to the European Commission R&D Scoreboard.[43] Samsung has strategic resources that competitors find hard to replicate, such as substantial economies of scale, which drive down per-unit cost. The company has a very favorable cost structure because of its great efforts in vertical integration. Samsung has an aggressive pricing strategy and allocates a large amount of resources toward marketing expenditures. The company is a dominant force in the Android operating system. With Android, consumers purchase and download multiple applications, similar to Apple's app store. Samsung sells products to authorized distributors, mainly through mobile network carriers or large electronic outlets like Best Buy. Samsung offers a wide range of smartphones with low, medium, and high price points.

Future of BlackBerry

Although BlackBerry no longer calls itself a smartphone company, its licensing partner, the Chinese consumer-electronics company TCL, introduced a version of the BlackBerry Key2 device. "It's very important that we don't detach entirely from the phone; it is part of our heritage and brand," CEO John Chen told Barron's in a March 2019 interview in San Francisco.[44] The smartphone industry experienced rapid development and high growth during the past decade. There were over 1.44 billion units of smartphones sold worldwide in 2018 with total sales revenue reaching $522 billion.[45] Although that is a remarkable number, new trends show that the smartphone industry growth rate has started declining. The biggest driver of the 2017 shipment downturn was the saturated market in China, which saw its smartphone market decline 4.9 percent year-over-year. Tough times are expected to continue, as IDC (global market intelligence firm) forecasts consumption in China to decline another 7.1 percent before flattening out in 2019.[46]

There is also low growth in North American and Western European markets. Most individuals in these countries already have smartphones, so growth was driven by replacement sales due to a low number of first-time buyers. Despite BlackBerry's smartphone demise, and the end of the BBM platform in 2019, the company still refers to itself as a pioneer in mobile messaging. After suing Facebook in 2018, alleging patent infringement, BlackBerry also sued Twitter for the same in 2019. The suit claimed that Twitter "created mobile messaging applications that co-opt BlackBerry's innovations, using a number of the innovative user interface and functionality enhancing features that made BlackBerry's products such a critical and commercial success in the first place."[47]

By moving away from hardware, BlackBerry is focusing attention on company strengths in software and services. In 2018, BlackBerry announced that its QNX software is embedded in 120 million cars.[48] The auto industry is expected to transform through 2030. According to PwC, there are five main trends that will influence this transformation. The trends are electrified, autonomous, shared, connected, and yearly updated. [49] As cars get smarter, BlackBerry will experience more demand in the auto industry.

BlackBerry is playing in both the Internet of Things and enterprise mobility management segment of the cyber security market. With its acquisition of Cylance, BlackBerry adds to its arsenal of cybersecurity solutions that help enterprises intelligently connect, protect, and build secure endpoints. "BlackBerry . . . and their now approved acquisition of Cylance makes this a critical game changing moment for the company and the IoT industry. In today's hostile world, security isn't an option, it is a requirement," said Rob Enderle, a technology analyst.[50]

Competing with big players such as Microsoft, Symantec, and Cisco in the Internet of Things market, BlackBerry prides itself on being an ideal fit for lightweight devices while companies like Cisco and Symantec are geared more toward large networked systems. "I don't mind going after a market with a lot of big players," CEO Chen said. "That means the market is appealing. Better that than to go after a market with no big players."[51] Jack Gold, principal analyst at J. Gold Associates, said, "BlackBerry is 'a born-again startup'. Their approach is let's take what's left of the DNA, and let's go after industries that need heightened security such as health care, Wall Street, and government agencies."[52]

ENDNOTES

1. Limitone, J. 2019. Blackberry morphs into billion-dollar AI cyber company. Fox Business, March 13, https://www.foxbusiness.com/technology/blackberry-morphs-into-billion-dollar-ai-cyber-company.
2. List of Blackberry acquisitions on Crunchbase.com. https://www.crunchbase.com/organization/blackberry/acquisitions/acquisitions_list https://www.blackberry.com/us/en/company/newsroom/press-releases
3. Press Release. 2019. BlackBerry completes acquisition of Cylance. Blackberry, February 21, https://www.cylance.com/en-us/company/news-and-press/press-releases/blackberry-completes-acquisition-of-cylance.html.
4. Cybersecurity Company Awards–Winners and Finalists. 2019. https://cybersecurity-excellence-awards.com/2019-cybersecurity-company-awards-winners-and-finalists.
5. Blackberry. 2019. Annual Report.
6. Swartz, J. 2019. BlackBerry is looking to its past to find a new future. Barron's, March 11, https://www.barrons.com/articles/blackberry-stock-revival-comeback-phones-51552083659.
7. Forrester research, Inc. 2018. The Forrester WaveTM: Unified Endpoint Management, Q4.
8. Maclean, J. 2018. Blackberry's future still unclear, Christine Poole says. Cantechletter, December 13, https://www.canechletter.com/2018/12/blackberrys-future-is-still-unclear-christine-poole-says/.
9. Breen, B. 2001. Rapid motion. Fast Company, July 31, https://www.fastcompany.com/43377/rapid-motion.
10. Gillette, F., Brady, D., and C. Winter. 2013. The rise and fall of BlackBerry: An oral history. *Bloomberg*, December 9, https://www.bloomberg.com/news/articles/2013-12-05/the-rise-and-fall-of-blackberry-an-oral-history.
11. CBC News. 2014. BlackBerry timeline: A tech titans roller coaster ride. CBC/Radio-Canada, March 17, http:// www.cbc.ca/news2/interactives/timeline-rim/.
12. Reuters. 2013. BlackBerry timeline: From RIM to RIP? *The Telegraph*, August 12, http://www.telegraph.co.uk/technology/blackberry/10237847/BlackBerry-timeline-from-RIM-to-RIP.html.
13. Research in Motion. Annual Report Fiscal 2000. http://us.blackberry.com/content/dam/bbCompany/Desktop/Global/PDF/Investors/Documents/2000/2000rim_ar.pdf.
14. Romero, S. 2001. The right connections; The simple BlackBerry allowed contact when phones failed. *New York Times*, September 20, https://www.nytimes.com/2001/09/20/technology/the-right-connections-the-simple-blackberry-allowed-contact-when-phones-failed.html.
15. The Atlas.com. 2016. Global Smartphone Market Share Held by RIM (BlackBerry) from 2007 to 2015. *The Atlas*, September 27, https://www.theatlas.com/charts/4kkGhxGWx.
16. Blackberry. The Enterprise of Things.
17. Pathfinder Report. 2017. Securing the Enterprise of Things. Blackberry, 451 Research.
18. Press Release. 2019. At 7% CAGR, endpoint security market size is expected to surpass USD 7.5 billion by 2024. *Market Watch*, March 19, https://www.marketwatch.com/press-release/at-7-cagr-endpoint-security-market-size-is-expected-to-surpass-usd-75-billion-by-2024-2019-03-19.
19. Lerner, S. 2018. To UEM, or not to UEM, that is the question. Enterprise Mobility Exchange, September 4, https://www.enterprisemobilityexchange.com/eme-managed-mobility/news/unified-endpoint-management-enterprises-benefits-uem.
20. Forrester research, Inc. 2018. The Forrester WaveTM: Unified Endpoint Management, Q4.
21. Q4 Earnings Report. 2019. BlackBerry. March 29.
22. Lopez, M. 2019. 2019: The road ahead for BlackBerry extends beyond auto with EoT and security. *Forbes* January 24, https://www.forbes.com/sites/maribellopez/2019/01/24/2019-the-road-ahead-for-blackberry-extends-beyond-auto-with-eot-and-security/#758acaec63c3.
23. Ibid.
24. Arthur, C. 2012. RIM chiefs Mike Lazaridis and Jim Balsillie's best quotes. *The Guardian*, Friday 29, https://www.theguardian.com/technology/2012/jun/29/rim-chiefs-best-quotes.
25. Vara, V. 2013. How BlackBerry fell. *The New Yorker*, August 12, https://www.newyorker.com/tech/annals-of-technology/how-blackberry-fell.
26. Gillette, F., Brady, D., and C. Winter. 2013. The rise and fall of BlackBerry: An oral history. *Bloomberg*, December 9, https://www.bloomberg.com/news/articles/2013-12-05/the-rise-and-fall-of-blackberry-an-oral-history.
27. Silcoff, S., Mcnish, J., and S. Ladurantaye. 2018. How BlackBerry blew it: The inside story. *The Globe and Mail*, April 7, https://www.theglobeandmail.com/report-on-business/the-inside-story-of-why-blackberry-is-failing/article14563602/.
28. BBM blog. 2019. Time to say goodbye. BBM.com, April 18, https://blog.bbm.com/2019/04/18/time-to-say-goodbye-english-version/.
29. Annual Report 2019. Blackberry.
30. Kastanes, J. 2018. BlackBerry under John Chen's leadership. Seeking Alpha, October 16, https://seekingalpha.com/article/4211973-blackberry-john-chens-leadership.
31. Paddon, D. 2019. BlackBerry stock soars as revenue and profit beat expectations. *The Canadian Press*, March 29, https://business.financialpost.com/technology/blackberry-reports-us51-million-q4-profit-beats-profit-and-revenue-estimates.
32. Annual Report 2019. Blackberry.
33. Forrester research, Inc. 2018. The Forrester WaveTM: Unified Endpoint Management, Q4.
34. Microsoft News Center. 2018. BlackBerry and Microsoft partner to empower the mobile workforce. Microsoft, March 19, https://news.microsoft.com/2018/03/19/blackberry-and-microsoft-partner-to-empower-the-mobile-workforce/.
35. Roszak, J. 2019. Dell and VMware transform how customers deploy, manage and secure PCs. VMware Blog, May 1, https://blogs.vmware.com/euc/2019/05/unified-workspace.html.
36. Forrester research, Inc. 2018. The Forrester WaveTM: Unified Endpoint Management, Q4.
37. News Release. 2010. Intel to acquire McAfee. Intel Newsroom, August 19, https://newsroom.intel.com/news-releases/intel-to-acquire-mcafee/#gs.bl7ep4.

38. Press Release, 2019. McAfee Cloud and Endpoint Security Solutions Recognized by CRN. McAfee, February 24, https://www.mcafee.com/enterprise/en-us/about/newsroom/press-releases/press-release.html?news_id=20190225005043
39. Calif, A. 2018. Wind River to be acquired by TPG. Wind River News, April 3, https://www.windriver.com/news/press/pr.html?ID=20982.
40. Wind River. 2019. Wind River ranked global leading provider of embedded operating systems. Wind River News, March 12, https://www.windriver.com/news/press/pr.html?ID=21909.
41. Elmer-DeWitt, P. 2019. In defense of Apple's $14 billion R&D budget. Ped30, March 10, https://www.ped30.com/2019/03/10/defense-apples-14-billion-rd-budget/.
42. Jackson, E. 2014. Apple isn't a hardware or software company–It's an ecosystem company. *Forbes*, June 3, http://www.forbes.com/sites/ericjackson/2014/06/03/apple-isnt-a-hardware-or-software-company-its-an-ecosystem-company/2/.
43. Hernández, H., Grassano, N., Tübke, A., Potters, L., Gkotsis, P., and A. Vezzani. 2018. The 2018 EU Industrial R&D Investment Scoreboard; EUR 29450 EN; Publications Office of the European Union, Luxembourg.
44. Swartz, J. 2019. BlackBerry is looking to its past to find a new future. Barron's, March 11, https://www.barrons.com/articles/blackberry-stock-revival-comeback-phones-51552083659.
45. Press Release, 2019. Global Smartphone Sales Reached $522 Billion in 2018. GfK Global, February 22, https://www.gfk.com/insights/press-release/global-smartphone-sales-reached-522-billion-in-2018/
46. Deans, D. 2018. Why the worldwide smartphone market continues to be sluggish.Telecoms Tech News, June 1, https://www.telecomstechnews.com/news/2018/jun/01/worldwide-smartphone-market-still-growing-slowly/.
47. Dickey, M. R. 2019. BlackBerry sues Twitter for patent infringement. TechCrunch, February 27, https://techcrunch.com/2019/02/27/blackberry-sues-twitter-for-patent-infringement/.
48. Press Release. 2018. BlackBerry QNX Technology now embedded in 120 million vehicles on the road today. BlackBerry News, June 6, http://blackberry.qnx.com/en/news/release/2018/7111.
49. Pwc Report. 2018. Five trends transforming the automotive industry. PwC. https://www.pwc.com/gx/en/industries/automotive/assets/pwc-five-trends-transforming-the-automotive-industry.pdf.
50. Blaize. 2019. BlackBerry's strategic acquisition of cylance is now complete. CrackBerry, February 21, https://crackberry.com/blackberrys-strategic-acquisition-cylance-now-complete.
51. Swartz, J. 2019. BlackBerry is looking to its past to find a new future. Barron's, March 11, https://www.barrons.com/articles/blackberry-stock-revival-comeback-phones-51552083659.
52. Ibid.

CASE 37

VENMO: WAR ON CASH?*

Venmo
/ˈvenmō/
verb

> Transferring money to someone through the mobile payment app called Venmo.
> "I'll pay for dinner. You can just Venmo me your share later."

The past couple of years, at the end of a restaurant meal or every month when splitting rent, some millennials began asking, "Do you use Venmo?" If the unfortunate friend answered negatively, there probably was a conversation extolling the convenience of the payment platform.[1] Venmo is a payment service based on combining a social network and a payment system. It gained momentum among millennials as a platform to exchange money, split a bill, and request money from their friends. It has nearly 23 million users, and a devoted generation of social media followers. "Just Venmo me the money" is a common phrase among millennials, making Venmo a genericized trademark like Google or Xerox. The reason why Venmo stands out among its numerous competitors is after every transfer, the exchange appears on everyone's social feed so they know who's getting lunch or a drink with whom. These transactions are often included with tasteful emojis that let users personalize their experience of transferring money. Although its target demographic is the younger crowd, the appeal of peer-to-peer payment method is gaining popularity among other age groups.

One of the reasons why the app might be appealing to the younger audience is because, for the most part, it is free. Venmo's revenue stream is reliant on either the fees levied on merchants, sending money from credit cards, and instant money transfer to bank accounts. The financial technology (FinTech) company, responsible for the funds transfers, functions primarily using a Customer to Customer (C2C) model. They managed to gain consumers with their direct network effects**—more users made the service more valuable. However, they found it considerably harder over the past couple of years to leverage indirect network effects—increasing value by adding businesses to the network. Venmo's free money-transfer model, with money streaming in only from credit card payments, limited the company's revenue generation. After acquiring Braintree, Venmo's parent company, PayPal invested significantly to strengthen Venmo's Business to Consumer (B2C) market. PayPal Holdings Inc. said that more than two million U.S. retailers will be able to accept payments through its mobile app Venmo.[2]

As Venmo became popular, large banks felt threatened, and a consortium of banks including Bank of America, Wells Fargo, JP Morgan Chase, and several others developed Zelle in September 2017. Like Venmo, Zelle is a peer-to-peer payment service allowing U.S. banks to enter the financial technology marketplace. Zelle lacked a social dimension, but the backing of the financial services powerhouses, who were strongly motivated to protect their sources of revenue, helped it gain popularity. In 2018, Zelle processed payments of $122 billion, surpassing Venmo at $62 billion. However, one of the key differences between Venmo and Zelle remains the social feed and loyal customer base that Venmo possesses (see Exhibit 1). Along with Zelle, long time competitor Square, Inc. poses a threat via their Cash App (released in October 2013).

Venmo is widespread in the United States and enjoys broad support from its younger audience. Although doing well monetizing its customer base in comparison to its social media counterparts, such as Twitter and Snapchat, its financial performance does not seem to measure up to

EXHIBIT 1 Mobile Phone P2P Payment Users by Platform (millions of users)

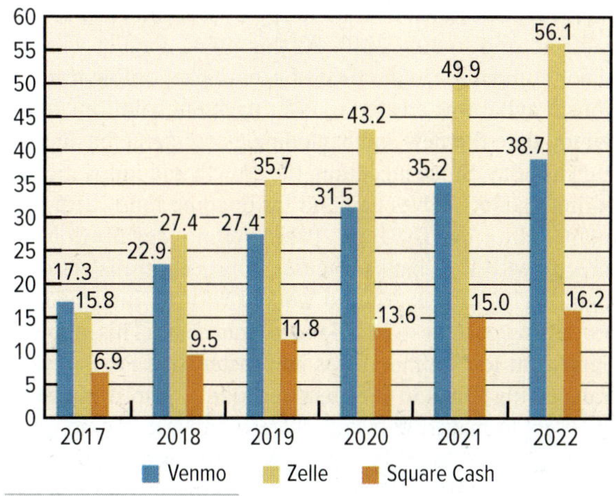

Source: eMarketer, May 2018

* This case was prepared by Professors Patrick J. McGuigan, Alan B. Eisner, and John C. Byrne, Pace University, New York. Special thanks to graduate assistants Jihane Mendard, Sushmitha Mudda, and Christoph Kirsch. This case was solely based on library research and was developed for class discussion rather than to illustrate either effective or ineffective handling of an administrative situation. Copyright ©2019 Alan B. Eisner.

** Network effects are the incremental benefit gained by an existing user for each new user that joins the network. Direct network effects are also known as same-side effects. The value of a service simply goes up as the number of users goes up. With indirect network effects, the value of the service increases for one user group when a new user of a different user group joins the network. You must have two or more user groups to achieve indirect network effects.[38]

its reputation. With a growing list of competitors (Cash App, Zelle, ApplePay, Google Wallet, Samsung Pay, Android Pay), and lack of a global presence, how does Venmo plan to remain relevant in today's dynamic market? Will their social-savvy feature provide enough differentiation to prevail in a crowded market space?

PayPal CEO Dan Schulman asserted that: "Instead of trying to compete we are going to open our platform to partner with tech companies and become allies in this war on cash."[3] Is a war on cash necessary? Is cash a strategic threat to developing the peer-to-peer payments market? It is critical that PayPal develop an effective strategy to monetize, grow, and sustain Venmo as a business. Fundamentally, irrespective of if Venmo is an app or a business, its growth must be addressed. It has been established that peer-to-peer payments are a viable market, but just how important is it that payments be socially connected? Mike Vaughan, Venmo COO, explained about Apple coming into the payments space: "you always have to pay attention to when Apple does things, there is a certain aspect of legitimizing what's happening in that space that can benefit everyone in the space, but we stay focused on what we can do because we can't affect what Apple is going to do. What we can do is build great products and great experiences in our brands."[4] Whether Venmo can harness the momentum Apple brings to the space remains to be seen, but with a desire to partner, Venmo does not seem to bring much to the table Apple does not already have. It is easy to see what is in partnership for Venmo, but benefits to the partners are harder to identify.

Company Background

Co-founders Andrew Kortina and Iqram Magdon-Ismail founded Venmo, LLC in April 2009. Because of Magdon-Ismail forgetting his wallet and having to borrow and pay back money to Kortina, the idea of a peer-to-peer payment service came into mind. They saw a need for quicker payment solutions as opposed to writing checks or returning cash later. By September 2009, the company raised $100,000 in debt financing from four investors.[5] This allowed Kortina and Magdon-Ismail to work full time, hire an engineer and launch its iPhone app by December 2009 and Android app in July 2010. At this point, PayPal was the major competitor in the field of peer-to-peer online transactions. PayPal was created to offer payment solutions to accommodate the new and exploding e-commerce businesses such as eBay. Since inception, the growth and innovation in online markets drives demand for ongoing innovative payment solutions. By June 2011, Venmo began working directly with U.S. banks in order to process transfers overnight (prior to this, Venmo worked with an intermediary processing partner to handle bank transfers). This step was significant for Venmo; it was now faster than PayPal when transferring funds to U.S. bank accounts, inspiring ex-PayPal users to make the switch, thereby growing Venmo's customer base. At this point Venmo was processing approximately $10 million in payments every month, with a 30 percent growth in users on a monthly basis,[6] however going public posed a burden for Kortina and Magdon-Ismail. With the rapidly growing number of processed payments, expenses grew exponentially and almost put the company out of business. In August 2012, four months after being released to the public and two weeks before going bankrupt, Venmo, LLC was acquired by Braintree Payment Solutions, LLC (a company that specializes in mobile and web payment systems for e-commerce companies) for $26.2 million. This acquisition would allow Braintree to extend its payment platform to consumers and allow Braintree to make it even easier for e-commerce companies to accept payments on mobile devices. At the time of acquisition, CEO of Braintree Bill Ready said, "The addition of Venmo to Braintree's offering will make it even easier for developers . . . to offer the most elegant, frictionless, mobile and social purchasing experiences. . . .Braintree and Venmo [together] will provide a set of tools as important to the next 10 years of e-commerce."[7] In September 2013, Braintree Payment Solutions, LLC was acquired by PayPal, for $800 million; making PayPal the parent of Venmo.[8] Before closing the PayPal and Braintree deal, there was talk that Venmo was a key part of what attracted PayPal to Braintree.

PayPal became the ultimate parent officially in 2015 when eBay spun off PayPal into a separate publicly traded company. Separating eBay and PayPal made sense to the investors because it allows each business to enter into partnerships with firms that competed with the former partner. Thus, eBay can accept other forms of payment, and PayPal can enter into partnerships with competing retailers, vendors, and merchants. eBay reasoned that this would allow each company to reach their full potential independently. The new entity, PayPal Holdings, Inc., develops and markets a digital payments platform that is technology driven and user friendly. The PayPal businesses includes: PayPal, PayPal Credit, Venmo, Braintree, Xoom, and Paydiant. Each business serves a complimentary market niche that collectively allows PayPal to offer the most robust portfolio of payment solutions to both consumers and merchants. The company has continuously strengthened its platform, adding iZettle, a Swedish-based company, Fraud Services, and Bill Me Later, in 2018. The company operates in 200 markets around the world with 246 million active consumer accounts who can conduct business with 21 million merchants, resulting in PayPal processing $3.7 billion mobile transactions in 2018.[9]

Electronic payment solutions, and digital commerce in general, are trending. Global digital commerce volume is expected to double to $6 trillion by 2022, according to consulting firm McKinsey.[10] The growth rate in digital payments suggests excellent market potential for innovative companies; whether the market can reward investors remains to be seen. Investors appear to have confidence in Pay Pal, as evidenced by their valuation, but some argue that PayPal is simply reinventing the wheel, and the company might be overvalued.[11] Whether Pay Pal's commitment to Venmo is justified is unknown. The market is growing and investors are interested. The U.S. Department of the Treasury reports that demand for cash is strong and growing, suggesting that cash has not yet been replaced by electronic funds transfer (EFT). PayPal is always thinking about what is next and working to stay relevant in this fast-changing marketplace. PayPal has a strong history of innovation and creative thinking, but there are some serious competitors that will need to be addressed. Alipay, WeChat Pay, and Square continue to see record growth, signing up merchants concerned with mobile payments, but PayPal is well positioned to put up a good fight.[12] The recent decision by eBay to abandon PayPal, its former subsidiary, for Adyen, a small payments startup located in the Netherlands, is a sure sign that the fight for dominance in the e-commerce and mobile payments space will be brutal and unpredictable. eBay announced that Adyen can provide merchants with greater flexibility and lower cost while allowing all transactions to be managed via eBay.[13] The one stop, one-click approach is exactly the type of innovation that PayPal needs to drive!

Industry Landscape

The financial services industry, more specifically the FinTech industry is growing substantially. This sector includes financial and nonfinancial service companies that develop innovative technological solutions to evolve from the traditional financial methods. Additional sectors within FinTech include Asset and Wealth Management, Banking, Insurance, and Payments/Transfers. Financial services institutions are embracing the disruptive nature of FinTech by learning to collaborate.[14] A major example of this is the combining of Early Warning Services and clearXchange in January 2016 by several U.S. banks. In a joint prepared statement in October 2015, the CEOs of Bank of America, BB&T, Capital One, JPMorgan Chase, US Bank, and Wells Fargo said, "we are combining our collective, bank-owned digital payments network (clearXchange) with our fraud, risk and authentication assets (Early Warning), to further ensure that our customers can send money confidently . . . via their financial institutions."[15] By September 2017, clearXchange ceased and became Zelle, an app allowing transfer of funds via several partnering U.S. banks. In the fourth quarter of 2018, Zelle saw a record $35 billion in payments on 135 million transactions. Year-on-year payments value soared 61 percent, while transaction volume shot up by 81 percent.[16] Paul Finch, CEO of Early Warning Services, the network operator behind Zelle, said "Already, customers of more than 5,100 financial institutions are using the Zelle Network, whether it's through their financial institution's mobile banking app, or by registering their debit cards in the Zelle mobile app."[17]

Business Concept

Venmo's business model is service based. It simplifies money transfers between person-to-person and person-to-business transactions via a mobile application.[18] In addition, Venmo provides a social networking aspect with customer's transactions. It is a combination of a wallet and a social network. In their 2018 financial statements, PayPal's total revenue increased by $2.3 billion, or 18 percent. The percentage growth in total payment volume (TPV) was up 27 percent from 2017 at $578 billion based on 9.9 billion payment transactions completed, also a 27 percent increase from the previous year (see Exhibits 2 to 4). Peer-to-peer payments

EXHIBIT 2 Summary of PayPal's Active Customer Accounts, Number of Payment Transactions, TPV, and Related Metrics

	Year Ended December 31,			Percent Increase/ (Decrease)	
	2018	2017(1)	2016(1)	2018	2017
	(In millions, except percentages)				
Active accounts(2)	267	229	199	17%	15%
Number of payment transactions(3)	9,871	7,769	6,295	27%	23%
Payment transactions per active account(4)	36.9	34.0	31.6	9%	8%
TPV(5)	$578,419	$456,179	$359,928	27%	27%
Percent of cross-border TPV	19%	21%	22%	**	**

Source: Annual Report. PayPal Holdings, Inc, December 31, 2018.

All amounts in tables are rounded to the nearest million except as otherwise noted. As a result, certain amounts may not recalculate using the rounded amounts provided.

(1)Prior period amounts were revised to reflect updated definitions of active accounts and TPV discussed above.

(2)Reflects active accounts as of the end of the applicable period. An active account is an account registered directly with PayPal or a platform access partner that has completed a transaction on our Payments Platform, not including gateway-exclusive transactions, within the past 12 months.

(3)Number of payment transactions are the total number of payments, net of payment reversals, successfully completed on our Payments Platform or enabled by PayPal via a partner payment solution, not including gateway-exclusive transactions.

(4)Number of payment transactions per active account reflects the total number of payment transactions within the previous 12 month period, divided by active accounts at the end of the period.

(5)TPV is the value of payments, net of reversals, successfully completed on our Payments Platform or enabled by PayPal via a partner payment solution, not including gateway-exclusive transactions.

** Not meaningful.

EXHIBIT 3 **PayPal Income Statement**

	Year Ended December 31,		
	2018	2017	2016
	(In millions, except for per share amounts)		
Net revenues	$15,451	$13,094	$10,842
Operating expenses:			
Transaction expense	5,581	4,419	3,346
Transaction and loan losses	1,274	1,011	1,088
Customer support and operations	1,482	1,364	1,267
Sales and marketing	1,313	1,128	969
Product development	1,071	953	834
General and administrative	1,451	1,155	1,028
Depreciation and amortization	776	805	724
Restructuring and other charges	309	132	—
Total operating expenses	13,257	10,967	9,256
Operating income	2,194	2,127	1,586
Other income (expense), net	182	73	45
Income before income taxes	2,376	2,200	1,631
Income tax expense	319	405	230
Net income	$ 2,057	$ 1,795	$ 1,401
Net income per share:			
Basic	$ 1.74	$ 1.49	$ 1.16
Diluted	$ 1.71	$ 1.47	$ 1.15
Weighted average shares:			
Basic	1,184	1,203	1,210
Diluted	1,203	1,221	1,218

Annual Report. PayPal Holdings, Inc, December 31, 2018.

appear to be valuable, as consumers flock to open accounts, but the willingness of users to pay for the social aspect of the product must be determined and verified. There is a general sense of momentum; established players like Apple's entry into the marketplace indicate that something very real is going on! The challenge is determining the market scope and the potential profitability of the marketplace to support new business models in the payment space. Dan Schulman described "the secret sauce of Venmo was turning a transaction into an experience."[19] The problem is that the secret sauce is usually put on the main dish to enhance the flavor. People will still get the main dish with or without the condiment. Is Venmo just a condiment?

Cash Transfers and Withdrawals

The company's revenue comes from credit card fees, instant transfer processing fees, and various automated teller machine (ATM) withdrawal fees. Although most customers link a debit card or bank account to their Venmo account, credit cards are another option but at a cost of 3 percent per total value of that credit card transaction. Standard processing time for transfers are free of charge. If a customer wants funds processed instantly, 1 percent of the value is deducted from the total transfer amount for each instant transfer made, with minimum fee being $0.25 and maximum being $10. For ATM withdrawal of funds from a customer's Venmo balance, the daily limit is $400 at MoneyPass® ATMs in the United States. For non-MoneyPass® ATMs, there is a $2.50 ATM Domestic Withdrawal Fee and possible additional fees charged by the ATM's operator. There is a $3.00 Over the Counter Withdrawal Fee if a signature is required to obtain cash back at a bank or other financial institution.

Mid-2018, Venmo launched the Venmo card, which bridges the gap between the digital app and the real world.

EXHIBIT 4 PayPal Balance Sheet

	As of December 31,	
	2018	2017
	(In millions, except par value)	
ASSETS		
Current assets:		
Cash and cash equivalents	$ 7,575	$ 2,883
Short-term investments	1,534	2,812
Accounts receivable, net	313	283
Loans and interest receivable, net of allowances of $172 in 2018 and $129 in 2017	2,532	1,314
Loans and interest receivable, held lor sale	—	6,398
Funds receivable and customer accounts	20,062	18,242
Prepaid expenses and other current assets	947	713
Total current assets	32,963	32,645
Long-term investments	971	1,961
Property and equipment, net	1,724	1,528
Goodwill	6,284	4,339
Intangible assets, net	825	168
Other assets	565	133
Total assets	$43,332	$40,774
LIABILITIES AND EQUITY		
Current liabilities:		
Accounts payable	$ 281	$ 257
Notes payable	1,998	1,000
Funds payable and amounts due to customers	21,562	19,742
Accrued expenses and other current liabilities	2,002	1,781
Income taxes payable	61	83
Total current liabilities	25,904	22,863
Deferred tax liability and other long-term liabilities	2,042	1,917
Total liabilities	27,946	24,780
Commitments and contingencies (Note 13)		
Equity:		
Common stock, $0.0001 par value; 4,000 shares authorized; 1,174 and 1,200 shares outstanding as of December 31, 2018 and 2017, respectively	—	—
Treasury stock at cost, 91 and 47 shares as of December 31, 2018 and 2017, respectively	(5,511)	(2,001)
Additional paid-in-capital	14,939	14,314
Retained earnings	5,880	3,823
Accumulated other comprehensive income (loss)	78	(142)
Total equity	15,386	15,994
Total liabilities and equity	$43,332	$40,774

Annual Report. PayPal Holdings, Inc, December 31, 2018.

It lets the customer use their Venmo balance at any shop where MasterCard is accepted. The card is ATM-friendly in the United States, specifically designed for the customers who want to use cash to try that cash-only food truck in town.[20] The cards come in six different colors, which is appealing to the younger crowd. It is easy to track the transactions as they are recorded under the transaction history on the Venmo app.

Social Feeds

Another important aspect of Venmo's business model is the social network feed.[21] This is what makes the company stand out from competitors. A consumer who provided a review of the app mentioned the following: "It's like Facebook and PayPal combined–only a better version of both of those things."[22] This social feed is the "secret sauce" that Schulman described. At the December 2015 Business Insider's Ignition conference, Schulman said, "Venmo users open the app four or five times a week . . . to see, 'What did you buy?' . . . The secret sauce on Venmo is one, the ease of use, but two, that it's tied into your social network."[23]

Despite the appealing nature of the social feed, there are privacy concerns and criticism about the amount of information displayed publicly. By default, Venmo's social feeds are public. The Venmo user would have to update their settings manually to change transaction activity settings to private. Note: the amount of money spent by users is not visible publicly. However, the visible transaction descriptions with emojis and time stamps say a lot. A report created by privacy researcher Hang Do Thi Duc, included an examination of 207,984,218 public transactions posted on Venmo in 2017.[24] Duc's report detailed life stories and personal habits of several users with data gleaned in the analysis. In February 2018, the Federal Trade Commission made a settlement with PayPal over a complaint about the company's handling of privacy disclosures in the Venmo app. Venmo was required to offer clear disclosures, discontinue misrepresentation of its services, provide privacy setting explanations to new and existing users, and include third party assessment of its compliance every other year for 10 years.

Fraud and Controversy

Earlier in 2018, Venmo was hit by a surge of payment fraud that helped push losses higher than the company previously expected and prompted it to shut down some user features to control the damage.[25] The company recorded an operating loss of about $40 million in the first three months of 2018. Fraud can occur in many different ways when it comes to payment platforms like Venmo. For example, stolen credit cards can be used to create new Venmo profiles and send money or hackers can take over accounts of existing Venmo users and syphon off their money.

After the fraud surge, Venmo management blacklisted tens of thousands of users and removed its feature of instant transfers to bank accounts. This was followed by angry users whose legitimate transactions were declined.

Cash App and Zelle

Cash App

Cash App is a mobile payment service developed by Square, Inc. (long time competitor of PayPal) in October 2013. It allows users to transfer money to one another via a mobile app or its online website. Most customer accounts use a debit card or bank account free of charge. However, like most other companies, credit card transactions require a 3 percent fee. Standard deposit times (usually next day) are free of charge, but instant deposits require a 1.5 percent fee of the total transfer amount. Cash App offers a virtual card and a physical debit card to use online, at retail stores and/or ATMs. An interesting feature of the card is the ability to obtain cash back rewards when used at certain merchants. For businesses that accept Square payments, fees start at 2.75 percent per swiped transaction and 3.5 percent plus 15 cents for manually entered transactions. A recent feature of Cash App allows customers to have direct deposits sent straight to their account balance.[26] In January 2018, Cash App expanded to support bitcoin trading through its app in most U.S. states, and supported bitcoin trading in all U.S. states by August 2018.

Zelle

Zelle is a mobile payments app created by several U.S. banks (Bank of America, BB&T, Capital One, JPMorgan Chase, PNC Bank, US Bank. and Wells Fargo) with partnerships with dozens of other U.S. banks. The app, introduced in September 2017, allows users of the respective banks to send and receive money from each other. Zelle's creation was a result of U.S. banks feeling the threat from digital payment apps. Financial institutions introduced Zelle as a way to enter the financial technology market, and keep and attract millennials. According to a Zelle spokesperson, "the goal is to broaden digital payments from millennials to mainstream."[27] Zelle has the capability to capitalize on older demographics because those customers are already banking with one of the partnering U.S. banks.

App Rankings

The best mobile payment system or who has the best P2P payments App varies from ranking to ranking, which is expected, as consumers have a lot of choice in the payments space.

As of December 2017, the total dollar amount of transactions processed for the fourth quarter were as follows: Zelle took the lead with $75 billion, followed by Cash App with $17.9 billion, then Venmo with $10.4 billion.[28] Although Venmo came in last place, it's year over year increase for the quarter was up by 86 percent with continued expectations of periodic growth.

According to the Apple App Store for iOS and Google Play Store for Android, top charts for finance apps display the following as of August 2018:[29]

- For Apple, Cash App is #1, Venmo is #2, PayPal is #3, and Zelle is #9.

EXHIBIT 5 Comparing Different Payment Platforms

	PayPal	Google Pay	Venmo	Square Cash	Apple Pay Cash
Compatibility	Android, iOS, Web	Android, iOS, Web	Android, iOS, Web	Android, iOS, Web	iOS
Payment methods	Credit, debit, bank transfer	Credit, debit card, bank transfer	Credit, debit card, bank transfer	Credit, debit card	Credit, debit card
Credit fee	2.9% + $0.30	2.9%	2.9%	3%	3%
Debit fee	2.9% + $0.30	Free	Free (25 cents for instant transfers)	Free	Free
Bank transfer fee	Free	Free	Free	N/A	N/A
Withdrawal speed	Up to 1–2 business days	Up to 1–3 business days	Up to1 business day	Up to 1–2 business days	Up to 1–3 business days
Transfer limits	$10,000	$9,999	$3,000	$2,500	$3,000
Special features	PayPal.me shareable links	Integration with other Google services	Quick transfers to banks	No need to set up an account	Automatically available in iOS

Looper, Christian de. PayPal vs. Google Pay vs. Venmo vs. Square Cash vs. Apple Pay Cash. Digital Trends, May 02, 2019

- For Android, Cash App is #1, PayPal is #2, Venmo is #3, and Zelle is #9.

Venmo's position has an indirect correlation with a top average app rating of 4.8 stars between Apple and Google Play. Lagging behind, average app ratings for PayPal, Cash App, and Zelle, are 4.6, 4.3 and 3.5 stars respectively. With the exception of PayPal and Venmo, all other platforms offer free instant transfers (see Exhibit 5). In regard to social media followings (Facebook, Instagram, Twitter, and LinkedIn), Cash App stands out above the rest, with 92,000 more followers than Venmo and 162,000 more followers than Zelle.

According to Consumer Reports, Apple Pay is actually the best P2P payment system (see Exhibit 6), however Apple Pay requires later-generation iPhones to use it. That makes it difficult to split a bill with friends, unless they are all loyal iPhone users. After Apple Pay, Venmo came in second, followed by Cash and Facebook P2P Messenger, with Zelle in last place.

EXHIBIT 6 Consumer Reports Analysis of Mobile Peer-to-Peer Payment Services

Worse ⟶ Better

MOBILE PEER-To-PEER PAYMENT SERVICES

Service	Overall Score	Payment Authentication	Data Security	Data Privacy	Customer Support	Broad Access
Zelle (standalone app)	50					
Facebook P2P Payment in Messenger	63					
Cash App (Square)	64					
Venmo	69					
Apple Pay	76					

Source: Stanger, Tobie. Why Apple Pay Is the Highest-Rated Mobile P2P Payment Service. Consumer Reports, November 21, 2018.

Moving Forward

Expansion into brick and mortar locations puts Venmo on the same level as competitors such as Cash App, who introduced their debit card in 2013. Rachel Huber, a payments analyst at Javelin Strategy and Research, states, "A card familiarizes [Venmo's] brand with merchants as a payment mechanism—and merchants are going to be the biggest factor in Venmo achieving profitability. Think marketing and loyalty tie-ins, integration fees, and promotional deals. Venmo has access to an extremely desirable consumer segment—expect them to use that to Venmo's advantage."[30] Venmo's social feed is of particular interest to retailers. Transactions via the debit card are logged into Venmo's user history, adding possibilities to promote retailers' sales activities. It is also an opportunity for companies to gain social endorsements from the Venmo feed and push targeted advertisements to users based on their behavior. Recent merchant partnerships for Venmo include Uber, GrubHub, Seamless, Eat24, and Abercrombie & Fitch. Morningstar analyst Jim Sinegal said, "The unique social aspects of Venmo could provide a path to advertising revenue—few other payment platforms make it fun for users to share their payment activity with friends."[31] Similar to other social networks (Facebook, Twitter, Instagram, and Snapchat), advertising revenue would become a major source of their income.[32] Most of these well-known social media companies started out with minimal revenue streams and spent many years making a name for themselves. Eventually they expanded in their markets with clever strategies that led to acquisitions, IPOs, and other business transactions. Such strategies include the following: Google IPO in 2004, Facebook IPO in 2012, Facebook's acquisition of Instagram in 2012, Twitter IPO in 2013, Facebook's acquisition of WhatsApp in 2014, Snapchat IPO in 2017, and the list goes on.[33]

Venmo's debit card acts like an intermediary, as users already have a linked bank account or credit card. Now very active Venmo users can keep their money in their Venmo account and spend it in the "real world" (one of the brand's email headlines reads, "How to spend your Venmo money in the real world").[34] For example, roommates who use Venmo to pool money for a utility bill can pay that bill with the debit card. The obvious question for Venmo is, what's next? Will it launch a co-brand credit card, like its parent company PayPal?

Although Venmo has succeeded in becoming a ubiquitous way for young people to send money back and forth, it is less successful at being a sustainable business, however Schulman is confident that Venmo will eventually make money. At the Morgan Stanley Technology, Media & Telecom Conference in February 2018, Schulman stated, "I have full confidence that we will monetize Venmo. We are clearly seeing the network effects of Venmo."[35] Whatever steps Venmo decides to take, all data and information acquired thus far should steer them in the right direction for future decision models. In its third quarter earnings, PayPal mentioned that it is accelerating momentum across all of Venmo's monetization efforts. Since its launch, more than 24 percent of all Venmo users have participated in a monetizable action, while payments with Venmo monthly active users increased approximately 185 percent month-over-month from August to September 2018. With PayPal's dive into monetization strategies and the Venmo card, will the company be able last in the long run? Or will Venmo succumb to the competition who offer similar services without a middleman?

The *Wall Street Journal* announced on April 19, 2019 that Venmo is working with banks to launch a Venmo branded credit card; this seems to be a tacit acknowledgement that creating a sustainable business is more difficult than previously believed.[36] The commentators were unanimous in expressing their confusion with respect to this move. Shulman explained that the firm wanted to be "very thoughtful about a multi-brand strategy—multi-brands don't intimidate us as long as they are focused at a particular segment, or a particular need multi-brand is fine."[37] Is the move to create a Venmo credit card a true multi-brand approach, or is it simply cannibalizing PayPal's existing business—do we have something new, or is this a disaster for PayPal?

ENDNOTES

1. Yang, A. 2015. Venmo: Building direct network effects and then . . . nothing happened? *HBS*, October 19, https://digital.hbs.edu/platform-digit/submission/venmo-building-direct-network-effects-and-thennothing-happened/.
2. Irerra, A. 2017. PayPal rolls out Venmo payments to its U.S. retailers. *Reuters*, October 17, https://www.reuters.com/article/us-paypal-hldg-venmo/paypal-rolls-out-venmo-payments-to-its-u-s-retailers-idUSKBN1CM1GH.
3. Goldman Sachs. 2017. Talks at GS–Dan Schulman: The Democratization of Finance. August 2, https://www.youtube.com/watch?v=4q_jVu5T80g.
4. Recode. 2017. Venmo's Chief Operating Officer Mike Vaughan | Code Commerce Fall 2017. September 15, https://www.youtube.com/watch?v=y9oQzpKChCo.
5. Baker, K. 2013. The story of how Venmo was started: The story behind every millennial's favorite app for paying back their friends is one of uncertainty, friendship, and perseverance. *The Hustle,* March 6, https://thehustle.co/how-venmo-started.
6. Caraway, M., Epstein, D.A., and Munson, S.A. 2017. Friends Don't Need Receipts: The Curious Case of Social Awareness Streams in the Mobile Payment App Venmo. PACM on Human-Computer Interaction, Vol. 1, No. 2, p. 28.
7. Businesswire.com. 2012. Braintree acquires mobile payments platform Venmo. *Business Wire*, August 17, https://www.businesswire.com/news/home/20120817005685/en/Braintree-Acquires-Mobile-Payments-Platform-Venmo.
8. Fintech.com. 2016. Mobile peer-to-peer payments. *Fintech Ranking*, April 11, http://fintechranking.com/2016/04/11/5608/.
9. https://www.paypalobjects.com/digitalassets/c/website/marketing/global/shared/global/media-resources/documents/Q4_2018_PayPal_Global_Scale.pdf
10. Bansal, S., Bruno, P., Denecker, O., and M. Niederkorn. 2018. Global payments: Expansive growth, targeted opportunities. *McKinsey & Company*, October 2018, https://www.mckinsey.com/industries/financial-services/our-insights/global-payments-expansive-growth-targeted-opportunities.
11. Markman, J. 2019. How PayPal muscled to the top of the digital money stack. *Forbes*, February 2, https://www.forbes.com/sites/jonmarkman/2019/02/24/how-paypal-muscled-to-the-top-of-the-digital-money-stack/#4e21d87f6779.

12. Reeves, J. 2018. PayPal vs. American Express – who will own the future of payments? *Market Watch*, July 2, https://www.marketwatch.com/story/paypal-vs-american-express-who-will-own-the-future-of-payments-2018-07-23
13. Brown, R. 2018.Why eBay abandoned PayPal for a smaller European competitor. *CNBC*, February 1, https://www.cnbc.com/2018/02/01/why-ebay-abandoned-paypal-for-a-smaller-european-competitor.html.
14. Kashyap, M. 2017. Redrawing the lines: FinTech's growing influence on Financial Services. PWC Global FinTech Report, https://www.pwc.ch/en/insights/fs/global-fintech-report-2017.html.
15. EarlyWarning. 2015. U.S. banks unite to form industry leading secure real-time payments network. October 26, https://www.earlywarning.com/press-release/us-banks-unite-form-industry-leading-secure-real-time-payments-network.
16. Finextra. 2019. Bank-backed P2P payments app Zelle reports strong take-up. January 25, https://www.finextra.com/newsarticle/33259/bank-backed-p2p-payments-app-zelle-reports-strong-take-up.
17. Larkin, M. 2019. The Big Banks' Answer To Venmo, Square Cash Accelerates Growth Rate. *Investor's Business Daily*, January 24, https://www.investors.com/news/zelle-answer-paypal-venmo-square-cash-record-quarter-growth/.
18. Nath, T. 2018. How safe is Venmo and why is it free? *Investopedia*, July 12, https://www.investopedia.com/articles/personal-finance/032415/how-safe-venmo-and-why-it-free.asp.
19. Fortune. 2016. This Is Venmo's Secret Sauce, July 13, https://www.youtube.com/watch?v=LwyT9ANqw1A.
20. PayPal Holdings, Inc. Annual Report, 2018.
21. Pinsker, J. 2017. How in the world does Venmo make money? *The Atlantic*, July 18, https://www.theatlantic.com/business/archive/2017/07/venmo-makes-money-banks/533946/.
22. Roller, E. 2013. The spawn of Facebook and PayPal: Why everyone should be using the wallet app Venmo. Slate, August 5, https://slate.com/technology/2013/08/venmo-review-the-wallet-app-is-light-years-ahead-of-paypal.html.
23. D'Onfro, J. 2015. Venmo's 'secret sauce' keeps users checking the app even when they're not making payments. *Business Insider*, December 9, https://www.businessinsider.com/venmo-social-feed-is-its-secret-sauce-2015-12.
24. Paul, K. 2018. The scary reasons you should make your Venmo account private. *MarketWatch*, July 17, https://www.marketwatch.com/story/the-scary-reasons-you-should-make-your-venmo-account-private-2018-07-17.
25. Rudegeair, P. 2018. Venmo caught off guard by fraudsters; A spike in fraudulent activity earlier this year led to higher losses than the payments company had expected. *Wall Street Journal*, November 24, https://www.wsj.com/articles/venmo-caught-off-guard-by-fraudsters-1543068120.
26. Mukherjee, S. 2018. Cash App review and its working strategy. *LuckScout*, March 12, https://www.luckscout.com/cash-app-review/.
27. Salinas, S. 2018. A mobile payments app from US banks is less than a year old, but rivals Venmo's volume. *CNBC*, August 23, https://www.cnbc.com/2018/02/23/mobile-payments-zelle-has-rival–paypals-volume-in-under-a-year.html.
28. Salinas, Sara, "A mobile payments app from US banks is less than a year old, but rivals Venmo's volume," cnbc.com, https://www.cnbc.com/2018/02/23/mobile-payments-zelle-has-rival–paypals-volume-in-under-a-year.html
29. Rankings from Apple App Store and Google Play Store websites.
30. Fortney, L. 2019. How the Venmo debit card may save PayPal. *Investopedia*, August 26, https://www.investopedia.com/investing/how-venmo-debit-card-may-save-paypal/.
31. Bhattacharyya, S. 2018. With debit card, Venmo eyes retail partnerships as path to monetization. *Digiday*, June 28, https://digiday.com/retail/debit-card-venmo-eyes-retail-partnerships-path-monetization/.
32. Campbell, S. 2010. How do social networks make money, *MakeUseOf*, April 20, https://www.makeuseof.com/tag/how-do-social-networks-make-money-case-wondering/.
33. Mittal, T. 2018. From Alibaba to Google, here are the 10 biggest tech IPOs of all time. *YourStory*, February 28, https://yourstory.com/2018/02/biggest-tech-ipo-of-all-time.
34. Bhattacharyya, S. 2018. With debit card, Venmo eyes retail partnerships as path to monetization. *Digiday*, June 28, https://digiday.com/retail/debit-card-venmo-eyes-retail-partnerships-path-monetization/.
35. Verhage, J. 2018. PayPal CEO says he's confident Venmo will make money someday. *Bloomberg*, February 2, https://www.bloomberg.com/news/articles/2018-02-27/paypal-ceo-says-he-s-confident-venmo-will-make-money-eventually.
36. Rudegeair, P., and A. M. Andriotis. 2019.Venmo's latest effort to turn a profit: Credit cards. *Wall Street Journal*, April 19, https://www.wsj.com/articles/venmos-latest-effort-to-turn-a-profit-credit-cards-11555666201.
37. PayPal Holdings, Inc. 10-K Filing Report 2018.
38. Loeb, S. When Venmo was young: the early years. Vator News. January 1, 2018.
39. See https://www.applicoinc.com/blog/network-effects/ for more information.

CASE 38

FLIPKART: WINNING IN INDIA?*

In 2019, India's Internet users were expected to deliver double-digit growth, reaching 627 million, driven by rapid Internet expansion in rural areas.[1] This sharp rise is the result of increasing acceptance of online payment gateways, the critical mass of Internet users, the rising middle class with disposable income to spend, and most importantly, the widespread adoption of low-cost smartphones and data plans. India's e-commerce revenue is expected to jump to US $120 billion in 2020, growing at an annual rate of 51 percent, the highest in the world.[2] As a result, the number of e-commerce businesses has grown rapidly in India. Flipkart and Amazon are the two main players in the Indian e-commerce industry, each with a 30 percent market share in 2018.[3]

The electronic retail màrket, commonly known as the e-tailing, was hardly known by Indian consumers before Flipkart. Started in Bangalore in 2007 by two former Amazon employees, its online shopping platform offers Indian customers a wide variety of product categories, such as consumer electronics, fashion, and lifestyle products. Since its inception, the company has grown significantly, with over 100 million registered users, 8 million shipments per month, 100,000 sellers, and 21 warehouses. This tremendous success has illuminated the potential of the Indian e-commerce sector to businesses around the globe.

Since Amazon's entry to India in 2013, the global giant has flourished. With its deep pockets and aggressive marketing campaigns, Amazon has almost matched Flipkart, becoming one of the few top e-commerce giants in India. In response, Flipkart has taken many steps to expand its market share and compete with Amazon: Flipkart completed mergers and acquisitions, changed its business model, and launched an innovative and secure payment system. But questions remain. How can Flipkart survive the increasingly tougher and well-capitalized competition? Can it keep up with Amazon's pace of innovation? Can it ever beat Amazon?

An Indian Home-Brew

Flipkart was the brainchild of Mr. Sachin Bansal and Mr. Binny Bansal (not related), both alumni of the Indian Institute of Technology, Delhi. The two Bansals worked for Amazon and eventually quit to start their new venture–Flipkart Online Services Pvt Ltd. The company is headquartered in Bangalore and operates exclusively in India. Bangalore, known to be the Silicon Valley of India, is one of the country's most progressive and well-established cities. Due to governmental regulations on foreign direct investment in business to consumer firms in India, Flipkart is registered in Singapore by a holding company.[4]

Sachin and Binny started out using a modest investment of about US $6,000 to build the Flipkart website. Following in Amazon's footsteps, they began by selling books online. Soon, they began to offer product across many categories including electronic goods, air coolers, air conditioners, stationery supplies, lifestyle products, and e-books (see Exhibits 1 to 3). Since its launch, the company has raised US $3 billion worth of capital. Now offering over 80 million products across over 80 categories, the company is credited with establishing the e-commerce market in India.[5] Its website is among the 10 most-frequented websites in India.[6]

Evolution of E-Commerce in India

Traditional Indian Retail Culture

Indian consumers have historically preferred shopping at small retail stores rather than online. India has over 14 million small shops, most of which are smaller than 600 square feet in size. India's Foreign Direct Investment (FDI) government regulations are structured to protect these local shops. Traditional retail shops also complement India's cash economy; many people in the country think e-commerce to be overly difficult and time consuming.

The experience of walking into a small Indian retail shop is unlike that of any American retail shop. For Indians, chai (tea) is an integral part of their lives. Businesses, whether small or large, incorporate tea into the shopping experience. Customers walk into a store and expect to be offered a cup of tea or light refreshment with no cost or expectation of purchasing a product. The customer then begins to leisurely look at products offered by the shopkeeper. If a substantial amount of time has passed, the customer may even be offered snacks from nearby food carts. The intent is hospitality–to put the customers first and make sure their needs are met. After selecting items that a customer is interested in purchasing, the negotiation commences. In India, listed prices are a mere suggestion or starting point. People negotiate in practically every transaction, whether it be for individual grocery items, clothes, or even taxi fares.[7]

* This case was prepared by Professor Alan B. Eisner, Pace University and Professor Helaine J. Korn of Baruch College, City University of New York. Special thanks to graduate assistants Saad Nazir, Sushmitha Mudda, Christoph Kirsch, and Lisa Feldstein, Pace University. This case was based solely on library research and was developed for class discussion rather than to illustrate either effective or ineffective handling of an administrative situation. Copyright © 2019 Alan B. Eisner.

EXHIBIT 1 The Journey of Flipkart

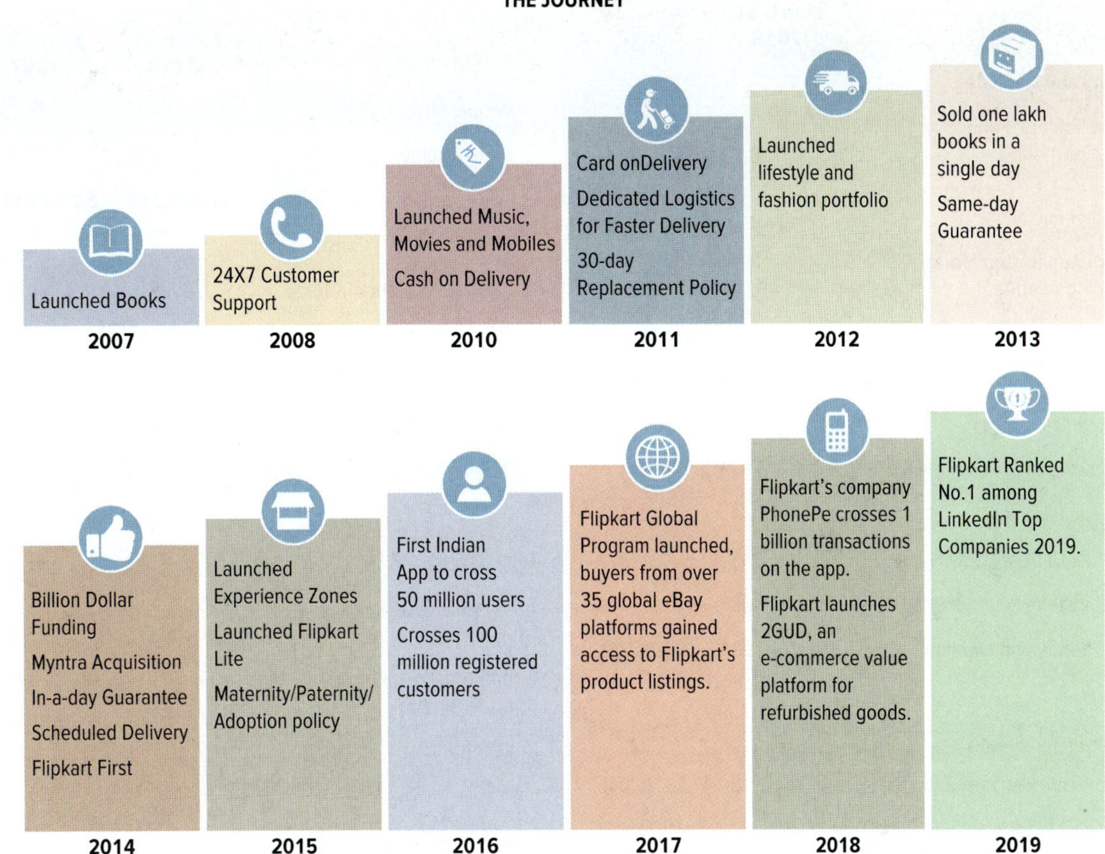

Source: The Flipkart Story. Flipkart Internet Private Limited, October 2007. Flipkart.com

Growth of E-Commerce in India

The e-commerce market in India has undergone exceptional growth, as the majority of the Indian population is gaining access to personal computers, smartphones, tablets, and high-speed Internet services. Demographics rule the destiny of online business in India, where 75 percent of the adults are between 15 and 34 years old, an age group more likely to be proficient at utilizing modern technology, ultimately making digital commerce in India very attractive. According to Bain & Company, e-commerce in India is projected to grow four times faster than the total retail market over the next five years (see Exhibit 4)[8]. Businesses have expanded the e-commerce consumer base by employing strategies such as online shopping websites, establishment of online marketplaces for third-party transactions, business-to-business buying and selling, online data gathering through social media, publishing online newsletters, and retailing novel products to prospective clients.

While the current retail market in India is predominantly served by traditional brick and mortar stores, which form 90 percent of the total market, sales from e-commerce are expected to reach 17.5 percent by 2021.[9] E-tailing will grow at a fast rate, from the present US $0.6 billion to US $76 billion by 2021, which is over a hundredfold. The acceleration in growth will be due to improvements in the market-enabling environment and ecosystem formation for e-tailing. Overall, a larger adaptation of e-commerce in India will offer numerous gains to the Indian economy, aside from the advantages it will bestow upon consumers. [10]

Becoming Big

In the early years, Flipkart faced many challenges in the e-commerce industry. Flipkart co-founder, Sachin Bansal, admitted in an interview that initially the idea of creating the company seemed absurd and that most of his peers believed Flipkart was a ridiculous idea.[11] One key operational challenge was supply chain management; ensuring that goods are punctually delivered is integral to the success of an e-commerce company. Flipkart's logistical infrastructure and supply chain were not initially prepared to handle the volume. Additionally, with its user base growing year after

EXHIBIT 2 Flipkart Balance Sheet (figures in thousand US$*)

	March 31, 2018	March 31, 2017
Equity and Liabilities		
Shareholders' Funds		
Share Capital	$ 103	$ 77
Other Equity	903,038	560,683
Share Application Money Pending Allotment		
Non-Current Liabilities		
Long-Term Provisions	1,083	806
Current Liabilities		
Short-Term Borrowings	32,482	
Trade Payables	408,041	325,183
Other Current Liabilities	318	821
Short-Term Provisions	1,468	1,460
Total Equity and Liabilities	**$1,404,293**	**$905,231**
Assets		
Non-Current Assets		
Property, Plant and Equipment	$ 16,118	$ 20,045
Capital Work-in-Progress	1,953	1,472
Goodwill	259	259
Intangible Assets	5	18
Investments	81,160	
Loans		211
Other Financial Assets	128,544	17,984
Other Assets	2,255	1,618
Current Assets		
Inventories	320,269	247,787
Investments	228,600	109,509
Trade Receivables	175,634	126,910
Cash and Cash Equivalents	9,987	109,989
Short-Term Loans & Advances	44,588	189,753
Other Current Assets	125,985	28,411
Total Assets	**$1,404,293**	**$905,231**

*Original data in INR converted *at* USD $1 = INR 70.35

Source: Tofler, Business Research Platform.

EXHIBIT 3 Flipkart Income Statement (figures in thousand US$*)

	March 31, 2018	March 31, 2017
Revenue from Operations	$ 3,047,427	$ 2,169,783
Other Income	31,132	43,332
Total Revenue	**$3,078,559**	**$2,213,115**
Cost of Materials Consumed		
Purchases of Stock in Trade	$ 3,363,310	$ 2,238,566
Changes in Inventory	72,482	45,907
Employee Benefit Expenses	47,128	23,691
Finance Costs	3,322	1,428
Depreciation and Amortization	8,847	7,988
Other Expenses	21,942	22,136
Total Expenses	**$3,372,067**	**$2,247,903**
Total Revenue Less Total Expenses	**$ 293,508**	**$ 34,788**
Profit From Continuing Operations	**(293,508)**	**(34,788)**
Net Profit/Loss	**(293,508)**	**(34,788)**

*Original data in INR - converted at USD $1 = INR 70.35

Source: Tofler, Business Research Platform.

year, maintaining optimal user experience was becoming a challenge.

Nevertheless, New York-based private equity firm Tiger Global Management LLC–Flipkart's biggest investor at the time–believed in the idea and its founders, as did others. With external investment of substantial funds, Flipkart was not only able to improve its supply chain and logistics, but also to expand and grow through several strategic acquisitions (see Exhibit 5).[12]

In 2014, Flipkart acquired Myntra, a leading fashion e-commerce company in India. Myntra increased Flipkart's margin in the e-commerce sector, giving the company an important advantage over rivals Amazon and Snapdeal. The acquisition also helped Flipkart, a formerly generic e-commerce company, scale and endure in the ecosystem. Pradeep Udhas, Head of Technology Sector at KPMG India, stated: "Firms lacking scale or a niche presence will find it tough to survive in the sector." Moreover, Flipkart and Myntra could experience enormous cost savings since both companies pursue a similar customer and demographic base.[13]

The co-founders of Myntra believed that the two companies together could better challenge a big player like Amazon. "It was an aligned viewpoint between founders of the two

EXHIBIT 4 India's e-Commerce vs. Total Retail Growth

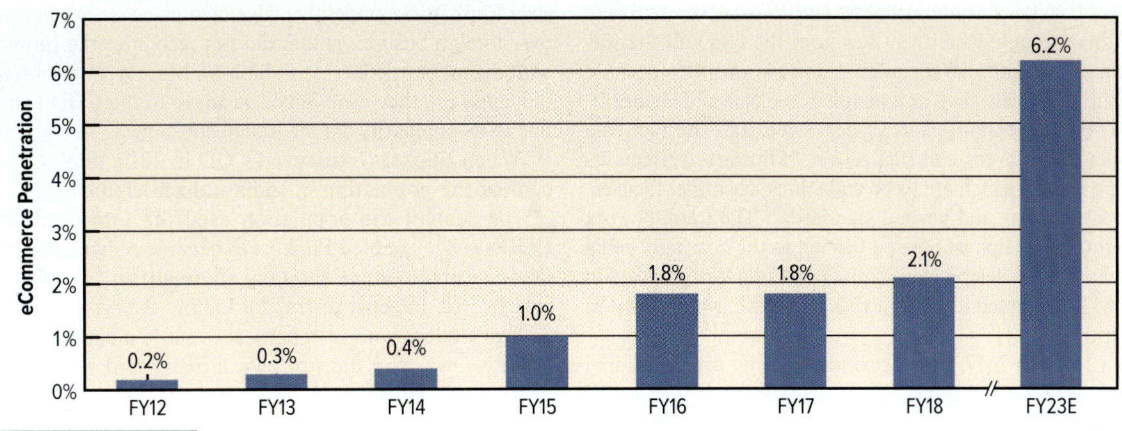

Source: Walmart-Flipkart Group Investor Presentation. Walmart, May 9, 2018.

EXHIBIT 5 Flipkart Acquisitions (2010–2018)

Year	Acquisitions
2010	WeRead, a social book discovery tool, which extended Flipkart's categories to include music, movies, electronics, mobiles, and games.
2011	Chakpak, an online Indian entertainment community. Flipkart acquired the rights to Chakpak's digital catalog. Flipkart has categorically said that it will not be involved with the original site and will not use the brand name.
2011	Mime360, a digital content platform company that links content owners with content publishers.
2012	LetsBuy.com, an Indian e-retailer in electronics. Flipkart has bought the company for an estimated US $25 million. Letsbuy.com was eventually closed down and all traffic to LetsBuy diverted to Flipkart.
2014	Acquired Myntra, a fashion e-commerce company, in an estimated $310 million deal.
2014	Flipkart purchased a majority stake in Jeeves, which offered maintenance, repairs, and product guarantees.
2015	Ngpay, which is a mobile payment gateway company.
2015	Appiterate, a mobile marketing start-up, which Flipkart acquired to help strengthen its mobile platform.
2015	FXMart is a payment services company.
2016	Flipkart's Myntra acquired rival fashion shopping site Jabong. They both have separate identities today but operate under Flipkart's umbrella.
2016	PhonePe, which is a revolutionary payment start-up.
2017	In April, in exchange for an equity stake in Flipkart, eBay agreed to make a $500 million cash investment in Flipkart and sell its eBay.in business to Flipkart; however, according to a company statement eBay.in would continue to operate as a separate entity from Flipkart.

Source: A Timeline of Flipkart's Acquisitions.http://techseen.com/2017/04/10/flipkart-acquisition-ebay-weread/

companies," stated Ashutosh Lawania, co-founder of Myntra. Lawania's Myntra co-founder, Mukesh Bansal (not related), said "both companies had a strong cultural fit. Flipkart would bring many things to the table to accelerate Myntra's growth, which would also help Flipkart to fight competition."[14] The fact that both companies had common investors made acquisition easier and helped improve synergies. Following the acquisition, Flipkart's valuation was estimated to be around $15 billion, five times more than its previous valuation.[15]

Organization

Flipkart believes that its success is due, in large part, to its employees. Smrithi Ravichandran, Senior Director at Flipkart, stated, "Innovations are only unique for a small duration of time, but its people are what make the business thrive. That killer attitude, that we will do whatever it takes to see this through, which you see from the CEO all the way down to the entry- level staffer–I don't know if it's because we hire people like that, or if people come here and change."[16]

The culture at Flipkart is pervasive, and the fact that Flipkart employees call themselves "Flipsters" reflects its strong values, which are to be audacious, customer-focused, unconventional, and beyond standards.[17] The friendly work environment Flipkart created has led to the company being rated the most desirable workplace in India for two years in a row. It surpassed its biggest rival, Amazon, which came in second.[18]

In January 2017, Flipkart underwent an organizational restructuring by creating an umbrella over all of its units, calling it Flipkart Group Organization. Through this process, founder and then CEO of Flipkart, Binny Bansal, became the Group CEO. Bansal planned to concentrate on constructing a high-growth portfolio of new businesses and on capital allocation across group companies. Kalyan Krishnamurthy, who joined Flipkart in June 2016 from Tiger Global Management as head of the Category Design Organization, became the CEO of Flipkart. Krishnamurthy oversaw customer experience, talent management, and overall profit and loss for Flipkart.

The Flipkart Game Changer—Cash On Delivery

Infosys co-founder Nandan Nilekani stated in his post in the *Economic Times of India,* "One of the reasons Flipkart took off was that they brought in cash on delivery,"[19] people pay for goods when they are delivered rather than in advance. Many Indians did not have a method for completing online transactions, since India had traditionally been a cash-based economy, so this innovation was a game changer for Flipkart. He went on to say that the cash on delivery (COD) system gave Flipkart a competitive edge over its rivals, particularly over foreign businesses that did not recognize the problem with digital payments (see Exhibit 6). Moreover, when rivals did catch on, they were forced to adjust to the COD system due to its popularity among Indian consumers.[20]

When Flipkart introduced COD in 2010, only 0.5 percent of the population in India utilized credit cards and 7.5 percent of the population used the Internet.[21] The COD service enabled Flipkart to become remarkably popular and made online shopping more attractive and trustworthy for its customers. Suddenly, everyone from a college student without a bank account to a person from a remote town who did not own a debit card was able to purchase goods with just a click.

Factors that aided the growth of Cash on Delivery payments in India included:

- Convenience
- Experience with cash payments
- Population of unbanked consumers
- Small amount of credit/debit card users
- Scarcity of secured payment gateways
- Consumer hesitancy in online payments, due to lack of trust
- Apprehension of online scams,bcs_lb.last.

Consumer Convenience

Flipkart continued increasing its customer base with the announcement of an easy return policy. Many consumers in India were reticent to shop online because they want to be able to physically see and examine the products. In order to address this, Flipkart offered a no-questions-asked return/exchange policy, wherein customers could return goods that did not meet their expectations. Making purchases online

EXHIBIT 6 Online Payment Methods Used in India

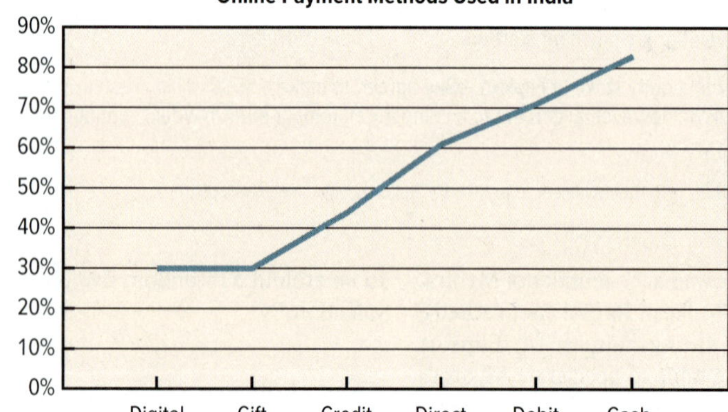

Source: Nielsen Global Connected Commerce Survey.

through Flipkart became extremely appealing to Indian consumers because brick and mortar stores never offered the same deal.

Flipkart also recognized that mobile network connectivity was not homogeneous throughout India, prompting the creation of Flipkart Lite, similar to Flipkart yet designed for a mobile experience. The mobile browser, developed within 45 days by five engineers, was easier to use while in areas with an inconsistent network. In addition, Flipkart Lite enabled users to access shopping search history. Flipkart Lite was considered very innovative and other companies such as LinkedIn began using similar technology.[22]

Flipkart Business Model

The introduction of a marketplace system changed the way Flipkart conducted its business, transforming its website portal into a "virtual mall" allowing consumers to shop different sellers and brands on a single platform. No longer required to maintain an inventory of its own, Flipkart greatly reduced overhead, while retaining control of the sales, with delivery completed by Flipkart's logistics and supply chain division. The model can be compared to eBay India, Tradus, or Amazon. Since foreign companies in India are restricted from multi-brand e-tailing, Flipkart sells its products through WS Retail, a private limited e-commerce company in India (see Exhibit 7).

Online marketplaces have several sources of revenue. A listing fee is charged to the seller. This charge can be one-time or on an annual basis. Sellers who wish to feature their products can pay for advertisements on the site. Sales commissions provide Flipkart a profit on each purchase transaction. The commission charged by online marketplaces varies by product type. In June 2019, Flipkart revamped its fee structure, significantly reducing the percentages that sellers must pay. The timing of this change suggests it is a strategic move to inspire seller loyalty, as competition heats up. Amazon is doubling down on investments in India, after finally admitting defeat and pulling out of China.[23]

EXHIBIT 7 **Flipkart Business Model—Current Marketplace Facilitation**

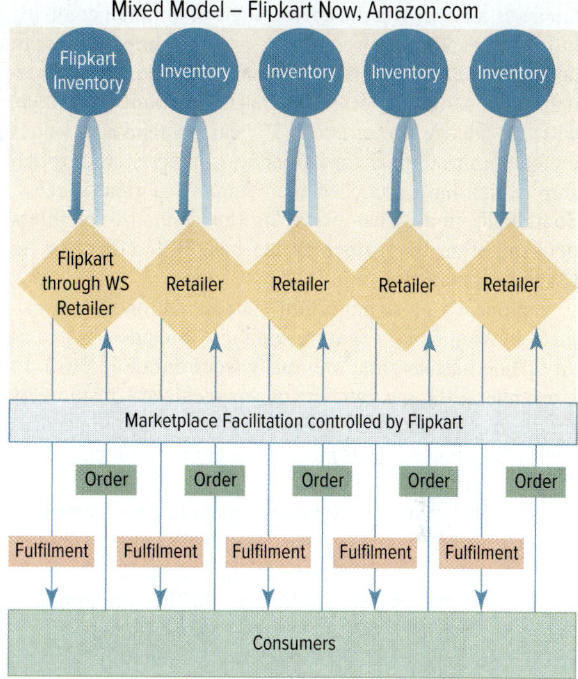

Source: What is the difference between the marketplace model and the warehousing model related to e-commerce? *Quora,* October 9, 2014. https://www.quora.com/What-is-the-difference-between-the-marketplace-model-and-the-warehousing-model-related-to-e-commerce

Flipkart Competitors

Flipkart has faced several competitors throughout its decade-long battle in the Indian e-commerce industry. The major competitors included Myntra, Jabong, Snapdeal, eBay, Paytm, and its strongest competitor, Amazon. Flipkart remained in the spotlight in the Indian e-commerce industry through frequent mergers and acquisitions, acquiring most competitors and increasing market share in an effort to compete with Amazon.

Paytm

Paytm, an acronym for Pay Through Mobile, is the largest mobile payment platform in India. It is owned by One-97 Communications, and its headquarters is located in Uttar Pradesh, India. Back in 2010, the company initially offered mobile recharge and utility bill payments. Today, Paytm provides a full marketplace through its mobile apps. The company has over 100 million registered users and gets approximately 60 million orders per month. Paytm offers the option of recharging a secure online wallet, Paytm-cash, enabling customers to shop from any location.[24] Paytm can also be accessed from a browser, and the Paytm app is accessible on mobile devices compatible with Android, Windows, and iOS operating systems. Paytm has attracted many notable investors, including Tata of India and Alibaba Group of China. Transactions completed on Paytm are completely free with no concealed charges.[25]

Paytm Mall has over 17 fulfillment centers across the country and over 40 courier partners for sellers.[26] In 2017, Flipkart cut the commission that it collected from sellers to combat Paytm Mall. Reliance Capital invested about $41 million in Paytm, increasing valuation for Paytm's parent company, One-97 Communications. Paytm's valuation is estimated to be approximately $5 billion, whereas Flipkart's is $5.39 billion.[27] In March 2019, Paytm took on Amazon and Flipkart as it launched its subscription-based loyalty program, Paytm First. Through this program, the company aims to offer exclusive benefits over and above the regular Paytm cashback offer, while looking to promote further usage (of its platforms) and to increase customer retention.[28]

Snapdeal

Snapdeal, founded by Kunal Bahl and Rohit Bansal (not related), is another rapidly developing e-commerce company in India. Snapdeal evolved from a group coupon business to an online marketplace that eventually turned into a billion-dollar company. Snapdeal has a relatively young workforce, with an average age of about 25 years. Snapdeal's values include innovation, change, openness, honesty, and ownership, which have propelled the company to great success. Snapdeal's impressive growth is the result of relentless determination to prosper as the best B2C (Business to Customer) marketplace in India.

Snapdeal's most important success factor was investment by Vani Kola, a venture capitalist. Snapdeal began as an offline business and eventually went online in 2010. In November 2011, the founders of Snapdeal were inspired by the success of Jack Ma's Alibaba and wanted to develop a somewhat analogous business. Hence, Snapdeal exited the deals business and moved into the online marketplace. The decision was risky since Snapdeal held a large market share in the deals business. However, Snapdeal's value is now estimated to be around $1 billion, and, currently, there are more than 50,000 sellers and approximately 5 million products on Snapdeal.[29] The company has grown through acquiring several companies since 2014 (see Exhibit 8).

Amazon India

Amazon, founded by Jeff Bezos in 1994, is an American e-commerce company based in Seattle, Washington. It is the largest Internet-based company in the United States. Amazon started as an online bookstore, but shortly diversified, offering compact discs, VHS, video and MP3 downloads and streaming, software, video games, electronics, apparel, furniture, food, toys, and jewelry. Amazon has individual retail websites for countries all over the world, including: United States, United Kingdom and Ireland, France, Canada, Germany, The Netherlands, Italy, Spain, Australia, Brazil, Japan, China, India, and Mexico. Amazon provides international shipping to other specific countries for selected products. In June 2013, Amazon started its Amazon India marketplace. One month later, Amazon publicized that it would invest US $1.85 billion in India to expand its business, seemingly in response to news that Flipkart decided to invest US $1 billion in expansion.[30]

Amazon came into the Indian market with the reputation of being the king of e-commerce. Initially, Amazon's success in India was uncertain, as Indian consumers are considerably different from the rest of the world. Amazon lags behind Asian e-commerce companies such as Alibaba, overwhelmed by competitors in China, with no indication of catching up. Amazon believes that the failure in China was because the company did not spend enough. That is why Amazon is investing more in India.[31] Amazon's CEO Jeff Bezos enlisted Amit Agarwal to lead Amazon's India business. Agarwal told Forbes, "Amazon's entry into India is big, we can add significant customer value, and we can generate significant cash flows."[32] Amazon already committed to spend $5 billion for Amazon India, and Bezos has indicated additional investments will be made as time goes by.[33]

One of the main reasons why Amazon stands out among Flipkart's competitors is because Amazon is customer-centric, similar to Flipkart's business strategy. Amazon has an edge in terms of reputation and brand recognition. The company is admired and well-known for providing excellent customer service internationally. People are confident making purchases with Amazon due to product replacement offerings and after-sales services.[34]

Flipkart has expanded by mergers and acquisitions. It has been trying to become self-sustained by developing its own payment gateway and logistics services. However, Amazon is also acquiring companies in India, although not on as grand a scale as Flipkart. For instance, in 2016, Amazon acquired Emvantage Payments Pvt. Ltd., an Indian payments company, to facilitate online payments.[35]

EXHIBIT 8 Snapdeal Acquisitions (2014–2019)

Date	Acquisitions
April 2014	Fashion products discovery site, Doozton.com
December 2014	Gifting recommendation site, Wishpicker.com
March 2015	E-commerce management software and fulfillment solution provider, Unicommerce.com
April 2015	Mobile-payments company, FreeCharge.com
May 2015	MartMobi, an innovative mobile technology company
June 2015	Letsgomo Labs, a mobile-focused technology company
September 2015	Reduce Data, a programmatic display advertising platform
February 2016	TargetingMantra, a tech marketing company
July 14, 2016	GoJavas, a supply chain solutions company

Source: Crunchbase. https://www.crunchbase.com/organization/snapdeal/acquisitions/acquisitions_list#section-acquisitions.

Home-Brewed Company versus International Giant

Flipkart definitely used home advantage by adapting to the Indian environment quickly. In 2015, Flipkart launched Flipkart One Stop (F-1 Stop) to provide sellers services such as training, registration, cataloguing, packaging, and financial assistance. The support services aim to help first-time merchants get their businesses up and running online.[36]

Even though Amazon only entered the Indian e-commerce market in 2013, it aggressively marketed itself to catch up.

Amazon launched the Chai Cart campaign to connect with small sellers. As mentioned earlier, India has a very strong chai (tea) culture, and Amazon found a way to capitalize on it. A chai cart operated by Amazon associates would move around various Indian markets and share with local sellers the advantages of online selling, over a cup of chai. It created a safe space for local sellers to raise questions and concerns about growing their businesses online. It also helped create brand recognition. Within four months, the Amazon Chai Cart team traveled 9,495 miles across 31 cities, served 37,200 cups of tea and connected with more than 10,000 sellers. The campaign was innovative and successful with Indian consumers.[37]

Looking at the Future–Flipkart's PhonePe App

India is swiftly evolving into a digital giant (see Exhibit 9). The increasing use of smartphones and Internet access has enabled Indian consumers to remain continuously connected. Consumer behavior and preferences are changing. This is only the beginning of digital payments in India, since a large portion of the population remains an untapped market. Digitization of cash will be faster over the next few years. In addition, non-cash payment transactions are estimated to surpass cash transactions by 2023. Overall, the proportion of cash transactions in the total consumer spending in the country has dropped from 78 percent in 2015 to 68 percent in 2017.[38]

EXHIBIT 9 India is Becoming a Digital Country

		2015	2020
People	#2 in the world	1,250 mn	1,350 mn
Mobile phone users	#2 in the world	1,000 mn	1,200 mn
Internet users	#2 in the world	300 mn	650 mn
Smart phone users	#2 in the world	240 mn	520 mn

Source: *Digital Payments 2020 - The Making of A $500 Billion Ecosystem in India,* The Boston Consulting Group & Google

It is projected that the total payment transactions through digital payment tools will be around US $500 billion by 2020. Person to merchant (P2M) transactions compelled by digital payments at the physical point of sale, trailed by business to business (B2B) and peer to peer (P2P) transactions, are predicted to be key suppliers of growth.[39]

Flipkart currently offers several payment options, which include cash on delivery, Internet banking, or payment by credit and debit cards. Flipkart's most recent offering, the PhonePe wallet app, developed in partnership with YES Bank, is revolutionizing payments. PhonePe enables customers to connect bank accounts securely to their smartphone through the encrypted software of the National Payments Corporation of India, which makes PhonePe especially attractive to Indian consumers. In the earlier stage of its launch, Flipkart's cash on delivery option drove success, as Indian consumers were not ready to commit to online payments. However, with the PhonePe app, Flipkart offers secure transaction options for almost all types of payment methods. The PhonePe app permits users to carry out transactions at no cost and users can exchange or return items to Flipkart and receive reimbursement in the PhonePe wallet.[40]

PhonePe is based on the government-backed Unified Payment Interface (UPI) platform. UPI permits consumers to transfer money between any two parties' bank accounts via secure unique identifiers. This means that the exchange of bank account details is not necessary. This makes it stress free to send or receive money. In addition, customers can pay straight from their bank account to both online and offline merchants. It eliminates the necessity of entering credit or debit card details or a one-time password.

India: The E-Commerce Frontier

Amazon may be the largest online e-retailer in the world but it is not yet the market leader in India. While that honor still belongs to Flipkart, Amazon is determined to conquer India. Amazon has a multibillion-dollar plan to dive into the online grocery business in India. Reduction in government restrictions allows online retailers to sell domestic products such as processed foods and groceries directly to consumers. The Ministry of Commerce and Industry is prepared to let Amazon create a nationwide network to stock and distribute such groceries.

Flipkart is choosing instead to focus on artificial intelligence (AI). Flipkart's research team is based in the United States, working at F-7 Labs, located in Silicon Valley. The company believes that investing more in AI will help Flipkart advance its business processes and customer interactions. "There is an understanding at Flipkart that, to deliver at scale, we will need artificial intelligence and that the Valley is the place where the cutting-edge research is being done," says Mihir Naware, Director, Product Development at F-7 Labs.[41]

Amazon can also afford to undercut Flipkart by offering a wider variety of services and more discounts; this may be enough to attract Indian consumers used to the tradition of negotiating prices. On the other hand, Indians are known to be nationalistic, and Flipkart has utilized this to their advantage. Other domestic start-ups have sought government intervention to give Indian businesses a formal edge over competition. While protectionist policies have helped create world-class technology companies like Alibaba, Tencent, and Didi in China, with Indian Prime Minister Narendra Modi courting foreign capital from the Silicon Valley companies, protectionist policies do not seem to be a realistic scenario in India at this point of time.[42]

The battle is intense because the stakes are high. What makes India so attractive is its huge population and growing consumer market. Growing Internet and mobile permeation are increasing the use of online payments. The e-commerce sector in India is expected to grow by four times its current size and is anticipated to go over $100 billion within the next five years. If so, e-commerce in India has the potential to add more than 4 percent to India's GDP.[43] Mobile commerce (m-commerce) is developing rapidly as a steady complement to the e-commerce industry. The government's "Digital India" project intends to promote the sector by bringing Internet and broadband to secluded corners of India. Supported by an investment of approximately $17 billion, this initiative will help make India a more connected economy. It will lead to additional investment in electronics manufacturing, creating millions of jobs.

During this time the American multinational retailer, Walmart, had been struggling to come up with a play for India. However, that ambiguity ended in August 2018, when Walmart invested $16 billion to acquire a 77 percent stake of Flipkart. While Flipkart's management team would lead the India business, Walmart would finally have a platform for business in India. Walmart would also infuse $2 billion into Flipkart to grow the business.[44]

In November 2018, three months after its celebrated acquisition by Walmart and following a probe into an allegation of "serious personal misconduct," Flipkart Group's CEO Binny Bansal left the company.[45] Flipkart underwent a management reshuffle, where several top and mid-level executives moved to new roles, and Kalyan Krishnamurthy became Group CEO. Krishnamurthy looked to tighten firm performance across all units and reduce Flipkart's reliance on smartphones, which continues to generate more than 50 percent of Flipkart's overall sales.[46]

Walmart remains extremely optimistic about Flipkart. Walmart's President and CEO Doug McMillon said, "I got to visit our teams in India and China a few weeks ago. I continue to be excited about the opportunity I see with Flipkart and PhonePe. I'm impressed with the team and their ability to innovate for customers with speed."[47] The company said that its plans for India includes investments that "support national initiatives and will bring sustainable benefits in jobs creation, supporting small businesses, supporting farmers, supply chain development, and reducing food waste."[48] Walmart is investing in the future of Flipkart, however, Walmart has not mentioned a hands on management approach yet. Armed with a $2 billion USD equity investment from the new owners Flipkart should be ready to compete.[49]

ENDNOTES

1. IBEF. 2019. E-commerce industry in India. India Brand Equity Foundation. March, https://www.ibef.org/industry/ecommerce.aspx.
2. Ibid.
3. Koetsier, J. 2018. Report: Amazon India worth $16B with 30% market share, will hit $70B GMV in 2027. *Forbes*, May 18, https://www.forbes.com/sites/johnkoetsier/2018/05/18/report-amazon-india-worth-16b-with-30-market-share-will-hit-70b-gmv-in-2027/#22f869b56b95.
4. Sen, S. 2013. Bansal's divest risk, move Flipkart to Singapore for growth. *Economic Times*, February 13, https://economictimes.indiatimes.com/blogs/Whathappensif/bansal-s-divest-risk-move-flipkart-to-singapore-for-growth/.
5. https://www.flipkart.com/about-us?otracker=undefined_footer_navlinks.
6. Top Sites in India. 2019. The sites in the top sites lists are ordered by their 1-month Alexa traffic rank. http://www.alexa.com/topsites/countries/IN.
7. Ferriss, T. 2017. How to negotiate like an Indian—7 rules. Huff Post, December 7. https://www.huffpost.com/entry/how-to-negotiate-like-an_n_79602.
8. Fabre, C., et al. 2019. E-commerce in MENA: Opportunity beyond the hype. February 19, https://www.bain.com/insights/ecommerce-in-MENA-opportunity-beyond-the-hype/.
9. Financial Express. 2018. Retail: Why bricks and mortars are still relevant. Financial Express, August 17, https://www.financialexpress.com/industry/retail-why-bricks-and-mortars-are-still-relevant/1283071/.
10. Mehra, Atin, IMT, Ghaziabad. 2015. E-commerce industry in India.
11. Soni, A. 2014. 7-yr-old Flipkart's evolution through the eyes of Sachin Bansal. YourStory, August 6, https://yourstory.com/2014/08/sachin-bansal-flipkart-journey.
12. Techseen Bureau. 2017. A timeline of Flipkart's acquisitions. Techseen, April 10, https://techseen.com/2017/04/10/flipkart-acquisition-ebay-weread/.
13. Borpuzari, P. 2014. Flipkart acquires Myntra: Here is why it makes sense. Economic Times, May 22, https://economictimes.indiatimes.com/tech/internet/flipkart-acquires-myntra-here-is-why-it-makes-sense/articleshow/35471764.cms.
14. Ghosh, D. 2016. Bansal's next adventure: CEO of India's largest fashion retailer makes an exit. Forbes Asia, April 27, 2016, https://www.forbes.com/sites/forbesasia/2016/04/27/bansals-next-adventure-ceo-of-indias-largest-fashion-retailer-makes-an-exit/#1db83bdb6372.
15. Press Trust of India. 2015. E-commerce to change face of Indian merchandise business: Ratan Tata. News18, July 15, https://www.news18.com/news/business/e-commerce-to-change-face-of-indian-merchandise-business-ratan-tata-1020869.html.
16. Money Control. 2017. How Flipkart's 8,000-plus team is working hard to stay ahead of Amazon. Moneycontrol.com, May 8, https://www.moneycontrol.com/news/business/startup/how-flipkarts-8000-plus-team-is-working-hard-to-stay-ahead-of-amazon-2273541.html.
17. Be Among The Ambitious. http://www.flipkartcareers.com/welcome.php.
18. Gilchrist, K. 2019. These are the best companies to work for in India in 2019, according to LinkedIn. CNBC, April 2, https://www.cnbc.com/2019/04/03/linkedin-top-companies-to-work-for-in-india-2019-flipkart-amazon-oyo.html.
19. Nilekani, N. 2016. Flipkart took off because it brought in cash on delivery: Nandan Nilekani. Economic Times, April 4, https://economictimes.indiatimes.com/small-biz/startups/flipkart-took-off-because-it-brought-in-1ash-on-delivery-nandan-nilekani/articleshow/53533483.cms.

20. Ibid.
21. World Bank. http://www.worldbank.org/
22. Dubey, T. 2017. These disruptions made by Flipkart over ten years helped it lead the e-commerce sector. Business Insider, June 1, https://www.businessinsider.in/These-Disruptions-made-by-Flipkart-over-Ten-Years-Helped-it-Lead-the-E-commerce-Sector/Cash-on-Delivery-2010/slideshow/58951487.cms.
23. Business Today. 2019. Flipkart cuts commissions. June 11, https://www.businesstoday.in/current/corporate/flipkart-cuts-commissions-shipping-fee-seller-numbers-rates-effective-june-24-e-commerce-company/story/355192.html.
24. Paytm Website. https://paytm.com/about.
25. Paytm Success Story. https://successstory.com/companies/paytm.
26. PTI. 2017. Paytm launches Paytm Mall marketplace against Flipkart, Snapdeal and Amazon. Hindustan Times, February 27, https://www.hindustantimes.com/business-news/paytm-launches-paytm-mall-marketplace-against-flipkart-snapdeal-and-amazon/story-PepJDrXNSNYi3dcxnTkqXO.html.
27. Choudhary, K. 2017. At $5 billion, Paytm is close to Flipkart in value. Business Standard, March 8, https://www.business-standard.com/article/companies/at-4-bn-paytm-close-to-flipkart-in-value-117030700830_1.html.
28. Bhalla, Tarush. 2019. Paytm takes on Amazon, Flipkart as it launches subscription-based loyalty programme 'Paytm First.' YourStory, March 5, https://yourstory.com/2019/03/paytm-first-launch-amazon-flipkart-rm5oijkglg.
29. Choudhary, K. 2017. At $5 billion, Paytm is close to Flipkart in value. Business Standard, March 8, https://www.business-standard.com/article/companies/at-4-bn-paytm-close-to-flipkart-in-value-117030700830_1.html.
30. Economics of Business and Labor. http://www.encyclopedia.com/social-sciences-and-law/economics-business-and-labor/businesses-and-occupations/amazoncom.
31. Walt, V. 2015. Amazon invades India. Fortune, December 28, http://fortune.com/amazon-india-jeff-bezos/.
32. D'Onfro, J.2015. Amazon's next big challenge: Winning India. Business Insider, July 24, https://www.businessinsider.com/amazon-growth-in-india-2015-7.
33. Sen, A. 2017. Jeff Bezos hints at more investments, says Amazon fastest online marketplace in India. Livemint, April 29, https://www.livemint.com/Companies/ZFlqjOUtZN3FFYpmpdlk2J/Jeff-Bezos-hints-at-more-investments-says-Amazon-fastest-on.html.
34. Schneider, L. 2018. Overview of Amazon.com's history and workplace culture. Balance Careers, February 18, https://www.thebalancecareers.com/amazon-com-company-research-2071316.
35. Rao, L. 2016. Amazon just acquire this payments company. Fortune, February 16, http://fortune.com/2016/02/16/amazon-acquisition-india/.
36. Agarwal, S. 2015. Flipkart to offer merchant support services. Business Standard, August 20, https://www.business-standard.com/article/companies/flipkart-to-offer-support-services-to-merchants-through-f-1-stop-115081900875_1.html.
37. Joshi, O. 2016. Amazon Chai Cart: Winning sellers' hearts and now a GOLD award, all over a cup of tea. Amazon Services, April 7, https://services.amazon.in/resources/seller-blog/amazon-chai-cart-won-gold.html.
38. Roongta, P., and A. Shah. 2018. The top five trends in India's digital payment landscape. Livemint, October 1, https://www.livemint.com/Technology/ACHEI1t6mB34c4xM5DiTsN/The-top-five-trends-in-Indias-digital-payment-landscape.html.
39. *Digital Payments 2020 - The Making of a $500 Billion Ecosystem,* The Boston Consulting Group & Google.
40. Flipkart Phone App. https://stories.flipkart.com/phonepe-app-flipkart/.
41. BI India Bureau. 2017. For strong Silicon Valley presence, Flipkart is focusing on products based on Artificial Intelligence. Business Insider, June 1, https://www.businessinsider.in/For-strong-Silicon-Valley-presence-Flipkart-is-focusing-on-products-based-on-Artificial-Intelligence/articleshow/58941338.cms.
42. Dalal, M. 2016. Flipkart, Ola look for govt protection against US rivals that once inspired them. Livemint, December 8, https://www.livemint.com/Companies/hwSiftzz7F8KWPmBan26II/Flipkart-Ola-look-for-govt-protection-against-US-rivals-tha.html.
43. Oberoi, T. 2016. Decoding the future of B2B e-commerce in India. India Retailing, October 12, https://www.indiaretailing.com/2016/10/12/retail/decoding-future-b2b-e-commerce-india/.
44. Walmart news. 2019. https://news.walmart.com/2018/08/18/walmart-and-flipkart-announce-completion-of-walmart-investment-in-flipkart-indias-leading-marketplace-ecommerce-platform.
45. Bahree, M. 2018. Flipkart CEO Binny Bansal resigns after probe into personal misconduct. Forbes. November 13, https://www.forbes.com/sites/meghabahree/2018/11/13/flipkart-ceo-binny-bansal-resigns-after-probe-into-personal-misconduct/#327aaad45ac3.
46. Sen, A. 2018. Flipkart conducts first major management reshuffle since Walmart buyout. Livemint, December 7, https://www.livemint.com/Companies/WRMRUEk0apbJsRdrGCnGCI/Flipkart-conducts-first-major-management-reshuffle-since-Wal.html.
47. Poojary, T. 2019. Excited about opportunity with Flipkart and PhonePe: Walmart CEO. YourStory, May 16, https://yourstory.com/2019/05/walmart-financial-results-flipkart-phonepe-india.
48. Russell, J. 2018. Walmart completes its $16 billion acquisition of Flipkart. TechCrunch, August 20, https://techcrunch.com/2018/08/20/walmart-flipkart-deal-done/.
49. Ibid.

COMPANY INDEX

NAME INDEX

SUBJECT INDEX